SO-AYA-315

Windows NT® Server 4

Second Edition

Jason Garms, et al.

SAMS
PUBLISHING

201 West 103rd Street
Indianapolis, IN 46290

UNLEASHED

This book is for my wife Marion, who has encouraged and supported me in the pursuit of my dreams.

It is also for all the people in the world who selflessly devote their time and energy to making this world a better place, even in the face of great adversity. I have been fortunate to have many such people as my teachers.

Copyright © 1998 by Sams Publishing

SECOND EDITION

All rights reserved. No part of this book shall be reproduced, stored in a retrieval system, or transmitted by any means, electronic, mechanical, photocopying, recording, or otherwise, without written permission from the publisher. No patent liability is assumed with respect to the use of the information contained herein. Although every precaution has been taken in the preparation of this book, the publisher and author assume no responsibility for errors or omissions. Neither is any liability assumed for damages resulting from the use of the information contained herein. For information, address Sams Publishing, 201 W. 103rd St., Indianapolis, IN 46290.

International Standard Book Number: 0-672-31249-2

Library of Congress Catalog Card Number: 92-82090

00 99 98   4   3   2   1

Interpretation of the printing code: The rightmost double-digit number is the year of the book's printing; the rightmost single-digit, the number of the book's printing. For example, a printing code of 98-1 shows that the first printing of the book occurred in 1998.

Composed in AGaramond and MCPdigital by Macmillan Computer Publishing

Printed in the United States of America

Trademarks

All terms mentioned in this book that are known to be trademarks or service marks have been appropriately capitalized. Sams Publishing cannot attest to the accuracy of this information. Use of a term in this book should not be regarded as affecting the validity of any trademark or service mark.

Windows NT is a registered trademark of Microsoft Corporation.

Executive Editor
Laurie Petrycki

Acquisitions Editor
Sean Angus

Development Editor
Nancy Warner

Technical Editor
Tom Borenberger

Manging Editor
Sarah Kearns

Project Editor
Tom Dinse

Copy Editors
Gayle Johnson
Howard Jones
Tonya Maddox

Indexer
Tim Wright

Cover Designer
Tim Amrhein

Book Designer
Gary Adair

Production Team Supervisor
Andrew Stone

Production
Betsy Deeter
Cynthia Davis-Hubler
Brad Lenser
Chris Livengood
Shawn Ring
Becky Stutzman

Contents

Acknowledgments

On a project as large as this, it is impossible to name all the people who have contributed to making this book possible. However, I would first like to thank two very special people from Sams Publishing, Kim Spilker and Sunthar Visuvalingam.

Kim got me involved in this project, and has been a continual source of support and encouragement throughout this project. She also deserves an award for working with me and my coauthors to coordinate all the schedules that have brought this book together in a timely manner.

Sunthar deserves a special thanks for having faith in my work and making contributions that developed this manuscript into an excellent resource. I would also like to thank both Sunthar and Kim for understanding and accepting my idiosyncrasies, and listening to me and taking action when things were not right.

Special thanks go to my coauthors for providing excellent material under extremely tight deadlines. These fine authors each bring a slightly different perspective to this book, providing a nice amount of variety. Without their support, it would have been impossible to keep the tight deadlines necessary to bring a book of this size to market in a timely fashion. I look forward to working with all of them on future projects.

I'd also like to thank the people at Microsoft, in particular the Windows NT development team for creating a superior product that does things the right way, and for their commitment to continuously making it better.

Most importantly, I'd like to thank my wife Marion for her support and understanding, even when the promise to spend only "one more hour" usually turned into four or five more hours. Also, to the rest of my family and friends, I am grateful for their understanding and continued encouragement, even when I was unable to return their calls, or visit as promised.

—*Jason Garms*

Windows NT Server Security Product Manager

About the Authors

Dan Balter

Dan Balter is a senior partner in Marina Consulting Group, a Microsoft Solution Provider located in Thousand Oaks, California. Dan works as an independent consultant and trainer who has been involved with several different network operating systems and PC application programs throughout his 12-year career. Dan takes pride in turning complex, technical topics into easy-to-understand concepts. He has specialized in integrating tax and accounting software into networked environments. Dan is certified as a Novell NetWare Engineer (CNE) and is very close to completing his certifications as a Microsoft Certified Systems Engineer (CSE) in addition to attaining the Certified Network Professional (CNP) designation as awarded by the international Network Professionals Association (NPA). Dan graduated from U.S.C.'s School of Business in 1983 and has been featured in more than 25 personal computer training videos, including Windows NT, and Windows 95, for KeyStone Learning Systems Corporation. Dan can be contacted by phone at 805-497-6100 or via the Internet at 73361.1611@compuserve.com.

Weiying Chen

Weiying Chen (v-weiyc@microsoft.com) is a software developer working for Microsoft Corporation. She specializes in developing Windows NT software, including custom server applications, OLE controls, and the container applications. Her current technology focus is OLE and ActiveX.

Jason Garms

Jason Garms (jason.garms@gsfc.nasa.gov) is the Windows NT Server Security Product Manager for Microsoft Corporation. He began working in the computer industry more than ten years ago and has been working with computers for longer than that. A Microsoft Certified Professional for both Windows NT Server and Workstation and a Microsoft Certified Systems Engineer, he also works extensively on other platforms, including MS-DOS, Windows 3.1, Windows 95, UNIX, and Macintosh systems. Jason has worked in a wide range of fields, including health care and medical services, the banking industry, various government agencies and contracting firms, and the publishing industry. His special topics of interest in Windows NT Server include Windows NT security, Windows NT architecture, and Macintosh connectivity. In addition to network engineering, Jason enjoys programming, graphics design, and researching the latest technologies for use in foreign language acquisition. He also contributed to *TCP/IP Unleashed* (Sams Publishing).

Joe Greene

Joe Greene has been playing with some of the best toys in the computer industry for more than a decade now. He has been lucky enough to draw assignment after assignment to learn and make those new, often experimental technologies work. Such was the case with Windows NT. After having worked for a while with Oracle databases and UNIX operating systems, he was assigned to make a Windows NT/Windows 95 workgroup environment support an Oracle Workgroup Server database for multimedia application development. After many hours experimenting with beta test software, a very productive environment was created that cost a small fraction of what it would have in other computer environments. He works in Pittsburgh, with a long-suffering wife who sees too much of the back of his head as he sits at the computer terminal writing books, working overtime, and testing new software. He is the author of the *Oracle DBA Survival Guide* and a contributing author of *Oracle Unleashed,* both from Sams Publishing.

Arthur Knowles

Arthur Knowles is president and founder of Knowles Consulting, a firm specializing in systems integration, training, and software development. Art is a Microsoft Certified System Engineer. His specialties include Microsoft Windows NT Server, Windows NT Workstation, SQL Server, Systems Management Server, Windows 95, and Windows for Workgroups. Art is the author of *Microsoft BackOffice Administrator's Survival Guide* (also by Sams Publishing), and has served as a contributing author to several books, including *Designing and Implementing the Internet Information Server* (Sams), *Windows 3.1 Configuration Secrets, Windows NT Unleashed* (Sams), and *Mastering Windows 95.* He is the forum manager of the Portable Computers Forum on The Microsoft Network. You can reach Art on the Internet at webmaster@nt-guru.com or on his Web site at http://www.nt-guru.com.

Terry W. Ogletree

Terry W. Ogletree is a consultant who divides his time between Atlanta, Georgia, and Raleigh, North Carolina. For over twenty years, he has worked with Digital's VAX/VMS systems and network products, and he has been involved with Windows NT since it was first released. He is the author of Windows NT Networking (vol. 4 of the *Windows NT 4* and *Web Site Library* book set) and he has contributed to other Sams titles, including *Windows NT Server 4 Unleashed Professional Edition* and *Peter Norton's Maximizing Windows NT Server 4.* You can reach Terry at togletree@mindspring.com.

Robert Reinstein

Robert Reinstein is a Microsoft Certified Systems Engineer. He is Senior Network Applications Manager at Manchester Equipment Company, Inc., a major systems integrator in Hauppauge, New York. He is also the author of a few popular shareware programs, a computer hobbyist, and loves the Beatles. Robert would like to thank his family—Lisa, Justin, Kevin, and Stephen—for their patience and support during the many weekends he spent writing this book. He would also like to thank Kathy Kelly for introducing him to the world of data processing way back in 1983, and Microsoft Corporation for producing great software. Contact Robert at robertr@mecnet.com or drop by his home page at http://ourworld.compuserve.com/homepages/r_reinstein.

Ken Rumble

Ken Rumble is a Microsoft Certified Trainer, Systems Engineer, and Solution Developer. He is currently emloyed by ObjectArts, an international technical training company specializing in Microsoft products. Mr. Rumble has 14 years teaching experience at both the college and corporate levels, and five years practical experience with Microsoft Windows NT operating system. He is a member of a team of dedicated trainers/consultants at ObjectArts who counsel a diverse collection of national an international corporations in the implementation of effective Microsoft Solutions. Mr. Rumble is based out of the company's New York office and can be reached at Krumble@ObjectArts.com.

David Wolfe

David Wolfe is an online techno-junky obsessed with all forms of telecommunications. He has written many telecommunication titles for John Wiley Publishing and is a regular feature writer for *Sysop News*. He has recently turned his attention to Windows NT's RAS feature, and his own Web site can sometimes be reached at http://pandy.com if he happens to have his Windows NT Server connected to the Internet. As a telecommunications developer for Core Technology in Indianapolis, he spends his days setting up RAS solutions for company clients. During his off hours, he spends his time setting up RAS solutions for private clients. David is the only known living person who can actually dial a phone by using his voice to mimic DTMF tones. (He's still working on pulse dialing.) He can be reached via email at dwolfe@iquest.net.

Tell Us What You Think!

As a reader, you are the most important critic and commentator of our books. We value your opinion and want to know what we're doing right, what we could do better, what areas you'd like to see us publish in, and any other words of wisdom you're willing to pass our way. You can help us make strong books that meet your needs and give you the computer guidance you require.

Check out our World Wide Web site at http://www.mcp.com.

> **NOTE**
>
> If you have a technical question about this book, call the technical support line at (317) 581-3833 or email us at support@mcp.com.

We welcome your comments. You can fax, email, or write us directly to let us know what you did or didn't like about this book—as well as what we can do to make our books stronger. Here's the information:

FAX: 317/817-7448
Email: networking@mcp.com
Mail: Comments Department
        Sams.net Publishing
        201 W. 103rd Street
        Indianapolis, IN 46290

What You Should Know Before Reading This Book

The goal in writing *Windows NT Server 4 Unleashed* was to provide you with a complete resource for basic to advanced features of Windows NT Server. In essence, it is meant for *anyone* who wants to learn about Windows NT Server. However, it does assume you've used a computer before in your life, and in particular, you have some background in using Windows 95. It assumes that you understand basic graphical user interface (GUI) terms such as *clicking* and *dragging*, as well as manipulating windows and pull-down menus. It also assumes you have some experience using a command-line system, such as DOS. Additionally, you are expected to have an interest in learning about Windows NT.

How This Book Is Organized

Most of the chapters in this book were intended to stand on their own as sources of information about a particular subject. Most of the chapters contain step-by-step procedures for accomplishing specific actions with Windows NT Server. Also included is theoretical and technical background knowledge that you must understand to properly install and make the most of Windows NT.

If you are new to Windows NT, and need to use this book to get up and running quickly, you might want to go directly to Chapter 4, "Installing Windows NT Server." This chapter will help you get a Windows NT Server system installed and will point you to specific chapters to gain more in-depth information on specific areas, such as configuring the TCP/IP protocol, which is covered in detail in Chapter 10, "Installing and Configuring Microsoft TCP/IP." But to fully understand the Windows NT environment, you should eventually go back and read Chapters 1 and 2, "Introduction to Windows NT," and "Building Blocks of Windows NT." These chapters will teach you why Windows NT does some of the things it does, from a historical, as well as a technological perspective.

Icons

In addition to providing notes, tips, and cautions, this book makes extensive use of icons to draw your attention to specific pieces of information that will help you understand what is going on, or simply provide supplementary information:

The architecture icon points you to text that describes the internal workings of Windows NT.

The networking icon shows you tips, techniques, or in-depth information about network connectivity.

The performance icon highlights a variety of optimization techniques.

The technical note icon shows you how to isolate a problem and decide exactly what to do.

The troubleshooting icon's text provides you with a tool or workaround for solving a particular problem.

The Windows NT Resource Kit icon highlights tools, information, and other resources available in the Windows NT Resource Kit.

The Version History icon points to text that explains the changes made to a feature over successive versions of Windows NT.

The third-party tools icon alerts you to information about Windows NT third-party tools and independent software vendors.

The security icon alerts you to security-related issues throughout the book.

The Registry icon highlights information for altering the Windows NT Registry settings so you can fine-tune various Windows NT services and fully configure its applications.

The command-line icon points out times you might want to use the DOS prompt instead of a graphical user interface.

Fundamentals of Windows NT Server

PART

I

Introducing Windows NT

by Jason Garms

IN THIS CHAPTER

CHAPTER 1

"He brought Windows to the World." The year is 2046. I just finished reading an interesting account of the evolution of the computer user interface. This quote hangs below an animation of Bill Gates lauding the release of "Cairo" at a conference in 1998. As everyone now recognizes, Bill Gates and Windows were the driving forces behind the 3-D interactive interface we all use today.

While this might sound funny, no one can deny that Microsoft's Windows family of products has changed the course of computing. I am not trying to be a revisionist by denying the existence of other graphical user interfaces (GUI), without which Microsoft Windows would never have been conceived. In fact, I have used with differing degrees of satisfaction so many different GUIs that I can't even count them with all my fingers.

However, it is definitely to Microsoft's (and Bill Gates') credit that Windows has survived a very unstable childhood and grown into the incredibly robust and stable operating system called Windows NT.

NOS, OS, But No DOS: An Introduction to Windows NT

Last week (we are now back in 1996!) I was leafing through the *Washington Post* Sunday Employment section, as I do occasionally to see what people are looking for, and everywhere I looked, I saw advertisements looking for people with Windows NT expertise. Not much longer than a year ago, most technical recruiters—and many IT specialists—didn't even know what NT was. Now, it is all the rage.

Why is that? To try to answer this question, let's look at what Windows NT is, and examine it in the context of 16- and 32-bit versions of Windows. Additionally, we'll take a look at how Windows NT is related to (or not related to) MS-DOS.

What Is Windows NT?

In 1988, Bill Gates commissioned the creation of a new operating system. The premise for the design of this new operating system was portability, security, compliance and compatibility, scalability, extensibility, and ease of internationalization. This meant that the system would need to run on different hardware platforms with minimal changes; it could be locked down through software, meeting NSA's C2-level criteria; it would be POSIX-compliant and run existing Windows applications; it would support symmetric multiprocessing (SMP); it could be easily expanded on by writing to a well-defined application programming interface (API); and it could easily be ported to run in numerous different languages and writing systems, with minimal modifications to the software. (See Table 1.1.)

1

Table 1.1. Foundation of Windows NT.

Premise	Description
Portability	The system would need to run on different hardware platforms with minimal changes.
Security	It could be locked down through software, meeting NSA's C2-level criteria.
Compliance and compatibility	It would be POSIX-compliant, run existing Windows applications, and support open international standards.
Scalability	It would support symmetric multiprocessing (SMP).
Extensibility	It could be easily expanded on by writing to a well-defined application programming interface (API).
Ease of internationalization	It could easily be ported to run in numerous different languages and writing systems, with minimal modifications to the software.

To design this system, Microsoft hired David Cutler, an operating system designer with Digital Equipment Corporation (DEC), and a group of his coworkers from DEC. David was renowned for his work on DEC operating systems, including RSX-11M (which helped turn DEC's PDP-11 mini-computer into a great world-wide success), and on his work with the VAX architecture.

It wasn't until almost five years and hundreds of millions of dollars later that Windows NT came to the market. The original version of Windows NT was called 3.1, which indicated its relationship to the Windows 3.1 user interface and its capability to run many Windows 3.1 programs. The similarities, however, stopped there.

The internals of Windows NT were written from scratch and centered around a microkernel-style architecture similar to UNIX. This microkernel gave Windows NT preemptive multitasking. Additionally, Windows NT made use of process *threads*—an idea popularized by Carnegie Mellon's MACH operating system—to support symmetric multiprocessing.

Using this microkernel as the foundation, Cutler's team added a number of features and services, including an integrated security subsystem, an abstracted, virtualized hardware interface, robust multiprotocol network support, fault tolerance, integrated GUI management tools, and much more.

When NT was finally released, Microsoft came to market with two different versions, Windows NT 3.1 and Windows NT Advanced Server 3.1. While these two products represented a tremendous achievement, their lack of compatibility with existing Windows programs and their steep hardware requirements prevented them from making significant in-roads in the network operating system environment, which was dominated by Novell's NetWare product.

In autumn 1994, Microsoft released NT 3.5. This release incorporated a number of important changes and enhancements, such as multiprotocol remote access services using the Point-to-Point Protocol (PPP), a reduced memory footprint, extensive bug fixes, a rewritten TCP/IP stack, and much more. Additionally, Microsoft renamed the products to Windows NT Workstation and Windows NT Server, which, coupled with a further optimization of the internal architectures, helped to better define the exact role of each product.

It was with this release that Windows NT began to legitimize its claim in the server market. The computer press began to turn out favorable reviews of NT Server and some people even began to predict that it could challenge Novell's market dominance.

Now with the 4.0 release of NT, Microsoft has made a concerted effort to make Windows NT the standard by which all others are judged. NT Server 4 includes not only the Windows 95 user interface, but a host of other features, such as Network OLE, Internet Information Server (IIS) 2.0, RAS multilink and RAS autodial, Point-to-Point Tunneling Protocol (PPTP), fully integrated DNS and WINS, integrated multiprotocol router, expanded driver support, improved performance, and much more.

16-bit and 32-bit Operating Systems

If you ask about the differences between a 16-bit and a 32-bit operating system, you'll get all kinds of responses. Very often they try to compare apples and oranges and mix them together with unrelated, but seemingly important "facts."

The essential difference between 16-bit and 32-bit operating systems is the way they handle internal structures. Additionally, some processors are optimized to work with structures of a particular size.

> **NOTE**
>
> Recently, Microsoft announced they would work on a pseudo-64-bit version of NT. Although the new system will not be fully 64-bit, it will permit 64-bit data structures and a 64-bit flat memory space. One area that will greatly benefit from this change will be databases. Using 64-bit addressing, you can support extremely large databases.

I'm not saying there isn't a difference. In fact, when we're talking about Microsoft Windows operating systems, there is a *big* difference between 16-bit and 32-bit versions. For example, one of the features of the 32-bit Microsoft operating systems is support for a 32-bit protected, flat memory model, which provides cleaner memory management than 16-bit Windows, and allows programs to create and address very large data structures.

The base of 32-bit Windows operating systems is a complete 32-bit kernel. The kernel does things such as system scheduling and memory management. Additionally, the 32-bit OS enables us to use 32-bit device drivers, which, among other advantages, enable the operating system to communicate with devices faster.

Most of the other features that come from 32-bit Windows operating systems come from their support of the Win32 API. This API set can only be fully implemented on a 32-bit kernel, such as Windows NT and Windows 95. Some of the advantages of the Win32 API are long filename support, 32-bit installable file systems, and better management of system resources.

No More DOS

Perhaps one of the greatest accomplishments for Windows NT was to get rid of DOS completely. In fact, when Microsoft first began work on the NT project, there were no firm plans to enable NT to run DOS *or* Windows applications. This, along with the fact that NT was conceived and designed by a group of programmers new to Microsoft, should be a convincing enough reason to believe that there is *no DOS* in Windows NT.

> **NOTE**
>
> Windows NT contains no DOS code in the operating system. Everything is done through emulation of standard DOS calls. Windows 95, in comparison, still relies on actual DOS code to run DOS applications. Windows 95 is actually two full operating systems in one package: Windows 4.0 and DOS 7.0.

Although there is no DOS, Windows NT is still able to run the vast majority of DOS programs as long as they don't try to directly access the hardware or require special device drivers. It does this by creating a virtual DOS environment called the NT Virtual DOS Machine (NTVDM). The DOS program runs in this emulated DOS environment. NT traps the DOS calls and converts them to standard Win32 API calls. In fact, this process means that certain DOS programs, such as disk intensive programs, can actually run *faster* in Windows NT than on a standard machine running DOS. Additionally, because the NTVDM provides emulated support for things like mouse drivers, network drivers, and CD-ROM drivers, you can actually get more free "conventional" memory in an NTVDM than would ever be possible running real MS-DOS.

Design Objectives of Windows NT Server

As mentioned previously, there was a definite set of goals in mind when Microsoft began developing Windows NT. These goals played a fundamental role in making NT the product it is today, and no discussion of Windows NT could be complete without addressing them.

Client/Server Operating System

When David Cutler was first brought to Microsoft to design the operating system that became Windows NT, he was sold on the idea that the operating system should be based on a client/server design. Under this paradigm the entire operating system would be divided into small self-contained units and would communicate with each other by passing well-defined messages back and forth. A unit that needed a service would pass a message to a unit that could provide the service. The requestor is the client and the provider is the server.

User programs, for example, would usually be the clients. They would request services from the protected subsystems, which in this case would be the servers. The protected subsystem would in turn play the part of a client and request services from other parts of the system.

The idea here is that each small portion of the operating system would run in its own protected memory space and would be isolated from interference from errant or invasive programs running on the system. Additionally, if a single server went down, it would not take down the rest of the system.

Flat, 32-bit Memory Model

Remember DOS? DOS was designed as a 16-bit operating system. This meant that memory structures could be addressed 16 bits at a time. Okay, so what does that mean? Well, two examples of where this 16-bit limit has created crippling effects on Windows 3.x today is in memory addressing and also in the file allocation table (FAT) scheme used for storing disk data.

With memory management, the 16-bit nature of DOS required that everything be written to 64KB (16-bit) code segments because you couldn't address anything larger than that. This process made writing software more difficult and cumbersome.

With the FAT, the 16-bit limit meant that only 65,536 clusters could be addressed on a single volume. Because at the time DOS was developed disks were very low capacity, this was not an issue. However, with today's high-capacity hard drives, this is a problem that results in enormous amounts of wasted space on large drives.

> **NOTE**
>
> To maintain compatibility, the NT version of FAT, called VFAT, still uses a 16-bit address for addressing clusters, limiting a FAT volume on FAT under NT to 65,536 clusters. Windows NT's solution to this limitation was to introduce a new file system—NTFS. Microsoft is also introducing a new 32-bit version of FAT for Windows 95 that corrects this problem, but the 32-bit version of FAT is incompatible with almost all existing disk tools.

Because Windows NT is a 32-bit operating system, it uses 32-bit addresses to access objects. This results in many advantages, one of which is NT's use of a 32-bit flat memory model as opposed to DOS's 16-bit segmented memory model. The 32-bit flat memory model enables NT to address 4,194,304KB (four gigabytes) of memory.

Reliability Through Protected Memory Model

One of the other concepts NT introduced into the Windows product family is the protected memory model. Windows 3.x inherited its memory structure from DOS. In this model, all programs essentially had access to any memory location, including memory segments belonging to the operating system itself. This meant that if an application misbehaved, it could accidentally write to a memory location belonging to another program, or even to the operating system itself. This resulted in a great deal of the instability of the Windows 3.x products. One misbehaved application could, and usually did, bring down the entire system.

In addition to accidental problems, the other down-side of this model was that any application could read information belonging to another, and thus no data was secure. A virus, for instance, could be written to snatch information, such as passwords, as the user entered it.

In Windows NT's memory model all processes get their own 32-bit address space. This 4GB space is divided in half, and the application can only really use the lower 2GB of space. The upper 2GB is for interfacing with other parts of the system. In this way, every process effectively thinks it is the only thing running. There is no way for a process to read or write outside of its own memory space, either accidentally, or intentionally. This has two very positive results. First, it prevents 90 percent of the system crashes that occurred in Windows 3.x. Second, it provides security for each process.

> **NOTE**
>
> Some 16-bit applications expect to run in a shared memory space with other programs, and some even rely on this to work properly. For this reason, Windows NT runs 16-bit applications in a shared memory space by default. This means that one 16-bit application could potentially interfere with other 16-bit applications in the shared memory space.

Preemptive Multitasking

There are two major types of operating system multitasking: cooperative and preemptive. The most common form on personal computers is cooperative multitasking, which is used by Windows 3.x and Apple's Mac OS.

In a cooperative multitasking environment the operating system gives control of the system to a particular application so it can run. When that application is finished, it returns control of the system to the operating system, which then gives control to the next application. Windows 3.1 uses a message queue to signal when an application was supposed to give up control. Applications were supposed to be written to check this queue regularly.

In this methodology, applications are expected to be good citizens, keeping control of the system only as long as necessary before passing control back to the OS. The downside here is that a single misbehaved application can seize control of the system, leaving everything else, including the operating system itself, starving for CPU time. Additionally, if a program crashes without returning control to the operating system, the entire system can hang.

In contrast to this is the preemptive multitasking model. The most common foundation for preemptive multitasking is a microkernel design, such as Windows NT and UNIX. With preemptive multitasking, the microkernel always maintains control of the system. It gives processes specific slices of time in which to run. At the end of that allotted time, the microkernel *preempts* the running process, and passes control to the next process.

An additional factor that needs to be addressed when discussing multitasking is the presence of non-re-entrant code. In a multitasking system there is often the need for a single segment of code to be simultaneously executed by more than one process, or even by multiple threads in the same process. Code that is written to support this is known as re-entrant code, while code that was not designed with this in mind is called non-re-entrant. Thus, in order to support full multitasking, the operating system code and the application code must be fully re-entrant. *All* the operating system code in Windows NT is re-entrant.

> **NOTE**
>
> For comparison, note that although Windows 95 provides a preemptive multitasking environment, large portions of the GDI and User routines are non-re-entrant. This was done to maintain full backward compatibility. The result is that Windows 95 "turns off" preemptive multitasking whenever an application accesses a piece of the non-re-entrant code. It has to do this to prevent possible application deadlock where two or more processes fight for access to the same piece of non-re-entrant code. Windows NT does not have this limitation.

Portability

Two years ago or so, public opinion in the computing industry was that Intel's x86 architecture, which included the 8086, 80286, 80386, i486, and Pentium processors, would eventually run out of steam. Intel's newer microprocessors would have to devote an increasing amount of valuable silicon and transistors to maintain compatibility with the older chips. The prediction was that eventually this would reach a point of diminishing returns. DOS and Windows were tied to this Intel chip family both because of the programs that were written to run on them, and also because of the reliance on assembly language programming to squeeze speed out of the operating systems.

Intel has spent lots of money and come up with some very creative chip designs to prove the naysayers wrong and help keep the x86 family alive. The Pentium Pro processor is just the latest example of their ingenuity. However, ultimately, as the programs themselves become more and more portable, the need for hardware compatibility with the older architecture diminishes.

The ultimate design, then, would be a portable operating system—one which could be quickly and easily moved to new chip architectures as they became available. Recognizing the importance of this, and hedging their bets about the future of the Intel x86 microprocessor family, Microsoft made portability one of the original design goals in Windows NT.

It is this portability that enables Windows NT to run not only on Intel x86 microprocessors but also on RISC chips, such as the DEC Alpha AXP, the MIPS R4400, and Motorola PowerPC.

Part of the key to Windows NT's portability is the hardware abstraction layer (HAL), which hides the difference in actual hardware from the higher level operating system software. The HAL makes all hardware look essentially identical to the rest of Windows NT.

Scalability

As it relates to Windows NT, scalability is used to refer to NT's capability to take full advantage of multiple processors in a single system. The key to scalability in Windows NT is symmetric multiprocessing (SMP). The SMP design in Windows NT Server enables you to run it on system with from 1 to 32 processors with up to four gigabytes of memory. NT dynamically assigns system and application threads for execution on different processors. The internal operations of Windows NT are designed to take full advantage of SMP systems.

Scalability, however, is not limited by the design of the operating system alone. Both the application software and hardware play a key role in determining the benefits of SMP. If an application is not designed to make effective use of the SMP environment, you might not gain worthwhile performance improvements by using SMP hardware. Likewise, the quality of the SMP hardware can greatly affect the performance of your system.

Personality/Compatibility

Personality is the key to compatibility. Most operating systems, such as DOS, are limited to a single personality. DOS can only run DOS programs. However, Windows NT was designed to support multiple simultaneous personalities. When Microsoft first began working on NT, they planned that it would support the OS/2 Presentation Manager interface as its primary personality. However, as the project continued, and the success of Windows grew, the Windows interface became the primary personality. In addition, Windows NT supports a POSIX personality, an OS/2 personality, and a DOS/Windows personality. Additional personalities such as a full UNIX personality can easily be added.

Localization

Microsoft recognizes the value and importance of products that integrate into the global marketplace. Windows NT is available in localized versions for Brazilian, Chinese, Danish, Dutch,

Finnish, French, German, Italian, Japanese, Korean, Norwegian, Portuguese, Russian, Spanish, and Swedish. In each of these versions, Microsoft has taken efforts to ensure that NT not only communicates in the particular language, but also employs standard idiom, uses correct punctuation in lists, dates, time, and numerical and currency output.

To support this localization, Windows NT uses the Unicode standard instead of the ASCII standard for representing characters. While the ASCII standard is popular in the United States, it lacks the capability to properly handle many of the characters needed in the international computing world. Unicode is a standard developed by a consortium of industry leaders, including Microsoft, Lotus, IBM, and Borland. While ASCII recognizes only 8-bit characters, meaning that a code-set can only contain 256 characters, the Unicode code-set is based on 16 bits, which means that it can represent 65,536 different characters.

NOTE

Windows 95 also supports Unicode. However, although Windows NT uses Unicode exclusively for storing internal data, Windows 95 still uses a substantial amount of non-Unicode fields in order to maintain backward compatibility.

NOTE

Even the next generation of the Mac OS, code-named Copland, will support the Unicode standard.

Although Windows NT provides full support for the ASCII code-set, Windows NT stores and manipulates all internal data structures using Unicode. This enables Microsoft to quickly and easily localize Windows NT for different languages and regions, including full support for Japanese Kanji and Chinese traditional and simplified character sets.

Security

When creating Windows NT, it was important that it meet a certifiable security standard. In this case, Microsoft chose to create Windows NT to meet the United States National Security Agency's C2 level evaluation criteria. By creating Windows NT based on a defined security model, Microsoft was able to guarantee that Windows NT would meet the most demanding corporate security needs. After all, the security of proprietary corporate data often translates directly into a monetary value for many corporations.

To enforce system security, NT has a robust security model that permeates every level of the operating system. This is unlike the flimsy security provided on other operating systems (including Windows 95), which is merely an easily broken wrapper on top of the operating system.

Fault-Tolerance

In order for Windows NT to be accepted as an enterprise workstation and server product, it was important to enable it to gracefully handle abnormal conditions. This is the essence of fault-tolerance. Windows NT has many features that provide varying levels of fault-tolerance for the system. Included in NT's list of fault-tolerant features are NT's journal-based, recoverable file system (NTFS), disk mirroring and disk striping with parity (RAID 1 and RAID 5), disk sector sparing, and support for an uninterruptible power supply (UPS).

Network Operating Systems

Windows NT is both an operating system and a network operating system. With LAN Manager, OS/2 was the operating system and LAN Manager was the network operating system. This integration of the OS and the NOS has proved to be a formidable combination in Windows NT.

What Is a Network Operating System?

A network operating system has traditionally been a method for describing the methods and protocols used by network clients when communicating with a network server. The most common transactions involved here are file and print services. This is a very simplified description, but it demonstrates the typical mentality used when designing these systems. Effectively, the NOS is centered at the server or servers.

Microsoft, however, has traditionally had a different approach to this concept, which has been heavily promulgated by Novell. Most of Microsoft's network-related products have obscured the line between operating system and network operating system. Windows NT is definitely no exception to this.

As we move into a period in computing when the network becomes more and more an integral part of the entire environment, the concept of and the need for a network operating system will disappear or, if you prefer, simply swallow up the underlying standalone operating system.

Summary

This chapter presented a high-level overview of Windows NT, discussing the premises upon which Windows NT was founded. You saw exactly how the designers of Windows NT implemented these goals in the final product.

You also saw how Windows NT represents the next generation of operating system, as well as a network operating system through its robust 32-bit design. You learned a little about the history of Windows NT, which shows that its designers took great care in crafting NT to be a true enterprise solution.

Building Blocks of Windows NT

by Jason Garms

IN THIS CHAPTER

The previous chapter gave you a pretty good idea about where Windows NT came from as well as some of its design objectives, such as scalability, portability, reliability, and compatibility. To meet these objectives, Microsoft had to first design a robust core that could handle not only today's needs, but could also be easily extended to support future needs.

This chapter discusses NT's architecture and how it is leveraged to achieve these goals.

An Overview of Windows NT's Architecture

The two major buzzwords to remember when talking about Windows NT's architecture are *modular* and *client/server*.

Modular means that the core internals are broken down into small, discrete units that serve clear and well-defined purposes, as shown in Figure 2.1. Modularity is a very desirable goal in all aspects of computer programming, and operating systems are no exception. Modular code is much easier to maintain because it has a clearly understood purpose, and entire code segments can be replaced without affecting routines that rely on it for services.

The modular design concept contrasts with the monolithic design methods used more often by earlier operating systems. In the monolithic design, the operating system runs in a privileged processor mode (discussed shortly) and blocks of code often provide many functions with little clear delineation, as shown in Figure 2.2. This allows for smaller and tighter code, but also makes the system less adaptable.

FIGURE 2.1.
The modular operating system design.

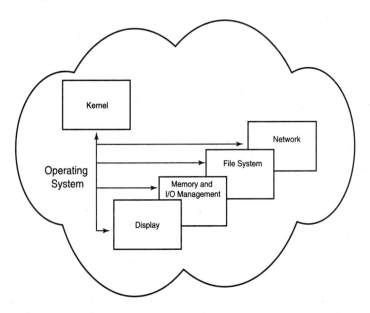

2

BUILDING BLOCKS
OF WINDOWS NT

FIGURE 2.2.

The monolithic operating system design.

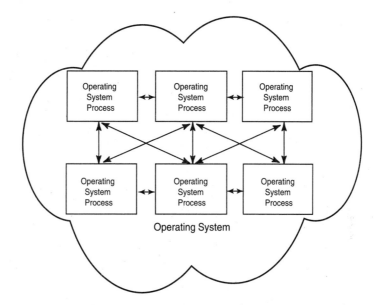

When people hear that Windows NT is a client/server operating system, they often assume this refers to NT's capability to be used in client/server database or network systems. While NT is an excellent choice for these applications, this is not what is meant when referring to NT's architecture. What is meant is that the internal pieces of NT communicate based on a client/server paradigm. More specifically, client/server refers to the organizational layout of NT's modular components, as shown in Figure 2.3. When a piece of code needs something, it is considered the client. The piece of code that fulfills the request is the server. For example, a user program that needs to draw a picture on the screen is a client. It uses a clearly defined message to ask another piece of code (in this case probably the Win32 subsystem) to draw the picture. The Win32 subsystem in this case is the server—thus, client/server.

FIGURE 2.3.

The client/server operating system design.

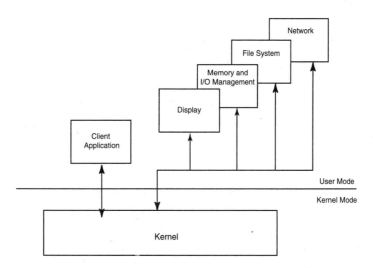

User Mode Versus Kernel Mode

One thing that NT shares with most advanced operating systems today is the division of the operating system tasks into multiple categories, which are correlated with actual modes supported by the microprocessor. Most microprocessors today support multiple modes, sometimes called rings, where programs can run. These modes provide the programs running inside them with different levels of privileges to access hardware and other programs running on the system. Windows NT uses a privileged mode and an unprivileged mode, usually referred to as kernel mode and user mode, respectively. Components that run in kernel mode have direct access to hardware and software resources on the system. Under Windows NT, only key pieces of the operating system are permitted to run in kernel mode. This is done to ensure the security and stability of the system. The NT Executive—which includes the microkernel, the hardware abstraction layer, and device drivers—is the only piece of Windows NT that runs in a processor's privileged kernel mode.

> **NOTE**
>
> Kernel-mode applications are protected from accidental or intentional tampering by the actual design of the microprocessor, while user-mode applications are protected from each other by the design of the operating system.

All programs not running in kernel mode run in user mode. The majority of code on Windows NT runs in user mode, including the environment subsystems, such as the Win32 subsystem and POSIX subsystem, and all user applications. These programs only have access to their own 32-bit memory addresses and interface with the rest of the system through client/server messaging, which will be described later.

With Windows NT, the creators tried to run as much of the operating system as possible in user mode. This helped to ensure the stability and security of the system, while at the same time simplified their job when they had to make modifications to underlying components.

Windows NT 4 brings a major architectural change to the NT operating system. They have moved two of the major subsystems, the USER and GDI code sections, into the NT Executive, which runs in kernel mode. While this was done to increase performance, and lower overhead, some people argue that the penalty will be reduced reliability. More on this design change is discussed later in this chapter.

NT Architecture Components

In order to understand how and why Windows NT works, it is important to take a look at the different pieces of the operating system and how they interact. Now that we understand a little about the premises behind NT, let's delve a little deeper. Figure 2.4 shows the major layers of Windows NT and their logical relationships.

FIGURE 2.4.

The Windows NT architecture.

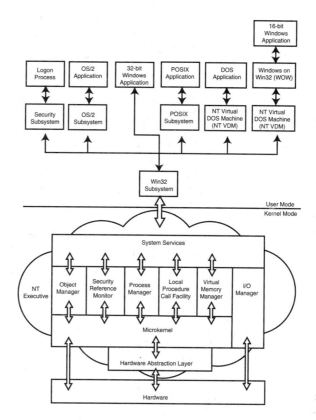

The four major pieces of the NT architecture follow:

- Hardware Abstraction Layer (HAL)
- Kernel
- NT Executive Services
- Environment Subsystems

Each piece in this model plays a well-defined role in making Windows NT work.

Hardware Abstraction Layer

The Hardware Abstraction Layer (HAL) is a software interface between the hardware and the rest of the operating system. The HAL is implemented as a dynamically linked library (DLL) and is responsible for shielding the rest of NT from hardware specifics such as interrupt controllers and I/O interfaces. This abstraction makes NT more portable because the rest of the operating system does not care what physical platform it is running on. Each hardware platform that NT runs on requires a specialized HAL. The design intent is that when NT is ported to a new processor architecture, the HAL gets rewritten for the new processor, but the rest of NT can simply be recompiled, thus making NT extremely portable.

The HAL also provides the interface for symmetric multiprocessing (SMP). NT Server ships with two HALs for each processor architecture (Intel, MIPS, PowerPC, and Alpha). The first HAL is used for supporting a single processor, while the second HAL supports up to four processors. Additional HALs are available from hardware vendors and can provide support for up to 32 processors on NT Server.

For each physical processor that resides in the computer, the HAL presents a *virtualized* processor to the microkernel. The intent is that this virtualized processor hides all the special characteristics of the processor itself from the operating system. For example if you had two multiprocessor systems, one running with Intel Pentium processors, and the other running with DEC Alpha AXP processors, the HALs on each system would be different, but the virtualized processor that the HAL presents to the microkernel would be identical in both cases. On an SMP system, for each physical processor in the system, the HAL presents one virtualized processor to the microkernel which represents a three-processor Intel Pentium system.

Although the intent of the HAL is to reduce the number of hardware dependencies and make NT more portable, in reality, it's not always quite so simple, but by minimizing the dependencies on physical hardware characteristics the designers of NT have reduced the time and effort needed to move the operating system to a new platform.

> **NOTE**
>
> During the initial development phase for Windows NT, all initial coding was done on hardware powered by Intel's I860 RISC chip. However, because of dwindling support for the chip by Intel, as well as design problems encountered during development, the chip was abandoned and the development effort was moved to the MIPS chipset with minimal problems. This is a perfect example of the portability of the NT operating system.

The HAL can only be accessed by components of the NT Executive, and is never called directly by user-mode programs. Also, the HAL is intended to be the only piece of software on an NT system that is permitted to talk directly to the hardware. The advantage is that rogue programs cannot purposefully or accidentally write information to the hardware and cause a system crash. Also, preventing programs from reading information directly from the hardware helps to support NT's security model.

Although the goal in Windows NT is to have all hardware-related calls go through the HAL, the reality is that a small number of device driver and kernel calls bypass the HAL and directly interact with the hardware.

The downside of the HAL model is that it is the biggest single cause of incompatibility with older DOS and Windows programs, which were in the habit of reading and writing directly to hardware. However, this incompatibility is a small price to pay for the protection and portability afforded by the HAL.

Kernel

The kernel in Windows NT is like the President of the United States. The kernel is ultimately responsible for all actions on the system, and almost all functions on the system pass through the kernel. Windows NT uses a *microkernel*, which essentially means that the kernel was pared down to the basics necessary to function.

> **NOTE**
>
> Do not confuse the *kernel*—or *microkernel*—with *kernel mode*. While they are related, they are not the same thing. The *kernel* is a discrete piece of code that makes up the core of the operating system. *Kernel mode* is a privileged state of operations supported by the microprocessor. In Windows NT, the *microkernel* runs in *kernel mode*, which means that it runs in a privileged processor mode, where the microprocessor is responsible for protecting the kernel from harm.

This microkernel design in Windows NT assigns many of the functions normally assigned to the kernel in traditional operating systems to a group of programs called the NT Executive. The NT Executive, of which the NT microkernel is a part, runs in the processor's privileged kernel mode. The NT microkernel communicates with the NT Executive through a set of low-level operating system primitives.

> **NOTE**
>
> *Threads* and *processes* are defined later in this chapter in a section titled "Process Manager."

The major role of the kernel in Windows NT is to dispatch and schedule threads. A thread is a code segment belonging to a particular process. Each thread is assigned a priority number from 0 to 31. The kernel dispatches threads to run on available processors based on their priority numbers. The kernel then allows the threads to execute for a particular amount of time before *preempting* them and allowing another process to run.

> **NOTE**
>
> Sometimes you see it written that the kernel schedules *processes*. While this is not technically correct, it is commonly stated this way for ease of explanation. The kernel does not actually schedule processes, it only schedules *threads in the context of a process*. For more on the distinction between processes and threads, see the section "Process Manager," later in this chapter.

It is this procedure that makes preemptive multitasking possible. Because it is the kernel that schedules the execution of all code on the system, it *cannot* be preempted. It also cannot be paged to disk for any reason.

On a multiprocessor system, a copy of the kernel actually runs on each processor. These kernel segments are used to maintain coherency of shared system resources that need to be accessed by threads running on all processors.

The kernel is also responsible for handling system interrupts from physical devices such as I/O devices, processor clocks, or timers. Normally, when there is a system interrupt, the kernel will preempt a running thread to process the interrupt.

Additionally, the kernel handles processor exceptions. These exceptions occur when the processor is made to do something it doesn't permit, such as writing to a locked portion of memory or dividing by zero.

The final use of the kernel in Windows NT is to provide support for power failure recovery. If the NT system is equipped with an intelligent uninterruptible power supply (UPS), the kernel is notified when a power failure is detected. The kernel then coordinates an orderly shutdown of the system, which includes notifying I/O devices of the power failure and allowing them to reset accordingly.

> **NOTE**
>
> Because the kernel is involved in almost every action taken on an NT system, critical portions of the kernel are written in assembly language. This ensures that it can run as fast and efficiently as possible. For this reason, kernel optimization is a critical factor of performance when NT is ported to different architectures.

The NT Executive

Continuing the analogy that the NT kernel is like the President of the United States, the NT Executive is like his direct staff. (The President is the head of the Executive branch, much like the kernel is the head of the NT Executive.) The NT Executive takes care of the important tasks that are vital to the entire system, but that the kernel is too busy to address directly.

A clear, concise definition is that *the NT Executive provides the operating system fundamentals that can be provided to all other applications running on the system.* This includes services such as object management, virtual memory management, I/O management, and process management.

> **NOTE**
>
> Remember, the NT kernel is actually *part* of the NT Executive.

The NT Executive runs exclusively in kernel mode and is called by the protected environment subsystems when they need services. Because of the hierarchy of Windows NT, user applications do not call pieces of the NT Executive directly, but rather request services from the environment subsystems, such as the Win32 and POSIX subsystems, which then in turn call the NT Executive components.

There are functions inside the NT Executive that are not exposed by existing API sets. This is because the designers of Windows NT tried to include hooks—or placeholders—in the operating system to provide room for future growth.

Aside from the kernel itself, the major pieces of the NT Executive are as follows:

- Object Manager
- Process Manager
- Virtual Memory Manager
- Local Procedure Call Facility
- Security Reference Monitor
- I/O Manager

Let's take a few moments to look at these other pieces of the NT Executive and see what they do and how they interact.

Object Manager

The Object Manager piece of the NT Executive is used to create, modify, and delete objects used by all the systems that make up the NT Executive. Objects are abstract data types that are used to represent operating system resources. It also provides information on the status of objects to the rest of the operating system.

Objects can be concrete, such as a device port, or they can be more abstract, such as a thread. When an object is created, it is given a name by which other programs can access the object. When another process wants to access the object, it requests an *object handle* from the Object Manager. The object handle provides a pointer that is used to locate the actual object, as well as access control information that tells how the object can be accessed. This access control information is provided by the NT security subsystem.

The Object Manager also makes sure an object does not consume too many resources (usually system memory) by maintaining quotas for different object types.

In addition, the Object Manager is responsible for cleaning up orphaned objects that seem to have no owner. This is known as garbage collection. Lack of a similar facility in Windows 3.x was a major cause of trouble. In Windows 3.x, if a program crashed, or if it didn't handle system resources properly, the system resources it consumed would not be properly returned to the available system pool, resulting in an error message about the lack of system resources. In effect, this was a memory leak.

Process Manager

The Process Manager is responsible for creating, removing, and modifying the states of all processes and threads. It also provides information on the status of processes and threads to the rest of the system.

> **NOTE**
>
> A *process*, by definition, includes a virtual address space, one or more threads, a piece of executable program code, and a set of system resources. A *thread* is an executable object that belongs to a single process and contains a program counter, which points to its current position in the process's executable code segment, two stacks, and a set of register values.

The Process Manager, like all members of the NT Executive, plays a vital role in the operation of the entire system. When an application is started, it is created as a process, which requires a call to the Process Manager. Because every process must have at least one thread, the Process Manager is invoked again to create a thread, as represented by the flow diagram in Figure 2.5.

The Process Manager is used to manage threads, but it does not have its own set of policies about how and when processes and threads should be scheduled. These policies are determined by the microkernel itself.

FIGURE 2.5.

Flow diagram showing the calls to the Process Manager when an application is started.

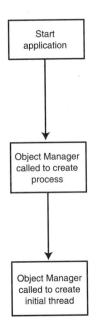

Virtual Memory Manager

The Virtual Memory Manager (VMM) provides management of the system's virtual memory pool. Virtual memory is a scheme that allows disk resources to be used instead of physical system memory by moving *pages* out to disk when they are not in use and retrieving them when they are needed. This is an integral piece of Windows NT, which allocates a 32-bit address space to each process regardless of the actual amount of physical memory in the system.

Each process is allocated a 4GB virtual memory space. Of this space, the upper two gigabytes are reserved for system use, while the lower 2GB are for the process's use. The process addresses memory as if it were the only thing around. The Virtual Memory Manager is responsible for translating the process's memory addresses into actual system memory addresses. If the process's memory address refers to a piece of memory that has been paged to disk, the VMM retrieves the page from disk.

Local Procedure Call Facility

The Local Procedure Call (LPC) facility is integral to the client/server design of Windows NT. It is the interface between all client and server processes running on a local Windows NT system.

The LPC structure is very similar to remote procedure calls (RPCs), except that it is optimized for—and only supports—communication between client and server processes on a local machine. More specifically, the LPC is a mechanism that enables two threads in different processes to exchange information.

Remember we said that the Win32 subsystem is a user-mode application and runs in its own memory space. When a program wants to communicate with the Win32 subsystem to request services, it calls a stub function from the appropriate DLL file. This stub function then uses the LPC facility to pass the request to the Win32 subsystem process, which processes the request and performs the requested action and returns any completion message through the LPC.

Security Reference Monitor

The Security Reference Monitor (SRM) is the bedrock of all security on a Windows NT system and is responsible for enforcing all security policies on the local computer.

It does this by working together with the *logon process* and *local security authority* runtime subsystems. When a user logs onto the Windows NT system and his or her credentials are verified, the logon process subsystem requests a *security access token* (SAT) for the user. The SAT contains a list of the user's privileges and group memberships. This is used as a key for that user during this logon session. Whenever the user wants to do something, the SAT is presented and used to determine if the user can perform that action.

This is where the SRM works closely with the Object Manager. Each time a user tries to access an object, the Object Manager creates a handle for accessing the object and calls the SRM to determine the level of access to be granted by the handle. The SRM uses information contained in the user's access token, and compares it to the access control list on the object to see whether the user should be granted the requested level of access to the object. In this way, the SRM has control over the security of all object access in Windows NT.

I/O Manager

The I/O Manager is responsible for coordinating and processing all system input and output. It oversees the device drivers, installable file systems, network redirectors, and the system cache.

The I/O Manager takes care of the black magic that is often necessary to make various devices talk to each other and live together in peace. It removes the traditional monolithic method of designing I/O drivers and presents a layered approach that supports mixing and matching of components as necessary.

Protected Environment Subsystems

Two of the design goals of Windows NT were *personality* and *compatibility*. These are both achieved through the protected environment subsystems.

Personality essentially means that Windows NT exposes multiple sets of application programming interfaces (APIs) and can effectively act as if it were a different operating system. Windows NT comes with a POSIX and OS/2 personality in addition to its Win32, Win16, and DOS personalities.

Although having multiple personalities in people is considered a bad thing, in operating systems it provides an effective way for the system to maintain compatibility. Windows NT would not have been such a success if it had been completely unable to run any existing DOS and Windows software.

In Windows NT, there are three protected environment subsystems:

- Win32 subsystem
- POSIX subsystem
- OS/2 subsystem

> **NOTE**
>
> Although you might see the Win16 and DOS personalities included in a list of protected environment subsystems, they are actually both part of the Win32 subsystem.

The protected environment subsystems act as mediators between the user-level applications and the NT Executive.

Remember we said that the NT Executive and all its components live in kernel mode, while essentially everything else lives in user mode. This includes all environment subsystems, which function *completely* in user mode. When an application makes a call to an environmental subsystem, it is passed through a system services layer to the NT Executive.

Each environment subsystem keeps track of its own processes and works independently of the other subsystems. Each application can run only in the subsystem for which it was designed. When you launch an application in Windows NT, it looks at the image header for the file and determines which subsystem to run the application in.

Let's take a look at how each of these subsystems work.

Win32

Win32 is the native and primary subsystem for Windows NT. The basis for this subsystem is the Win32 set of APIs, which were written during the development of the NT product. Many of these APIs are direct extensions of their Win16 counterparts.

> **NOTE**
>
> Win32 is the name of both the API and the NT subsystem for services in Win32 API-related calls.

> **NOTE**
>
> For the first year and a half of its design, the OS/2 Presentation Manager was scheduled to be the default and primary subsystem for Windows NT. However, with the success of Windows 3.x, Microsoft decided to use the Windows interface and related APIs as the primary personality.

In the client/server model we discussed previously, the Win32 subsystem acts as a server for all the other environment subsystems supported on Windows NT. The other environment subsystems act as clients and translate their API calls into the appropriate Win32 APIs, which are serviced by the Win32 subsystem.

The Win32 subsystem is responsible for all user input and output. It owns the display, keyboard, and mouse. When other subsystems, such as OS/2 or POSIX, need to take advantage of these devices, they request the services from the Win32 subsystem.

When originally designing the Win32 subsystem, NT's creators tried to make its overall functioning as close as possible to Windows 3.x. This resulted in a design with five major pieces: the window manager (often called USER), the graphics device interface (GDI), the console, operating system functions, and Win32 graphics device drivers, as shown in Figure 2.6.

FIGURE 2.6.

*The original Win32
subsystem in
Windows NT.*

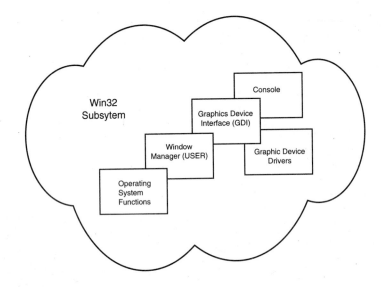

However, in Windows NT 4 the organization of the Win32 subsystem has changed. You'll notice in the preceding figure that the graphics device interface (GDI) and window manager (USER) are included inside the Win32 subsystem.

Because we've already identified that all other subsystems use the Win32 API for user input and output, the NT team removed the GDI and USER sections from the Win32 subsystem and moved them into the NT Executive.

This helped to reduce the overhead for all processes on the system that took advantage of any services requiring these code servers.

There has been a lot of speculation about what this move has done to the stability of Windows NT. Many people criticize this move, arguing that allowing more code to run in kernel mode increases the likelihood of system crashes, because kernel-mode processes have access to system resources.

I don't think this is true. With the original model—where the GDI and USER were in the Win32 subsystem—all programs that relied on the GDI or USER services would fail to respond if there were problems, which resulted in the entire user interface locking up.

However, by moving these two pieces entirely into the NT Executive, the kernel can keep an eye on them. If they fail to respond, rather than having the system lock up, the kernel can issue a bug check (the NT blue screen of death), and allow the system to reboot.

In most instances, this is a more desirable result because allowing the NT kernel to reboot the system when an essential service fails is considerably better than having the system lock up and be completely unusable.

There are people who argue the pros and cons for both methods. However, the ultimate decision about the stability of this new model will be decided by time and testing of Windows NT 4.

MS-DOS and Win16

One of the keys to success for Windows NT is the capability to run most Windows 3.x and DOS applications. During the initial development period for Windows NT, there were some mixed feelings between the design team and Microsoft management about whether Windows NT should be able to run these programs.

Microsoft management recognized that if Windows NT were not backward compatible, users would have to make a tremendous investment to upgrade their current software. This alone would make Windows NT prohibitively expensive. So the decision was made to support 16-bit Windows programs as well as DOS applications.

The decision to support these personalities was easily accommodated by NT's robust design.

Some of the goals were as follows:

- To enable DOS programs to run without modification
- To provide the capability to run the majority of 16-bit Windows applications without modification
- To protect the system and other 32-bit applications from interference from the 16-bit and DOS programs
- To enable the RISC platforms to run 16-bit Windows and DOS programs
- To provide a mechanism for the sharing of data between 32-bit and 16-bit Windows programs

Many people think of Windows 3.x as an operating system. Technically, it is not a true operating system, but rather a user interface that sits on top of DOS—the true operating system.

So, the first step in providing compatibility was to create a DOS environment. The DOS environment in Windows NT is called the *virtual DOS machine* (VDM), also referred to as the NTVDM. The VDM is a full 32-bit user-mode application that requests services from the Win32 subsystem and occasionally directly from the NT system services layer. It is based on DOS 5.0 and provides compatibility as such.

Windows NT enables you to run as many DOS applications as you want, and each application runs in its own VDM. Because the VDMs are nothing more than normal processes under Windows NT, they are preemptively multitasked along with other processes on the system. Therefore, it can be said that Windows NT allows for the preemptive multitasking of DOS programs.

One of the additional features of the VDM is that it gives the user over 620KB of free "conventional" memory. The miraculous thing about this is that it also gives the DOS application full mouse, network, and CD-ROM support. This is more free memory than you could ever hope to get on an equivalent DOS system with the same services loaded.

Much as Windows 3.x relies on the services provided by DOS, the Win16 subsystem on Windows NT relies on the Windows NT VDM. The 16-bit Windows emulator in a VDM is called WOW, which stands for *Windows on Win32*. Because it lives inside the VDM, it requests most of its services from the VDM the same way that standard Windows 3 requests services from DOS. The VDM then converts most of these calls directly into calls that are sent to the Win32 subsystem.

When a 16-bit Windows program makes a Win16 API call, the WOW subsystem uses a process called *thunking* to convert this call to an equivalent Win32 API call, which is then passed through to the Win32 subsystem. Likewise, when data from a Win32 call needs to be returned to a Win16 application, it must also be thunked.

Thunking is necessary because there must be a standard set of rules when converting from 16-bit data formats to 32-bit formats and vice versa. Going from 16-bit to 32-bit is easy because you simply pad the extra 16 bits with zeros. However, going from 32-bit to 16-bit by simply dropping 16 bits would surely result in data loss. The thunking process is actually performed inside the Win32 subsystem, as shown in Figure 2.7.

FIGURE 2.7.

Thunking converts 16-bit API calls to 32-bit API calls, and vice versa.

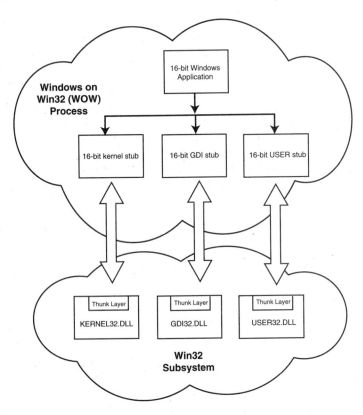

Because the Windows 3.x environment uses a shared memory model, many programs were written to expect, and even require, this shared address space. To help maintain compatibility with these applications, all 16-bit Windows programs are run in a single VDM.

The WOW subsystem is not multithreaded, and 16-bit Windows applications are cooperatively multitasked against each other, just like they would be on a real Windows system.

> **NOTE**
>
> Okay. I lied. Each time you launch a 16-bit Windows application, a new thread is created, so effectively the WOW is multithreaded. However, the microkernel schedules these threads in a different way than the rest of the threads on the system.

Normally, the NT kernel schedules threads based on priority. When a running thread is preempted, the kernel passes control to the next thread based on priority. The kernel treats the WOW threads differently. When it preempts the currently running WOW thread, it runs other threads just as it normally would. However, it will not schedule execution for any other WOW thread until this WOW thread gives up control.

So while the WOW actually has more than one thread, they are not actually taken advantage of. Remember, this is not a design flaw, but was done very carefully to maintain compatibility with existing 16-bit software that would break if it were preemptively multitasked against its fellow 16-bit applications.

Also, because all the applications in the WOW run in a single, shared memory space, if one 16-bit Windows application fails, it can cause all the 16-bit Windows applications running in that WOW subsystem to fail. However, it would not in any way affect the system itself, or any 32-bit applications running on it.

> **NOTE**
>
> Remember the difference: All DOS programs are run in separate VDMs and are preemptively multitasked. 16-bit Windows applications, on the other hand, are run in a single VDM and are cooperatively multitasked against each other, but preemptively multitasked against the rest of the system.

Because the DOS and Windows 3.x applications make heavy use of Intel assembly language code, it was tricky to get these programs to work unmodified on RISC systems supported by Windows NT. However, this was accomplished with a little ingenuity. The VDM breaks down all calls into an *instruction execution unit* (IEU). On the Intel architecture, these calls can be directly executed by the processor. On RISC systems, they are converted by an Intel emulation routine written by Insignia Solutions, Ltd. (These are the same people who write SoftWindows for the Macintosh.)

In versions of Windows NT prior to 4, the emulation code was based on a 286-class processor. This caused problems in that 16-bit Windows programs that required 386 enhanced mode could not be run on Windows NT under the WOW emulation on RISC processors. For example, programs like Microsoft Office, which requires 386 enhanced mode, could not run on RISC platforms.

One of the major advancements of Windows NT 4 is that this emulation routine was upgraded to include full compatibility with the 486 instruction set.

POSIX

As I have identified in other places, Microsoft paid close attention to various open systems standards when developing Windows NT. They recognized the value of supporting open systems as a method for gaining acceptance of their new advanced operating system into the market.

One of the most frequently cited standards supported by Windows NT is its POSIX compliance. POSIX stands for *portable operating system interface* and was developed by the IEEE as a method of providing application portability on UNIX platforms. However, POSIX has been integrated into many non-UNIX systems.

There are many levels of POSIX compliance ranging from POSIX.0 to POSIX.12. These levels represent an evolving set of proposals, not all of which have been ratified as standards.

The POSIX subsystem in Windows NT is POSIX.1 compliant. POSIX.1 compliance requires a bare minimum of services, which are provided by Windows NT. When a POSIX application runs on Windows NT, the POSIX subsystem is loaded and it translates the C language API calls—required for POSIX.1 support—into Win32 API calls, which are then serviced by the Win32 subsystem.

Because of the limited nature of POSIX.1, the POSIX subsystem on Windows NT does not provide any support for networking or system security.

Some of the features required by POSIX.1 follow:

- Case-sensitive filenames, which are supported by the NTFS file system.
- Multiple filename support (hard links), which are also supported by NTFS.
- File system traverse checking, which is controlled by the user right *bypass traverse checking*. In order to enable POSIX compliance for a particular user, you must remove this user right from that user.

Each POSIX application runs in its own memory address space, and is preemptively multitasked.

Different people have different opinions on why the POSIX subsystem was included with Windows NT. Some people think that it was done to increase application availability for end users. Some people think it was done in the noble pursuit of conforming to open systems standards. Yet others think it was done to demonstrate the interoperability of NT with UNIX platforms.

My take on this is different. While I accept that the POSIX subsystem is well implemented, I personally think the entire reason for the inclusion of the POSIX subsystem was to meet government buying criteria. For those of you not familiar with the process, it is not uncommon for government agencies to require that a particular system meet criteria based on various open system standards. One such example is the *Federal Information Processing Standards* (FIPS). By including the POSIX subsystem, Windows NT can be sold into large markets where it might easily have been excluded from for lack of support for this standard.

So you see, it's really a marketing ploy to increase NT's market penetration and to prevent people from using sometimes irrelevant purchasing criteria to exclude Windows NT from their environment.

NT is a great operating system. While the ease with which the POSIX subsystem was included with NT is indicative of NT's power and flexibility, don't be fooled into making too much of the POSIX subsystem.

OS/2

Windows NT was originally slated to be the next generation of OS/2. As such, it would have included the OS/2 Presentation Manager interface as its primary interface and would have run all standard OS/2 applications, including character-based and GUI-based programs.

However, when the decision was made to give NT the Windows interface and to build it as the successor for the Windows platform, the emphasis on OS/2 support was diminished.

The result was an OS/2 subsystem capable of running standard OS/2 1.x character-mode applications. It cannot run OS/2 2.x graphical applications.

NOTE

The OS/2 subsystem only works on Intel-based systems, not on RISC platforms.

The OS/2 subsystem is implemented as a protected environment subsystem, much like the POSIX subsystem. It translates OS/2 API calls into Win32 API calls that are serviced by the Win32 subsystem.

The OS/2 subsystem and each OS/2 application runs in their own 32-bit protected memory spaces and are preemptively multitasked in respect to each other and in respect to other applications running on the system.

In addition to a core set of OS/2 APIs, the NT OS/2 subsystem implements many LAN Manager APIs, including NetBIOS, mailslots, and named pipes. In this way it differs from the POSIX subsystem, which exposes no API support for networking.

Summary

Windows NT is a modular and well-planned operating system that provides a robust structure for today's most demanding applications. In addition, it provides room for growth, while adhering to its original design goals. This chapter presented you with an introduction to the architecture of Windows NT, and an insight into what makes Windows NT the best enterprise platform for both small businesses needs and mission-critical client/server applications.

The chapter began with an overview of the components of the NT architecture, as well as an introduction to some concepts required for discussion of the NT architecture, such as the difference between the privileged *kernel mode*, and unprivileged *user mode*. It continued with a more in-depth look at the NT components, including the Hardware Abstraction Layer (HAL), the NT kernel, the NT Executive services, and the protected environment subsystems.

In each of these sections, you saw the subcomponents and how they worked together to provide a rich client/server environment. For example, you saw the interoperation of the members of the NT Executive, including the Object Manager, Process Manager, Virtual Memory Manager, Local Procedure Call Facility, Security Reference Monitor, and I/O Manager, and how they provided services to NT's microkernel, as well as to the protected environment subsystems.

The chapter ended with a look at each of the protected environment subsystems, Win32, POSIX, and OS/2. When looking at the Win32 subsystem, you saw its key relationship to the rest of the NT environment, and how it supported not only Win32 applications, but also 16-bit Windows applications, DOS applications, and I/O services for the POSIX and OS/2 subsystems.

This architecture is what sets Windows NT apart from Windows 3.x and Windows 95, which, for compatibility reasons, could not build a new architecture from the ground up, but rather had to build on the crippled and antiquated foundation of DOS. It is also from this architecture that NT gets its incredible performance and reliability that make Windows NT Server such a desirable server and network operating system.

Windows NT Workstation Versus Windows NT Server

by Jason Garms

CHAPTER 3

IN THIS CHAPTER

Why Two Products?

When Microsoft introduced Windows NT in 1993, they offered two products: Windows NT 3.1 and Windows NT Advanced Server 3.1. The problem was that the exact roles of these two products had not been clearly defined in Microsoft's marketing strategy. This led to confusion about which product should be used in what environments.

With the introduction of 3.5 in late 1994, Microsoft changed the product names, their feature sets, and gave a clear indication of what roles each product was designed for. Windows NT became Windows NT Workstation, and Windows NT Advanced Server became Windows NT Server.

Windows NT Workstation was designed as a robust, 32-bit multithreaded, multitasking operating system that was capable of running high-end engineering or mission-critical client/server applications.

Windows NT Server became the cornerstone of Microsoft's enterprise-class network operating system. Windows NT Server was designed to provide file, print, and application services to diverse clients.

Features Common to Both Windows NT Server and Windows NT Workstation

Windows NT Workstation and Windows NT Server are both built using the same core technologies, resulting in products with more similarities than differences. Some of the features common to both Windows NT products are

- High-performance client/server platform
- Network foundation
- GUI management tools
- NetWare integration
- Robust TCP/IP services
- Remote Access Service (RAS)
- Integrated C2-level security
- Built-in backup
- Advanced file systems

High-Performance Client/Server Platform

The Windows NT platform was designed to provide a powerful operating-system platform capable of scaling from the simplest file and print services network, to the largest enterprise network providing file and print services to thousands of users, as well as advanced messaging and application services.

To achieve this, Windows NT was designed with a microkernel capable of preemptively dispatching threads to up to 32 processors. This provides scalability, both for servers and for high-demand workstations. Furthermore, by providing preemptive multitasking, NT can prevent any single process from monopolizing the processor.

Windows NT is a true 32-bit operating system, with no internal 16-bit code, unlike Windows 95, which still has a considerable amount of 16-bit code under the hood for compatibility with older versions of Windows. As a result, Windows NT is capable of taking full advantage of the powerful features of today's most advanced microprocessors, including Intel's new Pentium Pro processor.

In order to properly fit the role of a mission-critical operating system, Windows NT provides memory protection for all user-level processes. The NT kernel runs in its own 32-bit, virtualized address space. Additionally, every 32-bit program runs in its own address space. With 16-bit Windows programs, you have the option of running each process in its own memory space, or in a memory space shared by other Windows programs. In any case, programs cannot write to another program's address space, preventing an errant program from stepping on other programs or on the operating system itself.

On the hardware side, NT supports 4GB of RAM per system and 2GB of virtual memory per application. Additionally, it can address up to 402 million TB of data storage per system. With the capability to take advantage of this kind of hardware, NT is fully capable of meeting the needs of enterprise-level client/server.

Additionally, Windows NT, unlike Windows 3.x and Windows 95, is capable of running on many different processor architectures, although Windows 3.x and its descendants are supported only on the Intel x86 platform. Windows NT will also take full advantage of powerful RISC processors such as the DEC Alpha AXP, MIPS R4400, and IBM/Motorola PowerPC processors. This means that no matter how much processing power you need, Windows NT will be able to accommodate you.

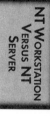

Network Foundation

The core networking components are virtually identical between NT Server and NT Workstation. As mentioned in Chapter 1, "Introducing Windows NT," networking was built into Windows NT from the beginning; it is one of the fundamental elements of the NT architecture.

For many people coming from an MS-DOS/Windows networking background, file and print services are traditionally based on either a client/server model or a peer-to-peer model. Windows NT is more like a hybrid of the two. Essentially, an NT Server is optimized to act as a server, but you can also use it as a workstation. Likewise, NT Workstation is optimized as a desktop workstation, but it can also be used as a server. This differs greatly from the Novell model, wherein you have dedicated servers and dedicated clients that are built on completely different architectural models.

Windows NT uses the NDIS 3.0 standard to support numerous transport protocols. Support is built into the product for TCP/IP, NetBEUI, IPX/SPX, DLC, and AppleTalk. Windows NT can provide traditional Microsoft file and print services over TCP/IP, IPX/SPX, and NetBEUI. DLC is supported for printing to network-connected printers and IBM mainframe connectivity. AppleTalk is supported on NT Server for providing Macintosh file and print services and on NT Workstation for administering NT Servers running file and print services for Macintosh.

Both NT Server and NT Workstation provide standard TCP/IP utilities, including Telnet and FTP clients. Additionally, an FTP Server service can be installed to provide TCP/IP-based file transfer between NT and UNIX hosts or any other system with an FTP client.

GUI Management Tools

Windows NT includes a full set of powerful GUI tools for administering most parts of the operating system. These tools include

- **User Manager:** This utility allows you to create and manage user accounts and groups, as well as user rights, and system-wide password and auditing policies. On an NT domain controller, it is also used for setting up inter-domain trust relationships, which allow user accounts in other domains to be granted access to local resources. This application actually comes in two flavors: *User Manager* and *User Manager for Domains*. User Manager is installed on NT Workstations and stand-alone NT Servers, and is used for administering the local user account database. User Manager for Domains has all the features of User Manager and includes features related to domain management. Another advantage of the User Manager for Domains is that it permits you to remotely manage the user account databases on other NT systems. It is installed by default on all NT Servers installed as domain controllers. Additionally, it can be installed on NT Workstations, and NT Servers that are not configured as domain controllers. A version is also available for Windows 3.1x and Windows 95. The User Manager and User Manager for Domains are discussed in greater depth in Chapter 17, "User Administration."

NOTE

An NT domain is a group of workstations and servers that can be administered together. A common user account database resides on the NT domain controllers, which provide user authentication services for other members of the domain. This enables a user to have a single account for logging on to all computers in the domain. Furthermore, trust relationships can be set up between domains that enable you to grant access to a local resource to user accounts from a trusted domain. More information on NT domains can be found in Chapter 4, "Installing Windows NT Server," and Chapter 16, "Administering the Server."

- **Server Manager:** The Server Manager is a GUI utility used for checking and controlling many server-related functions of an NT system. It can be used to check the status, start, pause, or stop services. It can also be used to obtain a list of currently logged-on users, including what files they have open. You can also use the Server Manager to send broadcast messages to logged-on users. The Server Manager is the utility that is used to create domain system accounts for NT Workstations, stand-alone servers, and domain controllers. Although Server Manager is installed by default only on NT Servers configured as domain controllers, it can also be used to administer NT Workstations and NT Servers not set up as domain controllers. Additionally, it can be installed on NT Workstations, and a version is also available for Windows 3.1x and Windows 95. The Server Manager is discussed further in Chapter 16.

- **Disk Manager:** Disk Manager is used to create and format disk partitions, as well as set up advanced disk partitioning, including volume sets, striped sets, and mirrored sets. This utility is installed on all Windows NT systems and can be used only to configure local drive systems. The Disk Manager is discussed in greater depth in Chapter 5, "Windows NT File Systems Management."

- **Performance Monitor:** This is a very powerful application in Windows NT. Although NT is very good at dynamic performance tuning, it is not able to do everything on its own. Performance Monitor enables you to graphically view hundreds of performance counters to ensure that your system is operating at its peak. You can use Performance Monitor to view the performance counters in real time, log counters for later reference, or even send administrative alerts or run external programs when certain thresholds are met. Performance Monitor is installed on all Windows NT systems. A great feature of the performance monitoring system in NT is that the performance counters are fully extensible, meaning that applications can be written to make their own performance counters available to the Performance Monitor applications. So, depending on the way your system is configured, you might have more performance counters than a baseline system. For instance, if you install the TCP/IP protocol stack *and* the SNMP service, you will get additional counters for TCP-, IP-, and ICMP-related information. Performance Monitor can be used to monitor the events on both the local and remote system simultaneously. Using the Performance Monitor to optimize system performance is discussed in Chapter 20, "Performance Tuning and Optimization."

- **Event Viewer:** The Event Viewer enables you to view the system log, application log, and security log. These logs keep you informed of the status of various system events, and, if you are auditing security-related events, the Event Viewer can be used to keep track of these as well. The Event Viewer is also used to set the maximum size for each event log and configure how the system should respond if the log fills up. The Event Viewer is installed on all Windows NT systems and can be used to view events on the local or on remote systems. A version of the Event Viewer for remotely viewing the event logs of an NT system is available for both Windows 3.1x and Windows 95 systems. Using the Event Viewer is discussed in Chapter 14.

- **RAS Admin:** This administrative utility is installed as a component of the Remote Access Service (RAS), which enables users to use a modem, or other supported communications device, to connect to the network as a standard network node. The RAS Admin enables you to designate which users are allowed to dial into the RAS server. RAS Admin can also be used to configure the dial-back capability of the RAS server on a user-by-user basis. The RAS Admin utility can be used to configure the local RAS server or a remote RAS server. You can find more information about RAS in Chapter 21, "Using Remote Access Services."

- **DHCP Manager:** Use the DHCP Manager program to administer the DHCP Server service, which enables DHCP-enabled network clients to dynamically obtain TCP/IP configuration information at startup. This program can be used to create and configure DHCP scopes, as well as administer leases. The DHCP Manager is installed with the DHCP Server service, and can be used to administer local and remote DHCP servers.

- **WINS Manager:** The WINS Manager is used for managing the WINS Server service, which provides NetBIOS name registration and resolution services on a TCP/IP network. The WINS Manager can be used to graphically manage push and pull replication partners, as well as the mapping of static address and other WINS-related features. The WINS Manager is installed along with the WINS Server service. It can be used to manage either local or remote WINS databases.

NetWare Integration

Microsoft has gone to great lengths to ensure that Windows NT integrates well with other desktop operating systems and network operating systems. Making both NT Workstation and NT Server fit seamlessly into a NetWare environment was a high priority. NetWare integration is primarily provided by the following two components:

- **NWLink:** NWLink is a high-performance, NT-native IPX/SPX-compatible protocol that Microsoft designed for Windows NT. This stack is fully compatible with the IPX/SPX specifications, including SPX II.

- **Client Services for NetWare:** Microsoft provides a Novell NCP requester with NT Server and NT Workstation. This service, called Client Services for NetWare (CSN), allows an NT system with NWLink installed to access file and print resources from Novell 3.1x and Novell 4.x servers. You can even run many of the Novell DOS-based administration tools over CSN.

Robust TCP/IP Services

Microsoft recognizes that TCP/IP is unarguably the most important network protocol in use today. The world is continuing to advance toward a worldwide computer network infrastructure, and the primary protocol for that network is TCP/IP.

Traditionally, Microsoft services were built on NetBEUI, which, although small and fast, is more suited to small networks due to its high level of network broadcasts and its inability to be routed. To make its software more universal, Microsoft has virtualized its entire networking platform so that you can mix and match protocols, requesters, and services. This means that you can use the traditional Microsoft networking services over NetBEUI, IPX/SPX, or TCP/IP and the result is the same to the user. It is now possible to build your entire Microsoft-based network using TCP/IP—or IPX/SPX. Having a single networking protocol can make network management easier. Additionally, it can improve client performance by not requiring each workstation to load multiple network protocols for communicating with different services.

Recognizing the importance of TCP/IP, Microsoft expended great effort to ensure that the TCP/IP implementation in Windows NT was robust and as fast as possible. The results are a highly optimized, 32-bit stack, the core of which is similar in its Windows For Workgroups 3.11, Windows 95, and Windows NT implementations. In addition to focusing on the speed of the stack, Microsoft has tried to provide TCP/IP-based services to make the stack more functional. The following are some of the features of the TCP/IP stack in Windows NT:

- **NetBIOS interface:** The Windows NT TCP/IP stack supports NetBIOS for establishing session-level logical names on the network, as defined in Request for Comments (RFCs) 1001 and 1002. Additionally, this interface provides support for network dynamic data exchange (Network DDE), which allows the sharing of information embedded within documents.

- **Dynamic Host Configuration Protocol (DHCP) client:** Windows NT can use a DHCP server to dynamically acquire TCP/IP configuration information such as IP addresses, DNS addresses, netmasks, and gateway addresses. This makes it easier to configure TCP/IP on client workstations and enables you to make enterprise-wide TCP/IP configuration changes without having to modify each workstation by hand. Configuring NT Server as a DHCP client is discussed in Chapter 10, "Installing and Configuring Microsoft TCP/IP."

- **Windows Internet Name Service (WINS) client:** WINS provides dynamic naming services for Windows network clients. This eliminates the need for static name resolution provided by LMHOSTS files. It also provides a dynamic name service for machines running DHCP. Configuring NT Server as a WINS client is discussed in Chapter 10.

- **Common TCP/IP connectivity utilities:** Windows NT includes Telnet, FTP, TFTP, rsh, rexec, RCP, and finger clients to allow you to take advantage of standard TCP/IP-based services. These utilities are discussed in Chapter 10.

- **TCP/IP diagnostic utilities:** The Windows NT TCP/IP stack includes arp, hostname, ipconfig, nbtstat, netstat, ping, route, and tracert for performing diagnostics and troubleshooting of your system and network. These utilities are discussed in Chapter 10.

- **TCP/IP printing support:** If you choose to install the optional support for TCP/IP printing, you will be able to print to queues on UNIX machines or network printers that accept Berkeley-style LPR requests as defined by Request for Comment (RFC) 1179. Additionally, Windows NT's TCP/IP Print Server service can accept LPR print jobs. NT includes the lpr and lpq utilities for sending remote print jobs from the command line and for querying the status of a print queue on a remote TCP/IP print device. TCP/IP printing support is examined more closely in Chapter 14, "Configuring TCP/IP Printing."

- **SNMP Support:** The SNMP agent allows your Windows NT system to be remotely monitored and administered though SNMP management software such as HP's OpenView, IBM's SystemView, or Sun's SunNet Manager.

- **Performance monitoring:** When you install the TCP/IP protocol and the SNMP service on a Windows NT system, additional TCP/IP-related objects will become available in the Performance Monitor application. This allows you to track numerous different TCP/IP performance counters and statistics for your system—a tremendous aid in locating bottlenecks and identifying potential problems before they occur. You can find out more about performance monitoring in Chapter 20.

Remote Access Service

The Remote Access Service (RAS) in Windows NT is a very robust tool for creating WAN connections to support today's advanced client/server computing environments. RAS enables remote users to gain dial-in access to the network using the NetBEUI, IPX, or TCP/IP protocols. RAS uses the Point-to-Point Protocol (PPP) to support network connections over standard modems, ISDN, and X.25 WAN links.

RAS is fully integrated with the NT security database so that users can use their standard NT user account and password for authentication. If a greater degree of security is necessary, RAS can take advantage of third-party security hosts.

RAS is compatible with UNIX systems via PPP, NetWare, Shiva LanRovers, Windows, Windows For Workgroups, Windows NT Server, Windows NT Workstation, and LAN Manager.

One of the exciting new technologies supported in Windows NT 4 is called Point-to-Point Tunneling Protocol (PPTP), which is supported through the RAS service. PPTP enables you to create virtual private networks (VPNs) across any type of network link. One of the VPNs is security. You can tell NT to encrypt data using RSA Data Security Incorporated's RC4 encryption algorithm. This provides data security and enables you to use the Internet as a secure "private" network. A second advantage of the VPN concept is that you can easily and securely use any Internet Service Provider (ISP) to dial into, while still maintaining data security.

For more information on RAS and PPTP, see Chapter 21.

Integrated C2-Level Security

When Microsoft designed Windows NT, the corporation concentrated on making it secure. Because NT was intended for use in enterprise environments, it was vital that NT be able to prevent unauthorized access to business-critical information. Microsoft deemed that designing the system to meet and exceed the U.S. National Security Agency's criteria for C2-level secure systems would result in a product that would satisfy the needs of the commercial sector as well. Additionally, by going through the lengthy C2 certification procedure, Microsoft would have a certifiable security metric that could be used to demonstrate the security of their system.

As part of the security system, Windows NT requires that the actions of all users, both local and remote, be verified against a built-in security database. So access to any part of the system would only be granted after a user provides a valid user account and password.

Furthermore, NT provides mechanisms to protect its built-in security database. One such mechanism is that, by default, NT does not allow passwords to be sent in clear text over the network. Additionally, no user or process can directly modify the system's security database. All interactions with this database are done through well-defined messages that are passed between the various software components. Additionally, you can create a password policy that requires users to have passwords of a certain length, or even create a policy that disables accounts after a designated number of failed logon attempts.

To protect the data stored on the system, NTFS, Windows NT's preferred file system, uses access control lists (ACLs) to provide file and directory protection on a user-by-user basis. Each object also has a owner, who is the ultimate authority when it comes to granting or denying access an object.

For more information on taking advantage of NT security, see Chapter 28, "Advanced Security Guidelines."

Built-In Backup

Security is important for protecting your data from accidental or intentional mishandling; however, regular backups are important for protecting your data from other kinds of problems. Recognizing this, Microsoft includes a full-featured, graphical tape backup utility with Windows NT. This utility, called NT Backup, was made for Microsoft by Arcada Software and is very similar to Arcada's commercial software package, Backup Exec.

> **NOTE**
>
> Arcada was recently acquired by Seagate and rolled into a division of Seagate called the Seagate Storage Group.

NT Backup can take advantage of any tape device supported by Windows NT. It can perform typical backup operations, including normal, copy, incremental, differential, and daily. With NT Backup you can have a backup set span multiple tapes, or include multiple backup sets on one tape.

Additionally, NT Backup supports NT's integrated security model through the use of user rights, and by allowing you to back up and restore files and directories with or without the access control lists (ACLs). NT Backup can also be used to back up NT's Registry and has full support of long filenames.

If you want to schedule regular backups, you can build batch jobs and use NT's built-in system scheduler to run the jobs as necessary.

Advanced File Systems

Windows NT supports two major files systems:

- NT File System (NTFS)
- File Allocation Table (FAT)

These file systems are discussed in greater depth in Chapter 5.

> **NOTE**
>
> One of the big surprises in Windows NT 4 was the discontinuation of support for the High-Performance File System (HPFS), originally developed for OS/2, and supported on NT 3.1, 3.5, and 3.51.

NTFS

To build a truly robust operating system, you must make sure that all components of the system are up to the task. So when designing Windows NT, Microsoft's engineers chose to develop a new file system that fit in line with NT's goals: performance, stability, scalability, and reliability. The result was NTFS.

NTFS is an advanced file system that uses journaling—a concept similar to logging—to provide recoverability. In fact, the transaction-processing concepts used in NTFS, combined with its relational database model, make NTFS look more like a high-performance database than a traditional file system. To provide improved speed, NTFS was built on a "lazy-write" model, rather than the "careful-write" model that is used by the traditional FAT file system.

NTFS is the only file system in Windows NT that supports file-level security permissions. This is done through an access control list (ACL), which contains the details of exactly what users are granted permissions to a resource and what level of permissions they have been granted.

In addition, NTFS supports many other advanced features, including:

- Long filename support
- Support for software-level sector sparing for fault tolerance
- Support for international filenames through the use of Unicode
- File-level compression through the use of an attribute bit
- Support for multiple data forks in a file, which is necessary for supporting Macintosh files

FAT

Windows NT supports FAT primarily to provide backward compatibility. However, the FAT implementation in NT differs somewhat from the implementation in DOS. One difference is that Windows NT allows for long filenames—up to 255 characters.

> **NOTE**
>
> Both Windows NT and Windows 95 support FAT in the same way.

There are many disadvantages of using FAT under NT. For example, FAT does not give you the recoverability provided by NTFS. Additionally, FAT does not support ACLs, so you cannot assign security permissions to individual files or directories.

There are times in NT where you must use the FAT file system. For instance, FAT is the only file system support on floppy drives. Also, because of their design, the boot partition on RISC computers running NT must be FAT.

There are some things in FAT's favor, though. Because of overhead involved in keeping the journal log under NTFS, there are situations in which FAT might be faster for writing information.

Additional Features in Windows NT Server

The features discussed above are shared by both the NT Workstation and the NT Server products. There are many features available in the NT Server product that are not available in the Workstation product. Some of the most important features are

- Increased server capacity for servicing more simultaneous connections
- Fault-tolerant disk driver for supporting disk mirroring and disk striping with parity (RAID 1 and RAID 5)
- Enhanced TCP/IP server services, such as DHCP, WINS, and DNS
- Internet Information Server 2.0

- Additional NetWare integration tools
- Unified domain-based security model
- Network client administrator
- Directory replication
- Services for Macintosh
- Remoteboot (RPL) for clients
- Client-licensing manager
- BackOffice suite integration
- Network Monitor Tool

Increased Server Capacity

Whereas NT Workstation is limited to 10 incoming network connections, Windows NT Server has no such limitation. In fact, there is no software-defined limit to the number of clients that can simultaneously connect to an NT Server. The limit of 10 network connections in NT Workstation is not simply a whimsically chosen number. After careful benchmarking and analysis, Microsoft determined that NT Workstation and NT Server performed similarly up to about 10 simultaneous incoming network connections. After that, NT Server was much more capable of handing the load. This has to do with differences in the internal optimization of the two products, including the pageability of the server code and the difference in the number of system worker threads.

Fault-Tolerant Disk Driver

Because NT Server is designed to meet the needs of high-end, mission-critical systems, Microsoft has included a fault-tolerant disk driver, called FTDISK.SYS, with NT Server. This driver uses a redundant array of inexpensive disks (RAID) levels 1 and 5 to handle fault-tolerant disk configurations such as disk mirroring, disk duplexing, and disk striping with parity.

- **Disk Mirroring:** Disk mirroring is a process in which a partition is exactly duplicated on two separate physical disks. This process is commonly known as RAID 1. By having an exact duplicate on a second disk, if the primary disk fails, the fault-tolerant driver will automatically use data from the backup drive, thereby virtually eliminating unscheduled downtime caused by drive failure. Disk mirroring can be used with any file system type—FAT, HPFS, and NTFS. Mirrored partitions do not need to be created on drives with the exact same geometry; so if a drive fails, you do not need to worry about replacing it with the exact same model. An obvious advantage to disk mirroring is 100 percent data redundancy. Additionally, if the hard drive controller is able to issue multiple simultaneous disk requests, disk mirroring can provide a speed improvement when reading data. One of the disadvantages of mirroring is that it requires twice the amount of drive space compared to the actual storage. When building large drive arrays, this can be quite costly.

- **Disk Duplexing:** Disk duplexing works the same way as disk mirroring, except that duplexing uses a separate disk controller for each drive. In the definition of the different RAID levels, there is no categorical difference between disk mirroring and disk duplexing, so they both fall under the category RAID 1. Disk duplexing can protect not only against drive failures, but also against controller failures, which, although uncommon, do occur. Additionally, disk duplexing can provide increased performance because one controller can handle a read request while the other controller is busy servicing a separate request.

- **Disk Striping with Parity:** The disk striping with parity that Microsoft includes with NT Server is classified as RAID level 5. With this feature you can spread the contents of one logical volume across from 3 to 32 physical drives. NT spreads information and a parity byte across all drives in the array. If there is a failure on any one drive, NT can reconstruct the data on the defective drive from the data and parity information stored on the remaining drives. With disk striping with parity, the drives can be on the same or on multiple controllers. It is important to realize that this method protects only against a single point of failure. If there is a failure in more than one of the physical drives, the data cannot be recovered. Additionally, depending on the speed of the hardware and the number of devices involved in the stripe set, writing to a RAID 5 volume can take longer because of the overhead involved in NT calculating the parity bits.

> **NOTE**
>
> Both Windows NT Server and NT Workstation can take advantage of hardware-based RAID solutions, which can provide increased performance, compared to NT Server's software solution.

You can find more information about RAID 1 and 5 in Chapter 25.

Enhanced TCP/IP Server Services

There are three major TCP/IP-related enhancements provided by Windows NT Server. These are

- **DHCP Server service:** The Dynamic Host Configuration Protocol (DHCP) is a client/server-based system that allows dynamic assignment of IP addresses and configuration information from a centralized server. This method of assigning IP information offers many advantages over the traditional static method. First, it allows you to move a computer to any location on the network and it will automatically configure itself with the appropriate settings for its new subnet. This can greatly cut down on the administrative headaches associated with incorrectly configured computers. Second, it allows you to quickly and easily make global changes for either a specific subnet or for an entire network. For instance, if the address of a DNS server changes, you can make a single change to the DHCP server and all DHCP clients will be made aware of the new server when they renew their IP lease. In a traditional, static environment, you would most likely have to go to each computer on the network and make the change.

■ **WINS Server service:** The Windows Internet Naming Service (WINS) provides dynamic NetBIOS name registration and resolution on a TCP/IP network. It is often configured to work hand in hand with the DHCP service. Without WINS, DHCP would not be as effective. This is because WINS can provide dynamic name services for computers that are assigned a dynamic IP address by a DHCP server. In the traditional TCP/IP realm, IP addresses were assigned to a particular machine, so the static naming system used by DNS servers was sufficient. However, with dynamic IP addresses, a more flexible solution was needed—hence WINS. Additional benefits include no longer needing LMHOSTS files for NetBIOS name resolution, reduction of IP broadcast traffic in Microsoft internetworks, and inter-subnet browsing.

■ **DNS Server service:** The Domain Name System (DNS) is a standard TCP/IP service that provides static name resolution on a TCP/IP network. The DNS Server Service included in NT Server 4 provides integration of the DNS service with the WINS service—providing the best of both worlds, called *dynamic DNS*. Dynamic DNS permits a standard DNS client to resolve IP addresses for computers that get their IP addresses dynamically from a DHCP server.

Internet Information Server 2.0

One major difference between Windows NT Server and NT Workstation is a very fast Internet server that is at the foundation of Microsoft's Internet strategy. It supports the Hypertext Transport Protocol (HTTP), which is the fundamental transport protocol of the World Wide Web, as well as support for FTP and Gopher services.

> **NOTE**
>
> Microsoft includes a service in NT Workstation, called Peer Web Services, which appears to be virtually identical to the IIS. However, the greatest limitation to Peer Web Services is that it only accepts 10 incoming connections, limiting its use for anything but the smallest application.

Through the use of the Internet Server API (ISAPI) programming interface, the IIS service can be extended to provide other services, such as a full-text search engine, like the forthcoming product Microsoft product code-named Tripoli.

You can find more information on IIS, and using NT as an Internet server in Chapter 31, "Using Windows NT as an Internet Server."

Increased RAS Server Capability

Although the RAS client in NT Workstation and NT Server are virtually identical, the RAS server service provided in Windows NT Server has two major features that set it apart from its NT Workstation sibling:

- **Up to 256 simultaneous RAS connections:** The RAS server service in NT Workstation allows only a single incoming call, whereas NT Server can handle up to 256 simultaneous RAS connections. This enables NT Server to provide enterprise-level communications services. With the introduction of the Point-to-Point Tunneling Protocol (PPTP) in NT, this allows you to create up to 256 Virtual Private Networks (VPNs).

- **Support for third-party security products:** Windows NT Server has an extensible API set that allows it to be integrated with third-party security products, such as Security Dynamics' ACE server, which requires users to provide an additional level of authentication by entering a code from an electronic credit card–like device they carry with them.

You can find more in-depth coverage of the Remote Access Service in Chapter 21.

Additional NetWare Integration Tools

Microsoft has realized that the most effective way to challenge Novell in the networking world is to make its products integrate as easily as possible with Novell networks. NT Server adds two main utilities that help narrow the once insurmountable chasm between the two products. The following two Novell-related services are provided in NT Server:

- **Gateway Service for NetWare:** By using the Gateway Service for NetWare, built into NT Server, you can provide standard Microsoft clients access to Novell NetWare servers without installing IPX/SPX or Novell client software on the client workstations. The gateway functions by translating the Server Messaging Blocks (SMB) requests between the NT Server and client to NetWare Core Protocol (NCP) requests that can be serviced by the Novell server. The Novell server responds, and the NT Server converts the NCP requests back to SMB and forwards them to the client.

  The magic of this service is that it allows you to make Novell-based disk and printer resources available to Microsoft clients without the additional overhead required for running the IPX/SPX stack and Novell client software.

- **NetWare Migration Tool:** If you are migrating a large Novell network to Windows NT, you might find the NetWare Migration Tool of some use. This tool enables you to migrate NetWare user and group accounts, logon scripts, files and directories, and security and permissions to your new NT Server. Migrating this information from the NetWare server can save you a tremendous amount of time by not requiring you to re-create all the accounts and configuration information. The Migration Tool gives you a quick and easy route to getting your NT Server up and running.

> **NOTE**
>
> Microsoft sells an add-on product for NT Server, called File & Print Services for NetWare, which makes an NT Server look exactly like a Novell 3.x server.

These NetWare-related tools are discussed in greater detail in Chapter 25, "NetWare Connections."

Unified Domain-Based Security Model

One of the foremost features included in NT Server, but not in NT Workstation, is the capability for NT Server to act as a domain controller. Without a Windows NT Server on your network to act as the primary domain controller, you would lose all of the functionality provided by a domain structure. Some of these additional features are

- **Server-based user profile storage:** When logging on to a Windows NT or Windows 95 system that is a member of an NT domain, you can store your user profile on the NT Server. The benefit of this is that when you log on to other workstations in the domain, you will get the same desktop and set of preferences. These are called *personal profiles*.

  Additionally, you can chose to use mandatory profiles, which cannot be changed by the user and can be used to limit the user's activities. Any changes made to the desktop or other settings by the user during an interactive logon session are not saved when the user logs off.

- **Netlogon service for processing logon scripts:** If you set up a domain, users who log onto Windows 3.x, Windows 95, and Windows NT systems can be made to use a logon script. These scripts are stored on the domain controllers and can be used to perform such actions as connecting drive and printer assignments, or even to run programs such as a virus scanning program.

- **Trust relationships:** In an NT Server–based network, the domain is the logical administrative unit for user accounts and server permissions. One of the great features of the NT domain structure is that it allows you to set up trust relationships between domains. These trust relationships enable you to grant access to your resources to users with accounts in trusted domains. This enables users to access resources in different domains without needing a separate account for each domain.

- **Single network logon:** Under NT's domain structure, you create a single account for a user, and this account can be used to log on or access resources anywhere within the domain. Additionally, if you set up trust relationships, this account could potentially be used to access resources throughout an entire enterprise. This is beneficial over many other systems that require you to create a separate account on each server.

Network Client Administrator

The Network Client Administrator is a tool that many people just don't seem to know what to do with. It was introduced in version 3.5 to make a system administrator's job easier when installing client-end software. This utility generates a boot disk that when booted in a client system can be used to automatically install Microsoft client software over the network from the server. The Network Client Administrator can be used to install the following client software which Microsoft has included on the NT Server CD:

- Windows For Workgroups 3.11
- Windows 95
- 32-bit TCP/IP for Windows For Workgroups 3.11
- NT administration tools for Windows 3.1 or Windows 95
- Network Client for MS-DOS 3.0
- RAS for MS-DOS 1.1a
- LAN Manager for MS-DOS 2.2c
- LAN Manager for OS/2 2.2c

The Network Client Administrator is discussed in-depth in Chapter 24, "Network Client Administrator."

Directory Replication

The Directory Replication service in Windows NT allows you to maintain identical copies of files and directories on multiple computers. When you make changes to any of these files or directories, the change is replicated to other computers configured to import replication changes.

Both Windows NT Servers and NT Workstations can be configured to import directories. However, only Windows NT Servers can act as directory replication export servers.

The Directory Replication service is useful for replicating logon scripts among all the Windows NT logon servers in a domain.

Services for Macintosh

Out of the box, Windows NT Server is able to act as a file and print server for Macintosh clients as well as print to AppleTalk-based printers. This makes it easier than ever to support both Macintosh and Windows networking clients from a single server product. There are five major services that are provided by NT's Services for Macintosh (SFM):

- **File Services for Macintosh clients:** With SFM installed, you can make any NTFS partition available to users with Macintosh computers. Protection is provided for these resources using NT's integrated user database, so no special accounts need to be created for Macintosh users. Additionally, Microsoft provides a User Authentication

Module (UAM) that uses encrypted passwords to enable the Macintosh client to negotiate a secure logon with an NT Server.

One of the problems commonly encountered with integrating PC and Macintosh systems is the 8.3 limit on filenames imposed by DOS. Because SFM files are hosted on an NTFS partition, which is capable of handling files with 255-character names, NT is easily able to accommodate the Macintosh's 32-character filenames.

In fact, in many ways NT provides far more robust Macintosh services than any current Macintosh product. To test the scalability of NT Server's SFM services, Microsoft has performed limits testing with more than 1,000 simultaneous Macintosh connections. This is good evidence of the robustness of NT as a Macintosh file server solution.

- **AppleTalk routing:** NT Server has native support for AppleTalk routing. This means that NT Server is able to forward data between AppleTalk subnets and can fully participate in an AppleTalk internetwork. Additionally, NT Server is capable of acting as an AppleTalk seed router for creating new AppleTalk zones.

- **Print services for Macintosh clients:** With SFM, all print devices created on your NT Server are automatically made available to Macintosh users. This feature, along with the capability to print PostScript code to non-PostScript printers and its capability to print to printers on an AppleTalk network, make NT Server a robust printing platform for Macintosh computers.

- **Printing PostScript to non-PostScript printers:** SFM includes a Macintosh print processor service that uses Microsoft's TrueImage raster image processor (RIP) for converting PostScript language code into bitmapped images that can be sent to non-PostScript printers. Because PostScript is the most common page description language for printing on Macintosh computers, the RIP enables you to print from Macs to non-PostScript devices connected to your NT Server. You can also use this service to print PostScript code from *any* system, including PC and UNIX machines, to non-PostScript printers attached to your NT Server.

- **Printing to AppleTalk-based printers:** An additional feature provided by SFM is the capability for an NT Server to send print jobs to printers using the AppleTalk protocol. This can be done if the printer is connected to the same Ethernet network as the server, or if the NT Server has a LocalTalk card installed and is connected to the same LocalTalk network as the printer. In either case, the NT Server can either simply print to the AppleTalk printer or *capture* the printer to prevent other computers from printing directly to it. You might want to do this to force people to use the NT Server as a print server or for job auditing purposes.

In-depth coverage of the Services for Macintosh is provided in Chapter 9, "Working with Macintosh Clients."

Remoteboot (RPL) for Clients

The Remoteboot service enables you to boot an MS-DOS, Windows 3.1, or Windows 95 workstation over the network from a shared software installation located on your NT Server. The client's network card must have a remote program load (RPL) chip. Remoteboot can give you increased workstation security, software, and operating system version control and decreased workstation costs.

The Remoteboot service is covered in Chapter 18.

Client-Licensing Manager

Microsoft offers two methods of client licensing for BackOffice products: per server or per seat. To help system administrators enforce its licensing policy, Microsoft has begun including the Client-Licensing Manager applet with NT Server. This program is the forerunner of a more sophisticated license monitoring software expected later this year.

The Client-Licensing Manager allows you to designate the number of licenses you own for various BackOffice applications and enforces the licensing policy by denying services to users if all available licenses have been exhausted. You can use this application to manage licenses for all BackOffice products on your network from a single location.

The Client-Licensing Manager also keeps track of license usage statistics, enabling you to view the highest number of current connections. This is extremely valuable for capacity planning.

The Client-Licensing Manager also supports local, domain, or enterprise-based license metering. You can set up central servers that will act as repositories for all licensing information. You can choose how frequently Windows NT replicates information to the master license server.

An additional use for the Client-Licensing Manager is for generating historical reports of when new licenses were purchased, and for which products.

Network Monitor Tool

Windows NT 4 now includes the Microsoft Network Monitor Tool, which enables you to directly view network traffic as it passes across the network wire. This tool was previously only available as part of Microsoft's Systems Management Server (SMS) package, but is now included with NT Server 4. The Network Monitor Tool is a very important troubleshooting device, because it permits you to actually disassemble the packets that are passed across the network and isolate where problems are occurring. For example, if you are having trouble getting a DHCP client to locate a DHCP server on the network, you could watch to see where the communications are getting held up, and quickly resolve the problem. Without being able to look at the raw network data, problems like this are often based on a tremendous amount of guesswork and can be very time-consuming.

Optimization of NT Server and NT Workstation

Windows NT Server and Workstation have more differences than just their feature sets. The actual code that controls the internals of each system is optimized so NT Workstation performs best as a desktop operating system for client/server and mission-critical applications, whereas NT Server provides a robust, fault-tolerant operating system capable of being the foundation of an enterprise-level network by providing application, file, and print services.

The following differences have been made to the two products to make each best fit its intended market:

- Write-throttling cache in NT Server
- Pageability of the server code
- Preloading of the Virtual DOS Machine (VDM) in NT Workstation
- Difference in the number of system threads
- Adjustable optimization for file/print services or application services in NT Server

Write-Throttling Cache in NT Server

To better meet their particular roles, Windows NT Server and NT Workstation handle the flushing of dirty cache data differently. This mechanism, known as write-throttling, essentially results in NT Server holding dirty information in cache longer than NT Workstation. This allows NT Server to better perform its role as a server. NT Workstation, on the other hand, flushes its cache more frequently, resulting in a smaller memory overhead for the cache.

Pageability of Server Code

SRV.SYS is the driver in Windows NT that is responsible for processing high-level file system requests and then passing them to the appropriate low-level device driver. In Windows NT Workstation, SRV.SYS is highly pageable, which translates to a lower memory footprint, but might result in additional paging. In NT Server, this driver is less pageable, meaning a larger dedicated memory footprint. This is part of the reason that NT Server needs more memory than NT Workstation. By not allowing parts of the SRV.SYS code to be paged out, NT Server is better able to respond quickly to requests.

Preloading of Virtual DOS Machine in NT Workstation

When you interactively log on to a Windows NT Workstation, the system preloads the Windows NT Virtual DOS Machine (NTVDM). Preloading the NTVDM allows NT Workstation to load 16-bit applications faster but results in a slightly longer logon time. Also, preloading the NTVDM consumes more memory if you will not be running 16-bit code. Because NT Server is not intended to be a regular logon workstation, there is no need to preload the

NTVDM. If an interactively logged-on user on an NT Server starts a 16-bit application, NT Server will load the NTVDM and then dispose of it when the application is exited.

Differences in the Number of System Threads

NT Server creates more worker threads than NT Workstation. These worker threads provide access to key system resources and ensure that access to these resources is handled in an equitable manner. By using more threads, the core services of Windows NT Server are more responsive to incoming user requests and are better able to distribute the system load across processors in an SMP system. Using a smaller number of system threads in NT Workstation results in a smaller system overhead, leaving more resources for user-based applications.

Adjustable Optimization for File/Print Services or Application Services

Windows NT Server allows you to choose whether you want to optimize your server for file and print services, or as an application server. This provides you the option of targeting which services you want to receive the highest priority. Because NT Workstation is not designed to be a high-performance server, it does not allow for this optimization.

IN THIS PART

II
PART

Installing Windows NT Server

Installing Windows NT Server

by Robert Reinstein and Terry Ogletree

IN THIS CHAPTER

CHAPTER 4

Installing Windows NT Server can be as simple as installing any other Windows application. If the target computer already has an operating system (MS-DOS or any Windows OS), you need only run a setup program (WINNT.EXE or WINNT32.EXE) to begin the process. From that point on, the Setup program queries you for information it needs to complete the process. If you are installing Windows NT Server on a computer that doesn't already have an operating system installed, you can use the three setup diskettes and CD-ROM provided with Windows NT Server to boot the computer and start the installation process.

After reviewing hardware prerequisites, this chapter covers the basic installation process, using the startup diskettes and the distribution CD. Next, variations on the procedure such as using a network share for the distribution are discussed. Instructions also are given for using a Network Client Start Disk (see Chapter 24, "Network Client Administrator") to boot a computer and install NT from a file share using an unattended answer file to automate the process. This method is particularly suited for situations when you must install the operating system on a large number of PCs.

Finally, this chapter contains hints and tips that can aid you in performing a non-standard installation or in using hardware that is not currently supported by Microsoft.

Hardware Considerations

Windows NT 4.0 can be installed on any of the following hardware platforms:

- Intel x86 based computer (486 or above)
- Digital Alpha RISC computer
- MIPS RISC computers
- PowerPC based computer

If you are purchasing new hardware, however, you should be aware that after version 4.0 of Windows NT, the MIPS and PowerPC platforms will no longer be supported. In other words, while you might want to use existing MIPS or PowerPC computers to maximize their value, you should think twice about buying new systems because you won't be able to upgrade them to future versions of Windows NT. Also note that if you choose to use an Intel 486 platform, you should probably do so only for a test system. The performance level of Windows NT 4.0 on such a platform is insufficient for most medium to large network requirements.

Performance factors should also be considered when making hardware purchases. For example, if you want to mirror your boot disk, you must have a RAID disk subsystem that can perform mirroring at the controller level. Windows NT Server cannot use software disk mirroring the boot disk, because it must first boot and then load the mirroring software.

ry requirements for Windows NT Server are documented by Microsoft to be a mini- 16 MB of RAM. However, for most purposes this minimum amount is unsatisfac- ough NT Server operates with this amount of memory, you should probably use a alue of 32 instead to get acceptable performance.

The amount of memory you require depends heavily on the use to which you put the server. If the server is used as a backup domain controller, for example, and users don't use it for file or print sharing, then little memory is required. For a server running an application such as Microsoft SQL Server (which requires a server with a minimum of 64 MB of RAM), however, you will find that the more memory you have, the better performance will be. It isn't uncommon to find SQL servers with 128 or 512 MB of RAM, or more. After you install NT you can use the Performance Monitor administrative tool to evaluate the Server's performance to see if additional RAM will improve performance.

The wide range of hardware platforms on which NT runs enables you to scale the operating system in your network from a small desktop server to large multiprocessor computers that can be used in enterprise networks. The fastest platform you can use at this time is the Alpha platform from Digital, for which a 64-bit version of NT is under development. You also can cluster Alpha or Intel based platforms using software from Microsoft called Microsoft Cluster Server (formerly known by the code name "Wolfpack") or Digital ("Digital Clusters for NT"), as well as from other hardware and software manufacturers.

When you execute Setup, you need to have a non-compressed FAT partition of at least 124 megabytes to use as a temporary storage area for files during the installation (you need 158 MB if you're installing on a RISC computer). After the installation has finished, you can use the CONVERT/FS:NTFS command to convert the partition to NTFS if you choose. If the computer's local hard drive contains unformatted partitions, or unpartitioned space, Setup enables you to partition and format a space during the installation process.

The actual amount of disk space you should have for your system disk should be larger than the minimum of 124 MB needed to perform the installation. If you're going to partition a disk to have a small system partition and a larger one to use for application software, you need to leave more room on the system partition than just the space required for the Windows NT Server files. For example, Windows NT is a virtual memory operating system and uses a paging file on disk as a backing store for pages of memory that have been swapped out. You need to leave enough space for the paging file also. In general, Microsoft recommends you size the paging file to be about 12 MB larger than the amount of physical memory installed on the server.

There are many other reasons why you need more space on the system partition. Disk fragmentation occurs much more rapidly on a smaller partition that is almost full. During the lifetime of the server you will probably install one or more service packs to correct bugs in the operating system or to add new features. Some third-party utilities may add files to the system disk even though they enable you to specify a path to another disk for the bulk of the installation. If you ever experience severe system crashes, you can use the memory dump that Windows NT Server creates on the system disk for troubleshooting purposes.

> **TIP**
>
> For performance reasons, it's sometimes a good idea to put the paging file on a disk other than the system disk. If you locate the page file on a disk that isn't used by the system or other applications, or if you create several paging files on several different disks, you can improve system performance. Note, though, that putting paging files on separate partitions that reside on the same physical disk does not improve performance, because the same device must be accessed for each file and concurrent accesses cannot be made. Also, placing different paging files on disks that are on different controllers can improve performance because multiple controllers can execute disk access command simultaneously.

Using the Hardware Compatibility List (HCL)

Before you decide to install Windows NT Server on a computer, you should be sure that the computer and any devices attached (disks, modems, and so on) are compatible with the operating system. Although Windows NT comes with a printed version of the Hardware Compatibility List (HCL), you should check the most current version of the list, which is maintained on the following Web site:

```
http://www.microsoft.com/isapi/hwtest/hcl.idc
```

It should be noted that items found on the HCL have been tested to perform with Windows NT. It isn't feasible, however, to test all possible combinations of listed hardware with each other. Thus, although a device may be listed in the HCL, it still doesn't guarantee you that you will be able to use it in your system in the combination you have put together. Be sure to let your hardware vendor know this before you sign on the dotted line for a large purchase.

You also should be aware that the HCL covers a large list of computer systems that have been certified to run Windows NT. Just because a system is certified, however, does not mean that it will run Windows NT, other BackOffice applications, or third-party applications. For example, you are going to find it difficult to run SQL Server on a Pentium 60mz system using a 300 MB disk drive, though you can certainly install Windows NT Server on such a system.

Carefully pick your hardware for the performance you expect from it. It's a good idea in larger configurations to select hardware that can be added to or reconfigured. The ability to add additional CPUs to create a multiprocessing system, for example, would be a highly desirable feature in a system used to support a large database.

Using Unsupported Hardware

If you are going to use hardware that isn't on the HCL, then you should consult the manufacturer to see if a driver is available for this version of Windows NT. In some cases you can use unsupported hardware and use a default generic driver. For example, many modems that don't appear on the HCL can be made to work by choosing a generic driver during the installation (for example, Standard 28800 bps modem). When using a generic driver, be aware that if the device works, it may not be fully functional.

It also is a good idea to periodically check with a device manufacturer to see if an updated driver has been released. The driver that comes on the Windows NT Server distribution CD may be months or years old by the time you purchase it. Manufacturers usually release updates to correct bugs or add features.

Information You Need During Setup

Before you begin the installation process, it's a good idea to first gather all the information that you will need during the setup process. What information that is depends, of course, on the type of installation that you're performing. You need networking information, for example, for any server you plan to deploy on your network. If you decide to use the Windows NT Server as a domain controller, then you need additional information, such as the domain name and possibly an administrator-level password to join the domain.

Determining the Installation Type

Before you attempt to install Windows NT Server, you should be aware that you have several options that might make your job easier if you prepare in advance. If you jump in and begin the installation without adequate preparation, you may find yourself performing a reinstall later, after realizing you haven't configured the system correctly. For example, you can only create an NT domain controller (PDC or BDC) during the installation process. If you go ahead and perform an install and designate the computer to be only a member server, you will have to reinstall the operating system to create a domain controller. You cannot change this network role after installation.

The following are questions that you need to ask before performing the installation:

- Are you performing a new installation, or are you upgrading an existing PC?
- Where are the distribution source files located?
- Will you use the three setup diskettes to start the installation or will you connect to a network share and run the setup program directly?
- Are you planning to use the computer in a dual-boot mode?
- If upgrading, do you have a backup of the current system that is sufficient to perform a recovery if something goes wrong?
- Will the server be used to offer network file or printer shares? If so, what security measures will you use to protect these resources? Will you use share-level security or choose to format your disk partitions with NTFS to gain a finer granularity of security control on files and directories?

The next few sections of this chapter cover some other issues you should think about before you start the installation process.

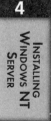

Choosing the License Information

Locate the paperwork that documents the number of licenses you have purchased and store it in a safe place after the installation. Before you start the installation, decide if you want to use *per seat* or *per server* licensing. This decision shouldn't be made lightly. After installation, you are allowed to make a change in the licensing mode *only once*, from per server to per seat. If you wish to change it again, you can do so only by reinstalling Windows NT Server.

> **CAUTION**
>
> Although Microsoft supports converting per server licensing to per seat licensing, it prohibits the reverse.

Why is this decision so important? You first need to understand the difference between per seat and per server licensing, and make the choice depending on the configuration of your network servers and clients.

Per server licensing means that the number of licenses you have are assigned to a particular server and are used as clients make connections to the server. After a client disconnects, the license becomes available for another client's use (after a timeout period of approximately 15 minutes). During that 15-minute interval, the same client that had disconnected can reconnect and continue to use the same license. This represents *concurrent* connections. There may be more clients on the network, but not all clients need to connect to the server at the same time. In an environment of several servers, a license is required for each server the client needs to access.

Per seat licensing means that licenses are assigned to individual clients. That particular license is used by the client for whichever server to which it makes a connection.

Obviously, if you have only one server in your network, then using the per server option is appropriate. If you have multiple servers on your network, however, and clients need to connect to more than one server, you may find it more economical to use per seat licensing.

To figure out which is best for you, do the math. First, figure out the total number of client computers that will access any of the servers in the network. For example, if you have two servers and 10 clients that will access the first server and 20 clients that will access the second server, then the value to use is 20. Next, multiply the number of servers times the number of simultaneous client connections that will be made at any one time. If the result is greater than the first value, then you should probably use per seat licensing.

One of the things that can make it complicated to determine how many licenses you will need for your network is understanding what type of situation uses a license. Some of those include the following:

- File share and Print share connections to a Windows NT Server that use SMB (Server Message Block).

- Using the same username to connect to an NT Server from two different client computers counts as two connections, thus, two licenses are used (in per server mode only).
- Using the /U command line switch with the NET USE command can cause additional licenses to be used if you use a username that is different from the domain username you are logged in with.
- Connections to print shares using the UNIX LPD service.
- Windows 95 clients that authenticate on a Windows NT Server domain.
- System Management Server (SMS) when it inventories a client server.
- Clients connecting to a Microsoft Exchange Server on an NT server.
- When NT Backup connects to a remote server to perform a backup of its files, it uses a license. This does not happen when NT Backup is used to backup local files on the system on which it resides.
- Connections using Service for Macintosh each use a license.
- Connections using File and Print Services for Netware (FPNW) each use a license.

There are some situations that you might think would constitute a license usage, but do not. For example, when you use many of the server administrative tools (such as User Manager for Domains, Server Manager, or the Performance Monitor) to connect to a remote computer, a license is not used. When you log onto a server locally at its keyboard, a license is not used. Also, you can generally use TCP/IP client utilities such as FTP and Telnet to make connections and these don't use a license unless they connect to an application that uses up a license.

Understanding the Network Role

Windows NT Servers can take on the role of domain controller or standalone server during the installation process. If you install Windows NT Server and do not elect to make it a domain controller, then after the installation process you *cannot* promote or upgrade the server to be a domain controller. You will have to reinstall Windows NT to accomplish that.

If you are installing Windows NT Server to be a standalone server, then you need to specify a password for the server's local Administrator account, just as you would if you were installing Windows NT Workstation. If you are making the server a domain controller, then it will not have a local security database (it will use the domain security database) so you do not have to provide any additional information.

Providing Network Information

Windows NT supports a wide variety of industry standard networking protocols. You should make a list of the protocols you will be selecting for installation, along with any pertinent configuration information for the protocols. If you are installing TCP/IP, for example, you need to have the correct IP address, subnet mask, and other optional information such as a DNS server or default gateway, if applicable. If you are going to use NetBEUI, you don't need to provide any additional configuration information.

In addition to protocol information, you also need to know if your network uses other configurable network services, such as the Windows Internet Naming Service (WINS).

Regardless of which protocol you use to connect to the network, you need to provide a unique computer name to identify the computer on the network.

Selecting the File System

Unless you use the three Setup floppy diskettes to start the installation, you need to have a FAT partition available during the initial installation for the setup program to use for temporary storage. You can elect during the installation to convert the system partition to NTFS. Because NTFS provides a more reliable file system than FAT does and because it offers a greater granularity of security permissions and auditing, you should probably choose to convert to NTFS unless you have a specific need not to. If you are going to dual-boot the computer between Windows NT Server and Windows 95, for example, you should leave the partition as a FAT partition because Windows 95 cannot access an NTFS partition or install NT on a separate partition that can be converted to NTFS.

If you're installing Windows NT on a RISC platform, then you have to have at least one FAT partition of 2 MB to use as the boot partition. However, this partition need only contain the files needed to boot the computer (such as the hardware abstraction layer and the Osloader program). The directory you plan to use for the remainder of the system files can be placed on an NTFS partition during the installation if you choose to do so.

Windows NT Components

Many of the components and accessories that comprise Windows NT are optional. A thorough reading of the documentation can assist you in deciding beforehand which components you need to install. For example, in a business environment, you may elect to not install any of the games that are provided as accessories. You may have employees who can be more productive by installing one or more of the accessibility options that are available.

If you decide after the installation that you need a component you didn't install, you can use the Add/Remove Programs applet in the Control Panel to reconfigure the computer.

As was discussed at the beginning of this chapter, you should locate and have available any additional or updated device drivers that you need during the installation. You also may need information about the specific devices, such as interrupt level, that the device uses. When you're installing Windows NT Server on a new computer, it's a good idea to document any important device setup information.

Tasks to Accomplish Before Running Setup

Although the Setup program walks you through the process of configuring the hardware and software components of the operating system, you may find it necessary to perform other functions to get the hardware ready before you do the install. For example, if you are using a hardware-based RAID disk subsystem, you should consult the documentation for that hardware to configure the disks (that is, setup mirror or stripe sets), before you install Windows NT. If you are going to install the operating system to a local hard drive on the computer that is not on the subsystem, then you can configure the disks later, after you have finished the installation.

Because creating a domain controller or joining a domain requires that the computer be connected to the network during the install process, check to be sure that network adapter card(s) are installed and that the proper cable has been used to connect it to the network.

Following the Basic Installation Process

The installation process for Windows NT Server consists of two basic parts: text-mode setup and GUI-mode setup. The installation begins in text-mode, prompting you for the information it needs to build a minimal system, and then continues in GUI-mode using the more familiar Windows interface.

Text-Mode Setup

The first portion of setup is called text-mode setup. This is where the setup program detects the attached hardware devices, loads the hardware abstraction layer (HAL) for the computer's platform, and runs the setup program. In addition, a large number of files are copied from the distribution source to temporary storage on a local hard disk. This portion of setup is called text-mode (or character-based setup) because the Setup screens are text-based. During the last part of the installation, after enough components have been installed to support it, the graphical interface portion of Setup is performed. During the GUI-mode Setup, a bare-bones stripped-down version of Windows NT is loaded to provide the graphical interface needed to continue the installation.

To begin the setup process on a new computer, complete the following steps:

1. Insert the first startup disk in the computer's A: drive and power-up or reboot the computer. The NTDETECT program, HAL, and other setup information files are loaded into memory.

2. When prompted, insert the second setup disk into the floppy drive. Additional files (such as keyboard drivers and the FAT file system) are loaded.

3. After the appropriate files have been copied, a blue, full-screen Setup menu is displayed.

   The menu offers three selections:

   ■ Press ENTER if you want to continue to setup Windows NT.

   ■ Press R if you want to repair a previous installation of Windows NT that has become corrupt (see the section "Repairing a Windows NT Installation Using the Emergency Repair Disk" later in this chapter).

   ■ Press F1 to get help on the setup process.

If you want to abort the installation, press the F3 key. To continue the installation, press ENTER.

4. Next, Setup attempts to detect attached mass storage devices, such as CD-ROM drives or SCSI adapters. Note that most floppy and ESDI/IDE drives are automatically detected. However, on occasion Setup has problems detecting SCSI devices and some other controllers.

   At this screen you can press ENTER if you want Setup to detect any additional devices.

   If you have had problems during this detection phase and have restarted the installation, you should manually install drivers (see the section " Manual Installation of Undetected Drivers" later in this chapter). To do so, press the S key to skip the detection phase.

   After you press ENTER, Setup prompts you to insert the third setup diskette.

5. Setup now attempts to detect mass storage devices and disk controllers by loading drivers and testing them, and makes a list onscreen showing each device as it is found.

6. After detection has finished, Setup prompts you to either continue with the installation (by pressing ENTER), or press the S key if you want to add additional drivers that weren't detected. Again, press the ENTER key. For more information on manually adding drivers, see the section "Manual Installation of Undetected Drivers" later in this chapter.

7. Setup continues to load additional files from the third diskette (such as the NTFS file system) and then presents you with a screen that displays the license agreement. Microsoft expects you to read this agreement. You cannot get past this installation screen until you use the Page-Down key to get to the end of the agreement, at which time you can press the escape key if you don't want to continue, or the F8 key to indicate that you accept the license agreement.

8. Setup then searches the local hard disks to see if it can find a previous installation of Windows NT. If it finds a previous installation, it prompts you to either upgrade that installation or create a new installation. Press ENTER to upgrade the existing NT installation or press the N key to install a new version. If no previous version of Windows NT is found, this screen is not displayed.

> **NOTE**
>
> If you choose to upgrade a previous Windows NT installation, Setup preserves the security information (such as user accounts and trust relationships) that exist in that installation. However, because many factors can cause an installation to fail, you should ALWAYS have a good, reliable (that is, tested) backup of your system before upgrading or performing any other system maintenance on it.

9. The next Setup screen displays a list of all the hardware and software components that Setup has found. To change an entry, you can use the UP and DOWN ARROW keys to highlight it and press ENTER. This takes you to a screen that is specific to the type of entry (disk controller, CPU type, and so on) and enables you to choose from a list of entries that Setup knows about, or to use a manufacturer's disk to install additional components.

   When you're sure that the listing is correct for your computer, highlight the entry that says The Above List Matches My Computer and press ENTER.

10. Setup next displays a screen showing the disk partitions it has found on your system. You can use the UP and DOWN ARROW keys to select the partition you want to use. Press the ENTER key when you have made your selection. At this screen you also can perform other disk maintenance functions. For example, you can use the UP and DOWN ARROW keys to select a partition and then delete it. If you select Unpartitioned Space, you can press the C key to create a new partition in that space. If you choose an Unformatted Partition, Setup displays a screen that enables you to select to format the partition using either FAT or NTFS. Highlight the type of file system you want to use and press ENTER. Setup assigns a drive letter to the partition and then formats it.

11. After you have chosen a partition, Setup next prompts you to enter the name of the directory you wish to use to install Windows NT. The default is \WINNT, and this is appropriate for most situations. If you are planning to install more than one bootable version of Windows NT on this computer, using the same disk, you may want to change this directory name to something that makes it obvious what the directory contains. For example, if you are going to dual-boot between Windows NT Workstation and Windows NT Server, you might make one directory \WINNTWK and the other \WINNTSRV. After you have entered the directory you want to use, press ENTER.

CAUTION

If you're planning to dual-boot between Windows NT Server and Windows 95, do not install Windows NT Server into the same directory that you use for the Windows 95 files. Although you can install Windows NT on a system running Windows 95, you cannot upgrade Windows 95 to Windows NT and maintain your programs and other settings. You can upgrade previous version of Windows NT.

NOTE

The directory that you decide to use for the system files does not have to already exist. Setup creates the directory for you.

4
INSTALLING
WINDOWS NT
SERVER

12. Setup now asks you if you want it to perform an intensive examination of your hard disk to look for corruption. You can press ENTER to allow this to happen, or you can press the escape key to skip this examination.

13. Finally, at the end of this text-mode phase of Setup, a list of files to be copied is built and Setup copies a large number of files from the temporary disk area to the partition on which you have chosen to install Windows NT.

After the file copy has completed, you are prompted to remove any floppy disks and/or CD-ROM disks from the computer. After you have done this, press ENTER to reboot the computer.

GUI-Mode Setup

The computer reboots into GUI-mode setup. Although the operating system is not yet completely installed, the rest of the process looks like the Windows interface you are used to.

> **NOTE**
>
> During the GUI-mode setup phase you are usually prompted to enter data and click the Next button to continue. In addition, there is a Back button you can use on each window to backup to the previous window, making it possible to correct errors without having to perform a re-install.

The following steps continue the installation process in GUI-mode:

1. Setup prompts you to put the Windows NT source distribution CD into the CD-ROM drive. Alternatively, you can specify an alternate source for the distribution files. In either case, click the OK button.

2. The next dialog box enables you to choose the path for the distribution. It defaults to the CD-ROM drive that Setup has detected. You should make sure that your path points to the correct subdirectory for your CPU platform. If you're using an Intel platform, for example, you would enter E:\i386, provided that E: was the CD-ROM. The subdirectories for other platforms are: Alpha, Mips, and Ppc. If you are unsure about the location of the distribution files, select the Browse button to aid in your search. When you finish, click the OK button and Setup copies a few files to the computer's local hard drive.

3. Next, the Windows NT Setup Wizard dialog box prompts you through the rest of Setup. Click the Next button to continue.

4. The next dialog box prompts you to enter your name and the name of your organization. Although you can leave the organization field blank, you must enter something in the Name field before Setup continues. The text you enter for these fields is used for descriptive identification purposes only. If you're installing Windows NT Server on a computer that will participate in a network, you are prompted during network

setup to enter a computer name to identify the computer on the network. When you have finished, click the Next button.

5. The next dialog box asks you to enter the 10-digit CD Key (usually found on the jewel-box case that the distribution CD came in). This key is used to help prevent software piracy and you cannot leave this field blank. When you have finished, click the Next button.

6. The Licensing Modes dialog box (see Figure 4.1) then appears. Enter the type of licensing you are going to use (per server or per seat). If you choose per server, then you need to indicate the number of licenses you have purchased in the field next to the selection. You can highlight the field with your cursor and type in a number, or you can use the scroll arrows to adjust the number of licenses in this field. If you're going to use per seat licensing, then you need only select it. You have an opportunity after the installation is completed to use the License Manager administrative tool to enter client licensing information. When you're finished with this dialog box, click the Next button.

FIGURE 4.1.

Think carefully before deciding on the licensing mode to use. You can only change it once—from per server to per seat—after the installation.

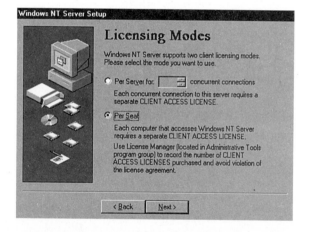

NOTE

If you choose the per server licensing option and enter zero for the number of licenses, Setup warns you that after the installation is complete, you can log in locally at the server. But, file and print services, along with remote access services, will not function for your clients until you have entered licensing information. Again, you can use the License Manager administrative tool to do this if you do not have the licensing documentation handy when you are performing the installation.

7. The next dialog box prompts you to enter a computer name for this computer, which must be unique on your network. You can enter from 1 to 15 characters. Click the Next button when you're finished.

4

INSTALLING WINDOWS NT SERVER

8. Next, the Server Type dialog box (see Figure 4.2) gives you three options:

   ■ Primary Domain Controller

   ■ Backup Domain Controller

   ■ Stand-Alone Server

   Select the appropriate option and click the next button.

FIGURE 4.2.

You can create a domain controller only during the installation process.

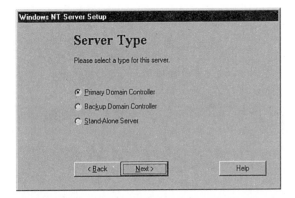

CAUTION

Remember that in order to create a primary or backup domain controller for your network you must do so in the Server Type dialog box. If you select Stand-Alone Server at this point, then after the installation you will not be able to make the computer a domain controller *without reinstalling Windows NT Server!*

Also, you cannot create a backup domain controller on the network unless you have first created a primary domain controller. If you choose to make the computer a backup domain controller (after networking is started by the Setup program) Windows NT looks for the primary domain controller on the network so that it can join the domain. If there's no primary domain controller available, Setup does not continue.

Conversely, if you select to create a primary domain controller during the installation, Windows NT looks on the network to make sure that a primary domain controller for the domain name that you select doesn't already exist. If it does, Setup doesn't continue until you either choose to create a BDC for that domain, or select another domain name.

---

9. Next, you are prompted to enter the password to be used for the Administrator account. If you are creating a primary domain controller, then this is a domain Administrator account. If you are creating a standalone server, this is the Administrator account for the local security database on just this computer. If you are creating a backup domain controller, you are not prompted for a password. This is because for an existing domain, the Administrator account already exists—on the primary domain

controller for this domain. The password is not displayed as you enter it. To ensure that you do not make any mistakes, you have to enter the password twice.

10. Next, you are prompted to create an Emergency Repair Disk (ERD). This is a disk that stores certain files and registry hives that can be used to help restore a Windows NT installation should it become corrupted.

    Each time you change the configuration of your server (by adding or removing hardware or software components), you need to re-create or update your ERD. Because most server installations are followed by installation of software applications, it's probably best to just elect not to create the ERD at this time. However, it is very important that you do so when you have fully configured the server for production use.

    If you select to create the ERD during the installation, Setup prompts you during the process to insert a blank, formatted floppy disk into the disk drive. After you make your selection, click the Next button to continue.

11. The Select Components dialog box (see Figure 4.3) next enables you to tailor your configuration of Windows NT. The components you can choose to install fall into six categories:

    - Accessibility Options
    - Accessories
    - Communications
    - Games
    - Multimedia
    - Windows Messaging

    If you are installing Windows NT Server as a production file or print server, you may want to choose not to install the games, or some of the accessories. For example, on such a server, would you need to install all the screen savers or mouse pointers? Would you need to install the Paint accessory? You might choose to eliminate the entire category of Multimedia from a production server. By tailoring components that will not be used, you will not only save a meager amount of disk space, but you also will prevent them from being used on a server where their execution could interfere with the server's main role.

    In this dialog box, in the Components section, you can select the checkbox next to a category to select all of the components of that category. Or, you can highlight a category and then click the Details button. This second option brings up another dialog box that presents a listing of the components for that category. It enables you to select each component that you want to install by using the component's checkbox. When you're done selecting from the components listing, click the OK button.

    On the Select Components dialog box, you may note that some of the checkboxes have a checkmark in them, but the background of the box is gray instead of white.

This is to indicate that some of the components of this category were selected, but not all. If all components for a category are selected, then there is a checkmark in the checkbox, and the background is white.

FIGURE 4.3.

You can decide to add or remove components of Windows NT during installation.

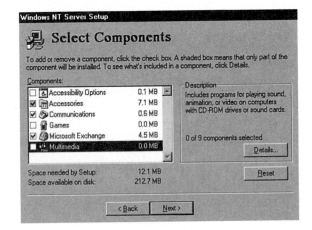

When you're finished selecting from all of the categories, click the Next button.

12. The next Setup dialog box (simply titled Windows NT Setup) informs you that networking components are about to be installed. Click the Next button to continue.

13. Setup needs to know if you want to set up networking for a direct connection to the network, or by using remote access, or both. The next dialog box gives you a checkbox for each choice. If you are connected to a network using a network adapter or an ISDN adapter, then select Wired To The Network. If you will be using a dial-up line to connect to the network, select Remote Access To The Network. You can select both checkboxes if you want to install networking components for a local LAN using your adapter and install the Remote Access Service for remote communications as well. When you have made the selection, click the Next button to continue.

14. Windows NT 4.0 Server includes version 2.0 of the Microsoft Internet Information Server (IIS). It is an easy-to-use Internet Web server kit that includes a World Wide Web (WWW) server, an FTP server, and a Gopher server. The next dialog box prompts you to install this server. If you choose to do so, select the checkbox and click the next button. Note that IIS v2.0 is a simple, easy-to-use Web server, but updated versions already exist on Microsoft's Web site at the following URL:

```
http://www.microsoft.com/iis/default.asp
```

15. Setup attempts to detect any network adapter cards you have in your system (see Figure 4.4). You can start the search by clicking the Start Search button. Setup is able to detect a large number of different network cards, but you may not be so lucky. If you want to select the card yourself, or if you have a manufacturer's driver diskette and want to manually install the network card software, click the Select from list button.

FIGURE 4.4.

You can let Setup detect your network adapter or you can specify it yourself.

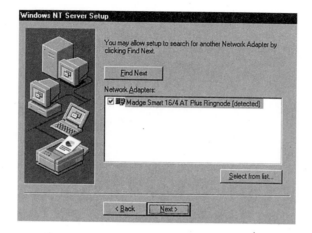

16. If you elected to have Setup search for your adapter card, it may take a few minutes. If it finds any cards, it lists them under the Network Adapters box. If you have more than one adapter installed in the computer, use the Find Next button after Setup finds each adapter to instruct it to find the next adapter.

    Setup also informs you if it doesn't find any adapters and you can then use the Select from list option to designate the card type yourself or manually install a driver from a diskette. When all of the cards for your server have been detected or selected, click the Next button to continue.

17. If you choose to select your network adapter, a dialog box that lists the network adapters that have drivers on the distribution CD pops up. You can scroll through the list and click the OK button if you find your adapter. Or, you can click the Have Disk button to install new software from floppy disk.

18. If you have selected the Have Disk option, the Insert Disk dialog box pops up to prompt you for the path to the software. The path defaults to the A: drive. However, you can change this to any valid path combination of disk and directory, to indicate where the files reside. When you have filled in the correct path, click the OK button, and when you are returned to the previous dialog box, click the OK button there to continue with the networking portion of Setup.

19. The next dialog box displays the networking protocols that you can install during Setup. These include TCP/IP, NWLink IPX/SPX Compatible Transport and the NetBEUI protocol. After you select the network protocols to install, click the Next button.

4

INSTALLING WINDOWS NT SERVER

> **NOTE**
>
> Windows NT supports a number of industry standard network protocols, including Point to Point Tunneling Protocol and DLC. However, during Setup you can install only TCP/IP, NWLink IPX/SPX Compatible Transport (Microsoft's implementation of IPX/SPX), or NetBEUI. These three protocols are used for network authentication browsing purposes and are needed for your computer to join a workgroup or domain. The remaining protocols are specialized to perform specific functions. For example, DLC can be used for printing to networked printers or for the Remote Boot service. If you want to install additional network protocols, you can do so using the Network applet in the Control Panel after you have finished the installation.

20. The next dialog box shows you the network services that will be installed by default. You can choose at this time to install additional network services by clicking the Select from list button, or you can click the Next button to continue the Setup process.

21. If you selected additional network services, a dialog box with a list of services you can scroll through appears. On this page you need to highlight a service and then click the OK button to add it to the install list. You'll have to return to this window using the Select From List button for each additional service you want to install. Unfortunately, you cannot use the Control key to select multiple services at a time. When you have finished selecting network services, click the Next button to continue.

22. The next dialog box simply informs you that Setup is about to proceed with the installation of the networking configuration you have chosen. Click the Back button if you want to make any changes, or the Next button to continue. During this portion of Setup, the prompts that appear depend on the components you have chosen to install. For example, Setup prompts you for configuration settings for your network card. If you are installing NWLink IPX/SPX, it prompts you for network information.

23. If you chose to install TCP/IP, Setup asks you if you want to use a DHCP server to request TCP/IP configuration information. A DHCP server is a service that *leases* network configuration information to clients on a network. This type of service eliminates the need to manually configure TCP/IP information each time a computer is moved to a different subnet or other addressing information changes. Click the Yes button if you're going to use a DHCP server, or the No button if you're going to manually enter static TCP/IP information.

> **NOTE**
>
> You can use DHCP if you are installing Windows NT Server as a standalone server. If you are installing it as a domain controller, then you must assign a static address to the computer. For more information on DHCP, see Chapter 11, "Dynamic Host Configuration Protocol (DHCP)."

24. If you chose to install the Remote Access Services earlier in this process, Setup prompts you to add a modem and then prompts you through configuring the modem, RAS and, if you selected it, IIS.

> **NOTE**
>
> For more information about installing your modem or RAS, see Chapter 6, "Integrated Networking." For information about the dialog boxes for configuring the network protocols that you choose to install, see Chapter 10, "Installing and Configuring Microsoft TCP/IP."

25. After configuring network protocols, Setup presents a dialog box in which you can alter the order of binding for network protocols, services, and adapters. You can use the Show Bindings for drop-down menu to select services, protocols, or adapters. To change the binding order, highlight an entry in the list for whichever category you use and click the Move Up or Move Down button. You also can use the Enable or Disable buttons for any entry.

26. When all of the network configuration information has been entered, Setup prompts you to start networking. Click the Next button to continue.

27. The next dialog box you see depends on the role you have chosen for the computer on the Network.

    If you chose to create a Primary Domain Controller, the Setup prompts you to enter the name of the domain you want to create. This name must be unique on your network. If a primary domain controller for the domain name you enter already exists on the network, Setup does not continue. You need to enter the domain name to create and click the Next button.

    If you chose to create a Backup Domain Controller, the Setup presents you with a dialog box to enter the domain information so that the computer can join the domain. Setup displays the computer name you have chosen in the computername field. You must then enter the name of a valid Windows NT domain on your network in the Domain field. To join a domain as a backup domain controller, you'll next have to enter the name of a domain account that has administrator level privileges and the password to that account. This security measure is meant to prevent unauthorized computers from trying to join the domain as a domain controller. Click the Next button after you have entered the necessary information.

> **TIP**
>
> You can create a computer account for a new workstation or Windows NT Server computer before you begin the installation process by using the Server Manager administrative tool. See Chapter 16, "Administering the Server" for more information about using the Server Manager.

4

INSTALLING
WINDOWS NT
SERVER

28. Setup next pops up a window telling you that you're in the final phase of installation. Click the Next button to continue. Several informational dialog boxes will inform you of the progress of setup.

29. If you chose to install IIS 2.0, you are prompted at this time to configure it. Use the checkboxes in this dialog box to select the Web services you want to install. You can select:

   ■ Internet Service Manager

   ■ World Wide Web Service

   ■ WWW Service Samples

   ■ Internet Service Manager (HTML)

   ■ Gopher Service

   ■ FTP Service

   ■ ODBC Drivers & Administration

   In this dialog box, you also can choose the Change Directory button to change the root directory that the IIS service will use for files needed in the operation of the service you configure. At the bottom of this dialog box you can see the amount of available disk space and the amount that your selections will use. This is to aid you in configuring services appropriate to the disk space you have. Click the OK button to continue.

30. To finish the IIS installation, you are next prompted by dialog boxes to enter the root directory path for each of the three main Web services: WWW, FTP, and Gopher. You can use the Browse button to locate a directory, or use the keyboard to edit the directory path yourself. If you specify a directory that doesn't exist, Setup prompts you and then creates it for you. Click the OK button when you're satisfied with the directory paths. Setup then creates directories and copy files for the IIS service.

31. The Date/Time Properties dialog box next appears (see Figure 4.5) and from this you can use the drop-down menu to select a time zone. Also on the Time Zone tab you can select a checkbox to enable Windows NT to automatically adjust the computer's time when it changes for daylight savings time. The Date & Time tab enables you to adjust the date and time down to the second. When you're finished, click the Close button to continue with Setup.

NOTE

You can change the time zone or modify the date/time after installation has completed. Use the Date/Time applet in the Control Panel.

FIGURE 4.5.

Select the correct time zone for your location from the Date/Time Properties dialog box.

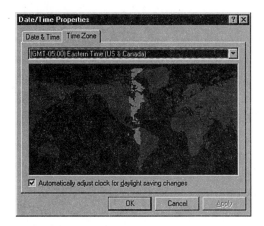

32. Installing the correct driver for your display monitor is very important. The Setup process doesn't want you to select a driver that doesn't work, because if it doesn't work, you're stuck trying to change it back because you can't see the screen. The next dialog box tells you the type of driver NT has detected, enables you to change or configure it, and then makes you test the display before continuing. If you don't use the Test button, you won't be able to continue with Setup.

TIP

When you boot Windows NT, note that in the boot menu there's an option to boot Windows NT in VGA mode. Although NT forces you to test a display monitor configuration, it doesn't prevent you from selecting one that won't work. If you do that by mistake, reboot the computer and select the VGA boot option. This boots Windows NT in a basic VGA mode and from there you can reconfigure the display settings. You also can use the recovery option Use Last Known Good Settings to recover.

Using this dialog box you can change many options for your display. The Display Type button shows you information that NT has detected about your display. However, the dialog box that it pops up does not allow you to change the display type or its configuration during Setup. To do that, you have to use Display applet in the Control Panel after you have finished the installation.

You can, however, change the Color Palette, Refresh Frequency and the Desktop Area options. After you have made your selections, click the Test button. The Setup program displays a color-bar display using your configuration for about five seconds. It then asks you if you were able to see the display. If so, click Yes. If not, click the No button. You can continue to change the display configuration and use the Test button until your display is correct. After you click the Yes button to indicate you have been able to correctly see the display, you can use the OK button on the main Display Properties dialog box to continue with Setup.

33. Setup now copies files from the temporary directory (WIN_NT.~LS and subdirectories) to the system path you specified earlier in the installation process. It then creates Registry settings for your configuration (the Saving Configuration window).

34. If you chose to create an Emergency Repair Disk, Setup prompts you to insert a floppy disk into the computer's A: drive. After you have done so, click the OK button. The diskette is formatted and important Registry and configuration files are copied to it.

35. Setup removes the temporary files it used for the installation.

36. If you chose to make the computer a BDC, a dialog box is displayed showing progress as security information from the primary domain controller is copied to the server. This may take some time if the domain has a large security database.

37. Finally, Setup informs you with a dialog box that Windows NT has been successfully installed. You can click the Restart Computer button to finish the installation.

The server reboots and you can log in and begin to install applications or configure network resources for clients.

Manual Installation of Undetected Drivers

If Setup does not detect one or more of your mass storage devices, you can install it manually during Setup. This is done near the beginning of the installation process after you use the S key to skip the detection phase. When Setup then presents a list of the adapters it has found, you again press the S key. This time it presents you with a screen listing additional drivers.

If you see only one entry on this screen

```
Other (Requires disk provided by a hardware manufacturer
```

use the UP and DOWN ARROW keys to bring other selections into view. If you have a diskette from the manufacturer, however, the Other selection is the one you should take. If you do select Other, Setup prompts you to insert the diskette into the floppy drive. The appropriate files are then copied by Setup and, if the device is properly configured on your computer, Setup continues. After Setup loads the driver file(s) it attempts to communicate with the device. If that fails, it informs you and does not install the driver.

If you have a SCSI driver that worked in previous installations of Windows NT Server, but you cannot get Setup to detect it, the problem may be that some drivers were moved from the base operating system and put into the \DRVLIB directory with the release of Windows NT 4.0. This is not the \DRVLIB.NIC subdirectory that is found under each platform-specific binary directory. It is a top-level directory on the source CD.

If you find the driver you need is in a subdirectory of \DRVLIB on the Windows NT Server source CD, you can create a floppy disk with the driver information to use to manually install the driver during setup:

1. Format a 3.5-inch floppy disk.
2. Set default to the directory:

   `\drvlib\storage\retired\cpu_type`

   cpu_type is x86, for Intel platforms, or MIPS or ALPHA if you are using a RISC platform.
3. Copy all the files from this subdirectory to the blank floppy disk.
4. Use this driver diskette to manually install the driver as described earlier in this section, by using the Other option and providing this diskette.

You don't have to reserve this method for just undetected drivers. You also can install newer drivers from manufacturers during the installation process. Quite often, a new hardware system ships with newer drivers on diskettes that you can load in this manner during setup. In that situation you can choose to install the driver during setup or, if an older driver is on the Windows NT source, you can finish the installation and manually load the driver afterwards.

Reviewing After the Installation

When you reboot your server after the Setup process has finished, you may notice a few things. First, if you forgot to remove the ERD from the floppy drive, you'll get an error when the computer tries to boot. Remove the floppy and reboot.

Changing the Default Timeout Value for the Boot Menu

The next thing you will notice is that when the boot menu is presented, the timeout value for this menu is set to 30 seconds. In most cases you probably don't want to wait that long for a reboot if there's no one present to hit the ENTER key when the computer is rebooted. To change this value, use the System applet in the control panel. In Figure 4.6, you can see that Startup/Shutdown tab has been selected.

While you're in the System applet you may want to examine other configuration properties. You can use the Startup drop-down menu to change which operating system is the default selection in the boot menu. If you are dual-booting between Windows 95 or other versions of Windows NT, select your primary operating system here. Changes you make for the default operating system and the number of seconds to display the menu are stored in a hidden, read-only file on your boot disk called boot.ini. If you're familiar with the contents of this file, you can edit it directly with an ASCII text editor. However, it's best to use the Control Panel System applet for these minor changes.

FIGURE 4.6.

The Startup/Shutdown tab in the System applet enables you to change the timeout value for the boot menu.

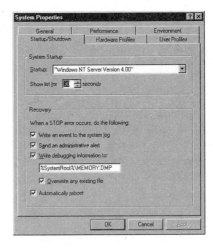

Checking the Paging File

You can use the System applet to configure many other properties of the operating system. This applet is referred to throughout this book in chapters appropriate to the configuration parameters you find here. However, after you complete the installation, you might want to check the size and location of the paging file that was created. Microsoft recommends that the size of the paging file be about 16 MB larger than the amount of physical memory. Thus, if you have 64 MB of memory installed, you would create a paging file of about 80 MB.

To do this, use the Control Panel System applet and select the Performance tab (see Figure 4.7).

FIGURE 4.7.

Click the Change button to change the size or location of the paging files.

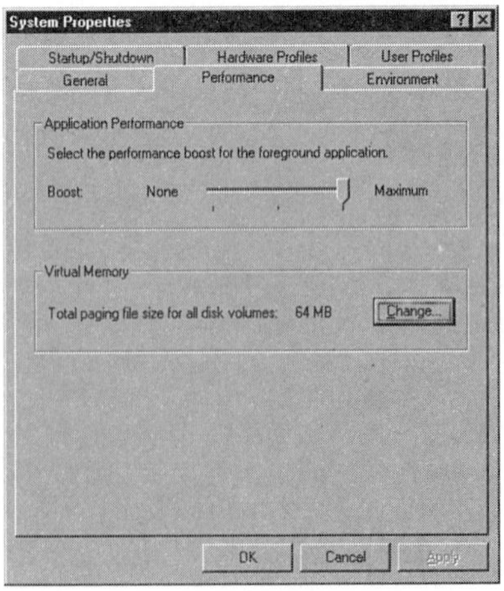

When you click on the Change button, the Virtual Memory dialog box pops up (see Figure 4.8). This dialog box can be used to change the size of the paging file, or add or delete additional page files.

FIGURE 4.8.

You can use the Virtual Memory dialog box to make modifications to the paging file.

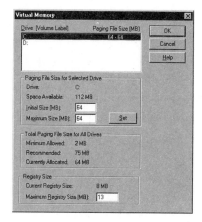

Use your mouse to highlight the disk drive you want to use, use the Initial Size (MB) and Maximum Size (MB) fields to set the size of your paging file, then click the Set button. If you're going to create multiple paging files on separate disks, do so one at a time, selecting the disk and setting the sizes for each file. When you're finished, click the OK button. After you exit the System applet you are prompted to reboot the computer if you have made any changes to the paging file configuration. Until you reboot, the changes you made will not take effect.

It can be difficult to know just what size or location is best to use on any particular system for the paging file. You should use the system Performance Monitor to track usage of the paging files and use that knowledge to adjust the configuration as your server undergoes a normal workload.

Creating the Emergency Repair Disk

Don't forget that after you finish installing applications on your server or configuring it to be a resource server on the network, you should create or update the Emergency Repair Disk using the RDISK utility. See Chapter 16 for instructions on using this important utility.

You also should remember to update this disk every time you make a configuration change on the server and keep the disk in a safe place. After you install a service pack on Windows NT, for example, you should update the ERD. The ERD, along with a good backup of the system disk, can be used by the Setup program to recreate or repair a damaged Windows NT installation. For instructions on how to use the ERD with Setup to restore a system, see the section "Repairing a Windows NT Installation Using the Emergency Repair Disk" later in this chapter.

Converting the Files System to NTFS

If you're going to use Windows NT Server on a network, then you will most likely want to take advantage of the performance enhancements and security features and reliability inherent in using the NTFS file system. If you use FAT partitions you will only be able to limit network access at the level of file shares. If you use NTFS, you can still use file share access, but you can then assign permissions and audit access on a file or directory level. You can read more about how Windows NT works with the different file systems by reading Chapter 5, "Windows NT File Systems Management."

If you have installed Windows NT Server on a FAT partition, you can use the CONVERT command to change it to NTFS:

```
CONVERT/FS:NTFS C:
```

Because the operating system has files opened on the system drive (C:, in this example), the conversion cannot take place at this time. You will get an informational message telling you that the conversion will be done the nest time you reboot the computer. You can, however, use the CONVERT command to change the file system of other drives on the system.

> **NOTE**
>
> If you decide to convert your file system to NTFS, it is a one-way conversion. The CONVERT command does not let you change an NTFS partition back to a FAT partition. You can, however, make a tape backup of the data on the disk, reformat it as a FAT partition, then perform a restore.

Checking Your Licenses

After you have installed the operating system and the applications that you will run on it, you should not put off registering your software licenses with License Manager. Click the Start button, then Programs\Administrative Tools\License Manager. Figure 4.9 shows the License Manager with BackOffice and Windows NT Server Licenses registered.

If you have problems getting clients connected to a new server you have just set up on the network, don't forget to check your licensing to be sure that you haven't forgotten something in the rush to install. As you can see, the License Manager shows you not only the number of licenses you have purchased, but also how many have been used.

FIGURE 4.9.

The License Manager administrative tool is used to record purchases and modifications to licenses.

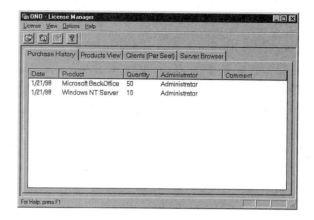

Installing Windows NT Server Service Packs

Microsoft periodically releases updates to Windows NT called Service Packs. Because these updates fix bugs that users find in the operating system as well as enhancements that Microsoft has added, it is a good idea to read the release notes from the service packs as they are issued and consider applying them to your system. You can download the current Windows NT 4.0 Service Packs from Microsoft's Web site using the URL:

```
http://www.microsoft.com/msdownload/default.asp
```

On this Web page, downloads are categorized by type. Select Support Drivers, Patches & Service Packs to get to the section that has the Windows NT Server 4.0 Service Pack downloads.

When you download a Service Pack, read the Readme file before attempting to install the pack. This is an ASCII text file you can download to read before you install the Service Pack. You can find information there that may be helpful in making your decision about whether or not to install the pack. It is highly recommended that you review the information in this file.

The executable file that you download for the current Service Pack 3 for Windows NT Server 4.0 is named NT4SP3_I.EXE. Because Service Packs are cumulative, if you install this Service Pack you don't need to first install pack 1 or 2.

To install Service Pack 3, download the file from Microsoft's Web site and use Microsoft Explorer to start the program or enter the command NT4SP3_I from the MS-DOS Command Prompt. The first dialog box (see Figure 4.10) reminds you that it's a good idea to update your Emergency Repair Disk before you continue, because the update makes changes to the Registry and system files. Should the update fail, or cause some component to malfunction, you can use the Emergency Repair Disk to help recover your system.

4

INSTALLING
WINDOWS NT
SERVER

FIGURE **4.10.**

The Welcome dialog box of the Service Pack setup program reminds you to create an ERD before continuing.

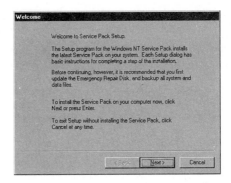

After you click the Next button you will see a dialog box containing the Software License Agreement. Read this and click the Yes button if you accept the terms and want to continue. If you don't accept the license agreement you won't be able to install the Service Pack.

The Service Pack Setup dialog box (see Figure 4.11) prompts you to continue and install the Service Pack. If a previous Service Pack is installed, you can uninstall it at this point. This can be useful if you wish to rollback the installation after testing it. After you make your selection, click the Next button.

FIGURE **4.11.**

You can choose to install the current service pack or you can choose to uninstall a service pack.

The next dialog box enables you to create an uninstall directory (see Figure 4.12). This is necessary if you want to be able to uninstall the service pack (using that option from the previous dialog box) at a later time. Make your selection and click the Next button to continue.

Finally, the Setup program gives you one last chance to either continue or abort the Service Pack installation. Click the Finish button to continue.

The Setup program inspects your system, copies the appropriate files to the uninstall directory (if you so specified), and copies the new files to the correct system directories. When finished, Setup prompts you to reboot the computer before the changes take effect. You should be sure to perform the reboot at that time, or at least before you attempt to install any additional software, to prevent inaccurate entries from being made in the Registry.

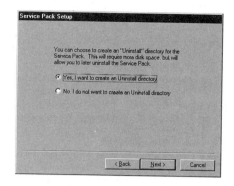

FIGURE 4.12.
You need to create an uninstall directory if you want to be able to rollback the Service Pack (if you encounter problems with it).

The closing dialog box of the install program reminds you that if you install other Windows NT components in the future, you should reapply the Service Pack. This is because when you reinstall Windows NT Server components from the distribution CD, you may be reinstalling older versions of files that were replaced by the Service Pack.

Starting the Installation Process Without the Setup Diskettes

The three setup diskettes that can be used to boot a computer and start the installation process are necessary only if the computer doesn't already have an operating system on it. If the computer is bootable into MS-DOS, Windows 95, or another installation of Windows NT, then you can run the Setup program directly.

There are several methods you can use to run the Setup program directly:

- Execute the Setup program directly from the CD, or copy the files to the computer's hard drive and execute the Setup program from there.
- Connect the client to a network share and run the Setup program from there.
- In a variation on the previous method, you can use an unattended answer file to automate the installation if you're connecting to a network share. Using the answer file eliminates the need for the administrator to sit at the computer and respond to some or all of the installation prompts.
- Again, building on the previous method, you can use an edited version of a Network Client Startup Disk to boot a computer into the network so it can attach to a file share for the installation. The computer doesn't need to have an operating system already installed because you are booting from the floppy disk, but it does require a FAT partition to handle the temporary setup files.

To start the installation you need to run the Setup program. There are two versions of the program: Winnt.exe and Winnt32.exe. If you are installing Windows NT from MS-DOS or Windows 95, use the Winnt 16-bit executable. If you are installing on a computer that already

4

INSTALLING WINDOWS NT SERVER

has a Windows NT installation on it, then you should use the 32-bit version of the program, Winnt32.exe.

The syntax for either command is as follows:

```
WINNT or WINNT32 [/S[:]sourcepath]
[/T[:]tempdrive]
[/I[:]inffile]
[/O[X]] [/X ¦ [/F] [/C]] [/B] [/U[:scriptfile]]
[/R[X]:directory] [/E:command]
```

The syntax is described as follows:

/S[:]sourcepath	Specifies the source location of Windows NT files. Must be a full path of the form x:\[path] or \\server\share[\path]. The default is the current directory.
/T[:]tempdrive	Specifies a drive to contain temporary setup files. If a drive is not specified, Setup attempts to locate a drive for you.
/I[:]inffile	Specifies the filename (no path) of the setup information file. The default is DOSNET.INF in the same folder as winnt or winnt32.
/OX	Create boot floppies for CD-ROM installation, but do not start and installation.
/X	Do not create the Setup boot floppies.
/F	Do not verify files as they are copied to the Setup boot floppies.
/C	Skip free-space check on the Setup boot floppies you provide.
/B	Floppyless operation (requires /s).
/U	Unattended operation and optional script file (requires /s).
/R	Specifies optional directory to be installed.
/RX	Specifies optional directory to be copied.
/E	Specifies command to be executed at the end of GUI setup.

Starting Installation From the CD or the Local Hard Drive

A simple way to start the installation is to insert the distribution CD into the CD-ROM drive and execute the WINNT command from a DOS prompt. If you are booted into Windows NT, you can use the WINNT32 command in an MS-DOS Command Prompt Window. When using this method use the /b switch to prevent Setup from prompting you for the three setup floppy disks. Instead, temporary storage for setup files is placed on the computer's hard disk.

To do this, set default to the correct subdirectory for your hardware platform and enter the following:

```
E:\I386> WINNT32 /B
```

In this example, the platform is Intel. The Setup program runs and prompts you through the process as described earlier in this chapter.

You also can use Windows NT Explorer to browse the network and start the program. By double-clicking the Winnt32 Setup program, you can start the installation program.

A similar method that is preferred is to copy the distribution files (the \i386 directory, for example) to the hard drive local to the computer. If you do this, the files will be available later on when you decide to alter the computer's configuration. You may, for example, want to add new printer drivers to a print server as you add new clients to the network. If the distribution source files are on the server's local hard drive, you don't have to locate the CD when performing this system maintenance chore.

Because each platform's subdirectory on the installation CD also contains subdirectories, you should use the Xcopy command with the following syntax when copying the files to the computer's hard drive:

```
XCOPY/S E:\I386 C:\I386
```

For example, the /S switch causes the subdirectories to be copied along with the main directory. To begin installation, use Microsoft Explorer or set default to the directory on the local drive and execute the Winnt32 command (or the Winnt command if booted into MS-DOS).

> **NOTE**
>
> If you choose to use the Explorer application to copy the files, be sure to use the Options selection on the View menu to set the application to Show All Files. By default Explorer doesn't show hidden files, for example. The problem comes when you attempt to use the Explorer to copy files. If a file isn't displayed by Explorer (that is, it's hidden), then it won't be copied.

Starting Setup From a Network File Share

This method is useful in a large network where it is impractical to have a CD-ROM drive on each computer. Instead, you can boot computers into MS-DOS or any Windows operating system and attach to a network file share to run the installation program. Connect to the file share using a simple LAN Manager command if you're booted into MS-DOS:

```
C:> NET USE ?: \\SERVER\SHARE
```

Use the following LAN Manager command if you're booted into Windows 95 or Windows NT:

```
C:> NET USE * \\SERVER\SHARE
```

Note that the ?: and * wildcard characters allow the networking software to assign a drive letter to the share. Set default to this drive, locate the correct subdirectory for the CPU platform you want to install, and execute the Winnt or Winnt32 command to begin the Setup program.

A nice feature that you can take advantage of when using a network share for your distribution files is the unattended answer file setup. Using an answer file enables you to start the setup and walk away from the computer while Setup uses the data in the answer file to run.

Using a Network Client Startup Disk to Install Windows NT Server

Another method you can use to begin the installation process is to use the Network Client Administrator tool (described more fully in Chapter 24). You can use this utility with an MS-DOS bootable floppy disk to create a diskette that boots a computer, connects it to the network, and starts the installation from a network file share.

To do this, you should use the following utility with the option Make Network Installation Startup Disk (see Figure 4.13):

```
Start\Programs\Administrative Tools\Network Client Administrator
```

FIGURE 4.13.

Use the Make Network Installation Startup Disk option of the Network Client Administrator utility to create a bootable disk to install Windows NT.

Click the Continue button and a dialog box appears (see Figure 4.14) asking you to designate a path for client files.

The Network Client Administrator utility isn't normally used to install NT, but instead to install other operating systems and client networking software. If you haven't used the utility before, it enables you in this dialog box to copy the client files from the CD source to a hard drive and share the new directory. Because you are creating a diskette to install Windows NT, none of these files is necessary. To get past this dialog box, insert the Windows NT source CD into the CD-ROM drive, select Share Files in the dialog box shown in Figure 4.14, and in the Path box fill in the drive letter for the CD.

The path you give here is placed in a line in the diskette's Autoexec.bat file. This is edited to connect to the Windows NT source files after the utility has created the diskette.

FIGURE 4.14.

You do not need to copy files and create a new share when using the Network Client Administrator for this purpose.

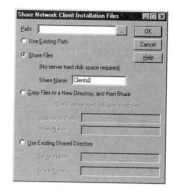

Next, the utility prompts you to specify the floppy drive type, the operating system of the client, and the type of network adapter card (see Figure 4.15). Select Network Client v3.0 for MS-DOS and Windows, along with the appropriate floppy disk size and network adapter. Click the OK button to continue.

FIGURE 4.15.

Use the MS-DOS option in the Target Workstation Configuration dialog box.

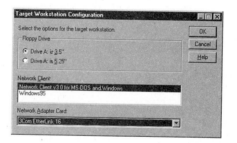

In the next dialog box (see Figure 4.16), you need to fill in a unique computername to be used when the computer boots using the install diskette. The values for the User name and Domain fields should reflect a valid administrator level user account in the domain that contains the file share that holds the distribution files. The TCP/IP protocol should be used. If you have a DHCP server on your network, you can use the checkbox Enable Automatic DHCP Configuration, or if you uncheck this box you must fill in at least the IP address and Subnet Mask fields. Click the OK button when you're ready to continue.

Next, you are prompted to insert a floppy disk in the floppy drive. What the prompt doesn't tell you is that it must be a floppy disk that has been formatted under MS-DOS to be a bootable system disk. You cannot use the FORMAT command at the MS-DOS Command Prompt window under Windows NT to create this diskette. You need to boot MS-DOS on computer to use the command FORMAT/S to create this type of floppy disk.

After you click the OK button, a dialog box appears showing a summary of the actions the utility will take in creating the diskette. Click the OK button. You see onscreen progress reports as the disk is created. When the process is finished, exit the utility and use a text editor to

4

INSTALLING WINDOWS NT SERVER

edit the Autoexec.bat file on the newly created floppy disk. From the MS-DOS Command Prompt, enter the following:

```
EDIT A:\AUTOEXEC.BAT
```

FIGURE 4.16.

The information in the Network Startup Disk Configuration dialog box is used to make the connection to the distribution file share.

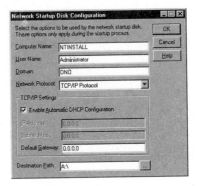

The following is an example of the file created by the Network Client Administrator:

```
path=a:\neta:\net\net initializea:\net\netbind.coma:\net\umb.com
a:\net\tcptsr.exe
a:\net\tinyrfc.exe
a:\net\nmtsr.exe
a:\net\emsbfr.exe
a:\net\net start
net use z: \\BCATST\Clients0
echo Running Setup...
z:\msclient\netsetup\setup.exe /b
```

As you can see, after the computer has been booted and the network started, a connection is made to the file share for the network client software. Edit this line so that it connects to the file share you will use for the Windows NT source files instead. Then edit the last line to run the Winnt Setup executable. Changes to this example file would look like the following:

```
path=a:\net
a:\net\netinitialize
a:\net\netbind.com
a:\net\umb.com
a:\net\tcptsr.exe
a:\net\tinyrfc.exe
a:\net\nmtsr.exe
a:\net\emsbfr.exe
a:\net\net start
net use z: \\BCA1\NT4SRC
echo Running Setup...
z:\i386\winnt /b
```

In this example, the server \\BCA1 is where the file share is located and it is called NT4SRC. The last line executes the Winnt Setup program using the /b switch (to tell Setup it does not need to create boot floppies).

To make this type of installation even more appealing, you can use the /U switch to specify an unattended answer file. If you do this, then you can simply insert the floppy into the computer's A: drive, power it up, and let the installation proceed automatically. The next section covers the use of an unattended answer file.

Using an Unattended Answer File to Install Windows NT

When you are installing a large number of computers (Windows NT Workstation or Windows NT Server), using an unattended answer file can save time and help make the process more accurate. You can establish a few template answer files that you use for basic types of computer installations in your network and then use these templates to create answer files for specific computers.

In addition to saving time in the installation configuration process, answer files can be saved for later use as documentation for each install or can be used to recreate a server that has become corrupt.

To use an unattended answer file with the Winnt setup program, use the /U switch. Use a colon (:) character after the switch and then specify the file name of the answer file. You also use the /S switch to designate the location of the source files.

You can find an example of an answer file on either the Windows NT Workstation or Server distribution CDs in the platform-specific directory (\i386 for example). The file is named Unattend.txt.

The answer file contains sections that have headers delineated by square-bracket ([]) characters. Following the section header are parameter keywords and values you assign to them. The following shows the [Userdata] section where you can specify the unique computername that the server will use on the network:

```
[Userdata]
FullName = "t.w.ogletree"
OrgName = "Business Communications Associates, Inc."
ComputerName = "NTSERVER1"
```

You can instruct the Setup program to install specific network adapters or to detect the adapter installed in the computer. You can specify network protocol information such as TCP/IP configuration information or instruct Setup to configure the computer to use DHCP. The complete list of sections and parameters you can use in an answer file can be found in Microsoft's Knowledge Base. You can access the Knowledge Base at the following URL:

```
http://www.microsoft.com/support/
```

Search the database for Windows NT Server for article number Q155197, which is titled "Unattended Setup Parameters for Unattend.txt File." In addition, the Knowledge Base contains other articles to help you use an unattended answer file, such as how to install a non-supported network adapter during unattended installation.

As was discussed in the preceding section, you can use the winnt command with an answer file to automate installing Windows NT using a Network Client Startup Disk. Following is an example of the command line that would be used to do this:

```
WINNT /u:z:\unattend.txt /s:z:\i386 /b
```

Here the Z: drive has been mapped to the file share. The file Unattend.txt is the name of the answer file, and it resides at the top level of the file share directory structure. The /s switch is used to indicate that the source files for the installation are in the \i386 subdirectory on the Z: file share. Finally, the /b switch instructs Setup not to create the boot floppies. After this line is executed in Autoexec.bat, the Setup program runs uninterrupted, provided you have given it sufficient information in the answer file.

> **TIP**
>
> It is possible to perform an almost-unattended installation using an answer file. For example, if you don't have available the information needed by Setup to install the network adapter when you create the setup file, you place a line in the answer file instructing Setup to prompt you when it gets to this phase, just as it would during a normal installation. In this type of situation, the answer file can still be used to automate most of the installation process, thus cutting down on the employee time needed to set up computers on the network.

Using the Sysdiff Utility From the Resource Kit To Customize Installations

In the Windows NT Workstation or Server Resource Kit, you can find a utility called Sysdiff that you can use to customize an installation. Sysdiff enables you to take a snapshot of the installed system, install applications, and then create a file of the differences. You can then use the Sysdiff utility to apply the differences file to a newly installed system. By using this technique, you can install applications on multiple servers or workstations without having to run the actual setup programs for each application.

It should be noted that Sysdiff does not work for all applications. It won't correctly install programs that run as Windows NT services, for example. You should test your specific configuration to determine if it will suffice for your purposes.

Before you can use the Sysdiff utility, you must create a text file called Sysdiff.inf. This file contains information needed by Sysdiff, such as directories or Registry keys that should be excluded. You can find an example of a Sysdiff.inf file in the Windows NT Workstation Resource Kit documentation. Note that if you have the Server resource kit, it also includes the complete text for the Workstation version of the resource kit.

To use Sysdiff, you first install Windows NT Server on a new computer and create a snap-shot file:

```
SYSDIFF /SNAP
  [/log:log_filename]snapshot_path/filename
```

Sysdiff creates the snapshot file using the path and filename you give it. Figure 4.17 shows an example of Sysdiff performing a snapshot.

FIGURE 4.17.

The Sysdiff utility first takes a snapshot of the initial system.

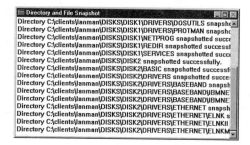

A small dialog box will inform you when the snapshot is complete.

NOTE

Sysdiff doesn't always terminate correctly when it is finished. After you click the OK button, you may find the Sysdiff utility still on the computer screen, but unresponsive to your mouse or keyclicks. If this happens when you are using Sysdiff, don't worry. Just use the Task Manager to kill the process. To bring up the Task Manager, right-click the task bar and select Task Manager from the pop-up menu. Select the Applications tab and highlight Sysdiff, then click the End Task button.

After you create the snapshot file, you then install the applications on the server. After you have installed and configured the applications, use Sysdiff to create a differences file. Sysdiff compares the system as it is to the record of it stored in the snapshot file, and produces the differences file that can be used to customize other systems.

```
SYSDIFF /DIFF [/log:log_filename]
snapshot_filename difference_filename
```

In this command you substitute the actual snapshot filename for the first filename parameter and then specify the name of the differences file to create.

To apply the differences file to another Windows NT Server installation, use the Sysdiff /apply command:

```
SYSDIFF /apply /m difference_filename
```

This is a simple introduction to the Sysdiff utility. The Resource Kit documentation describes other functions you can perform using this utility and gives examples.

The resource kits also contain other time-saving deployment methods you can use for installing Windows NT. You can create specific OEM directories for an unattended answer file to use to perform application installations after the operating system has been installed. This can be used when Sysdiff fails to accomplish the goal.

Repairing a Windows NT Installation Using the Emergency Repair Disk

The Emergency Repair Disk (ERD) is a very valuable resource. If your Windows NT Server becomes corrupt or unstable, you can use the disk to re-create the server. The ERD is not a bootable disk. It must be used with the Setup program to repair the system.

The ERD does *not* contain all the files needed for an NT installation, obviously. You cannot use it alone to bring up an NT system. Instead, it contains information from the Registry that can be used to correct an installation that has become unusable.

To use the ERD, you need to use the three Setup floppy diskettes to boot the system. When Setup prompts you to either install Windows NT or repair a damaged system, enter R for repair.

> **TIP**
>
> If you're unable to find the original setup floppy disks, you can re-create them on another computer using the Setup program. The syntax is: WINNT /ox. You are prompted for the location of the Windows NT source files (the CD-ROM, for example), and then for three blank, formatted floppy disks.

A text menu similar to the following will appear:

```
[x]     Inspect Registry files
[x]     Inspect startup environment
[x]     Verify Windows NT system files
[x]     Inspect boot sector
        Continue (perform selected tasks)
```

You can clear or set each option by setting or clearing the X character in the bracketed field. When you are ready to continue, click Continue.

Depending on the selections you made, Setup performs repair actions.

Inspecting Registry Files Option

Setup presents you with a list of the Registry files that it can repair using the ERD. You can select any or all of them:

```
[x]     SYSTEM (System Configuration)
[x]     SOFTWARE (Software Information)
[x]     DEFAULT (Default User Profile)
[x]     NTUSER.DAT (New User Profile)
[x]     SECURITY (Security Policy) and
        SAM (User Accounts Database)
        Continue (perform selected tasks)
```

Here you can again place an x in the brackets next to the items you want to repair, and then click Continue.

Inspecting Startup Environment

This option is used to check and see if the correct files are on the system partition that is needed to start Windows NT. For example, on an Intel based system, the boot.ini file must be present. It also replaces any missing files on the boot partition by copying them from the source CD.

Verifying Windows NT System Files

This option reads the Setup.log file from the ERD and use it to determine if any system files need to be replaced, by comparing the checksum for files listed in the Setup.log file with the actual files on disk. If any are deemed to be different, Setup prompts you before it replaces a file. This option also checks that certain files (such as the OS loader file and the NT kernel) are correct on the boot partition and replaces them if necessary.

Inspecting Boot Sector

On Intel-based systems, this option checks to be sure the boot sector points to the NTLDR program and replaces the boot sector if it doesn't.

When Setup is finished, it prompts you to reboot the computer.

Summary

Windows NT Server is a complex operating system. Installing it, however, doesn't have to be a chore, provided you understand the process and gather the information you need before you start. You should be sure that the hardware you're purchasing has been certified to be compatible with NT and you should be sure to test the configuration before you commit to a large purchase.

The installation program is very flexible. You can start it using the boot floppy disks that come with Windows NT, or you can start the Setup procedure by using the Winnt[32].exe programs. The source files can reside on a CD, or they can be on the computer's local hard drive or a network share the computer can access.

When you have finished installing Windows NT Server, you should consider installing the most current Windows NT Service Packs after you read the release notes.

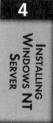

4

INSTALLING
WINDOWS NT
SERVER

Windows NT File Systems Management

by Robert Reinstein and Jason Garms

IN THIS CHAPTER

CHAPTER

5

Windows NT offers a wide array of file systems to meet the needs of any application. It does this by using installable file systems, which can easily be modified and replaced as necessary by either Microsoft or third-party vendors. Out of the box, Windows NT provides a great degree of flexibility by providing an advanced version of the File Allocation Table (FAT) file system format, the advanced NT File System (NTFS), and the CD File System (CDFS). Use of the FAT file system is mostly recommended when backward compatibility with DOS systems is a requirement. It also provides support for floppy disks and other removable media. The NTFS file system is the recommended file system for use with Windows NT. It supports robust fault-tolerance, provides excellent support for large volumes, and provides security and auditing capabilities.

Versions of Windows NT prior to 4.0 also supported the High-Performance File System (HPFS), which was used predominantly by the OS/2 operating system. This support was included primarily for users who were upgrading from OS/2, and support for HPFS has been removed from Windows NT 4.0. More on this topic is discussed later in this chapter.

Having knowledge of the different file systems and how to manage them is an important matter to consider before you install Windows NT Server.

This chapter reviews the FAT file system and introduces you to Windows NT's NTFS and the tools used to manage file systems under Windows NT, most notably the Disk Administrator utility.

Understanding Partitions

This section gives a brief overview of how disk partitioning works, which is important to getting the most out of your server system.

Each hard drive has a reserved section for a table called the Master Boot Record (MBR). This table can record four entries, which tell the operating system where to locate the partitions. These partitions are called *primary partitions*, and there is a maximum of four primary partitions on a drive. The information necessary to load Windows NT (NTLDR, NTDETECT.COM, BOOT.INI, and any special device drivers) must be located on a primary partition. Each primary partition will be assigned a drive letter, and it must be formatted.

A second type of partition that can be recorded in the MBR is called an *extended partition*. You can only have one partition on a hard drive. The extended partition is effectively a container that can be used to create *logical drives*. Because the MBR can only keep track of four partitions per disk, extended partitions give you a place to create additional partitions, which are in turn managed by the operating system itself. You can create as many logical drives inside the extended partition as the operating system will permit. As far as the MBR is concerned, all logical drives within the extended partition are part of the same volume. It cannot see the logical differentiation. You do not need to format the extended partition, nor is it assigned a drive letter. However, when you create logical drives inside the extended partition, the logical drives are assigned drive letters and must be formatted.

An extended partition is recorded in the MBR the same way as a primary partition, so if you create an extended partition, you can in fact only create three additional primary partitions.

NOTE

If you will be using a disk to boot from, you must have at least one primary partition on it. Only primary partitions can contain the system information need to bootstrap a computer.

CAUTION

Be careful when creating partitions on a drive that you don't consume your four allotted partitions and that you still have free space remaining. If, for example, you had a 1GB drive and you created four primary partitions of 200MB each, you would *not* be able to allocate the remaining unused 200MB. In order to use this remaining 200MB, you would need to remove the last partition and either create a 400MB primary partition or create a 400MB extended partition, inside of which you could create multiple logical drives.

Working with File Systems

Before we discuss how to effectively implement and use the file systems in Windows NT, it is important to understand the background of these file systems. I'll discuss a little history of the file systems, as well as their pros and cons.

The FAT File System

The FAT file system was named for the file allocation table, which is used to store information about the disk, such as the areas that are used and unused, the areas that are bad, and the location of the last cluster in each file. The FAT file system was designed at a time when floppy disks were the most common form of storage media, and hard drives had capacities of around 10 megabytes.

Because of this, FAT was not designed with larger capacities in mind. To meet the needs of ever-growing storage devices and new operating systems, FAT has continued to evolve. Furthermore, the original FAT was only designed to support small numbers of files with relatively simple directory structures. However, because of its original design limitations, there were only so many improvements that could be made.

To provide some minor degree of recoverability, the FAT actually keeps two copies of the file allocation table, called FAT1 and FAT2. FAT1 is the primary copy, but if it becomes damaged, the structure of the volume can still be read from FAT2. All FAT volumes are organized in the same manner. The beginning of the volume contains the partition boot sector, followed by FAT1, followed by FAT2, followed by the root folder, followed by all other files and folders.

The Root Folder

On a FAT volume, the root folder is a special section of the disk. It is the only folder on the volume that has a finite, predefined limit. The root folder on every FAT volume is in exactly the same location and has enough room for 512 folder and file entries.

> **NOTE**
>
> When we speak of the root folder of a volume, we are speaking of the top-level part of the volume. For example, on a standard drive denoted as drive c, the root would be the section called c:\.

> **NOTE**
>
> The limit of 512 entries in the root folder of a FAT volume can be a problem, particularly when dealing with long filenames. See the discussion on long filenames later in this chapter. This limit *only* applies to the root folder.

On a FAT volume, each folder has a 32-byte entry for each file and folder contained within it. The root folder can hold 512 entries, which means that the size of the root folder is 16KB on the FAT volume.

Clusters

Partitions formatted with FAT are broken into clusters. The type of FAT that is in use today is typically called FAT16, or 16-bit FAT. This means that there is only enough room in the file allocation table to define 65,536 (2^{16}) clusters. There is also a version of FAT called FAT12, which supports 2^{12}, 4096, clusters. In addition, Microsoft has developed a newer version of FAT called FAT32, which will support up to 4,294,967,296 clusters. This enables systems using FAT32 to access very large volumes—much greater than the 2GB limit on FAT16 volumes.

> **NOTE**
>
> At this point Microsoft will only be making FAT32 available with a special version of Windows 95 called OEM Service Release (OSR) 2. FAT32 is incompatible with FAT16 and will only work with operating systems that have special FAT32 drivers. This means that

FAT32 volumes will be unreadable with all versions of DOS, Windows NT, OS/2, and even the versions of Windows 95 prior to OSR2. Most utilities that directly access the hard drive, such as Norton Utilities, will no longer work with FAT32. Newer versions of these programs that specifically support FAT32 will need to be used.

Microsoft designed FAT32 because the size of hard drives has been growing so rapidly. At the time of this writing, most systems are shipping with drives greater than 2GB. In order to take advantage of this increase, you need a 32-bit file system.

So why not write FAT32 for Windows NT? Who knows. Microsoft might do that some day, but third-party vendors could also write it for Windows NT. However, because Windows NT already has NTFS, which is a 32-bit file system, there is no compelling need for FAT32.

As for why Microsoft didn't simply port NTFS to Windows 95, instead of writing a new file system, there are two reasons. First is that of compatibility with third-party applications, such as Norton Utilities. It is very easy for these utility vendors to modify their applications to support FAT32 because FAT32 is structurally identical to FAT16, with the exception of 32-bit clusters. However, if Microsoft had used NTFS on Windows 95, these utility vendors would have had to completely rewrite their applications because NTFS is very different from FAT. The second reason is that NTFS has a higher memory overhead than FAT32. The DOS real-mode drivers that would be needed to support NTFS would consume far too much conventional memory. Under Windows 95, that's not a problem. However, when you boot Windows 95 in its DOS compatibility mode (for example, for troubleshooting or games), you would not have enough conventional memory left to run most programs.

The cluster size for different sized FAT volumes is shown in Table 5.1.

Table 5.1. Cluster size for different sized FAT volumes.

Partition size	Cluster size
0 MB - 32MB	512 bytes
33 MB - 64MB	1KB
65 MB - 128MB	2KB
129 MB - 255MB	4KB
256 MB - 511MB	8KB
512 MB - 1023MB	16KB
1024 MB - 2047MB	32KB
2048 MB - 4095MB	64KB

NOTE

Under DOS and Windows, FAT partitions cannot be larger than 2047MB, regardless of the cluster size.

So what's the big deal? Why are large cluster sizes so bad? The answer lies in the way FAT records file and folder locations. Each cluster can only hold a single file because files are only located in the FAT based on their cluster number. This means that if you had a 1.6GB volume, it would be using 32KB cluster sizes. If you create a new Notepad document, type a few characters and save it, that would consume a whole cluster, which in this case is 32KB. So, you'd have over 31KB of wasted space that could not be used.

After the 16KB allocated to the root folder, the rest of the volume has no fixed organization. Files and folders are simply added as necessary and as room permits. As mentioned earlier in this chapter, each file and folder must be defined somewhere. The root folder is always in the same place, but it contains 32-byte entries that tell it about the files and folder that reside in it. These 32-byte entries contain the information shown in Table 5.2.

Table 5.2. Information stored in a file or folder reference.

Item	Size Allocated
Name	11 bytes
Attribute byte	8 bits
Create time	24 bits
Create date	16 bits
Last access date	16 bits
Last modified time	16 bits
Last modified date	16 bits
Starting cluster	16 bits
File size	32 bits

TIP

Because the overhead of using the FAT file system grows as partition size increases, it is advisable to not use FAT on partitions that are greater than 200 megabytes. Under Windows NT, you *cannot* use a FAT partition for a volume greater than 4GB.

So let's look at what happens when you want to locate a file and open it with Notepad. If you tell Notepad that you want to open `c:\users\this.txt`, then the file system will look first at `c:\`, which is in a predefined place on the disk, because it is the root folder. It will look through the entries in `c:\` to find a folder called users. The entry for users will tell it the starting cluster for users in the file allocation table. It will then look up the cluster for the folder users, and when it is found, it will look through the entries in users and try to find a file called `this.txt`. The entry for `this.txt` contains the starting cluster number for `this.txt`, which is where we find the file, and Notepad opens it for us.

So what happens when a file is larger than the cluster size? Well, if we had a 1.6GB FAT volume, the cluster size would be 32KB. This means that we could fit 32KB of information before worrying about another cluster. When the file grows larger than 32KB, the file system looks for the next available free cluster on the volume. It then records this new cluster number at the end of the previous cluster, so we're forming a chain. When we fill the second cluster, the file system locates a third cluster and records its address at the end of the second cluster. The file keeps on growing in this fashion, consuming as many clusters as necessary.

Fragmentation

This leads us to another problem of the FAT file system: It's prone to fragmentation. Fragmentation is the result of data being written to noncontiguous (non-sequential) clusters, which can slow down the read/write process. FAT writes files to the first available cluster it can find, and then skips ahead past used clusters to complete writing a file. The slower a computer's processor and hard drive subsystem are, the more the system will be affected by fragmentation.

The amount of actual fragmentation on a system can also be affected by the type of data that is stored on a system and the cluster size. For instance, if the majority of the files on your system are small text files and you have 32KB clusters, you might not be too concerned about fragmentation because most of the files will fit into their own clusters. However, if most of your data is larger than the system's cluster size, and you tend to copy, delete, and modify this data regularly, then you are more likely to suffer from a fragmented volume.

> **NOTE**
>
> Windows NT 4.0 does not provide a defragmentation utility, so you will have to shop around for a third-party product. You can find defragmentation utilities and much more on the Windows NT Magazine Resources page at
>
> `http://www.winntmag.com/resources/index.html`

5

WINDOWS NT
FILE SYSTEMS
MANAGEMENT

Long Filenames on FAT Volumes

Beginning with Windows NT 3.5 and Windows 95, Microsoft came up with a way to do long filenames (LFNs) on FAT volumes. This was a major convenience for users because the

255-character long filenames are much more user-friendly than the traditional 8-dot-3 character names that were traditionally the bane of many DOS users. In Windows NT 3.1, you could only use long filenames on NTFS or HPFS volumes. With DOS, there is no method for using LFNs on FAT volumes.

Windows NT and Windows 95 use the same method for recording LFNs on FAT partitions. Consequently, floppy disks that contain LFNs created by Windows 95 can be read by Windows NT without a problem. The converse is likewise true. In addition, you can dual-boot between Windows NT and Windows 95 and still use long filenames.

Because LFNs are stored in a special way on the FAT volume, you can even read a FAT volume that uses LFNs on a system that doesn't understand LFNs—such as DOS. However, if you modify the volume, you run the risk of damaging the LFN data because DOS doesn't know that it should update the LFN information when a change is made.

CAUTION

Some third-party disk defragmenters—such as pre-Windows 95 versions of Norton Utilities—do not support LFN. Using one of these products to defragment your FAT volumes can result in losing all LFN information, and Windows NT will not be able to locate some of the files on reboot.

When Windows NT saves a file with a long filename to a FAT partition, it saves an 8-dot-3–generated filename in the FAT, as would normally be expected. It then saves the long filename for the file by creating *special folder entries* to record the LFN data. It uses one of these special folders for each of the 13 characters of the long file name. These folders are *special* because Windows NT marks the *volume, read-only, system,* and *hidden* file attribute bits of the folder entry. Under normal usage, these four bits should *never* all be set, so other operating systems that support FAT, such as DOS and OS/2, will ignore these folder entries.

NOTE

If you're paying attention here, you might be wondering how you can fit 13 Unicode characters (26 bytes) into the same space that's normally used by 11 eight-bit characters (11 bytes). Actually, what's happening is that a directory entry is always given 32-bytes, of which 11 bytes are reserved for the filename. However, in this sneaky LFN method, you don't need to preserve the attributes, date, and timestamp information in each of the LFN file entries. So Windows NT actually uses the bytes normally reserved for these other file properties for storing pieces of the filename. The traditional FAT entry for the file that contains the generated 8-dot-3 name also then has all the file attributes. Each of the secondary entries used for the LFN contains only LFN data.

Therefore, if you were to create a file named Jason's long file name.txt (26 characters), it would consume three 32-byte entries for the file name—one for the 8-dot-3 name, which would be JASON'~1.TXT, and two for the LFN.

So how are the 8-dot-3 names generated from the long filenames? The 8-dot-3 version of a long filename of, for example My Report, would be MYREPO~1. Note that the imbedded space has been stripped out and only the first six characters of the filename have been used. The following tilde character and the number one have been added in case there was another filename that started with the same first six characters. If another long filename existed named My Report For September, that file under DOS would be seen as MYREPO~2, and so on. Spaces are not the only characters that will be removed from a long filename. Any other special character that is not supported in 8-dot-3 filenames will be replaced in the conversion by an underscore.

Long filenames on FAT use the 16-bit Unicode character set, which contains many special characters as well as support for most international special characters. Because many of these characters are deemed illegal by DOS file naming standards, these characters are also stripped in generating the 8-dot-3 filenames.

You can disable the generation of LFNs on FAT volumes by changing the Registry Win31FileSystem parameter to 1. This parameter is located in HKEY_LOCAL_MACHINE\ System\CurrentControlSet\Control\FileSystem. Setting this value prevents the creation of new LFNs on all FAT volumes but does not remove existing LFNs.

Disk Compression with FAT

Windows NT does not support disk compression with FAT volumes. Any FAT partitions that use DOS-based disk compression (such as Stacker or DriveSpace) will be inaccessible when running Windows NT. Only the "host drive" that houses the compressed data volume will be visible. If you want to upgrade a Windows 3.x or Windows 95 machine to Windows NT and you are using volume-compression software, you will need to remove the compression software before you can upgrade. If the software cannot be removed, you will need to reformat the entire volume.

Partitions formatted using special partitioning software designed for DOS will also not be recognized by Windows NT. If you want to upgrade a Windows 3.x or Windows 95 machine to Windows NT and you are using special partitioning software, you will most likely need to reformat the volume.

The HPFS File System

HPFS was introduced in 1990 as part of OS/2 version 1.2. HPFS allowed for greater capacity hard drives and instituted technologies that would help prevent the occurrence of fragmentation. Such technologies included the use of physical sectors instead of clusters, and implemented a data structure called a B-tree, which allows for directory searches to occur in a more logical manner, as opposed to FAT's linear structure. HPFS also tries to leave physical space between files, giving each file room for expansion, which would then result in less fragmentation except when the volumes were allowed to fill up. HPFS also introduced long filenames of up to 255 characters, along with other attributes, such as the same attributes kept by FAT, and an access control list (ACL).

Of course, HPFS was designed with OS/2 in mind, and it is the file system of choice for that operating system. At one point, when Microsoft and IBM were co-developing OS/2, another file system, HPFS386, was introduced that took advantage of the then-new 386 processor and was available for use on Microsoft's LAN Manager product. HPFS386 is back again in the most recent version of OS/2.

> **NOTE**
>
> Previous versions of Microsoft Windows NT Server came with native support for HPFS. Microsoft Windows NT Server 4.0 does not come with a driver for HPFS.

> **TIP**
>
> If you are running HPFS under Windows NT 3.5x and you want to upgrade to NT 4.0, you must first convert your HPFS volumes to NTFS using the CONVERT.EXE command. After converting the HPFS volumes, you may upgrade to Windows NT 4.0.

The NTFS File System

With the introduction of Windows NT in 1992, Microsoft took the advanced capabilities of HPFS and went many steps further. A major part of the security model that NT offers is based on the NTFS file system. While shared directories can be set up on an NT server regardless of the file system used, it is only with NTFS that individual files can be assigned permissions. These rights, which also include rights to a directory, can be assigned permissions, whether or not they are shared. Every attribute of the NTFS is kept as a file.

NTFS is the preferred file system for Windows NT because it allows you to use all of NT's security features. A system, however, can use all three of the available file systems at the same time. Of course, only the NTFS partitions will have the advantages of individual directory and file security. Usually HPFS partitions will be kept on a non-dedicated NT server to allow for dual booting of both NT and OS/2. However, the access control lists associated with the data on the HPFS partitions will not be recognized by NT's implementation of HPFS. If the server is a dedicated server, the existing HPFS partitions can be converted to NTFS using the CONVERT.EXE utility. The CONVERT.EXE utility is discussed later in this chapter in the section titled "Converting to NTFS."

NOTE

All floppy disks formatted with Windows NT use FAT. This is because the basic overhead of the NTFS file system would consume too much space on the floppy disk, effectively making the disk worthless for storing user data. Therefore, NTFS is not a supported format on floppy disks.

TIP

Many Windows NT services either require or work better with NTFS volumes. In particular, Services for Macintosh requires an NTFS volume in order to share files with Macintosh clients. Also, the Internet Information Server requires NTFS if you want to be able to implement file-level security for Web clients.

File descriptions on an NTFS volume are stored in a Master File Table (MFT), which is also a file. Besides the several records that contain data about the MFT itself, the MFT contains a record for each file and directory, as well as a log file. A mirror of the MFT is also kept, as well as pointers to the MFT and its mirror, which are stored in the boot sector of the disk. A copy of the boot sector is stored in the logical center of the disk. With this many copies of the MFT, data recovery becomes even easier. That is why NTFS is known as a "recoverable file system."

Figure 5.1 shows the general format of the Master File Table. The Master File Table contains pointers that refer to external continuations, which are referred to in this diagram as extents.

FIGURE 5.1.
NTFS's Master File Table.

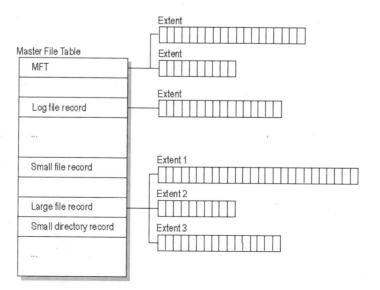

5

WINDOWS NT
FILE SYSTEMS
MANAGEMENT

When a file is called for on a FAT partition, a pointer to a list of sectors is read. NTFS cuts out one of these steps by having the sector map contained within the MFT. In cases of small files, it is possible that only a single record in the MFT can contain all the information for that one file. Larger files require that extents are read, and directories will require that the B-tree structure is read. This all makes for a very speedy file system.

When a partition is formatted as NTFS, numerous system files are created that keep track of certain attributes of that partition. These system files are documented in Table 5.3.

Table 5.3. NTFS system files.

Filename	System File	Description
$Mft	Master File Table	The MFT.
$MftMirr	Master File Table2	The mirror copy of the MFT.
$LogFile	Log File	A file activity log that can be used to help rebuild information in case of a failure.
$Volume	Volume	The name of a volume, along with other volume information.
$AttrDef	Attribute Definitions	A table of attribute names, numbers, and descriptions.
$.	Root Filename Index	The root directory.
$Bitmap	Cluster Bitmap	A representation of the volume, showing allocation units that are in use.
$Boot	Boot File	If this partition is bootable, a bootstrap is included here.
$BadClus	Bad Cluster File	Pointers to all the bad clusters on this volume.
$Quota	Quota Table	Quota information on the volume for all users. This is currently unused.
$Upcase	Uppercase Table	Table for mapping lowercase Unicode characters to their uppercase equivalents.

The attributes of a file on an NTFS volume may contain all or some of the items listed in Table 5.4.

Table 5.4. NTFS file attributes.

Attribute	Description
Standard Information	Includes timestamps, link count, and so on.
Attribute List	Lists all other attributes in large files only.

Attribute	Description
Filename	The long filename (up to 255 characters) and the MS-DOS–compatible short filename.
Security Descriptor	Contains permissions for the file, along with the owner's ID.
Data	Various data attributes which may include unnamed attributes that are identified by keywords.
Index Root	Required for directories.
Index Allocation	Required for directories.
Volume Information	The volume name and other information required by the volume system file.
Bitmap	Pointers to records in use on the MFT or directory.
Extended Attribute Information	Not used by NT, but contains data that can be used by OS/2 systems.
Extended Attributes	Not used by NT, but contains data that can be used by OS/2 systems.

NTFS Filenaming Concerns

The NTFS file system uses the 16-bit Unicode character set, which allows for the use of some special characters, including support for characters of non-Roman character sets, such as Chinese, Japanese, and Korean characters. Also, NTFS preserves both upper- and lowercase letters of the alphabet. Therefore, a filename of My Document will retain the uppercase characters in its name. NTFS, however, will not differentiate between files that use the same characters with different cases. For instance, my document may coexist in the same directory as My Document, but if you use Notepad to open the My Document file, the contents of my document will appear in Notepad. This anomaly can create havoc for some users, which is why it is important that you standardize how you name files.

> **NOTE**
>
> Interestingly enough, although NTFS can handle filenames of up to 255 characters, files created from the command line can only have filenames up to 253 characters. This limitation is created by the command line itself.

The following special characters cannot appear in an NTFS filename:

? " / \ < > * | :

When copying files from NTFS to either HPFS or FAT using command-line utilities such as XCOPY and COPY, you may receive errors. This could occur because although these utilities can handle long filenames, the receiving file system may "choke" on embedded spaces or other illegal characters. To get around this, use the /N switch on those commands, and then the short filename will be used. For example, to copy the contents of directory C:\My Documents from an NTFS partition to the directory D:\DOCS, located on a FAT partition, use the following syntax:

```
XCOPY "C:\My Documents\*.*" D:\DOCS /N
```

Special attention must also be used when creating shortcuts to programs using file associations. If a type of file is associated with a 16-bit program, and the long filename is being used, the 16-bit program will not know how to interpret the filename and not be able to load the file. This will not be a problem on a system that is running all Windows NT- or Windows 95-compliant programs.

> **WARNING**
>
> Using any 16-bit program—such as the Windows 3.x File Manager or a DOS utility such as Norton Commander—to manipulate files that have long filenames will destroy the long filenames! If this is on an NTFS volume, all the security information will be eliminated as well! Only use 32-bit programs that support long filenames when moving or copying files on an NTFS volume.

Because generating short filenames does create a certain amount of overhead on the server, you can disable this feature.

To disable short filename support, use the Registry Editor, REGEDT32.EXE, and locate HKEY_LOCAL_MACHINE\System\CurrentControlSet\Control\FileSystem. Change the value of the key value NtfsDisable8dot3NameCreation to a value of 1; short filename generation will be disabled.

The Recoverable File System

Of course, the main purpose of file systems is to keep track of data stored on hard storage media (usually hard drives) and to facilitate the reading and writing of this data. NTFS's recoverable file system is a great enhancement on FAT's careful-write file system and the lazy-write file system used by UNIX and FAT as implemented on Windows NT.

FAT's careful-write file system allows writes one at a time and alters its volume information after each write. This is a very secure form of writing. It is, however, also a very slow process.

The lazy-write file system uses a cache. All writes are performed to this cache and the file system intelligently waits for the appropriate time to perform all the writes to disk. This system gives the user faster access to the file system and prevents holdups due to slower disk access. It is also possible that if the same file is modified more than once within a short period of time, it may never actually be written to disk until the final modification is made and then flushed from the cache. Of course, this can also lead to lost data if the system crashes and unwritten modifications are still held in the cache.

NTFS's recoverable file system provides the speed of a lazy-write file system along with recovery features. The recovery features come from a transaction log that keeps track of which writes to disk have been completed and which have not. In the recovery process, this log can assure that only a few moments after a reboot the file system's integrity is back to 100 percent—without the need to run a utility such as CHKDSK, which requires the entire volume to be scanned. The overhead associated with this recoverable file system is less than the type used by the careful-write file system.

The recoverable file system can also ensure that an NTFS partition will always remain accessible, even if the partition is not bootable and the bootstrap has been damaged. In this instance, you can boot from another drive or from floppy disk and still have access to the volume.

NTFS supports hot-fixing as well. Instead of FAT's notorious Abort, Retry, Fail? message, NTFS will attempt to move the data in a damaged cluster to a new location in a fashion that is transparent to the user. The damaged cluster is then marked as unusable. Unfortunately, it is possible that the moved data will be unusable anyhow, because the chance of corruption is very likely unless fault tolerance is enabled, and then the replicated data from the nondamaged cluster will be used in its place.

> **NOTE**
>
> This feature is known as *sector sparring.*

The way that NTFS processes file actions as transactions is the key to its high degree of recoverability. Each write request to an NTFS partition generates redo and undo information. The redo information tells NTFS how to re-create the intended write. The undo information tells NTFS how to rollback the transaction in the event that the transaction is incomplete or has an error. After the write transaction is complete, NTFS generates a file update commit. Otherwise, NTFS uses the undo information in order to rollback the request.

The type of commit that NTFS performs is called a *lazy commit.* This is similar to a lazy write in the sense that it will cache these file commits and write them to the transaction log when system resources are high. This feature allows NTFS's high reliability features to have less overhead, overall, on the system.

In the case of a system crash or unexpected shutdown of NT (such as someone accidentally powering off the server before a clean shutdown is performed), NTFS will perform a three-pass system check upon restarting.

As with most transactional-type logs, checkpoints are created once all log transactions since the last checkpoint have been confirmed. Checkpoint creation occurs every few seconds. The first pass that NTFS makes after a system restart is called the *analysis pass*. In this pass, NTFS compares items in the transaction log, since the last checkpoint, to the clusters those transactions dealt with. A second pass, called the *redo pass*, performs all the transaction steps since the last checkpoint. The third pass, which is the *undo pass*, performs a rollback on any incomplete transactions.

> **NOTE**
>
> Whenever you start Windows NT, the NTFS volumes are checked to see whether they are "dirty." If it detects a potential problem, Windows NT will automatically run CHKDSK /F.
>
> If the CHKDSK utility finds orphaned files or directories, they are moved to special directories named FOUNDnnn. (If no other FOUNDnnn directories exist, the first one created will be FOUND000, the next is FOUND001, and so on.) Directories are named DIRnnn.CHK, and if they have files associated with them, those files will be placed within that directory. Orphaned files are named FILEnnn.CHK.
>
> If you want to run CHKDSK /F from the command line, run it from a drive other than the one you are checking. For example, to check the C: drive from a command prompt, run CHKDSK C: /F. If CHKDSK cannot check the drive because it is in use, it will ask you whether it should run automatically the next time you reboot.

NTFS File Compression

Available only to the NTFS file system on Windows NT is file-level compression. This form of compression is unlike the more familiar DOS-based programs such as Stacker or DriveSpace.

These DOS device driver-based programs such as Stacker and DriveSpace create one large file that contains all the files in the drive that you compressed. This single file is a mountable volume that a DOS device driver mounts as its own drive. This drive is then viewed by DOS as a standard DOS FAT volume.

Windows NT uses Explorer and the COMPACT.EXE utility to compress files individually. These compressed files are then decompressed in real time when the files are opened.

> **NOTE**
>
> NTFS file compression is not available on NTFS volumes with cluster sizes greater than 4KB.

Windows NT's type of compression is much safer than the DOS method, as it is possible that a corrupted compressed volume on DOS could result in the loss of the entire volume. As with all file-compression techniques, there is a certain amount of overhead for the decompression and recompression of these files.

With Windows NT's compression scheme, each file is handled separately. Therefore, any corruption will only affect that one file.

Again, this compression is only available for partitions formatted as NTFS.

> **TIP**
>
> I personally use Windows NT's file compression and have not had any bad experiences or noticeable lags due to compression. I would advise the following:
>
> ■ Feel free to use the compression for seldom-used files or archived data.
>
> ■ Large documents compress very well.
>
> ■ Do not use file compression for files that are already compressed, such as JPEG format graphics or archive files such as PKZIP or ARJ files.
>
> ■ Do not use compression on files that are part of a highly critical application.
>
> ■ Back up. Back up. Back up. Whether or not there are compressed files, always keep a current backup.

Disk Quotas

Disk quotaing is the ability for a system administrator to specify how much disk space a particular user or group may consume. One of the largest complaints about Windows NT and NTFS is the lack of built-in capability to track disk quotas. When comparing features of Windows NT with that of Novell, this is one of the only places where Novell, in my opinion, actually wins out. It's important to understand what this means for your environment, and how to mitigate the problems that this might create.

For instance, a system administrator has no means to say "user JasonG may only use 10MB of space on this volume." For some environments, this might not be a problem, such as a small cooperative workgroup, or on systems with very large storage capacities. However, in many large enterprises it can be a problem, particularly when the information systems department has to manage 100 or 1,000 users with a finite amount of disk space.

This problem crops up in many different areas, but is most common when looking at user home drive space or shared group directories. You can work around this problem in a couple of ways. One method is to create multiple file system volumes and assign groups of users to each volume. This puts a hard limit on the total size of the group, and can make individual control a little more manageable. When the group needs more disk space, you can use NTFS's ability to create volume sets to grow the volume. I don't particularly recommend this case because it can be the most unmanageable in large environments. However, you might be able to take your most disk-hungry users and put them together in their own volume. This way they mainly affect each other. You can think of this as prison for the heavy disk users. This works best when there is a definite company or organizational policy that limits the amount of disk space per user, but people don't follow it.

Another possibility is that many people simply don't know how much disk space they consume. It's not something that jumps in their face every day, and very often when there is a policy stating how much space a person can use and they don't obey it, it's because they don't realize they're overusing their space. In this case, if you make a policy to alert users once per week about how much disk space they're using, it could have a positive effect. Like anything else, having upper management approval and support for establishing policies is extremely important for this to work. You can use a tool like DIRUSE.EXE from the Windows NT Resource Kit to determine exactly how many megabytes are consumed in different directories. This is particularly useful for generating reports of user home directories.

A third possibility is to use a third-party product that limits the amount of disk space the users can consume. These work well for many environments, but after looking pretty hard at a few different products, I'm not terribly impressed with any of them. These products usually run as a background service in NT and watch specific folders that you specify. When users pass certain thresholds, the software will change the NTFS access control rights to prevent the user from adding anything to the folder until some files are removed and they drop back under the threshold. The first concern I have with these products is that, for large environments, they can be very expensive. They also don't provide the level of granularity that is often necessary. A third concern of mine is that although it's clever to use the NTFS security to enforce quotas, this is not the purpose of NTFS security. Programs such as the quota software should not be making changes to these permissions, because *they often do it wrong*.

The good news is that Microsoft has already hinted that it will have quota control in Windows NT 5.0.

Converting to NTFS

The CONVERT.EXE utility is a command-line utility that can convert FAT partitions to NTFS. However, it *will not convert from NTFS to FAT*.

> **NOTE**
>
> In previous versions of Windows NT, the CONVERT.EXE utility would also convert from HPFS to NTFS. However, since Microsoft removed HPFS support from Windows NT 4.0, the CONVERT utility no longer supports converting from an HPFS volume. If you are upgrading to

Windows NT 4.0 from an earlier version of Windows NT, you must convert an HPFS volume to NTFS before upgrading.

The proper syntax for the CONVERT.EXE utility is

```
CONVERT drive: /fs:ntfs [/v]
```

where *drive* is the drive letter for the partition you want to convert, and the /v switch indicates that CONVERT should run in verbose mode. You cannot convert the boot partition while it is active, so if the CONVERT command is used on the boot partition, the conversion process will run the next time the system is booted. Figure 5.2 depicts an actual conversion of a 300-megabyte FAT volume into an NTFS volume. For this size partition, only 3K additional space was needed to perform the conversion.

FIGURE 5.2.

Converting FAT to NTFS using CONVERT.EXE.

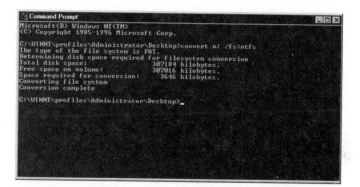

CAUTION

There is no non-destructive method to convert a volume from NTFS to FAT. If you need to do this, you must back up the data on the NTFS partition, reformat the partition as FAT, and restore the data. However, you will lose all NTFS security descriptors, as well as all other benefits of NTFS.

TIP

Whenever possible, use NTFS as your file system. Its security and reliability are too good to pass up. Also, the file compression for NTFS is another great advantage. (Refer to the previous section for a discussion on NTFS's unique file compression.)

5

WINDOWS NT FILE SYSTEMS MANAGEMENT

If you are using a RISC-based system and want to use NTFS, you must still create a 1MB FAT partition for the system files. The remaining volumes can then be formatted as NTFS.

> **CAUTION**
>
> Because RISC-processor-based machines require the FAT file system on the boot partition, never attempt to convert the boot partition on a RISC machine to NTFS. If you do, the machine will no longer be bootable, and you will need to use the program ARCINST.EXE, located on the NT CD-ROM, to reformat the boot partition.

Support for Removable Media

While Windows NT supports formatting removable media, such as Bernoulli drives, it requires that the system is rebooted in order to change media. It is recommended that the FAT file system be used to avoid this inconvenience. Of course, if the security of NTFS is required, this routine must be used.

> **NOTE**
>
> Rumor has it that Windows NT 5.0 will include dramatically improved support for removable media. Also, some removable media vendors write special device drivers to improve the usefulness of removable media under Windows NT.

Disk Administrator

During the installation of Windows NT, the option of creating, deleting, and formatting partitions is your first exposure to NT's file systems configuration. Windows NT's Disk Administrator utility is the primary utility for handling your physical and logical hard drives after the installation of NT.

Disk Administrator is only available to members of the Administrators group on the NT server.

Disk Administrator is usually used when adding a new physical drive to the server. It is also used to modify existing drives and for implementing fault tolerance.

As seen in Figure 5.3, Disk Administrator presents a graphical representation of the physical hard drives and CD-ROM drives. You can see at a glance the different partitions and their sizes, the volume names, the file systems in use, the drive letter assignments, and the amount of free space that is available for creating new partitions.

Essentially, Disk Administrator is a graphical and more advanced version of DOS's FDISK utility.

FIGURE 5.3.

Disk Administrator.

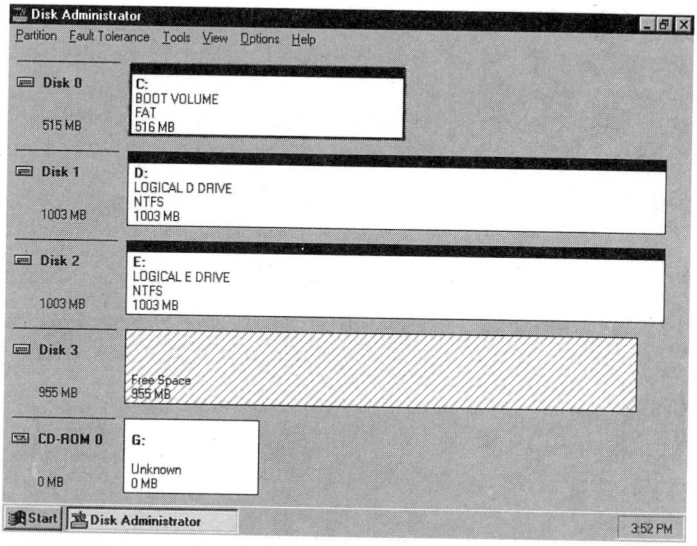

> **TIP**
>
> Speaking of DOS, if you've ever tried to use DOS's FDISK utility to delete an NTFS partition, you've probably noticed that not only does it not recognize the NTFS partition, it can't even delete it. This can be quite frustrating. However, Windows 95's version of FDISK knows what an NTFS partition is, and *it can even delete them.* Make yourself a bootable floppy disk with Windows 95 and include FORMAT.COM and FDISK.EXE on the floppy. This is useful when you need to wipe an NT system clean and start over again.

Disk Administrator's menu choices give you the following options:

- Create a partition
- Create an extended partition
- Delete a partition
- Create a volume set
- Extend a volume set
- Create a stripe set
- Mark a partition active
- Save or restore a disk configuration file
- Establish a mirror set
- Break a mirror set
- Create a stripe set with parity

- Regenerate a member from a missing or damaged stripe set with parity
- Format a partition
- Assign a drive letter
- Eject a drive
- View and change a partition's properties
- Choose a physical or logical view for Disk Administrator
- Customize Disk Administrator's toolbar

> **NOTE**
>
> Whenever using Disk Administrator to alter disk information, you should run the RDISK.EXE utility after you've made your changes. The RDISK utility enables you to create or update your Emergency Repair Disk.

Starting Disk Administrator

You start the Disk Administrator by choosing Disk Administrator, which is located in the Administrative Tools program group on the Start Menu. You can also start Disk Administrator by executing the program WINDISK.EXE.

The first time you start Disk Administrator, you will be prompted to allow Disk Administrator to write a nondestructive signature to each of your hard drives (see Figure 5.4). This signature is written to an otherwise inaccessible part of the hard drive, and is used by Windows NT to identify if a change of hardware has occurred. You should choose OK on this dialog box, unless you are using only a temporary drive. This prompt will appear each time you add a new hard drive to your system.

FIGURE 5.4.

Prompt to write a signature to the hard drives.

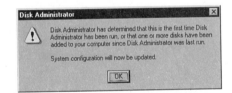

Configuring Disk Administrator

Disk Administrator uses visual cues to enable you to easily identify the size and type of partitions on your hard drives. Different colors and patterns are used as a legend to identify a primary partition, a logical drive, a stripe set, a mirror set, and a volume set. Free space is also identifiable by not having a color bar associated with it; instead, it uses diagonal lines as a background. This legend is customizable by using and choosing Colors and Patterns from the Options menu. These options are shown in Figures 5.5 and 5.6.

FIGURE 5.5.
Color options.

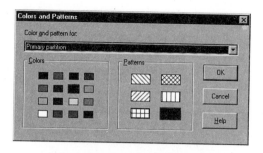

FIGURE 5.6.
Region display options.

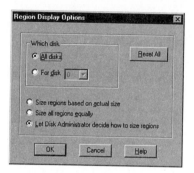

The Options menu also has choices for whether or not to show the status bar at the bottom of the Disk Administrator, and how to size the disk regions. Disk Administrator will size these regions in a fashion that is easy to read and identify. You have the option to use proportionate sizing for the length of the individual bars, which represent the individual hard drives and the partitions or free space blocks (see Figure 5.7).

FIGURE 5.7.
Disk display options.

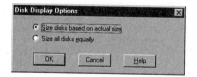

In all cases, an active partition is identified by an asterisk in the upper-left corner of the disk region. On x86-based computers, marking a partition as active identifies it as the *system partition*, the partition where the hardware-specific files reside that need to load NT. Only one active system partition at a time can be marked as active. RISC-based computers, on the other hand, do not require partitions to be marked active. On these systems, you need to use the hardware configuration program that came with the system to specify the active partition. Furthermore, on RISC-based systems, the system partition must be formatted for the FAT file system.

> **NOTE**
>
> The system partition can never be part of a stripe set or volume set.

Another configurable option for Disk Administrator's display is the capability to customize the Disk Administrator toolbar. The Customize Toolbar dialog (see Figure 5.8) is shown when you choose Customize Toolbar from the Options menu.

Every menu item from Disk Administrator can be added as a button on the toolbar, which can make configuring your storage media even easier because you won't need to hunt through the many menu items that Disk Administrator offers.

FIGURE 5.8.

Customize Toolbar dialog.

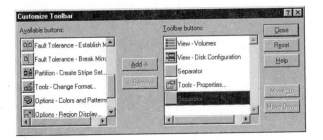

Changing the View

Besides the "bar chart" representation of hard drives, removable media, and CD-ROM drives, the View menu item enables you to switch to a grid-like listing of the different volumes that exist on the server (see Figure 5.9). This is done by choosing Volumes from the View menu. This listing ignores unpartitioned space and shows a logical view of the server's storage devices. You can switch back to a physical view of the storage media by choosing Disk Configuration from the View menu.

Working with Partitions

As with any operating system, there must be a way to manage your hard drive, or hard drives. The Disk Administrator gives you a graphical way to look at the partitioning schemes that you have implemented on these drives. It makes it that much easier to work with these partitions, or unpartitioned space, when you are able to view the entire drive or set of drives.

Existing Partitions

In the case of a new server in which no partitions existed on the hard drives prior to the installation of Windows NT, there should be no problems for Disk Administrator. However, if you are installing Windows NT onto a hard drive that already has an existing installation of DOS or another operating system, there are cases where Windows NT will not be able to understand the existing disk partitioning. This happens when a partition table does not comply with the strict requirements that Windows NT enforces. When this occurs, you must first boot from the operating system that created the disk partitions. Then back up any information that you would like to retain from those partitions. Once completed, delete the partitions by using FDISK under DOS, or Disk Administrator with Windows NT.

FIGURE 5.9.

Volume view.

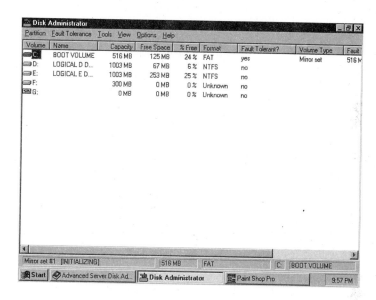

To re-create the partitions, you can use a recent version of DOS, Windows 95, or even simpler, you can use the Windows NT installation program. Otherwise, you can boot Windows NT and use Disk Administrator to re-create the partitions.

CAUTION

Using an older PC as a server with today's large IDE hard drives usually causes problems with Windows NT. This is because not all the cylinders of an IDE hard drive that is greater than 540 megabytes will be recognized by the setup program for the PC.

Working with large hard drives will be much easier if you either use SCSI hard drives with a supported SCSI controller or use a server that has built-in support for large IDE hard drives.

The latest version of On Track's Disk Manager does come with Windows NT drivers. However, this software implementation of cylinder translation should probably not be used on mission-critical servers due to its unnecessary overhead.

Creating a Partition

When creating a partition, you need to first decide on the method that you want to use.

DOS allows for only two types of partitions: a primary partition that is usually used for the operating system, and an extended partition. The Master Boot Record (MBR) on most hard drives will only support up to four partitions, one of which may be an extended partition. An extended partition can contain one or more logical partitions. If you create a primary partition that is formatted as FAT, DOS and Windows 95 will be able to recognize this as a FAT drive. Any extended partition containing logical drives that are also formatted with the FAT file system will also be recognized by DOS and Windows 95 as a valid drive. A nonextended partition beyond the first FAT drive will not be recognized as a valid drive under DOS or Windows 95, nor will any partitions that are formatted as NTFS or HPFS. Be sure to keep this in mind if you are planning to dual-boot the server with Windows NT and another operating system, such as DOS or Windows 95. Even FAT partitions may not be recognized by DOS or Windows 95 if the partitioning scheme is not one that is DOS compliant (see Figure 5.10).

FIGURE 5.10.

A message regarding the creation of a non-DOS compatible primary partition.

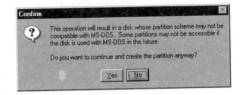

Usually, drives will contain more than one non-DOS partition if you are planning to dual-boot NT and UNIX or OS/2.

To create a primary partition, select the hard drive by clicking on the representation of the drive that is noted as free space, as shown in Figure 5.11. Then choose Create from the Partition menu. A dialog appears which displays both a minimum and a maximum number of megabytes that can be used for this partition. You will be prompted to enter the number of megabytes that you would like to use (see Figure 5.12). If this is the only partition that you would like on this drive, you may use the maximum. If you also plan to create additional partitions, which may or may not include an extended partition, be sure to leave enough space for the other partitions you may create. After you finalize your decision, the new partition will appear on the graph. These changes will not take effect until you commit them—either by choosing Commit Changes Now from the Partition menu, or by exiting Disk Administrator and then confirming the changes. Once completed, you may create more partitions (space allowing). As soon as you create a nonextended partition, a drive letter is assigned to that partition.

FIGURE 5.11.

Free space.

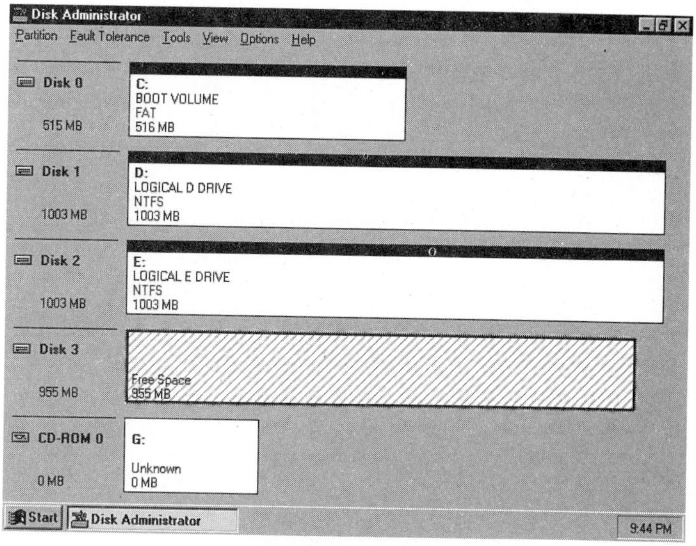

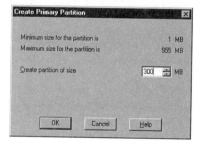

FIGURE 5.12.

Creating a primary partition.

Formatting a Partition

After creating a partition and committing the changes, the new partition can be formatted. This is accomplished by selecting the new partition and then choosing Format from the Tools menu (see Figure 5.13). Choose the appropriate type of file system (note that the choices are NTFS and FAT in Figure 5.14) and click the OK button to start the format process. There is also a checkbox, which enables you to choose whether to perform a quick format. This type of format will bypass checking the physical drive during the format process. It is recommended that you do not use this option unless you have recently formatted the same partition without incident. Before proceeding, a confirmation dialog box will appear for you to confirm that you wish to format the selected partition. While formatting, the progress is displayed in a status box, shown in Figure 5.15.

5
WINDOWS NT
FILE SYSTEMS
MANAGEMENT

FIGURE 5.13.
The Tools menu.

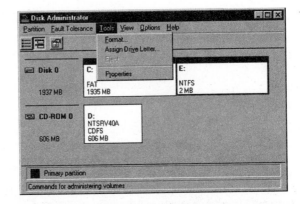

CAUTION

You may cancel the format from within this status box, but be aware that any data previously stored on the partition will be destroyed.

FIGURE 5.14.
Formatting a partition.

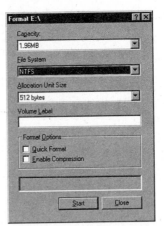

NOTE

In Figure 5.15, the formatting that is taking place is a *Quick Format*. Only use the Quick Format if you have previously formatted that area of the hard drive.

During a normal format, Windows NT performs an exhaustive check of the physical hard drive. By selecting Quick Format you bypass that check.

FIGURE 5.15.

The Format Status dialog.

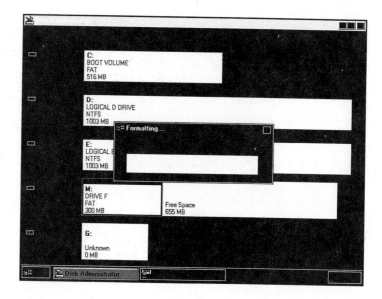

If you would like to change the drive letter that was automatically assigned by the operating system for the new partition, or for any other existing partition, select the partition and then choose Assign Drive Letter from the Tools menu. A drop-down box that has a choice of unused drive letters will appear (see Figure 5.16). Choose the drive letter you would like to use and click the OK button. That drive letter will be assigned to the selected partition instantly.

You can also use this option to change the drive letter that is assigned to CD-ROM drives, as shown in Figure 5.17.

CAUTION

When you add or remove options, many Microsoft applications look for the drive that they were installed from. You will receive an error if you modify the drive letter of your CD and then try to add or remove one of these options. To fix the problem, edit the registry to point the application in the right direction or fully reload the application using different options.

Marking an Active Partition

An active partition is a primary partition from which the system can boot. In most cases, the active partition will be the first partition on the first hard drive. It is possible to have different operating systems installed on the same computer, however, and allow the computer to boot from different partitions.

FIGURE 5.16.
Changing a drive letter.

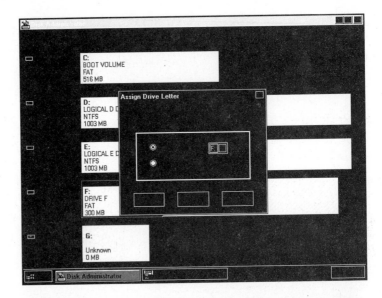

FIGURE 5.17.
Changing a CD-ROM drive letter.

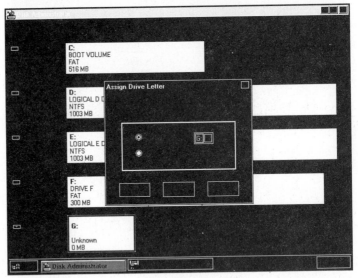

A good example of why you would alter the active partition on your first hard drive is if you should install Microsoft Windows NT Server onto a computer that already has the OS/2 Boot Manager installed. By default, Microsoft Windows NT Server marks as active the partition that contains the NT system files. Prior to the installation, the OS/2 Boot Manager partition had been marked as active. The only way to re-enable Boot Manager would be to use Disk Administrator. You would do this by highlighting the Boot Manager partition, and then clicking the Partition menu. Choose Mark Active from that menu, and you see the confirmation message shown in Figure 5.18. The next time the system restarts, the Boot Manager will appear.

FIGURE 5.18.

The Mark Active confirmation message.

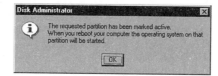

Creating an Extended Partition

Creating an extended partition is similar to creating a primary partition, except that you have the option afterward to create logical partitions within the extended partition.

> **NOTE**
>
> For a more detailed description of the differences between primary and extended partitions, see the section "Understanding Partitions," earlier in this chapter.

To create an extended partition, select a free space on a hard drive that already has an existing primary partition. Next choose Create Extended from the Partition menu. You are prompted for the size of this partition, as shown in Figure 5.19. Enter the size and click the OK button to create the partition. Once completed, the extended partition appears as free space. The status bar at the bottom of the screen indicates that it is an extended partition. You may now create logical partitions within the extended partition.

FIGURE 5.19.

Creating an extended partition.

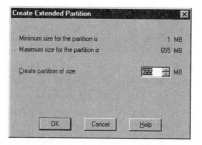

> **CAUTION**
>
> Do not confuse "creating an extended partition" with "extending a volume set." They are two totally different concepts, although they are often confused because of their similar names. An extended partition is a method of defining partition structures on the hard drive. Because a volume can only hold four primary partitions, you have to make an *extended partition* if you need more partitions on a single drive. In contrast, *extending* a volume set is what happens when you take an NTFS partition and *grow* it using an area of free space. I've seen too many strange things happen because these terms got confused.

Creating Logical Partitions

To create logical partitions within the extended partition, first choose the extended partition; then choose Create from the Partition menu. The dialog box shown in Figure 5.20 enables you to choose the size of the logical partition. The maximum size displayed is the amount of free space within the extended partition. After entering the size, click the OK button and the logical partition will be created. As with primary partitions, a drive letter is instantly assigned.

FIGURE 5.20.

Creating a logical partition.

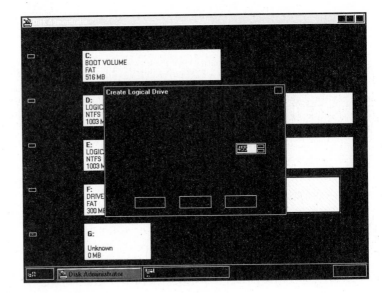

Deleting Partitions

To delete a partition, select the partition you want to delete, and then choose Delete from the Partition menu.

CAUTION

Be sure to back up all the information on the partition before you proceed with the deletion.

When you attempt to delete a partition, a confirmation dialog appears that warns you about the loss of data that will occur. If you are sure that you want to continue, click the OK button, and the partition will then be shown as free space. As with all the options within Disk Administrator that permanently alter a hard drive's partition map, the final changes to the affected partition will not occur until you choose to commit these changes. The changes can be manually committed by choosing the Commit Changes Now menu item, or they will be made automatically when exiting Disk Administrator. After choosing to commit the changes, Disk Administrator will warn you that the changes will be permanent. Choose the OK button to continue. If you choose OK, you will see the dialog box shown in Figure 5.22.

FIGURE 5.21.
Deleting a partition.

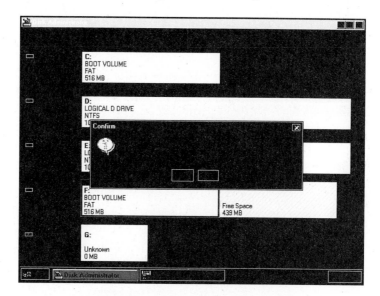

FIGURE 5.22.
Committing changes.

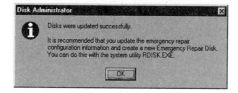

Partition Properties

In Disk Administrator, you can examine the properties of any volume attached to the system. You can access the drive properties by selecting Properties from the Tools menu, or by right-clicking on the volume and choosing Properties. These properties are exactly the same as when you examine the properties of a drive from the Explorer.

The Properties window will have up to four tabs, depending on the type of partition you've selected:

■ **General:** Available for all partitions, including NTFS, FAT, and CDFS. This tab tells you basic information about the volume, including its name, format type (NTFS, FAT, CDFS), amount of free space, amount of used space, and total capacity. This is shown in Figure 5.23.

- **Tools:** Available for NTFS and FAT partitions. The Tools tab has three main features: check for errors, backup, and defragment. When checking for errors, the system uses the same basic routine as the CHKDSK.EXE utility. When selecting the Check Now option, you will be presented with a dialog box. This dialog box gives you the choice to not fix file system errors automatically, fix file system errors automatically, or perform a complete disk scan, which will search for physical damage. Clicking on the Backup Now button will launch the Windows NT backup utility to back up the selected volume. Unless you've installed a third-party defragmentation utility, such as Executive Software's DiskKeeper, the Defragment Now button will be grayed out.

- **Sharing:** Available for all partitions that can be shared, including NTFS, FAT, and CDFS. This tab enables you to create share points for that volume to share it to the network. It also enables you to specify the permissions on the shares.

- **Security:** Only available on NTFS partitions. This enables you to set NTFS-level security permissions.

FIGURE 5.23.

The General property tab for a disk volume.

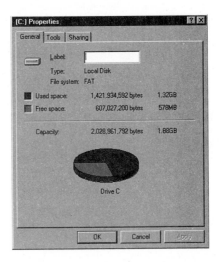

When you specify a volume to be checked for errors, if you select a volume that is busy, and it cannot be locked for inspection, you will receive a warning message (see Figure 5.24). You can choose to have the volume checked the next time the system is started or you can choose to cancel the Check Now option.

If the volume can be locked, the disk check will proceed. Once the disk check is complete, you see a summary of events that occurred during the disk check in the event log (see Figure 5.25).

FIGURE 5.24.
Disk Locked warning message.

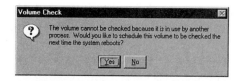

FIGURE 5.25.
Results from checking a disk for errors.

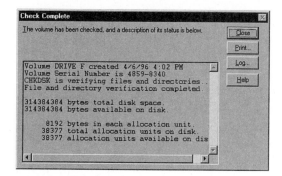

Disk Volumes

A Windows NT Server disk volume is comprised of one or more partitions on one or more hard drives that are formatted with a file system and can be assigned a drive letter.

With DOS, a volume was simply a partition on one hard drive, but with Windows NT Server, you can create different types of volumes that offer greater flexibility and fault tolerance.

Working with Volume Sets

A volume set is created by combining free space from between 1 and 32 hard drives into a single logical volume that is seen by the operating system as one partition. In reality, after the first segment of a volume set is used, the file system continues on the next segment of the volume set. One advantage of using a volume set is that you can save drive letters by combining areas on different hard drives, as opposed to assigning a drive letter to each individual area (partition). You may also run across a partitioning scheme that ends up with small empty areas at the end of multiple hard drives. These can easily be combined to form one volume.

To create a volume set, select all the free areas you want to include in the volume set. Do this by clicking on the first area you wish to include. Then, hold down the Ctrl (Control) key and select the next area for inclusion. Continue this until all the free space areas that will comprise the volume set are selected. Next, choose Create Volume Set from the Partition menu. Just as shown in Figure 5.26, you will be prompted to enter the amount of disk space you would like to allocate to this volume. Clicking the OK button then creates the volume set.

FIGURE 5.26.

Creating a volume set.

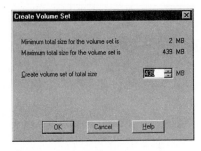

You can also extend a single NTFS partition by selecting an NTFS partition, holding down the Ctrl key, and selecting free space. Then, choose Extend Volume Set from the Partition menu and type the number of megabytes from the free space that you would like to append onto the current NTFS partition (see Figure 5.27). Click the OK button and the chosen free space appears as part of the NTFS volume. Note that the color bar on all the included partitions will now share the color that has been designated as signifying a volume set.

FIGURE 5.27.

Extending a volume set.

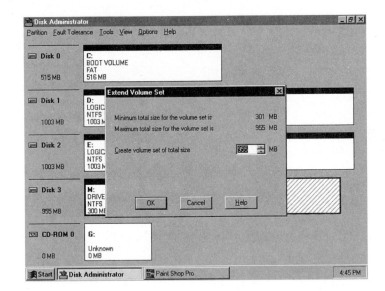

Also, you cannot extend the volume where Windows NT's system files reside. Attempting to do so will result in the message shown in Figure 5.28.

FIGURE 5.28.

Attempting to extend a volume with Windows NT system files.

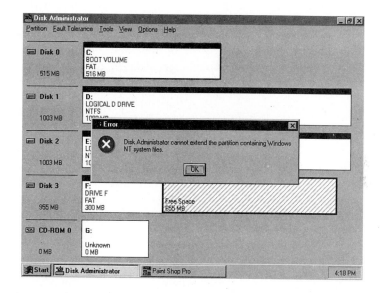

You may delete a volume set by selecting any of the regions that are part of the volume set and then choosing Delete from the Partition menu.

NOTE

You can only create volume sets with NTFS. In addition, the system partition *cannot* be on a volume set.

CAUTION

Be sure you back up all information on the volume set before deleting it.

A confirmation dialog (see Figure 5.29) then enables you to proceed or cancel the deletion.

FIGURE 5.29.

Deleting a Volume Set.

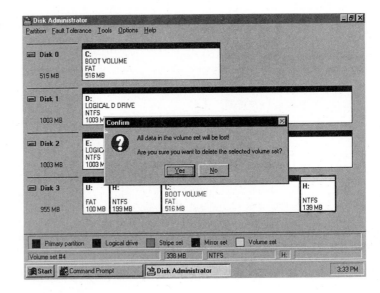

Working with Mirrored Partitions

Mirroring enables you to create a mirror image of a partition on another drive. This form of fault tolerance is also known as RAID 1. You will want to mirror all critical partitions on a server so that in case of a drive failure you have a complete copy of all the data that was once on the primary volume.

To mirror a partition, select the partition that you would like to mirror. Hold down the Ctrl key and click once on the free space that you would like to contain the mirror.

> **NOTE**
>
> The free space that you select for the mirror must be as large as, or larger than, the partition you want to mirror.

Choose the Establish Mirror option from the Fault Tolerance menu, and a partition that is the same size as the original partition will be created. Both of these partitions will share the same drive letter.

As shown in Figure 5.30, when mirroring the boot partition you will be instructed to create a boot floppy that will be needed when replacing the mirror drive for the mirrored drive.

After the mirror has been established, a message on Disk Administrator's status bar indicates that the mirroring process is in progress (see Figure 5.31). In addition, the mirror partition's statistics appear in red until the mirror has finished initializing. After it is initialized, the mirror partition is a usable partition in case of an emergency.

FIGURE 5.30.
Mirroring a boot partition.

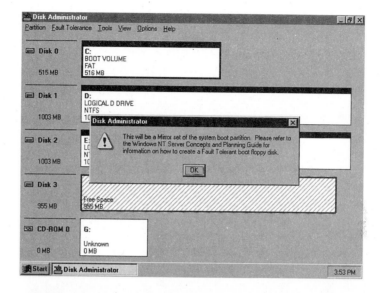

FIGURE 5.31.
Mirror initialization.

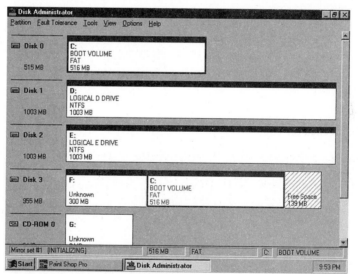

NOTE

If a power failure or other catastrophic problem occurs during the mirror initialization process, Windows NT will recover the mirror initialization process when it reboots.

Figure 5.32 shows the entry that is written to the System Event Log after the mirror starts to initialize. After the mirror initialization has completed, the entry shown in Figure 5.33 is also written to the System Event Log.

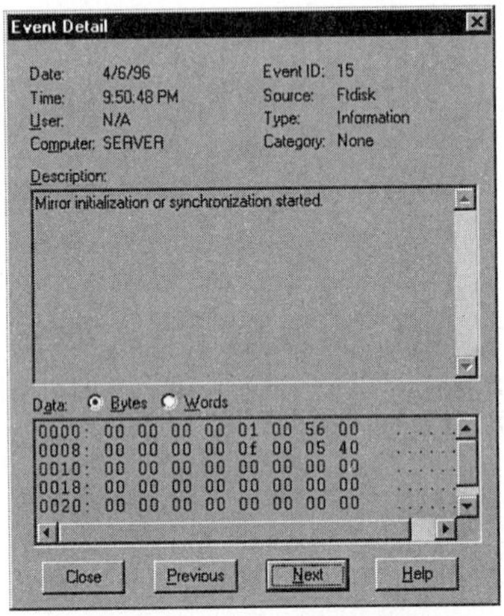

FIGURE 5.32.

The System Event Log entry for the start of a mirror initialization.

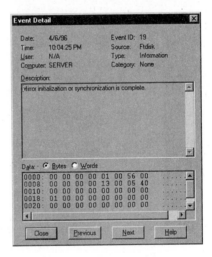

FIGURE 5.33.

The System Event Log entry for a completed mirror initialization.

Whether to reclaim disk space, remove a hard drive, or just to rearrange your partitions, you may find yourself in the position of needing to break a mirror. To break a mirror, select one of the partitions that participates in the mirror and choose Break Mirror from the Fault Tolerance menu. As shown in Figure 5.34, you will first be warned that breaking the mirror will result in two separate partitions. Once confirmed, the mirror will be broken. The primary partition from the mirror (the partition that existed before the mirror was formed) will retain the drive letter of the mirror. The slave partition (the partition that was originally added to create the mirror) will now have a new drive letter assigned to it. Both partitions will now contain the same data; they will be *mirror* images of each other. If you want to reclaim the space, you may now delete or reformat one of the partitions.

FIGURE 5.34.

Breaking a mirror.

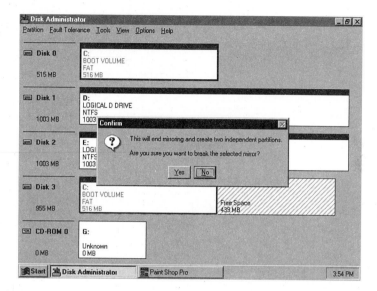

In some cases, the mirrored volume will not be able to be broken because a system service is actively using that volume. A message, shown in Figure 5.35, will let you choose whether to break the mirror the next time the system starts, or you can choose to cancel the breaking of the mirrored set.

FIGURE 5.35.

A mirror set cannot be locked.

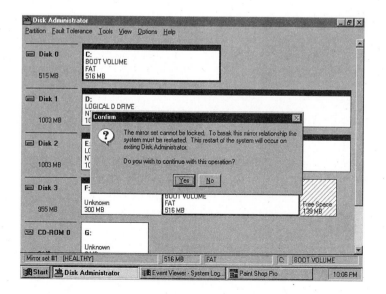

Once the mirror is broken, the next available drive letter will be given to the mirror partition (see Figure 5.36).

FIGURE 5.36.

The result of a broken mirror.

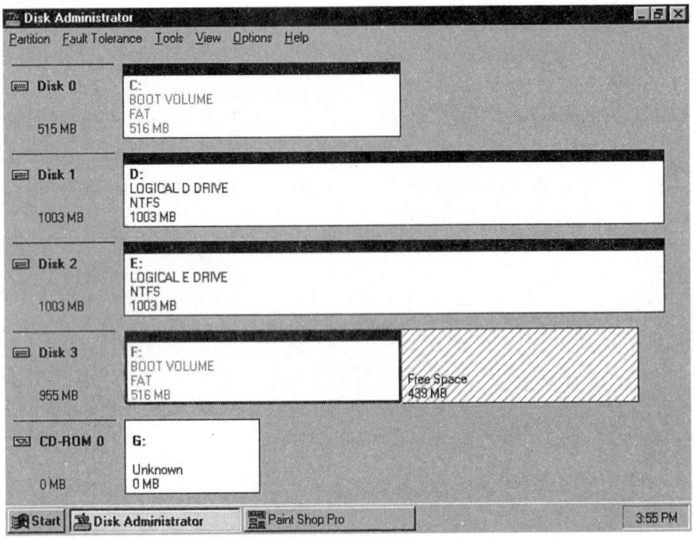

Working with Stripe Sets

While offering no-fault tolerance, disk stripe sets offer increased performance. Disk striping will evenly distribute a volume across multiple physical hard drives. This allows reads and writes to a single striped volume to be broken up into separate instructions that can be executed simultaneously by multiple hard drives and controllers without queuing. Between 2 and 32 drives can participate in a disk striping array.

This type of disk striping without parity is called RAID 0. Disk striping with parity, which is RAID 5, is the preferred method because it offers both a performance increase and fault tolerance.

CAUTION

While a stripe set without parity is a cost-efficient way to increase disk performance, the entire volume can be lost if any of the hard drives that contain parts of the stripe set has a failure.

TIP

Very often people unfamiliar with Windows NT's different disk volume options have trouble determining when to use *disk striping* and when to use *volume sets*. Here are a few tips: You must determine a permanent size for a disk stripe set when you create the set. A disk stripe requires an equal amount of contiguous space on all drives in the stripe set. Only one piece of contiguous space on a physical drive may participate in a given stripe set. Data is written in chunks evenly across all members of a stripe set. Under most circumstances, you can get good speed improvements from disk striping. If you want to grow a disk stripe, you must back up the data, remove the stripe, and re-create it—either by using larger contiguous amounts of disk space on each physical drive or by adding another drive to the stripe.

In contrast, volume sets are much more flexible with regard to *growability*. You can start off with an NTFS volume that includes a single disk partition on a single drive. If you want to grow the volume, you can simply add blocks of free space on the same physical disk, or from other physical disks. Each piece of a volume set can be of a different size. Data is written in a relatively linear fashion across a volume set, so you will rarely realize a disk performance increase by using a volume set. However, you also won't usually realize performance degradation.

So use disk stripes when you are comfortable setting the maximum size of the volume and want a performance improvement. Use volume sets when you need to grow an existing NTFS partition without the hassle of backing up and reformatting.

To create a stripe set, select the free space areas on each drive that will participate in the mirror. Click on the first free space region, and then hold down the Ctrl key and select the remaining free space regions you would like to include in the stripe set. Select Create Stripe Set from the Partition menu. The minimum and the maximum size of the stripe set that can be created appears. If you want to use the maximum size, just click the OK button. Otherwise, alter the size, and then click the OK button. Windows NT will then allocate the appropriate slices from the free space regions to build the stripe set. Once completed, these members of the stripe set will be identified by a color bar and background that symbolizes stripe sets—by default, this is green for both. Exit Disk Administrator, and you will be prompted to shut down and restart the server. After rebooting, your stripe set will be available for use.

NOTE

Because all the regions used for the stripe set must be the same size, the smallest free space region will determine the factor for the size of the stripe set volume. For example, if you have two drives, one with 250MB free and the other with 300MB free, the striped array will be 500MB large (250 × 2). Likewise, if you have three volumes with 400MB, 550MB, and 800MB free, the final striped array will be 1200MB large (400MB × 3).

5

WINDOWS NT FILE SYSTEMS MANAGEMENT

To remove a stripe set, select one of the members of the stripe set. Select Delete from the Partition menu. After confirming that you want to remove the entire stripe set, those regions are then marked as available. Commit your changes to allow these sections to be reused.

CAUTION

Be sure to back up all the information on the stripe set before you proceed with the deletion.

Disk Striping with Parity

Of Windows NT Server's choices for a software RAID solution, disk striping with parity at RAID level 5 is the most secure and robust form of disk fault tolerance available. A stripe is written across multiple hard drives, with a parity stripe interleaved within them.

Disk striping *with* parity is functionally very similar to disk striping *without* parity in that it stripes information across multiple hard drives. However, while the standard disk striping only requires a minimum of two partitions, striping with parity requires a minimum of three (and will support a maximum of 32). If there are three volumes in the stripe with parity, the first two contain the data and the third contains a parity set created by the first two drives. This way, if one of the two main hard drives fails, the remaining drive and the parity information can be used to recalculate the lost information and place this information back onto a newly installed and working hard drive. If the disk that contains the parity information fails, no data is lost but you lose your protection until the drive is replaced.

To create a stripe set with parity, select free space regions on at least three drives and choose Create Stripe Set with Parity from the Fault Tolerance menu. The minimum and maximum sizes of the stripe set that can be created appear. If you want to use the maximum size, just click the OK button; otherwise, alter the size, and then click the OK button. Windows NT then allocates the appropriate slices from the free space regions to build the stripe set with parity. Once completed, these members of the stripe set will be identified by a color bar and background that symbolizes stripe sets—light blue by default.

Exit Disk Administrator, and you will be prompted to shut down and restart the server. After rebooting, your stripe set will be available for use.

NOTE

As with stripe set without parity, all the regions used for the stripe set must be the same size. Therefore, the smallest free space region will determine the size of stripe set volume.

To remove a stripe set, select one of the members of the stripe set. Select Delete from the Partition menu. After confirming that you want to remove the entire stripe set, those regions are then marked as available. Commit your changes to allow these sections to be reused.

> **CAUTION**
>
> Be sure you back up all the information on the stripe set before you proceed with the deletion.

Regenerating a Stripe Set

With a stripe set with parity, you have protection if there is a single hard drive failure. When this occurs and you replace the hard drive, one of the first tasks you should do is to regenerate the stripe set.

After installing your new hard drive and restarting Windows NT Server, the autocheck phase will determine that the stripe set has been broken, and the stripe set will be locked. To re-enable the stripe set, you must start the Disk Administrator program and select one of the regions that belongs to the stripe set with parity. Once selected, hold down the Ctrl key and select the new empty region that you would like to replace with the missing stripe set partition. Next, select Regenerate from the Fault Tolerance menu, and the system will acknowledge the new member of the set. Exit Disk Administrator and restart the system to enable the stripe set again.

> **TIP**
>
> While Microsoft Windows NT Server's Fault Tolerance options are greatly useful, a hardware implementation of fault tolerance generally is a better way to run your server. This is because the disk controller will take over and provide the necessary processing, leaving the CPU(s) to handle other tasks. Of course, this solution will cost you more, and in some cases, might not be an option.
>
> Another reason to go with hardware fault tolerance is that the newest breed of controllers allows you to increase storage on a RAID system without requiring you to reinitialize the volume. This feature enables you to leave the server active while upgrading the disk space.

Saving Disk Configuration Information

Disk Administrator enables you to save and restore disk configuration information, such as drive letter assignments, stripe set, mirror, and volume set information.

You can save this information to a floppy disk by selecting Configuration from the Partition menu, and then selecting Save from the submenu. The system prompts you to insert a floppy disk into the A: drive on the server. This information is very important to keep available, should you accidentally make changes in Disk Administrator and need to restore the correct settings. It can also be used if you have to reinstall Windows NT Server, because reinstalling will reset your disk configuration information to its default state. If you decide to perform a fresh installation of Windows NT Server, this information could save you a lot of time in reconfiguring disk information.

To restore the information from disk, select Configuration from the Partition menu, and then select Restore from the submenu. The system prompts you to insert the disk configuration information disk into the A: drive on the server. After a confirmation, the information is restored. You should then restart the system to allow all the disk configuration changes to take effect.

Command-Line Tools for Managing Disk Partitions

In addition to the graphical Disk Administrator, a number of command-line tools are useful for administering disk partitions under Windows NT. These tools are as follows:

- `FORMAT.EXE`—Formats volumes
- `CONVERT.EXE`—Converts FAT volumes to NTFS
- `CHKDSK.EXE`—Drive diagnostic utility
- `LABEL.EXE`—Assigns a name to a specified volume

FORMAT.EXE

The `FORMAT` utility enables you to format a disk under Windows NT.

The syntax for the `FORMAT` command is

```
FORMAT [/FS:FAT|NTFS] [/V:label] [/Q] [/A:size] [/C]
FORMAT drive: [/V:label] [/Q] [/F:size]
FORMAT drive: [/V:label] [/Q] [/T:tracks /N:sectors]
FORMAT drive: [/V:label] [/Q] [/1] [/4]
FORMAT drive: [/Q] [/1] [/4] [/8]
```

`/FS:FAT|NTFS` specifies the file system that should be used to format the volume (FAT or NTFS).

`/V:label` identifies a label that should be assigned to the volume. The maximum is 15 characters.

`/Q` performs a quick format, which does not perform an in-depth analysis of the media during the format. Quick formats can format 4GB in seconds.

/C specifies that files created on the volume should be compressed by default. This applies only to NTFS volumes.

/A:*size* specifies allocation unit size, overriding the default settings. This should only be done under very special conditions. NTFS supports 512 bytes, 1KB, 2KB, 4KB, 8KB, 16KB, 32KB, and 64KB. FAT supports 8KB, 16KB, 32KB, 64KB, 128KB, and 256KB. NTFS compression is not supported for allocation unit sizes above 4KB.

/F:*size* specifies the size of the floppy disk to format (160, 180, 320, 360, 720, 1.2, 1.44, 2.88, or 20.8). This is used only for formatting floppy disks.

/T:*tracks* specifies the number of tracks per disk side. This is used only for formatting floppy disks.

/N:*sectors* specifies the number of sectors per track. This is used only for formatting floppy disks.

/1 formats a single side of a floppy disk. This is used only for formatting floppy disks.

/4 formats a 5.25-inch 360KB floppy disk in a high-density drive. This is used only for formatting floppy disks.

/8 formats eight sectors per track. This is used only for formatting floppy disks.

CONVERT.EXE

The CONVERT utility converts existing FAT volumes to NTFS.

The syntax for the CONVERT command is

```
CONVERT drive: /FS:NTFS [/V]
```

drive: specifies the drive that is to be converted.

/FS:NTFS specifies the file system that should be converted to NTFS. This parameter *must* be included.

/V specifies that the procedure should be run in verbose mode.

CHKDSK.EXE

The CHKDSK utility performs disk maintenance tasks.

The syntax for the CHKDSK command is

```
CHKDSK [drive:][[path]filename] [/F] [/V] [/R] [/L[:size]]
```

drive: specifies the drive that should be checked. If left blank, the current drive will be used.

filename, if included, specifies the file to be checked for fragmentation. When specified, CHKDSK will first perform normal drive diagnostics, and then it will check the specified file for fragmentation. For example, CHKDSK C:\PAGEFILE.SYS will check PAGEFILE for fragmentation. This works only on FAT partitions.

/F specifies that CHKDSK should fix any errors it finds on the disk.

/V specifies that CHKDSK should run in verbose mode. When running in verbose mode, it checks the full path of every file on the volume.

/R specifies that CHKDSK should perform a full surface scan of the volume to discover any bad sectors. Then CHKDSK should try to remap the data and retire the bad sectors.

/L:*size* is used to display and change the size of the NTFS transaction log. If you don't specify *size*, the current log size setting is displayed. If you specify *size*, the log size setting is changed. This applies only to NTFS volumes.

LABEL.EXE

The LABEL utility assigns names to disk volumes.

The syntax for the LABEL command is

```
LABEL [drive:] [label]
```

drive: specifies the drive that is to be converted. If this parameter is left blank, the default drive is used.

label is the name that you want to assign to the volume. If it is left blank, you will be prompted for the name.

Summary

After you have determined the most appropriate file system configuration, you are ready to configure and implement the rest of your Microsoft Windows NT Server network.

It is no coincidence that using the NTFS file system on your server will give you the most flexibility in implementing security and fault tolerance.

Be careful using Disk Administrator. One wrong move and you'll wipe out a partition. Remember that it is practically the same as using DOS's FDISK; do be sure to make your plans in advance of making changes.

And use the RDISK.EXE utility. If you do make a mistake and remove a partition by accident, you can restore a saved configuration. While you may have made your Emergency Repair Disk during installation, any changes made to your disk configuration should be updated on that disk, and using RDISK.EXE will keep that disk up-to-date.

One last time: *back up your data!*

Integrated Networking

by Joe Greene

IN THIS CHAPTER

CHAPTER 6

Not too many years ago, networking was an afterthought to most computer users. Personal computers were sitting on desktops, and people exchanged information via disks or printed reports. Then a number of vendors started to network their computers together. It started with the technical computer communities, which tended to use VAX and UNIX computers. They had to ship large files between machines and developed computer utilities that could use network cards to transfer this information.

Once these networking utilities evolved from being laboratory grade to production grade, people were able to build a case for networking office computers together. Initially, it was just to share printers and ship a few files around. Next thing you know, people were developing ways to store software on servers and meter out usage licenses to individual PCs and all sorts of other useful utilities. Some organizations even started to store key corporate information in digital form and make it available in a centralized location on the network.

Windows NT was developed after this push to networking really gained momentum. The Microsoft team recognized that this trend was here to stay and built networking in as a central component of the operating system (similar to many UNIX systems that are out there on the market). Most PC systems in the past (such as Windows 3.1) came without any built-in networking. People had to purchase add-on packages from various vendors. Each vendor had a vision of how networking was to be implemented, and you had to spend a lot of time and effort learning their systems. Also, in many ways these packages always seem to be an add-on and not really part of the operating system itself (for example, memory management, which was always a nightmare when you had several network drivers loaded).

Windows NT has taken networking to heart and built networking in as an integrated part of the operating system. You still have a choice on drivers and services, but there is a standard interface between the operating system and the network that all vendors are writing to. Also, because Windows NT is a 32-bit operating system that supports better memory management and multitasking, it is much easier to implement network drivers and services. This is especially true of those network services such as FTP servers, which have to continuously monitor the network in the background to see if there are any requests for information from other computers on the network.

This leads me to the purpose of this chapter. From its title, you see the focus is installing the networking components that come as part of the Windows NT server operating system itself. There are still a number of add-on packages made by Microsoft and third-party vendors. Examples of these products include Telnet servers and World Wide Web servers. However, this chapter covers installation of the basic components, which are actually fairly robust and tend to meet the vast majority of the business needs that I have run across.

Overview of Windows NT Networking

Let me start by going over what makes up Windows NT's integrated networking. Previous chapters have covered some of the technologies (such as NetWare services and FTP) at the technology level. This section is devoted to presenting an integrated picture of the networking components and how they all fit together. Perhaps the easiest way to start this task is with a picture. (See Figure 6.1.)

FIGURE 6.1.
Windows NT networking overview.

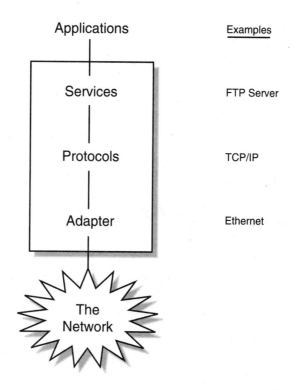

Applications	Examples
Services	FTP Server
Protocols	TCP/IP
Adapter	Ethernet

The Network

You need to understand these components and how they fit together before you can start configuring your network. The basic goal is to get data from a user application (such as Explorer or a client/server database application that you develop locally) to the networking wire running out of your machine. For purposes of this discussion, I have divided the networking hierarchy into three components:

■ **Services and programs:** This layer is a series of services that handle the high-level functions that users and applications require. Examples of services would be File and Print Sharing for Microsoft Networks. Windows NT Server also has some services that run in the background and are available whenever they are started (even if no one is logged in to the server console). Examples of these services would include the FTP server or the remote procedure call server. Finally, there are a series of applications that are run in the foreground that provide specific networking services such as checking to see if other TCP/IP computers are available (Ping) or to log on to a remote computer (Telnet).

- **Protocol:** This is the language and format of the communication signals. This really gets into some dirty, gut-level communications parameters, but for the purposes of most system administrators, all you have to worry about is that you are using the same protocol on all machines that you want to communicate with. You should be careful with NT, which allows multiple protocols to be available at a given time to ensure that you have the appropriate protocols for all of the applications and remote machines supported by your NT Server.

- **Adapter:** This is the device that connects the logical signals that you formed in the protocol portion of the hierarchy to the physical wires (or electromagnetic emissions, because there are some wireless networks out there) that connect your computer to other computers. Windows NT considers a modem to be a network adapter (although it also provides additional control panel icons to set it up completely), and you also have to set up protocols and services for the modems.

Standards Implemented in Windows NT 4

Following up on a point made in the previous section, the key to connecting workstations together for network communications is standards. Of course, the industry has a number of players who think that they are, by definition, the standard. (I am not just talking about Microsoft.) Therefore, your ability to connect to other workstations is limited by the standards that your computer supports. Fortunately, Windows NT supports a wide range of computers through its built-in networking protocols and services. Because almost everyone is building operating systems that connect to the Internet, TCP/IP is the most common communications protocol in use today and Windows NT supports it as part of the standard delivery (no extra products or options to buy).

Therefore, before I go into the actual configuration procedures for Windows NT networking, it might be helpful to review the list of options that you have that relate to network standards. These standards include not only the protocols that you will use to configure your network but also several interface standards that will allow applications that you purchase to interface with the NT networking services to communicate with remote systems:

- TCP/IP protocol for communications with the Internet and UNIX worlds.
- NetBEUI protocol for communications with traditional Microsoft networks such as those under Windows for Workgroups.
- IPX and SPX protocols, which allow communications with Novell NetWare networks using their own language (not a gateway or interpreter).
- Remote access services (a Microsoft standard) allows you to dial in from compatible Microsoft remote computers to your server and from your server to other Microsoft remote computers (such as Windows NT and Windows 95).

■ The Telnet program allows you to connect to remote servers (such as UNIX computers) that have a Telnet server active. You effectively become a terminal on that computer through this program.

■ FTP services allow other workstations that have FTP to connect to your workstation and your computer to connect to other FTP servers.

■ Remote procedure calls (RPCs) allow you to execute programs on other computers that support RPCs.

■ Named pipes allow you to connect two Windows applications together to communicate.

■ Open Database Connection (ODBC) enables client/server applications to communicate with databases for queries and results.

■ Object Linking and Embedding (OLE) allows applications to communicate with and use one another in a cooperative fashion. OLE can be used for simple functions such as embedding a spreadsheet in the middle of a document or complex functions such as communications between a client application and a database server.

Working with the standards listed above are dozens of other lower-level items such as the EtherNet and Token Ring transmission standards associated with a given network card. However, for our purposes, the preceding list can be thought of as a basic laundry list of services that you would install under Windows NT networking. These standards make it easy to integrate Windows NT Servers and workstations into existing networks. This is especially true of the NetWare connectivity and TCP/IP (hence UNIX) connectivity components. You might still have to work out the details of the connection, but it is a good start to know that communication is possible and relatively easy in the NT environment.

Common Networking Protocols

Many of the acronyms in this chapter end in the letter P and the P usually stands for protocol. I like to think of a protocol as an agreed-upon standard that ensures that I can communicate my information with others. This section focuses on a specific set of protocols that determine who can receive your signals on the network. These transmission protocols set standards that allow computers on the network to determine whether the packets are intended for them and then determine what should be done with the information.

There are entire books devoted to the details of these protocols from Sams Publishing and the Windows NT Networking Guide in the Resource Kit provides some more detailed discussions on protocols. I have chosen to focus this section on providing an overview of these protocols that covers the information that a system administrator (not a network engineer) would want to see. This includes:

■ An overview of the history of the protocol

■ The basics of how the protocol transmits signals

■ A discussion of the pros and cons of this protocol

TCP/IP

Let me start with a discussion of TCP/IP. What is it that makes TCP/IP an important protocol for today's system administrators? It is the protocol that drives the Internet, for one thing. It is also a protocol that can be routed (signals sent only to those network segments that need them as opposed to being broadcast throughout the entire network) which keeps overall network traffic loads down. It is also a robust protocol that incorporates transmission reliability features and a capability to interface applications to sockets for specialized forms of communications (such as FTP or client/server database communications).

The TCP/IP protocol was originally developed by the United States military. This protocol was soon adopted by universities and other government agencies as a standard. A large boost came when the Berkeley UNIX world started to emphasize networking and adopted TCP/IP as its standard. Over the years, the Internet and its protocol suite has developed a sort of life of its own. There are working groups composed of industry experts and concerned users who are working to evolve the standards to meet the new requirements that are coming up. An example of this is the work being done to address the issue of the rapid expansion of the Internet, how additional addresses can be made available and how to improve traffic routing.

The acronym TCP/IP can be broken down into TCP (Transmission Control Protocol) and IP (Internet Protocol). My rough distinction between these two is that TCP handles the details of the message while IP provides a means to provide a route address for each computer. There are a number of other standard supporting protocols that are grouped into the TCP/IP family in common practice. Examples of this would include Ping to see if a remote server is responding to the network or FTP to transfer files between computers.

The pros and cons of this protocol (from the system administrator's point of view) include:

- It is the most accepted protocol in the world. Almost all major computer operating systems support this protocol. A huge suite of software (from Internet Web browsers to client/server database tools) is built to use this protocol.

- It is robust enough to support demanding communications. For example, it is extremely difficult to get reliability and performance for client/server database communications in the Oracle database management system by using NetBEUI, but things work very smoothly under TCP/IP.

- You can route TCP/IP, thereby segmenting your network into segments that carry only the traffic that is applicable to their users. Also, with a well-defined set of application-specific interfaces (sockets), you can control what type of traffic is allowed on to a network segment. This is one of the keys to security devices such as firewalls.

- It is a multi-purpose transmission protocol. Therefore, it is not optimized to simple file and printer sharing services, although it gets the job done.

- It requires a fair amount of configuration work to get everyone talking to one another. You absolutely need a plan and control mechanisms before you implement a TCP/IP network.

NetBEUI

NetBEUI sort of falls at the other end of the spectrum in terms of standardization and robustness. Windows NT uses the NetBEUI Frame (NBF) protocol, which is an extension of the old NetBIOS Extended User Interface (NetBEUI) protocol. IBM introduced NetBEUI in 1985 to support its PC network communications. It was intended to be simple and optimized for simple network functions such as printing and file sharing, which are common to PC networks. NBF's main enhancement is that it allows you to have more than the 254 sessions that are permitted under NetBEUI.

Back when NetBEUI was invented, this seemed a very reasonable limit for local area networks. A more telling limitation is the fact that NetBEUI was not designed to provide reliable connectionless communications. The Windows NT Networking Guide provides an interesting discussion of this topic, but what it basically means is that it does not get a confirmation that the message has made it to the sender. This is not a big problem for a print job (if you do not get your printout, you re-send it), but it could be a severe problem for a large financial database transaction sent over the network.

The summary of pros and cons, as viewed by system administrators, of NetBEUI include

- It cannot be routed. Therefore, you cannot segment your network without losing the ability to communicate between certain computers or using another protocol such as TCP/IP.

- It is small and efficient for the tasks that it was designed to accomplish. Most of your basic workgroup and small domain processing fits into this category.

- It is supported on a wide range of Microsoft and IBM PC operating systems (which make up the majority of computers installed today).

- It is not robust enough to handle demanding messaging needs such as client/server database transactions.

- It is really simple to configure and would be a good choice for a small, simple local area network.

IPX/SPX

IPX/SPX is the protocol suite that forms the basis for the majority of Novell NetWare installations that are out there today. Novell has recently provided you with the option of using TCP/IP for your Novell network. IPX stands for Internetwork Packet Exchange. It is designed to have a low overhead and is optimized for local area networks. SPX stands for Sequenced Packet Exchange and it functions like NetBIOS for IPX/SPX networks. It is connection-oriented (both sides talk to one another about the transmissions they are making).

As with the previous two protocols, there are books on the subject that can take you into the details of the packets, addressing, and so on. However, the key points to take away from this chapter about IPX/SPX are:

- It is the most common way to interface with Novell NetWare networks. It is impressive at how smoothly you can integrate NT into a Novell environment and share resources.
- It is a routable protocol.
- It is a fairly robust protocol and able to handle some more demanding network applications.
- It is small and efficient for the types of communications it was designed for (file and print sharing).
- It is simple to configure.

Configuring Networking in NT 4

As with most Windows NT components that are integrated with the operating system, networking is configured by using the Control Panel, which can be accessed from the My Computer desktop icon or from the settings option of the start menu. As you can see in Figure 6.2, there are a number of Control Panel icons that relate to networking: FTP Server, Modems, ODBC, Services, and the one that we are interested in for this chapter—Network. This icon is the key to setting up your networking functionality, and you need to complete this setup before you can set up the other functions.

FIGURE 6.2.

Windows NT Control Panel and Network icon.

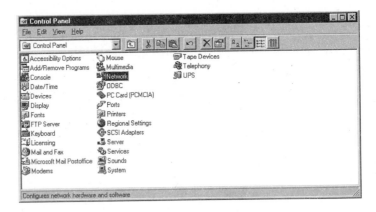

When you double-click on the Network icon, you will be presented with the new Windows NT 4 setup panel. (See Figure 6.3.) Based on my observations of Windows NT 4 and Windows 95, Microsoft seems to be moving heavily toward the tabbed dialog interface for configuring items, so it would be useful for you to get comfortable with this interface. It is relatively simple to work with; there are a number of tabs across the top, each of which corresponds to a data entry or display panel that you need to work with. The items that are being configured are listed in a window similar to the one showing network adapters in Figure 6.3. The plus sign indicates that if you click the icon, you will get an expanded list of items that are associated with the item that you just clicked (an expanding list). Finally, there is a series of buttons (such as Add, Remove, and Configure) that allow you to perform the allowable actions on the list.

FIGURE 6.3.

Network setup panel.

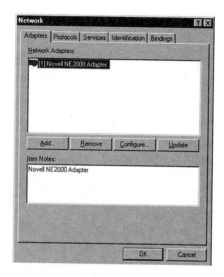

The tabs correspond to the items in the hierarchy discussed earlier in this chapter. In this case, you build your network from the bottom up, starting with the adapters. Next, you select the protocols and then the services. To connect this all together, use the Bindings tab. Finally, an Identification tab that lets you specify how your computer is identified on a Microsoft network. Each of these tabs builds upon the others to form the complete network picture, so you have to work with all of them to set up your network.

When you set up networking, you are probably going to have to reboot your computer after you are done entering the new settings. This is because networking is tightly integrated into the operating system itself. At the end of the setup, you will receive a prompt that asks if you want to reboot the system now. I like to choose a time when I can do the reboot immediately after my work so that I can check to see if everything went okay. (A little mistake could deactivate your client/server database connection, for example.) Also, if I were to click the wrong button (Yes) when prompted for the reboot, the system will be shut down and restarted. Therefore, I do not do this work on a production server during production hours. Users of a network-based computer system get really sensitive when their server goes down unexpectedly.

Back to configuration. One of the things that some people were hoping for in Windows NT 4 was what Microsoft and others refer to as Plug and Play. Unfortunately, that will not be completed in this release. Under Windows 95, the system has a reasonable chance of recognizing the existence and type for a large number of cards and peripherals that you might connect to your system. It will then take you through a series of wizards to set things up (hopefully) correctly. It is not perfect but makes life much easier when it works.

Network Adapter Setup

Under version 4 of Windows NT, you still have to go through and manually tell the operating system what components you have installed. Therefore, you start the networking section with the network adapters. You might be thinking that Windows NT 4 is more like Windows 95. Even though modems are part of networking under Windows NT, they do not show up as a network adapter like they do under Windows 95. However, you will find bindings to the RAS wrappers later in the network setup, so RAS is not a totally separate subsystem.

Now let me focus on your options in the Adapters tab on the Network setup panel. (See Figure 6.3 again.) As you can see, it lists my network adapter. It would list multiple network adapters and allow you to configure each of them individually. Let us now examine what setting up an adapter involves. If you added a new adapter to your system, you would click the Add button on the Adapters tab of the Network setup panel. NT would then present you with a list of adapters that it supports (that are distributed on the Windows NT operating system CD) and allows you to choose one of them, as shown in Figure 6.4. This list is not very long when compared with that of, say, Windows 95, so it is important to check that your adapter is supported by Windows NT *before* you buy it. If it is not one of the ones that Microsoft provides drivers for on the NT operating system CD, you can use the Have Disk button to allow NT to read a disk or CD drive that contains drivers given to you by the manufacturer.

FIGURE 6.4.

Adapter selection panel.

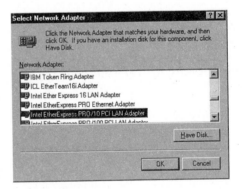

Once you have selected the adapter that you are going to use, you need to configure it. Here is where all of that hardware stuff can be a challenge for an operating system type who just wants to get things up and running quickly. The various adapter manufacturers have different ways to configure an adapter. Some use jumpers located on the card itself, and others use software utilities which will allow you to set it up programmatically. Whatever the method, you may have quite a challenge in front of you to select settings for this network card that do not conflict with other hardware components that you might have installed such as serial ports, drives, or sound systems.

There are two key addresses that you need to worry about when setting up an Intel-based machine, which is the most popular platform for NT, by far. The first address is known as the

IRQ level, which is also referred to as the interrupt number. It is one of 16 addresses that are available to get the attention of the operating system at the hardware level. You may think that 16 is a lot of addresses, but the machine that I am typing on has all 16 addresses used up between network cards, modems, a sound card, and the motherboard itself (which takes up four or more addresses before you put the first card on the system). The next address is usually referred to as the I/O port address. It is a section of the memory of your computer that is used for transferring data from the various installed cards and components.

When you buy workstations based on the MIPS or Alpha architectures, they usually have fixed addresses for their various components and your task is to figure out what these standard addresses are and just use them. The unfortunate part of the Intel world is that the operating system fixes a couple of addresses for such things as the system clock, and then throws the rest up for grabs with only some suggestions as to what should be used for what purpose. To make matters more complex, certain peripheral devices support only a few of the many possible combinations of IRQ and I/O port address. You will need to have this worked out before you start working on your server or else schedule plenty of time for you to try out all of the possible combinations. Finally, don't feel bad if it takes a while. I have found several machines that, no matter what combinations we tried, could not make certain components work and we had to replace them with others that were more compatible with the other components in the system.

Now back to the actual configuration task itself: You will be asked to set the addresses and possibly some additional configuration parameters for the adapter that you have chosen. You may choose poorly and be informed that your networking services did not start up because of some addressing conflict. Your task is to then adjust the settings of your adapter card, both through its jumper settings or setup utility and through the Network setup panel. On the Network setup panel, you select the Adapters tab and then choose the Configure button. You will be presented with a panel similar to Figure 6.5, which will allow you to alter the settings.

FIGURE 6.5.

Network adapter configuration settings.

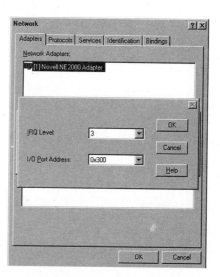

Perhaps you have gathered from the tone of my writings that this can be a very frustrating part of setting up a system. I can always tell in my group when one of us is setting up the hardware on a computer system. He is usually staring intently at his monitor with a mean look on his face or yelling at his system (I dread the day when it can yell back). There are a few tips that may help when you are trying to get through the installation and configuration of hardware:

- Keep all of your hardware manuals and read them.
- Look at your boards that have jumpers and record what their settings are.
- Make a chart that shows the addresses used by your various system components so that you can figure out what is available.
- If you are really stuck and comfortable with Windows 95, try installing Windows 95 on this machine first to see if the Setup Wizards in Windows 95 can figure out a workable combination of settings for the hardware in your machine.

After that, you're working a puzzle to see if you can get all of the pieces to fit together.

Network Protocol Setup

The next step in configuring your network is to decide which protocols you need to support. Usually, you will have these dictated to you by corporate standards, places you need to connect to, and so on. There are a few general suggestions for you to consider when deciding:

- If you might be using the Internet, you need to load TCP/IP.
- If you are going to be doing a lot of client/server database work, you should seriously consider using TCP/IP or IPX, not NetBEUI.
- If you just need a simple Microsoft network, NetBEUI is probably the easiest protocol to set up.
- If you are going to be coexisting with Novell NetWare systems, the IPX/SPX protocol is needed.

To set up protocols in your system, you will use the Protocols tab on the Network setup panel. (See Figure 6.6.) The nice thing that you will notice is that it looks very similar to the previous Adapters tab. That is the real benefit to this common interface for property setting. Basically, you have to add protocols from the list of available protocols (you can even add protocols from third-party manufacturer disks, but I have never had to use more than what is provided on the NT distribution CD). The complexity comes in when you go to configure the protocols. NetBEUI is relatively simple to configure and IPX/SPX usually works with the minimal default settings. However, TCP/IP usually requires some work to get running properly.

The reason that TCP/IP is so complex to set up comes from some of its ambitious design goals. It connects millions of computers worldwide through a logical network made up of many thousands of other networks. To make this all work together, software and hardware vendors have built up a scheme started by the United States military that allows you to map the hardware address (the EtherNet address which is a set of hexadecimal numbers assigned by the network card manufacturer) to a set of numbers that correspond to your organization (the Internet address or IP address). Therefore, the first key to remember is that an IP address is your key to getting on the Internet and therefore all of the TCP/IP software is designed to work with this address (even if you do not plan on surfing the Internet).

FIGURE 6.6.

Protocol setup.

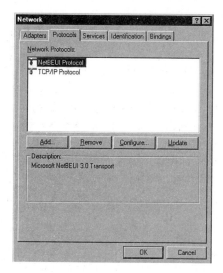

Figure 6.7 shows you the panel that will pop up when you go to configure TCP/IP. It is far more complex than the protocol setup panel and also requires that you understand a little bit about the fundamentals of TCP/IP systems before you can answer all of the questions. There are a number of considerations that you would use in making your decision, but let me list a few of the more common ones here:

- IP addresses are made up of a series of four numbers (bytes) ranging between 0 and 255 that are separated by periods (such as 123.123.123.123).

- If you are on an isolated network that you do not intend on connecting to the Internet, then you can make up your own addresses (by convention, you should use addresses in the 10.x.x.x range). Keep all of the addresses that you want to communicate with one another starting with the same first number.

- If you are on a network connected to the Internet, then you have to have someone (usually in the network group) who parcels out official addresses. Otherwise, they are coordinated by someone responsible for your local network.

- The subnet mask parameter is designed to help you ignore addresses that are not of concern to you (outside of your group and therefore the responsibility of a gateway if you have one). The subnet mask is a bit-pattern comparison (255 in one of the digits means that the address incoming has to match, while 0 means let everything in this digit pass). For example, 255.0.0.0 as a subnet mask means pass everything that has the same first number as my address and reject everything else.

■ Gateways are computers or network devices that allow you to communicate outside of your local network to the bigger world. When you define a gateway (or multiple gateways), TCP/IP traffic that is outside of your subnet mask is routed to the gateway(s) to see if they can resolve the address and transmit the information to the remote computer. You may actually go through a series of gateways when transmitting to distant computers.

■ Domain name servers are computers that allow you to use text names instead of IP addresses to describe remote computers. These are officially assigned names that are coordinated through the various Internet agencies and reflect the purpose and country in which the computer is located. (For example, aol.com references America Online; com identifies it as a commercial organization and the lack of a country suffix indicates that it is in the United States.) Windows NT can act as a domain name server or use it to translate IP names for your users. You are allowed to have primary and backup name servers in case one of these computers is unavailable.

■ WINS stands for Windows Internet Naming Service, which allows you to enter the IP addresses for your local computers and have other computers use these central lookup tables to translate a name into an address. This product now works together with DNS to resolve names on networks with both local and larger scopes. Again, NT can act as a WINS server or use its services.

■ The Routing tab determines whether your workstation will forward packets that it receives that are intended for other TCP/IP computers that it can communicate with (for example, act as a router). This can be useful if you have multiple networks and want to use one of your servers to forward traffic and connect the two networks together, but only transmit those packets that need to cross between the networks.

FIGURE 6.7.

Configuring the TCP/IP protocol.

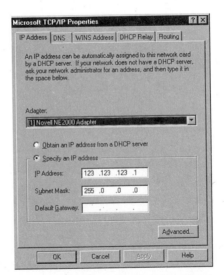

Let's just say that you want to keep things simple and get a basic TCP/IP network up and running. You do not plan on getting on the Internet. What I usually do is specify an explicit set of IP addresses similar to those shown in Figure 6.7 (the `10.x.x.x` family is reserved for internal assignments). I set the simple subnet mask of `255.0.0.0`. I then set up a special file used by most TCP/IP configurations known as the hosts file (which is a local file which resolves names to addresses similar to the WINS and DNS servers). Figure 6.8 provides a sample hosts file. It is a simple mapping between IP address and a name that is easier for people to type. As you can see, it would be impossible to maintain this table for the millions of people on the Internet, but it works well in small workgroups. You need to place this file under your Windows NT directory in the `system32\drivers\etc` subdirectory. (Mine is in `d:\winnt35\system32\drivers\etc` because I upgraded to 4 from 3.51.) This file should also be distributed to all clients so that they can work with these easy names.

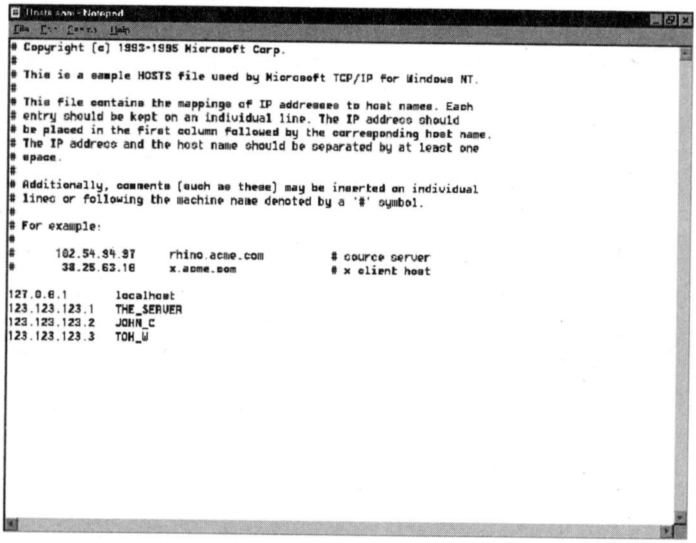

```
# Copyright (c) 1993-1995 Microsoft Corp.
#
# This is a sample HOSTS file used by Microsoft TCP/IP for Windows NT.
#
# This file contains the mappings of IP addresses to host names. Each
# entry should be kept on an individual line. The IP address should
# be placed in the first column followed by the corresponding host name.
# The IP address and the host name should be separated by at least one
# space.
#
# Additionally, comments (such as these) may be inserted on individual
# lines or following the machine name denoted by a '#' symbol.
#
# For example:
#
#      102.54.94.97     rhino.acme.com          # source server
#       38.25.63.10     x.acme.com              # x client host

127.0.0.1       localhost
123.123.123.1   THE_SERVER
123.123.123.2   JOHN_C
123.123.123.3   TOM_W
```

FIGURE 6.8.
Sample hosts file.

There are a lot of additional considerations with TCP/IP networking. Chapter 10, "Installing and Configuring Microsoft TCP/IP," goes over the configuration process in much more detail. The key to remember is that every computer that is running on a TCP/IP network at a given time should have a unique IP address. When this type of network is set up correctly, I have found it to run well and provide you with connectivity and service that is hard to beat.

Network Services Setup

So far, you have laid the foundation for networking, but you do not have much that is useful to the end user. For those of you who labored hours to set up a working IRQ setting on your network card, this may not seem fair. However, now is the time when you get to install the services that will allow your network to be used by the end users to get things done. I have found the services to be relatively simple to set up and configure once the networking basics are out of the way. So without any further ado, let me present the Services tab of the Network setup panel. (See Figure 6.9.)

FIGURE 6.9.

Network Services setup.

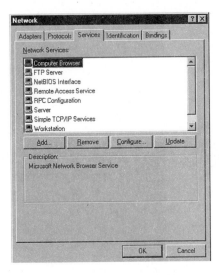

To add to the services that you have installed, choose the Add button. It gives you a list of available services and the option to add additional services from separate CDs or disks (the magic Have Disk button). The most difficult task is understanding what services are available to you (and there is quite a list of services that come off of the operating system CD):

- **Computer Browser:** This service allows you to see a list of computers that are available on the network.
- **NetBIOS Interface:** This is the basic interface to the Network Basic Internal Operating System.
- **Server:** This allows your machine to act as a network server.
- **Workstation:** This provides the services that you will need when using your server as a workstation.
- **BOOTP Relay Agent:** This was the predecessor of DHCP; use it if you already have such a network or else stick with the newer DHCP service. (You never know when they'll drop support on older products.)
- **FTP Server:** This service allows your computer to provide access to its files to other computers using the file transfer protocol common to UNIX and other computers.
- **Gateway (and Client) Services for NetWare:** This is your door into the world of Novell NetWare providing you with file sharing, print sharing, and other common Novell services.

■ **Microsoft DHCP Server:** This service, the dynamic host configuration protocol, allows your computer to act as a master repository for IP addresses so that you do not have to assign them manually to each computer.

■ **Microsoft DNS Server:** This allows your computer to act as a TCP/IP domain name server.

■ **Microsoft TCP/IP Printing:** This allows your computer to use UNIX TCP/IP print job transfer services (LPR/LPD).

■ **Network Monitor Agent:** This allows your computer to perform basic monitoring on the network.

■ **Network Monitor Tools and Agent:** This provides tools to allow your computer to monitor the network via the Simple Network Monitoring Protocol (SNMP).

■ **Remote Access Service:** This is the modem interface under Windows NT that allows you to dial in to the server.

■ **Remoteboot Service:** This allows your server to serve as the boot drive for remote computers with compatible remote boot software.

■ **RIP for Internet Protocol:** This allows your computer to route TCP/IP traffic between segments on your network (i.e., act as a router).

■ **RIP for NWLink IPX/SPC Compatible Transport:** This allows your computer to determine routes for IPX/SPX (Novell) traffic on your network.

■ **RPC Configuration:** This allows you to execute remote procedure calls (a standard way of executing jobs on other computers in the UNIX world).

■ **RPC Support for Banyan:** This allows you to execute jobs on computers using Banyan networks.

■ **SAP Agent:** This Service Advertising Protocol allows remote computers to determine the network access points on your computer.

■ **Services for Macintosh:** This provides you with a gateway into the world of Macintosh AppleTalk networks. (See Chapter 9, "Working with Macintosh Clients," for further details.)

■ **Simple TCP/IP Services:** This provides you with the basic services that you need to participate in a TCP/IP network (many other services require this service before they can start).

■ **SNMP Services:** This allows your server to provide basic operational information on load, availability, and so on, using the Simple Network Monitoring Services protocols that can be read by a number of monitoring packages.

■ **Windows Internet Name Service:** This allows your server to resolve IP addresses for clients on your network.

Many of these services are just installed. There are no configuration chores that you have to perform on them. For those that do require some form of configuration, you will be presented with a panel similar to Figure 6.10 that is specific to that particular service. For details on what the various options on this panel mean, you can refer to other chapters of this book and, of course, the Microsoft help system and documentation.

FIGURE 6.10.

Remote Access Setup panel.

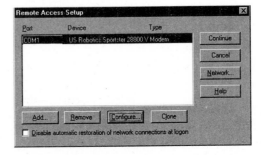

As you can see, there is a wide range of services available under Windows NT. The key to something that is implemented as a service is that it will be a background process that is in continuous operation once started, which usually occurs at system startup. Therefore, it is available even though there are no users logged in at the console and running programs. They are essential to Windows NT Server 4 being able to serve clients on the network.

Network Identification Setup

After the long discussion of options when setting up TCP/IP networking and the many services available under NT Server, it is refreshing to see a relatively simple tab on the Network setup panel—the Identification tab. (See Figure 6.11.) This tab sets what other computers on the Microsoft network will see when they are looking for computers. The key components are the Computer Name, which is just a unique identifier for the computer that should make sense to everyone else in your workgroup or domain. The next box for workgroups is your workgroup name. (You would be asked to identify your domain if you chose the Domain option when setting up your Microsoft network.) The workgroup and domain names are names made up by administrators to refer to a particular group of computers. In the domain environment, it has special meaning in that you can teach domains to trust one another and grant privileges to members of other domains. If you are looking for a more detailed discussion of domains and workgroups, the Windows NT Networking Guide in the Resource Kit provides some good material.

Network Bindings Setup

So far, we have covered the various options that are available when you set up networks. Now consider the possibility that you would want to set up multiple network adapters and remote access services that would use different sets of protocols and services, and perhaps even different configuration parameters for those protocols and services. It may seem like an unusual setup to some, but I have run across several examples of this being needed. A classic example would be a server acting as a gateway between two network segments. You may have Novell and TCP/IP machines on one side which your network administrator has assigned the IP address range of 123.123.1.*xxx*. The other network segment might have Microsoft networking (NetBEUI) and TCP/IP clients, but they use the IP address range of 123.123.2.*xxx*. In this manner, you can isolate and balance network traffic between different network segments. You would use the Adapters configuration tab to set up the IP addresses for the two adapters, but you would then have to use the Bindings tab (see Figure 6.12) to configure which protocols went where.

FIGURE 6.11.
Network identification.

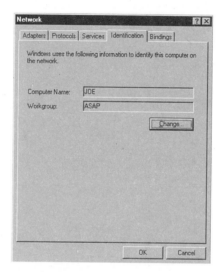

FIGURE 6.12.
Network bindings.

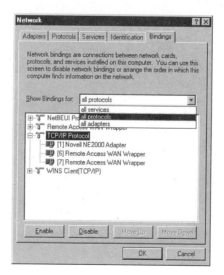

There are three ways to sort the list of bindings. The one that you choose depends on how you think of things and what problem you are working on. As you can see in Figure 6.12, I have linked the TCP/IP protocol to my network card and the Remote Access Server. If I wanted to remove this connectivity or add in additional connectivity, I would use the Enable and Disable buttons. You would be careful where you are when you start disabling bindings. The key is knowing what protocols, services, and adapters depend upon one another to ensure that you do not disable others things that you want when you disable a particular binding.

Remote Access Service (RAS)

Under Windows 95, Dial-Up Networking (the modems) is considered an integral part of networking and is set up pretty much the way you would set up any other adapter. Of course, it has its own property pages that take into account the unique setup parameters of a modem (all of the bit settings and whether you have to display a terminal screen before and after dialing a number). Windows NT Server 4 has not quite embraced this philosophy yet. Although you do bind the network wrappers (connections between the computers connected with the modem to computers connected via your network cards) using the Network setup panel, you do most of your other work setting up these connections by using the Modems option on the Control Panel. The actual modem connections and privilege setup (who can dial in, for example) is set up through the Remote Access Administration utility accessible from the Startup Menu, Programs selection, and Remote Access Service selection. (It is actually easier to show you Figure 6.13 than to describe it.)

FIGURE 6.13.

Accessing the Remote Access Service utilities.

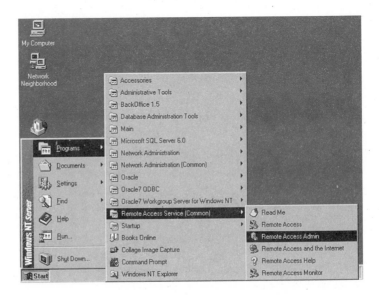

The first thing that you need to set up RAS is to have a modem properly configured. This might involve some of the same painstaking work described above for network adapters (such as getting drivers loaded for your modem and resolving IRQ/memory addresses). Figure 6.14 shows you the basic modem setup screen. You have to add a modem type that is supported by Windows NT 4 (again, see the hardware compatibility list or get an NT 4 driver from the modem vendor). You then have to identify a communications port to which that modem is mapped (yet another address when dealing with serial communications devices on Intel PCs).

FIGURE 6.14.

Modem configuration panel.

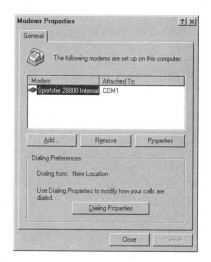

Once you have your basic modem set up, you may have two additional panels to set up. The Properties button gets into the communications details (see Figure 6.15) associated with the modem and its connection (speed, speaker volume, and all of those bit settings common to modem communications take the defaults whenever you can on these items). The Dialing Properties button lets you set up the details of dialing such as whether you need to dial a 9 to get an outside line.

Once your modem is set up, you are ready to use the Remote Access Admin utility that is located in the Remote Access Service program group shown in Figure 6.13. This utility is based on a pull-down menu system that allows you to perform the following useful services:

■ Start/Stop your remote access service (such as stop picking up incoming calls). Note that you might need to do this to allow other applications to access your modem because RAS tends to monopolize the modem even when it is not actively processing a call.

■ Grant permission to users to dial in from remote locations.

■ Show users who are currently connected to RAS.

FIGURE 6.15.

Modem Properties panel.

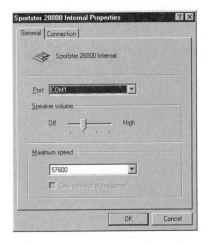

With the number of people who are accessing networks from remote locations (other groups that you work with or *road warriors* who travel a lot), RAS connectivity and modem pools are an important part of the Windows NT networking architecture. After having set up similar functions under UNIX and earlier versions of Novell, the RAS configuration is relatively simple, and I have found it to be very reliable. I have set up my home PC to dial in to the server and perform functions ranging from simple file transfers from my work PC to interacting with client/server databases using ODBC. If you have a modem, take some time to learn how to use it as a remote administrator. It could save you a trip into work in the middle of the night when your server has a few problems.

Network Client Setup

There are a lot of network clients out there (Windows NT Workstation, Windows 95, Windows for Workgroups, Macintoshes, and so on). This can present a challenge to administrators who have to support these clients accessing their NT Server. The fundamental problem is that you need compatible and working configurations on both ends of a network before communications can take place. It is useful to come up with standard setup procedures for each of the types of clients that you support that contain specifics such as the Internet address of your servers.

Useful Networking Utilities

One of the challenges with working and providing services in a network environment is that most users only see the end result. For example, they install a new client/server application on their PCs and complain that they can't access the database which is on your server. What is the problem? (I can't tell you how many error messages read something like, I couldn't talk to the server.) Going back to earlier discussions, the many layers and bindings involved have to be set up correctly on both ends to make communications happen. You also have to worry about logon IDs and passwords being set and used correctly to provide access to resources that are password protected.

With all of the things that can go wrong, I like to follow some basic checks from the client end to troubleshoot problems.

If anyone has trouble accessing the server, I usually try accessing the server from my workstation by using the My Computer icon or File Manager. (Note that File Manager and Explorer allow you to enter explicit network paths that may be available, but somehow the network browsing function does not detect when looking at the available nodes.) You can also use the NET VIEW command at the command prompt (for example, NET VIEW \\joe). This proves the server is up and accepting at least NetBEUI communications.

If I am troubleshooting a TCP/IP link from the user workstation, I go to the DOS prompt and type ping followed by the IP address of the server. If this works, you can try the ping command with the name to see if your problem lies in the name resolution process. Together, these utilities test the basics of TCP/IP networking on the server.

The tools that are available depend to a high degree on your environment. However, if you keep the fundamental principles in mind and start testing the various types of communications from the lower levels (such as ping and File Manager) and then work your way up in the chain (such as ODBC connections or trying to access a shared directory using the user's logon ID and password), you can usually spot the problem. If all else fails, try doing the same things, using the user's logon ID from a similar workstation in the same area and see if that clears up the problem.

Summary

This chapter has taken on the somewhat ambitious task of describing the basic setup of Windows NT Server's networking. The operating system comes with a large variety of networking support built in to the basic product. Your challenge is to map out which of the services and protocols are needed in your environment. You might also have to change these services over time as your network world evolves. Most networking is controlled from the control panel or the Remote Access Service utilities. I would like to leave you with my observation that I have found it relatively easy to use NT Server to connect to a wide variety of network types (UNIX, Novell, and the Internet) and achieve a high degree of reliability with minimal maintenance once things are set up.

Configuring and Installing Print Services

by Joe Greene

IN THIS CHAPTER

CHAPTER 7

It used to be quite a challenge to get access to a good printer. It seemed the best or closest printers were always on someone else's desk, and it was always a special favor to get access to that printer. Then people started to use network printers connected to PCs that were distributed throughout the building. They were nice, but users were always confused about print queues on various servers and all of those other details. Things got easier when printers started to get connection boxes and internal cards that allowed them to be connected directly to a network.

Today, the only printer that I use that is not connected to my PC via a network is the one I have on my desk at home (and I have to share that one with my wife via a switch box). With almost all of the printers connected to the network, it is easy to find one that is close to your desk and that has the capabilities (speed, duplex, graphics resolution, and color printing) that meets your needs. Printers have become more sophisticated, offering multiple trays for different types of paper and even envelope feeders that you can select.

Now step back to just a few years ago when Windows NT was just entering the market. Novell had the file and print server market fairly well locked up. They used a combination of file servers and special print servers (PCs whose sole job was to manage print queues) to spool print jobs to both local-attached and network-attached printers. The only difficulty was running all of those special Novell utilities to figure out what printers were available and then mapping to them in your login scripts. It was not a bad solution, but Windows NT had to do it better to gain market share.

The boys in Redmond came up with a pretty good solution. Mapping to printers was just about as easy as mapping to shared network directories. Users had a browser to search the network for available printers and then clicked on them to start the selection process. If the printer owners and administrators were nice, they would even give users a hint about what type of printer it was in the name (such as MKTG_4SI). If it was exported and you had the right permissions, you can grab it and start using it. Windows NT 4 takes this process one step further in that it provides Wizards (a series of screens that ask simple questions and provide you with lists to select from) to help ensure that you set up your printers correctly. Now if you monitor the Windows NT newsgroups (such as `comp.os.ms-windows.nt.misc`) on the Internet, you will find a number of old-time NT types who hate the idea of Wizards and do not want to bother with a long series of questions. However, for those of you who like a series of simple questions, you'll like the new setup.

This chapter covers the basics of setting up printers in Windows NT. Let me be a little more specific: It covers setting up directly attached printers (those connected to a port on your computer) and those on Microsoft and Novell network computers. There are two other possibilities which are covered in separate chapters. First, Macintosh printing is covered in Chapter 9, "Working with Macintosh Clients." Printing to LPR/LPD (such as to UNIX TCP/IP) printers is covered in Chapter 14, "Configuring TCP/IP Printing." I have found that the most useful printers are usually located on your office automation network, which means that most of your printers can be set up using the techniques described in this section. These setup techniques are relatively easy and I have found them to provide reliable printing services to the people on my network.

Printing in a Network Environment

There are a few considerations that you should be aware of before you start configuring a network of printers connected to your NT Servers and other workstations. The first extra consideration involves scheduling access to the printer. When you have a single-tasking operating system such as DOS accessing a locally attached printer, there is no problem figuring out who has access to the printer. You print directly to the printer with the only job that is running at the time. When you have an operating system such as Microsoft Windows, you have the possibility of queuing up several print jobs that run effectively in the background while you are doing other processing.

Now imagine a whole network of workstations printing to a series of network printers. When you send your print job, you have no idea as to whether the printer is turned on or working. Therefore, it becomes important to have printing utilities that can determine the status of the printer and feed that back to the users if there are problems. Another issue is how you coordinate the printing of a number of clients to a printer. If the print queue was located on each of the clients, there would be a question as to who gets the printer next when the current print job completes. This is typically solved by designating the computer to which the printer is attached as a print server which manages the print queue (a list of files waiting to be printed).

Finally, in many organizations you have to consider issues such as who gets to use a particular resource. In some organizations these limitations may be based on such real concerns as security restrictions or access to sensitive information. However, in many cases you have to deal with a group or person who does not want to share. Whatever the reason, network operating systems have to be able to control access to printer resources.

Printing in the NT World

The Windows NT environment provides a convenient set of services to allow users to access local and network printers. The thing that impresses me most about the way this environment is set up is that access to these resources is built directly into the operating system and is therefore really easy to configure and access. However, there are a few things that have to be in place to make this happen. I have come up with a simplified picture of this in Figure 7.1.

The first key is having a client that is capable of generating the information to print (or plot) in the correct format for the desired printer. Printer manufacturers have come up with a number of print control languages (such as HP PCL and PostScript). It is therefore the client's responsibility to have the correct printer driver for the type of printer being used. Since the Windows NT Server product has to act as both a server and a client (such as when you want to print logged information), you need to install the printer driver for the printers that you will be using. This applies whether the printer is directly attached to your server or is accessed over the local area network. The good news is that the Windows NT Server CD comes with printer drivers for the vast majority of printers out there. You can also get printer drivers from the manufacturer for those printers that are a little less common or if you want enhanced performance.

FIGURE 7.1.

A simplified view of Windows NT printing.

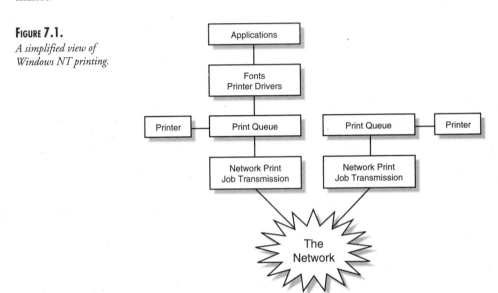

A side note on the last paragraph concerns fonts. DOS and early versions of Windows did not store fonts or printer drivers as part of the operating system. Therefore, when you had an application such as WordPerfect for DOS, you had to get a set of fonts and printer drivers from the application vendor. If you changed printers, you often had to live with a different set of fonts which meant you had to reformat your document to look good. Windows NT, like Windows 3.1 and Windows 95, has fonts built directly into the operating system. The operating system therefore becomes responsible for translating the text into the appropriate control sequences to get you the look that you want (such as the shape of the letters and boldness). The TrueType fonts extend this further by providing an even higher degree of control over the look between different printers. While you are typically not sensitive over the font on batch printouts of audit reports from a server, you may consider installing a wider array of fonts on a server that has to serve in the dual capacity as a personal workstation.

After the printer drivers have translated the desired information into the correct series of bits and bytes for your printer, it is time to transfer the information either directly to the printer or to the server which controls the queue for the printer. Once again, these utilities are built directly into the operating system. Later in this chapter, I will show you how to use the printers utility to control the queue (for example deleting jobs and stopping the printer). The key to this printer setup is the ability to communicate between computers and between the print servers and the printers themselves to keep things flowing smoothly. Gone are the days when you spooled a bunch of print jobs only to stand by the printer wondering where your work is in the system.

Since Windows NT came on the market after the established vendors had a large install base, it was in Microsoft's best interest to fit in well with existing organizations. It helped eliminate the argument that a company could not start using NT because they would have to throw out a huge investment in the other vendor's products. It is impressive the way Windows NT integrates with printers on a Novell network. You log on to the Novell network when you start your computer and then the Novell printers appear on the same list as the printers that are connected to computers on the Microsoft network. In addition, the Macintosh services component of Windows NT allows you to access printers on the AppleTalk network. Finally, if you have UNIX resources out there, Windows NT provides LPR/LPD services which allow you to send print jobs to many different types of UNIX computers that are connected to your network.

Before I leave this section, let me throw one more thought at you. Many organizations like to name their printers cute names such as naming them after planets or *Star Trek* characters. While this may make it interesting to people going to select a printer, it may be more practical to name your printers with names that contain two bits of information. This is important in larger organizations which may have dozens or even hundreds of printers attached to their network. The first bit of information is the location of printer. This may include group, floor, or building and floor. The next important bit of information is the type of printer. Remember, the remote user is going to have to configure the appropriate printer driver to send the appropriate job streams to this printer. An example of a good name for a larger network printer might be something like MAINT_4SI. This identifies the printer as being in the maintenance department and it is an HP LaserJet 4SI printer. You would have to change the name of the printer if you moved it to reflect the new location and some organizations may not want to do this. This is just a thought, but something that you should at least consider.

Windows NT Printer Configuration Utilities

I mentioned earlier that printing is an integral part of the Windows NT operating system. As such, the logical place to look for it would be under Settings-Control Panel on your startup menu. You will also notice a direct shortcut to printers on the Settings menu. Either way, you get to the same location which is the Printers control utility. Now I personally like the way things are set up under Windows NT and Windows 95. If I want to do something to a printer, I have one place to go. There is not a printer setup utility and then a printer queue management utility and a separate printer queue monitoring utility (for those Novell users who do not have administrator privileges over the printers). No, this is one-stop shopping.

Figure 7.2 shows the window that will greet you when you select the Printers option from the Settings menu. It looks very much like the My Computer or Control Panel utilities, which is nice because you probably already know what each of the buttons does for you. You will always find at least one icon on this display which is the Add Printer icon. This starts the Printer Setup Wizard (a series of panels that ask specific questions to guide you through the printer setup process).

FIGURE 7.2.

Printers control utility.

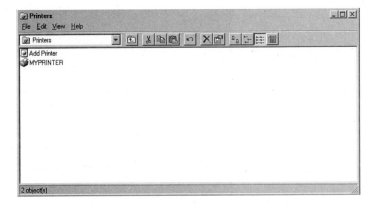

You will also see icons for any of the printers that you have already configured. The trick to the Windows 95/Windows NT 4 interface is that to change the configuration of a given printer, you right-click on the icon for that printer and select Properties from the menu that appears. This will bring up a tabbed dialog (yes, you see a lot of this type of interface for properties settings under 95 and NT) which lets you set all of the properties for this printer. Figure 7.3 shows a sample of this Properties dialog for an HP LaserJet attached to my server. Notice that it lets you perform a wide range of configuration tasks (these printer drivers get more sophisticated every day) including updating the printer driver if you receive a new one. It also allows you to print a test page which can be very helpful if you are having problems.

FIGURE 7.3.

Properties dialog for a printer.

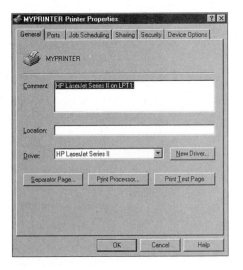

Finally, if you double-click on a printer icon on the Printers control utility, you will be given a window that allows you to control jobs and the print queue itself for that printer. Figure 7.4 shows this window. This panel allows you to stop the printer queue, delete jobs, or set up which printer is the default on your system. Therefore, while the Properties page lets you tell the system about the type of printer that you have and what you want your print jobs to look like, this utility lets you control the print jobs that are actually being processed by the system.

FIGURE 7.4.

Print queue control utility.

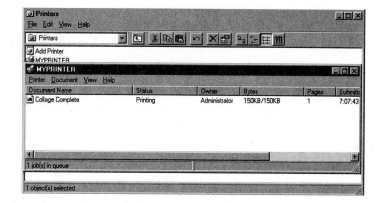

Configuring a Locally Attached Printer

Next I want to go over the printer configuration process in a little more detail. One of the first things that hit me when reading articles on the Windows NT Internet newsgroup was the violent reaction some of the old-time NT administrators had to the use of Wizards in the 4 version of NT. The main complaint was that they wanted to get things done quickly and that it took time to go through all of the panels in a Wizard. These are probably people who are so familiar with the process that they could enter parameter settings on a DOS command line from memory. However, if you are not one of these gurus, then Wizards can be a very friendly way to go through a configuration task, especially if you do not do this task every day.

You start the Add Printer Wizard by double-clicking on the Add Printer icon in the Printer control utility. The first Wizard panel that you will see is where you tell Windows NT whether the printer that you are setting up is attached to a port on your computer or whether it is a network resource that you are accessing. This will determine which panels you are presented with and also whether the printer queue is set up to be managed locally or transmitted to another computer on the network for printer management. Figure 7.5 shows you the Local/ Network Printer selection panel.

Because this section is devoted to configuring locally attached printers, we will assume that you selected the My Computer radio button on the Local/Network Printer selection panel and clicked the Next button. Note that you can click on the Cancel button on any panel in this Wizard and cancel your printer setup. The next panel that you will see after indicating that you want to configure a local printer asks you to tell Windows NT the computer port to which your printer is connected. (See Figure 7.6.) In the Intel world, these are referred to as LPT1 to LPT3 for parallel printer ports and COM1 to COM4 for serial ports. Hopefully your computer manufacturer was good to you and labeled the ports or at least documented them in one of the manuals. Anyway, all you normally have to do is check the box next to the appropriate port and click the Next button. I have never had to add a port or configure the port for Windows NT, but there are option buttons for this. The Configure Port button lets you set the transmission retry interval which could be required for some systems, but don't worry about it unless you have problems or a manual tells you to change it.

Figure 7.5.

Local/Network Printer selection panel.

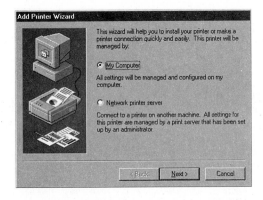

Figure 7.6.

Printer Port selection panel.

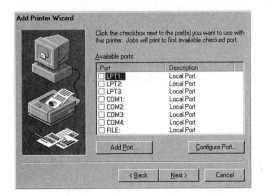

The next Wizard screen you see allows you to specify the type of printer that you are connecting to and lets you scroll down through a list of manufacturers on the left side and select a particular model of printer made by that manufacturer. Windows NT supports a wide range of the more popular printers, but if you cannot find your printer on the list, you might be able to get a printer driver for Windows NT from the printer manufacturer. If this is the case, you would click the Have Disk button and tell NT where this driver is located (usually A: for your floppy disk drive). If you are using a printer driver from the Windows NT CD-ROM, you should have this CD in the drive at this time. After you have selected your printer, you can click the Next button to go to the next panel. You should also note that there is a Back button at the bottom of all but the first screen in this Wizard. This allows you go to the previous Wizard panel if you realize that you made a mistake and need to change something. (See Figure 7.7.)

FIGURE 7.7.

Printer Driver selection panel.

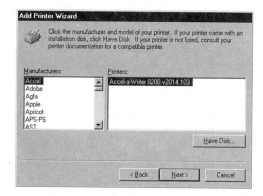

7

CONFIGURING
AND INSTALLING
PRINT SERVICES

> **NOTE**
>
> What do you do if you cannot find a driver for your printer on the Windows NT CD or the driver has bugs or lacks some features which you desire? The best answer is to get a Windows NT (not Windows 3.1) driver disk from the manufacturer when you buy the printer. Another alternative is to see if you can download a driver from the vendor's or Microsoft's (www.Microsoft.com) Web pages. Finally, you can try drivers for older versions of the printer made by the same manufacturer (such as a LaserJet 3 driver for an HP LaserJet 4 printer).

The next panel is really pretty simple (again, this is the type of panel that some people complain about being too simple and therefore making Wizards too slow). Figure 7.8 illustrates what I call the Printer naming panel. It lets you enter a name for your printer. You get to pick a name that suits your local tastes and standards. I would recommend using meaningful names (location and type of printer) in large organizations; however, you can name your printers after craters on the moon if that is what suits you. You also have radio buttons on this panel to indicate whether this will be the default printer for users who use the server as a workstation (like you, the administrator). When you have entered this data, you can press the next button to move onwards in this Setup Wizard.

The next (and next to last) panel in this Wizard lets you set up sharing for this printer. By default, a printer connected to your server will only be available to people who log on at the console. Now with everyone conscious about capital expenditures for computer equipment, the pressure is usually on to have people share printers that are located in convenient locations (or maybe in locations that are not so convenient). Sharing a printer is easy (see Figure 7.9).

Finally, you are given the opportunity to print a test page before you commit the new printer to your system. I always like to print the test page because it does not really take all that long and it can catch little oddities with drivers or port connections. Figure 7.10 shows the panel used to print the test page. The Finish button actually configures the operating system to use this new printer.

FIGURE 7.8.
Printer naming panel.

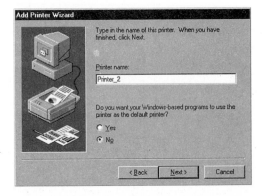

FIGURE 7.9.
Printer sharing panel.

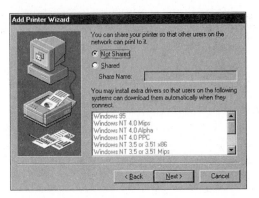

FIGURE 7.10.
Finishing screen for printer setup.

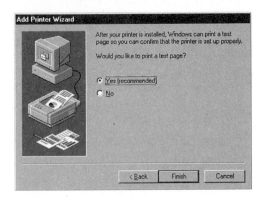

Welcome to the new world of Microsoft Setup Wizards. There are Wizards all over the place in Windows 95 and Windows NT. I have found that once you get used to them, it is relatively quick to just keep clicking Next, especially on a machine that is hefty enough to act as a server (even though NT Server is optimized for background speed versus user interaction, but more on that later). Perhaps if you are an administrator for a large network of servers, it could get tedious to set up two dozen printers on ten servers. There are a few key points about this printer Setup Wizard that I would like to reiterate to make sure they are clear:

- You can use the Back button up to the point where you click the Finish button to go back to previous screens on which you may want to change some of your input.

- You can use the Cancel button to stop the setup process without creating a printer that is half set up (it is only collecting information and executes the setup commands when the Finish button is clicked).

- In most cases, the defaults are usually good to follow (except, of course, when selecting printer models).

Every now and again, you will need to set up some of the fancier features of your printers (such as special trays for envelopes) or change some of the settings that you made. (I have a printer with limited memory and had to reduce the resolution to 150 dots per inch to print graphics.) Remember from the discussion around Figure 7.3 that you could call up property pages for an existing printer by right-clicking on the icon for that printer and selecting the Properties option (right-clicking is another one of those new interface standards that you have to get used to). This property sheet contains six tabs that give you an amazing amount of control over your network printer.

The first property page shown in Figure 7.3 is the general property page. One of the key items is that this page lets you install a new, updated driver for your printer. Also, it lets you set up separator pages for printers that handle jobs from a number of different users. Finally, a button that I am personally looking forward to is the Print Test Page button. As I will discuss in the section on printer problem resolution, I like to try to work the problem in a systematic manner and the ability to print test pages directly from the server utilities is a good start.

The next property page is ports used for locally attached printers. Figure 7.11 shows this tab. It looks very much like the Wizard page and is pretty self-explanatory. About the only thing that I could think of that would cause you to use this is if you want to switch ports—say to locate your printer farther than traditional parallel port connections support—and therefore you switch to a serial cable.

The next panel reminds me of the print queue setup utilities on larger computers such as mainframes. As you can see in Figure 7.12, you can activate printers at only certain times. This can be useful in preventing people from spooling sensitive information to a printer and allowing the printout to sit out all night where prying eyes could look at it. This panel even presents you with the option to speed up printing from the program's point of view and other advanced controls. Panels like this are finally giving you the control over your computer environment that you have had in older computer environments.

The next tab is another simple one (see Figure 7.13). It just lets you determine whether you are going to share your printer with other users. If you choose to share the printer, you get to give it a text name that hopefully makes sense to the people who might be attaching to it. This just indicates that you are planning to share the printer. The next tab will let you control who is allowed to access it.

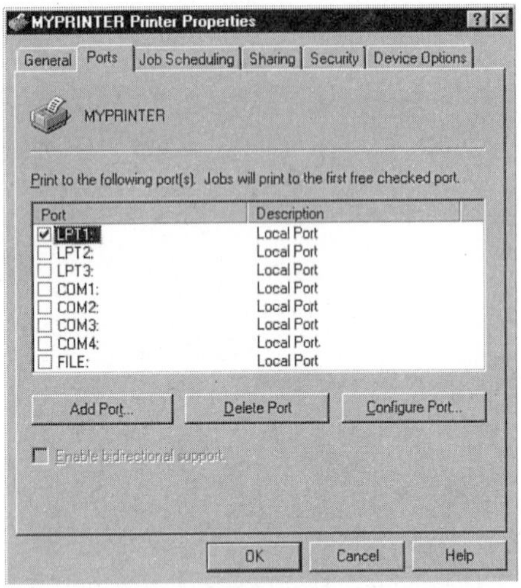

FIGURE 7.11.

*Ports tab of the Printer
Properties dialog.*

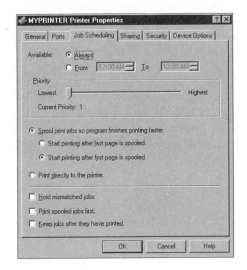

FIGURE 7.12.

*Job Scheduling tab
dialog.*

The next tab allows you to control and monitor the use of your printers. (See Figure 7.14.)
The concept of ownership may be foreign to some of you, especially if you do not use NTFS
file systems. Basically, ownership allows a person to gain control of a set of resources under NT
and be the one who must be contacted for access to those resources. This allows you to have
someone in the department take ownership of the printer and coordinate access to it. Access
can be granted to groups of individuals using the Permissions button on this tab. Finally, you
can set up auditing options to monitor usage of your printer using the Auditing button. All in
all, this is a fairly complete set of controls for printer resources.

FIGURE 7.13.
Sharing tab.

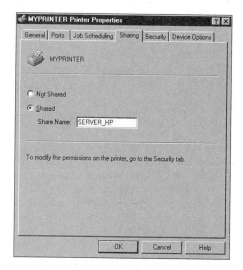

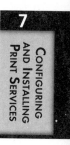

FIGURE 7.14.
Security tab.

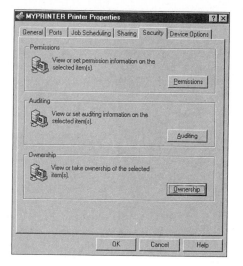

The final tab under Printer Properties controls device options. Figure 7.15 shows a sample of how this page looks for my laser printer. The items that you can control are dependent on your printer and the printer driver that you are using. If you have features that are supported by the printer, but do not appear to you on this display, you should check for an updated NT driver from Microsoft (check their Web page) or the printer manufacturer. As you can see, there are a number of tray options for printers that support multiple trays, font cartridges, and so on. I have seen some larger printers set up with multiple trays—one for normal paper, one for company letterhead, and one for envelopes. All the users had to do to print on a specific type of paper was to select the appropriate printer options under printer setup in their application and send the job off. It can save a large amount of time shifting trays around, manually feeding envelopes (the wrong side up), and so on.

FIGURE 7.15.

Device Options tab.

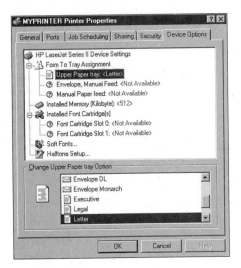

Configuring a Printer on Another Networked Computer

For those of you who flipped right to this section heading by looking it up in the table of contents, you need to read the section on configuring a local printer. That is because I am not going to repeat my discussion on the Printer Setup Wizard in this section. Instead, I am going to discuss the one panel that is different between the local and network printers. This book is already heavy enough as is without me adding unneeded pages.

This does illustrate a good point about the interface design of Windows NT. It tends to keep interface details similar between different utilities and it handles the technical details of these differences (such as the operating system software used for sending print jobs to a local printer versus that used to send to a network printer) behind the scenes. Figure 7.16 shows the key panel that is different when setting up a network printer.

As you can see, you get an Explorer-type view of the devices on your network. If you have both Novell and Microsoft network devices available, you will be able to see both networks. This and other such features let you drop an NT network in the middle of a Novell environment with relatively little pain. The convenient thing about this type of display is that you go down through the workgroups to individual servers and finally pick individual printers all by reading their names. You are not required to know the exact name of the print server and printer. All you have to do is be able to find it on a list. Note that you will be verified to be on the list of users (or a member of the appropriate group) that has access to this printer.

Finally, there are other utilities not covered by this section that allow you to access other printers. If you have a Macintosh AppleTalk network, you can access those printers using the Services for Macintosh option. Macintosh connectivity is covered in Chapter 9. Also, if you have a number of useful printers on a UNIX network or other computers that support the LPR/ LPD (line printer requester/line printer daemon) protocol over TCP/IP networks, you can attach to them via the Microsoft TCP/IP Printing service. The TCP/IP printing features are covered in Chapter 14.

FIGURE 7.16.

Network Printer Connection dialog.

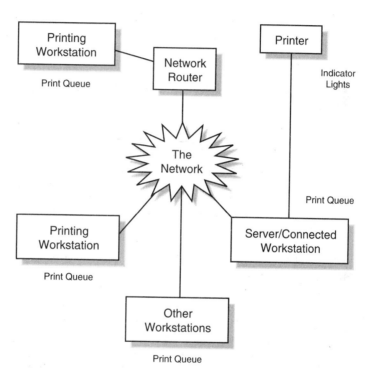

Print Queue Management

I covered the basics of controlling a printer queue earlier in this chapter. Basically, all you have to do is select Settings-Printers from the Start menu and then double-click on the printer that you wish to manage. You will get a screen similar to Figure 7.4 which displays the current print queue (jobs that have been submitted for print or are in the process of being printed). While this is a good start, I wanted to point out a few additional concepts to help you manage your printers a little bit better.

Multiple Queues: If you are using Windows to access a network printer, the application will actually print the job to a local print queue. The operating system will transfer this print job to the machine to which the network printer is attached. The job will then be printed from this remote print queue. It usually takes much less time to transfer a job from your computer to the network print queue than it does to actually print the job. You need to be aware that once the job disappears from your PC's print queue, you need to use the printer control utilities on the machine to which the printer is attached if you wish to stop or cancel the job.

Printer Memory: Most modern printers have a fairly significant amount of memory in them. This allows their host computers to rapidly transmit most simple print jobs to them and then get on with other tasks. When you cancel a print job in the printer control utility, you stop the server from transmitting any additional information to the printer. You do not erase what has already been transferred to the printer. Therefore, your printer may continue printing for some time unless you reset it.

Turning Printer Off in the Middle of a Job: Sometimes the only way that you can stop your printer from printing dozens of useless pages is to cycle the power switch off. You need to be aware that when you do this, you may jam paper inside the printer which you will have to remove manually (watch out for that toner getting on your clothing). Also, you need to ensure that the server is no longer sending print information. If you do, the printer will often reset to a default print (losing the font control information that you sent at the beginning of your print job) and start printing in a really strange manner (sometimes one letter per page). Also remember that you may have several other print jobs stored in the memory of the printer that would be lost if you turn the printer off.

Dealing with Printing Problems

The real challenges as a system administrator come not when everything is running well, but when everything is falling down around your feet. The number of problems that can occur with printers are as varied as the printers that are available on the market. When you add in the complications of networks and a variety of operating systems, it can be downright challenging. What I propose to discuss in this section is my generic approach for investigating server printer problems that should at least narrow down where the problem is for further investigation.

The underlying concept in my approach is to understand the path that the print job follows and try to isolate where the problem is occurring first. For networked printer environments, it is useful to have a diagram of the network. It may be tricky to extract one of these from your network staff, but often they will sit down with you and draw one up on a sheet of paper if you refuse to go away until it is done. What I then like to do is mark up this drawing to let me identify the places that are useful to help me determine where the problem lies.

My approach to troubleshooting is usually something like this:

The first thing to check is the printer queue on the workstation creating the print. If the job is not leaving the print queue on the workstation that is generating the print job, check network connectivity to the print server using Network Neighborhood, Explorer, or File Manager. See if you can connect to disk drives on the remote computer to prove that the network is correctly transmitting signals between the two computers.

If you cannot see the print server from the file connection utilities, go to other workstations that are on the same part of the network as the workstation having the problems and see if they can see the print server.

Check to see that the print server can see other resources on your network. Are there any segments of the network that you cannot see (such as all the workstations on that segment are missing). Based on these checks, you can determine if network connectivity is your problem. If you cannot see anything, you may have to check your network setup and possibly reboot the print server.

Check the print queue on the print server to see if jobs are getting stuck in its queue. If so, check lights and indicators on your printer to see if any information is getting to the printer. This isolates the problem between the printer and the print server.

After you have run these basic checks, you now get into the printer-specific, network-specific, and operating-specific problems. There are any number of them, but it helps to narrow your focus. I have found the print queues to function quite reliably once they are set up correctly. Occasionally you will have to reboot machines or servers that have become confused, but this is relatively infrequent. Most of the problems that I have run across deal with the printers themselves jamming, running out of paper, or just plain getting dirty.

Summary

This chapter was designed to introduce you to the basics of setting up the most common form of Windows NT printing—locally attached printers and printers accessed through Novell or Microsoft networks. The new Wizard utilities make it relatively easy to set up a new printer or access a network printer. Good naming conventions, combined with the network browser interface used to attach to network printers, make it easy to figure out which of the many printers on the network you want. Finally, a disciplined approach to troubleshooting is helpful for those times when your printers are acting up.

Working with Clients

by Robert Reinstein

IN THIS CHAPTER

CHAPTER 8

Introduction

With almost every NT Server there are NT clients. These clients must be defined to the NT Server domain before the clients can have access to the domain. Once defined, the clients must be configured to access the network.

In certain cases a Windows NT Server might be sitting on a LAN offering services for which client software is not necessary, but more often than not, the Windows NT Server will have clients that require an authenticated logon, or at least access to the file and print services that an NT Server has to offer.

In order for client computers to be able to attach to the Windows NT Server, they must have the necessary software and proper configuration. This chapter discusses the client software available with Microsoft Windows NT Server, which one to use, and how to configure them. The administrative tasks required on the server side are covered in detail in Chapter 16, "Administering the Server."

The Windows NT Server CD-ROM includes the client software for MS-DOS, Windows 3.1, and OS/2. The Windows NT Workstation client software is included as part of Windows NT Workstation and is available only on the Windows NT Workstation CD-ROM. The Windows 95 client software for NT networks is included with Windows 95. Windows for Workgroups also includes its own NT client software, and must be purchased separately.

I will also be mentioning the Network Client Administrator, which is a Windows NT Server utility that deals with the installation of client software for Windows NT Server. The Network Client Administrator can, among other things, create installation disks for Windows NT clients. A detailed discussion of the Network Client Administrator appears in Chapter 24, "Network Client Administrator."

In all cases of installing Windows NT Server domain client software, you must be sure that both the servers and the client are running the same protocols. More precisely, the client must be running at least one of the protocols that are active on the Windows NT Server domain controllers for authentication, and any other Windows NT Server that has resources that the client requires. In planning the entire network, one or more common protocols should have been selected.

Configuring the Windows NT Server

Before you can have client workstations attach to your NT network, you must perform certain tasks on the NT Server. This includes establishing standards and conventions before actually adding the user accounts through the NT administrative programs.

User Accounts

Each client on a Windows NT network must first be established with an account in the Windows NT domain. This is accomplished using the User Manager for Domains (see Figure 8.1).

In general, users are established by identifying their user name, password, permissions, and group memberships. Other configuration properties for each user are customized user profiles, logon scripts, home directories, logon hours, and ability to utilize Remote Access Services (RAS) for logging on to the domain.

FIGURE 8.1.

User Manager for Domains.

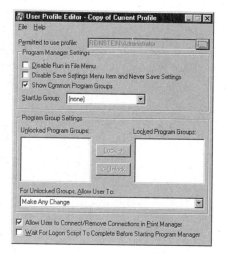

A user profile can be assigned to a user if the user is running Windows NT as a workstation operating system.

A logon script can also be assigned to a user running any operating system. The logon script can be either a batch file (.BAT or .CMD) or an .EXE file. The specified logon script is executed on the client's computer at the time of logon authentication. Examples of logon script commands include the execution of an anti-virus scanning on the client's local hard drive, calling another batch file, and attaching to network resources, as well as any other process specific to the user name that should be executed each time the client logs on to the domain.

Table 8.1 shows the variables that can be set from within a logon script.

Table 8.1. Logon script environment variables.

Variable	Description
ComSpec	Directory for CMD.EXE
LibPath	Directories to search for Dynamic Link Libraries (DLLs)

continues

8

WORKING WITH CLIENTS

Table 8.1. continued

Variable	*Description*
OS2LibPath	Directories to search for Dynamic Link Libraries (DLLs) under OS/2 subsystem
Path	Directories to search for executable program files
WinDir	Directory in which Windows NT is installed

Following is a sample batch file that can be used as a logon script:

```
net use o: \\server\c-drive
net use p: \\server\e-drive
net use lpt2: \\server\hp
net use n: \\server\d
net use m: \\server\maildata
call \\server\netlogon\landesk\netbios.bat
```

Logon scripts are created using any text editor, such as Notepad, and must be saved as unformatted ASCII files.

> **TIP**
>
> You might decide not to use logon scripts because persistent drive attachments and printer attachments might be sufficient to handle logon requirements.

> **TIP**
>
> Logon scripts should be created in a subdirectory called SYSTEM32\REPL\IMPORT\SCRIPTS under the main NT directory. If your domain has more than one domain controller, the contents of the IMPORT\SCRIPTS directory should also be placed in the SYSTEM32\REPL\EXPORT\SCRIPTS directory and replication should be set up to distribute these logon scripts to the other domain controllers.

A home directory can be specified for users that are running Windows NT as their operating system.

A user's home directory is a directory on an NT Server or NT Workstation that the user can choose to store files and programs in. When a home directory is assigned to a user through the User Manager for Domains, this directory will become the current directory whenever the user brings up a File Open or File Save dialog box. It also becomes the current directory when the user opens a command prompt or runs a program that does not have a working directory assigned to it.

Home directories can be shared by multiple users, but it is in the administrator's best interest to keep a separate directory for each user in case the user leaves the domain. The administrator needs to either migrate the contents of the directory to another domain, or, if the user is no longer part of the infrastructure, the entire directory can be deleted.

A properly implemented home directory can make it easy for a user to back up all of his or her data files. In most cases this directory should be on the user's local hard drive; however, if the user's hard drive space is limited, a network share should be created to allow the user to use space on a server's hard drive.

By default, Windows NT Server creates a USERS\DEFAULT directory on the Windows NT Workstation. If no home directory is specified by the administrator, this directory is used as the home directory.

System environment parameters are assigned for home directories, and can be used in batch files and logon scripts. Table 8.2 shows these parameters.

Table 8.2. Batch file and logon script parameters.

Parameter name	Definition	Default value
%homedrive%	Drive where the home directory is located	Drive where the Windows NT system files are installed
%homepath%	Pathname of the home directory	\USERS\DEFAULT
%homedir%	Redirected drive letter on the user's computer that refers to the share point for the user's home directory	No default value
%homeshare%	UNC name of the shared directory containing the home directory, or a local or redirected drive letter	No default value

Additional environment parameters are available that have values already assigned by Windows NT. Table 8.3 shows these, which can be used in batch files and logon scripts.

Table 8.3. Additional batch file and logon script parameters.

Parameter	Description
%os%	The operating system of the user's workstation
%processor_architecture%	The processor architecture (such as Intel) of the user's workstation
%processor_level%	The type of processor (such as 486) of the user's workstation
%userdomain%	The domain containing the user's account
%user name%	The user name of the user

Special Considerations When Configuring the Server for Windows NT Workstation Clients

For clients running Windows NT Workstation, each individual workstation must be added to the domain in order to participate in authentication by a domain controller. This is accomplished by using the Server Manager from the Windows NT Server Administrative Tools.

From the Computer menu in Server Manager, choose Add To Domain. This dialog enables you to add Windows NT Workstations, Windows NT Servers that have been installed as servers, and Windows NT Servers that have been configured as backup domain controllers. Enter the computer name of the Windows NT Workstation client and click Add. Once this is completed, that Windows NT Workstation client will be able to log on to the domain.

Things to Know Before You Set Up a Client for Microsoft Networking

Regardless of the operating system that the potential Windows NT Server client is running on his computer, there is information that will be needed in advance of running the client configuration procedures.

The following subsections describe these items, which should be researched.

The Client's Computer Name

This name can be up to 15 characters in length and cannot contain any spaces. This name will be used to identify the computer, not the user/client, to Microsoft Networking. This name must be unique to the network.

The Domain or Workgroup Name

With a Windows NT network, the domain name will be used; however, both Windows for Workgroups and Windows 95 have dialogs that will ask for a workgroup name. The domain name should be substituted for the workgroup name. Workgroups are used for peer-to-peer networking.

A Computer Description

This is a free-form text description for the computer. This will be displayed along with Computer Names as a more descriptive way to identify the computer.

Type of Network Adapter

The brand name and model of the network adapter are needed for all of the client setup programs. An alternative to installing a network adapter would be using the Remote Access Services client. This discussion will assume that a network adapter card is being used in each client machine.

> **TIP**
>
> Windows 95, Windows for Workgroups, and Windows NT Workstation ship with a plethora of drivers for network adapter cards; however, I have found that it might be necessary to obtain more recent drivers directly from the hardware manufacturer to ensure a smooth installation of the network adapter card.
>
> Before setting up clients, I usually call CompuServe and use the PC File Finder (GO IBMFF) to hunt for updated drivers. Sometimes a recently purchased card comes with a disk or CD-ROM that contains updated drivers. However, using an online service such as CompuServe or the hardware manufacturer's own BBS or Web page will usually offer the most recent drivers available.

Network Adapter Hardware Settings

For network interface cards that aren't plug and play, the proper settings, such as IRQ, DMA, and ROM address, are needed to allow the Microsoft Networking client to work with the adapter.

Each of the different clients might require additional information, but what I have discussed in this section is the primary data that must be known in advance of the installation of client software.

Windows NT Server Client Setup

> **TIP**
>
> In all of the following scenarios for setting up clients for a Windows NT Server domain, I explain the various utilities available to connect to shared printers and drives. Although these utilities are very useful, I have always found that it is a good idea to be familiar with the command-line option of connecting to these resources. For troubleshooting purposes, it might be necessary to bypass the GUI utilities or pop-up utility and use the NET USE command to test connectivity or permissions.

The MS-DOS and Microsoft Windows 3.x Clients

Microsoft LAN Manager was at one time Microsoft's only network operating system. This form of networking used networking concepts that are still being used in Windows NT Server. Curiously enough, the MS-DOS/Windows 3.x client software for Windows NT Server is the same client software that would be used to attach to a Microsoft LAN Manager 2.1 server, and is clearly identified as such in the README.TXT file that accompanies it.

Current users of Microsoft LAN Manager will be able to keep their client software unless they are not running the latest version. They should upgrade it if it is not the latest revision, which is, at the time of this writing, version 3.0.

In order for a DOS, the Microsoft Workgroup Add-on for MS-DOS, or Windows 3.x client to log on to a Windows NT Server, it is necessary to run the Network Client Full Redirector. (See Figures 8.2 and 8.3.) This redirector loads DOS drivers that occupy about 100KB of memory. It is because of this overhead that the DOS redirector is the least preferred method of attaching into an NT Server.

FIGURE 8.2.

Setup for the Microsoft Network Client v3.0 for MS-DOS.

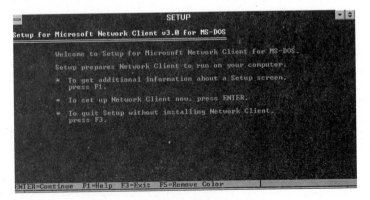

FIGURE 8.3.

The default path for installing the Microsoft Network Client v3.0 for MS-DOS.

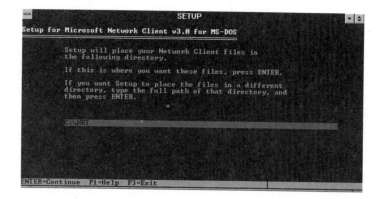

The software required for the Network Client Redirector is located on the Windows NT Server CD-ROM in the CLIENTS\MSCLIENT directory. You can also install the required software to a share on the server created by the Network Client Administrator.

Install the client software by running SETUP.EXE from the disk, network share, or CD-ROM.

> **NOTE**
>
> The Network Client Administrator program can copy the Microsoft Client for DOS installation files to your server and create a share point so that clients can do the install from the server itself. The Network Client Administration program creates a boot disk that will load the appropriate drivers and run the right commands to get your client attached to the server and give access to the share point that has Microsoft Network Client for DOS installation files.

The first screen, shown in Figure 8.2, welcomes the user and identifies the client software. After proceeding, the setup program prompts for a target directory to install its files into. As shown in Figure 8.3, by default the directory name is C:\NET. Before the files are copied to the client's hard drive, a list of settings is displayed. Move the light bar to each line and press Enter to choose the appropriate settings (as shown in Figure 8.4). First, enter the name of the user. This user name must be added to the user list on a Windows NT domain controller before the client can obtain an authenticated logon to the network. Next are basic setup options (as shown in Figure 8.5), which include choosing the proper redirector to load.

> **NOTE**
>
> To be authenticated by the server, you must load the Network Client Full Redirector. The Network Client Basic Redirector, which uses only half the memory of the Network Client Full Redirector, is sufficient enough to allow clients to attach to shares and print queues on the server, but gives them limited capabilities.

8

WORKING WITH CLIENTS

FIGURE 8.4.

Settings for the Microsoft Network Client v3.0 for MS-DOS.

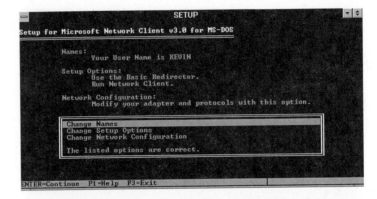

FIGURE 8.5.

Startup options for the Microsoft Network Client v3.0 for MS-DOS.

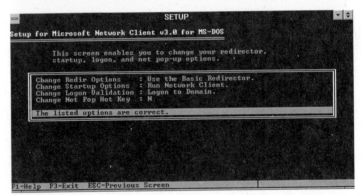

You must specify whether you want to load the Network Client on bootup (see Figure 8.6) if you want an authenticated logon. (If not, the guest account will be used on the domain, but only if the guest account is enabled.) You must also specify whether the hot key for the Net pop-up box will be changed. (See Figure 8.7.)

FIGURE 8.6.

Changing the startup options for the Microsoft Network Client v3.0 for MS-DOS.

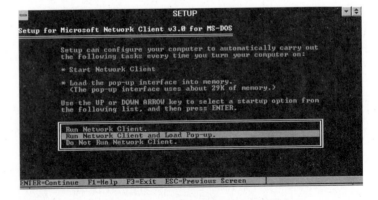

FIGURE 8.7.

Domain logon options for the Microsoft Network Client v3.0 for MS-DOS.

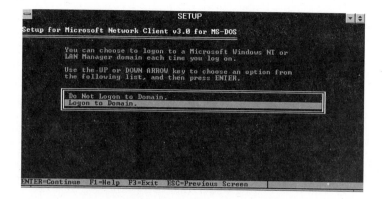

You must specify the type of network card you are using (see Figure 8.8), which will load drivers that come with NT Server or from a disk that you have gotten with your NIC. These settings are saved in the directory containing the client software in the SYSTEM.INI and PROTOCOL.INI files. Protocols are also chosen here. The protocols that are available are NetBEUI, NWLink (IPX-compatible), Microsoft DLC, and TCP/IP.

FIGURE 8.8.

Adapter selection screen for the Microsoft Network Client v3.0 for MS-DOS.

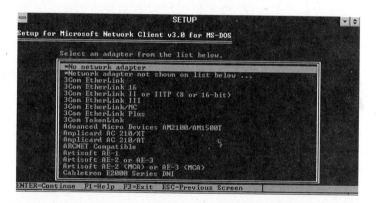

8

WORKING WITH CLIENTS

CAUTION

The network adapter drivers that ship with the DOS/Windows client software are very limited, so be sure to have drivers obtained from the hardware manufacturer if you want to ensure a clean installation.

The modifications made to the DOS startup files are

- IFSHLP.SYS is added to CONFIG.SYS.
- NET START is added to AUTOEXEC.BAT.

After you set up the parameters, the files are copied to the workstation's hard drive. Upon completion of the installation of the Microsoft Network Client for DOS, the status of the installation will be displayed. In the example shown in Figure 8.9, a PC that had used the multiconfig feature of MS-DOS 6.x could not have its configuration files modified by the setup program. In this case, the appropriate commands were put into copies of AUTOEXEC.BAT and CONFIG.SYS in the target directory. These commands would then have to be inserted manually into the AUTOEXEC.BAT and CONFIG.SYS in the root directory of the C: drive. Otherwise, the commands would have been placed in the AUTOEXEC.BAT and CONFIG.SYS directly.

FIGURE 8.9.

Completion screen for the Microsoft Network Client v3.0 for MS-DOS.

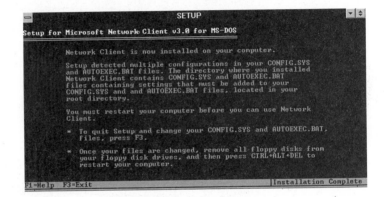

These modifications will then enable you to log on to the server. After you reboot the PC, the client software can be enabled.

Starting the Network Client Basic Redirector is handled by using the NET START command. For an authenticated logon, the NET START FULL command must be issued. The NET command, which has many parameters (that are all discussed later), can be used alone to start the basic redirector, which is also known as the workstation service. The NET command by itself brings up the Workstation Client pop-up interface. This utility allows you to point and click to attach to shares and print queues. When you use the NET START WORKSTATION command, you will make a non-authenticated attachment to the server, and not bring up the NET utility program.

The first dialog to appear when using the NET command is Disk Connections (see Figure 8.10), which allows the client to make attachments to shared drives on NT servers, and other PCs that have Microsoft drive sharing enabled. Pressing Ctrl+S will bring up the Printer Connections dialog (see Figure 8.11), which allows for redirecting the output of printer ports to network printers. Pressing Ctrl+S again causes the Disk Connections dialog to be displayed again. Pressing the Esc key causes the NET pop-up box to unload. The NET pop-up can also be configured as a 29KB TSR that is accessible from any DOS application.

FIGURE 8.10.

The NET *pop-up utility—Disk Connections.*

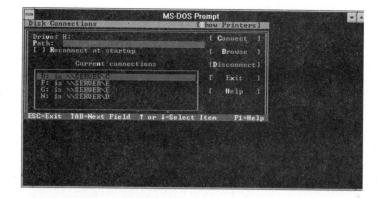

FIGURE 8.11.

The NET *pop-up utility—Printer Connections.*

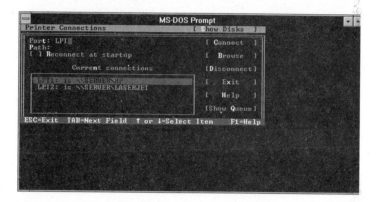

8

WORKING WITH
CLIENTS

> **NOTE**
>
> With the Network Client Basic Redirector, attachments to drives and printers before starting Windows 3.x will remain in effect during the Windows 3.x session; however, no other attaching can be done from within Windows 3.x.

To start the full redirector, which is necessary for full functionality under Windows 3.x and also allows for a domain logon, use the NET START FULL command. If the NT Server has been configured with a logon script, that script will now be executed.

Also included with the Microsoft Network Client for DOS is the DOS-based Remote Access Services (RAS) client. A batch file, RASCOPY.BAT, will appear in the Microsoft Network Client for DOS directory. The files that it is looking to copy are located on the Windows NT Server CD-ROM in the CLIENTS\RAS directory.

Besides using the pop-up utility for DOS to connect to shares and print queues, you should become familiar with the NET command. The NET command gives you all of the functionality that is in the Workstation Client pop-up utility plus more, but it is totally command-line driven. This allows you to create batch files to run various network utilities. The NET command will allow you to

- Load the Workstation Client pop-up utility as a TSR
- Test the hardware connection between two computers running the DOS Network Client Redirector
- Display information about the Network Client Redirector version
- Load protocol drivers and network adapter drivers without binding them to the Protocol Manager
- Log on to the server and reconnect to persistent connections
- Log off from the server
- Change your password
- Check the status of print queues
- Unload the Network Client Redirector
- Synchronize your system clock with the server's clock
- Attach to shares or redirect LPT ports to a print queue
- View a list of available shared resources on the network

Although the Network Client Full Redirector is the only way to be fully authenticated by an NT Server domain controller, the Network Client Basic Redirector uses DOS conventional memory sparingly—yet still allows for basic functionality. Resources on the server that are available to NT Server's guest account will also be available to Basic Redirector clients. If the client running the Network Client Basic Redirector has permissions giving them access to shared resources that are not available to the guest account, those resources will not be available. Non-secure environments can use the Network Client Basic Redirector for their clients; however, more secure environments will want to load the Network Client Full Redirector for full authentication.

This is mainly because the guest account might be removed in a more secure environment. It is also necessary to use the Network Client Full Redirector to allow for network functionality under Windows 3.x. Without the Network Client Full Redirector, Windows 3.x will not recognize that the client is connected to a network, therefore disabling all network functions.

In Windows 3.x, it is necessary to install support for Microsoft networking. This is done by using the Windows Setup, which can be invoked either through the DOS-based SETUP.EXE or the Windows Setup icon in the Main program group, and specifying that you are using Microsoft LAN Manager. This will give you full functionality of attaching to shares and print queues through the Windows-based client software that will be installed after making this selection.

As shown in Figure 8.12, choose Microsoft LAN Manager 2.1 Enhanced for the Network setting.

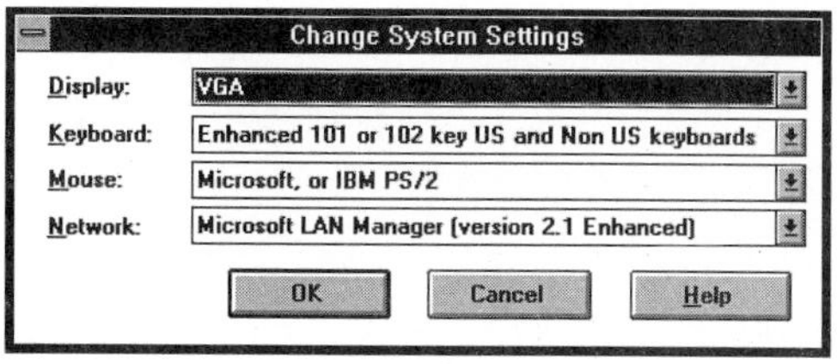

FIGURE 8.12.

Adding Microsoft networking support to Windows 3.1.

The Windows 3.x client for Microsoft Networks, even with the Network Client Full Redirector, is limited in its features compared to the client software for Windows for Workgroups, Windows 95, or Windows NT Workstation.

To attach to network drives under Windows 3.x, use the Disk menu in File Manager and choose Network Connections. The Network Connection dialog (see Figure 8.13) will allow you to choose the drive letter to use, but you must manually type in the UNC for the share you are connecting to.

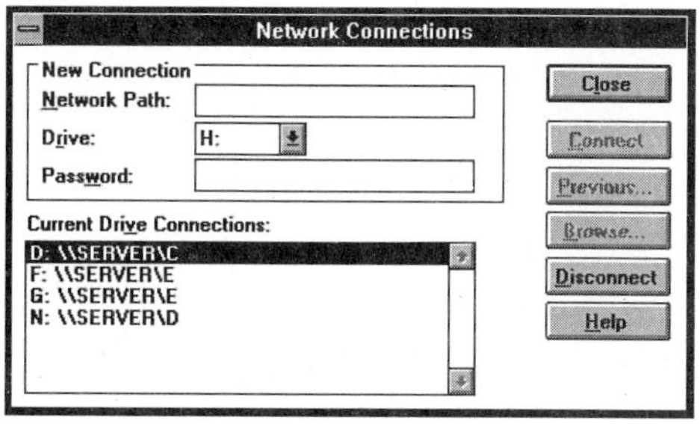

FIGURE 8.13.

Network connection in Windows 3.1.

8

WORKING WITH
CLIENTS

This lack of point-and-click ease of use makes this client software a poor example of what usually makes the Windows environment shine.

The Network Connections dialog in Print Manager (see Figure 8.14) is similar to the drive connections in that you can choose a printer port, but must manually type in the UNC for the shared printer name.

FIGURE 8.14.

*Attaching to a printer
in Windows 3.1.*

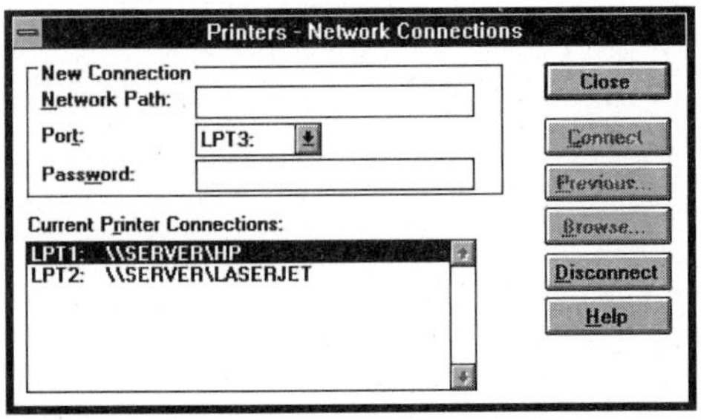

NOTE

I highly recommend that any DOS or Windows 3.x client is upgraded to Windows for Workgroups, Windows 95, or Windows NT Workstation. These operating systems have client software that truly exploits the Windows environment and makes accessing the NT Server much easier. Besides that, the 100KB overhead that the DOS/Windows 3.x client has is one big chunk and cannot be loaded high, so you don't have a chance of running your client workstation on more that 540KB. In my experience, this makes Windows 3.x much less stable and the chance of opening multiple applications, regardless of the amount of extended memory on the PC, is almost nonexistent.

Be aware that DOS and Windows 3.x clients cannot see the long filenames that might be stored on the Windows NT Server. They will instead see the eight-character, three-character extension DOS filenames that are generated for DOS clients.

The only other network settings available in Windows 3.x are through the Network icon in the Windows Control Panel. These settings (see Figure 8.15) allow you to state preferences regarding restoring connections through Windows whenever Windows is started, therefore not needing to use the tedious Network Connections dialogs or the NET pop-up utility, and the ability to suppress warnings if Windows is started before starting the Network Redirector.

FIGURE 8.15.

*Control Panel network
settings in Windows
3.1.*

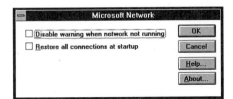

The Windows for Workgroups Client

One of the major enhancements on Windows 3.x that appears in Windows for Workgroups is the full support for Windows NT Server clients. Besides the peer-to-peer networking that is inherent in Windows for Workgroups, the Windows NT Server client comes on the Windows for Workgroups installation disks.

> **NOTE**
>
> Be aware that there are updated files on the Windows NT Server CD-ROM that fix certain problems related to speed on the network. If you are installing Windows for Workgroups from the shrink-wrap version or using a pre-installed OEM copy, you will need to copy the few files that are on the Windows NT Server CD-ROM in the CLIENTS\UPDATE.WFW directory to your WINDOWS\SYSTEM directory.

From within the Windows for Workgroups installation program or from the Network Setup program in the Network program group (see Figure 8.16), you need to tell Windows for Workgroups that you want to install support for Microsoft Networking. The Network Setup program (see Figure 8.17) gives you the ability to add network support, add network adapter drivers, enable file and printer sharing, and install protocols.

FIGURE 8.16.

The Network setup icon for Windows for Workgroups.

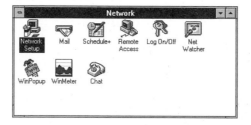

FIGURE 8.17.

Network setup program for Windows for Workgroups.

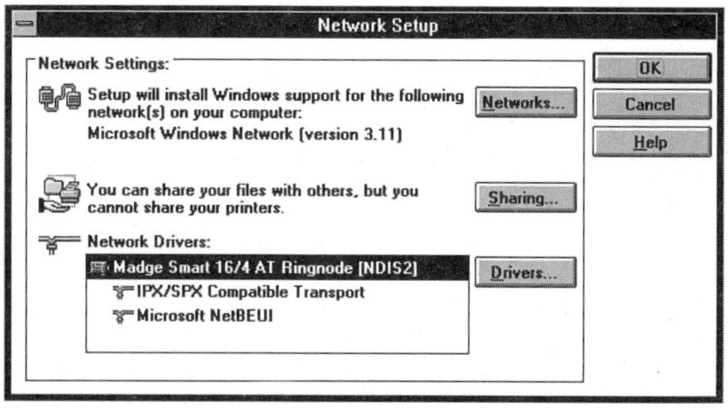

By clicking the Networks button, another dialog (see Figure 8.18) pops up that will allow you to choose Install Microsoft Windows Network.

Because Windows for Workgroups includes support for peer-to-peer networking, you can choose to create shares on the client computer and make printers attached to the client available to the network. Sharing a printer this way can allow you to create a print queue on the NT Server that people will use instead of the Print Manager running on the client's computer. This is a great option, because this will place the print spool on the NT Server instead of on the client computer. You can choose to share files and printers by clicking the Sharing button and clicking the checkbox for the options you want to enable. (See Figure 8.19.)

FIGURE 8.18.

Choosing network support in Windows for Workgroups.

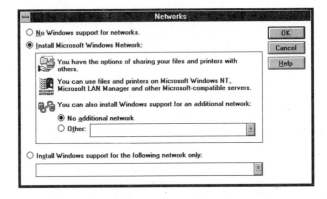

FIGURE 8.19.

Sharing options for Windows for Workgroups.

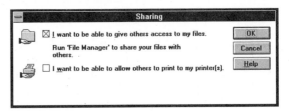

Clicking the Drivers button allows you to install Network Interface Cards and protocols. (See Figure 8.20.) Choose from the list of included NIC drivers (see Figure 8.21), or use the driver that came with the client's NIC. The installable protocols (see Figure 8.22) include NetBEUI, which is the default for Microsoft Networking on the client side, and NWLink, which is Microsoft's IPX-compatible protocol. The Windows NT Server CD-ROM also includes the 32-bit version of Microsoft's TCP/IP, which is installable through this dialog by selecting the item Other and then, when prompted, pointing to the CLIENTS\TCP32WFW directory on the Windows NT Server CD-ROM.

FIGURE 8.20.

Network Drivers setup for Windows for Workgroups.

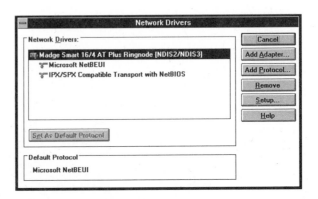

FIGURE 8.21.

Choosing network adapters for Windows for Workgroups.

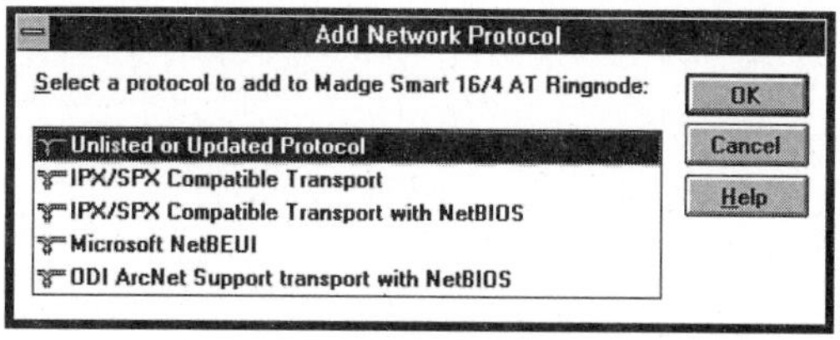

FIGURE 8.22.

Protocol selections for Windows for Workgroups.

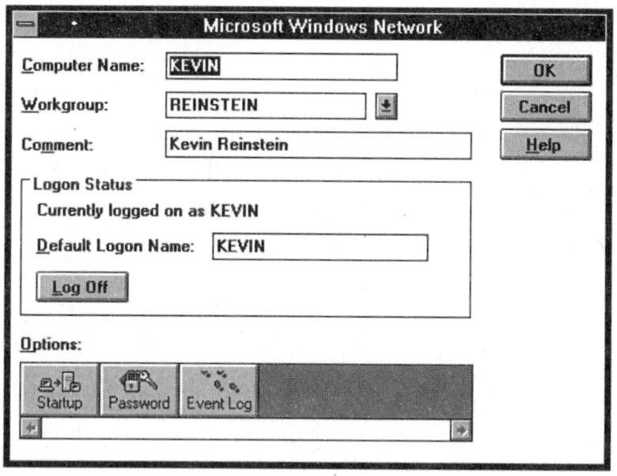

FIGURE 8.23.

Identifying the client to the network in Windows for Workgroups.

Once the network drivers are configured, Windows for Workgroups needs to be configured to log onto the Windows NT domain.

This is done through the Networks icon located in the Windows for Workgroups Control Panel. This dialog, shown in Figure 8.23, allows the user to change his or her computer name, include a description, and also change the workgroup.

The client's computer name should be something that is meaningful to you as an administrator. When browsing through the computers on your domain, you will see all of these computers listed. A descriptive name will enable you to identify the computer easier. The description field should also be used to properly identify the client. I would suggest using the client's full name for this description. Or, in the case of clients using different computers, use the description and name to indicate the physical location or purpose for the computer.

8

WORKING WITH CLIENTS

The workgroup is a virtual workgroup that can be used by clients running the Microsoft Network Client. By naming a common workgroup, clients can have access to disk drives, CD-ROM drives, and printers that have been designated by the clients that are running the appropriate client software that allows them to share these resources.

NOTE

When installing Microsoft Networking on a Windows for Workgroup client, the default value for the workgroup name will be WORKGROUP. Remember this when you browse the network for computers and find a few of them in their own little workgroup named WORKGROUP. This will probably mean that they have not been configured correctly. The default value for the computer name is the first eight characters in the name that was used during the installation of Windows for Workgroups. For example, my default computer name would be ROBERTRE. This should also be reviewed and changed if necessary.

It is from this dialog that a client can also log on to or log off from Microsoft Networking. The row of buttons at the bottom of the dialog are used to configure various other options for networking.

The most important, from the standpoint of Windows NT Server, is the Startup button. Clicking this button will bring up the Startup Settings dialog. (See Figure 8.24.) This is where the client can configure these items:

- Logging on to Microsoft Networking when Windows for Workgroups first starts
- Enabling Network DDE services
- Ghosted, or nonestablished, network drive connections
- Starting the Win pop-up dialog service
- Logging on to either a Windows NT Server domain or a Microsoft LAN Manager domain
- The Microsoft NT or LAN Manager domain name
- The display of a confirmation dialog for logging on to a server
- Changing a password
- The CPU time slice given up for sharing resources on the client's computer

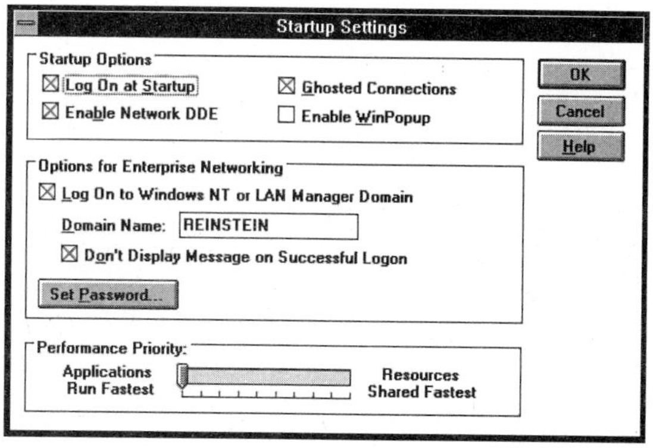

FIGURE 8.24.

*Startup options for
Windows for
Workgroups.*

Specific to Windows NT Server is checking the box that states Log On to Windows NT or LAN Manager Domain. Having this box checked will force Windows for Workgroups to authenticate a logon to the named domain whenever Windows for Workgroups is started.

If an authenticated logon takes place and the box that states Don't Display Message on Successful Logon is left unchecked, a confirmation dialog indicating the user name and level of authentication will appear each time Windows for Workgroups is started. At this point, if a logon script is defined for the client, the logon script will run within a DOS window.

As with the MS-DOS and Windows 3.x client software installation, the client's modifications made to the DOS startup files are

■ IFSHLP.SYS is added to CONFIG.SYS.

■ NET START is added to AUTOEXEC.BAT.

In addition, changes are made to the SYSTEM.INI file in the WINDOWS directory and a PROTOCOL.INI file is created in the WINDOWS directory.

Attaching to shared resources on the server can be done either through the command line with the NET USE command, or by using File Manager and Print Manager.

Clicking the Disk menu in File Manager and choosing Connect Network Drive allows the client to see a list of servers and workstations on the network that have file sharing enabled. The client can then choose an available drive letter and select a share to associate with that drive letter. (See Figure 8.25.)

8

WORKING WITH
CLIENTS

FIGURE 8.25.

Connecting to a network drive in Windows for Workgroups.

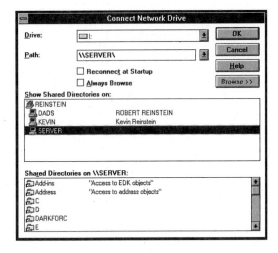

In Print Manager, you can associate a network printer with a printer port by clicking the Printer menu and then selecting Connect Network Printer. The resulting dialog (see Figure 8.26) shows a list of printer ports, and, if the Browse button is chosen or the Always Browse checkbox is checked, all of the available network printers will be listed.

FIGURE 8.26.

Connecting to a network printer in Windows for Workgroups.

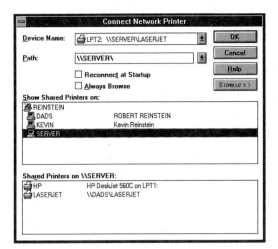

CAUTION

Be aware that Windows for Workgroups clients cannot see the long filenames that might be stored on the Windows NT Server. They will instead see the eight-dot-three DOS filenames that are generated for DOS clients. If you have implemented the use of long filenames via an NT Workstation or Windows 95 PC, you should upgrade all of your networked PCs to these advanced operating systems.

The Windows 95 Client

With Windows 95, Microsoft has integrated its Windows NT Server client in such a way that makes it truly part of the operating system.

Windows 95 also opens up many options for installation, and can be pre-configured using the Windows 95 Setup Editor. I will discuss this type of setup later, but first I will explain the ways to manually set up a Windows NT Server client running on Windows 95.

As with the other clients, Windows NT Server's Network Client Administrator can create a share point on the Windows NT Server for the installation of Windows 95. A startup disk can be created as well that gets the client onto the server and points to the Windows 95 installation files directory. If the client is already a Microsoft Networking client running an earlier version of Windows, the upgrade to Windows 95 can also be performed using this directory as the source of the Windows 95 files. And lastly, the commercial issue of Windows 95 can be used as well.

If the client is running Windows for Workgroups or Windows 3.x and is already configured for Microsoft Networking, the current settings will be carried over to Windows 95.

If Windows 95 is a new installation, the installation program will ask the client if support for Microsoft networking should be installed.

The installation process of the client software is very similar to the Windows for Workgroups client support installation; however, Windows 95 was designed to better fit into heterogeneous networks, and Microsoft Networking is only one of many types of network support that can be installed through the network setup portion of the Windows 95 installation.

As you can see, the Windows 95 dialog boxes for setting up the network client are similar, though more advanced than Windows for Workgroups.

When installing Windows 95, the user is asked for a logon name and password for Windows 95. This is the first item that needs to be considered when readying a client for access to a Windows NT domain. To use Microsoft's single logon feature, the Windows 95 user name should be the same as the user name set up on the Windows NT Server. This way, when the client logs on to the network, the same user name will be used for logging on to the actual workstation. Additionally, if support for other networks is going to be installed, using the same user name for all networks and for the Windows 95 workstation will enable the single logon feature.

> **NOTE**
>
> If these user names are not synchronized between the Windows 95 logon, the Windows NT Server logon, and any other network logons, the user will be prompted for the user name for each attachment wherein that user name does not exist. This is not necessarily the case for clients that have different user names for Windows 95 and Windows NT Server, but this will be addressed in the discussion of the Primary Network Logon later in this chapter.

The Windows 95 Control Panel has an icon titled Network that contains all of the settings that are pertinent to setting up the user for access to a Windows NT domain, among other networks. It is also the place to install and configure networking protocols, peer-to-peer networking, and other networking services that are offered by Windows 95 and third-party developers.

The following description of the Network configuration dialog includes tasks that can be performed during the initial installation of Windows 95 or after Windows 95 has been installed.

Windows 95 introduces the Network Component. These components include Network Clients, Network Adapters, protocol stacks, and network services.

Windows 95 uses the protected-mode virtual device driver VREDIR.VXD to allow the Windows 95 workstation to communicate with any Microsoft Networks–compatible computer. This includes other Windows 95 workstations, Windows NT Servers and Workstations, Windows for Workgroups workstations, and DOS computers running the Workgroup Add-on For MS-DOS.

The Network dialog in Control Panel has three tabs. (See Figure 8.27.) The first tab, Configuration, is the tab that needs to be selected for adding support for a Windows NT network.

To add support for a Windows NT network, use the Add button in the Network dialog. This will display the Select Network Component Type dialog. (See Figure 8.28.) Select Client from the list and click Add. Windows 95 has many choices for network clients, including Novell, Banyan, and SunSoft clients. Choose Microsoft from the Manufacturers list (see Figure 8.29) and highlight Client For Microsoft Networks in the Network Clients list. Click the OK button, and the Client For Microsoft Networks will appear on the list of installed network components. Repeat the process to add a network adapter and to add additional protocols. (See Figure 8.30.)

For clients of a Windows NT domain, when you are adding a protocol, be sure to select Microsoft as the manufacturer. The protocols listed for Microsoft are all included with Windows 95 and are compatible with Windows NT Server.

FIGURE 8.27.

Windows 95 Network Control Panel applet.

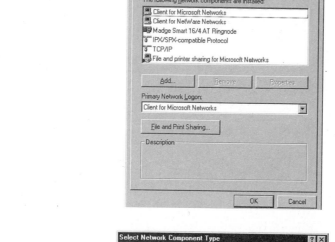

FIGURE 8.28.

Selecting a network component type to add for Windows 95.

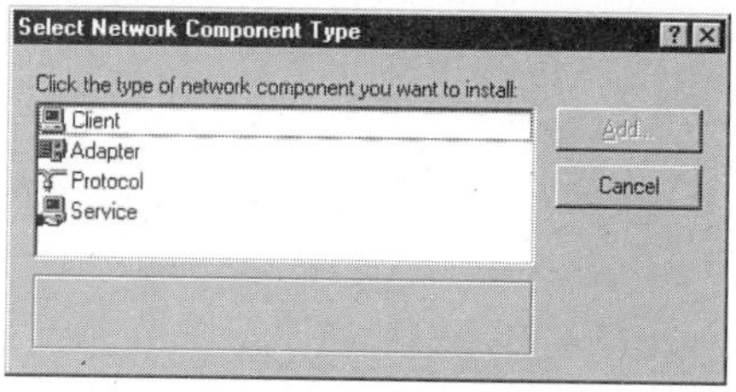

FIGURE 8.29.

Selecting the Network Client.

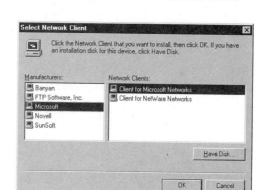

FIGURE **8.30.**

*The Windows 95
Protocol Selection
dialog.*

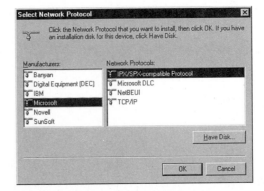

> **NOTE**
>
> In addition to the steps I've described, you can also add services (see Figure 8.31) such as File and Printer Sharing for Microsoft Networks, which enables the built-in, peer-to-peer functionality in Windows 95. In the context of this book, the only reason you might want to enable this is if you have upgraded from a workgroup environment and still want to give access to a printer connected locally to your computer, or access to your local hard drive(s).

FIGURE **8.31.**

*Adding a network
service to Windows 95.*

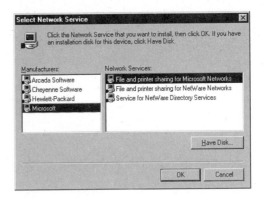

After the Client for Microsoft Networks has been installed, you need to configure it to allow the client to log on to the Windows NT domain each time Windows 95 is started.

You can accomplish this by highlighting Client for Microsoft Networks in the list of installed Network Components. Click the Properties button to bring up the Client for Microsoft Networks Properties dialog. (See Figure 8.32.) This dialog lets you tell Windows 95 to log you on to the named Windows NT domain, and how to restore persistent connections, each time Windows 95 is started.

FIGURE 8.32.

*Settings for Microsoft
networking on
Windows 95.*

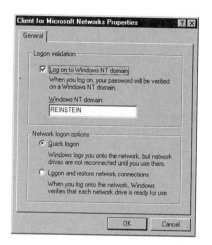

When you choose Quick Logon, the Network Client will not verify attached drives until you actually try to use the network shares. This will slow down the first time you go to access a network share, but speeds up the logon process. Click the OK button to save these settings, and you're well on your way to establishing yourself as a network client.

NOTE

Password caching must not be disabled as a system policy for Quick Logon to work.

After the appropriate client, protocols, and network adapter have been identified, click the Identification tab and identify the computer to the network.

The Identification dialog (see Figure 8.33) is where you name your computer, or rename your computer. The Workgroup field can be used for peer-to-peer networking; however, in this case you would name the Windows NT domain that you are going to be participating in. The last field, Description, is strictly a comment field and will help the NT administrators to further identify your computer.

The third and final tab, Access Control, is used only when you have installed the File and Printer Sharing for Microsoft Networks. This will allow you to specify whether or not you want to use the user list and group list from your Windows NT domain to identify security on the shared resources on your computer.

FIGURE 8.33.

*Identifying the
computer to the
network.*

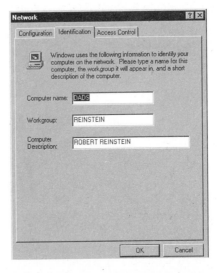

TIP

If you do want to share a locally attached printer but do not want other users spooling their print jobs to your computer, thus hogging your CPU cycles, the user-level access control is essential. This will prevent users from going directly to your computer.

By granting permission only to the administrator for use of the printer, it is then up to the Windows NT administrator to issue permissions for the shared queue on the server. This way the administrator will pass along print jobs from other clients from its print queue and will pass the data directly to your printer.

NOTE

If you are installing support for other networks in addition to Microsoft Networks, you must designate Microsoft Networks as the Primary Network Logon if you want to take advantage of user profiles and system policies stored on a Windows NT Server. Having the Primary Network Logon as Microsoft Networks will also make sure that the Windows NT Server domain logon script, if available, will be run after any other network's scripts.

Connecting to Windows NT Server domain resources in Windows 95 can be accomplished in many different ways. The easiest way is to open up the Network Neighborhood folder and view the resources that are available. First, choose the server that contains the resource the client wants to connect to. Right-mouse-click on the desired resource, and the client is prompted with a menu that will include the appropriate choice, including Map Network Drive or Capture Printer Port.

TIP

In Windows 95, it is possible to access network shares without assigning a drive letter to them. Further information is in the Windows 95 online documentation.

The Windows NT Workstation v3.51 Client

During the installation of Windows NT Workstation v3.51, the client has the choice of identifying itself to the domain and handling all aspects of adding protocols, network adapters, and certain services, much like the network configuration for Windows 95 and Windows for Workgroups. If an administrator for the domain or a user with permission to add a computer to a domain is performing the installation, the Windows NT workstation can be added to the domain during installation. Otherwise, the computer must be added to the domain after installation, either from the workstation or by using the administrative tools for Windows NT Server (as described above in the section titled "Special Considerations on Configuring the Server for Windows NT Workstation Clients"), in order to gain an authenticated logon to the Windows NT Server domain.

After installation of the operating system, you can enable the workstation to log on to a Windows NT domain by opening the Windows NT Workstation Control Panel. Double-click the Network icon to open the dialog that allows you to add, remove, or configure all of the networking protocols, services, and adapters.

At the top of this dialog, shown in Figure 8.34, is the Windows NT Workstation Computer Name that was defined during installation. If a workgroup was joined during installation, that workgroup name will show up as the current workgroup. However, if during installation a Windows NT Server domain was specified, that domain will appear instead of a workgroup name.

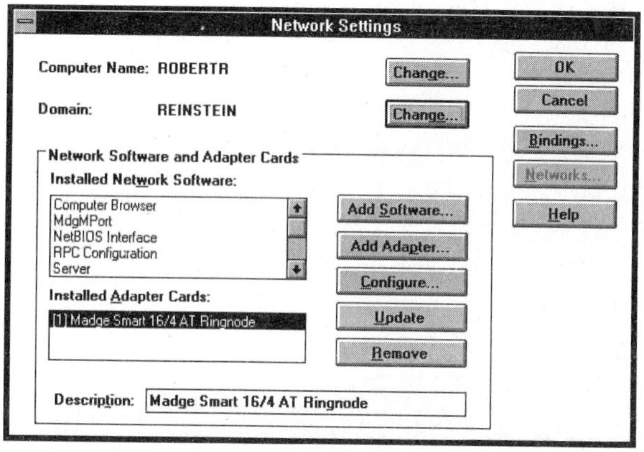

FIGURE 8.34.

Network settings for Windows NT Workstation v3.51.

Clicking once on the Change button next to the workgroup or domain name will bring up the Domain/Workgroup Settings dialog. (See Figure 8.35.) It is here that you need to specify the Windows NT Server domain name. This is accomplished by first clicking within the Member of: area on the radio button that reads Domain. Then enter the name of the domain in the associated textbox.

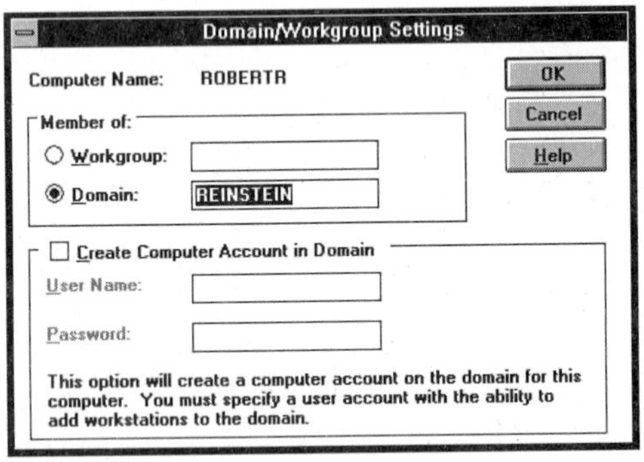

FIGURE 8.35.

Joining a domain or workgroup on Windows NT Workstation v3.51.

If the computer had been added to the domain via the Windows NT Server Manager, that is all the configuring that is necessary to allow an authenticated logon to the Windows NT domain; however, if the computer has not been added to the domain yet, it can be done from this dialog.

When you check the box next to Create Computer Account in Domain, an authorized user can add the computer to the domain from within this dialog. The fields for user name and password must be filled by a user with the authority to add a computer to a domain.

And that's it. Just log off of the Windows NT Workstation and press Ctrl+Alt+Del when prompted by the Welcome dialog. If the Windows NT Workstation had been previously associated with a workgroup, the From: field will become a drop-down listbox that will allow you to select either the workgroup name or the domain name. Logging on to the domain name will give the Windows NT Workstation an authenticated logon to the Windows NT Server domain.

The Windows NT Workstation v4 Client

With Windows NT Workstation 4, the client setup is very similar to the Windows 95 client configuration.

If an administrator for the domain or a user with permission to add a computer to a domain is performing the installation, the Windows NT Workstation computer can be added to the domain during installation. Otherwise, the computer must be added to the domain after installation, either from the workstation or using the administrative tools for Windows NT Server in order to gain an authenticated logon to the Windows NT Server domain.

From the Windows NT Workstation Control Panel, double-click the Network icon. The resulting tabbed dialog (see Figure 8.36) will allow you to enter all of the information needed to enable a Windows NT Workstation to log on to a Windows NT Server domain.

FIGURE 8.36.

The Networks Control Panel for Windows NT Workstation 4.

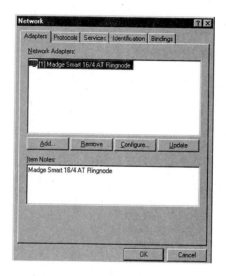

The first tab is Adapters, which allows you to specify one or more network adapter cards. Click the Add button for a list of drivers that ship with Windows NT Workstation. In most cases you can simply scroll down the list and choose the appropriate card; however, as I stated previously, you might do better using updated drivers obtained directly from the hardware manufacturer. In that case, you would choose the Have Disk button and point to the path that has these newer drivers. Once you have configured the card, you can proceed to the next tab.

The Protocols tab (see Figure 8.37) allows you to specify one or more protocols that you will use to communicate with servers, and if necessary, other workstations. In my example, I have added both NWLink, which is the IPX/SPX-compatible protocol, and Microsoft's TCP/IP.

The next tab is Services (see Figure 8.38), which will have some options already chosen for you. These predetermined services will be sufficient to give the client connectivity to the domain.

In order to identify your computer to the Windows NT Server domain, you must have a unique name for the computer and specify whether you are going to log on to a workgroup or a domain. The Identification dialog (see Figure 8.39) allows those specifications to be made. When first entering this dialog, the original choices, made during installation, will be displayed. Click the Change buttons to modify the current entries. Here, you will again get a choice of which type of logon should be made when logging on to the workstation, and the option to change the computer name. This computer name should already be defined as part of the domain; however, if this is not already done, a user with permission to add workstations to the domain may click the checkbox that will add the computer to the domain.

FIGURE 8.37.

Protocol selection for Windows NT Workstation 4.

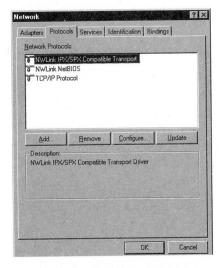

FIGURE 8.38.

Installing Network Services on Windows NT Workstation 4.

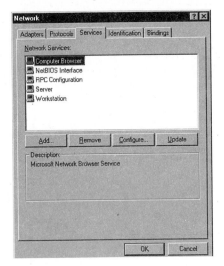

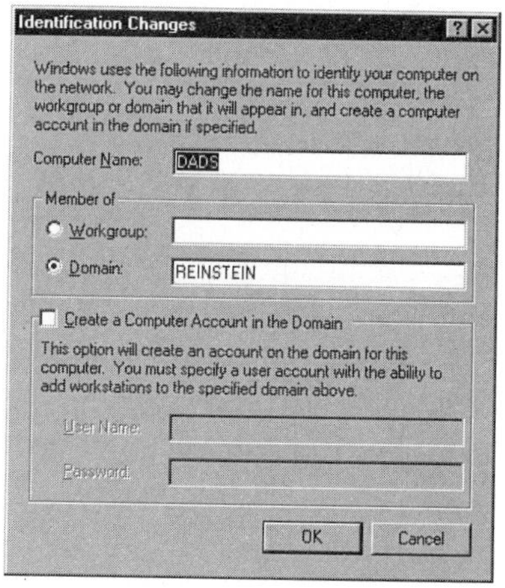

FIGURE 8.39.

Identifying the Windows NT Workstation 4 computer to the network.

The final tab allows you to configure the Bindings. (See Figure 8.40.) By default all protocols are bound to all network services. You can disable or change the order of binding through this tab.

The OS/2 Client

The Microsoft Client for OS/2 is the LAN Manager for OS/2 client software. As with the DOS/Windows 3.1 client, this is a character-based tool and offers no functionality within the OS/2 GUI environment. The tools must be run from an OS/2 command prompt and cannot be accessed through a DOS or Win-OS/2 session within OS/2. This client software is a hold-over from the days when Microsoft packaged OS/2 under its own name.

FIGURE 8.40.

Bindings Configuration for Windows NT Workstation 4.

8

WORKING WITH CLIENTS

The Network Client For OS/2 is installed from the CLIENTS\LANMAN.OS2\DISKS directory of the Windows NT Server CD-ROM. Within this directory are subdirectories for each of the individual disk images. SETUP.EXE can be run directly from the DISK1 subdirectory, or by copying these disk images to individual disks. The installation program is essentially the same as the MS-DOS version.

The current version of the Microsoft Client For OS/2 is 2.2c. This version does support domain names; however, it does not have support for DHCP services. Refer to the section on the MS-DOS client installation for more information on this installation.

Macintosh Clients

By enabling the Windows NT Services For Macintosh on the Windows NT Server, a Macintosh client, running version 6.0.7 or greater of the Macintosh operating system, will be able to see the Macintosh-compliant resources available on the NT domain.

On the client itself, it is necessary only to ensure that connectivity has been installed via enabling AppleTalk. When the client opens up Chooser and selects the appropriate AppleTalk Zone that the Windows NT Server has joined, the Windows NT Server will appear. The client can then log on to the NT domain, and have access to shared printers and Macintosh-accessible volumes.

Windows NT Server domain clients can be easily configured, as long as you have the proper information in advance. In all cases, be sure that you know what type of adapter card you are working with, the IRQ and memory settings for the card, a unique name for the computer you are installing the client software on, the name of the domain you want to log on to, the protocol required by the servers or workstations that have resources you want to use, and any other additional services that you might want to install.

Working with Macintosh Clients

by Jason Garms

IN THIS CHAPTER

CHAPTER 9

One of the most remarkable features that Microsoft included with Windows NT Server is the capability to act as a fully functional file server for Macintosh clients. Services for Macintosh, which provides this functionality, turns Windows NT into not only a fully compliant AppleShare file server that can support an unlimited number of Macintosh clients, but also a Macintosh print server and a native AppleTalk router.

This chapter examines the pieces that compose the Services for Macintosh, as well as the tools that are used to administer them. I've included some concepts of how to plan and implement your NT network to include Macintosh clients, and provided essential information for NT administrators new to the Macintosh world. I've also tried to make it useful for people coming from a Macintosh world who are new to NT Server by presenting the chapter in a capsulized format.

AppleShare File Server

Windows NT Server enables Macintosh and PC users to access the same files, which provides a true cross-platform, collaborative environment. When running Services for Macintosh, DOS and Windows users connect to the server as they normally would. They see no evidence that they might be sharing files with Macintosh users. Additionally, Macintosh clients see and connect to the NT Server in the exact same way they would connect to any other standard AppleShare server.

To create an enterprise-level solution for Macintosh clients, Microsoft leveraged many of the features integral to NT's architecture when designing Services for Macintosh. NT Server provides exceptional compatibility, performance, scalability, fault-tolerance, and security. For instance, part of the Macintosh file server portion, known as the AppleTalk Filing Protocol (AFP) server, runs inside the NT Executive, which provides significant speed benefits. Also, because the AFP server is multithreaded, it can fully leverage NT's capability to run on multiprocessor hardware. You can also take advantage of the software RAID options in Windows NT to provide increased performance and reliability. Furthermore, Services for Macintosh fully integrates with the NT security model to provide the same level of high security available to all Windows NT clients.

> **NOTE**
>
> The AppleTalk Filing Protocol (AFP) is a protocol that resides in the presentation layer of the ISO's OSI Reference Model. It is responsible for handling the logistics of accessing files and directories on a remote computer system.

There is no hard-coded limit as to the number of simultaneous Macintosh clients that can connect. To demonstrate the extensibility of Windows NT Server as a Macintosh file server, Microsoft has conducted real-world testing where they created over 1,000 simultaneous Macintosh connections to a single NT Server.

TIP

Because of the scalability of NT Server, it provides the most powerful Macintosh file and print services on the market—even better than any system Apple currently sells. In fact, a recent alliance between Microsoft and Apple should bear fruit in the near future, and there is a good likelihood that Apple will sell NT Server-based solutions under its own label.

AppleTalk Print Server

In addition to acting as a standard file server, Windows NT can also act as an AppleTalk print server. This leverages three important pieces of Windows NT's print architecture. First, Windows NT permits Macintosh clients to print to *any* printers available on the NT Server. It even allows the Macintosh clients to print to non-PostScript printers by providing a PostScript interpreter that generates a bitmapped image that can be sent to any non-PostScript printer. Second, Services for Macintosh leverages NT's capability to print to a number of remote network printers, including network printers using DLC, TCP/IP, and AppleTalk. Third, it exploits NT's capability to print to almost 2,000 different models of printers.

AppleTalk Router

To complement the file and print services, NT also includes a full AppleTalk router. This provides you with the ability to natively participate in an AppleTalk inter-network. The router can be configured to route AppleTalk between any standard network card supported by Windows NT, including Ethernet, FDDI, Token Ring, and even LocalTalk.

NOTE

Windows NT supports the Daystar Digital LocalTalk adapter.

You can also use the AppleTalk router to create new AppleTalk zones on local subnets, through a process known as *seeding*, which provides logical organization of the AppleTalk network.

Understanding the Macintosh

There are mostly two types of people who will read this chapter:

- ■ The Windows-oriented LAN administrators who often begrudgingly have to support Macintosh clients on their LAN.
- ■ Macintosh network administrators with minimal NT and Windows experience, who needed a file and print server that could support a large number of clients.

I have written this chapter to be as useful as possible to both audiences. No matter which category you fit into, or even if you don't fit into one of these two categories, you'll probably find a discussion of the differences between the two platforms useful.

> **NOTE**
>
> A little terminology review is definitely in order. Traditionally in the MS-DOS and Windows environment, files were stored in *directories* and *subdirectories*. Macintosh nomenclature has always referred to *folders* and *subfolders*, which are functionally identical. With the introduction of the Windows 95 interface, Microsoft has begun using the terms folders and subfolders to replace the traditional directories and subdirectories. In this chapter and elsewhere in this book, I use the terms interchangeably.

AppleTalk and Apple Networking

It would be impossible to cover all the concepts of Macintosh networking in a single chapter, but there are a few important concepts that should be understood before continuing. This section will be especially useful for a person with minimal Macintosh background to hit the ground running with Services for Macintosh.

AppleTalk, LocalTalk, EtherTalk, TokenTalk, and FDDITalk

If you're new to the Macintosh arena, you'll quickly recognize that Apple is very big on using the word *Talk* in naming its communications products and technologies. Of course, since networks are used to communicate, Talk is an appropriate word. However, keeping all these terms in order and using them to describe the appropriate technologies and products can often take a little practice, so let's do a quick review:

■ **AppleTalk:** When Apple designed the Macintosh, it recognized the need to be able to interconnect the computers for sharing files and printers. It developed hardware and software, collectively called AppleTalk, for performing this communication and built it into every single Macintosh computer ever made. Originally the term AppleTalk referred to both the hardware that was used to connect the computers as well as the protocol suite that provided a language and set of rules for the computers to communicate. However, in the late 1980s, Apple separated the hardware from the software. The software component—the protocol suite—retained the name AppleTalk, while the hardware component was renamed to *LocalTalk*. This is often a great source of confusion, and people still use the terms interchangeably. However, AppleTalk only properly refers to the AppleTalk protocol suite.

- **LocalTalk:** All Macintosh computers have the built-in capability of supporting LocalTalk. To connect two Macintosh computers in a LocalTalk network, you can simply plug a LocalTalk connector into the printer port on the back of each computer and connect the two with a LocalTalk cable. LocalTalk is a synchronous RS-422 bus that transmits data at 230,400 bps (bits per second). When the Macintosh was first introduced in 1984, this speed was acceptable for most applications, however, today LocalTalk is not considered fast enough for anything more than basic small file transfers, or for sharing printers.

> **NOTE**
>
> Macintosh computers traditionally use the printer port as the designated LocalTalk port, although newer Macintosh computers and newer versions of the Mac OS actually permit you to use either the printer port or the modem port.

- **EtherTalk:** EtherTalk is the name for running the AppleTalk protocol over an Ethernet network. The AppleTalk stack defines four link access protocols (LAPs) at layer 2 of the ISO's OSI Reference Model. The EtherTalk Link Access Protocol (ELAP) was the first of these to be introduced. The other three are LLAP (LocalTalk Link Access Protocol), TLAP (TokenTalk Link Access Protocol), and FLAP (FDDI Link Access Protocol).
- **TokenTalk:** The name for running AppleTalk on a Token Ring network.
- **FDDITalk:** The name for running AppleTalk on a FDDI network.

AppleTalk Phase 1 and Phase 2

When Apple first designed AppleTalk, there were a number of limitations, which as networks grew, began to cause problems. This original release of AppleTalk is now known as AppleTalk Phase 1. In 1989, Apple redesigned the AppleTalk protocols to support larger and more complicated networks. The new version of AppleTalk is known as AppleTalk Phase 2.

> **NOTE**
>
> Windows NT Server only supports AppleTalk Phase 2.

The original version of AppleTalk only permitted 254 nodes on an entire physical network, because nodes were addressed using a single 8-bit node ID. However, with the revamped AppleTalk Phase 2, you could now address over 16 million network nodes on a network. Each node is addressed using an 8-bit node ID, and a 16-bit network address.

9

WORKING WITH MACINTOSH CLIENTS

With *extended addressing* you can use multiple network addresses on a single network cable. This means you could have 500 clients on a single network segment, using two or more network addresses. This extended addressing is supported under EtherTalk, TokenTalk, and FDDITalk. It is not supported, however, under LocalTalk. This means that you can still only have a single network number per LocalTalk cable segment, limiting the number of clients to 254 per segment.

There were many other changes to the AppleTalk protocol with the introduction of AppleTalk Phase 2. These changes include modifications to the way AppleTalk devices acquire their dynamic node IDs when they start up, changes in the AppleTalk routing scheme to reduce network traffic, and the inclusion of directed broadcasting, which uses multicast addresses to prevent non-AppleTalk clients from being impacted by AppleTalk broadcast packets.

The most significant changes for many people was the incorporation of networking standards, such as the IEEE 802.3 and 802.5 standards for Ethernet and Token Ring, respectively.

AppleTalk Protocols

The AppleTalk protocol suite defines a number of other protocols that operate at different levels of the OSI Reference Model. The more important of these protocols are listed in Table 9.1.

Table 9.1. AppleTalk protocols matched with the OSI Reference Model.

Protocol	OSI Level	Description
RTMP	Transport Layer	Routing Table Maintenance Protocol. The RTMP is responsible for maintaining a list of all the routers on the AppleTalk network, as well as providing the rules for how routers exchange routing information. Each entry in the routing table consists of a network range, a distance in hops to the remote router, a port number on the remote network, the AppleTalk node ID of the next router on the path to the destination network, and the status of each port on the network. This is similar in functionality to the RIP protocol in the TCP/IP protocol suite.
AEP	Transport Layer	AppleTalk Echo Protocol. The AEP provides a protocol similar to ICMP in the TCP/IP suite. It supports sending an echo datagram from the requestor to the echo port on a destination computer, which then responds with an echo response datagram. This can be useful for detecting if a particular host is reachable.
ATP	Transport Layer	AppleTalk Transaction Protocol. The ATP is used to set up a transaction-based conversation between two computers. Although ATP does guarantee delivery of

Protocol	OSI Level	Description
		packets, it does not guarantee they are received in any particular order. When one machine sends an ATP request datagram, it waits for the second machine to respond with an ATP response datagram before it can proceed. When all the data has been sent between the two machines, an ATP release datagram is sent to indicate the transaction session is complete. The ATP is not intended for transporting large amounts of information, nor for establishing sessions that need to be kept open for long periods of time.
NBP	Transport Layer	Name Binding Protocol. The NBP is important to the working of the AppleTalk protocol suite. The network itself sends packets by using a numeric address to identify network entities. However, AppleTalk itself uses names internally to locate resources. The NBP is responsible for resolving the AppleTalk names into the node ID that is required for locating the machine on the network. AppleTalk stores names internally in the format `name:type@zone`, where `name` is the AppleTalk name of the resource, `type` is the resource type, such as LaserWriter, and `zone` is the name of the AppleTalk zone where the resource resides. An example of a complete AppleTalk name is `Jason's Macintosh:AFPServer@Home`.
ADSP	Session Layer	AppleTalk Data Stream Protocol. ADSP is similar to the ATP in that it provides guaranteed delivery of network packets. However, unlike the ATP, which is intended for small and quick data exchanges, the ADSP is intended for transmitting larger amounts of data, and for supporting long sessions. While the ATP does not guarantee the order in which packets are received, the ADSP ensures that packets are received in the order they were sent. Another advantage of the ADSP protocol is that it supports full duplex communications, meaning that both network entities can speak to each other at the same time. The ADSP protocol also supports flow control, which ensures that one of the network entities is not bombarded by more network traffic than it can handle.

9

WORKING WITH
MACINTOSH
CLIENTS

continues

Table 9.1. continued

Protocol	OSI Level	Description
ASP	Session Layer	AppleTalk Session Protocol. The ASP provides session-level communications between a client and a workstation for sending command streams. While ATP and ADSP are used to send raw data, the ASP is used to initiate a session control mechanism between a client and the server. Also, in ATP and ADSP, the two network entities are connected in a peer-type relationship, whereas the ASP clearly defines a client, which must initiate a session, and the server. With ASP commands can be sent from the client to the server, but the server is not permitted to send commands to the client. The only thing the server can send to the client is data requested by the client, and an alert packet to notify the client of a problem.
PAP	Session Layer	Printer Access Protocol. The PAP is used for communicating with AppleTalk print devices. It is responsible for opening a session with a PAP server (printer), transferring the print job to the printer, performing flow control to prevent the client from sending too much data too fast to the printer, and reporting printer status back to the client. The PAP actually uses ATP datagrams for communicating on the network.
ZIP	Session Layer	Zone Information Protocol. The ZIP is responsible for creating and maintaining the Zone Information Table (ZIT), which is stored in each AppleTalk router. The ZIT is a map that is used to link the friendly zone names back to the unique network numbers that are used to actually locate what subnets a zone actually resides on. The Zone Information Protocol is responsible for working with the RTMP protocol to keep the ZIT up-to-date.
AFP	Presentation Layer	AppleTalk Filing Protocol. The AFP is the high-level protocol that is used for sharing files from one computer with other machines on the network. AFP's primary focus is on providing a mechanism to control user access to folders, as well as how these permissions are displayed to the user. AFP is also designed to deal with naming inconsistencies between different operating systems and

Protocol	OSI Level	Description
		file systems, which support different allowable naming schemes. AFP relies on the ASP protocol for handling the logistical portion of setting up connections between the client and server.

Services for Macintosh supports all of these protocols and like the Mac OS itself, addresses each of them in different pieces of software. RTMP, AEP, ATP, NBP, ADSP, ASP, and ZIP are all addressed in the AppleTalk protocol loaded in Windows NT, along with related drivers that are loaded with the AppleTalk protocol. The PAP protocol is addressed in the Print Server for Macintosh service, and support for the AFP protocol is located in the File Server for Macintosh service, and related kernel-mode driver.

Macintosh File Structure

Macintosh files are different than PC files. Most computers use file structures in which all the file's data is stored as a single *stream* of information. This is the way MS-DOS, Windows, and Windows NT work. Additionally, there is no set method of identifying what program created the file or indicating what kind of data is contained in the file. The only standardized method of identifying a file's type is by using the filename extension, which is not always reliable.

NOTE

Microsoft is beginning to use OLE objects within files. This provides even more flexibility than multiforked files, because the OLE objects can be defined and included only as necessary. Future OLE-based file systems could potentially support Macintosh files by storing each fork in a separate OLE container.

NOTE

When discussing files, the terms *fork* and *stream* are used interchangeably to indicate discrete containers within the file. Fork is the term in common use in the Macintosh lexicon, while stream is the term used by Microsoft to describe the identical ability in the NTFS file system.

In contrast to this single fork approach, the Macintosh uses two file forks—the data fork and the resource fork. The data fork is directly analogous to a standard PC file. However, Macintosh computers also have a resource fork. This is where special information about the file is stored.

A resource fork can contain icons, bitmaps, fonts, small blocks of code, menus, window definitions, and other things.

> **NOTE**
>
> Not every Macintosh file contains both forks. Some might contain only a data fork, others might contain only a resource fork, and others might contain *both*.

Additionally, Macintosh files attach supplementary file properties not included on standard PC files. Of particular importance is the *creator* and *type* information. These are both four-digit codes that allow the Macintosh operating system and other applications to identify the program that created the file as well as the nature of the data contained in the file.

> **NOTE**
>
> Apple maintains a registry of creator types for Macintosh files. If a new software vendor wants to make a Macintosh version of their program that creates files, they must register a unique creator type with Apple. This ensures that no two vendors use the same identifier codes, which could cause the wrong application to launch when a user tries to open a file. Microsoft's registered creator code is MSFT.

Because NTFS offers native support for multiple data streams in a single file, it has no problem supporting Macintosh resource and data forks. This is in comparison to NetWare 3.1x, which tries to provide Macintosh file support by splitting the data and resource forks into two separate files. The problem with this approach is that a lookup table is used to provide mappings between the resource forks and data forks of all the files on the Novell partition. If this lookup table fails, all the Macintosh files on the partition would be destroyed. An additional advantage of providing native support for multiple file forks is that if a non-Macintosh user deletes a Macintosh file, both forks will be deleted, which is not guaranteed under a system using a non-native lookup table.

Long Filenames

Macintosh files support filenames of up to 31 characters. Additionally, Macintosh filenames permit characters, such as the backslash (\), that are forbidden in standard DOS-style 8.3 names. Furthermore, the Macintosh OS permits virtually unlimited nesting of folders within folders, whereas there is an effective limitation of 255-character path names in Windows NT (and Windows 95). This means that the full name of the file, which includes its entire path, cannot exceed 255 characters. This limitation is actually created by the Win32 API calls that are used to handle file references. In fact, NTFS will allow Macintosh users to nest folders within folders to their hearts' content. The problem is that if you try to use the Explorer or File Manager to look at or manipulate those files, you will get an error. To make matters worse, because most backup programs rely on the Win32 API to access files, you will not be able to back up any file that has a full path name of greater than 255 characters.

Because NTFS supports 255-character filenames, and Macintosh users can only use 31 characters, it is important to realize how the filename translation works.

If the Macintosh user views a file or directory whose name is 31 characters or shorter, the Macintosh user will see the full NTFS long filename. If the name is longer than 31 characters, however, the user will see the short 8.3 name that is created automatically for all NTFS files and directories.

> **NOTE**
>
> If a Macintosh client opens a file using its 8.3 filename and then saves the file, the long filename will be preserved, even though the Macintosh user cannot see it. This is done through a technique called tunneling. However, some applications copy the file you open to a temporary file and make all your changes to the temporary file. When you save it, the original file is deleted, and the temporary file is renamed as the original file. In this case, if the file was opened with the 8.3 filename, the long filename will *not* be preserved.

> **WARNING**
>
> If you copy a Macintosh file containing a resource fork to a FAT partition, the resource fork will not be copied, and thus the copy will be effectively useless.

Working with Macintosh Permissions

Macintosh folder permissions on Services for Macintosh are based on NTFS file and directory permissions. Under AppleShare, access restrictions can only be made on a folder-by-folder basis.

You can use the MacFile menu in the File Manager to set permissions on a particular folder on a Macintosh-accessible volume.

> **NOTE**
>
> You must use the File Manager interface or the MACFILE command-line tool to set permissions on Macintosh-accessible volumes. There is no Explorer interface for performing this action.

NOTE

If you try to set permissions on a folder that is not part of a Macintosh-accessible volume, you will get an error message.

The way that Macintosh computers assign permissions to folders is dictated by the AFP protocol. It permits the security permissions for a folder to include permissions for an *owner*, a *primary group*, and *everyone* else. These permissions are set with the File Manager as shown in Figure 9.1.

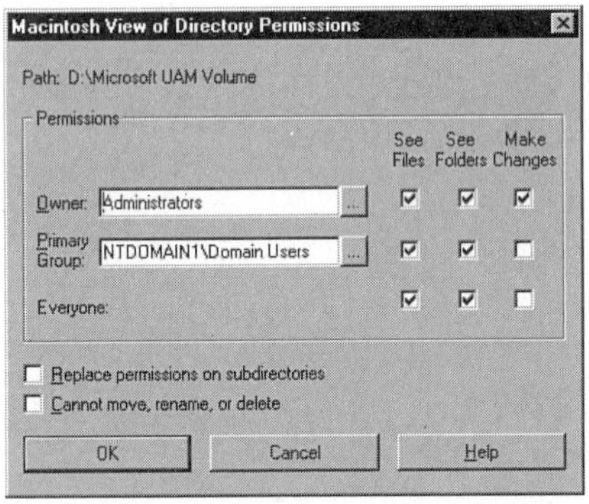

FIGURE 9.1.

The File Manager provides an interface for setting permissions on a Macintosh volume.

TIP

You can also log on from a Macintosh workstation to modify permissions.

Notice that for each of the three access control entries (ACEs)—Owner, Primary Group, and Everyone—AFP only permits three levels of permissions: *see files*, *see folders*, and *make changes*. When you apply these AFP permissions to a folder shared as a Macintosh volume, NT converts the AFP permissions into NTFS permissions and applies them to the selected folder as well as all files within the folder.

CAUTION

When you change the AppleShare permissions on a folder, it has a direct effect on the NTFS permissions for the folder and for any files within the folder.

Let's look at some of what happens when you choose different options and how this affects the NTFS permissions and attributes.

First of all, when you set the Macintosh permissions for a folder, NT will add the Owner, the Primary Group, and the Everyone group to the NTFS permissions for the folder, as well as all the files contained in the folder. The way that NT translates the Macintosh permissions into NT permissions is shown in Table 9.2.

Table 9.2. Translation of Macintosh permissions into NTFS permissions.

See Files	See Folders	Make Changes	NTFS Permissions
X			RX
	X		RX
		X	WD
X	X		RX
	X	X	RWXD
X		X	RWXD
X	X	X	RWXD

> **NOTE**
>
> You'll notice that many of the different Macintosh permissions translate into equivalent NTFS permissions, so you'll be unable to identify the exact Macintosh permissions by looking at the NTFS permissions.

In addition to the permissions listed in Table 9.2, the owner also gets the (P) and the (O) permissions on all of the preceding combinations. If the owner has all three permissions, the owner will be assigned the NTFS Full Control permission. This is not so with the Primary Group, or the Everyone group.

Remember, the NTFS permissions are as follows:

- Read (R)
- Write (W)
- Execute (X)
- Delete (D)
- Change Permissions (P)
- Take Ownership (O)

You'll also notice that the see files and see folders options actually appear to have the same effect on the NTFS permissions. Although it is not reflected in the visible permissions, NT honors these two flags for Macintosh clients. When a Macintosh user does not have the see files permission, a little file icon with a slash through it appears in the upper-left corner of the window. Likewise, if the user does not have permissions to see folders, the icon will be a small folder with slash through it. The icon that indicates a user does not have the see folders permission is shown in Figure 9.2.

FIGURE 9.2.

The little icon of the folder with a line through it indicates that the user does not have permission to see folders.

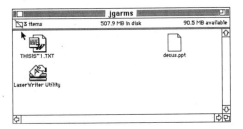

Here are some things to be aware of when working with these permissions:

- **Permissions are cumulative.** Essentially you can mix and match rights from each category. For instance, if *only* the Owner has see files permission, and *only* the Primary Group has see folders permission, and if *only* the Everyone category has make changes permission, and if I'm the owner, and I'm a member of the Primary Group, do I have all three rights?

- **The owner has built-in rights.** Even if you remove all three rights (see files, see folders, and make changes) from the owner, the owner still retains the change permissions (P) and take ownership (O) rights.

- **Discrepancies in permissions between PC and Macintosh clients.** PC clients do not honor the see folders and see files permissions the same way as Macintosh clients. This can result in discrepancies in what a Macintosh and a PC user can see.

- **Changing ownership changes the ACL.** When you use the MacFile permissions option to change the owner of a file, the old owner will be removed from the folder's access control list (ACL)—and likewise from all files within the folder. For example, if JGARMS is the owner and I change the owner to JSMITH, not only will the NTFS owner change to JSMITH, but JGARMS will be completely removed from the NTFS ACL.

- **The AFP permissions keep placeholder entries for the primary group and Everyone.** If you use the MacFile Permissions option to remove all three AFP permissions from the Primary Group or the Everyone group, they still retain placeholder access control entries (ACEs) in the NTFS access control list.

  For instance, if you remove all the AFP permissions from the owner, the Primary Group, and Everyone, the resulting NTFS permissions on the folder will list the owner with special access (PO), and will list the Primary Group and Everyone with special access (), which is essentially no specified access. This is shown in Figure 9.3.

FIGURE 9.3.

When you remove Macintosh permissions, place-saving entries are retained in the NTFS access control list (ACL).

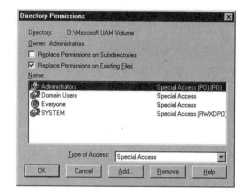

- **You can set the owner of the folder to a group—it does not have to be an individual user's account.** This is in sharp contrast to the normal operations of Windows NT, where the Administrators group is normally the only group that can own files.

- **Existing ACEs are preserved when replacing permissions on subdirectories.** When you choose the option to Replace Permissions on Subdirectories, only the NTFS permissions for the owner, the Primary Group, and the Everyone group will be changed. All other access control entries (ACEs) in the ACL will remain unchanged. This is quite different from the usual behavior of the NT Explorer and the File Manager, where the entire ACL of each subdirectory is replaced.

- **NT supports the AFP *Cannot Move, Rename, or Delete* option.** When you choose the option Cannot Move, Rename, or Delete, NT sets the read-only attribute on the folder, but not on the files within it.

Understanding Macintosh Guest Logons

When a Macintosh user connects to an AppleShare file server, there are normally two methods of logging in:

- As a guest
- As a registered user

To illustrate this point, Figure 9.4 shows the Macintosh user validation screen.

When the user logs on to an NT Server running Services for Macintosh as a registered user, they can use a standard Windows NT user account and password, much as would be expected. This is very straightforward.

The problem, however, is when the user tries to log on as a Macintosh guest. I often run into people that don't quite understand how this works, and they often encounter problems because of it.

9

WORKING WITH
MACINTOSH
CLIENTS

FIGURE 9.4.

Macintosh users can log on as a guest, or as a registered user.

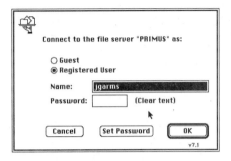

There are two basic things to remember, and everything else will fall into place:

- The Macintosh guest logon is *completely unrelated* to the Windows NT guest user account.
- The file-level access for a Macintosh guest is controlled by the NTFS privileges assigned to the pseudo-group Everyone.

NOTE

The pseudo-group Everyone is unrelated to the NT guest user account. The reason I call it a pseudo-group is that you cannot directly control membership in this group the same way as other groups. The actual membership of the Everyone group could be simply defined as *every non-disabled user account in this domain and all trusted domains.*

So what does this mean? Well, it means that you can disable the NT guest user account and Macintosh guests can still connect. Many people don't believe this until they've tried it, so feel free to go ahead and try it. Now that we've gotten over that, let's move on and figure out how the Macintosh guest access really works.

First of all, if you absolutely don't want guest access from Macintosh users, you can disable it by going to the MacFile Control Panel, choosing Attributes and then deselecting the Allow Guests to Connect option. This will prevent all Macintosh guest access, no ifs, ands, or buts.

However, you might want to rethink this strategy. There is a reason Macintosh guest access is there, and there is a reason it is enabled by default. When you install Services for Macintosh, NT creates a read-only, Macintosh-accessible volume called *Microsoft UAM Volume* and enables guest access. By default, when Macintosh users connect to NT Servers, their passwords are sent in clear-text over the network, which creates a security problem. However, the Microsoft UAM allows Macintosh clients to connect to the NT Server using encrypted passwords.

The catch-22 is that the users must be able to log on to the server to download the UAM. So the theory goes that they should connect to the server as a guest, which doesn't require a password and download the UAM. Because the volume is marked as read-only, it cannot be tampered with. Additionally, rather than disabling Macintosh guest access globally, and preventing people from downloading the UAM, you can restrict Macintosh guest access on a volume-by-volume basis—and leave it enabled for Microsoft UAM Volume.

So where does that leave us? Well, we now know how to restrict Macintosh guest users from accessing an NT Server running Services for Macintosh. Once they've been allowed to connect to the server, access to particular files and folders is dictated by the permissions set for Everyone at each folder level.

If you remove permissions for Everyone from a particular folder, a Macintosh guest will not be able to access files in that folder.

> **NOTE**
>
> The Everyone group that shows up when you set the AppleShare file permissions is exactly the same as the NT Everyone group that shows up when you set NTFS permissions.

Who Is the Macintosh Guest, Really?

This section is for the techie folks who really want to understand what's going on. We've identified in this chapter that Macintosh guest users do not in fact use any standard NT user accounts. If this is true, how can we explain the fact that NT requires all system events and processes to be auditable to a single user? Well, the answer is that when a Macintosh guest logs on, he or she is logged on as a special ANONYMOUS LOGON account that is built into Windows NT.

We can see this account by enabling auditing of user logons. Figure 9.5 shows the audit event that gets registered in the Security Log when a Macintosh guest logs on.

Well, at least we know how the user logs on. Just remember, the NT AUTHORITY\ANONYMOUS LOGON is built into NT and cannot be disabled. However, the rights of the ANONYMOUS LOGON are based on the privileges assigned to the Everyone group for a particular resource.

FIGURE 9.5.

A Macintosh guest generates logon events as the user NT AUTHORITY \ ANONYMOUS LOGON.

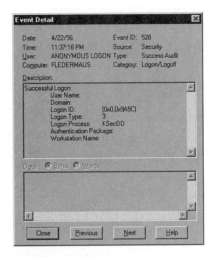

Installing and Configuring Services for Macintosh

Enabling Macintosh support for Windows NT Server is exceptionally simple. In fact, it is just as straightforward as installing almost any other service. There are essentially five steps:

1. Install the Services for Macintosh service.
2. Configure the File Server options.
3. Configure the AppleTalk router options, if desired.
4. Create any Macintosh Volumes and assign appropriate permissions.
5. Install the Microsoft User Authentication Module (UAM) on Macintosh clients, if desired.

Installing Services for Macintosh

When you install Services for Macintosh on your system, there are a number of changes that take effect. These include the following:

■ Installing the AppleTalk protocol and binding it to the default network adapter

NOTE

After installing Services for Macintosh, the AppleTalk Protocol will not be listed in the list of installed protocols in the Network Control Panel.

- Adding a MacFile icon to the Control Panel, and extensions to the File Manager and Server Manager that enable you to configure and manage Services for Macintosh

- Adding an option to the Print Manager and printer creation Wizard for printing to an AppleTalk printer

- Installing the PostScript Raster Image Processor (RIP) that enables you to print PostScript jobs to non-PostScript printers

- Adding two services, File Server for Macintosh and Print Server for Macintosh

- Adding Performance Monitor objects for AppleTalk and MacFile Server

- Creating a Microsoft UAM Volume directory on the first available NTFS volume and creating a Macintosh shared volume for it

- Installing the `MACFILE.EXE` command-line utility for managing and configuring Macintosh services

NOTE

In order to install Services for Macintosh, you must have at least one NTFS volume.

To install Services for Macintosh you should be logged on as a member of the Administrators group and follow these steps:

1. From the Control Panel, double-click the Networks icon.

2. Click the Services tab. This brings up the Services page, which lists all the services currently installed on your system.

3. Click the Add button. This brings up a window that lists all the services that can be installed on your system. Scroll down to Services for Macintosh and select it, as shown in Figure 9.6.

FIGURE 9.6.

Select Services for Macintosh from the Select Network Service window to install Macintosh client and printer support.

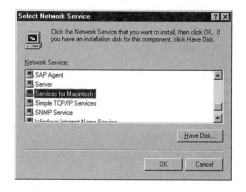

When you have highlighted Services for Macintosh, click OK.

4. You might be asked to provide the location of the Windows NT Server installation files. If so, enter the full path, such as `f:\i386`, where `f:` is the CD-ROM drive. Click the Continue button.

   NT Setup will copy files from the distribution media and make modifications to your system. This might take a few moments. When it is completed, it will return you to the Services page on the Network Control Panel. Services for Macintosh should be listed under Network Services, as shown in Figure 9.7.

FIGURE 9.7.

Once you have installed Services for Macintosh, it will appear in the list of Network Services in the Network Control Panel.

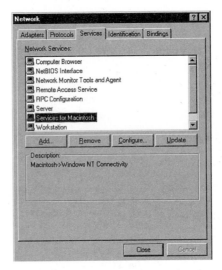

5. Click OK to close the Network Control Panel window and complete the installation process.

   NT Setup will review the network adapter binding and services. This might take a few minutes. Once this is completed, the Microsoft AppleTalk Protocol Properties window will appear, as shown in Figure 9.8.

   This window is used to configure the AppleTalk protocol options.

6. The default network adapter for your system will be listed in the field Default Adapter. This is the physical network on which the NT Server will advertise its services. If you have more than one adapter, you can choose which physical network segment you want your system to advertise on. This will make a difference if AppleTalk routing is not enabled.

7. The second field here, Default Zone, is the zone where the NT Server will advertise its services. Each AppleShare server can advertise itself in only one zone. If you don't already have an AppleTalk router on the network, this pull-down list will be empty. If you do have an existing AppleTalk router, the designated default zone on the router will be listed in the Default Zone entry. If you want the NT Server to appear in a different zone, choose it from the pull-down list.

FIGURE 9.8.

The Microsoft AppleTalk Protocol Properties window is used to configure the AppleTalk protocol necessary to support Macintosh clients.

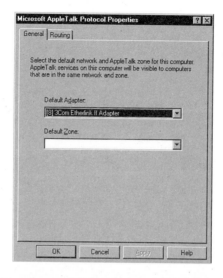

NOTE

AppleTalk zones are similar to NT workgroups, except that zones also contain routing information and workgroups do not.

For information on configuring NT Server as an AppleTalk router, see the section "Configuring Windows NT Server as an AppleTalk Router," later in this chapter.

8. Click OK to continue.

NT Setup will finish making internal configuration changes. This might take a few minutes. When it is completed, you will need to restart the system before any changes will take effect.

9. Click Yes when prompted to restart the system.

NOTE

When the system restarts, all printers created on the NT Server will become available to Macintosh clients.

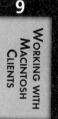

Configuring Services for Macintosh

You can configure Services for Macintosh by three different methods. The most common is to use the MacFile Control Panel, as we will do here. However, you can also use the Server Manager or the MACFILE command-line utility to perform the same functions.

To configure Services for Macintosh using the MacFile Control Panel, follow these steps:

1. Open the Control Panel. Notice the MacFile icon, shown in Figure 9.9. This was installed with Services for Macintosh.

FIGURE 9.9.

The MacFile icon in the Control Panel is used to configure the Services for Macintosh options.

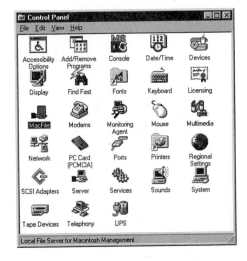

2. Double-click the MacFile icon. The MacFile Properties window appears, as shown in Figure 9.10.

FIGURE 9.10.

The MacFile Properties window displays file usage and information on logged-on users.

3. Click the Attributes button. The MacFile attributes window will appear, as shown in Figure 9.11.

The options for the MacFile Attributes window are as follows:

- **Server Name for AppleTalk Workstations.** This is the name the server will appear as on the AppleTalk network. By default this will be the same as the standard NT name of the computer. However, if you want to, you can choose to have your computer appear with a different name. This can be 1 to 31 characters long.

FIGURE 9.11.

From the MacFile Attributes window, you can configure global options for Macintosh services on your NT Server.

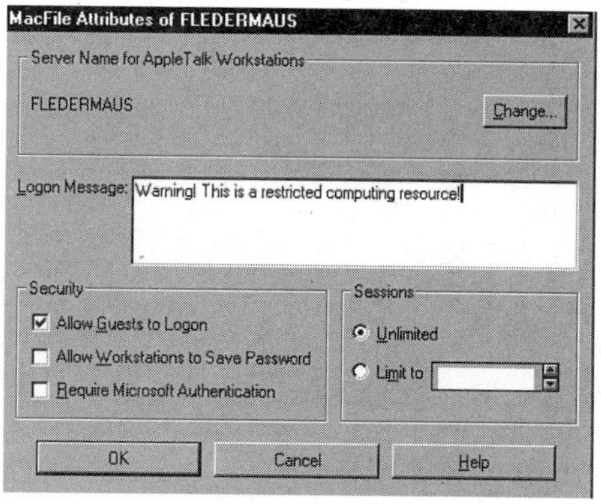

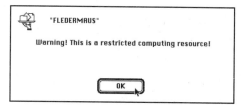

Logon Message. This message will appear on the Macintosh workstation when a user connects to the NT Server. The ability to receive these logon messages is built in to the standard AppleShare client for the Macintosh 2.1 and above. An example of this message is shown in Figure 9.12.

FIGURE 9.12.

NT supports the capability to send logon messages to Macintosh clients.

By default, no logon message is sent to Macintosh clients.

Allow Guests to Logon. By default, Macintosh users are allowed to connect to the NT Server as guests—even if the NT guest user account is disabled. To disallow Macintosh guests from logging on to the NT Server, deselect this option. For more information about guest Macintosh users see the section titled "Understanding Macintosh Guest Logons," earlier in this chapter.

Allow Workstations to Save Password. For Macintosh clients, the capability to cache server passwords is controlled by each server. This differs from standard Windows clients, where the caching of passwords is controlled by each individual client. By default, Services for Macintosh does not allow the Macintosh client to cache its password. Enable this option if you want Macintosh clients to be permitted to cache passwords.

■ **Require Microsoft Authentication.** By default, when a Macintosh client connects to an NT Server, the password is sent in clear text over the network. If you need a higher level of security, check this option and clients will be required to use the Microsoft User Authentication Module (UAM) to log on. For more information on the MS UAM, see the section titled "Installing the Microsoft Authentication Module on a Macintosh Client," later in this chapter.

> **WARNING**
>
> Even if you have the Require Microsoft Authentication option checked, users can still log on as guests, provided the Macintosh guest access is not disabled. This permits users to connect to the Microsoft UAM Volume and download the MS UAM. Because the guest access does not require sending a password, there is no security problem with this configuration.

■ **Sessions.** You can use this option to limit the number of Macintosh clients who can simultaneously connect to the NT Server. By default, there is no limit. If you want to limit the number of users, you can enter a value between 1 and 4,294,967,293.

> **NOTE**
>
> In Windows NT Advanced Server 3.1, there was a physical limit of 255 simultaneous Macintosh connections that was due to the design of the Services for Macintosh. However, with NT Server 3.5, Microsoft removed that limit. In fact, Microsoft has actually done internal testing of NT Server 3.51 with 1,000 simultaneous Macintosh clients without a problem.

> **TIP**
>
> Two other methods of configuring the Macintosh Services options are using the Server Manager and using the MACFILE command-line utility. Additionally, both of these methods enable you to configure Services for Macintosh on remote machines.

Configuring AppleTalk Routing on Windows NT Server

You can configure AppleTalk routing either during the Services for Macintosh installation process or at a later time. To configure the options at a later time, make sure you are logged on as a member of the Administrators group and start at step 1. If you want to configure AppleTalk routing during the Services for Macintosh installation process, start at step 4.

1. Open the Control Panel and double-click the Network icon.

2. Click the Services tab. The Services page should appear. It lists all the installed network services.

3. Find Services for Macintosh on the list and double-click it. This will open the Microsoft AppleTalk Protocol Properties window.

4. Click the Routing tab on the Microsoft AppleTalk Protocol Properties window. This will display the AppleTalk Routing page, as shown in Figure 9.13.

FIGURE 9.13.

The options on the Routing page can be used to configure NT Server as an AppleTalk router.

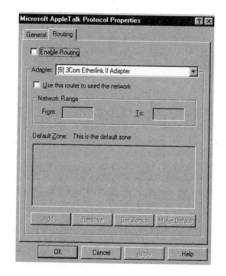

5. By default, AppleTalk routing is disabled, so all other options on the page should be grayed out. To enable AppleTalk routing, check the box next to Enable Routing.

   Enabling AppleTalk routing does two things. First, it routes AppleTalk packets between any Ethernet, LocalTalk, and Token Ring network interfaces on your computer. Second, it enables you to seed the AppleTalk network to create zones.

6. You can configure the seeding of AppleTalk networks individually for each network interface. If you have more than one network interface, choose the one you want to configure for AppleTalk seeding from the Adapter pull-down list.

7. Click the option Use this Router to Seed the Network. The Network Range field and the Default Zone listbox should now be enabled (not grayed out).

9

WORKING WITH
MACINTOSH
CLIENTS

8. Enter a valid AppleTalk zone range into the From and To fields. The AppleTalk zone range is used to identify different physical networks. If you are attached to a larger network, check with the person in charge of the AppleTalk protocol to obtain the correct ranges. For more information on AppleTalk zone ranges, see the section titled "Understanding the Macintosh" earlier in this chapter. Acceptable values are between 1 and 65,279. It is also acceptable to use the same value in the From and To fields.

9. Use the Add button to add zone names for the specified network segment. The first zone you enter will become the default zone for the network segment. If you want to change the default zone, select it from the zone list box and click the Make Default button.

10. If there are other AppleTalk routers on this physical network, you can click the Get Zones button to import the zone list. If you do this, all zones you entered manually will be replaced. NT will ask you to confirm that you want to replace the zone list, as shown in Figure 9.14.

FIGURE 9.14.

If you click the Get Zones button, NT asks you if you want to replace the zone list you entered manually with a list it acquires from existing AppleTalk routers.

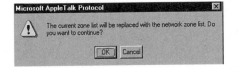

Figure 9.15 shows sample configuration information for AppleTalk routing.

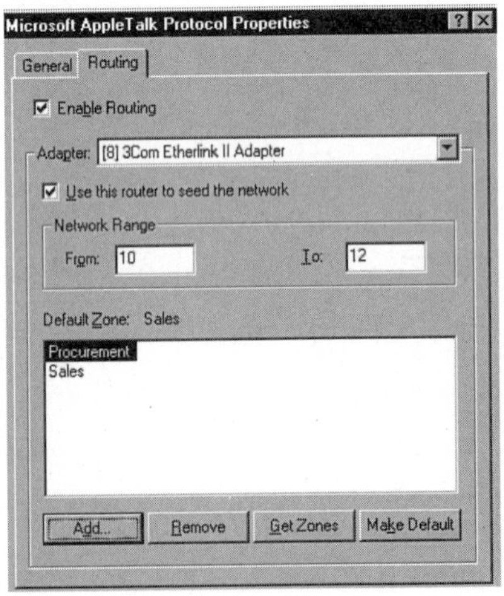

FIGURE 9.15.

These configuration settings indicate that the NT Server will act as an AppleTalk router and seed the local network segment with network values 10 through 12. Additionally, zones Sales and Procurement are on the local network segment.

11. When you are finished entering AppleTalk routing information, click the General tab at the top of the screen.

12. You can now use the Default Zone list to select the zone where you want your server to appear. When you are finished, click OK.

13. A window will appear notifying you that the AppleTalk protocol has been successfully configured. Click OK. You will be returned to the Network Control Panel.

14. Click OK. Restart the computer to ensure the changes take effect.

When to Use AppleTalk Routing

If you're not intimately familiar with AppleTalk routing, it might be hard to determine when you need to use it and how best to configure it. There are two basic configurations where AppleTalk routing might be useful to you:

- When you are using your NT Server to connect two physically separate AppleTalk networks. In this sense, you are using AppleTalk routing in the traditional sense of routing.

- When you have an AppleTalk network and you want to logically divide the network into zones. This provides for easier browsing and is not necessarily consistent with the traditional use of the word routing.

In both cases, you can use the NT Server as a seed router, depending on the existence of other AppleTalk routers on the network.

> **NOTE**
>
> You need to have a seed router for each zone that you want to appear on a subnet.

Let's address these scenarios separately.

Routing AppleTalk Between Two Physically Separate Networks

Let's say that you are working on a large, private network, with 1,000 Macintosh clients spread around the network. You have five major zones: Sales, Procurement, Tech Support, Administration, and General. You have a new suite of 20–30 Macintosh computers served by an NT Server running Services for Macintosh that you need to connect into the existing network backbone.

Of course, one option would be to connect the computers directly to the network backbone, as shown in Figure 9.16.

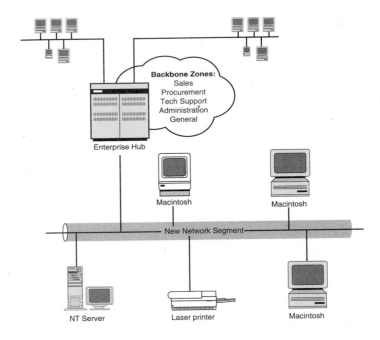

FIGURE 9.16.

Connecting a series of Macintosh clients served by an NT Server directly to the network backbone.

In this case, the Macintosh clients in the group of computers we just added can communicate with the NT Server, as can any Macintosh clients on the rest of the network. Additionally, the newly added clients can become part of any of the zones available on the backbone.

As far as the NT Server goes, you don't need to enable AppleTalk routing, because there is no need for actual routing, nor do you need to seed a new zone.

While this might seem nice and simple, there are two problems. First the minor one. You might not want the clients on the newly added network to be able to join any of the zones on the network. For instance, if the people in the newly added group of computers only need to be part of the Procurement and Sales zones, you might want to be able to restrict them to these zones. In this example, there are only five zones, so this might seem unnecessary. However, it is not uncommon for larger enterprises to have dozens and even hundreds of zones, where being able to restrict groups of computers to certain zones could be a necessity.

The second reason that the network architecture in Figure 9.16 is not adequate is that the users on the newly added computers will share all network bandwidth with the rest of the users on the network. This single-segment approach can have a negative impact on network performance.

To help alleviate both of these problems, you can use the NT Server as an AppleTalk router, as shown in Figure 9.17.

To make this scenario work, you need the following:

FIGURE 9.17.

In this scenario, the NT Server is used as an AppleTalk router between the local subnet and the rest of the network.

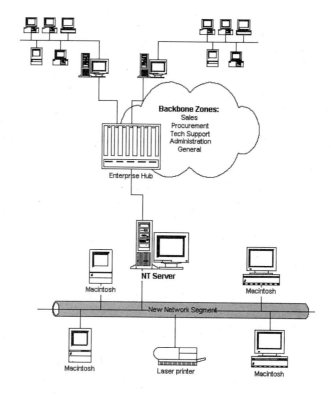

Backbone Zones:
Sales
Procurement
Tech Support
Administration
General

Enterprise Hub

NT Server

Macintosh

Macintosh

New Network Segment

Macintosh

Laser printer

Macintosh

- a second network card for the NT Server
- a unique range of network numbers for the new subnet

Let's say you will use the network range 36–38, since it's not being used elsewhere on the network.

To configure NT properly for this scenario, you would use the following steps:

1. Open the Control Panel.
2. Double-click the Network icon.
3. Click the Services tab.
4. Double-click the Services for Macintosh.
5. Click the Routing tab. This is where the real work begins.
6. Click the Enable Routing checkbox.
7. From the Adapter pick-list, choose the network adapter that is connected to the *new subnet*.
8. Select the option Use this router to seed the network.
9. Enter 36 in the From field, and 38 in the To field.

9

WORKING WITH MACINTOSH CLIENTS

10. Click the Add button. The Add Zone window appears. Type `Sales` and click OK. Repeat this step to add the Procurement zone as well.

> **NOTE**
>
> Make sure you enter the AppleTalk zone names exactly the same as they appear elsewhere on the network. Be especially careful to include exact spacing, punctuation, and case.

Because you entered the Sales zone first, it appears as the default zone. This means that all Macintosh clients will appear in this zone automatically, unless you manually configure them to use a different zone.

Figure 9.18 shows the configuration options discussed in the preceding steps.

11. Click the General tab at the top of the Microsoft AppleTalk Protocol Properties window.

FIGURE 9.18.

Services for Macintosh is now configured for AppleTalk routing.

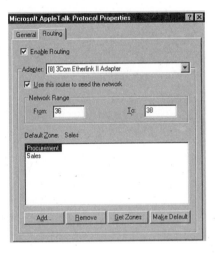

12. From the Default Adapter pick-list, choose the adapter that is connected to the new subnet. This is the same adapter you chose in step 7.

13. From the Default Zone pick-list, choose the zone you want the NT Server to appear in. The only choices will be Sales and Procurement, because these are the zones you chose to seed on the new subnet.

14. Now click OK a few times to get out of the Control Panel, and then restart the computer.

When the computer comes back up, it will be configured properly to support the routing scenario depicted in Figure 9.17.

Using AppleTalk Routing to Create Zones

The second common scenario is to use the AppleTalk routing capabilities to create AppleTalk zones on the network. My experience is that this is what the vast majority of people using NT Server's Services for Macintosh use AppleTalk routing for.

Remember, in the Microsoft world, there are workgroups and domains that provide logical grouping of computers. These logical groupings make locating a resource on the network easier.

In the Macintosh world, you can use an AppleTalk router to create zones, which are used to logically group machines and resources on the network. In a smaller network, full-fledged routing is often not necessary, but it is still often useful to create zones for organization of resources. Windows NT Server enables you to do this.

Let's use an example. Let's say that you have a small network that has 45 Macintosh computers and a couple of networked AppleTalk printers. You want to logically group your network into five zones: Development, Production, Advertising, General, and Printers.

You can use the AppleTalk routing capabilities of NT Server to do this. While it won't make your network any faster, it does help you to organize a little better.

To configure NT properly for this scenario, you would use the following steps:

1. Open the Control Panel.
2. Double-click the Network icon.
3. Click the Services tab.
4. Double-click Services for Macintosh.
5. Click the Routing tab.
6. Click the Enable Routing checkbox. Although this example only includes one network card on the server, so there won't be any real routing, you still need to enable this feature.
7. Select the option Use this router to seed the network.
8. Because this machine is the only AppleTalk router on the network, you can use whatever values you want to seed the network. For now, enter 10 in the From field, and 11 in the To field.
9. Click the Add button. The Add Zone window appears. Type Development and click OK. Repeat this step to add the Production, Advertising, General, and Printers zones as well.

   Because you entered the Development zone first, it appears as the default zone. This means that all Macintosh clients (and even printers) will appear in this zone by default.

   Figure 9.19 shows the configuration options discussed in the preceding steps.

9

WORKING WITH
MACINTOSH
CLIENTS

10. Click the General tab at the top of the Microsoft AppleTalk Protocol Properties window.

11. From the Default Zone pick-list, choose the zone you want the NT Server to appear in. Because it will be used by everyone, put it in the General zone.

FIGURE 9.19.

These options will create five zones on the AppleTalk network.

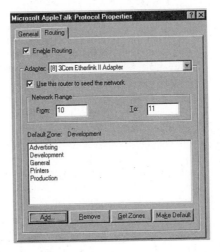

12. Now exit the Control Panel and restart the computer.

When the server comes back up, it will create the five zones specified earlier in the example. Now you'll be able to see the zones on your Macintosh clients, and you'll be able to move them into the appropriate zones.

Creating Macintosh-Accessible Volumes

In the AppleShare world, network volumes are the resources that are made available on an AFP file server for network users to connect to. They are logically the same as network shares, share points, or mount points in the Windows networking world. The process of creating a Macintosh-accessible volume with NT Server is similar to that of creating a standard network share that would be accessed by Windows networking clients.

NOTE

There is one major difference between Macintosh volumes and standard Windows shares, which you should be careful of. With Windows shares, you can create shares within shares. Let's take a look at an example. If you had a file structure that looked like the one shown in Figure 9.20, you could create a share-point for the Divisions folder. You could also create separate share-points for each of the folders in the Divisions folder, Accounting, Advertising, General, Procurement, and Sales. If a user attached to the Divisions share-point, he or she would be able to see the folders beneath that folder, given the correct permissions, of course. Likewise, if a user attached to the Accounting share-point, he or she could see the things below that level, but could not see anything else in the Divisions folder. This provides for a useful method of organization.

However, with Services for Macintosh, you cannot create Macintosh-accessible volumes within other Macintosh-accessible volumes. This would preclude you from setting up an environment like the one described above. You could either create a volume for each division, or you could create a single volume that contained all the divisions, but *not* both.

FIGURE 9.20.

Sample Windows directory structure showing shares within shares.

There are four tools you can use to create Macintosh-accessible volumes in Windows NT:

- File Manager
- Server Manager
- MACFILE command-line utility
- Administrative Wizards

9

WORKING WITH
MACINTOSH
CLIENTS

The easiest of these options is to use the Administrative Wizards, which we'll discuss in this section. We'll also look at using the File Manager for creating Macintosh volumes. The Server Manager interface for creating Macintosh volumes functions in almost the same manner as the File Manager interface. The syntax for using the MACFILE utility is listed at the end of this chapter.

> **NOTE**
>
> Microsoft did not include a method for creating Macintosh shares from the NT Explorer interface.

> **NOTE**
>
> NT Server automatically creates a Macintosh-accessible volume—called Microsoft UAM Volume—when you install Services for Macintosh. This volume is created on the first NTFS partition on your server.

Using the Administrative Wizards to Create a Macintosh-Accessible Volume

One of the new features of Windows NT Server 4 is the inclusion of a set of Administrative Wizards that simplifies common administrative functions. There are eight basic Administrative Wizards, one of which is called Managing File and Folder Access. This Wizard permits you to specify files and folders on the local server or on a remote server that should be shared to the clients—including Macintosh clients—on the network.

To use the Administrative Wizards to create a Macintosh-accessible network volume, follow these steps:

> **NOTE**
>
> You must be logged on as a user with administrative privileges to create network shares.

1. From the Start menu, choose Programs, Administrative Tools, then Administrative Wizards. The Administrative Wizards main window is shown in Figure 9.21.

FIGURE 9.21.

The Administrative Wizards permit you to perform a variety of common administrative tasks.

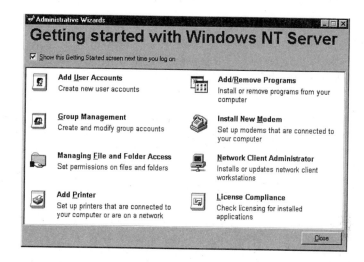

2. Click on Managing File and Folder Access. This will open the Share Management Wizard.

3. You will be asked if you want to provide network access to files and folders located on the local computer, or on a remote computer, as shown in Figure 9.22.

FIGURE 9.22.

You can use the Share Management Wizard to create network shares on the local computer, or on a remote NT system.

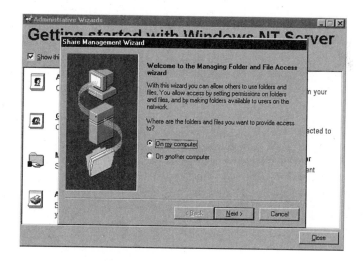

9

WORKING WITH
MACINTOSH
CLIENTS

4. By default, the share will be created on the local computer. Click the Next button to continue.

5. You will be given a list of all the local drives, as shown in Figure 9.23. Choose the drive that contains the files and folders you want to share. The drive will expand and you can see the files and folders contained on the drive. Locate the folder you want to share as a Macintosh volume, then click the Next button.

FIGURE 9.23.

*You need to specify
which local drive
contains the
files and folders you
want to make available
to the network.*

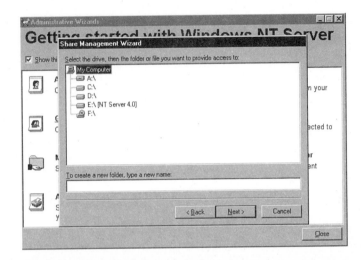

FIGURE 9.23.

*You need to specify
which local drive
contains the
files and folders you
want to make available
to the network.*

TIP

If you know the exact path of the folder you want to share, you can enter it in the field at the bottom of this screen, rather than browsing for it.

6. You will now be shown the current directory permissions on the folder you specified, as shown in Figure 9.24. Set the permissions to what you want, then click the Next button to continue.

FIGURE 9.24.

*The Share Manage-
ment Wizard permits
you to specify the
permissions on the
folder you specified.*

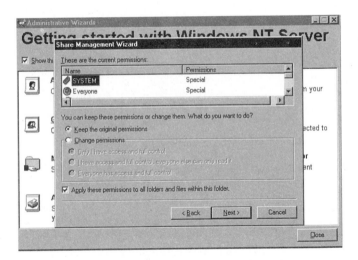

CAUTION

The Share Management Wizard is not a very robust tool and is probably best used by beginners who are just beginning to learn about Windows NT. However, if you are a more advanced user and commonly change permissions on files withholding subfolders, and want a fine level of granularity when specifying permissions, you should not use the Share Management Wizard.

7. You will be asked if you want to share the folder with network users. Click Yes.

8. The Share Management Wizard will ask you for a name for the share, a comment, and what kind of clients you want to share the folder with, as shown in Figure 9.25.

FIGURE 9.25.

You need to specify a name for the network share, as well as what kind of clients should be able to connect to it.

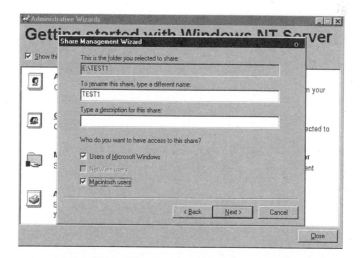

NOTE

Each shared volume on an NT Server must have a unique name. If you enter a name that is the same as an existing share name, NT will advise you that the name is already in use and ask you to choose a new name for the share.

NOTE

If the Macintosh users option is grayed out—indicating that you cannot share the folder with Macintosh users—then either you selected a folder located on a FAT partition, or you don't have Services for Macintosh installed on your NT Server.

9. Click the checkbox for Macintosh users to access the share. If you don't want to make the share available to Windows clients, you should uncheck the button for Users of Microsoft Windows. Click the Next button.

10. The Share Management Wizard presents a summary page indicating the name of the share you created, its network path, and what clients it will be shared with. Click Finish.

The share should now be available for users on the network. You can change Macintosh permissions for the file using the File Manager, or the MACFILE command-line utility.

Using the File Manager to Create a Macintosh-Accessible Volume

To create a Macintosh-accessible volume using the File Manager, follow this procedure:

1. Open the File Manager.

> **NOTE**
>
> The easiest way to get into the File Manager in NT 4 is to click the Start menu, choose Run and then type winfile and hit Return.

2. Find and select the directory you want to share as a Macintosh volume, such as D:\USERS, as shown in Figure 9.26.

FIGURE 9.26.

Select the directory you want to make accessible to Macintosh clients.

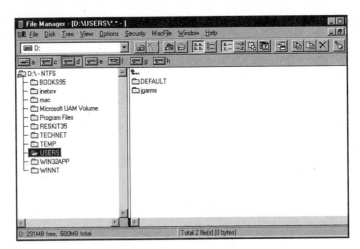

3. Choose Create Volume from the MacFile menu. The Create Macintosh-Accessible Volume window appears, as shown in Figure 9.27.

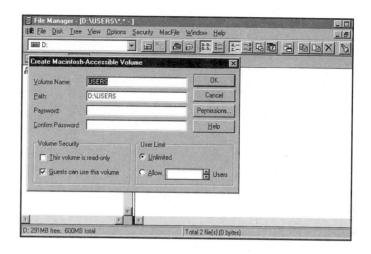

From here, you must specify the following:

- **Volume Name.** This is the volume name the Macintosh clients will see. It must be 27 characters or less. You can create a maximum of 255 Macintosh volumes on a single server. By default, this is the name of the folder you are sharing.

- **Path.** This is the path of the folder you want to share. It must be on a local volume, and it must be NTFS or CDFS.

NOTE

Services for Macintosh allows you to create Macintosh-accessible volumes on a CD-ROM.

- **Password/Confirm Password.** You can specify a password here and any Macintosh will be required to enter this password when connecting to this share. This security is provided in addition to any additional folder- and volume-level permission you might have set.

- **This volume is read-only.** If you check this box, the volume will be marked as read-only. Any Macintosh user who connects to the volume will be unable to make changes to the volume, regardless of what additional privileges he or she might have.

- **Guests can use this volume.** If you select this option, Macintosh users will be able to connect to this volume as a guest. If guest access is disabled from the MacFile Control Panel, this option has no effect. Note: Guest access from Macintosh clients has nothing to do with the NT guest account. For more information on Macintosh guest access, see the section titled "Understanding Macintosh Guest Logons," earlier in this chapter.

■ **User Limit.** You can use this setting to limit the number of simultaneous Macintosh clients that can access this volume. NT Server has no built-in practical limitation on the number of Macintosh clients it can serve. Note: The sum of the number of users of all the Macintosh-accessible volumes cannot exceed the Macintosh user limit in the MacFile Control Panel.

4. When you are finished entering the volume information into the Create Macintosh-Accessible Volume window, click the Permissions button to specify the access permissions for the volume. The Macintosh View of Directory Permissions window is shown in Figure 9.28.

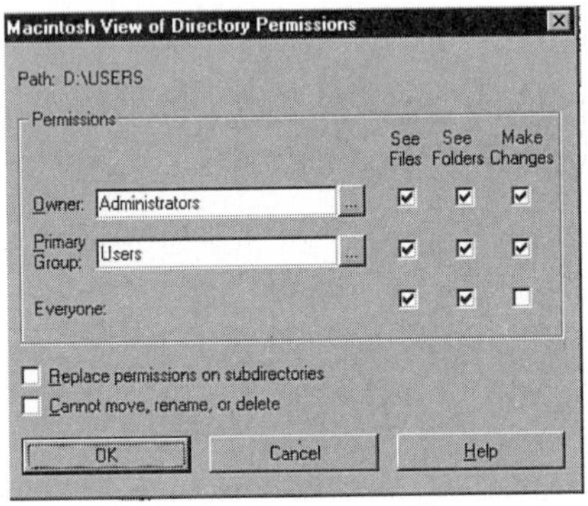

FIGURE 9.28.

You can use NT to specify the Macintosh permissions exactly as you would on a standard AppleShare server.

From here you can specify the permissions for the Owner, Primary Group, and Everyone. Additionally, you can change the Owner and Primary Group.

For more information on setting Macintosh permissions, see "Working with Macintosh Permissions," earlier in this chapter.

WARNING

It is very important to realize that Services for Macintosh does not distinguish between share permissions and file folder permissions. Standard Windows NT shares have their own permissions, which are different from the permissions set on the files and directories contained within. However, the volume permissions for a Macintosh are *exactly the same* as the folder where the volume begins. This means that if you change the permissions when you create a Macintosh volume, the NTFS permissions will *directly and immediately* reflect the change.

5. Click OK to close the security window.

6. Click OK again to create the share.

Macintosh users should now be able to access the share.

Viewing and Modifying Macintosh-Accessible Volumes

You can use the MacFile option in the File Manager to view and modify the settings for Macintosh-accessible volumes.

Any changes you make to the volume, including setting or clearing the read-only flag, will take effect immediately. However, if you remove guest access for the volume by clearing the Guests can use this volume option, it will not affect any users currently logged on as guests. This is because this option is only checked at logon.

Removing Macintosh-Accessible Volumes

You can remove Macintosh-accessible volumes by using the Remove Volumes option under the MacFile menu in the File Manager.

If there are any Macintosh users accessing the share, you will be warned that removing the share could result in the connected users losing data, as shown in Figure 9.29.

FIGURE 9.29.

You will be warned if you try to remove a Macintosh-accessible volume with active users.

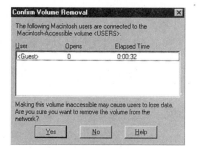

You can wait until the users have logged out, or you can click Yes to proceed and remove the volume anyway.

The Microsoft User Authentication Module (MS UAM)

When a Macintosh client connects to an AppleShare file server, it uses a user authentication module (UAM) to handle the authentication of the user by exchanging user name and password with the server. Macintosh computers running System 7.x (or System 6.0.7 and above, running AppleShare 2.1 or greater) have a built-in Apple authentication module. When communicating with other Macintosh computers running System 7.x, or with Apple's AppleShare servers, this allows the user's password to be encrypted before being sent over the network.

However, because of the way Windows NT stores passwords, it cannot take advantage of the Apple encryption method, called Apple Random Number Exchange. This means that when a Macintosh client wants to connect to an NT Server running Services for Macintosh, it sends the password in plain text over the network. Passing the password in clear text over the network results in a situation where anyone on the network could *see* the password as it goes between the network client and the server, thus sacrificing the security of the user's account.

Additionally, Apple's built-in UAM only supports passwords of up to 8 characters, while NT Server supports passwords of up to 14 characters. If a user has a password longer than 8 characters, he or she *will not* be able to log on to the NT Server from a Macintosh client using Apple's standard authentication module.

Thus, there are two occasions when you would want to install the Microsoft UAM:

- When you don't want user passwords to be sent in clear text over the network.
- When users have passwords longer than 8 characters.

Understanding the MS UAM

To help rectify the security problem, Microsoft created the Microsoft User Authentication Module (MS UAM). This module must be installed on each client that wants to use it. It interfaces with the Chooser and provides for encrypted user verifications, using Microsoft's Challenge Authentication Protocol (MS-CHAP). In addition, it supports up to 14-character passwords.

When you install Services for Macintosh on an NT Server, it automatically creates a directory called Microsoft UAM Volume on the first available NTFS partition. It then shares this directory as a read-only Macintosh volume and grants guest access. Macintosh clients can then connect to this share to obtain the MS UAM and install it on their systems.

> **NOTE**
>
> The reason the Microsoft UAM Volume is created with guest access enabled is so that Macintosh users do not need to sacrifice their passwords in order to obtain the UAM!

The MS UAM might seem like a great thing, and worthwhile to rush off and install it on all your systems. However, before you do this, let's take a look at the downside.

In the README.UAM file that is installed with Services for Macintosh, Microsoft writes, "Microsoft encourages you to install Microsoft Authentication (MS UAM) only if you need increased security on your Windows NT computer."

The reason for the caveat is that installing the Microsoft User Authentication Module adversely affects two major functions on Macintosh computers:

- The UAM cannot be used to connect to volumes at startup.
- The UAM cannot be used to connect to remote resources through aliases.

> **NOTE**
>
> For those not well versed in Macintosh terminology, file aliases are very similar to shortcuts in the Windows 95–style interface.

When Macintosh users connect to AppleShare file servers, they have the option of designating that certain shares should be reconnected automatically at startup, as shown in Figure 9.30.

FIGURE 9.30.

Macintosh users can designate certain network volumes to be reconnected at startup.

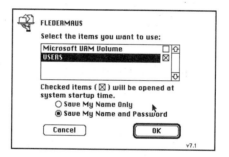

This is similar to the persistent connections option on Windows systems.

However, because of problems internal to Apple's system software, the Macintosh cannot use alternative UAMs to reconnect at startup. This means that either one of a couple of things will happen, depending on the server's configuration:

- If the server is configured to allow users to connect without the MS UAM, the user will be able to log on to the server at startup, using the standard Apple UAM. The problem is that this defeats the increased security of the MS UAM.
- If the server is configured to require MS UAM authentication, and the volumes the user is mounting permit Macintosh guest access, the Macintosh user will connect to the volumes as a guest.
- If the server is configured to require MS UAM authentication, and the volumes the user is mounting do not permit Macintosh guest access, the volumes will not be mounted.

The second problem with the MS UAM has to do with the way it interferes with reconnecting to file aliases located on network resources. Very often Macintosh users will create aliases to

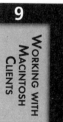

files or folders on remote file servers. If a user double-clicks an alias and is not currently connected to the file server where the file is located, the Macintosh tries to connect to the server. This is considered a great feature by many Macintosh network users. However, the problem is that the alias will always try to connect using the standard Apple UAM. The results are the same as listed previously, when users automatically connect at startup.

However, there is one slight saving grace. Once the user is attached to a network volume, the aliases will work. This is because the user authentication process is dealt with only when you first connect to the resource. While this doesn't provide a solution for connecting to systems at startup, it does mean that your users can use the MS UAM to attach to a Macintosh-accessible volume on the NT Server, and then use their aliases.

This leaves the system administrator, you or me, in a very unenviable position. It means that you can either forfeit the security provided by the MS UAM, or you can cripple the functionality of your users' systems. The correct solution to this problem must be handled on a site-by-site basis. If you choose to require the MS UAM, I encourage you to not turn it into a PC versus Macintosh argument.

> **NOTE**
>
> I want to make one thing clear. This problem is mostly because of defects in the Macintosh OS. All custom UAMs, including the NetWare UAM provided by Novell, have this same problem. Hopefully Apple will resolve this problem by adding full support for custom authentication modules sometime in the near future. As for the question of why can Macintosh clients use encrypted authentication with other Macintosh computers, including Apple's AppleShare servers, it is because Apple uses a different encryption method that requires the clear text password to be available at both ends. NT Servers do not store user passwords in a form that can be decrypted.

Installing the MS UAM on Macintosh Clients

Installing the Microsoft UAM on Macintosh clients is straightforward. If you are going to require users to use the MS UAM, you need to install it on all Macintosh clients.

> **NOTE**
>
> Don't be too concerned about the size of the MS UAM. It's only about 30KB.

To install the MS UAM on a Macintosh client, use the following procedure:

1. From the Macintosh client, open the Chooser from under the Apple menu.
2. Click the AppleShare icon in the upper-left corner of the Chooser.

3. Select the zone where you installed the NT Server running Services for Macintosh. Find the NT Server in the list on the right and double-click it.

   If you have already configured the NT Server to require Microsoft authentication, you will only be able to log on as a guest. However, if you have also disabled Macintosh guest access, you will get an error, as shown in Figure 9.31.

FIGURE 9.31.

If you require Microsoft authentication and have disabled guest access, you will get an error.

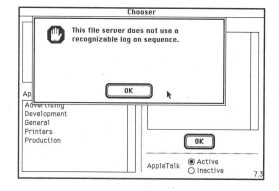

4. Select the option to log on as a Guest and click OK. The next screen appears, which lists all the Macintosh-accessible volumes on the NT Server, as shown in Figure 9.32.

FIGURE 9.32.

You can copy the Microsoft UAM from the Microsoft UAM Volume, which is created on the NT Server when you install Services for Macintosh.

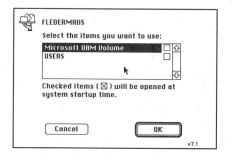

5. Double-click the Microsoft UAM Volume entry.

NOTE

Be sure *not* to put a check mark in the box at the right side of the entry. If you check this box, the Microsoft UAM Volume will automatically appear on your desktop the next time you restart the Macintosh.

If you have a logon message configured, it will appear now. Click OK to continue.

The Microsoft UAM Volume should now appear on the desktop.

6. Close the Chooser.

7. Open the Microsoft UAM Volume. There should be a folder called AppleShare Folder inside, as shown in Figure 9.33.

FIGURE 9.33.

The AppleShare Folder contains the MS UAM file needed to provide secure logons.

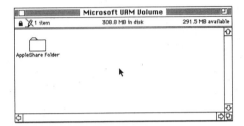

8. Drag-copy the AppleShare Folder into the System Folder on the Macintosh Client.

CAUTION

By default, there is no folder called AppleShare Folder inside the System Folder. However, if you have other UAMs installed, such as the NetWare UAM, the AppleShare Folder will exist and you will receive a message asking if you want to replace the AppleShare Folder. *Do not* do this. Simply open the AppleShare Folder on the NT Server and copy the MS UAM file inside into the existing AppleShare Folder on the Macintosh client.

---

9. Reboot the Macintosh to take advantage of the MS UAM.

Using the MS UAM on Macintosh Clients

Using the Microsoft User Authentication Module on the Macintosh is just as easy as installing it. Here's an example of connecting to an NT Server using the MS UAM:

1. From the Chooser, locate an NT Server to log on to and double-click it.

2. If the NT Server does not require Microsoft authentication, you will be asked if you want to use Microsoft authentication or standard authentication. Choose Microsoft authentication. The Microsoft authentication window will appear.

   However, if the server is configured to require Microsoft authentication, you will not be given a choice, but rather the Microsoft authentication windows will appear automatically.

3. Enter your user name and password. If the user account comes from a trusted domain, enter the name of the trusted domain, a back-slash, and then the user name (procurement\jgarms, for example).

4. Click OK.

5. Select the volumes you want to mount. If you want to select more than one volume, use the Shift key when you select the additional volumes.

6. Click OK. Volumes will appear on the desktop.

7. Close the Chooser.

Printing to an AppleTalk Printer

After you install Services for Macintosh, you can create an NT printer that sends jobs to any printer on an AppleTalk network. This is quite a neat feature, because even if you don't have Macintosh computers on your network, you might still have a printer that takes advantage of AppleTalk networking. If this is the case, you can use NT to allow Windows and DOS clients to print to this printer exactly as they would any other printer on an NT Server.

To create a printer on the NT Server that sends jobs to a printer device on an AppleTalk network, use the following procedure.

> **NOTE**
>
> In order to print to a printer using AppleTalk, you must have Services for Macintosh installed. See the section titled "Installing and Configuring Services for Macintosh," earlier in this chapter, for more information.

1. Make sure you have Services for Macintosh installed and are logged on as a member of the Administrators group.

2. From the Start menu, choose Settings, and then Printers. This will open the Printers window, which shows all currently created NT printers.

3. Double-click the Add Printer icon to start the Add Printer Wizard. The Add Printer Wizard is shown in Figure 9.34.

4. Choose the option for My Computer and click the Next button to continue.

> **NOTE**
>
> It might not seem obvious to choose the My Computer option, because you are in fact connecting to a computer on the network, so let's take a quick look at this. You can choose the Network Print Server option only when the printer has been created on another NT or Windows for Workgroups system, or on a Novell system if you have the Client or Gateway Services for Novell installed. For stand-alone network printers that you print to using AppleTalk, DLC, or TCP/IP, you must create the printer on your system. This is why you choose the My Computer option.

FIGURE 9.34.

The Add Printer Wizard is used to create or connect to an NT printer.

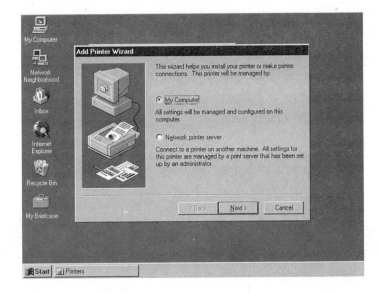

5. You now need to specify the port you want to add to. By default, you should see a number of LPT ports and COM ports listed. Click on the Add Port button to specify the location of the AppleTalk printer. This will bring up the Printer Ports window.

6. Choose AppleTalk Printing Devices from the list of available print monitors, as shown in Figure 9.35. Click OK.

FIGURE 9.35.

Choose the AppleTalk Printing Devices option.

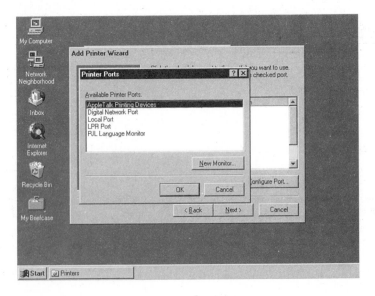

NOTE

If the AppleTalk Printing Devices option does not appear in the list of available print monitors, then you have not installed Services for Macintosh. See the section titled "Installing and Configuring Services for Macintosh," earlier in this chapter, for more information on installing Services for Macintosh.

7. The Available AppleTalk Printing Devices window will appear, as shown in Figure 9.36. This window is similar to the standard Windows network browser and is used to locate the AppleTalk printer on the network.

FIGURE 9.36.

The Available AppleTalk Printing Devices window is used for browsing the network to locate an AppleTalk printer.

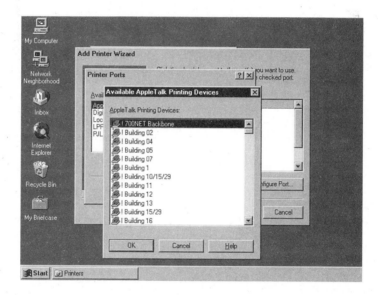

8. Double-click on the zone where the AppleTalk Printer you want to connect to is located. This will search for and display all available AppleTalk printers in the zone, as shown in Figure 9.37.

9. From the list, choose the printer you want to connect to and click OK.

NOTE

An AppleTalk name must be unique in its zone. However, you can have the same name used in multiple zones without problems, since AppleTalk resources are identified and located by both their name and their zone.

FIGURE 9.37.
When you expand the AppleTalk zone, all AppleTalk printers in the zone will be displayed.

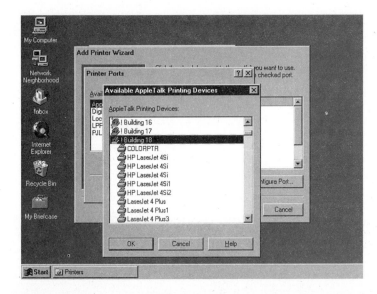

NOTE

You cannot use NT to change the actual name of an AppleTalk printer. If the printer is an Apple printer, you can use the LaserWriter Utility program that came with the printer to rename it.

---

10. A window will appear asking if you want to capture the AppleTalk printer, as shown in Figure 9.38. If you capture the printer, no one will be able to print directly to the printer. Rather, they will be forced to print through the NT print spooler. If you don't capture the printer, people can bypass the NT printer spooler and print directly to the printer.

TIP

For security reasons, you should capture the AppleTalk printers. The first security issue is that if you permit people to print directly to the printer, you have no method of auditing and tracking printer usage. The second, more critical problem is that if you don't capture the printer, someone else could capture the printer and deny everyone else access to it. Even in a smaller network where this might be easy to troubleshoot, this denial of service could result in lost productivity and angry users.

FIGURE 9.38.

You can capture an AppleTalk print device, which prevents people from printing directly to it.

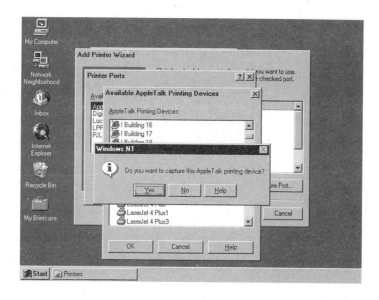

11. Click Close to close the Printer Ports window. The port identifier for the printer you just specified should appear in the list of available ports, as shown in Figure 9.39.

FIGURE 9.39.

The AppleTalk printer you specified will appear in the list of available ports.

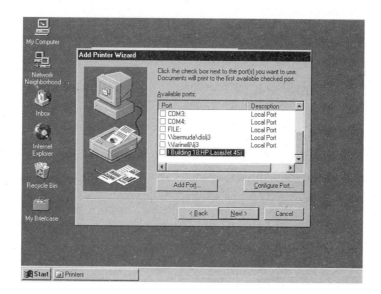

12. Make sure there is a check mark in the box next to the port, and click the Next button.

13. Choose the correct make and model for the printer. For example, an HP LaserJet 4Si, as shown in Figure 9.40.

FIGURE 9.40.

You must specify the make and model of the printer.

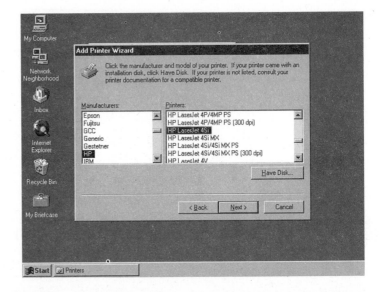

NOTE

It is important that you choose the correct make and model for the printer so that NT knows exactly what features the printer includes and how to work with it. Choosing the wrong printer can often cause unpredictable results.

14. Give the printer a name, as shown in Figure 9.41. You also need to tell NT whether or not you want to make this your default printer. Since this is a server, if you already have other printers created, you probably want to select No.

15. Click the Next button to continue. This will take you to the screen where you specify that you want the printer to be shared to the network.

16. Click the Shared button, as shown in Figure 9.42. Specify the name you want the printer shared as. If you have MS-DOS or Windows 3.x clients, you should make the share name 8 characters or shorter. If you will have Windows 95 or NT clients that need to print to the printer, you should specify the appropriate printer drivers to be installed.

17. Click the Next button. This will take you to a screen where you are prompted to print a test page. Click Yes to print a test page and click the Finish button.

18. You will be prompted for the NT Server distribution media. Enter the full path, or click the Browse button to locate the necessary files.

FIGURE 9.41.

Give the printer a name and specify if you want it to be the default printer when printing jobs from the server console.

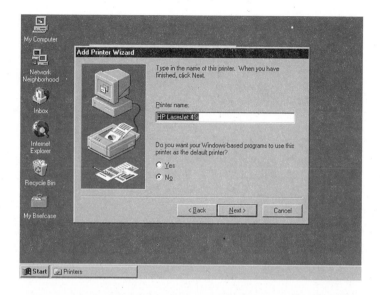

FIGURE 9.42.

Give the printer a share name and choose the additional operating system drivers to install on the server.

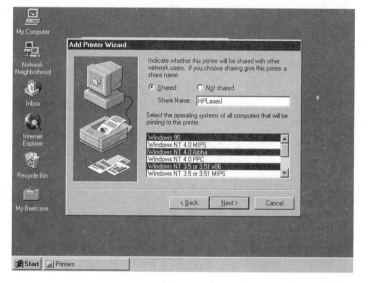

19. As the final step, NT will display the Properties page for the newly created printer, as shown in Figure 9.43.

    You should take the opportunity to enter any comments about the printer, as well as the location. If you want to change scheduling, sharing, security, or device settings, you can do it now, or later as necessary. For more information on these options, refer to Chapter 7, "Configuring and Installing Print Services."

    Click OK when you are finished configuring the printer.

FIGURE 9.43.

The Printer Properties page is used to change various settings once the printer has been created.

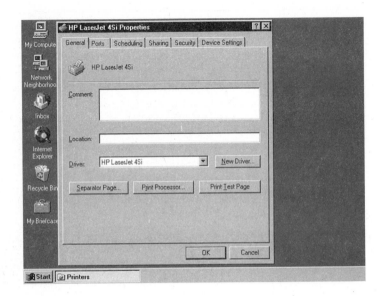

The printer you just created and shared on the network is capable of receiving print jobs from *any* Windows NT client. This means that standard Windows clients, other NT clients, Macintosh clients, Novell clients (with File and Print Services for NetWare), and UNIX clients (using LPD and TCP/IP) can all print to this printer through the NT Server. The strength in this feature is that the clients don't need to have AppleTalk installed; only the server *must* have AppleTalk installed.

Printing from Macintosh Clients to an NT Server

One of the truly remarkable aspects of NT Server is how seamlessly Services for Macintosh is integrated with the rest of the system. Perhaps this is seen best in how easy it is for Macintosh clients to print to printers through an NT Server.

When you install Services for Macintosh, NT automatically makes all printers on the NT system available to Macintosh clients. This means there is nothing that needs to be done for your Macintosh users to begin printing. All printers created on the NT Server will appear in the same zone as the NT Server.

NOTE

It is extremely important when you create printers on NT Server that you choose the correct printer type. NT knows from the printer type exactly what features are supported by the printer.

With Macintosh clients, it is important to know which printers have PostScript and which don't. For example, with HP printers, all printers with an M in the model name have PostScript. The M is HP's standard designation that lets you know the printer is made to work with Macintosh computers. (It also means the printer has a built-in LocalTalk interface.) If you have an HP LaserJet 4M Plus, you should be certain to select this when configuring the printer. If you choose HP LaserJet 4 Plus instead, NT will think the printer does not support PostScript and will rasterize the PostScript and send the bitmapped image to the printer, resulting in reduced print quality.

From a Macintosh client, you use the Chooser to select a printer on an NT Server exactly the same way you would to any other AppleTalk network printer.

NOTE

The PostScript interpreter built into Windows NT Server emulates an Apple LaserWriter Plus v38.0.

Administering Services for Macintosh

There are three major places you will need to go to for configuring Services for Macintosh:

- **MacFile Control Panel.** This applet enables you to get current statistics on Services for Macintosh, including a list of the current users, what files are in use, and what volumes are shared. Also, you can use it to send alerts to Macintosh users. It also enables you to configure the properties for Services for Macintosh, including the server's name on the AppleTalk network, a logon message for Macintosh clients, and the global policy for Macintosh guests.

- **File Manager.** The File Manager is used to create, view, modify, and remove Macintosh-accessible volumes. It can also be used to set Macintosh folder-level permissions, and associate MS-DOS–style extensions with Macintosh creator and type information. From here, you can also access the online help for Services for Macintosh.

- **Network Control Panel.** From the Services page in the Network Control Panel, you can configure the AppleTalk routing and zone information for Service for Macintosh.

Additionally, there are two other places that enable you to manipulate the Services for Macintosh options:

- **Server Manager.** You can use the Server Manager to do everything that the MacFile Control Panel does. Additionally, you can use it to create, view, modify, and delete volumes. The big advantage for Server Manager is that it can be used to configure remote systems.

- **MACFILE Command-Line Utility.** The MACFILE command-line utility can do everything—except configure AppleTalk routing and send alerts to Macintosh users. It even works on remote systems.

Identifying Logged-On Macintosh Users

If you need to identify which Macintosh users are logged on, what volumes they are accessing, and what files they have open, you should use the MacFile Control Panel.

> **NOTE**
>
> When Macintosh users connect through Services for Macintosh, they will not appear under the list of active users in the Server Control Panel. The Server Control Panel lists only users who connect using the standard Microsoft networking.

The MacFile Control Panel, shown in Figure 9.44, provides four different sets of information that enable you, as the system administrator, to find out who is accessing what files through Services for Macintosh.

Figure 9.44.

The MacFile Control Panel enables you to get information about which Macintosh users are connected to the NT Server.

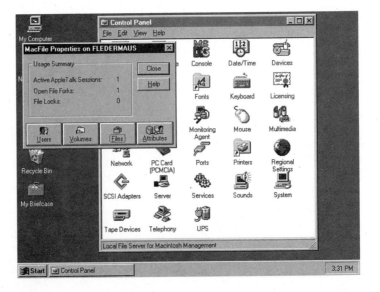

This screen gives you a summary of connections provided by Services for Macintosh. Included are the number of connected users, the number of open files, and the number of file locks. File locks typically occur when files are opened with write access.

The other connection-related information that can be obtained from the MacFile Control Panel is as follows:

■ **Connection Information by User.** The Users button from the MacFile Control Panel enables you to get statistics about the users currently connected to Services for Macintosh, as shown in Figure 9.45.

FIGURE 9.45.

You can find out to what volumes a particular user is connected.

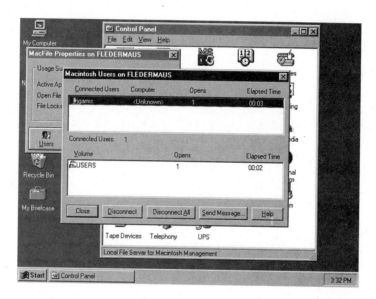

The top box includes a list of all the current Macintosh users, their computer names, how many files they have open, and how long they've been connected. When you click a user, the bottom window will show the volumes that the user is connected to, the number of open files the user has on that volume, and how long the user has been connected to that file.

While you have a user selected in the top window, you can select the Disconnect button at the bottom of the screen. If the user has no open files, you will be asked if you want to disconnect the user. Click Yes if you really want to disconnect the selected user. This will disconnect the user from *all* Macintosh volumes.

However, if the selected user has files open, NT will warn you that the user has open files and could lose data if you disconnect the user. It then asks you to confirm that you really want to disconnect the user. Click Yes to disconnect the user. This will disconnect the user from *all* Macintosh volumes.

If you want to disconnect all users, you can use the Disconnect All button.

■ **Connection Information by Volume.** With the Volumes button, you can get information about which volumes are being accessed by which users, as shown in Figure 9.46.

The top window shows all the Macintosh-accessible volumes on the local server. It also includes the number of open files on each volume and the actual path where the share is located.

TIP

If the path for a particular volume does not fit in the window, as with the Microsoft UAM Volume in Figure 9.46, you can double-click the volume name and NT will display a window containing the full path to the volume.

When you click a volume from the top window, the bottom window displays all the users attached to that volume, including how long the user has been connected and whether or not the share is in use. The definition of "in use" in this case refers to whether or not the user has file locks in that volume.

If you click a user and click the Disconnect button, NT will ask you to confirm the request. If you click Yes, the user will be disconnected from the *selected volume only*. If you click the Disconnect All button, all users on that volume will be disconnected. This will have no effect on user connections to other volumes.

FIGURE 9.46.

You can find out what users are connected to a particular volume.

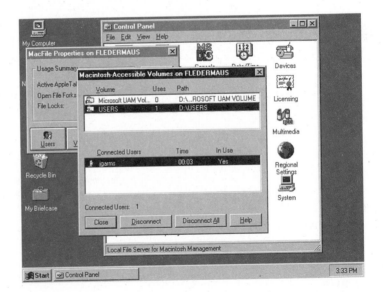

■ **Connection Information by File.** If you simply want a list of all the files that are being accessed by Macintosh clients, you can use the Files button. This gives you a list of all the in-use files, including the name of the user accessing the file, whether the file is opened for read or read/write access, the number of locks the user has on that file, and the full pathe to that file on the local server. This information is shown in Figure 9.47.

FIGURE 9.47.

You can get a list of all files that are currently in use by Macintosh clients.

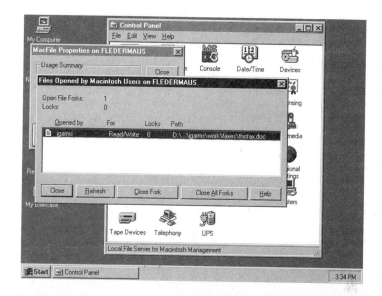

TIP

More often than not, you will not be able to read the full path of the files listed in this window. If you want to know the full path to a file, you can double-click the file name and NT will display a window containing its full path.

You can use this screen to close a user's access to particular files. This can be done by clicking on a file fork you want to close and then clicking on the Close Fork button. NT will ask you to confirm this action. If you click Yes, the user will be disconnected from the particular file.

However, if you click the Close All Forks button, all files open by Macintosh users on this server will be closed.

Sending Messages to Macintosh Clients

Windows NT's Services for Macintosh supports the capability to send alert messages to Macintosh users. This requires a Macintosh client running AppleShare 2.1 or above (built-in to System 7.x), and requires that the client be logged into the server. This differs from standard Microsoft clients, which aren't required to be logged on to a server to receive alerts.

NOTE

The NET SEND command and the Server Control Panel applet cannot be used to send messages to Macintosh users. So, if you have Services for Macintosh installed, be sure to send any important server alerts to your Macintosh clients as well.

Alerts can be sent from the MacFile Control Panel. From the MacFile Control Panel applet, simply choose the Users button. This brings up a window that displays all the currently connected Macintosh users, as shown in Figure 9.48.

FIGURE 9.48.

You can send messages to Macintosh users from the Users button in the MacFile Control Panel.

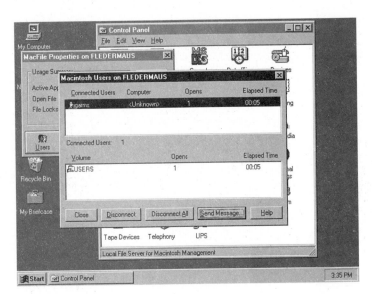

Simply select the user you want to send a message to and click the Send Message button.

TIP

If you want to send a message to more than one user, you can hold down the Control key while selecting additional users.

This will bring up a window where you can enter the message, as shown in Figure 9.49.

FIGURE 9.49.

You can send messages to selected users or to all users.

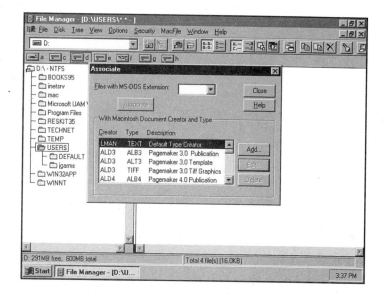

From here, you can also choose to send the message to all the users on the Macintosh local computer. You can enter up to four lines of text. Once you have entered the message, click OK and it will be immediately sent to the selected users.

NOTE

While the current AppleShare client for Macintosh supports sending messages from the server to connected clients, there is no provision for sending messages to clients who are not connected, or from client to server, or from client to client.

9

WORKING WITH
MACINTOSH
CLIENTS

Mapping File Extensions to Macintosh Creator and Type Fields

As described earlier in this chapter, creator and type information is very important for Macintosh files. This information allows the Macintosh Finder to know what application to launch when a user double-clicks it. It is also used to filter what a user sees when he or she tries to open a file.

Windows NT comes with a set of default mappings, as well as an extensive list of common Macintosh creator and file types.

To view the current mappings, or to set and create new ones, you'll need to use the Associate option from the MacFile menu in the File Manager. The Associate window is shown in Figure 9.50.

The pick-list at the top of the screen contains approximately 60 of the most common MS-DOS file extensions.

FIGURE 9.50.

The Associate window is used to set DOS extension to Macintosh creator and file type mappings.

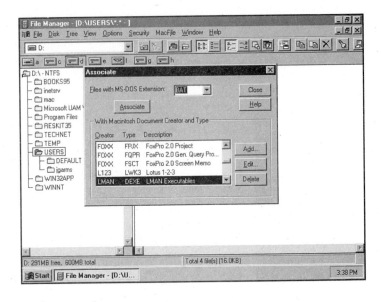

The scroll list at the bottom of the screen contains almost 70 common Macintosh creator and file types. For instance, you can scroll down and see the Microsoft Word 6.0 documents have creator MSWD and type W6BN. If you want to add new creator and file types, use the Add button. Likewise, you can select an existing entry and use the Delete button to remove it.

Let's take a look at how this works. From the list of MS-DOS extensions, choose BAT. You'll see that files with the BAT extension will be mapped to LMAN/DEXE and are LMAN executables, as shown in Figure 9.51.

FIGURE 9.51.

MS-DOS files with the BAT extension are mapped to Macintosh file type LMAN/DEXE.

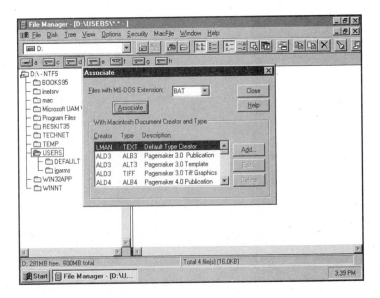

Now if we wanted to change that, we could simply choose a different creator/type combination from the list and click the Associate button. For instance, if we wanted Macintosh users to be able to double-click MS-DOS batch files and open them in a text editor, we could select the LMAN/TEXT option from the top of the creator/type list and click the Associate button, as shown in Figure 9.52.

FIGURE 9.52.

Now Macintosh clients will automatically open MS-DOS batch files with a text editor.

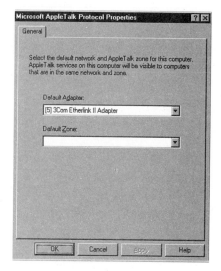

Now, from a Macintosh client, all files with the BAT extension will be recognized as text files and can be opened in any program that recognizes text files.

So why is it important to establish these associations? Well, normally the Macintosh stores and maintains these all by itself. However, if the file originates on a PC, it does not contain the creator/type information. The Macintosh then does not know what to do with the file. For instance, let's say that you used the Windows version of Microsoft Word 6.0 to create a file and saved it to an NT Server. Now if you went to a Macintosh and used Microsoft Word to look for the file on the NT Server, if the file associations were not created properly, the document would not even show up in the open list on the Macintosh. This is because the Macintosh can't find a valid creator/type for the file. However, with file associations, as long as you named the file with a DOC extension, the Macintosh version of Word would recognize it because NT Server would provide the creator/type information to the Macintosh.

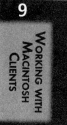

Administering Services for Macintosh from an NT Workstation

Although you can't set up NT Workstation as an AppleTalk file and print server, you can use an NT Workstation to administer NT Servers running Services for Macintosh. In order to do this, you need to install the AppleTalk protocol on the NT Workstation. In addition to enabling you to use Server Manager to manage Services for Macintosh on NT Servers, there are two other benefits for installing AppleTalk on an NT Workstation:

- You can use the NT Workstation to print directly to an AppleTalk printer.
- You can use third-party products that take advantage of the WinSock-compatible AppleTalk stack to communicate with other devices on the AppleTalk network. Possible products could include client software that allows NT Workstations to access files from an AppleShare server.

To install the AppleTalk protocol stack and administer remote NT Servers running Services for Macintosh, follow these steps:

1. On the NT Workstation, make sure you are logged on as a member of the local Administrators group.
2. Install the Server Tools for Windows NT. This can be found on the NT Server CD-ROM, and includes utilities such as Server Manager, User Manager for Domains, and others. For more information on installing these tools, see Chapter 9, "Working with Macintosh Clients."
3. Open the Control Panel and double-click the Network icon.
4. Click the Protocols tab. This takes you to the Protocols page, which lists all currently installed network protocols.
5. Click the Add button. This will present you with a list of all available network protocols.
6. Select AppleTalk Protocol, and click the OK button.
7. You might be asked to provide the location of the Windows NT Workstation installation files. If so, enter the full path, such as f:\i386, where f: is the CD-ROM drive. Click the Continue button.

    NT Setup will copy files from the distribution media and make modifications to your system. This might take a few moments. When completed, it will return you to the Protocols page in the Network Control Panel window. You should see the AppleTalk Protocol in the list of installed protocols.

8. Click the Close button to continue. NT will review the network bindings information and start the AppleTalk protocol so you can configure it. The Microsoft AppleTalk Protocol Properties window will appear, as shown in Figure 9.52.

9. Choose the Default Adapter and Default Zone for your NT Workstation.

   Your network adapter should be listed in the Default Adapter list. If you have more than one network adapter, the default adapter should be listed. If you have any third-party utilities that allow your NT Workstation to take advantage of the AppleTalk protocol, this is the adapter they will be bound to.

   Additionally, if you have an AppleTalk router on the network, the default AppleTalk zone should appear in the Default Zone. For most uses, this is really pretty unimportant, because NT Workstations do not publish services by default. However, if you have any third-party utilities that enable your NT Workstation to publish services to the AppleTalk network, this is the zone where they will appear.

10. Click OK to continue. A message will appear telling you that the AppleTalk protocol has been configured.

11. Click OK. You will be prompted to restart your computer.

12. Click Yes to initiate a system restart.

When the system restarts, the AppleTalk protocol will be fully installed and you will be able to use the Server Manager utility to manage NT Servers running Services for Macintosh.

Additionally, you can use the Add Printer Wizard or the Print Manager to create a local printer that can be used to print directly to an AppleTalk printer on the network.

NOTE

The MACFILE.EXE command-line utility will not be installed on the NT Workstation. If you want to use this utility to administer remote NT Servers running Services for Macintosh, you can copy the MACFILE.EXE executable from an NT Server with Services for Macintosh installed onto the NT Workstation.

Using the MACFILE Command-Line Utility

When you install Services for Macintosh, you also get a command-line utility called MACFILE.EXE. This utility performs four major functions. While three of these can be done from a graphical front end, with the MacFile Control Panel applet, or with the Server Manager, the fourth function, FORKIZE, can only be done through the MACFILE utility. Additionally, it's nice to have a command-line tool for appropriate tasks, such as writing batch files.

NOTE

Even if you're not interested in command-line utilities, look at MACFILE FORKIZE. This command has no graphical equivalent, and deserves careful attention.

One of the additional benefits of the MACFILE command is that it enables you to configure remote NT Servers running Services for Macintosh.

The MACFILE utility is broken down into four basic commands:

- MACFILE VOLUME
- MACFILE DIRECTORY
- MACFILE SERVER
- MACFILE FORKIZE

MACFILE VOLUME

The MACFILE VOLUME command enables you to add, remove, or change network-accessible Macintosh volumes.

The syntax for the MACFILE VOLUME command is

```
macfile volume /add [/server:\\computername] /name:volumename /path:directory
[/readonly:[true ¦ false]] [/guestsallowed:[true ¦ false]] [/password:password]
[/maxusers:number ¦ unlimited]

macfile volume /remove [/server:\\computername] /name:volumename

macfile volume /set [/server:\\computername] /name:volumename /path:directory
[/readonly:[true ¦ false]] [/guestsallowed:[true ¦ false]] [/password:password]
[/maxusers:number ¦ unlimited]
```

Parameters:

/add—Specifies that you want to add a Macintosh-accessible volume.

/remove—Specifies that you want to remove a Macintosh-accessible volume.

/set—Specifies that you want to change options on an already existing Macintosh-accessible volume.

/server:\\computername—Specifies the name of the NT Server running Services for Macintosh that you wish to administer. If this switch is omitted, changes will be made to the local computer.

/name:volumename—Specifies the name of the Macintosh-accessible volume you wish to create, remove, or modify. This can be between 1 and 27 characters and should be enclosed in quotation marks if it contains any spaces or special characters.

/path:directory—Specifies the path to the directory to be shared on the AppleTalk network. Only include this when creating a new share.

/readonly:[true ¦ false]—If true, users cannot make changes to any files located on the volume, regardless of additional rights given to them on particular folders within the volume. If false, user access to particular files is determined on a folder-by-folder basis. If this switch is not included when creating a volume, changes to the volume will be permitted (readonly=false).

/guestsallowed:[true ¦ false]—If set to true, Macintosh users can connect to the volume as a guest. If false, users will not be able to connect to the volume as a guest. When creating a new volume, the default is for guests to be able to log on (guestsallowed=true). Note: This is independent of the Windows NT guest user account. For more information on this, see the "Understanding Macintosh Guest Logons" section from earlier in this chapter.

/password:*password*—Specifies that users need to enter a password when connecting to this volume. If you don't use this switch, all access control is based on their user accounts and users will not be required to type an additional password when logging on. Using this option along with /guestsallowed:true enables you to effectively create a resource with share-level permissions, instead of user-level permissions.

/maxusers:*number* ¦ unlimited—By using this switch, you can restrict the number of users that can connect to a particular share. If you don't specify this switch when creating a volume, there is no limit placed on the number of users who can connect.

MACFILE DIRECTORY

The MACFILE DIRECTORY command is used to set the owner, group, and permission information on a directory in a Macintosh-accessible volume.

The syntax for the MACFILE DIRECTORY command is

```
macfile directory [/server:\\computername] /path:directory [/owner:ownername]
[/group:groupname] [/permissions:permissions]
```

Parameters:

/server:*computername*—Specifies the name of the NT Server running Services for Macintosh that you wish to administer. If this switch is omitted, changes will be made to the local computer.

/path:*directory*—Specifies the path to the directory in a Macintosh-accessible volume where you want to modify permissions, owner, or group information. Remember, Macintosh file permissions are designated on a per-folder, not a per-file, basis.

/owner:*ownername*—Specifies the new owner of the folder. If you omit this switch, the ownership will not change.

/group:*groupname*—Specifies the new primary group for the folder. If you omit this switch, the primary group will not change.

/permissions:permissions—This switch indicated the permissions to be set on the specified folder. With this switch you can set standard Macintosh folder permissions, which include the ability to see files, see folders, and make changes. You can set each of these options for the Owner,

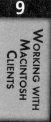

the Primary Group, and Everyone (also called world). In addition, this switch can be used to designate that the folder cannot be renamed, moved, or deleted. You can specify that the changes should be applied to all subdirectories within the specified directory. This switch is used by specifying an 11-digit string of ones (1) and zeros (0). A one (1) is used to grant the permission, and a zero (0) is used to revoke the permission, following this pattern:

Position	Permission
1xxxxxxxxx	Allows the Owner to see files
x1xxxxxxxx	Allows the Owner to see folders
xx1xxxxxxx	Allows the Owner to make changes
xxx1xxxxxx	Allows the Primary Group to see files
xxxx1xxxxx	Allows the Primary Group to see folders
xxxxx1xxxx	Allows the Primary Group to make changes
xxxxxx1xxx	Allows Everyone to see files
xxxxxxx1xx	Allows Everyone to see folders
xxxxxxxx1x	Allows Everyone to make changes
xxxxxxxxx1x	Specifies that the directory cannot be renamed, moved, or deleted
xxxxxxxxxx1	Specifies that changes should be applied to the current directory and to all subdirectories

MACFILE SERVER

The `MACFILE SERVER` option enables you to change default server configurations, such as the server's name as it appears on the AppleTalk network, guest access permissions, and the maximum number of users.

```
macfile server [/server:\\computername] [/maxsessions:number ¦ unlimited]
[/loginmessage:message] [/guestsallowed:[true ¦ false]]
```

Parameters:

`/server:\\computername`—Specifies the name of the NT Server running Services for Macintosh that you wish to administer. If this switch is omitted, changes will be made to the local computer.

`/maxsessions:number ¦ unlimited`—Specifies the maximum number of Macintosh users that can be simultaneously connected to the server.

`/loginmessage:message`—Specifies a message that will be sent to Macintosh clients when they connect to the NT Server. This is supported by all AppleShare 2.1 clients and greater (includes all System 7 clients). If left blank, no message is sent to clients when they connect.

/guestsallowed:[true ¦ false]—Specifies whether or not Macintosh clients can connect as guests. If this parameter is set to true, guests are able to connect to Macintosh-accessible volumes. However, you can restrict guest access to volumes on a volume-by-volume basis by using the MACFILE VOLUME command. Additionally, if this switch is set to false, *all* Macintosh guest access will be denied, regardless of the settings on individual volumes. By default, Macintosh computers can connect as guests. Note: This is independent of the Windows NT guest user account. For more information on this, see the "Understanding Macintosh Guest Logons" section from earlier in this chapter.

MACFILE FORKIZE

The MACFILE FORKIZE can be used to join two separate files together into a single Macintosh file with a data fork and a resource fork. Additionally, it can be used to set the file's creator and type information.

> **NOTE**
>
> The true usefulness of this command is in its capability to set the file's creator and type information. While the capability to join two separate files together into a single Macintosh file is useful, most people will not need it.

```
macfile forkize [/server:\\computername] [/creator:creatorname] [/type:typename]
[/datafork:filepath] [/resourcefork:filepath] /targetfile:filepath
```

Parameters:

/server:*computername*—Specifies the name of the NT Server running Services for Macintosh that you wish to administer. If this switch is omitted, changes will be made to the local computer.

/creator:*creatorname*—This specifies the program that was used to create the file. When a Macintosh user double-clicks a file in the Finder, the creator information is used to determine what program to start. It can be up to four characters. Every company that writes software for the Macintosh is required to register their creator code with Apple to ensure its uniqueness.

/type:*typename*—This specifies exactly what the file is. This helps the program that is called by double-clicking the file to determine how to handle the file.

/datafork:*filepath*—Specifies the name of the file you want to use as the data fork.

/resourcefork:*filepath*—Specifies the name of the file you want to use as the resource fork.

/targetfile:*filepath*—If you are joining two files into a single Macintosh file, this specifies the name of the file you want to create by combining the resource and data forks. If you don't specify the /datafork and /resourcefork switches, this is the file whose information you are modifying. This file must reside on an NTFS volume on the server specified by the /server switch.

Shortcomings and Problems

If you read through this chapter and the rest of the book, you will catch glimpses of where I point out the limitations of Services for Macintosh. I thought this was important enough for people to understand, however, so I created this section to bring them together in one place.

Some of these limitations are because of a lack of features, and others are just things to be aware of. They are as follows:

- **NT Server cannot read Macintosh CD-ROMs.** Although you can create a Macintosh-accessible volume on a Windows CD-ROM, NT is completely unable to read Macintosh CD-ROMs. This is because most Windows CD-ROMs use the ISO 9660 format, whereas most Macintosh CD-ROMs use the High Sierra format.

- **NT RAS does not support dial-in AppleTalk clients.** The standard remote networking for Macintosh clients is AppleTalk Remote Access (ARA). This is not, however, supported at this time by NT Server. Macintosh clients can, though, dial into an NT Server using TCP/IP over PPP. This usually requires a third-party add-on such as MacPPP. When Macintosh clients dial in using this method, however, they cannot access the Macintosh volumes on the NT Server because this requires the AppleTalk protocol. Microsoft expects to have ARA support in NT Server soon.

- **The Microsoft UAM is not fully integrated with the MacOS.** If you use the Microsoft UAM, you cannot take full advantage of aliases in System 7.x. This can be an extreme inconvenience to Macintosh users. This is discussed at greater length earlier in this chapter.

- **Services for Macintosh requires an NTFS partition.** In order to install Services for Macintosh, you need an NTFS partition. This is because the installation process creates a Macintosh-accessible network volume that contains the Microsoft UAM. Due to the dual-fork nature of Macintosh files, they cannot be stored on a FAT or HPFS partition.

- **AppleTalk printers do not support user authentication.** Under Windows NT, you can restrict access to printers based on a person's user account. However, the AppleTalk Printer Access Protocol (PAP) does not provide authenticated information on the user who submitted the print job. Additionally, by default Macintosh clients can print to *any* printer created on the NT Server. With Macintosh clients, all print jobs are submitted using the built-in SYSTEM account. This means that you cannot control printer access for individual Macintosh users.

- **Using NT as a PostScript interpreter is limited.** One of the most amazing features about Windows NT is that it can enable clients to send PostScript jobs to any NT printer, even printers that don't understand PostScript. While this is a great feature for Macintosh clients, because the standard laser printer driver is PostScript, there are limitations. Probably the most obvious is that when NT converts the PostScript code into a bitmapped image that can be printed to any printer, it does so at 300 dpi. Until recently, this might not have been a real problem, but today, with even the cheapest laser printers supporting 600 dpi, the difference is noticeable. If print output is of high concern, be sure to use a real PostScript printer.

- **Macintosh guest access is unrelated to the guest user account.** Even if you have the NT guest account disabled, Macintosh users can still access Macintosh-accessible volumes as guests. For more information on this, see the section "Understanding Macintosh Guest Logons," earlier in this chapter.

- **Services for Macintosh allows for a breach in NT file security.** Although by its very nature NT is not supposed to allow you to assign ownership of files to other users, there is a way around this. If Services for Macintosh is installed, an NT user can use the Macintosh permissions to assign ownership of files to a different user, which is normally *not* permitted. For more information on this, see Chapter 28, "Advanced Security Guidelines."

Summary

This chapter discussed using Windows NT Server as a complete server solution for networks with Macintosh clients. We looked at the core Macintosh services provided by NT Server, including the ability to act as an AFP-compliant file server, as well as providing Macintosh print services and native AppleTalk routing.

We looked at the structure of a Macintosh file and how it differs from a standard PC file. In addition, we looked at how NT Server provides on-the-fly translation of long filenames for Macintosh clients. We continued by looking at the Macintosh AFP permission structure for restricting access to network resources, as well as the differences between a Macintosh guest user and a PC guest user.

The chapter continued with a step-by-step installation guide for Services for Macintosh, including a guide to setting up AppleTalk printing. We also took a look at how and when to set up AppleTalk routing by looking at two common network scenarios.

We also took a close look at the Microsoft User Authentication Module (MS UAM) and how it can be used to strengthen the security of your network. We also saw that the MS UAM has some pitfalls that prevent Macintosh users from performing certain functions.

Next, we looked at tools that are used to administer Services for Macintosh, such as the File Manager, the Administrative Wizard, the MacFile Control Panel applet, the Print Manager, and the MACFILE command-line utility. Included in this discussion was information on administering Services for Macintosh from a remote NT Server, as well as NT Workstations.

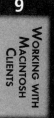

9

WORKING WITH
MACINTOSH
CLIENTS

Finally, the chapter ended with a look at some of the limits of NT Server's Services for Macintosh. While NT provides a robust and powerful server platform for supporting Macintosh clients, it can't do everything, and it is important to understand the limitations.

Installing and Configuring Microsoft TCP/IP

by Jason Garms

IN THIS CHAPTER

For many people coming from a background steeped in DOS and Windows, TCP/IP might still remain something of a mystery. Traditionally, DOS and Windows people only had to deal with TCP/IP when accessing services from a larger network, such as accessing a corporate UNIX system or even connecting to the Internet. Often, configuring the system involves using addresses and numbers that are provided by some other organization, such as InterNIC, or maybe the group responsible for your company's network backbone.

With Microsoft's recent recognition of the importance of TCP/IP and its push to provide all services over a TCP/IP protocol stack, TCP/IP is becoming more and more common in the Windows environment. You can now run a Windows-based network with TCP/IP as the only transport protocol. This is made possible by the availability of the fast and robust TCP/IP stacks that Microsoft provides with Windows for Workgroups, Windows 95, and Windows NT. With this strong support for TCP/IP, it becomes even more important for anyone designing or administering a Windows-based network to understand how TCP/IP works and how it can benefit your network.

> **NOTE**
>
> TCP/IP is continuing to grow in importance for Windows NT networking. With the tighter integration with Internet technologies, such as the World Wide Web, as well as increased support for open standards, Microsoft has made a firm commitment to the TCP/IP protocol. When the next generation of directory services for Windows NT is released with the next version of Windows NT, you will need to use the TCP/IP protocol to take full advantage of these advanced directory services. Smaller environments that do not want to use or cannot use TCP/IP will still be able to use NetBEUI or NWLink—Microsoft's IPX/SPX-compatible protocol.
>
> However, to take advantage of all the features of the new directory service, you will need TCP/IP.

This chapter begins with a discussion of TCP/IP on the Windows NT platform. This includes a discussion of how this TCP/IP integration enhances connectivity with Windows for Workgroups and Windows 95 clients. The chapter continues with an explanation of how to install and configure TCP/IP on Windows NT Server. I have included additional sections to discuss many of the optional TCP/IP-related services. Some TCP/IP-related services (such as WINS, DHCP, DNS, and TCP/IP printing) are important and substantial enough to warrant their own chapters.

Preparing to Install the TCP/IP Protocol

Before installing TCP/IP on your NT Server, let's take a few minutes to identify some of the things that will be required during the configuration process.

If you will be using DHCP for TCP/IP configuration, you won't need much information. However, if you won't be using DHCP, you need the following:

- The IP address and subnet mask for each network card onto which you will bind TCP/IP. If you want to configure any adapters as logically multihomed (multiple IP addresses for a single adapter), you also need any additional IP addresses and subnet masks.

- The IP addresses of the default gateway and any backup gateways for each network card onto which you will bind TCP/IP.

- The IP addresses for any Domain Name System (DNS) servers you will be using. In addition, if your computer is part of an IP domain, you need the full name of the IP domain (such as xyzcorp.com or USAcollege.edu).

- If you will be accessing a WINS server to obtain NetBIOS naming information, you need the IP address for the primary and, if available, secondary WINS servers.

In addition to this information, you might want to think about which IP-related services you want to install. The following is a list of additional TCP/IP-based services that can be installed after you install the TCP/IP stack:

- DHCP Relay Agent
- DHCP Server
- DNS Server
- Internet Information Server
- TCP/IP Printing
- RIP for Internet Protocol
- Simple TCP/IP Services
- SNMP Service
- WINS Server

Installing the TCP/IP Protocol on Windows NT

You can install TCP/IP during the NT Server installation process or add it later. In either case, the installation process is essentially identical. The follow set of procedures specifically details how to install TCP/IP on an existing NT Server.

> **NOTE**
>
> If you are installing a domain controller, you will need to install at least one network adapter and a transport protocol in order to complete the setup process.

> **NOTE**
>
> Make sure you are logged on to the server with an account that has administrative permissions.

1. Open the Control Panel, and double-click the Network icon. The Network window will appear, similar to that shown in Figure 10.1.

FIGURE 10.1.

The Network Control Panel permits you to change network-related configuration information.

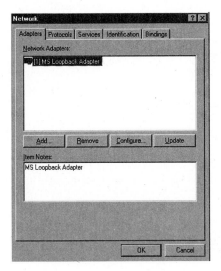

2. Click the Protocols tab. The list will show any currently installed network protocols. The Network Protocols dialog is shown in Figure 10.2.
3. Click the Add button. Windows NT will build a list of all available network protocols and display these in a new window, shown in Figure 10.3.
4. Select the TCP/IP Protocol and click OK.
5. You will now be asked if there is a DHCP server on your network and if you want to get your TCP/IP address automatically from this server. This message is shown in Figure 10.4.

    In this example, you should choose No. If, however, you were configuring a Windows NT Server and you did want it to dynamically obtain its IP address from a DHCP server, you would choose Yes.
6. You might be required to provide a path to the Windows NT Server distribution media so that Windows NT can install the necessary software components. If you are using a local CD-ROM, indicate the drive letter and path. If you are installing from a

network, indicate the UNC location (for example, \\NTSERVER1\NT40INST\i386) of
the Windows NT Server distribution files. Click OK once you have identified a valid
Windows NT distribution media set.

Windows NT will copy files from the distribution media to the local system directory.

FIGURE 10.2.

*The Network Protocols
dialog shows the
currently installed
network protocols.*

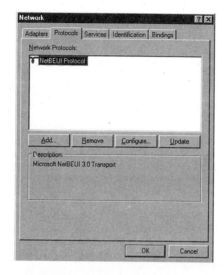

FIGURE 10.3.

*The Select Network
Protocol dialog lists all
available network
protocols that you can
install.*

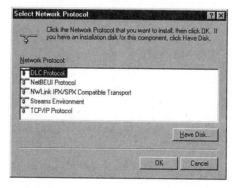

FIGURE 10.4.

*You can specify if you
want to act as a DHCP
client.*

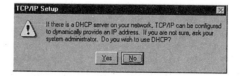

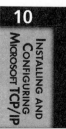

7. You will be returned to the Protocols tab of the Network window. You should see TCP/IP Protocol listed in the Network Protocols list, as shown in Figure 10.5.

Figure 10.5.

TCP/IP will appear in the Network Protocols list.

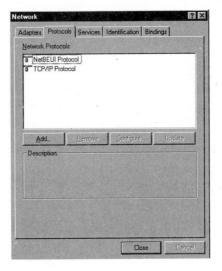

8. Click the Close button at the bottom of the Network window.

Windows NT will go through an automatic process to review the bindings on the network adapter. Windows NT will display the Microsoft TCP/IP Properties window so you can provide specific TCP/IP configuration information, which is necessary to complete the binding. The Microsoft TCP/IP Properties window is shown in Figure 10.6.

Figure 10.6.

Microsoft TCP/IP Properties page is used to configure the TCP/IP settings.

9. If your system is multihomed (you have more than one network adapter in your system), you can use the Adapter pick list to select the adapter you want to configure.

   If you chose in step 5 to use a DHCP server to acquire your TCP/IP information, the Obtain an IP address from a DHCP server option will be selected. The IP Address, Subnet Mask, and Default Gateway text boxes will be grayed out.

10. You should enter the IP address, subnet mask, and default gateway for your network card into the appropriate text boxes.

11. This is the minimal amount of information you need to provide to get your system up and running with TCP/IP. Click OK at the bottom of the Microsoft TCP/IP Properties window. Windows NT will complete the adapter binding process and tell you that you need to restart your computer before your changes can take effect.

Advanced TCP/IP Options

The Advanced TCP/IP settings option under the Microsoft TCP/IP Properties window allows you to configure your multiple IP addresses for a single network card or to specify multiple IP gateways for each network card in your system.

Logically Multihomed Adapter

Configuring more than one IP address for a single network card is known as configuring a logically mulihomed network adapter. Windows NT allows you to assign multiple IP addresses to a single network adapter. (I've done as many as 40 IP addresses on a single system.) This is known as a logically multihomed network adapter. Compare this to what is traditionally called a multihomed system, where you have multiple physical network interfaces on a system, each with its own unique IP address. There are advantages and disadvantages to a logically multihomed configuration.

One of the advantages of a logically multihomed system is very apparent when used in conjunction with the Internet Information Server (IIS) that is included with NT Server 4.0. IIS can be configured to respond to a default Hypertext Transfer Protocol (HTTP) request in different ways, depending on which one of the logically multihomed IP addresses is accessed. If you want to run three Web sites from your server, logical multihoming makes this easier and cleaner. For instance, if you wanted to host xyzcorp.com, USAcollege.edu, and greenfood.com from your server, you would simply designate a different IP address for each site and then bind all three IP addresses to a single network adapter. Then when someone uses a Web browser to connect to xyzcorp.com, he or she will get the home page for xyzcorp; if connecting to USAcollege.edu, the user will get the default page for USAcollege.

The disadvantage of using logically multihomed adapters is that NetBIOS over TCP/IP (NetBT) will only be bound to the first IP address of a logically multihomed adapter. If you want multihomed support with NetBT, you need to install multiple network adapters with a single IP address bound to each adapter.

Multiple IP Gateways

If you need to use TCP/IP to communicate with a computer outside of your subnet, the communication needs to be done through an IP gateway. Many smaller LANs include only a single gateway between subnets. However, for additional levels of fault tolerance, many larger and more stable networks are designed with multiple IP gateways between their major subnets.

Windows NT enables you to take advantage of these multiple gateways to provide fault tolerance in case the default gateway becomes unavailable. For each network card onto which you bind TCP/IP, you can also specify as many backup gateways as you have available. When you specify additional IP gateways, if the default gateway fails, Windows NT uses a mechanism called Dead Gateway Detection to determine when to switch to a secondary gateway. This is enabled by default in Windows NT 4.0.

Dead Gateway Detection in Windows NT is done with the TCP protocol. If, after several attempts, the default gateway doesn't respond to TCP requests, Windows NT decides that the gateway must be dead and automatically switches to a backup gateway. Windows NT implements the Dead Gateway Detection process, described in RFC 816.

> **NOTE**
>
> It is important to note that Dead Gateway Detection only works with TCP packets, not with UDP or Internet Control Message Protocol (ICMP) packets. This means that a failed ping attempt will not trigger the Dead Gateway Detect feature because ping uses ICMP packets.

Under certain circumstances, the Dead Gateway Detection process can fail to restore Windows NT to the original gateway when the original gateway comes back online. This is because Windows NT expects that the network routers (gateways) will inform it when the default route should change again. This requires the use of an intelligent (dynamic) routing protocol, such as Routing Information Protocol (RIP).

The following is a summary of what happens when Dead Gateway Detection works correctly. The failed gateway does not respond to TCP requests from the Windows NT system. After a number of retries, Windows NT automatically switches to a backup default gateway, as configured in the Microsoft TCP/IP configuration on the Windows NT system. When the failed gateway comes back online, it notifies the other gateways via an intelligent routing protocol, such as RIP, that it is back online. The next time Windows NT tries to use the backup gateway, the backup gateway notifies Windows NT via an ICMP redirect that the correct default gateway is back online. Then Windows NT can begin using the correct default gateway again.

If there is no intelligent, dynamic routing protocol in use, Windows NT will have no way of detecting when the default gateway is back in service. It will continue using the alternative gateway until Windows NT is restarted or the alternative gateway goes down.

The current default gateway can be verified by issuing the `ipconfig/all` command at the Windows NT command prompt.

PPTP Filtering

Windows NT 4.0 includes a new technology called Point-to-Point Tunneling Protocol (PPTP), which allows you to create multiprotocol virtual private networks (VPNs). PPTP uses Windows NT Remote Access Service (RAS) to communicate with another RAS/PPTP-enabled NT Server. PPTP establishes a connection over the network instead of the usual RAS dial-up modem-to-modem connection.

PPTP filtering is an important security feature in that it enables you to prevent your system from responding to any non-PPTP traffic on the network, thus isolating it from the "public" network it is physically connected to. This reduces the risk of somebody attacking your local network through a Windows NT Server acting as a PPTP gateway.

TCP/IP Security

One of the new features of Windows NT 4.0 is the ability to filter network traffic by TCP or UDP port number, as well as IP protocol value. This allows you to control the type of TCP/IP traffic that your server will respond to, providing a higher level of security. For instance, if you were running a SQL Server on your system, you might want to permit access only to the ports to which your databases listen.

The filtering mechanism built into TCP/IP with Windows NT 4.0 is not very configurable. However, if you need more control over TCP/IP filtering, you can install the new multiprotocol upgrade for Windows NT (codenamed Steelhead). This will greatly extend the kind of filters you can establish. For example, with the new multiprotocol upgrade, you will be able to filter on individual source and destination addresses for either incoming or outgoing packets, or for both. Additionally, it will permit an individual set of filters for each logical network interface.

Configuring Advanced TCP/IP Options

If you need to configure additional IP addresses or IP gateways once TCP/IP is installed, use the following procedure:

1. Make sure you are logged on as an administrative user.
2. Double-click the Network icon in the Control Panel. This will display the Network window.
3. Click the Protocols tab and then double-click TCP/IP Protocol. This will display the Microsoft TCP/IP Properties window.
4. Click the Advanced button located in the bottom-right corner of the window. This will bring up the Advanced IP Addressing window, shown in Figure 10.7.

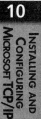

10

INSTALLING AND
CONFIGURING
MICROSOFT TCP/IP

FIGURE 10.7.

Advanced IP
Addressing allows you
to enter multiple IP
addresses or gateway
addresses, as well as
enable TCP/IP security.

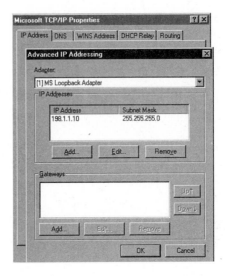

5. If you have multiple physical network adapters, you can use the Adapter pick list to choose the adapter you want to configure.

6. Use the Add button in the IP Addresses window to add additional IP address and subnet mask pairs for the current network adapter.

7. Use the Add button in the Gateways group to add any additional IP gateways that are available on your network.

8. If you are using PPTP and want to restrict network access to PPTP only, select the Enable PPTP Filtering option.

9. If you want to do IP or port-level filtering, select the Enable Security option, and then click the Configure button. This brings up the TCP/IP Security window as shown in Figure 10.8.

FIGURE 10.8.

Use the TCP/IP
Security Window to
restrict access based on
TCP, UDP, or IP
protocol information.

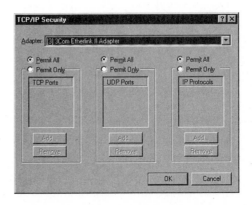

10. If you want to enable only certain TCP or UDP ports, select the Permit Only option above the appropriate field, and then click the Add button to add the TCP or UDP port addresses you want to allow. Valid TCP and UDP port addresses are between 1 and 65535.

11. If you want to enable only certain IP protocols, select the Permit Only option above the IP Protocols field, and then click the Add button to add the IP protocol values you want to allow. Valid IP protocol values are between 1 and 255.

12. When you have finished entering the filtering information, click the OK button to return to the Advanced IP Addressing window.

13. Click OK to return to the Microsoft TCP/IP Properties window, and then OK again to return to the Network Control Panel. Click OK one more time to exit the Network Control Panel. You will be prompted to restart the server.

Once the system has restarted, the changes you made will take effect.

Configuring Windows NT to Use an Existing DNS Server

You will want to configure your Windows NT Server to take advantage of the DNS servers in your organization or if you are connected to the Internet.

> **NOTE**
>
> There are so many acronyms in the computer industry, it's difficult to keep them all straight. A commonly mistaken acronym is DNS. Many people think it stands for Domain Name *Server* or Domain Name *Service*, when in fact it stands for Domain Name *System*. The "ultimate" authority is Request for Comments (RFC) 1034 and 1035, where DNS is defined.

The following set of procedures explains how to configure the items in the DNS tab of the Microsoft TCP/IP Properties window:

1. Make sure you are logged on as an administrative user.

2. Double-click the Network icon in the Control Panel. This displays the Network window.

3. Click the Protocols tab and then double-click TCP/IP Protocol. This displays the Microsoft TCP/IP Properties window.

4. Click the DNS tab. This displays the DNS configuration options for TCP/IP, shown in Figure 10.9.

FIGURE 10.9.

DNS options for TCP/IP properties.

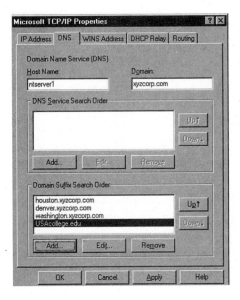

5. Enter the TCP/IP DNS *hostname* and the DNS *domain name* into the appropriate fields. By default, the computer's name as registered with the NT domain is automatically entered into the Host Name field.

NOTE

A common problem point is that people don't understand how the computer name and domain information entered into this screen differ from the computer and domain information entered when Windows NT was installed. Here are some tips:

- There are two name resolution processes at work here: the Windows/NetBIOS naming process and the DNS naming process. You should make every effort to use the same name here as the name registered for your system with the Windows NT domain.

- You should make sure the name registered with the DNS for the IP address you are using is the same as the name you typed into the *Host Name* field. You can ping the root name server and request the A records for the IP address in question. This record is retrieved using the ping -a command to verify the hostname on the DNS. For more information on the ping command, see the section titled "Diagnostic Utilities" later in this chapter.

- The domain name entered into the Domain field is the DNS domain name for your network. This is *rarely* the same as the Windows NT domain. Typically it is something such as xyzcorp.com or campus1.USAcollege.edu.

For more information on this topic, see Chapter 13, "Domain Name Service (DNS)".

6. If you are using a DNS server on your network, use the Add button to add the address of the DNS server. You can specify up to three DNS servers. Use the up and down arrows to change the order in which they are queried. The way this works is if the first DNS fails to properly resolve a name, Windows NT will try the second DNS, and finally the third.

7. You can also specify default domain suffixes by adding them to the list at the bottom of the window. You can assign up to six default domain suffixes. For instance, you might configure the domain suffix search order as shown in Figure 10.10.

FIGURE 10.10.

The domain suffix search order.

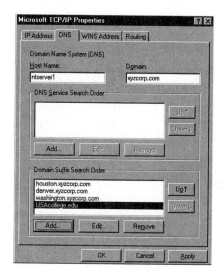

Given this setup, if you typed `ping server1` at the command prompt, NT would first try to locate a machine called `server1.xyzcorp.com` because `xyzcorp.com` is the DNS domain. If a machine by this name is not found, it would try `server1.houston.xyzcorp.com`, `server1.denver.xyzcorp.com`, `server1.washington.xyzcorp.com`, and finally `server1.USAcollege.edu` until a valid machine is found. If no machine is found at this point, you will get an error message.

Windows Internet Name Service (WINS) Address Configuration

The WINS Address tab in the Microsoft TCP/IP Properties window allows you to configure your NT system to take advantage of any WINS servers available on the network. Additionally, it provides more methods of Windows name resolution, such as using DNS for Windows name lookups and lmhosts files.

If you want to configure any of these options on your system, use the following set of procedures:

1. Make sure you are logged on as an administrative user.

2. Double-click the Network icon in the Control Panel. This displays the Network window.

3. Click the Protocols tab and then double-click TCP/IP Protocol. This displays the Microsoft TCP/IP Properties window.

4. Click the WINS Address tab. This displays the WINS configuration options for TCP/IP, shown in Figure 10.11.

Figure 10.11.

WINS configuration options.

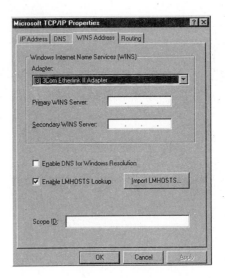

5. Windows NT allows you to specify different primary and secondary WINS servers for each network card on which TCP/IP is configured. If you have only one network card installed, it will appear by default in the Adapter pick list. If you have more than one adapter, you can use the pick list to select which network card you are currently configuring.

   Enter the IP addresses for the primary and secondary WINS servers on your network.

6. Check the Enable DNS for Windows Name Resolution option box if you want to use a DNS server to provide resolution for NetBIOS names.

   In order for this function to work, you must have your system configured to use at least one DNS server. See the "Configuring Windows NT to Use an Existing DNS Server" section earlier in this chapter for information about setting up Windows NT to use DNS servers.

7. If you want to use an lmhosts file for Windows name resolution, check the box Enable LMHOSTS Lookup. You can use the Import LMHOSTS button to import an existing lmhosts file. The lmhosts file is located in the `%SystemRoot%\system32\drivers\etc` directory. By default, this file does not exist, but Microsoft does provide a sample file called `Lmhosts.sam` as a template for creating your own.

8. If your network uses NetBIOS scopes for limiting NetBIOS traffic over TCP/IP, you can enter the scope into the `Scope ID` field. Typically, this field is left blank. The NetBIOS scope is a string that is appended to the computer's NetBIOS name. You can communicate only with computers that have the same NetBIOS scope as your system. The NetBIOS scope allows you to effectively have two physical computers on the network with the same NetBIOS name because the NetBIOS name is actually a concatenation of the computer's name and its NetBIOS scope. Most networks do *not* use NetBIOS scopes. Do not confuse this with DHCP scopes; they are unrelated.

> **NOTE**
>
> From the TCP/IP Properties window, you used to be able to enable Windows NT as a WINS proxy agent. However, because too many people didn't understand what this meant and enabled it, Microsoft removed the option from the GUI in the final release of NT 4. Improperly configuring WINS proxy agents can have a serious, negative impact on your network. In order to enable the WINS proxy agent, you must now set a Registry entry.

Enabling IP Routing

Windows NT Server has always supported static IP routing (IP forwarding) on multihomed systems. Until the 4.0 release, it was capable of only *static* IP routing. This allowed you to configure Windows NT to work with other static IP routers on the network. Under this configuration, you needed to use the `route` command to create static routes. However, with Windows NT Server 4.0, Microsoft includes an RIP agent that allows Windows NT Server to perform dynamic routing using the standard RIP protocol. RIP is used to collect RIP information from other routers on the network.

To configure your Windows NT Server as an IP router, use the following procedure:

1. Make sure you are logged on as an administrative user.

2. Double-click the Network icon in the Control Panel. This will display the Network window.

3. Click the Protocols tab. This will display a list of currently installed network services.

4. Double-click TCP/IP Protocol. This will bring up the Microsoft TCP/IP Properties page. Then click on the IP Routing tab. The IP Routing tab is shown in Figure 10.12.

FIGURE 10.12.

Enabling static IP routing.

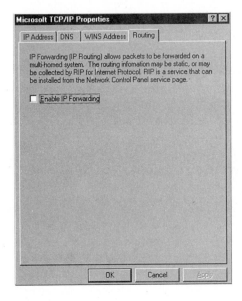

5. If you want to enable static IP routing (IP forwarding), click the Enable IP Forwarding option box.

6. Click OK. This returns you to the Network Control Panel window.

If you also want to enable dynamic RIP routing, you must install the RIP for Internet Protocol service. Continue with the following procedure to install this service as well:

1. Click the Services tab. This will display a list of all the currently installed services.

2. Click the Add button. Windows NT will generate a list of all available services for installation.

3. Scroll down the list and click the RIP for Internet Protocol entry, shown in Figure 10.13.

4. Click OK.

5. You might be required to provide a path to the Windows NT Server distribution media so that Windows NT can install the necessary software components.

   Windows NT will copy files from the distribution media to the local system directory.

   Once NT has finished copying the necessary files, you will be returned to the Network window.

6. From the Network Control Panel window, click the Close button. Any changes you made will not take effect until you restart your system. You will be asked if you want to restart your system.

FIGURE 10.13.
Selecting the RIP for
Internet Protocol entry.

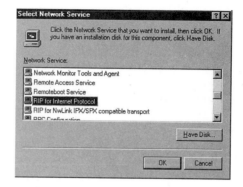

Installing Simple TCP/IP Services

Windows NT includes an optional service called Simple TCP/IP Services. This service allows Windows NT to respond to a number of network utilities that are found in the UNIX world. These include Character Generator, Daytime, and Quote of the day.

Simple TCP/IP services are all based on the UDP protocol and provide support for the following:

■ **Chargen**: When the chargen (character generator) service receives any input, it generates and returns a stream of data and sends it back to the sender. There is no relationship between the data received by the chargen service and the data it returns to the sender, although the data is usually a recognizable pattern. The use of chargen is defined in RFC 864.

■ **Daytime**: When this service receives input, it (defined in RFC 867) returns the current date and time.

■ **Discard**: This service accepts any incoming data and then throws it away. It does not return anything to the sender. Discard is defined in RFC 863.

■ **Echo**: Echo is defined in RFC 862. It takes UDP packets directed at it and returns them to the sender.

> **NOTE**
>
> Although it might seem that the ping diagnostic utility would probably use the Echo service, it does not. You do not need to install the Echo service to support ping. The Echo service uses UDP packets and operates at a much higher level than ping, which uses ICMP packets.

■ **Quote**: Quote is a quote-of-the-day service. When the quote service receives an incoming packet, it discards this packet and then returns a quote from a predefined quote file. The default quote file is installed in `%SystemRoot%\system32\drivers\etc`. This file can be modified to add new quotes so long as the quotes are less than 512 characters. The quote utility is defined in RFC 865.

Diagnostic Utilities

Microsoft has included a number of TCP/IP diagnostic utilities with Windows NT. Many of these utilities, such as `ping` and `tracert`, are functionally identical to common implementations on other platforms, including most UNIX systems. Other utilities, such as `nbtstat`, are more specific to Windows environments and do not have direct analogues on non-Windows systems.

All the diagnostic utilities listed in this section were automatically installed when you installed TCP/IP on your system. They are all located in the `%SystemRoot%\system32` directory.

arp

The `arp` command is used to display or modify the IP address to physical network address lookup table maintained by Windows NT. This table is called the address resolution protocol (ARP) table.

The syntax for the `arp` command is

```
arp -a [IP_addr] [-N [if_addr]]
arp -d IP_addr [if_addr]
arp -s IP_addr mac_addr [if_addr]
```

-a displays the current ARP table. If *inet_addr* is included, the IP and physical addresses for only the specified computer are displayed. If there is more than one network interface using TCP/IP, the ARP table is displayed for each.

-N *if_addr* displays the ARP entries for the network interface specified by *if_addr*.

-d deletes the ARP entry specified by *inet_addr*.

-s is used to manually add an entry in the ARP table. Typically, ARP entries age out of the table after a period of time. When you manually add an ARP entry, however, the entry will be permanent.

mac_addr specifies the physical address of the network adapter. It is represented as eight hexadecimal pairs separated by dashes.

IP_addr specifies an IP address.

if_addr indicates the address of the network adapter on which the ARP table should be updated.

hostname

The hostname command returns the name of the computer as defined in the DNS tab of the TCP/IP configuration window. There are no options to this command.

ipconfig

The ipconfig utility is useful for getting a quick look at a system's TCP/IP configuration. It is especially useful when your system receives its IP configuration from a DHCP server.

The syntax for the ipconfig command is

```
ipconfig [/all ¦ /release [adapter] ¦ renew [adapter]]
```

If you run ipconfig without any switch options, it returns the IP address, subnet mask, and default gateway for all network adapters bound with TCP/IP.

/all causes ipconfig to return additional IP configuration information for all network adapters running TCP/IP. This information includes the TCP/IP hostname, list of all DNS servers, node type, NetBIOS scope ID, state of IP routing (IP forwarding) on your system, state of WINS proxy on your system, and if your system will use DNS to provide NetBIOS name resolution. Additionally, for each network adapter using TCP/IP, it will provide the physical address of the adapter, whether or not it gets its information from a DHCP server, its IP address (or IP addresses if it's logically multihomed), its subnet mask, default gateway, and any WINS servers it uses.

/renew [adapter] is useful only when your system acquires its IP information dynamically from a DHCP server. If you use the switch without specifying an adapter, it will attempt to renew the DHCP lease for all adapters. If you only want to renew the lease for a specific network adapter, you can do that by typing its name. If you do not get your IP information from a DHCP server but you use this switch, it will return an error.

/release [adapter] is functionally the opposite of the /renew switch. If you use the switch without specifying an adapter, it will attempt to release the DHCP lease for all adapters. If you only want to release the lease for a specific network adapter, you can do that by typing its name.

nbtstat

The nbtstat command is used to display the status of NetBIOS over TCP/IP (NetBT).

The syntax for the nbtstat command is

```
nbtstat [-a hostname] [-A IP_addr] [-c] [-n] [-R] [-r] [-S] [-s] [interval]
```

-a displays the remote computer's NetBIOS name table given its NetBIOS hostname.

-A displays the remote computer's NetBIOS name table given its IP address.

10

INSTALLING AND
CONFIGURING
MICROSOFT TCP/IP

-c displays the NetBIOS name cache of the local computer, including the name and IP address for each entry.

-n displays the NetBIOS names of the local computer.

-R purges the NetBIOS name cache on the local computer and reloads the lmhosts file.

-r displays statistics for Windows name resolution. If you are using a WINS server for Windows name resolution, this option returns the number of names resolved by broadcast and the number of names resolved by a WINS server.

-S displays statistics and session information for workstation and server services. This information is listed by IP address.

-s displays statistics and session information for workstation and server services. It lists information by hostname if the IP address is listed in your Hosts file. Otherwise, it is listed by IP address.

interval, if specified, will result in nbtstat continuously redisplaying the statistics, pausing *interval* seconds between each update. If no interval is specified, the information will be displayed once.

netstat

netstat can be used to examine the statistics for all TCP, IP, and UDP connections.

The syntax for the netstat command is

netstat [-a] [-e] [-n] [-s] [-p *protocol*] [-r] [*interval*]

If you run netstat without any switch options, it displays all active TCP connections.

-a tells netstat to display all the current connections and listening ports.

-e displays the network statistics. These statistics are cumulative since the last time the computer was reset. The total number of bytes, the number of unicast and nonunicast packets, the number of discarded packets, and the number of errors are included.

-n results in (by default) netstat displaying the IP hostname and port names. This switch causes netstat to instead display the IP address and port number.

-s displays the statistics for each of the protocols, TCP, IP, ICMP, and UDP. You can combine this with the -p *protocol* option if you only want the information for a single protocol.

-p *protocol* specifies that connections and statistics should be shown only for a specific protocol. Valid values for *protocol* are TCP, UDP, IP, and ICMP.

-r causes netstat to display the active routes from the routing table.

interval results in netstat continuously updating the statistics, pausing *interval* seconds between each update. If no interval is specified, the information will be displayed once.

ping

`ping` is one of the fundamental diagnostic utilities. It can be used to verify if a host is reachable. When troubleshooting TCP/IP connectivity problems, `ping` should be the first tool to use. `ping` uses the ICMP echo packets to do its job.

The syntax for the `ping` command is

```
ping [-t] [-a] [-n count] [-l length] [-f] [-i ttl] [-v tos] [-r count]
[-s count] [[-j host_list] ¦ [-k host_list]] [-w timeout] destination_list
```

By default, `ping` sends four 64-byte ICMP packets with a one-second pause between each packet.

   `-t` indicates that `ping` should continuously send packets until you press Ctrl+C.

   `-a` is used to resolve the IP address to the DNS hostname.

   `-n` *count* indicates that `ping` should send *count* number of ICMP packets. The default is 4.

   `-l` *length* indicates the length of the ICMP packet. The content of the ICMP packet is a periodic sequence of alphabetical characters. The default packet size is 64 bytes, and the maximum is 8192. However, Ethernet networks have a maximum data size of 1512 bytes. Choosing a value larger than this causes the packets to become fragmented.

   `-f` sets the do-not-fragment flag on the packet. If you use the `-l` switch to indicate a packet size that is larger than the maximum packet size of one of the routers the packet must pass through, the packet will be returned with an error. You can use this switch along with the `-l` option to discover the largest packet you can send from your computer to a remote host without it being fragmented.

   `-i` *ttl* sets the time to live (`ttl`) field on the packets. *ttl* is the maximum number of router hops the packet can go through before being discarded. Valid values are between 1 and 255. The default is 30.

   `-v` *tos* sets the type of service field to the value specified by *tos*.

   `-r` *count* records the route of the outgoing and returning ICMP packets in the Record Route field. A minimum of 1 to a maximum of 9 hosts must be specified by *count*.

   `-s` *count* specifies the time stamp for the number of hops specified by *count*.

   `-j` *host_list* routes packets by means of the list of hosts specified by *host_list*. Consecutive hosts may be separated by intermediate gateways (loose source routed). The maximum number of hosts allowed is 9.

   `-k` *host_list* routes packets by means of the list of hosts specified by *host_list*. Consecutive hosts may not be separated by intermediate gateways (strict source routed). The maximum number of hosts permitted is 9.

   `-w` *timeout* specifies a time-out interval in milliseconds.

   destination_list specifies the remote hosts to `ping`.

route

The `route` command is used to manage the local TCP/IP route table.

The syntax for the route command is

```
route [-f] [print¦add¦delete¦change [destination] [MASK netmask] [gateway]]
```

-f flushes the routing table of all entries and resets it to its default values. If this option is not used alone, the route table is flushed before performing the other command.

print, used without *destination*, displays the entire route table. When used with *destination*, it prints the route table entry for that destination only.

add adds a permanent static route.

delete deletes the route specified by *destination*.

change modifies an existing route specified by *destination*.

destination specifies the destination in the route table and is expressed in standard IP dot notation.

MASK, if present, specifies that the next parameter is the *netmask* parameter.

netmask, when used with the add or change command, specifies the subnet mask to use for the route entry.

gateway, when used with the add or modify command, specifies the IP gateway to use when forwarding packets to *destination.*

tracert

`tracert` is an extremely useful utility that determines the path taken between your system and a target system. If you are experiencing connectivity problems, this utility can be useful for pinpointing the location of the problem.

tracert uses ICMP echo packets to accomplish its job. First, it determines the number of router hops to its destination. Then it sends a number of ICMP echo packets equal to the hop count. On the first packet, tracert sets the time to live (TTL) to 1. On each successive packet, tracert increments the TTL by 1. Each time a packet goes through a router, the router decrements the TTL by 1. When the TTL reaches 0, most routers send a message back to the sender indicating the packet has been discarded. This means the first echo packet sent (with a TTL of 1) will be returned by the first router. The second echo packet (with a TTL of 2) will be returned by the second router, and so on. The returning router's IP address is on the discard notification it returns to the packet's originator. This makes it easy to identify all the routers in the path.

The syntax for the route command is

```
tracert [-d] [-h max_hops] [-j host_list] [-w timeout] destination
```

-d specifies not to resolve IP addresses to hostnames, which is done by default.

-h *max_hops* specifies the maximum number of hops to search for *destination*.

-j *host_list* specifies the loose source route along *host_list*.

-w *timeout* specifies a time-out interval for each packet in milliseconds.

destination specifies the hostname or IP address of the destination computer.

Connectivity Utilities

Microsoft included a couple of standard TCP/IP connectivity utilities with Windows NT. These utilities include telnet, ftp, finger, and tftp.

Telnet

Windows NT includes a graphical Telnet utility that can be used to connect to any system running a standard Telnet server, as described in RFC 854. The Telnet utility can be found in the Accessories program group or can be started by typing telnet at the Run prompt.

> **NOTE**
>
> Windows NT Server does not include a Telnet server component. If you want to use Telnet to connect to your Windows NT Server, there are many third-party companies that make Telnet server components. There is also a beta version of Telnet called Telnetd in the Windows NT Resource Kit. While this freeware will work, it is not robust or tested well enough for serious Telnet use.

The Telnet application is fairly simple, but includes features such as logging the Telnet session to file, vt-100/ansi emulation, and configurable screen settings.

ftp

Windows NT includes a relatively simple, command-line ftp client. This utility can be invoked from the Run prompt or from the command line by typing ftp. Once in the ftp utility, you can get a simple level of help by typing help or ? at the ftp> prompt. ftp file transfers are governed by standards defined in RFC 959.

finger

Also included with Windows NT is a finger client utility. This command-line utility can be used to get user information from any system running a standard finger service.

The `finger` command can be used in one of two ways:

- `finger @hostname`
- `finger username@hostname`

The first syntax usually returns a list of users logged on to the hostname's system. The second syntax usually gives information about the specified user, such as full name, office phone number, or address. Additionally, many `finger` servers accept partial usernames and will return all matches.

> **NOTE**
>
> Windows NT Server does not include a `finger` server service. A `finger` server service for NT is available from the European Microsoft Windows NT Academic Centre (EMWAC). EMWAC can be contacted at `http://www.emwac.ed.ac.uk`.

tftp

The trivial file transfer protocol (`tftp`) command allows you to transfer files to or from a computer running a `tftp` server, as defined in RFC 783.

The syntax for the `tftp` command is

`tftp [-i] host [GET | PUT] source [destination]`

> `-i` indicates a binary file transfer. You must specify this switch when transferring binary files.
>
> `host` is the name of the remote machine.
>
> `GET` transfers the file from `host` to the local machine.
>
> `PUT` transfers the file from the local machine to `host`.
>
> `source` is the full name of the file to be transferred.
>
> `destination` is the name the transferred file will have when the transfer is complete. If `destination` is not included, the destination filename will be the same as the source.

Summary

This chapter presented a look at TCP/IP on the Windows NT platform. It included how Microsoft implemented TCP/IP on NT, as well as the steps taken to ensure that Windows NT can take full advantage of standards-based networking through the implementation of services such as WINS, DHCP, DNS, LPR/LPD, and other TCP/IP protocols.

You also saw how TCP/IP integration enhances connectivity with Windows for Workgroups and Windows 95 clients through a robust implementation of NetBIOS over TCP/IP. The chapter finishes with an explanation of how to install and configure TCP/IP on Windows NT Server, including an explanation of how to install and configure additional TCP/IP-related services, such as IP routing and Simple TCP/IP Services.

Dynamic Host Configuration Protocol (DHCP)

by Art Knowles and Jason Garms

CHAPTER 11

When Microsoft first introduced WINS and DHCP with Windows NT 3.5 in the fall of 1994, it was popular belief that they were both proprietary Microsoft protocols. However, that belief is inaccurate, although even today it is still believed. The Dynamic Host Configuration Protocol (DHCP) is an open-standard protocol that is defined by the Internet Engineering Task Force (IEFT) as an Internet standard. The Windows Internet Name Service (WINS), which is covered in the next chapter, is a service that is based on a set of open standards. Thus, it is standards compliant.

Introduction to DHCP

DHCP is not a completely new development. It is actually an extension to the BOOTP protocol (originally defined in RFC 951), which had been the standard for assigning dynamic IP addresses and remote-booting diskless workstations. Contrary to popular fiction, DHCP is not a "Microsoft protocol," although Microsoft was a major instigating force behind DHCP. Indeed, Microsoft's interest in making TCP/IP administration wasn't unique. There was a general agreement in the Internet community that a sophisticated method of dynamic IP allocation was necessary. Not only would such a system simplify the initial configuration of client computers, but it would dramatically reduce the administrative overhead necessary for maintaining the IP addresses and related information, such as subnet mask and default gateways. It would also permit roving, mobile users—a growing part of the computing population.

These were but some of the thoughts that brought DHCP into existence. DHCP is fully defined in the following Requests for Comments (RFC):

- RFC 1533: DHCP Options and BOOTP Vendor Extensions
- RFC 1534: Interoperation between DHCP and BOOTP
- RFC 1541: Dynamic Host Configuration Protocol (DHCP)
- RFC 1542: Clarifications and Extensions for Bootstrap Protocol

> **NOTE**
>
> The most interesting of these is RFC 1541, which defines the core structure and functionality of DHCP. This document can be obtained from `ftp://ds.internic.net/rfc/rfc1541.txt`.

Because DHCP is a client/server system, to have a fully functioning system, you must have at least one machine running the DHCP Server service and one machine with a DHCP-capable TCP/IP stack. In most scenarios, including our discussion here, the DHCP Server will be a Windows NT Server with its built-in DHCP Server service.

Dynamic Host Configuration Protocol (DHCP)

CHAPTER 11

323

11

DYNAMIC HOST
CONFIGURATION
PROTOCOL

> **NOTE**
>
> The number of available DHCP Server products is growing fairly quickly. Many third-party TCP/IP product vendors are developing DHCP Server software for Windows NT, Windows 3.x, Novell, and even most UNIX systems.

This discussion of the DHCP service begins with some of the design goals of the service and then moves on to planning your installation, installing the service, and using the DHCP Manager to administer the DHCP service. Administering your DHCP service consists of creating or deleting scopes and configuring individual scope properties. A scope is nothing more than a collection of IP addresses grouped into a single component for ease of administration. A scope can include all the IP addresses in a single subnet if desired, or you can subdivide a subnet into multiple scopes. Finally, this section looks at the DHCP database management required from time to time to improve performance. You also will learn about some of the Registry keys that cannot be configured directly by using the DHCP Manager.

> **NOTE**
>
> A *DHCP* scope is a collection of IP addresses grouped into a single component for ease of administration.

Looking at Design Goals for the Microsoft DHCP Protocol

All companies have definite goals they must reach prior to releasing their products into the market, and Microsoft had definite goals in mind for implementing DHCP for its operating systems. The primary concern was making Microsoft TCP/IP-based networks easier to implement and maintain. Because TCP/IP is playing an ever-increasing role in Windows NT-based networks, simplifying administration of these networks reduces implementation and maintenance costs. This has a direct influence on the likelihood that more people will deploy Windows NT networks over other, more difficult-to-install network solutions. Incidentally, simplifying TCP/IP administration also makes it easier for the Microsoft Product Service Support (PSS) group as well, because TCP/IP is one of the most widely implemented protocols in larger enterprises.

The TCP/IP protocol is recommended for medium to large local area networks, it is the preferred protocol for wide area networks, and it is required for integration with most UNIX networks, as well as the Internet.

Some of the goals for the Microsoft DHCP implementation follow:

- **Centralized administration of your TCP/IP IP subnets.** All your IP addresses, along with the configuration parameters for each, are stored in a central database located on your DHCP Server.

- **Automatic TCP/IP IP address assignment and configuration.** As a client computer starts up and accesses the network for the first time, it is automatically assigned an IP address, subnet mask, default gateway, and WINS Server IP address. If the client computer then moves to a different subnet, such as often happens with portable computer users, the original IP address and related configuration information are released back to the original pool of available IP addresses. Then, the client is assigned a new IP address and related configuration information for the new subnet.

- **The return of unused IP addresses to the available pool of IP addresses.** Normally, IP addresses are allocated statically by a network administrator, and these IP addresses are stored on a piece of paper or a local database. However, often this list can become outdated as clients move between subnets or new IP addresses are allocated without updating the list of IP addresses. This means that some IP addresses will be lost, so they cannot be reused. DHCP uses a time-based mechanism, called a lease, which a client must renew at regular intervals. If the lease expires and the client does not renew it, the IP address is returned to the pool of available IP addresses.

Understanding How a DHCP Lease Works

Leases are fundamental to the entire DHCP process. Every IP address offered by a DHCP Server has an associated *lease period*. "Lease" is an accurate term, because the DHCP Server is not giving the IP address to the client, but rather is allowing the client to use the information for a specified period of time. Also, the server or the client can terminate the lease at any time.

Because one of the goals of DHCP is to provide dynamic IP addresses, there must be a method of returning these addresses to the address pool, also called a *scope*. The lease period is defined independently for each scope. Lease periods can be anywhere from a few minutes to a few months to forever. Different lease periods are useful in different scenarios, and there is no single lease period that fits all needs. However, I don't recommend that you use unlimited lease periods, even if you are using DHCP to statically assign your IP addresses. Make the lease periods a few months long instead.

A DHCP client computer steps through one of six transition states in the process of establishing a valid IP address for use by the client computer:

- **Initializing:** When the TCP/IP stack on the client is started, it binds with an address of 0.0.0.0 because every machine on an IP network needs an address. It then sends out a DHCP Discover packet to its local subnet. This is a broadcast packet to UDP port 67, which is the DHCP/BOOTP server port.

Dynamic Host Configuration Protocol (DHCP)

CHAPTER 11

325

11

DYNAMIC HOST
CONFIGURATION
PROTOCOL

■ **Selecting:** Every DHCP Server on the local subnet receives the DHCP Discover packet. Each DHCP Server that receives the request checks to see if it has a valid free address for the requesting client. It then responds with a DHCP Offer packet containing the valid IP address, subnet mask, IP address of the DHCP Server, lease duration, and any other configuration details specified for the DHCP scope. All servers that send a DHCP Offer reserve the IP address they offered. This address cannot be assigned to another client until it is unreserved. DHCP Offer packets are broadcast to UDP port 68, which is the DHCP/BOOTP client port. The response must be sent by broadcast, because the client does not have an IP address, which is required for it to be directly addressed.

■ **Requesting:** The client usually selects the first offer to come in and responds by broadcasting a *DHCP Request* packet. This packet tells the server, "Yes, I want you to service me. I accept the DHCP lease you are giving me." Also, because it is broadcasted, all the DHCP Servers on the network see it. Any other DHCP Server that made an offer which the client did not accept returns the reserved IP address to its pool of available addresses. The client also can use the DHCP Request to ask for additional configuration options from the server, such as DNS or gateway addresses.

■ **Bound:** When the server receives the DHCP Request packet, it responds to the client with a *DHCP Acknowledge* packet, which provides any additional information the client might have requested. This packet is also sent by broadcast. It essentially says "Okay. Just remember you are only leasing this and you can't keep it forever! Oh, and here's the other information you requested." Okay, so it's not really quite so polite!

■ **Renewing:** When a client notices that its lease is 50 percent up, it tries to renew the lease. It does this by sending a directed UDP packet to the server it got its original information from. This packet is a DHCP Request, which asks if it can keep the TCP/IP configuration information and renew its lease. If the server is available, it would normally agree to the request by sending a DHCP Acknowledge packet back to the client.

■ **Rebinding:** When the lease reaches approximately 87.5 percent of its expiration time, the client attempts to renew the lease once again—if it could not be renewed in the preceding attempt. If this fails, the client tries to contact any DHCP Server to obtain a valid IP address. If another DHCP is able to assign a new IP address, the client enters the bound state once again. If the lease on its current IP address expires, the client must give up the IP address and re-enter the initializing state, at which point it repeats the entire process.

NOTE

When a DHCP client initially tries to acquire an IP address, only four network packets are exchanged across the network: DHCP Discover, DHCP Offer, DHCP Request, and DHCP Acknowledge. Each packet is less than 400 bytes. So you can see, the network overhead associated with DHCP is relatively small.

Planning Your DHCP Installation

If you have a small network in which all your TCP/IP hosts can take advantage of DHCP, it will be fairly easy to install the DHCP Server. However, this does not mean that you can just install the DHCP Server components and forget about it; it just means that there are fewer issues to contend with in your network installation. When you begin your planning, there are two types of network configurations to consider: The first is a simple network with only one subnet, and the second is a network with multiple subnets. The most common configuration is one with multiple subnets, and that is the focus of this discussion.

A single subnet is the easiest to work with. All the DHCP and WINS Servers are located on the same subnet, so very little maintenance is required. Maintaining the lmhosts files is not difficult unless you have many MS-DOS or Windows 3.*x* clients that use the Microsoft Network Client 3.0 software. Because these computers are all on a single subnet, you can use broadcast name resolution and bypass WINS configuration and lmhosts file maintenance all together. However, it pays in performance to use the same techniques that will be described for your network just as if you did have multiple segments. It also pays off if your network grows and must be divided into separate segments.

For a multiple-segmented (subnets) network, you must do some planning before installing DHCP on your server and implementing DHCP on your clients. Some issues to consider include the following:

- Routers
- WINS configuration
- Multiple DHCP Servers
- Static IP addresses
- Lease expiration
- DHCP Server maintenance

Routers and Relay Agents

If you don't plan to have a DHCP Server on each subnet, your routers must support RFC 1542, commonly known as BOOTP/DHCP relay support. This means that the router can properly forward the DHCP packets from a subnet without a DHCP Server to a remote subnet that can answer the DHCP request. For some older routers, this might require an upgrade. If your routers do not support this RFC, they will discard the network packets required for DHCP operation. If your routers do support this RFC but you have connectivity problems, check the documentation to see whether the default configuration passes or drops these packet types.

TIP

If your routers do not support RFC 1542, you can use the DHCP Relay Agent included with NT Server. For more information on BOOTP/DHCP relay, see RFC 1542, which can be found at `ftp://ds.internic.net/rfc/rfc1542.txt`.

Using DHCP with WINS

In a Windows NT environment, DHCP is often used in conjunction with WINS. Indeed, the services are complementary; however, they provide completely independent functions, and each can be run without the other.

DHCP allows you to dynamically assign IP addresses to clients. The synergy between DHCP and WINS comes from WINS's capability to locate the clients by a friendly name. With the more traditional static IP addresses, it was usually sufficient to maintain a list of all the IP addresses with their associated names. In the traditional NetBIOS world, this was the `lmhosts` file. Alternatively, clients could use name broadcasts to locate the IP address of network resources. However, for anything but the smallest networks, broadcast resolution is impractical. Furthermore, with DHCP's dynamic IP addresses, a static list for resolving hostnames to IP addresses is inadequate—thus, the synergy between WINS and DHCP.

When using WINS with DHCP clients, you need to make sure to specify a couple of client options that are returned by the DHCP Server. In particular, you need to be sure to use option 44, "WINS/NBNS Servers," which returns an array of IP addresses that specify the WINS Servers a client should use. Additionally, you should be sure to include option 46, "Node Type." A node type specifies the mechanism the TCP/IP protocol uses to resolve NetBIOS name requests to a TCP/IP address.

NOTE

These options are discussed in the "Working with DHCP Scopes" section later in this chapter.

Supported node types include the following:

- **B-node (Broadcast mode):** Resolves names by using broadcast messages. This option is the worst possible one to use, because it can flood your network segment with broadcast messages, lowering your network's capability to carry data over the network and effectively lowering your network bandwidth on the segment. Broadcasts also are not forwarded by routers, so if the requested resource is on the other side of a router, it will not be found. I recommend this type for a small network with a single subnet, one that does not have a dedicated network administrator to maintain the network. (Using broadcasts can essentially eliminate the need to maintain an lmhosts file or WINS database, and for a small network, very little network bandwidth is eaten by the broadcasts.) Another good reason to use B-node is that computers located on the same segment still can find each other, even if the WINS Server or DNS Server is down or unavailable.

- **P-node (Point-to-point mode):** Resolves names with a NetBIOS name server (NBNS), such as WINS, using point-to-point communications. Point-to-point communications are based on an IP-address-to-IP-address communication linkage. This is an efficient mechanism, but if the NBNS goes down, clients will be left without any method of locating other machines on the network.

- **M-node (Mixed mode):** Uses B-node first (broadcasts) to resolve the name and then uses P-node (name queries) if the broadcast fails to resolve a name. This method works, but it has the same problem as a B-node because it can flood the network with broadcasts.

- **H-node (Hybrid mode):** This is the default node type when configuring TCP/IP manually, unless the WINS IP address field is left empty. It uses P-node first (name queries) to resolve the name and then B-node (broadcasts) if the name service is unavailable or if the name is not registered in the WINS Server's database. I recommend this node type because it first uses a point-to-point connection to find a resource's IP address; it uses a broadcast to find the resource only if that fails. This is the most efficient node type to use, and it practically guarantees that the resource will be found even if the lmhosts file or WINS database does not contain the requested resource's IP address.

Using DHCP with DNS

With the growing importance of the Domain Name System (DNS) in Windows NT networking, you need to know a little about how DNS and DHCP interoperate. In Windows NT 4.0, you need to use WINS in order to provide DHCP and DNS integration. Furthermore, the DNS Server must be running on a Windows NT 4.0 Server. This combination together provides what is commonly called *dynamic DNS*.

The reason for the complicated interaction has to do with the status of dynamic DNS with regards to the Internet Engineering Task Force (IETF). There have been a couple of competing standards for how to provide dynamic DNS, but as of the release of Windows NT 4.0, there was no single standard for Microsoft to implement. Microsoft chose to provide the functionality through the existing Windows NT WINS structure, which many customers already had in place. The actual standard for dynamic DNS is expected to enter the standards track

with the IETF. Microsoft has commented that it is committed to providing complete support for that standard as soon as the IETF signs off on it.

If you use DHCP to always provide the same IP address to each client, you can use static DNS without a problem. In this scenario, you can still benefit from the administrative savings provided by DHCP, even if you can't benefit from a more flexible address pool.

Static IP Addresses

Any static IP addresses—such as those used by other DHCP Servers, non-DHCP computers, routers, and non-Microsoft Remote Access Software (RAS) clients that do not support a dynamically assigned IP address and are using PPP (point-to-point protocol) to connect to your network—must be excluded from the DHCP scope. If you forget to exclude these IP addresses, an address conflict probably will occur and could prevent your clients from communicating or even cause your entire network to fail, such as in the case of a router.

Lease Expiration

The minimum lease expiration should be twice the maximum expected server downtime. If you plan to upgrade the server over the weekend, for example, the expiration time should be at least four days. This prevents a client from losing its lease and IP address, which would prevent the computer from communicating with other resources on the network.

A good lease minimum should be based on your network turnaround. If you have many portable computer users, frequent computer upgrades, or many users passing between subnets, you should have a lease time of about two weeks. This returns the unused IP addresses back to the pool, quickly making them available for reassignment. However, if you have a pretty static network, lease times of six months could be used. The one lease to avoid is an unlimited lease because these addresses will never be released automatically and returned to the IP address pool.

Another factor to consider in determining lease duration is the ratio of machines to IP addresses. For instance, if you have more machines on the network than IP addresses, you should consider using a much shorter lease duration, such as an hour or 30 minutes. This situation might occur if you connect your office to the Internet and have a limited number of IP addresses that must be shared among all machines on the network.

Partitioning DHCP Address Spaces

When planning your DHCP environment, one important activity is determining the number of DHCP Servers and how to divide your IP address pools. In most environments, it is advisable to install more than one DHCP Server that handles a single address space. This allows for fault tolerance in the event that one DHCP Server is unavailable. Remember, if a DHCP client is brought online for the first time, or its lease expires and there is no available DHCP Server, the DHCP client will be unable to start.

> **NOTE**
>
> Each DHCP Server must have a statically assigned IP address. These IP addresses must be excluded from the DHCP scope that you create.

In subnetted environments, it is unnecessary to have one DHCP Server on each subnet when you use DHCP relay agents. To provide some degree of fault tolerance, you can split each IP address space over two servers. In most cases, it is unnecessary to split it over more than two servers. Windows NT's DHCP Server does not support a shared IP address database. This means that if you want multiple DHCP Servers to provide addresses from a single IP address space, you have to partition the space and put a portion of the addresses on each server. A good rule of thumb is to put 75 percent of a scope's addresses on the DHCP Server that is closest (least expensive path) to the clients. Then, put the remaining 25 percent of the addresses on a second DHCP Server.

> **CAUTION**
>
> If you configure DHCP Servers with overlapping IP ranges, you can end up with multiple clients with the same IP addresses. This definitely causes problems on your network because each IP address must be unique.

DHCP Client Configuration Options

If you are planning to implement your Microsoft DHCP Server service in a mixed environment, such as with a third-party UNIX DHCP Server service, you should be aware that not all the DHCP configuration options are supported by the Microsoft client. Specifically, the Microsoft DHCP clients only use the configuration options as specified in Table 11.1. Any other options received by the client are ignored and discarded.

Table 11.1. Microsoft DHCP client configuration options.

Number	Name	Data Type	Description
1	Subnet Mask	Subnet Address	Specifies the TCP/IP subnet mask to be used by DHCP clients. Note: This value can be set only when you create a scope or when accessed from the DHCP Options	Scope Properties menu option.

Number	Name	Data Type	Description
3	Router	IP Address Array	Specifies a list, in order of preference, of router IP addresses to be used by the client. A locally defined gateway can override this value.
6	DNS Servers	IP Address Array	Specifies a list, in order of preference, for DNS name servers for the client. Note: A multihomed computer (a computer with more than one installed network adapter) can include only one IP address, not one IP address per adapter.
15	Domain Name	String	Specifies the DNS domain name the client should use for DNS hostname resolution.
44	WINS/NBNS	IP Address	Specifies a list, in array order of preference, of NetBIOS Name Servers (NBNS).
46	WINS/NBT Node Type	Byte	Specifies the node type for configurable NetBIOS clients (as defined in RFC 1001/1002). A value of 1 specifies B-node, 2 specifies P-node, 4 specifies M-node, and 8 specifies H-node. Note: On a multihomed computer, the node type is assigned to the computer as a whole—not to individual network adapters.
47	NetBIOS Scope ID	String	Specifies the Scope ID for NetBIOS over TCP/IP (NBT) as defined in RFC 1001/1002. Note: On a multihomed computer, the Scope ID is a global resource and is not allocated on a per-network adapter basis.
50	Requested Address	IP Address	Specifies that a client's preset IP address be used.

continues

Table 11.1. continued

Number	Name	Data Type	Description
51	Lease Time	IP Address	Specifies the time, in seconds, from the initial IP address allocation to the expiration of the client lease on the IP address. Note: This value can be set only in the DHCP Options | Scope Properties menu option.
53	DHCP Message Type	Byte	Specifies the DHCP message type where the message type is 1 for DHCPDISCOVER, 2 for DHCPOFFER, 3 for DHCPREQUEST, 4 for DHCPDECLINE, 5 for DHCPACK, 6 for DHCPNAK, and 7 for DHCPRELEASE.
54	Server Identifier	IP Address	Used by DHCP clients to indicate which of several lease offers is being accepted by including this option in a DHCPREQUEST message with the IP address of the accepted DHCP Server.
58	Renewal (T1) Time Value	Long	Specifies the time, in seconds, from the initial IP address assignment to the time when the client must enter the renewal state. Note: This value cannot be specified manually because it is based on the lease time as set for the scope.
59	Rebinding (T2) Time Value	Long	Specifies the time, in seconds, from the initial IP address assignment to the time when the client must enter the rebinding state. Note: This value cannot be specified manually because it is based on the lease time as set for the scope.
61	Client ID	Word	Specifies the DHCP client's unique identifier.

Dynamic Host Configuration Protocol (DHCP)

CHAPTER 11

333

11

DYNAMIC HOST
CONFIGURATION
PROTOCOL

Something to be aware of is that the Microsoft DHCP client and server do not support DHCP option overlays. An *option overlay* is the process of using free space in the DHCP option packet to contain additional DHCP options. So if you are using a third-party DHCP Server instead of the Microsoft DHCP Server, you should make sure that your important configuration options are listed first; otherwise, they might be discarded. Microsoft clients are also limited regarding the size of the DHCP packet they can properly process. This limit is 312 bytes, so you must make all the options you choose fit within this allocation. The same consideration applies if you are using the Microsoft DHCP Server to support your third-party DHCP clients: Choose your most important configuration options first. And although you can use the additional configuration options (listed in Table 11.2) to support your third-party DHCP clients, these options will not be used by your Microsoft DHCP clients.

Table 11.2. Third-party DHCP client configuration options.

Number	Name	Data Type	Description
0	Pad	Byte	Specifies that the following data fields will be aligned on a word (16-bit) boundary.
2	Time	Long	Specifies the Universal Coordinate Offset Time (UCT) in seconds.
4	Time Server	IP Address Array	Specifies a list, in order of preference, of time servers for the client.
5	Name Servers	IP Address Array	Specifies a list, in order of preference, of name servers for the client.
7	Log Servers	IP Address Array	Specifies a list, in order of preference, for MIT_LCS User Datagram Protocol (UDP) log servers for the client.
8	Cookie Servers	IP Address Array	Specifies a list, in order of preference, of cookie servers (as specified in RFC 865) for the client.
9	LPR Servers	IP Address Array	Specifies a list, in order of preference, for Line Printer Remote (as specified in RFC 1179) servers for the clients.

continues

Table 11.2. continued

Number	Name	Data Type	Description
10	Impress Servers	IP Address Array	Specifies a list, in order of preference, of Imagen Impress servers for the client.
11	Resource Location Servers	IP Address Array	Specifies a list, in order of preference, of RFC 887-compliant Resource Location Servers for the client.
12	Hostname	String	Specifies the hostname (maximum of 63 characters) for the client. Note: The name must start with an alphabetic character, end with an alphanumeric character, and can contain only letters, numbers, or hyphens. The name can be fully qualified with the local DNS domain name.
13	Boot File Size	Word	Specifies the default size of the boot image file in 512 octet blocks.
14	Merit Dump File	String	Specifies the ASCII path of a file in which the client's core dump can be stored in case of an application or system crash.
16	Swap Server	IP Address	Specifies the IP address of the client's swap server.
17	Root Path	String	Specifies a path (in ASCII) for the client's root disk.
18	Extensions Path	String	Specifies a file that includes information that is interpreted the same as the vendor extension field in the BOOTP response, except that references to Tag 18 are ignored. Note that the file must be retrievable through TFTP.

Dynamic Host Configuration Protocol (DHCP)

CHAPTER 11

335

11

DYNAMIC HOST
CONFIGURATION
PROTOCOL

Number	Name	Data Type	Description
19	IP Layer Forwarding	Byte	Specifies that IP packets should be enabled (1) or disabled (0) for the client.
20	Nonlocal Source Routing	Byte	Specifies that datagram packets with nonlocal source route forwarding should be enabled (1) or disabled (0) for the client.
21	Policy Filters Mask	IP Address Array	Specifies a list, in order of preference, of IP address and mask pairs that specify destination address and mask pairs, respectively. Used for filtering nonlocal source routes. Any source routed datagram whose next hop address does not match an entry in the list is discarded by the client.
22	Max DG Reassembly Size	Word	Specifies the maximum size datagram that a client can assemble. Note: The minimum size is 576 bytes.
23	Default Time to Live	Byte	Specifies the TTL that the client will use on outgoing datagrams. Values must be between 1 and 255 hops.
24	Path MTU Aging Timeout	Long	Specifies the timeout, in seconds, for aging Path Maximum Transmission Unit values. Note: MTU values are found using the mechanism defined in RFC 1191.
25	Path MTU Plateau Table	Word Array	Specifies a table of MTU sizes to use when performing Path MTU (as defined in RFC 1191). Note: The table is sorted from minimum to maximum value.

continues

Table 11.2. continued

Number	Name	Data Type	Description
26	MTU Option	Word	Specifies the MTU discovery size. Note: The minimum value is 68.
27	All Subnets are Local	Byte	Specifies whether the client assumes that all subnets in the network will use the same MTU value as that defined for the local subnet. This option is enabled (1) or disabled (0), which specifies that some subnets may use smaller MTU values.
28	Broadcast Address	IP Address	Specifies the broadcast IP address to be used on the client's local subnet.
29	Perform Mask Discovery	Byte	A value of 1 specifies that the client should use ICMP (Internet Control Message Protocol) for subnet mask discovery, whereas a value of 0 specifies that the client should not use ICMP for subnet mask discovery.
30	Mask Supplier	Byte	A value of 1 specifies that the client should respond to ICMP subnet mask requests, whereas a value of 0 specifies that a client should not respond to subnet mask requests using ICMP.
31	Perform Router Discovery	Byte	A value of 1 specifies that a client should use the mechanism defined in RFC 1256 for router discovery. A value of 0 indicates that the client should not use the router discovery mechanism.
32	Router Solicitation Address	IP Address	Specifies the IP address to which the client will send router solicitation requests.
33	Static Route	IP Address Array	Specifies a list, in order of preference, of IP address pairs the client should install in its routing

Number	Name	Data Type	Description
			cache. Note: Any multiple routes to the same destination are listed in descending order or in order of priority. The pairs are defined as destination IP address/router IP addresses. The default address of 0.0.0.0 is an illegal address for a static route and should be changed if your non-Microsoft DHCP clients use this setting.
34	Trailer Encapsulation	Byte	A value of 1 specifies that the client should negotiate use of trailers (as defined in RFC 983) when using the ARP protocol. A value of 0 indicates that the client should not use trailers.
35	ARP Cache Timeout	Long	Specifies the timeout, in seconds, for the ARP cache entries.
36	Ethernet Encapsulation	Byte	Specifies that the client should use Ethernet version 2 (as defined in RFC 894) or IEEE 802.3 (as defined in RFC 1042) encapsulation if the network interface is Ethernet. A value of 1 enables RFC 1042, whereas a value of 0 enables RFC 894 encapsulation.
37	Default Time to Live	Byte	Specifies the default TTL the client should use when sending TCP segments. Note: The minimum octet value is 1.
38	Keepalive Interval	Long	Specifies the interval, in seconds, for the client to wait before sending a keepalive message on a TCP connection. Note: A value of 0 indicates that the client should send keepalive messages only if requested by the application.

continues

Table 11.2. continued

Number	Name	Data Type	Description
39	Keepalive Garbage	Byte	Enables (1) or disables (0) sending keepalive messages with an octet of garbage data for legacy application compatibility.
40	NIS Domain Name	String	An ASCII string specifying the name of the Network Information Service (NIS) domain.
41	NIS Servers	IP Address Array	Specifies a list, in order of preference, of IP addresses of NIS servers for the client.
42	NTP Servers	IP Address Array	Specifies a list, in order of preference, of IP addresses of Network Time Protocol (NTP) servers for the client.
43	Vendor Specific Info	Byte Array	Binary information used by clients and servers to pass vendor-specific information. Servers that cannot interpret the information ignore it, whereas clients that do not receive the data attempt to operate without it.
45	NetBIOS Over TCP/IP NBDD	IP Address Array	Specifies a list, in order of preference, of IP addresses for NetBIOS datagram distribution (NBDD) servers for the client.
48	X Window System Font	IP Address Array	Specifies a list, in order of preference, of IP addresses of X Window font servers for the client.
49	X Window System Display	IP Address Array	Specifies a list, in order of preference, of IP addresses of X Window System Display Manager servers for the client.
64	NIS + Domain Name	String	Specifies a list, in order of preference, of NIS + domain names.

Number	Name	Data Type	Description
65	NIS + Server	IP Address Array	Specifies a list, in order of preference, of NIS + servers.
255	End	Byte	Specifies the end of the DHCP packet.

Installing the DHCP Server Service

You can install the DHCP Server service through the Control Panel Network applet. Before you install the service on your current server, check for the existence of other DHCP Servers on the network. These could be other Windows NT Servers, a Novell NetWare server, or even a UNIX Server. You also need to make sure you have a unique range of addresses to define a scope on the DHCP Server.

NOTE

You must be sure that the range of addresses used for the scope is not in use elsewhere on the network. If any addresses in the range are in use elsewhere, you must *exclude* them from the scope; otherwise, you will have multiple machines with the same IP addresses—a recipe for trouble.

To install the DHCP Server service, follow these steps:

1. Make sure you are logged on as a member of the Administrators group and launch the Control Panel Network applet.
2. Click the Services tab, and then the Add button.
3. Select Microsoft DHCP Server from the list of network services.

NOTE

If you don't have TCP/IP installed already, TCP/IP will be automatically installed when you install the DHCP Server service.

TIP

To use SNMP to configure the DHCP Server service remotely, install the SNMP service as well.

4. Click the OK button. When prompted, enter the path to the Windows NT distribution files (that is, f:\i386) and click the Continue button. Setup warns you that DHCP Servers cannot also be DHCP clients and any network adapter configured as a DHCP client must be reconfigured. This message is shown in Figure 11.1.

FIGURE 11.1.

Network adapters on a DHCP Server cannot be configured to dynamically obtain IP addresses.

If any adapters are using DHCP to obtain an IP address, they are now required to use a static IP address. Press Close on the Network Control Panel and the TCP/IP Property Sheet will be displayed allowing you to enter an address.

OK

5. Click the OK button and then click Close to close the Network Control Panel.

6. If one or more adapters on your server was configured to obtain its IP address from a DHCP Server, or if you are installing TCP/IP at the same time as the DHCP Server service, you will be prompted to configure TCP/IP settings for each adapter on your system.

7. Now restart your system. After the system restarts, the DHCP Server service should be activated. If not, check your system event log for any error messages.

You will now need to define at least one DHCP before the DHCP Server can do anything useful.

Managing Your DHCP Server with the DHCP Manager

Your interface to managing the DHCP service is the DHCP Manager (DHCPADMN.EXE). It is installed in the Administrative Tools program group when you install the DHCP service and requires administrative privileges to use. With the DHCP Manager, you can do everything but stop or start the DHCP service. To stop or start the service, use the Control Panel Services applet and specify the Microsoft DHCP Server as the service to control. Or, you can issue the following commands from a Windows NT command prompt:

```
net stop dhcpserver
net start dhcpserver
```

Managing DHCP Scopes

The DHCP Manager's primary function is to work with *scopes*. This section discusses creating, deleting, activating, and deactivating scopes. Next, we discuss how to manage your DHCP clients. This includes managing your client leases and reservations, as well as setting individual

DHCP properties for reserved clients that differ from those defined for the scope as a whole. Finally, this section discusses the DHCP database administration required from time to time. This should provide you with a well-rounded education and prepare you for your duties as a network administrator so that you can manage your TCP/IP-based network.

Before you can use the DHCP Server to assign IP addresses and relevant configuration options to your DHCP clients, you must create a DHCP scope. A scope is the heart of your DHCP Server service. It is based on an IP address range, or subnet, if you prefer. It can include only a single subnet, but within that subnet, you can define the IP range to be used as the basis for your DHCP client's IP address assignment, the subnet mask, any IP addresses to exclude from the scope, a lease duration, a name for the scope, and a comment that describes the scope. This section discusses how to create, delete, activate, and deactivate DHCP scopes. Next, it moves on to configuring global, local, or default scope properties.

When you run the DHCP Manager for the first time, it does not have any scopes defined, although it does include a listing in the DHCP Server's window for the local machine. Before you start creating scopes, I suggest that you add the additional DHCP Servers on your network to the DHCP Manager. When you do, your DHCP Manager includes a listing in the window of each DHCP Server on your network (see Figure 11.2). This gives you the capability to manage your other scopes, and you can use these additional scopes as a reference point when creating new scopes.

FIGURE 11.2.

The Microsoft DHCP Manager with multiple DHCP Servers and scopes.

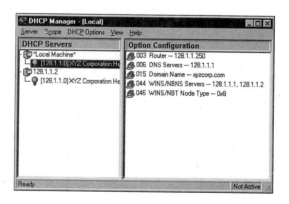

To add DHCP Servers to your local DHCP Manager, follow these steps:

1. Choose Add from the Server menu, or press Ctrl+A to display the Add DHCP Server to Server List dialog box.

2. Enter the IP address of the DHCP Server in the DHCP Server field and click the OK button. The IP address appears in the DHCP Server window.

NOTE

The DHCP Manager deals with TCP/IP FQDN (fully qualified domain name)-compliant hostnames—also called DNS names. It does not recognize NetBIOS names.

3. Repeat these steps for each DHCP Server you want to add to your local DHCP Manager.

NOTE

Because the DHCP Server service does not replicate its database and configuration information to other DHCP Servers, you must configure the DHCP Manager on each server in order to manage all the DHCP scopes from any computer with the DHCP Manager installed on it.

Working with DHCP Scopes

Working with DHCP scopes consists of four possible functions:

- **Creating a scope:** This is the beginning process to automating your DHCP client TCP/IP configuration.
- **Activating a scope:** Before you can use a newly created scope, you must activate it. When you have an active scope, your DHCP clients can be assigned an IP address and relevant TCP/IP configuration information from the scope.
- **Deactivating a scope:** Before you delete a scope, you should deactivate it. Deactivating a scope prevents a client from renewing its current lease and forces it to obtain a lease from another DHCP scope. This is a means of migrating clients to a new scope without manual intervention.
- **Deleting a scope:** After you finish using a DHCP scope, you can delete it.

To create a scope, follow these steps:

1. Select the DHCP Server in the DHCP Server window where you want to create the new scope. If you are creating a new scope on the computer running the DHCP Server service, this entry will be Local Machine; otherwise, it will be an IP address.
2. Choose Create from the Scope menu. The Create Scope dialog box appears, as shown in Figure 11.3.
3. In the Start Address field, enter the beginning IP address of your subnet.
4. In the End Address field, enter the last IP address of your subnet.

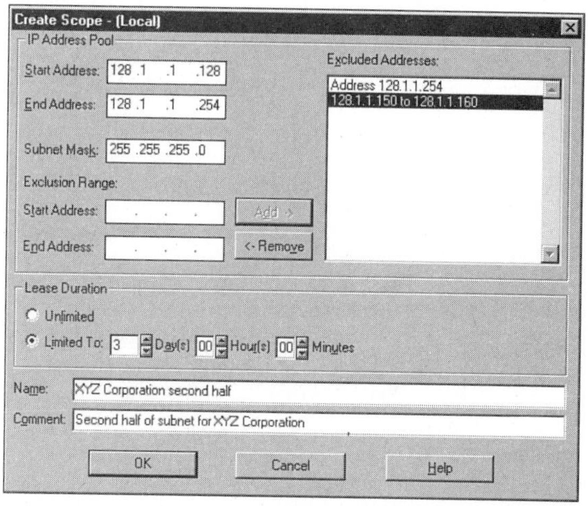

FIGURE 11.3.

The Create Scope dialog box.

TIP

If you are not planning to divide your subnet between two DHCP Servers, enter the complete IP address range of your subnet. However, if you are planning to split your subnet (as I have), enter only half of your IP address range in the Start and End Address fields. This is easier to work with and prevents complications with the second DHCP Manager's defined scope.

5. In the Subnet Mask field, enter the subnet mask to be assigned to your DHCP clients.

6. If your scope includes statically assigned addresses, such as those assigned to your network adapters in the computer or to the Remote Access Service, enter these addresses in the Exclusion Range group. To exclude a single IP address, enter the IP address in the Start Address field and click the Add button. To enter more than one consecutive IP address to be excluded, enter the beginning IP address in the Start Address field and the last IP address in the End Address field; then click the Add button. This places the IP address range in the Excluded Addresses box.

   To modify or remove an address range, select it in the Excluded Addresses box and click the Remove button. This places the range in the Exclusion Range fields where you can modify and later add it back to the Excluded Addresses box.

7. In the Lease Duration group, choose the Unlimited or Limited To radio button to specify the lease type. If you choose Limited To, which is the default, specify the length of time for your DHCP clients to keep their assigned IP addresses. By default the lease expiration period is set to 3 days.

Choose your lease time on the basis of the frequency with which your computers are upgraded, replaced, or moved between subnets. If you have a high movement of computers, choose a lease of approximately two weeks. If you have an extremely low movement of computers, choose a monthly, trimonthly, or biyearly lease.

> **WARNING**
>
> Do not assign the `Unlimited` lease type unless you are absolutely sure that no computers will ever be upgraded, replaced, or moved. I can assure you that it is very improbable that you will be in this situation. If you choose an unlimited lease, you cannot automatically recover IP addresses that have been assigned to a DHCP client.

8. In the Name field, enter a name for the scope. Your name can be a floor or building location, or a description for the type of subnet. This name, along with the scope address, is listed in the DHCP Server window. It can be up to 120 characters.

9. In the Comment field, enter a description up to 120 characters long for the scope. You should make this comment as descriptive as possible.

> **TIP**
>
> To modify the scope properties for an existing scope, just double-click it. This displays the Scope Properties dialog box, which is identical to the Create Scope dialog box (aside from its name, of course). You can change any of the options described in the earlier steps.

10. Click the OK button. A message box appears, prompting you to activate the scope. You should not activate the scope now, however, unless all your default scope properties are correct, as described in the "Configuring DHCP Scope Options" section.

11. Repeat these steps for each new scope you want to create.

> **CAUTION**
>
> Activate a scope only after you have configured it; otherwise, clients might get invalid configuration information. Also, be sure to make any necessary lease reservations before activating the scope; otherwise a client other than the intended recipient might take the IP address.

To activate a scope, choose Activate from the Scope menu.

Before you delete a scope, you should deactivate it. To do so, choose Deactivate from the Scope menu. When the scope lease time expires and you are sure that no DHCP clients are using a lease from the scope, you can delete it.

To delete a scope, follow these steps:

1. In the DHCP Server window, select the DHCP Server containing the scope you want to delete. If you are deleting a scope on the computer running the DHCP Server service, this entry is Local Machine; otherwise, it is an IP address.
2. The scopes for the server are listed. Select the scope you want to delete.
3. Choose Delete from the Scope menu. A warning message informs you that clients may still have active leases. Click OK to delete the scope.
4. Repeat these actions for each scope you want to delete.

TIP

If you delete a scope with active clients, you can force the client to discontinue using its current lease and obtain one from another DHCP Server by issuing the IPCONFIG /RENEW command at a command prompt on the client workstation. On a Windows 95 computer, you can use the GUI WINIPCFG program. Click the Renew button to release the active lease and obtain a new lease. WINIPCFG is also available for Windows NT on the Windows NT Resource Kit CD from Microsoft Press.

Configuring DHCP Scope Options

Scope options are divided into two classes: You can have a *global* scope setting, which applies to all scopes for the DHCP Server, or a *local* scope setting, which applies only to a specific scope. Local scope properties override global scope properties. This enables you to define common properties that apply to all scopes you create. Each scope can then be customized as needed.

Suppose that you define the global router setting to contain the IP addresses for your routers using subnets. After you create a new scope, you can delete the first entry in this list and then add it back. This places the IP address entry at the end of the list. In effect, it changes the order of router preference so that the router closest to the user is used first. You can repeat this sequence to continue moving the router addresses for each subnet you create without having to type each router address manually.

To modify a scope property, follow these steps:

1. In the DHCP Server window, select the DHCP Server containing the scope you want to modify. If you are modifying a scope on the computer running the DHCP Server service, this entry is Local Machine; otherwise, it is an IP address.

2. After the connection to the DHCP Server has been established, the scopes for the server are listed. Select the scope you want to modify.

3. Choose Global from the DHCP Options menu to display the dialog box shown in Figure 11.4. Here, you can set global properties for all scopes. Or, you can choose Scope from the DHCP Options menu to set local scope properties.

FIGURE 11.4.

The expanded DHCP Options dialog box.

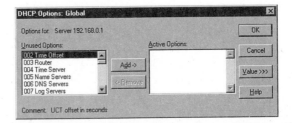

NOTE

The dialog box displayed by choosing the Scope option from the DHCP Options menu has the same format as the dialog box displayed by choosing the Global menu option.

---

4. In the Unused Options drop-down list box, select the option that you want to modify, and then click the Add button to move the highlighted option to the Active Options drop-down list box.

5. Click the Value button to expand the dialog box and display the edit field, where you can click the Edit Array button to modify an array of IP addresses or just edit the field for a single entry type.

6. Repeat steps 3–5 for each option to modify. When you finish modifying the options, click the OK button.

TIP

To modify an existing option, select it in the Active Options list box and then click the Value button to expand the dialog box.

Creating New DHCP Scope Options

Not only can you modify the predefined scope properties with the DHCP Manager, but you also can modify the name, unique identifier, and comment of existing configuration options.

And if your DHCP clients can use them, you can even create new scope options to be assigned to your DHCP clients. However, just because you can modify an existing configuration option or create new ones, it doesn't mean that you should do so arbitrarily. Only do so if absolutely necessary.

To change an existing configuration option default value, follow these steps:

1. Choose Defaults from the DHCP Options menu to display the DHCP Options dialog box, as shown in Figure 11.5.

FIGURE 11.5.

The DHCP Options: Default Values dialog box.

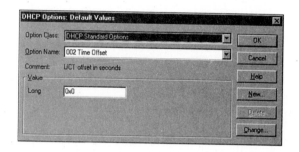

2. In the Option Class drop-down list box, select the class for the option you want to modify. The default is DHCP Standard Options.
3. In the Option Name drop-down list box, select the entry for the option class to modify.
4. In the Value group, specify the new value for the option.

To change a configuration option's name, unique identifier, or description, follow these steps:

1. Repeat steps 1–3 of the preceding procedure.
2. Click the Change button to display the Change Option Type dialog box.
3. Now change the name of the option in the Name field, the DHCP unique identifier number in the Identifier field, or the description in the Comment field.

WARNING

Changing the name or identifier may prevent a DHCP client from functioning properly. Only an expert who is aware of the consequences should modify any of these settings.

4. After you complete all changes, click the OK button.
5. Repeat these steps for each option you want to change.

To add a new configuration option, follow these steps:

1. Repeat steps 1–3 for the procedure to change an existing configuration option default value.
2. Click the New button to display the Change Option Type dialog box.
3. In the Name field, enter a name for the new option.
4. In the Data Type field, specify a data type. This can be one of the following:

   - `Binary`: An array of bytes.
   - `Byte`: An 8-bit unsigned integer.
   - `Encapsulated`: An array of unsigned bytes.
   - `IP address`: An IP address (4 bytes) in the form of ###.###.###.###.
   - `Long`: A 32-bit signed integer.
   - `Long integer`: A 32-bit unsigned integer.
   - `String`: An ASCII text string.
   - `Word`: A 16-bit unsigned integer.

   If the data type is an array of elements, enable the Array check box.
5. In the Identifier field, enter a unique number between 0 and 255.
6. In the Comment field, enter a description for the new option.

WARNING

Adding a new configuration option should be performed only by an expert who is aware of the consequences. It must support non-Microsoft DHCP clients that require the additional options.

---

7. After your changes are complete, click OK.
8. Repeat these steps for each option you want to add.

Managing Client Leases on the DHCP Server

Managing your DHCP client leases, for the most part, consists of informational displays. When you select an active scope and choose Active Leases from the Scope menu, the Active Leases dialog box appears, as shown in Figure 11.6.

You can perform the following actions in the Active Leases dialog box:

- **View the active or reserved leases for the scope.** By default, all the leases are displayed in the dialog box. However, if you enable the Show Reservations Only check box, only the reserved leases are displayed.

FIGURE 11.6.

*The DHCP Manager
Active Leases dialog
box.*

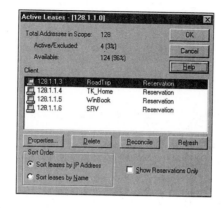

■ **View the client properties.** Select an IP address/computer name in the Client list and click the Properties button. The Client Properties dialog box appears, as shown in Figure 11.7. This can be a useful dialog box, because it displays the Media Access Control (MAC) adapter address in the Unique Identifier field, and there are several Windows NT Server applications, including the DHCP Manager (when reserving a lease, for example), that require a MAC address.

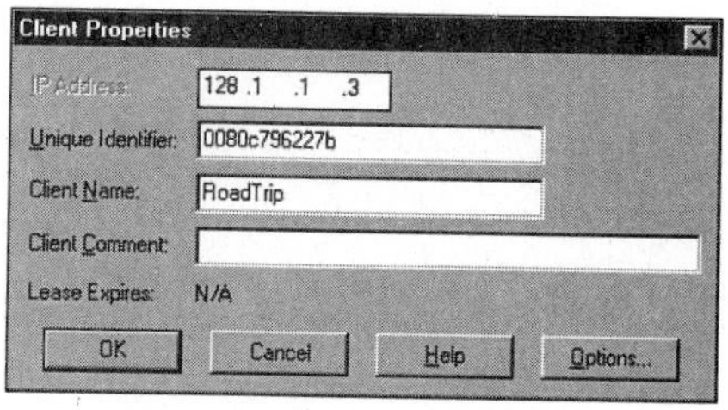

FIGURE 11.7.

*The Client Properties
dialog box.*

■ **Update the DHCP database after a restoration from a backup database copy.** If, for some reason, your DHCP database must be restored from a previous backup (automatically updated by the system or manually updated by you), click the Reconcile button to update the database. This adds lease entries for any leases that are not in the database.

TIP

You can delete a lease by selecting the lease in the Client list and clicking the Delete button. However, this is not an action to be taken lightly, because you could wind up with a duplicate IP address on the network if the original lease is still in use by another computer. Suppose that you delete an active lease because you want to move the client to a new IP

continues

> *continued*
>
> address. As soon as you delete the lease, reserve it (as described in the "Managing Client Reservations" section) to prevent the client from reusing the same IP address. Then force the client to establish a new lease by issuing the IPCONFIG /RENEW command on the client workstation. Or use the WINIPCFG command on a Windows 95 client and then click the Renew button to obtain a new lease.

Managing Client Reservations

Client reservations can be more useful than your average lease because you can preassign an IP address for a DHCP client. You also can change the DHCP configuration options for a DHCP client with a reserved lease. This is a pretty powerful option because it enables you to define global and local scope options for the majority of your DHCP clients when you create the scope, and then specify the specific DHCP options for those special DHCP clients that are the exception to the rule.

To create a reservation for a client, follow these steps:

1. In the DHCP Server window, select the DHCP Server containing the scope you want to modify. If you are modifying a scope on the computer running the DHCP Server service, this entry is Local Machine; otherwise, it is an IP address.
2. Select the scope where you want the client reservation to occur.
3. Choose Add Reservations from the Scope menu to display the Add Reserved Clients dialog box.
4. In the IP Address field, enter an IP address from your current DHCP scope to be assigned to the client.
5. In the Unique Identifier field, enter the MAC address (the network adapter's unique identifier) for the client's network adapter.
6. In the Client Name field, enter the client computer name.
7. In the Client Comment field, enter an optional description for the client computer.
8. Click the Add button.
9. Repeat steps 3–6 for each reservation to be added to the scope.

Changing the configuration options for a reserved lease requires a little more work. To change a configuration option, follow these steps:

1. In the DHCP Server window, select the DHCP Server containing the scope you want to modify. If you are modifying a scope on the computer running the DHCP Server service, this entry is Local Machine; otherwise, it is an IP address.
2. Select the scope you want to modify.

Dynamic Host Configuration Protocol (DHCP)

CHAPTER 11

351

11

DYNAMIC HOST
CONFIGURATION
PROTOCOL

3. Choose Active Leases from the Scope menu to display the Active Leases dialog box.

4. Select the reserved lease you want to modify and click the Properties button. If there are too many leases to scroll through, enable the Show Reservations Only check box. The Client Properties dialog box appears.

5. Click the Options button to display the DHCP Options dialog box. This dialog box is exactly the same as the other DHCP Options dialog box.

6. In the Unused Options list box, select the option you want to modify and then click the Add button to move the option to the Active Options list box. If the option to be modified is already in the Active Options list box, just select it.

7. Click the Value button to expand the dialog box and display the edit field, where you can click the Edit Array button to modify an array of IP addresses, or a field to edit the existing value.

8. Repeat steps 4–6 for each option to be modified. When you finish modifying the options, click the OK button.

9. Repeat steps 3–7 for each reservation you must modify. When you finish modifying all the reservations, click the OK button.

Managing the DHCP Database

Windows NT has always used the Jet database engine for the DHCP and the WINS services. With Windows NT 4.0, Microsoft updated the database engine to use the Jet 5.0 database engine (the same engine that is used as the basis for the Microsoft Exchange message store). This newer database engine provides much better performance with less system overhead. As such, Windows NT 4.0 is a more capable DHCP Server than its predecessors.

These databases for DHCP are located in the `%SystemRoot%\System32\DHCP` directory and include the following files:

■ `DHCP.MDB`: The DHCP database in Jet file format.

■ `DHCP.TMP`: A temporary file created by the DHCP Server for indexing operations.

■ `J50*.LOG` files: Files that contain transaction records for the Jet database engine. DHCP uses this transaction log to recover in the event of system failure.

■ `Backup`: This folder contains a backup of the database. DHCP automatically makes a backup on a regular basis (every 60 minutes by default.)

NOTE

The DHCP database in Windows NT 4.0 is different than the database in previous versions of Windows NT. When looking in the DHCP folder in previous versions of Windows NT, the filenames will be different from those listed.

Compacting the DHCP Database

As your DHCP Server operates day in and day out, the databases may grow or shrink as records are added or deleted. The DHCP Server service in Windows NT 4.0 automatically compacts the DHCP database on a regular basis to ensure that it is operating optimally. The automatic compacting is a new feature in Windows NT 4.0.

In previous versions (3.5 and 3.51), the database needed to be compacted by the system administrator on a regular basis. The most convenient way to do this is to automate the process by using the command scheduler (AT.EXE). You can create a batch file that stops the DHCP Server service (NET STOP DHCPSERVER), compacts the database with JETPACK, and then restarts the service (NET START DHCPSERVER).

To compact the database of a Windows NT 3.5 or Windows NT 3.51 Server system, follow these steps:

> **NOTE**
>
> Windows NT 4.0 DHCP databases do *not* need to be manually compacted with the JETPACK utility.

1. Stop the DHCP Server service from the Control Panel Services applet or issue the net stop dhcpserver command from a Windows NT command prompt.

2. From a command prompt, run the JETPACK.EXE program located in your %SystemRoot%\System32 directory. The syntax for this program follows:

   JETPACK *DatabaseName TemporaryDatabaseName*

   DatabaseName is the name of the database to compact, and it can be a fully qualified path name.

   TemporaryDatabaseName is a name to use as a temporary database. It also can be a fully qualified path name.

3. Start the DHCP Server service from the Control Panel Services applet or issue a net start dhcpserver command from a Windows NT command prompt.

> **TIP**
>
> Because failure is possible with the compact utility and data corruption is possible on your %SystemRoot% partition, you should back up your DHCP databases regularly and definitely before you compact them. Just stop the DHCP Server service temporarily and copy the files in the %SystemRoot%\System32\DHCP and %SystemRoot%\System32\DHCP\backup\Jet directories to another directory, or even occasionally to another computer.

Backing Up and Restoring the DHCP Database

To make it easier to recover in case of failure, Windows NT uses a transaction-based process for all modifications to the DHCP database. However, sometimes this is not enough to protect from serious problems. To help add a further degree of recoverability, Windows NT automatically saves a backup of the database every 60 minutes. The backup is saved into the directory %SystemRoot%\System32\DHCP\backup.

This is an important process; DHCP.MDB cannot be copied normally because it is always in use by the system. Nor, in fact, can it be backed up by backup software, such as the NT Backup utility included with Windows NT. Thus, the backup directory that DHCP automatically creates is important for restoring the DHCP Server's configuration if the entire system must be restored from tape.

You might also consider copying this directory to another location regularly to ensure you have a stable backup.

The database backup previously mentioned is controlled by the Registry value:

HKEY_LOCAL_MACHINE\SYSTEM\CurrentControlSet\Services\DHCPServer\Parameters\BackupInterval

If you need to restore a DHCP Server from tape, or from another backup, follow these steps:

1. Log on as a user with administrative permissions.
2. Stop the DHCP Server if it is running (NET STOP DHCPSERVER).
3. Delete J50*.LOG from the %systemroot%\system32\DHCP directory.
4. Copy a good version of the DHCP.MDB file from a backup location (tape).

> **NOTE**
>
> If you restore a DHCP.MDB file from a backup taken before upgrading to Windows NT 4.0, it will automatically be converted to the new database format when you start the DHCP Server service.

5. Restart the DHCP Server service (NET START DHCPSERVER).

Moving the DHCP Database

Even the best made plans sometimes need to be changed. Fortunately, the database maintained by the DHCP Server service is relatively portable, which helps in case you need to move it to a new system.

If you need to move the DHCP database, you only need the DHCP.MDB file. Shut down the original DHCP Server service (NET STOP DHCPSERVER), copy the DHCP.MDB file to the

`%systemroot%\system32\DHCP` directory on the new server (you must have the DHCP Server service installed already and make sure it is shut down), and start the DHCP Server service on the new system.

> **CAUTION**
>
> When you move the DHCP database to a new server, make sure you don't use the original DHCP database anymore. Otherwise, you will have duplicate scopes defined with duplicate IP address ranges. This will cause problems on your network.

On the new system, you should reconcile the DHCP database. Use the Reconcile option under the Active Leases menu option in the DHCP Manager utility to do this.

Registry Keys for the DHCP Server

Like most Windows NT services, the configuration information for the service is contained in the Windows NT Registry database. For the most part, you should use the DHCP Manager to modify your configuration. These listed Registry keys are not configurable from the DHCP Manager, and instead require that you use the Registry Editor (`REGEDT32.EXE`). The Registry Editor can be a dangerous tool to use. If you are administering a remote computer with a configuration problem so severe that the service cannot be started, you can modify the Registry and restore the database configuration remotely. After these changes are made, you can restart the service by using Server Manager.

The Registry keys are stored in the `HKEY_LOCAL_MACHINE\Systems\CurrentControlSet\Services\DHCPServer\Parameters` subkey. If you modify any of these keys (aside from the `RestoreFlag`), you must restart the computer for your changes to be applied.

The keys of interest include the following:

- `APIProtocolSupport`: This key's value specifies the transport protocol to be supported by the DHCP Server. The default is `0x1` for RPC over TCP/IP protocols. However, it also can be `0x2` for RPC over named pipe protocols, `0x4` for RPC over Local Procedure Calls (LPC), `0x5` for RPC over TCP/IP and RCP over LPC, or `0x7` for RPC over all three protocols (TCP/IP, named pipes, and LPC).

- `BackupDatabasePath`: This key specifies the location of the backup copy of the DHCP database. The default is `%SystemRoot%\System32\DHCP\Backup`. For additional fault tolerance, you can specify another physical drive in the system. Note: You cannot specify a network drive because the DHCP Manager does not support remote drives for backup or recovery.

- BackupInterval: Specifies the default backup interval in minutes. The default is 60 minutes (0x3C).

- DatabaseCleanupInterval: Specifies the interval in minutes for the time to remove expired client records from the database. The default is 1440 minutes (0x5A0)—24 hours.

- DatabaseLoggingFlag: Specifies whether to record the database changes in the J5*.LOG file. This file is used to recover the database if a system crash occurs. The default is 1 (enable logging), but if your system is extremely stable, you can set this value to 0 to disable logging and increase overall system performance slightly.

- DatabaseName: Specifies the database filename to be used by the DHCP Server service. The default is DHCP.MDB.

- DatabasePath: Specifies the location of the DHCP database files. The default is %SystemRoot%\System32\DHCP.

- RestoreFlag: This key specifies whether the DHCP Server should restore the DHCP database from its backup copy. Set this value to 1 to force a restoration, or leave it at 0 to continue to use the original database file. Note: If you change this value, you must stop and then restart the service for the changes to be applied.

DHCP Relay Agent

Because DHCP relies so heavily on broadcast methods, you can run into problems when using it in a routed environment. This is because routers are typically configured to filter out broadcast messages, restricting the range of the message to the local subnet.

However, DHCP uses the well-known UDP ports originally reserved for BOOTP, ports 67 and 68, so DHCP has an advantage. BOOTP is a method used for supplying an IP address and information necessary to allow a diskless workstation to boot from the network. People needed to provide this support across subnets, so router vendors began providing mechanisms for passing UDP ports 67 and 68 to remote subnets. This *relay* support is commonly known as BOOTP/DHCP relay support and is defined in RFC 1452. Not all routers support this and, on routers that do, the default state of the relay mechanism differs.

Not all routers provide this functionality, and others require upgrades, which are not always free. Therefore, Microsoft provided a DHCP relay agent with Windows NT. This agent runs as a service on a Windows NT 4.0 Workstation or Server and listens to UDP port 67 for *DHCP Discover* packets on the local subnet. When it detects such a packet, it passes this packet to one or more DHCP Servers configured when you set up the Relay Agent. When the DHCP Server receives the packet, it responds with a *DHCP Offer*, but instead of broadcasting this offer, as it would normally, it addresses it back to the DHCP Relay Agent. The agent then sends the offer to the client, on behalf of the DHCP Server. In fact, the client doesn't even realize it's talking to an intermediary, rather than directly to the server.

Installing the DHCP Relay Agent

To install the DHCP Relay Agent service, follow these steps:

> **NOTE**
>
> You must be logged on as a member of the local Administrators group to install the DHCP Relay Agent.

1. Open the Network Control Panel applet.
2. Click on the Services tab.
3. Click the Add button, and select DHCP Relay Agent.
4. If prompted, enter the path to the Windows NT distribution files (that is, `f:\i386`) and click the Continue button. This will bring you back to the Network Control Panel. DHCP Relay Agent should now be listed as an installed service.
5. Click the Continue button to exit the Network Control Panel.
6. You will receive a warning message, such as that shown in Figure 11.8, telling you that you must configure at least one DHCP Server address before the DHCP Relay Agent can be activated. Click Yes to bring up the Microsoft TCP/IP Properties page.

FIGURE 11.8.

Setup will warn you that you must configure at least one DHCP Server before the DHCP Relay Agent can be started.

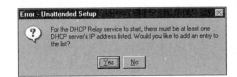

7. From the Microsoft TCP/IP Properties page, click the DHCP Relay Agent tab. This displays the DHCP Relay Agent configuration page, shown in Figure 11.9.
8. Use the Add button to enter the addresses of the DHCP Servers you want to service the local subnet.
9. Change the Seconds threshold and the Maximum hops as necessary for your particular network.

> **NOTE**
>
> For most networks, you can leave the Seconds threshold and the Maximum hops values at their defaults, which are 4 seconds and 4 hops, respectively.

FIGURE 11.9.

The DHCP Relay Agent is configured from the Microsoft TCP/IP Properties window.

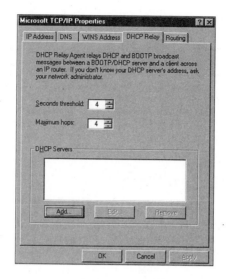

10. Click OK to close the Microsoft TCP/IP Properties window.

You must restart your computer for the changes to take effect.

Changes to DHCP in Service Pack 2

Microsoft made a number of changes to the DHCP Server service in Service Pack 2 (SP2) for Windows NT Server.

The following functionality was added or changed with SP2:

- New Database Format
- Address Conflict Detection
- Switched Network Support
- DHCP Server Activity Logging
- BOOTP Client Support
- Superscope Support

> **NOTE**
>
> Before installing SP2, you should make sure to back up the contents of your DHCP database.

New Database Table Format

Service Pack 2 implements a new database format for the DHCP Server. While it is still based on the Jet 5.0 database engine, the new DHCP database has a different table definition. When you install SP2, DHCP will convert the database the first time it is used.

There is always the possibility of problems occurring during the conversion process. As such, you should back up the DHCP database before upgrading to SP2. Follow the directions for backing up the database earlier in this chapter.

Address Conflict Detection

One of the significant new features in DHCP that is introduced in SP2 is Address Conflict Detection. In all previous versions of the DHCP Server Service, the DHCP Server assumed it had exclusive control over the IP address space defined in its scope. As such, it would never check to see if an IP address was in use before offering it to a client. While this should always be a safe assumption, the reality is that too often clients on real-world networks are not always configured the way the administrator expects.

When the DHCP Server hands out an IP address that is illegally used by a static client on the network, it is often difficult to troubleshoot and locate the offending host. However, while the administrator is trying to locate the offending host, the client to whom the IP address was legitimately issued through DHCP is out of commission.

Address conflict detection permits you to specify that the DHCP Server should check to see if an IP address is actually (and usually illegally) in use before offering it to a client. It uses ping (ICMP packets) to determine if the address is in use. Furthermore, you can specify the number of times that the DHCP Server should try to ping the IP address before offering it.

By default, this functionality is disabled because it has an impact on the DHCP Server's performance. Also, because a DHCP client will usually accept the first address offered to it, if there are two servers providing IP addresses, configuring the address conflict detection feature on only one server will prevent its IP offers from being accepted.

If a conflict is detected, the machine name in the scope list will be indicated by BAD_ADDRESS.

Switched Network Support

In many switched networks, it is not uncommon to use a client's own IP address as its default gateway. In this kind of scenario, IP knows it's on a subnet, as defined by its subnet mask, but there is no router to provide access to the other subnets. Instead, it is the job of the network switch to provide this service. As such, the client is expected to use address resolution protocol (ARP) for the target's MAC address in the same way as it normally would for a local resource.

In previous versions of the DHCP Server, it could only return a fixed, preset value for the gateway address (DHCP option value 3). This was a problem for environments where each system uses its own IP address as the gateway because each client has a different gateway address.

With the DHCP Server in SP2, you can now specify that the DHCP Server should return the same address for option value 3 (the TCP/IP gateway) as it returns for the client's IP address.

This feature can only be enabled in the Registry. To enable it, create the value `SwitchedNetworkFlag` under the Registry key and set it to 1:

```
HKEY_LOCAL_MACHINE\SYSTEM\CurrentControlSet\Services\DHCPServer\Subnets\a.b.c.d
```

DHCP Server Activity Logging

An exciting new feature of the DHCP Server in SP2 is the introduction of DHCP activity logging. Traditionally, it's been very difficult to track down problems with DHCP because of lack of information about what the DHCP Server has actually been doing. Now, with this new feature, the service will keep track of all activity.

This data is logged to a file called `DHCPSRV.LOG`, which is a comma-delimited log with the following fields:

- ID
- Date
- Time
- Description
- IP Address
- Host Name
- MAC Address

Most of these fields are self-explanatory. The ID field is an event code that indicates what action was performed. The event codes that the DHCP Server tracks are listed in Table 11.3.

Table 11.3. DHCP Server event log IDs.

Event ID	Meaning
00	The log was started.
01	The log was stopped.
02	The log was temporarily paused due to low disk space.
10	A new IP address was leased to a client.
11	A lease was renewed by a client.

continues

Table 11.3. continued

Event ID	Meaning
12	A lease was released by a client.
13	An IP address was found to be in use on the network.
14	A lease request could not be satisfied because the scope's address pool was exhausted.
15	A lease was denied.
20	A BOOTP address was leased to a client.

The DHCPSRV.LOG file cannot be copied or backed up while the DHCP Server process is running. To copy the log or make modifications, you must first stop the log.

If the system runs low on disk space, the DHCP Server will pause the log until disk space is freed up.

BOOTP Support on the DHCP Server

DHCP was designed to provide a superset of the functionality of BOOTP, while at the same time taking advantage of the infrastructure tools in place for BOOTP. Despite this overlap and sharing of basic protocol designs, the DHCP Server in Windows NT is not actually capable of being a BOOTP Server. In Service Pack 2, the Windows NT DHCP Server is now capable of acting as a BOOTP Server.

One major difference between BOOTP and DHCP is that BOOTP clients assume that when they are given an IP address, they are given it forever. There is no concept of lease lifetimes. Because of this "limitation" of BOOTP, in this initial release of BOOTP support, you must statically reserve IP addresses for each BOOTP client. Microsoft claims that this is a temporary limitation and that future versions of the DHCP Server will support dynamic assignment of BOOTP clients.

> **NOTE**
>
> When the DHCP Server service receives a BOOTP request, it looks to see if a static lease assignment has been made for the client address. If no static reservation has been made, the BOOTP request will be ignored. If a static reservation has been made, the DHCP Server will offer the IP address to the BOOTP client.

By default, when a BOOTP client requests an IP address, Windows NT returns only the following options if they are defined in the scope (see Table 11.4).

Table 11.4. Default BOOTP options.

Option Number	Description
1	Subnet Mask
3	Router
5	Name Server
12	Host Name
15	Domain Name
44	NetBIOS over TCP/IP Name Server
45	NetBIOS over TCP/IP Datagram Distribution Server
46	NetBIOS over TCP/IP Node Type
47	NetBIOS over TCP/IP Scope
48	X Window System Font Server
49	X Window System Display Manager
69	SMTP Server
70	POP3 Server
9	LPR Server
17	Root Path
42	NTP Servers
4	Time Server

When making a BOOTP request, some BOOTP clients are capable of requesting additional information. This is done by specifying option 55 in the BOOTP request. The BOOTP Server will return as many additional options as can fit in the response packet.

Some BOOTP clients require that a BOOTP Server return a filename or file server name for additional boot support. If this is the case, you can use DHCP option 66 to specify a Boot Server Host Name and option 67 to specify a Bootfile Name.

BOOTP lease reservations are made by using the same procedure as creating normal DHCP lease reservations.

Superscope Support

A large number of customers requested that Microsoft add support for a special type of DHCP scope called a DHCP *superscope*. This functionality was added into the DHCP Server in Service Pack 2.

There are many somewhat conflicting definitions of DHCP superscopes. Based on the way Microsoft implemented it, a DHCP superscope provides a way to manage multiple logical IP subnets on a single physical subnet. In most smaller environments, each subnet contains only a single range of IP addresses on the physical wire. However, in more complex environments, such as switched environments, some organizations have multiple IP subnets on a single wire. Because DHCP Server traditionally uses the physical subnet to determine the scope, all users on a single physical subnet are expected to belong to the same logical subnet. DHCP superscopes changes this assumption.

To create a DHCP superscope, follow these steps:

1. Log on as a user with administrative privileges.
2. In the DHCP Manager application, choose the Superscopes option from the Scope menu.
3. Click the Create Superscope button.
4. Enter the name of the DHCP superscope and click OK.

Once you've defined a superscope, you need to add actual scopes into the superscope. In order to add a scope to the superscope, use the following procedure:

> **NOTE**
>
> You must define a normal DHCP scope before it can be added to a superscope.

1. Log on as a user with administrative privileges.
2. In the DHCP Manager application, choose the Superscopes option from the Scope menu.
3. Select a scope from the list of defined scopes and click the Add button. You will see the scope added to the Child Sub-Scopes list.

Managing DHCP Clients

The DHCP client is built into all current Microsoft networking clients, including all versions of Windows NT 3.5 and greater, Windows for Workgroups (upgrade to the current networking updates from the Windows NT Server CD), Windows 95, the LAN Manager 2.2c client, and the Microsoft networking client for DOS 3.0. None of these clients need additional software in order to take advantage of a DHCP Server on the network.

Managing your DHCP clients consists of working with client leases and client reservations on the DHCP Server and forcing the client to release or renew its lease on the client workstations. On a Windows NT client, the main method of configuring DHCP is through the command-line program IPCONFIG.EXE.

The syntax for IPCONFIG follows:

```
IPCONFIG [adapter] /all /release /renew
```

Explanations of the syntax for this command follow:

- [adapter]: An optional component that is the specific adapter to list or modify the DHCP configuration. Use IPCONFIG with no parameters to obtain the adapter names.

- /all: Lists all the configuration information. This includes the hostname, DNS Servers, node type, NetBIOS scope ID, whether IP routing is enabled, whether the computer is a WINS Proxy Agent, and whether the computer uses DNS for name resolution (instead of WINS). It also includes per-adapter statistics, which include the adapter name and description, the physical address (network adapter Ethernet address), whether the DHCP client is enabled, the IP address, the subnet mask, the default gateway, and the primary and secondary WINS Server IP addresses.

- /release: Releases the current DHCP lease. If specified for all adapters (or if there is only one adapter), TCP/IP functionality is disabled.

- /renew: Renews the lease. If no DHCP Server is available to obtain a valid lease, TCP/ IP functionality is disabled.

TIP

Use the /renew option to manually force a client to obtain a new lease from a new DHCP Server or a new DHCP scope.

NOTE

Windows 95 does not include IPCONFIG; instead, it includes a Windows GUI application called WINIPCFG.EXE.

If executed with no parameters, the current DHCP configuration is displayed. This can be useful for determining the installed adapters and IP addresses. The following output is displayed on my WinBook XP, for example:

```
Windows NT IP Configuration
Ethernet adapter Elnk31:
IP Address. . . . . . . . . : 128.0.0.254
Subnet Mask . . . . . . . . : 255.255.255.0
Default Gateway . . . . . . :
Ethernet adapter NDISLoop9:
IP Address. . . . . . . . . : 129.0.0.1
Subnet Mask . . . . . . . . : 255.255.255.0
Default Gateway . . . . . . :
```

Summary

This chapter focuses on implementing the DHCP service on your Windows NT Server network. The design goals for this service, as well as its relationship to the BOOTP protocol, were discussed. We then looked at basic planning issues, including an investigation of the factors that affect the deployment of DHCP Server. This was followed by detailed instructions focusing on the installation of the DHCP Server service on Windows NT Server.

Once the fundamentals were covered, we continued by looking at issues surrounding DHCP Server management. We focused our attention on working with the DHCP management tool, DHCP Manager. We also looked at how to back up and restore the DHCP Server database, as well as other administrative activities. This was followed by a discussion of the DHCP Relay Agent support that has been included with Windows NT 4.0.

The final section focuses on significant upgrades that Microsoft made to the DHCP Server service with Service Pack 2 for Windows NT 4.0.

Windows Internet Naming Service (WINS)

by Jason Garms

IN THIS CHAPTER

CHAPTER 12

Now that you've looked at Dynamic Host Configuration Protocol (DHCP), you should have a good foundation for exploring Windows Internet Naming Service (WINS). Although DHCP is *not* required for running WINS, they complement each other well. The major impetus behind the creation of WINS was the need for a dynamic name resolution method that would work with DHCP. Because DNS in its standard form only supports static name resolution, it wouldn't have provided the level of necessary functionality.

So there you have it: WINS's primary job role is NetBIOS name *registration* and *resolution* on TCP/IP.

> **NOTE**
>
> WINS is based on RFC 1001 and 1002, which define NetBIOS name resolution over TCP/IP. WINS is fully interoperable with other NetBIOS Name Servers (NBNS). These RFCs can be found at `ftp://ds.internic.net/rfc/rfc1001.txt` and `ftp://ds.internic.net/rfc/rfc1002.txt`.

But wait, you might be saying. How do DNS and WINS really compare? One major note is that whereas DNS is designed for resolving TCP/IP hostnames to *static* IP addresses, WINS is specifically designed to resolve NetBIOS names on TCP/IP to *dynamic* addresses assigned by DHCP.

> **NOTE**
>
> It is important to understand the distinction between a NetBIOS name (usually referred to as the *computer name*) and a computer's TCP/IP *hostname*. A discussion of this can be found in the "WINS Versus DNS" section later in this chapter.

Another point worth noting is that whereas DHCP is truly a cross-platform service, WINS is primarily focused on the Windows (and DOS) platforms. This is because NetBIOS is a Windows (and DOS) artifact.

NetBIOS is a session-layer protocol that is actually capable of communicating over three different transport protocols in Windows NT—NetBEUI, NWLink, and TCP/IP. The WINS service specifically addresses issues that occur with NetBIOS on TCP/IP. You do not need WINS if you are not using TCP/IP.

This discussion of WINS begins with some of the design goals of the service. It then moves on to planning your WINS Server installation and a look at the actual installation steps required to install the service. Then we will move on to managing and configuring the WINS Service and, because a major portion of WINS involves client-related administration, you will see how you can manage your WINS clients. Finally, you will look at managing your WINS database.

Design Goals for the WINS Service

The primary purpose of the WINS Server Service is to make an administrator's job easier by automating the process of mapping computer names to IP addresses for NetBIOS name resolution in a TCP/IP-based network. In short, WINS maintains a database on the WINS server. This database provides a computer name to IP address mapping, enabling other computers on the network to connect to it simply by supplying a machine name. In many respects, WINS is like DNS, except it is designed for NetBIOS name resolution. There is more to WINS than just automating the name resolution process, however.

The WINS design also includes the following:

- **Centralized management:** Along with the WINS Server Service, Windows NT Server also includes the WINS Manager. With the WINS Manager, you can administer other WINS Servers and set up replication partners. You'll learn more about replication partners in the section titled "Planning Your WINS Installation," later in this chapter.

- **Dynamic address mapping and name resolution:** Every time a WINS client starts, and at specified intervals thereafter, the WINS client registers its name with the WINS Server. When the WINS client terminates, such as when the computer shuts down, it tells the WINS Server and the name is released. This gives a client computer the capability to change subnets or its IP address and still be accessible from other computers. It also alleviates the manual modifications to host files required by a UNIX DNS service. These three stages (registration, release, and renewal) operate in the following manner:

    Registration: A name registration request is sent to the WINS Server to be added to the WINS database. The WINS Server accepts or rejects a client name registration on the basis of its internal database contents. If the database already contains a record for the IP address under a different computer name, the WINS Server challenges the registration. A challenge is a means of querying the current holder of the IP address to see whether it is still using it. If it is, the new client request is rejected. If the current holder of the IP address is not using the IP address, the new client request is accepted and is added to the database with a timestamp, a unique incremental version number, and other information.

    Release: Whenever a computer is shut down properly by the user (that is, it did not crash or have a power failure), it informs the WINS Server, which marks the name entry in the database as released. If the entry remains marked as released for a specific period of time, the entry then is marked as extinct and the version number is incremented. Version numbers are used to mark a record as changed so that changes to WINS partners are propagated to all WINS Servers.

    If a record is marked as extinct and a new registration arrives at the WINS Server with the same name but a different IP address, the WINS Server does not challenge the registration. Instead, the new IP address is assigned to the name. This might occur with a DHCP-enabled portable computer (or another DHCP-enabled computer) that is moved to a different subnet, for example.

Renewal: When half the renewal time has expired, a WINS client reregisters its name and IP address with a WINS Server. If the renewal time expires completely, the name is released, unless the client reregisters with the WINS Server.

- **Domain-wide browsing:** If you are using WINS Servers, your clients (Windows NT, Windows 95, Windows for Workgroups, LAN Manager 2.x, and MS-DOS computers using the Microsoft Network Client 3.0) can browse for computer resources on a Microsoft network across a router without needing a Windows NT domain controller on each subnet.

- **Reduction of broadcast traffic:** A WINS Server decreases the number of broadcast messages by supplying an IP address when a name query message is received for a computer name from its local database on a WINS Server or from its cache on a WINS Proxy Agent. A broadcast occurs on the local subnet only if the name query request fails.

WINS Proxy Agents

As indicated previously, WINS is a relatively new service. Therefore, you might still have several NetBIOS over TCP/IP clients that cannot act as WINS clients. This is particularly true of older software and non-Microsoft NetBIOS networking clients, such as LAN Manager and other older OS/2-based clients. To enable these non–WINS-enabled clients to interact with a WINS service, Microsoft provides the capability to run WINS Proxy Agents.

A WINS Proxy Agent listens to the local network for clients trying to use broadcasts to resolve NetBIOS names. The WINS Proxy Agent picks these requests off the network and tries to resolve them. First, the Proxy Agent will look in its own local cache. If no match is found there, it forwards the lookup request to the WINS Server, which responds to the proxy with the resolved IP address. The WINS Proxy Agent then provides this information to the client requesting the name resolution.

The neat thing about this process is that no changes must be made to the non–WINS-enabled client. In fact, it is completely unaware that the name resolution has been provided by the WINS service.

> **NOTE**
>
> It is important to realize that the WINS Proxy Agent is only for resolving name requests for NetBIOS clients. It does not provide any name resolution for UNIX or other systems that do not use NetBIOS.

The WINS Proxy Agent will hold the names of all the hosts it resolves for six minutes before discarding them. This caching enables better performance with less need for the proxy agent to continuously re-resolve addresses.

You can use Windows NT 3.5 and higher or Windows for Workgroups as WINS Proxy Agents.

> **NOTE**
>
> In Windows NT 3.5 and 3.51, you could enable the WINS Proxy Agent easily from the TCP/IP properties user interface. However, when configured improperly, the WINS Proxy Agent can cause serious problems on your network. In fact, so many people configured it improperly that in Windows NT 4.0, you can no longer enable the WINS Proxy Agent from the user interface. You must now enable it from the Registry.

In order to configure a Windows NT 4.0 system to act as a WINS Proxy Agent, you must set the following Registry value to 1.

```
HKEY_LOCAL_MACHINE\SYSTEM\CurrentControlSet\Services\Netbt\Parameters\EnableProxy
```

WINS Versus DNS

The relationship between DNS and WINS (and even DHCP) is complicated and would require a lot of space and time to fully explore, but understanding this concept is key to getting the most from WINS and DNS on a Microsoft network.

> **NOTE**
>
> This section clarifies the overall concepts behind WINS, DNS, NetBIOS names, DNS hostnames, and so on. To make this as useful as possible, I'll gloss over certain less relevant (more in-depth) parts of the puzzle. So remember, it's the overall scheme that's important here.

As discussed repeatedly throughout this book, standard TCP/IP utilities (such as FTP and Telnet) use IP addresses for establishing connections between the client and server services. Recall also that people hate to remember long IP addresses, thus hostname to IP address mapping facilities have been developed. Local Hosts files and DNS services are the two most popular.

Whereas standard TCP/IP utilities must resolve the hostname to an IP address to locate the host on the network, Microsoft networking (a.k.a. NetBIOS networking) works differently. It does not use an actual address for locating a network resource; rather, it uses the NetBIOS name. NetBIOS is a session layer interface protocol developed in the early 1980s for IBM. It exposes a set of networking APIs that enable user applications to obtain and provide network services. It also provided a primitive transport protocol called NetBIOS Frames Protocol (NBFP), which evolved into NetBIOS Extended User Interface (NetBEUI) a few years later. NetBEUI's sole purpose was to efficiently transport NetBIOS traffic across small local area networks (LANs).

For many years, NetBEUI was the standard transport protocol for Microsoft networks. Today, many people still get mixed up about the role that NetBEUI and NetBIOS play. NetBEUI is inextricably linked to NetBIOS. NetBIOS, however, can be abstracted and applied to other transport protocols, such as IPX/SPX and TCP/IP, which, of course, is our interest here. But first, let's look quickly at the operation of NetBIOS over NetBEUI.

Remember that NetBIOS is a session layer protocol. However, it doesn't fully comply with the ISO OSI model, so the addressing takes place inside the NetBIOS layer. Also, the addressing is done by name and not by an address, like TCP/IP.

To see why this is significant, let's look at what happens when an application requests network services with NetBIOS over NetBEUI. Some NetBIOS application decides it wants to connect to a network resource. To do this it *must* know the NetBIOS name that identifies the resource on the network. The application says, "Okay, I want to connect to the network resource called SERVER." It speaks this command into the NetBIOS API interface. The NetBIOS layer then instructs the NetBEUI transport to find the resource on the network. "NetBIOS to NetBEUI. Please find the network resource called SERVER on the network." The NetBEUI transport does this by broadcasting to the network asking for the specified network resource to identify itself. "Hello out there. Is anyone out there called SERVER? If you are, would you please respond to me with your MAC address?" If the specified resource is on the network, it will respond with its MAC address. "Yeah, I'm SERVER. My MAC address is…" NetBEUI then uses this MAC address for passing packets back and forth between the two machines.

So you can see that it is imperative that you know the NetBIOS name of the resource you want to connect to. NetBEUI is a small and fast protocol, but because it relies heavily on broadcasts and it cannot support internetwork routing, it doesn't scale well past a small workgroup (fewer than 100 machines). That's probably a little more about NetBEUI than you wanted to know, but it is key to understanding the evolution that brought us the confusion between WINS and DNS name resolution.

As mentioned previously, Microsoft wanted to begin running NetBIOS applications over other protocols, such as IPX/SPX and TCP/IP. This would enable Windows users to participate more extensively in large networks and perform WAN communications. Also, users who wanted to connect to standard TCP/IP-based services as well, such as FTP and Telnet servers, would only have to install a single protocol stack, which would reduce overhead.

It was simple to create a TCP/IP implementation on DOS or Windows that acted like a normal TCP/IP stack for supporting standard TCP/IP connectivity. However, the problem was how to interface NetBIOS with TCP/IP. Remember, although NetBIOS is a session-layer protocol, it uses its own resource location system based on the NetBIOS name. TCP/IP, on the other hand, relies on the IP address for resource location. The problem was getting these two to work together. The idea is quite simple, but the method can be tricky.

> **NOTE**
>
> All current Microsoft stacks support NetBIOS over TCP/IP. However, many third-party TCP/IP stacks developed for the DOS and Windows environments still do not.

12
WINDOWS
INTERNET NAMING
SERVICE (WINS)

The essence of how NetBIOS interfaces with TCP/IP follows. The NetBIOS applications says, "I want to connect to a network resource called SERVER." The NetBIOS API interface then takes this information and passes it through a NetBIOS "helper" interface. This interface resolves the NetBIOS name into an IP address, which is required for locating the resource on a TCP/IP network. Remember, this step was not required under NetBEUI, because the NetBIOS name was actually used for locating the resource on the network.

This is the step where all the confusion usually occurs, and this is also where WINS plays its biggest role. Recall that there are four main methods of resolution: B-node, P-node, M-node, and H-node. They refer to the differing methods the NetBIOS client uses to register and resolve names on a TCP/IP network. We will look more closely at each of these in the next section.

When the NetBIOS to TCP/IP interface has resolved the NetBIOS name into an IP address, the remainder of the process works the same way as standard TCP/IP. The IP address is resolved into a MAC address, either of the actual resource or of the router that can be used to locate the resource, and communications take place.

So the real question becomes, "How does this interface translate the NetBIOS name into an IP address?" Before WINS was developed, the three most common ways of performing this resolution were as follows:

■ The interface can use broadcasts for name to IP address resolution, just as NetBEUI resolved the names. It broadcasts the NetBIOS name onto the TCP/IP network and waits for a response. However, this is not a terribly friendly thing to do to the network, so except in small LANs, it is undesirable.

■ You can use an LMHOSTS file. The LMHOSTS file is a text file, similar to HOSTS, and is used to link NetBIOS names to their corresponding IP addresses. When the NetBIOS application asks to connect to a network resource, the NetBIOS to IP interface looks up the NetBIOS name in the LMHOSTS file and passes the resulting IP address down through the layers. Traditionally, this has been the most popular method of supporting NetBIOS name resolution on large TCP/IP networks.

- The newer TCP/IP stacks from Microsoft have an option to use the DNS service for resolving NetBIOS names. The caveat here is that the NetBIOS name for the resource *must* be the same as the DNS hostname or you'll have problems. Also, it only works when connecting to machines at the same level of the DNS hierarchy as the client. For example, if my computer is called `ntserver.xyzcorp.com` and I have the DNS resolution option set, I can use the File Manager to connect to any NetBIOS resource in the domain `xyzcorp.com` by using DNS for the name resolution.

    The way this works is the NetBIOS application (in this case File Manager) requests a connection to the resource by its NetBIOS name. The NetBIOS to IP translation layer looks up the resource's name in the authoritative DNS server for the `xyzcorp.com` domain and gets an IP address back.

Although all these options have their advantages and disadvantages, none of them addresses how to deal with name resolution for dynamically assigned IP addresses. This is the primary reason WINS was created. Although WINS can be used as the only method of name resolution, it is more commonly used in conjunction with the previously listed methods.

When you use WINS on your network, WINS clients register their current IP addresses and their NetBIOS names with the WINS server. Then when someone on the network wants to resolve the NetBIOS name for a network resource, he or she can ask the WINS Server. Even if the IP assignment is obtained dynamically with DHCP, this process still works because every time a DHCP client gets a new address, it registers the change with the WINS Server.

I addressed why NetBIOS names are important and how NetBIOS name resolution works on TCP/IP networks. One area that remains to be explored is how WINS and DNS can be integrated. WINS works well for NetBIOS name resolution. This means that I can use the File Manager or other NetBIOS application (such as the Network ClipBook viewer) to connect to a machine registered in the WINS database.

Let's look at an example to explore the need for integration between WINS and DNS. I have an NT server called SERVER. I have a Windows for Workgroups (WfW) workstation called WORKSTATION. If the WfW machine wants to connect to a network drive on SERVER, it uses the NetBIOS name SERVER when it tries to connect. It uses whatever resolution method is available for resolving the NetBIOS name to the IP address. If I am also running an FTP server on the machine called SERVER, and I want to connect to that, things work differently. FTP is not a NetBIOS-based application. FTP really wants the actual IP address of the host in order to connect. This means that if the machine named WORKSTATION wants to connect to SERVER using FTP, it must be given the IP address of SERVER, or WORKSTATION must be given a name that can be resolved in the IP address using a local HOSTS (not LMHOSTS) file or a DNS service. Let's throw in a monkey wrench. Let's say that the machine called SERVER gets its IP address *dynamically* from DHCP. Neither the HOSTS file nor the DNS solution is capable of resolving names to dynamic IP addresses, and WINS is capable only of resolving NetBIOS names.

This is where the concept of interfacing WINS and DNS becomes important. Let's extend the example to see how this interfacing works. Imagine I run a mostly Windows-based network of 100 clients with a few NT servers. All resources receive their IP addresses dynamically with DHCP, except one NT server, which is the WINS and DHCP server. I also run an FTP server on one of the NT Servers on the network, which also gets its address dynamically. Suppose there is a UNIX box on the other side of the world that wants to FTP into the NT Server. One way to connect is to discover what the current IP address is for the server and use this to connect. The disadvantage is that the IP address might change, and you'll need to rediscover it.

There's no other way to connect, right? Well, that's what DNS to WINS integration is for. It works by running the Microsoft DNS Server service on Windows NT. This lets the DNS server request a name to IP resolution request from the WINS server.

> **NOTE**
>
> We've just spent all this space talking about the differences between NetBIOS names and TCP/IP hostnames; yet in the last paragraph, you get the feeling the distinction became blurred. You're right. Fortunately for us, TCP/IP hostnames and NetBIOS names use a compatible set of conventions, so when using this service, the NetBIOS name and the TCP/IP hostname can be used interchangeably.

To continue our example, the UNIX client on the other side of the world, let's say in Timbuktu, tries to connect to an NT Server called `NTFTP.xyzcorp.com`. Remember, this NT Server gets a dynamic IP address from a DHCP server. The UNIX client asks its local DNS server to resolve the name `NTFTP.xyzcorp.com`. The local DNS server then looks to the InterNIC for the IP address of the authoritative DNS server for domain `xyzcorp.com`. The InterNIC returns the authoritative server, which is the NT Server running the Microsoft DNS server and WINS server. The Microsoft DNS server is then asked for the identity of the machine called NTFTP. The Microsoft DNS server, in turn, asks the WINS server for the IP address of a machine called NTFTP. The IP address is ultimately returned to the UNIX machine in Timbuktu, which completes the connection now that it has an IP address for `NTFTP.xyzcorp.com`. This is an effective example of the integration between WINS and DNS.

Planning Your WINS Installation

For a small Microsoft-based network, all you really must do for your WINS installation is install the WINS Service on each domain controller. This provides the means to configure your TCP/IP-based network clients to fully interoperate with any other server or client on the network. This recommendation is based on the fact that a single WINS Server can accommodate about 1,500 name registrations and 760 name query requests per minute. In theory, this means that you can use one WINS Server with a backup WINS Server for every 10,000 clients. However, I prefer to use a WINS Server per logical grouping to provide additional fault tolerance and load balancing.

> **NOTE**
>
> These name query requests can be routed to other WINS Servers and WINS Proxy Agents to ensure that a request eventually will be fulfilled. If you enable replication of your WINS databases, however, each WINS Server will have a complete listing of every WINS client name and IP address. Then, when a name query request is received, an IP address will be returned without broadcasting on the network. This mechanism provides the capability to decrease the amount of broadcast traffic on the subnet.

This logical grouping should be based on the physical layout of your Windows NT Server domain controllers or servers. A logical group could be based on domain controllers or servers in separate physical buildings or floors. It could even be based on domain controllers on the other side of a WAN link or similar property. For every three to five domain controllers or servers, I like to install the WINS Service. This provides for fault tolerance, in case of required maintenance or a WINS Server failure, and also limits the load on a single WINS Server. At the very least, you should have two WINS Servers on your network supplying NetBIOS name resolution to prepare for a failure of the primary WINS Server, just as you should have a primary and backup domain controller to provide logon authentication in case of a primary domain controller failure.

This scenario works well for Microsoft-based networks that use the Microsoft TCP/IP protocol stacks, but it will fail if you use third-party TCP/IP protocol stacks that do not support WINS on your network clients. This does not mean that you cannot use WINS in this situation, however. It only implies that you also must install WINS Proxy Agents. A WINS Proxy Agent should be installed on each subnet, to provide a link between your non-WINS clients and the WINS Servers. Your WINS Servers also should share their database to provide complete coverage of the entire network. This sharing process is provided by WINS replication, which is discussed in detail later in this section.

> **NOTE**
>
> You also can create static mappings, which add a permanent computer name to IP address mapping in the WINS database to support your non-WINS clients.

You must have a WINS Proxy Agent per subnet because broadcast messages are not normally passed across routers. When a non-WINS client tries to find another computer, it uses a broadcast message to get the IP address of the requested computer. If the computer is on the same subnet, the request succeeds, but if it is on a different subnet, the request fails (unless you have domain controllers on both sides of the routers). This is where the WINS Proxy Agent comes into play.

Client #1 is a WINS client, Client #2 is a non-WINS client, Client #3 is a WINS Proxy Agent, and Server #1 is a Windows NT domain controller running the WINS service. When the WINS Client #2 attempts to access WINS Client #1 by broadcasting to obtain the IP address for Client #1, the request fails because Client #1 and Client #2 are on different subnets. The broadcast is intercepted by Client #3, however, which then caches this name and IP address. Client #3 also returns the IP address for Client #1 to Client #2 so that a TCP/IP connection can be established. If another WINS client on a different subnet attempts to access Client #2 by issuing a name query request, the cached IP address for Client #2 that Client #3 has stored is returned to the requesting client.

A WINS Proxy Agent will not store information obtained from a broadcast in the WINS Server's database. You therefore must have a WINS Proxy Agent on each subnet that contains non-WINS clients. In this case, the WINS Proxy Agent can respond to name query requests from WINS clients or WINS Servers, and then broadcast on its local subnet to find the non-WINS client. After the non-WINS client is found, the IP address can be passed to the WINS client or Server that issued the name query request.

When a WINS client requires access to another computer, it issues a name query request. This request can be routed to WINS Servers, but this occurs only if the primary or secondary WINS Server for the WINS client does not contain a registration for the requested computer. If the routed name query request cannot be resolved by any WINS Server, the WINS client then issues a broadcast message. Both broadcast messages and routed name query messages eat network bandwidth that could be used to pass data. If your WINS Servers have a complete listing of the computer names and IP addresses, however, the primary WINS Server then can respond to the name query request, limiting the number of routed name query requests and broadcast messages.

This leads to the next performance and planning tip, which is that every WINS Server on a network should replicate its database to other WINS Servers on the network so that every WINS Server has a complete listing of every WINS client's name and IP address. This method provides the fastest mechanism for resolving names to IP addresses and limiting broadcast messages and routed name query messages.

WINS Servers provide two mechanisms for replication:

- **Push partners:** This is a WINS Server that sends update notifications to its pull partners. After the pull partner receives this update message, it requests the changes from the push partner. The push partner then sends a replica of its database to the requesting pull partner.

- **Pull partners:** This is a WINS Server that requests updates from its push partner, and when the push partner responds, it receives the database replica.

As you can see from the description of push and pull partners, these are part of a circular process. To replicate the WINS database one way, one WINS Server must be a push partner and the other must be a pull partner. To completely replicate a WINS database between two or more WINS Servers, each WINS Server must be a push and pull partner of the other. This is a two-way nonlinear chain, which can be used to replicate every WINS database to every other WINS database. Some WINS Servers receive update notifications from more than one WINS Server, which can lead to increased network traffic.

A better method, although a bit slower, is to create a linear chain where one—and only one—WINS Server is the push or pull partner of another WINS Server. Only at a WAN link is this rule broken, where the WINS Server on the LAN side is a push and pull partner of a WINS Server on the LAN, and where it is also a push and pull partner of a WINS Server on a WAN link. This leads to another point: How often should you replicate? My basic methodology is based on the distance between replication points and the speed of the link. For your LAN, 10–15 minutes is a good choice because the network throughput is quite high. For local, heavily used WAN links, you should limit the replication period to 30–60 minutes. Decrease the rate only if you have a high turnover rate. For longer WAN links, choose a value of 45–90 minutes. And for intercontinental WAN links, choose 6–12 hours and schedule it for the non-peak hours. The idea here is that the more heavily the link is used, the lower the replication frequency (or the higher the number of scheduled minutes between replication attempts).

Installing the WINS Service

You use the Control Panel Network applet to install the WINS Server Service.

> **NOTE**
>
> To install the WINS Server Service, you must be a member of the Administrators group on the computer on which you want to install the service.

Follow these steps to install the WINS Server Service:

1. Launch the Control Panel Network applet.
2. Click the Services tab and then the Add button.
3. Select Windows Internet Name Service from the list of network services.

> **NOTE**
>
> If you don't have TCP/IP already, it will be automatically installed when you install the WINS Server Service.

> **TIP**
>
> To use SNMP to configure the WINS Server Service remotely, install the SNMP Service as well.

4. Click the OK button. When prompted, enter the path to the distribution files (that is, f:\i386) and click the Continue button.

5. Click the Close button to close the Network Control Panel.

6. When prompted, restart your system. After the system restarts, the WINS Server Service should be activated. If not, check your system event log for any error messages.

Configuring the WINS Server Service with the WINS Manager

The first time you use the WINS Manager, it displays only the WINS Server on the local computer. To add WINS Servers to the WINS Manager, choose Server | Add WINS Server and then supply the IP address or computer name in the Add WINS Server dialog box. To delete a WINS Server from the WINS Manager list, select it and then choose Server | Delete WINS Server. After adding your WINS Servers to the local WINS Manager, you should configure the local WINS Server for optimal performance. This includes setting your WINS Server configuration, replication partners, and preferences. Each of these options performs a slightly different task, which this section covers.

The first recommended option is to choose Server | Configuration, which displays the WINS Server Configuration dialog box, shown in Figure 12.1.

FIGURE 12.1.

The expanded WINS Server Configuration dialog box.

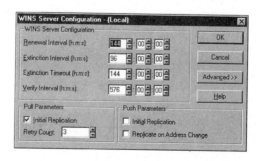

You can set the following options in the WINS Server Configuration dialog box:

■ **Renewal Interval:** Specifies how often a WINS client has to register its name with the WINS Server. The default is 6 days.

- **Extinction Interval:** Specifies the time interval between when a record is marked as released and when it is marked as extinct. The default and maximum time is 6 days.

- **Extinction Timeout:** Specifies the time interval between when a record is marked as extinct and when it is scavenged from the database. The default is 6 days and the minimum is 1 day.

NOTE

The extinction interval and extinction default for a fully configured WINS Server is based on the renewal time and whether the WINS Server has replication partners on the replication time interval.

TIP

You can manually scavenge the database by choosing Mappings | Initiate Scavenging. This process removes outdated records from the database.

- **Verify Interval:** This specifies the time interval in which a WINS Server must verify that old names owned by another WINS Server are still valid. The default (24 days) is dependent on the extinction interval. The maximum is 24 days.

- **Pull Parameters:** The pull partner replication interval is set in the Preferences dialog box, as described later in this section. If you want the replication to be triggered when the WINS Server Service starts, enable the Initial Replication checkbox and specify a number in the Retry Count list box.

- **Push Parameters:** To configure push partner configurations, you can enable these checkboxes:

  Initial Replication: If this setting is enabled, push partners are informed that a change has occurred when the WINS Server Service is started.

  Replicate on Address Change: If this setting is enabled, push partners are informed whenever an entry in the database changes or when a new entry is added.

- **The Advanced Button:** You can access the following options by clicking the Advanced button to expand the WINS Server Configuration dialog box:

  Logging Enabled: This specifies that the WINS Server Service will log database changes and inform you of basic errors in the system event log. The default is enabled.

  Log Detailed Events: This specifies that detailed events will be written into the system event log. It should be used only for a limited time, such as when you are troubleshooting WINS Server problems, because it can consume considerable resources and affect system performance. The default is disabled.

Replicate Only with Partners: This allows replication only with push or pull partners. If this option is disabled, you can replicate data from any unlisted WINS Server. The default is enabled.

Backup on Termination: This automatically backs up the WINS database whenever the WINS Server Service is shut down. It does not perform a backup whenever the system is shut down, however. The default is enabled.

Migrate On/Off: This enables or disables the treatment of static or multihomed records as dynamic whenever they conflict with a new registration or replica (data copied from another WINS Server). This option should be enabled if you are upgrading a non-Windows NT System (such as a LAN Manager Server) to a Windows NT Server. The default is disabled.

Starting Version Count: This specifies the highest database version number. Normally, you do not need to change this value; however, if you restore the WINS database from a backup because your primary database is corrupted, you should increment this value to a number higher than any other copy of the WINS Server partners to ensure proper replication.

> **NOTE**
>
> You can display the current value by choosing View | Database. To see the version numbers on other WINS Servers, choose the WINS Server before making the menu selection.

Database Backup Path: This specifies the full path to use for the backup copies of the WINS Server database.

I suggest setting your preferences for the WINS Manager and default settings for the WINS Server Service. You can access these preferences by choosing Options | Preferences to display the dialog box, shown in Figure 12.2.

FIGURE 12.2.

Specifying the WINS Manager preferences and WINS Server Services defaults.

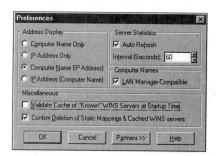

You can take the following actions from this dialog box:

- Specify how the WINS Manager displays the names for the WINS Servers it is connected to and, incidentally, the mechanism used for connecting to the service. These options include the following:

    Computer Name Only: Specifies that the computer name is displayed and uses named pipes to connect to the WINS Server.

    IP Address Only: Specifies that the IP address is displayed and uses TCP/IP to connect to the WINS Server.

    Computer Name (IP Address): Specifies that the computer name is displayed first and then the IP address, and uses named pipes to connect to the WINS Server.

    IP Address (Computer Name): Specifies that the IP address is displayed first, followed by the computer name; also specifies that TCP/IP is used to connect to the WINS Server.

- Specify the refresh interval for updating the WINS Manager display. If you enable the Auto Refresh checkbox, you also should specify a value (number of seconds to wait before updating the display) in the Interval field.

> **NOTE**
>
> The WINS Manager display is also refreshed automatically whenever you initiate an action with the WINS Manager.

- Specify the NetBIOS name compatibility. If the LAN Manager Compatible checkbox is enabled (the default setting), NetBIOS names are limited to 15 bytes to contain the name, whereas you are limited to 16 bytes for a special code for static mappings. If you use other applications that require a 16-byte NetBIOS name, such as Lotus Notes, this option should be disabled. The special codes include the following:

0x0	Specifies that the NetBIOS name is used by the Redirector.
0x1	Specifies that the NetBIOS name is used by the master domain browser.
0x3	Specifies that the NetBIOS name is used by the messenger service.
0x20	Specifies that the NetBIOS name is used by a LAN Manager Server.
0x1B	Specifies the master browser name that clients and browsers use to contact the master browser.
0x1E	Specifies that the NetBIOS name is used for a normal group.
0x1D	Specifies that the NetBIOS name is used for client name resolution when an attempt is made to contact the master browser for server lists.

0x1C Specifies that the NetBIOS name is an Internet group name. An Internet group name contains the addresses of the primary and backup domain controllers for the domain. This name is limited to 25 addresses.

- Specify the miscellaneous support options:

Validate Cache of "Known" WINS Servers at Startup Time: If this option is enabled, whenever you start the WINS Manager, it attempts to connect to all WINS Servers you have added. If a WINS Server cannot be contacted, you are prompted to remove the WINS Server from the list of connected servers. The default is disabled.

Confirm Deletion of Static Mappings and Cached WINS Servers: This option, if enabled (the default), prompts you with a message box whenever you attempt to remove a static mapping or cached WINS Server. I find the constant message boxes a bit annoying and usually disable this setting. However, before you do so, I suggest that you become familiar with the WINS Manager.

- If you click the Partners button, the dialog box expands and allows you to set defaults for the partner replication.

New Pull Partner Default Configuration: The entries in this group specify the default replication settings for new pull partners that you create for the currently selected WINS Server. These options include the following:

Start Time: The time to start your WINS Server database replication. There is no default, although I like to start at 12:00 a.m.

Replication Interval: The interval at which to repeat the WINS Server database replication. There is no default, although I generally choose a 15-minute interval for LAN WINS Servers.

New Push Partner Default Configuration: The entry in this group specifies the number of changes that must occur in the WINS Server database before a push notification is sent to the push partners that you create for the currently selected WINS Servers.

Update Count: This specifies the number of changes that must occur before a push notification is sent. There is no default, although I recommend a value of 1000.

I suggest that you set the replication settings for the local WINS Server by choosing Server | Replication Partners. This displays the Replication Partners dialog box, shown in Figure 12.3. Click the Add button to add the WINS Servers to be configured as the local push or pull partners. You can choose to replicate to any or all WINS Servers in a nonlinear fashion, or you can choose to pull from one WINS Server and push to another in a linear fashion. These techniques were described in more detail in the section titled "Planning Your WINS Installation."

Figure 12.3.

Specifying the WINS Server replications partners.

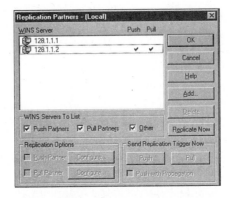

> **NOTE**
>
> To remove a WINS Server from the WINS Server list, select it and press the Delete key.

After you add your WINS Servers, you can take the following actions:

- Specify the WINS Servers to display in the WINS Server list by enabling or disabling the options in the WINS Servers To List section. These options include the following:

    Push partners: If enabled (the default), push partners of this WINS Server are displayed.

    Pull partners: If enabled (the default), pull partners of this WINS Server are displayed.

    Other: If enabled (the default), any nonpartner of this WINS Server is displayed.

- Specify the individual settings for the currently selected WINS Server to be a push, pull, or both partner in the Replication Options section. When you select a WINS Server that is already configured as a push or pull partner, the following Configure buttons are enabled:

    Push Partner: This specifies that the selected WINS Server is a push partner. You can then click the Configure button to display the Push properties dialog box, where you can view or set the update count.

    Pull Partner: This specifies that the selected WINS Server is a pull partner. You can then click the Configure button to display the Pull properties dialog box, where you can view or set the start time and replication interval.

> **TIP**
>
> If you specified the default values in the Preferences dialog box, these settings are set automatically for new push or pull partners. If you are configuring a push or pull partner across a WAN link, however, you should set higher values, as described in the section titled "Planning Your WINS Installation."

■ Initiate a replication trigger immediately instead of waiting for it to occur on the basis of the replication times set in the Configuration dialog box by setting the following values in the Send Replication Trigger Now group:

   Push: This initiates a push trigger to send to the selected WINS Server.

   Pull: This initiates a pull trigger to send to the selected WINS Server.

   Push with Propagation: This modifies the Push message to indicate that changes sent to the selected WINS Server should be propagated to all other pull partners of the selected WINS Servers.

> **TIP**
>
> You can initiate a complete replication to the selected WINS Server by clicking the Replicate Now button.

Managing Your Non-WINS Clients

Managing your non-WINS clients consists of creating static mappings, which is a permanent computer name–to–IP address record, and viewing your current database records. When you create a static mapping, it is also a good idea to create a reservation (as described in the section "Managing Client Reservations") for this IP address to provide a more manageable environment. You can add static mappings by choosing Mappings | Static Mappings, which displays the Static Mappings dialog box, shown in Figure 12.4. After you click the Add Mappings button, the Add Static Mappings dialog box appears. Here, you can enter a computer name, IP address, and type that will be added to the WINS Server database. Table 12.1 describes the special names the WINS Server uses and how WINS manages these names. You can delete a static mapping by selecting the mapping in the Static Mappings dialog box and then clicking the Delete Mapping button.

FIGURE 12.4.

*The Static Mappings
dialog box.*

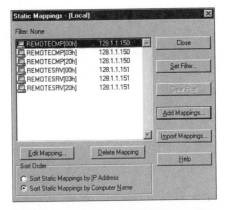

TIP

You can import a series of static mappings by importing a host file from a DNS Server to support your non-WINS computers.

Table 12.1. WINS Server special names.

Type	Description
Unique	A normal name, implying that only one computer name will be associated with the IP address.
Group	Does not have an associated IP address. Instead, when a group name is registered with the WINS Server and a name query request for this name is received, the WINS Server returns the broadcast address (FFFFFFFF) and the requesting client issues a broadcast message to find the requested computer.
Multihomed	A name that has multiple IP addresses associated with it. A multihomed device contains two or more network adapters that can register each IP address associated with the computer by sending a special name registration packet. A multihomed group name can contain a maximum of 25 IP addresses.
Internet	A group name that contains domain controller IP addresses. WINS gives preference to this name registration to the closest 25 addresses. After a request is received for the domain, the domain controller address and the additional 24 (maximum) IP addresses are returned to the client.

Managing WINS Databases

Because your WINS Server also uses the same database format (a modified Access database), it has the same basic issues as the databases for the DHCP Server. As records are added and deleted, the database grows. The WINS databases are located in the `%SystemRoot%\System32\WINS` directory and include the following:

- `WINS.MDB`: The WINS database
- `WINSTMP.MDB`: A temporary file created by the DHCP Server
- `JET.LOG`: Contains transaction records
- `SYSTEM.MDB`: Contains structural information about the WINS databases

The database growth affects the performance of the WINS Server. As your `WINS.MDB` database approaches the 30MB limit, you should compact it. To do so, follow these steps:

1. Stop the WINS Server Service from the Control Panel Services applet, or issue the `net stop wins` command from a console prompt.

2. From a console prompt, run the `JETPACK.EXE` program, which is located in your `%SystemRoot%\System32` directory. The syntax for this program follows:

   `JETPACK DatabaseName TemoraryDatabaseName`

   Here, `DatabaseName` is the name of the database to compact. It can be a fully qualified path name.

   `TemporaryDatabaseName` is a name to use as a temporary database. It also can be a fully qualified path name.

WARNING

Do not compact the `SYSTEM.MDB` file. If you do, the WINS Server Service will not start. If this occurs, restore your configuration from a previous backup.

---

3. Start the WINS Server Service from the Control Panel Services applet, or issue a `net start wins` command from a console prompt.

TIP

Before you back up or compact the database, choose Mappings | Initiate Scavenging to delete old records that are no longer needed.

> **TIP**
>
> Because the potential for failure or just plain data corruption on your %SystemRoot% partition is possible with the compact utility, you should back up your WINS databases regularly, and definitely before the databases are compacted. You can do this by choosing Mappings | Backup Database. Be sure to perform a full backup by disabling the Perform Incremental Backup option if you plan to use this copy to restore your configuration.

Monitoring the WINS Server Service

Although the WINS Manager displays the same statistics as those used by the Performance Monitor, the WINS Manager can display only the statistics for the currently selected WINS Server. If you use the Performance Monitor, however, you can monitor multiple WINS Servers simultaneously. This can be of enormous benefit when you are comparing the performance of multiple WINS Servers. Table 12.2 lists the available WINS Server performance object counters that you can use to monitor your selected WINS Server.

Table 12.2. The Performance Monitor object types and object counters for the WINS Server.

Object Counter	Description
Failed Queries/sec	Total number of failed queries per second.
Failed Releases/sec	Total number of failed releases per second.
Group Conflicts/sec	The rate at which group registration received by the WINS Server resulted in conflicts with records in the database.
Group Registrations/sec	The rate at which group registrations are received by the WINS Server.
Group Renewals/sec	The rate at which group renewals are received by the WINS Server.
Queries/sec	The rate at which queries are received by the WINS Server.
Releases/sec	The rate at which releases are received by the WINS Server.
Successful Queries/sec	Total number of successful queries per second.
Successful Releases/sec	Total number of successful releases per second.
Total Number of Conflicts/sec	The sum of the unique and group conflicts per second. This is the total rate at which conflicts were seen by the WINS Server.
Total Number of Registrations/sec	The sum of the unique and group registrations per second. This is the total rate at which registrations are received by the WINS Server.

Object Counter	Description
Total Number of Renewals/sec	The sum of the unique and group renewals per second. This is the total rate at which renewals are received by the WINS Server.
Unique Conflicts/sec	The rate at which unique registrations and renewals received by the WINS Server resulted in conflicts with records in the database.
Unique Registrations/sec	The rate at which unique registrations are received by the WINS Server.
Unique Renewals/sec	The rate at which unique renewals are received by the WINS Server.

TIP

To get a feel for how well your WINS Server is performing, monitor the total number of conflicts, registrations, and renewals. You also should monitor the failed queries and releases.

Using WINS Server Registry Keys

The WINS Server Service also stores its configuration information in the Registry, just as the DHCP Server Service does. And, once again, you may need to modify the Registry to change one or more configuration settings if you cannot set them from the WINS Manager or you are administering an inactive WINS Server. I am issuing this warning again because if improperly used, the Registry Editor can damage your system beyond repair.

The following primary Registry keys are located in the `HKEY_LOCAL_MACHINE\System\CurrentControlSet\Services\WINS\Parameters` key:

- `DbFileNm`: This specifies the full pathname to the locations of the WINS database file. The default is `%SystemRoot%\System32\WINS\WINS.MDB`.

- `DoStaticDataInit`: If this item is set to 1, the WINS Server initializes its database with records from one or more files in the Datafiles subkey. This initialization is performed at the time the process is executed and whenever a change to a key in the Parameters or Datafiles subkey occurs. If set to the default, this initialization does not occur.

- `InitTimePause`: If this entry is set to 1, the WINS Server starts in the paused state. It stays in this state until it replicates with its partners (push or pull) or fails in the replication attempt (at least once). If this entry is set to 1, the `WINS\Partner\Pull\ InitTimeReplication` subkey should be set to 1 or removed from the Registry for proper operation. A value of 0 (the default) disables this option. Note: You can set the `InitTimeReplication` key value by choosing Options | Preference and clicking the Advanced button to expand the dialog box.

- `LogFilePath`: This specifies the location for the WINS Server log files. The default is `%SystemRoot%\System32\WINS`.

- `McastIntvl`: This specifies the time interval, in seconds, for the WINS Server to send a multicast and announce itself to other WINS Servers. The minimum and default value is 2400 (40 minutes).

- `McastTtl`: This specifies the number of times a multicast announcement can cross a particular router. The default is 6, and the range is 1 to 32.

- `NoOfWrkThds`: This specifies the number of worker threads used by the WINS Server. The default is one per processor on the system, with a range of 1 to 40. Note: You can change this value and place it into effect without restarting the WINS Server.

- `PriorityClassHigh`: If set to 1, this entry enables the WINS Server to run in the high priority class. This prevents other applications and services running in lower priorities from preempting the WINS Server. The default is 0. Note: If you choose to enable this setting, make sure that you monitor the system with the performance monitor to ensure that the WINS Server is not using too much processor time and that other applications and services continue to function properly.

- `UseSelfFndPnrs`: This option is used to configure the WINS Server to automatically find other WINS Servers and configure them as push and pull partners. Set this entry to 1 (to enable it) or 0 (to disable it). The default is 0. If the push and pull partners are configured manually with the WINS Manager, the partnership information no longer is maintained automatically when a change occurs.

NOTE

If the `UseSelfFndPnrs` option is enabled, the WINS Server Service only configures WINS Servers as push and pull partners across routers if the routers support multicasting. Otherwise, only WINS Servers found on the local subnet are configured automatically as partners. If your routers do support multicasting, `UseSelfFndPnrs` can be a useful item to set because it relieves you of the burden of configuring your push and pull partners manually.

You can configure the following Registry keys by choosing Server | Configuration and modifying the entries in the WINS Server Configuration dialog box:

- `BackupDirPath`: This specifies the full pathname to the location to be used to back up the WINS database.

- `DoBackupOnTerm`: If enabled (1), the WINS database is backed up whenever the WINS Server Service is terminated. If disabled (0), the database is not backed up when the service is terminated. The default is 1. Note: The backup does not occur if the system is shut down. A backup occurs only when the service is stopped manually.

- `LogDetailedEvents`: If enabled (1), verbose logging of WINS events occurs. The default is disabled (0).

- `LoggingOn`: If enabled (1), WINS messages are placed in the event log. If disabled (0), no events are placed in the event log. The default is 1.

- `RefreshInterval`: This specifies the time, in seconds, for the client to register its name with the WINS Server. The default is 0x54600 (4 days).

- `RplOnlyWCnfPnrs`: This enables (1) or disables (0) the capability to replicate a WINS Server from a WINS Server that is not a partner. The default is 1.

- `MigrateOn`: This enables (1) or disables (0) the treatment of unique and multihomed records as dynamic when a registration conflict is detected. The default is 0.

- `TombstoneInterval`: This specifies the time, in seconds, between when a client record is released and when it is marked as extinct. The default is 0x54600 (4 days).

- `TombstoneTimeout`: This specifies the time, in seconds, between when a client record is marked as extinct and when it is scavenged from the database. The default is 0x54600 (4 days).

- `VerifyInterval`: This specifies the interval in which the WINS Server must verify that old names, which it does not own, are still valid. The default is 0x1FA400 (24 days).

The following Registry keys for partner replication are located in the `HKEY_LOCAL_MACHINE\System\CurrentControlSet\Services\WINS\Partners` key:

- `PersonaNonGrata`: This specifies IP addresses for WINS Servers from which you do not want to replicate data. This key is useful for administrators to block replication from WINS Servers that are not under their control.

- `Pull\<IPAddress>\MemberPrec`: This specifies the preference order of addresses in an Internet group. Values can be 0 for low precedence or 1 for high precedence. The default is 0. Note: This entry appears under an IP address (of a WINS Server).

12

WINDOWS
INTERNET NAMING
SERVICE (WINS)

Summary

This chapter's focus was on implementing the WINS services on your network. We discussed the design goals for the services, basic planning issues, and the management options available for manipulating your WINS clients.

This chapter also discussed specific issues for utilizing WINS in a mixed Windows NT and UNIX environment, and, where prudent, how to prepare for the possibility of a failure with the services database, some Registry keys you can use to configure otherwise unconfigurable options, and some basic performance tips.

Domain Name Service (DNS)

by Art Knowles and Jason Garms

IN THIS CHAPTER

- Using the Microsoft Domain Name System Server   392

The DNS server included with NT Server 4.0 permits your NT Server to act as a standard domain name system (DNS) server for resolving hostnames to IP addresses. Although this is often the most used feature of a DNS server, other uses include reverse name resolution, in which a client can request the hostname that belongs to a particular IP address, as well as mail exchange information, which provides the location of mail hosts for machines listed in the DNS domain. Windows NT Server's DNS server supports all these standard DNS services. One unique feature of the Microsoft DNS server is the integration of DNS and WINS. It provides this feature with a built-in interface that enables the DNS server service to look up names in a WINS database. It can then use this information to provide name-to-IP resolution.

> **NOTE**
>
> Microsoft first provided a DNS service with the Windows NT 3.5 Resource Kit utilities. However, it was difficult to configure, not very robust, and considered to be unstable. The DNS server that ships with NT Server 4.0 is a complete rewrite and is designed to handle large loads. It is also much easier to configure, thanks to the new graphical DNS Manager utility.

The goal of this chapter is to provide you with an understanding of these services so that you can properly implement the DHCP and WINS services on your network. This chapter discusses design goals, installation, configuration, and management of these services, which covers most of the administrative issues. Specific discussions regarding interoperability with existing UNIX services, tips to get the maximum mileage from these services, and some of the possible problems (gotchas) to avoid are also discussed.

Using the Microsoft Domain Name System Server

Unlike WINS and DHCP, which are barely two-years-old, the DNS is a relative old-timer in the TCP/IP arena. The primary purpose of a DNS is to supply friendly computer names instead of an IP address to locate a resource. This process is often referred to as name resolution. The DNS was developed a number of years ago to solve the problems of dramatic growth in the Internet and is defined in RFCs 1034 and 1035. Because its development centered around the Internet, which has no single authority, DNS utilizes a hierarchical architecture that allows the distribution of the name database and the decentralization of administrative tasks.

WINS and DNS share many similarities, but they also have numerous differences, in both the scope of their jobs and their actual implementation. Whereas WINS provides dynamic name resolution, DNS is based on static configuration files. DNS, on the other hand, allows hierarchical naming, whereas WINS, because of its ties to NetBIOS, only provides for a flat filename space. The major job of WINS is to provide name registration and resolution, whereas DNS also provides other services, such as mail exchange information that enables electronic mail to be properly routed for the entire domain. On a more bit-pushing level, DNS uses UDP port 53, and WINS uses UDP ports 137 and 138, which are reserved for NetBIOS name services.

CAUTION

Do not confuse the TCP/IP domain with the NT domain. DNS uses a hierarchical naming system, which is composed of a computer name and a domain name. The domain name provides information for locating the computer. An NT domain, in contrast, is a security database for managing an NT network. The computer's NT domain name, which follows a flat-file naming scheme, is always different from the DNS domain name, which follows a hierarchical naming scheme. For example, an NT system might be a member of the XYZ-PROCURE NT domain, but its TCP/IP DNS domain name is xyzcorp.com.

The Design Goals for the Microsoft DNS Service

Although you can use other DNS servers on your network, the Microsoft DNS Service that ships with NT Server 4.0 is the only one that can integrate with the WINS service to provide *dynamic DNS*. This feature is the real difference between the Microsoft DNS implementation and other DNS servers that run under Windows NT. The Microsoft implementation fully supports WINS, which in turn is aware of DHCP. If you use DHCP, WINS, and DNS together, then you also have the following capabilities:

- Utilizing DHCP, your clients automatically receive dynamic IP addresses and TCP/IP configuration information. You can centrally administer IP assignments, provide support for roaming, clean up IP allocation by automatically returning unused IP addresses to the available pool for reuse, and enjoy all the other benefits of DHCP.

- Utilizing WINS, machines automatically register their NetBIOS computer name and IP address every time they start up. If the computer moves between subnets, this information is automatically updated as well.

- Utilizing DNS, your clients can find any non–WINS-aware resources through the static mappings maintained in the configuration files. This also works in reverse. Any non–WINS-aware client that uses DNS to resolve names and has a static mapping to your DNS service can locate a WINS client, even if the IP address is dynamically assigned with DHCP.

This combination of DHCP, WINS, and DNS provides additional benefits as well. Dynamic address allocation also means dynamic address recovery. When a new IP address is allocated to a client on another subnet, then the old address is released back to the DHCP scope's address pool. This can prevent the confusion caused by duplicate IP addresses on the network. The only thing DHCP and WINS does not do for you is make it easy to get on the Internet. One of the requirements for registering your Internet domain with the InterNIC is that you maintain two or more DNS servers on your network so that clients that want to connect to your server, most likely through your WWW page, can find you. You'll find that many Internet service providers (ISPs) don't know how to deal with, or support, DHCP and WINS. You might as well get used to using a DNS server if you plan to connect to the Internet, but you don't have to go through all the hassle of modifying your configuration files every time you move or add a client to your network if you also use DHCP and WINS.

Another benefit of using a DNS server is that it can provide some additional name resolution capabilities that WINS cannot. A DNS server includes e-mail name resolution by supporting the MX record type, which associates an e-mail address with a hostname. When a DNS server cannot resolve a name locally, it refers the name query to another DNS server higher up the chain in a effort to resolve it.

Planning Your DNS Installation

First, consider who will be in charge of maintaining the configuration files. DNS is not a simple subject to be taken lightly. Entire books have been written discussing all the nuances associated with configuring DNS servers. Fortunately, Microsoft included a graphical configuration tool, the DNS Manager, for working with the DNS service in NT Server 4.0. This utility enables you to forgo the archaic process of editing configuration files by hand. If you use the Microsoft DNS service, you are not forced to use the graphical configuration tool. But if you prefer, you can edit the configuration files by hand.

> **CAUTION**
>
> A duplicate hostname, or IP address, on your network can cause serious problems. Make sure your administrators are aware of this and that your registration plan includes the capability to register a name and IP address before it is reassigned. You can use an ACCESS database to maintain information (hostname, IP address, filename, and so on) about your network and query the database to verify that the hostname and IP address are not in use.

First and foremost, make sure that everyone who makes modifications to the DNS service has the proper training to understand the consequences of their actions. It took a lot of people with doctoral degrees quite some time to make DNS as complicated as it ended up!

You have three main ways to configure your DNS service:

■ The *primary name server* for a domain holds the master copy of the name database. This database contains the records for all hosts in the zone, as well as records for all the subdomains.

- *Secondary name servers* hold a copy of the record database for the domain and subdomains. When changes are made to the domain, they are made to the primary DNS, and the updated database is replicated to all secondary DNS servers.

- A *caching name server* does not actually contain a copy of the record database. Instead, it is configured with the address of either a primary or secondary DNS for a particular domain. When a caching name server receives a name query request, it asks the other name server to resolve the request. It then caches this information so that when it is requested again, it is already cached. Effectively, the caching name server holds all the frequently visited locations, and the size of its cached database grows with time and use.

On a larger network, you might consider running multiple DNS servers to serve different subnets. This is an effective means of providing load balancing, fault tolerance, and improving network performance by limiting network traffic associated with name resolution.

Installing the Microsoft DNS Server Service

You can install the DNS Server service through the Network Control Panel applet. Follow these steps:

> **NOTE**
>
> To install the Microsoft DNS Server service, you must be a member of the Administrators group on the computer on which you want to install the service.

1. Launch the Control Panel Network applet.
2. Click the Services tab and then the Add button.
3. Select Microsoft DNS Server from the list of network services.

> **NOTE**
>
> If you don't have TCP/IP already, when you install the DNS Server service, TCP/IP is automatically installed.

5. Click the OK button. When prompted, enter the path to the distribution files (that is, `f:\i386`) and click the Continue button.
6. Click the Close button to close the Network Control Panel.
7. Restart your system.

When you restart your system, the DNS Server starts automatically.

Managing the DNS Server with the DNS Manager

Your interface to managing the DNS Server is the DNS Manager. It is installed in the Administrative Tools program group when you install the DNS service. You must have administrative privileges to use this program. With the DNS Manager, you can do everything but stop or start the DNS Server. To stop or start the service, use the Control Panel Services applet and specify the Microsoft DNS Server as the service to control. You can also issue the following commands from a console prompt:

```
net stop dns
net start dns
```

The DNS Manager enables you to work with the DNS *zones*, the administrative unit in the DNS. This section discusses how to create a zone, create domains and subdomains within the zone, and manage hosts and other records in a domain. You will also explore and learn more about the configuration files that form the heart of the DNS database. We also demonstrate how to configure the Microsoft DNS Server service to take advantage of the WINS Server for name resolution.

Creating a Zone

A *zone* is the administrative unit in the domain name system, so the first thing to do when you install the DNS service is create a zone. A zone represents a subtree of the DNS, such as xyzcorp.com. For example, you can configure your system such that the domain xyzcorp.com, the subdomain eng.xyzcorp.com, and the subdomain admin.xyzcorp.com are all part of a single administrative zone configured by one organization. A separate organization can then be responsible for maintaining a zone that consists of the subdomains research.xyzcorp.com and testing.xyzcorp.com. This is part of the distributed nature of DNS.

The interface of the DNS Manager is similar to that of the DHCP Manager and the WINS Manager. The first time you launch the DNS Manager tool, it shows the address of the local machine, as shown in Figure 13.1.

FIGURE 13.1.

By default, the DNS Manager focuses on the local machine.

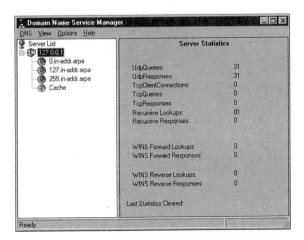

If you have other NT Servers on the network running DNS, you can add them to the DNS Manager display using the following steps:

1. Choose New Server from the DNS menu.
2. Type the fully qualified domain name or the IP address of the NT Server you want to administer.
3. Click OK. The IP address or hostname appears under the Server List.
4. Repeat these steps for each NT Server running the DNS service you want to administer from your local machine.

> **NOTE**
>
> You can only use the DNS Manager to administer NT Servers running the DNS service. As nice as it would be, you cannot use the DNS Manager to configure non-NT DNS servers, such as those running on the UNIX platform.

To create an administrative zone, follow these steps:

1. In the Server List, click the DNS Server you want to administer.
2. Choose New Zone from the DNS menu. The Create New Zone window appears.
3. Choose Primary, and click the Next button.
4. Give your zone a name, such as xyzcorp.com. You must also enter a filename for the zone. All the information for this zone is stored in %systemroot%\system32\dns*filename*, where *filename* is the name of the file you enter here.
5. Click the Next button and then click the Finish button.

The zone is now created and should appear under the listing for your server, as shown in Figure 13.2.

FIGURE 13.2.

The xyzcorp.com *zone now exists as an administrative unit on the local server.*

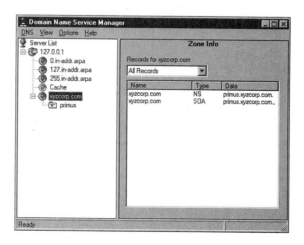

13

DOMAIN NAME SERVICE (DNS)

By default, two records are created in the domain, an NS entry and an SOA entry. The NS record specifies the selected machine as a name server in the domain, and the SOA record is known as the Start of Authority. Every domain must contain an SOA, which details the name server that is the best source of authoritative information for the zone, as well as the e-mail address of a contact responsible for the domain.

Enabling WINS Resolution for the Zone

You can enable WINS resolution on a zone-by-zone basis. When the DNS is asked to resolve a DNS name and it can't find an entry for the name anywhere in the DNS database, the NT DNS service takes the left-most part of the hostname (the characters up to the first period) and passes this to the WINS server for resolution. If the WINS server has a matching NetBIOS name in its database, it returns the corresponding IP address to the DNS service, which returns it to the client. The client can then attach to the resource. As you can see, this is an effective means of permitting the DNS service to resolve even dynamically assigned IP addresses because the WINS server understands dynamic addressing.

> **NOTE**
>
> The NT DNS Server only attempts to use WINS for resolution if it cannot find a matching hostname anywhere in its database.

To enable WINS resolution for a particular zone, follow these steps:

1. Click the zone for which you want to enable WINS resolution.
2. Choose Properties from the DNS menu.
3. Click the WINS Resolution tab.
4. Check the box for Use WINS Resolution.
5. Enter WINS Servers in the order they should be queried, as shown in Figure 13.3.
6. Click OK to close the Properties window for the zone.
7. A WINS Server record should appear in the zone information list for each WINS server you configured, as shown in Figure 13.4.

Creating Subdomains

The DNS is a hierarchical naming system. This means that you can create nested domains to divide the network into administrative units. For most standard configurations, especially those connected to the Internet, your zone name is the same as your base domain. For example, my company is called XYZ Corporation, so the domain is xyzcorp, but it is part of the .com hierarchy. My complete domain name is xyzcorp.com. I can subdivide that domain into additional units by creating subdomains. For instance, if I want to use different domains for our administrative group and our testing group, I can call them `admin.xyzcorp.com` and `testing.xyzcorp.com`.

Figure 13.3.

Enter WINS Servers in the order they should be queried.

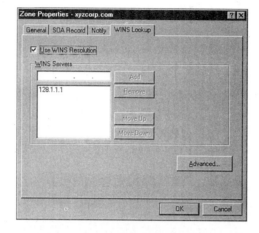

Figure 13.4.

A zone record is created for each WINS Server to be used for resolution.

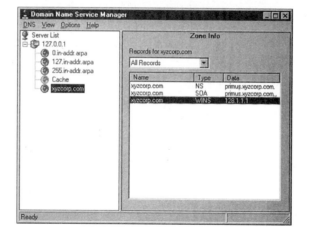

To create subdomains, use the following procedure:

1. Click the zone where you want to create a subdomain.
2. Choose New Domain from the DNS menu.
3. Enter the name for the subdomain, such as `admin` or `testing`, and click OK.
4. The new subdomain appears under the selected zone in the DNS Manager, as shown in Figure 13.5.

FIGURE 13.5.

Subdomains appear under their respective zones.

> **TIP**
>
> You can create hostnames with the same name as a subdomain. For instance, `admin.xyzcorp.com` can refer to a machine name, but it can also refer to a subdomain that contains other machines, such as `ftp.admin.xyzcorp.com`.

Adding Hosts to a Domain

Once you create a domain, you can add hosts to populate it. To add a host, follow these steps:

1. Click the domain (zone) or subdomain where you want the host to reside, such as `xyzcorp.com`.
2. Choose New Host from the DNS menu.
3. Enter the hostname and IP address, such as `secundus` and `128.1.1.2`.
4. To create an associated PTR record, click the Create Associated PTR Record button. A PTR (Pointer) record is essentially an A record for reverse address to name lookup.
5. Click the Add Host button and then click the Done button.
6. A new record of type A is created for the host, as shown in Figure 13.6 for secundus.

Adding a New Record

As mentioned earlier, the DNS provides many more services than just simple name-to-IP-address resolution. Other services are provided by adding appropriate records to the domain. For instance, to specify a server to handle incoming e-mail for computers in the domain, you can create an MX record to identify the mail server.

FIGURE 13.6.

*A record of type A is
created when you add a
new host.*

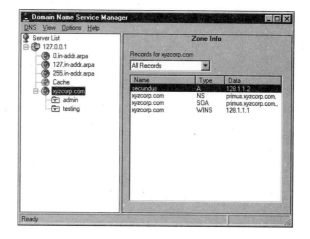

To add records to the domain, follow these steps:

1. Click the zone or subdomain where you want to create the new record.
2. Choose New Resource from the DNS menu. The New Resource Record window appears.
3. Select the type of record you want to create, such as an MX record. A description of the selected record type appears at the bottom of the screen, and the fields on the right change depending on the requirements of the particular record type, as shown in Figure 13.7.

FIGURE 13.7.

*The MX record type is
used to specify a mail
exchanger for the
domain.*

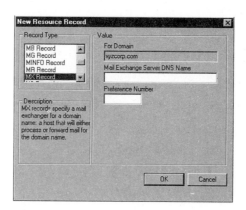

4. Enter the remaining information required for the particular record type, such as the mail exchanger's DNS name and preference number in the case of an MX record type.
5. Click OK.

The new record now appears in the domain listing.

The DNS Service Configuration Files

If you are the kind of person who likes to look at the nuts and bolts to see how things work, you actually have the option of directly viewing and editing the DNS configuration files. They are stored in the `%systemroot%\system32\dns` directory. The configuration files used with the Microsoft DNS server can be replaced by those from a UNIX BIND installation if you are migrating or interoperating with a UNIX system—although you might need to modify the files if you are using some outdated BIND commands.

> **NOTE**
>
> Before editing the DNS files directly, make sure they are up to date by issuing the Update Server Data Files command from the DNS menu in the DNS Manager application.

The configuration files for BIND are divided into four basic types:

- The BOOT file controls the startup behavior of the DNS server. It includes information on the default directory where the configuration files reside, the cache filename, the domain name the DNS server will service, and the domain name for secondary DNS servers.

> **NOTE**
>
> You can configure the Microsoft DNS service to store the boot information in either the boot file, located in the `%systemroot%\system32\dns` directory, or the Registry.

- The CACHE file contains information for Internet connectivity.
- The PLACE.DOM file contains information on hostnames in the domain. It also includes references to reverse lookup filenames and WINS servers.
- The ARPA-###.REV files (there is one per subnet) include information to resolve an IP address to a hostname.

BOOT

The BOOT file supports very few commands, so the syntax for the commands, as summarized in Table 13.1, is fairly easy to remember. A sample BOOT file for a simple network, such as the one in my office, looks like this:

```
;   DNS BOOT FILE - Master configuration for DNS service
directory       %System32%\system32\dns
cache   .       cache
primary xyzcorp.com     xyzcorp.dom
primary 127.in-addr.arpa        arpa-127.rev
primary 128.1.1.in-addr.arpa    arpa-128.rev
```

Table 13.1. Applicable commands for the BOOT file.

Command	Required	Description	Note
;	No	Starts a comment.	Avoid using unnecessary comments because the file is parsed line by line. Each comment added to the file slows down name resolution for any name not in the cache.
directory *PathName*	No	Describes the location of the DNS configuration files where *PathName* is a fully qualified path. The default if it's not specified is %SystemRoot%\System32\DNS.	If the directory cannot be found, the DNS service does not start.
cache *FileName*	Yes	Describes the location of the cache file used to find additional name servers, where *FileName* is the name of the file.	If the file cannot be found, the DNS service does not start.
Primary *DomainName* *FileName*	Yes	Specifies a domain name for which this DNS server is authoritative and a configuration filename that contains information for the domain.	

continues

Table 13.1. continued

Command	Required	Description	Note
Secondary *DomainName* *HostList* [*FileName*]	No	Specifies a domain name and associated IP address array from which to download zone information.	If a filename is specified, then the zone information specified, then the is downloaded and used if the domain DNS server, or alternate, cannot be located.

CACHE

The cache file is used for additional name resolution. When your DNS server cannot resolve a name, it queries the additional name servers listed in this file. If you are using this DNS server to resolve names on the Internet, your file should look similar to the following code:

```
;     DNS CACHE FILE
;     Initial cache data for root domain servers.
;     YOU SHOULD CHANGE:
;          - Nothing if connected to the Internet.  Edit this file only when
;            update root name server list is released.
;             OR
;          - If NOT connected to the Internet, remove these records and replace
;            with NS and A records for the DNS server authoritative for the
;            root domain at your site.
;     Internet root name server records:
;          last update:    Sep 1, 1995
;          related version of root zone:    1995090100
; formerly NS.INTERNIC.NET
.                         3600000   IN  NS      A.ROOT-SERVERS.NET.
A.ROOT-SERVERS.NET.       3600000       A       198.41.0.4
; formerly NS1.ISI.EDU
.                         3600000       NS      B.ROOT-SERVERS.NET.
B.ROOT-SERVERS.NET.       3600000       A       128.9.0.107
; formerly C.PSI.NET
.                         3600000       NS      C.ROOT-SERVERS.NET.
C.ROOT-SERVERS.NET.       3600000       A       192.33.4.12
; formerly TERP.UMD.EDU
.                         3600000       NS      D.ROOT-SERVERS.NET.
D.ROOT-SERVERS.NET.       3600000       A       128.8.10.90
; formerly NS.NASA.GOV
.                         3600000       NS      E.ROOT-SERVERS.NET.
E.ROOT-SERVERS.NET.       3600000       A       192.203.230.10
; formerly NS.ISC.ORG
.                         3600000       NS      F.ROOT-SERVERS.NET.
F.ROOT-SERVERS.NET.       3600000       A       39.13.229.241
; formerly NS.NIC.DDN.MIL
```

```
.                        3600000      NS    G.ROOT-SERVERS.NET.
G.ROOT-SERVERS.NET.      3600000      A     192.112.36.4
; formerly AOS.ARL.ARMY.MIL
.                        3600000      NS    H.ROOT-SERVERS.NET.
H.ROOT-SERVERS.NET.      3600000      A     128.63.2.53
; formerly NIC.NORDU.NET
.                        3600000      NS    I.ROOT-SERVERS.NET.
I.ROOT-SERVERS.NET.      3600000      A     192.36.148.17
; End of File
```

> **NOTE**
>
> You can find an updated version of this file at the InterNIC FTP site `ftp.rs.internic.net`. Just log on anonymously, change to the *domain* directory, and download the file `named.root`.

If this DNS server is not used for Internet name resolution, then replace the name server (NS) and address (A) records with the authoritative DNS server for your domain.

PLACE.DOM

PLACE.DOM is the heart of your DNS server's operation. It contains several record types to provide name resolution for the domain. Because the sample file included with the Microsoft DNS service contains information for a nonexistent domain, you should rename the file and modify it as appropriate for your domain. The following is a copy of my replacement file called xyzcorp.dom. I use a naming convention of *DomainName.dom*, and I recommend you do so as well. This is particularly useful when administering multiple domains.

```
@    IN SOA     primus.xyzcorp.com. admin.primus.xyzcorp.com. ( ;source host
e-mailaddr
                           1                         ; serial number of file
                           10800                     ; refresh interval
                           3600                      ; retry interval
                           604800                    ; expiration interval
                           86400 )                   ; minimum time to live
@                IN  NS    primus.xyzcorp.com.          ; name server
for domain
primus           IN  A     128.1.1.1                 ; IP address of
name server
@                IN  WINS  128.1.1.1 128.1.1.2       ; IP address of
WINS servers
localhost        IN  A     127.0.0.1                 ; loop back
@                IN  MX    10      primus            ; e-mail server
primus           IN  A     128.1.1.1                 ; IP address of
e-mail server
ftp              IN  CNAME primus                    ; alias name for
FTP service
www              IN  CNAME primus                    ; alias name for
WWW service
gopher           IN  CNAME primus                    ; alias name
for Gopher service
```

The first entry in the file must be an SOA record. This record includes parameters that describe the source host (where the file was created); an e-mail address for the administrator of the file; a serial number (or version number) of the file; a refresh interval (in seconds), which is used by secondary servers to determine when a revised file should be downloaded; retry time (in seconds), which is used so that secondary servers wait before attempting to download the file in case of error; and expiration time (in seconds), which is used by secondary servers to determine when to discard a zone if it cannot be downloaded. Then, your name servers (or DNS servers) for the domain should be listed, followed by their IP addresses. Next, include the LocalHost identifier, which is used for loopback testing, the name and address of any mail servers, and hostname aliases. A hostname alias is used to provide a host (such as my server primus) with more than one hostname. This is particularly useful when you want your WWW site to be accessible in the commonly used format www.*DomainName*.com (www.xyzcorp.com, for example) rather than *ServerName*.*DomainName*.com (primus.xyzcorp.com, for example).

> **NOTE**
>
> When you specify a fully qualified domain name (FQDN), it must be appended with a period; otherwise, the domain name is appended to the hostname for resolution and can cause the name query to fail. For example, I might have specified my domain name as xyzcorp.com in line 7 instead of xyzcorp.com. Then, when trying to resolve the hostname primus.xyzcorp.com, the domain name of xyzcorp.com would be appended once again (primus.xyzcorp.com.xyzcorp.com). Because there is no host by that name, the query would fail.

Table 13.2 summarizes the record types for PLACE.DOM that are used to provide name resolution for the domain.

Table 13.2. Supported domain name records.

Identifier	Record Type	Description
A	Address	Specifies the IP address of the associated hostname.
CNAME	Class name	Specifies an alias for the associated hostname.
MX	Mail	Specifies the e-mail server hostnames.
NS	Name server	Specifies the DNS servers in the domain.
SOA	Start of authority	The first record in any configuration file, used to specify name.
WINS	WINS	Specifies the IP addresses of WINS servers used for additional name resolution.

ARPA-###.REV

`ARPA-###.REV` is used for reverse lookups of hostnames within a domain. Instead of resolving a name to an IP address, a reverse lookup resolves an IP address to a hostname. For example, for my domain, which only has one subnet (`128.0.0.0`), the reverse lookup file is as follows:

```
@   IN  SOA     primus.xyzcorp.com. admin.primus.xyzcorp.com. ( ;source host
e-mailaddr
                            1                   ; serial number of file
                            10800               ; refresh interval
                            3600                ; retry interval
                            604800              ; expiration interval
                            86400 )             ; minimum time to live
@       IN  NS      primus.xyzcorp.com.         ; name server for domain
@       IN  NBSTAT  xyzcorp.com.                ; domain name to
append for NBSTAT lookups
1       IN  PTR     primus.xyzcorp.com.         ; primus at 128.1.1.1
99      IN  PTR     winbookxp5.xyzcorp.com.     ; WinBook XP5 at
128.1.1.99
```

Once again, the first record should be an SOA record. The next record lists the name (or DNS) server for the domain, followed by an NBSTAT record and then the individual PTR records for each host in the domain. These records and their usage are summarized in Table 13.3. What is generally most confusing is the PTR records. Instead of supplying a complete IP address (such as `128.1.1.1`) for the host, you only supply the last digit of the IP address (such as `1`) followed by the fully qualified hostname (host + domain name).

Table 13.3. Supported reverse lookup records.

Identifier	Record Type	Description
NBSTAT	NBSTAT	Specifies the domain name to append to any hostname found by an NBSTAT lookup.
NS	Name server	Specifies the DNS servers in the domain.
PTR	Pointer	Specifies an IP address for a host.
SOA	Start of authority	The first record in any configuration file, used to specify name.

Summary

This chapter's focus was on implementing the DNS services on your network. We discussed the design goals for the service and basic planning issues.

Configuring TCP/IP Printing

by Jason Garms

IN THIS CHAPTER

CHAPTER 14

As you have seen demonstrated in almost every aspect of the product, Windows NT is able to work in a diverse networking environment. This flexibility extends to network printing as well. In an effort to support Internet standards, including TCP/IP-based services, and to provide smooth integration with UNIX platforms, Microsoft included a set of TCP/IP printing utilities with Windows NT.

These utilities enable Windows NT to print to TCP/IP network printers as well as to receive and process incoming TCP/IP print jobs. These functions are provided using the Line Printer Remote (LPR) protocol for sending print jobs and the Line Printer Daemon (LPD) for receiving them. Windows NT also implements a third common protocol, the Line Printer Query (LPQ), which enables you to query the status of a TCP/IP print device.

> **NOTE**
>
> The TCP/IP Printing service in Windows NT is based on the Berkeley remote printing protocols commonly called Line Printer Daemon (LPD) and Line Printer Remote (LPR). These protocols are the most prevalent protocols in use today for TCP/IP-based printing and are defined in Request for Comment (RFC) 1179.
>
> There is an interesting distinction worth noting, especially for people who don't often read RFCs. Although LPR, LPD, and their related control protocols are defined by RFC 1179, these protocols are not actually designated as official Internet standards. Just because there is an RFC documenting something, it is *not automatically* an official standard. Of particular interest is the first paragraph of RFC 1179, which states, "This memo is for informational purposes only, and does not specify an Internet standard. Please refer to the current edition of the 'IAB Official Protocol Standards' for the standardization state and status of this protocol."
>
> This explains why there is often so much complexity surrounding TCP/IP-based printing. While many vendors attempt to ensure their product will work with others, proprietary interpretations or implementations are not uncommon. If you are going to use LPR and LPD to print in a multiplatform environment, you should budget in time to understand and work around the subtleties of each environment.
>
> Microsoft has tried hard to ensure that TCP/IP printing with Windows NT will interoperate with as many other platforms as possible and has even increased its compatibility with Windows NT 4.0.

> **NOTE**
>
> Many versions of UNIX based on System V do not support the Berkeley-style remote printing features and will not be compatible with the TCP/IP Printing service in Windows NT. In particular, TCP/IP Printing on Windows NT is not compatible with LPSCHED, another relatively common method used for printing over TCP/IP.

The LPD feature—the capability to receive and process a print job—under Windows NT is implemented as a Windows NT service, which quietly listens for incoming print jobs and submits them to the appropriate NT-based printer. There is no front-end interface that can be manipulated, with the exception of starting and stopping the TCP/IP Printing service.

The LPR support—the ability to send a job to a remote machine for processing—is handled in Windows NT by the LPR port monitor, which is accessed from the standard printer interfaces (either the Print Manager or the Printer Wizard). You can also submit an LPR print job directly from the command-line interface using the LPR.EXE utility.

If you want to get status information from a remote LPD print queue, you can use the third utility, LPQ, which is only available in the form of the LPQ.EXE command-line utility.

This chapter explores how to install the TCP/IP Print Services, as well as how to configure Windows NT as a TCP/IP printing client, and as a TCP/IP print server. It also discusses using the LPR.EXE and LPQ.EXE command-line utilities and their proper syntax. Finally, it takes a close look at how LPR/LPD really works by examining actual network traces. Understanding the techniques for network analysis is extremely useful when trying to troubleshoot TCP/IP printing in a multiplatform environment.

CAUTION

When you install the Microsoft TCP/IP Printing service and start the TCP/IP Printer Service, you make *all* printers currently created on your system available—*even if they are not shared*. Because the LPD service accepts all incoming jobs from *any* LPR client, you have no mechanism for restricting access to these printers.

NOTE

Under Windows NT 3.5 and 3.51, the TCP/IP Printing service was the source of a tremendous number of calls to Microsoft's Product Support Services (PSS). This is because some of the documentation on the TCP/IP Printing service was incomplete and occasionally inaccurate, leading to a lot of customer confusion. If you are going to use TCP/IP printing, I recommend you review this chapter thoroughly.

Installing the TCP/IP Printing Service

The TCP/IP Printing Service is not installed by default with Windows NT. Additionally, before you can install the TCP/IP Printing Service, you must first install TCP/IP. Please refer to Chapter 10, "Installing and Configuring Microsoft TCP/IP," for more information on installing TCP/IP.

> **NOTE**
>
> The Microsoft TCP/IP Printing Service is available on both Windows NT Servers and Windows NT Workstations. There is no difference between the NT Workstation and NT Server version of this service. This means if you are working in a small environment, an NT Workstation can act as an LPD print server supporting other clients.
>
> However, if you use this service on an NT Workstation, you are still limited by the 10-connection limit on incoming connections, as imposed by the NT Workstation license agreement.

> **NOTE**
>
> A very common misunderstanding stems from confusion between printing with LPR/LPD over TCP/IP and printing using NetBIOS (or SMB) over TCP/IP. If you have a Windows environment running TCP/IP, you probably do *not* need to install the Microsoft TCP/IP Printing service—even if TCP/IP is your only network transport protocol.
>
> You only need to install the Microsoft TCP/IP Printing Service if you need to send a print job to a UNIX workstation or a stand-alone network printer that uses the LPR/LPD protocols (RFC 1179). You will also need to install the Microsoft TCP/IP Printing Service if you need to enable your Windows NT system to accept print jobs from UNIX clients, mainframe hosts, or other network entities that send RPF 1179-compliant print jobs.

> **NOTE**
>
> You must be logged on as a member of the local Administrators group in order to install the Microsoft TCP/IP Printing Service.

After you have TCP/IP installed and configured, use the following procedure for installing the TCP/IP print services:

1. Open the Control Panel and double-click the Network icon.
2. Select the Services tab. You should see a list of all the network services currently installed on your system, similar to those listed in Figure 14.1.
3. Click the Add button and a list of all available network services will appear.
4. Select Microsoft TCP/IP Printing, as shown in Figure 14.2. Click OK.

FIGURE 14.1.

The Services tab of the Network Control Panel shows all currently installed services.

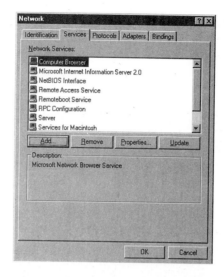

FIGURE 14.2.

The Microsoft TCP/IP Printing service is installed using the Network Control Panel applet.

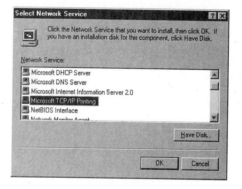

5. You might be asked for the location of the Windows NT distribution media. Enter the correct path or insert the CD-ROM into the appropriate drive. Click OK. Windows NT will now copy necessary files from the distribution media. When it is completed, you are returned to the Network Control Panel window.

6. Click the Close button. Windows NT will analyze and update the network bindings. When it is finished, you will be asked if you want to reboot your system.

7. Click Yes to restart the system.

NOTE

To be quite honest, unless you installed the TCP/IP protocol at the same time as the TCP/IP Printing service, you shouldn't need to restart your system after installing the latter. I've tried *not restarting* on many systems configured in different ways and I've always been able to get the TCP/IP Printing service to work without restarting first.

If you want to print to remote TCP/IP print devices, your installation is complete. However, if you want to use Windows NT as a TCP/IP print server, you must *also* start the TCP/IP Print Server service. For more information on this, please see the section "Setting Up Windows NT to Accept TCP/IP Print Jobs."

Setting Up Windows NT to Print to a Remote TCP/IP Printer or Print Queue

Once you've installed the Microsoft TCP/IP Printing service, Windows NT can print to any device capable of accepting Berkeley-style LPR jobs, as described in RFC 1179. In order to print to a TCP/IP print server, you must first create a Windows NT printer (print queue) and tell it where to send its print jobs. The process for creating a TCP/IP-based printer is exactly the same as creating a printer directly connected to the server through the LPT or similar port. The only difference is that you must first create a LPR port for the destination print device.

Once you have set up a Windows NT printer and told it the address and name of the remote TCP/IP print server, you can share the newly created printer, exactly as you would any other Windows NT printer. This enables *any* computer capable of sending print jobs to your Windows NT system—including Windows 3.1, Windows 95, and Macintosh clients—to print to the TCP/IP print server using your Windows NT system as an intermediary. This is possible *even if the client does not have TCP/IP installed.*

One of the additional benefits you gain from using Windows NT as an intermediary device (print queue) between a print client and a TCP/IP print server is security. There is no user authentication model included in RFC 1179, which defines TCP/IP printing with LPR. So if you configured your clients to print directly to the printer using LPR, you would be *unable to manage any real security* for the printer. By creating a Windows NT printer and making clients access the printer by means of the Windows NT print queue, you gain all the functionality of Windows NT printing, including print job auditing and user-level printing permissions. In addition, you could ensure that clients can't bypass Windows NT by configuring the LPD server to only accept print jobs from the Windows NT print server's IP address. Many stand-alone network printers support this kind of IP-level filtering.

To create a Windows NT printer that sends its jobs to a TCP/IP print server, follow these directions:

> **NOTE**
>
> In order to create a Windows NT printer that prints to the LPR port, you must be a member of the Administrators or the Server Operators group. This is more restrictive than creating a normal printer, which can also be done by members of the Print Operators group.

1. From the Start Menu, choose Settings, then Printers. This opens the Printers window, as shown in Figure 14.3.

FIGURE 14.3.

The Add Printer icon in the Printers window starts the Add Printer Wizard.

2. Double-click the Add Printer icon. This starts the Add Printer Wizard, shown in Figure 14.4.

FIGURE 14.4.

Use the Add Printer Wizard to create a new printer or to connect to an existing printer on the network.

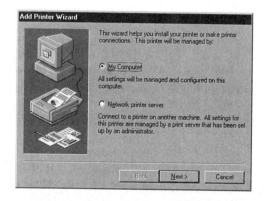

3. Select the option for My Computer and click the Next button to continue.

NOTE

Using the My Computer option might seem a little strange because you are in fact connecting to a printer on the network. The option for Network print server only works if you are connecting to a printer on the network shared by a Windows for Workgroups 3.1x, LAN Manager, Windows 95, or Windows NT system (any SMB-based print device).

When you print to a remote TCP/IP printer using the LPR Port Monitor, you actually need to create a Windows NT printer on your local computer, which is responsible for forwarding the job to the network printer. For stand-alone network printers that you print to using AppleTalk, DLC, or TCP/IP LPR/LPD, you must create the printer on your system.

This is why you choose My Computer instead of Network print server.

14

CONFIGURING
TCP/IP PRINTING

4. You now need to specify the port you want to print to. By default, you should see some LPT and COM ports listed. Click on the Add Port button to specify the location of the TCP/IP printer. This will bring up the Printer Ports window.

> **NOTE**
>
> Windows NT 4.0 includes much better support for remote print queues. However, you cannot use the printer wizard to create ports remotely. This needs to be done at the console of the Windows NT system where you are creating the LPR printer. I'm sure this oversight will be solved by a future service pack.

5. Choose LPR Port from the list of available print monitors, as shown in Figure 14.5. Click OK.

FIGURE 14.5.
Choose the LPR Port option.

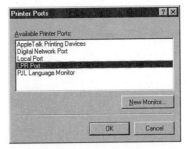

> **NOTE**
>
> If the LPR Port option does not appear in the list of available print monitors, you have not installed the Microsoft TCP/IP Printing service. Refer to the "Installing the TCP/IP Printing Service" section earlier in this chapter for more information.

6. The Add LPR Compatible Printer window will appear, as shown in Figure 14.6.

FIGURE 14.6.
Enter the printer's IP address and print queue name into the Add LPR compatible printer window.

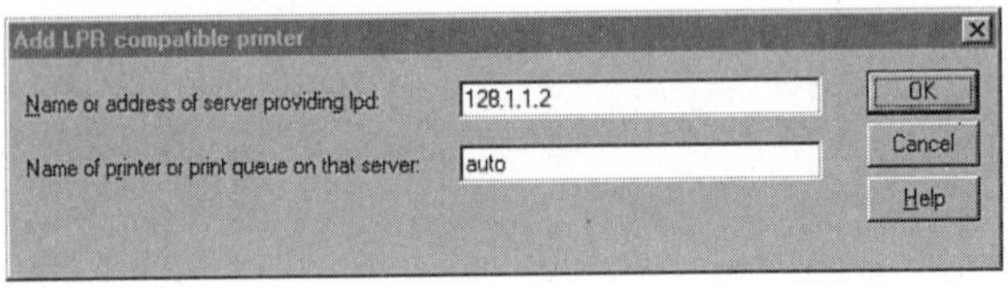

In the first field, enter the hostname or IP address of the computer that is providing the TCP/IP print server (LPD) service. If the host is a computer, such as a UNIX system, you would enter the DNS name or IP address of the UNIX system. If you have a printer connected directly to the network that accepts LPR print jobs, you would enter its IP address, or its DNS name, if one has been assigned.

In the second field, enter the name of the printer as defined on the host system. If the print server is a UNIX system running LPD, you would enter the printer as it is named on that system. If the host is a printer connected directly to the network, consult the manufacturer's directions for the appropriate name to use.

> **NOTE**
>
> If you're getting overloaded with the word printer, you're not alone. In the previous paragraph, you are asked to enter the printer on the LPD print server. RFP 1179 provides for *multiple virtual or physical printers* that are serviced through a single LPD print device. If you can't find your printer's instructions, you can try leaving this field blank because most printers support a default value.

8. Click the OK button to continue. Windows NT will send an LPD test command to the print server you specified. If it fails, you are warned that Windows NT could not establish communications with the LPD server, as shown in Figure 14.7. If you are sure that the information is correct—maybe the printer is turned off—then click OK to continue.

FIGURE 14.7.
Windows NT will give you an error message if it cannot find the LPD server you specified.

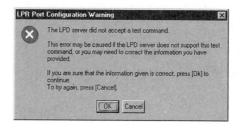

9. Click Close to close the Printer Ports window and return to the list of available ports in the Add Printer Wizard. The port identifier for the LPD server you just specified should appear in the list of available ports, as shown in Figure 14.8.

10. Make sure there is a check mark in the box next to the port, and click the Next button.

11. Choose the correct make and model for the printer—for example, HP LaserJet 4Si, as shown in Figure 14.9.

FIGURE 14.8.

The newly created port appears in the Add Printer Wizard.

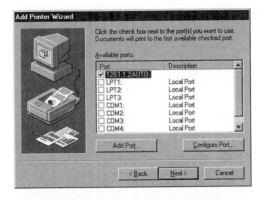

FIGURE 14.9.

You must specify the make and model of the printer.

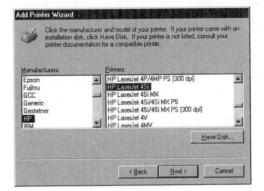

> **CAUTION**
>
> It is important that you choose the correct make and model for the printer so that Windows NT knows exactly what features the printer includes and how to work with it. Choosing the wrong printer can often cause unpredictable results.

12. Give the printer a name, as shown in Figure 14.10. You also need to tell Windows NT whether you want to make this your default printer. Because this is a server, you probably want to select No if you have other printers created.

13. Click the Next button to continue. This will take you to the screen where you specify that you want the printer to be shared to the network.

14. Click the Shared button, shown in Figure 14.11. Specify the name you want the printer shared as. If you have MS-DOS or Windows 3.*x* clients, you should make the share name eight characters or shorter. If you will have Windows 95 or Windows NT clients that need to use the printer, you should specify the appropriate printer drivers to be installed.

FIGURE 14.10.

Give the printer a name and specify if you want it to be the default printer when printing jobs from the server console.

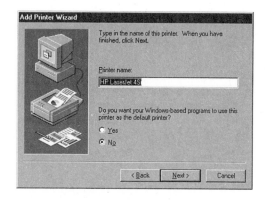

FIGURE 14.11.

Give the printer a share name and choose the drivers to install on the server.

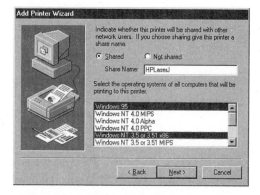

> **NOTE**
>
> You should be sure to specify the OS correct drivers to load for each printer because both Windows NT and Windows 95 clients are capable of automatically loading print drivers from a Windows NT Server. This will save you from the trouble of having to install print drivers on each computer on your network. Also, after you upgrade the drivers on the Windows NT Server, the next time a Windows NT or Windows 95 client tries to print, it will detect the new drivers and automatically install them.

15. Click the Next button. This will take you to a screen where you are prompted to print a test page. Click Yes to print a test page and click the Finish button.

16. You will be prompted for the Windows NT distribution media. Enter the full path, or click the browse button to locate the necessary files.

17. As the final step, Windows NT will display the Properties page for the newly created printer, as shown in Figure 14.12.

FIGURE 14.12.

The Printer Properties page is used to change various settings once the printer has been created.

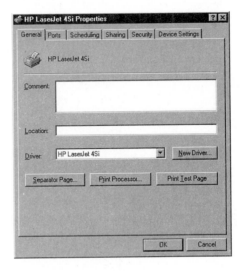

You should take the opportunity to enter any comments about the printer, as well as the location. If you want to change scheduling, sharing, security, or device settings, you can do so now or later, as necessary. For more information on these options, see Chapter 7, "Configuring and Installing Print Services."

Click OK when you are finished configuring the printer.

The printer you just created and shared on the network is capable of receiving print jobs from *any* Windows NT client. This means that standard Windows clients, other NT clients, Macintosh clients, and Novell clients (with Services for NetWare installed) can all print to this TCP/IP printer through the Windows NT system. The strength in this feature is that the clients *don't need to have TCP/IP-based printing tools installed*. For more information on printing strategies, please see Chapter 7.

Setting Up Windows NT to Accept TCP/IP Print Jobs

Setting up Windows NT to act as a TCP/IP print server is actually very simple. Use the following procedure to enable Windows NT to accept incoming TCP/IP print jobs from UNIX or other systems using Berkley-style LPR print utilities:

1. Install the Microsoft TCP/IP Printing Service as described earlier in this chapter.

2. Make sure you are logged on as a user with administrative rights. Open the Control Panel and double-click on the Services icon.

3. Select the TCP/IP Print Server entry from the list of installed services. The TCP/IP Print Server entry is shown in Figure 14.13.

FIGURE 14.13.

The TCP/IP Print Server service can be controlled from the Services Control Panel.

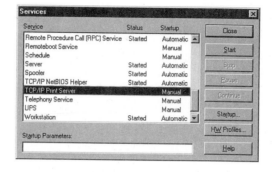

4. Click the Startup button. The Service control window for the TCP/IP Print Server will appear.

5. Choose Automatic from the Startup Type control group, as shown in Figure 14.14, and click OK.

FIGURE 14.14.

Set the TCP/IP Printer Server to start automatically.

This will set the TCP/IP Print Server to automatically start each time Windows NT is booted.

6. If you want to use the TCP/IP Print Server service before the next time you restart Windows NT, you should click the Start button to start the TCP/IP Print Server service now.

7. Close the Services window and the Control Panel.

You can now use your system as a TCP/IP print server to accept Berkeley-style LPR print jobs for any printer created on your Windows NT system.

14
CONFIGURING
TCP/IP PRINTING

NOTE

There is no mechanism to enable you to configure the TCP/IP Print Server service on a per-printer basis. This service runs with the built-in SYSTEM account and cannot be configured to run under a different user context. Because the Spooler service also runs with the built-in SYSTEM account, there is no mechanism that can be used to deny access to the TCP/IP Print Server service without also interrupting other necessary system functions.

This means that if you install the TCP/IP Print Server service, anyone can print to any printer connected to the system without any reliable level of auditing and access restrictions.

Additionally, the TCP/IP Print Server will accept jobs for *any* printer created on your server, even *if the printer has not been shared!*

Using the LPR Utility to Print to a Remote TCP/IP Printer

If you want to send a simple text file to a remote TCP/IP printer that is running an LPD service, you can use the LPR command-line utility.

The syntax for the LPR command is

```
lpr -S server -P printer [-C Class] [-J Jobname] [-o Option] [-x] [-d] filename
```

-S *server* is the DNS hostname or the IP address of the LPD print server.

-P *printer* is the name of the printer or queue on the host.

-C *Class* specifies the content of the banner page for the class.

-J *Jobname* specifies a name for the job. This name shows up if someone views the print queue status on the print server.

-o *Option* indicates the type of file. By default, the LPR.EXE command sends files with the TEXT datatype. You can also use -o 1 for binary files, such as PostScript.

-x indicates that the file is being sent to a print server running SunOS version 4.1.*x* and earlier.

-d specifics that LPR should send the LPR data file before the LPR control file. By default, the control file is sent first.

filename is the name of the file you want to print.

For example, to print a file C:\TEST.TXT to a printer called HPLaserJet on a UNIX system called unixServer.xyzcorp.com, use the command:

```
lpr -S unixServer.xyzcorp.com -P HPLaserJet c:\test.txt
```

Using the LPQ Utility to Check the Status of a TCP/IP Print Queue

The LPQ utility enables you to query the queue status of an LPD print server.

The syntax for the LPQ command is

```
lpq -S server -P printer [-l]
```

`-S server` is the DNS hostname or the IP address of the print server.

`-P printer` is the name of the printer or queue on the host.

`-l` requests a detailed status. Most LPD servers, including Windows NT, will ignore this switch.

For example, to find out the status of a printer called HPLaserJet on a UNIX system called `unixServer.xyzcorp.com`, use the command

```
lpq -S unixServer.xyzcorp.com -P HPLaserJet
```

Changes to TCP/IP Printing in Windows NT 4.0

Several changes were made to the Microsoft TCP/IP Printing service in Windows NT 4.0. The major changes are the following:

- Support for multiple data files per control file.
- The source TCP port for LPR jobs is now between 512 and 1023, inclusive.
- The hostname parameter is preserved when Windows NT is used as an intermediary print spooler.

Multiple Data Files per Control File

When an LPR print job is sent according to RFC 1179, there are at least two data structures defined in the print job. These are called the *control file* and the *data file*. The control file defines how the data file will be treated, and the data file contains the actual print job itself. RFC 1179 permits you to have a single control file control multiple data files. For instance, a client might need to print six documents. It could send these all together with a single control file. This actually can reduce the amount of network traffic.

Windows NT does not send multiple data files with a single control file when you use it as an LPR client. However, beginning in version 4.0, it is able to receive and properly process LPD jobs that contain multiple data files.

14

CONFIGURING
TCP/IP PRINTING

Source TCP Ports for LPR Jobs

Section 3.1 of RFC 1179 defines that LPR print jobs *must* be sent from an available TCP port between 721 and 731 (11 ports total). It also states that the LPD server *must* listen for jobs of TCP port 515. The problem is that under Windows NT 3.51 and earlier, when more than 11 jobs were sent via LPR in quick succession, all available outgoing ports might already be tied up. This could result in a logjam until Windows NT timed out an open port between 721 and 731. This could take a couple minutes.

To help alleviate this problem, Microsoft chose to deviate from the RFC in Windows NT 4.0. The new version of LPR on Windows NT—including both the LPR.EXE utility and the LPR Port Monitor—will send print jobs from any *available* TCP port between 512 and 1023, inclusive. This virtually eliminates any problems that could cause the print jobs to be held because there is no available port.

However, there is a potential downside to this. If you're running network filtering mechanisms, such as a firewall or a host filter product like TCP Wrapper on a UNIX box, you *might* encounter problems. Because the RFC says that all compliant print jobs should be between source ports 721 and 731 and destination port 515, some firewalls and TCP/IP filtering products might be set up to filter out everything else. If you have trouble printing, you might see if this isn't part of the cause.

Host Name Preservation in Print-Through Mode

Windows NT can be used as an intermediary print spooler, where the client prints to the Windows NT system using LPR, then Windows NT passes the job on to another printer server using LPR. In previous versions of Windows NT, the final print server that Windows NT passed the job to would think that the Windows NT system was the original source for the document. However, Windows NT 4.0 has been changed so that Windows NT will preserve the name of the original host and pass this on to the final print server.

Analyzing TCP/IP Printing

In order to understand what is happening with Windows NT, it is often beneficial to understand what is really happening on the network. This section looks at the network traffic that is generated with Windows NT using the LPR protocol to print different types of jobs. We'll look at the size of the jobs as well as the nature of the data. In order to do this, let's use the Windows NT Network Monitoring service.

I've included this section because printing with LPR/LPD can often be an excruciating ordeal, particularly for newer administrators, and troubleshooting can be extremely difficult. However, if you understand the protocol a little more and watch the traffic on the network, you can use this additional information to accurately troubleshoot and locate problems that would otherwise have been nearly impossible to solve. Not to mention that working at this in-depth level will help you get a firm grasp on the subject.

I've purposefully gone into more detail than one would expect in a Windows NT handbook because TCP/IP printing generates huge numbers of questions, yet no one has attempted to provide in-depth coverage of this topic. However, I hope that after reading this section you'll be able to solve some of those more intricate problems that seemed too elusive before.

> **NOTE**
>
> You should acquaint yourself with the Windows NT Network Monitoring Service.

In order to perform this experiment, I've configured two Windows NT Server systems on a single, isolated Ethernet network segment. I've installed the Microsoft TCP/IP Printing service on both machines. The machines are called GARLIC and TOMATO. In this experiment, GARLIC is the server (the LPD server) and TOMATO is the client (LPR client). I've configured it so that these two machines belong to two completely separate domains, share no common user accounts, and have no trusts. Additionally, the guest accounts are disabled on both machines. GARLIC has an HP LaserJet 5L printer directly attached to its LPT1 port. This device is *not* shared, as shown in Figure 14.15.

FIGURE 14.15.

The direct-attached printer called HP5L is not shared on the Windows NT Server called GARLIC.

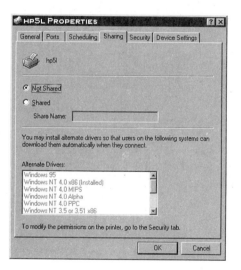

14

CONFIGURING TCP/IP PRINTING

I have started the TCP/IP Print Server service on the server called GARLIC because it will be our LPD server, but I have not started it on the machine called TOMATO because it will merely be a client.

For the first test, let's try sending a simple text file using the LPR.EXE command line utility from TOMATO to GARLIC. In this case, I'll send the file C:\BOOT.INI by typing the command LPR -S GARLIC -P HP5L C:\BOOT.INI. Both servers have Hosts files that include each others' IP addresses, so there should not be any name resolution issues. However, for the record, GARLIC is using IP address 128.1.1.35 and TOMATO is using IP address 128.1.1.9.

GARLIC is running the Network Monitoring tool and capturing all network traffic. When the above LPR command is entered on TOMATO, 18 packets are sent across the network from TOMATO to GARLIC. Looking at the print queue for HP5L on GARLIC, a print job has indeed arrived, as shown in Figure 14.16. I've paused the print queue on GARLIC so the job won't go through and we can look at some of its other properties.

Figure 14.16.

The LPR print job from TOMATO *arrived in the print queue for HP5L on* GARLIC.

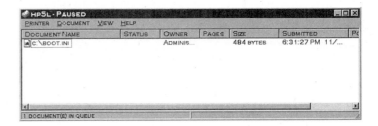

If you've been following along, you might be saying, "Now wait a second; the printer HP5L is not shared." That's absolutely correct. As mentioned earlier in this chapter, when you install and start the TCP/IP Print Server service on Windows NT, it makes *all* printers created on the NT system available to *any* LPR client on the network—even if the printer is not shared. This means that there is no way to provide selective control to printers when you install the LPD service (TCP/IP Print Server service) on your Windows NT system—so install it with care.

Now, let's take a look at some of the statistics. The file I sent, BOOT.INI was 484 bytes—according to dir command on TOMATO. If you look back at Figure 14.16, you'll notice that the queue for HP5L agrees that the file is in fact 484 bytes large. It's always nice when things work out this way!

In Figure 14.16, you'll also notice that Windows NT has managed to preserve the document name and the owner of the original print job. I was logged on as the administrator on TOMATO when I sent the print job.

At this point, you can find out a little more about the print job by looking at its properties, as shown in Figure 14.17.

There is some interesting information here that is worth noting. First, notice that the datatype for the print job is TEXT because the Windows NT LPR.EXE command-line utility marks jobs as text by default. This corresponds to the f control code defined in section 7.19 of RFC 1179.

FIGURE 14.17.

The properties of the print job show additional information, including how the print job will be processed.

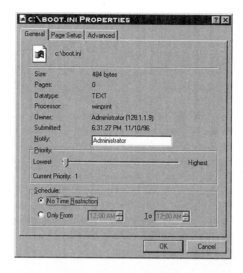

> **NOTE**
>
> RFC 1179 can be obtained from `ftp://ds.internic.net/rfc/rfc1179.txt`.

In Windows NT terms, when a job is marked as datatype TEXT in the queue, it will be processed by the Windows NT print monitor and converted into a standard text document. It uses whatever print driver is defined for the Windows NT printer to determine what kind of wrapper, if any, is necessary for the particular printer. For instance, if the printer was defined as an HP LaserJet 4M, a PostScript wrapper would be placed on it because Windows NT knows that the HP LaserJet 4M is a PostScript printer.

In Figure 14.17, you'll also notice that the Owner is Administrator of machine 128.1.1.9. This information was passed to the LPD service on GARLIC in the LPR control file. This information, however, cannot be deemed reliable as authentication data because there is no validation of this data by Windows NT.

Let's look a little more at what this print job looks like on the network. As mentioned earlier, the entire print job was 18 packets. This totaled 1596 bytes, and it took .310 seconds to complete. It might seem that 18 packets is a lot, but many of these packets were control packets. However, this protocol does not have a 3:1 overhead, as might be suggested by taking 1596 bytes to print a 484-byte file. Rather, there is a total LPR/LPD protocol overhead of just over 1000 bytes. (This doesn't take into account the average TCP overhead on top of the actual payload of the file—in this case BOOT.INI.) The actual network trace of the print job is as shown in Table 14.1.

Table 14.1. Network trace of an LPR print job.

Packet #	Source	Destination	Frame/Payload Size	Hex Payload	ASCII Payload
1	Tomato (TCP512)	Garlic (TCP515)	60/4	05 B4 00 00	.l..
2	Garlic (TCP515)	Tomato (TCP512)	58/4	02 04 05 B4	l
3	Tomato (TCP512)	Garlic (TCP515)	60/0		
4	Tomato (TCP512)	Garlic (TCP515)	60/6	02 68 70 35 6C 0A	.hp5l.
5	Tomato (TCP512)	Garlic (TCP515)	71/17	02 37 39 20 63 66 41 36 38 31 54 4F 4D 41 54 4F 0A	.64 cfA681TOMATO.
6	Garlic (TCP515)	Tomato (TCP512)	55/1	00	.
7	Tomato (TCP512)	Garlic (TCP515)	119/65	48 54 4F 4D 41 54 4F 0A 50 41 64 6D 69 5E 69 73 74 72 61 74 6F 72 0A 66 64 66 41 36 38 31 54 4F 4D 41 54 4F 0A 55 64 66 41 36 38 31 54 4F 4D 41 54 4F 0A 4E 63 3A 5C 62 6F 6F 74 2E 69 6E 69 0A 00	HTOMATO.Padministrator. fdfA681TOMATO. UdfA681TOMATO. Nc:\boot.ini..

Packet #	Source	Destination	Frame/Payload Size	Hex Payload	ASCII Payload
8	Garlic (TCP515)	Tomato (TCP512)	55/1	00	.
9	Tomato (TCP512)	Garlic (TCP515)	72/18	03 34 38 34 20 64 66 41 36 38 31 54 4F 4D 41 54 4F 0A	.484 dfA681TOMATO.
10	Garlic (TCP515)	Tomato (TCP512)	55/1	00	.
11	Tomato (TCP512)	Garlic (TCP515)	539/485	5B 62 6F 74 20 6C 6F 61 64 65 72 5D 0D 0A 74 69 6D 65 6F 75 74 3D 33 30 0D 0A	[boot loader]..timeout=30..
12	Garlic (TCP515)	Tomato (TCP512)	55/1	00	.
13	Garlic (TCP515)	Tomato (TCP512)	54/0		
14	Tomato (TCP512)	Garlic (TCP515)	60/0		
15	Garlic (TCP515)	Tomato (TCP512)	55/1	00	
16	Garlic (TCP515)	Tomato (TCP512)	54/0		
17	Tomato (TCP512)	Garlic (TCP515)	60/0		
18	Garlic (TCP515)	Tomato (TCP512)	54/0		

14
CONFIGURING
TCP/IP PRINTING

First, let me explain Table 14.1. The first column is self-explanatory. The second column is the name of the source machine and the TCP port from which the packet originated. The third column is the name of the destination machine and TCP port number. The fourth column is the total size of the Ethernet frame and the actual length of the data (payload). The next column is the hexadecimal contents of the payload, and the final column is the ASCII representation of the decimal values.

There are some interesting things to note from this trace. First, the print job originates on TCP port 512 on the client and is addressed to TCP port 515 on the server. According to section 3.1 of RFC 1179, port 515 is the port at which the LPD service is supposed to listen.

In addition, according to the same section of the RFC, the originating port *is supposed to be* any available TCP port between 721 and 731, inclusive. Yet, you'll notice that Windows NT seems to be using a different port. There is a good reason for this. In the version of Windows NT prior to 4.0, the LPR functionality strictly conformed to what was described in RFC 1179. However, if you attempted to print 12 jobs quickly with LPR, the twelfth job would appear to hang. This was because LPR would reserve an available port from 721 to 731, inclusive, for each job that was sent. These ports were not released for up to three minutes after the jobs were finished. Therefore, any further print jobs would have to wait for an available port. To prevent this problem, Microsoft chose to deviate from the RFC somewhat in Windows NT 4.0. Beginning with Windows NT 4.0, LPR will use any available port from 512 to 1023, inclusive. This is not a cause for concern and should not have any negative impact on most systems. The benefit is that you will be able to print virtually unlimited small documents in a short interval without print jobs being stalled while waiting for an available port.

> **CAUTION**
>
> If you are using LPR to print from a Windows NT system to a UNIX machine running TCP Wrapper or a similar product that restricts incoming TCP port usage, you might have an issue using Windows NT 4.0 as an LPR client. You will simply need to permit any incoming traffic destined for TCP port 515, regardless of its source address.
>
> Likewise, if you are using Windows NT LPR to print through a firewall to an LPD print server, your firewall will need to permit source TCP ports 512 to 1023, inclusive, to communicate with destination TCP port 515.

The second thing to note about the preceding trace is that most of the frames are control codes and acknowledgments. Frames 1, 2, 3, 6, 8, 10, 12, 13, 14, 15, 16, 17, and 18 are handshaking, most of which is defined in RFC 1179. For instance frames 6, 8, 10, 12, and 15 are responses from the LPD print server to tell the client that it has successfully processed the previous command. You'll notice the contents of these frames are simply hexadecimal 00, the null character. This is how LPD responds that everything went without an error. If there had been a problem, it would have responded with some other character, which in the language of the

LPD server means that something didn't go right. There is no way for the LPR client to know what didn't go right because this level of interaction is not provided by RFC 1179.

Frames 4, 5, 7, 9, and 11 are where all the work gets done. Let's take a quick look at these.

You'll notice that frame 4 begins with hexadecimal value 02, which, according to section 5.2 of RFC 1179, tells the LPD print server to prepare to receive a printer job. The characters that follow frame 4, ending with a line feed (hexadecimal 0A), specify the name of the print queue the job will be sent to. In this case, you can see that the job is sent to print queue hp5l.

Now the LPD print server is ready to receive a job from the client. In frame 5, the LPR client tells the print server to get ready to receive the control file for the LPR job. This is specified by the hexadecimal value 02 and is defined in section 6.2 of RFC 1179. Following this is 64 cfA681TOMATO, concluded with a line feed (hexadecimal value 0A). This "command" has two operands. The first one, 64, in this case, specifies the size of the control file. This tells the LPD server how many of the next bytes it receives should be treated as the control file. The second operand, cfA681TOMATO, is the name of the control file. This will always begin with cfA followed by a three-digit number and the name of the machine where the job originated.

Frame 7 is the contents of the control file. This control file contains a number of directives to the print server. These are defined in section 7 of RFC 1179.

> **NOTE**
>
> All control file directives are case sensitive.

In the example, there are five directives. The first one is H, which specifies the name of the computer where the print job originated. All control files *must* contain this directive. In our case, the print server is told the job comes from a host called TOMATO. The next directive, P, indicates the name of the user requesting the print job, which in our case is Administrator. All control files *must* contain this directive. The f directive is followed by a filename. This specifies that the data file specified, in this case dfA681TOMATO, should be printed as a plain preformatted text file, providing page breaks as necessary. All ASCII control characters other than hard tab (HT), carriage return (CR), form feed (FF), line feed (LF), and backspace (BS) are filtered out. The U directive tells the LPD print server that when it can discard the data file specified—in this case, dfA681TOMATO. The final directive, N, tells the LPD print server the name of the file it was sent. This information is used to name the print job if no formal title has been given. In this case, you can see the file is c:\boot.ini. For information on other valid directives, see section 7 of RFC 1179.

So far, so good. The print server knows that the control file should be finished now because it has processed the number of bytes specified in frame 5. It responds to the LPR client with an acknowledgment—frame 8. It now awaits another command from the LPR client.

14
CONFIGURING TCP/IP PRINTING

Frame 9 begins with a hexadecimal value 03, which tells the LPD print server to get ready to begin receiving a data file. This is followed by two operands. The first is the size of the data file and the second is the name of the data file. The size of the data file in our case is 484, which happily coincides with the size of the original BOOT.INI file. The second operand gives a name to the data file. This will always begin with dfA, followed by a three-digit job number, then the name of the host file that constructed the data file. If the size of the data file is 0 (zero), the LPD server assumes that all remaining bytes transferred over the current TCP connection are part of the data file.

Frame 11 contains the actual contents of the data file. In Table 14.1, I've truncated the file for the sake of space. You'll have to trust me that the entire file was actually there. You'll see that this file starts immediately with the text of the file [boot loader]. There are no control characters or directives necessary at this point.

That's essentially all there is to this process. As you see in the preceding trace, by default the Windows NT LPR.EXE utility sends the control file before the data file. This is important to know when troubleshooting LPR-related printing problems. Again, referring back to RFC 1179, section 6 states that LPR clients *should* be able to send the control file and data file in *any* order; however, the LPD server *must* be able to receive the control file first. Think about this for a few moments. This means that all LPD servers will be able to receive the control file first, which is why LPR.EXE defaults to that. The RFC continues by adding that the LPD server *should* be able to receive the data file first. Notice that there is no *must* here. In another words, an LPD server manufacturer would be foolish not to do this, but it's not required.

Using Windows NT LPR.EXE, you can easily specify that the data file should come first. This is done by specifying the -d switch on the command line. The following is the trace of sending the same file, C:\BOOT.INI, but this time the trace is sent with the data file before the control file. The command used was LPR -S GARLIC -P HP5L -d C:\BOOT.INI.

continues

Table 14.2. This trace is sent with the data file before the control file.

Packet #	Source	Destination	Frame/ Payload Size	Hex Payload	ASCII Payload
1	Tomato (TCP512)	Garlic (TCP515)	60/4	05 B4 00 00	.|..
2	Garlic (TCP515)	Tomato (TCP512)	58/4	02 04 05 B4	...|
3	Tomato (TCP512)	Garlic (TCP515)	60/0		
4	Tomato (TCP512)	Garlic (TCP515)	60/6	02 68 70 35 6C 0A	.hp51.
5	Tomato (TCP512)	Garlic (TCP515)	72/18	03 34 38 34 20 64 66 41 36 38 31 54 4F 4D 41 54 4F 0A	.484 dfA514TOMATO.
6	Garlic (TCP515)	Tomato (TCP512)	55/1	00	
7	Tomato (TCP512)	Garlic (TCP515)	539/485	5B 62 6F 6F 74 20 6C 6F 61 64 65 72 5D 0A 74 69 6D 65 6F 75 74 3D 33 30 0D 0A	[boot loader]..timeout=30..
8	Garlic (TCP515)	Tomato (TCP512)	55/1	00	
9	Garlic (TCP515)	Tomato (TCP512)	54/0		
10	Tomato (TCP512)	Garlic (TCP515)	71/17	02 37 39 20 63 66 41 36 38 31 54 4F 4D 41 54 4F 0A	.64 cfA514TOMATO.

14
CONFIGURING TCP/IP PRINTING

Table 14.2. continued

Packet #	Source	Destination	Frame/Payload Size	Hex Payload	ASCII Payload
11	Garlic (TCP515)	Tomato (TCP512)	55/1	00	.
12	Tomato (TCP512)	Garlic (TCP515)	119/65	48 54 4F 4D 41 54 4F 0A 50 41 64 6D 69 5E 69 73 74 72 61 74 6F 72 0A 66 64 66 41 36 38 31 54 4F 4D 41 54 4F 0A 55 64 66 41 36 38 31 54 4F 4D 41 54 4F 0A 4E 63 3A 5C 62 6F 6F 74 2E 69 6E 6E 0A 00	HTOMATO.Padministrator. fdfA514TOMATO. UdfA514TOMATO.Nc:\boot.ini..
13	Garlic (TCP515)	Tomato (TCP512)	55/1	00	.
14	Tomato (TCP512)	Garlic (TCP515)	60/0		
15	Garlic (TCP515)	Tomato (TCP512)	55/1	00	.
16	Garlic (TCP515)	Tomato (TCP512)	54/0		
17	Tomato (TCP512)	Garlic (TCP515)	60/0		
18	Garlic (TCP515)	Tomato (TCP512)	54/0		

You'll notice that the only change from the original trace is that frames 9 through 12 from the original trace (these frames define the control file) were effectively cut and moved before frame 5. You'll also notice that the file control number that is used for naming the files—the 514 in cfA514TOMATO and dfA514TOMATO—changed from the first trace to the second trace. This control number is dynamic and will always change.

Now you'll notice, LPR is used to send a file containing pure text to the LPD server. The LPD server received the file and because of the f option (in frame 7 of the preceding first trace), it knew the file should be treated as simple, preformatted text. In Figure 14.17, the file appeared in the Windows NT print queue as type TEXT.

If you need to send data types other than text, they need to be sent with different options. The most common alternative is to designate the file as a binary file that should be passed to the print device without any further processing. This is usually done for preformatted files, such as a PostScript file. For instance, suppose I have a PostScript file called FILE1.PS that was generated by some piece of software, such as a page layout program like PageMaker or QuarkXpress. I want to send it to a PostScript printer (an HP 5M in this case) attached to an LPD server. If I just sent it by typing LPR -S GARLIC -P HP5M C:\FILE1.PS, I might be in trouble. When the LPD server got the file, it would say, "Gee, this is supposed to be text, and I know I'm printing to a PostScript printer, so let me put a simple PostScript wrapper around this file so it prints properly." The problem is, there is already a PostScript wrapper around it, and you'll get something ugly from the printer. The following is the first couple of lines of the file FILE1.PS. This is what the output would look like if you tried to print SLIDES.PS to using HP5M without letting the LPD server know it was PostScript:

```
%!PS-Adobe-3.0
%%Creator: Windows PSCRIPT
%%Title: PowerPoint - FILE1.PPT
%%BoundingBox: 14 9 597 784
%%DocumentNeededResources: (atend)
%%DocumentSuppliedResources: (atend)
%%Pages: (atend)
%%BeginResource: procset Win35Dict 3 1
/Win35Dict 290 dict def Win35Dict begin/bd{bind def}bind def/in{72
mul}bd/ed{exch def}bd/ld{load def}bd/tr/translate ld/gs/gsave ld/gr
/grestore ld/M/moveto ld/L/lineto ld/rmt/rmoveto ld/rlt/rlineto ld
/rct/rcurveto ld/st/stroke ld/n/newpath ld/sm/setmatrix ld/cm/currentmatrix
ld/cp/closepath ld/ARC/arcn ld/TR{65536 div}bd/lj/setlinejoin ld/lc
/setlinecap ld/ml/setmiterlimit ld/sl/setlinewidth ld/scignore false
def/sc{scignore{pop pop pop}{0 index 2 index eq 2 index 4 index eq
and{pop pop 255 div setgray}{3{255 div 3 1 roll}repeat setrgbcolor}ifelse}ifelse}bd
```

The proper way to send this file is to use the following command line:

```
LPR -S GARLIC -P HP5M -o l C:\FILE1.PS
```

If you were to send this print job and capture the network traffic, you'd see that the information in the control file would contain the l directive instead of the f directive as in the first trace we looked at. For comparison, the contents of the control file packet from this capture here would look like this:

```
HTOMATO.Padministrator.ldfA711TOMATO.UdfA711TOMATO.Nc:\file1.ps..
```

Furthermore, it is interesting to look at how Windows NT as an LPD print server handles such a command. Look at the properties for this print job after the job has been received by the Windows NT print queue. In Figure 14.18, notice that it is marked as a datatype RAW, compared to TEXT in the earlier example. The RAW datatype tells Windows NT to take the contents of a print job and pass it bit-for-bit, byte-for-byte directly to the printer.

FIGURE 14.18.

Files sent with the l option are sent as RAW data that should not be processed by the Windows NT print processors.

You might be saying that's great, but I'm sure you realize that there are a few problems with LPR.EXE. One big question is probably, "So how do you get it to print from Microsoft Word?" Good question. You don't. At least that's not the most convenient way.

In Windows NT, there is also an LPR Port Monitor. This mechanism allows you to define a standard printer on your Windows NT system that processes jobs generated from normal programs such as Microsoft Word. The LPR Port Monitor is then responsible for sending these jobs across the network to an LPD printer. This leads us to the next section.

The LPR.EXE Versus the LPR Port Monitor

We've examined the LPR.EXE command and taken a look at some examples and network traces. Now, it's important look at the differences between using LPR.EXE from the command line to print a file and using the LPR Port Monitor in Windows NT. The LPR Port Monitor enables you to create a standard Windows NT printer that you can use to print the same way you would print to a locally connected printer. The directions for creating this printer are presented earlier in the section, "Setting Up Windows NT to Print to a Remote TCP/IP Printer or Print Queue."

This section looks at the more technical side of how this method of printing differs from using the LPR.EXE command.

Let's use the same hardware and software configuration described in the previous printing examples. There are two Windows NT Servers and each is the PDC of its own domain. The guest accounts have been disabled and there are no trusts or common user accounts on the two domains. The machine we will use as the LPR client is called TOMATO, and the LPD print server is GARLIC.

Following the instructions in the section, "Setting Up Windows NT to Print To a Remote TCP/IP Printer or Print Queue," I've created a new printer on TOMATO to print to the LPD print server on GARLIC. Figure 14.19 shows the Ports property information for this printer on TOMATO.

FIGURE 14.19.
The printer HP5L is configured to print to the LPD print server on GARLIC.

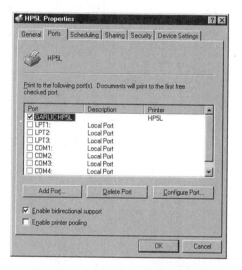

NOTE

The Enable bi-directional support option has no effect when printing to an LPR port because the LPR protocol does not define any complex two-way communications for returning messages from the printer.

Because we've defined this as a standard Windows NT printer, we've also defined a printer type—in this case, HP LaserJet 5L. This means that Windows NT knows about the capabilities of the printer it is printing to (provided you've chosen the correct printer). Most importantly, it knows whether it is PostScript or not.

Let's take a look at what the network traffic looks like when we send a job. As before, I've paused the print queue on GARLIC and I'll use Notepad to open the same BOOT.INI file that we were using before on TOMATO. For the record, it's still 484 bytes.

When I printed it to the new print queue, I captured the network traffic so we could analyze it.

The results are *very* different from the results of the earlier example where we simply printed the file using the standard LPR.EXE command. Before we look at the network trace, let's take a quick look at the properties on this document when it arrived in the print queue on GARLIC (the LPD print server). Figure 14.20 shows the properties of this print job.

FIGURE 14.20.

The properties of the BOOT.INI *file sent with the LPR Port Monitor are different from the properties when sent with* LPR.EXE.

There are a couple of important things to notice here. The first, and most superficial, is the name of the document. The Windows NT print client, TOMATO, reported not only the name of the document being worked on, but also the name of the program that printed it. The second thing to notice is that the file is *much* larger than before. It's 6347 bytes, rather than the 484 bytes when sent with the LPR.EXE. The third thing to notice from the properties is that the datatype is now RAW by default. Remember, with the LPR.EXE command, the default datatype was TEXT. However, when using the LPR Port Monitor on the client (TOMATO), the client prepares the document for the final destination printer. In this case, TOMATO knew that the destination printer was an HP5L, so it put a Page Command Language (PCL) wrapper around the text. We can expect to see that in the network trace. Let's take a look at that now. Table 14.3 shows the trace of this print job.

continues

Table 14.3. Network traffic for an HP LaserJet 5L print job.

Packet #	Source	Destination	Frame/ Payload Size	Hex Payload	ASCII Payload
1	TOMATO (TCP514)	GARLIC (TCP515)	44/4	05 B4 05 B4	.|.|
2	GARLIC (TCP515)	TOMATO (TCP514)	44/4	05 B4 02 04	.|..
3	TOMATO (TCP514)	GARLIC (TCP515)	40/0		
4	TOMATO (TCP514)	GARLIC (TCP515)	46/6	02 48 50 35 4C 0A	.HP5L.
5	GARLIC (TCP515)	TOMATO (TCP514)	41/1	00	.
6	TOMATO (TCP514)	GARLIC (TCP515)	57/17	02 39 31 20 63 66 41 39 37 37 54 4F 4D 41 54 4F 0A	.91 cfA977TOMATO
7	GARLIC (TCP515)	TOMATO (TCP514)	41/1	00	.
8	TOMATO (TCP514)	GARLIC (TCP515)	132/92	48 54 4F 4D 41 54 4F 0A 50 41 64 6D 69 6E 69 73 74 72 61 74 6F 72 0A 4A 62 6F 6F 74 2E 69 6E 69 20 2D 20 4E 6F 74 65 70 61 64 0A 6C 64 66 41 39 37 37 54 4F 4D 41 54 4F 0A 55 64 66 41 0A 4E 62 6F 6F 74 2E 4D 41 54 4F 0A 4E 62 6F 6F 74 2E 69 6E 69 20 2D 20 4E 6F 74 65 70 61 64 2E 2E 61 64 0A 00	HTOMATO.PAdministrator. Jboot.ini - Notepad. ldfA977TOMATO. UdfA977TOMATO.Nboot. ini - Notepad..

Table 14.3. continued

Packet #	Source	Destination	Frame/ Payload Size	Hex Payload	ASCII Payload
9	GARLIC (TCP515)	TOMATO (TCP514)	41/1	00	.
10	TOMATO (TCP514)	GARLIC (TCP515)	59/19	03 36 33 34 37 20 64 66 41 39 37 37 54 4F 4D 41 54 4F 0A	.6347 dfA977TOMATO.
11	GARLIC (TCP515)	TOMATO (TCP514)	41/1	00	.
12	TOMATO (TCP514)	GARLIC (TCP515)	1500/1460	1B 25 2D 31 32 33 34 35 58 40 50 4A 4C 20 53 45 54 20 50 41 47 45 50 52 4F 54 45 43 54 3D 41 55 54 4F 0A 40 50 4A 4C 20 53 45 54 20 52 45 53 4F 4C 55 54 49 4F 4E 4E 33 30 30 0A 40 50 4A 4C 20 45 4E 54 45 52 20 4C 41 4E 47 55 41 47 45 3D 50 43 4C 0A 1B 45 1B 26 2A 74 33 30 30 52 1B 26 75 36 30 30 44 1B 2A 72 30 46 1B	.%-12345X@PJL SET PAGEPROTECT=AUTO. @PJL SET RESOLUTION=300. @PJL ENTER LANGUAGE=PCL...E. *t300R.&u600D.*r0F.
13	TOMATO (TCP514)	GARLIC (TCP515)	1500/1460		
14	TOMATO (TCP514)	GARLIC (TCP515)	1500/1460		
15	TOMATO (TCP514)	GARLIC (TCP515)	1500/1460		
16	TOMATO (TCP514)	GARLIC (TCP515)	548/508		

Packet #	Source	Destination	Frame/Payload Size	Hex Payload	ASCII Payload
17	GARLIC (TCP515)	TOMATO (TCP514)	40/0		
18	GARLIC (TCP515)	TOMATO (TCP514)	41/1	00	
19	TOMATO (TCP514)	GARLIC (TCP515)	40/0		
20	GARLIC (TCP515)	TOMATO (TCP514)	40/0		
21	GARLIC (TCP515)	TOMATO (TCP514)	40/0		
22	TOMATO (TCP514)	GARLIC (TCP515)	40/0		

14
CONFIGURING
TCP/IP PRINTING

> **NOTE**
>
> To save space, I have truncated packet 12 and excluded the contents of packets 13, 14, 15, and 16. They all contained the PCL data information, which tells the LaserJet 5L how to print the document. Packet 12 shows the beginning of this job's header information.

As you can see, the majority of the packets are similar to what we saw in the earlier examples. The major difference you'll see, though, is in the actual payload packets—the packets that contain the information you actually want. There is now a lot more information that is passed across the network to the print server. This is because when we use the LPR.EXE command to send a print job, by default it is marked as simple TEXT and is sent device independent. It becomes the job of the print server to properly format the document—either put a PCL or a PostScript header on top. However, when using the LPR Print Monitor, it becomes the duty of the client to fully process the job and the print server, and then it simply sends the information bit-for-bit to the printer.

The LPR Print Monitor sends the LPR print job using the l option, which instructs the LPD print server that the job is binary and should not be formatted.

If you need to change the default print instruction that is sent to the LPD server, you can change it on a printer-by-printer basis using the following Registry key:

```
\HKEY_LOCAL_MACHINE\SYSTEM\CurrentControlSet\Control\Print\Monitors\LPRPorts\Ports\<portname>\
<IP Address or Host Name>:<Printer Name>
```

You must set the value PrintSwitch to the LPR control command you want to use. If you want all jobs set with the control code f, enter f without any other characters as the value for PrintSwitch. If you need to create the value PrintSwitch, it is of type REG_SZ.

Summary

This chapter explores how to use Windows NT to interoperate with UNIX systems and standalone print servers running LPR and LPD services. It discusses how to install the TCP/IP Print Services for Windows NT and covers some of the limitations of using LPR and LPD for remote network printing. You also saw how to configure NT Server as a TCP/IP printing client, in addition to configuring it as a TCP/IP print server. It also covers how to use the LPR.EXE and LPQ.EXE command-line utilities, including why and when to use them. Finally, you saw how to use the Network Monitor or other network packet analysis tools to troubleshoot TCP/IP printing.

Browsing on a Microsoft Network

by David Wolfe

IN THIS CHAPTER

Browsing a computer network is a lot like shopping in a large department store. Before you know what you can buy, you must find out what's available. Browsing a network is a process of just taking a look around to see what can be used. That's where the Microsoft browsing service comes in. With the new interface to NT, seeing what network resources are available has become a much more logical process. As with Windows 95, the primary network window for users to see what's available is the Network Neighborhood icon, which you always can find on the desktop if network services are enabled.

Because Windows NT and Windows 95 have excellent graphical interfaces to view the items available on the network, there is little need for users to resort to the text-based browsing methods that other networks are still mired in.

This chapter covers the principles and specifics of setting up browsing services on a Microsoft network.

Examining the Principles of Browsing

Browsing a Microsoft Windows network is like any other network element. It consists of a server side and a client side. In order for browsing to be successful, both sides must be correctly structured. Not to fear. Very little, if any, extra effort is needed to ensure that browsing on a Microsoft Windows network will succeed.

Looking at the Terms of Browsing

In order for you to understand the intricacies of browsing, you first must understand the terms involved. I have found that once people know the meaning of the words you are using, they generally have an easier time following your instructions. If you are an experienced network person, feel free to skip ahead to the next section. The following terms are used when discussing browsing on a Microsoft network:

- **Server:** Any computer participating on the network that allows other computers or users to link to devices on them. These devices can range from hard disks to printers to fax modems. All currently supported Microsoft environments and network software (NT, Windows 95, and LAN Manager) can act as servers.

- **Host:** This term is used primarily with TCP/IP-based networks to refer to any computer on the network. Even if a computer using the TCP/IP protocol is not offering any devices for use by other users, it still is labeled as a *host*.

- **Service:** A background application running on an NT Server or Workstation that performs a task needed by the network in general or by the NT machine on which it is running. The Windows Internet Naming Service (WINS), for example, runs on NT machines to resolve server names to IP addresses.

- **Datagram:** A network message packet that can be directed or broadcast over the network. Datagrams carry network configuration information between servers.

■ **Mailslot:** The port or socket through which datagrams are received. When servers want to send special configuration requests or messages to each other, they receive them through special network ports called *mailslots*.

■ **Network Segment:** A section of a TCP/IP-based network isolated from other segments via a router. Microsoft Windows network domains can span multiple network segments as long as the TCP/IP protocol is used.

■ **Resource:** Any item on a computer available for other users.

■ **Sharing:** Making a device on a computer available for others on the network to use.

■ **Using:** Linking a device on a remote network computer to a device label on a local computer. Examples include using a printer on a remote network computer as local device LPT1 or using a hard disk on a remote network computer as local disk drive M.

Understanding Workgroups Versus Domains

Many people become confused when talking about workgroups and domains. Both are very similar in nature. The difference is in security. *Domains* have a central security figure in the form of the primary domain controller (PDC), which always is going to be an NT Server. *Workgroups*, on the other hand, are simply a collection of computers on a network grouped together in name only. This action of grouping computers by a classification name (whether that name reflects a workgroup or a domain name) helps greatly when browsing the available network resources.

Try to imagine a large department store where the products for sale are not grouped together in a logical fashion. It would take hours to find the things you needed to buy. The same is true for networks that have no logical structure. Workgroups and domains, for browsing purposes, are the same except for the level of security involved.

Workgroup machines (Windows For Workgroups 3.11 or Windows 95) do not consult any higher authority when permitting a user to log on to them. Even though WFWG or Windows 95 prompts a user for a name and password when logging on, this information is not cross referenced against any central database. WFWG and Windows 95 store the user name and password locally. After a local logon name and password are defined, that information combination is kept and used only by the local machine to validate and permit that user to log on again in the future.

Consider this. A new user named Ben Franklin is logging onto a Windows 95 workstation for the first time. This workstation is set up as a workgroup machine only. Ben logs on when prompted to do so and enters a password of LIGHTNING. Windows 95 saves this information to the local drive in the form of a *.PWL file found in the default Windows directory (traditionally, C:\WINDOWS). If anyone wants to log on to this Windows 95 workstation in the future as Ben Franklin, he must enter the correct password that first was established.

15

In this scenario, just logging on to the Windows 95 workstation has done nothing as far as *network* validation goes. Old Ben has simply been given authorization to log on to the Windows 95 workstation in question. If Ben goes to another workgroup-based workstation, he can enter anything he wants for a user name and password. Workgroup machines do *not* share user names and passwords. All user names and passwords are for local use only.

Domains, however, are a lot different. If a WFWG or Windows 95 workstation is set to log on to a domain, all logons are validated by a central security machine called a *primary domain controller* (PDC). The action of a user logging onto a domain also establishes network authorization. Only NT Servers and NT Workstations have centralized security for resource management, however. WFWG and Windows 95 workstations simply do not have the capability to reference a domain controller in order to find out whether a network user has authorization to use one of their resources.

WFWG and Win95 workstations can use either workgroup- or domain-level authorization for user logons but have no capability to reference an NT PDC in order to find out if network users have authorization to use their resources even if they are set as domain participants.

The PDC of this small network is BOSS, and there are three workstations: Alpha, Beta, and Gamma. Alpha and Gamma are Windows 95 workstations, and Beta is an NT Workstation. All workstations are set to log on to the domain OFFICE. All user names and passwords therefore are validated by BOSS before anyone logging on is granted network permission.

The user Ben Franklin wants to log on to the network but is not a valid user of the domain OFFICE. This means that he is not in the user database that BOSS maintains. Ben is trying to log on from Alpha, one of the Windows 95 workstations. Ben is prompted for his name and password. He does not get validated with the user name Ben Franklin and a password LIGHTNING, so he clicks Cancel from the logon dialog box and proceeds to enter Windows 95 without network validation. At this point, Ben still can access resources on the other Windows 95 workstation of this small network because Windows 95 and WFWG workstations have very little resource protection. Ben cannot access resources on the NT Server and NT Workstation, however, because access to all resources on these computers is controlled by the PDC; because Ben is not validated by the PDC in this scenario, he is out of luck.

Of course, resources on Windows 95 and WFWG workstations can have access limitation placed on them in the form of passwords and allowed-user lists. When resources on workgroup machines are secured by password protection or they have a permitted-user list defined for them, the protection is only for the local resource. Workgroup machines do not have network-wide authority.

Browsing without proper network validation can produce mixed results because a user still might be able to see and use network resources of WFWG and Windows 95 workstations (unless resources on these machines are protected locally) and see but not have access to NT-based resources. Despite all of Windows 95's enhancements to networking, it is still very basic in the realm of security and internetworking cooperation.

Logging on as a Workgroup Member but Accessing the Domain

Even if a user logs on to a workstation that is set to only provide workgroup-level validation, he still can access domain resources if he has a valid domain name and password. If Ben Franklin had been a valid user to the PDC but the Windows 95 workstation he had been logging on to was set up as a workgroup machine, he still would be granted access to domain resources when he attempted to access or view them. NT machines demand validation of a workgroup user by a PDC using the current logon name and password from the workgroup machine. If the workgroup machine provides a valid user name and password (determined by the PDC), the user is granted permission to use a domain resource. This permission, however, is determined only at the point when the user attempts to access domain-controlled network resources. As stated earlier, just logging on to a workgroup machine does not provide network authorization at that point.

Using Trust Relationships

For a long time, trust relationships confused me. I understood only part of the principle involved when dealing with trusts. It sounds simple enough on the surface: Two domains can enter a relationship in which one trusts the other (and maybe vice versa) to properly validate network users and allow access to network resources. It's basically an *if you say the user is OK, then he's OK by me* situation.

Even if two domains have a two-way trust relationship, that does not by default mean that users of one domain have access to browse and use resources on the opposite domain. When I first began working with NT, I thought all I had to do to easily give users of one domain access to resources in another domain was to set up a trust between the two domains in question. Setting up a trust is only the first half of granting domain user rights to browse and access foreign domain resources.

After a trust is established correctly, the second part of setting up users in one domain as valid users of another is to modify the user group of one domain to be part of the user group of the other. This, in essence, makes the users of one domain able to access the resources of another domain without having to go through the hassle of ensuring that parallel and identical user accounts exist on both domains for every user needing access to both domain resources. Adding a user group from one domain to the user group of another domain is covered in greater detail in Chapter 19, "Understanding the Registry."

Examining the Pitfalls of Trust Relationships

When one domain trusts another domain, the PDCs of both domains talk to each other when a user from one domain attempts to access secured resources (resources on an NT Server or NT Workstation) on the other domain.

The two domains, Office and Home, are in a two-way trust relationship and the user groups of both domains have been adjusted correctly. Therefore, the two domain controllers BOSS and WORKER tell each other about their own users' access levels when users from one domain try to access resources on the other. When Karen Simpson from the Home domain wants to access the resources on Beta (an NT Workstation system that follows the security settings of the Office PDC), the Office PDC, BOSS, asks the Home PDC, WORKER, what sort of access Karen Simpson has. WORKER informs BOSS, and BOSS grants or denies access accordingly.

If Karen is on the Home network and, for some reason, the Home PDC, WORKER, goes down, she cannot access secured resources in the Office domain because her own PDC cannot tell the Office PDC about her security rights.

This scenario plays heavily in remote access situations in which one domain trusts another one but the two PDCs cannot communicate correctly. You might find that when attempting to access secured resources on a remote network, you are getting `Cannot Find Logon Server` error messages. This is due to the remote PDC not being able to locate the local PDC to gather user information.

Suppose that the two domains are not physically connected but the trust relationship has been established by connecting the two PDCs directly with the Remote Access Server (RAS) features built into Windows NT. After the trust is established and the RAS connection is broken, the trust still is active. Now, if Karen Simpson uses the network-dialer feature of her Windows 95 workstation to get a RAS network connection to the Office domain PDC, she cannot access any secured Office domain resources because the Office PDC still wants to talk to the Home network PDC, WORKER, to get security rights information. The network-dialer feature of Windows 95 *cannot* route network data back to the Home PDC. Just think of Windows 95 dial-up network connections as one-way only connections. The Windows 95 workstation can see the remote network but the remote network cannot allow the Home PDC WORKER to talk to the Office PDC BOSS. This means that the Office PDC requests for information from the Home PDC go unanswered and therefore Karen Simpson is not granted any access to secured Office resources.

The workaround for this situation is to simply not have a trust relationship between the two domains and to make certain that each domain has an identical user account for all users needing access to both domains. That forces the remote network to grant or deny access to remote resources based only on the security rights it finds for the user in question in its own user database. This solution is a little more work for the network administrator, but it ensures that users are granted access to resources when they need them.

Using the Network Neighborhood

To open the interface for browsing the resources a network has to offer, you double-click the Network Neighborhood icon on the Windows NT desktop. This has become the standard user interface for browsing network resources for both Windows 95 and Windows NT. And it's a good thing, too. Until this interface was developed, users had to use the File Manager to browse network resources or the command-line utility NET.EXE to browse. Figure 15.1 shows the Network Neighborhood window.

FIGURE 15.1.

The Network Neighborhood (browse client interface).

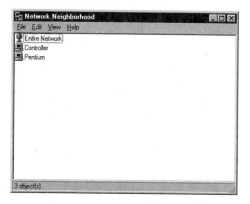

Other computers in the domain in which the current machine is a member are shown when Network Neighborhood is started. If the Network Neighborhood is started and you do not see all the members of your domain and you are certain that they are present on the network, many things could be occurring to prevent them from being displayed. Being present in the browse list (the display of systems on the network in the Network Neighborhood) and actually being on the network as a valid network member are two separate items. This chapter covers issues that deal with browsing network systems and resources.

Seeing Other Domains in the Network Neighborhood

The first entry in the browse list enables you to view the entire network, as shown in Figure 15.2. Keep in mind that a Windows NT Server can act as a gateway machine between many different network platforms. NT can talk to Novell networks, UNIX networks, and IBM mainframes. The proper term for the internal NT network platform is the *Microsoft Windows Network*. The next step after viewing the entire network is viewing other network platforms for which NT may be acting as a gateway. If no other network platforms are being gatewayed by an NT server, the only network platform listed is the Microsoft Windows Network.

Double-clicking the Entire Network entry in the Network Neighborhood enables you to browse all domains accessible to the current machine. Note that it is possible to see network systems and resources without actually having access to use them.

You can use a resource directly through the Network Neighborhood or by mapping a resource to a local drive letter or device name (such as LPT1, in the case of printer resources). When mapped to a local drive letter or device name, the resource becomes transparent to applications and services running on an NT Server. The main role of an NT Server is not to use resources but rather to give workstations access to them.

FIGURE 15.2.

Viewing your connections on the entire network.

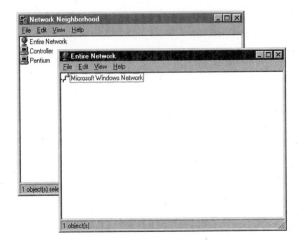

Using Master Browsers and Backup Browsers

On every network domain, a *Master Browser* exists. This is a system on the network responsible for keeping a list of all members on the network. This centralization of the domain member list helps increase network performance. Individual systems on the network don't have to continually broadcast their presence in order for the other machines on the network to see them. The Master Browser of a domain most likely is the PDC. If the PDC goes down, however, there are provisions for allowing other machines in the domain to take over the role of Master Browser.

These machines are called *backup browsers* and typically run concurrent to the Master Browser, maintaining the same member list of the domain, ready to take charge if promoted by the Master Browser or if certain network conditions arise that warrant a new Master Browser election.

Holding Elections

When an NT Server is brought online, an election is held. An *election* is a network process to find out which machine on the network is best suited to be the Master Browser. Typically, a PDC always must be the Master Browser for its domain. If a domain PDC is down, however, other machines can take over the roll of Master Browser.

When an NT Server is brought up, it sends out a network-wide notification indicating that a new election should be held. Every NT Server brought up on a network forces a new election unless that server's configuration is set so that it should never be a master or backup browser itself. The notification message NT Servers use is called an *election datagram*. Election datagrams are broadcast network-wide.

The term *election* is a little misleading because the servers on the network don't actually "vote" on who should be the Master Browser. These datagrams force every viable browser candidate to sum up its potential as a Master Browser and to report its result to the server that initiated the election. The server with the highest potential is elected as the Master Browser.

Included with the election datagram is information on the initiator's election version and election criteria. Receiving browser candidates compare their election version and criteria to the information sent to them by the new Master Browser candidate. If the new Master Browser candidate's election version is higher than any other potential browser's election version, the new candidate wins the election and becomes the new Master Browser. The server with the newest network software therefore always is the Master Browser for a domain. If the new candidate's election version is the same as the current Master Browser's election version, election criteria are summed up and the candidate with the highest criteria total wins.

When a new server is brought online in a network, a Master Browser already is running. An election is normally a process to see whether any newly started servers have the muscle to bump off the current king and take his place. Elections also are used to find a new king when the current king steps aside gracefully (is shut down properly) or does not respond to a browse client's request for a browse list (meaning that the current Master Browser was taken down hard via a crash or a power outage).

Browse clients talk to any available browser to gather a browse list. Clients typically talk to a backup browser to eliminate the burden of the Master Browser. If a browse client cannot find a backup browser, it polls the Master Browser for a list of available backup browsers. If it cannot find the Master Browser, the client issues a domain-wide request for an election.

Looking at the Election Procedure

When a new server is brought up or the current Master Browser cannot be found in a domain, an election takes place in the following manner:

1. The new server/existing backup browser initiates an election datagram. Included with the datagram is the election version and criteria of the new server.

2. All browse candidates receive the datagram and information. Normally, the only candidate the new server must run against is the current Master Browser (which is, by default, currently best suited to be the Master Browser). If there is no current Master Browser, it's a free-for-all situation.

3. The receiving browsers compare their election versions to the new server's. If the new server's election version is higher than any other election version on the network, the new server immediately is elected as the new Master Browser.

4. If the new server's election version is lower than the receiving browser's election version, the new server loses the election but still may become a backup browser. The

Master Browser is in charge of assigning backup browsers. The top candidates among the losers become backup browsers. On a Microsoft Windows network, there are at least one backup browser and one more for every 32 computers on a network segment. It is for this reason that all current browsers respond to the election datagram rather than just the current Master Browser. The Master Browser who wins the election chooses its backup browsers from the data it receives.

5. If, however, there is a tie and the current Master Browser and new potential browser's election versions match, the next step of weighing election criteria takes place.

6. Various election factors are examined. The browser with the best criteria for being the Master Browser wins and remains or becomes the new Master Browser. If there is a tie, the election goes to the next stage.

7. If a new Master Browser candidate and an existing browser are equal in election version and election criteria, the browser that has been running the longest wins. If there is still a tie, the browser with the alphabetically first name wins (Alpha would beat out Gamma if those were the two servers in contention, for example).

8. The browser that has tentatively won then reinitiates the election up to four more times and the process repeats. This is done to ensure that no other servers have just been suddenly brought up and missed the first round(s) of the election. The turn-around time between election cycles depends on the current role of the tentative winner. The cycle time follows:

   Master Browser: 200ms

   Backup browsers: 400ms

   All other browsers: 800ms

   Through this repeating of cycles, the network can handle a mass of new servers being brought up at once (perhaps because the power just came back on).

After a browser becomes the tentative winner of the election, all browsers enter a mode known as *running election*. During this period, the tentative winner reinitiates the election to ensure that it is the real winner. After a system loses an election, it does not broadcast any more cycles that may be left. A system also demotes itself to the status of backup browser if it loses an election. If no other browser on the network responds to the election request with better criteria, the tentative winner becomes the actual winner and the election is over.

Strange situations can occur during elections. The network might have a break in the communication lines and be functionally severed in half, for example. Each half might remain functional, but each half would have determined a Master Browser for itself. What if the two halves were rejoined? There would be two Master Browsers for a single domain. In this scenario, when a Master Browser receives a server announcement from another machine claiming to be a Master Browser for the current domain, it immediately demotes itself to the role of backup browser, sends out an election datagram, and starts a legitimate election.

Examining Election Criteria

If two potential Master Browsers have to duke it out by comparing capabilities, the elements listed in Table 15.1 are examined. These are hexadecimal values that are masked to obtain the end value.

Table 15.1. Election criteria.

Election Criteria Item	Election Value
Operating system type (Mask)	0xFF000000
Windows NT Server	0x20000000
Windows NT Workstation	0x10000000
Windows for Workgroups	0x01000000
Election version (Mask)	0x00FFFF00
Election criteria (Mask)	0x000000FF
Currently a PDC	0x00000080
Running a WINS client	0x00000020
Set as a preferred Master Browser	0x00000008
Currently a Master Browser	0x00000004
MaintainServerList is set to Yes	0x00000002
Currently a backup browser	0x00000001

As you can see, most of the election criteria tries to ensure that the Master Browser generally goes in this order:

1. The PDC of the domain, if available
2. Another NT Server
3. An NT Workstation
4. A Windows 95 Workstation
5. A Windows for Workgroups Workstation

Other factors, such as running a WINS client and being set as a preferred Master Browser, play minor roles if two machines are tied in the primary elements.

The MaintainServerList setting is a WFWG setting found in the SYSTEM.INI file in the [network] section. If this setting is set to True or Yes, the WFWG workstation maintains its own list of available servers on the network and is therefore a potential Master Browser. Setting this setting to No or False prevents a WFWG workstation from becoming a Master Browser. If this setting is not present, the value is Auto, which means that the WFWG machine still maintains a browse list but is not treated preferentially if an election is held.

15

BROWSING ON
A MICROSOFT
NETWORK

In networks in which there is a mix of NT machines and WFWG workstations, it is best to not allow WFWG workstations to be browsers. As mentioned earlier, WFWG machines do not have the same level of network security as NT machines. A situation could arise in which an election is held and a WFWG machine becomes a Master Browser, but it doesn't have the correct access privileges to correctly communicate with all members of the network. Remember that a WFWG machine has no network access at all if it does not have the correct login name and password. If a Master Browser goes down and a WFWG is placed in charge of the network browse list, the WFWG machine could have an incomplete list of available servers.

NT machines also have the `MaintainServerList`, which is found in the Registry in the section

`HKEY_LOCAL_MACHINE\System\CurrentControlSet\Services\Browser\Parameters`

This Registry key is a `REG_SZ` type value and can be set to `True` or `False`. The effect is the same as on a WFWG workstation.

A Master Browser election can be totally biased if a Registry key called `IsDomainMasterBrowser` is added to the section

`HKEY_LOCAL_MACHINE\System\CurrentControlSet\Services\Browser\Parameters`

This is a `REG_SZ` type key and can have a value of `True` or `False`. Setting this key to `True` ensures that the machine in question always is the Master Browser of a domain if no other servers are configured similarly.

Communicating Between Network Servers and the Browse Master

When a non-browser candidate server is brought up on a network, it sends out another type of datagram called a *server announcement*. This datagram is directed to the current Master Browser of the domain. After the Master Browser receives this datagram, the server name is added to the browse list. All Microsoft networking systems (WFWG, Windows 95, NT, and LAN Manager 2.x) send server announcements when they go online. It is at this initial stage that potential browsers are informed by the Master Browser whether they are backup browsers. The Master Browser also sends a list of backup browsers to any standard servers just joining the network as well at this point. Servers continue to announce themselves to the Master Browser when they first start at a rate of about once every minute. As they continue to operate, that announcement time gradually increases until it becomes once every 12 minutes. If the Master Browser does not hear from a server within three announcement periods, it removes the unresponsive server from the browse list.

If a new Master Browser has just gone online, it can force all servers on the network to reregister with it. This is done via a *request announcement datagram*—a network-wide broadcast to which all servers within the domain must respond. Servers are set to respond to this query with a *server announcement datagram* at a random time within 30 seconds. If a new Master Browser of a large network received responses all at once after just coming up, it might get swamped with responses. The randomizing of the response time by network servers helps keeps network traffic from becoming too heavy for the Master Browser to handle.

Using Backup Browsers

As already mentioned, the Master Browser is in charge of indicating which remaining potential browsers should be considered backup browsers. The general rule of thumb is one backup browser for every 32 workstations on the network, with at least one backup browser regardless of how few workstations are on the network. Potential browsers are tagged as backup browsers by the Master Browser when they come online. Thereafter, they contact the Master Browser once every 15 minutes to retrieve an updated browse list. If a backup browser is unable to locate the Master Browser, it immediately initiates an election. Backup browsers are the first to field browse-list requests by browse clients.

Spanning Subnets

Domains can span subnets, meaning that some of the servers on a domain can be separated by routers. The thing to keep in mind about routers is that they do not forward general network broadcasts. This means that networks that rely exclusively on the NetBEUI protocol do not work very well when routers are involved. Keep in mind that the NetBEUI protocol relies almost exclusively on network broadcasts to communicate. This is a simple method of network communication on non-subnetted domains.

The TCP/IP protocol can be routed across routers, however. Remote access connections also are considered to be routed connections and, therefore, the same restrictions apply. It always is best to have a second protocol enabled on a Microsoft Windows network other than NetBEUI. The logical choice currently is TCP/IP.

For each section of a domain that resides on a separate network segment, a Master Browser and a set of backup browsers exist. The PDC of the entire domain serves as an entity known as a domain Master Browser. A *domain Master Browser* is a browser that merges browse lists from all domain network segments into a single list and then redistributes that complete list back to the local segment Master Browser for it to use.

In order for subnetted browsing to function correctly, each segment of the domain must have an NT Server on it. Only NT Server can correctly route browsing datagrams over routers.

The following procedure is used during subnetted domain browser communication:

1. Local segment Master Browsers send announcements about themselves to the domain Master Browser in the form of *Master Browser announcement datagrams.* These datagrams are directed specifically to the domain Master Browser and therefore are sent correctly over a router.

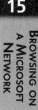

2. The domain Master Browser then collects all browse list members of all subnet segments by issuing a remote `NetServerEnum` API to the Master Browser on each subnet. The domain Master Browser does this every 15 minutes.

3. The browse lists are merged into a single list by the domain Master Browser.

4. The Master Browsers on each subnet then send a remote `NetServerEnum` API call to the domain Master Browser to retrieve the complete list of domain servers.

If a network segment becomes severed from the rest of the network, the Master Browser for that segment continues to operate, but the browse list entries from the rest of the network segments eventually are cleared. The local Master Browser continues to try to reach the domain Master Browser every 15 minutes.

Using Multiple Domains in the Browse List

A browse list can contain other domains as well as servers from the current domain. In order for a Master Browser to have information about other domains, *domain announcement datagrams* are used. These datagrams are broadcast by the Master Browser of a domain. The broadcast datagrams contain information about the Master Browser of the broadcasting domain and are received by foreign domains, which then add the domain name to their own browse list. The datagrams also contain information about the name of the Master Browser for the domain in question and what type of Windows NT the Master Browser of the domain is running (Server or Workstation). If the Master Browser of the domain is an NT Server, the datagram also contains information indicating whether the Master Browser is a PDC.

Master Browsers make domain announcement datagram broadcasts once every minute for five minutes and then once every 15 minutes thereafter.

A domain Master Browser queries any available WINS server for information on registered domain NetBIOS addresses to supplement its domain list obtained by domain announcement datagrams. WINS servers help out greatly when dealing with subnetted domains.

Using Browse Clients

Now that you have some basic understanding of how the server side of browsing works, take a short look at what happens from the client side. Remember that the primary browsing client interface for both Windows 95 and NT 4 is the Network Neighborhood on the desktop.

When a client first requests a browse list from the network, it must retrieve a list of available backup browsers from the Master Browser. Clients do this by means of the *query browsers servers datagram* directed to the Master Browser of the domain. The Master Browser responds with a list of available backup browsers for the client from which to choose. All backup browsers should have an up-to-date copy of the Master Browser's browse list (at least a copy no older than 15 minutes). The client chooses up to three backup browsers to query for future needs.

The client then randomly chooses a backup browser to use for browse-list requests. Each time the client needs a browse list, it randomly chooses one of the three backup browsers on which it has information. This approach to browsing the network spreads out the load placed on all browsers. The Master Browser's primary role is to make sure that all backup browsers have up-to-date information.

If a client cannot contact one of the backup browsers it has information on, it tries another one. If it fails to contact any of the three backup browsers it knows about, it queries the Master Browser for a new list of backup browsers. If it cannot contact the Master Browser for the domain after three attempts, it issues a *force election datagram*, which begins the election process for all potential browsers.

Using the Browse List

Many situations can occur that cause the information displayed in the browse list to be incorrect. Keep in mind that it can take some time before a crashed server is removed from the browse list.

At their longer intervals, for example, servers announce themselves to the Master Browser once every 12 minutes. Three non-contact cycles must occur before the Master Browser removes a server from the list. That means a Master Browser might not remove a server from display for 36 minutes.

To make matters worse, backup browsers retrieve a new browse list once every 15 minutes. So, if things are timed badly, it might take 51 minutes before a server is removed from the browse list.

The same principle can work in reverse. Simply because a server is not visible on the browse list does not mean that the server is not present on the network. A Microsoft Windows network is sometimes flighty when it comes to correctly showing who is online. It is particularly bad with RAS connections and dealing with workgroups without NT PDC.

If you want to test whether a server is on the network, but you do not see the server in the browse list, you always can use the NET.EXE program from within a command shell to try to manually locate it.

Looking for a Server on the Network

If the browse list does not show a server that you are certain is up and running, you can use NET.EXE to view and/or connect to resources on that server. NET.EXE most easily is used from within a command shell. NET.EXE is an application in both NT 4 and Windows 95.

To view resources on a non-visible server, you use the following command line:

```
NET VIEW \\ServerName
```

If the name of the server in question contains a space, you must enclose the double backslash name string in quotation marks.

To actually connect to resources on a server that is not visible in the Network Neighborhood, you use the following command line:

```
NET USE x: \\ServerName\ServerResource
```

Again, if the `ServerName` or `ServerResource` contains any spaces, you must enclose the final string in quotation marks. `x:` specifies the local drive letter to which you want to link the network resource.

`NET.EXE` supports a wide range of network commands that are useful when troubleshooting browse problems.

Hiding Resources from the Browse List

Although there is no way to keep a server that is a member of a domain from being displayed in the browse list, there is a way of hiding shared resources while still making them available for use. When assigning a share name to a resource, you can append a dollar sign to the end of the share name to keep the resource from being displayed in the browse list. The $ is an actual part of the share name. When resource share names are appended with a $, the only way to link to them from a remote network site is to know the name of the resource and to use the `NET.EXE` command from within a command shell to perform the mapping. An example of using a hidden resource follows:

```
NET USE S: \\controller\backdoor$
```

`backdoor$` can be a share name for the root directory of drive C on the server `controller`. Use hidden resource names if you need to have a publicly available resource but you don't want the majority of network users to know about it.

Manually Adding Domains to the Browse List

You can double-click the Network icon in the Control Panel to alter the browse service of an NT Server to manually include foreign domains for browsing purposes. To add a foreign domain to the browse list, follow these steps:

1. Open the Control Panel.
2. Open the Network control element.
3. Select the Services tab at the top.
4. Highlight the Computer Browser entry in the Services list.
5. Click the Configure button.
6. Type the name of the domain you want to have automatically included in the browse list of the domain of the current NT Server. (See Figure 15.3.)

FIGURE 15.3.

Adding a foreign domain to the browse list.

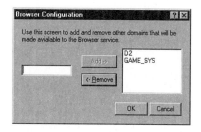

7. Click Add to add the domain to the browse list.

8. To remove an entry in the list, highlight the domain you want to remove and click the Remove button.

9. Click OK until you have exited the Control Panel.

The added domains are available immediately for browsing (assuming that they are accessible to the current domain) by clients. Normally, it takes several minutes before a newly connected domain is visible to the current domain browsers. Adding the domain names in this manner ensures that browse clients do not have to wait before the foreign domains have correctly announced themselves.

Browsing with LAN Manager

LAN Manager 2.x is another, older, Microsoft network environment. It behaves very similarly to Windows NT, but there are some small differences you might have to work around in order to get an NT Server to correctly interact with a LAN Manager 2.x system.

The first problem that arises is the fact that LAN Manager and NT use slightly different announcement formats for certain network activities. You can tell NT to issue LAN Manager–compatible announcements to LAN Manager clients by doing the following:

1. Open the Control Panel.

2. Open the Network control element.

3. Select the Services tab at the top.

4. Highlight Server.

5. Click Configure.

6. Enable the Make Browsers Broadcasts to LAN Manager 2.x Clients checkbox.

7. Click OK until the Control Panel closes.

You must restart the server in order for the changes to take effect.

Some special provisions must be made in order for NT browsers to see LAN Manager servers as well. Follow the same steps you used to manually add domains to the browse list. You can add up to four LAN Manager domains in this manner.

Summary

This chapter looked at the principles involved with browsing on a Microsoft Windows network. It showed how both the server side and client side of browsing works. You should now be familiar with the principles of elections and their purposes within a network environment.

Knowing all of this should allow you to more easily troubleshoot any problems you may be experiencing if browsing services on your network are not functioning as they should.

IN THIS PART

PART

Managing Windows
NT Server

Administering the Server

*by Art Knowles and
Jason Garms*

IN THIS CHAPTER

As a network administrator, your primary duties consist of constantly adding new computers and users, or modifying existing user accounts, configuring both server and client workstations, and troubleshooting all sorts of problems.

In this chapter we look at many of the features NT Server provides for administering the local server. Of primary importance here is the Server Manager application. We also look at how to use this application to perform administrative functions such as creating computer domain accounts and synchronizing the domain controllers. We then discuss managing services and shares on the server.

We then move to a discussion of how and why to use the Directory Replication service and configuring the server to alert you if there are problems. This is followed by a look at how to use the Event Viewer to troubleshoot problems, as well as a method of simply monitoring what is going on your server.

This chapter also looks at the Repair Disk utility (RDISK.EXE) and how to use it to help recover the server in the event of a system failure.

A section on using the workgroup version of the Microsoft Mail service explores how to use NT Server out of the box as a basic electronic mail server for small workgroups. Finally, we look at using the Remote Boot Service, which enables you to boot Windows 3.x and Windows 95 workstations from the network.

Interspersed throughout this chapter are command-line alternatives to managing your network in case you prefer to use the command line for your day-to-day activities.

Using Server Manager

Server Manager is a wonderful administrative tool. It encapsulates the manipulation of a remote computer's resource management into a single application. With it, you can manage your network client (Windows NT only) computer's shared resources and even determine which shared resources your other network clients are using. You can also use this tool to create computer accounts and to synchronize your backup domain controller's database with your primary domain controller. And you can perform all this from your own server or workstation.

> **NOTE**
>
> To enable a Windows NT Workstation, Windows 95, or Windows 3.x client to perform these tasks, first you must install the software. You can find this software in the \CLIENTS\ SRVTOOLS directory on the Windows NT Server CD-ROM. You also can install the software from a network share. You can create this share and copy the installation software by using the Network Client Administrator, as explained in Chapter 24, "Network Client Administrator." For more information on using other machines to administer your server, see Chapter 18, "Remote Administration."

NOTE

For purposes of this discussion, we assume that you are using the local domain for your administration. If you want to administer a different domain, just choose Select Domain from the Computer menu, and then choose the domain to administer in the Select Domain dialog box.

The Server Manager is installed in the Administrative Tools program group by default. The main Server Manager window, shown in Figure 16.1, lists all the computer accounts created in the domain.

FIGURE 16.1.

The Server Manager lists all computer accounts in the domain.

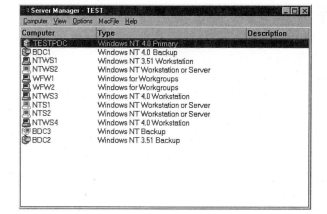

Each entry listed in the Server Manager is associated with an icon that lets you know at a glance what role the computer plays in the domain structure. The three icons are for the primary domain controller (PDC), the backup domain controller (BDC), and a workstation.

In addition, some icons might appear grayed out. This occurs when a computer is turned off or otherwise inaccessible.

Creating Computer Accounts

In a Windows NT domain structure, one of the most important tasks of server management is the creation of computer accounts. A computer account must be the same as the computer name of a client computer. A client can be a Windows NT Server backup domain controller (BDC), a Windows NT Server configured as a member server, or a Windows NT Workstation, for example. This component is used to establish the trusted connection between your domain controller and your client. This trusted connection is the beginning of the network authentication process for domain members.

NOTE

This idea of creating an account for both the computer and the user is new to the world of Microsoft networking. Before Windows NT, the user account was the only real means of authentication. Now the identity of the workstation or server itself can also be authenticated. This allows you to control what computer a user is allowed to use to log on to the network, but more importantly it allows the NT network—in particular the domain controllers—to trust the identity of an individual computer.

NOTE

You only need to create computer accounts for NT Workstations and NT Servers in the domain. You *should not* create computer accounts for other systems on the network, such as Windows 95, Windows 3.x, and Macintosh computers. Because these other clients will not take advantage of this computer account, someone could bring up an NT Workstation or NT Server configured as a domain controller, and make use of that computer account.

For a Windows NT Workstation or Server to join an existing domain, it *must* have a computer account. Furthermore, the creation of this account requires administrative permissions in the domain. This prevents an average user from bringing up an NT system in your domain without your permission.

There are two ways in which you can create the computer account: either from the Server Manager, or during the installation process of an NT Workstation or NT Server.

The major benefit of creating the computer account with Server Manager is that by precreating the computer account, you also can specify the computer name on the client. This enables you to regulate the naming convention of client workstations on your network. So instead of having names like FRODO, SUPERMAN, and JUNGLE_JIM, you can have responsible and descriptive names like FRED_WARD, ACCOUNTING, or MARKETING. Using Server Manager provides another important benefit: You don't have to give out an administrative password (which you would have to change afterward) to a user, and you don't have to physically go to the location of the client computer and enter your administrative account and password in the Control Panel Network applet's Domain/Workgroup Settings dialog box.

When an NT Workstation, or NT Server configured as a member server, joins a domain, the Domain Admins global user group is added to the client computer's Administrators local group. This provides you, the domain administrator, with administrative capabilities on the client machine locally or remotely. Also, the Domain Users global group is added to the client's local Users group.

WARNING

On a network with two-way trust relationships, if you do not have a computer account, you are not a trusted member of the domain, and you have no access to a domain controller. This means that even if you have a user account on the domain controller, without a computer account, you cannot be authenticated at the user level. And if you cannot be authenticated, you cannot access network resources. On a network with no trust relationships or with a one-way trust relationship, a user account can be mapped to a user account on the remote computer. This local user account-to-remote user account mapping provides limited access to network resources.

You can also use computer accounts to restrict a user's ability to access your network to a specific set of workstations. This possibility and the creation of user accounts are discussed in the section titled "User Manager for Domains" in Chapter 17, "User Administration."

To create a computer account, follow these steps:

1. Open the Server Manager from the Administrative Tools program group.
2. Choose Add to Domain from the Computer menu. The Add Computer To Domain dialog box appears, as shown in Figure 16.2.

FIGURE 16.2.

Specify the name of the computer account to create.

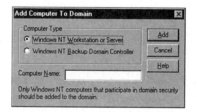

3. Select the computer type. A computer type can be a Windows NT Workstation or Windows NT Server configured as a member server, or a Windows NT backup domain controller. Enter the computer name in the Computer Name field.
4. Click the Add button.
5. Repeat steps 2 through 4 for each computer account you want to create. Then click the Close button.

Deleting a computer account with Server Manager is as simple as selecting the computer account and pressing the Delete key. Alternatively, you can choose the Remove from Domain command from the Computer menu. Before the computer account is deleted, you will be warned and asked to confirm the action, as shown in Figure 16.3.

FIGURE 16.3.

Removing computer accounts deletes the associated security identified.

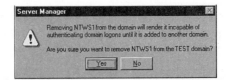

WARNING

Computer accounts have unique security identifiers (SIDs). If you delete an account and then re-create it, the client computer user must rejoin the domain. If you move a computer from one domain to another and then attempt to rejoin the original domain using the original computer account, the attempt will fail. If you change the client computer's configuration from a domain to a workgroup and then attempt to rejoin the domain using the original computer account, the attempt will fail. If you change the computer's name without creating an account for the new computer name, the attempt will also fail. The moral of this story is that whenever you change a computer's domain or name, you must create a new account for it.

TIP

Adding or deleting computer accounts from the command line is an easy task. As with most network-related commands, it begins with the NET command.

This version of the NET command is available only on Windows NT Server computers:

```
NET COMPUTER \\ComputerName /ADD /DEL
```

Explanations of the syntax follow:

ComputerName: Name of the computer account you want to create.

/ADD: Specifies that you want to create the computer account and add the computer to the domain.

/DEL: Specifies that you want to delete the computer account and remove the computer from the domain.

Synchronizing the Domain Database

The master domain database, which includes your computer and user accounts, physically resides on the primary domain controller (PDC). Changes to this database are replicated to your BDCs at periodic intervals, as defined by a setting in the Registry. Sometimes this replication process fails due to a poor network connection or other problems. You can use Server Manager to force an immediate replication of this database to all BDCs in the domain, or only to a specific BDC.

To synchronize all the BDCs with the PDC, follow these steps:

1. Open the Server Manager from the Administrative Tools program group.
2. Select the PDC in the main window of Server Manager.
3. Choose Synchronize Entire Domain from the Computer menu.

   You receive a message indicating that the process may take several minutes to complete, as shown in Figure 16.4. Click Yes to continue.

FIGURE 16.4.

Synchronizing the domain takes a few minutes.

You receive this message because synchronizing the account database can use quite a bit of network bandwidth and can affect your network performance. So you should use this command only if you absolutely must during peak network usage hours, particularly if you have a large number of accounts and users to replicate to the BDC.

4. Click the OK button to proceed.
5. Next you are informed that you should check the event log of the PDC and BDC to make sure that the replication process succeeded. The idea here is to make sure that the PDC and the BDC sent and received the same number of accounts. This information is contained in the system event log Net Logon.

If you have a number of backup domain controllers, you might only need to synchronize a particular one. This occurs most often when the BDCs and the PDCs are geographically dispersed and connected by wide area network (WAN) lines. To synchronize a specific BDC with the PDC, follow these steps:

1. Select the BDC in the Server Manager main window.
2. Choose Synchronize with Primary Domain Controller from the Computer menu. You will see a message that the process may take several minutes to complete. Click the OK button to proceed.
3. Next you are informed that you should check the event log of the PDC and BDC to make sure that the replication process succeeded.

Because all computer accounts and user accounts must be created on the PDC's database, if the PDC fails and goes offline, you cannot make any account modifications. If this occurs, you can promote a BDC to a PDC temporarily to make account modifications. After you solve the problem with the PDC, you can bring it back online. There are several items to consider when a failed PDC is restored or when promoting a BDC to a PDC:

- When you promote a BDC to a PDC, all client connections on both domain controllers are terminated. This could cause a loss of data for your network users. Because of this possibility, you should warn your users to disconnect prior to promoting a BDC.

- You will not be able to synchronize a domain if you are attached to the network through an NT RAS server running on a domain controller of the domain you wish to synchronize. This is because when you synchronize the domain, the RAS connection will be terminated before the role change is completed. When you lose connection to the network, NT terminates the synchronization request, which is then rolled back and the backup domain controller is not promoted.

- If you promote a BDC to a PDC and you bring a failed PDC back online, you now have two PDCs on the domain. This prevents you from making any changes to the account database. To correct the situation, you must demote one of the PDCs to a BDC.

- Before you bring your PDC back online, you should keep a few considerations in mind. Never use a domain controller that has stale data as a synchronization source. To prevent this from occurring, demote your failed PDC to a BDC. Then force the synchronization of the BDC with the current PDC. Then you can promote the BDC (the original PDC) back to a PDC and return to your original configuration. Synchronizing the database first ensures that the account database update will be successful (because you can check the event logs to make sure) and that any changes you made while the original PDC was down will be maintained. If you fail to synchronize the database prior to demoting the current PDC, you might overwrite your user databases on the backup controllers with an older copy (the one on your failed PDC) and lose any account modifications that occurred while the original PDC was down.

To promote a BDC to a PDC, follow these steps:

1. Select the BDC in the Server Manager main window.

2. Choose Promote to Primary Domain Controller from the Computer menu. You see a message telling you that the process may take several minutes to complete and warning you that all connections to the existing PDC and the BDC you are promoting will be closed. This warning is shown in Figure 16.5. Click the OK button to proceed.

3. After the account synchronization completes, the BDC is displayed as a PDC, and the old PDC is displayed as a BDC in the main window, as shown in Figure 16.6, where you'll notice the icon and the description on the old PDC, called TESTPDC, and on the new PDC, called BDC1, have changed.

FIGURE 16.5.

All network connections to the existing PDC and the machine being promoted to PDC will be closed.

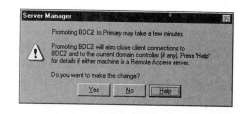

FIGURE 16.6.

Promoting a BDC to PDC demotes the existing PDC.

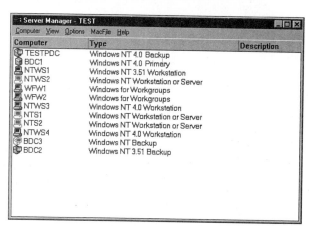

TIP

You can synchronize the entire domain account database by running the following command from a command prompt:

`NET ACCOUNTS /SYNC /DOMAIN`

Descriptions of this syntax follow:

/SYNC: Synchronizes the entire domain if it is executed on a PDC, or just the BDC with the PDC if it is running on a BDC.

/DOMAIN: Synchronizes the entire domain regardless of where the application is executed. Normally, this switch is used only when the command is executed on a Windows NT Workstation or Windows NT Server running as a member server.

Managing Remote Computer Resources

You can use Server Manager to manage your local or remote computer resources. I find this capability to manage remote computer resources highly useful in my day-to-day administrative activities because I do not have to leave my desk. With Server Manager, you can stop, start, pause, continue, or configure system services on a remote computer running Windows NT Workstation or NT Server. You can also use it to create new shares or to modify or delete existing shares. You can use it to determine who is connected to the remote computer, or even to determine which shares are available on the remote computer.

Managing Services

One method of controlling services on a Windows NT computer is to use the local computer's Control Panel Services applet. With this tool, you can stop, start, pause, or continue the execution of a service. You can also use it to specify if the service should be automatically started at boot time and to configure which user account privileges the service uses to do its job.

You can use Server Manager to perform these same tasks by selecting the computer in the Server Manager's main window and then choosing Services from the Computer menu. The Services on PRIMUS dialog box appears, as shown in Figure 16.7.

FIGURE 16.7.

The Server Manager can be used to control services on an NT system.

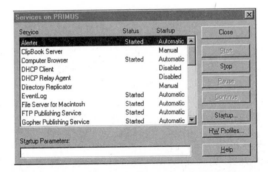

TIP

Before you stop a service that a client may be using, you should pause it. This prevents any new clients from connecting to this service. You can then send a message (by choosing Send Message from the Computer menu) to the connected users to inform them of your intention to shut down the service. The clients then have the opportunity to save their data before you shut down the service.

The buttons you can click to perform selected functions:

- **Start:** Starts a service that is not executing. Any command-line parameters entered in the Startup Parameters field are passed onto the service when it starts executing.

- **Stop:** Stops a service that is currently running.

- **Pause:** Prevents new connections to a service (if it is a network-aware service, such as the Server service), while still providing support to currently connected users.

- **Continue:** Continues the operation of a paused service.

- **Startup:** Changes the start-up characteristics for a service. The available options provided in the Services dialog box are the Startup Type and Log On As fields. The Startup Type entry can be Automatic, Manual, or Disabled. Log On As can specify that the service should use the default system account or a user account that you created with User Manager for Domains. If you specify a user account, then you must also specify a user password.

Managing Shares

Just as you can manipulate a remote computer's service control manager database with Server Manager, you can also manipulate a remote computer's network shares.

First, select the computer in the Server Manager main window to highlight it. Then choose Shared Directories from the Computer menu. The Shared Directories dialog box appears, as shown in Figure 16.8.

FIGURE 16.8.

The Server Manager can be used to view the current shares on an NT system.

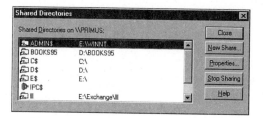

You can create a new network share by clicking the New Share button. The New Share dialog box appears, asking you to specify the share name, path, comment, and number of users that can connect to the share. By clicking the Permissions button, you can specify the share level permissions.

You can modify an existing share by highlighting a shared directory and then clicking the Properties button. The Shared Directory dialog box appears, which is similar to the New Share dialog box.

To remove an existing network share, highlight the shared directory and click the Stop Sharing button.

WARNING

Clicking the Stop Sharing button in the Shared Directories dialog box immediately stops sharing the directory. There is no confirmation message. Before you do this, check to see who is using the share. This is discussed in the next section, "Performing Resource Accounting."

Performing Resource Accounting

To determine which users are connected to a computer, the network shares available on a computer, or the shares in use on a remote computer, double-click the computer in the Server Manager's main window, or select the computer in the main window and then choose Properties from the Computer menu. The Properties dialog box appears, as shown in Figure 16.9. This is the same dialog box displayed in the Control Panel Server applet.

FIGURE 16.9.

The Server Manager can be used to view how many users are logged on and how many resources are being accessed.

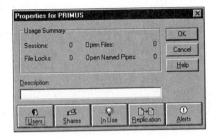

The Properties dialog box enables you to access the following functions:

- **Usage Summary:** This lists the number of sessions, file locks, open files, and named pipes in use on a computer. The number of sessions actually reflects the number of users connected to the computer because each connected computer uses one session.

- **Users:** This displays the User Sessions dialog box, shown in Figure 16.10, and determines which users are connected to the computer and what resources they are using. The upper box lists the connected users, the name of the computer they are connected from, the number of open files, the total connection time, the total idle time, and whether the users have connected with Guest privileges. The lower box lists the resources the selected user is connected to, the number of files in the resource opened by the selected user, and total amount of time the user has been connected. To disconnect a specific user, highlight the user and click the Disconnect button. To disconnect all users from all resources, just click the Disconnect All button.

- **Shares:** This performs an action similar to the Users button. After you click this button, the Shared Resources dialog box appears, as shown in Figure 16.11. The emphasis here is on the shares. The upper box lists the shares by name, number of connections, and physical path of the shared directory. The lower box lists the connected users, total connection time, and whether the connection currently is active. To disconnect all users from a specific share, highlight the share and click the Disconnect button. To disconnect all users from all resources, just click the Disconnect All button.

FIGURE 16.10.

The Server Manager can be used to see which resources a user is attached to.

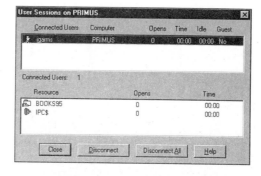

FIGURE 16.11.

The Server Manager can be used to see which users are attached to a particular share.

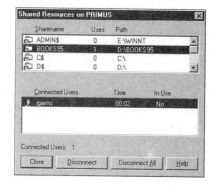

■ **In Use:** Clicking In Use displays the Open Resources dialog box, as shown in Figure 16.12. This lists the resources that currently are open, such as files, named pipe connections, print jobs, and links to LAN Manager communication devices. It also includes information about the user who has opened the resource, the permission granted when the resource was opened, any locks, and the pathname to the open resource. To disconnect all users from a specific resource, highlight the resource and click the Close Resource button. To disconnect all users from all resources, just click the Close All Resources button.

FIGURE 16.12.

The Server Manager can be used to display a list of all resources that are currently open.

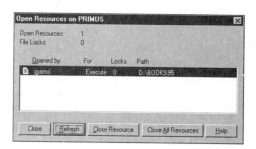

NOTE

Replication and alerts are discussed later in this chapter in the sections titled "Configuring the Directory Replicator Service" and "Configuring Alerts."

CAUTION

If you disconnect a user, any files that have been opened by the user will not be closed properly, and the user may lose data. Disconnecting a user in this fashion also does not prevent him from reconnecting. If the user or the user's application attempts a reconnect, it will be granted, unless you paused the Server service, as discussed earlier in the "Managing Services" section of this chapter.

Configuring the Directory Replicator Service

Use the Directory Replicator Service to copy directories and files from a Windows NT Server to another server or workstation. The service consists of an export component specifying the root directory to export and an import component used to specify directories and files to copy from the export server. The export server is limited to a single directory tree, which consists of the root directory and a maximum of 32 nested subdirectories. To configure the replication service, you must perform the following tasks:

- **Create the logon account for the service.** You can create this account with User Manager for Domains, and it must have the following properties:

    It must be a member of the Backup Operators group.

    It must have the Password Never Expires option enabled.

    It must have no logon hour restrictions.

    For specific information on these settings and how to add user accounts to groups, refer to Chapter 17.

- **Configure the replication service start-up values.** The Directory Replicator Service's start-up values must be changed to start up automatically and to use the This Account option in the Log On As field. The account specified must be the account you created in the previous step.

- **Set the logon script path.** The replication service is really designed to copy your logon scripts from one domain controller to your other domain controllers. Generally, this directory is your %SystemRoot%\System32\REPL\Import\Scripts path, which is where your logon scripts are stored, where %SystemRoot% is the root directory where you installed NT—usually, C:\WINNT. To import your scripts to a different directory path, just change the Logon Script Path entry in the Directory Replication dialog box to the directory path you want to use. (See Figure 16.13.) This path is used by your domain controller to locate your logon scripts during the user authentication process. Do not leave a blank entry in the Logon Script Path field, or your logon scripts will not be found when your network clients log onto the network.

FIGURE 16.13.

The Directory Replication window can also be used to specify the location of your logon scripts.

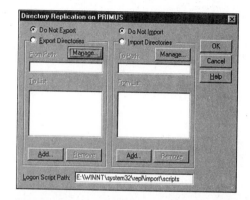

NOTE

When you configure the replication service to start, it creates a special share, called REPL$, based on the directory you specify as the logon script path. Generally, this is %SystemRoot%\System32\REPL\Export.

■ **Configure the server to export a directory tree.** This process is a bit complex and is covered in the following section, "Configuring the Export Server."

■ **Configure the client to import a directory tree.** This is similar to configuring for an export server. This is discussed later in this chapter in the section, "Configuring the Import Server."

Configuring the Export Server

To configure your Directory Replicator Service to export a directory tree, use Server Manager. Just double-click the name of the server to display the Properties dialog box, and then click the Replication button to display the Directory Replication dialog box. Then follow these steps:

> **NOTE**
>
> Windows NT Servers can be configured as both import *and* export servers. Windows NT Workstations can *only* be configured as import servers. Also, Windows NT Workstation cannot change the default replication path from `%SystemRoot%\System32\Repl\Import\Scripts`.

1. Enable the replication service by enabling the Export Directories radio button.

2. Add computers to replicate the To List box by clicking the Add button at the bottom left of the screen. The Select Domain dialog box appears.

3. Select the individual domains and computers to which you want to export. Then click the OK button. You are returned to the Directory Replication dialog box. To add more computers, repeat steps 2 and 3.

> **NOTE**
>
> By default, the local domain is always included as an export partner, unless you add an entry in the To List box. If you do add an entry, the local domain no longer is automatically included. To continue to export to the local domain, add the domain name to the To List box.

4. Specify the export path (if the default is not acceptable, although in most cases you will not need to change this entry) in the From Path field. Generally, this is the `%SystemRoot%\System32\Repl\Export` directory.

5. Add the subdirectories from the root export directory. Click the From Path Manage button, which displays the Manage Exported Directories dialog box (see Figure 16.14).

FIGURE 16.14.

The Manage Exported Directories window is used to specify subdirectories to export, as well as monitor replication locks.

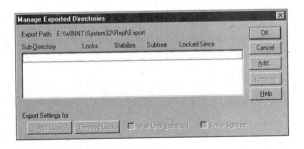

6. Specify the subdirectories to export by clicking the Add button. The Add Subdirectory dialog box appears, in which you can specify the subdirectories of the

root export path to export. For each subdirectory you select, you must specify whether you want to wait until the files in the directory have been stable (no changes have been made for 2 minutes) by enabling or disabling the Wait Until Stabilized checkbox, and whether you want any subdirectories to be copied by enabling or disabling the Entire Subtree checkbox. Remember that you must repeat this step for each subdirectory you want to export.

For each subdirectory entry, you can see some status information by looking at the following columns:

■ **Locks:** Specifies the number of active locks on the subdirectory.

■ **Stabilize:** Indicates whether the files must be idle for 2 minutes before replication can occur (which can prevent partial replication changes if the files are very active).

■ **Subtree:** Indicates that all subdirectories are to be replicated.

■ **Locked Since:** Indicates that a subdirectory has been locked since a specific date/time.

TIP

If you are going to be making a lot of changes to a subdirectory you have marked for export, use the Add Lock button to lock the directory. This prevents the directory from being replicated until all the locks are released.

Configuring the Import Server

This process is quite similar to exporting a directory tree. From the Directory Replication dialog box, follow these steps:

1. Enable the replication service by enabling the Import Directories radio button.

2. Add computers to replicate to in the From List box by clicking the Add button at the bottom right of the screen. The Select Domain dialog box appears.

NOTE

By default, the local domain is always included as an import partner unless you add an entry in the From List field. If you do add an entry, the local domain is no longer automatically included. To continue to import from the local domain, you must add the domain name in the From List field.

---

3. Select the individual domains and computers to which you want to import. Then click the OK button. You are returned to the Directory Replication dialog box. To add more computers, repeat steps 2 and 3.

4. Add the subdirectories from the root import directory. Click the To Path Manage button, which displays the Manage Imported Directories dialog box. (See Figure 16.15.)

FIGURE 16.15.

The Manage Imported Directories window is used to specify subdirectories to import, as well as monitor locks.

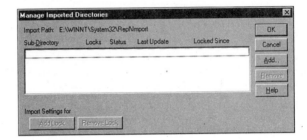

5. The only difference in the Manage Imported Directories dialog box is that the status information for each entry consists of the number of locks on the directory, the status (OK, which indicates that the directory is receiving regular updates; No Master, which indicates that no updates are being received; No Sync, which indicates that the directory has received updates, but the current data is outdated; and a blank entry, which indicates that replication has never occurred), the date/time the last update occurred, and the date/time of the oldest lock on the directory.

TIP

To prevent an import directory from being updated, just select it and click the Add Lock button. An import directory with a lock will not be updated.

CAUTION

If you are importing directories from a domain or server located on the other side of a WAN connection, the import may fail from the local domain. To ensure that this does not occur, manually add the domain or computer name in the From field of the Manage Imported Directories dialog box.

Configuring Alerts

Use alerts to notify an administrator of a serious problem that has occurred on a Windows NT computer. You can choose to send an alert to a particular domain user or a specific computer monitored by several administrators or support personnel.

To guarantee that the alert will be sent, you should also modify the system to start the Alert and Messenger services at system startup. This ensures that the services are functioning and available to send administrative alerts. If the services are left in their default start-up setting of Manual, then the services will attempt to send the alert but may fail due to unforeseen circumstances. If they fail, the alert will not be sent. A Windows NT Server computer has a default start-up setting of Automatic and does not have to be reconfigured. To *receive* an administrative alert, the messenger service must be running.

To configure the Alert service, use Server Manager. Just double-click the name of the server to display the Properties dialog box. Then follow these steps:

1. Click the Alerts button in the Server dialog box. The Alerts dialog box shown in Figure 16.16 appears.

FIGURE 16.16.

The Alerts section of the Server Manager is used to specify administrators who should be notified when something goes wrong.

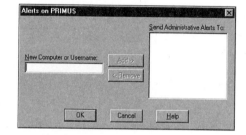

2. To add a new computer or user to be notified, enter the computer or user name in the New Computer or Username field and then click the Add button. The computer or user name then is moved to the Send Administrative Alerts To box.

3. To remove a computer or user, select the computer or user name in the Send Administrative Alerts To box and click the Remove button. This moves the computer or user name to the New Computer or Username field.

NOTE

You do not have to include the double backslashes (\\) for a computer name, as you do for just about every other usage involving a computer name. If you do, the double backslashes are dropped when the name is moved.

4. To add or remove more computers or users, repeat step 2 or 3.

5. When you finish entering or removing computer and user names, click the OK button to return to the Server Manager main window.

Using the Event Viewer

Use the Event Viewer to display status events that occur on your computer. These events are divided into three categories. Each category is contained in a specific log. The system log includes events related to running the operating system, the application log includes application-specific events, and the security log includes auditing events. These events are further divided into types that have specific icons associated with them.

> **NOTE**
>
> Use the Event Viewer to view your logs daily for your file servers, and at least weekly for workstations. If you do not review your logs in this time frame, you might be unaware of system errors that could result in a system failure, and you will not be aware of possible attempts to violate the security of your network.

Viewing Events

To view the events that have occurred on your system, first select the log to view. Access this information from the Log menu. You can select the application, security, or system log to view. Each event in a log is broken down into components that describe the event. Table 16.1 summarizes these event components. To get the details of an event, just double-click one and the Event Detail dialog box appears, as shown in Figure 16.17. What is important to note here is that the description contains a textual message in the Description box that describes the error condition, and if the event has any associated data with it, this is included in the Data box. This data list often contains information that you or Microsoft technical support can use to isolate and solve the problem.

FIGURE 16.17.

All events contain certain informational components.

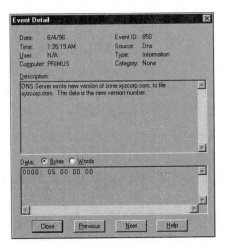

Table 16.1. The event components.

Component	Description
Icon	A quick indicator to the type of event.
Date	The date the event occurred.
Time	The time the event occurred.
Source	The name of the application, system service, or device driver that reported the event.
Category	A general classification of an event type. In most cases, categories are used only in the security log.
Event ID	An event number specific to the event source and associated with a specific error message.
User	An event can be associated with a specific user that triggered the event. In most cases, this is used only in the security log.
Computer	An event can be associated with a specific computer that triggered the event. In most cases, this is the name of the host (the computer where the log resides) computer.

Filtering Events

One of the problems you will notice over time is that so many events occur on your system that finding the trouble spots can be quite time-consuming. And if it takes too much of your time, then you probably will stop checking for these problems. Eventually, a problem will grow into a system-related failure that could cause you to lose your job. I would like to help you avoid that possibility. The easiest way to minimize the amount of data overload is to use the Event Viewer's filtering capabilities.

Follow these steps:

1. Choose Filter Events from the View menu to display the Filter dialog box shown in Figure 16.18.
2. In the View From section, select the Events On radio button. Then specify a date and time.
3. In the View Through section, select the Events On radio button. Then specify a date and time.
4. In the Types section, select the type of event to report. For a quick look, I suggest only looking for warning and error conditions.

FIGURE 16.18.

Event filtering is useful for finding desired items.

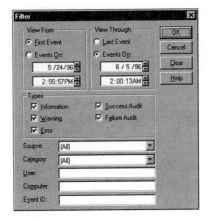

5. In the Source drop-down listbox, select the event source to view. This is useful for limiting the report to a specific application, system service, or device driver to determine how often the error has occurred.

6. In the Category drop-down listbox, select the event categories to view. In most systems, there will be only security-related categories, or possibly no subcategories. If you have categories, you can further limit the report to a particular category by selecting it from the list.

7. In the User field, enter the user account you want to use to further limit the report. This can be useful when you are checking events in the security log and have noticed a potential violation. By limiting the report to just this user, you can determine how often the user has attempted to violate your system security.

8. Enter the computer name in the Computer field to further limit events to just events that have occurred on the specific computer.

9. If you are looking for a specific event, enter the event number in the Event ID field. This can be useful to determine how often a specific event has occurred in the past.

NOTE

This is most useful when you already know the event ID you want to locate, such as when you want to find previous occurrences of an event you just found in the Event Viewer.

---

10. After you finish entering all your filtering characteristics, click the OK button to engage the filter. When a filter has been engaged, the title bar of the Event Viewer changes to include the word Filtered.

NOTE

After a filter has been specified, it remains in effect until you change it. If you enabled the Save Settings on Exit option, the next time you launch Event Viewer, the filter also remains in effect.

To remove a filter that you have created using these steps, just choose the View | All Events menu option, and all the events are displayed in the logs.

Archiving Events

Instead of just throwing away the events in your event logs when you fill them up, you should archive them. Then you can load them at a later date for comparison with current logs to isolate any potential problems. You also can use these logs with Excel or any database that can import a comma-separated value or ASCII text file. You can use this imported data to spot trends that can indicate a potential network trouble spot or hardware-related failure.

TIP

You can set the maximum size of the log by choosing the Log | Log Settings menu option to display the Log Settings dialog box. In this dialog box, you also can specify that you want the log to automatically wrap and overwrite events on an as-needed basis, to overwrite events after a specific number of days, or to manually clear the log to free space for further events.

To archive a log, follow these steps:

1. Choose Log Type from the Log menu, where Log Type is the Application, Security, or System log.

2. Choose Save As from the Log menu to display the Save As dialog box. In the Save File As Type field, select Event Log Files (*.EVT) to save the event file as a binary file that can be reloaded later into the Event Viewer. Or, select Text Files (*.TXT), which is a standard ASCII text file, or Comma Delim Text (*.TXT), which is a comma-separated value text file.

3. Enter a filename in the File Name field and click the OK button. If the drive or directory is not the one you want, change it before clicking the OK button.

Using the Repair Disk Utility

The Repair Disk Utility (RDISK.EXE) is used for creating and updating your system's Emergency Repair Disk (ERD). An icon is not automatically created for this utility when you install Windows NT. However, I find this tool to be so useful that I immediately create an icon for it whenever I install Windows NT Workstation or Windows NT Server, and I suggest that you do so as well. The ERD includes contents from your %SystemRoot%\Repair subdirectory, as well as copies of the NTLDR, NTDETECT.COM, and BOOT.INI files from your system. If you were unable to create a repair disk during the installation process, you should use this utility to create the ERD. Also, you should run RDISK regularly to update the ERD. The ERD is the most effective method of recovering your system in the event of a system failure.

NOTE

The ERD is not a bootable disk; instead, it is intended to be used with the three Windows NT installation disks that came with your copy of NT.

The ERD is also useful for restoring the Registry (which is what the repair information includes) when you make a mistake with the Registry Editor or install some software that prevents your system from functioning properly. If you have a recent copy of the repair disk, you can back out of the changes to your system just by running through the repair process and be up and running in minutes.

TIP

You can create the three boot disks by running WINNT32.EXE /OX from the CD-ROM in the \I386 directory. /OX specifies that you want to create the three installation disks that use floppy disks or the CD-ROM as the installation source medium. You can use /O instead of /OX to create the three boot floppy disks, which use the temporary copy of the installation directory (WIN_NT.~LS) that was copied to your hard disk from a WINNT.EXE (MS-DOS based) installation. The /S:*SourcePath* should be a UNC name (such as \\SRV\CD-ROM\ I386) or a local device name (such as E:\I386) for the installation media.

WARNING

Before you make any system modifications, you should use the Repair Disk Utility to back up your Registry. At the very least, you should update the local repair information, although I recommend that you also make a new repair disk. In fact, you should keep at least three repair disks so that you will always have one you can use to restore your configuration. Much as you have multiple backup sets, if you have multiple repair disks, you can restore your system to a known good state. At least one of these repair disks should contain a valid Registry to restore your Registry configuration.

Installing the Repair Disk Utility

To install the Repair Disk Utility, follow these steps:

1. Right-click the Start button and choose Open All Users. An Explorer window appears.
2. Double-click the Programs icon in the Explorer window, shown in Figure 16.19. This brings up another Explorer window.

FIGURE 16.19.

The All Users profile contains a Programs icon, which contains common Start menu items for all users on the system.

3. Double-click the Administrative Tools icon. This brings up an Explorer window that shows existing shortcuts to many of the NT administrative tools, shown in Figure 16.20.

FIGURE 16.20.

The Administrative Tools folder contains shortcuts to many of the NT administration tools.

4. From the File menu, choose New, and then choose Shortcut. The Create Shortcut window appears.

5. Type RDISK into the Command Line box, and then click the Next button. Click the Finish button.

6. Close all the Explorer windows.

RDISK now appears with all the other administrative tools in the Start menu, as shown in Figure 16.21.

FIGURE 16.21.

The shortcut to the RDISK utility now appears with the rest of the shortcuts in the Start menu.

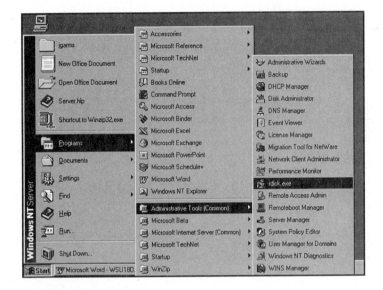

Using the Repair Disk Utility

After you create the program item for the Repair Disk Utility, it is a good idea to run it and back up your system configuration. When you run the application, the Repair Disk Utility dialog box appears, as shown in Figure 16.22.

FIGURE 16.22.

The RDISK utility is used to create and update the ERD.

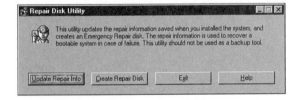

The Repair Disk Utility dialog box has four buttons:

■ **Update Repair Info:** This button updates the Registry information contained in the %SystemRoot%\Repair directory. After you click this button, you are asked whether you want to create a new repair disk.

■ **Create Repair Disk:** This button formats a high-density floppy disk and copies the same repair information as described for the Update Repair Info button. This repair disk is used by the repair process to restore your Registry.

> **TIP**
>
> If you have a 2.88MB floppy drive and experience problems creating a repair disk, insert a 1.44MB floppy and use this to create your repair disk.

■ **Exit:** This button exits the application.

■ **Help:** This button displays brief descriptions of the Repair Disk Utility buttons' actions.

The information contained in the `%SystemRoot%\Repair` directory consists of uncompressed copies of your `AUTOEXEC.NT` and `CONFIG.NT` files and the compressed files listed in Table 16.2.

> **TIP**
>
> If you have COMPRESS.EXE, which is included with several of the Microsoft SDKs and development platforms, as well as the NT Resource Kit utilities, you can compress the files in a format that is compatible with the Microsoft expansion program. EXPAND.EXE is included with Windows NT and is used to manually decompress these files. You might want to use the same format because you will have this program (EXPAND.EXE) on every system you use.

Table 16.2. Key components of the Registry.

Filename	Registry Key	Description
default._	HKEY_USERS\DEFAULT	The default system profile
sam._	HKEY_LOCAL_MACHINE\SAM	Your Security Account Manager
security._	HKEY_LOCAL_MACHINE\Security	The security database
software._	HKEY_LOCAL_MACHINE\Software	The software configurable settings
system._	HKEY_LOCAL_MACHINE\System	System-specific configuration settings

You will see one additional file not mentioned in the `%SystemRoot%\Repair` directory if you enable the Show Hidden/System Files option in the NT Explorer. This file is called `setup.log`, and it should never be deleted. This file is used by the Setup program during an upgrade. If the Setup program cannot find enough free space during the upgrade, it prompts you to delete some files from your current installation. The files listed in setup.log are the files that will be deleted to make room for the upgrade. If this file is missing and you have insufficient disk space, the Setup program can continue only if you reformat your hard disk. This is rarely an acceptable solution and could be quite dangerous to your continued health if this installation is your only domain controller (which contains all your account information), has critical data files, or contains similar nonrecoverable components. If this file doesn't exist or is unable to clear enough disk space to perform the installation, you will have to exit the upgrade process, manually delete enough files, and then rerun the upgrade program.

Working with a Workgroup Post Office

Windows NT Server and Windows NT Workstation can act as a workgroup electronic mail post office. When you run this post office service, any Windows 3.x, Windows NT 3.x, or DOS workstation running the Microsoft Mail client can connect to the post office. Windows 95 and NT 4 also include the Exchange client software, which comes with the Microsoft Mail connector. You can use this to connect to the NT 4 post office.

It does not offer all the functionality of the full-blown Microsoft Mail 3.5 or Exchange 4.0 mail servers, but if all you need are rudimentary e-mail services, it may be just the ticket for you.

Creating a Workgroup Post Office

Creating a post office is an easy task, but keep the following considerations in mind:

- Only the creator of the post office can administer it.
- A workgroup post office can display only personal or shared folders one at a time—not both simultaneously.
- If you have more than ten users, do not install the post office on a Windows NT Workstation computer because a Windows NT Workstation is limited to ten simultaneous connections.

To create your workgroup post office, follow these steps:

1. From the Control Panel, open the Microsoft Mail Postoffice applet. This will bring up the Microsoft Workgroup Postoffice Admin window.

2. Select the option to Create a new Workgroup Postoffice, as shown in Figure 16.23. There should be only one workgroup post office in your workgroup/domain. If you create more than one post office, the two post offices cannot exchange e-mails. You need the complete Microsoft Mail or Exchange package in order to support multiple post offices.

3. The next dialog box prompts you for the location of the WGPO (Work Group post office) directory.

FIGURE 16.23.

Use the Microsoft Mail Postoffice Control Panel applet to create a workgroup post office.

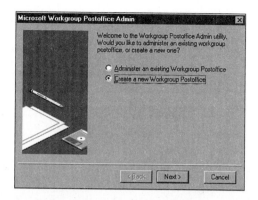

NOTE

You can only choose to install the WGPO into an existing directory, so you might have to use the NT Explorer to create a directory for the post office.

The post office should be installed on a partition with sufficient free space to handle all your client's mail data if you store the MMF (Microsoft Mail File) on the server. If you will have ten clients with a maximum of 10MB of mail per user, for example, you will need at least a 100MB partition.

WARNING

If you install your post office to a compressed NTFS volume, you may gain a bit of additional storage space, but you will decrease the performance of your mail server. This occurs because Microsoft Mail Files (MMFs) are already compressed. The overhead of trying to compress an already compressed file, or to uncompress these files as they are used, is rarely worth the effort.

4. After the WGPO directory is created, you are prompted to enter your Administrator account detail information, as shown in Figure 16.24. In this dialog box, enter a name (such as Mail Administrator), a mailbox name (such as Admin) with a maximum length of 10 characters, a password with a maximum length of 8 characters, and miscellaneous information (such as your phone numbers, office, department, and notes). Then click the OK button to create your account.

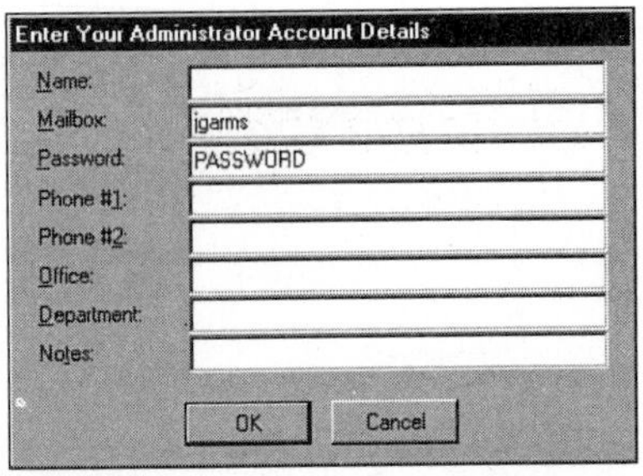

FIGURE 16.24.

An administrative user is created by default when you create a new post office.

NOTE

If you create an account and do not assign a password, the default is PASSWORD.

A confirmation dialog box appears, informing you of the location where the post office was created and reminding you to share the directory you just created.

And that's all there is to it. In addition to using File Manager to share the post office directory, be sure to create the share with at least Change permission, or the users cannot use their mail clients without errors.

TIP

I prefer to create the share with Full Control permissions for the Everyone group and then to set directory- and file-level permissions with File Manager. This way, I can set Change permissions for the Domain Users group, Read for Domain Guests (which provides limited functionality and does prevent them from deleting the entire directory), and Full Control for Domain Admins, which gives the Administrators the capability to run mail utility programs.

Managing Your Workgroup Post Office

Managing your workgroup post office does not involve very many options. In fact, the primary option you will use is to just create mailboxes for your network clients. This is accomplished by opening the Microsoft Mail Postoffice Control Panel icon and choosing the Administer an existing Workgroup Postoffice option. The Postoffice Manager dialog box appears, which you can use to display the details of a mailbox (click the Details button), create new mailboxes (click the Add User button), delete a mailbox (click the Remove User button), and look at the shared folders' usage summary (click the Shared Folders button).

Whenever you add a user, you must supply a mailbox name with a maximum length of 10 characters, a password with a maximum length of 8 characters, and miscellaneous information (such as the phone numbers, office, department, and notes). This procedure is just like the one you followed when you created your own account earlier. If you do not create the accounts, the individual users can create their own accounts the first time they run the 32-bit Microsoft mail client.

There are a few ways that you can make your post office a little safer:

■ You can specify that the user's MMF file be located locally on his computer or remotely on the server. To place the file on the server, each user must choose Options from the Mail menu. The Options dialog box appears. Click the Server button. The Server dialog box appears, in which the user can specify the storage group in which the MMF file should be placed in the post office or locally on the user's computer. If you store all your MMF files on the server, backing up these files becomes a relatively easy task.

TIP

You also can use the Options dialog box to specify that the inbox (where new messages are stored) be copied to the user's local MMF file when the user connects through remote access.

■ If the MMF is stored locally, the individual users must back up their own MMF files by choosing Backup from the Mail menu.

■ You can choose Export from the File menu to back up a single folder to a file, and you can choose Import from the File menu to restore a folder from a file.

■ To create shared folders, which enable your mail users to share a single folder, you can choose New Folder from the File menu. Shared folders can be limited to Read, Write, or Delete privileges for your connected users. By using a shared folder, you can save space in your workgroup post office. You can also use this command to create a new personal folder.

Using the Remoteboot Service

The Remoteboot service is used to support your network clients who boot their operating system from the server rather than from a local disk drive. This process uses a Remote Program Load (RPL) ROM located in the network adapter to load a boot block from the server. The boot block is the actual start-up code for the operating system. After this boot block is loaded, the rest of the operating system is loaded. Most of these network clients do not contain a floppy drive or a hard disk and are referred to as diskless workstations.

> **NOTE**
>
> To take advantage of the Remoteboot service in Windows NT Server, your clients must have Ethernet cards that support remote boot and have an RPL chip installed. This usually must be purchased separately, and not all Ethernet cards support it.

A diskless workstation can offer a few advantages for you and your enterprise:

- Diskless workstations can prevent the spreading of viruses because there is no mechanism to introduce them. Most viruses are spread from a bootable floppy disk inserted into a local disk drive on a user's computer.

- You can control the distribution of information and software on your network. This is because the network client does not have the capability to change its configuration for it cannot save any settings to the shared software installation. It can execute only the software you permit or save its configuration in a home directory that you provide. But as an administrator, you can control these options.

- Software upgrades are easier to perform because you only have to update the central configuration. The users automatically benefit from these changes.

- Computers without local floppy drives or hard disk drives are less expensive.

Of course, there are a few disadvantages to diskless workstations as well. They increase the traffic on the network because every user is accessing the same files. Windows performance suffers because any paging must be performed on the networked drive, and the loading of dynamic link libraries must be performed from this shared installation. You can offset some of these disadvantages by using a local hard disk. This hard disk can be used to create the paging file, and it contains the user's data files (and applications, if desired), while still giving you the benefits of easy operating system upgrades and the prevention of virus introductions.

> **NOTE**
>
> You can only remote boot DOS, Windows 3.1, and Windows 95 clients. You *cannot* remote boot Windows for Workgroups 3.11 or Windows NT clients.

> **NOTE**
>
> People often wonder why you can't remote boot NT. There are a couple of reasons, but the most understated, yet most important has to do with NT security.
>
> Each time you run setup to install NT, it creates a unique security identifier (SID). This SID is supposed to be unique through all time and space, and is used to set up trust relationships

with other computers and domains. This SID is created during the NT setup process and gets coded into many of the services, particularly the network-related ones. If you were to take an NT image and copy it file-for-file to another machine, you would end up with two machines with the same SID, and you would be begging for really big problems.

Likewise, if you were to permit multiple machines to run Windows NT from the same image (set of files), each machine would have the same SID, which cannot be permitted.

Installing the Remoteboot Service

Installing the Remoteboot service is a multipart process. First, you must install the service. Then you must copy the operating systems to the RPL root directories. And finally, you must use the Remoteboot Manager to set the security on these files and check the configurations. All this before you can create a profile. A profile contains the user configuration. You might have a profile for MS-DOS 5.0 or MS-DOS 6.x, for example, with both of them being able to run Windows 3.x from the shared installation.

NOTE

Before you install the Remoteboot service, you should be aware of two points: First, your server name cannot contain any spaces, or your MS-DOS clients will not be able to connect to it; and second, you should install the Remoteboot files to an NTFS directory because the FAT file system cannot support more than 100 Remoteboot clients and so that you can specify the correct permissions on the shared files.

NOTE

You must have the NetBEUI and DLC protocols installed before you can install the Remoteboot service.

To install the DLC and NetBEUI protocols, follow these steps:

NOTE

You must be logged on as a member of the Administrators group to install the DLC and NetBEUI protocols.

1. Open the Control Panel Network applet. The Network dialog box appears.

2. Click the Protocols tab.

3. Click the Add button to display a list of installable protocols.

4. Select DLC Protocol and click OK.

5. Specify the path to the NT distribution files, such as F:\i386.

    When NT is finished copying the necessary files, it returns you to the Network Control Panel. You should see DLC Protocol in the list of installed protocols.

If necessary, repeat steps 3–5 to install the NetBEUI protocol.

> **NOTE**
>
> After installing DLC and NetBEUI, you do not need to reboot before installing the Remoteboot service.

To install the Remoteboot service, follow these steps:

> **NOTE**
>
> You must be logged on as a member of the Administrators group to install the Remoteboot service.

1. Open the Control Panel Network applet. The Network dialog box appears.

2. Click the Services tab; then click the Add button to display a list of installable services.

3. Select the Remoteboot service and click the Continue button.

4. When prompted, enter a path to specify where you want to install the Remoteboot files. This should be an NTFS partition.

5. When prompted, enter a path to the location of the Remoteboot client files. These are stored in the \CLIENTS\RPL directory on your CD-ROM.

6. Click the OK button to exit the Network Control Panel window.

7. Click Close to exit the Network Control Panel.

8. Reboot when prompted.

The next step is copying the client files to your Remoteboot directory that you created in step 4 to install the Remoteboot service so that you can create a client profile. You can copy the MS-DOS system files and Windows 3.x system files to support an MS-DOS client and allow it to run the shared copy of Windows 3.x, for example.

To set up a client, follow these steps:

1. Find a copy of the version of MS-DOS you want to support. On the client workstation, log on to the network, and then connect to the Remoteboot shared directory (NET USE *X*: *ServerName*\RPLFILES, where *ServerName* is the name of your server and *X* is the drive letter you choose to use for the mapped drive).

2. Remove the attributes on the MS-DOS boot files. These files are IO.SYS and MS-DOS.SYS. Use these commands:

   ```
   ATTRIB -h -s IO.SYS
   ATTRIB -h -s MS-DOS.SYS
   ```

3. Copy these files to the appropriate subdirectory. If you are copying an MS-DOS 5.0 installation, copy these files to the BINFILES\DOS500 subdirectory, for example:

   ```
   COPY IO.SYS X:\BINFILES\DOS500
   COPY MS-DOS.SYS X:\BINFILES\DOS500
   COPY COMMAND.COM X:\BINFILES\DOS500
   ```

> **NOTE**
>
> Do not create any additional subdirectories in the BINFILES root directory. If you are installing any version of MS-DOS 6.2x, for example, it must be placed in the BINFILES\622 subdirectory. This means that you can support only one version of MS-DOS in a particular directory. You cannot install MS-DOS 6.2, 6.21, and 6.22 in the same directory.

> **NOTE**
>
> If you are copying files from an IBM version of PC-DOS, rename the files on the server from IBMDOS.COM to MSDOS.SYS and from IBMIO.COM to IO.SYS.

4. Replace the attributes on the MS-DOS boot files. These files are IO.SYS and MS-DOS.SYS. Use these commands:

   ```
   ATTRIB +h +s IO.SYS
   ATTRIB +h +s MS-DOS.SYS
   ```

5. Repeat steps 1–4 for each version of MS-DOS that you want to support.

The next step requires that you choose the Configure | Fix Security and Configure | Check Configurations menu options to set the appropriate permissions on the files and to verify that all the required boot files are present, including BOOTSECT.COM, IO.SYS, MS-DOS.SYS, and COMMAND.COM. If any of these files are missing, you cannot create a profile.

To create a profile, follow these steps:

1. Choose New Profile from the Remoteboot menu. The New Profile dialog box appears.

2. In the Profile Name field, enter a unique name containing up to 16 characters. This name cannot contain any spaces or backslashes (\).

3. In the Configuration field, select the operating system and network adapter. Select DOS 6.22 3Com Etherlink III to support clients with Etherlink III network adapters and to provide MS-DOS 6.22 as the operating system, for example.

4. In the Description field, enter a description for this profile if the default is not acceptable.

NOTE

If you enter a description before selecting the configuration, your description is overwritten with the default description. The default description is the same as the configuration you choose.

5. Click the OK button and your profile is displayed in the Profile Name field.

6. Repeat these steps for each profile you want to create.

Managing Your Remoteboot Clients

Now that you have created your profiles, it is time to add workstations to the Remoteboot service. This is accomplished with the Remoteboot Manager. There are two ways to create a new workstation record: You can do it manually, or you can automate the process a bit.

NOTE

You must have the network client for which you want to create a workstation record turned on and available to be queried by the Remoteboot Manager. Otherwise, the process will fail.

To create a new workstation record manually, follow these steps:

1. Choose New Workstation from the Remoteboot menu. The New Remoteboot Workstation dialog box appears, as shown in Figure 16.25.

2. In the Adapter ID field, enter the 12-digit hexadecimal adapter identification number of the network adapter. If you do not know this number, use the automatic installation procedure.

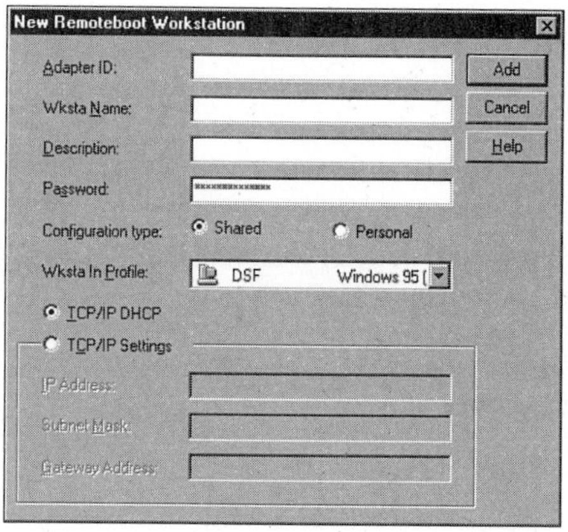

ADMINISTERING THE SERVER

FIGURE 16.25.

You must enter information about each Remoteboot workstation.

3. In the Wksta Name field, enter the computer name of the workstation.

4. In the Description field, enter a comment for the workstation.

5. In the Password field, enter a password.

> **NOTE**
>
> This password is not the user account password you created with User Manager for Domains. Instead, it is used by the Remoteboot service to authenticate the workstation and to enable users to set the permissions for the user configuration maintained by the Remoteboot service. In fact, a user account is created on the basis of the workstation name you supply, and the password for this account is the password you supplied in the Password field in the New Remoteboot Workstation dialog box.

6. Select a Configuration type option. This can be Shared or Personal. A shared configuration can be accessed by multiple users, although they cannot make any changes. A personal configuration is user-specific and can have user-customizable settings.

7. From the Wksta In Profile drop-down listbox, select a profile for the account. This is one of the profiles you just created in steps 1–6.

8. If you are using TCP/IP as your network protocol, select TCP/IP DHCP to use your DHCP server to provide an IP address (the preferred method). Or, to manually assign an IP address, a subnet mask, and a gateway address, enable the TCP/IP Settings option instead.

9. Click the Add button to add the workstation record.

10. Repeat these steps for each new workstation record.

To create a new workstation record automatically, follow these steps:

1. Boot the workstation client. When the workstation starts, it attempts to find an RPL server that will create an adapter record.

NOTE

An adapter record appears just like a workstation record in the Remoteboot Manager main window, but it doesn't have a workstation name associated with it. Instead, it has the 12-digit hexadecimal adapter identification number listed.

2. Select the adapter record. Then choose Convert Adapters from the Remoteboot menu. The New Remoteboot Workstation dialog box appears.

3. Repeat steps 3–10 of the preceding procedure to create a new workstation record manually.

TIP

To convert multiple adapter records one at a time, select each adapter record while pressing and holding down the Control key. Then choose Remoteboot | Convert Adapters. To convert all adapter records, just choose Remoteboot | Convert Adapters.

Now that you have created these configuration programs, you probably will want to install some software for them to use—maybe Windows 3.x or Microsoft Office.

First, you must install the application files on the server. For this example, use Windows 3.x. Follow these steps:

1. Boot the client workstation and sign on with an Administrator account.

2. Insert the Windows installation disk (or other application disk) and run the network version of the setup program. To run the Windows network installation program, for example, type setup /a.

3. When prompted for an installation directory, specify C:\WIN. This copies the expanded files into the RPLFILES\BINFILES\WIN subdirectory. For an application, specify C:\WIN\AppName, where AppName is a unique name.

TIP

If you are installing an application that is already expanded and does not require any network-configurable parameters, you can just copy the files without running through the network installation process.

Second, you must install the files in the client profile configuration. This configuration can be a shared configuration profile, in which case all users of the configuration profile benefit, or a personal configuration profile, which is unique to that individual. Follow these steps:

1. Boot the client workstation and sign on with an Administrator account.

2. Change to the Windows directory (type CD C:\WIN).

3. Type setup /n and press Enter to run the network client installation. Do not upgrade the installation; instead, just choose the Express installation.

4. Install Windows in the C:\WINDOWS directory.

5. Copy all the files in the C:\WINDOWS directory to the C:\WKSTA.PRO\WIN directory by using the following command:

```
XCOPY C:\WINDOWS C:\WKSTA.PRO\WIN /E
```

This copies the files to the configuration profile and enables all users of this profile to run the application.

TIP

To install additional applications, perform the same steps, but install to a subdirectory of the C:\WINDOWS directory. If you performed a network setup for Microsoft Office to the C:\WIN\OFFICE directory, for example, when you run Setup, specify C:\WINDOWS\OFFICE as the destination directory. Then copy the OFFICE subdirectory files to the C:\WKSTA.PRO\WIN\ OFFICE subdirectory.

Summary

This chapter covered many of the administrative duties you are required to carry out on a day-to-day basis. You first learned about Server Manager, which you use to create your computer accounts, synchronize the domain account database, perform remote management of your network clients' shared directories, perform remote service configuration (which includes enabling the Directory Replicator Service to copy your logon scripts to other servers), and perform remote resource accounting of your network clients.

You then learned about using the Event Viewer to keep track of system events that have occurred on your server. This chapter discussed the basic usage of this tool and provides a means for you to archive the data for future reference.

This chapter discussed the Repair Disk Utility, which is used to create and update the Emergency Repair Disk necessary for repairing failed NT installations.

Your final stop was a look at managing your workgroup post office, and using the Remoteboot service to support your diskless workstations.

User Administration

by Joe Greene

IN THIS CHAPTER

CHAPTER 17

Sometimes the fact that you have worked with older computer operating systems can be an impediment to using a new operating system such as Windows NT. There are many computer professionals who are not old timers in the computer industry, but they have worked with a number of systems dating from an old DEC PDP-8E through IBM mainframes and DEC VAX computers to the more modern UNIX and NT systems that they work on today. Many of the concepts that evolved in user administration on older systems can be useful even on modern systems like Windows NT.

The goal for this chapter is to merge an understanding of the fundamental techniques of user administration with the tools and functionality provided by Windows NT Server. By now, you have come to appreciate that one of the design characteristics of Windows NT is flexibility. In user administration, you will find a number of options available to you when you want to perform a task. This chapter covers those options and some of the rationale for various techniques. To accomplish these goals, this chapter is divided into the following sections:

- General topics related to user administration
- Windows NT user security
- Attributes of a user
- Windows NT Server's User Manager tool
- Windows NT Server's System Policy Editor
- Remote Access Service (RAS) security
- Resource access grants
- Routine monitoring

General Topics Related to User Administration

Earlier computer operating systems depended on a user ID coded on a control card in the card deck. They did not really control my access to the computer. This was controlled more by the person who accepted or rejected my card deck. Soon, however, billing considerations came into play and computer operating systems started to track user IDs to determine who gets the bill. Of course, when money is involved, you have to be concerned with access controls to ensure that the right person gets the bill. This was the beginning of passwords. It was somewhat hokey in that all you had to do was get access to a control card that someone stupidly threw away and you had all of the access that you needed.

It was almost painful, thinking back to those days of card decks. Productivity was low and costs enormous. I only had to use such systems a few times because many of the places I used for computer services tended to use DEC PDP and VAX equipment, which were some of the early terminal-intensive systems, although I did have my introduction to switch registers and paper tape (if you do not know what those things are, you probably need a history book since I have not seen any of these things around in years) on these systems.

Anyway, for a long time, access was so limited to computer types that setting up accounts remained relatively simple. The main attributes of an account were user ID, password, spending limit, and your status (computer center staff had absolute priority followed by professors, graduate students, and ultimately undergraduates). Because people did not have access to any real operating system functions (we were typing card decks into text files and then running them), there was little risk that key system features would be compromised. That is not to say that prehistoric hackers were not at work on these vintage systems; it was more that the potential damage was small and, therefore, not a big concern.

Computers started to catch on, however. After they got out of the information systems and academic environments, security suddenly became a very hot topic.

The big push for security initially was driven by money. Computers were still a long way from being able to display MPEG movies, but people figured out that computers were ideal for those complex financial systems that were so difficult to accurately track. When money started to flow in computer systems, there arose a great incentive to start doing illegal things (such as transferring a few million dollars to your personal account). At first, financial systems were still batch jobs that were run by trusted computer staff members, but as more people saw the power of these systems, those people wanted access. Operating system vendors came out with a number of security features designed to control not only whether you had access to a system, but which resources (files, disks, printers, and so on) you were allowed to use.

The next wave of security came from the military/intelligence community. The military/intelligence community faced the need to process huge volumes of classified material and keep it all straight. Their needs were even greater than the financial community in that if you caught someone taking money, you usually could recover it. If someone sold your top-secret war plans, you couldn't ask hostile governments to mail them back and forget about what they read.

This led the government to pour a lot of money into developing security systems that provided fine levels of control as to what you could see, when you could see it, a record of when you actually did see it, and so on. This money was in the form of research grants on security theory to purchases of those early secure systems that were primitive by today's standards, but helped move the industry along so that it got to where it is today.

Now most of you reading this chapter probably are not working for the Central Intelligence Agency or National Security Agency. Therefore, you probably are turned off by the idea of having to put in a huge amount of work just to configure every user account on your system. This is one of the challenges that Windows NT faces. The folks at Microsoft decided early on to implement a system that allowed for high levels of security.

NT Security Model

Windows NT is certified at the C2 level by the National Security Agency. For those of you not familiar with those terms, it means that NSA put Windows NT through a tough series of checks on security and determined that it had a very reasonable security system based on a set of standards published in what is known as the *Orange Book* (it has a typically long and boring title, but the cover is orange so that is how everyone identifies it). There are operating systems with the higher B-level security rating, but very few commercial applications will run on these operating systems because the security features usually get in the way of basic functionality. An alternative to this is to secure the network on which the computer is located with a firewall (a network device that filters out unauthorized traffic), which usually has a B-level rating.

The Windows NT team made a good decision when implementing their security model in that they allow you to degrade the security level of the operating system based on your needs. For example, the capability of the operating system to force you to change your password after a specified number of days and have a password with a controlled complexity (that is, 12345 does not cut it) is a requirement for certification. If you are in a wonderfully friendly environment in which security risks are low, you have the option of creating user accounts where the password never expires and users can even have a blank password. I would not recommend such a lax security environment, especially if you are connected to large networks or the Internet, but it is *your* choice. You can choose a tough security setup, a very lax one, or perhaps a reasonable compromise between the two, depending on your local needs.

This leads to your first task as a user account administrator. You have to design a security plan that will implement that "just right" security environment for your system. The start to this design process is a knowledge of the options that Windows NT affords you. This chapter covers the basic security model and the basic options from which you can choose in the next several sections. These sections prepare you for the remaining sections of this chapter, which show you how to actually implement your grand plans.

Windows NT User Security

This section discusses a few basics that should help you to understand how Windows NT approaches the task of security management. As with most computer functions, there are a number of ways to implement security. Figure 17.1 shows three of the more common models that you might run into. Each of these models has advantages and disadvantages, which will be covered so that you can better understand the strengths and weaknesses of the Windows NT security model.

Simple Access Security Model

Perhaps the simplest model is what I am calling the *simple access system*. It consists of a logon ID and password combination that allows you access into the computer.

After you are in the system, you have free range to access anything you want. The advantage of this type of system is that it is simple to administer and provides adequate security in very simple environments. The disadvantage of this system is that it allows anyone who can get in to roam freely and access all resources. This may not seem like a problem to PC users who are used to having full access to the system, but on a mainframe in which you have a large number of different systems (such as engineering, accounting, and human resources), you run into problems when access to sensitive data and other resources is available.

FIGURE 17.1.

Alternative security models.

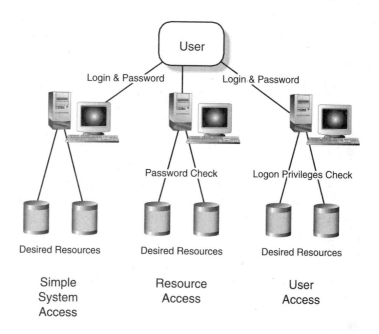

Resource Password Security Model

An alternative implemented in some environments is to assign a password to each resource (as can be used in Windows For Workgroups). For example, you would set a special password on a directory or printer and then only distribute that password to those people you wanted to have access to that system. I have called this *resource access* in Figure 17.1. The advantages of this system are that it provides control over access on a resource-by-resource basis and is relatively simple to set up. The disadvantage is that it can be difficult to maintain. Suppose that someone obtains access to the password for the human resources data or someone transfers out of human resources and, therefore, should have his/her access revoked. Your only alternative is to change the password on this data and distribute the new password to everyone who needs it.

User Access Security Model

Windows NT follows the model labeled *user access* in Figure 17.1. This starts with a logon ID and password that identifies you to the operating system. After the operating system knows who you are, it then checks your name against a list of access restrictions when you access resources. The most common examples of resources in a Windows NT environment are shared directories, printers, and remote access connections. This access model has the advantage of providing a fine level of control, although there are those additional administrative actions needed to not only authorize the user to access the system but also to authorize the user to use all the resources that are appropriate for him/her.

If you want this finer level of security, it is going to take more work. Windows NT provides you with some design features to make this job easier. These features come from observing the work of the typical system administrator.

The first thing that became apparent was that users who performed the same job function tended to need the same operating system security accesses to perform their tasks. The system administrator typed the same series of access grants repeatedly, for all these folks. Why not capture all these privilege grants into a series of buckets and then just grant one or more buckets of privileges to the users?

Creating Groups

This is the concept of groups in Windows NT and other operating systems. You create the name for the group, select the privileges for that group, and then determine who gets that group of privileges. This is a powerful feature, especially for system administrators who have a large number of users for which to care. To take full advantage of groups, however, you need to plan the way in which you are going to organize your groups.

Your first reaction might be to create a group for every type of user who will access your system. While this will work, it usually requires more work and that you create more groups.

Let me show you an example of how a building block approach can be useful. Suppose that your server is supporting the accounting, marketing, and engineering departments. You have accountants who need access to the accounting data files and an accounting supervisor who accesses accounting data, plus a management information system. Your marketing department users access marketing data and have a supervisor who accesses this data, plus the management information system. Finally, you have the engineers who access two project databases (electronics and mechanical) and a supervisor who requires access to the management information system, as well as both project databases. From my previous discussion, you might say that there are seven Windows NT user groups that should be formed: accountant, accountant manager, marketing, marketing manager, electronics engineer, mechanical engineer, and engineering manager.

You could create just five groups: accounting, marketing, electronics engineer, mechanical engineer, and management. You would grant the managers of the various departments two group privileges (such as accounting and manager). This is a simple example of a powerful concept.

Suppose that your organization is more loosely organized and you have people working on multiple project teams that have their own privilege sets. If you construct the basic privilege sets correctly, you can grant and revoke group access to these individuals as they come and go from the various project teams. The two points that should be emphasized are that you initially should spend some time planning your groups to save you work later on and that you re-evaluate your group structure from time to time, as the needs of your users evolve.

Now you have worked out a system whereby you can easily administer a server with a large number of users and still have time left over to catch up on your reading. Word of your skill has spread far and wide. The next thing you know, your management has decided that you should maintain not only your server, but all the servers in your company. There probably will not be any pay increase associated with this responsibility, but you still have to get the job done.

Building Workgroups

A typical network of PC servers includes machines running database management systems, acting as file servers, acting as mail servers, and so on. A given user may require access to many of these servers as time goes on (for example, I want to send a print job to the color laser printer on the second floor because it is the only one in the building and is attached to the second floor server). Keeping up with generating an account and assigning the correct privileges to a large number of users on multiple servers could become quite a burden.

This brings up another consideration. Because Microsoft uses nice graphical tools to list the other computers on the network when you are trying to access remote resources, what would that display look like in a company that has several thousand computers? Most administrators do not want to have to scroll down through several hundred items in the list to find the one that they want.

The solution to this problem is to group computers together into what Microsoft refers to as *workgroups*. A workgroup is one or more computers on a network that claim to have some logical relationship to one another. I say *claim* to have a relationship because you could take your computer, and via the Network Settings tool in Control Panel, join any group on your network, and it would appear to be a member of this group when people go to access network resources.

Building Domains

Now we return to the problem of maintaining a number of computers on a network. Just as user groups solved the problem of granting a large number of access privileges to users on a single server, grouping computers together is Microsoft's solution to administering a large number of servers on the network. As pointed out previously, however, the workgroup concept does not provide much in the way of security. Anyone can say that he or she is a member of the workgroup with a few simple settings changes on his or her computer.

The solution to this is what Microsoft refers to as a *domain*. One can think of a domain as a secure workgroup with centralized administration. Figure 17.2 shows the different security configurations for a Windows NT network. The key here is that there needs to be a centralized security configuration database that verifies who you are and then relays this information to any other nodes on the network from which you are requesting resource access. For those who serve as administrators, this has the side blessing of providing a single maintenance point for the entire network.

FIGURE 17.2.
Windows NT network configurations.

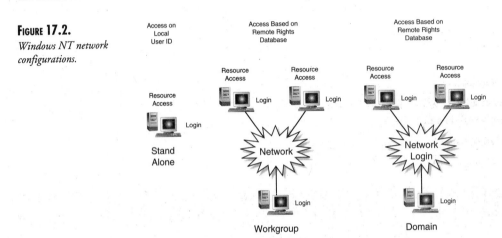

The domain is a nice concept, but how do you implement one? It is somewhat impractical to configure a system in which all security information is stored on every node on the network. Actually, that would be a disadvantage for security purposes because it would provide opportunities for hackers to tweak the local security database when they log on as administrators on their local machines. Microsoft domain networks use servers that are designated as domain controllers to store this security access information.

There are two types of domain controllers: primary and backup. Imagine a day when everything goes wrong with your server (crashes, failed hard disks, and so on). If only one domain controller existed on the network, you would have no way to validate users and allow them to access network resources. A *backup domain controller* enables the network to continue servicing your users until your primary domain controller returns to operation. The difference between primary and backup domain controllers revolves around the fact that when two servers disagree on a password (perhaps one server is down or is having a problem with a corrupted security file) or some other access privilege, someone has to settle the disagreement. The primary domain controller is the one that is right in this case.

Backup domain controllers have other functions in addition to providing authentication services when the primary domain controller is down. First and foremost is that they can authenticate users on the network. The primary controller ensures that everyone is synchronized with one another, but any domain controller can authenticate a user to the domain. Therefore, if your servers are on several different network segments, you can place a local domain controller on each network segment to support those users.

An important item to remember is that primary domain controllers are born, not made. By this I mean that you configure a machine as a primary domain controller during the installation procedure. You cannot change your mind later on and click a few buttons in the Control Panel to convert a regular machine to a primary domain controller. Also, a given domain on a given network can have only one primary domain controller. If two machines on a network claim to be the primary domain controller, a battle will ensue to see which one the rest of the network trusts as the primary domain controller. That unit will get control of the domain and the other will be prevented from joining the domain, which makes absolute sense from a security point of view.

Another important consideration is that other computers need permission to enter the domain. You cannot just change your Control Panel network settings to reflect that you now are a trusted member of the SALES domain. Instead, you need to have someone log on as domain administrator and authorize your entry onto the domain before you can participate in this security environment. This prevents someone from developing a program to gather security data from the network by sending and receiving authentication requests from a computer running an anything goes operating system, such as MS-DOS.

Now that you are an expert on Windows NT domains, there is another topic to challenge you with. Imagine that you are supporting a large company. This organization is so large that it actually has multiple system administrators in multiple locations. You could build a large, centralized computer center on which all the corporate servers reside and have a central administrative staff take care of these computers. This, however, is a clumsy architecture prone to slow long-distance communications circuits and has many components that could fail and take down the entire network. In reality, it usually makes sense to implement multiple domains that are matched up with the locations and organizations within your company.

Domain Trust Relationships

In this era of cooperation among different groups to achieve the overall organizational goals, however, a way to get accesses to services within another domain can come in quite handy. To make this happen, Microsoft implemented what it called *trust relationships* among domains. This works much like the way the name implies. You tell one domain that it should trust the security validations of another domain. It is not carte blanche access to all the resources in your domain by any user validated in the other domain. You still must grant access privileges to the users of that other domain in order for them to get access to any resources that you have not designated as being available to everyone.

This brings up yet another set of terms you must become familiar with in order to be a Windows NT domain system administrator: local and global groups. Within your domain, you can use *local groups* to assign privileges to access resources. In effect, you are saying that if a user can show credentials that he or she is a member of a group that has access to a resource (as determined by a domain controller), then the machine providing the requested resources should honor the request.

What do you do when other domain administrators create groups that have the same name that you have used (managers, for example)? The answer is that the groups you typically create are local groups that identify the user within your domain. If you want to identify a user to other domains with which you have set up trust relationships, you must create what Microsoft refers to as a *global domain*, whose name is coordinated with the trusted and trusting domains out there. The domain administrators in these domains then grant access to their resources to the global groups, which is how users in other domains get access to resources.

A few points need to be made about trust relationships. First, trust relationships are one-way, not two-way. If I trust you, that does not mean that you trust me. Second, both domain administrators must agree to the trust relationship. I cannot just say that I trust you and you cannot say that I trust you.

Finally, the relationships are not point-to-point and do not imply any hierarchy of trust relationships. By this I mean that if domain A trusts domain B, and domain B trusts domain C, this does not imply that domain A trusts domain C. This actually can be helpful to administrators. You might not be familiar with the trust relationships of another domain. That domain may have trust relationships with domains that you do not want to establish a trust relationship with for your domain.

Before finishing this general discussion on domain security, a few points need some attention. First, the Security Account Manager (SAM) for the domain server can only manage 16,000 user accounts. For most of us, that is a large limit and we will never even get close to it. It does, however, have implications for those large organizations that would like to use a large, centralized domain controller to serve as the master account controller for all users in the organization. It also affects how people structure their trust relationship hierarchy to ensure that all their groups work together. Figure 17.3 shows some of the alternative domain configurations.

FIGURE 17.3.

Alternative domain trust relationships.

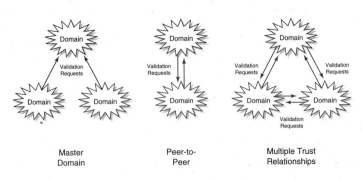

I provide three examples of domain configurations, which should cover most Windows NT networks. In the first case, which I refer to as master domain, you have a central domain which serves as the master security environment for the organization. Other domains provide services to the end users based on information obtained from the master domain. This allows more efficient administration and better control over security at the cost of being dependent that the master domain will always be accessible.

The next domain configuration example that I propose is what I call peer-to-peer. In this case, each domain has its own administration and controls granting access to its users. Users from one domain can access resources in the other domain, based on grants to foreign groups based on trust agreements between the domains. This provides localized control over security while allowing users to access resources in other domains. It is probably the simplest one to maintain.

The final example that I provide is what I call multiple trust relationships. While the master domain configuration is a parent-child environment and the peer-to-peer is an everyone-is-equal environment, the multiple trust relationships can be thought of as a complex web of security and access grants. Conceptually it is similar to the peer-to-peer in that everyone takes care of his or her own people. The difference here is that you grant access rights to a number of other domains. This can be complex to administer, but may be the appropriate solution in environments where local divisions control their networks and only allow other divisions to access their resources as needed.

There are a number of other domain trust architectures that could be thought up. The examples above are designed to illustrate some of the basic environments that you might run across. The peer-to-peer would probably be the simplest to implement if you are just starting out. For a more complete discussion of the domain environment and trust relationships, the books in the Windows NT Resource Kit provide several chapters that cover the concepts of networking and security in more detail.

After having taken up quite a number of pages in this chapter, this discussion merely is a summary of what could be said about the Windows NT security model. You can download a number of technical papers from the web and the various Microsoft CDs that provide additional detailed information about the intricacies of the domain and workgroup security implementations. There could be entire chapters devoted to the various authentication system components, such as NETLOGON. This chapter, however, has a more practical intent. This discussion was designed to prepare you for the next section, which discusses the controls that the system administrator has over a given user's account. Together, these two sections prepare you for the day-to-day chores of user administration and the how-to sections that make up the remainder of this chapter.

Attributes of a User

It would be extremely difficult for you to properly control user accounts if you did not know the various things over which you have control. This section discusses the components in what I call the *overall user environment*. Following is a simple summary list of control features:

- User account and password
- User group membership
- Account policies
- User rights

- User profile
- User home directory
- User logon script
- User logon times
- User logon capabilities
- Remote Access Service capabilities
- Access to applications

If you want to get fancy, you can find more to tweak, but from my experience, this is the set that will serve you in the vast majority of cases. The preceding items interact with one another to help you accomplish your goals. Each item is incomplete by itself and requires the other items to properly control the user's interactions with resources. The rest of this section provides an overview of each of these tools that you will need to understand in order to become a full-fledged Windows NT system administrator.

Logon IDs, Passwords, and Groups

The first topic is the user logon ID and password. The concepts actually are relatively simple and resemble those on most other operating systems. This is the first instance of how the various properties of the user environment will interact, however.

Many security types set limitations on the passwords that are selected in order to make them difficult to guess. The rule of thumb usually is "at least seven characters long." Even if you, as the administrator, create the user logon ID and password following this rule, what will stop the users from using the password change utilities to choose a password such as 12345? To prevent this, you will need to use the policy features of Windows NT.

The *group feature* has already been discussed as a powerful tool in the user administration process. The key here is that resource accesses can be given to either individuals or groups. When given to groups, a user who is made a member of that group automatically inherits all the privileges of the group itself. This enables you to quickly give users the privileges they need to complete their jobs. Another advantage of this is that you can choose the group names to be meaningful to you. This enables you to quickly scroll through the list of groups and determine which groups are appropriate for a new user.

Account Policies, Rights, and Profiles

The *account policy feature* is not always used by NT administrators, but can be quite powerful. The user policy under Windows NT sets up facets of the user operating environment other than the group privileges related to what the user is allowed to do on the system. This is where you set up the system to ensure that the password is complex and secure enough for your organization's security needs. Some of the features controlled by the user profile include the following:

- Password length
- Password age
- Password history
- Account lockout on failed logon attempts

A closely related set of policies made by the system administrator are *user rights*. These focus primarily on what the user is allowed to do with the operating system. This is discussed in detail in the User Rights section, but for now you should have a feel for a few of the functions of the User Rights tool.

- Access computer from the network
- Add computers to the domain
- Back up files
- Log on locally to this computer (such as using the local keyboard and monitor)

A closely related user control feature is the *user profile*. This feature specifies the available program groups. It also controls whether the Run command is allowed on the File menu. You can create a number of profiles and assign them to various users.

There used to be some confusion over having to work with multiple tools that were needed to set up the profile of operation for a given user. The good news about Windows NT 4 is that Microsoft has consolidated almost all of the user setup controls in the User Manager tool. When you call up the properties screen for a given user under User Manager, you will find a button labeled Profile that discusses many of the features discussed in the next couple of paragraphs. Some enhanced fine-tuning over the user's working environment can be made by using the System Policy Editor on the Administrative Tools menu. You get to control some low-level details such as which wallpaper graphic will be displayed as the desktop for a given user. The System Policy Editor allows you to assign a policy to a given user or group.

Home Directories, Logon Scripts, Logon Time, and Logon Capabilities

The next control feature of the user environment is the *home directory*. You have the option of specifying a directory that the user will access by default for all save operations that are directly controlled by the operating system. If you open up a DOS prompt, for example, the home directory will be the default. Note, however, that many applications (such as Microsoft Word) have their own Settings panel in which they set up the default storage and retrieval directories for their files.

Another useful environmental control feature is the *logon script*. Suppose that there is an action you want performed every time the user logs on, but you cannot find any operating system setting to accomplish your goal. An alternative is to create a batch file (or an executable program) that performs the action you want and then specify that file or program to be the logon script for a given set of users. This also is a nice alternative in environments in which you want to force the users into a menu program or perhaps even just a single application when they log on. In these cases, you can enhance security and usability by not allowing the users to get to the desktop and have the full power of the Windows NT operating system.

Rounding out the list of environmental control features, you come to the capability to control when a user can log on to the system. A major security concern in some organizations is that a user could come in after hours and access the system in an illegal manner. Other environments might contain large batch jobs or have system maintenance activities that occur during specified periods. If these maintenance activities require that all users be logged off, it would be helpful to have a utility that kept users from logging on during these periods. Windows NT provides such a utility in the User Manager tool that gives you a good degree of control over the hours that users can access the system.

Remote Access

You use the RAS administrative utilities to specify whether a given user has access to RAS. You also can implement additional security by requiring a call-back to a specified number when a user dials into your system. This way, the only way someone can hack in by using one of your user's IDs would be if they were calling from the user's house (add breaking and entering to the computer hacking crimes). Remote access to computer resources such as data files and electronic mail is a wonderful convenience; however, it can also be a major security hole. Anyone with a modem and telephone connection can dial up your server (assuming that they know the telephone number) and gain access to your network, bypassing all of the physical security controls of your building. You need to consider the impact of security against productivity when implementing RAS dial-in.

An interesting note for version 4 of NT is that RAS security is now integrated into the User Manager tool. In version 3.51, you set up the properties of your user (with the exception of remote access) by using the User Manager tool. You then had to use the RAS Admin tool to grant dial-in privileges (which were defaulted to prevent remote access). While you can still use the RAS Admin tool to set up dial-in privileges, the User Properties page allows you to set up dial-in permissions for the section user from within User Manager.

User Environment

Finally, the user environment is rounded out by rights and privileges set up for the applications provided on your server. Depending on the application, rights and privileges may simply enhance the environmental parameters you set up for the user as the Windows NT administrator, or they may form a complete environment of their own. If you are using a client/server architecture to access information on a Windows NT Oracle database, for example, the database will provide all security and control the user environment. In many cases, the user does not even need an operating system account to access the database.

Windows NT Server's User Manager Tool

This section discusses the practical nuts and bolts of Windows NT user administration. The main tool that enables you to control your users is the *User Manager tool*, which is available on the Administrative Tools menu. User Manager has one of two titles, depending on whether you are using a server, a workstation in a domain, or a workstation in a workgroup. The server always uses the User Manager for Domain tools (even when you are in a workgroup). The workstation uses User Manager (without the Domains) when you are in a workgroup, but will use User Manager for Domains if it is in a domain. In the domain environment, the updates are sent to the domain controllers rather than the local security database.

My first impression of the administrative environment in Windows NT 3.5 was based on the Control Panel mindset. When you have a function you want to perform, you build a small application to perform the function and slap it into a program group with the other administrative tools. I am impressed with the trend in Windows NT 4, and especially in the User Manager tool, towards building integrated tools. The User Manager tool sets almost all of the administrative properties for a user. It even integrates with Microsoft Exchange Server (the electronic mail system in BackOffice) to bring up properties pages to configure the person's electronic mail account when you add a new user to the operating system. With all of the power built into User Manager, I like to place a shortcut to the application on my desktop so that I have ready access to it.

Most of the tools in Windows NT 4 seem determined to use an Explorer-like tree control somewhere in their display. User Manager is one exception to this rule (at least for now). Its interface adheres to the basic premise of a relatively clean interface that provides access to all the necessary control features using pull-down menus and simple controls, such as double-clicking. Figure 17.4 shows the basic User Manager display.

This review of User Manager begins by going through the key pull-down menu items that you will be using. The first of these menus is the User menu. Here you will see a couple of clues to indicate that you are using a Windows NT 4 Server, which gives me the User Manager for Domains utility. The clues are that there are menu picks to add a New Global Group and Select Domain. These menu picks typically display a dialog box that enables you to fill in the details of the action you are taking or prompts you to confirm that you really want to do what you asked for (such as delete a user). The actions on these menus are taken for the user that is highlighted in the case of copy, delete, rename, and properties. The remaining items, such as New User, by their very definition imply that you should see a dialog box to create a new item or perform an action, such as select domain.

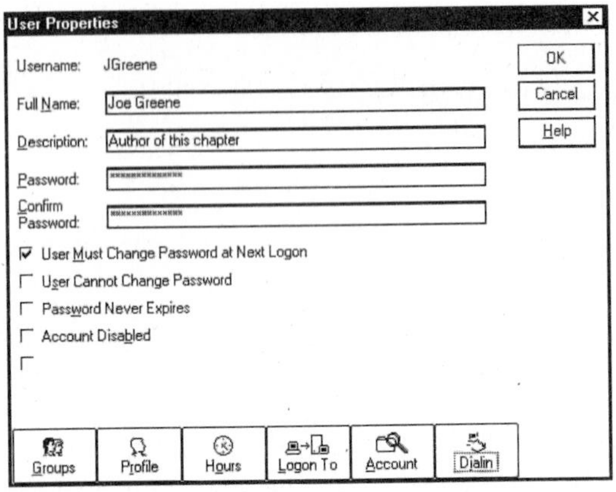

FIGURE 17.4.

The User Manager for Domains display.

The next menu is the Policies menu. The View menu was skipped because it is pretty much what you would expect (it controls the way in which items are sorted in the display and provides an option to refresh the lists). The Policies menu provides you with access to most of the user environmental parameters that do not involve resource access discussed in the last section. It also includes a function that enables you to set your trust relationships.

An extension of my last thought in the preceding paragraph is shown in Figure 17.4. Here you see the integration of the Microsoft Exchange Server with the User Manager. This integration goes a long way actually, in that when you add a user to your system that contains Exchange Server, you will be prompted to enter the information needed to create an electronic mail account. With the exception of RAS access, which is discussed in the "Remote Access Service (RAS) Security" section later in this chapter, User Manager is one place to perform almost all your user-management activities.

Groups in User Manager

Now it is time to go over some of the functions that are activated by these menus. The first function enables you to add or modify groups. You can add a new group by choosing either New Local Group or New Global Group from the User menu. To modify an existing group, highlight the group and choose Properties from the User menu or double-click the group name. Figure 17.5 shows the panel that appears when you modify the properties of an existing group. The only difference you will see when adding a new group is that you are allowed to enter the group name; otherwise the panels are identical.

The Group Properties pane is very simple with which to work. You have the group name, a text description to help you out in the future, and two sets of lists. The first list shows the users who are members of the group. The second list shows the users who are not members of the group. To move users between the members and non-members categories, highlight the user you want to move and click the Add or Remove buttons.

FIGURE 17.5.

Group Properties dialog box under User Manager.

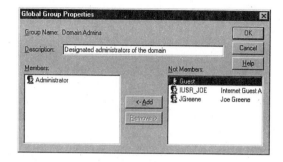

User Properties in User Manager

The User Properties panel is shown in Figure 17.6. It enables administrators to add or modify the basic logon properties of a user and, therefore, is one of the most commonly used tools in User Manager. As you can see, it is a simple panel that enables you to enter username (when adding users, this becomes a non-editable field when modifying the properties of an existing user), full name, description of the user, and two fields that enable the administrator to modify the user's password. In addition, the check boxes control the following features:

- Whether users must change the password next time they log on. This feature is useful when you create all accounts with some neutral or even a null password and then want to force the users to choose a password of their own when they log on.

- Whether users are prevented from changing their passwords. This reduces the user's chance of forgetting the password and making you reset it.

- Whether the password expires. This overrides the password aging functionality, which is described in the Policies section.

- Whether the account is disabled. You may want to disable a user's account when he or she goes on vacation or leaves the company. With the account disabled, you then have time to go through the user's data files and transfer them to other users who may need them.

- Whether the user's account has been locked out. A lockout typically occurs when someone fails to supply the correct password after a number of tries and no automatic reset time interval is specified for this account. A locked-out account can be an indication of hacking or merely an indication of a forgetful user. This is a good security feature in environments in which you have to be careful of hackers.

Group Memberships in User Manager

At the bottom of the User Properties page are important buttons with which you need to become familiar. These buttons access dialog boxes that enable you to set many of the other environmental parameters for the user's account.

FIGURE 17.6.

User Properties page of User Manager.

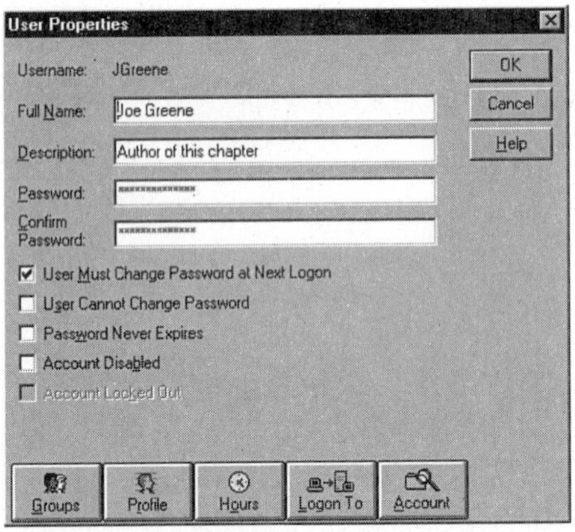

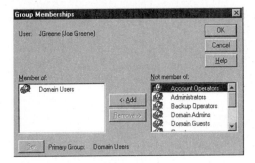

FIGURE 17.7.

Group Memberships dialog box of User Manager.

The first of these properties is the group affiliation of the user. Figure 17.7 shows the Group Memberships dialog box. As you can see, it provides you with two lists: one showing the groups to which the user belongs and one that shows the groups to which the user does not belong. The Add and Remove buttons enable you to move a group from one list to the other.

User Environment Profile in User Manager

The User Environment Profile is activated by the Profile button. Figure 17.8 shows the panel that appears. Be careful not to confuse this button with the User Profile Editor that is provided in the Administrative Tools Start Menu group. The Profile button enables you to select the user profile file (as edited by the User Profile Editor) that applies to this user. It also enables you to specify a logon script that runs every time the user logs on to the system or domain. At the bottom of this panel are fields that enable you to specify the home directory the operating system will use as a default for those times when the applications do not provide their own fully qualified path.

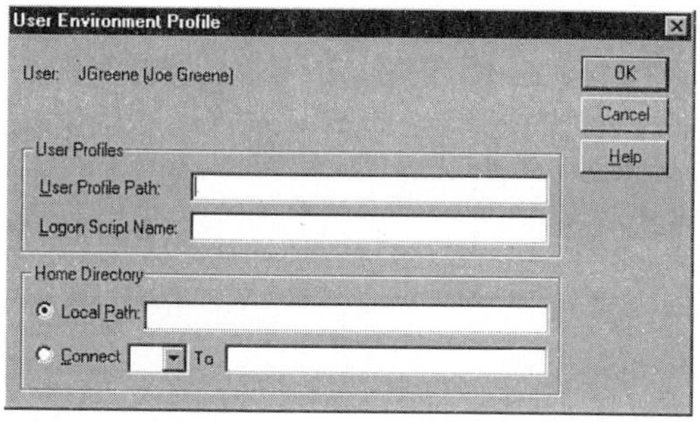

FIGURE 17.8.

User Environment Profile panel of User Manager.

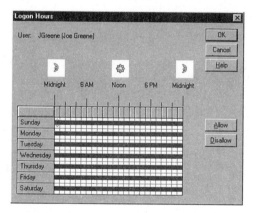

Logon Hours in User Manager

Continuing on with the user environmental parameters that are controlled from the buttons on the bottom of the User Properties page, you come to the Logon Hours panel (see Figure 17.9). To set the hours of operations, using your mouse, highlight the range of hours with which you want to work and then click the allow or disallow buttons. The sections with the blue lines through the middle are the allowed hours of operation. The sections that are black are the hours in which the user is not allowed to log on. The key here is that these are the hours when the system will allow the logon (connection) process to occur. It does not automatically log off users who are on the system if they are still on the system after the allowed hours.

FIGURE 17.9.

Logon Hours panel of User Manager.

Workstations Allowed in User Manager

Another useful feature on the User Properties page is the capability to restrict workstations from which a particular user is allowed to log on. Figure 17.10 shows the basic data entry panel, which is a very simple interface. You can allow the user to log on from all workstations in the domain or you can specify the list of workstations from which the user can log on. This is help-ful in operational environments where users should be at a specific console when performing certain critical tasks. You should ensure that people can log on to enough workstations to en-sure system access in the event of hardware or network failures.

FIGURE 17.10.

Logon Workstations panel of User Manager.

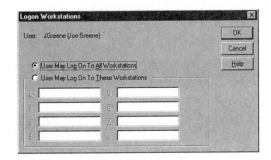

Account Parameters in User Manager

The next dialog box that you can access from the buttons at the bottom of the User Properties page controls certain parameters related to the user's account (see Figure 17.11). The first pa-rameter controls when the user's account expires. This usually is implemented as a safeguard to prevent you from forgetting to disable the account of a contractor or permanent employee when they leave. I tend not to use this parameter, but there are some environments in which this parameter might be mandatory (such as access to a computer that requires a security clearance to be updated at regular intervals so that access is not denied). The other parameter enables you to specify whether this is a global account (which is the normal account that you create) or a local account for users from non-trusted domains.

FIGURE 17.11.

Account Information panel of User Manager.

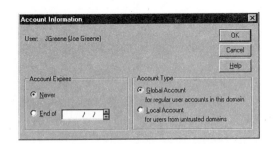

Policies

Next is a discussion of the attributes of the user environment that are controlled from the Policies pull-down menu. This is where you set the global policies for your domain or server as a whole, as opposed to the properties that you set for individual users. The first of these property pages is the Account Policy page (see Figure 17.12). Most of the features you see in this figure determine whether you are going to implement those complex security features that Microsoft had to put into Windows NT to receive that C2 security certification. The good news is that you can turn them all off, turn them all on, or select the features that will be operational, based on your needs. For further discussion of policies, see Chapter 28, "Advanced Security Guidelines."

FIGURE 17.12.

Account Policy dialog box of User Manager.

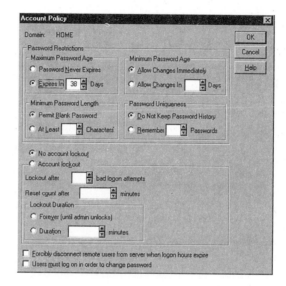

User Rights

The next policy editor in the Policies pull-down menu is the User Rights Policy editor that facilitates granting users and groups the capability to perform certain sensitive system functions. Figure 17.13 shows the dialog box that appears. You need to select the function that you wish to grant or revoke privileges on and then use the Add or Remove buttons to add or remove users or groups from this privilege. The following list discusses the privileges you can control with this dialog box:

- Access this computer from network. This is the basic use of Windows NT Servers to share files, printers, and so on. You might, however, build a database system on which users do not need to access anything except the database by using the database communications processes.

- Add workstations to domain. This is an important domain administrative function in that it controls who can make a workstation a trusted member of the domain.

- Backup files and directories. This gives the user access to the utilities and files to create a backup tape.

- Change the system time. This is a relatively minor function in terms of use, but it can have some serious security impacts (such as users altering file time stamps to hide illegal activity).

- Force a shutdown from a remote system. This is a useful feature when you want to perform a shutdown from a desktop workstation.

- Load and unload device drivers. This privilege enables you to reconfigure the devices attached to your system (such as CD-ROM drives and printers). You probably do not want everyone who performs operational tasks to have this level of access due to the possibility that they could damage your system.

- Log on locally. This enables you to log on to the system from the keyboard and monitor attached to the system. A good way to radically increase your security level is to keep all users off of the console except for the administrators.

- Manage auditing and security log. Some systems may prefer to have separate security administrators who have system privileges, but who do not get involved with backups or device driver changes.

- Restore files and directories. This is the opposite of the backup privilege. You may want to restrict this somewhat more than backups because, while it usually is not harmful to have someone create extra backup tapes, it can be disastrous if someone overwrites all the current disk files with old files.

- Shut down the system. This is the privilege enabling you to log on to the console and perform a system shutdown.

- Take ownership of files or other objects. Windows NT allows users to own files. This privilege enables you to take ownership of files owned by other users (which is needed to delete user files for which you do not have access).

FIGURE 17.13.

User Rights Policy dialog box of User Manager.

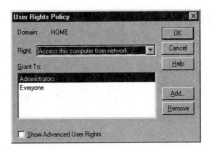

Auditing

The final policy editor that you will work with sets up the events to be audited by your system. Chapter 27, "Auditing Windows NT Server," discusses auditing in greater detail. For now, just look at Figure 17.14. As you can see, you have the option of disabling auditing (you still have the basic security and system event monitoring provided by Event Viewer) or activating only the pieces that interest you.

Before activating any of these menu choices, you need to think about the times per day the event you are going to audit occurs. For example, while security policy changes are rare (and also extremely important from a security point of view), use of user rights occurs many times per minute. Each time the event occurs, you will have a record written to the audit trail that you have to review (this also takes up space on your hard disk drives). It is a balancing act of getting enough information without creating more information than you can review or store.

FIGURE 17.14.

Audit Policy dialog box in User Manager.

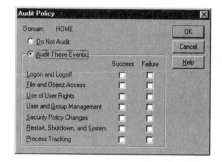

Trust Relationships

The Trust Relationships dialog box enables you to say that you trust another domain or that you permit another domain to trust you (see Figure 17.15). Remember that both sides must agree to a trust relationship (I trust you and you allow me to trust you) before anything happens with it. You should be sure that you are comfortable with the implications of trust relationships and discuss the setup with the other domain administrators before you set up trust relationships. The key to a successful multiple domain configuration is having an agreed-to plan before the network is implemented.

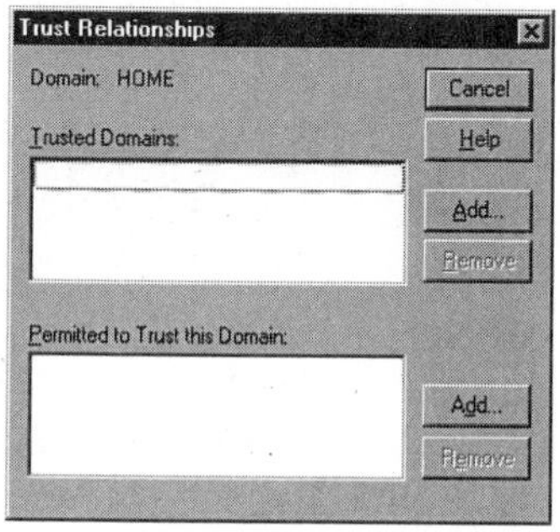

FIGURE 17.15.

Trust Relationships dialog box in User Manager.

Other User Manager Panels

There are a few other minor panels that you can find on the User Manager display, but the ones discussed in this section are the ones that you will need to get your day-to-day job done. Before moving on, there are a few topics to clean up. First are the following groups created by default when you set up a Windows NT 4 Server:

- Account Operators
- Administrators
- Backup Operators
- Domain Admins (domains only)
- Domain Guests (domains only)
- Domain Users (domains only)
- Guests
- Print Operators
- Replicator
- Server Operators
- Users

Predefined Accounts

You also will have the following accounts set up for you:

- Administrator (with full system privileges and a password you set during the installation process)
- Guest (an account that has very little in the way of privileges, but is a tool to allow casual access to your server by users who do not have their own account)

Windows NT Server's System Policy Editor

Almost all the properties of a user's environment are set by the User Manager tool. Microsoft has continued to enhance this feature so that it is a complete tool for administrators. The System Policy Editor (which is not yet integrated into User Manager) enables you to set a series of parameters that relate to the appearance of the user's desktop, which operating system functions (such as the Control Panel) they are allowed to access, and other very fine controls over user activity (see Figure 17.16). If you are running servers exclusively using a client/server architecture, you probably will not use the System Policy Editor often because your users will access the server through the network for shared resources. If you have a number of users who actually work on NT workstations, you might want to take the time to become familiar with the functionality that this editor allows you to control on your user accounts.

FIGURE 17.16.

System Policy Editor.

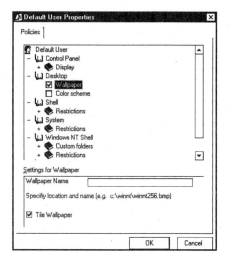

Remote Access Service (RAS) Security

The Remote Access Service (RAS) monitoring and configuration tool is accessed from the Administrative Tools menu. Its purpose is to control the service that monitors your modems for dial-in requests. It also allows you to specify which users are allowed to access the modems, although the User Manager tool can also be used in NT 4 to set up user access to RAS. Another key change in NT 4 is that the dial-out utilities are no long called RAS. Instead, they are located under the Dial-Up Networking tool in the Accessories menu or in the My Computer display. The Remote Access Admin tool has a simple display that shows you the status of the RAS server on the computer that you have selected, as shown in Figure 17.17. Note that you can control and monitor the RAS services on another computer by choosing the Server menu, Select Domain or Server option.

The first task you might want to accomplish is to start or stop the Remote Access Service. Stopping and starting RAS might be necessary to run other communication packages that will not run as long as your modem is dedicated to listening for incoming calls to RAS. The stop functions are located on the Server menu, along with a pause (which means don't take calls, but don't shut down the server or free up the modem). An interesting thing to note is that you can select the domain and server you are administrating when you are in a domain environment. This is another example of how Microsoft is integrating remote administration into its basic tools as opposed to building separate remote access tools. (Just wait until you see the next version of the operating system and applications that will integrate web access.)

How do you control who accesses your system via telephone lines? The Permissions menu item on the Users menu is the main access control tool (see Figure 17.18). It is relatively simple to understand. You select a user you are interested in and then specify a Grant dial-in permission to user whether the user has dial-in access. At the bottom of the dialog box is the option of setting whether the system calls back the user. Call backs are a security feature that limits the hacker's capability to log into the system. Suppose that your users only want access from home and you set up the system so that it automatically calls the user back at home after a successful logon. Even if a hacker successfully guesses the user's ID and password, the worst that will happen is that the user's PC at home will get a call back, thereby preventing the hacker from gaining any real access to your system.

FIGURE 17.17.

Remote Access Admin Display.

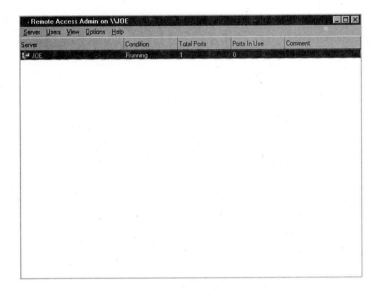

FIGURE 17.18.

Remote Access Permissions dialog box.

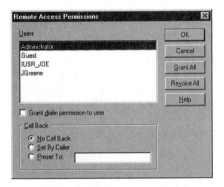

An innovation in NT 4 RAS is the fact that you now can specify the RAS access permissions for users from within the User Manager tool that was discussed in the User Manager section of this chapter.

There is one final topic left in my RAS discussion. Suppose that you see the lights on your modem and know that someone has dialed in. How do you find out who it is that is logged on? The Active Users menu item on the Users menu shows you who is connected, to which server the user is connected, and when that user's connection started (see Figure 17.19). The buttons at the right of the display enable you to get more information on the user account, send that user a message, (such as "the system is going down in 10 minutes"), or even disconnect the user. Chapter 23, "Implementing Routing and Remote Access Services," discusses RAS in more detail.

FIGURE 17.19.

Remote Access Users display.

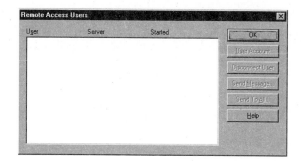

Resource Access Grants

So far, we have classified users into groups and set environmental parameters for them. However, they still have next to nothing in terms of shared network resources unless they are connected to their local machines. The other half of the user administration picture is the access grants to resources. This actually is quite simple under the new Windows NT 4 interface. For example, to grant a user access to a directory, you follow a simple two-step process. First, you select the directory that is to be shared by using Explorer or My Computer tools and create a share name for it (see Figure 17.20). The easiest way to create a share name is to highlight the directory of interest and then right-click your mouse and select the sharing option from the pop-up menu.

Step two in this process is to select the Permissions button on the Sharing tab and fill in the Permissions dialog box (see Figure 17.21). This functions like most of the other administrative control tools. To delete permissions, highlight that user and click the Remove button. To add permissions, click the Add button, select first the user or group to give the permission to, and then choose the type of access permission. For files, the permissions are Full Control, which allows directory modification; Read, which allows users to look but not touch; Change, which allows them to look but not change; and No Access, which does not allow them to even look at the list of files.

The concepts in the preceding paragraph apply to printers also. You select the Printers options of the Settings selection on the Start menu and then highlight the printer you want. Specify the Share Name under the Sharing tab of the tab dialogs that are presented to you when you right-click on that printer and select the Sharing menu option. You control who has access to the printer on the Security tab dialog. The enhanced NT 4 printer setup options provide the fine degree of printer control that is provided by mainframes and minicomputer systems, which is pretty impressive for a little PC-based server.

FIGURE 17.20.

Creating a share name for a folder.

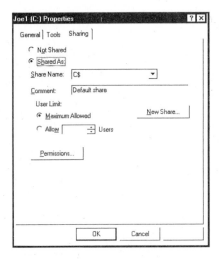

FIGURE 17.21.

Access Through Share Permissions dialog box.

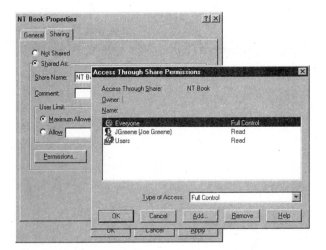

Routine Monitoring

This has been a long and challenging chapter because user administration is complex. It also is an important topic to administrators because it takes up a fair amount of their time. You probably are ready to take a break about now, but there is one more thing you need to know. Suppose that you set up the most perfect user administration scheme known to mankind (fantastic groups, the best policies, and so on). How long do you think things are going to stay the same? From my experience, change is the one thing that you can count on.

You will have users quit and others that take their places. People move between departments and get promoted. You have to keep up with these changes to ensure that everyone has the user environment that they need (and also that they do not have more than they need).

To do this, you need to have a system whereby the needs of the users are conveyed to you, the system administrator. Many companies have forms that personnel departments have filled out when people leave or change jobs. If you can get this form routed to you, it can save you time checking to see that everyone is where they are supposed to be. You also can make up user request forms (either paper or online) to change privileges after they have the appropriate approvals.

Finally, you need to periodically schedule some of your limited time to go through the settings that I have discussed in this chapter to ensure that things are still correct. To keep your system running smoothly, you have to look at it and tune it up occasionally.

Summary

This chapter covered a lot of ground. You must think about many things when dealing with Windows NT user administration. You first have to understand the basic security and user environment options that are provided for you. You next have to come up with a plan of how you want to administer your system. Finally, you have to understand the tools that Microsoft provides to perform these administrative tasks. This chapter is just a starting point for many of you. There are many technical papers, located on the Microsoft TechNet CDs, that cover the intricacies of the Windows network and NT security system. Before leaving this chapter, however, you should be comfortable with the basic concepts of NT user administration and be able to set up your basic server, workgroup, or domain.

Remote Administration

by Joe Greene and Terry Ogletree

IN THIS CHAPTER

The distributed nature of Windows NT security makes it impractical to force system administration to be done from a central location. Instead, many of the operating system's features, such as replication of the security database among domain controllers, imply that management and administration will also be distributed. The Administrator account for the domain comes with built-in rights that allow it to perform tasks related to domain management on the PDC and any BDCs, as well as workstations and server members in the domain, or in domains that trust that domain. The specific set of rights and permissions needed when trying to remotely administer another computer depend on the particular utility you are trying to use.

> **NOTE**
>
> You should be thoroughly familiar with Windows NT security when allowing remote administration capabilities on your network. See Chapter 28, "Advanced Security Guidelines," for an in-depth discussion about the impact of the rights granted certain user accounts and user groups. You need to be aware that if trust relationships exist with other domains, you need to be careful about the default access mechanisms granted certain groups from those domains.

> **TIP**
>
> When a workstation or server joins a domain, the Domain Admins global group is added to the computer's local Administrator group. It is through this group membership that the domain's Administrator account gains access to the computer. If you need to restrict access to a particular computer on your domain by domain administrators, you can use the User Manager on the local computer to remove the Domain Admins group from the local Administrator's group.

Many of the basic system administration tools have built-in capabilities for administering multiple computers or domains. These include:

- Server Manager
- User Manager for Domains
- Event Viewer
- Registry Editor
- System Policy Editor
- Performance Monitor

In addition, other commands (such as the AT command for the Scheduler service) and additional applications from the Windows NT Server 4.0 Resource Kit provide remote functionality. This chapter covers both the built-in capabilities of Windows NT utilities and components from the resource kit. Special attention is paid to the resource kit's Web administration tools, which allow you to administer Windows NT computers using a Web browser.

Using the Server Manager

This is perhaps one of the most important tools the network administrator has to work with. Using the Server Manager can quickly give you an overview of the computers on your network and their roles. In Figure 18.1 you can see that BCA1 is the primary domain controller for this domain, and that BCA99 is the backup domain controller. You can use the View menu to view either Windows NT workstations on the network or both workstations and servers.

FIGURE 18.1.

The Server Manager gives you an overview of the network.

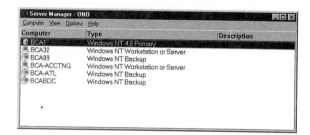

It is with the Server Manager that you create a computer account in the security directory database for a computer. All NT servers and workstations must have a computer account before they can join the domain. To do this you simply select Add To Domain from the Computer menu. You can also use the Remove From Domain option in this same menu when computers have been removed from the network and the account is no longer needed. This utility is also used when a primary domain controller is taken offline and you need to promote a backup domain controller to that role.

> **CAUTION**
>
> You should not use this function without being aware of the implications. For example, do you plan to bring the original PDC back online at a later time, or are you planning to replace it with a new server? Chapter 16, "Administering the Server," covers the process of promoting a BDC to become the primary domain controller and some considerations you should think about before doing so.

In Chapter 16 you can see that the Server Manager is a powerful tool that can be used for many other administrative purposes; the graphical interface makes it even easier. To administer a computer you need only highlight it on the Server Manager window and use the Computer menu to select a function. Double-clicking on a computer in this window is the same as using the Properties selection from the Computer menu. It brings up a dialog box that allows you to quickly get information about users and resources on the target computer.

18

REMOTE ADMINISTRATION

You can use Server Manager to access computers in other domains, provided you have a trust relationship with the domain or an account in that domain. You can also gain access if you are logged on to a domain using a username that exists, with sufficient rights, in the remote domain and if both accounts use the same password.

Use the Select Domain option from the computer menu and the Server Manager prompts you to either enter a domain name or select it from a list that it knows about (see Figure 18.2). In the Select Domain dialog box, you can put in a computer name instead of a domain name by preceding the computer name with two backslash characters.

FIGURE 18.2.

The Server Manager can be used to administer computers in multiple domains.

Using a Slow WAN Connection

If your connection to the domain is by a slow link such as a dial-up connection or a slow WAN connection, then you might want to set the Low Speed Connection check box (although the Server Manager can usually determine the speed of the connection and adjust this for you automatically). This prevents the automatic display refresh that the Server Manager performs periodically. If you have already connected to a computer in a domain and did not use this check box, you can later change it by selecting the Low Speed Connection entry from the Options menu in the main Server Manager window.

You can also start the Server Manager from the command prompt and tell it to use a low-speed connection by using the /l switch (or the /h switch for high-speed connection).

```
C:> Svrmgr Ono /l
```

You can either use the Svrmgr program directly from the command prompt or use it in a batch file. For example, you might want to set up a batch file to start the Server Manager with its focus set to a specific domain (the ONO domain in the preceding example), and then create a Desktop shortcut to run the batch file. Creating shortcuts like this can save time when you are managing multiple domains.

Using the Server Manager to Synchronize the Security Database

When you update user accounts or otherwise make changes to the domain security directory database, those changes are made on the copy of the SAM that resides on the primary domain controller. The PDC sends a message to its BDCs, telling them to request an update, at regular, staggered intervals. All changes that are made to the directory database are stored in a *change log* on the PDC. Each BDC requests only the changes that have been made since its last update request.

The important implication is that if you change a user's account (a password, for example) the change is actually being made to the database on the PDC and it will not be propagated immediately to the backup domain controllers. You can use the Server Manager to force the replication to begin immediately by selecting Synchronize Entire Domain from the Computer menu. When performing remote administration on any network, you should always keep in mind the type of information you are changing and where it is stored in the network. Understanding how important databases are replicated or distributed can save time when you have problems.

Promoting a BDC to Become the New Primary Domain Controller

Perhaps one of the most important functions you can perform using the Server Manager is promoting a backup domain controller to become the new PDC for a domain. This built-in fault tolerance for the domain security directory database is one you should take advantage of—even on a small network, where a BDC is not needed to help offload logon processing from the PDC. Having a database backup to use for recovery in the case of a fatal hardware or software crash on the PDC not only allows you to completely recover the directory database (minus any entries in the change log that have yet to be replicated to the BDCs), but it also allows your network clients to continue logging on to the network in the absence of the PDC.

There are several situations where you may want to use this function:

- *The PDC has become unavailable permanently.* The PDC has encountered hardware or software problems that render it nonfunctional, and you do not have an adequate backup or other recovery mechanism to rebuild it. In this case you promote an existing BDC to become the new PDC.

- *You are adding a new computer to the network and you want it to be the new PDC for the domain.* You can install Windows NT Server on a new computer, initially set it up as a BDC, and then promote it to PDC when the installation process is finished. When you promote a BDC to become a PDC, the existing PDC is automatically demoted to BDC status, since you cannot have more than one PDC for a domain on the network at any one time.

Perform the following steps to use the Server Manager to promote a BDC to PDC:

1. Bring up the Server Manager tool and highlight the BDC you want to promote.
2. From the Computer menu, select Promote to Primary Domain Controller.

3. A dialog box warns you that all clients who are connected to this BDC or to the existing BDC will be disconnected if you continue. Click Yes to continue or No if you want to postpone the process.

4. The Server Manager stops the Netlogon process on the existing PDC and restarts it on the newly promoted PDC after changing its status to PDC.

Managing Resources on Remote Computers

The Server Manager can be used to manage many different resources on remote computers. Chapter 16 discusses, in detail, the functions you can perform. Briefly, those functions include:

- Create and Remove Computer Accounts—This function allows you to create accounts for computers, so that they can join a domain or remove the computer account when the computer is no longer a member of the domain. For example, if you were replacing a computer with a new installation and wanted to use the same computer name, you would use this function to remove the computer name (and its associated SID) from the database, and create a new computer account with the same name.

- Managing Services—This function brings up the same dialog box (Services on *computername*) that you get if you were logged on locally at the computer and were using the Services applet in the Control Panel. You can start, stop, and disable services, as well as change their startup configuration.

- Managing Shares—You can view or change the properties of network file shares on a remote computer with this function. For example, you can change the permissions on a share or the connected users limit for the share. You can also create new shares on the computer or remove existing shares.

- Performing Resource Accounting—By using the Properties function in the Computer menu of the Server Manager, you can perform many functions related to resources on a remote computer. These include:

    Usage Summary   The number of connected sessions, open files, file locks, and opened named pipes on the computer.

    Users   Names of connected users along with the computer name of the client, number of open files, and other resource usage information.

    Shares   A summary of resource usage for the shares offered by the computer.

    In Use   A summary of all resource usage on the computer (user connections, named pipes, print jobs, and so on).

    Replication   The Directory Replicator Service can be used to replicate directories from one server to another. You use the Server Manager to configure and manage the import and export directories on a server. Replication is most often used for replicating users' logon scripts to other domain controllers.

Alerts   You can add usernames or computernames to a notification list that
Windows NT uses when it sends out an alert message. By configuring remote
servers to send alerts to your computer, you can quickly react to problems when
they arise on your network.

■ Send Message—The Send Message option on the Computer menu allows you to send
a text message to all users that are connected to the computer highlighted in the Server
Manager dialog box.

This section highlights the major functions you can perform using the Server Manager to remotely administer computers. See Chapter 16 for in-depth information on these capabilities
and how to perform the functions discussed.

User Manager for Domains

The User Manager for Domains administrative utility can be used to access the security directory database for the domain or the local security database on an NT workstation or stand-
alone server. In Chapter 17, "User Administration," you can learn about setting up user
accounts with this utility, as well as establishing trust relationships and configuring events to
audit for the security log files. You must be a member of the Administrators or the Account
Operators group on the computer in order to create or manage users. However, Account Operators are limited in the functions they can perform. For example, Account Operators cannot
modify the account of an administrator or other Account Operators, Server Operators, Print
Operators, or Backup Operators. Additionally, only administrators can assign user rights.

You can select the domain that you want to administer using the Select Domain option in the
User menu. The dialog box that appears is the same as that used by the Server Manager (shown
in Figure 18.2) and the selection method is the same. You can also enter a specific computer
name here to use the utility to administer the local security database of an NT workstation or
stand-alone server.

Managing User Accounts

The User Manager's main function is to create or modify user accounts for the domain. The
User menu's functions for this purpose are

■ New User—Brings up the New User dialog box, which you can use to provide
information necessary to create a new user, such as username, password, group
memberships, and logon restrictions, among other things.

■ Copy—You can select a user account by highlighting it on the main User Manager
dialog box and use the Copy function to create a new user by copying characteristics
from the existing user account.

■ Delete—You can highlight a user account in the User Manager and then use the
Delete function to remove the user account from the domain.

■ Rename—This function allows you to select a user account and change the username associated with it.

- ■ Properties—The Properties button brings up a properties dialog box (for the user account) that appears similar to the New User dialog box, with the exception that it shows the current user information and you can modify individual fields or use the buttons provided to change the user account properties.

See Chapter 17 for a more complete discussion of managing users with this utility.

Managing User Rights and User Groups

The User Manager administrative tool is the utility you use to grant or revoke rights from users and groups. You can use the User Manager to grant rights on an individual basis, which can be a time-consuming, tedious chore, or you can use the built-in global and local user groups to make granting rights easier. You can also use the User Manager to create new user groups if you find that the built-in groups do not match your needs.

To manage user rights, select User Rights from the Policies menu. The User Rights Policy dialog box appears. You can use this dialog box to select the specific right, and then use Add and Remove buttons to either grant the right to new users or groups, or to remove the right.

To manage groups, you can select the group from the display in the main User Manager dialog box and use the same User menu buttons that you used when managing users: Copy, Rename, Delete, and Properties. The User menu also has functions to create new global or local user groups.

Managing Trust Relationships

Trust relationships between domains are the prerequisite for granting rights in your domain to users from another domain, or vice versa. Trust relationships work in two directions—each domain has a list of other domains that it trusts, and it has a list of domains that trust it.

A domain administrator can grant access permissions and rights to a user from a trusted domain in the same way that he does for users of his domain. Once the trust relationship is established, dialog boxes used for granting user rights, group memberships, and access permissions allow you to select users from your domain; they also allow you to expand a list of users from trusted domains from which you can also select.

When a trust relationship exists, *pass-through authentication* takes place. This means that after the user is authenticated by the logon process in the trusted domain, then the trusting domain accepts the security token granted by that domain and doesn't require the user to authenticate again when she accesses resources in the trusting domain.

To establish a trust relationship between domains, it is best to establish the trusting side first. For example, if the administrator of Domain A wants to establish a trust relationship with Domain B, whereby Domain A will trust users in Domain B, then:

1. Domain B's administrator should use the User Manager for Domains to add the name of Domain A to the list of trusting domains.

2. Domain A's administrator then uses his User Manager for Domains to add the name of Domain B to his list of trusted domains.

If you perform step 2 before step 1, you will probably get a message saying that the trust relationship cannot be verified at that time. To prevent any confusion, it's best to do it in the order described.

Trust relationships are uni-directional. If you want to establish a relationship that has each domain trusting users from the other domain, then you have to create two trust relationships between the two domains, one for each direction (trusted-trusting).

Setting Account Policy with the User Manager

You can use the Account option on the Policies menu to set certain policies for enforcement on all user accounts. The types you can specify here include:

- Password Restrictions—Minimum and maximum password lifetimes, or "password never expires."
- Minimum Password Length—You can force users to utilize a minimum number of characters for a password, or even allow blank passwords.
- Password Uniqueness—You can control whether a password history list is kept and how many entries it should hold. Users cannot reuse a password until it has been removed from the password history list by being aged out.
- Account Lockout and Duration—You can configure a policy that locks out the use of a user account after a specified number of failed logon attempts, along with the duration of the lockout and the time interval that must pass before the failure count is reset.
- Disconnect Users—You can specify that users will be logged out if they are connected when their user account logon hours expire.
- You can force users to log on in order to change their password.

Setting the Audit Policy

Each Windows NT Server and workstation has an Event Viewer that you can use to view events stored in the System, Application, and Security log files. The User Manager allows you to set the events to be audited. Select Audit from the Policies menu to bring up the Audit Policy window. You can select to audit success or failure audits for each type of audit. The types of events you can select to audit using this dialog box are:

- Logon and Logoff
- File and Object Access
- Use of User Rights

■ User and Group Management

■ Security Policy Changes

■ Restart, Shutdown, and System

■ Process Tracking

Establishing auditing of some events can seem confusing at times. For example, if you enable success and failure auditing for File and Object Access events, you still need to use the Properties sheets; you need it for file or directory objects, to set up which types of access will be audited (read or write access, for example). You should also be aware that some audits are set using other utilities. To audit print jobs, you use the Security tab in the property sheet for a particular printer.

Before you let yourself become assured that you have adequately secured your network using appropriate grants of rights, group memberships, and auditing, you should become intimately familiar with Windows NT security. Reading Chapter 28 is an excellent step in that direction.

Low-Speed Connections

In most respects, the utility works the same no matter which security database you are working with. The exceptions come when you use a low-speed connection (such as a dial-up line or slow WAN). Because the user database itself can be extremely large in some cases (many thousands of users in some large companies), it is impractical for the utility to download all the entries to the local computer when administering the database over a slow connection. For this reason, the user list and the group list are not available in User Manager when you select low-speed connection (see Figure 18.3).

Figure 18.3.

The user and group listings are not available when using a low-speed connection to a remote computer.

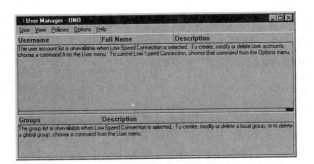

You can, however, manage a user account or a local group by using the commands available in the User menu:

■ New User

■ New Local Group

■ Copy

■ Delete

- Rename
- Properties

Note that the New Global Group option is not available when using a low-speed connection. You can, however, use the Delete option to delete a global group, and you can still manage user membership in groups by selecting a user to manage (User|Properties) and then using the Groups button.

The Select Users option is not available, since you need the user listing to use it.

The Policies menu (Account Policy, User Rights, Auditing, and Trust Relationships) can still be used in a low-speed connection. Anything you do with a low-speed connection may take longer, depending on the amount of data being transferred.

Using the Event Viewer

When a significant event occurs on a system, such as a disk becoming full or a hardware component failing, the system writes records to an event log that you can use to diagnose the situation. In addition to the operating system itself, applications can be coded to write application-specific event records. The Event Viewer allows you to examine the system log files from the local computer or other computers in the domain. The log files for each computer consists of three separate files:

- System Log File—Events logged by the operating system components. A driver's failure to load or initialize is an example.
- Security Log File—Events that you elect to audit by setting the Audit Policy via the User Manager for Domains are stored in this log file. You use this log file to diagnose failed logon attempts.
- Application Log File—Events that applications developers decide to audit are sent to this file.

For more information on using the Event Viewer, see Chapter 16.

The Event Viewer defaults to using the event log files from the local computer on which it is running. To select another computer, use the Select Computer option under the Log menu. The dialog box that appears, which is shown in Figure 18.4, is similar to the one used by the Server Manager and the User Manager. The only difference is in the title bar: Select Computer instead of Select Domain.

When you use the Event Viewer to access a remote computer's log files, you not only view the data in those files, but you can also perform maintenance functions on them. For example, when you select Log Settings from the Log menu to change the log file's characteristics (such as the size of the file or the Overwrite Events As Needed option), you are setting properties for the log file on the computer to which you have attached, not the local computer. When you select Clear All Events from the Log menu, you are clearing the log file on the computer to which you are attached.

FIGURE 18.4.

You can use this dialog box to select the computer you want to connect to using the Event Viewer.

The only exceptions to this are the Open and Save As functions in the Log menu, which use the file system on the local computer.

Using the Registry Editor

You can edit the Registry hives on the local computer or on other computers on the network with the Registry Editor. There are two Registry Editors included with Windows NT: `Regedit.exe` and `Regedt32.exe`. This section covers `Regedt32.exe`. If you need to edit a remote computer's Registry, you should use `Regedt32.exe`.

The reasoning for this is because `Regedit.exe` appears to allow you to connect to a remote computer when you select Connect Network Registry under the Registry menu. This brings up a dialog box that allows you to enter a remote computername or browse the network. However, an error message appears when you choose a computer (see Figure 18.5).

FIGURE 18.5.

You should not use the `Regedit.exe` *program to edit Registry files remotely.*

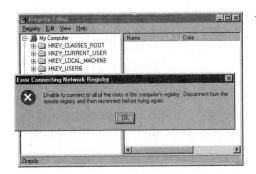

Although `Regedit` appears to let you edit a remote Registry, there is a bug in the program. You can use `Regedit` to edit the local Registry on a computer, but you must use `Regedt32` for remote Registry editing instead.

> **NOTE**
>
> In order to edit a Registry of another computer remotely, you must be a member of the administrator's local group or the Domain Admin global group.

Using Regedt32.exe

To start this editor, you can either enter its name at the command prompt or Start|Run and enter the name in the Run dialog box. For remote administration, use the Select Computer option from the Registry menu. A Select Computer dialog box appears, similar to the Event Viewer. You can enter the computername in the Computer field, or you can click on a computer listed in the Select Computer dialog box window.

When you edit a remote computer's Registry, only two more windows are added to the Registry Editor's display. In Figure 18.6 you can see that when using the Regedt32 to remotely edit the Registry for a server with the computer name RNC1, only two additional windows pop up in the editor: one for HKEY_LOCAL_MACHINE and one for HKEY_USERS.

FIGURE 18.6.

Only two additional windows are added to the display when remotely editing another computer's Registry.

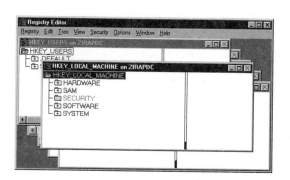

This is because the other roots simply point to subkeys of these two roots. You find them as follows:

Key	Look Under
HKEY_CLASSES_ROOT	HKEY_LOCAL_MACHINE\Software\Classes
HKEY_CURRENT_CONFIG	HKEY_LOCAL_MACHINE\SYSTEM\CurrentControlSet
	\Hardware\Profiles\<profiles number>
HKEY_CURRENT_USER	HKEY_USERS\<user SID>

> ## CAUTION
>
> Everywhere you look in Windows NT Registry documentation you are warned that even very slight changes to the Registry files can have disastrous results if you are not exactly sure of what you are doing. Your risk is compounded when you are using the Registry editor to edit files on remote computers, especially if you are separated from the remote computer geographically. You can quite literally crash a computer remotely and render it unusable—you would not be able to use remote administration techniques to fix it. As always, be very cautious when using the Registry Editor.

Using the System Policy Editor

The System Policy Editor administrative tool can greatly simplify the administrator's job; it does so by providing an easy-to-understand interface into selected Registry settings that are used to define resources, their availability, and access on the computer or throughout the domain. Things you can control using System Policies include the user desktop environment, the Start menu, and the ability to change the desktop's characteristics.

The System Policy Editor uses administrative files (which have the .ADM file extension in their filename) as templates to determine which Registry settings are exposed to the user of the editor. Additionally, third-party software developers can create policy files (which have the .ADM file extension) that can be added to the System Policy Editor to further extend the Registry parameters that can be accessed.

In Figure 18.7 you see that there are two icons in the editor's main window: Default User and Default Computer.

FIGURE 18.7.

The System Policy Editor allows you to edit portions of the Registry.

In this window the Default User icon allows you to make changes to keys stored in the HKEY_CURRENT_USER root. The Default Computer icon gives you access to the HKEY_LOCAL_MACHINE root of the local machine.

To use the System Policy Editor to edit the Registry on a remote computer, use the Connect command from the File menu. The dialog box that appears allows you to enter a computername; there is no browse button. What about policy files? The impact of remote registry editing is felt much more using policy files.

This utility can be used to make changes to the Registry without having to know the names of Registry keys and the data format they use. Instead, check boxes with descriptive titles are used to simplify the administrator's work. See Chapter 17 for further information on using the System Policy Editor.

Using the Performance Monitor

The Performance Monitor can be a great help in diagnosing resource problems on computers in the network. To view performance data from a remote computer, edit the Computer field in the dialog box that appears when you choose an Add To option from the Edit menu. In Figure 18.8 you see the Add To Chart dialog box.

> **NOTE**
>
> Several conditions must be met in order to use the Performance Monitor to monitor a remote computer. First, you must have access to the remote computer's Registry. By default, only administrators have this access level. You also need specific read access to the following Registry subkey:
>
> `HKEY_LOCAL_MACHINE\Software\Microsoft\WindowsNT\CurrentVersion\Perflib`
> `\LanguageID`
>
> *LanguageID* is a numeric code (`Perflib\009`, for example, would be for English). Secondly, you must have access to files that have names that match `Perfc*.dat` and `Perfh*.dat` (with the asterisk being replaced by a numeric language code; `Perfh009.dat` would indicate English), which are usually found in the `System32` subdirectory under the system root directory.

FIGURE 18.8.

You can change the computer in the Add to Chart dialog box to monitor performance information for remote computers.

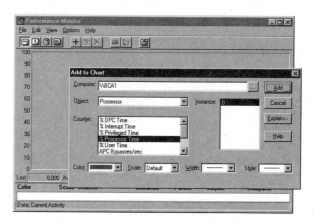

If you want to browse the network to select a computer, you can click the Browse button to the Computer field's immediate right. The button icon is three dots. Clicking this button brings up the standard Select Computer-type dialog box (refer to Figure 18.4, for example) that is discussed earlier in this chapter.

NOTE

You can use the Add To option for all four views you can get with the Performance Monitor: Chart, Alert, Log, and Report. The dialog box for each Add To option is similar to the Add to Chart example shown in Figure 18.8.

The nice thing about using the Performance Monitor to monitor remote systems is that you can put data on your display from several systems at the same time for evaluation. In Figure 18.9 you see that the counter % Processor Time is being monitored for both nodes BCA1 and BCA-ACCTNG. You can do comparison performance monitoring in this manner if you have several servers that are performing similar functions on your network and you are trying to locate which are the bottleneck.

FIGURE 18.9.

You can monitor data from more than one computer at the same time using the Performance Monitor.

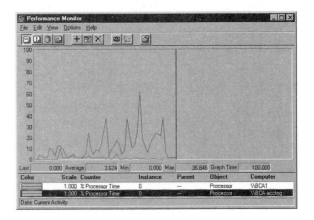

For more information on using the Performance Monitor, see Chapter 20, "Performance Tuning and Optimization."

Additional Utilities with Remote Administration Capabilities

There are a few other useful Windows NT commands that allow you to specify a remote computer as the target for execution. In addition, the Windows NT Server 4.0 Resource Kit includes several utilities that are remote-administration capable.

Scheduler Service (AT Command)

The Scheduler service allows you to perform batch processing under Windows NT. A *batch file* is an ASCII text file containing commands that can be executed by typing the filename at the command prompt or that can be run by submitting it to a batch queue using the Scheduler service. A batch file can contain not only system commands, but can also be used to start and run third-party applications. For this reason the Scheduler service can be a powerful command to use when you need to administer applications on remote computers.

The daily chore of performing backups is a perfect example. Rather than having to log in at each computer when you want to make changes to a backup procedure, you can create batch files for each computer and submit them to the Scheduler service; they will be run on their respective computers on the date and time you specify. You can also use the Scheduler service to start or stop services and perform other system administration chores. For example, you could write a batch file that closes all files for an application and takes it offline before a backup procedure executes.

The user interface into the Scheduler service is the AT command. The syntax for the AT command is as follows:

```
AT [\\computername] [ [id] [/DELETE] | /DELETE [/YES]]
AT [\\computername] time [/INTERACTIVE]
    [ /EVERY:date[,...] | /NEXT:date[,...]] "command"
```

> **NOTE**
>
> When composing a command line using the AT command, be sure to use the command-line options and parameters in the order they are listed in the command syntax.

As you can see, you can optionally place a computername directly after the AT command to specify a remote computer for execution of the command. The *command* value can be a valid command executed at the command prompt, or it can be an executable program or batch file to be run. For example, you could use the following to start a backup using a batch file called `backup.bat`:

```
AT \\BCA1 3:15 "c:\procedures\backup.bat"
```

The /INTERACTIVE switch for the AT command can cause the application to be run on the desktop. If you omit this switch, the application is run in the background. The flexible nature of the command-line switches allows you to schedule jobs not just for a specific time or date, but also to recur on a regular basis. For example, to schedule a command procedure to run every Tuesday, you would use the following syntax:

```
AT 23:00 /every:T BATCH.CMD
```

The syntax you should use to specify specific days of the week are:

- M   Monday
- T   Tuesday
- W   Wednesday
- TH   Thursday

■ F Friday

■ S Saturday

■ SU Sunday

To view entries that are waiting the batch queue, simply use the AT command by itself.

Enter AT /? at the command prompt to receive more help on the syntax for using the AT command's various command-line switches.

WinAT Command Scheduler

There is a graphical version of the command scheduler called WinAT Command Scheduler in the Windows NT Server 4.0 Resource Kit. You can see in Figure 18.10 the utility with a window showing a command that is waiting to execute the backup.bat command file at 5:00 p.m. that afternoon.

FIGURE 18.10.

The GUI version of the Command Scheduler simplifies the syntax for scheduling batch jobs.

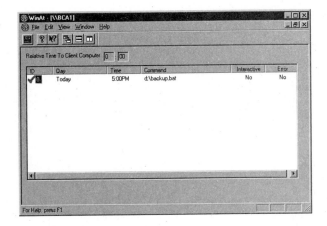

The WinAT Command Scheduler opens a separate window for each computer you want to administer, so that you can easily keep track of the commands for several computers on the same screen, at the same time.

The Edit menu is used in the utility to add, remove, or modify commands that you schedule. The Copy and Paste commands are very nice features on the Edit menu; you can use them when you are administering a large number of computers. You can highlight a command in one computer's window, select Edit|Copy, place your cursor in another computer's window, and select Edit|Paste. The pasted command is scheduled on the second computer system, just as if you had filled in the dialog box used by the Edit|Add command.

Still another nice feature is the Relative Time field, located near the top of the display. If you are administering computers that are located in different time zones, the difference between your zone and the target computer's zone is shown here. This can make deciding when to schedule jobs easier by reminding you of the time difference.

By default, the utility starts with a window open for the computer on which it is running. You use the New command from the File menu to add another computer to the display. The standard Add Computer dialog box (refer to Figure 18.4) appears, where you can type in a computername or browse the network to make your selection.

Shutdown Manager

The Shutdown Manager utility is also found in the resource kit. It comes in a command-line form and a GUI form. You can remotely shut down Windows NT Servers and Workstations on your network with this utility. The utility displays an alert message on the target computer's screen, informing the user that the computer is being shut down. A timeout interval, which you can configure, ticks down before the shutdown occurs, allowing you some time to abort the procedure if you change your mind. You can also specify that the computer be rebooted after the shutdown, and you can even enter a custom message to be displayed on the Alert dialog box that the user sees.

The syntax for the SHUTDOWN command is as follows:

```
SHUTDOWN [/?] [\\Computer] [/L] [/A] [/R] [/T:xx] ["Msg"] [/Y] [/C]

\\Computer      Computername of computer to shutdown.
/L              Shutdown the local computer.
/A              Abort the shutdown during the timeout period.
/R              Reboot after shutdown.
/T:xx           Number of seconds before shutdown (20 default).
"Msg"           Custom message to display to user before shutdown.
/Y              Answer all following questions "yes".
/C              Forces running applications to close.
```

CAUTION

When using this command, you should be aware that the /C switch causes the target computer to close all applications before shutdown, but it does not prompt the user to save any files that may be open, which a local shutdown normally does. Do not use this switch unless you are confident that no important data will be lost. If you do not use the /C switch, any applications with unsaved data prompt the user to save.

The GUI version of the Shutdown Manager (see Figure 18.11) makes the process even simpler.

To bring up the GUI version, you can locate it by clicking the Start button. Then select Programs | Resource Kit 4.0 | Management | Shutdown Workstation.

You can enter the name of a computer on the network in the Computer Name field, or you can use the Browse button next to that field (the button with the three dots on it) to bring up the standard Select Computer dialog box, which you can use to browse the network.

18

REMOTE
ADMINISTRATION

FIGURE 18.11.
*The GUI version of the
Shutdown Manager.*

You can also select the other shutdown options available with the command-line version, such as to kill the running applications without prompting the user to exit, or sending a message to the target computer. You can also enter a text message of up to 127 characters for display with the shutdown Alert dialog box. The Abort button can be used, of course, only during the shutdown timeout period (the Delay field). The remote user whose computer is being shut down cannot abort the shutdown. Only the administrator who has initiated the shutdown can abort it by using the Abort button.

> **NOTE**
>
> Although the GUI version is called Shutdown Workstation on the menu, it can be used to shut down either Windows NT Workstation or Server.

Administering Windows NT Server Using a WWW Browser

Remote administration of Windows NT Servers took a giant step forward when Supplement 1 to the resource kit was released. You find in this kit the Web Administration tools that you can install on a server running IIS 2.0 or higher. These Web Administration tools give you a limited amount of management tasks, which you can exercise over an Internet connection to your remote servers.

Installing the Web Administration Tools

When you perform the usual Install Resource Kit option, you do not install everything that is on the CD. In Figure 18.12 you can see that installation of the Web Administration tools is a separate task. Be sure that you have IIS installed and running, and then insert the supplemental CD into your computer; select Web Administration from the Autorun menu.

FIGURE 18.12.

Use the Windows NT Server 4.0 Resource Kit Supplement 1 CD to install Web Administration.

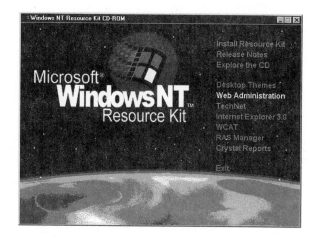

The Setup program copies files to your local hard drive, and it may prompt you with an error message for the `Scripts` and `WWW` directories. If this happens, be sure that the value you insert is as follows:

```
Scripts:        <IIS root>\Scripts
WWW Root:       <IIS root>\WWWroot
```

For example, if you took the default directory name when you installed IIS, the WWW root would be

```
C:>\Inetpub\WWWroot
```

It is important that you correctly specify these two directories; otherwise, the utility will not work.

You do not need to reboot your computer after the Setup program has finished. You should, however, stop and restart the WWW service. You can do this using the Services applet in the Control Panel or by using the IIS Internet Service Manager utility.

Using the Web Administration Tools

To administer an NT Server that is running the Web Administration tools, bring up your favorite Web browser and use the following URL:

```
http://<server name>/ntadmin/ntadmin.htm
```

`<server name>` is your IIS server's Internet domain name, or the IP address associated with your server.

You can see the main HTML page for the Web Administration tools in Figure 18.13. On the left side of the screen you have the following options:

- Introduction
- Accounts

- Devices
- Event Logs
- File System
- Maintenance
- Printers
- Services
- Sessions
- Status
- Help

FIGURE 18.13.

This is the home page for the Web Administration tools on your server.

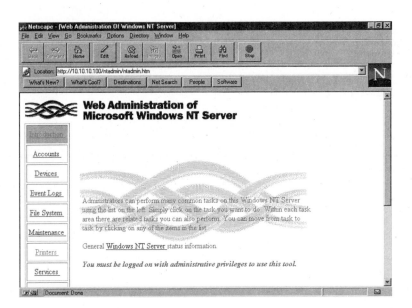

In addition to these hyperlinks on the left side of the screen, you find a link at the bottom of the screen that gives an overall general system status. The output for that display is shown in Figure 18.14.

Each of the selections on the left side of the main window take you to another window, which displays the tasks that you can remotely perform using these tools. In Figure 18.15 you see the main screen that is displayed when you choose, for example, the Accounts hyperlink.

FIGURE 18.14.

The General Windows NT Server Status link gives you an overview of the system resources.

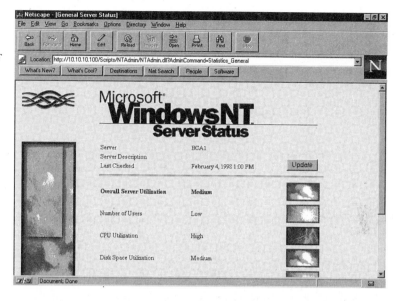

FIGURE 18.15.

The Accounts category allows you to manage user accounts, groups, and add workstations and servers to the domain.

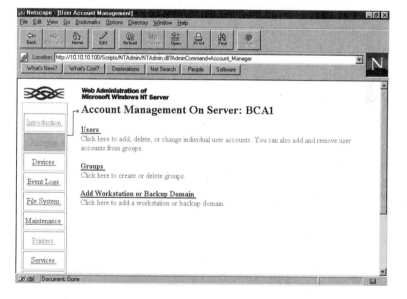

Accounts

You cannot perform all the functions using the Web Administration tools that you can with the actual User Manager for Domains. However, you can perform a large subset of the functions by using HTML forms for input. The subcategories you find under the Accounts category include:

- Users
- Groups
- Add Workstation or Backup Domain

The Groups selection allows you to create or delete local groups. The Add Workstation or Backup Domain selection allows you to add workstations and servers to the domain, including the ability to add a server as a backup domain controller.

The Users selection brings up functions related to User Account management. Large installations may notice one limitation: the number of usernames that will be downloaded and available in the scroll box is limited to 1,024 names. You can still use the Add function to add new names—however, no more than 1,024 will be available for you to select using the form provided. You can edit the following Registry key if you need to change the name limit size.

```
HKEY_LOCAL_MACHINE\Software\Microsoft\Inetsrv_NtAdmin
```

Select the `MaxUsersToDisplay` value. The number you need to use when changing this value should be expressed in hexadecimal.

In Figure 18.16 you can see the functional portion of the User Accounts screen, which is displayed when you select the Users hyperlink from the Accounts screen. The user accounts for the domain or server are shown in a scroll box, and the buttons to the right are used to perform functions on the name you select from the list.

Figure 18.16.

The Accounts screen allows you to perform some of the User Manager utility's functions.

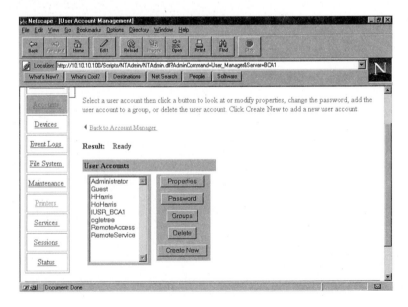

The functions you can perform here include:

- View and change user account properties, which include only Full Name, Comment, and Password Policy fields from the user database.
- Change a user's password.
- View or change a user's group memberships.
- Add or delete a user account.

Devices

This hyperlink takes you to a listing of all the devices on the system. You can select a device and choose to start or stop it. You can even use the Startup button on this screen to change the device's startup parameters (for example, boot, system, and manual).

Event Logs

The Event Log hyperlink brings up a dialog box that allows you to select the log file (System, Security, or Application). You can then enter the number of events to view per page (the default is 40) and then click the View Events button to get the event listing, or you can use the Clear Log button to clear the log file. Figure 18.17 shows the System Event Log. To get the detail for any entry, simply select that entry by clicking the button at the beginning of the entry and then clicking the Details button.

FIGURE 18.17.

You can view the event logs for any computer remotely.

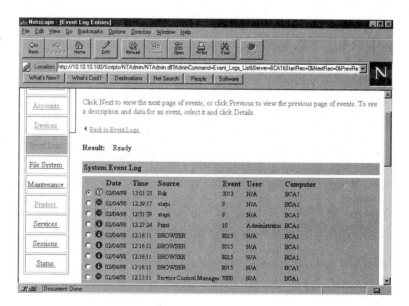

The Next and Previous buttons allow you to navigate through the log file. Figure 18.18 shows the display that results from using the Details button.

FIGURE 18.18.

*The Detailed Event Log
record display.*

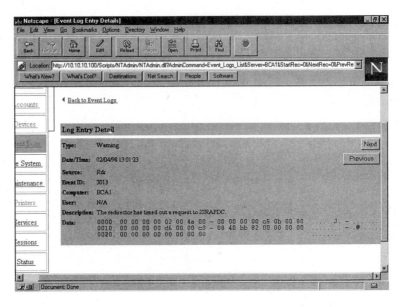

When you use the Clear button on the Event Log's main page, you are prompted by another page, on which you can continue and clear the log, or specify a filename to store a backup copy of the log file before it is cleared.

File System

This option gives you two categories from which you can choose functions:

- Shared Directories
- File and Folder Access for NTFS Partitions

When you select the Shared Directories option, a page that lists the server's shares with the path to the folders made available is shown (see Figure 18.19). The Properties button brings up a display where you can change the user limit or the comment associated with the share name.

The Permissions button allows you to add and remove permissions for users and groups. The Delete button can be used to delete the share and the Create New button allows you to create a new share on the target computer.

The File and Folder Access for NTFS Partitions selection, under the File Systems page, brings up a page that allows you to scroll through directory and file listings. You can then select a Permissions button to set NTFS permissions on entities by user or group.

FIGURE 18.19.

The Shares option shows you the shares on the target system.

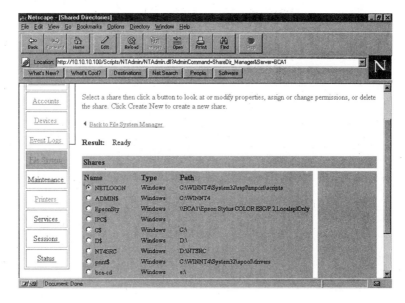

Maintenance

This function brings up a page that lists several useful utilities for use during remote administration. The options are:

- Broadcast Message—Use this to send a text message to all users in the domain. When the message has been sent, an informational message tells you how many logged-on users to which it was sent.

- Remote Console—This is a utility that performs a function similar to Telnet. You must install the Remote Console utility that is included in the resource kit. This function brings up a page that allows you to start or stop the Remote Console server or to download a client to use in accessing the server.

- Reboot Server—This option works similarly to the Shutdown Manager found in the Windows NT Server 4.0 Resource Kit. It allows you to send a text message to all users and set a countdown time limit before it shuts down the target computer.

- Web Administration Preferences—Here you can change values associated with the General Status Page display discussed at the beginning of this section (refer to Figure 18.14).

Printers

This page provides the capability of managing printers on your server and in the rest of the Domain. The first page lists the printers and gives you buttons to:

- Jobs—Pauses, resumes, or deletes individual print jobs (documents).
- Pause—Pauses the printer.

18

REMOTE
ADMINISTRATION

■ Resume—Resumes the printer after pause.

■ Flush—Flushes remaining documents from the printer queue.

Managing printers is an ongoing task that can consume a lot of an administrator's time. By allowing remote administration of printers attached to an NT Server, this job becomes somewhat easier. You can manage printers using a browser from another computer in your office, or from the other side of the world via the Internet.

Services

Figure 18.20 shows what you see when you select the hyperlink to get to the Services page. You can select any NT service on this page and use the buttons to stop or start it. You can also change the service's startup parameters by using the Startup button.

FIGURE 18.20.

The Services page allows you to manage services running on the target computer.

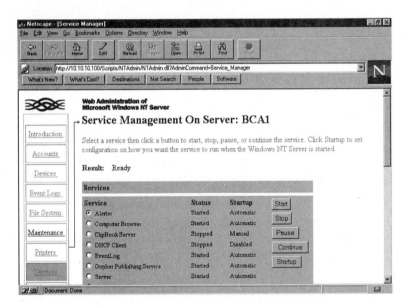

In Figure 18.21 you can see the Startup page for the Server service. Here you can modify a service to use a different user account, or you can disable the service while you are troubleshooting. You can make the same changes here that you can in the Control Panel's Services applet or the Server Manager.

CAUTION

Be sure you think before you stop services using the Web Administration tools for remote administration. If you stop the WWW service on the target server, for example, your Web Administration tools stop working!

FIGURE 18.21.

You can modify the startup parameters for any service running on the server.

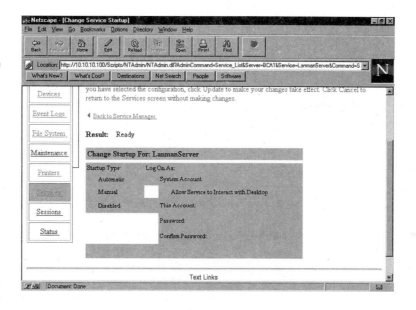

Sessions

This selection brings up a page showing the open sessions for the server. For each session you can use buttons for:

- Information—Brings up a page showing more details about the session, such as the resources it has open.
- Disconnect—This button disconnects a specific session.
- Disconnect All—Use this to disconnect all sessions on the server.

Status

This hyperlink allows you to gather more detailed information than the General Windows NT Server Status Information link. It allows you to view information in the following categories:

- Server Configuration—You can use this option to get extensive information about the server. This information is similar to what you get using the `Winmsd.exe` program (Windows Diagnostics). You can elect to choose a specific category of information or use the All Settings option to get everything in one large report. The categories include:

Operating System Version	Memory Resources
Drives	Port Resources
Services	DMA Resources
Drivers	Hardware
Memory	Environment
Interrupt Resources	

- Network—This option can be very useful to help desk personnel when trying to remotely diagnose problems with a computer.

- Performance Statistics—This option lets you select a Performance Monitor object, and then shows you a snapshot of the counters associated with that object. You don't get a continually updating display like you do with the regular Performance Monitor administrative tool, but this option can be useful when troubleshooting performance problems on a network.

- Server Statistics—This option gives you a page of miscellaneous information about the server, such as processor, memory, and paging file information.

Help

This selection brings up online help for the Web Administration tools. The help categories include installation tips, a brief introduction on how to use the tools, and some troubleshooting information. A Frequently Asked Questions (FAQ) is also provided.

Installing Windows NT Server Administrative Tools on Windows 95 and Windows NT Workstation

You can administer Windows NT Servers and Workstations using many of the administrative tools that usually are installed only on Windows NT Server from a Windows 95 or Windows NT Workstation client. The server tools that you can use on these clients are

▓ Event Viewer	Workstation/95
▓ Server Manager	Workstation/95
▓ User Manager for Domains	Workstation/95
▓ DHCP Manager	Workstation
▓ Remote Access Administrator	Workstation
▓ Remoteboot Manager	Workstation
▓ Services for Macintosh Manager	Workstation
▓ WINS Manager	Workstation
▓ User Profile Editor	Workstation

In addition, you will find on a Windows 95 computer that extensions have been added to the Windows 95 Explorer and Network Neighborhood after you install the server tools. Those extensions allow you to manipulate NTFS permissions on Windows NT Servers to which you have access.

NOTE

In order to use any of the server tools, you must be logged on to the network and have the correct administrative-level permissions on the computer that is the target of the utility's actions.

Source Files for the Server Tools

The source files for these tools are on the Windows NT source CD in the \Clients directory. You can use the CD to install the tools on each client, or you can create a network share for the tools when you have to do multiple installations. The simplest method for creating a shared folder is to work with the Network Client Administrator tool. You can see the opening dialog box for this utility in Figure 18.22. Simply select Copy Client-based Network Administration Tools, and then click the Continue button.

FIGURE 18.22.

The Network Client Administrator utility can be used to copy the server tools to a shared folder.

The next dialog box that appears is used to designate the destination directory you want to use for the shared folder (see Figure 18.23). Click the Copy Files to a New Directory option, and then click Share. Enter the disk and directory that you want the utility to create for the files in the Destination Path field. In the Share Name field, you can accept the default name or enter one of your choosing.

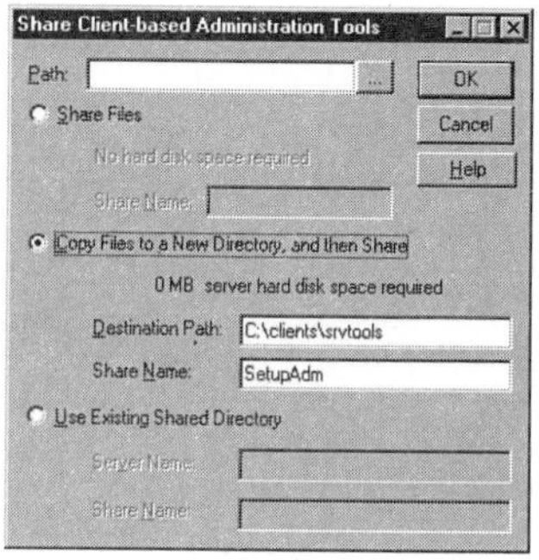

FIGURE 18.23.

Specify the location that will be used to store the files and the name for the share.

After you click the OK button, the utility copies the files and automatically creates the share on the server for you. You can then connect clients to this share when you install the server tools using the network.

18

REMOTE ADMINISTRATION

For more information on this see Chapter 24, "Network Client Administrator."

Installing the Server Tools

The process for installing the server tools on your Windows 95 or Windows NT Workstation clients is quite simple. You use the Add/Remove Programs applet from the Control Panel. You should first insert the Windows NT Server source CD into the computer's CD drive, or you should connect to the network share that holds the client files.

1. Double-click the Add/Remove Programs applet. When it appears, select the Windows NT Setup tab (see Figure 18.24).

FIGURE 18.24.

Installing the Server Tools using the Add/Remove Programs applet.

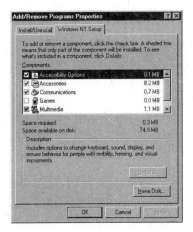

2. Click the Have Disk button. This brings up another dialog box, prompting you for the location of the source files. This should be *<driveletter>*:\clients\srvtools \win95 if you are using the CD. You should use the network share name if you are accessing the files that way.

3. The Setup program reads the .INF file in that directory and then allows you to select the programs to install. In this case (see Figure 18.25) there is only one choice: the Windows NT Server Tools. Select the check box, click the Install button, and click the OK button.

4. The Setup program then copies files and returns you to the Add/Remove Programs dialog box. Click the OK button to close this dialog box.

5. Windows 95 clients should now edit the Autoexec.bat file and add the following to the path variable: **c:\SRVTOOLS**.

6. Although you are not prompted to do so, you should now reboot the computer. The server tools are not available until you do.

FIGURE 18.25.
Select the programs to install.

To use the server tools, look under Start|Programs|Windows NT Server Tools. When you use them from an NT Workstation, you participate in NT authentication, so no further security information is needed. Windows 95 clients are prompted for a valid username and password, which are used to authenticate access in the domain.

Other Windows NT Tools

One of Windows NT's biggest strengths is its networking. Supporting multiple network protocols for different client types at the same time requires sophisticated management and configuration tools. The Dynamic Host Configuration Protocol (DHCP) and the Windows Internet Naming Service (WINS), along with the traditional Domain Name Service (DNS), help make it easier to connect clients and to locate computers on the network. The tools provided for these protocols and services can be used to administer them throughout the network. For example, the WINS service allows you to set up replication partners for WINS servers, so that they can exchange computer registration information.

Chapter 11, "Dynamic Host Configuration Protocol (DHCP)," Chapter 12, "Windows Internet Naming Service (WINS)," and Chapter 13, "Domain Name Service (DNS)," cover these three topics at great length. Although not strictly a remote administration topic, you should be aware of how these services operate and the management tools used with them.

System Management Server (SMS)

If you need further control over the computers in your network, you may consider the BackOffice component known as System Management Server (SMS). You need to also have installed Microsoft SQL Server to use SMS, so it's not an inexpensive or simple product. However, with SMS you can automate many of the most tedious system administration jobs, such as installing new software applications or performing a hardware and software inventory of your computers. You can automate these tasks to be performed remotely by using SMS.

Summary

This chapter covered the remote administration capabilities of many Windows NT Server administrative utilities, as well as other applications that can be acquired by installing the Windows NT Server 4.0 Resource Kit. You can do almost all major user and network administrative chores without having to be present at each individual computer. The Web Administration Kit even allows you to administer servers using a Web browser across a WAN. The BackOffice family of products includes System Management Server, which can also be used to further control computer administration remotely.

Understanding the Registry

by Jason Garms

IN THIS CHAPTER

The Registry is one of those pervasive items in Windows NT that plays an enormous role in making everything work. It is also often the biggest source of mystery for neophytes and experts alike. If you ever plan on doing anything more than a cursory amount of system administration, you will need to become familiar with the Registry, how it works, and how to make changes to it. The sooner you develop this knowledge, the more it will benefit you and the more proficient you will become at your job.

This chapter provides an overview of the Windows NT Registry, including how to examine and change data recorded in the Registry with programs such as the Registry Editor and Windows NT Diagnostics.

> **NOTE**
>
> The Windows NT Registry database contains thousands of items. For the best coverage of what each setting does, refer to the first volume of the *Windows NT Resource Kit*, the *Windows NT Resource Guide*.

By the end of this chapter you should have the tools and knowledge you need to be comfortable working with the Windows NT Registry database—one of the basic skills necessary for administering Windows NT systems.

The Windows NT Registry Database

Windows NT stores all its configuration information in a hierarchical database called the Registry. The Registry contains user, application, hardware, and operating system information, and replaces the .INI files from Windows 3.x. It also provides configuration security and multiuser support in a more extensible and adaptable framework than is provided in Windows 3.x.

The first thing you must know about the Registry is that making invalid changes to it can result in system instability or complete failure of the operating system to boot. Whenever Microsoft support personnel issue tech notes describing changes that must be made to the Registry to fix a problem or implement a desired feature, they are always careful to include a lengthy disclaimer indicating that making changes to the Registry could make a system unusable and should only be done by knowledgeable people. Most responsible authors also include such a statement by way of disclaimer.

> **WARNING**
>
> Using the Registry Editor to make changes to the Registry can result in unexpected results when misused. You should fully understand how to use the Registry Editor and the exact purpose of any changes before making them. Even if you fully understand what changes

you are making, there is still the possibility that you might make a mistake because the Registry doesn't use any form of syntax or validity checking when you make changes. Therefore, you should also have a recently updated copy of your system's Emergency Repair Disk (ERD), as well as an understanding of how to recover from failed attempts at editing the Registry, which is discussed later in this chapter.

Now that I've put in that disclaimer, I think it's also important to note that it is much easier to recover from mistakes while editing the NT Registry than it is while editing the .INI files with Windows 3.x. Also, many sources, including some Microsoft documentation, say that you should never need to make direct changes to the Registry because most changes that must be made can be effected through other, less perilous utilities. This is true of the average user. There is no reason that an average user should need to make changes. However, as a system and network administrator, you *must* understand how to make the changes, because you will need to edit the Registry occasionally to keep your system working properly.

NOTE

Many people are surprised when I tell them that Windows 3.x also contains a Registry. However, the Windows 3.x Registry is not very sophisticated and plays a much smaller role than does the NT Registry. The Windows 3.x Registry contains only information on the OLE classes, as well as associations that link file extensions (such as .DOC) to applications.

Looking at Design Goals for the Registry

When Microsoft programmers designed Windows NT, they recognized the need for a better way to manage configuration information than the simple .INI files used in Windows 3.x. In particular, they needed a means of providing certain functionality that could not be provided by the .INI files, including the following:

■ **Single repository for configuration information.** If you've been burdened with the task of managing Windows 3.x systems with many different software packages, then you're familiar with the trouble of locating the often buried and hidden configuration files for different parts of the operating system or software packages. For a particular application, the information might be stored in the SYSTEM.INI, WIN.INI, or an .INI file created by the application itself and stored in C:\WINDOWS, C:\WINDOWS\SYSTEM, or even in the application's own directory. Worse yet, configuration information for a particular application might even be stored in more than one location. The NT Registry database alleviates this problem by providing a single place for applications to register configuration settings.

■ **Support for multiple users on a single computer.** With .INI files, it is difficult to provide users with their own set of personalized options. With .INI files, all users on a single computer are forced to share configuration information, which often leads to a lot of annoyances; if one user makes a change to fit his or her preference, it affects all other users on the computer. NT's security paradigm requires a user to have a confidential set of preferences. The Windows NT Registry supports each user having his or her own preferences for both operating functions and applications.

■ **Granular security for configuration settings.** With Windows 3.x, many different configuration settings are set in a single .INI file. To provide security, or some degree of configuration management, you must choose one of two methods: Either protect the entire .INI file and prevent users from changing it, or don't protect the .INI file, permitting users to make *any* changes. There is no finer level of granularity. However, with the Registry, you can protect each entry in the Registry database with an access control list (ACL), which lists the exact rights granted to any users or groups to a particular Registry value, permitting you to grant read-only access to guest users but a higher level of access to domain users, for example.

■ **Multiple levels of hierarchy.** One of the restrictions of the .INI files is that they permitted only two levels of hierarchy. Within a specific .INI file, you can specify a *section name* and then include several *entries* under each section. There is no extensibility to provide further nesting of entries. For example, in the SYSTEM.INI file, there is a section called [boot], which contains several entries, such as shell, network.drv, drivers, and so on. You cannot create a new section that is subordinate to [boot], and this is a great limitation, especially as software is becoming increasingly complex. With the NT Registry, however, you can create deeply nested sections, so that you can organize configuration information in a more logical manner.

■ **Inclusion of rich data types.** With .INI files, you can use only standard ASCII text for all entries. This limits the type of data that can be stored in the .INI files, thereby limiting their usefulness. In contrast, the NT Registry supports extended data types, including not only standard human-readable text, but also binary data, which can even include executable code segments. In addition, Registry information can be stored in 16-bit Unicode format, instead of simple 8-bit ASCII representation.

NOTE

Windows NT still supports the use of .INI files, particularly for programs that are still not written to take advantage of the Registry. In particular, .INI files must be maintained for 16-bit Windows applications because the Win32 API is needed to access the Registry. Because Microsoft heavily favors the use of the Registry, and because Windows 95 also uses a Registry database, Microsoft has made it a requirement for programmers to use the Registry for storing information if they want the Windows 95 logo on their package.

Examining the Structure of the Registry

The Registry database uses a hierarchical format with five main branches. Before going any further, let's look at some of the vocabulary used when dealing with the Registry:

- **Root key.** There are five main, or root, *keys* in the Registry database. These contain information that is specific to either the user or the computer. Think of a root key as being similar to a partition on the local computer, that is, c:, d:, e:, f:.

- **Subkey.** Each root key contains one or more *subkeys*. If the root key is like a partition on the computer, a subkey is like a folder or directory on that computer. Each subkey can have one or more subkeys under it, similar to the nesting of directories on your hard drive.

- **Value entry.** Continuing our analogy, a *value entry* is like a file. Whereas root keys and subkeys are good for organizing information, it is the value entry that actually contains the data. Value entries contain three pieces of information: a *name*, a *data type*, and a *value*. These are discussed subsequently.

- **Hive.** A hive consists of a particular set of keys, with their dependent subkeys and value entries, contained in the Registry. The hive is stored in a single file in the %SystemRoot%\system32\config directory, along with an associated .LOG file.

> **NOTE**
>
> People commonly misunderstand the difference between a Registry hive and a root key. Quite simply, root keys are at the highest level and are made up of one or more hives. However, some root keys, such as HKEY_CLASSES_ROOT, HKEY_CURRENT_USER, and HKEY_CURRENT_CONFIG, don't actually have their own hives, but rather point to information stored in other hives.

Root Keys in the Registry

As mentioned previously, the Registry is made up of five root keys, each represented as a subtree of the Registry itself. Each root key contains subkeys and value entries that contain all the configuration information for the NT system and its users. The five root keys are listed and described in Table 19.1.

Table 19.1. Registry root keys.

Root Key	Description
HKEY_LOCAL_MACHINE	This is the root key that contains the most interesting information. It contains information on the hardware such as processor

continues

Table 19.1. continued

Root Key	Description
	type, bus architecture, video, and disk I/O hardware. It also contains software information for the operating system, including information on device drivers, services, security, and installed software.
HKEY_CLASSES_ROOT	This key is similar to the functionally limited Registry included with Windows 3.x. It contains information on file associations (matching a file extension to an application), as well as acts as the repository for OLE classes. This root key points to data stored in the HKEY_LOCAL_MACHINE\SOFTWARE\Classes subkey.
HKEY_CURRENT_USER	This key contains the profile information for the user currently logged onto the console. It contains user-level preferences for the operating system, as well as for applications installed on the computer. This key is a pointer to one of the subkeys stored in HKEY_USERS.
HKEY_USERS	This key contains a pointer to the hive for the user currently logged on at the console, as well as a pointer to the hive for the default user. In neither case does HKEY_USERS contain profiles for users who log on remotely.

> **NOTE**
>
> Functionality for this key has changed in Windows NT 4. In previous versions, this key contains the profiles for *all* users who had logged on at the console of the computer. However, because of the changes to the user profiles in NT 4, much of the functionality of this hive has changed, and its usefulness is now mostly to support backward-compatibility for programs that access this hive directly.

HKEY_CURRENT_CONFIG	This is a new root key in Windows NT 4. It contains the current hardware configuration information, as specified by the current hardware profile. It actually points to the same contents as the HKEY_LOCAL_MACHINE\SYSTEM\CurrentControlSet\Hardware Profiles\Current subkey.

Locating an Entry in the Registry

Whenever you need to make a modification to the Registry, you will need the path to the value entry, just as you would need to know the path to locate a disk resource. The Registry path for locating a resource contains the following:

- The name of the root key
- The name of each subkey
- The name of the value entry

For example, to locate the value that sets the current maximum size the Registry can grow to, you would need to know the following:

- The root key name: `HKEY_LOCAL_MACHINE`
- The name of each subkey:
  - `SYSTEM`
  - `CurrentControlSet`
  - `Control`
- The name of the value entry: `RegistrySizeLimit`

The path for locating this Registry value entry is commonly written as `HKEY_LOCAL_MACHINE\SYSTEM\CurrentControlSet\Control\RegistrySizeLimit`.

NOTE

This value entry might not exist on your system. If it does not exist, the default maximum Registry size of 12MB is used. This key might exist on Windows NT 4 computers on which you upgraded from previous versions of NT Server, or if you had previously used the System Control Panel to change the maximum Registry size.

Knowing this path permits you to locate the value entry. Each value entry has a *data type* and *value*. If a value entry already exists, you can use Registry Editor to see its data type. However, if you need to create a new value entry, you *must* know the correct data type. For instance, the data type for `RegistrySizeLimit` is `REG_DWORD`, and the value can be between 4MB and 102MB.

NOTE

Here is a perfect example of where you should *not* use the Registry Editor to make changes. The Registry Size Limit can be set using the System Control Panel, which is the method you *should* use. Because the Registry Editor does not perform any verification when you enter a new value, you could enter a value that causes problems. Fortunately in this instance, if you set the value too high, you won't cause any major problems, and if you set the value too low, NT will automatically default to 4MB, which is the smallest value permitted for this entry. However, making changes to many other value entries could cause system failure if you were to enter an invalid value.

19

UNDERSTANDING THE REGISTRY

The information for setting a value entry is often written in the format

```
name:data type:value
```

For instance, if you used the System Control Panel applet to change the maximum Registry size to 20MB, the complete information for the `RegistrySizeLimit` value entry would be as follows:

```
RegistrySizeLimit:REG_DWORD:0x1400000
```

> **NOTE**
>
> By default, the Registry Editor uses hexadecimal notation for displaying numbers, as indicated by the `0x` preface on the value `0x1400000`, which is equal to 20,971,520 bytes in decimal notation—or 20 megabytes. Remember, one megabyte equals 1,024 times 1,024 bytes. When using the Registry Editor, you can view numeric entries in decimal, hexadecimal, or binary format.

Windows NT recognizes five data types for Registry entry values. These values are shown in Table 19.2.

Table 19.2. Data types for Registry entry values.

Data Type Name	Description
REG_BINARY	**Binary.** A value entry of this data type contains machine-readable information. You should never have to edit this type by hand. Many of the value entries of type `REG_BINARY` have to do with hardware configuration on the system and appear under the `HKEY_LOCAL_MACHINE\HARDWARE` subkey. An example is `HKEY_LOCAL_MACHINE\HARDWARE\DESCRIPTION\System\Component Information`: `Component Information:REG_BINARY:00 00 00 00 ...`
REG_DWORD	**Double word.** The double word data type represents a number up to 4 bytes long (traditionally one *word* is 2 bytes). By default, this data type is displayed in hexadecimal format, although you can also display it in binary or decimal format. `HKEY_LOCAL_MACHINE\SYSTEM\CurrentControlSet\Control\RegistrySizeLimit` uses the `REG_DWORD` data type: `RegistrySizeLimit:REG_DWORD:0x1400000`

Data Type Name	Description
REG_SZ	**Readable text.** Values entries of type REG_SZ contain human-readable text and often involve a description or identification. This is a common data type. HKEY_LOCAL_MACHINE\SOFTWARE\Microsoft\Windows NT\ CurrentVersion\RegisteredOwner is an example of a value entry that uses a REG_SZ data type: RegisteredOwner:REG_SZ:Jason Garms
REG_EXPAND_SZ	**Expandable data string.** An expandable data string is similar to a standard REG_SZ, except that it contains a system variable that will be replaced when it is accessed by an application. For instance, HKEY_LOCAL_MACHINE\SOFTWARE\Microsoft\Windows\CurrentVersion \DevicePath is defined as type REG_EXPAND_SZ: DevicePath:REG_EXPAND_SZ:%SystemRoot%\Media When a program accesses this key, however, it will not get the string %SystemRoot%\Media but rather C:\WINNT\Media—if you installed Windows NT in the C:\WINNT directory.
REG_MULTI_SZ	**Multiple string.** A value entry of this type contains a list of values, separated by NULL characters. For example, HKEY_LOCAL_MACHINE\SYSTEM\CurrentControlSet\Services\EventLog \Application\Sources is of type REG_MULTI_SZ:Sources:REG_ MULTI_SZ:WinsCtrs Winlogon Userenv ...

NOTE

There is a sixth data type you might see in use in the Registry, REG_FULL_RESOURCE_ DESCRIPTOR. It is not listed in Table 19.2 because you cannot create value entries or edit existing values of this type. Most value keys of this type appear in the HKEY_LOCAL_ MACHINE\HARDWARE subkey. For example, HKEY_LOCAL_MACHINE\HARDWARE\DESCRIPTION\ System\Configuration Data, which is shown using the Registry Editor in Figure 19.1, is of data type REG_FULL_RESOURCE_DESCRIPTOR.

NOTE

The maximum size for any single Registry value entry is 1MB.

19

UNDERSTANDING THE REGISTRY

FIGURE 19.1.

You can't create or edit data types of REG_FULL_ RESOURCE_DESCRIPTOR.

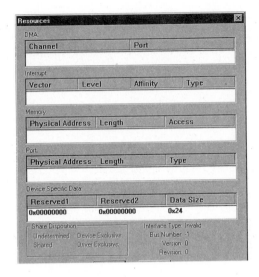

Registry Hives

A hive is a discrete set of keys, subkeys, and value entries contained in the Registry. Each hive is stored in a single file in the %SystemRoot%\system32\config directory, along with an associated .LOG file. Figure 19.2 is an Explorer window for %SystemRoot%\system32\config, showing the Registry hives and their log files.

FIGURE 19.2.

Each Registry hive corresponds to a particular file and .LOG *file in the* %SystemRoot%\system32 \config *directory.*

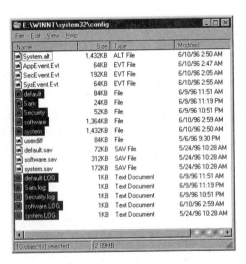

The Registry hives and their associated files are shown in Table 19.3.

> **NOTE**
>
> There is a Registry value entry that is used to point to the location of all the Registry hives:
> `HKEY_LOCAL_MACHINE\SYSTEM\CurrentControlSet\Control\hivelist`. It should not be modified.

Table 19.3. Registry hives and their files.

Registry Hive	Associated Files
`HKEY_LOCAL_MACHINE\SAM`	`%SystemRoot%\System32\config\SAM`
	`%SystemRoot%\System32\config\SAM.LOG`
`HKEY_LOCAL_MACHINE\SECURITY`	`%SystemRoot%\System32\config\SECURITY`
	`%SystemRoot%\System32\config\SECURITY.LOG`
`HKEY_LOCAL_MACHINE\SOFTWARE`	`%SystemRoot%\System32\config\SOFTWARE`
	`%SystemRoot%\System32\config\SOFTWARE.LOG`
`HKEY_LOCAL_MACHINE\SYSTEM`	`%SystemRoot%\System32\config\SYSTEM`
	`%SystemRoot%\System32\config\SYSTEM.LOG`
`HKEY_USERS\.DEFAULT`	`%SystemRoot%\System32\config\DEFAULT`
	`%SystemRoot%\System32\config\DEFAULT.LOG`
`HKEY_CURRENT_USER`	`%SytemRoot%\Profiles\%UserName%\NTUSER.DAT`
	`%SytemRoot%\Profiles\%UserName%\NTUSER.LOG`

> **NOTE**
>
> The `HKEY_LOCAL_MACHINE\HARDWARE` key is a dynamic subkey that is generated every time Windows NT is booted by the NT hardware recognizer (`NTDETECT.COM`) and the NT kernel. Although `HKEY_LOCAL_MACHINE\HARDWARE` is technically a Registry hive, it is stored as an internal structure in the system's memory rather than on disk. In the event of system failure, no valuable data is lost because it is reconstructed from scratch during each system boot.

19

UNDERSTANDING THE REGISTRY

> **NOTE**
>
> Sometimes people have a hard time relating the root keys to the Registry hives. Remember, there are five root keys, but they don't all have corresponding hives. This is because the root keys HKEY_CLASSES_ROOT, HKEY_CURRENT_USER, and HKEY_CURRENT_CONFIG actually point to information stored in other hives.

Fault Tolerance with the Registry Log Files

Each Registry hive has a corresponding log file, as shown in Figure 19.2. The log files are provided to ensure the stability of the Registry database, even in the event of a system failure during a Registry update. This procedure works in much the same way that NTFS ensures the stability of the file system in the event of a system failure.

When an update is made to the Registry, NT records the beginning of it in the appropriate hive's log. It then proceeds through the update by recording what change is being made, as well as how to roll back the change to the original state. This information is recorded in the log for each Registry property being updated. When all properties are updated, the change is committed and recorded in the log. At this point—and only at this point—is the transaction complete. If there is a power outage or system failure before the transaction is marked as being complete, when NT reboots or the system failure is repaired, NT uses the information in the hive's log file to roll back the transaction and restore the Registry to a stable state.

> **NOTE**
>
> Many people get mistaken ideas about what is being described here. When you make a change that affects multiple Registry entries, NT does not ensure that they will all be updated, or that none of them will be updated. What it does guarantee is that for any discrete transaction, either the *entire* transaction will succeed, or none of the transaction will succeed.
>
> For example, if you modify an existing key and the computer is turned off in the middle of updating the Registry, you will not get a new value with an old timestamp. Or, if you were adding several users to the ACL on a Registry value entry and the power failed, you would not end up with some of the users in the ACL to the exclusion of others. You would get none of them if the transaction failed, or all of them if the transaction was committed before the power failure.

The HKEY_LOCAL_MACHINE\SYSTEM hive is an important part of the NT boot process, so it cannot be left in an unstable state when the system is booted. To protect against this possibility, NT keeps an alternate copy of the HKEY_LOCAL_MACHINE\SYSTEM hive in a file called %SystemRoot%\System32\config\SYSTEM.ALT.

When you make changes to the Registry that affect the HKEY_LOCAL_MACHINE\SYSTEM hive, the changes are first applied to the actual system hive, then to the alternate hive. If there is a system failure during the updates to the alternate hive, there is no problem, and after the system boots, NT updates the alternate hive to again be an exact copy of the actual system hive. However, if there is a failure *during* an update to the actual system hive, when NT reboots it detects that the system hive is dirty, so instead it boots using the alternate hive, which is in an older but stable state. It then rolls back changes to the original system hive.

This kind of fault tolerance helps to ensure that NT will always boot up clean, no matter what might occur.

Recovering the Registry Using the Last Known Good Configuration

Much of the information necessary for Windows NT to start up is stored in the HKEY_LOCAL_MACHINE\SYSTEM\CurrentControlSet subkey. If you—or a program on your system—make invalid changes to one of the value entries in this subkey, your system could fail to boot. Alternatively, if it does boot, it could prevent you from logging on.

To help protect against these kinds of accidental problems, NT keeps copies of the HKEY_LOCAL_MACHINE\SYSTEM\CurrentControlSet in HKEY_LOCAL_MACHINE\SYSTEM\ControlSet001 and HKEY_LOCAL_MACHINE\SYSTEM\ControlSet002.

If your NT system fails during startup and you suspect it has something to do with a Registry change you just made or a device you just installed, you can tell NT to use the backup version of the control set by pressing the spacebar during the boot process when NT displays the message Press spacebar NOW to invoke Last Known Good Menu.

When you invoke this option, you lose any changes made to the Registry since the last time a user successfully logged on to the system.

> **NOTE**
>
> It is only after a user successfully logs on to the console of an NT system that the NT boot process is determined to be a success and the last known good configuration information is updated.

Using the Registry Editor

The Registry Editor is the primary tool used to directly manipulate the Registry database. By default, when you install Windows NT, no icon is created for the Registry Editor. In fact, to make things a little more complicated, Microsoft included two different Registry Editors with

Windows NT 4, REGEDT32.EXE and REGEDIT.EXE. For many common functions, you can use either of these tools; however, REGEDT32.EXE is the correct tool for use with Windows NT.

The REGEDIT.EXE tool is actually the same version of the Registry Editor that ships with Windows 95. Although it supports a few interesting features that you can take advantage of, it has numerous shortcomings for use with Windows NT. There are many occasions when you could even use both versions of the Registry Editor side by side.

NOTE

Actually, Microsoft programmers included two Registry Editors with Windows NT 3.5 and 3.51 as well. The difference is that, with 3.5 and 3.51, they included the Windows 3.x version of the Registry Editor. When an unsuspecting administrator looked for the NT Registry Editor and accidentally stumbled across the 3.x version instead, it was very noticeable, so he or she continued looking until they found the correct program, REGEDT32.EXE. However, with Windows NT 4, Microsoft included the Windows 95 Registry Editor, which looks very similar to the Windows NT Registry Editor, and it can even perform most of the actions that people need. Thus, the administrator might not notice the difference.

To make matters worse, if you upgrade to NT 4 from Windows 3.x, or from a Windows NT 3.x version that has been upgraded from a Windows 3.x version, NT 4 will leave the Windows 3.x limited Registry Editor, which is also called REGEDIT.EXE. If this happens and you want to install the Windows 95 version, you can copy it from the NT installation CD. You must copy REGEDIT.EXE, REGEDIT.HLP, and REGEDIT.CNT to the %SystemRoot% directory. This will replace the existing Windows 3.x version.

TIP

You should use REGEDT32.EXE to make any changes to the Registry database. However, there are uses for the Windows 95 REGEDIT.EXE program as well.

The two major advantages of the Windows 95 REGEDIT.EXE follow:

- **Enhanced find capabilities.** The REGEDIT.EXE program enables you to perform finds using information found in the key or subkey name, the value entry name, or even data contained in the value itself, as shown in Figure 19.3.

  This is far superior to the basic find support in the REGEDT32.EXE program, which only enables you to search for keys and subkeys. REGEDT32.EXE does not enable you to perform searches based on value entry names or actual data values.

FIGURE 19.3.

`REGEDIT.EXE` *has better find support than* `REGEDT32.EXE`.

- **Full Windows 95 user interface support.** The `REGEDIT.EXE` program takes full advantage of the Windows 95–style interface. It enables you to view all the root keys in a single window, much like the Explorer-style interface. This is unlike the `REGEDT32.EXE` program, which still uses the old Windows 3.1–style interface and displays each root key in a separate window. In addition, `REGEDIT.EXE` makes use of right-clicking. You can right-click a subkey to delete it, rename it, perform a find, and many other functions. One of the most useful features of right-clicking a subkey is the option Copy Key Name, as shown in Figure 19.4. This enables you to get all the spelling and punctuation correct if you need to copy the subkey to another location.

FIGURE 19.4.

You can right-click to copy the full name of the subkey with all the correct spellings and syntax.

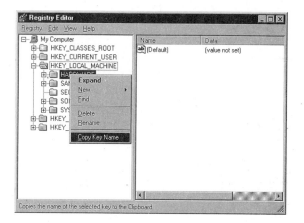

The three main limitations of the `REGEDIT.EXE` tool when used with Windows NT 4 follow:

- **Lack of security interface.** Because the `REGEDIT.EXE` tool was made for Windows 95, which lacks a means of protecting the Registry, the `REGEDIT.EXE` tool does not have any options for viewing or modifying Registry security provided by Windows NT. This also means that you have no means of configuring auditing for Registry data.

- **Lack of support for the `REG_MULTI_SZ` and `REG_EXPAND_SZ` data types.** Windows 95 does not support the `REG_MULTI_SZ` or `REG_EXPAND_SZ` data types. This means that if you use the `REGEDIT.EXE` utility to view value entries of type `REG_MULTI_SZ` or `REG_EXPAND_SZ`, they are displayed as type `REG_SZ`. Also, you cannot use the `REGEDIT.EXE` utility to create value entries of type `REG_MULTI_SZ` or `REG_EXPAND_SZ`.

19

UNDERSTANDING
THE REGISTRY

■ **Only basic printing support provided.** The printed output generated by the `REGEDIT.EXE` program is rudimentary at best. For better and more accurate Registry output, use `REGEDT32.EXE`.

Creating a Registry Editor Icon

As mentioned earlier, there is no icon created for either version of the Registry Editor when Windows NT is installed. You invoke the Windows 95 Registry Editor by choosing Run from the Start menu, and then typing `REGEDIT.EXE`. Alternatively, you can start the Windows NT version of the Registry Editor by choosing Run from the Start menu, and then typing `REGEDT32.EXE`.

To create an icon that is visible to all users who log on to the NT Server console, follow these steps:

1. Right-click the Start button and choose Open All Users. An Explorer window appears.
2. Double-click the Programs icon in the Explorer window shown in Figure 19.5. This brings up another Explorer window.

FIGURE 19.5.

The All Users profile contains a Programs icon, which contains common Start menu items for all users who log on to the system's console.

3. Double-click the Administrative Tools icon. This brings up an Explorer window that shows existing shortcuts to many of the NT administrative tools, as shown in Figure 19.6.

FIGURE 19.6.

The Administrative Tools folder contains shortcuts to many of the common NT administrative tools.

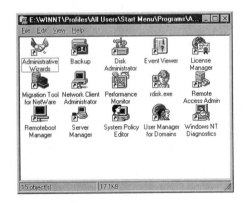

4. From the File menu, choose New, then choose Shortcut. The Create Shortcut window appears.

5. Type REGEDT32 into the Command Line box, then click the Next button. Click the Finish button.

6. Close all the Explorer windows.

REGEDT32 now appears with all the other administrative tools in the Start menu, as shown in Figure 19.7.

FIGURE 19.7.

The shortcut to the
REGEDT32 *utility now*
appears with the rest of
the shortcuts in the
Start menu.

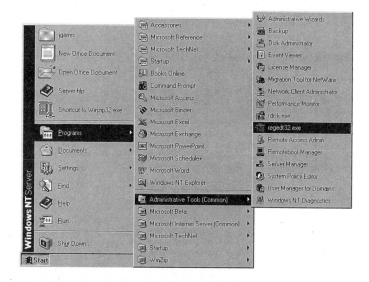

NOTE

To create a shortcut to the Windows 95 version of the Registry Editor, repeat this procedure and type REGEDIT instead of REGEDT32 in step 5.

Using the Registry Editor

Now that you have an understanding of some of the basic concepts behind the Registry, let's look at how to use the Registry Editor tool to browse through and make changes to the Registry.

19

UNDERSTANDING
THE REGISTRY

NOTE

Because REGEDT32 is the correct method of editing the Registry (rather than REGEDIT), this section focuses on using REGEDT32.

Open REGEDT32 from the shortcut you created in the previous section, or by choosing the Run option from the Start menu, and then typing REGEDT32. When REGEDT32 opens, it displays the five root keys, each in its own individual window, as shown in Figure 19.8.

FIGURE 19.8.

Each root key is displayed in its own window.

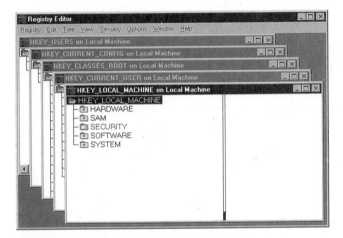

TIP

If you simply want to browse through the Registry without making changes, you could choose Read Only Mode from the Options menu to avoid making accidental modifications.

To see the Registry Editor in action, let's look at a real-world example. The most common use you'll find for the Registry Editor (aside from just looking around and seeing where everything is) is to change default settings in Windows NT to settings that are better suited to your particular environment.

By default, whenever you send a print job with Windows NT, it generates a print job audit in the System Log, as shown with the Event Viewer in Figure 19.9.

Perhaps in your particular environment, this is a nuisance and you'd like to disable it. Well, there is no simple method of making this change, at least not using the normal administrative tools such as Print Manager or the Printer Wizards. So you look it up in the Microsoft TechNet CD-ROM reference to see if there is a method of disabling this print audit, and you come across TechNet article Q115841, "Turning Off Print Job Logging in the System Log."

FIGURE 19.9.

Windows NT generates an audit each time a print job is completed.

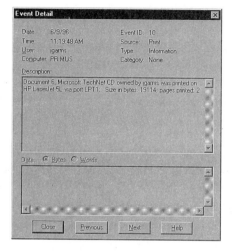

It tells you to go to the subkey `HKEY_LOCAL_MACHINE\SYSTEM\CurrentControlSet\Control \Print\Providers` and create a new value entry as follows:

`EventLog:REG_DWORD:0`

To make this modification, follow these steps:

NOTE

To perform the following procedure, you must be logged on as a user with local administrative rights.

1. Open the Registry Editor.

TIP

When you open REGEDT32, the root keys are each listed in their own window, and the windows are cascaded, as shown in Figure 19.8. However, for easier viewing, you should maximize the HKEY_LOCAL_MACHINE on the Local Machine window, by either double-clicking its title bar or clicking its maximize icon. The screen should now look similar to Figure 19.10.

FIGURE 19.10.

Maximize the root key window for easier viewing.

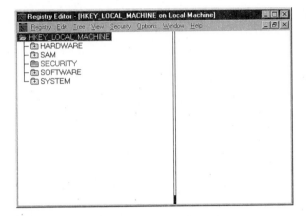

NOTE

The ability to display multiple document windows within a single program window, such as with the Registry Editor, is called the Windows Multiple Document Interface (MDI). I find that this is often a confusing point and worth pointing out. Often when I explain to someone that they should maximize the MDI child—the HKEY_LOCAL_MACHINE window in the example above—they mistakenly maximize the MDI parent window instead—the Registry Editor, in this case.

2. Now you must go down the Registry tree to locate the value entry specified in the TechNet article. Double-click the SYSTEM entry on the left side of the HKEY_LOCAL_MACHINE on the Local Machine window. Continue traversing the tree in this method until you end up at the HKEY_LOCAL_MACHINE\SYSTEM\CurrentControlSet \Control\Print\Providers subkey, as shown in Figure 19.11.

3. When you're there, make sure you've selected the Providers entry on the left side of the window. This displays a few entry values on the right side of the window, including the EventLog value key you are looking for.

4. One of the first things you'll probably notice is that the EventLog value entry already exists, although the knowledge base article said that you need to create it, don't worry. It is not uncommon for the knowledge base article to contain information that does not match your system. If you look back at the TechNet article, you'll see that it's pretty old and specifically covers Windows NT version 3.1. (My copy of the article is dated September 19, 1994.) This is a good lesson, because Microsoft continuously updates and makes changes to the default Registry settings. Although the article is old and Microsoft has since changed NT so that the EventLog value entry exists by default, the article is still good. This example demonstrates that it still works.

FIGURE 19.11.

Locate the
HKEY_LOCAL_MACHINE
\SYSTEM\CurrentControlSet
\Control\Print\Providers
subkey.

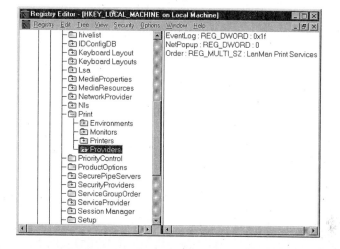

NOTE

Microsoft is continuously changing the default values in the Registry, as well as which keys exist by default and which do not. However, if you understand the process, you can determine the correct course of action when making changes to the Registry.

5. To gain experience working with the Registry Editor, go ahead and delete the existing value entry and re-create it. First, note the current value of the EventLog value entry. It is probably 0x1f (or 31 in decimal notation). Also note that the value entry is defined as a REG_DWORD data type.

6. Click the EventLog entry in the right side of the window. It should now be highlighted. Choose Delete from the Edit menu, or push the Delete key on the keyboard. You will be warned that the value entry will be deleted and asked to confirm the delete.

7. Click Yes. The entry value should be gone from the list on the right.

8. Now go ahead and create the new value entry. Make sure the Providers subkey is still highlighted in the left side of the window and choose Add Value from the Edit menu. The Add Value dialog box should appear as shown in Figure 19.12.

FIGURE 19.12.

The Add Value dialog box is used to specify the value entry name and data type for a new value entry.

19

UNDERSTANDING THE REGISTRY

9. Type `EventLog` in the Value Name field.

10. Take a quick look through the Data Type pick list. You'll see that you can define the value entry as one of five data types (see Table 19.2). Choose the type `REG_DWORD`, as per the directions in the knowledge base article. The completed Add Value dialog box is shown in Figure 19.13.

FIGURE 19.13.

The value name and the data type are entered using the information given in the TechNet article.

11. Click OK. This will bring up the DWORD Editor dialog box, shown in Figure 19.14. You can enter information here in hexadecimal, decimal, or binary.

CAUTION

By default, the DWORD Editor dialog box expects data to be entered in hexadecimal format.

FIGURE 19.14.

The DWORD Editor dialog box is used to enter the 4-byte DWORD value.

12. Type a 0 (zero) into the Data field, as specified by the directions in the TechNet article, and click OK.

The `EventLog` value entry with a value of 0 should now appear in the `HKEY_LOCAL_MACHINE` `\SYSTEM\CurrentControlSet\Control\Print\Providers` subkey, as shown in Figure 19.15.

Now test the system to see if the knowledge base article is correct. This change doesn't take effect right away because most system components only read their Registry configurations when they start up. You could restart the computer to see if it works, or you could simply stop and then restart the print spooler, which is the piece of software that generated the event log entries. At a command prompt, issue the command `net stop spooler` and then `net start spooler`.

FIGURE 19.15.

The newly created
EventLog *entry appears
on the right side of the
window.*

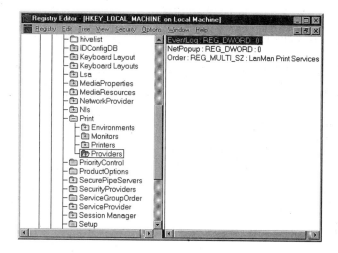

Open WordPad or Notepad, type a few characters, and then print the document. Next, open the Event Viewer and look at the System Log. Is there an entry for the print job you just sent? There shouldn't be. Next, restore the EventLog value entry to its original setting to see if the print job auditing returns. Follow these steps:

1. If you closed REGEDT32, reopen it and relocate the EventLog value entry.

2. Double-click the EventLog value entry. This brings up the DWORD Editor dialog box. The Data field should contain a 0. Change this back to 1f (that is, hexadecimal 1f, which is 31 in decimal notation), as shown in Figure 19.16.

FIGURE 19.16.

Change the EventLog
*value entry back to
hexadecimal value* 1f.

3. Click OK. You should see the change reflected in the right side of the Registry Editor window, which should show the following:

```
EventLog:REG_DWORD:0x1f
```

Let's find out if this has in fact re-enabled the print job auditing. From a command prompt, issue the command net stop spooler and then net start spooler.

Open WordPad or Notepad again, type a few characters, and then print it. Reopen the Event Viewer and look at the System Log, or if you still have the Event Viewer application open, press the F5 key to refresh the display. Was a print job audit created for the job you just sent? There should be one similar to that shown in Figure 19.17.

19

**UNDERSTANDING
THE REGISTRY**

FIGURE 19.17.

Setting EventLog *to* 0x1f *tells the print spooler to generate a print job audit.*

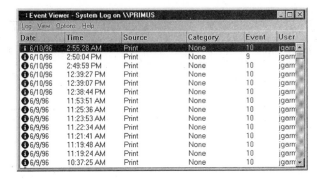

Finding Registry Information

Now that you've seen the basic workings of the Registry Editor, let's move on to something more advanced. The Registry is a large and complex database. It is not always possible to find things unless you know exactly where to look.

Fortunately, REGEDT32 includes a find facility, albeit an overly simplified one.

> **NOTE**
>
> When you are trying to locate a value entry but don't know the name of any of its parent subkeys, or if you are trying to find a value entry and you know only its data value, use the Windows 95 REGEDIT.EXE command. It includes a more full-featured find command.

In the previous example, you had to locate the HKEY_LOCAL_MACHINE\SYSTEM\CurrentControlSet \Control\Print\Providers subkey. Rather than navigating through the multiple subkeys, you could have simply used the Find Key option from the View menu to quickly locate it.

When you choose the Find Key option from the View menu, the Find dialog box appears, as shown in Figure 19.18.

FIGURE 19.18.

You can find a subkey using its whole name or a portion of it.

TIP

TIP

The find command works using your current location in the Registry database. It will search only the currently selected root key, and only from the point selected in the left side of the root key window. To search the entire root key, scroll to the top of the window and select the root key's name—HKEY_LOCAL_MACHINE, for example.

So if you want to locate the HKEY_LOCAL_MACHINE\SYSTEM\CurrentControlSet\Control \Print\Providers subkey, you could choose Find Key from the View menu and enter Providers in the Find what field. For a faster find response, select the Match whole word only option. If you are unsure of the exact subkey name, you could enter a portion of the name, in which case you would *not* select the Match whole word only option. Click the Find Next button. If you started at the top of the HKEY_LOCAL_MACHINE root key, then you would end up with HKEY_LOCAL_MACHINE\SOFTWARE\Microsoft\Windows\CurrentVersion\Telephony\Providers, which is not what you were looking for. So click the Find Next button again, and this time, the correct subkey is located, as shown in Figure 19.19.

FIGURE 19.19.

Find can be used to quickly locate a subkey.

Securing and Auditing Information in the Registry

As part of the Windows NT security system, you can also provide discretionary access control to discrete Registry value entries.

NOTE

You must use the REGEDT32 utility for creating and editing security settings in the Registry. The Windows 95 REGEDIT utility does not include the necessary support for Windows NT's security subsystem.

The security for Registry keys, subkeys, and value entries is supported regardless of the file system where the Registry database is stored.

19

UNDERSTANDING
THE REGISTRY

NOTE

You can secure Registry information even if the Registry files are located on a FAT partition.

WARNING

If the NT system files are located on a FAT partition, then anyone who is logged on to the system's console can delete any of the NT system files. Although they cannot make changes to or delete individual Registry entries, they can delete entire Registry hives.

Assigning permissions in the Registry Editor is similar to doing so in the File Manager or NT Explorer. To view permissions on a subkey, follow these steps:

1. Open the Registry Editor (REGEDT32.EXE).

2. Select HKEY_LOCAL_MACHINE from the Windows menu to bring the HKEY_LOCAL_MACHINE root key to the front.

3. Click the SOFTWARE subkey, as shown in Figure 19.20.

FIGURE 19.20.

Select the SOFTWARE *subkey.*

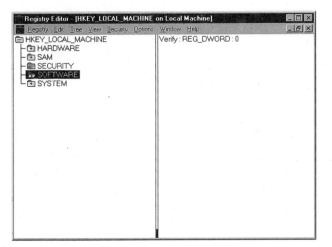

4. Choose Permissions from the Security menu. This brings up the Registry Key Permissions window, shown in Figure 19.21.

FIGURE 19.21.

The Registry Key Permissions window looks similar to the File Manager and NT Explorer interfaces for setting security permissions.

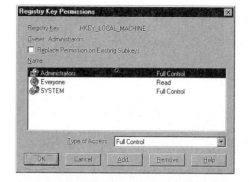

NOTE

Permissions in the Registry can be set only on keys and subkeys. They *cannot* be set for individual value entries.

For each user or group listed in the ACL, you can set the permissions to Read, Full Control, or Special Access. The Special Access permissions are shown in Figure 19.22.

FIGURE 19.22.

You can assign a discrete level of permissions using the Special Access setting.

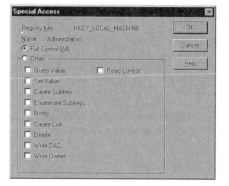

19

UNDERSTANDING
THE REGISTRY

5. Use the Add button to add users or groups to the ACL, or use the Remove button to remove existing access control entries (ACEs).

6. If you want the changes to propagate down the Registry tree, choose Replace Permission on Existing Subkeys.

WARNING

Making changes to the security permissions of Registry subkeys can result in system failure or other unpredictable problems.

7. When you have made the changes you want, click OK.

If you assign Special Access to subkeys in the Registry, you can specify any of 10 discrete settings, summarized in Table 19.4.

Table 19.4. Summary of Special Access permissions for Registry security.

Permission	Explanation
Query Value	Specifies that the assigned user or group can read the setting of a value entry located in the subkey.
Set Value	Specifies that the assigned user or group can set the value of a value entry located in the subkey.
Create Subkey	Specifies that the assigned user or group can create a subkey located in this selected Registry subkey.
Enumerate Subkeys	Specifies that the assigned user or group can identify all the subkeys in the selected subkey.
Notify	Specifies that the assigned user or group can receive audit notifications generated from this subkey.
Create Link	Specifies that the assigned user or group can create a symbolic link to the selected subkey.
Delete	Specifies that the assigned user or group can delete the selected subkey.
Write DAC	Specifies that the assigned user or group can modify the discretionary access control (DAC) list for the selected subkey.
Write Owner	Specifies that the assigned user or group can take ownership of the selected subkey.
Read Control	Specifies that the assigned user or group can read the security information associated with the selected subkey.

Auditing Registry Keys

With the Registry Editor (REGEDT32.EXE), you can also assign specify auditing on certain subkeys. This is done much the same way as enabling auditing on an NTFS partition using the File Manager or NT Explorer.

> **NOTE**
>
> To audit Registry subkeys, you must be auditing File and Object Access, as specified in the system's audit policy in the User Manager for Domains.

When using the Registry Editor to select a subkey, you can select Auditing from the Security menu to specify auditing on that subkey. This brings up the Registry Key Auditing window, shown in Figure 19.23.

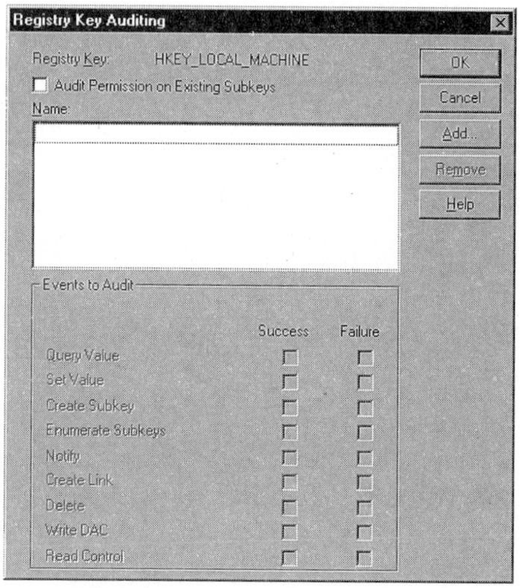

FIGURE 19.23.

The Registry Key Auditing window is used to specify auditing for a particular subkey.

If you select the Audit Permission on Existing Subkeys option, the audit properties you specify in this window will also be applied to all subkeys, beginning at the selected subkey.

You can use the Add button to specify users and groups from the local domain account database or from any trusted domains. When you have added all the users and groups you want to audit to the list, you can specify the events to audit for each user or group by clicking that particular entry and specifying events from the list of checkboxes, as shown in Figure 19.24.

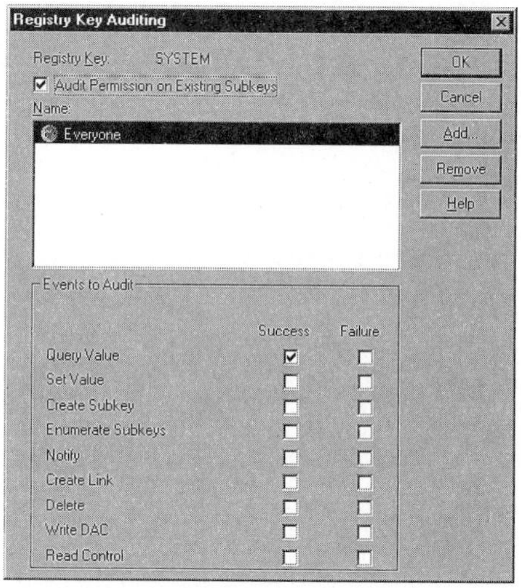

FIGURE 19.24.

Using these options, everyone on the system will generate an audit event when they access the HKEY_LOCAL_MACHINE\SYSTEM *subkey.*

> **CAUTION**
>
> For some applications, the Registry is accessed frequently. Auditing these subkeys might create sufficient system overhead that it could adversely affect system performance, not to mention that it will quickly fill up the Security Log.

Using the Registry Editor Remotely

One of the great strengths of the Registry Editor, and of Windows NT, is the capability to remotely access and edit the Registry database. From a Windows NT machine, you can use the Registry Editor (REGEDT32.EXE) to connect to a remote system running Windows NT.

Using REGEDT32, choose Select Computer from the Registry menu. This will display a browse window, enabling you to locate a remote computer.

Using the browse box, select the computer whose Registry you want to view, or type the computer's name into the Computer field.

You are now connected to the remote computer's HKEY_LOCAL_MACHINE and HKEY_USERS root keys.

> **NOTE**
>
> Remember, the other root keys are simply links to other subkeys, in either the HKEY_LOCAL_MACHINE or 4‡e HKEY_USERS root key.

When you are finished viewing or making changes to the remote computer's Registry, select Close from the Registry menu to close the connection to the remote Windows NT system.

> **NOTE**
>
> When you connect to a remote NT system's Registry, you are granted the level permission determined by your user account and the privileges granted to it on the remote system.

Summary

This chapter explained the Windows NT Registry, as well as the primary tool used for editing the Registry—the Registry Editor (REDGEDT32.EXE).

In learning about the Registry, you learned about the terminology used to describe the pieces of the Registry, including hives, root keys, subkeys, and value entries. In addition, you learned about the information that makes up a value entry. This chapter then showed you where the NT Registry hives are stored and how the hives and the root keys are related.

After a brief discussion of the fault-tolerant capabilities of the Registry database, the chapter continued with a look at the two Registry Editor utilities included with Windows NT and a discussion of which utility to use to get the job done right. You learned about using the Registry Editor for browsing the Registry database, as well as creating, deleting, and modifying Registry value entries through a hands-on example. You also learned how to use the find capabilities of the Registry Editor for locating subkeys.

Then you learned about setting security permissions and auditing on Registry subkeys. The chapter concluded with a brief look at using the Registry Editor to view and edit the Registry on a remote computer running Windows NT.

19

UNDERSTANDING THE REGISTRY

## CHAPTER 20

Performance Tuning and Optimization

by Joe Greene

IN THIS CHAPTER

Perhaps you have been given the largest DEC Alpha computer known to mankind to run your NT Server with a huge disk farm, the maximum memory configuration, and only 10 users who want to print a few simple reports each day. Now back to the real world. Most of the typically encountered operating systems (whether UNIX, VMS, or NT) start out with plenty of capacity, but people soon start to see what can be done with them and start using them more and more. Over the past several decades, one trend is very clear—applications continue to demand more processing capacity, more memory, and more disk space as time progresses. Be cheerful; this trend helps to keep us computer gurus employed.

The downside of this trend is that you have to be ready for the increased load that your users will be putting on your server and deal with performance problems that come up. Perhaps one of the features you liked when you first read about Windows NT was that line in the marketing materials about Windows NT being a self-tuning operating system. Yes, it is true that Windows NT takes much better care of itself than systems such as VMS and UNIX. Especially in older versions of UNIX, many of the parameters were poorly documented (if at all). The whole system could be brought to its knees if one of these parameters was not adjusted properly for the load applied to your specific system.

Having hired some of the folks who designed one of the best of the previous generation of operating systems (VMS, which was revolutionary for its day), Microsoft tried to take a logical scheme for allocating resources and make it one better with algorithms that help divert resources to where they are most needed. Windows NT does an admirable job (especially considering that it has not been out for all that many years) of getting the most out of your existing computer systems. However, there are a few real-world considerations that you need to factor in against your joy at having a self-tuning operating system:

- Your hardware has real limits. You can get only so much processing out of a 486/66 computer, no matter how well tuned it is. The same applies to all your disk drives, memory areas, and other hardware items.

- You can configure your system poorly so that no amount of automated tuning will help. An example of this would be a file server that has ten disk drives, only one of which contains information of interest to the users and is therefore the one that bears all the load for data transfer operations.

- You can have bad applications that either you write or you buy from a vendor. A relatively simple function (such as a device driver or financial database) can put a huge load on the system. You might not have as much control over this as the system administrator, but you might want to coach your developers or influence your users who are purchasing applications.

- Your server can be limited by the loading and performance of your network. Many experienced computer systems professionals still find all those wires, concentrators, and protocols to be a dark mystery. However, that mystery has a significant impact on the overall performance of client/server applications and network operating system services (such as file sharing and printing). Therefore, you need to be conversant with the capabilities of these networks and know when they are affecting your performance.

This chapter is devoted to arming you with the knowledge of when you need to intervene to help keep your system running at peak performance. This process starts with an introduction to the components of your hardware and operating system that relate to performance. It then introduces the monitoring tools that are used to help you figure out if your system is operating well and, if not, where the problems lie. Next, this chapter covers the various steps that can be taken to alleviate common problems. Finally, there is a discussion of capacity planning, which helps you ensure that you have the resources you need before you need them.

One final note is that there are entire books devoted to this topic (such as in the resource kit). The goal of this chapter is not to capture all the wisdom of these large volumes in a matter of a few pages. Instead, my goal is to present material that helps you understand the basics of the tuning, optimization, and capacity-planning processes. That, combined with an understanding of the most common problems, will equip you to handle the vast majority of NT Server installations out there. Finally, don't forget that not all the tuning responsibility lies at the operating system administrator level. Applications, especially complex databases and three-tier client/server applications, can humble the most powerful computer systems if they are not tuned properly. Therefore, system tuning might involve obtaining support from database administrators or application administrators to ensure that their applications are making efficient use of your system resources.

The Challenge of Performance Management

A common theme in most businesses today goes something like "more for less." Because you want to keep the salary levels of information systems professionals such as yourself high, it is preferable to cut costs in other areas. This is where performance management comes into play. Because you have little control over the prices charged by your hardware and software vendors, your job is to acquire tools that help you get the job done at a reasonable cost and then use those tools effectively. Performance management addresses the effective use of the tools you have been given.

Although performance management has it benefits, it can also be a challenge. Just as you should not open the hood of your car and start adjusting the carburetor if you are not familiar with engines, you cannot start tweaking the operating system until you understand both the basics of your hardware platform and the operating system itself. In the next section, this challenge is taken on, covering the basics of typical PC architecture. NT is delivered on other computer platforms, but this is not a book on comparative computer architectures, and the general concepts of the Intel world are not that alien to the other environments. Typically, they change the arrangement of the components and the names of the buses.

Once you are familiar with the basics of your computer and operating system, the next challenge is to know when to adjust things. Just as you could completely mess up a car that is working perfectly by making adjustments when they are not needed, you need to know when to make adjustments to your Windows NT Server. Coupled with knowing when to make the adjustment is the knowledge of what to adjust. Both of these subjects are answered by the performance monitoring utilities provided by NT.

Once you detect a problem, you need to know what has to be done about it. Sometimes you can make adjustments that fix the problem without having to buy additional hardware or software. You can become really popular with management if you can implement such cost-effective solutions. However, part of the challenge is knowing when to tune and when to buy. Shops that contract out for labor usually better appreciate the cost of an hour of a person's time. You don't win anything by spending a large number of hours (such as rewriting a large application for efficiency with a team of people) to fix a problem that could be solved just as easily by purchasing a $300 disk drive that splits the input/output load.

The final section in this chapter discusses capacity planning and routine performance monitoring. The basic philosophy behind this section is that knowing how to solve a problem is good. However, knowing how to avoid the problem altogether is even better. This section discusses how you can set up a program to keep an eye on the load on your systems. Based on this data, you can anticipate when your hardware capacity will be exceeded or when an application will grow to the point where it needs to be moved to another server.

Windows NT Components and Performance

This section is the starting point for my performance management discussions. My goal is to cover the typical hardware and software found on Intel-based servers running Windows NT. These concepts can easily be extended to the other hardware platforms on which NT runs. The first challenge when working in the PC server world is the number of vendors out there. This is good when it comes to keeping pressure on the vendors to innovate and offer products at a reasonable price. However, it does complicate things for administrators who have to keep up with these innovations and keep the systems running. It is not just a matter of dealing with the different transfer rates of different types of hard disk drives. It involves having disk drives that have completely different data transfer architectures and capabilities. The industry is committed to ensuring that you don't get bored with a lack of new technologies to keep up on.

Intel-Based PC Architecture

So what is the Intel-based PC architecture? Figure 20.1 presents a sample of such an architecture. It starts with a processor chip made by Intel or one of the companies that produces chips compatible with those made by Intel (Cyrix, AMD, and so on). This chip dictates several things about the architecture; it defines the interface between the processor chip, cache memory, and main random access memory. Intel numbers its chips with numbers ending in 86 (such as 80386 and 80486), although the later generations have been marketed by fancier names, such as Pentium. Whatever you call them, they define the hardware standard for Intel-based PCs and drive how Microsoft builds the versions of Windows NT that are designed to run on these processors. For purposes of this discussion, all the internals of these Central Processing Unit (or CPU) chips are skipped, because they don't contain anything you need to worry about related to tuning. Two of your most precious resources are connected to the processor chip by the highest-speed bus in your computer (which is 32 bits wide in the processors that run Windows NT 4). The first of these resources is the random access memory (RAM). This is the main memory in your computer, which enables you to hold the instructions that make up the programs you want to execute. The next resource, the second-level cache, is designed to make things a little faster. Conceptually, it is similar to random access memory, although it is faster. The goal is that if the operating system and processor guess correctly as to which is the next instruction or data element that needs to be retrieved and draws it into this cache, you can speed up the operation of the computer. It becomes important to you when purchasing systems that talk about cache in the specifications. Typically, computers that have more cache for the same processor speed operate slightly faster.

FIGURE 20.1.

Typical Intel-based PC architecture.

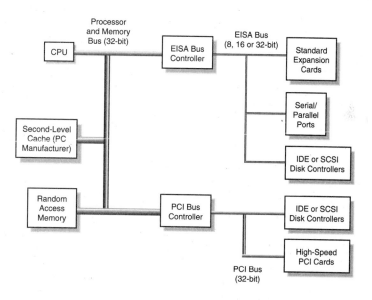

Because Windows NT operates on a variety of computer platforms, there is one thing related to the central processing units that needs to be discussed. The Intel 80x86 family of computers is what is known as a complex instruction set computer (CISC). This means that each instruction actually performs relatively complex tasks. This is in contrast to the reduced instruction set computers (RISC), such as the DEC Alpha, which process relatively simple tasks with each instruction. This becomes important when you consider the processing speed ratings that computer makers always throw at you. RISC computers almost always have higher speed ratings than CISC computers that perform the same amount of useful processing per unit of time.

Also, because the Intel family continues to evolve, later generations of Intel processors usually out-perform older processors that have similar speed ratings, assuming that the operating system is designed to take advantage of these features. Windows NT is one of the few operating systems in the PC world that exploits many of the advanced features of recent Intel chips such as the Pentium.

Now back to the discussion of the computer architecture. So far, this chapter has discussed the three main components (CPU, cache, and RAM) that are attached to the processor's wonderful, high-speed data transfer bus. To keep this bus available for the important transfers between memory and the CPU, lower-importance communications are split off onto other buses within the computer. This was not the case in the early PC days. What happened here is that the slow stream of data from the various peripherals impeded the communications of the more critical components. Designers learned from this and placed these other devices on their own buses.

Many of the modern PCs that you would be considering for server configuration actually have two types of supporting data transfer bus. The EISA (Enhanced Industry Standard Architecture) bus has been around for a while. Because of this, the majority of expansion cards on the market today support this architecture. It comes in two flavors: one uses an 8-bit or 16-bit wide data transfer bus and the other uses a 32-bit wide data transfer bus. This architecture was designed when processors and peripheral devices were much slower than they are today.

In recent years there have been several attempts to specify a new standard data transfer bus for the industry. The one that seems to be assuming this role is the PCI bus. This bus uses 32-bit wide data transfer rates. Some other technical design considerations also enable it to transfer data at much higher rates than the older EISA bus. What this means to you is that if your server has a PCI bus and you can find a peripheral (such as an SCSI disk drive controller card) that supports this structure, you get higher levels of performance. Be aware, though, that most of these cards cost more than their EISA counterparts. Also, some peripherals cannot use the higher performance capabilities of the PCI bus (floppy disk drives). Most of the servers I have configured recently have a mix of EISA and PCI slots. You typically guard the PCI slots for needs such as 100 megabit per second network cards that need the speed of the PCI bus.

So where does that discussion leave you? You have a processor chip that executes the instructions that allow the computer to process information. You have two forms of very high speed data and instruction storage in the RAM and cache that have a direct line to the CPU. You then have controllers that link the high speed processor and memory bus to slower peripherals. The lower speed data transfer buses come in several different flavors. The key is that you have to match the data transfer bus used in your machine with the type of card you want to add to your machine.

Now that you are comfortable with those basic concepts, there are a few other wrinkles you should be aware of before you jump in and start measuring your system performance in preparation for a tuning run. Some of the cards you attach to the EISA, PCI, or other lower speed data transfer buses are actually controllers for a tertiary bus in the computer. The most common example of this is hard disk drive controllers. Of course, there are several different standards for these controllers (SCSI, Fast-Wide SCSI, IDE, and others) that you have to get used to and that offer different performance characteristics. I cover a few of these just so you understand some of the differences.

IDE stands for Integrated Drive Electronics, which simply means that a lot of the logic circuits are on the drive itself and therefore provide a smarter drive that burdens the system less and is capable of supporting higher transfer rates than the older drives (MFM, RLL, and ESDI). These controllers can typically support two drives, which are referred to as master and slave (if one is a boot drive, it is typically the master). They are typically slower than SCSI controllers and support fewer drives per controller. This is by far the most popular drive architecture in today's PCs.

SCSI stands for Small Computer Standard Interface and was first commonly used in the UNIX world. As such, it was designed for a slightly higher transfer speed and also supported more devices (typically seven peripherals on a single controller). You can usually have multiple SCSI controllers in a system if you have really big disk needs. SCSI components cost a bit more, and the device drivers are a bit harder to come by, but many administrators prefer an SCSI bus for servers. You can also buy SCSI tape drives (my favorite is the 4 mm DAT tape drive), optical drives and a few other peripherals, such as scanners. The SCSI bus is an architecture designed for the more demanding data transfer requirements that used to occur only in UNIX worksta- tions and servers but today are being levied on Windows NT Servers.

Now that you are getting somewhat comfortable with SCSI, you should be aware that there are several flavors of SCSI. All those people out there who want to do more with computers each year keep driving vendors to bring out hardware and software that does more. The good news about SCSI is that there is a standard specification and you can almost always get SCSI devices from different vendors to work together. However, SCSI was designed for a kinder, gentler world several years ago, and it is time to push forward. Because the SCSI specification limits the technology that can be brought to bear on the performance needs of the users, ven- dors had to come up with newer forms of the SCSI standard. The most common version of this is fast-wide SCSI. It uses a data transfer bus that is twice as wide as the original. It can generally perform at twice the data transfer rate of basic SCSI. These controllers often enable you to install up to 15 peripherals on the SCSI bus. Also, be ready for an SCSI-3 standard. It might be the solution when PC servers running NT need large disk farms that have very high data transfer rates (everyone keeps pushing video and other demanding applications). For fur- ther information on SCSI, you can refer to Peter Norton's *Inside the PC,* published by Sams.

Other components also have their standards. Modems are often referred to as Hayes or US Robotics compatible. However, for the most part, these devices do their own thing, and it typi- cally has a lesser impact on the performance of the computer system. One area that does have an impact on the system performance is the video subsystem. Several graphics cards take high- level graphics commands and work the display details out on the graphics card itself using on-board processors and special high-speed graphics memory. NT can be set up to interface directly with these cards at a high level, or it can be asked to work out the display details using the main CPU, which increases the load on the system.

For those of you who have already exceeded your limits on hardware-related information, be brave. There is only one more hardware topic to discuss before moving on to the software world. The final topic is the components themselves. Memory chips have speed ratings, but because the data transfer rate is synchronized by the processor bus, all you have to worry about is that your memory chips are good enough for the clock speed of your computer. The performance effects that are most commonly considered are those associated with disk drives. You might have a fast bus, but if the disk drive is slow, your overall data transfer rate is reduced. Therefore, if you have a system that needs a lot of performance, you need to check out the performance characteristics of your peripherals as well.

I'm sure you found that discussion of server hardware components absolutely fascinating, but where does that leave you? Computer systems are a collection of hardware components that interact to perform the tasks assigned to them. Figure 20.2 shows a hierarchy of these components. These levels need to act together to perform services for the user, such as accessing data on a hard disk drive. Each of these components can be purchased from several vendors. Each of these products has varying levels of price and performance. The difficulty is finding that correct blend of price and performance to meet your needs.

FIGURE 20.2.

Hierarchy of hardware components.

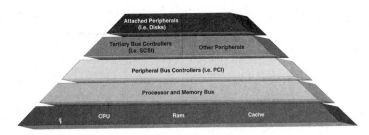

The Operating System and Its Interaction with Hardware

This section addresses the operating system and how it interacts with all this hardware. Chapter 2, "Building Blocks of Windows NT," provides a more detailed discussion of the NT architecture. Think of the way you set up a new computer. Typically, you set up all the hardware first and then you install your operating system. If your hardware doesn't work (the machine is dead), it really doesn't matter what the operating system can do. This is a good way to think of the interaction of the operating system with the hardware. The operating system is designed to interface with the various hardware devices to perform some useful processing.

The first interface between the operating system and your computer is pretty well defined by Intel (or your hardware vendor, such as DEC) and Microsoft. The operating system contains a lot of compiled software that is written in the native language of the CPU and related processors (a bunch of 1s and 0s). The low-level interface to the computer chips is segregated into a small set of code that is specific to the particular computer chip used (this helps NT port between Intel, DEC Alpha, and other host platforms).

Each of the other hardware devices (expansion cards, SCSI controllers, and disk drives) responds to a series of 1s and 0s. The challenge here is that different devices use a different set of codes to control their devices. For example, you would transmit a specific binary number to eject the tape on a 4mm DAT tape drive and another binary number to eject a CD-ROM from its drive. Walking through any major computer store and seeing the huge variety of hardware available gives me a headache just thinking about all the possibilities for controlling commands.

In the old DOS world, each application was pretty much on its own and had to worry about what codes were sent to each of the peripherals. That made the lives of the people who wrote DOS easier, but created great headaches for application developers. Realizing this problem, Windows (before Windows 95 and Windows NT) introduced the concept of device drivers. This enabled you to write your application to a standard interface with the operating system (part of the application programming interface, or API, for that operating system). It was then the operating system's job to translate what you wanted to have done into the appropriate low-level codes specific to a particular piece of hardware. The section of the operating system that took care of these duties was the device driver (sometimes referred to as printer drivers for printers).

It is now no longer your problem to deal with the hardware details as an application designer. You have a few other things to think about, though. Because different hardware devices have different capabilities (for example, some printers can handle graphics and others are text-only), the device driver has to be able to signal the applications when it is asked to do something that the attached device cannot handle. Also, because these device drivers are bits of software, some are better written than others. Some of these device drivers can get very complex and might have bugs in them. This leads to upgrades and fixes to device drivers that you have to keep up on. Finally, although Windows NT comes with a wide variety of device drivers (both Microsoft and the peripheral vendors want to make it easy for you to attach their products to your Windows NT machine), other devices might not have drivers on the NT distribution disks. New hardware or hardware from smaller vendors requires device driver disks (or CDs) for you to work with them. An excellent source of the latest device drivers is the Internet Web pages provided by Microsoft and most computer equipment vendors. The key to remember here is that you need to have a Windows NT–compatible (not Windows 3.1 or Windows 95) device driver for all peripherals that you will be attaching to your NT system. If you are in doubt as to whether a peripheral is supported under NT, contact the peripheral vendor or look at the NT Hardware Compatibility List on the Microsoft Web page (www.microsoft.com or CD-ROMs if you lack Web access).

Now that you have eliminated the low-level interfaces to all that hardware, you have a basis on which you can build operating system services that help applications run under Windows NT. Using the same logic that drove the developers to build device drivers, there are several common functions that almost every application uses. Microsoft has always been sensitive to the fact that you want a lot of great applications to run on your operating system so that it is useful to people and they will buy it. Rather than have the application developers spend a lot of time writing this code for every application, Microsoft engineers decided to build this functionality into the operating system itself. Examples of some of these services include print queue processing (killing print jobs and keeping track of which job is to be sent to the printer next) and TCP/IP networking drivers. This actually has the side benefit of enabling Microsoft engineers who are specialists in these components and the operating system itself to write these services and drivers. This usually results in more powerful and efficient processes than would be written by your typical application programmer who has to worry about the screen layout and all those reports that accounting wants to have done by Friday.

Finally, at the top of the processing hierarchy are the end-user applications themselves. One could consider a computer as next to useless if it lacks applications that help people get their jobs done. Remember, UNIX talks about its openness, Macintosh talks about its superior interface that has existed for several years, and the OS/2 folks usually talk about the technical superiority of the internals of their operating system. All Microsoft has going for it is a few thousand killer applications that people like. One thing you have to remember as a system administrator now that you are at the top of the performance hierarchy is that you still have the opportunity to snatch defeat from the jaws of victory. You can have the best hardware, the best device drivers, and the most perfectly tuned Windows NT system in the world, but if your applications are poorly written, your users will suffer from poor system performance.

Figure 20.3 provides a summary of what this chapter has covered so far in a convenient, graphical form. Obviously, this drawing does not depict the interaction of all the components. The operating system interfaces with the CPU, and some peripherals actually interact with one another. What this does show is that several components need to work together to provide good performance as seen by the end users. This can be a complex job, but fortunately Windows NT provides you with the tools that help you manage this more easily than most other server operating systems. That is the subject of the rest of this chapter.

FIGURE 20.3.

Hierarchy of hardware and software components.

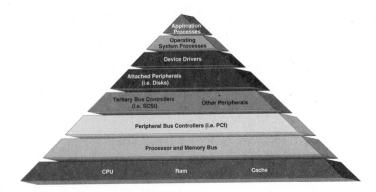

Determining Normal Efficiency Levels

You might be wondering how to figure out all the options and have any idea whether this complex array of components is functioning at normal efficiency. There are articles that go through the theory behind components and try to calculate values for various configurations.

However, because hardware technology continues to march on, and any configuration you might read about is quite possibly out of date by the time you read it, many prefer a more empirical approach.

Unlike most other operating systems, Windows NT is designed to handle most of the details of the interaction of its components with one another. You can control a few things, but I wouldn't recommend it unless you have a really unusual situation and a really serious need. You might do things that the designers never intended. Therefore, I start by accepting my hardware and operating system configuration. From there, I look for metrics that measure the overall performance of the resources that typically have problems and that I have some form of control over. For purposes of this chapter, I treat the vast complexity of computers running Windows NT as having five components that can be monitored and tuned:

- CPU processing capacity
- Random access memory and virtual memory capacity
- Input/output capacity
- Network transmission capacity
- Application efficiency

CPU Processing Capacity

The first component specifies the amount of processing work that the central processing unit of your computer can handle in a given period of time. Although this might depend on the clock speed, the type of instruction set it processes, the efficiency with which the operating system uses the CPU's resources, and any number of other factors, I want to take it as a simple limit that is fixed for a given CPU and operating system. You should be aware that different CPUs exhibit different processing capacities based on the type of work presented to them. Some computers handle integer and text processing efficiently, whereas others are designed as numeric computation machines that handle complex floating-point (with decimals) calculations. Although this is fixed for a given family of processors (such as the Intel Pentium), you might want to consider this when you are selecting your hardware architecture.

RAM and Virtual Memory Capacity

The next component is RAM and virtual memory. Applications designers know that RAM can be read very quickly and has a direct connection to the CPU through the processor and memory bus. They are under pressure to make their applications do more and, of course, respond more quickly to the user's commands. Therefore, they continue to find new ways to put more information (data, application components, and so on) into memory, where it can be retrieved much more quickly than if it were stuck on a hard disk drive or a floppy disk. Gone are the days of my first PC, which I thought was impressive with 256KB of memory. Modern NT Servers usually start at 24MB of RAM and go up from there.

With Windows NT and most other operating systems, you actually have two types of memory to deal with. RAM corresponds to chips physically inside your machine that store information. Early computer operating systems generated errors (or halted completely) when they ran out of physical memory. To get around this problem, operating system developers started to use virtual memory. Virtual memory combines the physical memory in the RAM chips with some storage space on one or more disk drives to simulate an environment that has much more memory than you could afford if you had to buy RAM chips. These operating systems have special operating system processes that figure out what sections of physical memory are less likely to be needed (usually by a combination of memory area attributes and a least recently used algorithm) and then transfer this data from RAM to the page file on disk that contains the swapped-out sections of memory. If the swapped-out data is needed again, the operating system processes transfer it back into RAM for processing. Obviously, because disk transfers are much slower than RAM transfers and you might be in a position of having to swap something out to make room and then transfer data into RAM, this can significantly slow down applications that are trying to perform useful work for your users.

Some use of virtual memory is harmless. Some operating system components are loaded and rarely used. Also, some applications have sections of memory that get loaded but are never used. The problem is when the system becomes so memory-bound that it has to swap something out, then swap something in, before it can do any processing for the users. Several memory areas are designated as "do not swap" to the operating system; these cause you to have even less space for applications than you might think. If you are using a modern database management system such as SQL Server or Oracle, be ready to have large sections of memory taken up in shared memory pools. Databases use memory areas to store transactions that are pending, record entries to their log file for later transfer to disk, and cache records that have been retrieved on the hope that they will be the next ones asked for by the users. They are probably the most demanding applications on most servers.

Input/Output Capacity

The next component to discuss is the input/output capacity of the computer. For today at least, you can simplify this to be the input/output capacity of your disk drives and controllers. Someday, not too long from now, you might be worrying about saturating your PCI bus with complex audio/video traffic. However, for now, I concentrate on disk drives. Typically, three components are involved with getting data from the high-capacity disk drives to the RAM memory where the CPU can use it. The first is the secondary data transfer bus controller, usually a PCI or EISA controller. The next is the actual disk drive controller, which is most often an IDE controller, with more reasonably priced SCSI showing up as time progresses. Finally, there is the disk drive itself. I discuss ways to measure the overall transfer capacity of the disk drive systems as if they were individual drives directly connected to the processor bus. This simplification treats the controllers and drives as a single entity and makes measurement and management easier. You still need to keep in the back of your mind the possibility that you might saturate the capacity of your disk drive controller even though you have not saturated the capacity of any of the individual disk drives attached to it.

Network Transmission Capacity

A very important component in many Windows NT Servers is the network transmission capabilities. Windows NT Server is a network-based computing environment. This is basically data input and output using a card similar to those used to attach disk drives, right? I separated my discussion of network I/O from other I/O for several reasons. First, the technologies are completely different and you have to get used to a different set of terminology. Also, you usually have to deal with a different group of engineers when trying to resolve problems. Second, unless you are also the network administrator, you typically do not completely own the network transmission system. Instead, you are just one of many users of the network. This means that you have to determine if you are the cause of the network bottleneck or if you are merely the victim of it. Finally, you end up using a different set of monitoring utilities when dealing with networks.

Network cards are an often overlooked component in a server. The networking world is somewhat deceptive because they quote transmission rates for the type of network you are using (for example, 10 million bits per second on Ethernet). This might lead you to think that it doesn't matter which network interface card you choose because the transmission rate is fixed anyway. Unfortunately, that is not the case. If you ran different network cards through performance tests, you would find that some are much more capable than others at getting information onto and off of a particular computer. Because most network cards on the market are designed for workstations that individually have relatively light network loads, you might have to look around to find a network interface card that is designed to meet the much more demanding need of a server that is continuously responding to network requests from several workstations.

Application Efficiency

Finally, I want to re-emphasize the idea of application efficiency as an important part of overall performance. Perhaps this is because I come from the perspective of the database administrator where you continuously run across developers who are complaining that "the database is too slow." I can't tell you how many times I have looked at their software only to find things such as if they want ten numbers, they put the program in a loop and make ten calls to the database over a heavily loaded network, as opposed to one call that brings back all the data at once. Perhaps they are issuing queries without using the indexes that are designed to make such queries run faster. By changing a few words around in the query, they could take a 30-minute query and turn it into a 10-second query. (I'm not kidding—I saw this done on a very large data warehouse many times.) Unfortunately, this is one of those things that requires experience and common sense. You have to judge whether the application is taking a long time because it is really complex (for example, a fluid flow computation with a system that has 10,000 degrees of freedom) or because it is poorly tuned (they want to retrieve 10 simple numbers and it is taking 30 seconds). Of course, you need to be certain before you point the finger at someone else. That is what the Performance Monitoring Utilities section is all about. It gives you scientific data to show that you are doing your job properly before you ask for more equipment or tell people to rewrite their applications.

In this section, I have tried to give an overview of how the hardware, software, and operating system interact to give an overall level of computer service to the users. The difficulty in this process is that a huge variety of hardware components, device drivers, and applications all come together to affect the performance of your Windows NT Server. I don't believe it is worthwhile to calculate out numbers that indicate the capacity of your system. Instead, I believe in measuring certain key performance indicators that are tracked by Windows NT. Over time, you will develop a baseline of what numbers are associated with good system performance and what are associated with poor performance. I have also simplified the vast array of components in the system to a list of five key components that you will want to routinely monitor. These are the ones that will cause your most common problems.

Self-Tuning and Windows NT

As I mentioned earlier, Windows NT is a self-tuning operating system—within limits. Don't get me wrong. Having worked with UNIX, I appreciate all the self-tuning that Windows NT does for you. What I want to ensure is that you don't think that NT can tune itself on a 486/ 33 to support thousands of users. With that caveat out of the way, I want to explore some of the things that Windows NT does to keep itself in tune for you and how you can affect this process. Once you understand what NT is doing to help itself, you will be in a better position to interpret monitoring results and therefore know when your intervention is required.

First, there are several things you do not want Windows NT to try to do for you. Moving files between disks to level the load might cause certain applications to fail when they cannot find their files. That is something you have to do for yourself. You also don't want NT to decide whether background services that have not been used for a while should be shut down. You might have users who need to use those services and applications and who cannot start the services automatically if they are currently shut down.

There are also some things Windows NT cannot do. It cannot change the jumper settings on your expansion cards and disk drives to reconfigure your system to be more efficient. It cannot rearrange cabling. Thankfully, it also cannot issue a purchase order to buy additional memory or CPU upgrades. Basically anything that requires human hands is still beyond the reach of Windows NT self-tuning.

So what does Windows NT have control over? Basically, it boils down to how Windows NT uses memory to improve its performance. There are several games it plays to try to hold in memory the information you will probably want to work with next. To do this it sets aside memory areas for disk caches and other needs. It also tries to adapt itself to your demonstrated processing needs. When changes in your needs are detected, it reallocates memory to try to best meet your needs. This is why you almost always find almost all your system memory used on a Windows NT Server even when you are not especially busy. Windows NT senses that there is a lot of memory available and it tries to apply it to best meet your anticipated needs rather than just having it sit around unused.

Another thing Windows NT can do automatically for you is adjust its virtual memory space. If your existing page file space (`pagefile.sys`) is not large enough to handle your needs, it can go after other space that is available on your disks to get additional temporary paging space. The downside of this is that the new page file space is probably not located next to the default page files on disk. Therefore, when you are writing to or reading from these page files, you will probably have extra delays as the heads on the disk drive move between the various files. Although disk drive transmission rates are relatively slow when it comes to paging, the physical movement of the arms that hold the heads is even slower, so it should be avoided whenever possible.

Although I'm sure that self-tuning is the topic of many of the white papers available on the Microsoft Web page or Technet CD, the previous page is good enough for these purposes. Although I spent only a page on the subject, do not underestimate the power of self-tuning. In UNIX, if you had to go in to tune the kernel, you were faced with a series of parameters that were ill-documented and had strange, unexpected effects on one another. I have more than once done more harm than good when changing UNIX kernel parameters to get applications such as databases going. However, self-tuning is not a magic silver bullet that solves all your problems. The next section starts the discussion of how you can tell when your system is having problems that self-tuning cannot solve and how to identify what the specific problem is.

Performance Monitoring Utilities

One of the more interesting things about coming to Windows NT after having worked on several other types of server platforms is the fact that several useful, graphical administrative tools come as part of the operating system itself. Although UNIX and other such operating systems come with tools that can get the job done if you are fluent in them, they are neither friendly nor powerful. My main focus in this section is the built-in utility known as Performance Monitor. This tool enables you to monitor most of the operating system performance parameters that you could possibly be interested in. It supports a flexible, real-time interface and also enables you to store data in a log file for future retrieval and review.

However, before I get too far into the tools used to measure performance, a few topics related to monitoring need to be covered. Although you could put your ear to your computer's cabinet to see if you hear the disk drives clicking a lot, it is much easier if the operating system and hardware work together to measure activities of interest for you. Windows NT can monitor all the critical activities of your system and then some. Your job is to wade through all the possible things that can be monitored to determine which ones are most likely to give you the information you need.

Activity Measurement

How does Windows NT measure activities of interest? The first concept you have to get used to is that of an object. Examples of objects in Windows NT performance would be the (central) processor or logical disk drives. Associated with each of these objects is a series of counters.

Each of these counters measures a different activity for that object, such as bytes total per second and bytes read per second. That brings me to a good point about counters. To be useful, counters have to measure something that is useful for indicating a load on the system. For example, six million bytes read does not tell you very much. If it were six million bytes per second, that would be a significant load. If it were six million bytes read since the system was last rebooted two months ago, it would be insignificant. Therefore, most of your counters that show activity are usually rated per second or as a percentage of total capacity or usage (as in percent processor time devoted to user tasks). A few items, such as number of items in a queue, have meaning in and of themselves (keeping the queue small is generally a good idea).

Another important concept when working with counters is that you have to measure them over an appropriate time interval. A graph showing every instant in time would produce an enormous amount of data very quickly. To control this, measurement programs such as Performance Monitor average the values over an amount of time you specify. You have to be somewhat careful when you specify the time interval. For example, if you average the data over a day, you can see long-term trends on the increase in usage of your system when you compare the various days. However, you would not notice the fact that the system is on its knees from 8 to 9 am and from 1 to 2 pm. This is what your users will notice; therefore, you need to be able to measure over a more reasonable interval, such as several minutes. I'll show you later how to turn monitoring on and off automatically, so you aren't collecting a lot of relatively useless data when no one is using your server.

Another important point about monitoring is that you need to monitor the system without influencing the data. For example, imagine setting up several dozen instances of Performance Monitor to measure all the parameters that could possibly be needed for later analysis using a time interval of one second and logging all this information to a single disk drive. The data you collected by this process would be heavily influenced by the load placed on the system to collect, process, and store the information related to monitoring. Your counters for the number of processes running, threads, and data transfer to that logging disk might actually reflect only the load of the monitoring application and not show any data about the use of the system by other applications.

A final term you need to get comfortable with that relates to Windows NT performance monitoring is that of an instance. Most of the objects monitored by Performance Monitor have multiple instances. An example of this is when you try to monitor the logical disk object: the system needs to know which of your logical disks (such as the C drive) you want to monitor. As you see later, Performance Monitor provides you with a list of available instances for the objects that have them.

In summary, monitoring under Windows NT is provided by a built-in, graphical utility known as Performance Monitor. This tool monitors many different types of objects (for example, processors). Each object has several possible attributes that might need to be measured. Windows NT refers to these attributes of the objects as counters (for example, percent processor time). Finally, there are more than one of many of the objects in your system. When there are multiple items of a given object, you need to tell Performance Monitor which instance of that object you want to have measured and for which of the counters. Figure 20.4 illustrates these concepts.

FIGURE 20.4.
Performance Monitor terminology.

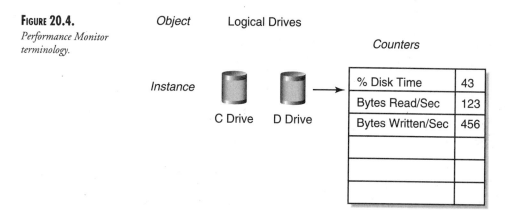

Activities that Can Be Monitored

As I alluded to earlier in my discussion, Windows NT provides you with a large number of counters to select from. I found the following objects, with the number of counters associated with them in parentheses:

- Browser (21)
- Cache (27)
- IP (17)
- Logical Disk (21)
- Memory (27)
- NetBEUI (39)
- NetBEUI Resource (3)
- Network Interface (17)
- NWLink IPX (39)
- NWLink NetBIOS (39)
- NWLink SPX (39)
- Objects (Events, Mutexes, Processes, Sections, Semaphores, and Threads)
- Paging File (2)
- Physical Disk (19)

- Process (18)
- Processor (10)
- RAS Port (17)
- RAS Total (18)
- Redirector (37)
- Server (26)
- Server Work Queue (17)
- System (24)
- TCP (9)
- Thread (12)

Now on to one of the really interesting features of Performance Monitor. Much as the Event Log can be used by applications to give you one place to look at for things that have happened (information and problems) on your system, applications can be interfaced with Performance Monitor to give you one place to look for performance information. One of the things I found useful is that the monitoring options appear on the list of objects only when you have the appropriate applications running. For example, the five Performance Monitor objects associated with SQL Server and the nine Performance Monitor objects associated with Exchange Server are listed only when you have those servers running. This does not prevent you from running Performance Monitor in multiple windows to monitor things one at a time. It does enable you to put the usage data for an application on the same graph as critical operating system parameters to see how the application is interacting with the operating system. Think of it as being able to put the blame on a particular application for bringing your server to its knees.

This brings me to my first bit of advice related to using the Performance Monitor built into Windows NT: Try it out. It can monitor numerous things, but the interface is fairly simple. It is not like the registry editor, where you are doing something risky. You might waste a little time playing with this utility when everything is going well on your system. Being comfortable with selecting the various counters and graphical options could pay you back in the future when things are not going well and you are under pressure to solve the problems quickly.

With all this performance theory and terminology out of the way, it is time to actually look at Performance Monitor and see how it can be used to get you the data you need. Figure 20.5 shows you how to access Performance Monitor in the Start menu hierarchy. As you can see, it is conveniently located with all the other administrative tools that you will come to depend upon to keep your server going.

FIGURE 20.5.

Accessing Performance Monitor.

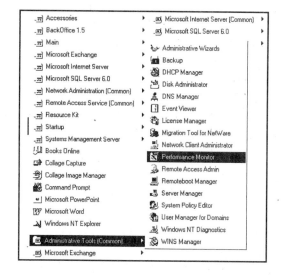

Performance Monitor

What does Performance Monitor do for you? Figure 20.6 shows my favorite means of displaying data: the line graph. It is a flexible utility that has other ways to capture data, but for now you can learn a lot about the tool using this format. Following is a description of the basic interface.

FIGURE 20.6.

Performance Monitor's basic interface.

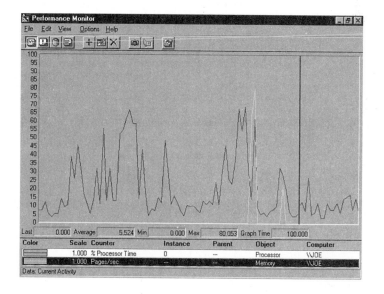

■ Across the top is a traditional Windows menubar that enables you to access all your basic processing options.

■ Underneath the menu is a toolbar that enables you to pick the most commonly used options with a single mouse click. The first four buttons enable you to select the type of display to be presented: chart view, alert view, log view, and report view. The next three buttons enable you to add, modify, or delete a particular counter from your list via a pop-up dialog box. The next button enables you to take a snapshot of performance data (for when you are not collecting data at predefined intervals). The next to last button enables you to write a comment (bookmark) to the log file at a particular time that might help jog your memory later when you are reviewing the data. The final button displays the Display Options dialog to enable you to set things up to your liking.

■ The majority of the display is consumed with the display of performance data. I will go over the various display formats shortly.

Before leaving the basics of the Performance Monitor display, I wanted to cover a few options that might appeal to some of you. Those of you who are comfortable with several windows or toolbars being open on your desktop at a given time so you can see everything that is happening can use a few control keys to minimize the Performance Monitor display. Figure 20.7 shows a Performance Monitor graph of CPU processor time use in a nice, graph-only window. To do this, I hit the following keys: Ctrl+M (toggles the menu on and off); Ctrl+S (toggles the status line on and off); and Ctrl+T (toggles the toolbar on and off). You can hit Ctrl+P to toggle a setting that keeps the Performance Monitor display on top of other windows on your desktop. All you have to do is set up Performance Monitor to monitor the items you want, trim off the menu, toolbar, and status window, then size the window and move it to where you want it.

FIGURE 20.7.

Trimmed Performance Monitor window.

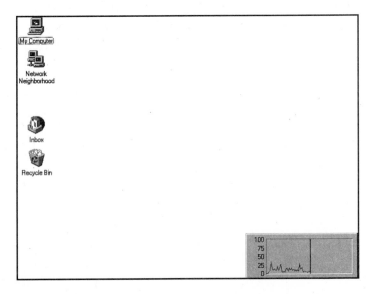

When you first start Performance Monitor, you notice that it is not doing anything. With the large number of monitoring options, Microsoft was not willing to be presumptuous and assume which counters should be monitored by default. Therefore, you have to go in and add the options, counters, and instances you want to get the system going. It is not at all difficult to accomplish this task. The first thing you do is click the plus sign icon on the toolbar. You are presented with the Add to Chart dialog box, shown in Figure 20.8. From here, all you have to do is select the options you want:

FIGURE 20.8.

The Add to Chart dialog box.

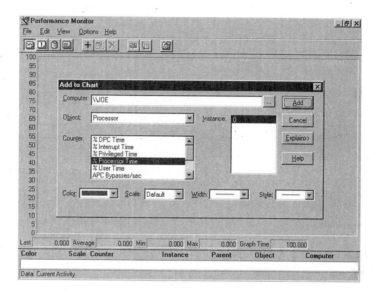

- ■ **Computer:** This box enables you to select which computer you want to monitor. This is a really nice feature because it lets you sit at your desk and use your terminal to monitor the world (at least that part of the world to which you have privileges). The selection box at the right helps you locate the computers that are available for you to monitor, or you can do it the old-fashioned way by typing a double backslash followed by the computer name.

- ■ **Object:** This is a drop-down listbox that enables you to select which object you want to monitor. The object selected drives the legal values that are displayed in the next two controls.

- ■ **Counter:** This is a scrollable list that enables you to choose which of the counters associated with your selected object you want to monitor.

- ■ **Instance:** To the right of the Object and Counter controls is a scrollable list of the instances of the object you have selected (which disk drive).

- ■ **Add:** To add the specified object counter instance you have entered to the list of counters monitored, click the Add button.

■ **Explain:** To get a more detailed explanation of the counter you are selecting, click the Explain button and you get some text at the bottom of the dialog box. (See Figure 20.9.) This text could be a little more detailed and easy to understand, but it can be useful in certain circumstances.

FIGURE 20.9.

The Add to Chart dialog box with the Explain option selected.

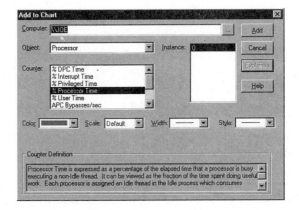

■ **Cancel:** When you are finished, click the Cancel button before you click the Add button, or click Done after you click the Add button. This takes you back to the main display so that you can see what is happening.

■ You should note that this same dialog box is used for all the types of monitoring (chart, alert, log, and report) that are supported by Performance Monitor. The last word in the title bar changes to correspond to the display option with which you are working.

■ Finally, you see Color, Scale, Width, and Style controls at the bottom of this dialog box. Performance Monitor automatically cycles through a predefined color and line pattern list as you add different counters, but you might want to take control of this decision to suit your artistic sense. These buttons let you do that.

Considerations for Charts

Here there are a few considerations for laying out this chart. So far I have presented relatively simple graphs to illustrate my points. However, now consider Figure 20.10 , which I intentionally made complex to illustrate a few new points. First, you might find it hard to distinguish which line corresponds to which counter. There are several lines, and they are all crossing one another. Very few people, even those comfortable with graph reading, can follow more than a few lines. You might want to keep this in mind when you take your wonderful charts before management to prove a point. Also, you might find it especially difficult to read the graphs presented here. That is because Microsoft uses different colors and patterns for the lines to help you pick out which line corresponds to which data element. Although there are shading differences between the various colors and there is the line pattern, you might want to keep the number of lines on your graph especially small if you are presenting it in black and white.

FIGURE 20.10.

A complex performance monitor chart.

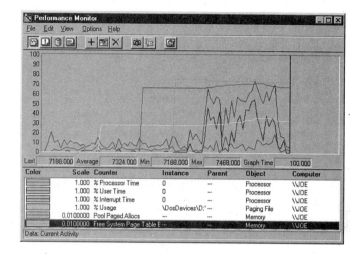

It can take some time to customize this display with the counters you want to monitor, the display options, and the colors that appeal to your sense of beauty. It would be a real pain if you had to go through this process each time you wanted to start up Performance Monitor. The boys from Redmond have not let you down. They have provided the Save Chart Settings option under the File menu in Performance Monitor (see Figure 20.11) for you to save your settings for the chart. You can also save all the settings for your charts, option menu selections, and so forth in a workspace file using the Save Workspace menu option. These features can be quite powerful. You can actually create a series of Performance Monitor settings files in advance when everything is working well. You can even record data for these key parameters that correspond to times when the system is working well. Then, when a crisis comes up, you can quickly set up to run performance charts that can be compared with the values for the system when it was running well. This up-front preparation can really pay off when everyone is running around screaming at you, so you might want to put it on your list of things to do.

If you develop applications in addition to administering an NT system, one of the things you are probably aware of is that report generation and presentation utilities are the ones that generate the most debate and interest in the user community. You can get away with a wide variety of data entry forms, as long as they are functional and efficient. However, when it comes to reports and presentation utilities, you will have users arguing with each other about which columns to put on the report, what order the columns have to be displayed in, and sometimes how you calculate the values in the columns. I have seen people go at it for hours arguing such little details as the font used and what the heading of the document should be. You are in the position of being the consumer of a data presentation utility (Performance Monitor), and Microsoft knows that everyone has slightly different tastes. Therefore, they give you several options for presenting the data. Not only are there basic format options such as alert reports versus the graphical charts I have been discussing, but they even let you get into the details as to how the data on a chart is collected and presented. The Chart Options dialog box is shown in Figure 20.12.

FIGURE 20.11.

Saving Performance Monitor settings to a file.

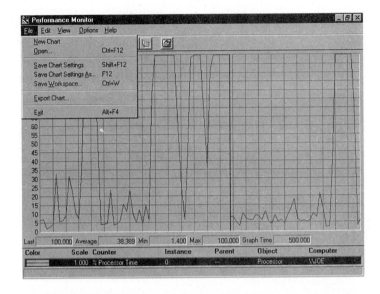

FIGURE 20.12.

The Chart Options dialog box.

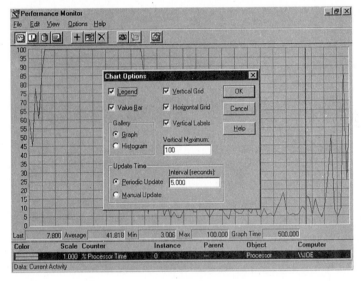

This dialog box enables you to set the following presentation options:

- **Legend:** This checkbox enables you to specify whether to take up part of the screen display with a legend (the section where you match a line color and pattern to a specified computer, object, counter, and instance). Unless this is absolutely obvious to anyone walking up to the display, I recommend keeping the legend available at all times.

- **Value Bar:** This checkbox controls whether the Last, Average, Minimum, Maximum, and Graph Time data displays are presented just below the graph itself (see Figure 20.12, which has this option selected).

- **Vertical Grid:** This checkbox controls whether vertical lines are drawn in the middle of the graph to help you see what the values of a given data point are. (Both horizontal and vertical lines were selected for the graph displayed in Figure 20.12.)

- **Horizontal Grid:** This checkbox controls whether horizontal lines are drawn in the middle of the graph to help you see what the times corresponding to a given data point are.

- **Vertical Labels:** This checkbox controls whether the scale of values for the vertical line is displayed.

- **Gallery:** This option contains radio buttons to select either Graph (a line graph where all the data points are represented as dots connected together with a line) or Histogram (a bar chart where each data point is represented as a vertical bar whose height corresponds to the value being measured).

- **Vertical Maximum:** This edit box enables you to control whether you display the whole range of values possible as determined by NT (0 to 100 percent) or you focus on a narrower range of data (such as 0 to 50 percent). This can be useful in situations where you want to see finer variations in data that is confined to a narrower range.

- **Update Time:** This section enables you to specify whether you want Periodic Update or Manual Update. Periodic Update is the default, in which Performance Monitor automatically collects a data point for the parameters being monitored at the interval (in seconds) specified in the edit box. Manual Update collects data manually, by clicking the Performance Monitor toolbar item that looks like a camera, by selecting the Options menu and Update Now, or by pressing Ctrl+U.

By now you should be impressed with the wide array of charting options Performance Monitor provides. You are probably a little uncertain as to which of the many options you will want to use in your environment. I give my list of favorite counters to monitor later in this section. Also, as I mentioned before, there is no substitute for sitting down and actually playing with Performance Monitor to get comfortable with it and see how you like the environment to be set up. What I want to cover now are the other data collection and presentation options provided by Performance Monitor. You have so far experienced only one of the four possible presentation formats. The good news is that although the format of the displays is different, the thinking behind how you set things up is the same, so you should be able to adapt quickly to the other three presentation formats.

The Alert View in Performance Monitor

Figure 20.13 presents the next display option Performance Monitor provides: the alert view. The concept behind this is really quite simple. Imagine that you want to keep an eye on several parameters on several servers to detect any problems that come up. The problem with the chart view is that the vertical line keeps overwriting the values so that you see a fixed time interval and lose historical information. You probably don't want to have to sit in front of your terminal 24 hours a day waiting for a problem value to show up on your chart, either. Later, I explain the log view, which lets you capture each piece of data and save it in a file for future reference. However, if you want to have a fairly reasonable time interval that enables you to detect response time problems for your users (for example, 60 seconds), you will generate a mountain of data in a relatively short period of time.

Figure 20.13.

The Alert Log display.

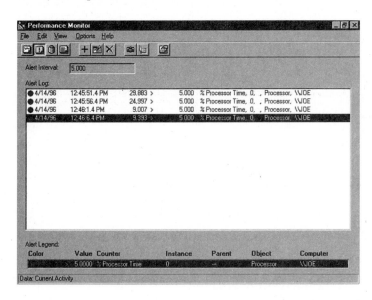

When you look at the data that would be captured in a Performance Monitor log file, the one thing that hits you is that the vast majority of the data collected is of no interest to you. It shows times when the system is performing well and there are no problems. Disk drives are relatively inexpensive these days, so it isn't that much of a burden to store the data. However, your time is valuable, and it would take you quite some time to wade through all the numbers to find those that might indicate problems. People are generally not very good at reading through long lists of numbers containing different types of data to find certain values. Computers, on the other hand, are quite good at this task. The alert view combines savings on disk space and the task of sorting through values that are of no interest into one utility. It lets you record data only when the values reach certain critical values that you tell Performance Monitor are of interest to you.

To set up monitoring with the alert view in Performance Monitor, you first select this view from the toolbar (the icon with the log book with an exclamation mark on it). Next, you click the plus sign icon to add counters to be monitored. The Add to Alert dialog box you get (see Figure 20.14) has the basic controls that you used to specify the counters under the graph view (Computer, Object, Counter, and Instance). The key data that is needed to make the alert view work is entered at the bottom of the screen. The Alert If control enables you to specify when the alert record is written. You specify whether you are interested in values that are either under or over the value you enter in the edit box. The Run Program on Alert control gives you the option to run a program when these out-of-range values are encountered. You can specify whether this program is to be run every time the alert condition is encountered or only the first time it is encountered.

FIGURE 20.14.

The Add to Alert dialog box.

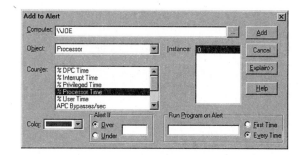

The alert view can be really useful if you want to run it over a long period of time (or continuously whenever the server is running). It collects only data that is of interest to you. You can specify values that indicate both extremely high load and extremely low load. You can even kick off a program to take corrective action or enable more detailed monitoring when you run across an unusual condition. You still have to make time to view the data, but at least you get to avoid reading anything but potentially interesting events.

The Log View in Performance Monitor

The next view provided by Performance Monitor is the log view. The principle behind this is simple—you write all the data to a log file. Later, you can open this log file using Performance Monitor and view the results or export the results to a data file that can be imported into a spreadsheet (like Microsoft Excel) for further processing, or you could even write your own program to read this file and massage the data. The log view is relatively simple to work with. First, you need to specify the parameters that you want to log using the plus sign toolbar icon. Next, you have to specify the file that is to contain the logging data and how often the data points are to be collected. Figure 20.15 shows the Log Options dialog box, which captures this information.

The Log Options dialog box contains your standard file selection controls. You can add to an existing file or make up a new filename. You can even keep all your log files in a separate directory (or on a network drive) so that it is easy to find them. Once you have specified the filename, your only other real decision is the update interval. Again, you have to be careful, because if you choose a 10-second interval, you will generate over 8,600 data points per counter selected per day. All that's left is to click the Start Log button to get the process going. The Log Options dialog is also used to stop the logging process. Note that you need to keep Performance Monitor running to continue to collect data to this log file. I will show you later how to run Performance Monitor as a service in background.

FIGURE 20.15.

The Log Options dialog box.

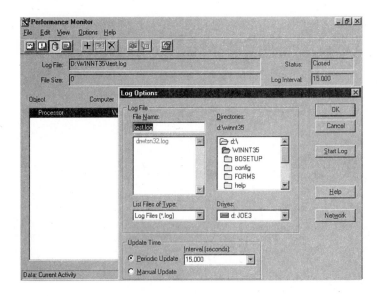

The Report View in Performance Monitor

Now for the final view provided by Performance Monitor: the report view. It is actually a very simple concept, as is shown in Figure 20.16. You specify a set of counters that you want to monitor, and it gives you a screen that lists the parameter and the value observed in the last interval. This is one view where manual data collection could be useful. Imagine a situation where you have an application turned off and everything is running fine. You collect a set of values for this normal-time and save them to disk. You can then start up the application that seems to be causing the problem and capture a new set of data to see what the differences are. This is yet another tool to add to your arsenal for those times when problems arise.

Selecting the Data Source in Performance Monitor

There is one more interesting feature of Performance Monitor to discuss before moving on. Performance Monitor has lots of nice display capabilities built into its graph view. However, the log option is useful for collecting data over a long period of time when you can't sit at your terminal and review the graphs before they are overwritten. A menu selection on the Options menu helps you with this situation. The Data From option brings up a dialog box (see Figure 20.17) that lets you select what you are graphing. The formal setting is to graph current activity (the counters that you have currently selected to monitor). You have the option of selecting one of the log files you built to be the subject of the graph for later review.

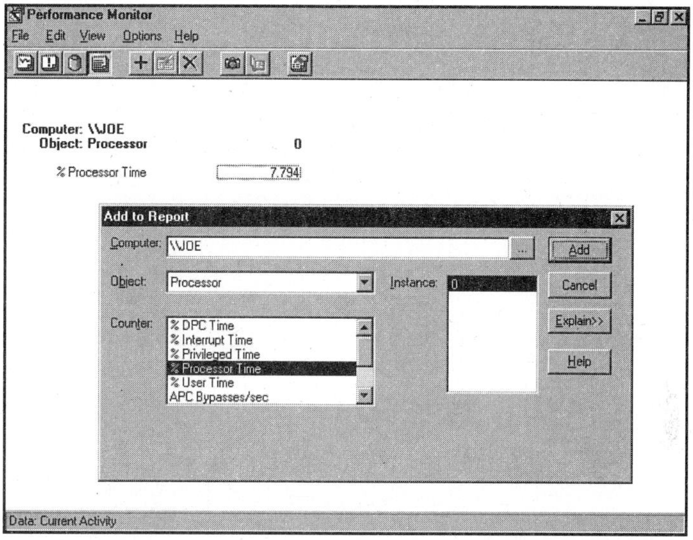

FIGURE 20.16.
The Add to Report dialog box.

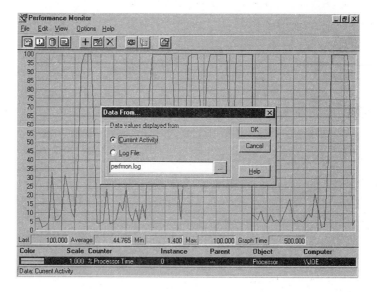

FIGURE 20.17.
The Data From dialog box.

So far I have covered the four views Performance Monitor provides that can be used to display data in different formats. One of these views should be what makes the most sense for you when you need to review data. I also covered how to set these monitors up and alter their display to your taste. You need to remember that if you set up to monitor a certain set of parameters in one view, these settings do not carry over to the other views. (For example, if you are monitoring logical disk transfer rates in the graph view, it does not mean that you can access this data and settings from within the report view.)

Other Performance Tools

What I want to cover next is a series of tools you might want to call into play when a performance problem is suspected. Performance Monitor is the main tool designed into the Windows NT environment to support performance monitoring, and it is quite powerful. It can measure far more data items than you would ever want to review (unless you are really bored). However, I would like you to consider data that you can obtain from the following tools that support your performance monitoring activities:

- Event Viewer
- Virtual Memory display in the Control Panel System applet
- Tasking display in the Control Panel System applet
- The Services applet in Control Panel
- The Server applet in Control Panel
- The Windows NT Diagnostics utility in the Administrative Tools program group

Event Viewer

First on this list is Event Viewer. This tool was basically designed to support auditing in Windows NT and is described in more detail in Chapter 27, "Auditing Windows NT Server." The Event Viewer audit trail records occurrences of certain situations that have been defined as being of interest for future review. This includes both problems (as in the case of a service that fails to start up or dies) and information messages (such as startups and shutdowns of the system). The Event Viewer can also record activities related to applications (such as SQL Server and Exchange Server) that have been designed to record such information. This time-stamped record can be very valuable when you are trying to figure out what was happening with your system when a problem occurred.

Imagine that users complained that the system was extremely slow around 12:45 today. I didn't have Performance Monitor running at the time, so I don't have any hard data related to key performance counters. I do, however, have the subjective data point from the users that performance was poor at a certain time of the day. The first thing I would do is look in the Event Viewer to see if there was anything special happening about that time.

Figure 20.18 shows the Event Viewer from my system. Looking at this, I can see that several print jobs were queued around the time that the users reported the performance problem. I might suspect that someone had queued a series of complex screen print jobs to that printer that placed a high demand on the system (which is what I was doing). I would then be able to run some tests and see if I could replicate the problem and then take corrective action to prevent it from happening again. The best thing about Event Viewer is that it is sitting there waiting for you to read it. You don't have to go out of your way to set it up.

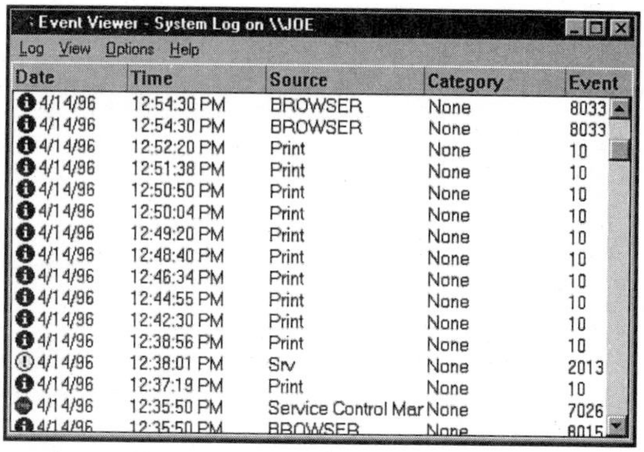

FIGURE 20.18.

An Event Viewer record used for performance monitoring.

Virtual Memory Display Applet

Next on my list of other tools that might come in handy is the Virtual Memory display in the Control Panel System applet. Figure 20.19 shows this display for my computer. Although this tool does not tell you why a particular application was slow this afternoon, it is one place to visit when you want to know how your paging files are set up. There are also some interesting bits of data at the bottom about the space taken up by drivers and the size of the registry. The display at the top can be useful because if you are observing a fair amount of paging and also a disk drive that is heavily loaded, you might want to check which disk drives contain paging files. Paging might cause the disks that contain the paging files to become heavily burdened.

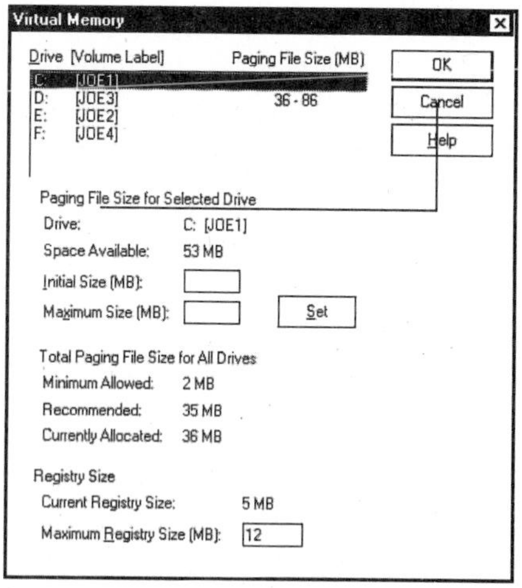

FIGURE 20.19.

The Virtual Memory display.

Tasking Dialog

Another interesting mini-tool you might want to use as a reference is the one that controls tasking priorities for Windows NT. This is one place where you get to influence those self-tuning algorithms. Windows NT Workstation is optimized toward providing a good response to user actions (in the foreground). Windows NT Server is optimized toward sacrificing some console responsiveness in return for doing a good job taking care of networked users through background services, such as the network services, print services, and database management system services. Figure 20.20 shows the Tasking dialog on the System applet accessed from the Control Panel. As you can see, you have three levels of control, ranging from heavily supporting foreground applications to a balance between foreground and background responsiveness. If you ever have to do a significant amount of processing on the system console of a less powerful Windows NT Server, you will become convinced that it is not balanced but instead is ignoring you in favor of those users who are connected through the network. Perhaps that is just my opinion or I am getting spoiled from using relatively good equipment.

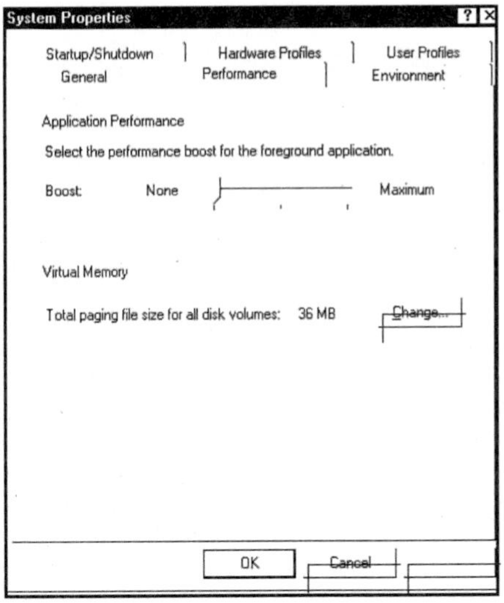

FIGURE 20.20.

The Tasking dialog box.

Services Applet

Another tool you might want to bring to bear on performance problems is the Services applet in the Control Panel. (See Figure 20.21.) This is the best place to look to see which services are actually running at the current moment. If you are experiencing performance problems, you might be able to find a few services that you are running that you no longer need. This is an ideal way to get more performance from your system without increasing your costs. Another possibility is that you have a series of services that you use only at certain times of the day. You can build a batch file that uses the net start and net stop commands to start and stop the services so that they run only when they are needed. This is shown in the following example, which stops an Oracle database instance service to allow a backup to be completed. (There are also a few calls to shut down the Oracle database and then reopen it in this script, but this is not a tutorial on Oracle.) The key to remember is that the Services applet is where you can go to see which services are running.

```
net stop "OracleServiceORCL" >> c:\scripts\backup.log
ntbackup backup c: /d"Daily Backup" /b /l"C:\daily_bk.log" /tape:0
net start "OracleServiceORCL" >> c:\scripts\backup.log
```

FIGURE 20.21.

The Services applet.

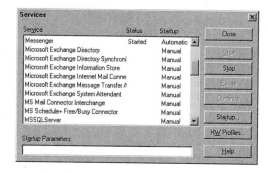

Server Applet

Next on my list of useful utilities is the Server applet (not to be confused with the Services applet) in the Control Panel. (See Figure 20.22.) This is a quick place to check several parameters that directly impact performance without setting up Performance Monitoring settings files. The items that are of interest to me are as follows.

FIGURE 20.22.

The Server applet.

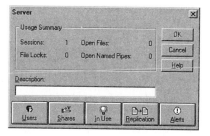

■ The number of users who currently have sessions on your server. You can click the Users button to get a list of these users. If you have an intermittent problem, it might be useful to see who is always logged on when the problem occurs. You can then explore what they are doing that might be causing the problem. This might seem a bit tedious, but it might be the only way to figure out those problems that crop up and then disappear before you have time to set up formal monitoring routines.

■ The number of files that are locked. Certain applications are very interested in maintaining data integrity. They therefore lock up their data files while a thread is in the process of updating that file. The problem is that other user applications that need to access those files might be stuck waiting for the first application to release the data file. This period of being stuck seems the same to an end user as a grossly overloaded CPU. It is just time sitting there looking at the hourglass cursor.

■ The other indicators might be interesting in certain cases. You might want to explore them when you get some time.

Windows NT Diagnostics Applet

My final item on the list of other useful monitoring utilities is the Windows NT Diagnostics panel. (See Figure 20.23.) This is not quite up to the functionality of the Windows 95 device control panels that let you see all those nasty internal parameters such as IRQs, memory addresses, and so forth that affect your system. If you have any questions about these parameters, this is one place to find the data.

FIGURE 20.23.

Windows NT Diagnostics utility.

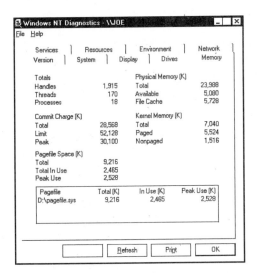

Final Points on Monitoring Utilities

With these utilities, you have a really good shot at tracking down most of the common problems that might rear their ugly heads. Before I leave this subject, I wanted to bring out a few final points that you should consider related to monitoring utilities:

■ The disk monitoring utilities require a bit of overhead to monitor them. (1.5 percent is the number you typically see.) Microsoft has therefore decided that it is best to leave disk monitoring turned off by default. To get those disk-related counters going, you have to run a utility from the command line (`diskperf -y`) and then reboot the computer whose disk drives you want to monitor. After that, you have data for those counters associated with the logical and physical disk drives.

■ You should keep in mind that monitoring an excessive number of parameters can weigh down your system. Most of the time it is beneficial to start monitoring for general problems and then activate additional counters that relate to specific areas when the general counters indicate potential problems.

■ You have the option of monitoring remote NT computers with Performance Monitor. This enables you to use your personal workstation to keep an eye on several servers. When set up in this manner, you have to look in only one place to check the performance of all the computers on your network.

Time-Based Performance Monitoring

Finally, you do not have to collect performance data all the time. In many organizations, you find very little processing during the evening or night hours. Why waste disk space collecting data from numerous counters when you know they are probably close to zero? The answer to this is a neat little utility included in the Windows NT Resource Kit that enables you to start performance monitoring in the background using settings files that you have previously saved to disk. You can configure multiple settings files to take averages every minute during the normal work day and collect averages every half hour at night when you are running fairly long batch processing jobs whose load varies little over time. The service to accomplish this function is `datalog.exe`. You turn this on and off at various times using the command line (and batch file) utility of NT and the `monitor.exe` command line utility. The following example would start the monitoring utility at 8:00 and stop it at 11:59 (the morning data run):

```
at 8:00 "monitor START"
at 11:59 "monitor STOP"
```

The Resource Kit provides more details about using the automated monitoring service. You still have to look at the log files to see what is happening with your system, but at least you don't have to be around to start and stop the monitoring process. It also has the convenience of letting you build and check out settings files interactively using Performance Monitor. This feature, combined with all the other monitoring functions discussed earlier, gives you a really powerful set of tools to track what is going on with your NT system.

Good news. My lengthy theoretical discussion of hardware, the Windows NT operating system components and the performance monitoring utilities is complete. I know that many of you would have preferred a simple list explaining "if you observe this, do that." If it were that simple, everyone would be doing it, and that would lower the pay scale. So I had to give you an understanding of what you were controlling. I also had to present all the tools you can use to help you when a problem comes up, as well as the basics of how to use them. I urge you to get comfortable with these tools before you actually have to use them to solve a problem with everyone breathing down your neck.

A Starting Set of Counters

There are many possible things you can look at and several tools you can use. Many of these counters are designed for very special situations and yield little useful information about 99 percent of the servers that are actually in operation. My next task is to present what I would consider to be a good set of counters to monitor to give you a feel for the overall health of your system. If one of these counters starts to indicate a potential problem, you can call into play the other counters related to this object to track down the specifics of the problem.

Going back to my earlier discussion, I simplified the numerous hardware and software systems on your computer into four basic areas: CPU, memory, input/output (primarily hard disk drives), and networking. Based on this model, I offer the following counters as a starting point for your monitoring efforts:

- **Processor: percent processor time.** If your processor is running continuously at near 100 percent load, you are probably nearing the limit of processing capacity for your computer. If you have multiprocessor systems, remember to look at the loads on all the processor instances. It might turn out that your system and applications are beating up on one processor while the rest remain idle (one of the areas Windows NT is working upon is splitting the load across multiple processors). Remember that processing naturally comes in surges (an application waits for a while for data to load from disk, then suddenly starts off in a burst of activity), so you have to consider the load measured over a reasonable period (10 seconds or more).

- **Memory: pages/second.** Some paging between physical and virtual memory is normal and happens even in periods of light loading. What you have to be sensitive about is when this paging becomes higher than normal and your system is spending all its time transferring information between the paging files and physical memory instead of servicing user processing needs. A number of 5 or less in this category is generally considered to be acceptable, but it varies between systems.

- **Physical disks: percent time.** Applications tend to like to have all their files located together so they can be found and segregated from the files created by other applications. This leads to a problem: when an application is running, especially when it is supporting multiple users, it tends to place a high load on the disk drive where the file is located, whereas other disk drives might be sitting idle. Because disk drives are one of the slowest components in most applications, this is an area where you can build up a bottleneck where applications sit and wait for data transfers for one user to be completed before the other users can access their data. In databases, this is usually the single biggest tuning activity that can improve performance. General wisdom usually states that if a drive has over 90 percent disk time, it is very busy and might be a candidate for a bit of load reduction.

- **Physical disks: queue length.** Another important indicator designed to catch the fact that several user processes are sitting idle while waiting to be granted access to a disk drive is the queue length. A good rule of thumb is that if the queue length is greater than 2, you should be investigating ways to lighten the load on this disk drive.

- **Server: bytes total/second.** The final component you need to keep an eye on is network transmissions. This is a tough one because there are so many monitors for each of the different protocols. Perhaps this is a sign that very few people truly understand networking to the point where they are one with the network and instantly know of problems. The server total bytes per second counter provides a good overall picture of when the network and/or network interface card is struggling to keep up with the load. Anything near the rated sustained limit for the type of network that you are using (3 million bits per second for Ethernet and either 4 or 16 million bits per second for Token ring) is an indication that the network itself is overloaded. This can be somewhat deceptive because you might be connected to a local network that can transmit signals at the speeds listed earlier, but you might be connected to other local networks by lines as slow as 56 thousand bits per second that might be your true bottleneck. Finally, your network might be within its rated transmission capacity, but your network card might not be. This varies between cards, so you have to get a feeling for the limit of your particular system.

These rules of thumb are fine for the industry in general, but they do not reflect the unique characteristics of your particular configuration. You really need to run your performance monitoring utilities when your system is running well to get a baseline as to what counter values are associated with normal performance. This is especially important for some of the counters that are not in the preceding list; it is difficult to prescribe a rule of thumb for them because they are very dependent on your hardware. For example, a fast disk drive on a fast controller and bus can read many more bytes per second than a slow disk drive on a slower controller. It might be helpful to run Performance Monitor with several of these other counters that make sense to you and write down what the normal values are.

You can take the preceding discussion one step further and use a utility found in the Resource Kit to simulate loads on your system to determine what counter values correspond to the limits of your system. This utility is relatively simple to operate. Your goal is to start with a moderate load and increase the load until performance is seriously affected. You record the values of the counters of interest as you increase the load and then mark those that correspond to the effective maximum values. This takes a fair amount of time, and you do not want to impact your users; however, if you are running a particularly large or demanding NT environment, you might want to have this data to ensure that you line up resources long before the system reaches its limits.

One final point is that each application has a slightly different effect on the system. Databases, for example, tend to stress memory utilization, input/output capabilities, and the system's capability to process simple (integer) calculations. Scientific and engineering applications tend to emphasize raw computing power, especially calculations that involve floating point arithmetic. It is useful for you to have an understanding of what each of the applications on your server does so that you can get a feel for which of the applications and therefore which of the users might be causing your load to increase. Remember, a disk queue counter tells you that a certain disk drive is overloaded. However, it is your job to figure out which applications and users are placing that load on the drive and to determine a way to improve their performance.

Common Problems: Detection and Correction

Unfortunately, your new-found knowledge of how to analyze the source of a Windows NT performance problem is not enough. You also need to know how to pinpoint the problem and fix it to get performance back up to standard. Armed with the magnificent array of data you collected from Performance Monitor, you should be able to have the system back to peak efficiency in a matter of minutes. Although you are well on the way to returning your system to health, you might still have a few hurdles to jump over along the way:

- Problems can tend to hide one another. For example, you might have a disk drive that is being used excessively. Unless you check all your indications and think the problem through carefully, you might miss the fact that this particular problem was caused by a high degree of paging that is occurring to a drive that also contains most of your database files. This is really indicative of a problem with both memory and the way you have your disk drives laid out. Therefore, it is always wise to check all the information available to you.

- You must also know what is running on your system when problems are observed in order to know what to adjust. This can be tough on systems that are processing a large number of users and a variety of applications. Just knowing that a disk drive is overloaded is not enough. You have to know which application is causing the problem so that you know what adjustments to make. (It could take a very long time if you moved files around one by one until you found the one that reduced the load to acceptable values.)

- There are differing opinions as to what is satisfactory response time. People who are used to working with simple PC applications usually consider instantaneous response time to be at least adequate. If you are searching for data in a database that contains a few hundred gigabytes of information, you have to be a little more tolerant as to how long it takes to search the data for your query. This is something that should be agreed to by your organization, preferably before the applications are built, so that you can obtain adequate processing resources. It can make the administrator's job extremely difficult if you have to spend all your time chasing after performance problems that you can do nothing about because users' expectations are unreasonable.

- You also have to be sensitive to the cost/performance trade-offs that have to be made. Although extra speed is a good idea in any system, it might not be worth devoting your efforts for several months to cut a second or two off user response time on a particular application. Most administrators have plenty of other work to do. Another trade-off that has to be made is whether it is cheaper to spend $400 on an extra 8MB of RAM or have a contractor come in at $50 per hour and spend a month tuning the system (at a cost of around $8,000). Technical people are often not trained to think about these considerations, but they probably should be.

- Finally, you should sometimes consider nontechnical solutions to your problems before you buy equipment or spend a lot of your time on tuning. One of the classic loading problems on servers is the fact that they experience peak loads for the first hour of the business day and the first hour after lunch. This is relatively easy to explain, because most people come in, get their coffee, and log onto the e-mail system to check their mail. The same thing happens after lunch, and possibly just before the end of the business day (which also might experience peak printing loads as everyone finishes off what they have been working on and prints it before they go home). Sometimes an e-mail (or memo) to your users explaining the situation and offering them greatly improved response times if they alter their habits a little can be enough to solve the problem without any drastic measures or purchases.

Performance Tuning Methodology

It is now time to go over the analysis and tuning process itself to see what steps are involved. In my approach to performance tuning, I start with the basic performance data collected by the tools discussed in this chapter. I combine this with knowledge of what is happening on the system (what jobs are running, is this a special time such as monthly closing of the books, and so on).

The next step is to combine the data you have gathered with your knowledge of your hardware platform and the Windows NT system. Your job is to come up with possible causes of the problem you are seeing. This is where it is especially helpful to have collected a baseline of performance data when the system is working well so that you can see relatively slight changes in the performance indicators, which might lead you to the problem. Sometimes it is useful to start by figuring out what is working correctly and narrowing down the list of things that could be causing the problem. It depends somewhat on how your brain thinks.

Once you have a list of possible causes to the problem, you might next want to collect a bit more data to confirm your theories. Also, the general performance data might not be sufficient to narrow down the problem. You might have to run additional performance counters while the system is running to get the data necessary to make a decision. This can be a challenge because users often want an immediate solution and might not understand when you take time to investigate things a bit further. Another real problem area is intermittent problems. Perhaps you are using the alert feature of Performance Monitor and come in one morning to find that the system had two nasty performance spikes yesterday. How do you re-create the circumstances that lead to those problems? You might have to run extra monitors for days or even weeks until the problem crops up again.

Once you have enough data, you need to come up with likely causes for the problem. Looking ahead to the next step, where you try to fix the problem, it is to your benefit to try to keep the list of possible causes to those that are reasonable. It is also useful to rank the items on your list in order of likelihood that they are the cause of the problem. Because your time is valuable, it would be nice if you solved the problem with your first or second try. It also keeps your users much happier.

Once you have done all the analysis you consider reasonable, it is time to actually solve the problem. Here is where you need to apply knowledge of your system to know what has to be done to solve a given problem. There are often alternative solutions to a problem. You have to use engineering judgment and experience to come up with the best solution for your environment. An important principle in scientific experiments that you need to apply to your problem-solving efforts is to change only one thing at a time on your system. If you move all the files on every one of your disk drives around, you might solve the first problem you found but create several more in the process.

So much for the basic problem-solving method. What I want to devote the rest of this section to is a list of common problems that come up on servers and some alternative solutions you might want to consider. Please remember that thousands of things could go wrong in a modern computer. The list I am presenting could never cover every possible problem and solution. I am just listing a few of the more common solutions to stimulate your creative processes when you are working on your problems.

Typical Performance Problems

CPU capacity problems are the first area I want to consider. This is an area where you have to be somewhat careful in your analysis. Adding an extra disk drive is becoming a relatively insignificant expense that will probably be needed in the future anyway, with the growth in data storage needs and application sizes. However, you are talking serious expense and effort to upgrade to a higher capacity CPU in most cases. Some servers have the capability of just plugging in additional processors, but most do not. Therefore, you better be absolutely sure you have exhausted all other possibilities before you bring up buying a new CPU as a solution. Some things to consider when you think you might have a CPU problem include the following:

- Is the load placed on the CPU reasonable for the applications that are being run? This might be tough to assess for individuals who are not experienced in the computer industry. However, if you have a 150MHz Pentium processor that is being overloaded by running an e-mail system for 10 users, I would say that you have a problem with the application or other tuning parameters; this is not a load that would typically require a more powerful processor.

- Do you have any new or uncommon hardware devices in your computer? A poorly written device driver can waste a lot of CPU time and weigh down the processor. You can check to see if the vendor has seen this problem before and possibly has an updated device driver that is kinder to the CPU.

- Do you have monitoring data from your capacity planning efforts (which I discuss later) that backs up your claim that the user's demand has grown to the point where a new processor is needed? Have any new applications been loaded on the system that might need tuning or be the cause of the problem that forces you to upgrade the CPU?

The next area of concern is memory. One of the main complaints PC users have about Windows NT is that it demands what seems to them to be a large amount of memory. As I discussed earlier, accessing information stored in memory is so much faster than accessing data located on disk drives that operating system and application designers will likely continue to write software that requires greater memory to perform more complex tasks and produce reasonable response times. Another point to remember is that many Windows NT self-tuning activities are centered around allocating memory space to help improve system performance. A few thoughts related to memory problems include the following:

■ Are your applications that use shared memory areas properly tuned? An Oracle database can be tuned by the DBA to use only a few megabytes of memory or almost one hundred megabytes (I did that once on a very large data warehouse). You should check to see that these applications are properly tuned (neither too much nor too little memory used) before you go out and purchase memory. It is also useful to check whether you have any unnecessary services running. With all these automated installation utilities, it is hard to remember whether you have cleared out old application services when new ones are installed. It doesn't hurt to scan through the list of services in the Control Panel just to be sure.

■ What is the configuration of your memory expansion slots? Typically you have a relatively small number of memory expansion slots in a computer. Also, hardware vendors often tie pairs of these memory slots together and require you to install the chips in this bank (as they call it) in matched pairs. If you are expecting to continue to expand the use of your server and its memory requirements, you might want to consider getting slightly larger memory chips now so that you don't have to remove older, smaller chips in the future to make room for chips that are large enough to support your needs.

Next on the list of problem areas are input/output problems related to disk drives. Working with a lot of database systems, I find this to be the most common problem. The good news is that with current disk drive capacities and prices, it is also one of the easiest to solve. Almost all the servers I have worked with have their disk requirements grow every year, so it isn't much of a risk that you will never use additional disk capacity. The risk you take is that you will spend extra money this year on a disk drive that has half the capacity and twice the cost of next year's model. Some considerations when you have a disk input/output problem include the following:

■ One of the easiest solutions to an overworked disk situation in a system with multiple disk drives is to move files around to balance the load. The basic process is to figure out which files are accessed frequently (or accessed at the same time by a given application) and put them on separate disk drives. The biggest tuning recommendation for an Oracle database that is performing poorly due to input/output is to place the tables and indexes on separate disk drives. You have to be sensitive to how the disk drives are connected together when you are doing this. You can split the load between several disk drives so that each disk drive is well below its data transfer capacity, but you might run into problems when you exceed the transfer capacity of the disk controller card to which these drives are attached. On very large disk farms with multiple levels of disk controllers, someone has to balance the load across controllers (and controllers of controllers) in addition to worrying about the load on individual disk drives.

- You will run into situations where your application load or other factors will not enable you to split the load across several disk drives (for example, all the input/output activity is centered around a single file). In this case, you might have to consider buying faster disk drives and controllers (such as fast-wide SCSI or even electrostatic disk drives) to handle these busy files and reallocate the other disk drives to other purposes (such as holding all the performance data you are going to have to log onto this heavily loaded system). You could also implement disk striping to split single data files across multiple disk drives.

- Depending on which of the NT file systems (FAT, NTFS, and so on) you have used on a given disk drive, you might run into a problem known as fragmentation. Back at the dawn of time in the computer world, all data in a file had to be located in a set of contiguous blocks on a disk drive. People had a lot of problems dealing with this as they tried to write applications such as word processors, where they would write a little bit on one document, do some other things, and then write a little bit more. The disk blocks at the end of the word processing document would get filled by other work, and it would take a lot of rearrangement of files to make space for the new, larger document. The solution to this was to allow files to be split into multiple sections on the disk drive with file access utilities that are smart enough to put all the pieces together when the user accessed the file. This can be a problem in many file systems when you consider the fact that the disk drives can transmit data much more quickly than they can move the mechanical arms to which the heads read and write data. Therefore, a file that is scattered all over the disk drive (known as a fragmented file) is much slower to access than one where all the data is located in one chunk. There is some debate over whether NTFS suffers from fragmentation, but there are utilities that can defragment different types of file systems, such as Executive Software with its Diskeeper product.

- An interesting situation relates to the fact that disk services have a lower priority than printing services. If you are really daring, you can go into the registry under the `service\lanman\server\parameters` key and raise the priority of the server from its default priority of 1 to 2 (add `ThreadPriority` of type `DWORD` with a value of 2).

- An alternative that is supported on many different types of disk drives enables you to scatter a single file across multiple disk drives. You can rely on either hardware or software to let you tie together sections of several disk drives and treat them as if they were a single logical disk drive. In a two-disk pair, for example, the first logical block would be on the first physical disk drive; the second logical block would be on the second physical disk drive; the third logical block would be on the third disk drive; and so on. This technique, known as striping, is actually just one form of a technology known as RAID (redundant arrays of inexpensive disks) that can be used to improve performance and reliability.

The final area in which you might encounter problems is the network. I have always found this to be a much tougher area to troubleshoot, because I do not own it all. Even the network administrators can have troubles because servers or workstations can cause the problems as often as a basic lack of network capacity or failed equipment. One of the keys to being able to troubleshoot a network effectively is to have a drawing of how things are laid out. This is difficult because it changes regularly and most people do not have access to these drawings, if anyone has even bothered to make one. A few thoughts on the area of network problem-solving are as follows:

- The best hope for quick and efficient solutions for network problems is to isolate the problem to a particular section of the network or even a particular machine. This often involves going around to friends on the various network segments and seeing how their systems are performing. Perhaps you have some of the advanced network monitoring technologies that will help you in this process. One of the most common problems on a wide area network is the limited transmission capacities of the links to remote sites. Although these network links might not be your problem to solve, you are often the first one to hear about it ("why is your server so slow today?") and you have to come up with some data to prove that it is not your problem and that someone else has to solve the problem.

- If the problem is actually with your server, you might try to reduce the number of network protocols that have to be monitored by the server. It is easy to just check every protocol when installing the server so that you don't have to worry about it in the future, but this can become a burden later.

- You might also want to rearrange the binding order for the various protocols to emphasize those that are more important (for example, TCP/IP for those database transactions that everyone wants to speed up) at the cost of increasing response time for those services that need speed less (the print jobs where the printout can always get to the printer faster than the user can).

- If all else fails, talk to network experts and see if they can recommend a network card that has better throughput than your current card. There is a wide variation in performance, with most PC cards designed for the relatively simple transmission requirements of workstations, not the more demanding needs of servers. It is less expensive than replacing your network with a faster network or altering the topology to provide better routing.

That is probably sufficient for this introductory discussion of performance problem-solving. Try not to feel overwhelmed if this is your first introduction to the subject. It is a rather complex art that comes easier as you get some experience. It is not easy, and there are people who specialize in solving the more complex problems. It is often a challenge just to keep up with all the available technology options. Windows NT will probably also continue to evolve to meet some of the new challenges that are out there, including Internet/intranet access and multimedia initiatives such as PC video. It could almost be a full-time job just to keep up with all the application programming interfaces that Microsoft releases to developers these days.

Network Monitoring

Many administrators find themselves on small local area networks that don't suffer from many performance problems. Others are attached to complex, global networks that place high demands on all parts of the system. The network monitoring utilities built into Windows NT are designed to meet the more simple needs of the smaller networks. They are designed to provide a reasonable amount of information to determine whether the problem lies with NT Server. They can even help isolate the protocol and possibly the application causing the problem.

More powerful tools can monitor the traffic levels and types of the various segments of the network itself. Many of them even run under Windows NT and are marketed by vendors such as the big network hardware vendors, Hewlett-Packard, and others. They provide convenient GUI interfaces and graphical displays of loads. They are definitely beyond the scope of this introductory discussion. You might want to keep them in mind for those times when you have proved that your server is providing adequate network transmission services but a problem somewhere in your corporate network is causing user response times to be unacceptable. Who knows, your company might already have this equipment located in one of those dark corners of the data center known only to the true network gurus.

Simple Network Monitoring Protocol (SNMP)

The Simple Network Monitoring Protocol (SNMP) started out with the goal of monitoring network-related information. However, it had the blessing of being a published standard as opposed to a proprietary tool that locked you into a particular network equipment vendor's hardware. I mention it here for two reasons. First, the use of this protocol has been expanded to monitor the functioning of devices on the network such as Windows NT Servers. You can install an SNMP agent to allow remote devices to find out how your server is doing. A second reason is that there are packages designed to collect the performance results from other devices on the network that run under Windows NT. One of your workstations or servers might be used to serve as a central network system monitoring computer.

Capacity Planning and Routine Performance Monitoring

Some people spend their entire lives reacting to what others are doing to them. Others prefer to be the ones making the plans and causing others to react to what they are doing. When you get a call from a user saying that the system is out of disk space or it takes 10 minutes to execute a simple database transaction, you are put in the position of reacting to external problems. This tends to be a high-pressure situation where you have to work quickly to restore service. If you have to purchase equipment, you might have great problems getting a purchase order through your procurement system in less than a decade (government employees are allowed to laugh at that last comment). You might get called in the middle of the night to come in and solve the problem, and you might have to stay at work for 36 hours straight. This is not a fun situation.

Although these reactive situations cannot always be avoided (and some people actually seem to prefer crisis management), I prefer to avoid them whenever possible. The best way to avoid crises is to keep a close eye on things on a routine basis and try my best to plan for the future. All the performance monitoring techniques presented in this chapter can be run at almost any time. You could be running some basic performance monitoring jobs right now. The key to planning is some solid data that shows trends over a significant period of time combined with information on any changes planned in the environment.

This process has been the subject of entire books. There are several detailed, scientific methodologies for calculating out resource needs and performance requirements. For the purposes of this book, I just want to present a few basic concepts that I have found useful and that can be applied with a minimal amount of effort by administrators who take care of small workgroup servers or large data centers of servers:

- If your program to track performance and capacity requirements takes too much time to complete, you are probably going to have trouble keeping up with it. I would recommend automating the data collection using Performance Monitor log files either started with the at command or run as a service. Make it one of your routine tasks to collect averages or maximum/minimum values from these log files and place them in a spreadsheet, database, or log book.

- You should present this data to management, users, and so forth on a routine basis. People tend to react poorly if you suddenly drop on them that they need to buy some new disk drives next month (which is the end of the fiscal year and all the budget for such things is already spent). You might want to tie your capacity planning into the budgeting cycle for your organization.

- I like to use a spreadsheet to store the data so that I can easily construct a graph showing load over time. People tend to get lost in a long series of numbers but can easily see that line of disk utilization progressing relentlessly toward its limits.

- Knowing what has happened and using it as a prediction for the future is often not enough. For example, based on past trends, you might have enough processor capacity to last for two years. However, you also know that your development group is developing five new applications for your server that are to be rolled out this summer. You need to find a way to estimate (even a rough estimate is better than none at all) the impact of these planned changes on your growth curves to determine when you will run out of a critical component in server performance.

Summary

I think most people would consider this a somewhat challenging chapter to read. It was a challenging chapter to write. It was a balancing act between presenting too much information (there are entire books devoted to Windows NT tuning) and too little. My goals for this chapter included the following:

- Provide information on the basics of server hardware as they affect performance.
- Provide an overview of the components of the Windows NT Server operating system that affect performance, including the self-tuning features.
- Discuss the monitoring tools that are provided with Windows NT.
- Go over the basic methodology used to troubleshoot a problem.
- Review some of the more common problems and their solutions.
- Present a few extra credit topics that you should be aware of, such as network monitoring, SNMP, and capacity planning. I would recommend getting in there and trying out the performance monitoring tools that are available under Windows NT. You will be more ready to solve problems when they come up and be able to worry less about your ability to determine exactly what is going on with your system. You might also consider taking a performance baseline every now and then so that you have a set of numbers that represent your server when it is working well. You can compare the numbers generated when the server is performing poorly to this baseline to see what has changed. Finally, you should at least try to store the performance monitoring data that you collect every so often so that you have data that you can use in case someone asks you to project when you will need equipment upgrades, and so on.

Using Remote Access Services

by David Wolfe and Terry Ogletree

IN THIS CHAPTER

CHAPTER 21

Before the Internet became the phenomenon it is today, most computer users used modems to connect to PC bulletin board services. The ability to use a CRT to dial into a computer system and establish a terminal session has been around even longer than the PC. Windows NT has an accessory that you can use for this purpose—it's called *Hyperterm*. Connecting to a corporate network or to the Internet over a phone line, however, requires a different type of connection.

When you dial in to a computer using Hyperterm, you are limited to executing programs on that remote computer or in using a file transfer protocol to upload or download a file.

When you use Remote Access Services (RAS) to establish a dial-up connection, however, you are not limited to communicating with a bulletin board type of program. Instead, the protocols used allow your computer to become a peer member on the network you are dialing into. These protocols include the Point-to-Point Protocol (PPP), Serial Line Internet Protocol (SLIP), and the Microsoft RAS protocol. Although communication is much slower on a standard dial-up telephone line, you should be able to perform most of the same functions through this link to the network that you could if your computer were directly attached to the network. Indeed, if you can afford an ISDN or higher connection instead of a standard telephone line, access is much faster.

For example, when you use a terminal session to dial into a computer on a network, you can run programs in the terminal emulation window that are executed on the target computer. When you use RAS to connect to a network remotely, you are able to browse the network and connect to file and print shares. Thus, using RAS, you can actually execute programs on your local PC that reside on disks attached to computers on a remote network.

This chapter covers the process of installing RAS and administering remote users, as well as how to use RAS's Dial-Up Networking features to connect a PC to a corporate network or to the Internet.

Understanding Windows NT RAS

Windows NT RAS provides functionality that can be used by the smallest business using a single modem to dial in to the office computer, or the largest NT servers using banks of modems for multiple users or X.25 and ISDN connections for high-speed remote connections. Multiple RAS servers (each with up to 256 remote clients) can be managed using a single utility, making RAS an enterprise-enabled application. Users connected to an NT network can gain the same access to network resources as users on the LAN, the only difference being the speed of access. You can, for security reasons, restrict RAS clients to accessing only resources on the RAS server they have dialed into.

Clients are authenticated using standard NT user accounts and can connect using PPP, SLIP, or the Microsoft RAS protocol. Client software is available for other Windows operating systems and even MS-DOS and LAN Manager clients. Most non-Microsoft PPP implementations can also be used to dial into an NT RAS server. As of version 4.0 of Windows NT, the Point-to-Point Tunneling Protocol (PPTP) is also supported. PPTP is a protocol that allows for private communications over the Internet or an intranet by encrypting and encapsulating other protocols and transmitting them. A virtual private network (VPN) is created between two computers to provide a secure exchange of data.

Microsoft has released a new version of software for remote access and routing that can be downloaded from http://www.microsoft.com. You greatly enhance RAS's capabilities by installing this update. Support for PPTP between servers is provided (only client-to-server PPTP is supported without the update), and so are standard routing protocols such as RIP, OSPF, and RIP for IPX, among others.

For more information on LAN, WAN, RAS, and routing protocols supported by Windows NT RAS, see Chapter 23, "Implementing Routing and Remote Access Services."

NOTE

PPP is the protocol of choice. It is the most widely used at this time, and provides better performance than SLIP. Windows NT RAS supports SLIP for clients to dial up to non-NT servers that use SLIP. However, support is not provided for SLIP clients to dial into Windows NT RAS. In other words, Windows NT provides your computer the ability to be a dial-up SLIP client, but not a SLIP server.

Using Dial-Up Networking

The term RAS is most often associated with the server side of remote access services. The client side, as of version 4.0 of Windows NT Server, is called Dial-Up Networking (DUN). The software interface for DUN now resembles the Windows 95 version, and is easy to configure and use. A wizard can be used to set up new connections and you can really make things easier by creating a desktop shortcut for your most often used connections.

Using X.25 Connections

This type of connection sends data through a packet-switched network. The X.25 protocol specifies an interface into the network and underlying transport mechanisms are invisible to the X.25 clients. A device called a PAD, which stands for Packet Assembler-Disassembler, is usually used to interface with the network, though many providers allow dial-up lines into a PAD for a packet-switched network. You can also use an X.25 Smart Card. For more information, see the Hardware Compatibility List (HCL).

NOTE

Although a printed copy of the Hardware Compatibility List (HCL) is provided with Windows NT Server 4.0, you can access the up-to-date online version at Microsoft's Web site: http://www.microsoft.com/isapi/hwtest/hcl.idc

X.25 networks can provide a bandwidth of up to 56K, and are more reliable than ordinary telephone lines. However, since ISDN can provide faster throughput, it is probably a better choice. X.25 is an older technology, which was very popular during the 1980s, before the Internet became a popular commercial network. In most cases, you are charged in a metered-use fashion, where you pay by the amount of data transferred. ISDN offers a digital connection at a higher rate of data transfer, and is provided as a non-metered service in most locations.

When using a dial-up X.25 provider, you may have to use the capability of RAS Dial-Up Networking to bring up a terminal window after a connection has been established, or to run a script file so that it can perform logon verification for access and billing purposes.

Using ISDN Connections

ISDN stands for Integrated Services Digital Network, and provides a fast and reliable communications channel for accessing remote computers or networks. Although the cost of an ISDN line (and the ISP access fees) makes this out of reach for most home users, it can be a good choice for businesses that need greater speed than can be provided by ordinary modems, but do not have the need to use T1 bandwidth. T1 lines allow for a data transfer rate of 1.544Mbps, and are usually used by businesses with large amounts of data or voice traffic, because they can be expensive. Medium-sized Internet service providers can make efficient use of T1 lines, because they can pool traffic from many different sources to use the bandwidth.

ISDN actually comes in two different forms, which vary in expense and bandwidth. Basic Rate Interface (BRI) consists of two 64Kbps "B" channels, which are used to carry the actual data, and a separate "D" channel, which is used for control signals between the ISDN hardware at both ends of the connection. Each B channel can be used separately or can be combined to achieve a greater bandwidth connection.

If you are going to combine both channels, you should be careful when configuring the hardware. If you use a Terminal Adapter (TA) that attaches to the serial port and you choose to aggregate the two B channels, you won't be able to get the full 128Kbps because the serial port is limited to 115.2Kbps.

Primary Rate Interface (PRI) service is similar to BRI, except that the number of B channels jumps to 23 (in the United States; up to 30 in some European countries).

Charges for ISDN lines can vary widely from one geographical location to another. Different telephone companies charge varying rates for installation and usage fees for ISDN. Some provide a flat monthly rate for an ISDN connection, while others charge by the amount of actual usage. One important reason rates can vary widely from one company to another is that an ISDN connection requires a good physical connection to the central office. Some locations have a better telephone networking infrastructure than others, and the cost of building new communications links is not inexpensive.

In addition, if you are planning to use an ISDN connection to attach your computer or network to the Internet, don't forget that the phone company's charges for the ISDN line are not the only large expense involved. An Internet services provider (ISP) charges a larger fee for connecting an ISDN line than it does when setting you up with a modem connection.

Using Modems

This is the most common device used for dial-up connections. Not many laptop or portable computers come with X.25 or ISDN adapters installed.

When deciding which modems to use for RAS, try to use the same make and model on each side of the connection, if possible. Slight incompatibilities may exist between manufacturers' products, especially when you get into the higher-speed modems that are still awaiting agreement on a final standard.

When configuring the COM port used for a modem, you should raise the speed at which the port communicates with the modem to be faster than the speed of the modem itself. For example, you should use a port speed of at least 57.6Kbps for a 28.8Kbps modem. The reason for the speed differential is that modems often compress information. The last thing you want to do when trying to improve performance is have a modem waiting for data from the computer (or vice versa).

There are manufacturers now making multi-port I/O boards, which allow you to attach up to 256 modems to an NT server. If you decide to go this route, be sure to use equipment that is on the HCL or is certified by the manufacturer to work with Windows NT RAS. In addition to making a large number of modems available for RAS, there are third-party software applications that can allow you to allocate a bank of modems as a modem pool for use by other network clients.

Installing Remote Access Services

Evaluate the hardware you plan to use for a RAS server and, if possible, be sure that every component is listed on the Windows NT Hardware Compatibility List (HCL); you can also test the components using manufacturer-provided drivers to be sure everything will function as you expect.

Before you start the installation of the Remote Access Service network component, you need to check to be sure you have already installed the networking protocols you will use with RAS. For example, if you are setting up a RAS server on an office LAN and you are using Netware for your networking, you should install IPX/SPX (or NWLink IPX/SPX Compatible Transport, as it's called in the Network applet in the control panel) on the server before you start the installation of RAS itself. Conversely, if you are going to use the Remote Access Service's Dial-Up Networking function to call up the Internet, then you would need to install the TCP/IP protocol before installing RAS.

You can run multiple protocols over RAS sessions under Windows NT Server. If you are using Microsoft networking on your LAN, you might want to allow both the NetBEUI and TCP/IP transport protocols to be used with RAS.

Beginning the Installation

You can install Remote Access Services during the initial installation of Windows NT Server, or you can choose to add the service after installation by using the Network applet in the Control Panel. Select the Services tab, which is shown in Figure 21.1, after you bring up the Network applet. If you do not see Remote Access Service displayed in the Services applet, you need to install it.

> **NOTE**
>
> You must be a member of the Administrators group in order to install RAS.

Figure 21.1.

*The Remote Access
Service is an NT service
that you add using the
Network applet in the
Control Panel.*

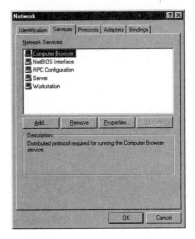

Complete the following steps to add a new service:

1. Click the Add button.

2. The Select Network Service dialog box (Figure 21.2) appears. Use the scrollbar on the right of this dialog box to scroll down until you see the Remote Access Service entry. Highlight the entry and click OK.

3. You are prompted for the location of the Windows NT Server source files. Enter the letter for your CD-ROM drive if you are using the CD, or enter a local or network path to the source files. When you are finished, click the Continue button. Files are copied to the local disk.

At this point in the installation procedure, you are prompted to select a communications device (such as a modem or X.25 PAD) to be used with RAS.

FIGURE 21.2.
*Find the Remote Access
Service and click OK.*

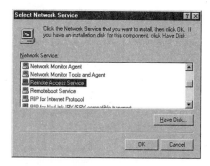

Adding a Communications Device to RAS

If you have already installed modems in the computer and added them to Windows NT using the Modem applet in the Control Panel, then you will be able to choose from here. If you have not added the devices yet, then the installation procedure allows you to do so at this time.

Complete the following steps to add a communications device to RAS:

1. If the service installation program detects that you do not have a suitable RAS communications device installed, it prompts you to do so (see Figure 21.3).

   If you receive this prompt, you should click Yes to invoke the Modem Installer Wizard to guide you through the process. If you already have a usable device installed, then the Add RAS Device dialog box appears (skip to step 8).

FIGURE 21.3.
*You will be warned if
no RAS-capable devices
exist on the computer.*

2. The Install New Modem dialog box (Figure 21.4) pops up as the first step in the wizard. Click Next if you want NT to attempt to identify the modem. Select the check box labeled Don't Detect My Modem, I Will Select It From A List if you know the modem type and want to specify it yourself (then skip to step 7).

FIGURE 21.4.
*You can choose to let
NT detect the modem
automatically, or you
can decide to specify the
modem yourself.*

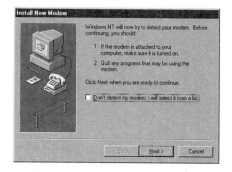

3. The next step in the Install New Modem dialog box appears if you elect to have
Windows NT attempt to detect the modem (see Figure 21.5). It queries the COM
ports on your PC and shows you all the devices that it has detected.

FIGURE 21.5.

*Windows NT queries
the COM ports on your
computer looking for
attached modems.*

NOTE

The modem detection method is not foolproof. If Windows NT is unable to determine your
modem type, or if it returns from the detection phase and indicates that it has chosen a
generic type of modem driver (such as the standard modem shown in Figure 21.6), you
can still choose to change the driver type by clicking the Change button.

FIGURE 21.6.

*Setup prompts you to
continue when it has
finished the detection
process.*

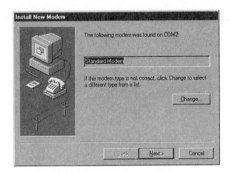

4. If you chose to select your own modem, you are prompted with the Install New
Modem dialog box (see Figure 21.7). Select the Manufacturer on the left side of the
dialog box. A list of models for that manufacturer appear in the list on the right. Select
the correct modem and click OK.

FIGURE 21.7.

You can select the manufacturer and model from this dialog box.

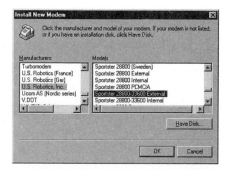

NOTE

If you do not find your modem in the manufacturer model list, but have a disk from the manufacturer with a driver that is compatible with Windows NT 4.0, click the Have Disk button. You are prompted to enter the location of the files (the A: drive or an alternate source). After the Setup program reads the information on your disk, it presents you with a list of one or more modem drivers found on the disk. Select the correct entry and click OK to continue.

5. When you are satisfied with the modem Windows NT has detected or that you have selected manually, click Next in the Install New Modem dialog box.

6. The Location Information dialog box appears (see Figure 21.8). Enter your telephone area code, any number your phone system requires to access an outside line, and whether to use pulse or tone dialing. Use Location Information when you use Dial-Up Networking to connect from different locations. Click Next to continue.

FIGURE 21.8.

Fill in your area code and other dialing information in this dialog box.

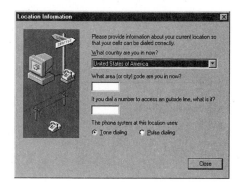

> **NOTE**
>
> The Location Information dialog box may not appear when you install RAS. This most likely happens if you are reinstalling RAS on the computer, or if you have used the Telephony applet in the control panel. Once you have used this dialog box, it does not appear again. Instead, you can use the Telephony applet in the control panel to add more locations.

7. The last dialog box informs you that the modem has been installed and returns you to the modem configuration process (the Add RAS Device dialog box) in the Remote Access Service setup.

8. The Add RAS Device dialog box shown in Figure 21.9 allows you to select the communications device you want to use from the RAS Capable Devices pull-down menu. You can also use this dialog box to add modems or X.25 devices by clicking on the appropriate button.

FIGURE 21.9.

You can select which modem to use from this dialog box, or choose to add devices.

9. If you chose to install an X.25 PAD, you are prompted to select the COM port to which it is attached, and to specify the type of device (see Figure 21.10).

FIGURE 21.10.

You can use this dialog box to add X.25 devices for use with RAS.

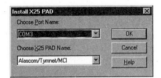

After you have decided which modems or other devices you are going to use for RAS, decide which network protocols you will use on each communications port and whether the particular port will be usable for dialing in (Remote Access Service) or dialing out (Dial-Up Networking).

Configuring Communications Ports for Use with RAS

When you are finished adding or selecting devices to use with RAS, the Remote Access Setup dialog box shown in Figure 21.11 appears. Complete the following steps to configure the communications ports:

1. In the Remote Access Setup dialog box, you can use the Add and Remove buttons to continue adding devices for use with RAS (or removing those not needed). When you select a modem to add, click the Configure button. The Configure Port Usage dialog box appears (see Figure 21.12). Here you should use the radio buttons to select how you will use RAS: for incoming, outgoing, or both incoming and outgoing calls.

NOTE

Using the Remote Access Setup dialog box's Remove option does not uninstall the modem on the server. It merely makes it unavailable for use by RAS.

FIGURE 21.11.

You use this dialog box to add or remove modems as RAS devices, or to configure the modems you have already selected.

FIGURE 21.12.

Use this dialog box to set your RAS service to accept incoming calls or place outgoing calls—or both.

2. If you plan to use the server only for users dialing into the system, select the Receive Calls Only option. If you plan to use the computer to dial out to other servers (Dial-Up Networking), select either the Dial Out Only or the Dial Out and Receive Calls options.

3. You can also use the Network button in the dialog box shown in Figure 21.11 to configure which network protocols will be used on RAS connections. In Figure 21.13, you can see the Network Configuration dialog box with only TCP/IP selected. If you want to use this feature, you can mark the Enable Multilink check box at the bottom of this dialog box. This feature allows NT to use two separate modem devices as if they were one.

FIGURE 21.13.

*You can select which
network protocols to
allow on RAS
communications.*

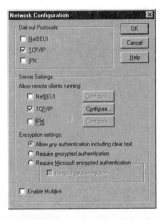

> **NOTE**
>
> If the network protocol you select here is not already installed on the server, then it is
> installed after the RAS setup concludes. In addition, if you have not installed a network card
> in the server, the Setup program automatically installs the Microsoft Loopback Adapter,
> which is a software module that emulates a network card; it allows you to perform basic
> network functions (such as browsing). This would be the case if you were setting up a PC at
> home so that you could dial in to it from work, rather than the other way around.

4. After you select a network protocol, use the Configure button next to it to bring up a
   dialog box that you can use to enter configuration information. In Figure 21.14 you
   see the RAS Server TCP/IP Configuration dialog box. At the top of this dialog box
   you can select to allow dial-in clients access to resources on just this computer, or to
   resources on the entire network.

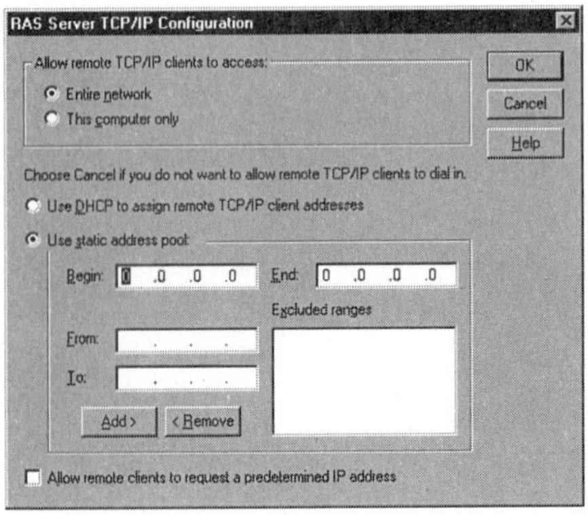

FIGURE 21.14.

*You can use this dialog
box to configure
properties of the TCP/
IP protocol as it is used
in RAS.*

5. If your network has a DHCP server on it and you would like to use it to assign TCP/IP configuration to clients that dial in to this RAS server, select the Use DHCP To Assign Remote Client TCP/IP Addresses option. If you do not have a DHCP server, then you have to provide a range of addresses that the RAS server can use when clients dial in.

Remember that all network clients need a unique address, even those dialing via RAS, as a RAS connection is indeed a network connection.

6. Click the Use Static Address Pool radio button and fill in a beginning and ending address for the range of addresses.

NOTE

You can use the Add and Remove buttons on the RAS Server TCP/IP Configuration dialog box to add or remove address ranges from RAS use. For example, if you specified the range of 10.10.10.10 through 10.10.10.50, but you were using 10.10.10.25 as an address assigned to another client, you could enter that address in the From field, with 10.10.10.26 in the To field, along with the Add button to exclude these two addresses from the range of addresses that RAS uses for dial-in clients.

7. Finally, you can allow clients to request their own address by using the Allow Remote Clients To Request IPX Node Number check box (at the bottom of the dialog box shown in Figure 21.15). This does not mean that all clients have to be preconfigured with an address. You can still use DHCP or a static pool of addresses. However, if a dial-in client wants to do so, it can request to use its own address if you select this check box.

8. When you are finished configuring the TCP/IP protocol for use with RAS, click OK to return to the previous dialog box.

9. If you are going to use the IPX/SPX protocol, the RAS Server IPX Configuration dialog box appears (see Figure 21.15). Here you can restrict clients to the RAS computer's resources or allow access to the connected LAN. You can let RAS allocate addresses automatically, or you can specify the range of addresses to allocate. Similar to IP configuration, you can let clients request an address by using the appropriate check box. If you choose to use the same network number for all IPX clients, you reduce the size of RIP announcements on the network.

If you decide to use IPX for RAS connections, then the RAS Setup program also installs the RIP for NWLink IPX network service. Windows NT RAS acts as an IPX router and SAP agent (Service Advertising Protocol) for RAS clients. If you let IPX clients have access to the network and let RAS automatically generate and assign an IPX network number for a client, then the RAS server uses the Router Information Protocol (IPX) for IPX to locate a network number that is not in use. You can manually override automatic generation of network numbers in the RAS Server IPX Configuration dialog box by letting clients request an address or by specifying a range of addresses to be used by the RAS server.

10. If you configure NetBEUI for use by RAS clients, then RAS acts as a NetBEUI gateway for those clients, translating packets to IPX or TCP/IP, depending on what is needed for the RAS server's connected LAN. These clients can access regular network file and print shares, but cannot run applications that depend on the client having TCP/IP or IPX installed.

FIGURE 21.15.

Use this dialog box to configure the IPX/SPX protocol for use with RAS.

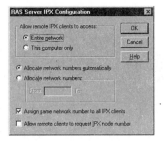

11. A dialog box informs you that you must grant dial-in permission to users. Click OK on this information dialog box, and you are returned to the Network applet's Services tab.

12. Click the OK button to finish the process. You are prompted to reboot the computer before the changes you have made take effect.

After you reboot the computer, you can use the Remote Access Admin tool in the Administrative Tools folder to manage your remote users.

Granting Dial-In Permission to Users

By default, no users are able to use RAS to dial in to your system until you grant permission. You can do this in one of two ways. You can use the Remote Access Admin tool or you can use the User Manager for Domains. If you are already in the process of adding new user accounts, it makes sense to grant the dial-in permission at that time—while you are still in the User Manager utility.

Using the User Manager Utility to Grant Permission

In Figure 21.16 you can see a user's typical properties sheet. The Dial-In button at the bottom right of the display can be used to grant the permission.

After you click on the Dial-In button a Dialin Information dialog box (see Figure 21.17) appears. The Dialin Information dialog box allows you to grant or revoke the permission, and to control whether call-back is used as a security or cost-control measure.

FIGURE 21.16.

Use the Dial-In button in the User Manager utility to grant this permission to users.

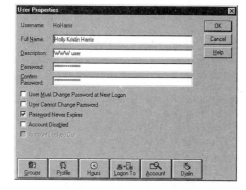

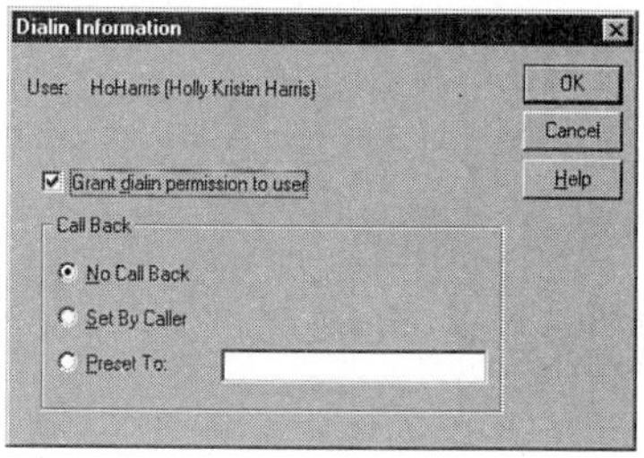

FIGURE 21.17.

You use this dialog box to control how a user is allowed to dial in to your system.

If you elect to use the Call Back option, the telephone line is dropped and the computer will call the user back after a user dials into the system and is authenticated. Why would you want to use this feature? There are two good reasons.

The first is security. If a user account is compromised and a hacker tries to dial in to your system using a stolen username and password, they would be foiled, as the computer would drop the line as soon as they are authenticated and call back to a preset number you enter here. The second reason for using the Call Back option is cost. If you have a traveling user, telephone rates can be expensive in some hotels or geographical locations. By using the Call Back option, the remote user only needs to pay long distance charges for the time it takes to be authenticated. The computer can then call back to a number specified by the user and use the company's long distance service instead.

Using the Remote Access Admin Utility to Grant Permission

The Remote Access Admin tool is the main utility the administrator uses to manage the Remote Access Service and its users. In addition to granting RAS users permissions via the User Manager for Domains, you can also perform this function using the Remote Access Admin tool. You can find the utility under the Administrative Tools folder. You see the main dialog box for this utility in Figure 21.18.

FIGURE 21.18.

The Remote Access Admin tool is used to manage RAS.

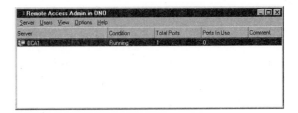

Select Permissions from the User menu to give users the right to dial in. The Remote Access Permissions dialog box pops up (see Figure 21.19). To grant permission to a single user, highlight that user's name, check the Grant Dialin Permission To User check box, alternatively select a Call Back option, and then click OK. If you are granting permission to multiple users, you need to do this for each user. You can, however, simplify the process if you want to grant the permission to all users that appear in the list of users in this dialog box. Just click the Grant All button. Another dialog box prompts you before continuing to grant the permission.

FIGURE 21.19.

Use this dialog box to grant dial-in permission using the Remote Access Admin tool.

Managing dial-in permissions is also easy. If you want to know if a user possesses the permission, simply highlight the user's name in this dialog box. If the check box for the dial-in permission is checked, the user has the permission. You can remove dial-in permission from a user by unchecking this check box and clicking OK. You can also remove the permission from all users in the list of users by using the Revoke All button.

Using the Remote Access Admin Tool

This utility allows you to manage all your remote users in once place—even when you are using multiple RAS servers. You can use Remote Access Admin to grant dial-in permission to users, as you saw earlier in this chapter. You can also use it to see which users are online and to view statistics about individual sessions or communications ports.

The Remote Access Admin tool's main window displays a list of the servers that you can work with using the tool. By default, you see the local computer listed if it is running RAS. You use the Server menu to add other computers. From that menu, use Select Computer or Domain.

Figure 21.20 shows the Select Domain dialog box, which allows you to view the domains visible on your network. You can double-click any domain to expand it to a list of servers in that domain. Alternatively, you can simply enter a domain name in the field provided in the box, and the utility browses the network for RAS servers for that domain.

FIGURE 21.20.

*Use the Select Domain
dialog box to add RAS
servers to the Remote
Access Admin tool.*

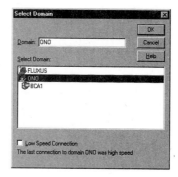

To administer RAS on a server after you have added it to your display in the Admin tool, simply highlight the computer and use the menu functions. If you simply double-click the computer entry in this dialog box, you get the Communications Port dialog box, from which you can monitor the status of the ports on the computer.

The Server Menu

The first menu in the Remote Access Admin tool allows you to perform the basic functions of this tool. Again, use the Server menu to select computers to add to the list of computers you want to administer. The other functions you can perform using this menu are:

- *Communications Ports*   Displays a list of the ports used by the particular server, as well as the username of the person who is logged in using the port and the time that the session began (see Figure 21.21).
- *Start Remote Access Service*   Starts RAS on the computer that you have highlighted.
- *Stop Remote Access Service*   Stops RAS on the computer that you have highlighted. All connected users are disconnected.
- *Pause Remote Access Service*   Connected users can continue working, but new connections are ignored.
- *Continue Remote Access Service*   When you resume the service, new connections are again accepted.

You can use the buttons on the right side of the Communication Ports dialog box to disconnect users and to send messages to users. You can get an error message if, when trying to use the Communications Port option, all of the communications ports set up for use with RAS are being used by dial-out users (see Figure 21.22).

FIGURE 21.21.

The Communication Ports dialog box shows you the ports on the RAS server, as well as the name of the connected user.

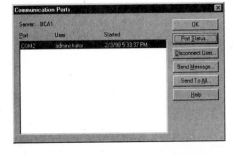

FIGURE 21.22.

If all ports are in use by dial-out users, you get this error message when trying to view communications ports for a RAS server.

If you want to view session statistics, you can highlight a port/user entry and use the Port Status button. This brings up a Port Status dialog box, which is shown in Figure 21.23. The dialog box gives detailed information about the port and the communications statistics, as well as information about the connected remote computer, such as the IP address it is using and the NetBEUI name of the workstation.

FIGURE 21.23.

The Port Status property sheet shows statistics about the selected port.

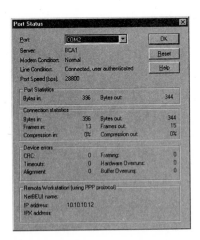

Important things you can learn from the Port Status property sheet are:

- The Modem Condition field should always read normal. If it doesn't, you may have a hardware problem with that port. Other possible values you can see in this field are:

    Modem not responding—Check the modem and its connection to the port.

Hardware failure—Unknown error, check the modem and the port for problems.

Incorrect modem response—Possibly unsupported modem, or you may have a problem in a modem configuration file.

Internal error—This indicates a software error. Stop and restart RAS.

- The Line Condition field reads `waiting for call` when the port is idle. Other text you may see in this field includes `Connected`, `User authenticating`, `Connected user authenticated`, `Calling back`, and `Line non-operational`.

- The Port Speed field shows the speed at which data is being transferred from the port to the modem. It is not the speed at which the modem is transferring data to another modem.

- In the Port Statistics fields (bytes in/bytes out), you see a raw reading of the number of bytes being transferred through the port. If any compression is being used, then these bytes represent the number of bytes of compressed data that is being transferred into or out of the port.

- The Connection Statistics fields show you the uncompressed bytes sent or received in this session. The Frames In/Frames Out fields show the number of frames sent or received; frame size is dependent on the network protocol being used. The Compression fields show the compression ratio for data sent and received.

- Device errors are listed for several types of errors. CRC (which stands for cyclic redundancy check) means that a garbled character was received. Timeouts occur when a character is not received when expected (for example, within a timeout period). If this happens, the program requests that the data be re-sent. Alignment errors usually indicate that a character has been lost or a timeout has occurred. Framing errors happen when a character is received and the start or stop bit is invalid. Hardware overruns indicate that the sending computer is trying to send data faster than the receiving computer's hardware can process it. Buffer overruns are similar, but represent a failure in the software to process the characters on the receiving end.

The User Menu

This menu has only two choices: Permissions and Active Users. The Permissions option is covered earlier in this chapter's "Granting Dial-In Permission to Users." The Active Users entry brings up a window that displays connection information similar to the Communications Ports option in the Server menu. Figure 21.24 shows this window with one user connected. You can see active sessions sorted by username instead of port, and you can see to which server the user is connected.

Another difference in the Ports view—and an important one—is that the Port view only shows users connected to the computer you are viewing. If you use the Active Users selection on the Users menu and are connected to a domain, then all users from that domain can be seen in this one window, making management much easier.

FIGURE 21.24.

*The User menu allows
you to show the active
users for all computers
in the domain.*

Using the Dial-Up Networking Monitor

The Dial-Up Networking Monitor is another administrative utility that can be used to manage remote connections. This is a convenient tool that can be used to show the statistics of connections and to configure preferences for the utility.

To bring up the Monitor utility, you can either double-click its icon in the Control Panel, or look in the system tray at the bottom-right of the toolbar. When you have installed RAS, there should be an icon consisting of two status lights (horizontal bars on top of each other), with a telephone sitting in front of them. If you double-click this icon, you bring up the Dial-Up Networking Monitor (as shown in Figure 21.25). You can also bring up the monitor using the More menu on the Dial-Up Networking utility.

FIGURE 21.25.

*The Dial-Up
Networking Monitor
shows statistics for
inbound or outbound
connections.*

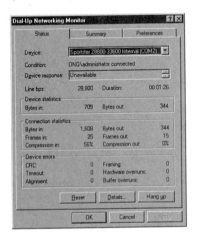

Displaying Statistics

On the Status tab shown in Figure 21.25, you can use the Device field's pull-down menu to select the communications device for which statistics will be displayed. The Condition field shows you for what the port is being used. The statistics on the rest of the page are the same as those you get when you use the Port Status dialog box under the Remote Access Admin utility. You can see the device statistics, connection statistics, and device errors. The Hang Up button at the bottom of this dialog box can be used to disconnect the current session and the Reset button can be used to reset the statistics counters.

> **NOTE**
>
> Using the Reset button does not disconnect a user. It only resets the Counter fields to zero. This can be useful during troubleshooting, when you want to get a clean start.

The Details button brings up the Details property sheet, which shows Network Registration information. You can see if the connection is being done by SLIP or PPP. You can also see addressing information for TCP/IP and IPX and naming information for NetBEUI.

Summarizing the Connections

The Summary tab shows a summary of the connections (see Figure 21.26). Use the +/- box to expand the listing under the connected user's name; the links that are forming the connection are displayed. If you double-click the entry or use the Details button, you get the Network Registration details property sheet.

FIGURE 21.26.

The Summary tab shows you the connections managed by the server.

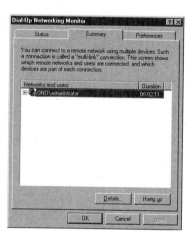

Configuring RAS Parameters

The final tab, Preferences (see Figure 21.27), allows you to configure certain RAS parameters. You can select the events for which the RAS server will make a sound, and whether the status lights icon is displayed on the desktop or in the system tray. You can also customize the display of the status lights, including making them always appear on top of other windows on the desktop.

FIGURE 21.27.

The Preferences tab allows you to set characteristics for RAS.

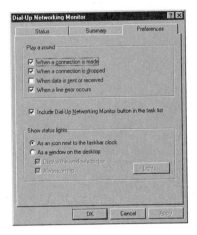

The check box labeled Include Dial-Up Networking Monitor In The Task List lets you determine whether the monitor shows up in the Task Manager list of applications. By default, this box is not checked, so the monitor utility does not appear in the task list. Figure 21.28 shows how the Dial-Up Networking Monitor appears when you elect to have it as a desktop icon rather than an icon in the system tray. To bring up the utility, simply double-click this icon.

FIGURE 21.28.

This is the Dial-Up Networking Monitor icon as it appears on the desktop.

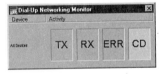

Using RAS as a Client

When you install the Remote Access Service, you also install the capability to use Dial-Up Networking—the client side of RAS. Look in the Accessories folder to start DUN. You can also find the icon under My Computer. In order to use Dial-Up Networking, you must first create entries in the Phonebook.

Creating a New Connection Using the Wizard

If you get the message shown in Figure 21.29, then you haven't installed RAS yet; DUN isn't available. Otherwise, if RAS is installed and working correctly, you will get a message saying the Phonebook is empty. Click OK to continue and DUN walks you through the creation of a new connection.

The New Phonebook Entry Wizard pops up next, with the dialog box shown in Figure 21.30. You should replace the text **MyDialUpServer** with the name you want to give to the connection you are creating. This descriptive name is for identification purposes and is displayed underneath the icon that is created for the connection. If you would rather use the Phonebook

directly to enter the data and bypass the wizard, select the I Know All About Phonebook Entries and Would Rather Edit the Properties Directly check box at the bottom of the dialog box. Click Next to continue.

FIGURE 21.29.

Dial-Up Networking is installed when you install the RAS service.

FIGURE 21.30.

A wizard can guide you through the process of adding a new connection.

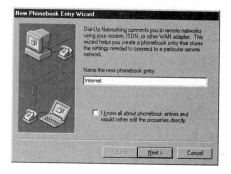

The Server dialog box (see Figure 21.31) has three check boxes from which you can select. The third concerns the method used to log onto the remote computer. Check this box if you will use a terminal screen or a script after a connection is made to the remote computer, so that you can provide logon information (or if your provider has given you fixed addresses that you need to enter before dialing). Check the first box if you are calling the Internet, and check the second if you are calling a non-Windows NT computer that doesn't accept an encrypted form of password authentication. When you have finished, click Next to continue.

FIGURE 21.31.

Select the appropriate boxes and click Next to continue.

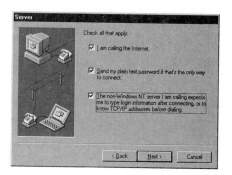

Protocols Must Be Enabled for Dial-Out

At this point, you may get an error message like the one shown in Figure 21.32. This message can be confusing. For example, you can get this error even if you do have TCP/IP installed on the computer. The important part of the message is the word `disabled`. If you follow the directions given by the error message and open the Network Configuration dialog box, you may get a property sheet like that shown in Figure 21.33.

FIGURE 21.32.

You need to either install TCP/IP or enable it for RAS if you get this message.

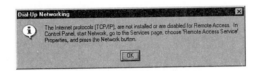

FIGURE 21.33.

The Network Configuration dialog box indicates that TCP/IP is not enabled for dial-out.

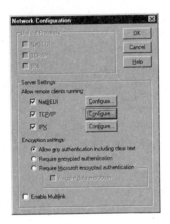

Note in this figure that TCP/IP is enabled for dial-in users, and that if you click the Configure button, you can see that it is configured properly. The problem lies in the fact that the top portion of the property sheet is grayed out. Why is this?

When you installed RAS, there was a Configure button present during the portion where you select the modem or other communication device. When you click this button, you are presented with the Configure Port Usage dialog box, which is shown in Figure 21.34.

FIGURE 21.34.

You need to select an option that allows dial-out in order to use Dial-Up Networking.

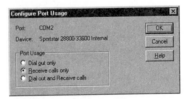

When you install RAS, the default for this dialog box is Receive Calls Only. If you don't select one of the other options, RAS is installed without prompting for dial-in information for that port—you have told it you are not going to use the modem for that purpose. To correct the problem, use the Configure Port Usage dialog box to change your selection. You see the dial-out network options available.

Entering Dialing Information

Provided you have correctly configured the dial-out protocols, the wizard prompts for the telephone number to dial (see Figure 21.35). You can use the Alternates button to bring up the Phone Numbers dialog box shown in Figure 21.36, and you can use the Use Telephony Dialing Properties check box. If you do select the Telephony check box, the dialog box changes to add new fields for the telephone number, as shown in Figure 21.37.

Figure 21.35.

Use this dialog box to enter telephone number information.

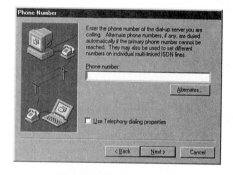

Figure 21.36.

Use this dialog box to add alternate phone numbers to be dialed for the connection.

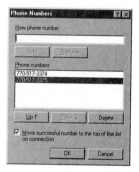

Figure 21.37.

The Telephony check box brings new fields to the dialog box.

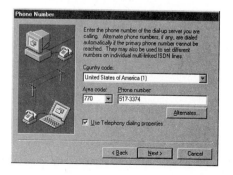

The Phone Numbers dialog box can be used to add telephone numbers that are dialed if a connection cannot be made using the first number. The check box at the bottom of the dialog box causes the phone numbers associated with successful connection attempts to be moved to the top of the list, ensuring a better chance of connection in the future. You can manually adjust the order by highlighting a phone number and using the Up, Down, and Delete buttons, or use the Add or Replace buttons to enter new phone numbers or modify existing entries.

Click Next when you have finished with this dialog box. A last dialog box tells you that you are finished, unless you selected the option at the beginning of this process to receive logon information.

ISP Information

The first dialog box, Serial Line Protocol, allows you to choose either PPP or SLIP (see Figure 21.38). Select one and click Next to continue.

FIGURE 21.38.

Choose the protocol your ISP uses in this dialog box.

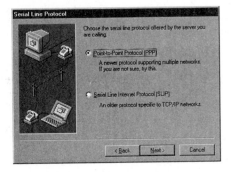

The next dialog box gives you the option of using a terminal window or a script file after the connection has been made. You can select None if you only need to enter addressing information. If you choose to use a script, you can use the pull-down menu to select from a few predefined scripts that come with NT, or a custom script you have written.

The next two dialog boxes are used to enter the fixed IP addressing information: the IP Address dialog box (see Figure 21.39) and the Name Server Addresses dialog box (see Figure 21.40). All entries are optional and should be set to zeros if you are not sure. Leave them at zeros if you are dialing into a computer that uses DHCP to provide addressing information, for example.

When you click Next, the wizard tells you that you are through, and you can click Finished.

FIGURE 21.39.

Enter a fixed IP address in this dialog box for a static address; enter zeros if you want to use DHCP.

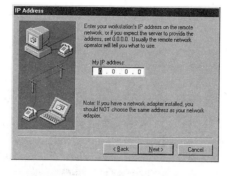

FIGURE 21.40.

Enter a domain name server address or a WINS server address in this dialog box.

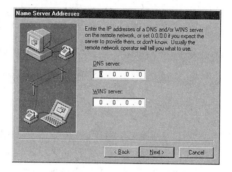

Creating a New Connection Using the Phonebook

If you select the check box in the New Phonebook Entry Wizard that allows you to edit the Phonebook entry directly (the I Know All About Phonebook Entries and Would Rather Edit the Properties Directly option), then you get the New Phonebook Entry dialog box shown in Figure 21.41. You can use the tabs to bring up different property sheets and enter the information directly. This bypasses the wizard altogether.

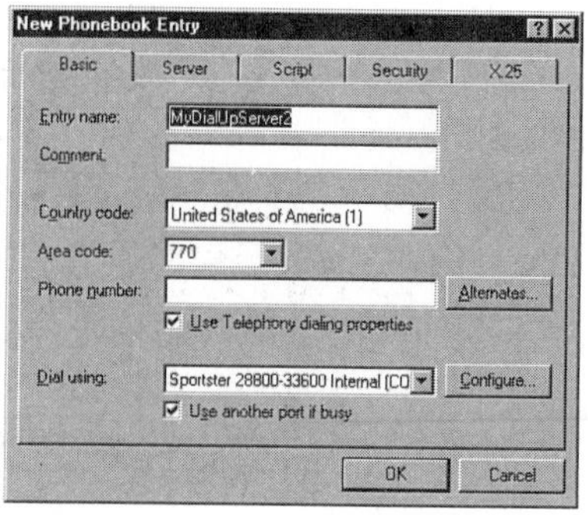

FIGURE 21.41.

You can enter Phonebook information directly and bypass the wizard.

You can use the Alternates button to bring up the Phone Numbers dialog box so that you can provide a list of phone numbers for use with the connection or to prioritize their order in the list. You can select the modem you want to use with a pull-down menu, and if you use the Configure button, you can use a Modem Configuration dialog box (see Figure 21.42) to make changes to the modem properties. Here is where you should be sure to set the port speed to something greater than the modem's speed; that ensures that the modem is not idle while waiting for input from the computer.

FIGURE 21.42.

You can make modifications to the modem's properties using this dialog box.

The Server tab, shown in Figure 21.43, allows you to enter dial-up server type (PPP or SLIP) and network protocols. Use the Configure button to enter addressing information for the TCP/IP protocol, if it has been selected for use.

FIGURE 21.43.

Use this dialog box to select PPP or SLIP, and to configure the network protocol.

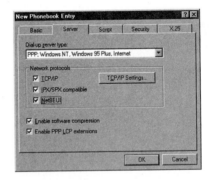

The Script tab allows you to specify a script file to be run after dialing via use of the Run This Script pull-down menu (see Figure 21.44). You can use the Before Dialing button to specify a script file to run before dialing, if you need to.

If you choose the Edit Script button, the Notepad accessory pops up with the script file loaded, so you can view it or make changes.

The Security tab, shown in Figure 21.45, is where you indicate the type of authentication (clear text or a form of encrypted authentication) to be used for the connection. If you have selected the Save Password check box on the main Dial-Up Networking dialog box, you can use the Unsave Password button found in this dialog box to clear that password.

FIGURE 21.44.

The Script tab can be used to run a script or bring up a terminal window.

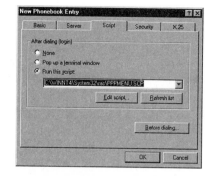

FIGURE 21.45.

The Security tab is used for authentication information.

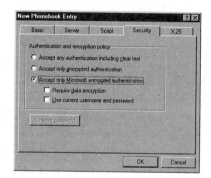

Finally, the X.25 tab can be used to enter the service provider, address, and user data needed for the service. Look at Figure 21.46.

FIGURE 21.46.

The X.25 tab is used to indicate the provider and provide logon information.

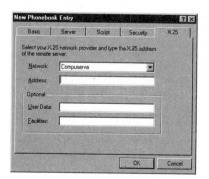

Using the Dial-Up Networking Dialog Box

Figure 21.47 shows the normal Dial-Up Networking dialog box that appears, if the Phonebook contains entries, when you bring up the application. You can select the Phonebook entry to dial or a location you have set up using the drop-down menus. You can place your cursor in the Phone Number Preview field and make edits to the phone number. The New button activates the wizard to walk you through creating a new connection.

FIGURE 21.47.

This is the Dial-Up Networking dialog box.

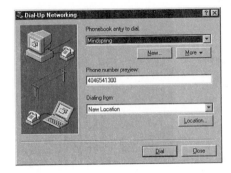

The More button brings up a menu that allows you to configure the entries you have created, and to view and configure setup and preferences information about Dial-Up Networking.

Edit Entry and Modem Properties

This Edit Entry and Modem Properties menu selection brings up the Edit Phonebook Entry dialog box. You should use the pull-down menu on the main dialog box to select the entry you want to edit before using this selection. One handy function found in the Security tab is a button—the button you need to unsave a password if you have used the Save Password feature and your password has changed.

Clone Entry and Modem Properties

The Clone Entry and Modem Properties menu option works like the Edit Entry option, but instead of changing the original entry you have selected to edit, you are creating a new entry. You can find this a timesaver if you are setting up new connections that are similar in most respects. The Clone Phonebook Entry dialog box looks exactly like the Add and Edit Phonebook Entry dialog boxes.

Delete Entry

Select an entry on the main Dial-Up Networking dialog box and then use this menu option to delete the entry. The application prompts you to be sure you really want to perform the deletion before continuing. Use this option to get rid of old entries and avoid confusion.

Create Shortcut to Entry

This menu option prompts you to create a shortcut for the Phonebook entry you have selected. Figure 21.48 shows the Create Dial-Up Shortcut dialog box that you use to select the shortcut's location.

The Desktop is the default. Use this function to create shortcut icons for the most used Phonebook entries.

FIGURE 21.48.

This is the Create Dial-Up Shortcut dialog box.

Monitor Status

This menu option brings up the Dial-Up Networking Monitor discussed earlier in this chapter. You can get a quick review of status and statistical information about devices, connections, and users with this utility.

Operator Assisted or Manual Dialing

This menu option can be toggled on or off. When this option is toggled on, you are prompted to perform the dialing operation yourself after you click the Dial button for this entry (see Figure 21.49).

FIGURE 21.49.

You can configure DUN to allow you to perform manual dialing.

When the final connection is made, click OK; DUN takes over the connection.

User Preferences

The User Preferences dialog box comes up when you select that option from the More menu. Figure 21.50 shows the dialog box with the Dialing tab selected. You can select the defaults for Phonebook entries here. If you have specified multiple locations when creating entries, they appear here.

You can specify what the application should do if a number is busy or if an error occurs during the initial dial-up attempt.

■ Number Of Redial Attempts—This is the number of times DUN dials the number to attempt a connection before giving up. If you set this to zero, then no redial is attempted if the number is busy.

■ Seconds Between Redial Attempts—This is the number of seconds DUN waits before it tries to redial if you have set the redial attempts to a non-zero number. You should specify a time long enough to give the remote device time to be reset if there was an error.

■ Idle Seconds Before Hanging Up—Set this to a non-zero value if you want DUN to hang up the connection after a specified amount of time (in seconds). This can be used to prevent long distance calls from mistakenly being connected too long.

■ Redial On Link Failure—If you select this check box, the link is redialed if it terminates for some reason. Use this if you are leaving the computer unattended and need to be sure that it stays connected for a length of time.

Figure 21.50.
The Dialing tab in the User Preferences dialog box.

The Callback tab allows you to enter callback information if the server you are calling uses that feature. The options are to skip the callback (the default), to ask each time if you want to use callback, or to use callback all the time. If you elect to use callback, you can select from the list of modems that have been configured in your PC for DUN, and use the Edit button for an entry to attach a phone number to that modem.

The Appearances tab allows you to configure some properties of the Dial-up Networking application, such as whether it should remain on the desktop or close after dialing, and whether the New Phonebook Entry Wizard should be invoked when you use the New button to create an entry. The Appearance tab is shown in Figure 21.51.

Figure 21.51.
Use the Appearance tab to configure DUN properties.

Finally, the Phonebook tab allows you to select the Phonebook used by DUN. You can select from the system Phonebook, your personal phonebook, or use the Browse button to use an alternate phonebook.

Logon Preferences

If you have DUN installed on your computer, you can select in the logon box a Logon Using Dial-Up Networking check box. The Logon Preferences menu option from the More menu in Dial-Up Networking is where you set preferences for this option (see Figure 21.52). The tabs for this dialog box are the same as those for the User Preferences (discussed in the preceding section). The exception is that the Appearance tab allows you to opt to edit the Phonebook entry or the location during the logon sequence.

FIGURE 21.52.

Use this dialog box to set preferences when using DUN to log onto the computer.

Routing and RAS

The basic RAS that you install from the NT source distribution can act as a static router for IPX or IP. It is very limited, however, in what it can do. RAS can route only between networks that it is directly connected to, and it does not understand the dynamic routing information that dedicated routers exchange. RAS can route between RAS clients and other servers on your LAN.

To set up routing between your LAN and the Internet using RAS as the router, you need to make two Registry entry changes. Locate the following key using the Registry editor (`REGEDT32.EXE`):

`HKEY_LOCAL_MACHINE\SYSTEM\CurrentControlSet\Service\RasARP\Parameters`

Add a new value to this key of type `REG_DWORD` and give it the name of `DisableOtherSrcPackets`. Set the value to 0. This tells RAS that packets from LAN clients, which are being routed through RAS to the Internet, should have their IP addresses in the packet header. If this value does not exist in the Registry, or if it is set to zero, then the packets sent out use the RAS server's IP address as their source address instead. If that happens, any response to the packets is sent back to the RAS server as the final destination, instead of to the client from which the communications started.

The next key to change should be done if the remote ISP uses the same network class address you use. It causes RAS to route traffic using the subnet rather than just the network portion of the address. Locate the next Registry key:

`HKEY_LOCAL_MACHINE\SYSTEM\CurrentControlSet\Services\RasMan\PPP\IPCP`

Locate the `PriorityBasedOnSubNetwork` value—create it if it does not exist—and give it a value of 1. This key allows RAS to correctly route traffic to the correct subnet, rather than routing all traffic through the RAS connection, which acts as the default gateway for all network traffic.

Troubleshooting RAS

Considering the combination of hardware that can exist on a RAS server, it is to be expected that you may encounter problems in configuring or using RAS. There are a few simple things you can do for quick troubleshooting.

Using the Device Log

You can troubleshoot problems with the modem by instructing RAS to write a log file of the interaction between itself and the modem. You need to change a `registry` parameter to do this. As always, remember that making any use of the Registry Editor can be dangerous, so always make sure that you have a good backup of your system and a recently updated emergency repair disk.

Locate the following key using the Registry Editor (`Regedt32` or `Regedit`):

`HKEY_LOCAL_MACHINE\SYSTEM\CurrentControlSet\Services\RASMan\Parameters\Logging`

The value for this key should be set to number 1 to turn on device logging. To turn it off, set this key back to 0.

The device log file is called `DEVICE.LOG`, and can be found in the `%SystemRoot%\system32\ras` directory. This log file shows the commands issued to the modem (such as the `ATDT` command to dial the modem), along with the modem's response. This log file can help you determine if you have correctly configured the modem that you are using as a RAS communications device.

Using a Terminal Window

When you are using Dial-Up Networking to connect and have problems, you can use the Hyptterminal accessory to troubleshoot many problems. If you can connect using Hyperterminal to a remote location, then you can be sure that the modem setup is working properly. Otherwise, you can use Hyperterminal to send `AT` commands to the modem for configuration or diagnostic commands.

Perform the following steps to use the Hyperterm accessory to diagnose problems with a modem:

1. Choose New Connection from the File menu. The Connection Description dialog box appears. Enter any name (such as "Test") in the field provided and click OK.

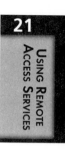

2. The Connect To dialog box appears. Click Cancel.

3. Enter commands to the modem for which you expect a response. For example, for a Hayes-compatible modem, enter the AT command to see if you get a response from the modem (a 0 or the word OK).

4. Try dialing out to any telephone number using documentation provided by the modem manufacturer. For example, you can use the ATDT command followed by a phone number to cause a Hayes-compatible modem to dial.

If you cannot get the modem to work using Hyperterm, be sure to review any hardware switches or jumpers covered by the manufacturer's documentation.

Using the Event Log to Monitor RAS Users

To help protect your network against intrusions, you should routinely audit user logon and logoff attempts and review the event logs. You can then use the Security log file to quickly scan for user names. You can also use the System log file to help diagnose logon problems. For example, a quick look into the System log file shows the reason that the user Administrator cannot log into the RAS server (see Figure 21.53).

FIGURE 21.53.

The Event Viewer can help you diagnose login failure problems for remote users.

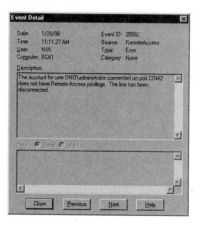

Use the Permissions option on the Users menu in the Remote Access Admin program to grant the user the permission.

You can also gather basic session information from the System log. In Figure 21.54, you can see that the event detail can show you the username used to log on, the time and date of logon and logoff, elapsed time, bytes sent and received, and port speed. The detail also shows the reason the user disconnected.

You can also use information from the Security log file to help troubleshoot logon problems. In Figure 21.55, you can see an example of a logon failure. You can tell that this failure audit is due to a user trying to get in using RAS because the Logon Process field has a value of MS.RAS. Although it is obvious from this that the username is correct and that the problem is probably a bad password, you can also use the Security event log to find out if the user entered the wrong domain name. This is a common mistake when Windows 95 clients dial in and their workgroup name is not the same as the RAS server's domain name.

FIGURE 21.54.

The detail of an event log entry can show a considerable amount of information about a user session.

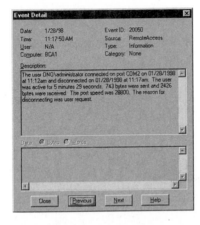

FIGURE 21.55.

Important information can be found in the Security event log file when diagnosing logon failures.

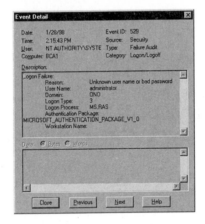

Finally, you can use the event logs to help determine the cause of failure of the RAS service itself. When you have hardware or software problems that prevent the service from starting, you usually find very detailed information in the event logs. In Figure 21.56, you can see an example from the System log that indicates that the service did not start due to a logon failure.

After reading this error message, you can then look in the Security log file and locate the error message for the logon failure (see Figure 21.57). In this case, the failure was due to a user account being created under which to run the RAS service instead of using the local system account, which is the default. The administrator forgot to grant the right logon as a service to the account. Thus, an error was generated in the Security log when the logon attempt failed, because it was being used to log on a service.

FIGURE 21.56.

Use the event logs to determine why RAS does not start.

FIGURE 21.57.

The RAS service was unable to start because the logon type (as a service) was not granted to this user account.

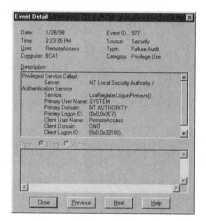

Using the Performance Monitor to Troubleshoot RAS

The Performance Monitor (which is covered in Chapter 20, "Performance Tuning and Optimization") can be used to track resource usage on computers acting as RAS servers. In addition to using counters that are already built into the Performance Monitor, new objects and counters are added to the utility when you install RAS. These objects include:

- *RAS Port* This object can exist for each instance of a communications port used by RAS. The counters associated with this object include Bytes Received, Buffer Overrun Error, Alignment Errors, and other counters related to communication port errors and performance. Instead of using the Remote Access Admin tool to view statistics about a communications port, you can use the Performance Monitor to get a real-time graphical view, or to log data to a file for later analysis or comparison.

- *RAS Total* This object tracks counters similar to those used by RAS Port, but provides server totals rather than breaking down the statistics by communications port.

Read through Chapter 20 to get more familiar with the Performance Monitor and how to use it to record data for later analysis and how to create charts, reports, and setup alerts.

Summary

This chapter briefly covered a wide range of topics involved in using Remote Access Services with Windows NT. Many of the topics are related to other parts of the operating system (such as networking or device management), and you can get more information from reading those chapters. However, after completing this chapter, you should be confident that you can set up Windows NT to operate as both a Dial-Up Network client and a remote access server for a LAN with few, if any, problems.

The new routing option package that Microsoft has released for Windows NT 4.0 (see Chapter 24, "Network Client Administrator") further extends the capabilities of Windows NT, as well as its use as a gateway or server on the Internet.

Point to Point Tunneling Protocol

by John White

IN THIS CHAPTER

This chapter examines the Point to Point Tunneling Protocol (PPTP) and its implementation within Windows NT. PPTP is a versatile protocol that allows for the creation of secure virtual private networks (VPN) for data transfer. Two systems can connect over a public network such as the Internet and transfer data using a secured channel between them. PPTP can tunnel NetBEUI, IPX, or TCP/IP packets over dial-up, LANs, or WANs.

Tunneling, or *encapsulation,* is the process of taking the packets that would normally be transferred over a network connection and placing them inside an outer wrapper, which is then used to deliver the contents across an external network connection. An analogy would be an inter-office mail system. You place correspondence inside an internal mail envelope for delivery. You write the recipient's name and department on the outside. The mailroom takes the envelope and delivers it to the destination. However, if that destination is in another building or city, the envelope isn't acceptable to the external delivery system. The mailroom will insert the correspondence into a U.S. mail or courier envelope, write an externally acceptable address on it, and hand it over to the external delivery system. When the correspondence arrives at its destination, the outer envelope is removed, and the inner envelope continues to its final destination.

PPTP can encrypt the inner envelope and the data it contains so that the external mail system can't even see the internal delivery address.

Understanding Point to Point Tunneling Protocol

Using tunneling, you can take a protocol such as NetBEUI—which isn't a routable protocol—encapsulate it in PPTP, route the PPTP packet, remove the PPTP layer, and deliver the NetBEUI packet to the destination network.

Several different competing technologies offer tunneling solutions. When IPV6 is finally standardized, it will contain a tunneling standard called IPSec. Novell also has an offering out for tunneling IPX packets by encapsulating the IPX with a UDP and IP header. One of the more interesting competitions has been between two corporate groups—one led by Microsoft and the other by Cisco.

Microsoft submitted PPTP for approval by the InterNIC committee as a tunneling standard. Cisco submitted L2F (Layer 2 Forwarding) to the InterNIC for approval as a tunneling standard. The InterNIC committee looked at the two competing standards, decided they were too similar to be separate standards, and sent them both back with instructions to combine them into one submission. The final standard will be called L2TP when the two groups have reached an agreement on how to combine the features of the two protocols.

Benefits of PPTP

PPTP offers network administrators many benefits when it comes to securing remote or local clients. A major point here is that PPTP is not used only for clients using a modem to dial in to the network. PPTP can be used in several scenarios to connect two systems.

Here are some of the benefits:

- Creates a secure channel over a public network
- Can reduce cost while still maintaining security for remote users
- Can route nonroutable protocols
- Open and multiprotocol
- Available for Windows NT and Windows 95
- Built into Windows NT and can be made available to all users without additional software
- Can complement existing security firewall systems without reconfiguration of the firewall system

The big reason to implement PPTP is the additional data encryption it can provide while using Windows NT across the Internet.

Using PPTP Connections

To set up a PPTP tunnel, you need a PPTP client on one end to place the call, a PPTP server on the other end to answer, and a connection medium in between. This connection could be over a network (Token ring or Ethernet), phone line, ISDN, Internet, T1, null modem cable, and so on—whatever option you have available to connect the two machines to allow the exchange of packets. Each end requires a RAS-capable device with the client end configured to dial out and the server end configured to receive dial-in calls. The server can have one or more network interfaces configured to forward the traffic after it has been delivered.

Installing PPTP on Windows NT

There are several scenarios under which PPTP can be implemented for Windows NT. However, a basic set of components needs to be in place in all cases. First we will examine how to install the software, and then we will deal with appropriate configurations based on the needs of each scenario.

PPTP is installed on both the client and the server. Along with the PPTP protocol, both client and server will require the RAS or dial-in networking software.

Preinstallation Hardware and Software Considerations

Prior to the installation of PPTP, several components need to be in place. PPTP uses Windows NT's Remote Access Server (RAS) and dial-up networking as the foundation to establish a connection and exchange data. RAS and dial-up networking must be installed before PPTP can be added. Configuration of RAS and dial-up networking will take place after all components are in place.

In order to communicate over RAS and dial-up networking, PPTP must use Virtual Private Network (VPN) devices. This is similar to what a modem would do for a regular RAS connection. Each VPN is configured as a RAS device for incoming or outbound connections. The server can have from one to 256 VPNs configured for incoming connections. If four VPNs are configured, only four simultaneous PPTP connections can be handled.

Hardware and software requirements for server and client are as follows:

- Windows NT 4.0
- RAS or RRAS and dial-up networking
- Clients must have the user right to use dial-up networking
- One or more modems or network cards
- Common transport protocol (TCP/IP, NetBEUI, and so on)
- Internet Service Provider account (only if using the Internet)

Once you understand these requirements, you can begin the installation of PPTP on Windows NT.

Installing PPTP on Windows NT

To begin installing PPTP on Windows NT, follow these steps:

1. From the Start menu, select Settings and then Control Panel.
2. Double-click the Network icon.
3. On the Protocol tab, click Add. A list of protocols will appear, as shown in Figure 22.1.

Figure 22.1.

The Add button on the Protocol tab of the Network icon lists the Point to Point Tunneling Protocol.

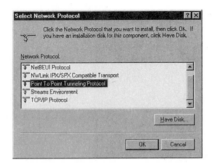

4. Select Point to Point Tunneling Protocol and click the OK button. Windows NT will then copy from the source files or prompt you for the location of the source files.
7. The PPTP Configuration dialog box, shown in Figure 22.2, appears. Select the Number of Virtual Private Networks to be created and click OK.
8. Click OK in the Select Network Protocol dialog box to return to the Setup screen and close the Network icon. The system will recompile the bindings and prompt you to restart the computer.

FIGURE 22.2.

The number of VPNs will control the maximum number of connections using PPTP.

At this point, the PPTP software is installed but not fully configured.

NOTE

These steps are required for both the client and server setup of PPTP.

Configuring PPTP on the Server

Once the system has RAS and PPTP installed, they need to be configured to work together. RAS will use the VPNs similar to using a modem. A VPN is not a physical device, so an underlying connection must be established before the VPN can be used. This connection could be a private LAN or across the Internet.

Each PPTP connection will require a VPN to be in place and configured with the appropriate protocol and security features. To do this, follow these steps:

1. From the Start menu, select Settings and then Control Panel.
2. Double-click the Network icon.
3. Open the properties of Remote Access Server (RAS) on the Services tab.
4. Click Add to set up a new device. You see the dialog box shown in Figure 22.3.

FIGURE 22.3.

The drop-down list offering all RAS-capable devices.

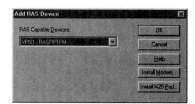

5. Once the new device has been added, it is listed with all the other RAS devices, as shown in Figure 22.4. As many VPNs can be configured as were added under PPTP.
6. Click the Configure button to identify the VPN's role on the system (see Figure 22.5). Dial out only will not be monitoring incoming requests. Servers and clients are configured differently.
7. Based on the previous choice, the Network configuration button will display appropriate information. Select the VPN to be configured and click the Network button.

FIGURE 22.4.

The VPN item is listed similarly to a modem in the Remote Access Setup properties box.

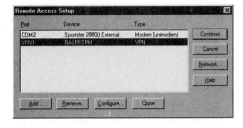

FIGURE 22.5.

Dial out only will not offer any further configuration items and should be used only on clients. Receive calls only or Dial out and Receive calls will provide server configuration items.

8. The Network Configuration dialog box, shown in Figure 22.6, uses the top section for RASs that have been configured to dial out only. The middle section is for receive-calls-only servers, and both sections will be presented to systems that have been set up for dial-out and receive calls. Data encryption on this dialog box is only for server configuration.

FIGURE 22.6.

This system presents both sections for configuration. Dial out and Receive calls would have been selected.

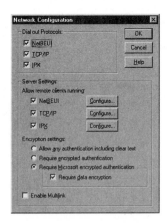

9. Select all transport protocols allowed for incoming or outgoing communication.

10. Click the Configure button to further specify the access permissions and configuration of any protocol.

The RAS and PPTP components are now set to work together. Still more items can be configured in order to provide even greater security. These will be discussed shortly.

Both server and client require the same basic system configuration. Configuration of the client will be different from configuration of the server. A system can be set up to act as both client and server.

Configuring the PPTP Server for Encryption

Additional security features can be put in place to avoid exposing data to an unprotected network. The encryption features in place by default wouldn't prevent someone with basic tools from capturing and reading information as it passed on the network. The risk is even higher when part of the network is the Internet.

Within the RAS implementation of PPTP, there are two areas in which encryption is used: logon authentication and data transfer. Logon authentication is encrypted using a modified version of the Challenge Handshake Authentication Protocol (CHAP), which is appropriately named MS-CHAP. Within the Remote Access Service, the Data Encryption Standard (DES) is used to encrypt logon information. All data that is transferred on a PPTP connection can also be encrypted, but it uses RSA Security Inc.'s RC4 encryption protocol.

To achieve the best security PPTP can offer, it is suggested that you use Microsoft encrypted authentication with data encryption. (See the bottom part of Figure 22.6.)

For Internet TCP/IP networks, an additional item can be put in place to eliminate any packet that isn't using PPTP. This is called PPTP filtering. Filtering is simply a mechanism used to hide or drop all packets that don't meet certain criteria. All packets coming from the Internet are filtered, and only packets using PPTP are let into the system. This will prevent some monitoring tools from gaining access to the private network.

By no means is this a completely safe system. These security features are methods used to reduce the risk of information's being captured and deciphered.

To configure the server to implement PPTP filtering, do the following:

1. From the Network icon in the Control Panel, select the Protocol tab.
2. Select TCP/IP and click the Properties button.
3. Click the Advanced Configuration button.
4. Select the Enable PPTP Filtering check box for the appropriate network card (see Figure 22.7).

FIGURE 22.7.

The advanced TCP/IP configuration dialog box offers PPTP filtering for any network card installed.

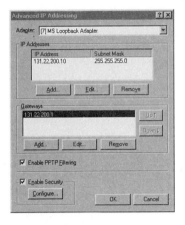

Configuring the RAS Server for Routing

A PPTP server can act as a router to the internal private network from the Internet. With standard RAS, Registry changes need to be implemented in order for this to work properly. The intent is to have the PPTP server act as a single point of entry into the private network and allow access to all resources as if the client were connected directly to the network. PPTP server will still maintain the basic security features discussed earlier on the outbound connection.

Three components are required to allow the PPTP RAS server to route TCP/IP packets properly:

■ IP forwarding must be enabled in the TCP/IP properties.

■ A Registry entry must be made to disable default routing tables.

■ A new routing table is created with static entries to handle the private network.

To enable IP forwarding, follow these steps:

1. From the Start menu, select Settings and then Control Panel.
2. Double-click the Network icon.
3. Select TCP/IP from the Protocols tab.
4. Click the Properties button and select the Routing tab.
5. Enable IP Forwarding.
6. Click OK twice and close the dialog box.
7. Restart the computer in order for routing to take effect.

For the second component, you need to edit the Registry. There are two Registry editors in Windows NT. Use either one.

To add a Registry entry for routing, do the following:

1. From the Start menu, select Run.
2. Type REGEDT32 to start the 32-bit Registry editor.

3. Add the entry `DontAddDefaultGateway` of type `REG_DWORD` value of `0` as shown here:

```
HKEY_LOCALMACHINE\SYSTEM\CurrentControlSet\Services\<networkadapter>\
➥Parameters\Tcpip\DontAddDefaultGateway
```

4. Close the Registry.

This will prepare the system to handle information coming from the outside network. A static routing table must be created to direct information to the appropriate intranet segments of the network.

A static route can be created on any Windows NT system to help with directing packets. If a route can't be found, the system usually refers to its default gateway. Windows NT Server with multiple network cards will create dynamic routes based on the machine's internal network cards. Static routes are added to extend the server's knowledge to the rest of the network.

Static routes will be lost when the system is rebooted. In this case, it makes sense to make these entries persistent using the `-P` switch on the `route` command.

You must first decide which network to include in the routing table and which route you would like the packets to take. The network's subnet mask is also required for this entry.

For example, a network ID of 207.6.153.0 accessible through the router 207.6.153.1 would require that an entry be added to the routing table with this command:

```
Route Add  207.6.153.0 Mask 255.255.255.0 207.6.153.1 -P
```

Here are the steps for creating a static route on the PPTP RAS server:

1. From the Start menu programs, open a command prompt.
2. Type `Route Print` to view the existing route table.
3. Type the following for each internal network serviced by the PPTP RAS server:

```
Route ADD network ID Mask subnet mask destination host -P
```

4. Type `Route Print` to view the new static routing table.

The PPTP RAS server is now ready to operate.

Installing a PPTP Client on Windows NT

Installing a PPTP client is also an extension of the Remote Access Service—in this case, the RAS client rather than the RAS server. Effectively, a VPN device is added as a RAS device the same way it was for the server. Make sure RAS is installed first, and then follow these steps:

1. From the Start menu, select Settings and then Control Panel.
2. Double-click the Network icon.
3. From the Protocol tab, click Add. A list of protocols will appear, as shown in Figure 22.8.

FIGURE 22.8.

The Add button on the Protocol tab of the Network icon lists the Point to Point Tunneling protocol.

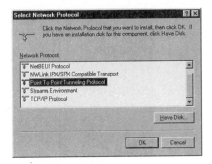

4. Select Point to Point Tunneling Protocol and click OK. Windows NT will then copy from the source files or prompt you for the location of the source files.

5. The PPTP Configuration dialog box appears, as shown in Figure 22.9. Select the Number of Virtual Private Networks to be created and click OK.

FIGURE 22.9.

The number of VPNs will control the maximum number of outbound connections using PPTP. The range is one to 256 VPNs.

6. Click OK to return to the Setup screen and close the Network icon. The system will recompile the bindings and prompt you to restart the computer.

At this point, the PPTP software is installed but not fully configured.

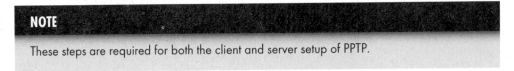

NOTE

These steps are required for both the client and server setup of PPTP.

Configuring PPTP on the Client

To configure RAS to use PPTP and the VPN, follow these steps:

1. From the Start menu, select Settings and then Control Panel.

2. Double-click the Network icon.

3. Open the properties of Remote Access Server (RAS) on the Services tab. You see the dialog box shown in Figure 22.10.

FIGURE 22.10.

*A VPN item is added
to the devices used for
RAS communication.*

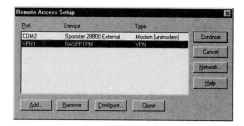

4. Click the Configure button to identify the VPN's role on the system. Dial out only will be used to enable the client (see Figure 22.11).

FIGURE 22.11.

*Dial out only will not
offer any further
configuration items and
should be used only on
clients.*

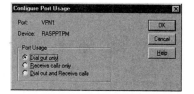

5. Based on the previous choice, the Network configuration button will display appropriate information. Select the VPN to be configured and click the Network button.

6. The Network Configuration dialog box offers the top section for only RASs that have been configured to dial-out systems. The middle section will not be displayed for receive-calls-only servers. Both sections will be presented to systems that have been set up for dial-out and receive calls. The protocols available are listed.

7. Select all transport protocols allowed for incoming or outgoing communication.

Connecting to a PPTP Server from a Windows NT Client

Once PPTP is installed on both the client and the server, a PPTP connection can be established. For the sake of demonstration, this section uses a Windows NT Server as a PPTP server and also uses a Windows NT Server as a PPTP client.

There are several different scenarios to set up a tunnel, and we will review some of them.

Using the Client-to-ISP-to-Server Tunnel

In this scenario, the client connects to the ISP using a standard PPP connection. The ISP establishes a connection through the Internet for the client to the enterprise network. The client then establishes a PPTP tunnel with the PPTP server. The data can be encrypted at the client, inserted into the tunnel, and transmitted to the ISP via PPP. The ISP forwards the packet over the Internet to the PPTP server, which decrypts the packet and places it onto the corporate network. This scenario needs two demand-dial interfaces at the client end: one for the PPP connection to the ISP, and another for the PPTP connection that will use the PPP interface to create the tunnel over.

The client will connect to the ISP with a RAS PPP connection. This is set up as a phone book entry using the ISP's phone number to connect.

Once the connection to the ISP is established, the client then must make a PPTP connection to the PPTP server using the PPTP VPN device defined earlier (see Figure 22.12).

FIGURE 22.12.

Each connection requires a phone book entry. This PPTP entry uses a VPN as the device type and a server name as the phone number.

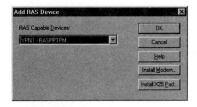

To make a phone book entry for the PPTP connection, do the following:

1. From the Start menu, select Programs, Accessories, Dial-up networking.
2. Enter a name to identify this connection. The PPTP server name could be used.
3. Select I am calling the Internet to set up PPP connection through the ISP.
4. Select the VPN device configured earlier instead of a modem.
5. Enter the IP address or host name of the PPTP server as the phone number. If a host name is used, a host file or DNS server must be available to the system to resolve the name.

Alternatively, the ISP might be configured as a PPTP server, so a second connection wouldn't be necessary. Contact your local ISP for more information.

In order for the PPTP server to be effective, it should have PPTP filtering enabled and Microsoft encryption for the connection and data in place. (See the earlier section "Configuring the PPTP Server for Encryption.") In order for the PPTP server to allow full access to the internal network, it should be configured as a routing RAS server. (See the earlier section "Configuring the RAS Server for Routing.")

Using the Client-to-Server Tunnel Over a LAN

This scenario has the tunnel created across the corporate LAN between the client and the server. Instead of using a modem, the client and server are connected by a null modem cable or the existing network infrastructure. This would create a secure channel between the two machines to prevent tampering with the data. This connection would be accomplished with dial-up networking. There is only one interface, and the phone book entry will use the IP address of the PPTP server as the telephone number.

Using the Server-to-Server Tunnel

In this scenario, one server is configured to dial out as a RAS server (to be a client) and to receive calls as a RAS server. The other server is configured to receive calls as a RAS server. The first server then initiates the call. Once the tunnel is created, encrypted data can be sent between the two sites.

This scenario is similar to a client-to-server over the Internet. Both servers are responsible for routing to their local networks.

Troubleshooting PPTP

PPTP is a simple process, but it relies on several factors in order to be successful. The following sections list items to check if PPTP appears to be misbehaving or simply not working.

RAS Installation and Configuration

Since PPTP depends on RAS and dial-up networking, you need to confirm that they are installed properly. Try to access other resources from RAS using a typical modem.

Is RAS installed on both the server and client? Check the Network's Services tab.

Is the RAS server configured with enough VPNs to accommodate the volume? If one VPN is created, only one connection can be established.

Windows NT Authentication

Windows NT's security is still in place when using RAS. Do your account name and password exist? The account name and password used to log on to the client machine must exist on the RAS server, or a domain controller must be able to authenticate the information.

Does your account have the appropriate dial-in privileges? Each user account needs to have the right to dial in. From the User Manager on the RAS server or domain controller, verify that the user account being used has dial-in permission. You can also do this from the Remote Access Admin tool, accessed through the Start menu's Administrative Tools group.

ISP Connection

Can you connect to your ISP? If you're planning on using the Internet to access your company's LAN, you first must be connected to the Internet through an ISP.

Are you getting an IP address? Use IPCONFIG /ALL. Even though you might be connected, you still need a valid IP address.

Can you ping the PPTP server? Use Ping. The PPTP server should be accessible on the Internet. With the Ping command you can verify that the server's address is valid and accessible from your client machine. The PPTP server's address must be a valid Internet address.

System Speed

Your system might appear very slow. There might not be a problem at all. Using the Network Neighborhood will cause your machine to run very slowly.

Avoid using the browsing tools. Try to use the UNC names instead. For example, the share reports on the server admin1 can be viewed with \\admin1\reports. You also can map drives to common shares using (as an example) Net Use Z: \\admin1\reports.

If you are unsure of a share name and you don't want to browse, use the Net View \\admin1 command to list all public shares on the server admin1. An IP address could be used instead of the server name.

Summary

This chapter examined the Point to Point Tunneling Protocol and its implementation within Windows NT. PPTP is a versatile protocol that allows for the creation of secure virtual private networks for data transfer. Two systems can connect over a public network such as the Internet and transfer data using a secured channel between them. PPTP can tunnel NetBEUI, IPX or TCP/IP packets over Dial-up, LANs or WANs. Using tunneling, you can take a protocol such as NetBEUI—which is not a routable protocol—encapsulate it in PPTP, route the PPTP packet, remove the PPTP layer, and deliver the NetBEUI packet to the destination network. In addition, PPTP offers many benefits to network administrators when it comes to securing remote or local clients. The big reason to implement PPTP is going to be the additional data encryption it can provide while using Windows NT across the Internet. The rest of the chapter covered how to install PPTP on Windows NT and how to troubleshoot it once you have it up and running.

CHAPTER 23

Implementing Routing and Remote Access Services

IN THIS CHAPTER

At the end of the second quarter of 1997 Microsoft filled a gap in its network offering by taking on some of the problems faced by mid-size corporations trying to route network traffic. Prior to this update release, the MPR (Multi-Protocol Routing) software bundled with NT 4.0 was suitable only for small business solutions with limited routing needs.

RAS (Remote Access Service), which has been a built-in feature for some time now, has some limitations that many administrators find restrictive. One such limitation is that RAS has no easy way to dial a connection automatically. If you have a client that needs only periodic dial-up access to the office, say to deliver a piece of critical e-mail on demand, it is very difficult to set up.

RAS has an additional problem—the PPTP (Point to Point Tunneling Protocol) offering allows only client-to-server connections. Many admins wanted to set up secure VPNs (Virtual Private Networks) between servers. No one really enjoyed maintaining static routing tables and not really knowing if the router in another building was still functioning. To make the administration job easier, Microsoft has released a new add-on product for the NT Server 4.0 operating system called Routing and Remote Access Service (RRAS).

Microsoft has tackled these problems with varying degrees of success. At the time of this writing, RRAS is still a newly released product and, like any new release, is having some growing pains. This chapter explains what the product has to offer, discusses basic operating instructions, and lets you know what to watch out for if you use RRAS. While every administrator may not need RRAS on his or her desktop, most of you will find some part of it useful. There are many different parts, but all are related to getting into and out of your subnet. If everything you do is in one subnet, then there isn't much of interest for you here, although you should still look at the demand-dial interface. It can come in handy.

Using Routing and Remote Access Service

The Routing and Remote Access Service offers LAN-to-LAN routing and remote office connectivity solutions to small and mid-size businesses. You can view and manage all of your Routers and RAS servers through the use of the RRAS Administrators Utility, a GUI-based tool. The designers of RRAS intended to make all the different administrative tasks required for network routing management easily accessible from one point.

RRAS enables you to establish and use secure virtual private networks (VPNs) over WAN connections and the Internet. Some of the features this product makes available are explained in the following list:

- Industry standard dynamic routing protocols, including Routing Information Protocol (RIP) Version 1 and Version 2 for IP, Open Shortest Path First (OSPF) for IP, DHCP Relay Agent for IP, RIP for IPX and IPX SAP (Service Advertising Protocol).
- PPTP support for creating VPNs from client to server and server to server.
- RAS and Demand Dial routing support over WAN links.
- IP and IPX Packet Filtering for performance tuning and security.

■ Radius Client Support to allow an existing RADIUS server to communicate with your NT router.

■ Simple Network Management Protocol (SNMP) version 1 management capabilities with several supplied MIBs (Management Information Bases).

■ Published API set for developers. Microsoft has made the Application Programming Interface specifications freely available online to encourage third-party developers to write add-ons for the Administration utilities, supported routing protocols themselves, and the Graphical User Interface.

■ A graphical user interface for remote monitoring and configuration of all of your NT routers.

Before getting too far into a discussion of these different features, it's time to make sure you understand the operations and problems that this product is designed to make more manageable.

Understanding Routing

This chapter assumes you already understand the basics of routing: the delivery of addressed packets across multiple network links. We will look at the process of how a router selects which route to use from its routing table. If you want more in-depth coverage, I refer you to W. Richard Stevens' book, *TCP/IP Illustrated, Volume 1,* for a detailed discussion of routing theory.

In brief, a router is a dedicated box (hardware router) or a general-purpose computer (software router) that is connected to two or more physical networks. When a host is ready to transmit information over the network, it breaks the data up into manageable packets. The host then adds to each packet a header containing its own physical (IPX) or logical (IP) address as the source address and the address of the host it is trying to reach as the destination address. If that destination address is on a different subnet or network, the host sends the packet a gateway or router.

The host might also have specific information about how to get there from here and direct the packet to a predetermined router instead of a default router. The router receives the information packet from the host via one of its connected interfaces, compares the destination network ID with an internal table, called a *routing table,* and decides how best to transfer the information to reach that destination.

These routing tables and how the entries are created, updated, maintained, and removed are what routing administration is all about. Transferring the information usually entails sending the packet out another one of the connected interfaces pointing at the destination network.

If a router can't find an entry in its table pointing to the destination network, it has what is called a *default route* in the table. This is the equivalent of saying "I don't know what to do with this packet, so I'll send it to another router and maybe it will know how to get there." If there's no specific route and no default route, the router attempts to return a destination unreachable error message to the sender using ICMP (Internet Control Message Protocol).

Routing Tables

A routing table is just a database of information on all known networks and hosts. The information stored in the table is used by the operating system to decide the best path to use to reach a destination address. The contents of the table change depending on the protocols being used and the operating system itself.

On an NT system with TCP/IP installed, routing tables can have four different types of entries. In the order in which they are searched for, they are Host, Subnet, Network, and Default. The host route is a route to a single, specific destination IP address. The Subnet route is used for any host on the specified subnet address. The network route is for any destination on the specified network ID and the Default route is used if no other match is found.

So what does a routing table look like? If you're sitting in front of a computer that has the TCP/IP protocol installed, run a command prompt and type route print. Your results will vary depending on what your computer has been doing lately. You should see output similar to that shown in Figure 23.1.

FIGURE 23.1.

The route command displays five columns of information.

The router compares the Network Address column with the destination address, after it has been masked, to see if it can find a match. The most correct match is the one selected in the order previously discussed.

In this example, if the destination address was 192.168.50.12, then table entry number 4 would be used. It is a better match than entry number 3, which matches all hosts on network 192.168.0.0, while entry number 4 applies to just the 192.168.50.0 subnet. If the destination was 192.168.50.172 then entry number 5 would be used, because that is the most correct down to the host level. Of course, that would mean I was sending to my own machine, which is why it's connected to the loop-back address 127.0.0.1. 224.0.0.0 is used for multicast addressing, discussed in the following section "Multicast Addressing," while 255 is used for broadcast addressing.

The Netmask column contains the subnet mask for the network address. The subnet mask is logically anded with the destination address in the packet to identify what part of the address is relevant for routing. Zeros turn off the part of the mask that is binary, and ones leave the binary equivalent parts in the destination address alone. 255 is 8 binary ones while 224 is three high-order binary ones.

For example:

```
                  Decimal        Binary equivalent
                  ¦ Network ¦host¦      ¦    Network       ¦ host  ¦
host address    192.168.50.172  11000000.10101000.00110010.10101100
and the mask    255.255.255.0   11111111.11111111.11111111.00000000
leaves network  192.168.50.0    11000000.10101000.00110010.00000000
ID only
```

If the bit in the address is a 1 *and* the bit in the mask is a 1, leave it on (1); otherwise, turn it off (0).

The Gateway Address is the address to which the packet is to be forwarded. This may be on the destination network or the next hop toward the destination network. Either way, sending to this address is going to get the packet closer to final delivery. The Interface is the network card to send the packet out on this machine to reach the next gateway or hop.

Metric is a measurement to quantify the cost of using this route. If there is more than one route to reach a destination, then the router selects the one with the lowest cost. The metric field is configurable on NT routers, but there are certain limitations, especially when using RIP, as we shall see. What can the metric represent? Depending on the implementation, it might represent the following:

- Hop count is a count of the number of physical routers that you must pass through to get to the final destination if you use this route. The higher the hop count, the more delays in delivery and the greater the chance of discarding the packet. With RIP, the hop count can be a maximum of 15 because 16 means destination unreachable.

- Delay is a measure of the time required to reach the destination network. This can be used to indicate the speed of the path (ISDN versus Direct Dial path), or it could be configured to show congestion on the route. (Don't use a busy router in Chicago—higher delay count—if a less busy router in Memphis is available—lower delay count.)

- Throughput represents the amount of data that a link can handle efficiently. A very busy Ethernet segment might be a poorer choice that an underutilized 64 kbps WAN link.

- Reliability is a measure of the uptime of the path.

If the route is learned of via a dynamic routing protocol, there is another relevant field that's not shown on the screen. That is the *lifetime* of the route. The route *lives* in the table for only a preset length of time and is then discarded if not used or updated. How this field is used and what values it contains varies with the protocol used to acquire routes.

23

IMPLEMENTING
ROUTING AND
REMOTE ACCESS

The preceding is not intended to be a definitive list of all available fields used by all available routers for every routing protocol. There are many proprietary solutions and other data is stored about routes by other common protocols. For example, IPX stores a *Tick Count* in the tables—the approximate time it takes to reach the destination router in 1/18-second increments (a Tick). The Tick count is used to break ties with the metric. These fields are the most relevant to our discussion.

Routes are called static routes if they are never automatically removed or updated in the routing table by the router. If you have static routes in the table, the administrator is responsible for updating them manually to keep them current. Generally, the static routes are loaded from text files when the router starts up. If there is a change in the network topology, the administrator must use the route command at the command prompt to update the routing tables when he becomes aware of the change.

Table 23.1 describes the entries found on every NT computer running TCP/IP. You may have other entries that are unique to your organization. The host assigned IP addresses should definitely be different.

Table 23.1. Default routing table entries.

Network Address	Description
0.0.0.0	The default gateway. If no other matching entry is found, send the packet out this interface to this gateway in the hope that it will know how to get there.
127.0.0.0	Loop-back address. Used for diagnostic and testing procedures to test the software stack.
192.168.50.0	Subnet address used for all hosts on this subnet.
192.168.50.172	Local host IP address. Packets sent to this address will be routed to the loop-back address.
192.168.50.255	Local subnet broadcast address. Packets that are to be sent to all local hosts on subnet 192.168.50.0 are sent to this address.
224.0.0.0	IP multicast address.
255.255.255.255	Limited IP broadcast address.

Multicast Addressing

With broadcast traffic, every host must examine the packet to see if it is of interest, and with unicast traffic, only the sending and receiving hosts see the packet. Multicasting fits in between when you have many hosts that need to see the packet, but not all.

When you assign a multicast address, an address starting with 224, you assign the same address to more than one machine. All machines with the same address form a group when they're started and then packets can be sent only to all of the group members. The non-group members can ignore the packets, so they don't get bogged down processing unnecessary traffic, and the OS doesn't have to coordinate multiple streams of unicast traffic to reach all of the many destinations.

Multicasting is the method workgroup programs like Netmeeting use and, for our purposes, both RIP (v2) and OSPF allow the routers to form a group and use multicasting to talk to each other.

You also have a routing table you can set up on a local host. For example, let's say you had a dedicated router (A) for Internet traffic and another router (B) for internal, company-only traffic. You would set up the host to run a batch file on boot containing static route commands. This batch file would configure the host to route all company subnet traffic to router B and then make router A the default gateway for all other traffic. That way, router A doesn't have to re-direct all internal traffic back to router B for it to handle.

Using Static and Dynamic Routers

With static routers, all table entries must be added and maintained manually. While this may work well for a small company with limited routes, it does not scale well. The routers do not inform each other of changes in the topology and any downed routes must be manually re-moved from the table. If you have only two or three routers on your network, you may find that static routers are the easiest solution for you to use.

> **NOTE**
>
> Static routes have an endless lifetime.

Dynamic routing is the process of having the routers communicate among themselves and inform each other of changes in the topology of the network. This is accomplished with a constant chatter of periodic or on-demand messages containing routing table information. Entries in the table that a router finds out about from another router are called *learned routes*. Each learned route has a finite lifetime before it is removed from the table, based on locally enforced routing policies. There are two different types of dynamic routing protocols: Distant Vector and Link State.

Using Distant Vector Protocols

The following are the distinguishing characteristics of Distant Vector Protocols:

- Unsynchronized and unacknowledged information exchanges
- Complete table sent by updates

- Potentially multiple entries in the tables if more than one route exists to a destination
- High convergence times (see the section "Routing Loops and Other Problems")

Even if there are no changes in the routing table during an update period, these routers send the entire contents of their table to all attached routers. The advantage of using this type of router is that to set up and configure them is nice and easy and fairly simple to understand. This protocol is good for a small to mid-sized company with a limited number of routers (5 to 10). Examples of Distant Vector Protocols are RIP, RTMP (Routing Table Maintenance Protocol for AppleTalk), and IGRP (Interior Gateway Routing Protocol).

Using Link State Protocols

These protocols are distinguished by storing only a single best route to each network in the routing table. They exchange only information that has changed since the last update period with synchronized, acknowledged packets. They maintain a database of available routes and use multicast traffic to limit host involvement in router exchanges.

Link State Protocols scale well and can greatly reduce the amount of router chatter on the network. The convergence time is faster than Distance Vector Protocols and they can be used to break very large networks into smaller, more manageable areas. The disadvantage is that they are more complicated to set up and larger corporations have to do a lot more planning and configuration up front if they want to use them. You would have to be a large to very large corporate environment before you could justify the extra demands to use a Link State Protocol. Examples of Link State Protocols are OSPF and NLSP (Novell Link State Protocol).

Routing Loops and Other Problems

When talking about routing, convergence occurs when all associated routers have the same information in their routing tables. Let's say we had five routers connected to the network and one of them finds out that a connected interface has gone down. The router marks the route through that interface as unreachable, then notifies all the connected routers that they can no longer send packets to be routed through that interface. When all five routers have updated their tables to reflect the new state of the network, we say that convergence has occurred. The faster convergence happens, the better for the network, because that router won't keep receiving packets it can no longer route. Also, the longer it takes for convergence, the greater the number of errors that can find their way into the routing tables. The link state protocols tend to have a much faster convergence time than distance vector protocols.

Routing loops are another problem that can cause errors in the routing tables. Routing loops occur when a router can see more than one other router and the completed path loops back on itself.

For the sake of example, say we have three routers: A, B, and C (see Figure 23.2). Each of them can see the other two routers. When A learns of a new route, say to the network office, it tells both B and C, "You can get to office through me." B receives this information and then tells

C, "You can get to office through me." What C doesn't know is that B is routing through A. C then in turn tells A that "You can get to office through me" and A dutifully adds that to its routing table. This creates a routing loop. If A loses its first route to network office, it selects the next best route, which is through C. C in turn forwards to B, which sends back to A and forms a loop.

Most routing protocols have built-in mechanisms to help prevent router loops from happening. As a safety feature, each packet has a maximum hop count (TTL) to prevent a packet from looping endlessly. Every router that forwards the packet decrements the hop count and, when it reaches zero, the packet is discarded. Router loops generally happen only if convergence has not occurred or the network is not correctly configured.

FIGURE 23.2.

An example of a routing loop.

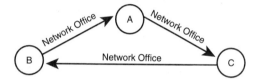

Preparing to Install RRAS

Before you try to install RRAS, there are several issues you should be aware of. Read through the section on System Requirements carefully before you start to make sure you have everything in place that you need, and that you've removed any potential conflicts.

Understanding System Requirements

The first thing you need is a computer running Windows NT Server 4.0 with Service Pack 3 installed. Sorry, no other configurations work at this time. Of course, you need to make it a multi-homed computer—two or more network output interfaces are necessary, be they network cards, WAN links, a dial-up connection, whatever. There must be at least two interfaces to route between. Otherwise, you don't need a router.

The computer itself needs to be powerful enough to run NT, which requires a minimum of 16 MB of RAM and at least 15 MB of hard disk space. With those requirements, you will get a 10- to 15,000-packet-per-second router. If you add more RAM, you will get better speeds, up to 40,000 packets per second with 64 MB.

CAUTION

Packets might be dropped on slower systems that are recalculating routing tables with OSPF. If you plan to use OSPF, you should exceed the minimum processor requirements because recalculating many OSPF routes can be processor intensive.

One of the quirks about RRAS is that, prior to installation, you need to install all of the networking protocols and services required. This means that if you want to use TCP/IP, NWLINK (IPX/SPX), PPTP, or SNMP after you install the product, they should be installed before you start. In the case of PPTP, that means you must install RAS to configure your VPNs first.

Of course, in true Microsoft style, you cannot have any of the components or services that RRAS replaces installed when you run RRAS setup. This includes RAS, DHCP Relay Agent, RIP for IP, and RIP for IPX. If any of these components are installed, you must remove them before you start the RRAS install. So if you want to use PPTP on a new server, you have to install the operating system, add all of the networking protocols, install RAS, configure your VPNs, and then uninstall RAS before you can set up RRAS to add the routing protocols and use the created VPNs.

Selecting and Installing a WAN Adapter

If you want to use RRAS with wide area technologies such as ISDN, X.25, Frame Relay, ATM, or T-carrier, then you have to make sure your adapter card is on the HCL (Hardware Compatibility List) for NT. Currently, there are about a dozen cards supported, including Eicon S94, Cabletron F70, and a group of Digi adapters.

You install the card per manufacturers' instructions and then add the drivers in the Adapters tab on the Network program in the Control Panel. RRAS detects the new adapter and allows you to add the interface.

Acquiring a Copy of RRAS

RRAS is available free of charge as a download from the Microsoft web site. As of this writing, the address is http://www.microsoft.com/ntserver/info/ntcomm.htm. It will be included in future versions of the operating system (NT 5.0) and in future service packs as well.

After you have connected to the web site, download the file Mpri386.exe for Intel processors or Mpralpha.exe for Alpha processors. This is a self-extracting zip file that when executed creates a temporary folder (c:\temp\ixp0000.tmp on Intel platforms) and extracts the compressed files to the temporary folder.

You are then prompted for the name of an install folder to expand the compressed files into, to act as the final installation point. It expands and copies the setup files into the installation folder. The temporary directory and files are removed at the end of this part of the setup, but the final installation files are left. You are asked if you want to continue the install or exit at this time.

> **TIP**
>
> Exit the RRAS installation after the temporary files are moved to an installation directory and perform a backup. That way, if anything goes wrong during installation, you can restore your system to the way it was before the problem occurred.

Keep those installation files handy. You will find you may have to add additional components later, refresh the install when routing protocols *disappear* from the GUI, and reinstall when things go badly wrong. Some services are not compatible with RRAS. Check the Microsoft web site for the latest updates and problem reports.

Installing RRAS

You have a choice about how you can complete the setup. You can run Mprsetup from the installation folder created during the copy files phase, or you can choose Add Services from the Control Panel, Network program, Services tab. Click the Have Disk button and supply the folder name created during the file copy phase.

During the installation process, you are asked which components you want to install, as shown in Figure 23.3. After the install, you have to shut down and reboot your computer to complete the process. If you choose not to install all of the components at this time, you can go back and install them later. You do this either by running the setup program again, or from the Control Panel, Network, Services, choose Add, and then select Routing and Remote Access Services from the dialog box.

FIGURE 23.3.

RRAS Installation Options.

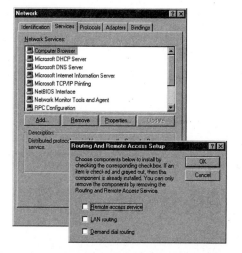

> **NOTE**
>
> Sometimes RRAS doesn't add itself to the Network/Services/Add Network Services dialog box. In that case, you must click Have Disk and point it at the installation folder again.

Once you have successfully installed the product, you will find it has added a Routing and Remote Access Manager into the Administrator's Tools menu. There also is a new service added to start RRAS automatically, which you can view in the Services program under the Control Panel.

Using the RRAS Administration GUI

The RRAS GUI has a typical Microsoft look to it, with two panes and many right-click options. The pane on the left side shows a tree-like hierarchy of objects and the right side shows the contents of the object that is selected in the tree (see Figure 23.4). The root of the tree is the router, followed by the LAN and Demand Dial Interfaces, which eventually contain all of your installed LAN and WAN adapters and any demand-dial interfaces configured (after you have added them).

The next branch of the tree is where you do all of the IP routing work. It is to this that you add protocols, interfaces, and static routes as you configure your router. If you have NWLink installed, then there will be an IPX routing branch, which contains all of the IPX routing configuration settings. The last branch is the Active Connections and Ports, where all the active demand-dial connections are listed. You can track and get detailed status information for these connections here.

FIGURE 23.4.

The RRAS Administration Utility.

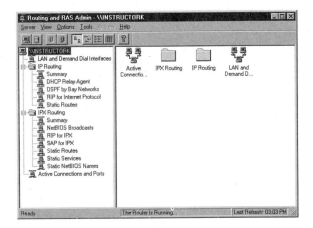

If you explore the menus, you will find the Server menu has options that enable you to connect to any remote NT router in the domain, start and stop the selected router, and load and save the router configurations.

> **TIP**
>
> Saving a completed router configuration to a disk file can save you a lot of rebuilding later if you have to reinstall.

The View menu has the standard Explorer view options. The Options menu enables you to set refresh options for the RRAS windows. You also can check the auto refresh option rather than repeatedly having to remember to press F5 to refresh the display.

A Telnet option on the Tools menu enables you to connect to a non-NT, non-RRAS, Telnet-based router to administer it. The Actions menu changes based on what is selected in the Tree or Contents pane. This generally gives you the same options you get on the right-click pop-up menus.

A word about the tool bar buttons: Most of the items on the Server and View Menus are available on the tool bar for easy access. There are buttons to change the view options, to select networks and routers, and to get help. There also is a button to start and stop the router. If the button shows a green light, that means your router is stopped—press the button to start it. If the button shows a red light, that means your router is running—press the button to stop it. The color of the icons indicates what will happen when you press the button, but does not reflect the state of the router.

If you have been observant during this quick overview of the menus, you may have noticed a couple of missing things. To add a routing protocol to IP, you right-click on the summary branch and choose Add routing protocol. If NWLink was installed when RRAS is added, an IPX Routing branch with all of the available routing protocols is automatically added.

One of the things you cannot do in the GUI is remove routing protocols. If you want to re-move a routing protocol from the RRAS utility, you run a command prompt and use the Routemon utility. In fact, everything you can do in the GUI, you can perform with the Routemon command line utility. This enables you to script, batch, and schedule most of the routine maintenance tasks we will talk about. After you run setup, you will find a document called the Administrator's Guide in the installation folder. Appendix B of this document contains all of the syntax for scripting the various Routemon actions. See the online NT help for instruction about how to schedule a batch file to run.

What if you want to administer your routers from your desktop but you're running NT Workstation 4.0 instead? You don't have to upgrade to NT server to do this, but you do have to do without some existing services. In the install folder, you run the following command:

```
Copyadmin.exe SourceFolder DestinationFolder
```

This command copies the Mpradmin.exe and all of the necessary DLLs onto your machine so you can run the GUI. Be warned that this action overwrites your current RAS DLLs (if you have it installed) and you can no longer use normal RAS on that machine. The DLLs are not compatible. This process does not copy the Routemon utility; you have to do that manually.

There are many times when the display does not accurately display the status of the router. There were times when we moved an OPSF router to a new area but the display did not reflect that fact and continued to report it in the original area. Remember to press F5 occasionally to update the display.

23

IMPLEMENTING ROUTING AND REMOTE ACCESS

> **TIP**
>
> Is your router "hung"? Does nothing appear to respond? Go to the task list and look for a background instance of Dr. Watson32. It will sometimes get invoked without actually displaying a message on the screen. You will probably have to shut down and reboot anyway.

Understanding RIP for IP

RIP (Routing Information Protocol) for IP (Internet Protocol) Version 1 was made an official specification in RFC 1058 in 1988. Previously, it had been unofficially used for years. RIP v1 uses UDP port 520 for the broadcast delivery of packets containing a copy of each router's complete routing table. This happens every 30 seconds by default. The packets aren't authenticated or acknowledged by the receiving router.

The metric used by RIP is a hop count that represents how many routers a packet has to cross to reach the desired network ID. The highest acceptable hop count is 15 because the RFC 1058 defines a hop count of 16 to mean infinity or destination unreachable.

If there are multiple routes to a destination, the RIP router typically stores only the best route, based on the lowest hop count. When building or maintaining a routing table, the router compares all of the routes in the received packet with its current routes. If there are any routes it does not already know about, it adds them to the table. If it finds a route with a lower (better) metric, it replaces the route in the table with the better one. If it finds a route with a higher (worse) metric, it has to determine whether it will use it or not. It checks the source router ID and if it's the same router that it learned this route from earlier, it replaces the route in the table with the new metric. If it's a different router, it discards the route. This is the cause of a problem discussed in the next section, where we talk about convergence problems.

Understanding RIP Operating Stages

There are four different stages of normal operation in RIP operations:

- Initialization
- Continuous Operations
- Triggered Updates
- Shutdown

There are two additional failure states: Interface Failure and Router Failure.

Initialization is when a router first starts up. The router builds the initial routing table from all of the locally attached interfaces. The router then sends a special request packet on all interfaces requesting the contents of the tables from all attached routers. This request packet contains a Network ID of 00000000 with a hop count of 16. It then starts to listen on UDP port 520 for other routers to broadcast. It adds any new routes to the routing table as it hears from each router, until it knows about all the available routes and we have convergence.

The router then enters a Continuous Operation stage where every 30 seconds it broadcasts the contents of its tables on all attached interfaces. Each RIP packet contains a maximum of 25 routes. If you have a large network with many routes, this can lead to a lot of network traffic.

What if you had five routers in a chain, one after the other, and you had a change in topology at the end of the chain? The first router makes the change in its routes and, at 30 seconds between each broadcast, it could potentially take two and a half minutes before the last router found out about the change. That is too long for convergence, so the next operating stage is called Triggered Update to resolve that problem. If a router makes a change to the table, it almost immediately starts the broadcast process to notify all the other routers that a change has occurred.

This notification is almost immediate because there is a brief built-in waiting period. Imagine if you had a router that was centrally connected to 10 other routers and it had a change to the table. It would notify all 10 by broadcast and, because their tables had changed, they in turn would immediately trigger an update and broadcast their tables. We would have a broadcast storm that could potentially cripple the network.

With all of those broadcast packets coming in from all of these routers at the same time, the chances are that one of them would start to drop work packets. The packets also are supposed to deliver normal network traffic through all of this. The Triggered Update delay gives all of the routers a chance to process the updates and catch up with their workload before the next round of updates arrives.

The fourth stage is router shutdown, where a router is gracefully shut down. Before leaving the network, the router changes all of the routes that were reachable through it to a hop count of 16 (infinity) and broadcast to all adjacent routers. That way, the other routers don't forward any more packets to the router because all of its routes are now unreachable.

A failed router or interface results in an ungraceful exit from the network. A failed router doesn't get a chance to tell the others it was leaving, so they still try to send packets to it. This is the reason for the lifetime field in the routing tables. When a route is added, its lifetime is set to 3 minutes by default. Each time the same route is seen in the update packets, its lifetime is renewed to 3 minutes.

If a route hasn't been heard within its lifetime, then it's marked as unreachable, causing a triggered update. This means that if we have a router that fails, it will be over three minutes before convergence, and a lot can happen in three minutes. There also could be a situation where just one interface fails on a router. If it is a WAN adapter, many of them have the capability to sense a failure and update the tables accordingly. Not many LAN adapters have this capability, though, so the routes through that interface have to be aged out of the tables.

Identifying Convergence Problems

We have already discussed several convergence issues, but the *count to infinity* problem is one that needs explanation. Let's look at a simple configuration with two routers and three networks as depicted in Figure 23.5.

FIGURE 23.5.

Two routers and the count to infinity problem.

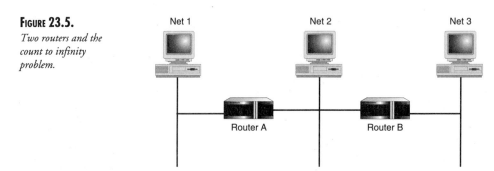

Let's watch these two routers build their routing tables as we have described RIP to understand what can happen here. The following shows the routing tables for both Router A and Router B:

```
Router A Table        Router B Table
Net 1 - 1 hop         Net 2 - 1 hop
Net 2 - 1 hop         Net 3 - 1 hop
```

In their first update, they tell each other about the networks they can't see directly. A tells B about Net 1 and B tells A about Net 3. The following shows the routing tables after the update. At this point, there is convergence:

```
Router A Table        Router B Table
Net 1 - 1 hop         Net 2 - 1 hop
Net 2 - 1 hop         Net 3 - 1 hop
Net 3 - 2 hops        Net 1 - 2 hops
```

During the course of the day, Router A loses the connection to Net 1. Router A modifies the tables and gives Net 1 a hop count of 16. Before it can issue a broadcast, though, it receives a regular update from router B stating it has a route to Net 1 with a hop count of 2. This is better than 16, so router A adjusts its tables to say there is a route to Net 1, using router B, with a hop count of 3 (it has to add one), and initiates a triggered update. Router B gets the update and looks at its table.

Now, because it first learned about this route from A in the first place, and this is a higher metric, it replaces the original entry in the table with a hop count of 4. These routers don't realize that they're updating each other with a dead route. This in turn causes B to fire a triggered update and it reports back to A that the hop count on that route has gone up to 4. Because A learned about this route originally from B, it again updates its tables to reflect a new hop count of 5 and fires a triggered update. The only way out of this loop is when both routers reach a hop count of 16 and agree that it is a destination-unreachable network.

This is called a count to infinity problem and is one of the reasons why unreachable was set at 16. Multiply this problem by the number of routers you have on your network, because each router that gets a triggered update will itself send a triggered update. This will cause a broadcast storm on the network until infinity is reached by all routers.

To address this problem, RRAS implements Split Horizons with Poison Reverse by default. Split Horizons means that a router that learns of a new route cannot advertise that route back to the router it learned about the route from.

In our previous example, Router B could not advertise back to Router A that it has a route to Network 1 because it learned of that route from Router A. Poison Reverse means that it includes the route in its update packets back to the original router, but with a hop count of 16, meaning you can't get there through me. This helps prevent the count to infinity problem and speeds up convergence on the network, but it also increases the size of the update packets. You now have not only valid routes in the update packets but also unreachable ones as well.

Dealing with Problems in RIP Version 1

In 1988, when RIP was standardized with RFC 1058, it met the needs of most networks. Since then, however, some problems with the original design have become evident. Foremost of these was the inability to include a subnet mask with the route advertisement. The router would assume either a default network mask or use the mask from the interface the advertisement arrived on. This means you could not use a variable length subnet mask on your network. This is a common practice in many modern businesses. Unfortunately, the lack of authentication also posed a security problem because anyone could modify your router tables. Last but not least, the broadcast updates can slow other network traffic.

To address these problems a new standard was proposed in RFC 1388 and updated in RFC 1723 for RIP Version 2. This was designed to stay compatible with Version 1, add a subnet mask field, a clear text password for authentication, and to use Multicast announcements instead of broadcast. These three changes resolved some of the problems with Version 1.

RRAS supports both RIP Version 1 and Version 2. If you're running both versions on routers that can see each other, there are some rules that have to be enforced to ensure the Version 1 routers aren't confused by and can see the Version 2 packets. Also, some Version 1 routers are configured to discard Version 2 packets, which they see as being corrupt because of the extra fields.

It is strongly recommended that you install only one RIP version. RRAS is designed to use Multicast Version 2 packets using IP address 224.0.0.9, so don't use that address in any other multicast groups you might have set up. For those of you who don't know about multicasting, all machines configured with the same multicast address form a group and talk to each other only when they send packets. This is a one-to-many broadcast instead of a one-to-all, the standard broadcast type.

Supporting RIP in RRAS

By using the RRAS Administration utility, you can configure an interface to use either Version 1, Version 2, or both. You can allow the interface to advertise and accept both default routes and host routes. This feature is disabled by default.

Updates use Split Horizons with Poison Update by default, which you can disable. You can configure the Advertisement Interval (30 seconds by default), the Triggered Update Interval (5 seconds by default), and the Routing Table Lifetime interval (3 minutes by default).

> **NOTE**
>
> You can set up a router to perform Silent RIP, which means it will listen to broadcasts and maintain a routing table but will not advertise any routes.

RRAS supports all of the RIP Version 2 options such as advertised subnet masks, authentication, and multicasting. You can set up filtering so that the router will either accept or reject routes from specified networks IDs, routers, protocols, or services.

Installing RIP

To add RIP to the RRAS Administration Utility, follow these steps:

1. Open the IP branch in the tree pane.
2. Select Summary and right-click.
3. Choose Add Routing Protocol from the pop-up menu.
4. Select RIP for IP when a list of all of the uninstalled routing protocols is displayed.

The RIP for Internet Protocol Configuration dialog box is displayed, which lets you configure Event Logging and Security features as shown in Figures 23.6 and 23.7. You can configure the global settings now or click OK and complete them later, as described in the next section.

Configuring RIP for IP

You can configure global RIP parameters by selecting the RIP for IP branch just added to the tree and right clicking. You will get a menu option to Configure RIP. This displays the RIP for Internet Protocol Configuration Sheet that is used to set global properties for the router.

On the General tab, you set the Minimum seconds between Triggered Updates and the level of event logging (see Figure 23.6). The event log messages are generally very informative and can be very useful in identifying a problem. Logging the maximum amount of information can be useful when troubleshooting, but make sure you reduce it back to Log errors when you have solved the problem.

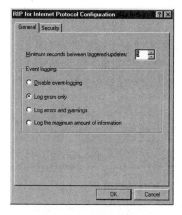

FIGURE 23.6.

*Configuring RIP—
General tab.*

CAUTION

Logging the maximum amount can be time-consuming.

On the Security tab, you control which routers take part in building the routing table. You create a list of router IP addresses and then select either to accept routes from these routers only or to ignore routes from these routers (see Figure 23.7). The default is to process announcements from all routers. You can create only one list of routers and then tell it to Accept only from this list or ignore anything from the routers in this list. You can't have it both ways and you can't have two lists. After you have entered the IP address of each router, make sure you click the Add button. Clicking OK before you click Add means it will discard the last one entered.

FIGURE 23.7.

*Configuring RIP—
Security tab.*

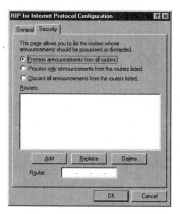

Now that you have set up the global properties, you have to add the interfaces you want this protocol to use. Select Rip for Internet Protocol on the left tree pane and right click. From the menu, select Add an Interface. A dialog box is displayed showing all of the available interfaces.

23

IMPLEMENTING
ROUTING AND
REMOTE ACCESS

Select the interface you want to add and it will appear in the contents pane on the right. After you have selected all of the interfaces you want RIP to use, you have to configure each one with interface specific properties. Right-click on the interface in the contents pane and select Configure Interface from the Menu. You should see the dialog box shown in Figure 23.8.

FIGURE 23.8.

RIP per interface configuration—General tab.

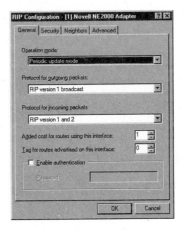

For each interface configuration, there are four tabs: General, Security, Neighbors, and Advanced.

Setting per Interface General Properties

On the General tab, you configure the basic properties for the interface. The Operation mode is Periodic Update by default if this is a LAN interface. If this is a demand dial interface, though, you don't want it to be dialed every update period (30 seconds) so the default becomes Auto-Static. This means the RIP tables are updated only when requested by the user. The user does this by selecting the Summary branch under IP routing and then right-clicks on the demand-dial interface in the contents pane. From the pop-up menu, the user selects Update routes. If this needs to be done regularly, you also can schedule this task by using the command line routman utility.

The Protocol for Outgoing Packets tells this interface what type of advertisements to make. The choices are RIP Version 1 Broadcast, RIP Version 2 Broadcast, RIP Version 2 Multicast, and Silent RIP.

If this interface is connected to a mixed environment of RIP 1 and RIP 2 routers, pick RIP 2 Broadcast or the RIP 1 routers never see the advertisements. Select RIP 2 Multicast only if all other routers connected to this interface are also configured the same as multicast group address 224.0.0.9. Silent RIP means no outgoing advertisements are sent.

Protocols for Incoming Packets identifies what this router expects to see from its neighbors. Choices include RIP Version 1 and Version 2, RIP Version 1 only, RIP Version 2 only, and Ignore incoming packets. This last means the router will not update its routes and becomes a static router.

The Added cost for routes using this interface is the metric to add to all routes learned of over this interface. The default is 1, but you can adjust this cost upward to discourage the router from using this particular interface. Remember that a total of 16 means unreachable, so don't adjust it too high.

Tag for routes advertised on this Interface are a way for you to identify the routes this router is advertising when looking at packets with a sniffer like Network Monitor. This field is used only with RIP Version 2 and some BGPs.

If you check the Enable Authentication check box, you can supply a case-sensitive password. Router advertisements are ignored unless all RIP Version 2 routers connected to this interface have the same password. With event logging turned on, the event viewer tells you if you have the wrong password. If you do, just capture a packet and see what it's supposed to be. It is passed in clear text so that it's easily seen. Look in the captured RIP packet for the field labeled Password.

Setting per Interface Security Properties

On the Security tab, you can specify Network IDs and then filter them (see Figure 23.9). The top drop-down box enables you to specify if this is when announcing routes or when accepting routes. You then specify whether to Process All Routes, Process Only Routes in the Ranges Listed, or Discard All Routes in the Ranges Listed. You can then add the starting and ending network IDs of the networks you want to filter. Make sure you click on the Add Button or the range won't be added.

FIGURE 23.9.

RIP per interface configuration Security tab.

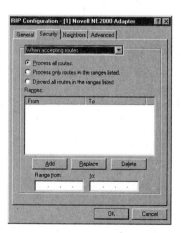

If you specify only your own network subnet IDs as a range and select Process only routes in the ranges listed, then you will only get your own internal networks in the routing tables. If you discard all routes in the listed ranges then you can list known problem networks on the external side and have them excluded.

Setting per Interface Neighbors Properties

The Neighbors tab is used if this interface is an NBMA, such as X.25, or a point-to-point connection, such as T1. You specify the ID of the neighbor routers you want this router to send updates to over this interface. If you chose Disable Neighbors-List, this interface uses the global announcement type, broadcast, or multicast. If you select Use Neighbors-List in Addition to Broadcast or Multicast, then the neighbors in the list get a unicast announcement of router tables and all others on this interface get the broadcast or multicast. If you select Use Neighbors-List Instead of Broadcast or Multicast, then only the routers listed get unicasts of the routing tables.

Setting per Interface Advanced Properties

On the Advanced tab, you set all the RIP timer options and select protocol options you want to enforce on this interface (see Figure 23.10). First you set the Periodic announcement timer to the number of seconds between routine announcements. The default is 30 seconds. You then set the lifetime for routes with the Route-expiration timer. The default is 180 seconds. You then set the Route Removal timer, which has a default of 120 seconds. After a route has been declared dead (the lifetime has expired), the route is marked in the tables with a hop count of 16 and is included in router updates. After the Removal timer has expired, the route is completely removed from the tables. This ensures that instead of just disappearing from the tables, the route is advertised as unreachable for two minutes before disappearing.

FIGURE 23.10.

RIP per interface configuration—Advanced tab.

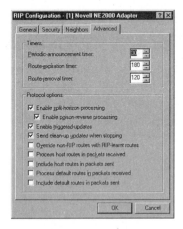

The Protocol Options include Enable split-Horizon processing, Enable poison-reverse processing, Enable triggered-updates, and Send clean-up updates when stopping, all selected by default.

Options not selected include Override Non-RIP Routes with RIP-Learnt Routes, which causes static routes or OSPF routes to be overwritten by RIP-learned routes. The Process Host Routes in Packets Received and Include Host Routes in Packets Sent are disabled by default.

When dealing with demand-dial and RAS connections, the host at the other end of the dialup line is classified as host route. These options must be enabled or static routes must be created throughout the company so that other networks can route to that host machine. Process Default Routes in Packets Received and Include Default Routes in Packets Sent are also disabled by default. You generally don't want one router's default gateway overwriting all the other default gateways just because it has a better metric.

The next thing you might need to do is add some static routes. These are required for your non-RIP-enabled routers or demand-dial networks so they can be routed to. In the left tree pane, right-click the Static Routes branch and select Add Static Route. The Static Route dialog box is shown in Figure 23.11. Type in the destination network ID, the Subnet mask, the Gateway to reach this network, and the Metric for this route. Select the correct interface that is to be used to reach the specified gateway and click OK. The route is added to the Contents pane.

It's fairly normal if the route isn't added to the right pane. You simply have to shut down your router, reboot, restart your router, then add the static route again. There seems to be a glitch in the interface that sometimes requires a restart.

FIGURE 23.11.
Adding static routes.

Understanding RIP for IPX

RIP for IPX is a distance vector routing protocol that uses simple broadcast to exchange routes across an IPX internetwork. The IPX router supplied with RRAS combines both an IPX routing agent and an SAP routing agent. The IPX routing agent uses RIP for IPX to route packets and maintain routing tables. The SAP agent collects and propagates SAP information using a similar process and responds to client SAP requests.

For anyone who is not familiar with IPX networking, an IPX address takes the format of Network.Node. The network portion is a four-byte hexadecimal number assigned by the network administrator during NWLink installation. The Node portion is the MAC (Media Access Control) address usually assigned to the physical network adapter by the manufacturer. On my machine, the Novell 2000-compatible adapter has a MAC address of 0000B4371824 and the Network Number I assigned to the physical network is 80000000. The IPX interface address is 80000000.0000B4371824.

When you install NWLink you are asked for both an Internal network number and a network number. Every IPX router requires a Virtual Internal Network, complete with Virtual

Network adapters, to communicate between the physical interfaces. The Internal network number I assigned to the router was 99000099.

The Virtual adapter on a Microsoft NWLink installation is 00-00-00-00-00-01. To start the router, you must change the Virtual Internal Network number from the default 00000000. The router doesn't work if you leave it at 0. You can assign any number you want to the internal network as long as it is not 0 and is different from your external networks. This Internal network often shows up in the RRAS IPX routing Contents pane. The network numbers can be set and changed through the Control Panel, Networks, NWLINK IPX/SPX properties.

As long as you have NWLink IPX/SPX Compatible Transport Protocol loaded before you install RRAS, IPX routing is automatically installed and enabled on all LAN interfaces. If you install NWLink after RRAS, you have to reinstall RRAS to pick it up. You cannot add a networking protocol to RRAS. If you use the Add a service, Have disk and specify the installation directory, you are shown the install screen with the currently installed options. Just click OK and the display is refreshed—you shouldn't lose any configuration information from your router.

IPX also allows packet filtering on source and destination addresses, sockets, and packet types. See the section later in this chapter on packet filtering for the details. RIP for IPX has three operating states and the same two unavailable conditions as IP. The following are the three operating states:

- Initialization
- Continual Operation
- Route Shutdown

Link Failure and Router Failure are the two unavailable conditions. RIP for IPX also supports triggered updates.

Initialization is the process of bringing the router online. The router builds its initial routing table from all of the attached Network IDs and broadcasts to all adjacent routers informing them of these routes with a RIP packet. The router then broadcasts a request for all other known routes on all of the local networks. It then rebuilds the routing table from the replies.

Continual Operations is the periodic broadcast of the contents of the routing table every 60 seconds using the Split Horizons algorithm, discussed under IP routing. Up to 50 routes can be contained in one IPX message.

Router Shutdown occurs when the IPX router is properly shut down. The router broadcasts to all adjacent routers that its routes are no longer available. They will in turn use triggered updates to propagate this change throughout the IPX internetwork.

If an interface is a WAN adapter and the hardware can sense a link failure, the routing tables are updated and sent out via triggered updates to notify the network. Most LAN adapters don't have this capability and the unavailable routes must be aged out of the tables.

If the router fails unexpectedly, then all of its routes must be aged out of the adjacent routers' tables. The default lifetime is three minutes before the route is marked as no longer available.

Analyzing the IPX Routing Table

The IPX routing table is similar to the IP table except that it uses Network Numbers instead of Network IDs, Next hop MAC address instead of Gateway, and Hop count instead of Metric. The Interface and Protocol columns are the same and there is no Network Mask column because IPX doesn't support them.

The one additional IPX column is the Tick Count, which is an estimate of how long it takes to reach the destination segment. A tick is 1/18 of a second in length. LAN links usually have a tick count of 1 while WAN links could be 6 or 7 ticks. If the Hop counts on two or more routes to the same destination are the same, the one with the lowest tick count is the one selected.

Configuring RIP for IPX

Because RIP for IPX will be automatically installed if NWLink was installed, there will be an IPX branch on the tree. Right-click either the Summary or RIP for IPX branches and choose Configure IPX or Configure RIP to configure Event Logging Levels. There are no other global settings for RIP for IPX.

Setting per Interface Timer and Protocol Parameters for IPX

Right-click on one of the installed interfaces and choose Configure Interface. The dialog box is shown in Figure 23.12. Selected by default are Enable RIP on This Interface, Advertise Routes, and Accept Route Advertisements. Clearing the Enable RIP on This Interface means RIP won't bind to this adapter. Clearing the Advertise Routes turns the router into a silent RIP router on this interface and clearing the Accept Route Advertisements turns the router into a static router on this interface.

FIGURE 23.12.
RIP for IPX Configuration per interface General tab.

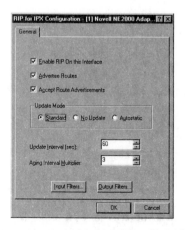

There are three update mode choices, Standard for LAN interfaces, No Updates to turn off updates on this interface, and Autostatic for Demand-Dial interfaces.

Setting the Update Interval Defaults to 60 Seconds

The Aging Interval Multiplier is the number of Update Intervals during which a route is aged out of the tables if it's not updated or heard from. Using the defaults, if the Update Interval is 60 seconds and the Aging Multiplier is 3, then 180 seconds will elapse before a route is aged out of the tables.

Using Route Filtering for IPX

If you click Input Filters or Output Filters in the dialog box in Figure 23.12, you can permit or deny specific network routes and groups of network routes from getting into the routing tables. See the discussion later in this chapter in the section "Understanding Packet Filtering" for a more complete coverage of the different filters that can be applied to an interface.

Using Static Route Configurations for IPX

If you right-click on Static Routes and select Add Static Route, you can create static IPX routes to destinations that are across Demand-Dial interfaces and to destinations that are non-RIP-enabled routers. The dialog box requests the Network Number in Hex, the Next Hop MAC Address in Hex, the Tick Count, the Hop Count to associate with the route, and which interface to assign it to.

Understanding SAP for IPX

SAP (Service Advertising Protocol) allows servers to advertise services and resources on the network and the IPX address where those services and resources can be taken advantage of. Servers include any machine sharing files, printers, or applications.

The SAP agent in the RRAS IPX router collects the service and address information into an SAP table similar to a routing table. Each SAP service has a service type number associated with it. The table contains the Service Type, Service Name, Service Address, Hop Count, Interface, and Protocol.

Using the table, a client process can learn the IPX address of the server offering the needed service. SAP tables are created, updated, maintained, and propagated the same way as IPX Routing Tables are with Periodic Updates, Aging Processes, Split Horizons, and Triggered Updates.

Understanding SAP Operations

To keep the SAP tables dynamic and accurate, the IPX router uses the same three operational procedures it does in IPX Routing (Initialization, Continual Operation, and Router Shutdown).

During Initialization, the SAP agent broadcasts a general request for information for all services available on all attached networks. From the responses it receives, it builds the SAP table.

While in Continual Operation mode, the contents of the SAP table broadcast on all locally attached networks every 60 seconds. All routers that receive the broadcast update their own SAP table with the contained information. SAP clients then query the router for the name and address of all servers offering a specific type of service. The client also can request the name and address of the nearest server supplying a specific service, such as Get nearest server.

When a Router Shutdown occurs, it sends an SAP broadcast on all locally attached networks, informing them that the services available through it are no longer available. The adjacent routers then use triggered updates to notify all their adjacent routers.

If a router were to suddenly and unexpectedly exit from the network (Router Unavailable), all SAP table entries have a lifetime to age them out of the tables. The default is 3 minutes. After this period, if a service has not been refreshed or heard from it is marked as no longer available, causing a triggered update to occur.

Setting SAP per Interface Configurations

You configure each interface in the IPX router for SAP after you have added it to the contents pane. Select SAP for IPX in the tree pane and then right-click the interface you want to configure. Select Configure Interface from the menu and you will see the dialog box shown in Figure 23.13.

FIGURE 23.13.
SAP for IPX Configuration per interface General tab.

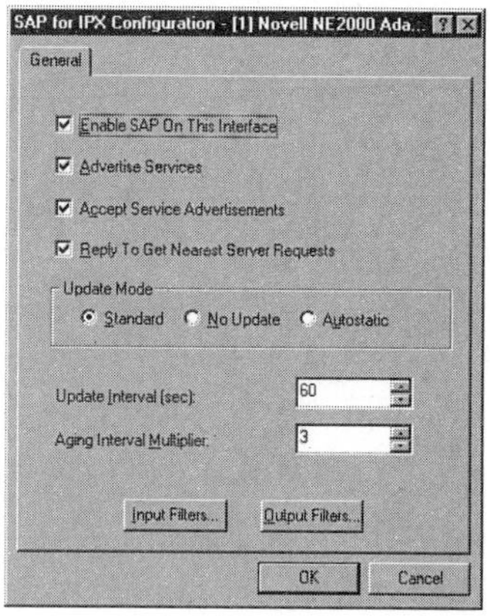

By default, the Enable SAP On This Interface option is selected. Also selected by default are the Advertise Services, Accept Service Advertisements, and Reply To Get Nearest Server Requests. If you want to disable any of these features, clear the appropriate check box.

The default update mode is Standard if this is a LAN adapter, and Autostatic if it is a Demand-Dial link. The update interval is 60 seconds by default and the Aging Interval is the number of Update intervals that occur before an SAP service is removed from the SAP tables if it is not updated or referenced.

Using SAP Filters

Clicking either Input Filters or Output Filters enables you to either Permit or Deny requests for specific types of services. The Filter dialog box asks you for the Interface, the Service Type, and the Service Name. By default, all service types are allowed. A service type of 0xFF also means all services.

Adding Static Service Entries

As with adding static routes to routing tables, you can add static services to your SAP tables. Right-click Static Services in the tree pane and select Add Static Service. The dialog box asks you for the Service Type, the Service Name, the Network Number and Node Address of the server offering this service, the Socket address to advertise, the Hop count to get there, and the Interface to use. All required numbers must be entered in Hex.

Configuring NetBIOS over IPX

In the absence of a Wins Server, most Microsoft networking processes use NetBIOS broadcasts to resolve computer names and services to destination addresses. These processes include Netlogin, Locate Server Name Query, NetBIOS Name Registration, Query, and Browser Host Announcements. If the network is functioning on IPX protocol, NetBIOS broadcast over IPX is enabled to allow these services to function correctly. Disabling this feature impairs the ability of Microsoft Operating Systems to perform their functions. By default, the Accept Broadcasts option is enabled on a LAN interface and disabled on a Demand-Dial interface.

Controlling NetBIOS Broadcasts

To control the way NetBIOS Broadcasts are performed, select the NetBIOS Broadcast branch in the tree pane. In the contents pane, right-click the interface you want to configure the broadcasts on and select Configure Interface. The dialog box is shown in Figure 23.14.

FIGURE 23.14.

NetBIOS Broadcast Configuration per interface.

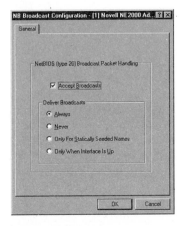

Clear the Accept Broadcasts check box if you want to completely disable broadcasts or select the appropriate radio button to control when broadcasts are to be delivered. The four choices are Always (default), Never, Only For Statically Seeded Names, and Only When Interface Is Up. Each is described as follows:

- *Always* means to propagate the NetBIOS Broadcasts to all interfaces except the one on which it was received. If this choice is selected on a Demand-Dial interface, the Interface attempts to connect each time it receives a NetBIOS broadcast.

- *Never* means to silently discard all NetBIOS broadcasts received. This is the default setting on a Demand-Dial interface.

- *Only For Statically Seeded Names* makes the router check the name against a table of statically defined NetBIOS names. If the name is in the list, then propagate the broadcast; otherwise, silently discard it.

- *Only When Interface Is Up* is used for Demand-Dial interfaces. When selected, the NetBIOS broadcasts are sent over the interface only if it is currently active.

By controlling the NetBIOS broadcasts on a per-interface basis, you can limit the traffic on your non-Microsoft networks that don't use NetBIOS names.

Adding Static NetBIOS Names

If you select Only For Statically Seeded Names, you have to create the table of Static NetBIOS names. To do so, select Static NetBIOS Names in the tree pane and right-click. Select Add NetBIOS Name from the menu. There are only three items to fill in: the Name (maximum 15 characters), the Type (a one-byte hex number), and the interface to propagate the broadcasts on for this name. Some common Service Types include

00	Client Workstation service or Workgroup or Domain Name
	Messenger Service
20	Server Service
1E	Group Name for Browser Elections
1B	Domain Master Browser
1C	Domain Controller
1D	Subnet Master Browser

To find out what names and service types you should statically seed, look in the Wins server database for the correct values or check Technet for a listing of service types.

Understanding OSPF

OSPF by Bay Networks is a link-state routing protocol that is compliant with OSPF Version 2.0 as defined in RFC 1583. An OSPF router calculates the shortest path between itself and all other nodes on the network and then adds the best route available to its routing table.

An Autonomous System (AS) is a network or networks under a single administrative authority. All routers in an AS use the same routing protocol. A dynamic routing protocol, used within an AS, is called an Interior Gateway Protocol (IGP). RIP and OSPF are examples of IGPs. The protocol that routers use to communicate between different Autonomous Systems is called an Exterior Gateway Protocol (EGP). Border Gateway Protocol (BGP) and EGP itself are RFC defined EGPs. Routes that are learned about from the EGPs are called AS External routes.

Understanding OSPF Areas

If an AS grows large with many networks and numerous routes, the OSPF calculations may require a substantial amount of processing time. The resulting routing table can be quite large and require extra machine memory to hold it. To reduce the time and size requirements, the AS can be divided into several smaller Areas and the routers within each Area will have to perform detailed route calculations for routes contained only within their own Area (IntraArea routes).

To the other Areas in the AS, each Area advertises only a summary of routes contained within. Routers in the outside Areas use this summary information to decide which Area contains the desired destination network and the best route to take to reach that Area. They then forward the packets to a router on the edge of the correct Area, called a border router. This router is responsible for the final delivery to the correct network host within its Area.

Defining Areas

An Area is defined as a collection of contiguous networks and hosts, together with the routers having interfaces on any one of the included networks. Each Area runs a basic link-state routing algorithm to create a topological database of all routes within the area. Each area is configured with a four-digit, dotted decimal notation ID, in the same format as an IP address. However the Area ID is separate from the IP address and is not used for routing data. It is simply used to identify this Area to other OSPF Areas. A sample Area ID might be 0.0.3.0. Figure 23.15 shows a sample autonomous system with five areas.

NOTE

You may choose to use the subnetted IP address of an area as the Area ID but it would simply be for administrative convenience. They are not in any way related within the structure of OSPF or routing.

How many routes and routers you should contain in an Area depends on your hardware specifications. If you're running RRAS on minimum requirement machines, then I wouldn't recommend more that 40 routes per area. If you have 500 mHz Alpha processors running on 128 MB of RAM, then you could probably have several more. A couple of hundred routes more shouldn't be an issue with that kind of hardware.

FIGURE 23.15.

Sample OSPF Autonomous System with five areas.

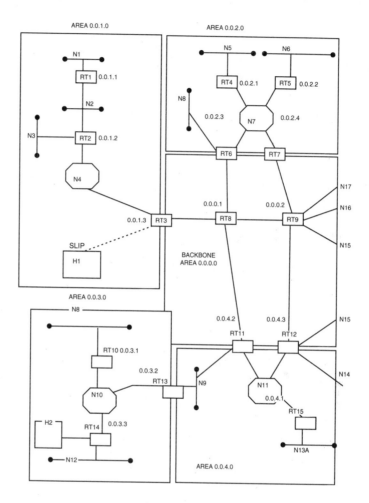

Defining Stub Areas

Stub Areas are defined as areas that have only one entry/exit point, or areas where the choice of exit point does not need to be made on a per-external-destination basis. This means that routers inside the Stub Area need to know only about a default gateway (the single exit point) for all routes outside of the area. They don't have to decide which is the best way out; there is only one. This has the effect of reducing the size of the Stub Area's routing tables if there are many external routes being advertised. In Figure 23.15, areas 0.0.1.0 and 0.0.3.0 are Stub Areas.

Defining Backbone Areas

If you have more than one area defined, then you must have a Backbone Area to connect all of the other areas. If you envision all of the ASs as a wheel, the Backbone is the hub and each different Area is a spoke. All areas must have a router with one interface connected to the Backbone. InterArea routes are advertised on the Backbone and InterArea traffic travels across the Backbone to get to other areas. The Backbone area must have an Area ID of 0.0.0.0.

23

IMPLEMENTING
ROUTING AND
REMOTE ACCESS

Understanding OSPF Routing Tables

The process of creating a routing table is much more complex under OSPF than RIP. OSPF routers do not exchange routing tables, like RIP, but Link State Updates. Each router maintains a database of all the available networks, routes, and routers in either its area, or the AS if there is only one area. This database is called the Link State Database.

When two routers agree to exchange database information, they become adjacent routers and they assume a Master/Slave relationship. The router with the higher router ID (described next) becomes the master and sends Database Description packets to the slave. These packets contain a list of abbreviated Link State Advertisements describing the current state of the database. The slave then acknowledges these packets with database description packets of its own describing its database. The master/slave relationship is just to decide who initiates this process and serves no other function. Which machine becomes the master and which will be the slave has no effect on the final outcome of the exchange.

The two routers compare the other router's descriptions with the status of their own databases. They then build a Link State Request packet. This packet contains a list of requests for Link State Advertisements that are newer on the other router.

A Link State Advertisement is a description of one entry in the database consisting of the Area ID, Type of advertisement, Link State ID, or network that can be reached by this advertisement, advertising router, age, and other information. Each Link State Advertisement also has a sequence number that is updated with every change to the information. This update is how the routers know which advertisement is newer. The Type of advertisement field contains Network, Router, Stub, Summary, or AS External, depending on the information being described by this entry.

When the two routers have built these Request packets, they send them to their adjacent router. That router returns a Link State Update packet with the requested information. All of these packet exchanges are acknowledged and synchronized as well. When the contents of the two Link State Databases are identical, then the routers are Fully Adjacent Routers and the next step in the process begins. The Link State Database can be viewed under RRAS.

The Link State Database is now submitted to the Shortest Path First Algorithm, which builds the Shortest Path First Tree. This is a binary tree structure where the branch points in the tree are routers and the links between branch points represent connecting networks. Each router places itself as the root of the tree, which is why each router must create its own copy of the tree. This answers the question of "How do I get there from here by all available routes?" The SPF Tree is created in memory and cannot be viewed. With each change in the database, information in the tree must be completely re-created.

The Routing Table is then generated from the SPF Tree calculations. Then, the least-cost route to deliver packets to each network is selected and added to the routing table. Routing tables are local to this router and are never exchanged with another router. Each time the SPF Tree is recalculated, the routing table is re-created. The routing table can be viewed under RRAS by right-clicking on Static Routes and choosing View IP routing table.

Designating OSPF Routers

Every router in an OSPF AS is identified by a four-digit, dotted decimal notation number that is in the same format as an IP address but is not used for routing packets. That's right; you will have a four-digit number to identify each area in your AS, a four-digit number to identify each router in each area in your AS and, if you are using IP, a four-digit IP address for each interface on each router in your AS. When it comes right down to packet delivery, though, only the IP address is used. The other numbers are just to identify what area the destination is in and what router is advertising it from that area.

You can number your routers based on their area ID, or you can choose not to do so. It doesn't matter to OSPF. Just remember that later, when you're troubleshooting, you may have to find out what router 1.2.3.4 sent to router 250.251.252.253. The more logical your numbering scheme, the easier it is to locate those physical machines later.

Each OSPF router is given a designation to describe its function or location in the OSPF AS. These designations are discussed in the following sections.

Using the Internal Router (IR) Designation

If all of the interfaces on a router are connected to networks belonging to the same area, then that router is declared an Internal Router. The interfaces will have a single Link State Database and SPF Tree. In Figure 23.15, in area 0.0.1.0, routers 0.0.1.1 and 0.0.1.2 are internal routers, while in the backbone area, routers 0.0.0.1 and 0.0.0.2 are internal routers as well.

Using the Area Border Router (ABR) Designation

A router that has interfaces in multiple areas is called an Area Border Router. It has at least one interface connected to a network in each attached area. There is a separate Link State Database and SPF Tree for each attached area. The Area Border Router summarizes the available routes in each area for advertisement outside of its area. In Figure 23.15, 0.0.1.3, 0.0.2.3, 0.0.2.4, 0.0.3.2, 0.0.4.2, and 0.0.4.3 are all ABRs.

Using the Backbone Router (BR) Designation

If you have more than one area in your AS, one of them must be a backbone area that connects all of the areas. A router that has one or more interfaces connected to the backbone area is called a Backbone Router. If a router has one interface in the backbone and at least one interface in another area, it is considered both an Area Border Router and a Backbone router. If a router has all of its interfaces in the backbone area, that router is considered both an Internal Router and a Backbone Router. In Figure 23.15, all six ABRs are Backbone Routers, as well as the two Internal Routers 0.0.0.1 and 0.0.0.2.

Using the Autonomous System Boundary Router (ASBR) Designation

A router that exchanges routing information with routers outside of the AS is called an Autonomous System Boundary Router. This router knows about routes external to the AS and advertises them into the AS. Every router in the AS has a route to each ASBR, so it knows the cost of getting out of the AS by those routes. In Figure 23.15, 0.0.0.2 and 0.0.4.3 are ASBRs.

Using the Designated Router (DR) Designation

When there is more than one router on the same network within an area, the timing of communication between the routers becomes an issue. As we saw under RIP, this is one way that routing loops and count-to-infinity problems occur. To eliminate these problems under OSPF, one router on the network is automatically selected as the Designated Router.

All route updates sent into and out of that network are sent to the Designated Router first and it then distributes the changes to all connected routers. The other routers on this network only listen for updates from their duly elected Designated Router. When a change happens on this network, the first router to notice it notifies the Designated Router and then it becomes the DR's responsibility to notify the rest.

When you set up your OSPF routers, you assign a Priority to each router. When the network is initializing, the Router Priority is used in the election process to select the Designated Router. If the router priority on more than one router is the same, then the router with the highest router ID is selected.

Using the Backup Designated Router (BDR) Designation

After the election is held and the Designated Router is selected, the runner-up is selected as the Backup Designated Router. In the event that the Designated Router were to go offline or disappear from the network, then the Backup Designated Router would assume that role. The BDR gets all of the updates at the same time as the DR, so it has the next most accurate copy of the database if the DR fails.

OSPF uses two multicast addresses. The Designated Router sends multicast updates on 224.0.0.5. All other routers are members of this multicast group. The DR and BDR are members of the 224.0.0.6 group. When a router notices a change in the topology, it sends a multicast on 224.0.0.6 so that both Designated Routers get it. The DR then sends the information to group 224.0.0.5 so that everyone else gets it.

Setting Up a Single OSPF Area

To set up a single OSPF area in the RRAS Administration Utility, right-click the Summary branch on the IP tree. Select Add a Routing Protocol from the menu and then select Open Shortest Path First by Bay Networks from the available protocols list. This adds an OSPF branch onto the tree. Right-click this branch and select Configure OSPF to set the General configuration options.

Configuring General Properties

The first thing you need to do is create your Router ID for this router. This 32-bit number uniquely identifies this router in your network. You can choose the router ID after one of the network interfaces it contains, the Area ID it is a member of, or four of your favorite numbers between 0 and 255. This is just to identify who is advertising which routes in the Link State Database, and is used in Designated Router elections if the Priority is equal.

Next, you click the Areas tab and create an Area ID. This is the 32-bit number that uniquely identifies this Area. The default is 0.0.0.0, but that makes this the backbone area.

Think ahead—will this be the logical backbone area after you expand the network to include multiple areas? If not, click the Add button and enter an Area ID for this area. You might choose to make the Area ID the same as the Network ID for the network contained within this area. If there is more than one network contained within, you might choose to create a number to represent all of the networks. Another scheme might be to create the Area ID in such a way that you can incorporate it into the router IDs. That way, you can tell at a glance to which Area each router belongs. Think ahead to how you're going to grow your network.

On this tab, you also can enable a clear-text password for the area routers. You actually set the password on the Per Interface Configuration dialog box General tab, but this is where you enable or disable the clear-text option. The default password is 12345678 and you can't see it on the configuration tab, so remember it. If you forget it, just capture a couple of packets and take a look—it's clear-text in the packets unless you have cleared the box.

You also can configure this area to be a stub area, which we previously discussed. This means there is only one entrance/exit router to this area. By default, summary advertisements from other areas don't flood into a stub area, but you can force it to propagate them by checking the Import Summary Advertisements box.

The Ranges tab is only used when you have multiple areas, so it is discussed later when we talk about multiple areas. After you have configured the new area, you can delete the default area, 0.0.0.0. You will be unable to delete this area until you have created a new one to replace it.

Setting OSPF per Interface Configurations

Once you have configured the Area router, you have to add the interfaces to use the protocol. Right-click the OSPF by Bay Networks branch and choose the Add Interface option from the menu. You should see the dialog box shown in Figure 23.16. The first thing you must do on the general tab is check off Enable OSPF on this interface box. Just because we added the interface doesn't necessarily mean we want it to use the protocol, right? This is not selected by default.

You then select the area you want this interface to be in from the drop-down list. The new one you just created should show if you deleted the default in the last procedure. You next set the Router Priority for the Designated Router elections for this network. The higher the priority, the greater the chances of being the DR. You then set the cost of using this interface. This cost is added to any routes learned of over this interface, to be advertised to the other routers. There is no upper limit on what a cost can grow to under OSPF, but this value must be greater than 0.

You can now change the default password from 12345678 if you want. All interfaces in the same area must have the same password or they won't accept router advertisements from their neighbors. The last thing on the general tab is to tell it the type of interface this is. The four choices are Broadcast, the default, Point-to-Point for T-Carrier or ISDN type, NBMA (Non-Broadcast Multiple Access); and X.25 or frame-relay type networks.

FIGURE 23.16.

The OSPF per interface Configuration General tab.

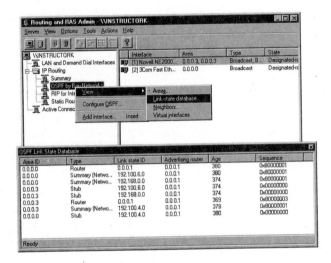

If you select either of the last two choices for this interface, you have to configure the Neighbor tab. On the Neighbor tab, you list the address of all of the Neighbor routers you want this router to communicate with over this interface. This is how the router knows whom to send router updates to down this pipe because it can't use broadcast or multicast to reach them. Assign a Priority to each router to describe its eligibility in the Designated Router process.

Setting Synchronization Parameters

The Advanced tab configures all of the synchronization parameters for this interface. It's important that all routers on the same network have the same parameters set here.

Starting at the top, the Transit Delay is an estimate of how long it takes to transmit a Link State Advertisement over this interface. The default for LAN links is 1 second, which is the minimum allowed. Point-to-Point might require longer transit times.

Next is the retransmit timer. If a packet has been sent to an adjacent router and not acknowledged within this time, then the packet is retransmitted. It should be set slightly longer than the round trip time between two routers on this interface. The default is 5 seconds.

The Hello interval is how often the router requests the database description packets from its neighbors. The router sends out a Hello packet, by default every 10 seconds on a LAN, which initiates the exchange of database information as previously described. The longer the Hello interval, the greater the convergence time. The shorter the Hello period, the more traffic that is generated. All routers on a common network must have the same Hello period. An X.25 connection might have a Hello period of up to 30 seconds.

The Dead Interval is how long a router will wait for a Hello packet from a neighbor it knows about before declaring that router dead. If a router has been declared dead, then all of its routes are removed from the Link State Database and the routing table is regenerated. The default is 40 seconds and should be set as a multiple of the Hello interval (4×10 sec. Hello interval). All routers on a common network should have the same Dead Interval set. On an X.25 network, this might be two minutes or more.

The Poll interval is used after a router has been declared Dead. Every Poll interval, the dead router is requeried by sending a Hello packet to it to see if it has come back online. The Poll Interval is set to two minutes on a LAN interface by default.

The MTU Size (Bytes) setting is the size of the OSPF packets sent on this network. This is to allow for larger packet sizes if the underlying network structure will handle it. On an Ethernet, it is set to 1500, but a token ring can handle packets up to 4000 bytes.

Setting Up Multiple OSPF Areas

Once the network has grown, or if it is already large enough, you can configure multiple Areas. As soon as you have more than one area, you need that Backbone Area with ID 0.0.0.0. All other areas must have an interface connected to this Backbone Area. Destinations in another area (InterArea) cross the Backbone Area to get there. The routers advertise complete routing information within their own area but summarize that information to advertise it to other routers in other areas via the Backbone. The Backbone Area must be contiguous. Routers with at least one interface in the Backbone Area are known as Backbone Routers as well as any other designation that they currently have. Many of these routers are Area Border Routers, but they do not all have to be. They also can be Internal Routers if all interfaces are within the Backbone Area, and ASBR routers also can be backbone routers.

You specify which interface on the router belongs to which area when configuring the router. If a router is an Internal Router, you have only one choice in the drop-down box. If it is an Area Border Router, then there needs to be one interface in each of the areas the router straddles.

You have to create all the area IDs that the router will have interfaces in before you can add them to the interfaces. Right-click OSPF by Bay Networks and select Configure OSPF. Select the Areas tab and choose Add. Type the new Area IDs. If the Area contains more than one network ID and the router is an Area Border Router, then you might use the Range Tab; otherwise, click OK and your new area is created. Repeat for each area that this router will connect.

Setting Area Range Configurations

The purpose of defining Ranges is to reduce the size of the Backbone Routing Table. To define a range, there must be more than one subnet ID in the Area and the subnet IDs must be addressable with the same subnet mask.

On an ABR, you may configure an Area Range for each connected Area that has more than one Subnet ID contained in it by specifying the first subnet ID in the range. You then specify the subnet mask to address all of the IDs you want to group. After you have defined the range, all of the network IDs within the configured range are advertised as just one route to the Backbone.

As an example, if you had four class C networks in this area with network IDs of 200.10.4.0, 200.10.5.0, 200.10.6.0, and 200.10.7.0, you would enter a range of 200.10.4.0 with the subnet mask of 255.255.252.0. This would enable the Area border router to advertise only one route to the backbone to reach all four of these networks. This helps to reduce the size of the routing tables on the backbone.

Using Virtual Links

What if you have a situation where you wanted to define an area, but it doesn't have a direct physical connection to the backbone area? This situation is shown in Figure 23.15, where router 0.0.3.2 doesn't have an interface in the backbone area.

Note that there are six routers that are Area Border Routers but only five Routers (0.0.1.3, 0.0.2.3, 0.0.2.4, 0.0.4.2, and 0.0.4.3) are Backbone Routers. Area 0.0.3.0 does not have a direct connection to the backbone, so Area 0.0.1.0 and area 0.0.2.0 won't know about its existence because it can't advertise itself on the backbone.

This situation requires a Virtual Interface or Virtual Link between the router in the remote area and a router with an interface on the backbone. In this case, we could set up a Virtual Link between Router 0.0.3.2 and Router 0.0.4.2. When 0.0.3.2 wants to advertise summary information on the backbone, it forwards the information to 0.0.4.2 across the virtual link and receives backbone information in return from 0.0.4.2. This way, it can still advertise its available routes and hear about all the other available routes. Area 0.0.4.0 becomes known as the Transit Area because all traffic destined for Area 0.0.3.0 must cross the networks in Area 0.0.4.0 to get there.

To set up the Virtual Link, you have to configure both routers to know of the Link. Right-click on OSPF by Bay Networks in the tree pane and select Configure OSPF. You first define all of the areas that the router is a member of. Select the Areas tab and Add the areas. In our example, we set up router 0.0.3.2 and configure it to be in areas 0.0.3.0, 0.0.4.0, and 0.0.0.0 (by means of the virtual link).

Next, you click the Virtual Interface tab and choose Add. The first dialog box asks for the Transit Area ID. This is the Area ID of the area with the physical connection to the backbone. In this example, it is Area 0.0.4.0.

The next field is the Virtual Neighbor Router ID. This is the ID of the router with the physical backbone interface. In our example, this is Router 0.0.4.2.

You now configure the timing for the Virtual Link the same as you did on the OSPF Area Advanced tab. These settings apply to this link. The transit delay and retransmit interval should be adjusted for the speed of the transit area. The Hello interval and Dead interval must have the same settings as the backbone area.

We now configure the other end of the link at Router 0.0.4.2 to be in Areas 0.0.4.0 and 0.0.0.0. Its virtual neighbor is Router 0.0.3.2 and the configuration settings are identical to 0.0.3.2. The virtual link is now set up.

Using Stub Areas

When there is only one route into or out of an ara, then any internal routers don't need to know about anything beyond that entry point. If they recognize a network ID as belonging within their area, they know the route to get there. If they don't recognize the network ID, they can then treat that single exit point as a default gateway and send all unknown traffic to it. With this configuration, the routing tables for the routers within the area are much smaller because there is only one entry for all InterArea routes. Such an area is called a Stub Area. The reason for setting one up is to reduce the size of the routing tables on the routers within the area.

In our previous example, Area 0.0.1.0 and Area 0.0.3.0 would be Stub Areas. The other Areas don't qualify because there are two different exit points and the contained routers need to decide which is the better one to use on the way out. In Stub Areas, there is only one choice, so it can be treated as the default for all contained routers.

To configure a Stub Area, right-click OSPF by Bay Networks, Select Configure OSPF, choose the areas tab, select the area that will be the Stub, and select Configure. On the General tab, check the Stub Area box and set the metric for this area. The Stub Metric is the cost of the default route that will be advertised into the area. After an area is configured as a Stub Area, your ASBR won't advertise any external routes into the stub area. You count on the default route and the ABR to forward external packets correctly.

> **NOTE**
>
> You can force the ABR to send summary advertisements from other areas into the Stub Area but it is not done by default.

Using External Routing

The last type of routing we have to deal with for OSPF is when you want to get out of your autonomous system completely. This usually means leaving behind your nicely configured OSPF network and going adventuring in someone else's RIP or Static route environment. This is where the last of the different types of OSPF routers comes into play—the Autonomous System Boundary Router.

As its name implies, this router sits on the edge of your configured environment and exchanges routes outside of the AS. All routes the ASBR learns about from outside get flooded into the AS as External Route Advertisements. In all areas, except Stub Areas, these routes are added into the Link State Databases via the backbone. Because the metric from an external route has a different meaning than an equivalent OSPF metric, there are two different categories of external metric types.

A Type 1 metric is added directly onto the OSPF metric when advertising the routes. Type 1 metrics are for external networks that are attached directly to the ASBR. A Type 2 metric is for a network that is not directly attached to the ASBR. Its metric is the external metric only.

To configure an ASBR, you call up the global properties dialog box by right-clicking OSPF by Bay Networks and selecting Configure OSPF. On the General tab of the dialog box, check off the box labeled Enable Autonomous System Boundary Router as shown in Figure 23.17. When you do this, another tab appears, enabling you to configure the ASBR just created.

FIGURE 23.17.

*Enabling an Autono-
mous System Boundary
Router.*

Selecting this tab displays the Router Protocols dialog box, as shown in Figure 23.18. At the top there are two radio buttons. Depending on the button selected, the router either processes routes from all protocols except those selected protocols, or ignores routes from all protocols except those selected protocols. That's right, you check off the ones you want to ignore if you leave the top button selected and check off the ones you want the router to accept if you select the bottom button. By default, all three protocols are processed, so all routes are learned from all three protocols.

After you have decided which protocols you want to process or ignore, you also can tell your ASBR which specific routes to process or ignore. Click the Routes button on the External Routing tab and you are presented with an OSPF External Route Filters dialog box. Again, the buttons are to Process all except those listed or Discard all except those listed. If you want to ensure some specific routes do not make it into your system, choose the Process button and add the routes you want to make sure are ignored. If you want to process only very specific routes, then choose the Discard button and add the routes you want.

FIGURE 23.18.

*Configuring an
Autonomous System
Boundary Router.*

Understanding Packet Filtering

Once you have your router up and operational, you can implement a minor form of security and traffic control by enabling packet filtering. You can apply filters to control input and output, IP and IPX traffic. This product is not a full-fledged firewall product. You cannot create user-defined filters and must work from the supplied interface options. You create the filters on a per-interface basis and can filter based on the following:

- Source and Destination IP and IPX address
- Source and Destination TCP and UDP Ports
- Source and Destination IPX Sockets
- ICMP message type and codes
- IPX Message Types
- SAP Service Types

When configuring filters, remember that RIP communicates on UDP Port 520 and PPTP communicates on Port 1723 and Protocol 47. If you filter these ports, your router will not work.

Understanding Relationships Between Protocols, Ports, and Sockets

When we break a packet open by the four layers in the TCP/IP model, the bottommost layer is the Network layer. This equates roughly to the Physical and Data Link layers in the ISO OSI seven-layer model. RRAS does no IP filtering at this layer.

The next layer higher is the Network layer where IP addressing is performed and ICMP messages originate. At this layer, you can filter those IP addresses and messages to control what packets get through and what messages get sent and received. Most of your diagnostic software depends on ICMP messages to respond, so be careful what ICMP and on what interface you

23

IMPLEMENTING
ROUTING AND
REMOTE ACCESS

filter. A simple command such as Tracert relies on ICMP Time Exceeded–TTL Expiration messages to perform its function.

At the Transport Layer, we have the different protocols (TCP and UDP) and their numerous ports. Each different service and many applications depend on traffic arriving on various ports for them to function. An FTP server sends and listens on TCP Port 20 and 21 while a DNS server needs UDP port 53 to function correctly. How can you tell what ports are what? A good place to start is in %windir%\system32\drivers\etc\services. This file contains a list of the well-known ports on the Windows NT system. In addition, if you run a command prompt and use the Netstat -a command, it shows you all the ports your server is currently monitoring. Otherwise, visit the InterNic site where there is an RFC of all of the well-known ports.

Sockets under IPX perform much the same function as Ports under TCP and UDP. They identify endpoints for a process to exchange information with another process or machine. Some well-known sockets under IPX include 453 for RIP, 452 for SAP, 455 for NetBIOS, and 451 for NCP server. These are hexadecimal numbers.

Enabling IP and IPX Packet Filtering

In order to enable IP or IPX packet filtering on the RRAS router, you right-click Summary under IP routing and select Configure IP Parameters. On the General tab, check Enable Packet filtering, as shown in Figure 23.19. It is disabled by default. Now, on a per-interface basis, you have to define your filters.

FIGURE 23.19.
Enabling IP and IPX packet filtering.

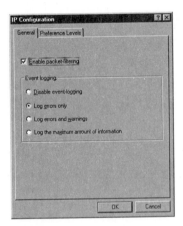

Configuring Input or Output Filters

Select the interface you want to set a filter on and right-click. Select Configure Interface from the menu. On the General tab, select Input Filters or Output Filters. You can configure both input and output filters on the same interface. Be aware of the full implications of the filters before you apply them. The IP Packet Filters Configuration dialog box is displayed as shown in Figure 23.20. If the buttons at the top are grayed out, that means you have not yet added a filter. Until you actually add a filter, you cannot tell it whether to receive, transmit, or drop the specified packets. Click on Add and the Add/Edit IP Filter dialog box appears, showing all of the available filters.

Figure 23.20.

Creating IP Packet Filters.

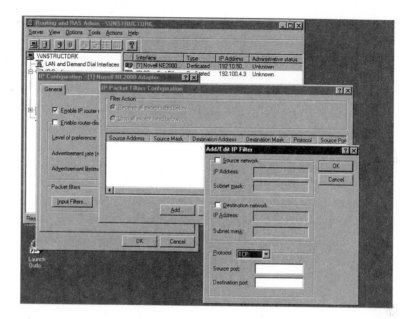

If you want to filter a Source Network or Source Host, check the Source Network box and enter in the Network or Host ID. If it is a network, then the Subnet Mask is the appropriate Subnet mask for all machines on that Network/Subnet, but if it is a Host ID, then the Subnet Mask is 255.255.255.255. The IP address cannot be more specific than the Subnet Mask. In other words, the subnet mask bits must encompass all of the bits used in the IP address field.

The same rule applies to the Destination Network filter fields. If you're filtering a specific protocol or part of a protocol, you use the third section of the dialog box. It is set to Any protocol by default. Drop the list and select the protocol you want to filter. If TCP or UDP are selected and you don't specify a port number, then the entire protocol is filtered. If you just want a specific port, then fill in the Source and/or Destination Port Number. Only one pair of ports (one input and one output) can be configured per filter.

If you select ICMP, then you can fill in the message type and code (see Table 23.2). If you leave the type and code fields blank, then that implies all ICMP messages. If you select other, you are asked what protocol number you want to filter. In the %windir%\system32\drivers\ etc\protocol file is a list of common protocols and their numbers.

Table 23.2. Commonly used ICMP message types and codes.

ICMP Type	ICMP Code	Description
0	0	Echo Reply
8	0	Echo Request
3	0	Destination Unreachable–Network Unreachable
3	2	Destination Unreachable–Protocol Unreachable
3	3	Destination Unreachable–Port Unreachable
3	4	Destination Unreachable–Fragmentation Needed and Don't Fragment Flag Set
3	5	Destination Unreachable–Source Route Failed
3	6	Destination Unreachable–Destination Network Unknown
3	7	Destination Unreachable–Destination Host Unknown
3	8	Destination Unreachable–Source Host Isolated
3	9	Destination Unreachable–Communications with Network Administratively Prohibited
3	10	Destination Unreachable–Communication with Host Administratively Prohibited
3	11	Destination Unreachable–Network unreachable for type of service
3	12	Destination Unreachable–Host unreachable for type of service
4	0	Source quench
5	1	Redirected datagrams for the host
5	2	Redirected datagrams for the type of service and network
5	3	Redirected datagrams for the type of service and the host
9	0	Router Advertisement
10	0	Router Solicitation
11	0	Time Exceeded–TTL Expiration
11	1	Time exceeded–Fragmentation/Reassemble Expiration
12	0	Parameter Problem
13	0	Timestamp Request

ICMP Type	ICMP Code	Description
14	0	Timestamp Reply
17	0	Address Mask Request
18	0	Address Reply

Using IPX Filters

To access the IPX packet filters screen, select Summary under IPX routing, right-click the interface, and select IPX configuration. You can then select either input or output filters and add the appropriate filters, as shown in Figure 23.21.

FIGURE 23.21.

Creating IPX Packet Filters.

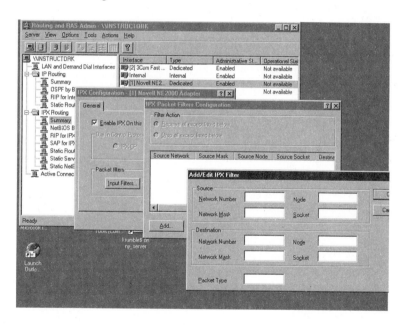

With IPX filters, there are four Source and Destination entries. The Network Number and Node are 4-byte and 6-byte hexadecimal numbers, respectively, used to identify specific networks or hosts to filter. You can add a Network Mask, which also is a 4 byte hexadecimal number, to express a range of network numbers. A Network Mask of FFFFFFF0 would filter networks numbered 0–15 decimal. You can then add a 2-byte hexadecimal Socket number for any specific socket you want to filter.

In addition, you can filter an entire Packet type. Some sample hexadecimal Packet types include the following:

RIP -01, SAP - 04, Normal IPX - 04, SPX - 05, NCP - 11, NetBIOS broadcast -14.

SAP Filters just request the Service Type Number and Service Name.

Using Demand-Dial Routing

If you are like a lot of computing professionals these days, you may have found yourself in a position where you are starting to set up a small home-based network. You have connected a desktop and a laptop or a couple of desktops together. The problem is that you have only one modem in one of the machines and only one telephone line—you would like to access and use the modem from any of the machines. Until now, you had to buy some third-party software and tinker with the Registry. Enter RRAS.

With this product, Microsoft has added a new feature for the home or small branch office to resolve this problem. Demand-Dial routing is sure to be a big hit with consultants once they realize the potential for this service. Once your RRAS router is installed and configured with the Demand-Dial interface, the router checks the IP address of the packet. If it is destined for the other side of a dial-up connection, the router automatically establishes the connection, transfers the data, and then hangs up the line, based on what you have configured it to do. No more paying to stay connected all day just in case you might need the line. No more having to remember to manually establish the connection before you can access the server. It all becomes automatic using a Demand-Dial interface. Of course, you do need another RRAS router to answer the call on the other end and complete the connection.

Identifying Application Problems with Demand Dial

If an application issues a request to the server, it assumes it has a direct connection to the server open all the time. With a Demand-Dial interface, the objective is to conserve costs by opening it only when needed and closing it as soon as it is no longer needed. These two different ways of operating might cause some problems.

One result could occur if the application is sending data at the server. It just merrily streams away while the router, realizing this is a Demand-Dial request, must establish the connection, exchange the handshake, negotiate the transfer speed, and acknowledge the connection. If the application isn't aware and doesn't use flow control, it overflows the buffers on the router and loss of data occurs.

Another problem occurs when the application requests data or resources. If the application isn't patient, it time-outs and reports an error while the router is trying to establish the connection. If you get an option to retry, waiting a bit and retrying usually meets with success.

Test each application you want to use across a Demand Dial to ensure it will perform as expected over the link. Until applications become aware of Demand-Dial interfaces and intelligent enough to monitor the connection being established, this connection is still best for only occasional access.

Authenticating Servers

You can set up either one-way or two-way authentication when you have an NT router establishing a connection to another NT router. With one-way authentication, the router being called confirms that the calling router has permissions to call in. The answering router checks the calling router's username, Domain, and password in the accounts database to validate it. With two-way authentication, the answering router validates the credentials of the calling router first. It next sends its credentials back to the calling router. The calling router then checks its domain accounts database to confirm that the answering router is who it claims to be.

For this to work, you must create a user account with dial-in permissions in each router's domain. The user account must have the same name as the interface you will create on this router. You create the Demand-Dial interface on each router, using the appropriate properties (phone number, security, and so on), to connect to the other router. The user credentials are the same as those of the interface on the other router, with the password that was assigned to the user account.

As an example of this process, we'll create a two-way authentication for the home-to-office connection. We'll call the router at home Homebase in the Home Domain, and the router at the office NYserver in the NewYork Domain. First, on the Homebase router domain, create a user account called NYserver. Next, create a Demand-Dial interface called Nyserver, with the correct properties to connect to the office server (we'll go through the exact steps to do this shortly). For the user credentials on this connection, specify Homebase in the New York domain with the appropriate password.

In the NewYork domain, create a user account called Homebase with dial-in permissions and a matching password. Next, create a Demand-Dial interface on NYserver, called Homebase, with the correct configuration to connect to the Homebase router. For user credentials, specify the user account NYserver in the Home domain. See the diagram in Figure 23.22 to keep the names straight.

FIGURE 23.22.

Setting up a Demand-Dial interface with two-way authentication.

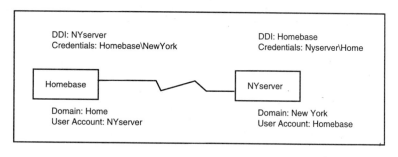

DDI: NYserver
Credentials: Homebase\NewYork

DDI: Homebase
Credentials: Nyserver\Home

Homebase — NYserver

Domain: Home
User Account: NYserver

Domain: New York
User Account: Homebase

*DDI= Demand-Dial Interface

23

IMPLEMENTING
ROUTING AND
REMOTE ACCESS

To test the connection, from the homebase machine you would start RRAS, right-click the Demand-Dial interface called NYserver, and choose connect. Because the credentials are for an account called Homebase in the NewYork domain, when NYserver gets the call it checks and validates that account with the Domain Controller for NewYork. When it is validated, it then searches for the Demand-Dial interface it has called Homebase, and returns the credentials for the account NYserver in the domain Home. The Homebase router then checks its security accounts for an account called NYserver and validates the credentials. Two-way authentication is taking place.

Configuring a Demand-Dial Service

Now that we have an overview of how Demand-Dial works, let's get into the details of how to set it up. Right-click the LAN and Demand-Dial Interface branch on the tree and select Add Interface. If the wizard is checked, it steps you through the process one screen at a time. Otherwise, you get the six-tab dialog box used to set up a RAS connection, as shown in Figure 23.23 (General, Protocols, Script, Security, X.25, and Dialing).

FIGURE 23.23.

Configuring the Demand-Dial Interface.

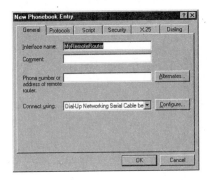

The first thing you need to do is Name the new Demand-Dial interface. The name must match the name of a user account in this domain. The next screen offers options for which networking protocols to route. Check a box if you want to automatically create a user account here so a remote router can call in, and to authenticate the remote router when calling out (two-way authentication). Then you get an option to send a plain-text password if that is the only way to connect. The last option is for occasions when you are calling a Non-NT router and have to log in to the system after connecting. Check the appropriate boxes and click next.

You are now asked which RAS-capable device this interface will use to connect. Select the modem or device you want to use from the list. If a device is missing from the list, go to the Control Panel, Network, Services, Routing and Remote Access Service, Properties. If the device is not listed, click Add and add it. If it is listed, select it, click Configure, and make sure the port usage is correct to allow it to dial out as a RAS Client and dial out and receive calls as a Demand-Dial router.

Once you have added the RAS device, you are asked to specify the phone number or address of the destination. If it is a LAN connection, Null Modem cable, or PPTP connection, supply the IP address of the destination router interface. If it is a modem connection, then supply the telephone number to connect. Click Next.

If you checked the box to create a user account in this domain for the remote router to call in, you are asked for the account details so it can be created. Next, you supply the credentials for the user account created in the remote domain for this router to use when it calls. The name must match the name of the interface/user account on the remote computer. Click next.

The interface is now created and you are asked which routing protocol you want to enable on this interface. The only options are Rip V2 and OSPF. You are presented with a series of screens to configure IP, IPX, NetBIOS Broadcasts, RIP for IPX, and SAP for IPX on this interface, depending upon which protocol you choose to forward packets over this interface. These screens offer the same options as already discussed under each of these topics earlier in this chapter.

Using Demand Dial

To manually test the demand-dial connection, select LAN and Demand-Dial Interface, right-clicking on the interface in the contents pane and selecting connect. The entry under the Connection State Column should go from Disconnected to Connecting to Connected. This might take a little longer than you would expect, so be patient. It could take more than two minutes to establish a connection using a null modem cable operating at 19200. Assuming you're successful, the next thing is to configure it to dial on demand.

In order for the router to know when it has to dial the interface, it has to know what's on the other side of the link. You have four choices to keep the router informed:

1. The first is to implement RIP on this interface and have it dial the connection every 10 minutes (by default) to update the tables.

2. The second is to *configure this interface as the default gateway* so that if there is no other route in the tables for a destination, it must be across the dial-up link. This would most likely be acceptable for the small branch office connecting to the head office with limited external connections. It would not be practical to implement the other way around.

3. The third method is to *create static routes*, specifying the Demand-Dial link as the interface, to connect to the networks across the link. You will configure the Destination Network, the Network Mask, the metric, and the interface as shown in Figure 23.11. The Gateway address is ignored because the demand-dial connection is assigned an IP address by the answering router—any entry will do; 1.1.1.1 is as good as any.

4. The fourth method is to use *autostatic updates*. In order to perform a manual autostatic update, select the Summary Branch under either IP or IPX, whichever routing table you want to update. Right-click on the Demand-Dial interface in the contents pane and select update routes from the menu. To automate the process, you can schedule the Routemon utility to perform an autostatic update at specified times. See the administrator's guide for Routemon syntax and the online NT help for the scheduler services instructions.

> **NOTE**
>
> If you are demand dialing IPX, it isn't possible to configure default routes, so you must either specify static routes or use autostatic updates for the remote router to learn about the available routes.

It might take a little tweaking to get things running correctly. Don't forget to add static routes/propogate host routes to get back to the remote host from networks across other routers. Once it's up and running, though, it makes a pretty good tool in the administrator's bag of tricks.

Understanding Point to Point Tunneling Protocol

Now that you have a dial-up connection and demand-dial interfaces in operation, you probably want to ensure that the data being sent across is secure from tampering and snooping. The simplest way to do this is to set up and configure a Virtual Private Network (VPN) using PPTP (Point to Point Tunneling Protocol). This protocol is supplied with NT 4.0, and then enhanced with the addition of RRAS. The standard version that ships with NT 4.0 enables you to create only client-to-server connections. The version that comes with RRAS enables you to create server-to-server pipes.

Defining Tunneling

Tunneling, or encapsulation, is the process of taking the packets that would normally be transferred over a network connection and placing them inside an outer wrapper, which is then used to deliver the contents across an external network connection. An analogy would be an inter-office mail system. You place correspondence inside an internal mail envelope for delivery. You write the name and department on the outside. The mailroom takes the envelope and delivers it to the destination. However, if that destination department is in another building or city, the envelope it is in isn't acceptable to the external delivery system. The mailroom inserts it into a U.S. mail or courier envelope, writes an externally acceptable address on it, and hands it over to the external delivery system.

When it arrives at the destination, the outer envelope is removed and the inner envelope then continues to the final destination.

NOTE

PPTP can encrypt the inner envelope and the data it contains, so the external mail system cannot even see the internal delivery address.

Using Tunneling, you can take a protocol like NetBEUI that isn't a routable protocol, encapsulate it in PPTP, route the PPTP packet, remove the PPTP layer, and deliver the NetBEUI packet to the destination network.

There are several competing technologies offering tunneling solutions. When IPV6 is finally standardized, it will contain a tunneling standard called IPSec. Novell also has an offering out for tunneling IPX packets by encapsulating the IPX with a UDP and IP header.

One of the more interesting competitions has been between two corporate groups, one led by Microsoft and the other by Cisco. Microsoft submitted PPTP for approval by the InterNIC committee as a tunneling standard. Cisco submitted L2F (Layer 2 Forwarding) to the InterNIC for approval as a tunneling standard. The InterNIC committee looked at the two competing standards, decided they were too similar to be separate standards, and sent them both back with instructions to combine them into one submission. The final standard will be called L2TP when the two groups have reached an agreement on how to combine the features of the two protocols.

Using PPTP Connections

To set up a PPTP tunnel, you need a PPTP client on one end to place the call, a PPTP server on the other end to answer, and a connection medium in between. This connection could be over a network, phone line, ISDN, Internet, T1, Null modem cable, and so on—whatever option you have available to connect the two machines to allow the exchange of packets. Each end requires a RAS-capable device with the client-end configured to dial out and the server-end configured to receive dial-in calls. The server can have one or more network interfaces configured to forward the traffic after it has been delivered.

You should have PPTP installed and the VPNs created before you install RRAS. You can create more VPNs using the PPTP properties in the Control Panel, Networks, and Protocols tab. You can assign only already-created VPNs to interfaces. After you have added the VPNs, the RAS Setup is automatically invoked. The Remote Access Setup dialog box enables you to add the newly created VPNs and configure them. See Chapter 21, "Using Remote Access Services," for a description of configuring RAS devices.

The following sections review the different scenarios for setting up a tunnel.

Using Client to ISP to Server Tunnel

In this scenario, the client connects to the ISP using a standard PPP connection. The ISP establishes a connection through the Internet for the client to the enterprise network. The client then establishes a PPTP tunnel with the PPTP server. The data can be encrypted at the client,

23

IMPLEMENTING
ROUTING AND
REMOTE ACCESS

inserted into the tunnel, and transmitted to the ISP via PPP. The ISP forwards the packet over the Internet to the PPTP server, which decrypts the packet and places it onto the corporate network. This scenario needs two demand-dial interfaces at the client-end: one for the PPP connection to the ISP and another for the PPTP connection that uses the PPP interface to create the tunnel over.

Using Client to Server Tunnel over a LAN

This scenario has the tunnel created across the corporate LAN between the client and the server. This creates a secure channel between the two machines to prevent tampering with the data. This connection would be accomplished with dial-up networking. There is only one interface, and phone book entry uses the IP address of the PPTP server as the telephone number.

Using Server to Server Tunnel

In this scenario, one server is configured to dial out as a RAS server (be a client) and to receive calls as a RAS server. The other server is configured to receive calls as an RAS server. The first server then initiates the call. Once the tunnel is created, encrypted data can be sent between the two sites.

Configuring the Phone Book Entry

If the connection is to be established over a modem or ISDN line, then the PPP connection must be completed first. Configure a phonebook entry to connect to the ISP as you did the demand-dial interface. Next, you create another demand-dial interface for the PPTP connection using the IP address of the PPTP server's Internet interface and select the VPN device as the device to use for dialing.

Using the DHCP Relay Agent

If your network is divided into subnets and you're using DHCP to assign IP addresses, a router sometimes can solve your problems. As explained in Chapter 11, "Dynamic Host Configuration Protocol (DHCP)," when a client machine is configured to get its IP address from a DHCP server, the process involves four broadcast packets. These four packets, in the order sent, are called Discover, Offer, Request, and Acknowledgment.

Until the client machine has the Acknowledgment, it does not have an IP address it can use, which is why the conversation is done with broadcasts. The problem with routers is that they are designed not to forward broadcast traffic. This means that the DHCP server never sees the broadcasts from clients on the wrong side of the router. The solution to this problem is to make your router a Bootp-compliant router so that it can forward the broadcasts to the server and return the replies to the client.

This is the purpose of the DHCP Relay Agent. Once this protocol is loaded on your router, it watches for DHCP broadcasts packets on the configured interfaces. If it sees a broadcast Discover or Request from the client, it modifies the packet to be a directed request to the server.

The DHCP Relay Agent includes the interface IP address so the server knows what scope to issue the IP address from, and then sends the modified packet to the server. The server directs the Offer and Acknowledgment replies back to the Relay Agent, which broadcasts them back to the client. With the Relay Agent enabled, your clients on the wrong side of the router can still get an IP address. See Chapter 11 for a detailed discussion of how to set up and configure the DHCP server with multiple scopes.

To install the DHCP Relay Agent, select Summary under IP routing and right-click. Choose Add Routing Protocol, select DHCP Relay Agent from the dialog box, and click OK. This adds a DHCP Relay Agent Branch onto the IP tree.

After it is installed, you have to supply the IP address of the DHCP server to which you want it to direct the packets. If you select and right-click this branch, the menu choice is Configure DHCP Relay Agent. On the General tab, type the necessary IP address and click Add. Next, you add the interfaces you want to listen for the broadcast traffic. Right-click the DHCP Relay Agent branch and select Add Interface.

After you have the interfaces, you can configure them. Right-click on the interface and select Configure Interface. There are only three options on the General tab that you can configure, as shown in Figure 23.24:

- Relay DHCP Packets Across This Interface—The first option can enable/disable the Relay agent on this interface, if you want to turn it off.

- Hop-Count Threshold—The second option can set the maximum hop count. Each time a relay agent forwards a request, it increments the packet hop count. If the hop count exceeds the limit you specify here, the packet is discarded. This is to prevent packets from being forwarded from Bootp router to Bootp router endlessly.

- Seconds-Since-Boot Threshold—This last option is most useful if you have multiple, backup DHCP servers configured. When you have more than one server, each on its own subnet, you can set up a secondary scope in each server that belongs to the other server's subnet. These addresses must be non-overlapping with the primary scope.

  Generally, a division of 75% of the available IP addresses in the primary scope and 25% in the secondary scope on the other server is suggested. Now we come to the reason for this option. When the Relay Agent picks up a broadcast discover packet, it waits the specified length of time (four seconds by default). If a server hasn't replied, the router forwards the request to the backup server on the other side. This way, if your primary DHCP server fails, the backup server can supply addresses until you get the primary fixed. If you have only one DHCP server, you might want to set this threshold down to 1 second so the relay happens right away.

Once the Relay Agent is installed, you can configure the DHCP servers to serve up IP addresses across the router. Just make sure you don't have multiple servers serving up the same range of IP addresses.

FIGURE 23.24.

Configuring the DHCP Relay Agent.

Summary

The Routing and Remote Access Service offers LAN-to-LAN routing and remote office connectivity solutions to small and mid-size businesses. You can view and manage all of your routers and RAS servers through the use of the RRAS Administrators Utility, a GUI-based tool. This chapter explained what RRAS has to offer, basic operating instructions, and what to watch out for if you use it. While this is not a product every administrator needs on his or her desktop, most will find some part of it useful. There are many different parts, but all are related to getting into and out of your subnet. We looked at the process of how a router selects which route to use from its routing table and the issues that you should be aware of when you install RRAS.

Network Client Administrator

by Robert Reinstein

IN THIS CHAPTER

Introduction

One of the greatest headaches in setting up a network, any network, is getting your clients connected to the network. If your clients are running Windows NT Workstation, Windows 95, or Windows for Workgroups, getting them onto a Microsoft Network is not quite as difficult, and usually just requires a little tweaking; however, the workstations that are still running DOS, DOS/Windows 3.x, or OS/2 require a lot of time and configuration. A lot of that time is spent installing the client software necessary to make that network connection.

The Windows NT Server Network Client Administrator is a tool that can help the administrator ease the installation of Windows- and DOS-based clients onto the Windows NT Server domain.

These tools include the means of copying all the client software contained on the Windows NT Server CD-ROM to a network share, the creation of disks that can be used to enable a client to attach to the network and access that share, and copy administrative tools that can be used on PCs that are not running the Windows NT operating system.

It also has features that can be modified to give you even more functionality than is explained in the documentation. Toward the end of this chapter, I will explain this.

Starting the Network Client Administrator

The shortcut for the Network Client Administrator is located in the Administrative Tools folder on the Windows NT Server Start menu.

This simple yet very effective application gives you four choices of functionality, although one of them is nothing more than an instruction to refer to a section of the Windows NT Resource Kit. (See Figure 24.1.)

The first two choices on the available tasks depend on the existence of copies of the Microsoft Network client installation software. The Windows NT Server CD-ROM contains a directory structure, located under the \CLIENTS directory, that contains Microsoft Network client software for MS-DOS, Windows 3.x, and OS/2. In addition to these, installable copies of Microsoft's 32-bit TCP/IP for Windows for Workgroups and Remote Access Services (RAS) for MS-DOS are included.

> **NOTE**
>
> At the time of this writing, the pre-release Microsoft Windows NT Server 4 CD-ROM did not contain the full version of Windows for Workgroups. A full version was included on the Microsoft Windows NT Server 3.51 CD-ROM. The full copy of Windows for Workgroups included on the Microsoft Windows NT Server 3.51 CD-ROM contains updated files that

are not found in the shrink-wrapped copy of Windows for Workgroups. If you are working with workstations that are already running Windows for Workgroups, you need to copy the files located in the `\CLIENTS\UPDATE.WFW` directory, which is on both copies of the Microsoft Windows NT Server CD-ROM.

FIGURE 24.1.
The Network Client Administrator.

Sharing the Network Client Installation Files

When starting either Make Network Installation Startup Disk or Make Installation Disk Set, you will be prompted to configure the network share that the client software can be copied from.

If this is the first time you have run either of these options, you can choose to create a new share on your server or specify another server that already has the client software share established. In Figure 24.2, the PATH field refers to the location of either the Microsoft Windows NT Server CD-ROM and the path where the client software can be copied from, or you can specify another location, such as a share on another server that has that same directory structure. Copying the client installation files to your server is optional. It can be very convenient, however, to not have to dig out the Microsoft Windows NT Server CD-ROM whenever you need client software.

NOTE

Unless you have another server on your LAN containing the Microsoft Network client software that you will access for the purpose of making client installation disks, you need to specify the PATH.

FIGURE 24.2.

The Share Network Client Installation Files dialog.

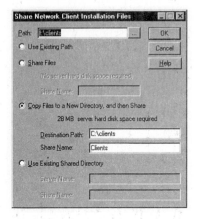

After filling in the PATH field, you need to specify whether you want to create a share that points directly to the source for the files, or you can create a new share. In Figure 24.2, I have opted to use the default setting of creating a new share called CLIENTS in the C:\CLIENTS directory.

Twenty-eight megabytes of files are then copied to the new directory. (See Figure 24.3.) After the copying has been completed, however, unneeded parts of the directory structure can be deleted. The subdirectories in the C:\CLIENTS directory are shown in Table 24.1.

FIGURE 24.3.

Copying files from the NT Server CD-ROM to a network share.

Table 24.1. Network client software directory structure.

Directory	Description
\CLIENTS\LANMAN	Microsoft LAN Manager for MS-DOS
\CLIENTS\LANMAN.OS2	Microsoft LAN Manager for OS/2
\CLIENTS\MSCLIENT	Microsoft Network Client for MS-DOS

Directory	Description
\CLIENTS\RAS	Microsoft RAS for MS-DOS
\CLIENTS\RPL	Remoteboot Service for Microsoft Windows NT Server
\CLIENTS\SRVTOOLS	Client-based network administration tools
\CLIENTS\TCP32WFW	Microsoft TCP/IP-32 for Windows for Workgroups
\CLIENTS\WDL	Windows Driver Library containing additional network card drivers

NOTE

The LAN Manager client is available because LAN Manager servers can be incorporated into a Windows NT Server domain.

Making a Network Installation Startup Disk

Installing Microsoft Network client software to a workstation that is running MS-DOS or Windows 3.x can be accomplished by either creating a network installation startup disk or using disks created by the Network Client Administrator.

Sometimes it is more convenient to create installation disks in advance, and keep them handy for future installations; however, the option Make Network Installation Startup Disk is geared toward a specific workstation, and cannot be reused.

This option will copy the necessary software to a single floppy disk, which will load the appropriate network interface card driver, attach to the network, connect to the share that has the Microsoft Network client software, and execute the setup program for the type of client that was specified when creating the disk.

The Target Workstation Configuration dialog (see Figure 24.4) lets you choose which type of network client software you want to install on the workstation. By default, only the MS-DOS/Windows 3.x client software is available for installation. I have illustrated here adding another choice to this dialog, but I will explain how to do that later. The two choices shown here, MS-DOS/Windows 3.x and Windows for Workgroups, are based on the existing configuration of the workstation, and whether or not you want to upgrade from MS-DOS/Windows 3.x to Windows for Workgroups.

FIGURE 24.4.

The Target Worksta-tion Configuration dialog.

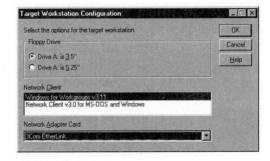

The client software for DOS and Windows 3.x does not need to be licensed and is included for part of the cost of the network access license that should have already been purchased.

The other option, Windows for Workgroups, is not included as part of the network client license and requires separate licensing. If the workstation is currently running Windows 3.x, there is upgrade pricing, known as the Workgroup Add-On for Windows. If the workstation is running DOS only, a full copy of Windows for Workgroups must be purchased to properly license the Windows for Workgroups installation.

> **TIP**
>
> Whenever possible, install Windows 95 or Windows for Workgroups. The built-in network-ing components of Windows 95 and Windows for Workgroups more than justify its price. A Windows 95 or Windows for Workgroups workstation does not require the Microsoft Network full redirector, which is a 100KB hog. The navigation tools, when connecting to a network printer or network share, are worth the price by themselves.
>
> Usually only a computer running on less than 4MB of memory, and/or having a 286 CPU should be excluded from being a Windows for Workgroups workstation. 8MB is sufficient for Windows 95. And, of course, Microsoft Windows NT Workstation is the best client of them all.

From a pick-list of available network interface card drivers, choose the workstation's network adapter card. This setting must be accurate, as the startup disk will attempt to load this driver.

The Network Startup Disk Configuration dialog (see Figure 24.5) asks for a unique computer name for the client workstation. Any user account can be used to access this share, so a pre-existing account must be entered into the User Name field. Enter the name of the domain that this workstation will join, and the initial protocol that will be used for the Network Client software installation.

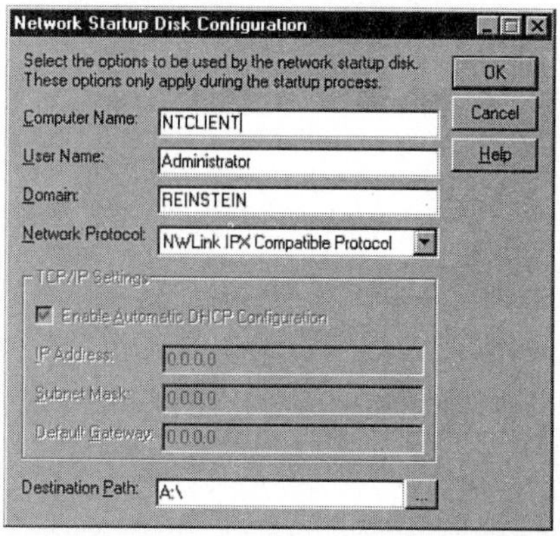

FIGURE 24.5.

The Network Startup Disk Configuration dialog.

> **NOTE**
>
> If there is a Windows NT Server in the entered domain that is running DHCP Services, you can opt to install TCP/IP and check the box that says "Enable Automatic DHCP Configuration." If this option is used, then the IP address and subnet mask for the DHCP server need not be entered.

The last field is specifying a target for the files that will be copied. This should be a drive letter associated with a floppy drive; however, you may wish to copy these files to a local hard drive or a network share for future use.

The floppy disk that is used as a network installation startup disk must be formatted and bootable.

On this disk, a CONFIG.SYS file and an AUTOEXEC.BAT file are created, along with a directory called NET.

As shown in Listings 24.1 and 24.2, the necessary drivers are loaded in CONFIG.SYS, the appropriate bindings are created in AUTOEXEC.BAT, a connection to the network share is made, and the SETUP.EXE program from the Windows for Workgroups directory is run.

Listing 24.1. A sample startup disk CONFIG.SYS.

```
files=30
device=a:\net\ifshlp.sys
lastdrive=z
DEVICE=A:\NET\HIMEM.SYS
DEVICE=A:\NET\EMM386.EXE NOEMS
DOS=HIGH,UMB
```

24

NETWORK CLIENT ADMINISTRATOR

Listing 24.2. A sample startup disk `AUTOEXEC.BAT`.

```
path=a:\net
a:\net\net initialize
a:\net\nwlink
a:\net\net start
net use z: \\SERVER\Clients
echo Running Setup...
z:\wfw\netsetup\setup.exe /#
```

TIP

Although there are a limited number of network interface card drivers that can be chosen from the Target Workstation Configuration dialog, it is possible to edit some of the files on the startup disk to reflect a driver that comes from a third-party driver disk. This is accomplished by editing files from the NET directory that have the extensions INI and INF. These files make references to the specific network interface card driver that was chosen in the Target Workstation Configuration dialog. To determine the appropriate changes, perform a manual installation from disks of the client software and indicate that you want to use another driver, rather than an included driver. Use the hardware manufacturer's driver disk, and once the installation is complete, note the netcard= entries made in SYSTEM.INI and PROTOCOL.INI. It will also be necessary to install the manufacturer's version of PROTMAN.DOS to the NET directory on the Startup Disk.

Once the necessary entries have been made, the Network Client Administrator will confirm your settings with a dialog (see Figure 24.6) that explicitly explains the type of disk that will be created.

FIGURE 24.6.

The Confirm Network Disk Configuration dialog.

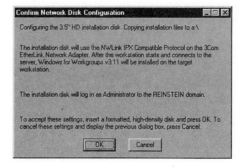

Making Network Installation Disks

When you choose Make Installation Disk Set from the Network Client Administrator dialog, you will first be prompted for the location of the client setup installation files. If this has been previously set up, those settings will be retained and shown for confirmation.

The available disk sets that can be made through this process are

- Microsoft TCP/IP-32 for Windows for Workgroups
- Microsoft Network Client for MS-DOS
- Microsoft LAN Manager for MS-DOS
- Microsoft LAN Manager for OS/2
- Microsoft RAS for MS-DOS

The Make Installation Disk Set dialog (see Figure 24.7) lists these items and allows you to choose the letter of the floppy drive you want to create the disks on. The number of disks required is also displayed (one disk each, except for the LAN Manager options, which are four disks each), as is a choice for the Network Client Administrator to format the disks before copying the chosen files to them.

FIGURE 24.7.

The Make Installation Disk Set dialog.

> **TIP**
>
> Although you might want to have a copy of Remote Access Services for DOS or TCP/IP for Windows for Workgroups, once you have connectivity to the server, it is just as easy to directly install these items from the CLIENTS share.

After choosing the drive and product that you want to make disks for, press OK and you will be prompted for the disks required.

Copying Client-Based Network Administration Tools

The third utility available in the Network Client Administrator is copying Windows NT Server administration tools that can run on Windows 3.x, Windows for Workgroups, and Windows 95.

The tools included here are non-NT versions of User Manager for Domains, Server Manager, and Event Viewer. These tools enable a client to administer certain functions on the server. The missing administration tool, Disk Manager, is rightly kept as a local tool that should only be used by a user at the server's console.

The minimum requirement on the workstation that runs these tools is 8MB of RAM and 3MB to 5MB of hard drive space. The extra 2MB of disk space is for the Win32s extensions, which may already be installed on the client workstation.

The Share Client-based Administration Tools dialog (see Figure 24.8) is similar to the Share Network Client Installation Files setup. A source path for tools needs to be identified. On the Windows NT Server CD-ROM, this is in the `\CLIENTS\SRVTOOLS` directory. If the tools had already been copied to another directory on a network share, click the radio button next to Use Existing Shared Directory, and type the server name and share name. This utility can be used to create a share that points directly to the CD-ROM or to create a share for a pre-existing directory on a network drive—or it can create a new directory on a network drive.

FIGURE 24.8.

The Share Client-based Administration Tools dialog.

If one of the latter two methods is chosen, the files are also copied to the new share.

The final function of the Network Client Administrator is actually not much of an option. As Figure 24.9 shows, choosing this option merely tells the user to refer to the Windows NT Resource Kit.

FIGURE 24.9.

View remoteboot client options.

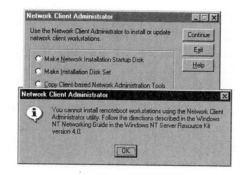

Modifying the Network Client Administrator

One of the great features of the Network Client Administrator is its capability to be modified to extend its functionality.

Because it can create a disk that will enable an over-the-network installation of Windows for Workgroups or the MS-DOS Client for Microsoft Networks, why not make it a way to implement an over-the-network installation of Windows 95 or Windows for Workgroups?

Actually, Microsoft must have planned to allow us to modify this file because there are entries in some of the sections of NCADMIN.INF that show that an over-the-network installation of Windows for Workgroups, Windows 95, and Windows NT Workstation was on their mind.

The driving force behind the Network Client Administrator is a file that is placed in the shared directory. The NCADMIN.INF file looks like a standard Windows INI file, using bracketed sections with values within each section. The only noticeable difference is that Microsoft uses the pound sign (#) for commented lines instead of semicolons (;).

Listing 24.3. The [OTN] section of NCADMIN.INF.

```
[OTN]
#
#       list of sub dirs of the client tree that should be presented
#       for creating an Over-The-Net install disk
#
# SubDirName=DisplayName
wfw=Windows for Workgroups v3.11
msclient=Network Client v3.0 for MS-DOS and Windows
win95=Windows95
winnt=Windows NT Workstation
winnt.srv=Windows NT Server
```

24

NETWORK CLIENT
ADMINISTRATOR

In Listing 24.3, the section called OTN (for Over-The-Net) lists the subdirectories that could be included in the share that contains the client software. The first two entries in the OTN section name directories created by the Network Client Administrator when you originally create the network share. The last three entries in the OTN section name directories that are not created by the Network Client Administrator but can be manually created by you, and then the contents of the respective products can be copied to those directories.

When you use the Network Client Administrator to create a Network Installation Startup Disk, it reads the OTN section of the NCADMIN.INF file, but then it checks to see which of these directories are available in the share. If it doesn't find a directory, it does not list the item in the list of possible client software installations to run.

For instance, if your network share is in the C:\CLIENTS directory on the NT Server, and you manually create a directory called Win95 and copy the contents of the \WIN95 directory from the Windows 95 CD-ROM into the C:\CLIENTS\WIN95 directory, Windows 95 will be a choice in the Network Client Administrator Target Workstation Configuration dialog. (See Figure 24.10.)

FIGURE 24.10.

A customized Target Workstation Configuration dialog.

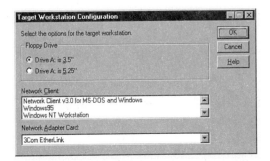

> **TIP**
>
> I previously mentioned that the best choice for DOS workstations is to upgrade to Windows for Workgroups. Using this method, however, you can give your clients the other options of other excellent Microsoft Network client software, Windows 95, and Microsoft Windows NT Workstation.

The next section that pertains to the Over-The-Net installation is the WarningClients section. (See Listing 24.4.) This contains the text that will be displayed whenever network client software is chosen for the network installation startup disk. This text may be modified, such as by adding additional instructions. See Figure 24.11 for an example of the resulting dialog, created by a modification to the WarningClients section. If any of the OTN values are not represented in this section, then there will be no dialog shown.

Listing 24.4. The `WarningClients` section of `MCADMIN.INF`.

```
[WarningClients]
# ClientDir_n = text string
#   where n is a decimal number
#   more than one string can be displayed in the warning popup by
#   adding more lines, each with an incremented decimal digit. The
#   strings will be concatenated before display.
#
wfw_caption="MS Windows for Workgroups Installation"
wfw_1="You have selected the option to install Windows for Workgroups on your
target workstation.\r\n\r\n"
wfw_2="You must purchase a separate license for Windows for Workgroups prior to
installing and "
wfw_3="using Windows for Workgroups.\r\n\r\nThe license accompanying Windows NT
Server does NOT contain a "
wfw_4="license to install and use Windows for Workgroups.\r\n\r\nIf you have
already acquired a separate "
wfw_5="license for Windows for Workgroups, select OK to continue. Select Cancel to
return to the Target "
wfw_6="Workstation dialog."
#
win95_caption="MS Windows 95 Installation"
win95_1="You have selected the option to install Windows 95 on your target
workstation.\r\n\r\n"
win95_2="You must purchase a separate license for Windows 95 prior to installing
and "
win95_3="using Windows 95.\r\n\r\nThe license accompanying Windows NT Server does
NOT contain a "
win95_4="license to install and use Windows 95.\r\n\r\nIf you have already acquired
a separate "
win95_5="license for Windows 95, select OK to continue. Select Cancel to return to
the Target "
win95_6="Workstation dialog."
#
winnt_caption="MS Windows NT Workstation Installation"
winnt_1="You have selected the option to install Windows NT on your target
workstation.\r\n\r\n"
winnt_2="You must purchase a separate license for Windows NT Workstation prior to "
winnt_3="installing and using Windows NT.\r\n\r\nThe license accompanying Windows
NT Server does "
winnt_4="NOT contain a license to install and use Windows NT Workstation.\r\n\r\n"
winnt_5="If you have already acquired a separate license for Windows NT
Workstation, "
winnt_6="select OK to continue. Select Cancel to return to the Target Workstation
dialog."
#
winnt.srv_caption="MS Windows NT Server Installation"
winnt.srv_1="You have selected the option to install Windows NT Server on your
target system.\r\n\r\n"
winnt.srv_2="You must purchase a separate license for each Windows NT Server system
prior to "
winnt.srv_3="installing and using Windows NT Server on that system.\r\n\r\nThe
license accompanying Windows NT Server does "
winnt.srv_4="NOT contain a license to install and use additional Windows NT
Servers.\r\n\r\n"
winnt.srv_5="If you have already acquired an additional license for Windows NT
Server, "
winnt.srv_6="select OK to continue. Select Cancel to return to the Target
Workstation dialog."
```

24

NETWORK CLIENT ADMINISTRATOR

FIGURE 24.11.

The result of a modified
`WarningClients`
section.

The next relevant section in NCADMIN.INF for the Over-The-Net installation is the SetupCmd section. (See Listing 24.5.) This provides the generated AUTOEXEC.BAT for the floppy disk, its final command, to kick off the setup program for the installed network client software. You might want to examine the different command-line switches included here, because they might not apply to what you want to accomplish.

Listing 24.5. The SetupCmd section of NCADMIN.INF.

```
[SetupCmd]
msclient=setup.exe /$
wfw=setup.exe /#
win95=setup.exe
winnt=winnt.exe /B /S:Z:\WINNT\NETSETUP
winnt.srv=winnt.exe /B /S:Z:\WINNT.srv\NETSETUP
Summary
```

The other sections in NCADMIN.INF should be examined as well. You will see that depending on the protocol stack selected for use on the Over-The-Net installation, there are different commands added to the AUTOEXEC.BAT on the floppy disk. You might want to add additional commands to this AUTOEXEC.BAT based on the topology of your network, or to adhere to certain standards.

> **TIP**
>
> For instance, you might want to have an antivirus program scan the client's hard drive at the time of installation. By adding an antivirus program to the list of files copied to the floppy disk, and adding the command to kick off the antivirus scan, you can make a customized version of the network installation startup disk.

When properly utilized, the Network Client Administrator program can be one of the best tools a Microsoft Windows NT network administrator can have.

CHAPTER 25

NetWare Connections

by Robert Reinstein

IN THIS CHAPTER

Introduction

Of course, Microsoft Windows NT Server is a great server and can handle all the file, print, and application server requirements for a small company or a large corporation. But still, other network operating systems also exist in the marketplace.

When the first version of Microsoft Windows NT Server was released, Novell NetWare held the greatest market share for network operating systems. At the time of this writing, NetWare still does, with Microsoft Windows NT Server catching up quickly.

Because of the huge installed base of NetWare servers, Microsoft decided, beginning with Microsoft Windows NT 3.5 Server, to incorporate some features that would enable Microsoft Windows NT Server to coexist with NetWare. Microsoft also offered tools that enable an easy migration from NetWare to Microsoft Windows NT Server.

This chapter discusses some of the built-in functions Microsoft Windows NT Server offers that give Microsoft Windows NT Server the capability to coexist with NetWare, and to replace NetWare. I'll also discuss a utility available from Microsoft that can actually make an NT Server appear as a NetWare server.

Microsoft and Novell

When Microsoft Windows NT Server was first released in 1993, it seemed as though there would never be connectivity between NT and NetWare. Microsoft didn't care to include its version of a NetWare client, and Novell seemed to have even less of an interest to allow NT PCs to see NetWare servers.

Perhaps this was because of the differences that Novell and Microsoft encountered with the release of Windows for Workgroups. If you're unfamiliar with this issue, Microsoft had included Novell's NetWare client for Windows in the first release of Windows for Workgroups. According to Novell, Microsoft had not asked permission to include this client software, and demanded that its software be removed from the product. This was the start of a feud that would be short-lived, but would result in a lack of a NetWare client for NT being produced in time for the release of NT.

As a user in a NetWare environment at the time, it was very frustrating having to live without network connectivity when running NT as my desktop operating system.

Due to customer demand, Microsoft decided to create its own NetWare client for NT. Apparently not wanting to be outdone by Microsoft, Novell released its own NetWare client for NT, albeit in beta form. Both of these clients offered nothing more than basic connectivity, and in my opinion, the Microsoft client was more solid than the Novell client, which appeared to be a rush job. Both products had no support for login scripts, and no GUI tools.

Both companies were then releasing their respective beta versions of the NetWare client for NT, each time adding a little bit more functionality.

Not until the release of Microsoft Windows NT 3.5 Server was there a client for NetWare built into the NT product. Microsoft's client depended on a NetWare bindery to gain access to a NetWare server. With the release of NetWare 4.x, with its new NDS tree, Microsoft's NetWare client for NT required NetWare 4.x servers to run in "Bindery Emulation Mode." Novell and Microsoft soon released their NDS client for NT, but this was only usable on a Windows NT Workstation. Not until Microsoft Windows NT 4 Server has Microsoft finally included the ability for an NT Server to log on to a NetWare NDS tree (although this functionality has been available for Windows NT Workstation, from both Microsoft and Novell).

The next section of this chapter discusses the feature built into NT Server called Gateway Service for NetWare, which has been revised for this new version of Microsoft Windows NT Server to allow for NDS logons.

Gateway Service for NetWare

Gateway Service for NetWare is an installable service that enables access to a NetWare server through the NT Server. This enables a client to run only the client software for an NT network and still have access to NetWare resources.

There are a few guidelines for using this service. First, this is not a way to bypass NetWare security. A client that uses the gateway must have an account on the NetWare server and must have permission to access whatever resources it tries to attach to. Second, Gateway Service for NetWare is not a replacement for making a direct connection to a NetWare server. Gateway Service for NetWare uses only one connection to NetWare and cannot achieve the same performance as a direct connection. In fact, if more than one user is utilizing Gateway Service for NetWare, the performance degrades even more. That is why it is strongly advised to use Gateway Service for NetWare only if the resources on the NetWare server are seldom used.

For instance, if a NetWare client decides to migrate to an NT domain and run only the client software for NT to avoid unnecessary overhead, there is a chance that there is a shared directory on the NetWare server that the user still wants access to. To retrieve an occasional document or to print to a NetWare print queue, Gateway Service for NetWare is the perfect tool. It should not be used for running applications. Yes, you can run an application, but again, there is a good chance that there will be a performance issue. Users who do want access to applications residing on a NetWare server should run native NetWare client software and make a direct connection.

Installing Gateway Service for NetWare

Before you install Gateway Service for NetWare, you need to do some setting up to enable it to install properly.

Configuring NetWare

In this example I use a NetWare 4.1 server. I am logged into the NetWare NDS tree, which enables me to run the NWADMIN.EXE administration program from Windows 95. I am using Microsoft's Client for NDS to get access to the NetWare server.

For a NetWare 3.x server, you use SYSCON to perform the same activities I describe here. With the earlier versions of NetWare you need to repeat the steps for each NetWare 3.x server you want to give your NT clients access to. NDS enables you to go through this routine only once.

One account used on NetWare functions as the service account for Gateway Service for NetWare. Using NWADMIN, you choose to create a new user object. The name of the user can be anything, but the same ID must exist in both NetWare and NT. For this example I use the name NTSERVER. (See Figure 25.1.)

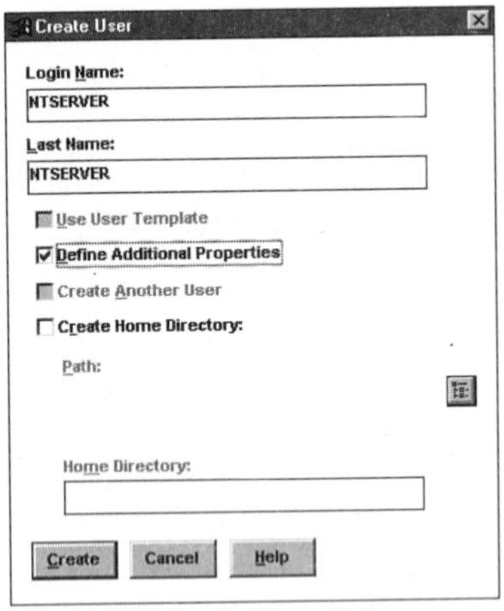

FIGURE 25.1.

Adding the Gateway Service for NetWare service account to NetWare.

Click the Define Additional Properties checkbox, because you want to continue configuring this account.

The next dialog, shown in Figure 25.2, has several configuration tabs to choose from. In this case, I add a description to the account so that someone else doesn't accidentally delete the account.

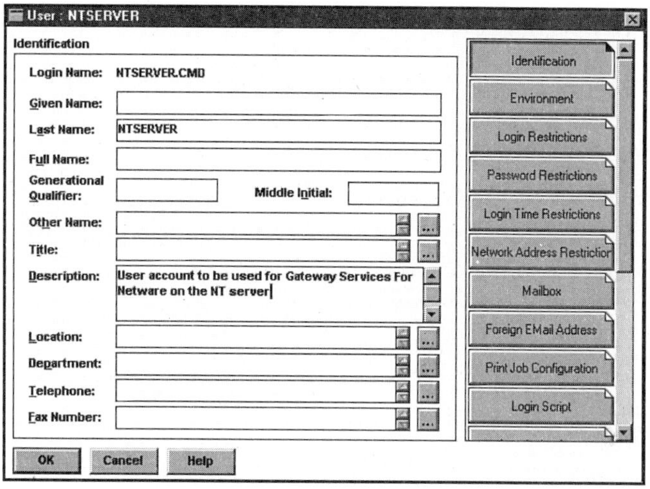

Figure 25.2.

User identification in
NWADMIN.

Click the Password Restrictions tab so you can set the password for the Gateway Service for
NetWare service account. (See Figure 25.3.)

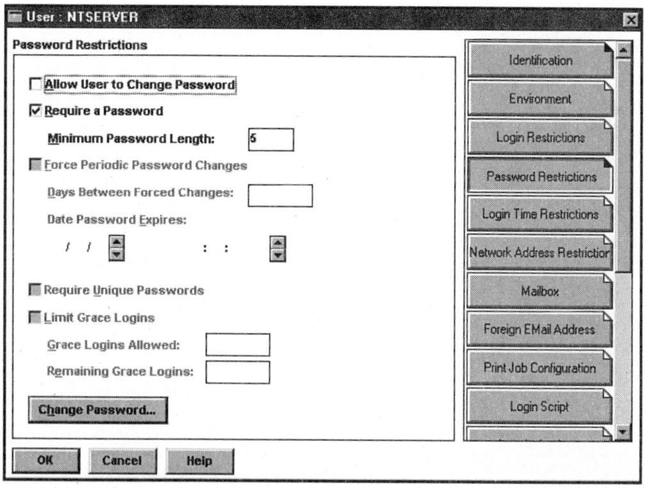

Figure 25.3.

Password restrictions in
NWADMIN.

> **TIP**
>
> As with all networks, having a password defined is highly advised. Chances are that you
> already have a default user profile set up that dictates the password standards for your
> organization. However, in the case of this service account, you don't want the user to be
> able to change the password, and you don't want the account or the password to expire.

Click the Change Password button to set the password. (See Figure 25.4.)

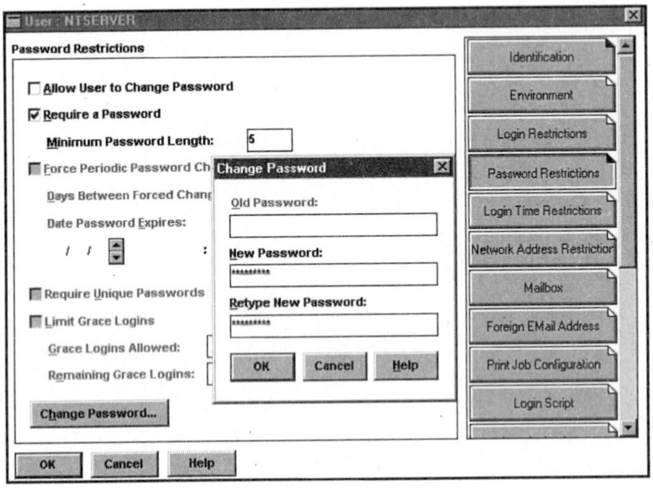

FIGURE 25.4.

*The Change Password
dialog in* NWADMIN.

Click the OK button and you have finished configuring the Gateway Service for NetWare service account in NetWare. You still need to create this account in the NT domain.

On the NT Server, create a user account as shown in Chapter 16, "Administering the Server." The Gateway Service for NetWare service account on NT must have permission to create shares, and it should have a password that never expires.

The next task you need to do on the NetWare side is to create a new group. (See Figure 25.5.) Call the group NTGATEWAY and click the Define Additional Properties checkbox for this group. (See Figure 25.6.)

FIGURE 25.5.

*Creating a new object
in* NWADMIN.

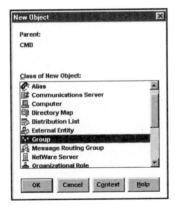

FIGURE 25.6.

Naming the new group.

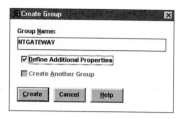

In the Identification page shown in Figure 25.7, you should type in a description for this group so that no one accidentally deletes the group. Without this group, Gateway Service for NetWare does not function at all.

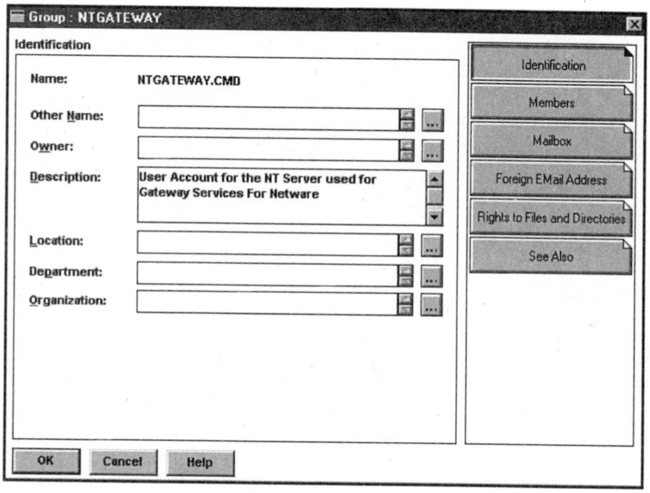

FIGURE 25.7.

Describing the NTGATEWAY *group in* NWADMIN.

Next, click the Members tab. Here is where you add the Gateway Service for NetWare service account to this group. (See Figure 25.8.)

Click the Add button and go through the tree to find the Gateway Service for NetWare service account NTSERVER.

Once the Gateway Service for NetWare service account has been added to the NTGATEWAY group, scroll down the tabs and click the Rights to Files and Directories tab (see Figure 25.9).

You can configure the NTGATEWAY group to have as much or as little access to NetWare as you like. Because the users still have access only to the files and directories that their own NetWare account has access to, you might want to give Supervisor rights to all the NetWare volumes. You also have the option to assign lesser rights to limit the usage of the Gateway Service for NetWare service account.

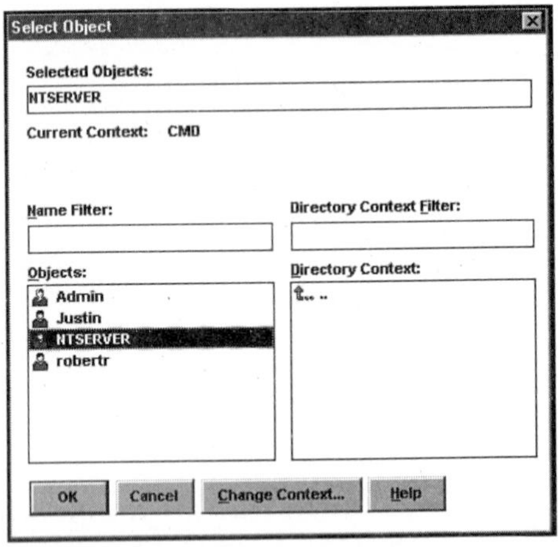

FIGURE 25.8.

Selecting the Gateway Service for NetWare service account for the NTGATEWAY *group.*

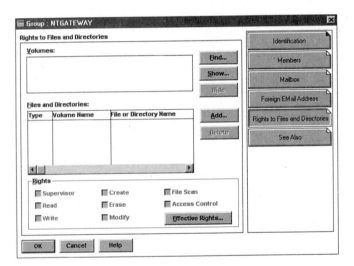

FIGURE 25.9.

The Rights to Files and Directories page in NWADMIN.

Click the Add button to find the volumes that are available in the NDS tree. Navigate through the tree, and when you see a volume you want to enable the Gateway Service for NetWare service account to access, highlight it, as shown in Figure 25.10, and click the OK button. Continue this until you have identified all of these volumes.

After you have added the last volume you want to make available, highlight each volume and assign the appropriate rights for that volume. To assign Supervisor rights for all the volumes, select all the volumes and click the Supervisor checkbox. (See Figure 25.11.)

Once these rights have been set, click the OK button, and your work configuring NetWare is complete. (See Figure 25.12.)

FIGURE 25.10.

Selecting volumes for the gateway.

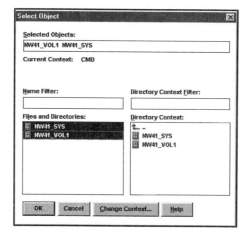

FIGURE 25.11.

Assigning Supervisor privileges for volumes.

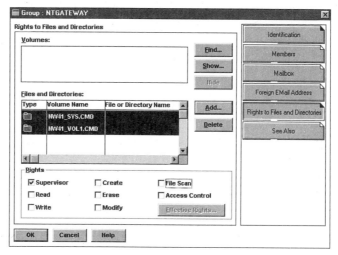

Configuring the NT Server

> **NOTE**
>
> If you already have another NetWare redirector installed, such as Novell's NetWare Services for NT, you must remove the existing redirector before installing Microsoft's Gateway Service for NetWare.

To install Gateway Service for NetWare on your NT Server, click the Start button, choose Settings, and click Control Panel. Double-click the Network icon. In the Network dialog, click the Services tab. A list of services that have already been installed appears. Click the Add button, and a list of installable services is displayed. This is the Select Network Service dialog.

FIGURE 25.12.

Completing the creation of the NTGATEWAY *group.*

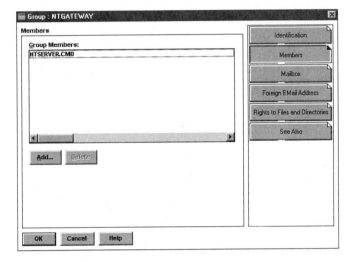

From the Network Service listing, highlight Gateway (and Client) Services for NetWare (see Figure 25.13), and click the OK button.

FIGURE 25.13.

The Select Network Service dialog.

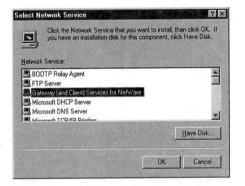

You are prompted for the location of the Microsoft Windows NT Server CD-ROM, and the appropriate files are copied to the Microsoft Windows NT Server directory. When the copy has completed, Gateway Service for NetWare appears on the installed services list. (See Figure 25.14.) Click the Close button, and you are prompted to restart your computer. (See Figure 25.15.)

FIGURE 25.14.

Gateway Service for NetWare has been installed.

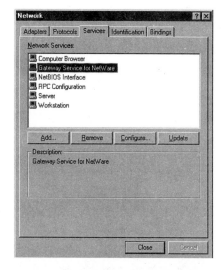

FIGURE 25.15.

Microsoft Windows NT Server must be restarted to start the new service.

> **NOTE**
>
> If you did not already have the NWLink IPX/SPX Compatible protocol installed, Gateway Service for NetWare will automatically install this protocol. If the NWLink IPX/SPX Compatible protocol is installed for you, you are prompted for configuration settings for the protocol before you are prompted to restart the server.

After the server has restarted, the user name used in the local logon must be a valid user on both the NT Server and the NetWare server where Gateway Service for NetWare is used. The user name must also have permission to create shares on the NT Server.

After logging on, the Select Preferred Server For NetWare dialog box, shown in Figure 25.16, prompts for either a server name, if you are connecting to a NetWare 3.x server or a NetWare 4.1 server in Bindery Emulation Mode, or a Tree and Context for attaching to an NDS tree on a NetWare 4.x server. In this example I have chosen to use the NDS tree for the logon.

25

NETWARE CONNECTIONS

FIGURE 25.16.

The Select Preferred Server For NetWare dialog.

> **NOTE**
>
> You have the option of choosing to execute a logon script when logging on locally; however, there really shouldn't be any reason to do that if your only intent is to create a gateway.

> **TIP**
>
> Select your preferred server quickly. After approximately 60 seconds, this dialog times out and logs you on to the NT domain and then attempts to log on to the first NetWare server found.

Once you have been logged on, you can proceed in configuring Gateway Service for NetWare.

After you install Gateway Service for NetWare, a new icon appears in the Control Panel. (See Figure 25.17.) Double-click the red GSNW icon, and the Gateway Service for NetWare applet appears. (See Figure 25.18.) You can change your preferred server choice here. You can also make printing configuration choices for NetWare when logging on locally in this applet. This configuration information applies only to the user name that appears at the top of the dialog.

By pressing the Gateway button, you enter the Configure Gateway dialog (see Figure 25.19). The first thing you need to do in this dialog is check the box that says Enable Gateway. That enables you to specify the Gateway Service for NetWare service account and password defined in NetWare. In Figure 25.19 you see that there are no shares defined. These shares are the same type of share you might already be used to as an NT Server administrator. The main difference is that the shares defined here point to volumes located on a NetWare server.

FIGURE 25.17.

The Control Panel with the Gateway Service for NetWare icon.

FIGURE 25.18.

The Gateway Service for NetWare applet.

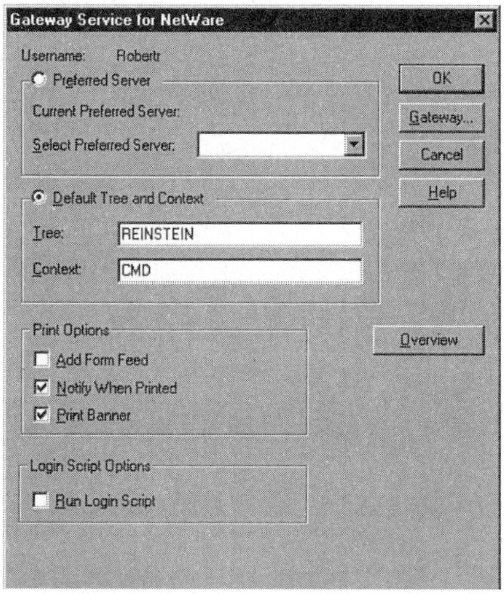

FIGURE 25.19.

The Configure Gateway dialog.

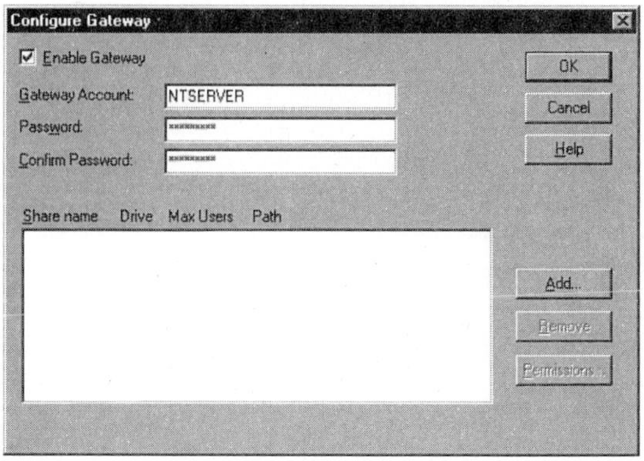

To create shares, click the Add button. The New Share dialog, shown in Figure 25.20, prompts you to enter the following.

FIGURE 25.20.

Creating a new share
for the gateway.

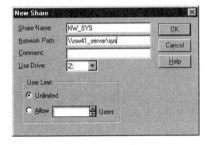

- ■ **Share Name:** Like the normal type of NT Server share, you should enter a name that is displayed to clients in a browse list. Names longer than eight characters are not accessible from MS-DOS workstations. If this is the case, you receive a warning, as shown in Figure 25.21. The share name can be no more than 15 characters long.

FIGURE 25.21.

Warning for non-
DOS–compatible share
names.

- ■ **Network Path:** Specify the volume to be used for this share using UNC (Universal Naming Conventions). In this example I am pointing to the server named NW41_SERVER and the volume SYS.
- ■ **Comment:** This is a description that appears in the resulting list of gateway shares.
- ■ **Use Drive:** An unused drive letter on the server is chosen for this share. Even though the gateway is active without a local logon, a currently available drive letter must be used to establish the gateway share originally.
- ■ **User Limit:** Enter the maximum number of concurrent connections that are allowed to access this share. Choose Unlimited to allow unlimited connections.

Click the OK button, and the share should be established.

> **TIP**
>
> You might receive an error message like the one shown in Figure 25.22. This is an interesting error message because it does not always mean what it says. You can get this error message if you have incorrectly specified a service account that was not set up properly under NetWare, or if you made a typo while entering an account name. In this case, I

created this error message by attempting to exceed the number of licensed connections available on the NetWare server. Incidentally, an incorrect or mistyped password results in an Incorrect Password message, and an incorrect or mistyped network path gets a Server Not Found or Network Path Not Found message.

FIGURE 25.22.

The User Does Not Exist error message.

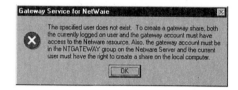

If the share was created successfully, the Configure Gateway dialog should now list your newly created share. (See Figure 25.23.)

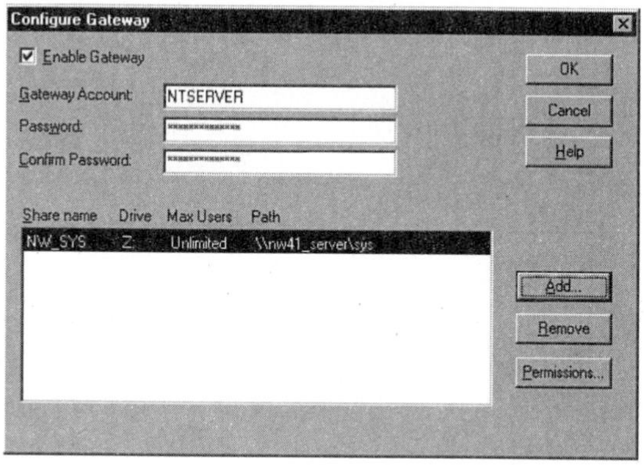

FIGURE 25.23.

The newly created share.

Now you can work on setting the permissions for this share. This is an interesting piece of configuring the gateway, because even if a user has full permissions on a NetWare volume, the permissions set on this share can lessen the user's actual permissions. For instance, if I have READ and WRITE permission on the \\NW41_SERVER\SYS volume, and the permission for the NW_SYS share gives Full Control to the Everyone group, I am still limited to READ and WRITE permissions, as set in NetWare. But if I alter the Gateway Configuration permissions to give the Everyone group only READ permission (see Figure 25.24), my access to that volume is now limited to READ only. Furthermore, if I have limited permissions set on the NetWare NTGATEWAY group, the user's permissions cannot exceed the permissions set for that group.

FIGURE 25.24.

Setting permissions for the new share.

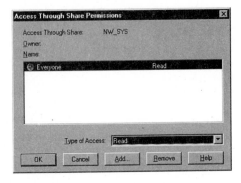

Click the OK button in the Configure Gateway dialog, and the share is available to the network. As shown in Figure 25.25, the share list for SERVER shows NW_SYS as one of the shares on that NT Server. Opening up the NW_SYS folder shows your standard NetWare SYS volume.

FIGURE 25.25.

The Gateway Share as seen by a client.

The Migration Tool for NetWare

Although Gateway Service for NetWare enables the integration of Microsoft Windows NT Server and Novell NetWare, the Migration Tool for NetWare enables you to upgrade from NetWare to NT. This is done by having both servers on the same network and performing an over-the-wire transfer of administrative information and data.

The Migration Tool for NetWare relies on the existence of a NetWare bindery. The bindery is the database of administrative information used in NetWare 3.x. NetWare 4.x uses NDS to hold its data, but there is a Bindery Emulation Mode for NetWare 4.x, and this emulation mode is required if you want to migrate from NetWare 4.x to NT using the Migration Tool for NetWare.

Another requirement is that your NT Server's system partition must be formatted as NTFS. This enables NT to take in the security information contained on the NetWare server.

Of course, you must match hard drive capacity on the NT Server or have more available, so you have enough space to bring over the information you want to migrate.

> **CAUTION**
>
> Usually, a NetWare server will be running not only the NetWare network operating system but also some utilities, such as backup software, anti-virus tools, or communications software. In most cases, the executable program for this software is a NetWare Loadable Module (NLM). NLMs are useless for a Windows NT Server and cannot be migrated. Before you fully migrate from NetWare to NT, be sure to purchase NT-compatible replacements for these programs.
>
> With backup software, the backup tapes created from an NLM backup program may not be compatible with an NT backup program. You might want to keep your original NetWare server and backup software available until you are sure that you no longer require it. Once you have migrated to NT, be sure to create a full backup. There is cross-platform backup software. (Cheyenne Software's ArcServe comes to mind.)

What is not transferred to the NT domain are any logon scripts and user account passwords. There is a way to configure the Migration Tool for NetWare to set passwords, but the only way to migrate logon scripts is to translate them manually into NT logon scripts.

See the section later in this chapter titled "File And Print Services For NetWare" to learn about an alternative strategy for migrating from a NetWare environment to an NT domain.

Preparing for the Migration

When you migrate NetWare servers to an NT domain, you have many choices to make. If you are migrating a single NetWare server to an NT domain, you will have a relatively easy time. If you are migrating multiple NetWare servers to a single NT domain, you run the risk of duplicate user accounts, groups, and data.

Along the path of setting up the migration, you are given options on how to handle potential problems.

> **TIP**
>
> Now might be the time to go through your NetWare servers and weed out unused groups, user accounts, and files. Why deal with these during the migration if you don't really need them?

Before you can run the migration utility, you must be logged on to your NT Server as a member of the Administrators group. You are also required to use a NetWare user account that has supervisory permissions.

Let's start preparing for the migration by starting the NWCONV.EXE program found in the SYSTEM32 subdirectory under your Windows NT directory.

The Migration Tool for NetWare starts out by displaying the Select Servers For Migration dialog. (See Figure 25.26.) Click the button next to the From NetWare Server entry field, and the Select NetWare Server dialog is displayed. (See Figure 25.27.) Highlight the first NetWare server you want to migrate, and click the OK button.

FIGURE 25.26.

The Select Servers For Migration dialog.

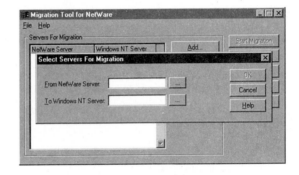

FIGURE 25.27.

The Select NetWare Server dialog.

Next, click the button to the right of the To Windows NT Server entry field to bring up the Select Windows NT Server dialog. (See Figure 25.28.) After you have selected the destination server, click the OK button to be returned to the Select Servers For Migration dialog. (See Figure 25.29.)

Click OK to add this set of servers to the main Migration Tool window. If your current NT logon name and password are not usable by NetWare, you are prompted for the user account on the NetWare server that gives you full access to the bindery and the volumes. (See Figure 25.30.) Once the appropriate information has been entered, click the OK button, and the pair of servers appears on the Servers For Migration list. (See Figure 25.31.)

FIGURE 25.28.

The Select Windows NT Server dialog.

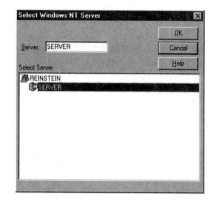

FIGURE 25.29.

The Select Servers For Migration dialog with selection results.

FIGURE 25.30.

The Enter Network Credentials dialog.

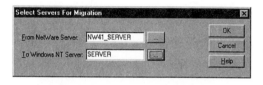

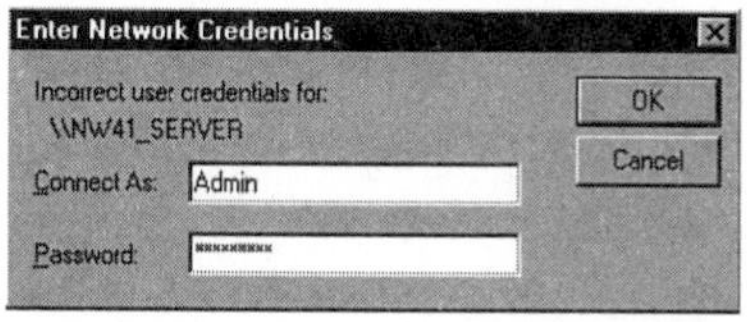

FIGURE 25.31.

The Servers For Migration list.

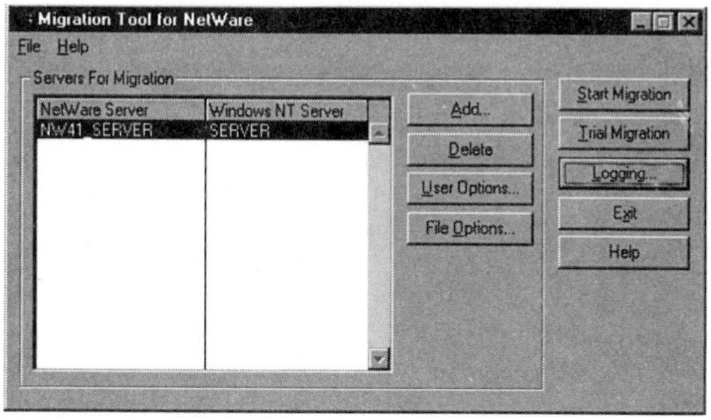

If you want to migrate more NetWare servers, repeat this process until you have identified all the servers you want to migrate to NT.

> **TIP**
>
> Even if you want to migrate more than one server from NetWare, you might want to handle them one at a time so that you don't have to handle several possible conflicts in one shot. A slow migration is sometimes best, although some people opt to perform the entire migration in one swoop, just to get it done quickly. Luckily, there is a trial migration mode that can identify these conflicts in advance.

After all the servers have been selected for migration, you can start configuring the different options.

Before you proceed with configuring your migration, you should be aware of some options that are available to you during the configuration process.

The File menu in the Migration Tool for NetWare main dialog enables you to save the currently configured migration. By default, when you exit the Migration Tool for NetWare dialog, all the configuration options you set during the last time you ran the program are saved and brought into the current session. You can also click the File menu and choose Save Configuration to save all the current options to a file with a file extension of .CNF. You can also restore previously saved settings by choosing Restore Configuration from the File menu. To start the Migration Tool for NetWare with a clean slate, just choose Restore Default Config from the File menu.

Now, back to configuring your migration.

First, the user and group options are configured by clicking the User Options button.

The User and Group Options dialog, shown in Figure 25.32, enables you to specify whether user accounts and groups will be transferred to the NT domain. If they will be transferred, you can configure how this transfer will be handled.

FIGURE 25.32.

The User and Group Options dialog.

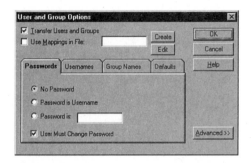

First, you can specify whether the passwords for all the migrated users should be blank, set to their user names, or set to a password you specify to be used for all user accounts. You can also specify whether the users are forced to change their passwords the first time they log on to the NT domain.

You can also specify how duplicate user names are handled during the migration. A duplicate user name can occur if an NT account has the same name as a NetWare account, or if you are migrating more than one NetWare server to the same NT domain.

The options available are to skip the duplicate user name and log an error, skip the duplicate user name and ignore the error, add information from the duplicate user to the existing user account, or add a prefix to the duplicate user name.

The same options are available for groups; however, you cannot add information from the duplicate group to the existing group.

You can also choose to add NetWare users that have Supervisor equivalency to the NT domain's Administrators group.

You also have the choice of overriding all the preceding settings by creating a mapping file. A mapping file is a text file with the file extension .MAP that tells the Migration Tool exactly how to handle each user name and group.

To create a mapping file, click the checkbox in the User and Group Options dialog labeled Use Mappings in File. Then, enter the name of the file you would like to create. Do not type in the file extension. In my example, shown in Figure 25.33, I used the name NW2NT for the mapping file. Click the Create button, and the Create Mapping File dialog appears. (See Figure 25.34.)

FIGURE 25.33.
The User and Group Options dialog.

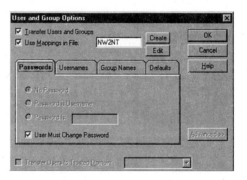

This dialog enables you to choose whether user names and group names appear in the mapping file. If user names appear in the mapping file, you can specify whether you want a default password put into the mapping file. In this example I opted to include both user names and groups. I chose to leave the password blank, because I want to fill in my own passwords for the users I want to migrate.

FIGURE 25.34.

*The Create Mapping
File dialog.*

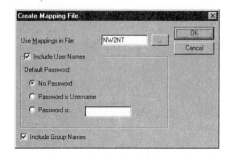

When these options have been completed, click the OK button. A file creation confirmation box asks whether you want to edit the mapping file. (See Figure 25.35.) Click Yes to bring your newly created mapping file into Notepad for editing.

FIGURE 25.35.

*Mapping file created
confirmation.*

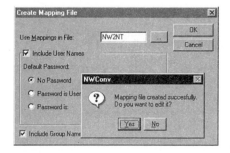

In Figure 25.36, you see that the options you chose (in this case, both users and groups) have been brought into this file, along with whatever password you have chosen (none in this case). The syntax for the mappings is OldName, NewName, and Password.

In Figure 25.37, I changed the NetWare user name JUSTIN to JUSTINR for the NT domain account. I also set that account's password to HOME. I also altered the NetWare KEVIN account and set a password for it. I left the other accounts alone because those accounts already exist in the NT domain and are flagged as duplicated. I decided to leave the group name alone as well. Exit Notepad normally to save the mapping file.

This text file is read by the Migration Tool when either the trial migration or actual migration is run. It can be altered at any time, even outside the User and Group Options dialog.

Now you are back to the User and Group Options dialog. If your settings here are completed, click the OK button to return to the Migration Tool for NetWare main dialog.

The next area of configuration is File Options. By clicking the File Options button, you can specify what volumes and files are migrated, and what their destinations are.

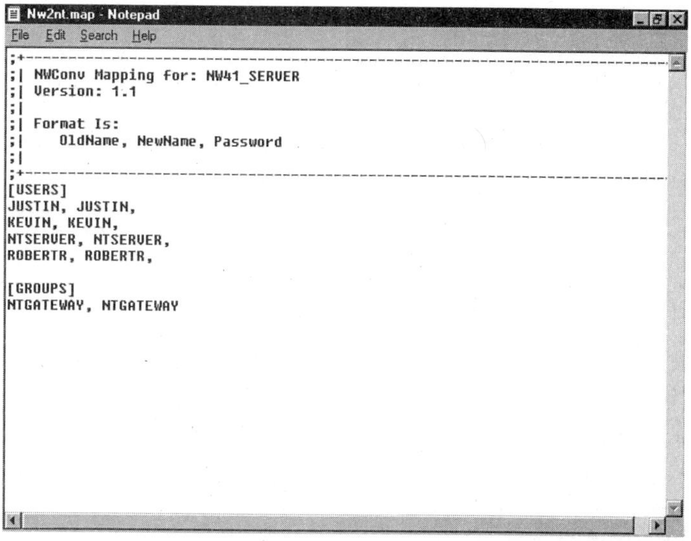

FIGURE 25.36.

The default mapping file.

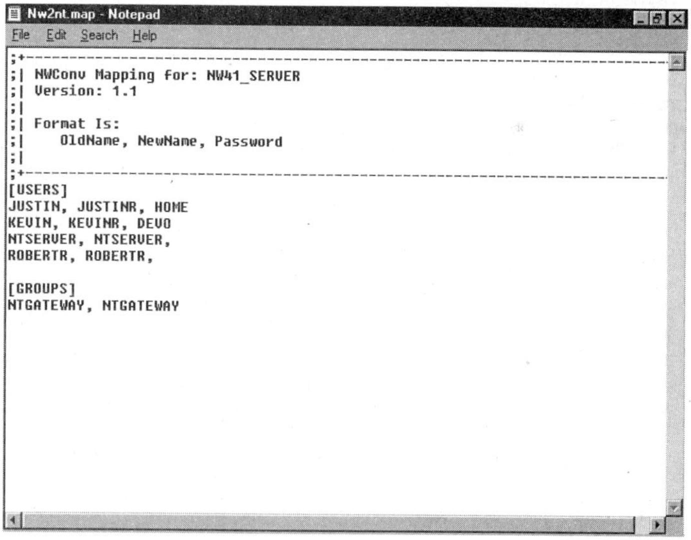

FIGURE 25.37.

The mapping file after editing.

25

NetWare
Connections

By default, if you choose to migrate the NetWare volumes, they are copied to the first NTFS partition found in drive letter order. A directory is created with the same name as the volume name, and the default share name is also the volume name. In the example, there are two volumes on the NetWare server: SYS and VOL1.

In the User and Group Options dialog, click the File Options button. The File Options dialog is displayed (see Figure 25.38), listing the volumes from the selected NetWare server. The first choice you are given is whether to copy these volumes to the NT Server. Because I have left the default, which is to migrate the volume, the NetWare volumes are listed and I can now specify the specific configuration options.

FIGURE 25.38.

The File Options dialog.

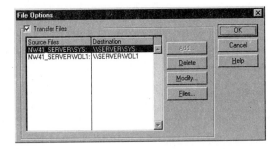

As shown in the Destination column, the shares that are created have the same name as the volumes. This is the default option, which can be overridden. You can also choose to remove one or both volumes from the list by highlighting the volume and clicking the Delete button. I wanted to change the destination of the SYS volume, so I highlighted the SYS volume and clicked the Modify button.

The Modify Destination dialog, shown in Figure 25.39, gives you the option to change the share name and the destination directory for the selected volume. I wanted to change both of these, so I clicked the New Share button.

FIGURE 25.39.

The Modify Destination dialog.

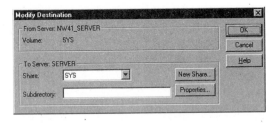

The resulting dialog, shown in Figure 25.40, enabled me to type in the share name I want to use, which is NW_SYS. I also changed the default migration directory, which was D:\SYS because my C drive is formatted as FAT, to a directory of my choosing on the E drive, named Old NetWare SYS Volume.

FIGURE 25.40.

The New Share dialog.

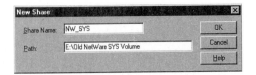

After you click the OK button, the File Options dialog is displayed, with the new information reflected in the Destination column. (See Figure 25.41.)

FIGURE 25.41.

File Options after changing the destination share.

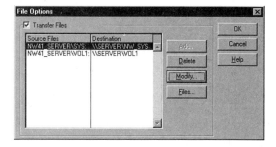

By clicking the Files button, you can choose individual files and directories contained on that volume that you want to migrate. As shown in Figure 25.42, by default the Files To Transfer dialog selects most of the non-NetWare–specific files and directories to be migrated. It is up to you to check the unchecked boxes next to the items the Migration Tool has automatically chosen to omit, or to uncheck the boxes of the files or directories you don't want to migrate. Because this migration is going to an NTFS partition, most of the file attributes travel along with it.

FIGURE 25.42.

The Files To Transfer dialog.

> **NOTE**
>
> Hidden and system files are not migrated by default. In the Files To Transfer dialog (refer to Figure 25.42), click the Transfer menu and choose Hidden Files to transfer all hidden files in the directories selected for transfer. To migrate system files, click the Transfer menu and choose System Files to transfer all system files in the directories selected for transfer.

The actual translation methods of file and directory attributes are shown in Tables 25.1, 25.2, and 25.3.

The effective rights for a directory are translated to the NTFS permissions shown in Table 25.1.

Table 25.1. Directory rights.

NetWare Directory Rights	NTFS Directory Permissions
Supervisory (S)	Full Control (All) (All)
Read (R)	Read (RX) (RX)
Write (W)	Change (RWXD) (RWXD)
Create (C)	Add (WX) (not specified)
Erase (E)	Change (RWXD) (RWXD)
Modify (M)	Change (RWXD) (RWXD)
File Scan (F)	List (RX) (not specified)
Access Control (A)	Change Permissions (P)

The effective rights for a file are translated to the NTFS permissions shown in Table 25.2.

Table 25.2. File access rights.

NetWare File Rights	NTFS File Permissions
Supervisory (S)	Full Control (All)
Read (R)	Read (RX)
Write (W)	Change (RWXD)
Erase (E)	Change (RWXD)
Modify (M)	Change (RWXD)
Access Control (A)	Change Permissions (P)

NOTE

The Create (C) and File Scan (F) rights are ignored when files are transferred.

NetWare file attributes are translated to the NTFS file attributes shown in Table 25.3.

Table 25.3. File attributes.

NetWare File Attributes	NTFS File Attributes
Read Only (Ro)	Read Only (R)
Delete Inhibit (D)	Read Only (R)

NetWare File Attributes	NTFS File Attributes
Rename Inhibit (R)	Read Only (R)
Archive Needed (A)	Archive (A)
System (SY)	System (S)
Hidden (H)	Hidden (H)
Read Write (Rw)	None, because files without the R attribute can be read and written to

NOTE

The following NetWare file attributes are not supported by NTFS and are therefore ignored:

Copy Inhibit (C), Execute Only (X), Indexed (I), Purge (P), Read Audit (Ra), Shareable (SH), Transactional (T), and Write Audit (Wa)

After you have set the options for the first volume, repeat the procedure for all the other volumes from the NetWare server you are migrating.

When all the file and directory options have been completed, click the OK button to return to the Migration Tool for NetWare main dialog.

You can now choose the logging options for your migration. Click the Logging button to display the Logging dialog (see Figure 25.43), which enables you to turn on or off three options.

FIGURE 25.43.

The Logging dialog.

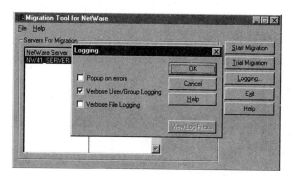

The first option, Popup on errors, is whether you want to have a message displayed whenever an error situation has been encountered. If you are running a trial migration, which simply creates a log and does not actually perform the migration, you might want to turn this option off. The intent is to run a trial migration and then make changes based on the error log.

The second option, Verbose User/Group Logging, gives you the option to have explicit logging of every translation performed on users and groups. If you require a complete record of the migration, turn on this option by checking the box.

The third option, Verbose File Logging, gives you a list of each file and directory that has been transferred from the NetWare volume to the NT Server. Again, if you require a complete log of your migration, turn this on by checking the box.

Regardless, all errors are placed in an error log.

Starting the Migration

You are now ready to perform your migration; however, you have the option of performing a trial migration first. This puts the Migration Tool for NetWare through the motions of an actual migration, using the options you have specified, without actually migrating users, groups, or volumes.

Kick off the trial migration by clicking the Trial Migration button. As shown in Figure 25.44, the migration is performed just as if it were the real migration. Users, files, and directories are examined. If any contentions are found, the Migration Tool reacts however the options have been configured. Figure 25.45 shows one such error, where a duplicate user name has been encountered. Here you are given the choice to manually give that user a new name (and then click the OK button to continue), abort the entire procedure, or cancel the migration of this particular user.

FIGURE 25.44.

A trial migration in the works.

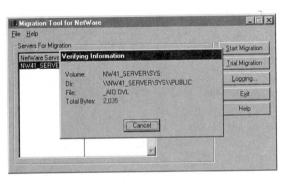

When the trial migration is complete, you are notified in exactly the same way you would be if this were the real migration. A summary of the migration gives you the vital statistics. (See Figure 25.46.) You can also choose to view the three log files in an application called LogView. (See Figure 25.47.)

FIGURE 25.45.

*An error transferring
user name.*

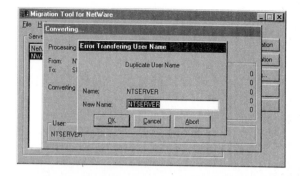

FIGURE 25.46.

*Trial migration has
completed.*

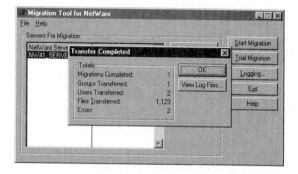

FIGURE 25.47.

*The LogView
application.*

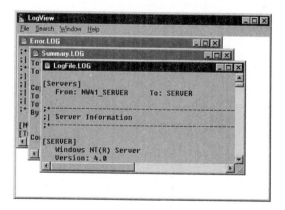

The Logfile.LOG file (see Figure 25.48) is where you would find detailed information about the actual conversions that have occurred. If you have chosen Verbose File Logging, this is where you will find it.

The Summary.LOG file (see Figure 25.49) gives you a brief account of what translations have been completed.

FIGURE 25.48.

The Logfile.LOG *file.*

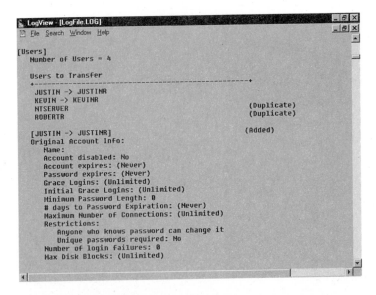

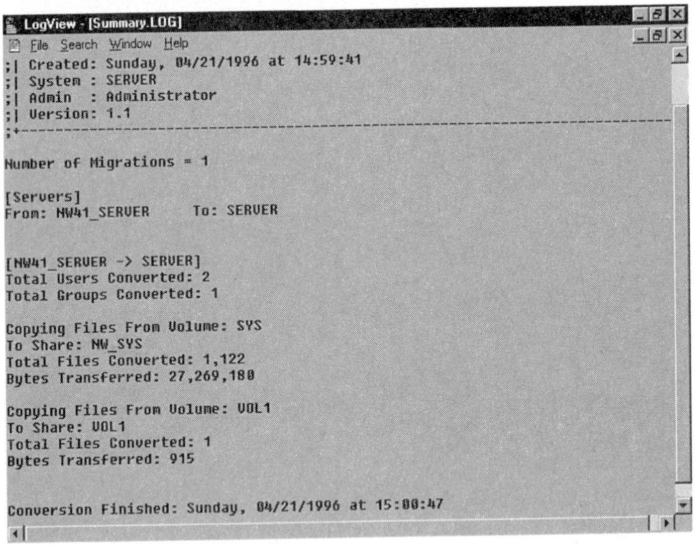

FIGURE 25.49.

The Summary.LOG *file.*

The Error.LOG file (see Figure 25.50) shows you what went wrong in the translation process.

Before you proceed with the actual migration, you should review these logs and make sure that what you are about to do is the right thing. The migration cannot be reversed—at least, not automatically.

After you have made changes to your mapping file or changed some of the logging options, you might feel comfortable with proceeding with the real migration. When you are ready, click the Start Migration button, and you will see exactly what you saw when you tried the trial migration. This time though, it's for real.

Figure 25.50.

The Error.LOG *file.*

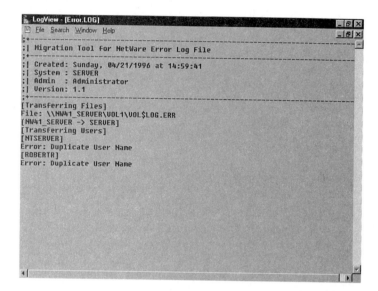

As you can see in Figure 25.51, the NetWare user JUSTIN has been transferred to the NT domain as JUSTINR. As you might recall, this transformation was dictated by the mapping file NW2NT.MAP. In the group listing, you can see the NTGATEWAY group that had been set up on the NetWare server to enable Gateway Service for NetWare to function. Figure 25.52 shows the NetWare-to-NT-translated NTGATEWAY group, which has retained its only member: NTSERVER.

Figure 25.51.

User administrator for domains with a newly migrated NetWare user.

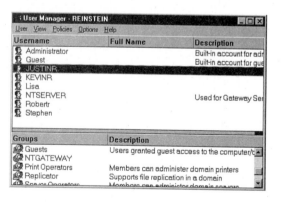

FIGURE 25.52.

A NetWare group after migration to NT.

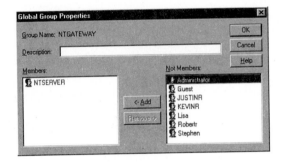

In Figure 25.53 you can see the new directory from the NT Server's E drive called `Old NetWare SYS Volume`. This translation was also configured through the use of the `NW2NT.MAP` mapping file.

FIGURE 25.53.

A NetWare SYS volume after migration to NT.

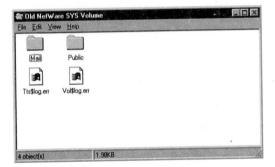

A mapping file is a very powerful way to have a NetWare migration run without errors and have the result look exactly as you would want. When you migrate multiple NetWare servers over to one NT domain, you will probably run into a lot of naming conflicts. Unless you are dealing with hundreds or thousands of users, which might make editing a mapping file too time-consuming, you can resolve most conflicts without having to deal with user intervention during the actual migration process.

File And Print Services For NetWare

Microsoft produces a tool that can be very helpful for easing NetWare to NT migrations: File And Print Services For NetWare. This exceptional product is sold separate from the Microsoft Windows NT 4 Server product.

The basic premise of File And Print Services For NetWare is allowing an NT Server appear to the network as a NetWare 3.x server. This is achieved by adding a service to an NT Server that emulates a NetWare bindery.

Two major uses for this product come to mind.

One is allowing an NT Server to coexist on a predominantly NetWare network, giving workstations running NetWare client software access to NT resources without having to run a Microsoft networking client.

Another reason would be to ease a migration from NetWare to NT, by making the NT Server emulate an existing NetWare server, making a switch from NetWare to NT transparent to the end user.

I will discuss scenarios for both of these reasons, but first I will tell you about installing the service.

Installing File And Print Services For NetWare

Installing File And Print Services For NetWare is the same as adding any other network service to Windows NT Server. Open the network applet in the Control Panel, and click once on the Services tab. Click on the Add button in the Services dialog. A list of installable services is shown in the resulting dialog; however, since File And Print Services For NetWare is not supplied with the Microsoft Windows NT Server product, click on the Have Disk button. You will be prompted for the location of File And Print Services For NetWare installation files. Enter the proper path and click on the OK button.

You now have the option to install the File And Print Services For NetWare service and administrative tools, or only the administrative tools. I chose to install the File And Print Services For NetWare service and administrative tools. You would install only the administrative tools if you already have this service running on another server in the same domain, and wish to add the File And Print Services For NetWare extensions to User Manager and Server Manager.

After files are copied, the installation dialog for File And Print Services For NetWare is displayed. It is here that you can give your pseudo-NetWare server a name, and you need to define a path for your SYS volume. The SYS volume on a File And Print Services For NetWare server will resemble the SYS volume on an actual NetWare 3.x server.

> **NOTE**
>
> If you do not create your SYS volume on an NTFS partition, you will be given a message. In order for you to be able to place permissions on the SYS volume in the same manner that you would on an actual NetWare server, the NTFS file attributes are absolutely necessary. If you do create the SYS volume on a FAT partition, you will be limited to only assigning Read or Read/Write permissions.

The directory structure for the SYS volume as the directory SYSVOL, contains the LOGIN, SYSTEM, MAIL, and PUBLIC directories that NetWare administrators are used to seeing on the SYS volume. The commands in the PUBLIC directory are Microsoft versions of the familiar NetWare commands. These commands are 100 percent compatible with their NetWare counterparts.

When the File And Print Services For NetWare service is installed, a SUPERVISOR account is created for the NT domain. This account is automatically added to the Administrators group. In this configuration dialog, you define the password for the SUPERVISOR user account. You can also fine-tune the service by choosing the amount of resources to be used to handle this service.

After you have finished the installation for File And Print Services For NetWare you are prompted to enter a password for the service account that will be created and used for File And Print Services For NetWare. Enter the password twice, and click on the OK button to finalize the installation of File And Print Services For NetWare. The newly installed service will now appear in the list of installed services. Click the Close button, and you will be prompted to restart the NT Server. Click on the Yes button, and your server will shut down and restart. When the server reboots, the File And Print Services For NetWare service will be active.

You can test the service by running the NetWare SLIST command from any NetWare client workstation. The Windows NT Server will appear on the list of NetWare servers, using the server name that you had specified in the installation dialog.

File And Print Services For NetWare Extensions

Both User Manager and Server Manager will have new menu items that can help you administrate the NetWare-compatible facilities that File And Print Services For NetWare has given your NT Server. These extensions allow you to perform tasks that are available through User Manager and Server Manager, and these extensions allow you to treat NetWare-compatible users as if they are logging into a separate NetWare server. I will go into detail on this in the next section, "Configuring File And Print Services For NetWare."

Configuring File And Print Services For NetWare

A new icon will appear in the Windows NT Control Panel. Double-click the File And Print Services For NetWare icon to bring up the File And Print Services For NetWare applet. This applet allows you to change the server name, define the server as an "open system," and define whether or not you want clients who have not specified a preferred server in their NET.CFG file to be allowed to log in to the pseudo-NetWare server. You can also gain access to the User Manager and Server Manager extensions that are also available through those administrative tools.

The User Manager extensions adds a checkbox that allows you to specify if a user account will maintain a NetWare-compatible logon. If this box is checked, you have access to the NW Compat button. Clicking on the NW Compat button brings up the NetWare Compatible Properties dialog. Here you can set attributes for a user account that are not available for native NT clients, but are found on genuine NetWare administration tools. This includes limiting the number of concurrent connections for a user, and editing a logon script. The logon script for a NetWare-compatible user uses the same syntax that is used on NetWare servers for logon scripts.

The Server Manager extensions give you a new menu item. An FPNW drop-down menu gives you the ability to access the FPNW Control Panel applet, manage NetWare-compatible volumes, and define NetWare-compatible print servers. You can also send NetWare-compatible messages to NetWare-compatible users.

When I mention NetWare-compatible, I mean that these are resources for which the NetWare-compatible commands can be used on, such as CAPTURE and MAP. These are also the commands that can be used to create NetWare-compatible logon scripts.

Creating and Maintaining NetWare-Compatible Volumes

Using the FPNW menu in Server Manager, you can create, delete, or alter NetWare compatible volumes that you create using File And Print Services For NetWare. The Volumes dialog appears after selecting Shared Volumes from the FPNW menu. The volume that is listed is the SYS volume that was created when installing File And Print Services For NetWare. To create an additional volume, click on the Add button. The Create Volume dialog prompts you for a volume name and an existing directory to use for the new volume. Permissions and user connection limits can also be configured here. The following section in this chapter, "Migrating from NetWare to NT Using File And Print Services For NetWare," will show you how to use this dialog for a smooth NetWare to NT migration.

Click the OK button to complete the creation of the new volume, and the resulting list of volumes will show both the original and the new volume.

Migrating from NetWare to NT Using File And Print Services for NetWare

One of the greatest benefits of using File And Print Services For NetWare can be realized when you are planning a NetWare to NT migration.

If you are in a NetWare environment, the workstations accessing NetWare are probably running different versions of the NetWare client, such as NETX and VLM, and running on different platforms, such as DOS, DOS/Windows, OS/2, Windows 95, and Windows NT. These workstations probably are running logon scripts that are handling their connections to printers and volumes. Changing from a NetWare environment to a native NT client workstation involves a lot of work and planning, especially when you are dealing with dozens, hundreds, or even thousands of client workstations.

The Migration Tool for NetWare does a beautiful job in assisting with this process, but it is possible to perform a phased migration, and that is where File And Print Services For NetWare comes in very handy.

Let's use a simple example. A NetWare server named NW_SERVER has two volumes, SYS and VOL1. VOL1 contains a directory called APPS that contains numerous applications, each in their own subdirectory. A system login script maps drives for users based on their group memberships.

Under normal circumstances, a NetWare to NT migration would entail using the Migration Tools for NetWare to copy user accounts, groups, and volumes. Then an NT logon script could be created that emulated the commands used in the NetWare system logon script. And finally, each workstation would require its NetWare client software changed over to a Microsoft networking client. Depending on the number of users, this could take hours, days, or months. It would also probably require leaving the NetWare server online while users are slowly migrated over to the NT environment.

Now picture this. Use the Migration Tool for NetWare to copy user accounts, group, and volume. Install File And Print Services For NetWare giving the pseudo-NetWare the name NW_SERVER. Now a login appears specifying that the preferred server would give the user the same login, but this time, it would be to the NT Server. Next is creating a directory on the NT Server, and placing the APPS directory from the NetWare server into this directory on the NT Server. Then create a volume named VOL1 using this directory as the path. The users would then still find their applications within the APPS directory on VOL1; only this time it's not on the NetWare server, but on the NT Server. All you have to do now is flag all of the users as NetWare compatible, and assign them their old system login script (after copying it over, of course). Follow the same logic for creating print queues with the same name as the original NetWare queues. Now you are free to bring down the NetWare server and have all of your users function the same as they had, without them even knowing that any type of change had occurred.

This would then give you time to slowly bring workstations over to Microsoft networking, by installing their new client software, creating an NT logon script or creating persistent connections to the network shares they require, and removing their User Manager attribute of being NetWare compatible.

Using File And Print Services For NetWare to Integrate NT into a NetWare Environment

Sometimes a NetWare shop will require the use of an NT Server because of one application that runs only on NT Server. Most of the NT Servers my company sells into NetWare environments are due to programs that need Microsoft SQL Server as their database.

Since an NT Server has a lot of power to offer and a company may not want to upgrade the hardware it is using for its NetWare servers, an ideal idea is to add new services to the NT Server.

For instance, we have had customers that decided to attach CD-ROM drives to an NT Server because they didn't want to invest in a dedicated CD server, or didn't want to attach any peripherals directly to their NetWare servers. File And Print Services For NetWare is the perfect solution for allowing current NetWare users access resources on an NT Server without having to change their client software. By adding users to the NT Server and flagging them as NetWare-compatible, they can map a drive, using their NetWare tools, to one of the CD-ROMs attached to the NT Server.

File And Print Services For NetWare creates resources that are so NetWare-compatible, they can even be seen as part of a Novell NetWare NDS tree. The NWADMIN program is used to administer a NetWare 4.x environment. I add an NT Server that is running File And Print Services For NetWare to the NDS tree. I am adding a NetWare-compatible volume to this same NDS tree.

A printer that is attached directly to an NT Server's parallel port can also be defined as a NetWare-compatible print queue and accessed by any NetWare client workstation.

Of course, anyone using these services on the NT Server must be licensed as an NT client, but the cost for this is minimal, and the benefits are great.

Summary

As you have just seen, Microsoft Windows NT Server makes it easy to integrate with NetWare, or even to migrate from NetWare.

The tools that are available, both with NT Server and as a separate product, can make your NetWare and NT integration easier than you probably thought.

Both Microsoft and Novell have been working to allow these two network operating systems to interact, and it seems that the ties are getting closer and closer.

Don't forget that migrating from one environment to the other requires a lot of planning. But if you get familiar with the tools I've just written about, you should be able to create a plan that will run very smoothly.

Protecting Windows NT Server

Protecting Your Server

by Jason Garms

IN THIS CHAPTER

CHAPTER 26

Windows NT Server is designed to be used as the cornerstone of enterprise-level networks. Other chapters have already discussed much of the functionality of NT that enables it to play this role so well. However, as strong as NT is, it is only as reliable as the hardware it runs on. Although the quality and reliability of today's PC hardware have greatly improved from 10 years ago, and will continue to improve in the future, the chance of something going wrong is always present.

Even if you are not using your system for mission-critical applications, it is important that your system be reliable, or the users will lose faith—and you might even lose your job. Never lose sight of the fact that most of the work you do is in support of the users. The network exists for the users, not for the sake of its own existence.

To help ensure that your system can be as reliable as possible, Windows NT includes a number of features that, when used properly, can help increase reliability and guarantee the integrity of your system. These features include the following:

- Fault-tolerant hard disk driver
- Built-in backup support
- Integrated UPS support

Fault-Tolerant Disk Systems

The technology used for manufacturing computer hard disks has developed rapidly over the past few years. Today, most hard drives have a *mean-time between failure* (MTBF) of 180,000 hours, or more. The MTBF rating is meant to give you a statistical reference as to the likelihood that your hard drive will encounter an error that could cause data loss. Sometimes people see the 180,000 hours, do the math and come up with 28.3 years, which seems pretty good. If your hard drive only crashed once every 28.3 years, you'd probably be pretty happy. However, this is only a statistic, and it's based on the drive running under fairly good conditions. If you have poor line power quality at your site, or your computer's power supply feeds the internal components with less-than-clean power, this expected lifetime drops dramatically.

A fault-tolerant disk system is intended to provide mechanisms for reducing the likelihood of data loss in the event of a failure. Windows NT uses three different techniques for providing fault tolerance for the hard drive subsystems. These are Redundant Array of Inexpensive Disks (RAID), NTFS recoverability, and sector sparing. Each of these features is described in this chapter, both in terms of how they are implemented in Windows NT, as well as how you can take advantage of them.

Understanding RAID (Redundant Array of Inexpensive Disks)

RAID is a technology that has been around for a few years now and is traditionally implemented in hardware. The concept behind RAID is rather simple. Disk drives are typically one of the areas in high-performance computers that have the most bottlenecks. They just can't read data from the drive fast enough. This is one of the problems RAID was designed to help resolve. The idea is that by using multiple disks and spreading the data across them all in parallel, you can get a performance increase. In addition to providing increased performance, RAID has provisions for providing data redundancy, either through mirroring or the use of parity information.

TIP

RAID is another one of those great acronyms that people sometimes pronounce in unexpected ways. The most common method, and in my book the correct one, is like the roach spray, *RAID*, or to *raid* the refrigerator. However, you might run into the occasional pronunciation of "rad," as in *rad*ical. If you choose to use this pronunciation, don't be surprised when people keep saying "hunh?"

The key to RAID is a technique called striping. When the system tries to write a block of information to the array, the array controller (in this case, NT) breaks the information into smaller chucks of a predetermined size and writes these chunks in parallel across all drives in the array.

There are six basic levels of RAID, although other levels have been defined or suggested:

- **RAID 0: Striping:** Some people do not consider this to be a true RAID level, because it does not provide any redundancy. This means that if a drive in a RAID 0 array goes bad, you lose the entire array.

  RAID 0 is useful for providing improved speed because the data is striped across all disks in the array. There is no need to calculate a checksum byte, so striping can offer improved performance over methods that use parity. Also, because you don't need a place to store the checksum byte, striping without parity requires less disk space—for each byte of physical data, you get one byte of logical data.

- **RAID 1: Mirroring and Duplexing:** Mirroring is accomplished by writing all data onto two separate physical disks, providing 100 percent redundancy. If information on one disk is corrupted, it can be automatically rebuilt using data on the mirrored partition. Additionally, mirroring can improve performance because the first available disk can be used to service a read request. Duplexing is where each device of the array is put on its own controller. As far as the RAID standards go, duplexing and mirroring are the same, although duplexing offers greater redundancy and reliability. RAID 1 provides robust redundancy, but its main disadvantage is that it needs twice the number of drives.

- **RAID 2:** RAID 2 is a proprietary architecture that has not been very successful. It requires numerous synchronized drives with multiple parity drives. It stripes data bit by bit across these drives in parallel and records parity information to the dedicated parity drives for complete redundancy without needing twice the number of drives, as required by RAID 1. It is best suited for applications that transfer large contiguous amounts of data such as those created by graphics and imaging packages. This method does not provide good performance with small files. Windows NT does not offer a RAID 2 implementation in software.

- **RAID 3:** This method is similar to RAID 2 but requires only one parity disk. Additionally, data is striped byte by byte, not bit by bit, across the array. Having only a single parity disk can create bottlenecks for writing because the parity information must be written before the next write can take place. Again, this method is most useful for applications that make large block transfers but is less effective with other applications, such as many databases that use small transactions. Windows NT does not offer a RAID 3 implementation in software.

- **RAID 4:** RAID 4 is set up similar to RAID 3 with only a single parity drive, but the drives are not synchronized, and the data is striped block by block, not byte by byte. This improves the performance for small reads but still does not address the bottleneck caused by the fact that write updates often have to wait to access the parity drive.

- **RAID 5: Striping with Parity:** RAID 5 solves the problem of accessing the parity drive. This is done by spreading the parity information equally across all the drives. If any drive in the array fails, missing information can be reconstructed from the remaining information and the parity information for that block. This provides the same level of redundancy as RAID 1 without incurring the cost penalty caused by needing 100 percent redundancy.

Windows NT includes software support for RAID levels 0, 1, and 5, which are the most common RAID implementations. Because RAID 0 does not provide any level of redundancy, it is not dealt with in detail in this chapter. For more information on disk striping, please refer to Chapter 5, "Windows NT File Systems Management."

One of the major advantages of RAID on Windows NT Server is that it does not lock you into proprietary hardware interfaces, which can be a problem with most hardware solutions.

If you want to find out more about the origins of RAID, a good starting place is *A Case for Redundant Arrays of Inexpensive Disks, or RAID*, published by A. Patterson, Garth Gibson, and Randy Katz, University of California at Berkeley, December 1987.

Fault-Tolerant Disk Sets in Windows NT

Windows NT Server includes a driver called FTDISK.SYS that provides fault-tolerant capabilities for NT Server. This driver actually performs many functions, but the primary purpose is to provide support for sector sparing and for RAID levels 1 and 5, also known as disk mirroring and disk striping, respectively. This driver is included only in Windows NT Server, and therefore these fault-tolerant options are not supported on NT Workstation.

NT Server can use three primary methods to ensure the integrity of your disk data:

- NTFS recoverability
- Sector sparing
- RAID levels 1 and 5

NTFS Recoverability

With traditional file systems such as FAT under DOS—and even HPFS on OS/2—the primary concern was with how fast the file systems performed, not necessarily with how reliable they were.

NTFS was built to provide the kind of data integrity assurances you need from an enterprise-level client/server system. When using FAT under DOS and Windows, if the system crashes, you end up with file system corruption. This corruption can lead to an entirely unusable system.

To prevent this problem, NTFS was created as a journal-based file system that records all disk transaction to a log before beginning. It includes in the log information necessary to roll back the transaction if needed. When the transaction is complete, NT marks it in the log. With NTFS, if the system crashes, all files that were currently being accessed are rolled back. This is done by consulting the log to find out what was going on and determine what actions were completed and what were not. The transactions that were not completed are rolled back to their previous state using information contained in the log. This transaction-based method of operating ensures that no matter what, the file system remains intact.

> **CAUTION**
>
> NTFS does not guarantee the protection of user data that was being updated during a system crash. It guarantees only the stability of the file system. This means that if the system crashed while a user was updating a database file, the data in that file might be corrupted as far as the database is concerned; however, the file system itself is intact. Sometimes this might not seem that important to some people, but the integrity of the file system is of paramount importance. If the file system itself becomes corrupt, you could lose *all* the data on a drive.

Sector Sparing

Sector sparing is the capability of a system to dynamically remap bad sectors as they are discovered during read or write operations. In Windows NT, sector sparing can occur at two different levels, either in the file system or with the fault tolerant driver, FTDISK.SYS.

Sector sparing in NTFS is discussed in greater detail in Chapter 5. Basically, if you are not using a fault-tolerant configuration and NTFS receives either a read or a write failure error, it marks the cluster as bad and remaps it to a good cluster—essentially destroying the information, but preserving the integrity of the file system. If the error is on a SCSI hard drive, NTFS tells the SCSI drive to remap the sector, and NTFS does not need to make any changes to the file system. If you are using an IDE, ESDI, or other drive that does not support cluster remapping, NTFS maps the cluster as bad at the file system level and reassigns it to a good, free cluster.

If you are using the fault-tolerant disk driver, FTDISK.SYS, NT can recover the data. Exactly how the remapping of the bad sector is done depends on your server's configuration.

If you are using a SCSI drive and it is part of a fault-tolerant array, FTDISK can recover the data. It doesn't matter which of the three NT files systems you use: FAT, HPFS, or NTFS. NT recovers the data either by using the mirrored copy (in RAID 1) or by reconstructing it from the other strips and parity information (RAID 5). FTDISK tells the SCSI drive to remap the bad sector, and FTDISK writes the salvaged information to the newly remapped sector. In this instance, the file system remains completely unaware of the problem.

If you are not using a SCSI drive, you must use NTFS to support sector sparing. Currently NT does not support file-system-level sector sparing on HPFS or FAT.

> **WARNING**
>
> If you are using a non-SCSI drive with FAT or HPFS and the disk encounters a bad sector, you will have file system corruption. Windows NT does not ship with any utilities that can help correct this problem.

If you are using a non-SCSI drive with NTFS and the system experiences a read or write failure, one of two things will happen:

- If the system is using the fault-tolerant disk driver, FTDISK reconstructs the information from the other drives in the array, notifies NTFS that the cluster is bad, and NTFS remaps the cluster on a file system level. FTDISK then puts the recovered data into the remapped sector.

- If the failed volume is not part of a fault-tolerant array, NTFS is notified of the error, and NTFS remaps the sector at a file system level. However, you will experience data loss, although the integrity of the file system is maintained.

> **TIP**
>
> If you want to provide maximum protection for data on your system, you should use only SCSI subsystems formatted with NTFS and configured in either a RAID 1 or RAID 5 configuration.

RAID in Windows NT Server

As discussed earlier, the FTDISK.SYS driver in Windows NT Server is used to support RAID levels 0, 1, and 5, as well as volume sets. Although RAID 0 and volume sets are not fault-tolerant systems, they still use NT's FTDISK.SYS driver. For more information on disk striping (RAID 0) and volume sets, please refer to Chapter 5.

One of the powerful features of RAID support in Windows NT Server is the capability to set up mirrors and stripes on a partition-by-partition basis, unlike hardware RAID solutions, where the minimum granularity is on the drive level, not the partition level.

> **NOTE**
>
> You can use the Performance Monitor to collect performance statistics for RAID subsystems in one of two ways. By default, if you enable disk performance monitoring, using the `diskperf -Y` option, the statistics that will be returned reflect the entire RAID subsystem. If you want statistics on individual drives in the RAID subsystem, you must use the `diskperf -YE` option to enable performance measuring for the physical drives.

Disk Mirroring and Duplexing

Windows NT Server enables you to create mirrors of any partition, including the boot and system partitions. Additionally, mirroring works with any of NT's three supported file systems: FAT, HPFS, and NTFS. Mirroring works by creating a complete copy of the primary partition onto a mirror partition. You can use disk mirroring to mirror any of NT's supported hard drives, including SCSI and IDE-based systems.

In addition to gaining the benefit of complete data redundancy, disk mirroring can provide increased performance for your system. The FTDISK.SYS driver dispatches reads to both halves of the mirror, and the first response is used. A scenario where this would provide a performance boost is when the primary partition is busy performing a write, and a read request comes in. In this case the latent drive can respond faster, thus improving performance.

> **NOTE**
>
> Although in theory you could have more than two disks in a RAID 1 system, you would not realize any significant improvement in speed or reliability. For this reason, disk mirror sets are typically limited to two drives, as they are in NT Server.

Because NT Server's mirroring is done on the partition level, the two drives in a mirror do not have to be the same geometry. Nor do the partitions have to appear in the same part of each drive. For example, the primary partition might be the first 250MB of a 1GB drive, but the shadow partition could be the last 250MB of a 2GB drive. The FTDISK.SYS takes care of all the details to make sure this works fine.

> **NOTE**
>
> If you create a mirror set using two disks of different makes and models, the size of the mirror partition might differ from the primary partition by 1MB. This is due to NT compensating for the differences in drive geometry.

> **NOTE**
>
> If one of the partitions of a mirror fails, the FTDISK.SYS issues an alert, but the system appears to continue functioning normally. When one member of a mirror dies, even if it is the primary partition, there should be no noticeable performance degradation.

Of course, one of the primary advantages of being able to use drives of different makes and models is that it makes it much easier to replace failed drives. In some proprietary hardware-based RAID solutions, the disk geometry needs to be identical, so failure in a partition could pose a problem. NT's software-based RAID solution helps solve this problem.

In addition to disk mirroring, Windows NT Server also supports *disk duplexing*. Disk duplexing works by placing the two drives of the mirror on different controllers. The can potentially provide additional drive performance by dispatching commands simultaneously to both controllers.

Disk Striping with Parity

Disk striping with parity in NT Server requires at least three disks and can support up to 32 disks. The stripes do not need to be on drives of identical geometry, but each partition must be exactly the same size.

> **WARNING**
>
> Although you can mirror NT Server's boot and system partitions, they cannot be members of striped disk sets—with or without parity.

Striping with parity gives you two basic features:

- It can provide increased performance by splitting disk I/O among the multiple drives in the set. The more drives, the greater the potential improvement in reads.

- It provides complete redundancy for all data without the storage overhead of mirroring. The actual storage overhead depends on the number of drives in the array. In a three-drive array, the overhead is one-third. In a four-drive array, the overhead is one-fourth. This continues up to a 32-drive array, where the storage overhead is one-thirty-second.

Although disk striping with parity can be useful, it does have its drawbacks. The major problem in some systems could be the overhead associated with calculating the parity information for writes. The more disks you have in the array, the more calculations are necessary to perform the XOR function used to calculate the parity. Although this overhead is still pretty small, your processor could become a limiting factor in the performance of the system—especially if it is already overburdened and if there are a large number of disks in the mirror.

An additional performance problem with disk striping with parity is that it is not very efficient for writing small blocks of data. If you primarily need a large number of small transactions, you might be better off using disk mirroring. However, disk striping with parity performs much better for large-block transfers, such as large graphics and audio files.

If one of the partitions in a striped set with parity fails, your system's performance is severely affected. Although everything continues working, FTDISK.SYS must use the information in the remaining stripes to regenerate the missing data on-the-fly. This means that reads from a striped set with parity where one of the partition has failed can take up to three times as long as normal.

Setting Up Mirroring and Striping with Parity on Windows NT

The Disk Administrator is used to set up both mirrored and striped with parity disk sets on Windows NT Server.

Creating a Mirror Set

CAUTION

When you create a mirrored partition, NT has to reboot before the configuration can take effect.

NOTE

To create a disk mirror, you must be logged on to the server as a user with administrative permissions.

Follow these steps to set up a disk mirror in Windows NT:

1. Start Disk Administrator (WINDISK.EXE) from the Administrative Tools program group.

2. If you have never used Disk Administrator, or if you have added a new drive since the last time you ran it, you are warned that it needs to write an identification tag to the hard drives. Choose OK.

   The Disk Administrator window will appear, as shown in Figure 26.1.

FIGURE 26.1.

The Disk Administrator shows you the allocation of hard drives and CD-ROM drives in your system.

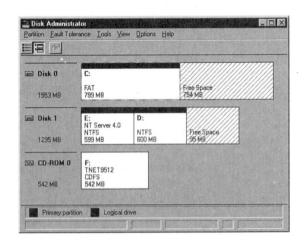

3. Click the existing partition that you want to create a mirror of.

   In our example, we are going to create a mirror for the 599MB system partition (drive E) located on disk 1.

4. Holding down the Ctrl key, click an area of free space on a different drive. The area of free space must be at least as large as the partition you want to mirror.

In our example we are going to click on the 754MB free space at the end of disk 0 because this is where we want the mirror created.

5. From the Fault Tolerance menu, choose Establish Mirror.

6. NT pops up a window asking you to confirm that you want to create the mirror. Read it, then click OK.

7. The drives should now have the same drive letter, E, and they should both have a purple border. The purple border is NT Disk Administrator's default way of indicating that the partition is a member of a mirrored set.

Figure 26.2 shows the 599MB system partition on disk 1 mirrored on disk 0.

FIGURE 26.2.

Disk Administrator is used to create a mirror of the 599MB system partition from drive 1 to drive 0.

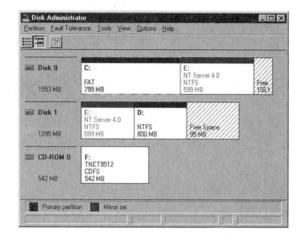

8. Exit Disk Administrator.

9. Disk Adminsitrator will now warn you that NT will have to restart after making the changes. Click Yes to continue.

WARNING

When you make these changes, NT will *require* the system to restart when you exit Disk Administrator, as shown in Figure 26.3. This is not like other operations where you are given the option of restarting or not.

10. Disk Administrator will display one more message asking you to confirm the disk update. Click OK.

11. Click OK to continue. NT will close all current applications and reboot the system.

For more information on the Disk Administrator, please refer to Chapter 5.

FIGURE 26.3.

*Disk Administrator
will force the system to
restart when you create
a mirror set.*

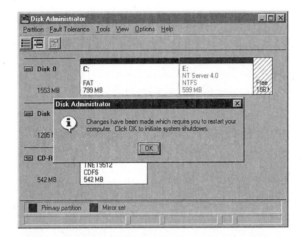

TIP

If you are creating a mirror of the system partition, then you should also create a fault-tolerant boot floppy, as described later in this chapter.

When you restart the computer, NT will begin to build the mirror, so you should see a flurry of disk activity. If you go back into Disk Administrator while the mirror is being created and click on any part of the mirrored volume, the status at the bottom of the screen will display INITIALIZING. Once the mirroring process is completed, the status should display HEALTHY.

WARNING

Update your emergency repair disk by running RDISK.EXE. For more information about using RDISK.EXE, please refer to Chapter 5. If you don't update the emergency repair disk and you need to restore your system from backups, you will lose your mirror!

Creating a Fault-Tolerant Boot Floppy

If you have created a mirror set for your system partition, you also need to create a fault-tolerant boot floppy. The purpose of the boot floppy is to enable the system to boot even if the drive that fails is the primary partition of the mirrored boot drive. Normally, the system begins to boot from the first primary partition installed by the BIOS. The NT bootstrap then begins loading NT from the ARC (Advanced RISC Computer) partition specified in the BOOT.INI file. The problem is that when the primary boot partition has failed, the partition referenced in the BOOT.INI file is invalid.

> **NOTE**
>
> Although the ARC convention for identifying system disk partitions was originally developed for RISC systems, Microsoft has adopted this naming scheme for Intel-based Windows NT systems as well.

The best method to solve this problem and allow your system to boot from the mirror of the system partition is to create a floppy disk with the NT bootstrap code that hands off boot control to a different ARC resource—the mirror copy.

To create a fault-tolerant boot floppy, use the following procedure:

1. Format a floppy disk on your NT system. This can be done by typing `format a:` at the command line, or right-clicking on the floppy drive icon in My Computer and choosing Format.

> **NOTE**
>
> You must use NT to format this disk because the bootstrap code created by formatting it with DOS is unable to load the NTLDR.

2. Now, you need to copy three files from your NT boot partition (usually the c: drive) to the floppy disk. These three files are hidden by default, so depending how you have your Explorer options configured, you might not see them. The easiest method to copy them is to use the `XCOPY /H` command from a command prompt. Open a command prompt and enter the following three commands:

```
XCOPY /H C:\NTLDR A:\
XCOPY /H C:\NTDETECT.COM A:\
XCOPY /H C:\BOOT.INI A:\
```

> **NOTE**
>
> If you have a system that boots from a SCSI controller that does not have its BIOS enabled you will also need to copy the `NTBOOTDD.SYS` file to your floppy disk. If this file does not exist on your hard disk, then you don't need it on the boot floppy.

3. Use the command `attrib -s -r -h a:\boot.ini` to make the `BOOT.INI` file on the floppy editable.

4. Edit the `BOOT.INI` on the floppy drive to point to the mirror partition instead of the primary partition. To do this, you must know the ARC name of the mirror partition. For example, if you have one SCSI adapter in your system and two hard drives, the first hard drive (SCSI ID=0) contains a single partition, which is the system partition.

The second hard drive (SCSI ID=1) contains only a mirror of the first hard drive. If you installed Windows NT Server into a directory called \WINNT, your BOOT.INI for booting to the mirrored partition would look like this:

```
[boot loader]
timeout=30
default=scsi(0)disk(1)rdisk(0)partition(1)\WINNT
[operating systems]
scsi(0)disk(1)rdisk(0)partition(1)\WINNT="Windows NT Server Version 4.0"
```

TECHNICAL NOTE

It is important to understand how to create the ARC naming path necessary for correctly identifying the proper partition. An ARC path takes the following form:

`type(x)disk(y)rdisk(z)partition(a)path`

type   Identifies the disk controller. If the disk controller is SCSI, the type is scsi. Other disk controllers, such as IDE and ESDI, are referred to as type multi. On some SCSI systems, you also use multi.

x   The number of the adapter in the order it is loaded by Windows NT. For computers with only a single adapter, x is always 0. Note that all buses of a multi-bus adapter are referred to with the same value for x. For example an Adpatec 2742AT controller has two SCSI buses. They are both referred to with the same x value, since they are part of the same controller card.

y   Calculated by multiplying the bus number (on multi-bus adapters) by 32 and adding the target ID of the drive. For controllers of type multi, y is always 0.

z   The device's logical unit number (LUN). For controllers of type multi, z is 0 for the master drive and 1 for the slave drive. For SCSI systems, this is always 0.

a   The number of the partition on the disk. To figure out the partition number you want, remember this: MS-DOS extended partitions (type 5) are not counted, nor are unused partitions (type 0). Starting with 1, count the primary partitions first, then the logical drives. If there is only one partition on the drive, this value is always 1.

path   The directory where you installed Windows NT Server, such as \WINNT, \WINDOWS, \WINNT40, or \WINNT35.

5. Write-protect the floppy disk to ensure that it is not accidentally modified or infected by a virus.

You should now test the floppy disk to make sure it does what you expect it to. Reboot the system and allow it to boot from the floppy disk.

WARNING

Remember that the only way for NT to catch a boot-sector virus is to start the system from a floppy disk. A boot-sector virus can totally destroy your installation of NT. For this reason, I highly encourage you to check the floppy disk for viruses before booting from it. After all, you are trying to protect your system from problems, not create new ones!

One of three things should happen:

- If the boot disk was created properly, the system should begin booting and you should get a blue screen with a STOP message, PROCESS1_INITIALIZATION_FAILED, or similar message. Believe it or not, this is a good thing.

  What you see here is the NT bootstrap handed off correctly to the mirrored drive and NT coming to life. However, at a certain point during the boot process, NT realizes that it is running from the mirror partition of a mirror set. At this point, NT looks to see if the primary partition of the mirror set is accessible. If the partition is available and appears to be good—as is the case in this little test—NT dies with the blue screen you have just seen. This is done in an attempt to preserve the integrity of the mirror. However, if NT cannot detect the primary partition of the mirror set, it assumes that something is definitely wrong and continues to boot.

  If you want to verify this for yourself, you can try unplugging the drive that contains the primary partition of the mirror and try booting from the floppy.

- If you enter the ARC path incorrectly, you receive the following message:

```
Windows NT could not start because of the following boot configuration
problem: Did not properly generate ARC name for HAL and system paths. Please
check the Windows NT documentation about ARC configuration options and your
hardware reference manuals for additional information. Boot Failed.
```

  To try to solve this problem, you should review the instructions earlier in this chapter for determining the correct ARC path.

- If the correct SCSI driver cannot be found, you receive the following message:

```
Windows NT could not start because of a computer disk hardware configuration
problem. Could not read from selected boot disk. Check boot path and disk
hardware. Please check the Windows NT documentation about hardware configura-
tion and your hardware disk configuration and your hardware reference manuals
for additional information. Boot Failed.
```

  To solve this problem, make sure the correct SCSI driver for your SCSI card is copied to the boot floppy. For additional help, you should contact the SCSI card's manufacturer.

Breaking a Mirror Set

There are two main reasons you might want to break a mirror set. First, you simply don't want the mirror any longer, or want to move the mirror to another drive. Second, one of the drives in the mirror has gone bad. In either case, the procedure for breaking the mirror is essentially identical. However, if you are breaking the mirror because one of the drives has failed, you should also refer to the section later in this chapter on recovering failed mirror sets.

The procedure for breaking a mirror is as follows:

NOTE

In order to create a disk mirror, you must be logged on the server as a user with administrative permissions.

1. Start Disk Administrator (WINDISK.EXE) from the Administrative Tools program group.
2. Click one of the partitions in the mirror set you want to break.
3. From the Fault Tolerance menu, select Break Mirror.
4. You are asked to confirm that you want to break the mirror. Select Yes to confirm.
5. From the Partition menu, select Commit Changes Now.
6. Disk Administrator prompts you to confirm your selection. Choose Yes.
7. The mirrored partition is assigned the next available drive letter.
8. Exit Disk Administrator.

NOTE

If you are breaking a mirror containing the system partition, you must reboot before the mirror can be broken.

When you break a mirror, NT does not delete any data. It simply breaks the mirror into two *identical* volumes. The primary part of the mirror retains the original drive letter, and the other half of the broken mirror gets the next available drive letter. If you want to re-create the mirror, you first need to delete the old mirror partition. You cannot simply rejoin the two broken halves together.

Creating a Striped Set with Parity

If you want to set up your system for disk striping with parity, follow these steps:

WARNING

When you create a striped set with parity, NT has to reboot before the configuration can take effect.

NOTE

In order to create a disk mirror, you must be logged on the server as a user with administrative permissions.

1. Start Disk Administrator (WINDISK.EXE) from the Administrative Tools program group.

2. If you have never used Disk Administrator, or if you have added a new drive since the last time you ran it, you are warned that it needs to write an identification tag to the hard drives. Choose OK.

3. The next step takes a little planning. Each of the stripes in a striped set must be exactly the same size, so the total size of the entire set can be only $n*(m-1)$, where n is the size of the smallest area of free space and m is the number of drives in the array. For example, if you have three drives with 50, 60, and 90MB of free, contiguous disk space, the total size of your set can be only 100MB—50*(3–1). Likewise, if you have six drives with 90, 100, 100, 110, 190, and 300MB of contiguous free space, the maximum size of your array is 450MB—90*(6–1).

4. Holding down the Shift key, click the areas of free space on each drive you will be using for the set.

5. From the Fault Tolerance menu, choose Create Striped Set with Parity.

6. NT asks you how big a disk you want to create. The default is the largest set you can make, as calculated by the formula in step 4. You can choose a smaller number, and the partition size that NT creates from the free space on each disk is $x/(m-1)$, where x is the total size of the set and m is the number of drives in the set. For example if you told NT to create a 400MB set on five drives, it would use a 100MB partition on each drive—400/(5–1).

   Enter the size you want and click OK.

7. The striped set should now appear with the same drive letter and a light blue border. The light blue border indicates that the partitions are members of a striped set with parity.

8. Exit Disk Administrator.

9. You receive a warning reminding you to update your emergency repair disk. Click OK.

10. Reboot the computer.

11. When the computer comes back up, log on again as a user with administrative rights and go back into Disk Administrator.

12. Click any partition in the striped set. All other partitions that are part of the striped set with parity will automatically be selected. Choose Format from the Tools menu. You can format the partition as FAT, HPFS, or NTFS.

13. When the format is complete, exit Disk Administrator.

The striped set with parity volume you just created is now available for use. For more information on the Disk Administrator, please refer to Chapter 5.

> **WARNING**
>
> Update your emergency repair disk by running `RDISK.EXE`. For more information about using `RDISK.EXE`, please refer to Chapter 5. If you don't update the emergency repair disk and you have a problem with your system, you could lose data!

Recovering Failed Sets

If one of the disks in a mirrored set or a striped set with parity fails, `FTDISK.SYS` logs an event to the system log. In both of these cases, the system continues to function as usual, as is the intent with fault-tolerant systems. However, exactly what effect this failed drive has on system performance and how to fix the problem depends on which fault-tolerant method you are using.

Recovering a Failed Mirror Set

When one disk of a mirror fails, you will probably not notice a significant difference. This is yet another reason why you should make sure to periodically review your logs using the Event Viewer.

When one disk fails, `FTDISK.SYS` automatically adjusts itself to compensate for the problem. If the disk that fails is not the primary partition of your boot partition, the danger consists of only a single major problem. If the second drive fails, you will experience data loss. For this reason, you should endeavor to fix the mirror as soon as possible.

However, if the drive that fails is the primary drive of a mirrored set containing the boot partition, you have a potentially more serious problem on your hands. If this happens and you allow your system to reboot, then NT cannot load, because the boot information contained in the BOOT.INI file is pointing to the wrong location.

If you have determined that one of the drives of a mirror has failed, and the drive that failed is not the primary partition of a mirror set containing the system partition, use the following procedure to repair the problem:

1. Using Disk Administrator, break the mirror as described earlier in this chapter.
2. Shut down the system and replace the failed drive.
3. Turn the system back on and use Disk Administrator to create a new mirror on the new drive.
4. Update the emergency repair disk.

If the primary partition of a mirror set containing the system partition has failed, you need to follow this procedure. For ease of understanding, I call the failed primary partition Disk 1 and the mirror Disk 2:

1. Boot the system with your fault-tolerant boot disk. Instructions for creating this disk are provided earlier in this chapter.
2. Use Disk Administrator to break the mirror by clicking Disk 2 and choosing Break Mirror from the Fault Tolerance menu.
3. Exit Disk Administrator, acknowledging any warnings.
4. Shut down the system.
5. Replace the failed hard drive, if necessary. I call this new drive Disk 1.
6. Boot the system again from the fault-tolerant boot floppy.
7. Open Disk Administrator. If you replaced the hard drive, Disk Administrator warns you that this is the first time it has seen this hard drive and that it will write a signature to the disk. Acknowledge this.
8. If you didn't replace the hard drive, you need to delete the failed system partition from Disk 1 and commit the changes.
9. Create a new mirror by clicking Disk 2. Then, holding down the Ctrl key, click the free space on Disk 1. Choose Establish Mirror from the Fault Tolerance menu.
10. Exit Disk Administrator, acknowledging any warnings.
11. Reboot the system again, still booting from the fault-tolerant boot floppy.
12. Go into Disk Administrator and wait until the status on the system partition mirror is reported as HEALTHY.

13. Break the mirror again. (See the following Technical Note for a discussion of why this is all necessary!)

14. Exit Disk Administrator, acknowledging any warnings.

15. Reboot the system again. This time allow it to boot by itself.

16. Go into Disk Administrator and delete the partition that contains the duplicate of the system data from Disk 2.

17. You should now follow the normal procedures for reestablishing the mirror for Disk 1.

Although it might seem senseless to keep rebooting the system and breaking and restoring the mirror, there really is a good reason.

Remember that a mirror set is really made up of a primary and a secondary partition. The primary is the real thing. In the preceding steps, the primary partition failed. The first thing you had to do was break the mirror. This left you with the primary partition as being bad, and the secondary partition as being good. You deleted the primary partition—or replaced the drive if necessary. Then you created a new mirror based on the information from the secondary partition. The problem is, it is now the primary partition. That's why you reboot the system and break the mirror again. You now have two good partitions, with perfectly good data. You have basically accomplished your job, which is to recover the primary system partition. This leaves you free to delete the partition that was the secondary partition of the original mirror—and that saved your life—and re-create the mirror, using the correct partition as the primary partition of the mirrored set.

Recovering a Failed Striped Set with Parity

Because the data in a striped set with parity is spread across all the drives in the array, you don't lose any data if a single drive in the array fails. However, your system does take a significant performance hit, because NT must re-create the lost data from the information and parity data spread across the remaining disks. Additionally, by having a single drive fail, you have lost the fault tolerance. If a second drive in the array fails, you lose all data on that volume. So, although NT can continue to function with a single drive failure, you should make every attempt to replace the failed drive as soon as possible.

Follow this procedure to recover from a disk failure in a striped set with parity:

1. If you need to replace a failed hard drive, shut down the system as normal, swap the drive, and bring the system back up.

2. Log on as a user with administrative privileges.

3. Start Disk Administrator. If you replaced the hard drive, Disk Administrator warns you that this is the first time it has seen this hard drive and that it will write a signature to the disk. Acknowledge this.

4. Click the stripe set with parity that needs regenerating.

5. Hold down the Ctrl key and select the newly replaced drive, or click on a drive that's not currently part of the set that has free space equal to or greater than the stripe size used on the other disks.

6. Chose Regenerate from the Fault Tolerance menu.

7. Exit Disk Administrator and reboot the computer.

   When the computer restarts, it automatically begins to regenerate the data onto the newly added partition. This might take some time.

   You can check the status of the regeneration by clicking the striped set with parity in Disk Administrator.

Backing Up Your Server

No matter how you implement fault-tolerant disk drives, there is always the possibility that data could get corrupted beyond repair, or even more common, that something could get accidentally deleted. Because there is no way to undelete files in Windows NT, it is very important that you maintain current backups of your system's data.

The damage caused by either failed hardware or accidental deletion ranges from minor nuisance to major catastrophe. To help protect your data, you should evaluate its importance and the impact data loss would have on your organization and then develop an appropriate backup plan.

In addition to deciding how often to back up your data, and what to back up, you should also consider making a policy on how user data gets restored. In most cases, if a system failure causes data loss, restoring the system is very high priority. But how do you deal with a user that comes and asks you to restore a file that he or she accidentally erased? It would be nice to be able to deal with this kind of situation immediately; however, in reality that's not always possible. That's why having a well-defined policy regarding restoring user data from tapes can be useful. It gives the user a statement of rights and provides the administrator the ability to prioritize.

How to Choose a Tape Drive

Choosing a tape drive is at least as important as choosing the other components that go into making your system. If you are going to use the backup software that comes with NT, you need to make sure the tape drive you use is listed on NT's Hardware Compatibility List (HCL).

When choosing a tape backup device, here are a few things to look at:

■ **Tape style:** If you have tape backup units in more than one machine, you should consider standardizing on a tape format. This allows you a much greater level of flexibility. Two of the most common and respected tape formats in standard use today are 4-millimeter (mm) and 8mm tapes. These are data-grade versions of the 4mm audio DAT and 8mm video cassette. They have gained acceptance because they are cheap (around $10 per tape for 4mm and $18 per tape for 8mm); they hold large amounts of information (between 2GB and 9GB per tape for 4mm and 4 and 25GB per tape for 8mm); and they are fast. Other common styles include the DC-6000 style and the DC-2000 format. Both of these styles have been around for years, and although they are made from heavy-duty materials, they are usually far more costly than 4mm and 8mm tapes and often orders of magnitudes slower.

TIP

One format that has recently been gaining widespread acceptance for its high transfer rates, long shelf life, and high capacity is the digital linear tape (DLT). DLT provides about three times the storage capacity of an 8mm tape (10GB to 40GB depending on compression and type of the DLT drive), not to mention three times the speed (between 2.5MB and 3.0MB per second sustained transfer with peaks up to 10MB per second), and more than five times the expected life span (tape shelf life of 30 years, and drive head life of 10,000 hours).

One of the other advantages of the DLT format is the use of a multi-track, serpentine tape path. Multi-track means that in the case of DLT-2000 and DLT-4000 drives, data is stored on 128 parallel tracks (or 64 pairs of tracks) on the tape. The tape is read by moving forward along one track, and when the end of the tape is reached, it moves to the next track and reads backward. When the beginning of the tape is reached it moves to the next track and changes direction again. This is what is know as serpentine recording. It provides quick access to any point on the tape—significantly quicker than a single-track, longer tape.

DLT was originally popularized by Digital Equipment Corporation, but it is an open solution. With the growing need for large and fast tape backup solution, more major tape drive vendors are offering solutions based on DLT. If you need fast tape backup for large amounts of data, DLT might be right for you.

- **Capacity:** When selecting a tape format, make sure you get one that meets your current needs but also will cover you as your system grows. Also be careful of the claimed data capacity of the device. Most drives now support built-in hardware compression routines, and the advertised data capacity is based on the drive's capability to compress the data as it's written to the tape. You can run into some potential problems here because if your system contains a significant amount of already compressed data, you will run into troubles with your backups. For instance, if you are using NTFS file-level compression, or you have a large number of zip archives, your system might report that you have 2GB of data used on your volume. However, you might find your system asking you for a new tape halfway through the backup. This is because the tape device is unable to further compress the already compressed data.

■ **Speed:** With 4mm tapes, you can easily achieve data transfer rates of at least 30MB/minute. With 8mm tapes, the transfer rates are usually much higher. This is in contrast to the 1MB to 5MB/minute transfer rates of most DC-2000 and DC-6000 devices. Imagine backing up 8GB of data at 5MB/minute. That would take almost a full day! So when choosing a backup solution, make sure you calculate how long the backups take to run. In some cases, where the amount of data is so great, you might find that you need to use multiple tape devices to back up in parallel. For this kind of configuration, you would need a third-party backup program.

■ **Cost of media:** You need to carefully consider the cost of media when purchasing a tape drive. Different styles of tapes can cost between $5 and $50 per cartridge. It is common for people to skimp on purchasing their hardware, by saying "I can't justify spending $1,000 on a tape backup, when I can get one of the same capacity for $300!" This logic often falls to pieces when you consider the cost of the media for many of these devices. It's not uncommon that the cost of media alone for a single year on some of these "cheaper" systems exceeds the combined cost of a good tape backup unit and equivalent number of tapes. You should always calculate this before you buy.

■ **Autoloader:** An autoloader is a magazine that holds multiple tapes, and the backup software can automatically access any tape in the magazine as needed. There are two major reasons to use an autoloader. First, if you need to back up an amount of data that won't fit onto a single tape, an autoloader eliminates the need to manually change tapes, thus allowing the job to run unattended overnight. Another common reason to buy autoloaders is to be able to put a whole week's worth of tapes in the system at a time. The backups then run as necessary, and everything remains online, so you have almost immediate access if you need to recover a file. If you want to use a tape autoloader, you need to purchase third-party backup software, because NT's backup software does not support autoloaders.

Developing a Backup Strategy

Every site is unique and this makes it difficult to provide a general formula for developing a backup strategy. However, here are a few things you should look at in determining your backup strategy:

What Should You Back Up?

This might sound like an obvious question, but you should determine exactly what you need to back up. More to the point, you should decide if you will only back up the server—or servers—or if you need to back up the client workstations as well.

■ **Servers Only:** Backing up only the servers on your network will certainly take less time and space. If you are only going to back up the servers, then you should make sure the users know that the contents of their workstations are not getting backed up. You might also want to adopt a policy that requires or encourages users to store their data on the server. This way if their workstations do have problems, their data is protected.

■ **Workstations and Servers:** In some environments it is critical that the workstations and servers all get backed up. With most workstations today shipping with 1- to 2-gigabyte hard drives, many people want to maximize the use of this storage. Also, some environments consider data to be more secure when stored on the workstation hard drive.

TIP

As tempting as it might seem to maximize the use of large capacity local hard drives, in anything larger than a small network, this can dramatically increase the work of the information technology staff. By storing all user data on the network, the user's workstation can be quickly replaced, or reloaded with a clean image when there is a problem. This dramatically cuts down on the diagnostic time required to isolate problems with a workstation.

In addition to determining what machines get backed up, you will have to decide what portion of the machines need to get backed up. For instance, if you keep a large clip-art gallery—or other static data source—loaded on the hard drive of one of your servers, you might not want to back it up. If you could simply reload it from CD-ROM, as necessary, the tape space it would consume, and the time it would take to regularly back it up might not be worthwhile.

Where Should You Put the Tape Drive

Another great question with many different answers deals with where you should put the tape drive—or tape drives. Again, this depends on the setup of your network, how much money you are willing to spend, and what you want to accomplish.

The two main places for the tape drive are in the server, or in a workstation.

NOTE

The backup program that comes with Windows NT does not support running the backup program on an NT Server and backing up the data to a remote tape drive. What you would do instead is mount the server at the client workstation and run a local backup program at the server, such as the backup programs that come with NT Workstation or Windows 95. However if you do this, you will not be able to back up the Registry database on the NT Server.

I always recommend having the tape device attached directly to the NT Server, because that ensures it will always be available when needed. If it's attached to a client workstation, if the workstation is turned off, the backups will not get done. Also, having the tape backup device directly attached to the server makes it easier to recover the entire server if there is a system failure and you need to restore from tapes.

However, the advantage of placing the tape backup unit on the workstation is that if there is a problem with the tape drive, it can be corrected without disturbing the server. However, if the tape drive were directly attached to the server, the server would have to be shut down in order to rectify the problem.

The other consideration when using a client workstation to back up a server—or using a tape drive in a single server to back up multiple servers—is what effect it will have on network bandwidth. Remember, backing up multiple gigabytes over the network can have a negative impact on other applications running over the network. And if you do a verify on the backup, you actually end up copying the data over the network twice!

How Often Should You Back Up

The foundation of a successful backup program is to implement a fixed schedule and keep up with it. Just like exercise programs, it doesn't do much good to do it here and there. Set a schedule and stick to it!

As part of the schedule, you should rotate the tapes you use. If you only have a single backup set, you can't go back to an older version if the tape set you are restoring from fails. Also, if you are in the middle of performing a backup, and the system crashes, how are you going to restore the system? If you have multiple backup sets, that will not be as much of a problem.

> **TIP**
>
> If you are backing up 1GB of data to an 8GB tape, don't get lulled into using the same tape to do a full backup each night of the week. You should always use a rotational schedule.

Also, sometimes you might not become aware of a problem, such as a viral infection, until weeks or months after it occurred. By keeping archived copies of your data, you can recover from these incidences better than if you always use the same tape set.

> **TIP**
>
> Tapes wear out. You should keep track of the number of times you use a tape, as well as the date of the first time you used it. You should retire tapes after they get too old, or have
>
> *continues*

continued

been used too many times. The exact life span of different tape types varies, and you should check with the manufacturer of the drive for recommendations. You might also check with the tape manufacturer, but they are often a little on the optimistic side because they want you to believe their products will last forever—or at least forever in *computer years*.

You will need to determine how often you want to run a backup by deciding how many days worth of data you can afford to lose. One common method of backing up is to perform a complete backup every Friday night, and then perform a differential backup each additional night of the week. The differential backup stores only the data that has changed since the full backup. Then, if you want to recover data, you would need the full backup tape, and one of the differential backup tapes. This is often good if your tape device cannot store all your server's data on a single tape.

TIP

Always make sure you label your tapes. This prevents accidentally using the wrong tape. It will also speed up the recovery process, should you need to restore your system from tape.

Ideally you would supplement this strategy with a good rotational method that also includes off-site storage for added protection. For instance every two weeks, or once each month, you might retire a full-backup take and take this tape off-site. Then in the event of a catastrophic accident, such as the building burning down, you will lose at most 2 to 4 weeks worth of changes. Of course, the frequency with which you send tapes off-site will increase depending on the value of your data.

CAUTION

NT does not encrypt data on the tapes when it does a backup, so be sure to put your tapes in *secure* places, both on-site and off-site. Anyone who gets possession of that tape will have a complete copy of everything stored on your system.

Installing a Tape Driver

The first thing you must do before you can use NT Backup is install a tape driver. NT Backup supports only backing up to and restoring from tapes, not floppy media or other hard drives.

To install a tape driver, use the following instructions:

NOTE

Make sure you are logged on as a user with administrative permissions before attempting to load a tape device driver.

1. Open the Control Panel, and double-click on the Tape Devices icon. This will open the Tape Devices window.

2. Click the Detect button. This will attempt to locate a compatible tape device attached your system.

   If this does not work and you have a tape drive attached to your system, or if you have a disk from the tape drive manufacturer that contains the necessary tape device driver, click the Drivers tab at the top of the window, then click the Add button. This brings you to a window where you can pick the tape driver you want to install.

3. Once NT has detected your tape device, or you have chosen it from the list, you might be asked for the location of the NT Server distribution media. Enter the appropriate path, and NT will copy the necessary files for your tape device.

4. When NT is done, it will ask you if you want to reboot your system. You must reboot your system before you can use the newly installed tape drive.

Using NT Backup

NT Backup is a simple but elegant backup solution that serves the needs of most smaller LANs. You can use NT Backup to perform selective backups and restores, for tape maintenance such as tape formatting and retentioning, and for backing up the local Registry.

Let's take a walk through a basic backup procedure.

When you start the NT Backup utility from the Administrative Tools group (NTBACKUP.EXE), you will see a screen similar to the one shown in Figure 26.4.

First, be sure to have a tape ready. Some DC-2000 and DC-6000 cartridge formats require that you format your tapes before you can use them. Other tape formats, such as standard 4mm and 8mm tapes do not need to be formatted. A simple way to tell if your drive requires you to format tapes is to insert a tape, and from within Backup, look at the Format Tape... option under the Operations menu. If Format Tape... is grayed out, you can safely assume the tape does not need to be formatted.

Notice the drive window in the figure above. This window will show *all* local volumes, including CD-ROMs, as well as any current network connections. Placing a check mark in the box next to any volume tells NT Backup that you want to back up the entire contents of that volume. Place a check mark next to any volume you want to back up.

In our example, we will back up our system partition, drive E. (See Figure 26.5.)

FIGURE 26.4.

The NT Backup utility is a full-featured tool for backing up and restoring data on your system.

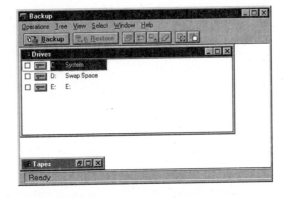

FIGURE 26.5.

The check mark next to Drive E shows that it is selected for backup.

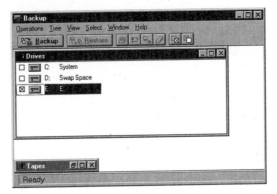

Once you have selected the drives you want to back up, click the Backup button.

The Backup Information Window

This window is used to configure the options for your backup. (See Figure 26.6.) Here is an overview of the various features provided on this window:

- **Current Tape:** This field will contain one of three things. If there is no tape in the drive this field will say "There is no tape in the drive." If the tape is blank, the field will read "The tape in the drive is blank." Finally, if the tape already contains information, the field will display the current name of the tape, such as "Wednesday backup of SAMSON server."

- **Creation Date:** If the tape in the drive currently has data, it will tell you the date that the first backup set was written to the tape. Otherwise, this field will be empty.

- **Owner:** If the tape in the drive already has information on it, this field will contain the name of the user who created the tape. If the tape is blank, this field will also be blank.

FIGURE 26.6.

The Backup Informa-tion window.

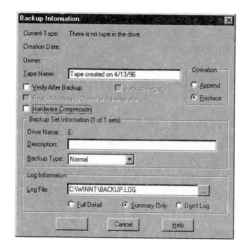

- **Tape Name:** If you are performing a replace operation, you will be able to assign the tape a name. By default the tape will be called "Tape created on" with today's date on the end. If you are performing an append operation, you will not be able to change the name of the tape.

- **Operation:** You have two options here: Append and Replace. If you choose Replace, all data currently recorded on the tape will be lost. If you choose Append, the system will write your current backup job after the end of the last job on the tape. This allows you to store multiple backup sets on a single tape. If you choose Replace, you will be unable to change the tape name, which is assigned by the first backup set on the tape.

- **Verify After Backup:** If you choose this option, NT will back up all the selected data according to the other options you selected. It will then read all the data back from the tape and compare it to the originals. Using the verify option typically takes twice as long, and if you are backing up a network share, it will create twice as much network traffic.

- **Backup Registry:** This option will be grayed out unless you select *at least one* file on the system partition to back up. Choosing this option will cause the Registry hives to be copied to the tape. Essentially this means it will copy all files meeting the criteria %system_root%\system32\config*. As a general practice, you should always back up the Registry whenever you back up your system partition.

- **Restrict Access to Owner or Administrator:** By checking this option, NT will write a header to the tape designating that its access should be restricted. Please note that the data on the tape *is not* encrypted and therefore it is possible the data on the tape could be read by alternative means. Using this option is not an excuse for lax protection of sensitive backup tapes. This option is only available when you are performing a replace.

■ **Hardware Compression:** If your tape device doesn't support hardware compression, this option will be grayed out. Some tape devices do not support mixing compression types on a tape, so if you are performing an append and this option is gray, although your device supports hardware compression, this is probably why.

■ **Backup Set Information:** If you are backing up information on different volumes, Backup treats them as different backup sets. You are told how many sets will be backed up. In our example, we are backing up two volume sets and the screen tells us "(1 of 2 sets)" and provides us a slider bar to view the options for each set.

■ **Drive Name:** This gives you the local mapped drive and the universal naming convention (UNC) name for the current backup set. If you are backing up data from more than one volume, remember that you should use the slider at the right to determine which backup set you are viewing.

■ **Description:** You can enter an individual description for each backup set. When you catalog a tape, this information will show up next to the backup set, allowing you to know exactly what it contains.

■ **Backup Type:** You can set the backup type individually for each backup set. You have five options here:

Full (Normal) Backup: All selected components are backed up and their archive bits are cleared.

Copy Backup: All selected components are backed up and their archive bits are not changed.

Incremental Backup: All selected components that have their archive bit set are backed up and their archive bits are then cleared.

Differential Backup: All selected components that have their archive bit set are backed up and their archive bits are not changed.

Daily Backup: All selected components that were modified today (regardless of the status of their archive bits) are backed up and their archive bits are not changed.

■ **Log Information:** You can tell NT where to save the backup log information. You should store the log files in a secure place since there is really no reason for this to be public information. By default the log is written to `%system_root%\backup.log`, which is not necessarily a secure location.

You can also set what kind of information the log records. By default, NT will record summary information only. The summary information consists of information such as the number of files backed up, the number of bytes backed up, the date and time the job started and when it finished, the elapsed time, the name of every directory that was backed up and a list of exceptions. If you choose the Full Detail option, NT will record the name of every file backed up. While to some people this might seem like a neat idea, don't forget that logs that contain full details grow *very* quickly. Of course if you don't want a log, then you should check the Don't Log option and no log file will be created.

Once you've finished configuring the backup options, click OK and NT will start the backup. A Backup Status window will appear showing the current progress of the backup.

If you wish to stop the backup at any time, click the Abort button and you will be prompted to confirm whether or not you really want to abort the backup.

If NT comes across any open files during backup, it will wait 30 seconds for the file to close. If the file does not close, then Backup skips over it and logs an exception to the backup log.

When NT is finished backing up all the files, the Backup Status window will remain on the screen. You can click OK to dismiss it and then you will be returned to the main Backup screen. (See Figure 26.7.)

FIGURE 26.7.

The Backup Status screen.

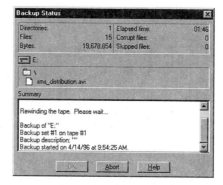

> **NOTE**
>
> NT Backup generates an audit entry to NT's Application Log when a backup set begins and when it completes. This means that if you back up two volumes, C and D for example, you will end up with four events logged in the Application Log.

Restoring Selected Files and Directories from Backup Tapes

To restore files created with the NT Backup program follow these steps:

> **NOTE**
>
> Make sure you're logged on as a user with permissions to access the tape you need to restore, as well as having permissions to the destination, and the Restore user right if you want to restore the files with their NTFS access control lists (ACLs) intact.

1. Start NT Backup (NTBACKUP.EXE).

2. Insert the tape you want to restore from.

3. Open the Tapes window by double-clicking on the Tapes icon, or by choosing Tapes from the Window menu. (See Figure 26.8.)

FIGURE 26.8.

The tape backup unit resides on a client workstation.

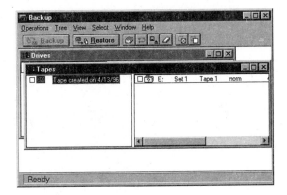

4. The Tapes window will now display a list of all backup sets available on the current tape.

   If you don't see a catalog of the current tape, choose the Catalog option from the Operations menu.

5. With NT Backup, you can choose exactly what you want to restore. If you want to restore the entire tape, place a checkbox next to each of the volume sets listed in the Tapes window. If you only want selected sets, click only next to the sets you want. If you want specific files within one or more of the volume sets, you can browse through the tape, selecting only the files you want to restore, as shown in. (See Figure 26.9.)

   Once you have selected all the files you want to restore, click on the Restore button, or choose Restore from the Operations menu.

FIGURE 26.9.

The Tape Devices Control Panel applet is used to install tape drivers.

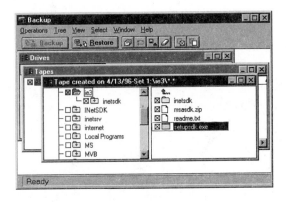

6. The Restore Information window appears. (See Figure 26.10.)

   If you are restoring more than one set, NT Backup displays the information for one set at a time and provides a scroll bar that can be used to view the restore information for the other sets.

FIGURE 26.10.

The Restore Information screen.

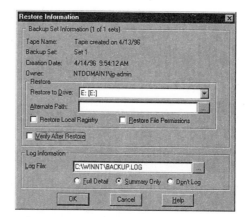

You are presented with the following information for each set being restored:

Tape Name: This is the name of the tape currently in the tape drive.

Backup Set: This is the ordinal number of the backup set on the tape. If you have backed up five volumes to the tape and restore files from the last set, the value for this field will be 5.

Creation Date: This is the date that the current backup set was created.

Owner: This is the name of the user account that created the backup tape.

Restore to Drive: Using this pick list you can specify any currently mounted, writeable volume to recover the files to. By default they will be recovered using the exact same directory structure from where they were backed up.

Alternate Path: If you don't want the restored files to use their original file structure, you can specify a path where Backup will create the restored files.

Verify After Restore: If you want to ensure that there were no problems restoring the data, you can have NT Backup verify the data. Selecting this option makes restoring files take roughly twice as long.

Restore Local File Permissions: You can select this option if you want files and directories restored with their NTFS permissions intact. You can only choose this option if the files were originally backed up from an NTFS partition and if you are restoring them to an NTFS partition.

Restore Local Registry: If you want to restore the system Registry, use this option. This option is only available if you are restoring from a backup of the system partition that was made with the Backup Local Registry option selected.

Additionally, you can specify the location of a restore log and the level of information that is recorded to the log.

7. Click OK and Backup will begin to restore the files.

   The status of the job is displayed during execution. (See Figure 26.11.)

   You can abort the restore job at any time by clicking Abort.

FIGURE 26.11.

The Restore Status screen.

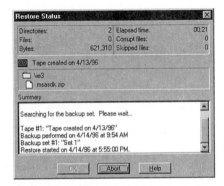

> **NOTE**
>
> NT Backup generates an audit entry to NT's Application Log when you begin to restore files from a backup tape and when the restore job is complete. If you restore files from more than one set, NT will generate an audit entry for the beginning and end of each set.

Restoring the Entire Server from Backup Tapes

If you need to restore the entire server from tape because of a system failure, use the following procedures:

1. If the system failure was due to a problem with the hard drive, replace the hard drive or do whatever is necessary to make sure it is functioning properly now.

2. Boot from the Windows NT Setup Disk 1 and perform a basic NT Server install from scratch.

3. Boot from the Setup disk again and perform a repair, using the system's Emergency Repair Disk. This restores part of the Registry.

4. Once the system reboots, use NT Backup to restore the last full system backup.

5. Restore any incremental or differential backups that were performed since the last full backup.

Running NT Backup from the Command Line

I have discussed how to use the GUI interface for NT Backup to perform backups and restores. However, in some instances you don't want to work with the GUI interface, so NT Backup provides a set of parameters that can be used to call NT Backup from the command line to perform different functions. The syntax for NTBACKUP is as follows:

```
NTBACKUP operation path [/a] [/v] [/r] [/d "text"] [/b] [/hc:{on¦off}] [/t
{option}] [/l "filename"] [/e] [/tape:{N}]
```

operation	Specifies whether NTBACKUP should perform a backup or a restore. Accepted values are BACKUP or RESTORE.
path	Tells NTBACKUP which file or path should be backed up or restored. You can enter more than one entry here.
/a	Use this option to have the backup appended to the end of an existing tape. If you don't specify this option, NTBACKUP starts at the beginning of a tape and replaces any previously backed up data contained on the tape.
/v	Specifying this option has NT verify all data after performing the backup. Using this option takes much longer, and if used to back up data from a network share it effectively doubles the amount of network traffic.
/r	Tells NTBACKUP to mark this tape as a restricted access tape. Tapes marked as such can be read only by the owner and by members of the Backup Operators and Administrators groups.
/d "text"	Supplying this uses the text in quotes as a description of the tape set. For instance, you might use this to mark your tape with an identifying number or with other information such as "Backup of FARINELLI workstation on 1/1/96."
/b	Including this option causes NTBACKUP to include a copy of the local registry on the tape. Note that this can be used only to back up the local registry. It cannot be used to back up the registry of a remote system.
/hc:{on¦off}	Supplying the switch /hc:on tells NTBACKUP to use hardware compression, which on many systems effectively doubles the storage capacity. Using /hc:off causes NT to disable hardware compression. To use this option, your tape device must support hardware compression. This option is not effective when used with the /a option, because if you are appending your backup to a tape, NTBACKUP automatically uses whatever compression option was used for the first backup job on the tape.

/t {option}	Tells NTBACKUP whether to perform a Normal, Incremental, Differential Backup, Copy, or Daily Backup. Accepted values for option are NORMAL, INCREMENTAL, DIFFERENTIAL, COPY, and DAILY.
/l "filename"	Tells NTBACKUP to save a log file for the job in file "filename." By default, NTBACKUP uses a file called %SYSTEM_ROOT%\XXX.
/e	Supplying this option causes only exceptions to be written to the backup log. Without this option, NTBACKUP includes complete backup descriptions for the job. When backing up large numbers of files, the backup log can grow extremely large. Using this option can help keep the log to a more manageable size.
/tape:{N}	NT supports up to 10 tape drives. Use this option if you have more than one drive installed. Tape drives are designated as 0 to 9. By default, NT uses tape device 0.

Using the NT Scheduler Service to Schedule Regular Backups

Although NT Backup does not have a built-in scheduling mechanism, you can use the Scheduler service built into the NT system to run regular backup jobs automatically.

Before you can do this, you need to make sure the Scheduler service has been started and the Scheduler user has the appropriate user rights on the local system and on any system you need to back up.

Let's assume your system has two volumes: C and D. To perform a full backup of your system every Friday night at 10:00 pm and a differential backup of your system every Monday, Tuesday, Wednesday, and Thursday night at 10:00 pm, you need two scripts, as follows:

backfull.bat:

```
ntbackup backup c: d: /v /d "Full System Backup" /b /t normal /l
"c:\users\backup\backfull.log" /e
```

backdiff.bat:

```
ntbackup backup c: d: /v /d "Differential System Backup" /b /t differential /l
"c:\users\backup\backdiff.log" /e
```

Create a directory for these scripts. c:\users\backup might be a good location. Now you have two files: c:\users\backup\backfull.bat and c:\users\backup\backdiff.bat.

You then set up the jobs in the system scheduler by issuing the following two commands:

```
at 22:00 /interactive /every:friday "c:\user\backup\backfull.bat"
```

```
at 22:00 /interactive /every:monday,tuesday,wednesday,thursday
"c:\user\backup\backdiff.bat"
```

Now you're all set. Each morning you can simply take out the tape from the previous night and insert a new tape.

Backing Up Remote Volumes

You can use the Scheduler service and NTBACKUP to back up remote volumes, but you must take some additional steps.

By default, the Scheduler user runs using the built-in SYSTEM account. When you run NTBACKUP from the Scheduler service, it runs in whatever user context the Scheduler service is using. The built-in SYSTEM account cannot make remote network attachments, so it cannot back up remote network shares.

If you want to back up remote network shares in this way, you need to run the Scheduler service with a user context that has both backup and restore user rights and has permission to access files on the remote system.

Once you have the Scheduler service running as a user with backup and restore user rights, and permissions to access the remote network shares you want to back up, you can create a batch file like the following to back up a share called CLIENTS from a machine called SAMSON:

```
net use k: \\SAMSON\CLIENTS

ntbackup backup k: /v /d "Backup of \\SAMSON\CLIENTS" /t normal /l
"c:\users\backup\samson.log" /e

net use k: /d
```

> **NOTE**
>
> Remember that if you tell NTBACKUP to verify data backed up from a network share, you double the amount of network traffic.

Assuming you save this batch file as c:\users\backup\samson.bat, you could have NT's Scheduler service run this batch file every weeknight at 10:00 pm by issuing this command:

```
at 22:00 /interactive /every:monday,tuesday,wednesday,thursday,friday
"c:\user\backup\samson.bat"
```

> **NOTE**
>
> If you include a /b switch in a backup command like the one contained in the batch file listed earlier, it backs up the registry on the computer that is running NTBACKUP, not the computer whose share it is you are backing up. Using NTBACKUP, there is currently no method to back up the registry on a remote machine.

Using an Uninterruptible Power Supply (UPS) with NT

Think of jumping out of the plane without a parachute. This is essentially what you are doing if you run your server without an uninterruptible power supply (UPS). This is one of the most important investments you can make to protect your server. I would consider it a crime comparable to treason to set up a server of any kind without providing an UPS device for protection against power problems.

> **TIP**
>
> There are two ways to pronounce UPS. If you have noticed that I write "an UPS," you probably realize that I pronounce it "ups" as a word. This is the most common way. You can also find people pronouncing the letters individually, "U-P-S."

Now that you realize how important UPS devices are, I will explain why. An UPS is a device that is plugged in between your computer and the wall and provides protection for your computer in the event of a power failure. Most UPSs also provide line conditioning to ensure the quality of power that actually reaches the computer. This translates into longer life for your computer's power supply, and for all of your computer's components. Also, since most servers rely heavily on disk caching—such as Windows NT's lazy write file system—you risk losing all data stored in a write cache.

> **NOTE**
>
> If you are using NTFS under Windows NT and the power goes out, you will not get file system corruption, however, you will lose the contents of the lazy write cache that has not been committed to disk.

In most cases an UPS is not intended to enable you to continue working through a lengthy power outage. Rather, it is intended to permit your server to shut down gracefully without losing data.

> **NOTE**
>
> Of course, in some mission-critical situations your system must be able to outlast long power outages, but the cost of UPS devices to support this kind of operation can be costly.

TIP

Buy an UPS for each of your servers. Now that you have that settled, let's talk about the rest of your network. Realize that if there is a major power failure, an UPS protects the machine attached to it, but what about the rest of your network? What about the routers? What about the hubs? Sometimes people put UPSs on their workstations and servers and think they are protected from catastrophe. Boom, the power goes out and they lose their network connections because their hubs are gone. These devices are important too! *Just remember to ask yourself what you need.* Do you just need to make sure that your server can shut down safely, or do you also want to make sure that your users do not lose data because their workstations die, too? If the latter is your goal, you need to put UPSs on their workstations, but also on all the network components.

Deciding What to Protect

One of the questions you need to answer is what you want to protect with your UPS—what is the *goal* for which you are installing the UPS. There are so many mitigating circumstances that it is almost impossible to list them all, but here are a few things to look at:

- **Server CPU:** Obviously you want the CPU itself on the UPS.

- **External Storage Devices:** Don't forget to plug any external storage devices into the UPS as well. This includes external CD-ROMs, hard drives, and tape backup units. It would even include many scanners, if they are plugged into a SCSI interface. If you lose power to any of these devices, it will cause problems with your system.

- **Server's Monitor:** In general, the larger the monitor, the more power it consumes. If your NT system will be performing a shutdown without your intervention during a power failure, you might not need to put the monitor on the UPS. However, if you need to monitor the events on the server, you're going to have to make sure to put the monitor on the UPS and determine the correct balance between the size of the monitor versus the power consumption and how that will affect your UPS budget.

- **Printers:** In general, you should not plug printers into UPSs, particularly laser printers. This is because of large amount of power these devices require when they actually print something will overload most UPSs that your would be using with an NT system.

- **Networking Hardware:** If you need to provide continued network access to coordinate remote shutdowns, you will need to ensure that all your networking hardware, such as bridges, routers, and hubs, is protected by an UPS.

- **Workstations:** If it is critical that users don't lose even a moment's work, you will need to put an UPS on each workstation. Then when there is a power failure, the server can send a message to all its clients indicating that it will be shutting down.

The users will have time to safely save and exit their applications. If you need to provide this level of support, then make sure you have your networking hardware protected as well, as listed in the previous bulleted item.

Choosing an UPS

As with any other component of your server system, you should give careful attention to buying an UPS. Of course, price is always going to be a factor, but here are some other things to think about:

- **Runtime:** You want an UPS that is going to support your system for *at least* five minutes under full load. You also need to consider what will happen if you have multiple shorter power outages in a row. Each outage drains from the UPS's battery, and the UPS might not have enough time to recharge before the next hit, so it will already be at a disadvantage. Always purchase your UPS with room to grow into. Remember, as you add more disk drives, CD-ROMs, and memory, the total power requirement of your system increases.

> **TIP**
>
> One of the most difficult tasks about buying an UPS is determining how large it should be. There is no simple rule that determines 100% accuracy, but for a conservative guess, you should add up the rated power consumption for all devices you will plug into the UPS. The rated power consumption on all electrical components is given in *watts*. Most UPSs are traditionally rated in *volt-amps* (VA), which measures the UPS's output capacity. The relationship between the two is determined by a *power factor*, which varies depending on the make and model of the UPS. However, a good rule of thumb would be that a 1000VA UPS can support a *maximum* load capacity of 600 to 700 watts. At the maximum load capacity the UPS will provide the least amount of runtime. The smaller the load capacity, the longer the runtime.
>
> Unfortunately there is no simple shopper's method that you can use across all UPS vendors for quick comparison. In order to determine your system's runtime at different load levels, you will often need to contact the UPS vendor for help.

- **Type of protection:** UPS protection is often classified into three categories, online, stand-by, and line-interactive.

    Online UPSs are the original type of UPS device, sometimes called a double-conversion UPS. With an online UPS, the computer is always feeding from the battery, so the battery is constantly charging. When the power fails, the UPS continues feeding the attached device, with no interruption or switching. These are also the most expensive type of UPS, and according to some people, unnecessary.

Stand-by UPSs are very common, particularly in the newer low-cost UPSs targeted for the home consumer market. Stand-by UPSs work by constantly monitoring the quality of the incoming AC power and when it detects a dip in voltage, the UPS provides power to the attached equipment.

> **NOTE**
>
> Remember a battery provides a type of electricity called direct current (DC), while the type of power you get from electrical outlets is alternating current (AC). The UPS is in essence a large battery and it needs to convert the DC power provided by the battery into AC power, which the computer's power supply expects to get. This process is called *inversion* and the UPS provides this through a built-in *inverter*.

The amount of time the UPS takes between the beginning of the voltage dip and when it begins providing power to the attached equipment is called the *transfer time*, and it varies depending on the make and model of the UPS, but is often between 2 and 10 milliseconds. The power supplies in most computer hardware are rated to be able to keep the system going for a minimum of 10 to 15 milliseconds after the loss of power. This is called the *hold-up* time for the power supply. In actual tests, though, most systems are not even affected by power losses of 50 to 100 milliseconds, or greater. However, you want to be sure to get an UPS with a low transfer time.

Line-interactive UPSs provide the functionality of stand-by UPSs, but they also provide enhanced line conditioning. They use voltage regulation methods to try to correct over- and undervoltages without changing over to the battery. This is usually listed as brownout protection and can help to increase the life of the UPS.

- **Intelligent serial/network communications:** For your server, you want to buy an UPS that is capable of communicating *intelligent messages* with NT, typically through the serial port. It is not enough to simply offer a serial port that reports when the battery has kicked in so that NT can shut down. A good quality UPS will also send NT messages about the quality of the line, battery charge levels, and other environmental conditions. Most cheaper models, especially those geared more for the home market, are not able to communicate *intelligently* with Windows NT. If you do nothing else, make sure to invest in an intelligent UPS with a serial interface. For a larger network, where you use Simple Network Management Protocol (SNMP) network monitoring packages, you might consider getting an UPS with a network card that supports SNMP monitoring and control.

- **NT-specific software:** Although NT provides its own built-in support for talking with UPS intelligent devices, the software provided by some UPS manufacturers often provides more robust and value-added enhancements. For example, some models are able to communicate information about the quality of the line to NT. When there is a brown-out, the UPS reports it to NT and NT logs the event in the system event log and tells you the line voltage. This can be useful for diagnosing and isolating bad lines so they can be fixed. Other software provides features such as paging and integration with various management packages, such as Microsoft's Systems Management Server (SMS). For example, American Power Conversion's (APC) PowerChute Plus software, which ships with their intelligent UPS devices, provides an SMS MIF file that records UPS events and status information in the SMS database.

> **NOTE**
>
> Before installing any software that comes with your UPS, you should ensure that it is designed for your version of NT, including any service packs you might have installed. I have had problems with this in the past. When in doubt, contact the vendor before installing the software.
>
> More than nine months after NT 3.5 had been shipping, I installed an intelligent UPS from a major UPS manufacturer—no names mentioned—along with its software, which was designed for NT. Nowhere in the instructions did it even mention which version of NT it had been designed for. After spending hours cleaning up its mess and subsequently contacting the UPS vendor to complain, I found out that the version I had been sent was only for NT 3.1.

- **Audible power failure indicator:** Many products provide an audible sound that indicates when something is wrong. Although it is a useful feature, it can sometimes be quite annoying, especially if your power is typically of poor quality.

- **Visual load indicator:** Many of the better UPS models provide a visual indication of how much power is being drawn by the attached equipment. This is done with either a thermometer-style indicator or a numeric display.

- **Visual time indicator:** Again, this feature is typically provided on many of the better UPS models. Usually it is displayed the same as the load indicator—with either a thermometer-style indicator or a numeric display. This is a particularly useful feature and well worth choosing a good model to get.

- **Site wiring indicator:** Some UPSs provide a visual and/or audible indicator to alert you to hazardous situations cause by improper electrical wiring, such as poor grounding or reversed line polarity. If you don't get an UPS with this feature, be sure to have your line checked by a licensed electrician (or at least someone competent in the subject) to ensure that the wiring at your site was done correctly.

- **Location of power switch:** This might seem silly if you have never dealt with an UPS before. An alarmingly high number of UPS devices—even many of the better ones—have simple on/off toggle switches or buttons located right on the front of the console. This is fine for access, but most people don't need to use them very often, so putting them in back, or providing a guard to protect against accidents, seems in order. In many environments, UPSs are kept on the floor, and more often than not, under desks. I have heard many cries from upset people who have accidentally kicked or knocked their switches and shut their whole systems down. At least give this some thought.

■ **Replaceable batteries:** Some UPSs have user-replaceable batteries. In a cheap, dumb UPS that is nothing more than a simple battery with inverter circuitry, the expense of the battery makes up most of the cost of the UPS. However, with more advanced, intelligent UPSs, the intelligence and other parts of the UPS begin to have a definite long-term value. Since UPS batteries don't last forever (typically two to five years, depending on usage), investing in an UPS with user-replaceable batteries can cut down on your long-term expenses.

■ **Test button:** You should test your UPS on a regular basis to ensure that it is functioning properly. Having a test button built into the front of the unit is an easy way to do this.

■ **Number of outlets:** Typically, the number of outlets provided with an UPS is related to its volt-amps rating. If you have any external devices, it's not uncommon to need more outlets than are provided, particularly on the cheaper models, which often come with only two outlets.

Installing Your UPS

Although NT has built-in support for intelligent UPS devices, some makes and models of UPS devices actually come with their own software, which usually provides more robust services than the built-in UPS service. If your UPS comes with its own software for NT, you should probably use it—just contact the vendor to make sure it supports Windows NT Server 4.

However, if your UPS does not come with its own software, you can use the UPS service built into NT. The UPS applet can be configured to work with most of the intelligent UPS devices on the market.

> **TIP**
>
> Before buying an UPS, you should be sure to consult the latest NT Hardware Compatibility List (HCL).

To install the UPS, you should follow the manufacturer's installation instructions for attaching the UPS to a serial port on your Windows NT system. Once the connection is established, use the following procedure for configuring the UPS service.

To do this, follow these steps:

> **NOTE**
>
> To configure the UPS service, you must be logged on as a member of the administrators group.

1. Choose the UPS icon from the Control Panel. A window appears. (See Figure 26.12.)

FIGURE 26.12.

The UPS window.

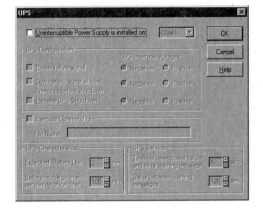

2. At this point the UPS service is disabled. You must check the box labeled Uninterruptable Power Supply is installed on and select the COM port before you can continue configuring the service.

3. The UPS service supports three common controls that can be sent by many intelligent UPS devices. These controls are as follows:

   Power failure signal: You should check this box if your UPS is capable of sending a signal to NT when it detects a power failure. You must also select whether your UPS sends a positive or negative voltage for this signal. This information can be found in the documentation for your particular UPS.

   Low battery signal at least 2 minutes before shutdown: Check this box if your UPS is capable of sending a signal to NT when it detects a low battery. Again, you should set the positive or negative value according to the documentation for your UPS.

   Remote UPS Shutdown: You should check this box if your UPS is able to respond to a signal to shut itself off. For example, if your UPS has a network interface and could receive a command from network management software to shut down, you would use this option. You must also select whether your UPS sends a positive or negative voltage for this signal. This information can be found in the documentation for your particular UPS.

4. If you want NT to run a particular command or batch file before the UPS service shuts the system down, check the Execute Command File box and enter a valid `.CMD`, `.BAT`, `.EXE`, or `.COM` file into the textbox.

5. The correct values in the UPS Characteristics section depend on the make and model of your UPS. You should consult your UPS directions for the proper value to enter here.

Expected Battery Life: Some UPS devices have a built-in load indicator that gives you a good indication of how long the system should continue running with the current system load. If you use this value for setting the expected battery life, you should make sure that all devices needed for the system, such as the monitor, are turned on when taking this reading. However, if your UPS does not have a method of indicating the current load, you should be sure to use the charts included in most UPS manuals to determine how long the battery should last. To do this properly, you need to know the power requirements for each device plugged into the UPS. The default for this value is set to a conservative two minutes, although you should definitely make sure to use the proper value discovered earlier. The UPS applet accepts settings between 2 and 720 minutes.

Battery recharge time per minute of runtime: This value is the number of minutes your UPS must recharge for each minute it provided power backup for your system. Properly filling in this value enables NT to keep track of the recharge state of the UPS so that if there are multiple short power outages, it can properly calculate the current battery level. You need to consult your UPS manual for this setting, and it depends on the amount of power drawn by the system connected to the UPS. The default for this setting is 100. This means that if the UPS was needed for two minutes, it would take 200 minutes (over three hours) to completely recharge. This setting can be set to between 1 and 250 minutes.

6. You now need to fill in the values in the UPS Service section of the dialog box. These values depend on your personal preference, and you want to choose values that make sense for your environment and how long your UPS can sustain the system.

Time between power failure and initial warning message: When the standard line power fails and NT must switch over to the UPS to supply power, NT sends an administrative alert. The value you specify here determines how long NT waits after the power fails before it sends the first administrative alert. You want to choose a value here that makes sense. For instance, you want to ensure that this value is low enough that NT has time to send the administrative alert before the power actually fails. It is best to keep this number fairly low. In general, the default value of five seconds is good for most environments. If you want to change it, values between 0 and 120 seconds are accepted.

Delay between warning messages: Once NT has sent its first message warning you that the UPS has kicked in, it continues to send warnings on a regular basis. The amount of time between warnings is set by this option. The default is 120 seconds and can be changed to anything from 5 seconds to 300 seconds. The default setting of 120 seconds is probably about right for most environments. There is no way to prevent these follow-up warning messages. If you don't want these alerts, the only thing you can do is set this value to its maximum, which is five minutes.

7. Once you have entered all these values, you can click OK, and NT takes care of the rest. It creates a Registry subkey for storing your configuration. It also starts the UPS service and sets it to start automatically in the future. You now want to test the UPS system to ensure that it works properly.

Testing Your UPS

You should definitely test your UPS on a regular basis. The simplest way to test an UPS is to unplug the UPS from the wall. You might not want to try this the first time with your live NT system. Some UPS devices do not actually switch to battery unless there is a load applied, so you should make sure to have something plugged into it—a monitor is good for testing. Or you can simply tell your NT system to shut down and when it tells you it is safe to shut off the computer, pull the UPS's plug from the wall.

> **CAUTION**
>
> If you are like most people, you probably got your new UPS and want to play with it right away. You should always make sure to allow your UPS time to fully charge (usually overnight) before using it.
>
> Failure to allow your UPS to fully charge before using it could prevent it from properly protecting you, because NT assumes that it is fully charged and makes its calculations based on this assumption.

Once you are confident that the UPS actually does what it is supposed to, you can turn your attention to how NT responds:

1. Make sure you are logged in as an administrative user.

2. Unplug the UPS from the wall, wait a minute or two, then plug the UPS back in. Did NT send you a message after the number of seconds you chose when configuring the UPS?

3. Open the Event Viewer and view the system log. You should see an event indicating that the system switched over to UPS support, and then a second event indicating the return to line power. If you double-click the event, it gives you more information.

4. You might also want to make sure that NT is able to shut down properly when the battery is depleted. To perform this test, rather than allowing your UPS to deplete, you might set the Expected Battery Life in the UPS applet to a much smaller value. If you do this, NT shuts down the system much faster. Realize that the system needs time to recharge after these tests before it can provide you with maximum protection.

Although you don't need to test all these features all the time, you should regularly test your UPS to make sure that everything is functioning properly. Most UPS models include a test button that is equivalent to momentarily unplugging the UPS.

UPS Entries in the NT Registry

When you install Windows NT, by default, no entries are created for the UPS service in the Windows NT Registry. However, the first time you run and configure the UPS applet in the Control Panel, NT creates an UPS subkey, which can be accessed through the following path: HKEY_LOCAL_MACHINE\SYSTEM\CurrentControlSet\Services\UPS.

For the UPS service to function properly, this subkey must exist and contain valid entries. If you uninstall the UPS service, this Registry subkey is not automatically removed.

Seven values can be set in this subkey that affect the functioning of the UPS service. (See Table 26.1.) All of these values can be set using the UPS applet.

Table 26.1. UPS subkey values.

Value Name	Value Type	Permissible Value	Default Value	Description
BatteryLife	REG_DWORD	2–720 minutes	2	The length of time the UPS battery should last during a power failure.
CommandFile	REG_EXPAND_SZ	a filename	none	When the UPS service must shut down your NT system, this is the command or batch file it runs before doing so.
FirstMessageDelay	REG_DWORD	0–120 seconds	5	During a power failure, Windows NT waits this number of seconds before sending a broadcast to notify the users.
MessageInterval	REG_DWORD	5–300 seconds	120	After sending the first broadcast message to users that the system is running from battery backup, NT repeatedly sends broadcast warnings every few seconds. The time between broadcasts is set by this value.
Port	REG_SZ	COM port name	COM1	The COM port that Windows NT expects to find the UPS attached to.

continues

Table 26.1. continued

Value Name	Value Type	Permissible Value	Default Value	Description
RechargeRate	REG_SZ	1–250 minutes	100	Specifies how many minutes it takes to fully recharge the UPS.

Summary

Windows NT was designed to provide the level of fault tolerance necessary for supporting large, mission-critical applications and server solutions. This chapter discussed three major fault-tolerance systems provided by Windows NT: disk fault tolerance, server backup, and support for uninterruptible power supplies (UPS).

You got to see how Windows NT provides fault tolerance for disks, including how it can work with the drive controller on a SCSI disk to perform sector sparing; the fault tolerance, including fault-tolerant disk support, such as sector sparing; as well as some of the recoverability features of NTFS, including support for sector sparing on non-SCSI disks. You also learned a little about FTDISK, the Windows NT driver that is used to support disk fault tolerance, including RAID. You had the opportunity to learn about the different levels of RAID, find out which are supported by NT, and what situations each is good for.

The chapter continued with a discussion about backing up Windows NT. You got some advice on what to look for in choosing a tape backup device for your server, as well as how to use NT's built-in tape backup program for backing up your server.

Finally, you learned about uninterruptible power supplies and what to look at when purchasing one for your NT Server. You also got to see how to configure the built-in UPS support for Windows NT and how it can be used to monitor power events to ensure the integrity of the data on your server.

Auditing Windows NT Server

by Joe Greene

IN THIS CHAPTER

Does auditing sound to you like something accountants do to you at income tax time? This chapter is about a different kind of auditing. Specifically, I discuss Windows NT's built-in functions to record certain events that might be of interest to you as a system administrator. Some examples of things that might be interesting to you include the following:

- Someone trying multiple times to log on to several of the accounts on your system (hackers?).

- A service that is routinely failing to start up when it is supposed to or stopping in an unplanned manner.

- Someone trying to use privileged system functions (those that you normally restrict to yourself).

- A person logging on or off the system at unusual hours.

- The number of people logging on or off the system at various hours, to determine the number of users you are supporting at different times of the day or days of the week.

- A person using a sensitive right (such as administrator privileges) that has been granted to him.

- Certain files or other resources (objects) being accessed by various individuals.

As you will see later in this chapter, Windows NT enables you to monitor a fairly large number of events that can occur in your system. However, in this era of information overload, you need to determine which events are important enough for you to monitor, given your particular security and reliability needs. In super top-secret environments, almost no effort is too much to expend on security. However, in a small company development environment, you might not have infinite amounts of time to devote to reading through log files.

This chapter is designed to address this central issue for auditing: What is good enough for you? The chapter starts with a general introduction to the concepts behind auditing. Next, I cover the things that Windows NT can monitor for you if you so desire. These first two sections prepare you for perhaps the most important section of this chapter, which deals with audit planning. Of course, for your plans to be useful, you have to implement them, and that is what the next section of this chapter is about. Finally, I put together some samples of how I might approach auditing in several different environments (not that I am necessarily right, but it does give you a couple different opinions to consider).

Introduction to Auditing

Certain people view auditing as strictly something designed to detect and potentially stop hackers and other security risks. Certainly that is the focus of several classified government agencies, and rightly so. Audit trails that are carefully reviewed can enable people to detect new ways users are probing the information in a computer that have never been used before. Hackers are just like virus writers; they sit up all night thinking of new ways to hack.

However, I would like you to also consider a broader use for auditing that might interest even those of you who implicitly trust everyone who has access to your server. The first audit records were not written by people trying to stop Internet hackers. Instead, they were people dealing with early computers that just halted in the middle of executing a program. Because there were no fancy computer monitors back in that era (or any monitors, for that matter), people had little idea where their program halted. After many frustrating attempts to solve problems by trial and error, people started to record progress that was being made in their applications to output devices such as printers (or paper tape). When applications crashed, they simply traced the progress through these checkpoints to determine where the problems occurred.

As operating systems grew and become more capable, the auditing capabilities were built into the operating system. This is especially important for multi-user operating systems, where you need to know who caused the problem and what they were doing at the time to prevent it from happening again. Eventually, auditing was expanded beyond the "finding who caused the crash" stage to provide additional helpful information. It became a tool to record usage of the computer and its various resources. It was also extended to perform the security monitoring tasks mentioned earlier.

A general purpose operating system distributed to a large number of users now has to support a wide range of auditing. It has to cover the security angle to meet the needs of those super-secret environments, but also provide usage metering for people concerned with efficiently using their resources and planning for the future. Others might be concerned with only a light level of security (who is using system administrator privileges). Windows NT has to meet this wide range of challenges and also enable the users to pick from various forms of auditing to suit their individual needs.

Auditing Features on Windows NT Server

This section discusses auditing as it is implemented under Windows NT. I like the way Windows NT implements auditing for the following reasons:

- It integrates all the various forms of auditing (operating system events, security events, and application events) into a single system for review and monitoring. It can be difficult to find time to review your log files, and having all the information in one place displayed by one user interface makes life much easier.

- It is highly automated, with a fair level of basic information recorded automatically using the default system installation procedures.

- It is highly customizable, enabling you to pick exactly what you want and need based on your environment.

- You can interface applications that you develop locally with the auditing subsystem, thereby extending auditing to meet specialized needs, or integrate all your auditing activity into a single system.

■ It is self-cleaning. I have gone into several computer systems where people have used up many tens of megabytes of disk space with logs that they never even knew existed (database and middleware log files, for example). These logs were so large that no one would ever bother to go through them (although UNIX does have utilities that let you see only the last *x* lines in the file).

For smaller server environments, it is often difficult to get a lot of formal training on your operating systems. What basic training you do get does not emphasize the finer features of the operating system, such as auditing. Therefore, I thought it would be useful to go over the auditing options that are available to you. The first set of events that are audited deal with operating system events:

■ Services that fail to start

■ Hardware conflicts detected

■ Start of key services such as the Event Viewer

■ Print jobs completed

■ Anonymous logon requests such as WWW

■ Disks nearing or completely out of space

■ Access requests to the CD-ROM drive when there is no CD in the drive

The second area you can monitor involves system security events such as these:

■ Activation of remote access server (RAS) processes

■ Use of special privileges by the users

■ User logon and logoff

■ Failed logons

■ Access to certain objects (for example, the auditing setup)

■ Policy changes

■ System shutdown and restart

■ User and group management activities

Finally, the most expandable area involves Windows NT's capability to audit events within applications on the system:

■ Setting up BackOffice applications such as Exchange Server or SQL Server

■ Starting up BackOffice components

■ Other events that you build into your applications or system scripts using the Software Development Kit (SDK) routines

Because the first thing you would want to do if you were trying to do something illegal is cover your trail, the auditing information in Windows NT is fairly well-protected inside the operating system (it doesn't have even the old, relatively obvious auditing Registry keys you had in

NT 3.51). The bad guys can't just delete a file and be done with it. You can, however, make a copy of the current log file to save error conditions or document unauthorized activity. This is especially important when you use the automatic overwrite features in the Windows NT auditing system.

Developing an Audit Plan

Now that you have at least a basic understanding of the sort of auditing information Windows NT can provide for you, it is time to figure out what you need to audit. It can be a somewhat tricky balancing act between controlling your volume of work (these logs can get very large on even a moderately active server), need for security (which you might not appreciate until you have a security problem), and the need to recover from problems. An absolute, simple answer would be nice; however, it turns out to be a balancing act that is unique to your particular situation, as shown in Figure 27.1.

27

AUDITING
WINDOWS NT
SERVER

FIGURE 27.1.

Balancing needs for auditing.

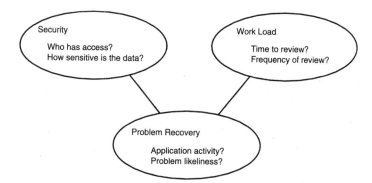

The way I like to approach any such planning task is to go through and list the factors that I considered in the front of the plan document (usually right after some form of introductory paragraph explaining what I am doing). This is useful because it forces me to put things on paper and strain a little bit to try to consider every possible angle and factor that might influence the actual plan itself. I then list what I plan to do. It is a good exercise to go back and review how well your actions satisfied the needs you identified in the factors section.

Let me start with some of the factors you might want to consider when making your audit plan. You will probably be able to come up with a number of additional factors that are more pertinent to your environment. Also, some of these might have absolutely no bearing on your environment. My suggestions for factors that you might consider include the following:

- Are you going to be connected to the Internet or another network that has users who are beyond your control and might possibly be hostile towards your computers or data (hackers and virus writers are hostile in my mind)? This would tend to lead toward much higher security monitoring than nice, isolated local area networks.

- What levels of access do your users have to your system? If all they access is a mail system or client/server database, your auditing requirements might be lighter than a server that has most of its directories exported or available through FTP. Even greater access security issues would come up if you let users actually log on to your server through utilities such as Telnet (see Chapter 17, "User Administration," for more discussion of user management topics).

- What are your chances of having hardware or other system problems that might not be noticed for some time? This might lead you to retain your audit information longer than in an environment where you are checking the logs daily for any indication of problems.

- How much time do you have to review audit information? You have to factor this reality check into any auditing plans you make.

- How important is it for you to document the usage of your server? In some organizations, information systems people are constantly required to justify their benefits to the company. In these environments, it might be important to record information on the number of logons per day, for example.

- Do you have a large number of servers under your care? If so, you might not be logged on to any one server very often. This might lead you to want more information in the audit logs so that you can look for performance or loading problems.

- How important is it for you to monitor the status of your applications? Some server administrators are also responsible for server-based applications such as databases or Web servers. In this case, it might be useful to build your applications to use the SDK to record information in the NT audit trail so that you can see application-internal problems or status messages.

- Do you need to record successful events (such as logons) or only times when these events failed? If you are not interested in usage statistics, failures might be all you need, and failures is a much shorter list to review than successes.

- Do you need to monitor system availability (up-time statistics)? If so, the shutdown and restart statistics can be very helpful at the end of the month when you are frantically trying to calculate up-time for the monthly report.

Finally, never underestimate the value of experimentation. Why not run full auditing on your server for a week or so and see how it goes? Look for those audit events that are most useful. Also look for those that occur frequently or convey little useful information. Try turning off a few parameters to see if this produces an audit trail that seems useful for you. Eventually, with a little bit of trial and error, you will get to an audit plan that meets your needs.

Implementing Audit Policies on Windows NT Server

Now that I have covered the "what to do" discussion of auditing, it is time for the "how to do it" discussion. The truly practical among you can rejoice that I am now leaving the theory world and getting down to business. A good place to start is what I consider to be the heart of auditing under Windows NT—the Event Viewer. You access the Event Viewer through the Start menu.

The Event Viewer both displays auditing results and enables you to perform most of the control functions for NT auditing. Figure 27.2 shows the Event Viewer interface. This is a clean, data-driven interface that focuses on the actual logged information. The control functions are located on the menu across the top. The columns you see here remain the same for all the event types that are monitored. You can maximize or minimize this display as desired.

FIGURE 27.2.

The Event Viewer interface.

Date	Time	Source	Category	Event	User	Computer
3/25/96	7:17:42 PM	Print	None	10	Administrator	JOE
3/25/96	7:05:10 PM	Server	None	2511	N/A	JOE
3/25/96	7:05:07 PM	Serial	None	11	N/A	JOE
3/25/96	7:05:07 PM	Serial	None	24	N/A	JOE
3/25/96	7:05:07 PM	Serial	None	24	N/A	JOE
3/25/96	7:04:44 PM	EventLog	None	6005	N/A	JOE
3/24/96	10:53:40 PM	BROWSER	None	8033	N/A	JOE
3/24/96	10:53:40 PM	BROWSER	None	8033	N/A	JOE
3/24/96	7:39:47 PM	Server	None	2511	N/A	JOE
3/24/96	7:39:44 PM	Serial	None	11	N/A	JOE
3/24/96	7:39:44 PM	Serial	None	24	N/A	JOE
3/24/96	7:39:44 PM	Serial	None	24	N/A	JOE
3/24/96	7:39:24 PM	EventLog	None	6005	N/A	JOE
3/18/96	11:25:26 PM	BROWSER	None	8033	N/A	JOE
3/18/96	11:25:26 PM	BROWSER	None	8033	N/A	JOE
3/18/96	11:20:05 PM	Server	None	2511	N/A	JOE
3/18/96	11:20:00 PM	Serial	None	11	N/A	JOE

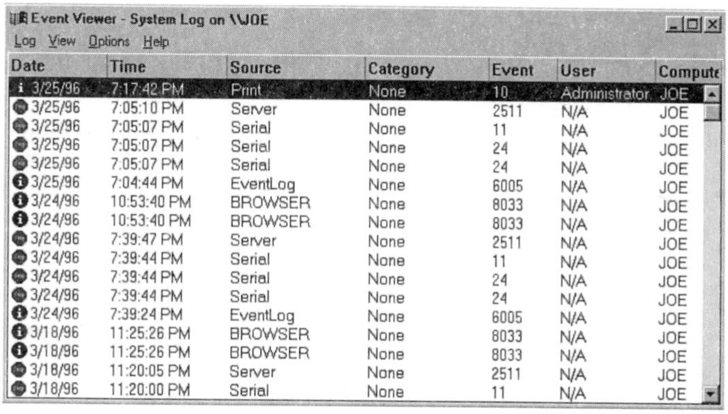

The following information is captured in these audit records:

- Date of the event
- Time of the event (to the second)
- Source of the event (for example, service)
- Category of the event (for those audits that have been categorized)
- Event number (a code you can reference)
- User ID that caused this event (not applicable on system start-up events and other events generated by the operating system with no user interaction)
- Computer identifier that caused the event (in multicomputer environments)
- Domain in which the event occurred

■ A reason for the event (such as a logon that failed because of an unknown user name or bad password)

■ Additional information specific to the event (such as the logon type attempted for a failed logon)

■ Type of event. This is not a text column; instead, the type of event is conveyed by an icon picture. The types of events you might see include errors, warnings, information, success audits, and failure audits.

The first key concept to grasp with the Event Viewer is that this one interface displays all three types of Windows NT audit records: system events, security events, and application events. You select which of these event types is displayed using the Log menu (see Figure 27.3). The Event Viewer remembers the type of log you were looking at the last time you used this utility and displays this same log type when you next start it. To determine which log is displayed at any given time, you simply look at the title. The title contains two useful bits of information. First is the type of auditing performed. The other is the machine whose audit log is being displayed. One of the nice features for administrators who are in charge of multiple systems is the ability to select various Windows NT computers for which you want to display the audit log. Of course, you must have the appropriate trust relationships established with these machines, but it is worth it if you have several systems to keep track of.

FIGURE 27.3.

The Log menu of the Event Viewer.

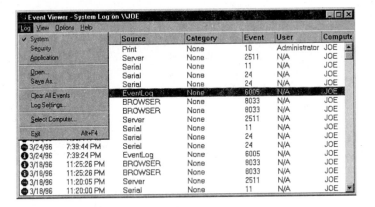

Although these columns provide a good deal of useful summary information, they are not everything you would want or need to solve a really nasty problem. They are useful to scan through quickly to see if you have any real problems or if your log is just full of routine information messages and expected conditions. To get the full details about a particular event that catches your interest, all you have to do is double-click that event. When you do, you see a detailed display dialog, as shown in Figure 27.4.

This dialog echoes the information contained on the summary display, along with several other useful bits of information. The exact details depend somewhat on the event encountered. For example, in Figure 27.4 where I intentionally typed in a bad password, you can see a text description of the reason and even the logon authentication package used. Some events display data in the bottom text area that can give you clues as to the state and activities that were occurring to cause the event. I always like to screen-print messages that I might have to take action on (or copy them down if screen printing is too much of a problem).

FIGURE 27.4.

The Event Detail dialog box.

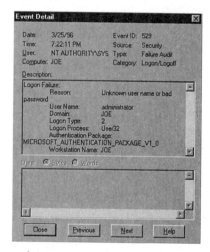

The next log to review is the security log, which is shown in Figure 27.5. Again, you see the same basic columns as in the system log. You get detailed information about a particular event by double-clicking it just as in the system log. The key differences for this log are the icons that you see at the left edge of the display, the use of the Category field, and the fact that the User column is often the most important bit of information displayed.

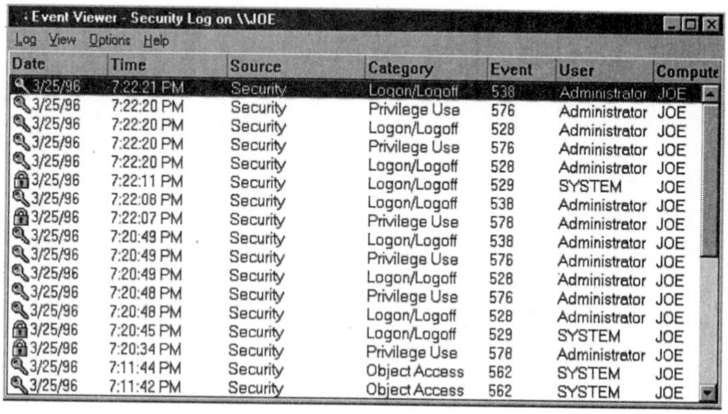

FIGURE 27.5.

The security log.

Date	Time	Source	Category	Event	User	Compute
3/25/96	7:22:21 PM	Security	Logon/Logoff	538	Administrator	JOE
3/25/96	7:22:20 PM	Security	Privilege Use	576	Administrator	JOE
3/25/96	7:22:20 PM	Security	Logon/Logoff	528	Administrator	JOE
3/25/96	7:22:20 PM	Security	Privilege Use	576	Administrator	JOE
3/25/96	7:22:20 PM	Security	Logon/Logoff	528	Administrator	JOE
3/25/96	7:22:11 PM	Security	Logon/Logoff	529	SYSTEM	JOE
3/25/96	7:22:08 PM	Security	Logon/Logoff	538	Administrator	JOE
3/25/96	7:22:07 PM	Security	Privilege Use	578	Administrator	JOE
3/25/96	7:20:49 PM	Security	Logon/Logoff	538	Administrator	JOE
3/25/96	7:20:49 PM	Security	Privilege Use	576	Administrator	JOE
3/25/96	7:20:49 PM	Security	Logon/Logoff	528	Administrator	JOE
3/25/96	7:20:48 PM	Security	Privilege Use	576	Administrator	JOE
3/25/96	7:20:48 PM	Security	Logon/Logoff	528	Administrator	JOE
3/25/96	7:20:45 PM	Security	Logon/Logoff	529	SYSTEM	JOE
3/25/96	7:20:34 PM	Security	Privilege Use	578	Administrator	JOE
3/25/96	7:11:44 PM	Security	Object Access	562	SYSTEM	JOE
3/25/96	7:11:42 PM	Security	Object Access	562	SYSTEM	JOE

The two icons you typically see are a key (indicating success, which could be bad in the case of a hacker accessing something he shouldn't have) and a lock (indicating that the system stopped the user from doing something). It is normal to see a few failures every now and again (for example, I have so many passwords that I have trouble keeping them all straight). What you are really looking for is several failures occurring in a short period of time, which might indicate hacking. You can also scan through the Category list for events that are of interest to you (for example, logon/logoff events). Finally, the User column can help you zero in on the activities of a particular user that you might be keeping your eye on.

One thing I considered a bit strange about the Event Viewer display was the fact that it did not allow you to sort on any of the categories in the multicolumn listbox display by simply clicking the column heading (such as Category). You can find this type of control on the My Computer utility on your desktop. This would make it really easy to sort the list by user, for example, and see who is being naughty and nice. You do have some of this functionality by using the Filter option on the View menu. This gives you a dialog (see Figure 27.6) that enables you to focus on a particular category, user, and so forth. You have to be somewhat careful because you don't see events that don't match your input criteria but might be important to you (use the Clear button on the Filter dialog to view all events). This is an interesting technique to keep in your inventory when you have to audit a large number of events.

FIGURE 27.6.

The Event Viewer Filter dialog box.

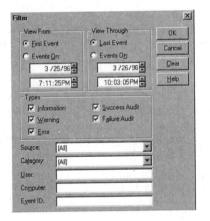

The final log is the application log, shown in Figure 27.7. This is perhaps the least-exploited log in its basic form. About the only applications I have loaded that make good use of this log are the Microsoft BackOffice applications, and even they could make greater use of it. I like the concept of being able to record application events in one central point as opposed to dozens of different log files scattered all over the system (I have had to deal with these files before, and they can be a bit of a pain). The software development kits from Microsoft enable programmers to interface to these audit files. You might want to consider this if you have any input into the application development at your facility.

The best way to get used to these logs is to run your system for a while and review the events that get recorded. You should be especially sensitive to the icons displayed on the far-left side of the list of events, because these help you sort out the problems from the routine items. The next issue you have to deal with is controlling the event log itself. The control over the size of the data and time it is retained is set using the Log Settings option of the Log menu (see Figure 27.8).

FIGURE 27.7.
The Event Viewer application log.

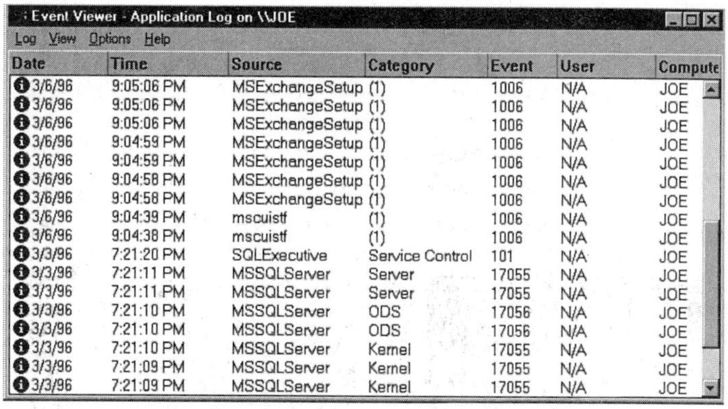

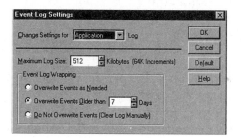

Event Viewer - Application Log on \\JOE
Log View Options Help
Date Time Source Category Event User Compute
3/6/96 9:05:06 PM MSExchangeSetup (1) 1006 N/A JOE
3/6/96 9:05:06 PM MSExchangeSetup (1) 1006 N/A JOE
3/6/96 9:05:06 PM MSExchangeSetup (1) 1006 N/A JOE
3/6/96 9:04:59 PM MSExchangeSetup (1) 1006 N/A JOE
3/6/96 9:04:59 PM MSExchangeSetup (1) 1006 N/A JOE
3/6/96 9:04:58 PM MSExchangeSetup (1) 1006 N/A JOE
3/6/96 9:04:58 PM MSExchangeSetup (1) 1006 N/A JOE
3/6/96 9:04:39 PM mscuistf (1) 1006 N/A JOE
3/6/96 9:04:38 PM mscuistf (1) 1006 N/A JOE
3/3/96 7:21:20 PM SQLExecutive Service Control 101 N/A JOE
3/3/96 7:21:11 PM MSSQLServer Server 17055 N/A JOE
3/3/96 7:21:11 PM MSSQLServer Server 17055 N/A JOE
3/3/96 7:21:10 PM MSSQLServer ODS 17056 N/A JOE
3/3/96 7:21:10 PM MSSQLServer ODS 17056 N/A JOE
3/3/96 7:21:10 PM MSSQLServer Kernel 17055 N/A JOE
3/3/96 7:21:09 PM MSSQLServer Kernel 17055 N/A JOE
3/3/96 7:21:09 PM MSSQLServer Kernel 17055 N/A JOE

FIGURE 27.8.
The Event Log Settings dialog box.

Event Log Settings
Change Settings for Application Log
OK
Cancel
Default
Help
Maximum Log Size: 512 Kilobytes (64K Increments)
Event Log Wrapping
Overwrite Events as Needed
Overwrite Events Older than 7 Days
Do Not Overwrite Events (Clear Log Manually)

You set each of the log record sizes separately as controlled by the drop-down listbox. The first thing you set is the maximum size of the log. Basically, I accept the default and adjust it only if I am retaining information for too long a period or too short a period. The next feature you set here is the one that controls the Windows NT auditing log self-cleaning feature. I really like this because I have seen some really huge log files that someone (like me) forgot to clean out. Your options are to overwrite as needed, to overwrite events only if they are more than a certain number of days old, or to never overwrite (to manually clear the log). Again, remember that you have to set this up for each of the three logs (system, security, and application) used by NT's auditing.

One final set of controls you have in the Event Viewer tool is shown in Figure 27.9. I have already covered the All Events and Filter Events options. This menu also gives you the option of displaying the events from earliest to latest or latest to earliest event. The Find dialog looks similar to the Filter dialog, but instead of limiting what is displayed, it takes you to the records that meet your input criteria. The Detail option is similar to double-clicking a particular event. Finally, Refresh updates the display with any new events.

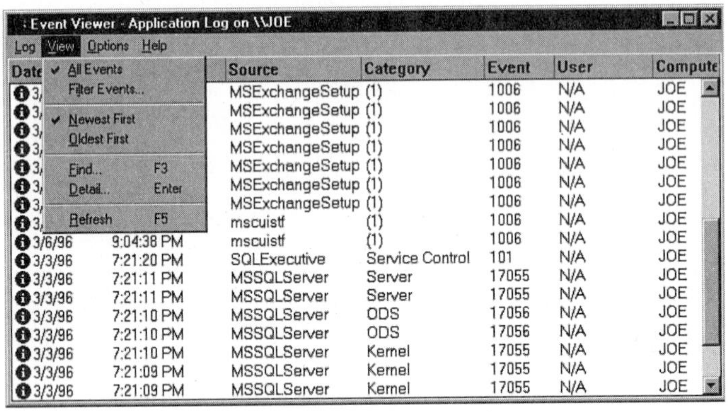

FIGURE 27.9.

*The Event Viewer's
View menu.*

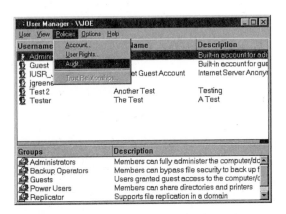

The system audit events are pretty clear as to what you would want to record (you almost always would want to know if your serial port has an interrupt conflict). The same goes for application events, because you would have to add them to your applications to get anything to go in there other than a few of the BackOffice products that are currently using this portion of the auditing system. However, the security logging mechanisms need finer control to accommodate the wide variety of environments that are out there. If you were to audit everything imaginable in security, your log file would be so large that you would have to write an application just to filter out the events that might possibly be of interest (which would not be all that difficult, actually). However, some groups that I work with do not even want to waste the disk space for security auditing because everyone has full access to all resources and therefore these records have no meaning (small software development environments can be fun in this regard).

NT's auditing system accommodates this wide range of needs through the User Manager utility. This is another of the administrative tools that are available to you. I guess it was a toss-up as to whether to put all auditing controls in the Event Viewer or to put all the features involved with user security in the User Manager. Microsoft chose the latter option. To access the controls for security auditing, choose the Audit option from the Policies menu in User Manager (see Figure 27.10).

FIGURE 27.10.

*Selecting the Audit
option in User
Manager.*

The Audit option displays the Audit Policy dialog shown in Figure 27.11. The radio buttons are important because they make the basic selection as to whether you perform any of these detailed security auditing functions. If you select to perform these security auditing actions, you are given two basic choices for auditing. The first column of checkboxes enables you to audit when users perform the functions listed successfully (such as logging on with the correct user ID and password). The second column of checkboxes enables you to audit when users fail when trying to perform a function. You can greatly reduce the number of events recorded if you look only for failures. This catches hackers or people trying to access a resource for which they lack permission. However, if you are trying to gather statistics on usage or logging all (legal) access to a resource, you would want to use the first column's checkboxes. Of course, if you want a lot of information, you can audit both successes and failures.

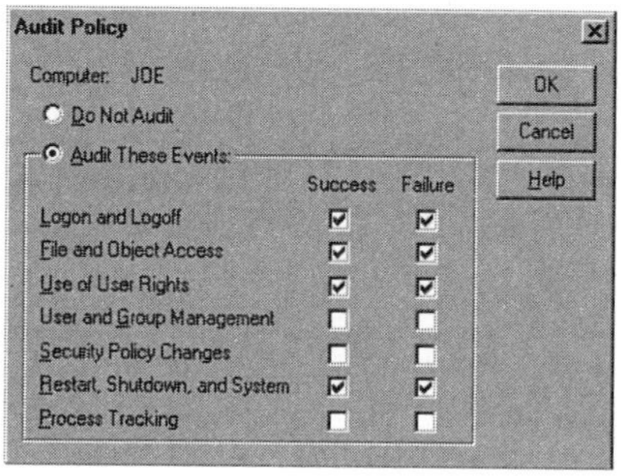

FIGURE 27.11.

The Audit Policy dialog box.

Splitting the security auditing features into these seven categories enables you to pick the items that meet your needs and ignore the others, which can also reduce the number of log file entries you have to review. The categories you have to choose from are as follows:

- **Logon and Logoff.**
- **File and Object Access:** This can be very detailed, but it works only for NTFS file systems that have access rights (FAT is a pretty open storage mechanism designed for nonsecure DOS environments).
- **Use of User Rights:** This refers to rights that have been granted to a user or group (for example, performing system administrative functions with a personal NT account).
- **User and Group Management:** This catches when someone alters the privileges of another account or creates an account to perform some bad activities and then deletes it.
- **Security Policy Changes:** This is another area where the whole security picture of your system can be changed and therefore is a common audit function.
- **Restart, Shutdown, and System:** This can be useful for recording downtime and determining when serious problems such as power outages occurred.
- **Process Tracking:** This captures some very detailed information such as process activation and indirect object access.

As you can see, you can set up a lot with NT auditing. The interface that controls and reviews the auditing information is also a clean and simple one. The challenge is often to make the time to review the log. In summary, your steps in setting up auditing on an NT Server should include the following:

1. Determine the factors that affect your auditing needs.
2. Develop an audit plan.
3. Use Event Viewer's Event Log Settings dialog to control the amount of information retained in each of the logs.
4. Use the User Manager's Audit Policy dialog to control which security auditing features are implemented on your system.
5. Make time to review the logs using Event Viewer.

Sample Auditing Implementations

Now that you are an expert in setting up auditing on Windows NT, here are a few sample auditing configurations that I might set up. Think of them as food for thought when you go through setting up your auditing. For purposes of this discussion, I construct three possible scenarios:

- The small server in a low effort environment.
- A middle-of-the-road corporate server with some sensitive information.
- A server with a fair amount of sensitive information.

For my first scenario, I consider a small server in an environment where not much effort can be expended on administering the server. Perhaps this is a nice, secure development environment that exists on an isolated LAN where everyone has access to all data that is stored on the server. You can limit the user's ability to access directories containing applications just so they don't accidentally destroy something. Also, you can use FAT file systems for compatibility with other operating systems loaded on this machine (for example, DOS/Windows 3.11).

Under this scenario, I recommend using the default audit settings in Windows NT. The log files take up 512KB each, which is not a lot in most server systems. The security auditing features under User Manager are turned off (set to Do Not Audit). However, this seems like a very good way of doing business for this low security environment. Note that you still get a full set of auditing on the system log recording problems that you might have with processes or conflicts. You also get whatever application log entries the applications you install on your system support.

The next scenario is a middle-of-the-road scenario. I think of this as a typical office server that might serve as a file server, print server, mail server, and application server. The information stored in the user's directories is not top secret or sensitive personnel information (perhaps just a bunch of spreadsheets and word processing documents). You want some form of security to ensure that hackers do not mess with another user's data (such as the marketing plans of a competing salesperson), but you don't have a lot of time to devote to this auditing function. Perhaps you are responsible for all the servers in your building, for example.

In this case, I would probably set up the NT auditing to maintain the default log size unless I run into problems with it. This is pretty good for most of the work I have done. I would set it up to keep log entries for 30 days on the Event Log Settings panel. The biggest changes from the default would be to set up some basic auditing functions in the Audit Policy dialog in User Manager. I would typically record failure of logons, failure of file and object access, success and failure of user and group management functions, success and failure of security policies changes, and restarts and shutdowns. This assumes that I have a good security setup (I am using NTFS and therefore can isolate user access to appropriate directories or have disabled the average user's ability to log on at the console) and that I just want to catch changes that might occur. I also want to catch any time there are several failures trying to log on to the system or access a particular resource. This might be a sign of someone trying to hack a password for another user's account (most of the places I have worked have standard naming conventions for accounts, so all the hacker needs to do is guess the password to gain access to information). Finally, I would plan a time once a week or so to review log information. Again, I would look at the icons on the left of the Event Viewer display to see stop signs and padlocks, which indicate potential problems.

The final environment you might have to support is a server that contains some really sensitive information. Perhaps you are dealing with top-secret government information. Perhaps you are dealing with bank or personnel records that must be safeguarded. Another possibility is that you are just processing sensitive company information on a server that is open to access from the Internet or is connected to a customer's network. In any event, you would be under a lot of pressure to make sure that you keep everything as safe as possible.

I would attack this problem by setting up the audit log to retain a few megabytes of information in the security log section. I would retain events for at least 30 days. You should check your local record retention requirements to see if you are required to retain the records for longer periods. I might also consider saving log files once a month to disk. That way you have the option of going back in time to see how long suspicious activity has been taking place and what the impacts on security might have been.

As to Audit Policies set up under User Manager, I would probably set up the full spectrum for at least the failure option. I would set up success auditing for at least the logon, user rights, user and group management, security policy change, and shutdown/restart options. This assumes that NTFS is being used for disk storage on disks that store sensitive information. It also assumes that you have set up your user and group structure correctly with emphasis on controlling access for such things as directories that are shared to only the appropriate groups. You might want to review your event log every day or two because you need to take action fairly quickly if you detect suspicious activity.

I hope these samples help you when you formulate your auditing setups. Remember again that these are just samples. Every environment has its own unique problems that need to be solved. Also, you might have more or less time to spend on the job than I typically do, so that has to be weighed against the information benefits of more detailed auditing. Finally, think of this as an ongoing process. If you find that you are getting too much or too little information, alter your policies until you have something that works for you. You should also review your auditing policy every time the use of your system changes. For example, if you add a personnel group or start keeping financial records in a new database, you might have to increase your auditing and security features.

Summary

Auditing brings up some interesting concepts that you have to consider as an NT Server administrator. You are not just a simple MS-DOS/Windows 3.1 PC user anymore without a care in the world about security. You are also not within a mainframe environment with its large staff of specialists, which usually includes a dedicated security staff. You are somewhere in-between. Often you are expected to provide the easy, intuitive access to data found on the Windows PC and the tight security found on mainframes. The auditing features of Windows NT make this task a little easier.

The key points to remember are that you use the Event Viewer to review results from all of the various forms of auditing: system, security, and application. It also sets up the retention parameters for the audit logs. The Audit Policy dialog in User Manager is used to set up most of the security auditing features under Windows NT. The application auditing feature can be designed into your applications if you want to have one central location for auditing information. Taken together, the environment is fairly easy to work with and provides a good deal of auditing information.

Advanced Security Guidelines

28

by Jason Garms

IN THIS CHAPTER

This chapter is not for the faint of heart. However, if you use Windows NT Server for anything more than tinkering, I strongly encourage you to look through this chapter so that you begin to understand how some of the changes you make (or don't make) can have a dramatic effect on the overall security of your system.

If you are an advanced administrator, this chapter will definitely interest you.

This chapter introduces some of the basic concepts behind computer security, including what it is and why it's important to you. It continues with an explanation of the U.S. government's computer security evaluation criteria, and how Windows NT evaluates against it. In particular, it focuses on what C2-level security is, and how Windows NT complies with the guidelines required for this rating.

The chapter then continues by going through all of the major components of Windows NT that impact the security of the system, including what you should do to increase the level of security, as well as the disadvantages of taking these actions. Remember, increased security often comes at a price, either in convenience or performance.

Some of the changes described in this chapter are not applicable to every environment. However, if you take the time to understand the implications and logic behind each section, you will end up with a much better understanding of how Windows NT works, as well as an increased ability to secure Windows NT in your particular network.

Therefore, let's start at the beginning. Before a practical security policy can be developed, you need to address some important questions.

What Is Computer Security?

Broadly defined, computer security involves the prevention of undesired or unintentional access to any part of a computer system. In an inclusive sense, this would include all aspects of hardware and software, servers, workstations, LAN devices and cabling, as well as computer operating systems, network operating systems, user programs, and the most important element—user data. Of course, this definition is far too expansive a subject to be addressed in a single chapter, so we focus on ways to use Windows NT to its fullest capability and how to lock down the operating system to prevent tampering.

What Are We Trying to Protect?

If we look back many years into the annals of computer lore, we learn that computer security originally focused on protecting the single most precious resource—the compute cycle. When people communicated with a central, massive computer through punch cards and dumb terminals, the compute cycle—the atomic unit of computing power—was in great demand. This valuable commodity was often the main objective of wayward hackers, who would attempt to find ways to divert a system's compute cycles for their own use. It became part of the job for a computer operator to protect his or her system from being compromised, so that each compute cycle could be accounted for and billed to the appropriate party. Although stealing compute cycles is still a concern for some people today, I would venture to say that the majority of us have other issues that we place higher on our list of worries. Because many people have computers on their desks that can run rings around the mainframes of yesterday, stealing compute cycles is just not something most people worry about.

> **NOTE**
>
> In this section, I use the term *hacker* to refer to a person who tries to break into or otherwise compromise a computer system. I use the term here specifically because it is the most common term used by law enforcement professionals to describe people who try to access electronic systems illegally. Additionally, although some other terms are coming into use, the name *hacker* is what most of these people call themselves.
>
> Unfortunately, there are also a great many other computer wizards who also call themselves hackers, but do not use their computers and skills to attack other systems. It is truly unfortunate that this term has taken on such a negative connotation and I apologize to the good guys for using this term here to describe computer intruders.

When computer networks began to emerge—mostly to link universities, research agencies, and the military—the target of computer hackers began to change. These networks presented a new and potentially more interesting subject for their attacks. Because it was widespread in large computing environments to establish inter-system trust relationships (such as rhosts files in the UNIX environment), hackers would try to break into a system, not for the data that was contained on that particular system, but rather to gain access to computers that trusted it. In other words, hackers began to try to steal the *identity* of a computer. They would ride this spiderweb-like trust relationship from computer to computer and sometimes it could lead them around the world. Some hackers would do this just for fun—to see where they could get. Others, however, had intentions other than joy riding.

Computer networks opened a new can of worms that was hard for many people to understand. People tend to discount the security-related consequences of computer networks because they represent such an intangible concept. While we've grown used to our electronic toys, such as televisions and radios that communicate in a *single* direction, we have not quite gotten used to people being able to connect to our computers from across the world and access our files. Up until the proliferation of personal computers, our telephones have been our only *two-way* communications devices. They were easy to deal with because we had to worry about one person at a time. It was impossible for someone to simply call our homes or offices and eavesdrop on us.

With computer networks, this has all changed. The scary part is not that someone *can* access our computers from across the world, but rather that it *happens all the time*! Additionally, whatever the chances are that someone is going to worm into your computer system from the other side of the world, the chances are even greater that you'll be attacked by a set of prying eyes from right down the hall. I've heard many people who are connected to the Internet explain with perfect logic that with the countless number of systems connected to the Internet, the chances of someone attacking their system is statistically nonexistent. Unfortunately, these kinds of people are often proved to be flat-out wrong. Security-in-numbers may be a nice concept, but it's not reliable.

Who Are the Bad Guys?

Often the concept of security begins with "us" against "them." This is definitely a good place to begin. However, as is often the case, the "us" and the "them" are not so easily defined.

When developing a security policy, you should consider all possible players in the security arena. You need to ensure that your security policies include considerations for protecting your system from not only the outside intruders, but also from accidental mistakes on the part of the local users and administrators. Additionally, you should consider intentional mischief from within your organization and from the most powerful adversary, a renegade administrator. Although you might not need to or even be able to fully protect your system from all of these, you need to consider that each is possible and evaluate how these kinds of attacks would affect your system.

Security and Windows NT

It's hard to have a coffee-table conversation about Windows NT without at least broaching the subject of security. Security is built into the core of Windows NT and represents an integral part of Microsoft's marketing strategy for its NT product line.

UNIX has been around for over two decades, and the number of books written about security from a UNIX point of view is overwhelming. Windows NT, on the other hand, has only been around a few years and there is still little extensive information published that focuses directly on Windows NT-specific security issues, such as the way that NT handles its user security database and network authentication. Reading a generalized treatise on computer and network security is useful for developing ideas that can be extended to the NT environment, but there are critical NT-specific issues that need to be addressed directly. Although there are architectural similarities between Windows NT and various flavors of UNIX, the complexities of computer security are directly linked with the intricacies of the operating system, such as how users are created, where and how the user database is stored, how you access files, and what privileges different processes have.

With more than two million copies of Windows NT on the market, coupled with an ever growing migration toward global connectivity through the Internet and other means, accurate information about building and maintaining a secure NT Server is imperative. These are the details that are dealt with in this chapter.

This chapter is *not* intended to be an in-depth discussion of the development of security policies or the end-all and be-all of risk analysis. There are numerous excellent books published on these subjects and they should be consulted for a more detailed and rigorous investigation of the subject. Additionally, if you are concerned about the security of your Windows NT system, you might want to consider getting help from a professional computer security specialist.

> **NOTE**
>
> If you are interested in learning more about computer security, a good place to begin is with NCSA, the National Computer Security Association. It can be found at `http://www.ncsa.com`, and should not be confused with National Center for Supercomputing Applications (NCSA), the developers of Mosaic.

I have tried to make this chapter as useful to as many people as possible. I have included basic concepts of security policy for people without a background in computer security. This is followed by a discussion of C2 security evaluation and concludes with a review of areas that system administrators should address to help make their systems as secure as possible. I have compiled a list of all the security-related problems and warnings that I've encountered while working with Windows NT systems. Windows NT has some wonderfully robust features that allow for very secure installations; however, like any complex system, there are many things that can go wrong. If I can communicate one thing in this chapter, it is that the most secure facility in the world can be compromised if the front doors are left open. Likewise, your NT system can be compromised if you don't fully understand the security implications of your actions, or even in some cases, your lack of actions.

Although many users still consider computer security to be something that they don't need to be concerned with, they couldn't be farther from the truth. The increasing appearance of computer networks in today's corporate environment requires that users begin to get more involved with this issue.

With a standalone computer, it is relatively easy to identify your potential attackers and develop means to protect yourself. However, as soon as you attach that computer to a network, you've just changed the nature of the game.

Security Through Obscurity

Security through obscurity is an important enough topic that I thought it deserved its own section. It's a simple concept that has tremendous significance on the strength of a security policy.

Quite simply, the security through obscurity policy is where certain facts are kept secret with the intent that doing so will provide some level of security for the whole system. Unfortunately, this does not work in computer security.

Under the principle of security through obscurity, the administrator assumes that just because a user does not have the proper instructions or documentation to perform a certain action, he or she will be unable to perform it.

I did some work for an organization where they used a homegrown accounting system for internal use. This accounting system was created in a commercial database package and used a standard text file to determine who would have what permissions in the accounting system. The problem with this file was that it had no security to prevent anyone from making changes to it. It was mixed in with literally hundreds of other files that occupied a dozen-or-so directories, so the likelihood of someone tripping across this *one file* was supposedly quite remote.

This is security by obscurity. If someone had wanted to gain access into this accounting system, they merely would have needed to change that file. When I addressed this concern, the response was, "Well, no one has done it yet, and who's going to go looking for it?" That's a common problem with security. Just because it is obscure and hasn't been noticed yet, doesn't mean that it will not or cannot be done.

Another example of security by obscurity is a situation where people feel that because the source-code for their software has not been released, people will not be able to analyze it and find flaws. Many flaws are found entirely by accident. Also, don't underestimate the ability of a dedicated hacker. Another example of something to avoid is developing an in-house security algorithm. Leave encryption to people trained in the subject. Security algorithms developed in-house are rarely secure. Just because you're convinced that it's safe does not make it so.

In the case of UNIX, most of the source code is readily available and anyone with the proper knowledge and desire can analyze its security value. The source code for Windows NT, on the other hand, has not been made public. For some people this is a sign that the security might not be as strong as Microsoft claims. Microsoft has implemented a number of effective encryption algorithms in Windows NT, including Data Encryption Standard (DES) and Rivest, Shamir, and Adleman's public-key encryption method (RSA), which have been proven to be effective. DES is currently a U.S. standard as declared by the National Institute of Standards and Technology (NIST), and RSA is the world's most-used public-key encryption method. However, just because an algorithm is known to be effective, does not ensure the accuracy of the particular implementation.

> **NOTE**
>
> For some people, it might seem strange that making source code available for review could actually increase the security of the entire system. This is true only where a system's security design has been based on architectural constraints rather than on obscurity. For example, if the system has a special password that it uses to perform certain internal actions, analyzing the source code will provide this information, which could be used by a hacker.

This type of system uses obscurity as pseudo-security. In a well-designed system, analyzing the source code would not reveal information that could be used against the system. Therefore, in theory, if you don't have any skeletons hiding in the system code, you should be willing to show it to anyone for scrutiny so that they can see that your code is secure and trustworthy. This is also important so people can see that the source code has no hidden back doors or other unwanted features that could be taken advantage of at a later time by the code's writer or someone else familiar with the code.

For this reason, the C2 evaluation process is an important certification for Windows NT. Although Microsoft's in-house development team worked with many independent, world-class security consultants during the development of Windows NT's security system, this is not enough for some people. There are many people who believe that the only way to test a system's security is to open the source code to public scrutiny. In Microsoft's defense, neither they nor any other commercially viable company can afford to release their source code to the general public.

The Data Encryption Standard (DES), originally developed by IBM, was first endorsed by the U.S. government in 1977. The important things to know about DES are that it uses a fixed-length, 56-bit key; is based on a private-key method; and uses a symmetric encryption algorithm. Now what does this mean? That it uses a fixed-length, 56-bit key means that there is no way to make the algorithm stronger by increasing the key length. The algorithm used in DES has undergone an extreme amount of scrutiny over the past decade and a half by encryption experts worldwide. Although some people believe the National Security Agency (NSA) might have had a back door built in, no one has been able to find a way to defeat DES except through brute force attacks. That DES is a private-key method goes hand-in-hand with using a symmetric encryption engine. Symmetric means that the same key you use to perform the encryption is also used to perform the decryption. This means if someone knows how to encrypt a file, he or she can also know how to decrypt it.

RSA (Rivest, Shamir, Adleman) is a patented encryption method developed by Ron Rivest, Adi Shamir, and Leonard Adleman in 1977. RSA is a public-key, asymmetric algorithm that can use variable length keys and can be used for both encryption and authentication. That a cryptosystem is asymmetric means that the key used to encrypt the data is different from the key used to decrypt the data. This lends itself to an approach called public-key cryptography. In a public-key cryptosystem everyone typically has a public key and a private key. The public key is what is used to encrypt the data and can be given to anyone. Your private key must be kept secret and can be used to decrypt information encrypted with your public key. This enables someone to send me a document in a secure way by using my public key to encrypt it. Because you need my private key to decrypt it, and only *I* have my private key, the transaction is secure. This is not possible in a private-key cryptosystem such as DES. Also, unlike DES, the algorithm used in RSA enables you to increase the size of the encryption key provided and thus gain additional security.

So which is better? DES and RSA are actually complementary, not competing cryptosystems. For many applications, DES is faster. RSA, however, provides functionality not possible with DES, such as digital authentication and the capability to conduct secure transactions over an unsecured channel.

The important thing to remember is that it's a fallacy to rely on a belief that just because you think that no one knows something, or you think they will not be able to figure something out, it's secure. I met an administrator who used to set up "invisible" administrative shares on his Window NT Server for the computer support staff. He would create shares with a $ on the end of the name, which would prevent them from showing up in the network browser. His belief was that because no one else knew the share names and could not see them in the browser, he didn't need to implement proper share-level permissions. Although securing the shares would have been trivially easy, he was just lazy. Of course he was surprised to find out that it was in fact extremely easy for anyone to get a list of these "invisible" shares. This is security through obscurity.

It might be argued that he didn't know that these shares could be seen, so it wasn't his fault. I don't agree. He made two serious mistakes. First, it's his system—he should make an effort to understand how it works. Second, it would have been simple for him to implement the share- or file-level permissions necessary to protect his resources. He chose to hide them, because it was easier. This is also security through obscurity. Don't do it.

Security Policies and Procedures

The key to today's marketplace is information. The vast majority of our information is now being stored electronically by computers. It's increasingly becoming true that control of this information is what gives an organization the competitive advantage necessary to succeed in the marketplace. It is this competitive edge that we are trying to protect by designing and implementing a robust security policy for our computer systems.

Many administrators seem to fall neatly into the two major extremes. The first group of people are those who think that implementing a strict set of computing guidelines is not necessary. They might feel this way because they are in a small company that is not connected to the Internet, or they feel that tight security policy gets in the way of the users. The rationalizations are numerous.

Of course you've probably already guessed the second type of administrator that completes my stereotyped pair. This administrator is the one who has security fever. The one that people often call "control freak" behind his or her back. This person often tries to lock down every door and control every aspect of the environment, which often results in an Orwellian style of administration.

For most organizations, an appropriate security policy would fall somewhere in the middle of these two extremes. Of course in some situations, such as banking, insurance, medical, and other industries where confidentiality is a concern, a security policy is always better on the more cautious side. I would never recommend any organization to completely neglect the development of a security policy. No network is too small or too unimportant to ignore creating and documenting a security policy.

Developing Policies and Procedures

When you develop your security policies and procedures document, you should be sure to address all parts that make up and interact with your system. This includes the hardware, the offices and building itself, the network cabling, the operating systems—both on the clients and on the server—and programs that are used on the systems. You should also address any actions relating to the systems, such as what precautions should be taken in the event of a hardware failure or upgrade, how backup tapes should be handled, and so on. Additionally, you should take into consideration the users, the administrators, and any additional facility staff, such as maintenance and housekeeping.

Of course it is likely that the greatest factor that will determine the depth of your security policy is the value of your data. If your systems are used primarily for simple office memos and fliers that have no lasting value, your data might not seem important enough to worry about. However, if your data has *any* lasting importance, or especially if it is of a proprietary or confidential nature, you need to take your security policies and procedures document very seriously.

When talking to users about computer security it is important to relate computer security to other security issues in their lives. Many people wouldn't think of leaving their cars unlocked, or leaving the front doors of their houses wide open, yet these same people don't want to protect their computer systems. Many people are afraid that everyone is trying to steal their credit card numbers, but yet they don't admit the reality of people breaking into their computer systems.

Also it is important not to alienate users by making them feel that they are not trustworthy or that they are being watched. When you discuss security issues with users, you should be careful not to create an adversarial relationship between the user and the security policy. Focus on the idea that the system is based on the principles that a user only gets access to resources they need for their work. Explain that this helps to avoid accidents as much as anything else.

Commitment to Security

It's fine for you and me as system administrators to sit around a table and discuss implementing a security policy. If there is no buy-in from upper management, we can preach from here to eternity about the importance of a security policy, but nothing will happen. Upper management must participate during the entire development period. Their input and endorsement is essential. In some cases, you as the administrator might even be part of upper management. In that case you might have an easier job.

I've seen too many instances where a well-developed security policy was ignored by all the users because the upper management didn't seem to care. Even worse is when management undermines its own policies by making exceptions for itself.

No one should be exempt from the security policy. It should be followed by one and by all. It is there for the protection of the system, and ultimately of your organization's data and resources.

Once a policy is developed, you must follow it. Like many other policies, a security policy can succumb to the fate of being nothing more than documentation that fills a binder in the office. No one reads it. No one cares. The policy should be followed with diligence. Users need to be reminded on a regular basis. Furthermore, the policy should be evaluated periodically to ensure its effectiveness, and modifications should be made when necessary.

Security Audits

In computer security jargon, a *security audit* is the procedure of checking all the subsystems of a computer or network to ensure that all known problems have been protected against and that the appropriate security devices have been properly enabled.

Additionally, NT provides a means to generate a log of almost all system activity, including when users log on or off, when a file is accessed and by whom, and even when print jobs are processed. This functionality is referred to as *auditing*.

Routine security audits of the entire network are a good idea to ensure that holes haven't accidentally been opened and gone unnoticed. In your security policy document, you should identify items that need to be checked and determine how often they should be checked. As part of this process, you should develop an audit check list for your system. This list should contain information on how your share permissions should be set, how the security on certain folders should be set, what privileges different users should have, and so on. It might not sound like a glamorous job, but it needs to be done. It's all too easy to set up a system and attempt to let it run itself. However, without constant attention, that system is likely to run itself into the ground. I've met quite a few system administrators who claim to have nothing to do, yet wouldn't be caught dead looking through their system to make sure everything looks okay. Be proactive, not reactive.

In organizations where the confidentiality of the data is essential, there should be formal policies in place to routinely audit the system to ensure that nothing has been compromised. In organizations such as these, you might want to designate an individual to be responsible for the auditing. This auditor would be tasked with using Windows NT's audit logs to verify the integrity of the data on the system. In financial institutions or other organizations that already have official internal auditors, these people should be trained to work with NT and to be able to read NT's audit logs for identifying potential problems.

Of course, the auditor and the administrator could be the same person, but there are many cases in which you would not want this. The first reason is that very often the administrator is confident that things are set up correctly and might tend to gloss over areas that might actually contain problems.

A second scenario in which the auditor and the administrator would be different people is if the auditing of your system is mandated by either law or corporate policy. A good example is a financial institution. Many of these organizations are required to provide audit trails that prove the integrity of the data. The audit features in NT allow you to know when the data—or the audit log—has been tampered with.

Additionally some organizations might not "trust" their administrators fully. This might be especially true in areas where proprietary trade secrets are involved. Also, in the government, for instance, when private contractors sometimes perform administrative tasks on servers that contain data they should not be viewing. In this case a government auditor can be assigned to verify what the administrator has done.

The most important thing to realize here is that NT allows you to enforce an environment where the administrator is not granted *carte blanche* access to the entire system, but rather is held accountable for his or her actions.

What Is C2 Security?

Listed prominently on Windows NT's list of features is that it meets the C2 computer security guidelines set by the U.S. government. As with many matters relating to the U.S. government and security, it is often difficult to figure out what this really means. In writing this book, I asked a number of administrators about Windows NT's security features, and they all ranted and raved about how secure of a system it is. Without fail, they all mentioned "C2" somewhere in their explanation about why Windows NT is so secure. However, when asked what the C2 meant, and what it meant to be C2-evaluated or C2-certified, they were stumped.

The National Computer Security Center (NCSC) publishes the two definitive texts on computer security. By "definitive," I don't necessarily mean the most complete, comprehensive, or accurate, but rather that these two texts dictate the outward position held by the United States Department of Defense with regards to qualifying computer systems for use in various critical environments. Although these guidelines must often be adhered to in many government agencies, there is no requirement that the private sector take any interest—unless they wish to do business with the government. Nonetheless, many people in the private sector do take great notice because the guidelines set forth in these documents are definitely good advice.

The Department of Defense's Trusted Computer System Evaluation Criteria (TCSEC)—also called the "orange book" for the color of its cover—provides security requirements for automatic data processing (ADP) systems. The companion to this book—called the "red book"— extends the interpretations for the evaluation of trusted systems to computer networks. These books were developed to provide users a metric for determining the degree of trust they can put in their computer system.

28

ADVANCED
SECURITY
GUIDELINES

I don't recommend running off and getting copies of these books for your bookshelf, as they are certainly not the most interesting bedtime reading material, unless you want something to put you to sleep! Although they might be a little dry, they are very important for explaining the evaluation criteria necessary to meet a specific security level. If you are interested taking a look, both texts are available in their entirety on the Internet by way of FTP, Gopher, and the World Wide Web.

The TCSEC is broken into four major divisions: Division D, Division C, Division B, and Division A, with Division D being the "least" secure and Division A being the "most" secure. Each division must meet the requirements of its predecessor and include additional features to provide enhanced security. Table 28.1 lists the different divisions.

Table 28.1. The divisions of the TCSEC security rankings.

Division	Name	Overview
D	Minimal Protection	Reserved for systems that failed to be evaluated for a higher class.
C1	Discretionary Protection	Requires user-level controls for protection of data from accidental loss. Expected to be a cooperative non-sensitive environment.
C2	Controlled Access Protection	Users are held accountable for their actions. System tracks all processes and records actions on a user-by-user basis. Prevents object reuse, and must ensure efficacy of system security monitor. Users can grant others access to their data.
B1	Labeled Security Protection	Requires development of an informal security policy. All data must be labeled as to sensitivity of data, and system must ensure consistency of labels as data is transferred across the system. Users cannot override mandatory security labeling.
B2	Structured Protection	Requires a structured, formal security policy. User authentication methods are strengthened to guarantee validity and security of authentication information.
B3	Security Domains	Requires security system to be as small as possible, and strip out any non-security-related code. This code is then subjected to scrutiny and testing. Additional facilities to signal administrators in the event of security-related

Division	Name	Overview
		actions is required. The system must be tamper-proof and highly resistant to penetration.
A1	Verified Design	Functionally equivalent to B3, except A1 systems must undergo rigorous and formal testing.

Division D: Minimal Protection

Division D, called Minimal Protection, is reserved for systems that have been evaluated, but have failed to meet the requirements necessary for a higher division. Last I heard, no systems have actually been rated as Division D, because having a system evaluated is extremely expensive and most vendors prepare their systems adequately to meet a higher class.

Division C: Discretionary Protection

Division C, called Discretionary Protection, provides for discretionary control of information, which can be accounted for by the use of audit facilities. This division is further broken into two classes, C1 and C2, with C2 being deemed the more secure.

Class C1 is called Discretionary Security Protection and requires that some form of controls are in place to enable users to protect private information from other users. Systems in this class require users to identify themselves by entering a unique identity and validate their identity by entering a password. Naturally the system is required to maintain the integrity of the user/password data by preventing unauthorized access. The system will use the user's authenticated credentials to control both reading and writing of sensitive information. Additionally, this class requires that the system within the computer responsible for authenticating the user is protected from external interference, which implies that a user should not be able to run a program to circumvent the security mechanism.

The second class, C2, is called Controlled Access Protection. This class includes all of the requirements of C1, but adds additional requirements. C2 class requires that a control mechanism be provided to grant or restrict access to data files on a user-by-user basis. Furthermore, access permission to an object to which a user does not currently have access can be granted only by authorized users. A further requirement of C2 class is that when an object or file is discarded, no part of that data may be retrieved either intentionally or accidentally. Although systems in class C2 are permitted to allow users access to data based on membership in a group, or access from a particular host, the systems must be able to identify and provide an audit record of exactly what user performed the action.

Division B: Mandatory Protection

With Division D and C, it was sufficient to provide mechanisms for restricting a user's access to data and to audit any security-relevant actions. Beginning with Division B, however, it becomes necessary to provide mechanisms to label the sensitivity of data and provide mechanisms that ensure that authorized users cannot pass sensitive information—either accidentally or intentionally—to users without a sufficient level of authorization. This level begins a requirement that the system must enforce object control on a mandatory, not merely discretionary, level.

Specifically, class B1 requires the implementation of this data labeling, which must be capable of including or excluding users to the granularity of a single user. Furthermore, the integrity of the labels and the capability of the labels to move with data as it is copied from one location to another must be enforced. The system must also mark the top and bottom of all printed or other human-readable output with sensitivity labels that appropriately identify the output. There are additional and very precise requirements about the capability of the system to authenticate and audit access to data based on multiple levels of security clearance.

Class B2 is essentially a strengthened version of B1, where its security system is required to control all aspects of the system environment. The security authority in the system must be designed in a carefully structured way and is subjected to considerably more scrutiny and review than lower-security classes. By way of review, this class is required to provide discretionary access control for all objects to the granularity of a single user. Furthermore, the capability to change access permissions on an object is restricted to authorized users. Objects that have been discarded or deleted cannot either accidentally or intentionally be recovered by any means. All ADP system resources must be capable of being labeled by the security system, which will provide mandatory access restrictions based on the sensitivity label assigned to the resource. Furthermore, the integrity of the labels must be ensured, even when passing the object over various I/O or other internal or external devices. The beginning and end of all human-readable output must be labeled with the appropriate sensitivity information. The security system must notify an interactive user of every change in security status during the course of the computing session. As with prior levels, B2 requires the security system to maintain a database of authorized users and passwords for authentication, along with a detailed listing of the users' security clearance authorizations. What is new in this level is the requirement of a guaranteed trusted path for the user's initial logon and authentication. Like the other levels, class B2 must support extensive auditing capabilities. Furthermore the architecture of the system must guarantee that the security system is a protected domain of its own, free from external influence or tampering. Both hardware and software shall be used to enforce this, along with a mechanism for routinely confirming that no breach has in fact occurred in this protected domain.

> **NOTE**
>
> The major difference between B1 and B2 is that B2 must include special trusted logon paths enforced through hardware and software to ensure not only that the user's password

cannot be compromised, but also that the system can guarantee the source of the logon request. For example, you cannot log on to a B2-class computer using a PC and modem at home because there would be no way to guarantee the source and security of the logon session.

Believe it or not, there's more. The B3 class system must satisfy the requirements that it mediate all accesses of subjects to objects, be tamperproof, and be small enough to be subjected to analysis and tests. To this end, the security system is structured to exclude code not essential to security policy enforcement, with significant system engineering during its design and implementation directed toward minimizing its complexity. A security administrator is supported, audit mechanisms are expanded to signal security-relevant events, and system recovery procedures are required. The system is highly resistant to penetration.

Division A: Verified Protection

Division A, called Verified Protection, has only a single category, A1: Verified Design. A system meeting this class must go through rigorous formal security verification to ensure that the system in fact functions exactly as intended. In order to be evaluated for this class, the system must be designed in a most exacting way and be presented with extensive documentation. Aside from meticulous testing, class A1 is functionally equivalent to class B3.

Windows NT and C2 Security

I can't count the number of times I've been asked what C2 certification meant. Other questions I've been asked over and over include why NT did not meet a higher level of security evaluation. For the way most people do business, C2 is about the most realistic level necessary—as far as NCSC goes. People needing additional security features should look for their criteria elsewhere, not in any of the rainbow-colored books.

Microsoft designed Windows NT from the ground up to meet the C2 criteria set forth in the Orange Book; the Red Book, an interpretation of the Orange Book for network systems; and the Blue Book, an interpretation of the Orange Book for other subsystems. They began working with the NCSC in 1992 to evaluate Windows NT for the C2 class.

In August 1995, Microsoft announced that Windows NT Server and Workstation 3.5 with service pack 3 passed testing and would be added to the official Evaluated Products List of C2-certified operating systems published by the National Security Agency. However, Windows NT is still being evaluated for the Red and Blue Book interpretations.

What does this really mean? It means that the stripped-down and bare-bones operating system of Windows NT has successfully been evaluated at the C2 level. However, the networking systems and other secondary parts of the operating system have not yet completed evaluation.

28

ADVANCED
SECURITY
GUIDELINES

Currently for an NT installation to be C2-compliant, it must *not* be connected to any kind of network. If you need to ensure that a system configuration meets the C2 guidelines, you should refer to a security expert who specializes in this topic.

> **NOTE**
>
> As stated earlier, the actual C2 certification process means little to most end users. Its real worth is for government agencies that are required to purchase systems that meet the C2 evaluation criteria.

If C2 security is important to you, the good news is that evaluation of Windows NT is continuing to advance. The full certification process simply takes time. As of the writing of this book, Windows NT is being evaluated for additional components, as well as for complete certification under the Red Book interpretations.

In each chapter of this book I have tried to address many of the security concerns about specific systems as they come up in their related areas. In this section, I would like to try to bring all those concerns together and address them in a single place.

First I will review the basic features in Windows NT that can be used to help you create and manage a secure system. This will be followed by a discussion of other security-related issues that all NT administrators will want to be aware of. I have tried hard to come up with all kinds of odds and ends relating to security that I have often tried to find in a single place. Furthermore, I hope to persuade those administrators who don't care too much about security to re-examine this extremely important topic.

Review of Requirements for Class C2 Security as Related to Windows NT

We've identified that Windows NT is in fact a product that has been evaluated to meet the C2 security rating based on the NCSC Orange Book. Let's review one more time the key criteria for C2 class systems:

- Discretionary Control: The operating system must enable the owner of an object (in most cases a file, print job, or process) to grant or restrict access to the resource. This discretionary control feature is implemented in Windows NT through access control lists, which provide single-user granularity for controlling object access.

- Object Reuse: Discarded or deleted objects must not be accessible, either accidentally or purposefully. Because all object assignments must pass through a single point, the Security Reference Monitor (SRM), the system guarantees that discarded objects cannot be accessed by any other process. For example, when a file is deleted under NTFS, the file's data cannot be retrieved, hence the lack of an undelete facility.

Additionally, when a process is allocated memory, Windows NT initializes this space, ensuring that no data from a prior process will be left behind.

■ User Identification and Authentication: Before being allowed to access the system, each user must identify him- or herself by entering a unique logon name and password. The system uses this data to validate a user's right to access the system. If the credentials are valid, the user is granted a security token, which is used to validate any object access during that particular logon session. Furthermore, the user's logon information can be used to track actions performed by the user.

■ Auditing: An integrated feature of Windows NT is its capability to audit all object access and security-related actions on the system and identify which user performed the actions. This capability to provide such a granular level of auditing is necessary for C2 compliance. Additionally, access to this audit data is restricted to authorized administrative users.

■ Protection: Windows NT prevents processes from accessing memory outside of its own 32-bit space, thereby removing the possibility that an application can read or write data from another process's memory space. The kernel itself runs in a protected 32-bit memory space. Processes can communicate with the kernel and with other processes through the use of a carefully defined message-passing system, which removes any need for a process to modify another process's memory. Additionally, because Windows NT prevents direct hardware access, no process can bypass the security model and directly access memory or hard disk information.

Physical Concerns

Most of what we will spend our time on is about how to secure Windows NT from the software side. However, it is important that I first spend some time discussing some of the physical security concerns you might want to address. Remember that no matter how secure you lock down the software, if someone has physical access to the server, there is an increased cause for concern.

Server

For servers where the data is not confidential or business critical, it might be okay not to spend too much attention on the physical security of your server. Basic hardware security is so simple, however, I encourage you to give it some serious attention.

Even if the data on the server is not of value to anyone else, there is still the chance that your office might get broken into and the server stolen just because it will fetch some money on the street. Even if you are insured, how much will the lost productivity cost?

Rule number one: Keep your server in a locked room. It shouldn't be kept in a highly trafficked location. By placing it out of the way, you remove many of the potential accidental problems such as tripping over cables and bringing the network down, spilling a drink or food into the machine, and so on. Furthermore, by restricting access to the computer you can limit the threat of someone gaining access to the power switch and the floppy drive. Most machines today enable you to use the CMOS to disable booting from the floppy drive. You can then password-protect the BIOS. In this way, you have taken a good step toward reducing the chances that someone can easily compromise the system. Remember, the floppy drive is dangerous. By booting from a floppy disk, someone can use low-level disk utilities to read the data directly off the drive, because Windows NT is not alive to protect itself. An even easier method would be to reinstall Windows NT and replace the security authority. In either case, this risk can be reduced by restricting the ability to boot from a floppy.

When buying systems, often the emphasis is placed on things such as the processor speed and memory capacity while ignoring the quality of the hardware itself—including physical security features. It is good practice to buy equipment made from physically strong materials that can discourage tampering. This includes having a lock that prevents people from opening the case, and, if at all possible, a locking door cover the power switch and reset button. If the case can be opened, the computer can be compromised. Again, remember much of this can be resolved by putting the server in a locked, secure room.

When choosing a secure room for the server, also look up and down. The floor and the ceiling are often the easiest ways to break into a locked room. Many computing facilities still have cooling and venting paths that run under the floor. Often these are not secure and it is easy to pull one of the tiles from the floor, crawl under the door, and enter a room. The ceiling path, however, is often the easier route. Most office buildings with drop ceilings are not usually planned with single-room security in mind.

I did some consulting for an organization that required that the server be located behind two locked doors. The first lock was at the front door to the office suite and the second was on the office itself. However, the server room was located with one wall adjacent to the men's bathroom, with no firewall in between. The building opened to the public at 6:00 each morning, but no one usually came around until after 7:00. It was extremely simple for anyone to enter the building undetected from the basement and take the elevator to the appropriate floor. From there they could enter the men's bathroom, climb over the wall and they were in the server room. Does this sound kind of like the movie *Sneakers*? Also sounds a little paranoid? Well, I don't think that it would have been a laughing matter if someone were to follow this little plan. To the best of my knowledge, nothing has been done to rectify this problem to this day. I won't say exactly what kind of data could have been compromised, except that it could easily have resulted in a lot of people losing a lot of money.

In fact I had a similar experience, where the customer had custody of sensitive social security data for statistical analysis. He insisted that the data could not be allowed to pass over their network of about 100 computers, because this would enable the possibility that someone could capture the data. When I asked what their suggestion for securing the data was, he replied that they would keep the computer in a locked room. When I pointed out that it was much easier to climb over the wall and access the computer than it would be to use a LAN sniffer to capture *over 20 gigabytes* of data, he refused to even entertain the idea that someone would climb over the wall. I guess that's just different perceptions of the world.

Restricting the Boot Process

You should use the BIOS to disable booting from a floppy drive. Not only will this prevent people from booting to a different operating system, which could enable them to circumvent NT's security facilities, but if the floppy boot is not disabled, the server will not be able to reboot from a system crash or a remote reboot if someone accidentally leaves a floppy disk in the drive.

> **NOTE**
>
> Configuring the system so that it cannot boot from floppy only helps to protect from accidents, unless you enforce this restriction by also using a BIOS-level password. If your hardware supports it, this password will prevent a potential intruder from simply booting a different operating system from floppy, or worse, booting from an NT setup disk and reinstalling the NT account database, thereby circumventing your system's defenses.

The additional benefit of disabling the boot-from-floppy option is the prevention of boot-sector viruses. While Windows NT is up and running, it cannot be infected by a boot sector virus. However, if you boot the system off an infected floppy, the virus will infect the system.

Also, you should make sure that no other operating system, especially DOS, is loaded on the computer. Some people recommend setting the timeout option for selecting an operating system during boot to 0 seconds. The theory is that this would prevent someone from tampering with the system. For example, if a person can boot to DOS, they could potentially modify the BOOT.INI, NTLDR, or NTDETECT.COM files, which could affect the functioning of your system. Additionally, if you have other system files or data stored on a FAT partition, booting to DOS would enable someone to tamper with these files.

If you set the timeout option to 0 seconds, you should definitely create a fault-tolerant boot floppy to enable you to boot Windows NT using various diagnostic features should a problem occur.

> **NOTE**
>
> Of course, if you need to use this fault-tolerant boot floppy, you would have to go into the BIOS and re-enable the boot-from-floppy option.

Network

The chief concern when putting computers onto a network is the division of sensitive information. The most common Ethernet configuration is an environment where the entire network is made of a single segment. In this environment, you are vulnerable because any other user on the network can tap and monitor all network traffic. If all users on the network are cleared for sensitive information, this might not be a problem, but typically this is not the case. Additionally, it is easy to create unauthorized wire taps for the sole purpose of capturing sensitive data. To help remove these problems, you should consider setting up a routed environment, dividing the network based on the level of secure information. This would prevent sensitive information from traveling the entire network. An additional option would be to run in a switched Ethernet environment. The price of switched Ethernet hubs has come down considerably and in many cases is considered more desirable than a routed environment. Not only do you gain the advantage that your sensitive information does not need to be transmitted everywhere, but the switched environment gives each node a dedicated bandwidth, resulting in better network performance.

> **NOTE**
>
> Many small- to mid-sized Ethernet networks today are set up as a single segment. What this essentially means is that network traffic between two devices on the network can be monitored from any point on the network. For instance, if your network spans two floors of a building, but is still set up as a single segment, and you have a computer on the first floor talking to the server in the next room over, the people on the second floor can also "see" the traffic.
>
> Because all this network bandwidth is shared, this kind of network topology is susceptible to problems caused by high volumes of network traffic. But more important to our discussion here are the security implications of this shared bandwidth.
>
> The demand for better network performance led to two different solutions for splitting up the network into segments and thereby reducing the number of devices that share a particular segment. These solutions are bridging/routing and switching. Fortunately, if they are implemented properly, they can also help to provide us increased security by preventing the conversation between our server and client on the first floor from being overheard by the client on the second floor. That's what's important to us here.

If you need to protect against unauthorized wire taps, you should consider using fiber cable. You can then use network management agents to determine instantly if there is a cable break and investigate. However, just running fiber does not necessarily remove the risk of a user monitoring the network from an authorized network drop.

If you are running a secure network and the cabling must run through an unsecured area, you should consider using encryption devices to encrypt the data before leaving the secure area and decryption devices when it again enters a secure area. This is especially important if you are using the Internet to connect WANs. If you are attached to the Internet, you cannot guarantee who is going to have access to your data. To ensure that the security of the data is not compromised, you need to use encryption.

Connecting your network to the Internet opens a whole additional can of worms. Not only do you have to worry about the security of data that you transmit across the Internet, but you need to worry about people coming into your network from the Internet. For more information about connecting to the Internet, see Chapter 31, "Using Windows NT as an Internet Server."

User Accounts

Because Windows NT was designed to meet the C2 criteria, which is based on user-level authentication, any security-related issue in Windows NT must first be looked at from the context of a user account. That makes a discussion of user accounts a good place to begin.

All objects have owners, and as we have already discussed in earlier chapters, almost everything in the Windows NT universe is an object. In fact, as future generations of Windows NT are developed, this object-based paradigm will continue to play a greater and greater role. The preliminary feature set of the next generation of NT, called Cairo, currently includes the implementation of an object-based file system.

Many administrators are hesitant to create multiple user accounts for a single user. Sometimes they will even create one user account to be used by various people (for instance, creating a single user account for a front-desk receptionist, which is used by three people). The password is then shared among many people and the account is used by anyone sitting at the front desk. The problem with this is that it provides no accountability. If data is erased or something else is done, there is no way to know who was responsible. Additionally, if you want to change the password on this account, you must then worry about informing all necessary users of the new password.

Both of these situations should be avoided. Every user should have at least one account. Some users, depending on need, should have more than one account—although rarely more than two. The thing that's important to remember is that Windows NT enables you to create as many user accounts as necessary. If people play multiple discrete roles, there is no problem in giving them multiple accounts with each account having the appropriate permissions for the particular role.

Creating multiple accounts with only the rights necessary to perform specific roles is a valuable thing. I personally try to avoid using privileged accounts whenever possible, especially for day-to-day activities. It's too easy to slip while in the NT Explorer or File Manager and delete the wrong directory. Slips of the fingers can be costly. To help alleviate this problem, you should consider using an NT Workstation for your administrative tasks. Because Windows NT can operate in multiple-user contexts, you can be logged on to your workstation as a normal user but connect to your server as a different user to perform your administrative tasks. This obviates the need to log out and log back on in order to perform administrative functions. For more on this, see the section "Use an NT System for Management" later in this chapter.

It's also useful for administrators to get a chance to understand what it's like to be a plain, mild-mannered user. It gives them a better perspective of what a user's life is really like, and they can better appreciate when users come complaining that they can't do this or that. Many administrators don't realize the limitations of a normal user's account. On many clients such as Windows 3.x, Windows 95, and Macintosh, these limitations are not very apparent. However, the limitations on a Windows NT Workstation are more noticeable. There are lots of things a normal user cannot do by default. Try playing the normal user and see what it's like.

User Accounts for Services

User accounts are not just for people. All processes in Windows NT run in the context of a user. As we'll discuss in a later section, many of the processes in Windows NT are set by default to run under the built-in SYSTEM account. This can pose security problems and I encourage you to consider making user accounts for some of these services and assign that account only the privileges necessary for the tasks it will perform.

> **NOTE**
>
> If you choose to allow a service to use the SYSTEM account, you need to understand the potential problems and pitfalls.
>
> To give you an example of a potential pitfall, let's take a look at the Scheduler service. By default, this account runs in the context of the SYSTEM user. Let's say, for instance, that you use the Scheduler service to regularly backup the local system using the backup utility that comes with Windows NT. The batch file you use to perform the backup is `c:\users\backup\backfull.bat`. This batch file contains a single line that invokes the NTBACKUP program with the appropriate switches.
>
> However innocuous this seems, there are two potential problems. First, if you don't have the permissions set correctly on the batch file and someone were to change it, they could add the line "net user administrator breakin," or some such line, to the batch file. This line is quite simple. It changes the password on the administrator account to "breakin." Because the batch file gets run with the SYSTEM account, and the SYSTEM account has the capability to perform account maintenance, you have a problem. Of course this can be prevented if the batch file is properly protected.
>
> A second potential hole that could be taken advantage of would be if you didn't call NTBACKUP by specifying its full path, such as `c:\winnt\system32\ntbackup.exe`. If you simply called NTBACKUP by using NTBACKUP /switches, someone might be able to place a file called NTBACKUP.EXE or even NTBACKUP.BAT somewhere in the path so that it gets called

instead of the NTBACKUP.EXE that you want to be called. This unknown program or batch file would then get called with the full privileges of the SYSTEM account. Of course this can be prevented by fully qualifying the path, and by properly defining the system's path.

You'll notice that both of these two problems I proposed can be rectified relatively easily, and I even pointed out the proper method to solve them. However, the point of this is that, unless you go through everything with a fine-toothed comb, there might be problems that someone can take advantage of.

Of course, the best way to solve this problem is to run the schedule service, or any service for that matter, with the level of privileges necessary to perform its job.

For a more in-depth discussion on this topic, see the section "Services" later in this chapter.

Good security policy includes a routine audit of all accounts, active and inactive, to ensure that they should still exist and that they have the correct privileges. It might sound ridiculous and time consuming, but I've seen it more than once when a system administrator looked through the group assignments and was surprised to find out who the other domain administrators were! Don't let this happen to you. See the section "Auditing" later in this chapter for more information.

Rename and Don't Use the Administrator Account

The Administrator account and the Guest account are two issues that need some special attention. It is often confusing to figure out how to best use these accounts and what, if anything, is particularly special about them. It is very important that you understand what these accounts are for and decide how best to use them. If you are familiar with the UNIX environment, the Administrator account is very similar to the root account, and should be used with as much caution. If you are familiar with Novell's NetWare, the Administrator account is similar to the Supervisor account. Although there are similarities to both of these other environments, there are also differences.

The Administrator account is the first user account created when you install Windows NT. It is the ultimate user authority on the NT system. As the name implies, it can be used to perform administrative activities on the system, such as account management, disk and printer management, and security policy administration. Although NT has user rights that can be assigned to any user to enable him or her to perform these activities, the Administrator account can do all of these things. Furthermore, whereas user rights can be removed from normal user accounts, the Administrator account cannot be stripped of its powers. The intent behind this is to prevent you from locking yourself out of your system because you removed administrative rights from all the users.

Because the Administrator account holds so much power, and this power cannot be removed, it is often a visible target for someone trying to break into your system. The Administrator account cannot be deleted, it cannot be disabled, but the good news is that it can be renamed.

One of the special features of this account is that even if the system policy is set to lock out user accounts after a certain number of failed login attempts, the administrator account can *never* be locked out.

> **TIP**
>
> Rename the Administrator account and do not use it except for emergencies, such as if you lock out all your other accounts with administrative rights, or you forget your password. Every administrative task that needs to be done can be performed by granting users the appropriate group membership.

When you rename this account, you can call it anything you want. Picking a normal-sounding user name is often a good place to start. Also, make sure you remove the comment indicating that this is the built-in administrative account. Because this account is the only account in Windows NT that cannot be locked out—even if the password lockout feature has been enabled—it is an extremely attractive target for hackers. Using the API set that is built into Windows NT, it is not a difficult task to create a program that continuously attempts to log on to the system using a systematic password-guessing algorithm. By renaming the Administrator account, and enabling the account lockout feature, you can make a hacker's job more difficult.

Furthermore, the built-in Administrator account is permanently a member of the local Administrators group. You cannot remove the privileges from this account, so you'd better make sure that you protect it properly.

You should refrain from using this administrative account as much as possible, so as to minimize the attention you draw to it. It is better practice to create privileged accounts for each user who needs to perform special administrative functions. Take advantage of the built-in NT groups to grant people varying degrees of access.

It is also important to inspect this account on a regular basis to ensure that someone else has not changed the password and that the account has not been compromised.

Although the Administrator account cannot be locked out, if someone attempts to log on with the incorrect password the number of times specified by the account lockout policy, Windows NT places a check mark in the account lockout box under the Administrator account in the User Manager for Domain, as shown in Figure 28.1.

This is, however, somewhat misleading, because the account has not, in fact, been disabled. To confirm this, simply try logging on as the Administrator. Furthermore, if you audit failed logon attempts, you can view the security log, which will confirm that the administrator user has not been disabled.

FIGURE 28.1.

The Locked Out check box is deceiving because the Administrator account cannot be locked out due to invalid logon attempts.

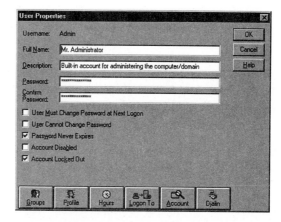

NOTE

I've tried to figure out why the system behaves in this manner. I can only think of one reason why this might be considered useful and not a bug. By having the system check this box, the system administrator has an easy way, aside from auditing, to see if someone has tried to break into the Administrator account.

28

ADVANCED
SECURITY
GUIDELINES

Version
History

Disable the Guest Account

The Guest account is the second built-in account that is automatically created when Windows NT is installed. The Guest account cannot be deleted, but it can be renamed. By default, this account is disabled.

In NT 3.51, the Guest account was disabled on domain controllers, but enabled on member servers and NT Workstations.

Naturally, the history of the Guest account is for systems that allow one-time or occasional access. However, there is a more important role that the Guest account plays. When someone attempts to log on to an NT system across the network, the client presents a set of user credentials. If these credentials don't match an account in the NT security database and the Guest account is enabled, the user is logged on as the Guest user. If you want to use the Guest account for this purpose, the password needs to be left blank. If users will only be accessing these resources from the network, you might want to revoke its Log On Locally user right to prevent someone from logging on to local machines with the Guest account.

NOTE

If you have installed Services for Macintosh and permit Macintosh clients to connect as guests, they are not authenticated with the Guest account. They are logged on using a special internal ANONYMOUS USER account. For more information on this, please see Chapter 9, "Working with Macintosh Clients."

Personally I think the Guest account should be disabled in all but the most open environments. Creating accounts in Windows NT is so easy and any functionality provided by the Guest account can be easily duplicated in a secure manner by creating a few accounts.

CAUTION

If the Guest account is enabled, anyone will be able to connect to your server over the network, browse through your Registry, and run Microsoft Diagnostics (WINMSD.EXE) against your computer. This can potentially give them more information about your computer than you might want them to have. This is of particular concern if you are connected to the Internet.

In Windows NT Advanced Server 3.1, the Guest account was a member of the Domain Users global group, which was a member of the Users group. This presented a security problem because any resource that granted access to the Domain Users or local Users groups also granted permission to guests. By default the Guest account was disabled, so it was not an immediate security problem. However, by enabling the Guest account, the system administrator could create a potentially serious security problem and not even realize it.

To help alleviate this problem, Microsoft made some changes beginning with Windows NT Server 3.5. A new global group, Domain Guests, was created, of which the Guest account is a member. The Guest account was removed from the global Domain Users group and is therefore no longer a member of the local Users group.

TIP

To regain the same functionality for Guest accounts as in Advanced Server 3.1, put the Domain Guests into the local Users account.

Implement Mandatory User Profiles

User profiles enable an administrator to customize aspects of a user's machine when logged on to Windows 95 and NT machines. The profile is loaded when the user logs on to a workstation and gives the user the same desktop on all workstations in the domain. You can use profiles to restrict a user's access to the command line, or prevent a user from changing certain program groups. If your network has NT Workstations or Windows 95, you should consider implementing mandatory profiles. For more information, see Chapter 17, "User Administration."

User Rights

Before making changes to user rights, you need to make sure you understand not only the security-related consequences, but also what effect these changes might have on the rest of the system. For most NT Servers installed as domain controllers, the default user rights are adequate for security purposes. Because the default user rights are different for domain controllers and member servers, however, you should consider making the following two changes to any NT Servers that are not domain controllers:

Right	Change
Log on Locally	Remove Everyone and Guest
Shut down the System	Remove Everyone and Users

Remember that the security setup on an NT Server that is not a domain controller, also called a *member server*, is essentially the same as an NT Workstation. By default, these systems enable Everyone and Guests to log on to the console and work. Furthermore, once logged on, these users can execute a system shutdown. Although this might not be such a big deal for an NT Workstation, it is a big deal for an NT Server configured as a member server.

At one place I did some work for there was a large multiprocessor DEC Alpha running Windows NT Server that was sitting in a high-traffic area. This machine ran Microsoft SQL Server and served a number of important production databases. The administrator of this was familiar with NT Advanced Server 3.1, where all servers were domain controllers. When he upgraded this machine to 3.5, he decided to make it a member server, because he didn't want the overhead associated with making it a domain controller. Unfortunately, he didn't understand the differences between the user accounts of a domain controller and a member server, so he did two things wrong.

First, he left the Guest account enabled, which had been the default (and is no longer the default for an NT Server). Second, he left the Log on Locally user right granted to Everyone and Guest. For months the server ran this way. One day I reviewed the configuration on the server and discovered this problem.

Essentially anyone could log onto the server with the Guest account, *any* user account from the domain, or trusted domain and have almost free access to the server. Because the machine was solely a SQL server, and not a file and print server, he hadn't bothered to make sure the NTFS file permissions were locked down. Essentially anyone who had physical access to the machine could have done almost anything to it.

So what is the lesson here? First, know your machine. But that's obvious. More importantly, if your NT Server is a member server, you should make a point to change the permissions listed to ensure an acceptable level of security at the console.

For a complete description of all the user rights, see Chapter 18 and Appendix C.

Understand the Bypass Traverse Checking User Right

Bypass Traverse Checking is a user right that is enabled for everyone by default in Windows NT, as shown in Figure 28.2. The problem is that most administrators do not fully understand what it does and why it's there.

FIGURE 28.2.

By default, the Bypass Traverse Checking user right is enabled for everyone.

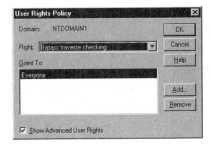

Having the Bypass Traverse Checking right tells NT to check the Access Control Lists (ACL) only on the file or directory a user is accessing—not on its parent directories up to the root. Although this sounds like a fairly easy concept, it has some ramifications that should be fully understood.

Leaving Bypass Traverse Checking enabled can be a big problem if users are not careful and aware of its security-related consequences. To illustrate what this right does, look at the security differences between moving a file and copying a file, as well as how and when access rights to a file are inherited. This example should give a clearer example of what this right does.

> **CAUTION**
>
> Remember, if you move a file, it keeps its existing permissions, whereas if you copy it, it will inherit the permissions from its parent directory. For more information on the differences between moving and copying a file, as well as its effect on the security permissions of the file, see Chapter 5, "Windows NT File Systems Management."

Consider the following scenario:

1. Use the NT Explorer to make two folders called E:\TEST1 and E:\TEST2 (assuming E:\ is an NTFS volume).

2. Assign Everyone Full Control permissions to the folder E:\TEST1 and tell NT to replace the permissions on all subdirectories. This is shown in Figure 28.3.

FIGURE 28.3.

Assign the Everyone group Full Control of the folder E:\TEST1.

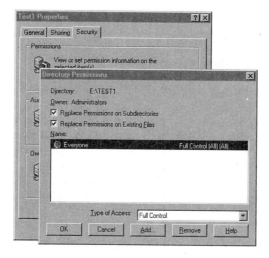

3. Assign Everyone Add permissions to E:\TEST2 and all subdirectories, as shown in Figure 28.4.

FIGURE 28.4.

Assign the Everyone group Add permissions of the folder E:\TEST2.

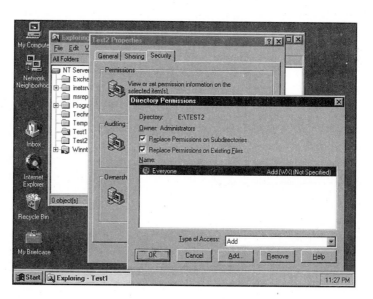

4. Use Notepad to create a text file. Just type a few random characters into the file—its contents are unimportant. Then save the file as E:\TEST1\MYFILE.TXT.

28

ADVANCED
SECURITY
GUIDELINES

5. Use the NT Explorer to examine the permissions on the file you just created—E:\TEST1\MYFILE.TXT. The permissions should be set so that Everyone has full control. No other access control entries (ACE) should be listed.

6. Now, using the NT Explorer, move MYFILE.TXT from E:\TEST1 into E:\TEST2.

7. Double-click on E:\TEST2 to get a directory. You should get an access denied error.

8. Now open Notepad, then using the Open menu item, type E:\TEST2\MYFILE.TXT and press Return. You will need to type the full name and path in the Open dialog box, because you will not be able to browse the directory tree. You should be able to see the contents of the file.

9. If you repeat steps 4 through 8 but this time *copy* the file rather than *move* it, you will be unable to view the file with Notepad because the restricted ACL will be inherited from E:\TEST2.

If you disable the Bypass Traverse Checking user right, and then repeat this exercise, you will be unable to open the file E:\TEST2\MYFILE.TXT regardless of whether you copied or moved it. This is because with this user right disabled, Windows NT checks to ensure that you have the appropriate privileges for *every* directory beginning with the root.

To further illustrate this concept, let's say you have a file E:\USERS\ADMINISTRATION\JGARMS\WORK\ FAXES\THISFAX.DOC. Assume the ACL on THISFAX.DOC grants Everyone Full Control. If a user has the Bypass Traverse Checking right (and remember all users have it by default), the user will be able to read, modify, or delete this file, regardless of what rights the user might—or might not—have to the parent directories that this file is nested in. If you removed all permissions from C:\, C:\USERS, C:\USERS\ADMINISTRATION, C:\USERS\ADMINISTRATION\JGARMS, and C:\USERS\ADMINISTRATION\JGARMS\WORK, the user could still read, modify, or delete this file.

However, if you remove the Bypass Traverse Checking right for this user, he or she would need rights to each directory in the path in order to access this file, even if he or she had Full Control permission on that file.

The ability to modify the Bypass Traverse Checking right is really included to provide strict POSIX compliance. You should disable this user right for any user or system that requires strict POSIX compliance. However, one of the downfalls is that enforcing traverse checking can cause some performance degradation since the ACL for each item in the path must be checked whenever a file is accessed.

> **CAUTION**
>
> Although you need to understand the existence of the Bypass Traverse Checking right and how it affects a user's ability to access certain files, Windows NT and many of its components, as well as many user applications, expect that the right to bypass traverse checking will be enabled. Removing this right without considering what programs are running on your system and what files they need to access on the system can cause problems.

Groups

The user account is the most granular level of user identification in Windows NT. Any action can be directly linked back to the user who initiated it. However, having to administer your entire system by assigning privileges to individual user accounts would be time consuming, especially if you have a large user base.

Groups provide you a tool for assigning user rights and privileges based on a common set of needs. For example, all users who need access to a certain printer might be put into a single group. That group would then be assigned the appropriate permissions on the printer and anyone who needed to use the printer could be assigned to the group.

Aside from the convenience this provides, it actually improves security. By assigning permissions based on group membership, you can see very quickly who has access to what resources. Furthermore, you can quickly validate that the permissions are set properly.

Consider this: In the previous example we talked about assigning rights to a particular printer. Say we had 40 users who needed to print to that printer. If you wanted to verify the permissions, you would have to review 40 access control entries (ACE) to ensure they are set properly. If you assigned the resource based on group membership, you would simply verify that the one ACE for the group was set properly and then review the membership list for the group.

By managing your resources this way, the security of your system can be enhanced by providing a much less error-prone way of assigning permissions.

> **TIP**
>
> Even though it might seem easier in the short run just to assign privileges directly to people as necessary, it will make long-term administration much easier if you create groups and assign privileges based on groups.

A more detailed explanation of using groups to simplify administration can be found in Chapter 16, "Administering the Server."

Managing Built-In User Groups

From a security perspective, you need to make sure that you understand the rights and restrictions provided by membership in the built-in computer groups. Windows NT creates different default user groups depending on the security role it will play in the domain. Many people think that the built-in user groups depend on whether the system is an NT Workstation or an NT Server. This is only partially correct and a potentially serious misunderstanding. Windows NT Workstation will always have the same built-in groups. However, the built-in user groups on an NT Server depend upon the role of the NT Server. If it is a domain controller (DC), it

28

ADVANCED
SECURITY
GUIDELINES

will not maintain its own local accounts database and will inherit the user database from the primary domain controller (PDC). What many people don't realize is that a Windows NT Server configured as a member server—not a domain controller—does not have the same built-in groups and user rights as the rest of the domain. This can be a serious problem. A Windows NT Server configured as a member server has the same default users, groups, and rights as an NT Workstation. For example, they both permit the Guest account, as well as domain users, to log on locally.

Consider the following configuration. You install a Windows NT Server as a standalone server and want to use it to run SQL Server. You run the system on a DEC Alpha server. If you don't realize that its local security database looks identical to an NT Workstation (because the NT Server is *a member server*, not a domain controller), you might not realize that you need to make some changes. For instance, by default anyone can log on to the server console using the Guest account. The level of potential damage is very high. Because this is a RISC system, its boot volume must be on a FAT partition and is therefore vulnerable. The intruder could delete the necessary files from your boot partition, rendering the server incapable of starting up. I actually know of a situation where this happened. Other actions the hacker could perform are equally damaging.

For this reason, it is important to realize that a Windows NT Server that is not configured as a domain controller has special needs and should be secured the same way as an NT Workstation.

For more detailed information on the built-in user groups, please refer to Chapter 16.

Making Optimal Use of Passwords

The password is everything. If a password is compromised, so is the account and anything the account has permissions to. Furthermore, an account that has been compromised to someone outside your organization, no matter what permissions the compromised account might have, is a building block that could allow further penetration. Remember, it is always easier to break into a system from the inside. This is why implementing a security policy based on least-needed permissions is a valuable choice.

Because most networks rely on shared bandwidth to connect systems, it is not at all difficult to get someone's password if it is sent in clear text over the network. For example, if you connect from your machine to an FTP server or Telnet server elsewhere on your internal network, or even across the Internet, do you know how many people could potentially "watch" your password go over the line? Because most people use the same password for everything—although this is not recommended—all their accounts would be compromised if someone got hold of their password.

Windows NT enables you to designate password-related account policy through the User Manager. Changes made to the account policy are global in that they affect all users of the computer or domain. It is important to realize, however, that modifying the account policy for the domain does not affect the account policy for local accounts on non-domain controller machines in the domain. Remember, these computers maintain their own local user accounts.

Avoid Clear-Text Passwords

It is important to understand why clear-text passwords should be avoided in all cases, unless there is a very good reason to keep the password in clear text and the repercussions are fully understood. Windows NT does not store users' passwords in clear text and the NT logon service never transmits passwords over the network in clear text. However, there are other things that need to be observed.

> **NOTE**
>
> When I say that NT does not store passwords in clear text, I mean that not only are the passwords stored in an encrypted form, but there is no way to decrypt the passwords. So what good are the passwords? NT uses a *hash* algorithm to encrypt the passwords. Then when it wants to validate a password entered by a user, it encrypts the user-entered password with the same algorithm and compares the result to the stored value. If these hash values match, then the password is validated.

You should refrain from entering passwords into batch files, shortcuts, or into Program Manager icons. Shortcut information and Program Manager icons can be easily accessed on Windows 3.x and Windows 95 machines and can also be accessed through the Registry in Windows NT. Any password entered into these places should not be considered safe.

There are third-party services that run on Windows NT that integrate with the security account database. If connections are accepted by this service from the network, Windows NT cannot ensure that these passwords are not being received across the network in clear text. One good example is the implementation of Post Office Protocol (POP) services. Under request for comment (RFC) 1227, which defines mailbox retrieval for POP clients, clients send clear-text passwords over the network. For example, the POP mail server created by European Microsoft Windows NT Academic Centre (EMWAC) integrates with the Windows NT user account database and accepts clear-text passwords from clients who connect to read mail. This password, which is the user's domain password, is then sent in clear text over the network. This is not NT's fault. It's not even really the POP server's fault. It's the definition of the protocol. Authenticated Post Office Protocol (APOP), a new version of POP that allows for encrypted password transport, is currently gaining a following. It requires updating both the POP clients and servers.

Setting Password Policy Through the User Manager for Domains

Password-related account policies that can be changed through User Manager include the minimum and maximum password age, minimum password length, password history, account lockout, and enforcement of logon hours. The screen used to control the account policy for the domain is shown in Figure 28.5.

FIGURE 28.5.

Account Password Policy is controlled through the User Manager.

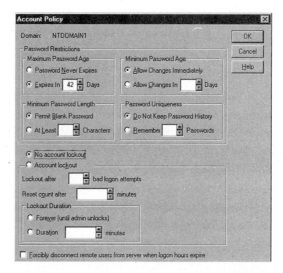

> **NOTE**
>
> This window does not completely fit on the screen using 640×480 screen resolution, so you might need to move it around to see the bottom of the window.

Maximum Password Age

By default, passwords never expire in Windows NT. However, even in environments with minimal security concerns, it is important to force users to change passwords on a regular basis, because the security provided by a password decreases the longer that password is in use.

If you check the maximum password age option, you can set the age to anywhere between 1 and 999 days. The maximum password age must be greater than the minimum password age. I find that 45 days is a reasonable length for most environments, although some people say this is a little conservative. Even if you don't want to be conservative, you should not allow passwords to last longer than 180 days.

Passwords can be prevented from expiring on a user-by-user basis by checking the Password Never Expires checkbox for the user's account in User Manager for Domains, as shown in Figure 28.6.

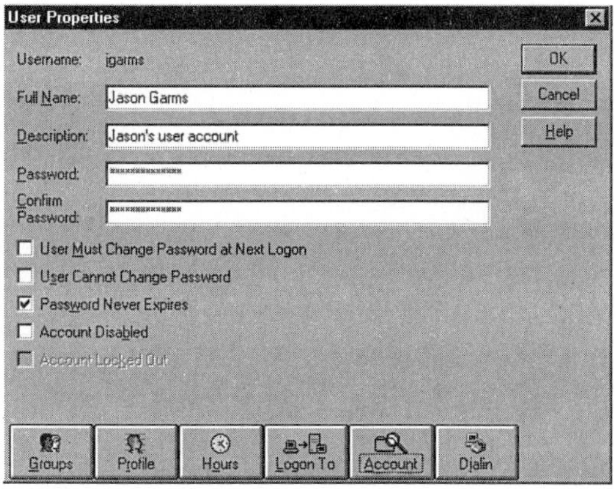

FIGURE 28.6.

Passwords can be prevented from expiring on a user-by-user basis, regardless of the overall system policy.

Remember, passwords are at the heart of your system's security. The more times a user types his or her password at a keyboard, the more likely it is that it will be compromised. However, if your boss comes to you and says, "I don't give a damn about *your* security problem, I don't want to have to keep changing my password!" then maybe you should check this option. As humorous as this might seem, it happens.

There is also a more practical and common instance where you would want to prevent a password from expiring. If you have accounts created for specific services, such as for the schedule service, you might want to prevent the password on these resource accounts from expiring by checking the Password Never Expires option.

Minimum Password Age

There are good reasons for implementing a minimum password age. One reason is to discourage users from changing their passwords so often that they forget them. A second and even more practical reason works in combination with the password uniqueness feature listed next. The minimum password age can be from 1 day to 999 days and must be less than the maximum password age.

Minimum Password Length

For the most part, the shorter the password, the easier it is break. By default, no minimum length is required and blank passwords are permitted. You should use passwords of no less than six characters and encourage your users to use good passwords, containing a mix of uppercase and lowercase characters, numbers, and punctuation. If you choose to enforce a minimum password length, you can choose a length from 1 to 14 characters. Windows NT does not permit passwords longer than 14 characters. Of course the minimum password length must be smaller than the maximum password length.

Password Uniqueness

Password uniqueness is useful for ensuring that a user does not use the same password over and over again, thus eliminating any security gains from making the user change the password. Password uniqueness is effectively used with minimum password age. If you do not enable minimum password age, a user could change his or her password a number of times in a row and end up with their original, again defeating the purpose of password uniqueness. Choosing a minimum password age of even one day would essentially remove this problem. You can set Windows NT to remember anywhere from 1 to 24 passwords. I have heard of no problems setting the number of remembered passwords to a high number, even in sites with thousands of users in their account database. A setting of five to seven should be sufficient for most environments.

Implement Account Lockout

It is a good policy to implement the account lockout feature. This prevents hackers from attempting to gain access by trying a sequential password-guessing program. However, unless security is of the utmost concern, you should be careful when implementing this feature so you don't increase the level of difficulty for the user. Many more conservative administrators recommend a setting from three to five. I would recommend a slightly higher setting of around seven, unless extremely tight security is critical.

The first reason you might want to increase this number is that when most Microsoft clients attach to other systems, they immediately try to authenticate themselves using the currently logged on user name and password. If the user name you're logged on as is the same as the machine you're connecting to, but the password is different, this will immediately result in one failed logon attempt. If you type your password incorrectly, the system will fail your logon attempt. That's two. If you attempt to logon again, it will try your current credentials again, that's three. If your lockout was set to 3, you'd now be locked out, although you only typed your password wrong once.

Here's a slightly different scenario. I'm working at my NT Workstation and am logged on using my standard user account, jgarms. I need to use my administrative account, jg-admin, to attach to the STUFF share on a server called \\PRIMUS to get a file. At the command line I could type net use * \\PRIMUS\STUFF /user:NTDOMAIN1\jg-admin. The problem is, although NT tries to authenticate me using the correct user name, it tries to pass my current password for authentication. This results in a failed logon attempt before I ever get a chance to type my password. One bad logon attempt is not a problem. However, if I do this enough times, and within the time period set in the User Manager, then I will lock out the account.

I know that there are people out there who are probably saying, "If you had typed net use * \\PRIMUS\STUFF /user:NTDOMAIN1\jg-admin * NT would have immediately prompted you for a password." That's correct. However, if you had been performing this action using the Map Network Drive in the NT Explorer, or with the File Manager, NT would have tried your current password first. The previous example is just to show that there are good reasons to carefully consider how you want to set these options. Most problems similar to this example would happen to administrators and power users.

> **TIP**
>
> Unless you have an ongoing problem, or the need for higher security, you might want to consider setting the account to lock out after seven bad attempts within 30 minutes and to lockout for 60 minutes. This is typically enough to discourage most systematic break-in attempts. Locking the account out forever just adds to the possibility of irate users and increases the work for the system administrator.

You can set NT to lock out an account after a specific number of failed logon attempts. The number of failed logon attempts before the lockout occurs can be anywhere between 1 and 999. You can also specify the windows of time during which the failed logon attempts must occur in order to lock out the account, as well as the duration for which the account will be locked out. These values can be set to between 1 and 99,999 minutes (almost 70 days), but the duration must be greater than or equal to the reset count.

For example, you might set the accounts to lock out after five failed logon attempts within a 60-minute period, and have the account stay locked out for five minutes. This would discourage a hacker from trying to break into a system by guessing passwords, but it will also enable a user to continue working without having to contact the administrator.

Forcibly Disconnect Remote Users from Server When Logon Hours Expire

When a user approaches the end of his or her permitted logon time, the server automatically sends a message to notify the user. If this option is enabled, the server will send a couple more notices before finally disconnecting the user. Even for environments where you don't care when your users access the server, you might want to force users to disconnect during the server backups to ensure that all files get backed up. If this option is disabled, users can still work on the server when their logon time ends, they just cannot make new connections. This might be desirable when it is not critical that users log out immediately and you don't want to risk possibly interrupting something they are doing.

Users Must Log On in Order to Change Password

Normally when a user's password is getting close to expiring, he or she receives a warning each time they log on that the password will expire in x days. The users are also asked if he or she wants to change the password at that time.

If this option is not selected, and the user allows his or her password to expire, the next time that user logs on, he or she will be told the password has expired and will be prompted to change it immediately.

28

ADVANCED SECURITY GUIDELINES

However, when this option is enabled, the user will not be able to change his or her password if it is allowed to expire. Instead, the user must go to the administrator to have the password changed.

Review of Password Policy

Implementing good password policy is very important. However, a good password policy does not end with deciding on the minimum password length, or password uniqueness, or password expiration. There are additional issues that require some attention.

It is important to realize how passwords are used and stored—both on your computers and on your network. We have discussed why it is important to decide if users should be allowed to include passwords in command-line batch files or Program Manager icons. You also need to consider what programs are in use on your network that require passwords. Most people will tend to use the same password for all applications. This is good and bad. The good of it is that it makes their lives a little easier. The bad, however, is that if one program does a poor job passing this password across the network, or storing it, all systems secured by this password are compromised.

Another example of where your password might be compromised is if you log on from a Macintosh using the standard Macintosh authentication method. Here, again, your password is sent in clear text over the network. Also, many in-house database and client/server applications use rudimentary logon procedures and often send these passwords and user names in clear text across the network.

So what's the big deal? Believe me, it's not just paranoia. LAN analysis tools are becoming a dime a dozen—in fact, NT Server now ships with one, called the Network Monitoring Tool. Additionally, anyone can go to their local computer software store and buy a program that will turn their tool into a packet catcher. And the programs are just getting better and better. The hardware on many users' desks are already of sufficiently high performance to take advantage of these programs. Furthermore, many smaller LANs are still single segments and many larger LANs often run as bridged environments. This means that any Ethernet tap on the network can be used to tap the entire network. Sounds pretty ugly, right? And it happens.

The last rule to remember about passwords is that just because an application uses a password, it's not necessarily protected. This is tied in to what was mentioned previously, but differs slightly. If anything in your network can be trusted, the algorithms in Windows NT's password mechanism can be. For the most part, you have no choice but to trust them. What is important is to allow them to do their job, and encourage the users to do their job, which is taking care to protect their passwords. However, there are many programs that put passwords on your files and some people feel this is sufficient. It rarely is. Unless you know from a reliable source (and the manufacturer is not a reliable source), these password-protection schemes should be considered to be little more than child-proof locks. Many of the algorithms used to "encrypt" files in standard commercial office suites use simple hashing algorithms, which are easily broken. In fact, there are many people on the Internet who seem to make it their hobbies to break these "encryption" methods and then post the method on the Internet for all to see.

What does this mean? It means I would rather trust a well-secured Windows NT system to keep my data safe than have a false sense of security from these simple password protection schemes.

Logging On

Logging on to the system is perhaps one of the most important security-related actions you take. It is during this process that the system compares your credentials to the NT's security account database and either denies you access or grants you an access token, which is used to validate all of your actions during that logon session.

Ctrl+Alt+Del Logon

When Windows NT 3.1 first came to market, a lot of people had a difficult time adjusting to the idea that you press Ctrl+Alt+Del to log on to a system. After all, coming from a DOS background, this would do no less than reboot your computer! So why did Microsoft choose this key combination as a logon sequence for Windows NT?

The main reason Microsoft used this keystroke is that nothing else ever uses it. They needed a keystroke combination that no other program would want to use as a hot key. The only really safe keystroke to use is Ctrl+Alt+Del. Trapping for this key combination is performed at a very low level in Windows NT, and no other application is able to trap it. This assures that when a user presses Ctrl+Alt+Del, the window that pops up is the logon process and not a Trojan horse.

I have heard people argue, and even read in many places, that another reason Microsoft chose the Ctrl+Alt+Del was that, because it usually resets MS-DOS machines, it would make it more difficult for someone to use a DOS-based computer to impersonate an NT logon process and thereby capture a user's password. I personally don't think this really played much of a role in the decision, because it is easy to trap Ctrl+Alt+Del on DOS-based computers and use the keystroke for other purposes.

The only caveat here is that if someone has had access to the NT-based computer, it is possible that they could have installed a DOS-based program that appears to be the Windows NT logon service—deleting NT from the machine if necessary—and captures your password, denies you access, reporting some bad-password error. The program could then even be written to trash the hard drive to remove evidence that it had been there. Sound unlikely? It happens. You might not think it could happen to you, but this is why your network is only as secure as the physical security precautions that guard it.

Hiding the Last User Name

If you've ever used UNIX before, have you ever gone up to the console and had it tell you at the logon prompt who the last person to log on was? Or have you ever used Telnet to connect to a computer and had it tell you that JohnD was the last user? I don't think so. Most people, even anti-UNIX bigots, would think such a thing would be absurd. Then shouldn't it also be considered absurd that Windows NT tells you the name of the last person to log on to the console?

Personally, I think so. However, Microsoft did it this way for ease of use, not to mention the tradition of all Microsoft network products that have always done it this way.

It is actually quite easy to prevent NT from telling the world the name of the last user. I always recommend doing this, for two reasons.

The first reason has nothing to do with security and is more geared for administrators of NT Workstations. Let's go back to the previous UNIX example. Could you imagine a UNIX user not knowing his or her logon name? Under certain circumstances when the user logs on with scripts, yes. But people who use the system on a daily basis for work? Seems strange. However, for some strange reason users in the Windows world seem to have problems remembering their user names. I can't count the number of users who are accustomed to having their user names already filled in and only have to enter their password. If you dare to log on to their system and your user name appears there, they will be totally lost and unable to figure out why they cannot log on. What's worse, if you have the account lockout feature enabled, you might get *your* account locked out before they figure out what's going on. I've had more than one irate user call to grumble and ask how I could expect them to remember both a user name *and* a password! If you're running for no other reason, disable this feature so that your users learn their user names.

If the first reason has nothing to do with security, the second reason has everything to do with it. If someone walks up to your server, they should not be able to get any useful information from it without authentication. Your user name can be considered important information, especially if you don't want people discovering the renamed administrator account. I had a user get upset when I disabled this feature. In addition to complaining about how much extra work it was for him to have to type his user name every time, he wanted to know when other people had been using his computer. If there is a concern about who is logging on to a computer, use the audit logs for tracking this. In fact, I highly encourage you to audit these logons and periodically review them. This audited information, unlike the last-logged-on-user information, is restricted to privileged users.

To prevent Window NT from displaying the last logged on user name, use the Registry Editor to assign the following Registry key value:

Hive: HKEY_LOCAL_MACHINE

Key: SOFTWARE\Microsoft\Windows NT\CurrentVersion\Winlogon

Value Name:	DontDisplayLastUserName
Value Type:	REG_SZ
Value:	1

Display Legal Notice

I highly encourage everyone to use this feature. Displaying a legal notice has long been considered an important feature to assist in the prosecution of people who attempt to gain illegal access to a machine. Many hackers have been set free because it was determined that the "Welcome" message displayed when they tried to log on was an indication that it was acceptable for them to log on. When deciding on what kind of text to put in this box, the most appropriate is usually some simple text that states that the computer system is for authorized use only. An additional statement that all use of the system is subject to various monitoring techniques without the user's permission might be a good addition. Typically, you'll want to refrain from making any threats about what might happen if users attempt to use the system without proper authorization. Of course, in a sensitive environment, you might want to consult a lawyer to assist with the actual text of the message. Many larger organizations and government agencies have developed stock messages that traditionally were used on mainframe or other multiuser systems, such as UNIX.

The legal notice includes a title for the legal window, which is usually something like "Warning!," that is followed by a body of text that is displayed in the pop-up window. This window will appear during logon, immediately after the user presses Ctrl+Alt+Del. The user must then click the OK button, which signals his or her acceptance of the terms in the legal warning. They cannot log on without clicking OK. Figure 28.7 is an example of what the legal warning window looks like.

28

ADVANCED
SECURITY
GUIDELINES

FIGURE 28.7.

You can set a warning that appears when a user tries to log on at the console.

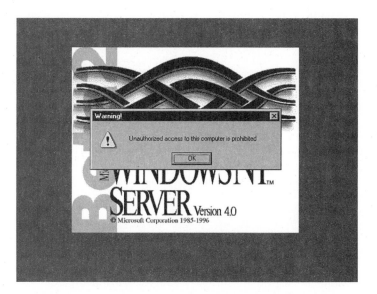

To implement the legal warning feature, you must make modifications to the Registry. There are two Registry entries that should be set. One is for the caption and the other is for the text. Both of these entries should already exist, but the strings are empty by default. If the keys do not exist or have been accidentally deleted, they can be created using the Registry definitions listed in the following example.

Hive:	HKEY_LOCAL_MACHINE
Key:	SOFTWARE\Microsoft\WindowsNT\ Current Version\Winlogon
Value Name:	LegalNoticeCaption
Value Type:	REG_SZ
Value:	The value for this key should be the desired caption of the legal warning.
Hive:	HKEY_LOCAL_MACHINE
Key:	SOFTWARE\Microsoft\Windows NT\Current Version\Winlogon
Value Name:	LegalNoticeText
Value Type:	REG_SZ
Value:	The value for this key should be the desired text of the legal warning.

For instance, follow these steps to create the legal warning shown in Figure 28.7.

1. Open the Registry Editor.
2. Traverse the HKEY_LOCAL_MACHINE hive to find SOFTWARE\Microsoft\Windows NT\CurrentVersion\Winlogon.
3. Double-click the LegalNoticeCaption entry and enter Warning! into the String Editor dialog box, as illustrated in Figure 28.8.
4. Double-click the LegalNoticeText entry and enter Unauthorized access to this computer is prohibited. into the String Editor dialog box.

FIGURE 28.8.
*Use the Registry Editor
to modify the*
LegalNoticeCaption
Registry key.

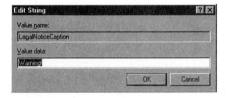

Time-Out when Entering Bad Passwords

When a user tries to log on locally to a Windows NT machine and fails five times in a row, the system will wait for 30 seconds before allowing the user to try again. This is very similar to many UNIX and other systems that allow console logons. It is intended to make password guessing at the console a painfully long process.

This time-out only occurs during an interactive logon attempt.

Use an NT System for Management

I keep talking about how security is a major element in Windows NT. Windows 3.x and Windows 95, however, do not provide anything approaching the level of security that Windows NT does. Despite the fact that Microsoft offers NT management tools for Windows 3.1 and NT Workstation, if you want to ensure the security of your system, you should only administer it from another NT machine.

Because we've already agreed your server should be somewhere in a locked room, which is not always convenient to run to all the time, you should consider using an NT Workstation for your regular administrative duties.

> **NOTE**
>
> What I mean here is that you should try to use only Windows NT Workstations or other NT Servers when you are administering your system. There are actually three reasons why you should consider only using NT systems for administration.
>
> 1. Microsoft does not make all the administrative tools available for Windows 3.x or Windows 95, so there are still things that can only be done on an NT system.
> 2. Windows 3.x and Windows 95 use Microsoft's encrypted password exchange (MS CHAP) for logging on to NT systems, which protects the password as it travels across the network. However, neither of these operating systems can guarantee any level of security against eavesdropping and rogue programs on the system.
> 3. Convenience. Using a Windows NT system for administration makes it easier to do things the way they should be done. This includes using a non-administrative account for day-to-day activities. This is described below.

Aside from getting NT's standard security features, which we've already discussed, there is another benefit from using an NT system for administration. Windows NT is often billed as a multiuser system. Many UNIX traditionalists have fought this point, but try as they might to discredit this claim, NT is truly a multiuser system—it just depends on what definition you use.

The difference in views as to whether or not NT is a multiuser system comes from a difference in perception of what multiuser really means. For many people, a multiuser system is that which is capable of having multiple people logged on to it at the same time, often through some form of terminal, and each performing individual tasks. Windows NT doesn't strictly adhere to this definition.

However, what's probably more important to use as a definition for a multiuser system is a system that is capable of running multiple processes simultaneously, each in its own user context, and each protected from the others. In this definition, NT excels.

So what's the difference? Obviously, the first definition is from a user's point of view, while the second is from a system's or process's point of view. Because of NT's architecture, it is fully capable of supporting the first classification, as well as the second classification. If Microsoft would have simply shipped a Telnet server with Windows NT, no one would have argued that NT is not multiuser. However, Telnet servers are available for NT, and actually, they are quite simple because they are merely extending the hooks that already exist.

One of the benefits that you get from using NT as your primary workstation is the ability to log on to different network resources with different user names. What does this mean? It means you can be logged on to your local workstation as an unprivileged user, and connect to and administer other systems using privileged accounts. This eliminates the need to log off and back on as another user to perform administrative functions. For more information on why you should use a nonprivileged account for your routine work, see the section "Rename and Don't Use the Administrator Account," earlier in this chapter.

Administering from Windows 3.x and Windows 95

If you use a Windows 3.x or a Windows 95 machine for administration, you run into a number of potential problems. These other operating systems do not provide mechanisms to prevent other processes from grabbing your password as you type it. This opens up the possibility of Trojan-horse applications stealing your password. To help protect yourself, you might want to avoid logging into non-NT systems with a privileged account. If you need to log on to other computers using this account, you should be sure to take precautions.

For more on using Windows 3.x and Windows 95 machines to administer NT Servers, see Chapter 8, "Working with Clients."

> **TIP**
>
> For additional protection, you should disable password caching features on all Windows 3.x and Windows 95 machines you log on to.

Use Microsoft's User Authentication Module for Macintosh

There are good security reasons to use Microsoft's User Authentication Module (MS UAM) for the Macintosh, and there are compelling user-oriented reasons not to use it.

First, the pros. Although Macintosh AppleShare clients support an encrypted password for connecting to AppleShare servers, Windows NT does not support this password encryption method. Without the MS UAM, a Macintosh client would be required to send its password in clear text over the network. As we've already discussed numerous times, this is a *big* problem.

Microsoft provides the UAM that can be installed on the Macintosh clients to provide a secure password transport between the clients and Windows NT Servers running Services for Macintosh. By default, users can connect from Macintosh clients using clear-text passwords. However, you can require that users only connect using the MS UAM. This can be done from the MacFile icon in the Control Panel as shown in Figure 28.9.

FIGURE 28.9.

You can require Macintosh users to connect using encrypted passwords instead of clear-text passwords.

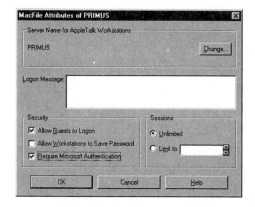

By checking the Require Microsoft Authentication option, Macintosh users must install and use the MS UAM to connect to your NT Server.

Now for the bad news. By doing this, you have a very good chance of upsetting quite a few Macintosh users. If you're not a Macintosh user, bear with me and try to see it from their side.

Why? In MacOS version 7 (actually back then it was called System 7) Apple introduced file aliases. These are very similar to shortcuts in Windows 95–interface jargon, except that Macintosh aliases keep better track of their targets. When you were attached to a file server you could create an alias to a file and place it on your desktop, much like you can with the new Windows 95–style interface. If you then removed your connection to the file server and tried to open the alias, the Macintosh would automatically go through the proper procedures for logging you on to the server so it could open your file. The only problem is that when the alias tries to open the file server, it will only use the default Apple UAM, not the MS UAM. Not to point fingers, but this is a problem with the MacOS. It also occurs when Macintosh users try to access NetWare servers using Novell's UAM.

You can get around this by telling people not to create aliases to items on the file servers, but I don't recommend this approach. This might not get too good of a response. Or you can tell people that they need to manually log on to the file server before opening the alias. Unfortunately, there is no acceptable workaround that will make everyone happy.

Use Password-Protected 32-Bit Screen Savers

Windows NT gives you the ability to have the workstation or server automatically secure itself after it has been idle for a specified period of time. This feature is implemented through the screen saver option. There are some important points worth mentioning here.

The console can be set to lock after a specified number of minutes without mouse or keyboard activity. This option is adjustable on a user-by-user basis and should be set through the Desktop icon in the Control Panel as shown in Figure 28.10.

FIGURE 28.10.

Screen savers with passwords can be used to protect your data when you step away from the computer.

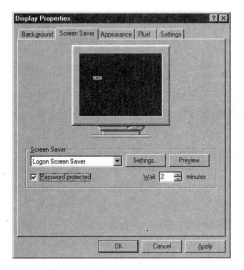

By checking the Password protected option box and setting an appropriate delay time, the security of your console can be increased. The delay can be set in single-minute increments from 1 to 99 minutes. (Actually, by using Registry Editor to change the ScreenSaveTimeOut entry in the user's ../Control Panel/Desktop subkey, you can set the delay in seconds, though this level of granularity should not be necessary.) The length of the delay that should be implemented will vary from environment to environment. I typically set all of my systems, including my primary workstation, to one minute. I do this primarily to ensure that if I am logged on with a privileged account and get distracted, the system is not compromised. For many environments, this might seem a little draconian. However, I find that it works rather well now that I'm used to it. I'd prefer to take precautions up front rather than clean up later after carelessness.

> **NOTE**
>
> When enabling a password-protected screen saver, you must first select a screen saver, and then you can select the Password protect option.

When choosing a screen saver, there are a couple of factors that need to be addressed. The first is to ensure that you have picked a 32-bit screen saver. When choosing a 16-bit screen saver, Windows NT will gray out the Password protect checkbox. The first reason this is done is because the 16-bit applications cannot use the Win32 API calls necessary to interface with the security subsystem to check the validity of a user's password. Second, even if you were allowed to enter a password for 16-bit screen savers, as with other 16-bit applications, they run in a shared memory space. Because this memory space is not protected, it's not too difficult to write a program that snatches the password from the screen saver when the user enters it, thus compromising your password. The lesson here is to only use 32-bit screen savers.

Additionally, you might want to avoid using third-party screen savers unless you are sure of their quality and have specific reasons for using them over the standard Microsoft-supplied ones. The code for the Microsoft screen savers has been checked by numerous sources to ensure that there are no holes that would allow the system to be compromised.

One other concern when choosing a screen saver is the performance degradation caused by running the more complex screen savers. I mention it again here to emphasize how important this is. Choosing a complex screen saver for your server, especially one of the OpenGL ones, can literally cripple your entire system. Again, for more information on this, please refer to Chapter 20, "Performance Tuning and Optimization."

Allowing Only Logged-On Users to Shut Down

By default, in order to initiate a restart or shutdown, Windows NT Server requires that a user be logged on and have the appropriate user rights, typically granted by group membership. For more information about user rights, see the section on user rights earlier in this chapter.

The default installation of Windows NT Workstation, however, permits the system to be shut down or restarted without a user first logging on. I would recommend that you disable this in any environment. As for why exactly Microsoft chose to set this as the default option, I can only guess that it was merely designed for convenience. If someone approaches a machine and is determined to shut it off, the power switch is always a last resort. Perhaps the reasoning is that by putting a shutdown option on the logon screen, maybe the person will safely shut the system down first. Go figure. I'm sure all the readers out there with UNIX backgrounds are probably saying that you would never find such a strange option on a UNIX workstation.

To require users to be logged on before shutting down a system, change the following Registry key value:

Hive:	HKEY_LOCAL_MACHINE
Key:	SOFTWARE\Microsoft\Windows NT\Current Version\Winlogon
Value Name:	ShutdownWithoutLogon
Value Type:	REG_SZ
Value:	0

Changing the value to 1 would allow the system to be shut down without a user first logging on.

Caching Account Credentials on Windows NT Systems

Windows NT caches the account credentials for the last 10 users. This is intended to allow a user access to the system even if all domain controllers are offline. In most environments, caching the credentials should not be a problem, because they are stored in the system's security database and cannot be compromised the same was as cached account information on a Windows 3.1 or Windows 95 system. It is fully possible, however, to abuse these cached credentials.

Consider the following situation. I am the administrator of a network of Windows NT Workstations connected to a Windows NT Server. Security is a concern and we have chosen Windows NT for the desktop because of its robust security system. User JohnS has been fired and I have been asked to disable his logon account to prevent him from accessing any of the computer systems and accessing any sensitive information.

The problem with the cached user credentials is that although I disabled his user account, he still can log on to his local NT Workstation and access files using his cached credentials. To do this, he would simply disconnect his computer from the network and log on. Windows NT will tell him that it cannot find the domain controller, but will log him on using cached credentials.

You can check to see what user profiles are currently cached on your system. Simply right-click the My Computer icon in the NT Explorer and choose the Properties option. Then choose the User Profiles tab. This screen displays the profiles currently stored on the system and allows you to delete cached profiles.

Files, Directories, and Shares

This section covers implementing file system security features to help secure your Windows NT Server. It does not include a detailed description of the features of NTFS and how to assign permissions. This information is covered in Chapter 6. Instead, I have tried to focus more on warnings about what you should and should not do to make your system as secure as possible.

Use NTFS for File- and Directory-Level Permissions

NTFS is the only file system in NT that supports file- and directory-level permissions. This alone makes it considerably more secure than either FAT or HPFS. The capability to set permissions, fault-tolerance, and access speed are all good reasons to use NTFS for all partitions. If you choose not to use NTFS, make sure you fully understand the security limitations that this will create.

NTFS does not provide an encryption facility. If a disk containing an NTFS partition is removed from a machine and installed in another machine, it is fully possible to extract data from the disk. NT, by default, will not allow you to read an NTFS disk made in another system. However, there are other means of accessing the information. The fact that other systems cannot *easily* read the data should be seen merely as a deterrent, not a means of protection.

Unlike most other operating systems that support the concept of ownership of objects, ownership of objects in Windows NT cannot be given away—it can only be taken. What does this mean? It means that each file and directory on an NTFS volume has an owner. By default the owner of a file or directory is the person who created it. By stating that ownership of objects cannot be given away means that even if you want to give someone else ownership of a file, you cannot—even if you are the administrator. What you can do, however, is give a particular person Full Control on the file, and then that person can voluntarily take ownership of the object.

For instance, I log on to my NT system using a non-administrative account, jgarms. I then create a file called MYTEXT.TXT. Naturally, this file is owned by my account jgarms. This can be confirmed by right-clicking on the file in the Explorer, choosing the Security tab, and clicking on the Ownership button. Now, let's say that I want to give ownership of this file to jsmith. There is no mechanism in NT that will enable me to assign ownership of this file to jsmith. Even if I logged on as the administrator, I would be unable to assign ownership of that file to jsmith. This is by design.

What I can do, however, is allow jsmith to take ownership of the file. Although nobody can forcibly assign ownership of an object in Windows NT, the owner of the object, in this case a file, can grant someone permission to take ownership of it. So, although I cannot give jsmith ownership of the file, I can *allow* him to take ownership by granting his user account Full Control of the file. Once I've given him Full Control rights to the file, he can choose to take ownership of the object.

Remember, if you create an object, you are the owner. If you copy a file, you become the owner of the copy. Additionally, ownership is not inherited from the directory into which you copied the file. The access rights are inherited, but you will be the owner.

This is an important concept because it is closely related to NT's security structure and concept of accountability. When using NTFS, the owner of an object has the ability to remove rights from it so that no one else can access it, not even the system administrator. However, if a user removes all access permissions from a file, the administrator can elect to take ownership of the file. This is an administrative right. Once the administrator has ownership of the file, the access permissions can be changed appropriately. However, the ownership of the file cannot be returned to the original owner. This creates a trail of accountability.

For those of you familiar with UNIX, this idea of not being able to give ownership of a file might seem a little odd. In UNIX, you can simply use the CHOWN command and assign ownership of a file to anyone you want—given adequate privileges. However, as you've seen, it doesn't quite work that way in NT.

However, you can get a CHOWN command for NT, but don't expect it to work the way you might expect. CHOWN.EXE comes with the Windows NT Resource Kit and runs in the POSIX subsystem.

While this command can be used to check the ownership of a file, and even to take ownership of a file, if you have the appropriate permissions, it cannot be used to grant ownership to a specific user, as it can be used in UNIX.

> **WARNING**
>
> Now that I've gone through so much to carefully explain how you cannot *assign* ownership of a file in NT, I'll tell you that I lied. Well, I didn't actually lie, I've only misled you a little.
>
> What I've explained is correct. However, Microsoft threw a monkey wrench into the pot. On a normal Windows NT system, everything I just wrote is correct. However, if you install Services for Macintosh, you can in fact use the Services for Macintosh tools to assign ownership of files that reside in a volume shared for Macintosh users to access. So, if you have Services for Macintosh installed on a system, you can use it to assign ownership of files. This assignment of ownership is recorded in the Event Viewer's Security Log if you turn on auditing in the User Manager.

Securing Your %SystemRoot%

Among the files and directories to be protected are those that comprise the operating system software itself. Microsoft has changed the default security permissions in NT 4, and the standard set of permissions on system files and directories provide a reasonable degree of security without interfering with the computer's usability. However, you might want to make the following changes *immediately* after Windows NT is installed. Be careful not to apply these permissions to subdirectories.

%SystemRoot%

Administrators: Full Control (All)
CREATOR OWNER: Full Control (All)
Everyone: Add & Read (RWX)(RX)
SYSTEM: Full Control (All)
Server Operators: Change (RWXD)

%SystemRoot%\FONTS

Administrators: Full Control (All)
CREATOR OWNER: Full Control (All)
Everyone: Add & Read (RWX)(RX)
SYSTEM: Full Control (All)
Server Operators: Change (RWXD)

`%SystemRoot%\HELP`

Administrators: Full Control (All)
CREATOR OWNER: Full Control (All)
Everyone: Add & Read (RWX)(RX)
SYSTEM: Full Control (All)
Server Operators: Change (RWXD)

`%SystemRoot%\INF`

Administrators: Full Control (All)
CREATOR OWNER: Full Control (All)
Everyone: Add & Read (RWX)(RX)
SYSTEM: Full Control (All)
Server Operators: Change (RWXD)

`%SystemRoot%\PROFILES`

Administrators: Full Control (All)
CREATOR OWNER: Full Control (All)
Everyone: Add & Read (RWX)(RX)
SYSTEM: Full Control (All)
Server Operators: Change (RWXD)

`%SystemRoot%\REPAIR`

Administrators: Full Control (All)
SYSTEM: Full Control (All)
Server Operators: Change (RWXD)

`%SystemRoot%\SYSTEM`

Administrators: Full Control (All)
CREATOR OWNER: Full Control (All)
Everyone: Add & Read (RWX)(RX)
SYSTEM: Full Control (All)
Server Operators: Change (RWXD)

`%SystemRoot%\SYSTEM32`

Administrators: Full Control (All)
CREATOR OWNER: Full Control (All)
Everyone: Add & Read (RWX)(RX)
SYSTEM: Full Control (All)
Server Operators: Change (RWXD)

28

ADVANCED
SECURITY
GUIDELINES

%SystemRoot%\SYSTEM32\DHCP

If you're not running a DHCP server on this system, you should delete this directory.

%SystemRoot%\SYSTEM32\LOGFILES

Administrators: Full Control (All)
CREATOR OWNER: Full Control (All)
Everyone: Read (RX)
SYSTEM: Full Control (All)
Server Operators: Change (RWXD)

%SystemRoot%\SYSTEM32\OS2

If you don't run any OS/2 programs, you should delete this directory.

%SystemRoot%\SYSTEM32\RAS

If you don't use RAS, you should delete this directory. If you do use RAS, you should restrict this directory to the RAS users.

%SystemRoot%\SYSTEM32\VIEWERS

Administrators: Full Control (All)
CREATOR OWNER: Full Control (All)
Everyone: Add & Read (RWX)(RX)
SYSTEM: Full Control (All)
Server Operators: Change (RWXD)

%SystemRoot%\SYSTEM32\WINS

If you're not running a WINS server, delete this directory. Additionally, on Intel-based systems you should modify the access permissions on the following system files:

\BOOT.INI

Administrators: Full Control (All)
SYSTEM: Full Control (All)

\NTDETECT.COM

Administrators: Full Control (All)
SYSTEM: Full Control (All)

NTLDR

Administrators: Full Control (All)
SYSTEM: Full Control (All)

```
\AUTOEXEC.BAT
```

Administrators: Full Control (All)
Everybody: Read (RX)
SYSTEM: Full Control (All)

```
\CONFIG.SYS
```

Administrators: Full Control (All)
Everybody: Read (RX)
SYSTEM: Full Control (All)

The \BOOT.INI and the \NTDETECT.COM are hidden files. To use the NT Explorer to change permissions on these files, you will need to open an Explorer window and choose the Options item under the View menu. Then choose the View tab and select the Show all files button. Now that you can see them, you can make changes to their permissions settings.

Moving Versus Copying

Be careful to set the permissions properly when you move files. Remember that when you move a file, it keeps its permissions, whereas when you copy a file, it inherits the permissions from its destination directory.

When copying or moving sensitive information, you should always verify the access control lists (ACLs) after copying the files.

SCOPY

The Windows NT Resource Kit provides a utility called SCOPY, which is intended to enable you to copy files and preserve their permissions. SCOPY only works when you copy files from an NTFS volume to an NTFS volume. It will not work with FAT or HPFS partitions, because these other file systems do not support security settings. Additionally, SCOPY requires that you have Backup and Restore user rights on both the source and destination computers.

The SCOPY command is just an example of how user rights can be used to circumvent security features. You need to make sure that you only give the Backup and Restore rights to users who really need it. Furthermore, because NT does not audit the use of Backup and Restore user rights by default, tracking the usage of the SCOPY command is difficult. For more information on how to force NT to track the use of Backup and Restore user rights, see the section "Auditing Backup and Restore Rights," later in this chapter.

The only other way to track usage of the SCOPY command is to track access to files about which you are concerned. For example, if you wanted to secure E:\CLASSIFIED, you could audit all read access to the directory by administrative users. Then if an administrator were to use SCOPY to copy files from the directory, it would show up in the security event, as shown in Figure 28.11.

FIGURE 28.11.

A read audit generated by SCOPY *indicates that the file was accessed using the Backup user right.*

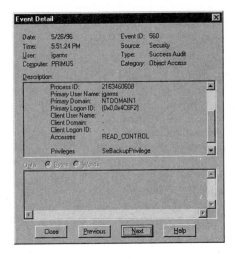

The syntax for the SCOPY command is

SCOPY *source destination* [/o] [/a] [/s]

/o copies the owner information.

/a copies the auditing information. This option requires you to have the Manage Auditing user right on the source and destination computers.

/s specifies that all files and subdirectories should be copied.

Note: Parameters *must* be entered in the order listed.

CAUTION

SCOPY has trouble copying files with ACLs that have a large number of ACEs. This is a good reason to make use of groups for assigning permissions. Also, the larger the ACLs, the longer the files will take to copy with SCOPY.

File Delete Child Permission

To provide POSIX compliance, Windows NT supports a hidden permission called the File Delete Child (FDC) permission on NTFS volumes. Users who have the Full Control permission to a directory also have the FDC permission.

Having FDC permission enables a user to delete files that are located at the root level below a directory, even when he or she has no permissions on the file itself. The FDC permission only gives a user the ability to delete files at the root level of a directory to which he or she has full control. It does not grant them the right to delete a subdirectory, or delete files that are nested within a subdirectory.

The FDC permission is useful because it's based on the concept that if you own a directory, you should be able to remove files that reside in it, even if they don't belong to you.

For most people, the FDC permission is not a big deal. It was really only included to provide an equivalent of the UNIX directory write permission for the POSIX subsystem. In UNIX, if a user has write permission to a directory, he or she can delete any file in the directory, regardless of the ownership or assigned rights of that particular file.

If you don't want to grant the FDC permission to a user, you need to avoid granting Full Control to the directory. Instead, you can use the Special permissions option and assign all permissions except Full Control.

To illustrate the use of the FDC permission, let's look at the default installation of Windows NT. When NT is installed, most of the files in `C:\WINNT` (or whatever your particular `%systemroot%` directory is) are given the following permissions:

> Administrators: Full Control (All)
>
> Everyone: Read (RX)
>
> Server Operators: Change (RWXD)
>
> SYSTEM: Full Control (All)

However, the actual directory `C:\WINNT` is given

> Everyone: Full Control (All)

The problem is that since everyone has full control of this directory, *anyone* can delete *any* file that resides directly inside `C:\WINNT` folder. An example would be the file `C:\WINNT\WINHLP32.EXE`, which has the default permissions:

> Administrators: Full Control (All)
>
> Everyone: Read (RX)
>
> Server Operators: Change (RWXD)
>
> SYSTEM: Full Control (All)

From the looks of things, only a member of the Administrators group, the Server Operators group, or the SYSTEM account itself would be able to delete `C:\WINNT\WINHLP32.EXE`. However, because of the FDC right, *anyone* can in fact delete this file. If you have the Guest account enabled, even the Guest could delete this file. This is why it is important to understand how the FDC right works and the consequences of giving someone Full Control access to directories.

28

ADVANCED
SECURITY
GUIDELINES

Share-Level Protection

When you create a share, it will default to granting Everyone Full Control to any file and directory accessed through the share. Remember, this is just a filtering mechanism. If you are using NTFS file- and directory-level permissions, the *share-level permissions cannot give you more permissions than granted by the NTFS permissions.* It can only reduce the level of permission. It does provide you, however, with a simple mechanism to help protect your system if the NTFS permissions are improperly set.

Here are a few points to remember:

■ If you connect to a network share that grants read-only access, you will not be able to change anything through this share *even if you are a member of the Administrators group.* For example, if you create a share called MEMO and the only permission you set is that Everyone gets read-only access to the share point, then if you connect to this share point, you will not be able to delete or change any files—*even if you have the appropriate NTFS file-level permissions.*

■ Don't rely solely on share-level permissions to protect your data. If a user logs on locally, the share-level permissions are not applicable.

■ The hidden administrative shares that Windows NT automatically creates can only be accessed by a member of the Administrators group. The permissions on these shares cannot be changed.

Hidden Shares Are Not Sufficient Protection in Themselves

When you browse a Microsoft network, shares that end in a $ are not displayed. This is a useful feature because it enables you to hide administrative shares so they don't clutter the browse list. However, you can usually use the Net Watch program to view the hidden shares on most NT computers. Additionally, anyone can still connect to a hidden share if they know it exists.

> **CAUTION**
>
> Do not hide a share and think that it is automatically protected. You should always implement appropriate share-, file-, and folder-level permissions to ensure that your system is protected.

Logon Script Shares

Windows NT Server domain controllers automatically create an administrative share called NETLOGON that is used to store users' logon scripts. By default this share allows everyone read-only permissions. To provide an additional level of security you should take the following two steps:

1. You should remove Everyone from the permissions on the NETLOGON share and add Domain Users with read-only permissions. Only domain users should need access to this share.

2. Implement file-level permissions on the individual logon scripts so that each user can only see his or her own logon script. There is no reason for any user to have access to another user's logon script.

For more information about configuring the logon service and creating logon scripts, please refer to Chapter 8.

Services

When you are looking at the security of an NT system, it is also important to look at the services that run under Windows NT. One of the places where Windows NT differs greatly from Windows 3.x and Windows 95 is that different processes can run on the system simultaneously as different user accounts. You learned this earlier in this chapter as being part of Windows NT's multiuser nature.

Because these processes usually run as user accounts that are different from the logged-on user, it is important to understand what services are running on a system, what user accounts they run as, and how they interact with the rest of the system.

> **NOTE**
>
> When you speak of a process running while using a particular user account, it is common to say that the process runs in the *context* of a particular user.

Win32 Services

By default most services under Windows NT run in the context of the local SYSTEM account, as shown in Figure 28.12.

This gives these services special permission to certain parts of the system. Some services, such as the Alerter, Computer Browser, and Event Log, cannot be made to run in anything except the SYSTEM account. If you try to configure the service from Control Panel/Services, the Log On As section is grayed out. Other services, like the ClipBook Server, Directory Replicator, and Scheduler services, can be configured to log on using an assigned user context. For most environments, the default way Windows NT configures most services is sufficient. However, there are certain processes that should not be run using the SYSTEM context because of the possibility of someone hijacking the process and making it do things it is not supposed to be doing.

FIGURE 28.12.

Most Windows NT services run using the SYSTEM *account.*

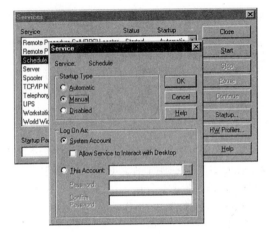

You can go about assigning user contexts to these services using one of two methods. First you could create a single nonprivileged user account to configure all of your services to run under. Or, you could create one user account for each service. As we've already discussed, Windows NT can handle almost any number of accounts that you want to create, so there is no reason why you should not create an account for each service. This enables you to grant each service's account only the permissions necessary to do its job.

The following are services you might want to consider running with a limited user account:

- Replicator Service
- Scheduler Service
- Almost any third-party add-on that runs as an NT service

CAUTION

If you have your security policy set so that accounts are locked out after a certain number of failed logon attempts, it is possible for a malicious hacker to try logging on using a service's user account so the account gets locked out. This would result in a denial of service to users. For example, Microsoft's Internet Information Server (IIS), which is included with NT Server 4, creates a user account for accessing Web pages. By default, this account is called IUSR_*computername*, where *computername* is the name of the computer. If this account is locked out, then all users trying to access IIS will be denied service.

This is one of those examples in which the security of the system needs to be weighed against the problems caused by potential denial of service.

Replicator Service

The Replicator service needs to be run in the context of a user more for practical reasons than for security reasons. The default SYSTEM account is prevented from accessing the network, so by creating a special user for this service, it can do its job.

Scheduler Service

Only members of the Administrators group can submit jobs to the Scheduler service. It is important that you create a limited user context for this service to run in. Because it is the specific job of the Scheduler service to spawn other programs, you need to ensure that programs that are run by the Scheduler service are secure.

Imagine scheduling your daily backups by using a batch file that calls the NT Backup program. If someone were to replace that batch file with something else, the Trojan program would be run with a privileged account. The severity of damage that could be done using this method is limitless.

To help reduce this risk, assign the Scheduler service to run as a user other than the SYSTEM account. Assign this user the minimum rights it needs to get the job done. The exact limit of these rights will depend on the needs of your individual environment.

Additionally, when calling programs from the Scheduler service, ensure that any files you call are safe and that no one could tamper with or replace them. Also, be sure to use fully qualified path names when calling programs from within a batch file that is run from the Scheduler service.

Third-Party Apps that Run as a Service on NT

You should always be careful when installing any program that runs as a service on your NT Server. By creating a user account to control the service, you can help to protect yourself from malicious Trojan-horse-style programs. Additionally, you can reduce the impact of potentially serious bugs caused by poor programming. If there is a bug in the service and it is running as the SYSTEM user, it could have serious consequences. However, if it only had limited system access, the risk is lessened.

To illustrate this point, there was a major software vendor that made its name in the Novell world. A few months ago it introduced its best-selling backup software to the NT market, but a critical bug was found. The backup software installed itself as a service and created a privileged user account with which to run the service. The mistake that was made—and hopefully this is one that was popularized enough that other software vendors have learned from it—was that the password for this user account was static and easily determined. This meant that virtually anyone could access your system using this privileged account. In all fairness, the software vendor quickly produced a patch to fix this problem. But this is a perfect illustration of why it is important to understand what services are installed on your system and what rights their associated user accounts have.

> **NOTE**
>
> The proper behavior for a program that needs to create a user account to run as is to create a randomly generated password for the account. This prevents anyone from guessing the password. For example, this is the method Internet Information Server (IIS) uses when it creates its Internet user account.

Internet Information Server

One of the major new features in Windows NT Server 4 is the inclusion of version 2.0 of the Internet Information Server (IIS). IIS enables you to publish content to the Internet—or to your intranet—through an FTP service, a Gopher service, and a WWW (HTTP) service.

Although this increased functionality can help to increase the usefulness of your NT Server, it can also have severe negative impacts on the security of your server.

IUSR_computername Account

When you install IIS, it creates an account called IUSR_computername, where computername is the name of the computer (for example, on my system it is called PRIMUS; the user is called IUSR_PRIMUS). This account is created with a randomly generated password and is intended to be used for guest access by the IIS FTP server, Gopher server, and WWW server.

You should understand which permissions are given to this account by default, and how that might affect your security equation. The IUSR_computername account is given membership in the Domain Users and local Guests groups. Additionally, the account is given permission to log on locally. That means that if you are installing IIS on a domain controller, the IUSR_computername account will be able to log on locally to *all* domain controllers. Because the password is generated randomly when IIS is installed, this probably won't be a concern. However, to make you feel even more comfortable, you might even want to change the password in the User Manager. If you do this, don't forget to tell IIS about the changes by using the Internet Services Manager.

> **NOTE**
>
> The security concerns associated with giving the Log on Locally right are discussed in a little greater detail under the heading "WWW Publishing Service."

FTP Publishing Service

This section discuses the general security-related issues surrounding the file transfer protocol (FTP). The FTP server service that shipped with NT 3.5x was difficult to set up properly, and many people ended up compromising the security of their systems without realizing it. However, the new FTP server included with NT 4 as part of the Internet Information Server (IIS) has made dramatic improvements that enable it to be configured in a more secure manner with relative ease.

> **CAUTION**
>
> Unless you have a compelling reason to continue using the 3.5x version of the FTP service, you should remove it and use the IIS version instead.

When you install the IIS FTP service, the default is to only allow anonymous connections. Even though to some people this might seem to be a security problem, in fact it is not. Because the FTP service integrates with the NT user database, you could easily enable users to log on with their standard NT user name and password. However, the FTP transport mechanism itself is not secure because it sends passwords in clear text over the network. As you've already learned, this is a problem because clear-text passwords can be easily intercepted and viewed without your knowledge.

The only real use for FTP service where it won't compromise security is as an anonymous file repository. This way users can come to the FTP site and log on using the name anonymous, enter any password, and the system will allow them access. With the IIS FTP service, when a user logs on using the name anonymous, he or she is really authenticated using the account specified in the FTP setup portion of the Internet Service Manager, as shown in Figure 28.13.

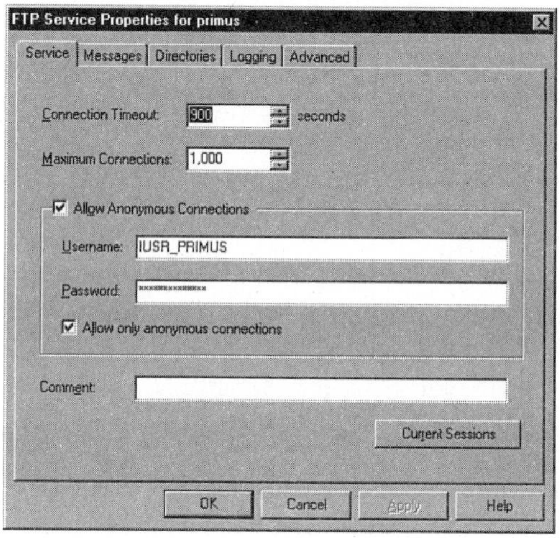

FIGURE 28.13.

"Anonymous" FTP users are really authenticated using the user account and password entered in the Internet Service Manager.

> **NOTE**
>
> There isn't really a user called anonymous.

If you uncheck either the Allow Anonymous Connections or the Allow only anonymous connections checkboxes, NT will warn you that what you are doing will compromise the security of the system. This error message is shown in Figure 28.14.

FIGURE 28.14.

The FTP server service warns you that FTP sends passwords in clear text across the network, allowing them to be captured by a packet analyzer.

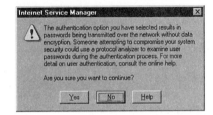

Do not take this message lightly. If anything, it's understated. It is intended to scare you into thinking about what you are doing, and to prevent people from complaining that Microsoft didn't adequately warn the users about the security risks of FTP.

WWW Publishing Service

There are two major security issues you should be aware of when you run the IIS WWW server on your system. The first has to do with permitting clear text authentication, and the second is the method that IIS uses to provide user-level discretionary control over documents it provides through the WWW server.

By default, IIS uses the IUSR_*computername* account for processing WWW requests. The WWW service is restricted as to what files on the system it is able to access. Normally this restriction is limited to the WWWROOT directory created when you installed IIS, and to any subdirectories. If this directory structure is located on an NTFS partition, you can deny the IUSR_*computername* rights to access any files you want. Then, if a user tries to access the file using a WWW browser, he or she will be required to enter a user name and password for authentication.

The problem is that unless you're using Secure Sockets Layer (SSL), WWW browsers send their passwords across the network in clear text, much like FTP clients. These passwords can be intercepted. So by default, IIS does not accept the standard user authentication methods from WWW browsers. However, it does support client authentication using the Windows NT Challenge/Response authentication, which encrypts the user's password before sending it across the network.

> **NOTE**
>
> At the time of this writing, the only WWW browser that supports the NT Challenge/Response handshaking is Microsoft's Internet Explorer.

This means that if you want to provide secure authentication of WWW clients without SSL, you should use only WWW clients that use the NT Challenge/Response authentication.

If you choose to permit Basic authentication using the Internet Service Manager, you will be warned that this could compromise the security of your system, as shown in Figure 28.15.

FIGURE 28.15.

If you enable Basic authentication, passwords will be sent in clear text across the network.

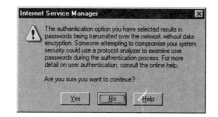

The second problem with IIS's WWW server is how it handles user-level authentication. As we already touched on when talking about the IUSR_*computername* account, IIS requires users who will access WWW pages with user-level access restriction to have the Log on Locally user right. When you install IIS, the IUSR_*computername* account is given this permission, which is not a problem because the password is unknown.

However, if you need to begin using IIS to restrict access to WWW pages for different users, then you need to give all those users rights to log on locally to your NT Server. This can be of particular concern because, as we've already discussed, you shouldn't allow people to log on to your NT Servers.

The only suggestion here is that if you must give user-level access permissions for people, then make sure your NT Server is physically locked away where no one can gain access to it.

Hopefully, Microsoft will get enough people complaining about this that it will change its authentication method in the next version of IIS. This is really a plain and simple design flaw.

The Domain

The domain structure used by Windows NT provides considerably more than a simple method of logically grouping together resources, like its workgroup counterpart. It also provides the foundation for a robust and secure networking environment. The domain contains a user account database that can be used across all resources in the domain. Additionally, the domain provides a guaranteed trust relationship, not only with other domains, but also among NT systems within the domain. This trust permits one NT machine to validate the identity of another computer system, instead of simply identifying the identity of the user on that system, which is all that is permitted with Windows 3.x and Windows 95 systems.

Joining a Domain

Unlike Windows 3.x, Windows 95, and Macintosh computers, Windows NT Workstations and NT Servers configured as member servers have the option of participating in the security structure of the Windows NT domain itself. This is done by having the NT Workstation or NT Server join the domain. However, before it can join a domain, a *workstation trust* account must be created in the domain. This can only be done by a member of the Administrators group. This account is used to perform pass-through authentication for users who log on to the system.

You can use the Server Manager to create a machine account for an NT system and you designate if the system will be a workstation/server or a backup domain controller (BDC). When you create the computer account, no password is initially assigned. When you bring an NT system to life and assign it the name of the account you just created, it will negotiate a "password" with the domain controller. This password is used to create a secure channel between the NT system and the domain controller, as well as to authenticate the system itself so that it cannot be impersonated. The NT system will regularly negotiate new passwords with the domain controller. Because of this, it is essentially impossible for another computer to impersonate an NT system once it has joined a domain.

> **NOTE**
>
> Because of the workstation trust that is created, NT machines configured in a domain are virtually immune to IP spoofing attacks. However, this only accounts for NT networking services, such as file and print services, and administration. It has no bearing on services such as FTP, HTTP, or any other standard TCP/IP service.

There is a security concern created whenever you create a computer account and then don't use it immediately. Someone could use that abandoned computer account to join your domain. Worse yet would be if you had created a domain controller account and forgot about it. This means that someone could bring an NT Server to life and join your domain as a BDC, thus obtaining a copy of your user database and other potentially damaging information.

For this reason, you should never create unused computer accounts. Furthermore, you should use Server Manager to periodically review your computer accounts and delete any old accounts that are no longer necessary.

Domain Trust Relationships

One of the greatest misconceptions about domain trusts is that by establishing the trust, you have given away some level of administrative rights. In fact, this is not true. Creating a trust between domains merely provides a guaranteed path between the PDCs of each domain that allow the trusted domain to certify a user's credentials to the trusting domain.

When you create a trust between two domains, there is no immediate change in administrative privileges. An action such as this must be explicitly done by the administrators of each domain.

TCP/IP Filtering

One of the new features of Windows NT 4 is its capability to use TCP/IP to set up security filtering at the protocol level. This permits you to grant and deny services based on either the TCP or UDP port numbers. This provides an effective packet filter somewhat similar to simple firewall systems.

This functionality is particularly useful if your server will be serving limited functionality on the Internet. For example, if you have a server with a network interface card that is connected to the Internet and you only want it to be able to act as a Web server, you could enable the appropriate port addresses. Or if you have a SQL database that you want people to access, you could include only the port addresses for the database.

> **NOTE**
>
> For those of you familiar with UNIX, this option is very similar to the TCP Wrapper utility.

You can modify this setting on an interface-by-interface basis, and it is done through the Network Control Panel. After you open the Network Control Panel, select the Protocols tab and double-click on TCP/IP Protocol. This brings up the Microsoft TCP/IP Protocol Properties page. Click on the Advanced button, and then click on the checkbox Enable Security. Finally, click on the Configure button to configure the ports you want to filter. The TCP/IP Security window is shown in Figure 28.16.

You will have to restart your system in order for these changes to take effect.

Well-Known Ports

Table 28.2 is a list of the more well-known port addresses in an NT environment. Because the port filtering feature in Windows NT only permits you to include ports on a port-by-port basis, instead of permitting you to deny them on a port-by-port basis, you must be aware of these well-known ports before you enable port filtering.

28

FIGURE 28.16.

You can select what TCP or UDP port addresses or IP protocols you want to permit your system to listen to.

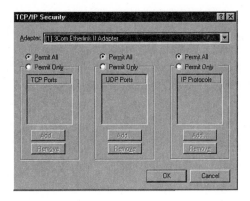

Table 28.2. NT port addresses.

TCP/UDP Port Address	Keyword	Description
7	echo	Echo
9	discard	Discard; alias=sink null
13	daytime	Daytime
17	qotd	Quote of the Day; alias=quote
19	chargen	Character Generator; alias=ttytst source
20	ftp-data	File Transfer [Default Data]
21	ftp	File Transfer [Control]
23	telnet	Telnet
27	smtp	Simple Mail Transfer; alias=mail
42	nameserver	Host Name Server; alias=nameserver
43	nicname	Who Is; alias=nicname
53	domain	Domain Name Server; alias=nameserver, dns
66	sql*net	Oracle SQL*NET
67	bootpc	DHCP/BOOTP Protocol Server
68	bootpc	DHCP/BOOTP Protocol Server
69	tftp	Trivial File Transfer
70	gopher	Gopher
79	finger	Finger
80	www	World Wide Web HTTP
90		Default WINS name server destination port
107	rtelnet	Remote Telnet Service
108	snagas	SNA Gateway Access Server

TCP/UDP Port Address	Keyword	Description
109	pop2	Post Office Protocol Version 2; alias=postoffice
110	pop3	Post Office Protocol Version 3; alias=postoffice
118	sqlserv	SQL Services
119	nntp	Network News Transfer Protocol; alias=usenet
123	ntp	Network Time Protocol; alias=ntpd ntp
137	netbios-ns	NetBIOS Name Service
138	netbios-dgm	NetBIOS Datagram Service
139	netbios-ssn	NetBIOS Session Service
161	snmp	SNMP; alias=snmp
162	snmptrap	SNMPTRAP
177	xdmcp	X Display Manager Control Protocol
178	nextstep	NextStep Window Server
194	irc	Internet Relay Chat Protocol

28

ADVANCED
SECURITY
GUIDELINES

Remote Access Service

The Remote Access service provides a powerful tool for creating multiprotocol, dial-up, and virtual WAN connections. However, this utility comes with a potentially hefty security cost. If you are going to implement a RAS server on your network, it is important to understand the security implications and how to protect your network from outside attack. This section covers some of the RAS server settings that affect your network's security. The RAS server is discussed in more depth in Chapter 23, "Implementing Routing and Remote Access Services."

When you install the server portion of the Remote Access service, you are prompted with some options that will affect the security of your RAS server. Those options are shown in Figure 28.17.

Password Encryption

The RAS Server in Windows NT supports three types of password authentication for dial-in clients. The first, Allow any authentication including clear text, is intended to support any third-party dial-in clients that employ the Password Authentication Protocol (PAP) method of authentication. With PAP, the passwords are exchanged in clear text and can be easily captured. This is considered the least secure authentication method.

FIGURE 28.17.

When you set up the Remote Access Service server, you can specify different options that will impact the security of your system.

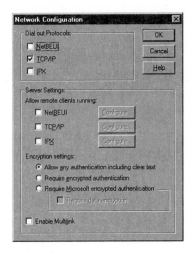

Regardless of which option is selected, Microsoft clients will always negotiate the most secure password-negotiation method supported by both client and server.

Selecting the Require encrypted authentication option provides support for more secure password authentication methods, including SPAP, DES, CHAP, and MS-CHAP.

Shiva Password Authentication Protocol (SPAP) uses two-way encryption to ensure password security when communicating with a Shiva LAN Rover client.

DES encryption for password authentication is supported on the RAS server to maintain backward compatibility with older Microsoft clients, such as the Windows for Workgroups RAS client.

The Challenge-Handshake Authentication Protocol (CHAP) uses a challenge with one-way encryption on the response for secure authentication. One of the features that makes CHAP secure is the capability to periodically verify the identity of the client by issuing a challenge, which changes every time. If the client does not respond properly to the challenge, the server disconnects. An additional feature of CHAP is the ability to use different encryption algorithms. MS-CHAP is Microsoft's variation of CHAP, which implements RSA Data Security Incorporated's MD4 encryption standard to provide the highest level of password authentication on NT's RAS server. The only clients that currently support the MS-CHAP authentication method are the Windows NT and the Windows NT RAS clients. These two systems will always use MS-CHAP when negotiating passwords with each other.

RSA's MD5-CHAP encryption method is one of the most popular authentication protocols supported by most third-party PPP clients and servers. It is supported by Windows NT's RAS client, but the Windows NT RAS server will not negotiate using MD5-CHAP. MD5 is considered to be a strong encryption method, but it requires passwords to be stored on the server in clear text, which Windows NT does not permit.

The option Require Microsoft encryption authentication will only authenticate users with MS-CHAP.

Data Encryption

To help ensure the security of your data when transmitted over public carriers such as the standard phone systems and X.27 networks, Microsoft has provided the capability to encrypt the data stream. If you use MS-CHAP, you will also have the option to require data encryption. This option will be grayed out unless the Require Microsoft encryption authentication option is selected.

When this option is selected, RSA's RC4 encryption algorithm is used to secure all data sent over the RAS line. This implementation uses a 40-bit key that is negotiated at call setup.

RAS Dialin Permissions

When you install the RAS server on Windows NT, you must still assign the right for users to dial in on an individual basis. This can be done using the User Manager or the Remote Access Admin program.

Using the User Manager to configure a user's ability to dial in to a RAS server is new to NT 4. In prior versions you had to use the Remote Access Admin.

In the User Manager, the Dialin option appears as a tab on the properties page for each user. When you select this tab, you can set the user's ability to dial in and be authenticated by this domain. You can also set the user's call-back options, as shown in Figure 28.18.

28

ADVANCED
SECURITY
GUIDELINES

FIGURE 28.18.

The User Manager can be used to permit users to dial in using the Remote Access service.

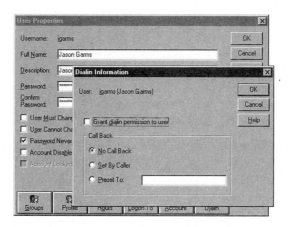

You can use the RASUSERS utility from the Windows NT Resource Kit to obtain a list of all users who have been authorized to dial in with RAS. You should check this list regularly to ensure that you know who is able to dial in to your system.

Call-Back Feature

I suggest you consider using the call-back feature to provide added security. For most users who dial in from home, it should not be a problem to preset RAS to call them back at their home phone number. This makes it almost impossible for someone to impersonate other users. You should definitely implement the call-back feature if you need a more secure means for authenticating a user.

Restricting Network Access

If you have decided to grant users Dialin access, RAS permits you to limit the extent of their access. You can specify that users can connect to the entire network, or if you want to provide higher security, you could limit their access to only the RAS server.

You do this when you configure the RAS service setup in the Network Control Panel. You can specify the level of restrictions as shown in Figure 28.19.

FIGURE 28.19.

When you set up the RAS server, you can specify that dial-in users can only access resources on the RAS server, but not on the rest of the network.

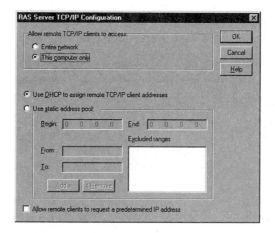

Unless your dial-in users specifically need access to network resources, you should limit their access to the local machine in order to reduce the consequences if there is a security breach.

Third-Party Security Hosts

Microsoft designed an open interface into Windows NT Server's RAS service that enables you to integrate a third-party security host. The capability to seamlessly integrate with additional security hosts enables you to enhance the security of your dial-in connection.

The security host is a device that provides an additional level of authentication before allowing the user access to the RAS server. When using these security hosts, authentication is provided by a hardware key in the possession of the user. Without the code generated by this key, the user will not be authenticated by the security host and cannot gain access to the RAS server. Windows NT currently supports a number of external security hosts.

The cost of installing a third-party security host is fairly expensive, so unless a high degree of security is a must they are probably unnecessary. As mentioned previously, the call-back feature provides a level of protection that should defeat most intruders. However, the third-party security hosts provide the added benefit that they don't require the user to dial in from a preset location.

Using the Point-to-Point Tunneling Protocol for Increased Security

Windows NT 4 introduces a new feature called Point-to-Point Tunneling Protocol (PPTP). PPTP is an extension of RAS that permits the creation of virtual private networks (VPNs). There are two major areas where PPTP can dramatically improve your security.

The first scenario would be if you need to communicate with another site across the Internet. You could use PPTP to set up an encrypted tunnel across the Internet, which can guarantee the privacy of all data.

The second scenario would be if you dialed into your corporate network through an independent Internet Service Provider (ISP). You could use PPTP to guarantee the security of your data between your dial-up location and your NT network.

The PPTP VPN uses RAS's built-in bulk data encryption method to ensure privacy of the VPN channel. This is based on RSA Data Security Inc.'s RC4 algorithm with a 40-bit key. The key is negotiated when the VPN connection is established.

PPTP makes secure network communication across the Internet possible.

The Registry

Protecting the Registry is a very important step to creating a secure system. Because the Registry contains the control parameters for the entire Windows NT system, gaining control of the Registry would essentially allow a hacker free run of the entire system.

> **NOTE**
>
> Microsoft has included two Registry editing tools with Windows NT 4, REGEDT32.EXE and REGEDIT.EXE. REGEDT32.EXE is the same program that was included with previous versions of Windows NT, and REGEDIT.EXE is the newer version, which is essentially ported from the Windows 95 version. As of the writing of this book, although REGEDIT.EXE has a nicer interface, it does not contain the necessary functionality to manipulate security on the Registry keys. For this reason, you will need to use REGEDT32.EXE when you edit access control lists (ACLs) or enable auditing on Registry keys.

28

**ADVANCED
SECURITY
GUIDELINES**

Protecting the Registry

The Registry, like everything else in Windows NT, is a set of files that makes up a hierarchical database. These files are stored in the system root area. The Registry does not need to be installed on an NTFS partition to enable you to set permissions and auditing on individual keys. However, if the system root is not on an NTFS partition, anyone with access to the Registry hives, located in C:\WINNT\SYSTEM32\CONFIG, has the ability to directly read and modify the hives. For this reason, you should always ensure that the system root is located on an NTFS volume.

Sensitive Information in the Registry

When determining your need to secure the Registry, you should consider the sensitivity of the information stored in the Registry. Remember, by default any user that can access the system, locally or remotely, has access to read large parts of the Registry. Unfortunately, securing the Registry is something more of an art than a science. You need to be especially careful when making changes to the Registry because various programs need access to read data from certain keys in the Registry, and blindly modifying the permissions on the hives would almost certainly cause unidentifiable problems with your system.

The flip side is that the Registry provides a wealth of information to which most users do not need access. The Registry permissions are set, by default, to prevent unauthorized users from changing things that should not be changed. However, they make no real attempt to prevent users from seeing information that they really have no business seeing.

For instance, everyone has read permissions to the entire HKEY_LOCAL_MACHINE\HARDWARE hive. This enables anyone to gain access to the complete hardware inventory of the NT machine. They can find out what kind and how many processors, how much RAM, what kind of network cards, what type of drive controllers, the make and model of all storage devices, and the type of video card. Additionally, the SOFTWARE and SYSTEM hives show the same lack of read security. From these hives a user can discover how the networking is configured on the server, including the protocols and bindings, what services are running and how they are configured, and a wealth of other information. This is the kind of information that can be used to discover and take advantage of security flaws in a system's configuration.

Unfortunately, securing this problem with the Registry is not very easy. Often, various software and services need access to this information and thus, changing the access can cause unpredictable results. If access to this information concerns you, you should carefully consider removing Everyone/read access from some of these hives. As of yet, Microsoft has provided very little information as to how to properly secure these keys.

The following is a method I use to secure keys that concern me. In the Registry Editor, enable full auditing for a select hive area, for instance HKEY_LOCAL_MACHINE\HARDWARE, as shown in Figure 28.20.

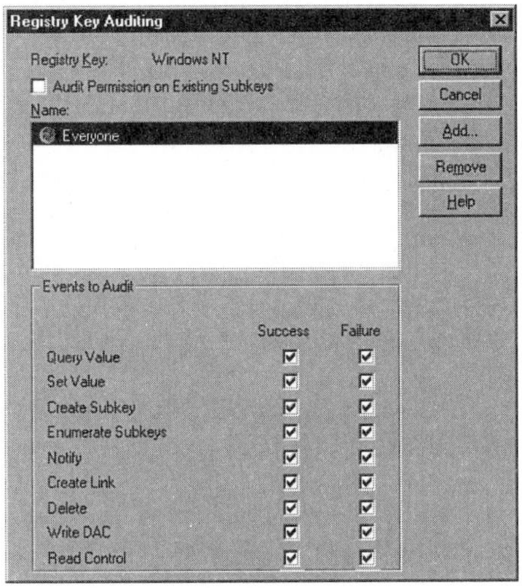

FIGURE 28.20.

You can use Windows NT's auditing facility to determine who, or what, is accessing specific Registry keys.

For the auditing to take effect, you must use User Manager to ensure that the File and Object audit events are turned on in the system's Audit Policy.

You can use the Event Viewer to monitor the Security Log and discover who or what is accessing the keys and decide what level of permission you need to assign them. If you choose to use this method, you need to make sure that the Security Log is large enough and you should definitely disable the CrashOnAuditFail feature discussed later in this chapter.

A slightly more risky, but thorough, approach would be to restrict Everyone/read access on keys that concern you and then enable auditing on failure to access these keys. This is certainly a more thorough approach than the method mentioned previously, but is not as safe. Restricting access to certain keys can potentially cause processes to crash when they are not able to access them. If you use this method, you should keep a very close watch on the Security Log.

Securing the Registry

If Registry security is of concern to you, there are a couple changes you can safely make that will increase the overall security of the Registry. You could change the following keys so that Everyone has only Query Value, Read Control, Enumerate Subkeys, and Notify access.

```
HKEY_LOCAL_MACHINE\Software\Microsoft\RPC

HKEY_LOCAL_MACHINE\Software\Microsoft\Windows NT\CurrentVersion

HKEY_LOCAL_MACHINE\SOFTWARE\Windows 3.1 Migration Status

HKEY_CLASSES_ROOT
```

When changing the access lists on these keys, be sure to note the permissions on any subkeys so that you don't propagate the wrong permissions. In particular, be careful with the permissions on the keys under HKEY_LOCAL_MACHINE\Software\Microsoft\Windows NT\CurrentVersion.

Printers

By default, shared printers created with Windows NT Server are available to any user on the network. Although the capability to print to a printer does not pose a direct security problem, it does create the possibility that someone can flood the queue and deny legitimate users access to the printer. Additionally, unauthorized printer abuse can cost you money. To help curb these problems you should consider adjusting the default printer permissions.

Printer Permissions

In order to create or modify a printer, you must be a member of the Administrators, Server Operators, or Print Operators local group. You can use the Printer Manager to adjust the permission on each printer. The default printer permissions are shown in Figure 28.21.

FIGURE 28.21.
By default, everyone can print to a shared printer.

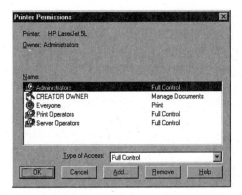

You should remove the entry for Everyone and replace it with whatever appropriate group of users need to be able to print to your printer. For more on setting printer permissions, see Chapter 7, "Configuring and Installing Print Services."

TCP/IP Printers

If you are connected to a large network, especially the Internet, you should carefully consider what protocols you use to print to your printers. If your printer is connected directly to the network, rather than directly to your server, you should consider not using TCP/IP to print to it. The common method of printing across TCP/IP is to use the Berkeley-style print daemons, LPR and LPD, as defined in RFC 1179. LPR/LPD do not support user-level authentication and therefore will accept print jobs from anyone. Thus, if you're connected to the Internet, anyone who knows the IP address of your printer could submit a print job. Of course you can always implement router-level filtering and some LPD implementation built into printers support a rudimentary level of filtering.

Rather than going through all the trouble to implement filtering mechanisms, it might be much easier to disable the TCP/IP features of your networked printer and use a nonrouted protocol to talk to your printer. There are other reasons for using protocols such as DLC or AppleTalk rather than TCP/IP for the connection between your NT Server and networked printer. For a more in-depth discussion on this topic, please refer to Chapter 7 and Chapter 14, "Configuring TCP/IP Printing."

Auditing Printers

If you are concerned about keeping track of who is printing to your printers, you should use Print Manager to setup printer auditing. In order to enable auditing of printers, you must first use the User Manager for Domains to enable auditing. See Chapter 16 and Chapter 27, "Auditing Windows NT Server," for more details on using the User Manger for Domains to change the system auditing policy.

Macintosh Clients

By default, any Macintosh user can print to any printer regardless of the permissions set on the individual printer. This is because the Macintosh print client has no support for user-level authentication. The Macintosh print service on Windows NT Server is set by default to log on using the SYSTEM account and therefore has access to all local print devices. It is not possible to grant print privileges to Macintosh clients on a user-by-user basis.

It is possible, however, to restrict print privileges to Macintosh users as a whole. To do this, follow these steps:

1. Use User Manager for Domains to create a Macintosh print user. You should pick a password for this user and check the User cannot change password and Password never expires options.

2. Using the Services icon in the Control Panel, set the Print Services for Macintosh service to log on using the account you created in step 1. Windows NT will warn you that the user has been granted the logon as a service user right.

3. Using the Printer Manager, give this user account whatever privileges you want the Macintosh print users to have.

Backups

Now we get back to the fundamental question: How important is your data? No matter how we answer this question, I think it really boils down to this: no matter how unimportant it is, you'd hate to have to do it over again. I think that most administrators would agree that backups are important, but very few organizations take appropriate care to ensure the security of their backup tapes. No matter what protection was assigned to your files and directories, the tape can be taken to a different system and restored without any controls. It is extremely good practice to carefully inventory your media and keep it under lock and key.

Backup Tapes Are Not Encrypted

NT Backup does not encrypt the data when it writes it to tape. For that matter, I don't know of any tape backup software for NT that offers an encryption option. Just realize what this means—anyone with an NT system and a tape device like yours can read your tapes and any confidential information on them. I've had numerous people argue about the usefulness of encrypting backup tapes. I have a couple of problems with this and personally think that encrypting backup tapes is a bad idea. One of the big questions is what would you use as a key for the encryption. Certainly not any system-level data. If you did, what would happen if the system crashed and you needed the backup tapes for restoring your data? If the unique system-level data was no longer available, you'd be out of luck. Likewise, if the user was required to enter a password and this were used as a key, what would happen if that password was lost? It would be terrible if you had a system crash and could not recover the data from tape because the password was lost.

Securing Backup Tapes

Rather than encrypt the data, securing the backups under lock and key and keeping copies off site is a more reasonable practice. You should follow a good tape-rotation scheme and keep careful inventory of the tapes. For more information on tape schedules, see Chapter 32, "Programming Windows NT Server."

Tapes should not be stored together with the computer system. If the system is stolen or damaged in a fire or other accident, the tapes might go with it. There are numerous organizations that provide off-site data storage services. Usually, for a nominal fee, you can schedule for them to come and pick up tapes on a regular basis for off-site storage. Don't always jump for the cheapest and make sure to check around, because, as with any organization, you need assurances that you can trust them with your confidential data. When shopping for such a service, find out in what kind of facility they store your tapes. What security precautions do they take to ensure that your data is safeguarded? Also, in an emergency, how fast will they get your tapes back to you so you can begin cleaning up?

Backup Operator

The backup and restore user right that is granted to the Backup Operators group is one of the most powerful rights in NT. Although NTFS file-level permissions can be used to deny an administrator access to a file or directory, the backup and restore user right can essentially be used to bypass this security. Although a user with this right cannot simply read files, he or she could use this right to back files up to tape, and restore them onto other systems to gain complete access. The problem is that this is not fully auditable. To ensure complete security for these files you must either acknowledge that the person running the backups should have clearance to see all the files contained on the tape, or you must physically separate the backup operator and the tape device. In this scenario, a trusted party would need to be responsible for the tape.

I bring this point up only because I've run into a few different environments where people had some very rigid rules regarding the permissions on their files. In one such environment, the administrator was denied access to all user data. This made things extremely frustrating. When I pointed out that if the administrator wanted access to the data, all he would have to do was back it up and restore it somewhere else, they complained that this was unrealistic and should be ignored. I argued that they should either trust their administrator and allow him to do his job, or if they were honestly concerned about security, they should keep the server and tape backup unit in a locked place and not allow the administrator to have access, except when accompanied by an individual trained to know what to look for. The point here is to make policies that make sense. Don't go halfway and stop. If there is a loophole, you should reconsider the policy. Don't bet on the fact that people won't notice the loophole.

Remember, only give the backup and restore rights to someone you trust!

Allocation of Tape Drives

Under Windows NT, any user on the system can use the tape device. For this reason, you should not leave tapes containing potentially sensitive data in the tape drive. If you want to stick a tape in the device before a regularly scheduled backup, make sure to erase the tape first. Also, you should have the tape eject as soon as the backup is complete. There is currently no way to restrict access to the device, like there is for the floppy and CD-ROM devices.

Auditing

Auditing is one of the fundamental security provisions in Windows NT. It enables you as the system administrator to identify what users are doing on your system. If reviewed properly, it is especially useful for identifying potential security breaches or break-in attempts.

This section briefly looks at the basic guidelines you should follow for using NT's auditing facilities as a tool for increasing your system's security. For a more in-depth look at auditing, see Chapter 27.

Implementing Security-Oriented Auditing

By default, Windows NT does not audit security-related actions. This is because auditing these events requires additional processor time and disk storage. You will need to enable your audit policy through the User Manager for Domains, as shown in Figure 28.22.

At a minimum you'll want to audit failed logon attempts. This will help warn you if someone is trying to break into your system. Additionally, you might consider auditing successful logon attempts and looking for user logons during your nonstandard times. For example, if your employees don't typically work at night, auditing successful user logons might tell you if someone, the night maintenance staff for instance, is trying to illegally access your system or perhaps even identify if a user is trying to access unauthorized information and hoping not to get caught by doing this during off hours.

FIGURE 28.22.

Security auditing can be enabled with the User Manager.

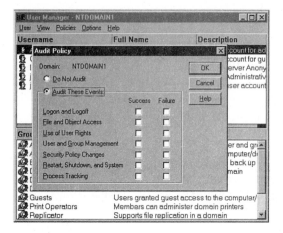

You should also consider enabling auditing of Use of User Rights, User and Group Management, and Security and Policy Changes. By having NT audit failures on these settings, you can see what people are trying to do on your system. It's natural for people to play around sometimes. Most people are inquisitive and will occasionally attempt to do something they shouldn't be doing. Other times, people do things without realizing what's happening. Auditing failures enable you to identify people in your organization that might need watching, or might just need help. Of course it will also identify major problems, such as attempted attacks.

For more detail information on each of these options, please see Chapter 27.

By auditing success on these items, you also provide a record of your actions that could prove useful later. Audit logs help to identify problems, but they also provide a true account of what really happened on the system.

I once had a user accuse me of changing the permissions on a confidential file of his. The audit logs backed up my claim that I did no such thing. In fact, we were auditing all file and object access and were able to show that he had in fact created the file in a different directory, whose rights mask it inherited, and then moved it to a secure directory. He insisted that he had checked the rights on the file and that it was secure. However, the audit trail doesn't know how to lie.

Unless you have a specific need, or if security is of the utmost concern, it's not necessary to enable Process Tracking. On a busy system this consumes a considerable amount of resources. Also, auditing unnecessary actions means there is less room in the security log for more important actions, which means that critical events might get removed from the security log faster than necessary.

Auditing File Access

In terms of security, it can be very useful to know who is trying to access certain files or directories. With Windows NT, you can choose to audit files and directories on a one-by-one basis. In order to implement this, you must enable the File and Object Access in the audit policy located in User Manager for Domains. If you don't enable the audit policy here, choosing to audit a file or directory from the NT Explorer or File Manager will have no effect.

What kinds of files and directories might you want to audit? Imagine that you have a directory, E:\CLASSIFIED, and you want to restrict access to it. Of course it's important to apply the appropriate file- or directory-level security measures under NTFS. But with auditing, you can see when and what people are doing to these files—(for instance, if the E:\CLASSIFIED directory is restricted to a very limited number of users). By auditing the access to the directory, you can know what users are doing to files in this directory.

This is also a good way to keep administrators clean and ensure that sensitive information is not being accessed without proper authorization.

If you have enabled File and Object Access auditing in the User Manager for Domains, you can use the NT Explorer or the File Manager to select which files you want audited. For each file or directory, you can select which actions you want audited for which users. For example, you could set up auditing on the directory E:\CLASSIFIED such that all access failures are audited for everyone, but successful Change Permissions and Take Ownership events are audited for the only members of the Administrators group, as shown in Figures 28.23 and 28.24.

FIGURE 28.23.

All access failures are audited on
E:\CLASSIFIED.

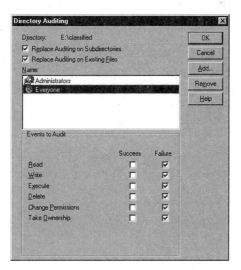

FIGURE 28.24.

Successful Change Permissions and Take Ownership events are audited for the Administrators group.

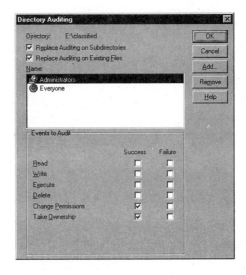

Security Log

When you implement a security policy as described previously, the audited events will appear in the security log, which is accessed by using the Event Viewer, shown in Figure 28.25.

FIGURE 28.25.

You can access the security log from the Event Viewer application.

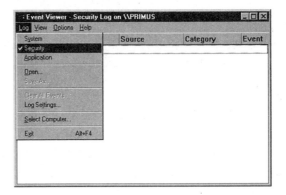

By default, the security event log is only viewable by members of the local Administrators group. You can enable other users to view and clear the security log by granting them the Manage Auditing and Security Log user right from User Manager for Domains.

As mentioned previously, when you install Windows NT Server, the Administrators local group is automatically granted this right. The ability for members of the local Administrators group to view and clear the security log is inherent in the Windows NT system itself. Even if you remove the Manage Auditing and Security Log user right from local Administrators group, they will still be able to view and clear the security log.

You should take some time to understand how the security log is organized and what your system's log looks like, so that you can better identify when there is trouble or you're under attack. You should review this log regularly. For most environments, once a week should be sufficient.

You also need to decide how long you want the security log to grow and how often items should be pruned. Ideally, you will review, save, and clear the log before it is full. How large the log should be allowed to grow to and how often it should be archived and cleared will depend entirely on what events you're auditing and the amount of use your system receives.

The log setting can be set in the Event Viewer, as shown in Figure 28.26.

FIGURE 28.26.

You can set how large the security log is permitted to grow.

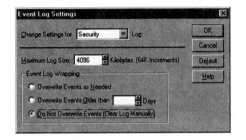

By default, the security log is set for a maximum size of 512KB, but you should definitely increase this amount. A log size of 4,096KB is typically acceptable for most environments. Rather than making the log larger than this, you might want to consider reviewing and archiving it more often. The amount of log space a security event uses depends on the nature of the event. This means that you can only make good predictions by analyzing your log over time as to how many events it will take to fill it up. For example, it takes approximately 270 failed logon attempts to fill a 64KB log size.

To see the current size of the security log, look under C:\WINNT\SYSTEM32\CONFIG\SECEVT.EVT. This is the security event log. You will not be able to open it, because it is open for exclusive use by the system. However, you will be able to check its size. It will always be in multiples of 64KB. By doing this you can check to see if your log is reaching its limit.

The security log is set by default to overwrite events older than seven days. For most environments, you should consider changing the setting to Do Not Overwrite Events. By making the log sufficiently large, you hopefully will have ensured that the log will not fill up. Again, you should review, archive, and clear this log regularly. By choosing this option, and properly setting the size of the log, you will most likely capture the more important actions of a hacker who tried to break into your system. If you allow the log to overwrite events, the hacker could simply perform some simple, repetitive action that would fill up your log and wipe out any trace of the damage that was really done.

28
ADVANCED
SECURITY
GUIDELINES

Causing the System to Crash When the Security Log Is Full

If you choose either Overwrite Events Older than *x* Days or Do Not Overwrite Events, you can also force your NT Server to crash when the event log is full. I only recommend this in environments where security is of higher concern than the availability of the server. By implementing this feature, you can ensure that no events will go unaudited. If you choose to use this option, be sure to set the size of your security log properly. However, if a hacker tries to generate a series of events in an effort to cover up his or her footsteps, this is a useful feature.

In most corporate environments this is really overkill, which is part of why Microsoft didn't provide a simple way to enable it. It is really provided for organizations where the audit logs are vitally important, such as a bank.

Although this measure might seem a bit draconian to most people, it is the *only way* to ensure that nothing is accessed without an appropriate audit trail.

To enable this feature, you must use the Registry Editor to create the following Registry entry:

Hive:	HKEY_LOCAL_MACHINE
Key:	SYSTEM\CurrentControlSet\Control\LSA
Value Name:	CrashOnAuditFail
Value Type:	REG_DWORD
Value:	1

Realize that when you implement this feature, the system will literally crash with a blue screen when the security audit log fills up. It will *not* warn users and gracefully shut down.

This feature will only bring the system down when the security log fills up. The application and system logs have no effect on it.

The system treats this crash like any other. If you are using this option to protect the audit log, you should probably consider disabling the Reboot on System Crash feature. Otherwise the system will reboot automatically. The security auditing is essentially disabled until you make some modifications to the system.

When the system crashes, it changes the CrashOnAuditFail value entry to type REG_NONE so that the system can reboot without immediately crashing again.

In order to restore a crashed system to a secure state, you must take the following actions.

1. Restart the computer.
2. Log on using an Administrative account.
3. Archive the events in the security log.
4. Clear the security log.
5. Delete the CrashOnAuditFail entry from the HKEY_LOCAL_MACHINE\SYSTEM\CurrentControlSet\Control\Lsa Registry subkey.

6. Recreate the `CrashOnAuditFail` value entry as describe previously.

7. Restart the computer.

Policy for Clearing the Security Log

No matter what size you choose for your log, or how often the data gets cleared, you should consider implementing an archive strategy for the old security logs. This is useful because, although you might not identify some action as being a problem today, it could be discovered to be a problem in the future. Having those old logs will greatly aid your work.

If security is a concern in your organization, you should develop a strict policy dealing with the clearing of those logs. Remember, the security log can also hold information about wrong-doings by the system administrators. Put a statement in your policies and procedures document about when the logs will be archived, when they will be reviewed, how they will be reviewed, who will review them, and for how long they will remain archived. It is also important to make it understood what actions, if any, will be taken for improperly clearing the event logs. Remember, this is the security document for your entire system!

Archiving the Security Log

The security log contains sensitive information that you don't want other people to have access to. It is very important to make sure that you save the archived security log files in a secure location. Create a directory on your server—under the `%SYSTEM_ROOT%` is a good location—and secure the directory so that only the administrators have access to it. You might also want to audit access to this directory.

When you use the Event Viewer to archive the security log, be sure to save it directly into the directory you created for these archives. This way it will inherit the proper NTFS file-level permissions.

Remember, if you save the log into some other directory, `C:\USERS\DEFAULT` for example, the file will inherit its permissions from this directory. When you move it to its archive location, it will retain these permissions. If the Bypass Traverse Checking user right is granted to Everyone (as it is by default), anyone with access to a share that contains that archive directory will be able to access the file! For more on this subject, see the sections on the Bypass Traverse Checking user right and security considerations when moving files, earlier in this chapter.

Auditing Backup and Restore Events

I've heard complaints that although the Windows NT Backup program does log its activity, you cannot log the use of the Backup and Restore user rights. From a security standpoint, this is a potential problem, because it is possible to create a backup program that does not log its events. Without the capability to audit the use of these user rights, you cannot truly secure your system.

The problem is when a user backs up files, NT verifies that the user has the Backup Files and Directories user right for every single file. Similarly, when a user restores files, the Restore Files and Directories user right is checked for every single file. Because auditing all these events would quickly flood the security log, Windows NT masks these events by default and prevents them from being written to the log. This means that it is merely infeasible, rather than impossible, to audit the backup and restore user rights.

If you choose to audit the use of backup and restore user rights, assign the following Registry key value using the Registry Editor:

Hive:	HKEY_LOCAL_MACHINE
Key:	SYSTEM\CurrentControlSet\Control\Lsa
Value Name:	FullPrivilegeAuditing
Value Type:	REG_BINARY
Value:	1

Unauditable User Rights

If you follow the procedures listed previously and create the `FullPrivilegeAuditing` key value, you might think that this will actually enable auditing for *all* user rights. The name of this value, however, is slightly misleading. There are some user rights under Windows NT that cannot be audited, no matter how this key value is set. The following is a list of user rights that Windows NT cannot audit:

- Bypass traverse checking
- Create a token object
- Create a new security context for a new logon
- Debug programs
- Generate security audits

Protecting Against Renegade Administrators

In many organizations, if someone were to suggest performing an analysis of the damage that a rogue administrator could cause, it would be tantamount to sedition. In some organizations, such as those that fall under certain federal jurisdiction—the banking industry, for example—it is not uncommon for an outsider to be brought in to perform a thorough check of the system to make sure that everything appears to be in order.

For the decision as to whether or not your company needs to take precautions against treachery from inside, you need to ask yourself the following questions:

- Are there government-dictated or other guidelines you must follow that require such precautions?

■ Does your network contain high amounts of proprietary trade secrets that represent your company's competitive advantage?

■ Do you have multiple administrators with varying degrees of responsibility and access needs?

Although it is difficult to impossible to fully protect your system from an administrator with ulterior motives, if your information is of a sensitive nature, you should at least devise a policy for regularly tracking the use of administrative privileges. This can be done using the Windows NT auditing features, discussed in Chapter 27.

Summary

Windows NT Server provides one of the most secure, generally available computing platforms on the market today. The security system is an integral part of Windows NT Server and you can't install NT Server without it.

Microsoft has tried to make NT Server as secure as possible by default, but sometimes it has placed ease of use over security. This is why it is imperative that all administrators understand how security works on Windows NT, so they can properly configure NT's security settings to fit their environment.

It is, however, such a complex product that it is extremely easy to make changes and not recognize the security-related consequences of your actions. This chapter has not only made you aware of the common, yet not-too-obvious, pitfalls, but also offered you a variety of strategies for ensuring the level of security you really need.

The Applications Server: Windows NT

V

PART

## CHAPTER 29

Microsoft BackOffice and Other Microsoft Products

by Joe Greene

IN THIS CHAPTER

As this book nears its end, there are a few topics that Windows NT users and administrators should be aware of. This chapter covers the Microsoft BackOffice product family and a few other products that are designed to flesh out the functionality of your NT system. What is BackOffice? I can see two possible answers. The first involves a listing of products—SQL Server, Exchange Server, System Management Server, and SNA Server. These are a series of products that are designed for the NT server environment.

Another answer to the question of what NT is lies more in the marketing and product strategy arena. In the PC world, Microsoft built DOS and Windows. They then branched out into the market of word processing, spreadsheets, and graphics packages. These products evolved and became quite powerful. People grumbled, however, about the difficulties involved with getting presentation graphics into word processing documents and other similar tasks. Microsoft engineered interfaces between their various products (using simple things such as the Windows Clipboard and complex things such as OLE 2 objects) and bundled them together into a tight product family known as Microsoft Office. They also provided some bundle price incentives. In any event, this family of office automation tools took off in the marketplace. People tended to favor a suite that worked well together over individual products which might do certain things better, but did not make the overall job easier. BackOffice is Microsoft's equivalent to Office for the server environment.

It combines the most common applications that run on Windows NT Servers—a database management system, a mail/groupware server, a mainframe connectivity package, and a software distribution/management system. Perhaps the software distribution/management system is not all that common today, but I think it is a promising technology that will help reduce the support nightmare faced by many corporations. Think of this component as a technology that will be one of the most common applications on servers in a year or two. Much like Microsoft Office, these products have been tied together to make interchanging information relatively easy. This begins with the underlying technologies that have been designed to use the same operating system functions, such as the Common Object Model and Object Linking and Embedding.

This chapter provides a quick overview of the components in the Microsoft BackOffice product line. It also covers a few other useful tools put out by Microsoft. The first is the Windows NT Resource Kit. These books and CD-ROM serve as a detailed technical reference for the guts of the Windows NT system. The CD-ROM contains a series of useful utilities that make life easier for the NT system administrator. I will also present an overview of the Internet Information Server. The chapter on NT as an Internet server (Chapter 30, "Windows NT as a Database Server") goes through the details of setting up this product, but I wanted to mention it here to show how it integrates with the BackOffice suite. Microsoft has announced plans to make its operating systems able to interface to Internet resources almost as easily as you would access a file on your local hard disk. Even applications such as Microsoft Word will be able to load Web documents from their File menus. I also introduce some of the resources available on the Microsoft World Wide Web pages that can be of use to NT users. Finally, I take a little bit of artistic license and speculate on the world of the future for BackOffice and Windows NT add-on products. (Hey, that's one of the fun things about being an author.)

Introduction to BackOffice

Once upon a time (not all that long ago), operating systems were barren shells that provided a place where applications could be run, but little else. Over the years, operating system vendors have kept adding services and utilities to operating systems to make them more capable in and of themselves (to gain market share, of course). Some of the more useful things that are now bundled as part of the operating system that used to be add-on packages include the following:

- Network protocol support (TCP/IP, NetBEUI, and SPX/IPX, for example)
- Network printing and file sharing services (FTP, LPD/LPR, and the basic Microsoft/ Novell file and printer sharing services, for example)
- Modem support and communications software (RAS)
- Graphical user interface support (remember that Windows was always an add-on package to DOS)
- Internet access tools
- Electronic mail clients
- Screen savers and desktop wallpapers
- Sound players—WAV, MIDI, and so forth
- Video presentation tools (Video for Windows or Active Movies, for example)
- Telephony support

It is impressive the number of services that are built into the operating system itself these days. I believe that some day, however, not too long from now, people will look at us oddly when we talk about operating systems that did not have built-in speech recognition and audio response systems. The rapid pace of development in this field makes even 36-year-old people like myself seem like old-timers when we relate stories of operating systems that fit on disks or were loaded from paper tape. In spite of the vast array of services built into operating systems such as Windows NT, there are still a number of other services that are common to many network environments that require additional products.

These services are not required by everyone and therefore would not make sense to be bundled with the operating system itself and therefore add to the cost of the operating system. However, they are used in enough applications as to require tight integration with the basic services that the operating system provides. What Microsoft is hoping is that you not only want tight bundling with the operating system, but tight bundling among these services. This is one of the main goals of BackOffice—to provide a tightly bundled set of add-on services for the Windows NT operating system.

So what are some of these applications that people would want to share among users and projects instead of creating them from scratch? This depends somewhat on your environment (engineers use different tools than accountants), but the following is a good start:

- Database management system—All modern operating systems support storing data in files on disk drives. However, it can be time consuming to read through large data collections in these "flat" files. To improve efficiency, people have developed a number of search and storage algorithms and techniques. It is much easier to use an existing system than write your own, and that is the market for modern database management systems.

- Electronic mail—One of the advantages of networked computer systems is the capability to transfer information between users. One of the most natural forms of information transfer for people these days is electronic mail. This has become a little more complex than quick notes in that most users now want to be able to attach word processing documents and spreadsheets to their mail messages. They also demand convenient viewers, the capability to store messages for later use, and many other features.

- Administrative tools—Because everyone is being asked to do more with less, system administrators tend to find themselves maintaining a much larger number of servers and other computer systems than in previous years. While some would say all that you have to do is work smarter and waste less time, I tend to favor the use of improved administrative tools to make life a little easier and to keep all of those scattered computer systems working properly. Microsoft's Systems Management Server is designed to provide improved tools for maintaining a large network of computers. This utility includes not only tools to take care of the servers, but to monitor, distribute software to, and store the configuration of the client workstations attached to the network.

- Gateways to other systems—You cannot and may not want to convert your entire computer environment over to one type of computer environment such as Windows NT overnight. Therefore, you need to communicate with a wide variety of other computer systems. Windows NT provides a high level of communication in the basic operating system to the large number of UNIX and Novell servers that are out there today. However, there are still a large number of shops who use IBM mainframe computers. While these computers can support TCP/IP communications, this is often an expensive solution. There needs to be a gateway that allows efficient access to these computers using IBM's native SNA protocols.

- Internet/intranet servers—The Internet stores an enormous amount of information. It is beneficial for a lot of organizations to get access to this information or even put out their own information using the Net. Even if you are not interested in the information that is out there from other organizations, you may want to use the convenient graphical tools that have been designed to support access to the information that is available on the Internet. In this case, you may want to set up your own intranet (network server[s] that use the same protocols and services as the Internet, but are limited to access within your organization) to disseminate information. I am not sure whether Microsoft is going to make this part of Windows NT itself (they are pushing their Internet products heavily), part of BackOffice, or a separate product family. Whatever the case, you should understand what these products are and what they can do for your organization as information distribution tools.

One of the concepts that you can pick up reading the BackOffice literature is that Windows NT Server is considered an integral part and is the foundation of BackOffice (see Figure 29.1). None of the other components other than Microsoft Mail (which has been around longer than NT) and SQL Server run on anything other than NT. Windows NT provides the following services to BackOffice:

- Connectivity to Windows desktop clients (DOS, Windows, Windows 95, and Windows NT Workstation)
- Connectivity to other computers such as Novell NetWare servers, UNIX servers, and Macintosh
- Access control (such as logon) facilities
- Management tools and utilities
- A multiprocessing operating system that allows specialized background processes and shared memory areas to be implemented to support the BackOffice applications

FIGURE 29.1.
Microsoft BackOffice.

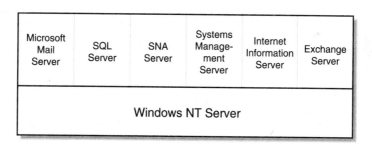

It is useful to take a look at the services that NT Server provides to BackOffice in a little more detail. Not only does it help you to understand BackOffice better, it also helps you to understand more about NT and how applications use it for support. The first set of services mentioned previously involve connectivity to the desktops that will be the clients of BackOffice and NT server. Some of the NT features that are used for this include the following:

- File and disk storage areas that contain applications and data to which the client workstations need access.
- Communications protocols and transmissions systems such as NetBEUI and TCP/IP. This frees the application designers from having to worry about these communications details—they merely call the services that are standard to NT.

29

MICROSOFT
BACKOFFICE

- Network services such as file and printer sharing. The file sharing enables you to implement directories containing software and data that is needed by multiple clients.

- Data transmission standards such as ODBC which provide higher level communications services such as database access.

- Communications services such as Remote Access Service (RAS) that enable you to interface clients to the server by way of modem much as if they were attached to the local area network. This saves application designers from having to deal with all of those annoying communications standards and details.

The next set of services that NT provides to BackOffice and other applications involves connectivity to other server and host computer environments. This deals with real-world situations where you have a number of different processors and operating systems, each of which meets a certain need. To be efficient, you often need to make these computer systems work together to exchange information or even process information cooperatively. The following NT features support these needs:

- NetWare connectivity products built directly into NT

- UNIX services such as TCP/IP, remote procedure calls, FTP, and TCP/IP printing services (LPR/LPD)

- AppleTalk networking software

 Access control facilities are also an important Windows NT feature used by BackOffice. While you could write your own access control utilities for databases and mail packages (which you still have to do with Microsoft Mail but not Exchange Server), why bother? Users get annoyed having to remember multiple user IDs and passwords. You have the extra burden of setting up all of these accounts and resetting them when the users forget them. One of the fundamental design features of the NT environment is the single logon ID for access to resources. If you are using a domain environment, you can even use the same logon ID to get access to resources located on multiple servers. The NT access control functionality supports BackOffice in the following manner:

- Single logon ID for access to BackOffice resources (excluding Microsoft Mail)

- Capability to control access to applications by client users

- Support for C-2 security (that is a U.S. government standard for security that few computer operating systems meet), which is discussed in Chapter 28, "Advanced Security Guidelines"

The next key feature of NT that BackOffice relies upon involves the system management tools and utilities. Much like user access control, each application could write its own management and maintenance utilities. Administrators would have to get into the mindsets of each of the people who wrote the various tools before they could become proficient in using them. However, because most of these tools perform the same conceptual functions (showing a log of warning messages and other events, or starting and stopping the processes associated with the applications, for example), it would be much easier on the administrators if they used one tool to maintain all these applications. BackOffice still has a few separate administrative tools that are unique to the various packages, but they do make use of a number of common utilities including the following:

- Event viewer (auditing)
- User manager (user accounts and privileges)
- Registry (configuration information)
- Remote access administrator (controlling who can access the server by way of modem)
- Disk administrator (prepare disk storage space for the applications)
- User profiles (control what each type of user can do and what restrictions exist on passwords and so forth)
- Performance monitor (determine if the system is functioning efficiently and locate any bottlenecks)
- Data backup (save all of that precious data to tape)
- Service manager (start and stop the services associated with the applications)
- Print manager (to control printed output from the applications)
- SNMP service permits the use of the Simple Network Management Protocol data collection mechanisms to capture both operating system and application management and monitoring information
- Standard installation and configuration utilities (use of Windows setup, a common NT/BackOffice installation screen, and features such as self-starting CD-ROMs to load the setup utilities automatically when these CD-ROMs are inserted)

Finally, coming from a database background, one of my favorite operating system services is the capability to run multiple processes in background and share memory areas. When you are in the business of moving lots of data around, the slowest point in the process is transferring information to and from the disk drives. If you have the option of caching information in memory, you can speed up the performance of databases and a number of other applications. Also, it is often much easier to design a complex application such as a database management system to be a series of processes (threads), each of which has its own specialized task. Windows NT provides the designers of the BackOffice applications with these two services which greatly speed applications up when they are moving large amounts of information around.

There are a few other interfaces between Windows NT and BackOffice that make NT an important part of the BackOffice architecture:

- The Windows application programming interface (API). This 32-bit interface eliminates many of the silly games that developers had to play when dealing with such things as memory management under older operating systems. This standard interface to the operating system and its services simplifies the task of developing software in the NT environment. This includes a number of supporting APIs such as telephony (TAPI), messaging (MAPI), licensing (LSAPI), Internet services (ISAPI), and others.

■ The standards that exist to communicate between applications. Chief in the current Microsoft list of hot topics is OLE and the Common Object Model (COM) that enable you to call functions of one application (MS Excel, for example) from within another application (such as MS Word). Microsoft has already extended this structure to work in the network environment with its distributed COM standards and operating system services.

■ Most of the interfaces to various hardware devices are through the operating system and a series of defined device drivers interfaces. This frees applications from having to be concerned with the nauseating details of the hardware itself.

With all of that said about Windows NT as the base of the BackOffice architecture, it is time to go over the products that make up BackOffice. I cover each of these in a little more detail later in this chapter, but a brief introduction is in order here. The oldest product in the BackOffice family is an extension of a product that has been around for some time—Microsoft's electronic mail system. The current official release is called Microsoft Mail Server. It is similar to many of the popular PC server mail packages in that it has a shared directory that contains a series of files that are used to transfer messages between users.

The mail server product has just been replaced in the BackOffice family by a more powerful product known as Exchange Server. Microsoft Mail has been around for some time and was never designed to handle the large networks of client workstations that are common today. It also lacks integration with the operating system, and some of the recoverability and backup features that many users want for the important corporate resource that electronic mail systems have become. Exchange Server, on the other hand, relies upon multiple background processes to execute the functions needed in a mail server. The architecture is designed to allow it to scale up to support a larger number of users. It also provides reliability and feature enhancements that users are now requesting. Some of the features of interest in this product follow:

■ Allows multiple users to exchange messages with one another

■ Supports attaching files (MS Word documents or a text file, for example) to the messages for transfer

■ Gateways to external mail systems such as Lotus cc:Mail or various Internet mail systems with the capability to transfer attachments in a number of different formats

■ Forms interfaces to enable you to transmit messages with standardized content

■ Application programming interfaces to enable you to send messages from your locally written programs

■ A group scheduling tool (Schedule+)

The next oldest product in this family is Microsoft SQL Server. You will also see the Sybase SQL Server product out there for both Windows NT and UNIX platforms. Microsoft and

Sybase collaborated for a number of years on the development of SQL Server, although they have now gone their separate ways on development. The SQL Server is a relational database management system (DBMS) that provides most of the features that you would expect from a DBMS:

- Utilities to store and retrieve data
- Capability to communicate between the server and client applications
- Utilities for administration of the database and the data
- Facilities for communication between databases
- Interfaces from various application development tools (ODBC-capable applications, for example)

The next product is not currently deployed in a large number of shops, as it is still fairly new, but I believe that tools such as this will become quite popular shortly. The Systems Management Server (SMS) enables administrators to not only manage a number of servers, but also a number of client workstations all from a central location. The features that make this product most interesting include:

- Capability to track (in an SQL Server database) the configurations of hardware and software on a network of client workstations running Windows, Windows 95, and Windows NT.
- Capability to deploy software automatically over the network. This support includes both simple file copy operations and those that require a little additional configuration work through custom scripts.
- A programmatic interface that enables you to extend the capabilities in the base SMS product to meet your unique needs (that is, you do not have to wait for Microsoft to think up all of the good ideas and implement them).
- Support tools for help desk staff to merge information on system configurations, technical product information, and even remote monitoring tools to provide more effective help desk services.

Finally, unless you have been in hibernation for the last year or so, you realize that the hottest topic in the computer industry is the Internet (at least it was the hot topic when this book was written, and there will surely be another hot topic to help sell products next year). Anyway, Microsoft is not known for passing up golden opportunities to sell products, and the Internet is no exception to this rule. Many of the early Internet servers ran on UNIX systems. However, because NT integrates networking tightly into the basic operating system much like UNIX, it is also an ideal candidate to serve as an Internet server. Microsoft's product on the server side of Internet tools (they have a number of products for client workstations also) is called the Internet Information Server, which was just recently released. Although there are other products out there with large market shares such as Netscape, you should be aware of what IIS can do for you:

- Act as a server to store and display information to World Wide Web (WWW) clients.

- Act as a file transfer server using the File Transfer Protocol (FTP). Note that this is a significantly enhanced (both from a security control and processing volume standpoint) FTP server when compared with the FTP server that comes as part of the Windows NT operating system (which was designed for local area networks).

- Act as a Gopher server providing the capability to look for resources on the Internet.

- Act as a domain name server (DNS) that translates the complex Internet address numbers (123.123.123.123, for example) into names that human beings can recognize (www.microsoft.com, for example).

One final comment on the Internet is in order. The Internet was developed by governments, universities, and commercial organizations around the world to provide an incredibly powerful information storage and access tool. Many companies and government agencies like having the ability to access these resources, but fear those nasty little kids out there who want to access information that they are not entitled to (yes, those nasty hackers and virus writers). There have been enough actual horror stories to make the more conservative information systems type swear off the Internet as a sure path to eternal damnation. They work hard to limit Internet access to mail and a few other limited services while adding protection through devices known as firewalls. Many computer vendors have sensed that many people are not ready to make the jump to the Internet, but they can benefit using the powerful and convenient information access tools developed for the Internet on an intranet (a network that is only accessible within your organization). Many feel that intranets will sell far more products over the next several years than the Internet in corporations, so you may be seeing requests to implement Internet Information Server or other Internet servers for intranet applications.

So much for the general introduction to Microsoft BackOffice. By now, you should be comfortable with the general concepts behind this product family—integration, services provided, and so on. I tried to convey some of the rationale for designing these products to make it easier to understand why things have been implemented the way that they have. In the next several sections, I want to go over the products in this family in just a little more detail. A complete discussion of BackOffice could fill up an entire book, but this introduction should make you at least conversant on what BackOffice is and what it means to your NT Server operating system.

SQL Server

Let me start my more detailed discussions with SQL Server. As I mentioned earlier, this was originally a joint development project with Sybase, but now Microsoft markets and develops its own product. The goal of this product is to provide a fully functional relational database management system server. Relational database management systems are the most common commercial databases. Their basic concept is that you have a series of tables containing different types of information. You can think of this data as being much like a spreadsheet with columns that have various attributes that describe the type of information that is stored in the table. The key to a relational database management system is that it can link these tables together to form an overall system of information.

SQL Server is not without competition. The largest database maker (depending on how you measure things, of course) is Oracle, which also makes a Windows NT product. Sybase also markets a Windows NT product, and there are numerous smaller database vendors that offer Windows NT products. While Oracle and Microsoft debate the feature set of their products (replication, scalability, and a number of other terms that only make sense to database types), the key discriminator is that Oracle has a number of applications that are built for Oracle, and SQL Server has other applications (including SMS) that are built to run with it. If you are building your own applications, you need to look at the current release of products from the various vendors and see which ones meet your cost/performance needs.

The basis of interaction with SQL Server, like most other commercial relational database management systems (IBM DB2, Oracle, and Informix, for example) is the Structured Query Language (SQL). This language has a few minor tweaks by each of the vendors who offer it, but for the most part the ANSI standard is followed well. This allows a high degree of portability for applications that seek to interact with multiple flavors of the database management system. Added to this is the built-in support and set of drivers for Open Database Connectivity (which is a Microsoft-sponsored standard) access to SQL Server. This gives you access to SQL Server from a wide range of development tools (Visual Basic, Visual C++, and others).

There are a number of features that could be covered related to Microsoft SQL Server. One that may be especially interesting to system administrators is the concept of replication and distributed databases. SQL Server enables you to make copies of tables contained in a large master database and distribute them to local, smaller databases. This replication feature is taken care of by SQL Server itself once you set it up so you avoid having to write complex duplication logic. This feature can help you in environments where people need frequent access to data that is stored at a remote site where the communications lines are a limiting factor. You may be able to make local copies of the data that you access frequently on less-expensive servers to satisfy some of your users' data needs.

Next, I would like to provide an overview of how SQL Server is implemented on your NT Server machine. The utilities that you will commonly use are arranged on the SQL Server program group on the Start menu as shown in Figure 29.2. As you can see, there are a number of utilities designed to help you work with the SQL Server system. For purposes of this chapter, I will focus on three of these utilities:

- SQL Service Manager to start/stop the database
- SQL Enterprise Manager to control the database configuration
- ISQL_w to access information in the database

29

MICROSOFT
BACKOFFICE

FIGURE 29.2.

SQL Server Utilities menu.

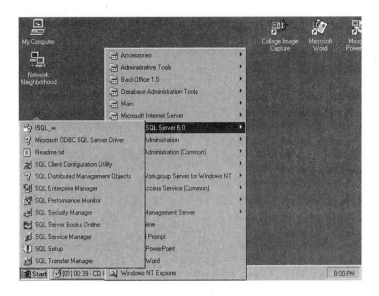

The first utility, SQL Service Manager, gets things going for you. There are two key services that you will want to have started before you begin using SQL Server. The first service is the MS SQLServer, which is basically the database processes themselves. If you do not have this service running, you will not have access to your database. The second service that you will be interested in is the SQLExecutive. This process enables you to schedule server tasks. Server tasks could include database replication events (keeping tables in sync across multiple databases), executing Transact-SQL statements, or executing other database commands. You can schedule (and modify the schedule of) events using SQL Enterprise Manager, which I will discuss next. Figure 29.3 shows the simple Service Manager interface. You select the service that you want to work with (and of course the server if you have more than one server running SQL Server), and then click on the appropriate text phase (stop, pause, or start/continue). The stop light shows you the current state of activity. I like simple interfaces that anyone who is licensed to drive a car can understand.

FIGURE 29.3.

Microsoft SQL Service Manager.

Next on the list of utilities that every NT administrator who supports SQL Server should know about is the SQL Enterprise Manager, which is shown in Figure 29.4. Again, you have a relatively simple interface that enables you to perform most of the functions you would need as an administrator. As it is becoming the norm with Microsoft products, you have an expandable tree control that shows all of the things that you can work with using this tool. This includes all of the things that you would expect, including the following:

- Jobs scheduled for SQL Executive
- Database and dump devices (your data files)
- The databases themselves
- Database objects such as tables
- Logons

FIGURE 29.4.

Microsoft SQL Enterprise Manager.

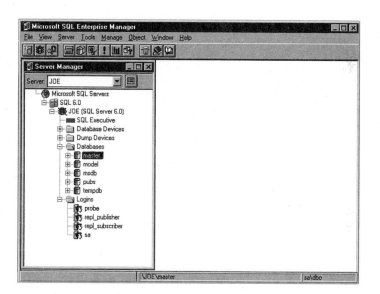

To work with any of the items mentioned previously, you open the appropriate branch on the tree control by clicking the plus sign to the left of it. Once you have located the object you want to work with, you double-click that object to display an editing dialog. Each type of tree member has an appropriate property page. Figure 29.5 shows the dialog that comes up for editing a logon (changing passwords, permissions, and so on). By the way, one thing I think is interesting is the stop light on the third line down in the tree control. You cannot see it in this book, but you get a red, yellow, or green light to indicate if you have the server started or not. You can activate SQL Service Manager by clicking the stop light in the toolbar.

Next on the quick tour of SQL Server is a utility that actually lets you work with the data stored in your database, which is called ISQL_w (interactive structured query language for Windows). It is not convenient for people who are not familiar with the structured query language (SQL), but for those who are, it is a quick way to get at your data. Figure 29.6 shows an example of an SQL query that you can type in quickly. When ready, you hit the green play button (the right

29

MICROSOFT
BACKOFFICE

I-

Part V

pointing arrow, which is the second item from the right on the toolbar). ISQL_w executes your query and then returns the results into the Results tab (see Figure 29.7). People who are interested in tuning queries can use the Statistics I/O and Showplan (the execution plan that is the way the database approaches the task of getting at the data) tabs. For those of you who are not interested in learning to write SQL statements, you might want to consider setting up Open Database Connectivity (ODBC) drivers (which are supplied with SQL Server) and using a GUI-based data access tool such as Microsoft Query (which comes with Visual C++ and Microsoft Office).

Figure 29.5.
SQL Enterprise Manager dialog.

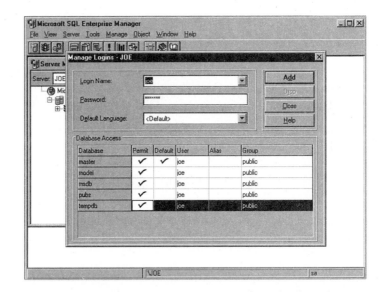

Figure 29.6.
An ISQL query.

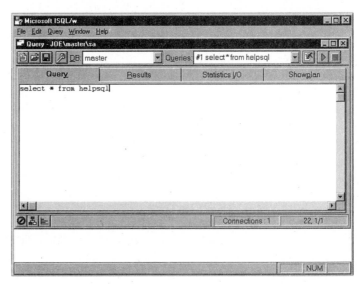

FIGURE 29.7.

The results of an ISQL query.

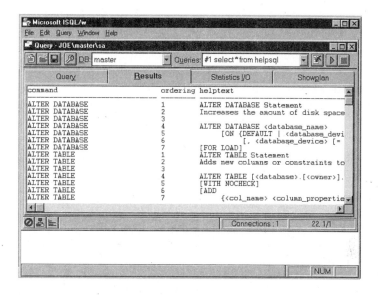

A final configuration control utility that you might want to work with is the SQL Server Setup utility (shown in Figure 29.8). This enables you to specify the paths for a few key items such as your master database and the location of your SQL Server files. A few other options of interest include options to automatically start your SQL Server and whether to use NT event logging to record database information. This can be nice in that it gives you one utility to look through to find events that are happening on your system.

FIGURE 29.8.

MS SQL Server Setup panel.

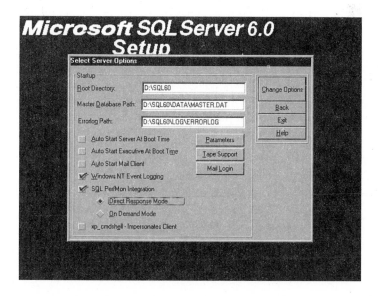

29

MICROSOFT
BACKOFFICE

Because this is a book about the Windows NT Server operating system, a few words on the impacts of running SQL Server on the operating system would be appropriate. First, databases make heavy use of memory for caching to speed up performance. Therefore, if you want to maximize performance, you will want to have sufficient memory in your server. Another factor to consider when setting up larger databases on PCs is that you may want to balance your input/output load across several disks. In SQL Server, you might want to set up multiple database devices that are on different disk drives, and locate your objects to balance the load. Most PC servers do not have the same high capacity data-transfer systems that you would find on something like a UNIX server, and therefore, this may be the first limit that you reach when implementing a database.

This has been a quick tour of the SQL Server product on Windows NT Server. It is not the only major database product for NT, although it is tightly integrated with BackOffice (especially SMS). It provides most of the features of a modern relational database management system. You may want to work with an expert if you need to implement a complicated database and want to learn which of the products best suit your needs. This section has gone over the major tools that are used to control SQL Server with a relatively easy-to-use interface.

Microsoft Mail Server

The next product in my discussion of Microsoft BackOffice is the old mail system from Microsoft—Mail Server. It has been around in various forms for a number of years, dating back before Windows NT was a glimmer in Bill Gates' eyes. It is not sophisticated compared to other modern mail systems, and it does not scale to the large number of users that may be found on larger NT Servers. It has, however, the blessing of being battle-tested for several years and is relatively easy to administer.

The main competitor to Microsoft Mail today is the Lotus cc:Mail product. This product is somewhat similar in structure to MS Mail (you have a post office directory on a disk that you have to share across the network). The interfaces exist for both DOS and Windows, just as with MS Mail. Lotus (now owned by IBM) implements some of the more advanced groupware features such as information sharing in its Lotus Notes products (which also leads the industry in installations). There are a number of other products in the PC network electronic mail and groupware fields. You may want to consider them, especially if your needs are modest as is your budget.

So what is Microsoft Mail Server all about? It is a client/server electronic mail system designed for networks of personal computers (Microsoft is not trying for the mainframe market). It is implemented through a series of data files that have to be accessible to all the client workstations and some application software that enables the clients to access that data. You can get this product in several ways. If you are using older Windows For Workgroups installations, you get the MS Mail client as part of the operating system. If you are using Windows 95 or Windows NT, you get the Exchange Inbox, which has the option of connecting to MS Mail servers and several other mail systems. Finally, you get a mail client as part of Microsoft Office. A component that integrates with this mail system is a scheduling package called Schedule + (which has recently moved to the Microsoft Office product line). This scheduling package allows both local calendars and calendars stored on the Microsoft Mail network data drive. If you choose the network drive storage option, you can implement group scheduling and coordinate your activities with others who keep their calendars on the network. Figure 29.9 illustrates this basic architecture.

FIGURE 29.9.

The basic architecture of Microsoft Mail Server.

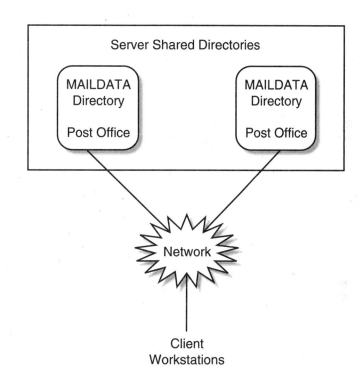

Now take a look at a sample of the directories that are used to store the mail data (the post office) in the Microsoft Mail Server. Figure 29.10 shows a directory listing for a Microsoft Mail Server that I have set up. As you can see, it is a series of files and folders that people have access to through a share name (in my case, I called it Maildata). What about the detailed contents of these folders? Actually, that is not your problem. You interact with these files through your Microsoft Mail client (or Microsoft Exchange on Windows 95 and NT 4) and the Microsoft Mail administration utility. You back these files up (we always do backups, right?) using normal operating system backup utilities. I have never had to go into these files and mess with them individually, and hope never to have to do it. I would not recommend doing such things unless you have a Microsoft Mail guru telling you to do so.

FIGURE 29.10.

Sample Microsoft Mail Server post office.

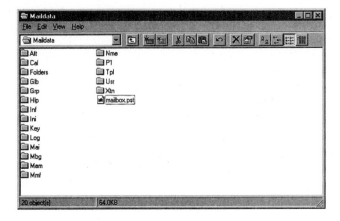

The other half of Microsoft Mail Server is the software that is used to access this post office data. As mentioned earlier, the Microsoft Mail client software is distributed through a number of forms, which include Windows For Workgroups, Microsoft Office, Windows NT 4, and Windows 95. For Windows NT 4 and Windows 95, you use the Microsoft Exchange client Inbox option, which has a Microsoft Mail Service available for you to set up to access your Microsoft Mail Server post office. With the right gateway software installed (optional and at extra cost, of course), you can access a number of different electronic mail systems, including Internet mail. The Microsoft Mail client (see Figure 29.11) basically enables you to compose and access mail messages. There are two basic types of messages that you can deal with. One is sent to you directly and is referred to as a private message. The other type of message is designed for group reading later on similar to a bulletin board. These group messages are stored in public folders. Note that all messages within Microsoft Mail allow you to attach a variety of other documents (such as spreadsheets or word processing documents) very easily (select attachments from the menu or the toolbar). This can be a very powerful way of routing complex information around the company. It usually takes the form of a quick cover note with an attachment for action and review.

Microsoft Schedule+ is also integrated with the Microsoft Mail system. This was one of the first electronic mail–enabled (a term meaning that it uses the electronic mail system for transmission services instead of making its own transmission system) applications. It uses the electronic mail system to distribute meeting invitations, cancellations, and confirmations. You can also set up a copy of your calendar on the server and grant others privileges to read or update it (as is the case when department administrators can schedule your time). One trick is that you can even create "dummy" users to represent your conference rooms (you give the mail user ID a name corresponding to the conference room, such as "Board Room"). You assign someone to respond to messages and log on as the conference room to coordinate schedules. I have seen some very efficient scheduling systems set up in even small workgroups with little effort using this system. A picture of the Schedule+ software (in this case the Windows 95 version which runs under Windows NT) is shown in Figure 29.12.

FIGURE 29.11.
Microsoft Mail client.

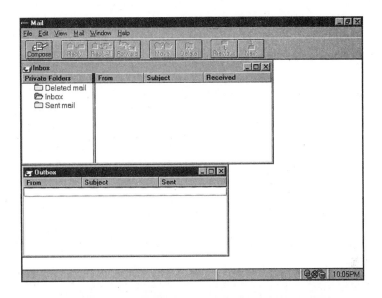

FIGURE 29.12.
Microsoft Schedule+.

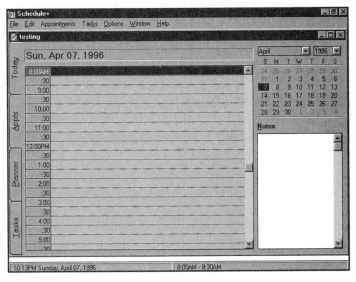

29

MICROSOFT
BACKOFFICE

Of course, someone has to administer this post office and he or she needs a tool to accomplish this task. The tool (admin.exe) is a relatively simple administration utility that is shown in Figure 29.13. Yes, it is a DOS-based tool that requires you remember how to use the Lotus-style menus of yesteryear. However, it gets the job done for adding users, modifying user accounts, and deleting users. One thing that I always found tricky was that you use the section of the Local Admin menu item titled *Recover* to change the user's password if he or she forgets it. You are not prompted for a value to set the password to; instead, it is one of the options that you set up for the local post office and whenever you recover any user, he or she is given that default password. Again, not very sophisticated, but it works (and that can be a blessing at times).

FIGURE 29.13.

The Microsoft Mail Admin utility.

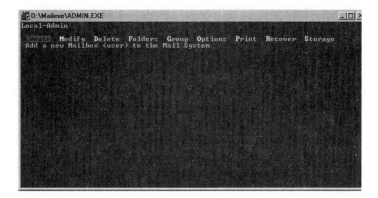

One of the major plusses related to PC mail packages is their integration with other applications. Microsoft started this process by providing the option to send mail from within applications such as Microsoft Word. The goal here was that you would normally compose a document and then want to route it to others in your group for review or approval. This saved you from having to exit from your word processor, load the mail software, compose a note, and then attach the document. In any event, Microsoft Mail is integrated with the Microsoft Office components and there is an applications programming interface (MAPI) that enables you to integrate it with your applications and BackOffice applications as well. You may want to keep this in mind if you are developing a hot new client/server application in an environment where people know how to use electronic mail efficiently.

Going back to the focus of this book, I would like to devote a few words to the effect of Microsoft Mail Server on your Windows NT Server. The good news is that while this package is not the most powerful one on the market, it is also relatively easy on your server in terms of resources. Basically, this package relies on you having two shared directories out there for the post office and the executables. NT Server does a fairly good job and is designed to handle the load of shared file systems, so that is about the limit of your impact, other than providing login accounts for all the people who will want mail boxes (they need both Windows NT access to get to the server and a Microsoft Mail Server account).

So concludes my discussion of the Microsoft Mail Server. Once again, it is a product that has been around for a number of years and works fairly well for smaller groups of users. Its main limitation is the fact that it is not designed to scale to the large number of users who are often being placed on a single PC server these days. It also lacks some of the fancy groupware interfaces that Microsoft Exchange Server is targeting. It is simple to set up, but you have to make sure that everyone has both an NT account and a mail account with which to access the system.

Exchange Server

Microsoft Mail resembles many of its competitors—shared files on a network drive that everyone accessed to see if they had new mail to read and wrote to when sending mail to others. Most of the technology was concentrated in the mail viewers located on individual PCs. This was okay for those brave souls who were first pioneering this new technology. A shortcoming, however, soon became apparent. As the number of mail users increased and their usage of the system also increased, the performance of these shared file mail systems decreased. Also, advanced features such as directory synchronization between servers and the like were extremely difficult to implement under this simple architecture. The trend towards more powerful PC servers also contributed to this problem in that more users were concentrated on fewer, larger servers for their network support. However, the power of these larger servers also provided a solution to this problem.

Microsoft decided that the way to get speed and scale up to support larger numbers of users was to look at how client/server database management systems performed a similar task. The key to this whole process is memory and a series of background tasks (services and threads) that transfer information between the memory areas and data files and also process the requests from users on the network. The series of processes that are implemented for the Microsoft Exchange Server are shown in Figure 29.14.

FIGURE 29.14.

Microsoft Exchange
Server Services.

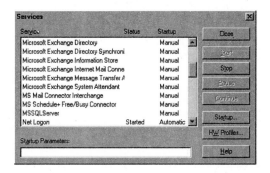

Now for the administrative side of the picture. The good news is that Microsoft Exchange Server is built right into the Windows NT security model and can access its security information. The bad news is that the Microsoft Exchange Server is built right into the Windows NT security model and requires that you implement a domain to handle security controls. Actually, it is only bad news for those folks who use workgroups instead of domains. You cannot convert a server from a workgroup server to a domain server. Unfortunately, you will have to completely re-install Windows NT Server. If you just try to upgrade from 3.51, it will take whatever configuration settings 3.51 had (you wanted a workgroup named xyz, for example). In any event, be prepared for this if you decide to implement Exchange Server. It is reaching for a goal that most system administrators would support: reducing the number of accounts that have to be set up for a single user in this database, this mail system, and that server.

29

MICROSOFT
BACKOFFICE

Exchange Server installs a number of items in its start menu group, as shown in Figure 29.15. I find this program group interesting in that, as opposed to many of the program groups that are filled with a large number of utilities, help files, and online book icons, this one has only a single application that performs most of the administration. It has a documentation entry and a few other minor tools. However, the majority of the group is devoted to performance monitoring tools and an optimizer utility. I think that these boys and girls are interested in speed and capacity. I at least found this to be interesting.

FIGURE 29.15.

Microsoft Exchange Server program group.

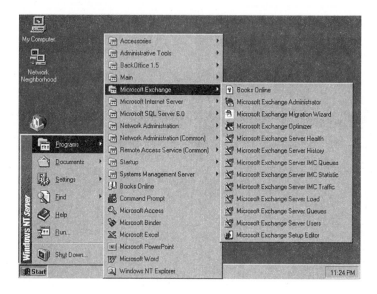

The administrator utility resembles many of the modern Microsoft Office products (and most of their other Windows 95 and Windows NT 4 applications). Figure 29.16 shows this interface. You start off with the traditional tree control on the left, which has a display on the right that displays the data that is appropriate for the items you have selected. There are a number of options available in the menu across the top, but most of the control functions can be accessed using the mouse and this tree control. You can select any number of servers to connect to (this is a multidocument interface application) and pick the parameters with which you want to work.

One of the things that is not obvious from the previous discussion is where this product is headed. Part of the answer can be found when looking at Lotus Notes, which is the leading groupware product (software that is designed to enable groups of people to exchange information and work together) on the market today. You see the beginnings of forms in this release of Exchange Server that let you use electronic mail to route information. You also see a programming interface that allows other applications to interface directly with Exchange Server to provide message routing capabilities. I think that you will also see a tighter integration with SQL Server to handle that information that is best suited to be kept in database table format as opposed to text document format.

FIGURE 29.16.

Microsoft Exchange Administrator.

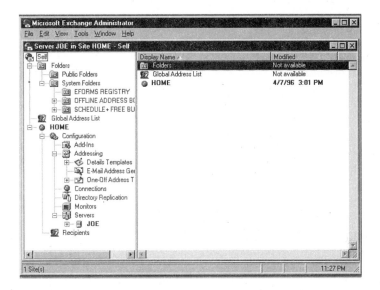

In return for all the benefits described in this chapter, there comes a price. You have to support a number of background services when running Exchange Server. Also, it uses a fair amount of memory to attain speed and support multiple users. The optimizer is designed to help you keep this consumption reasonable for your particular load, but you need to keep an eye on things (as described in the performance tuning chapter) to ensure that your resources keep up with your load.

One final note that I wanted to make about Exchange Server: If you have a number of Windows NT 4 or Windows 95 workstations that will be using the Microsoft Exchange client, you will be receiving a little nudge from Microsoft to upgrade to Exchange Server from Mail Server. Public folders have been supported under Mail Server for some time, and the old, primitive mail client supports access to these public folders, but the Exchange client does not support public folders when attaching to a Mail Server post office—only Exchange Server public folders are supported. This can be quite annoying if you have people getting these new operating systems and wanting to use the new tools, but you are not ready to upgrade to the new server. I know I was annoyed.

It will be interesting to see how Exchange Server performs in the field (I was working with release candidate software when writing this). It seems to be using an architecture for scaling that has been around for some time in the database world. This will increase demands on the server, but hopefully you have a budget for memory and processor upgrades. I think that it will be an architecture that can be extended well beyond the limits of the old shared file directory mail systems such as Microsoft Mail Server.

29

MICROSOFT
BACKOFFICE

System Management Server

The next product in the BackOffice family is also fairly new. It is designed to meet one of the more common complaints of PC system and network administrators—it is too hard to maintain a large network of computers with the current staff. Yes, more for less has certainly struck home in the information systems world where computers are often considered controllable expenses. (I guess that makes all the other expenses in business completely out of control.) Conceptually what has to be done is not difficult:

- You have to keep track of the hardware and software that you have deployed.
- You have to perform occasional software upgrades.
- You have to fix hardware and perform upgrades, especially when you upgrade to more demanding operating systems such as Windows 95 or Windows NT.
- You have to support your software and hardware configurations with telephone help desks, in-person visits, and so on.
- You have to support users who might have altered their configuration files (Registry, .ini files, and so on). They will usually swear that they never touched anything and that the system suddenly started acting funny completely on its own.

Relatively simple concepts, but the problems come in when you have a large number of PCs that are full-fledged computers that have all of the sensitivities of operating systems and a large number of things that can fail. The typical computer person's solution to such problems is to write some software that helps automate some of these functions. That is the purpose of the Systems Management Server or SMS in the Microsoft BackOffice family. In its current form, it provides the following services:

- The capability to automatically gather an inventory of the hardware and software on client workstations and your servers
- The capability to take control of remote workstations from the help desk for trouble-shooting
- The capability to distribute software over the network in an automated (that is, scripted) fashion
- The capability to provide basic-level network protocol analysis
- The capability to interface other applications to the SMS database and develop more sophisticated applications to meet special needs
- Support for application metering package interface to make sure that you do not run more copies of server-based software than your license supports (you know Microsoft was very interested in this feature)

The SMS program group contains the tools that you would use to access these functions. Figure 29.17 shows this program group. In this abbreviated overview of SMS, there are three items in this program group that I wanted to bring to your attention. The first is the Administrator, which is the main tool for controlling SMS. The second is the Books Online option. I sense Microsoft is moving more to using this to distribute documentation. You may want to take some time to get comfortable with their online documentation and help systems before a crisis strikes and you desperately need to get at critical information. The third thing that I wanted to point out is the Service Manager icon. Much like SQL Server and Exchange Server, SMS uses a series of background processes that are specialists in their respective areas that must be running to get access to these features. Figure 29.18 shows the background services associated with SMS.

FIGURE 29.17.

Systems Management Server program group.

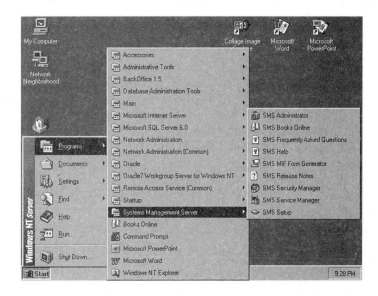

FIGURE 29.18.

Services associated with SMS.

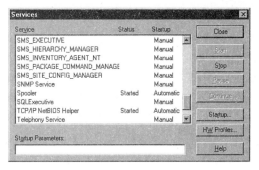

Systems Management Server is tightly integrated with Windows NT Server and other BackOffice components. As a matter of fact, you have to run SQL Server with a database set aside for SMS to store all the inventory and control data. Figure 29.19 shows the screen from the SMS setup on which you specify the SQL Server database properties. When it comes to integrating SMS with other applications, this typically takes the form of writing procedures to handle the unique installation requirements of each of these applications. There is a defined interface to SMS for building enhanced control utilities of your own, or you can simply use a report generator tool that works with SQL Server to provide customized reports on your network.

FIGURE 29.19.

SQL Server Setup for SMS.

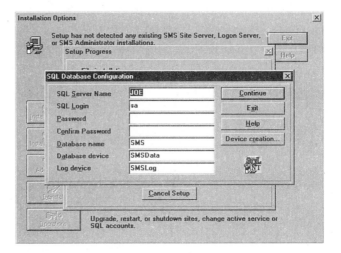

There are a number of existing and new competitors for SMS. Because SMS is such a broad product, these competitors fall into several categories. You will find a number of help desk support tools and automated configuration tracking packages that have been around for several years. The network monitoring and management market has a number of protocol analyzers and some more sophisticated network monitoring tools based on the Simple Network Monitoring Protocol (SNMP—you find acronyms everywhere). Finally, Oracle is among the competitors for the all-encompassing PC management tool vendors with a product that is similar to SMS that is scheduled for release in the summer of 1996. They, of course, use their own database instead of SQL Server. The number of products coming out in this field is a good indication that there is a need. Like most Microsoft products, I'm sure SMS will evolve to meet market needs as Microsoft drives to make it the number one product in the field.

Running SMS is much like running both a database and a server-based application at the same time. You have to have SQL Server running. In addition, there are all those SMS services that are running and using up memory areas. The stated requirement for an SMS server is 28MB (remember, that does not include any other uses that you might have for that server such as Exchange Server). I got it running on my test machine with 24MB, but I did not use it for production work, and I had to shut down several other services to keep the system from going into swap (it was horribly slow). Therefore, if you have the option, you may want to include a little bit more memory and processing capacity if you are planning to install an SMS server on your network.

One final note that I just had to throw in here. Figure 29.20 shows the installation status panel from the SMS installation. You can see that it has multiple status indicators. Much like the `winnt32.exe` installation used for Windows NT itself, the installation procedure uses multiple threads running at the same time to accomplish the installation. In the SMS case, the file installation is going in parallel with database configuration work. I really like it any time that people spend the time to make installation scripts an efficient use of the installer's time and not just an afterthought done the day before the product goes to the production group.

FIGURE 29.20.

Multiple threads in SMS installation.

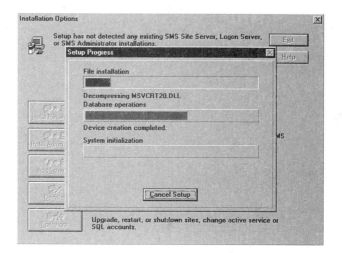

SNA Server

Gateways to IBM mainframes are a reality in many business environments. There is just too much code to convert, even if you wanted to convert it. The chief difficulty that I have found dealing with IBM mainframes is that they have their own way of doing just about everything. I can link together two UNIX computers without any difficulty, and I can make Novell and Windows NT Servers work together in a local area network environment. However, when it comes time to link to that mainframe, you usually have to do it the mainframe way, which usually means talking to them using their networking architecture, known as the System Network Architecture (or SNA).

To be fair, there are a number of solutions that can teach the mainframe to use protocols such as TCP/IP. These solutions work and some of them even come from IBM itself. However, I have run into two problems when trying to teach the mainframe TCP/IP. The first one involves getting the equipment and software set up. Mainframes tend to have 24-hour availability requirements, and their operating systems need to be rebooted for many of the changes to take place. It can take forever to get a reboot scheduled, and if your staff is not familiar with setting up these mainframe products; you may have to try several different times to get the configuration correct.

The next problem that I have seen with mainframe TCP/IP installations involves resource utilization. Few of the mainframe shops that I have seen have large amounts of excess capacity. The main hindrance to mainframe sales and loyalty has been their relatively high costs per unit of processing capacity. Therefore, every computer cycle on most of the mainframes that I have worked with is treated as a precious commodity. If not tuned correctly, or if used heavily by a wealth of new systems seeking data from mother IBM, your mainframe system can become quite heavily loaded with having to translate everything into that foreign language of TCP/IP. This can be tuned, and there are some mainframe TCP/IP solutions that are better at reducing performance problems than others, but be aware that this can be a problem for you.

Now to the other solution, which is teaching all the other computers to speak to the mainframe in its native language. Actually, there are multiple components to this language for file transfer, terminals, and so on, just as TCP/IP has FTP, Telnet, and so on, built on top of it. In addition, IBM has its own wiring scheme with its own connectors that you often have to deal with. For many installations, it is easier to translate the needs from users on the local network into IBM's terms and talk to the mainframe as if they were terminals or other types of components in the Big Blue world. This usually means mainframe emulation cards and IBM terminal network connections run throughout the building. This "second network" can be an additional design and maintenance headache with which to deal.

Microsoft's goal with SNA Server is to try and live in both worlds. It can, through the purchase of the appropriate supported hardware, connect to the mainframe in a variety of forms from a simple terminal connection line (which differs between the AS/400 and the other mainframes, wouldn't you know it) to channel attachments (which is the high speed internal bus on the mainframe that is so jealously guarded by the mainframe hardware types). On the other side, you have a wide variety of client LAN architectures and communications protocols to include TCP/IP, NetBEUI (Microsoft LANs), Novell, and AppleTalk. You can even use Remote Access Service to dial in and make a connection.

Any time you are connecting to that expensive mainframe or AS/400 system, you need to perform a lot of up-front analysis. A mistake can seriously affect your operations and your bottom line. You need to look at the products that are out there and weigh the total costs (wiring up all those mainframe coaxial cable connections versus the cost of the server and communications equipment). You may also want to take advantage of the fact that Microsoft SNA Server supports multiple smaller servers providing SNA services as opposed to one huge server doing all the work (imagine the outcry when that server has a failed hard drive and is down for maintenance). Anyway, SNA Server is an interesting product that may be a good contender if you are implementing a connection to those Big Blue mainframes or AS/400s.

Internet Information Server

Next in line is a product that is now a part of Windows NT Server itself. This product is the newly released Internet Information Server or IIS. The Internet and intranets (networks within a company that use standard Internet tools to disseminate information) are the hottest topic in all the trade magazines, and everyone is rushing to market with IIS products. I always hate anything that is surrounded by such a large wall of hype, but the Internet addresses many of the most useful things that computers can be used for and therefore merits consideration. The Internet and intranets can be used to provide the following:

■ Access to complex (text, graphics, sound, and video) information in an easy, graphical format. Better still, this format (the hypertext markup language or HTML) is an industry standard, so you are not signing your life away when you pick one particular vendor's products.

■ A convenient means to select files for downloading.

■ A means to access data from a database in a controlled format.

■ The capability of distributing objects (data and the associated software to run it) over a network.

■ A means to access data on millions of computers located around the world.

This section is just a quick product overview for those who have not yet read my more detailed discussion of Internet servers in Chapter 30. Basically, the Internet Information Server is a product designed to be tightly coupled with the Windows NT operating system and its networking infrastructure to provide some of the most commonly used services on the Internet:

■ World Wide Web (WWW)

■ File Transfer Protocol (FTP)

■ Gopher

The World Wide Web server is probably the hottest feature on the Internet. I have even found a number of business people listing their Internet addresses on their business cards and stationery. A Web server is a repository of documents that are written in HTML and a background service that responds to requests for information in the format of a standard Web server. Early results have shown IIS to be an efficient and powerful server product. I like the fact that you do not have to drop a bundle on hardware to get yourself going—a fair-sized NT Server does just nicely. Figure 29.21 shows a sample Web page for those of you who have not yet surfed the Web.

The File Transfer Protocol (FTP) service provided in IIS is a beefed-up version of the FTP that comes standard with Windows NT. It is designed to handle higher volumes of traffic from the Internet and the additional security considerations. The Gopher server dates back to the days before the World Wide Web had search engines to find what you are looking for. You can set up a Gopher server for your Web crawling if you are still primarily FTP- and Telnet-based.

Microsoft is not without competitors in this industry. Netscape leads the field of PC servers and also the browser market (the tools used to read Web pages). There are also servers from other big industry competitors such as Oracle. Also, the majority of servers out there still date back to the days when the Net was UNIX territory, and therefore they use UNIX versions of Web servers. When you get out onto the Net, you will find a number of shareware, freeware, and even home-grown products. That is the beauty of a fairly defined standard such as HTML—they can work together, at least for the most part. You will find "extensions" to the basic standards that are put out by Netscape and Microsoft, but you can still read almost all the pages on the Web with your basic browser.

FIGURE 29.21.

A sample Web page.

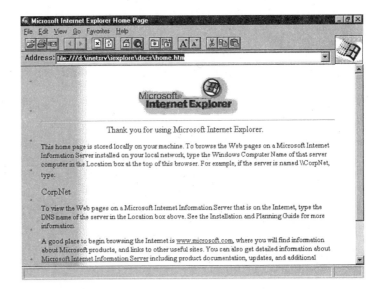

The Internet Information Server is controlled (started and stopped) by a relatively basic tool shown in Figure 29.22. In this case, I have only loaded the World Wide Web and FTP services (not Gopher). You select which of the services that you want to control and then click the controls that resemble your standard CD or VCR controls (start, stop and pause). Unlike many of the other BackOffice components, IIS does not put much load on your server until you have a lot of users accessing it (there are not a number of background processes that are running at all times or large memory areas allocated for processing). You will probably want to be most sensitive about the input/output loading on your server and split up files across multiple disk drives if you feel that you are going to run into heavy user loads.

A few words about the integration of IIS and BackOffice seem to be in order here. As with many of the new products that seem to be flooding the market these days, there is a new application programming interface (API) that is used to interface programs written in languages such as C++ to IIS. Also, there is the traditional method of using Common Gateway Interface (CGI) scripts, which can be thought of as the traditional programming language of Web pages, to interface operating system applications to Web and FTP services. This exciting area of programming focuses on such things as dynamically building the content of Web pages from data stored in a database. There are a number of good examples of this—for example, www.nasdaq.com, which Microsoft implemented to display current stock quotes to Web users, comes from an SQL Server database.

FIGURE 29.22.

Internet Service Manager.

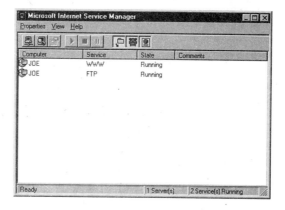

So much for IIS. It is a just-released product, so my comments made on other products earlier apply. Specifically, I expect that it will evolve and see a lot of research and development effort to become what Mr. Gates (driven by the computer consumer) wants it to be. I found it to be relatively easy to install and work with. This is as it should be. Your main focus when publishing a book is the content, not the mechanics of binding or paper types. When building a Web site, the content of the site should be your focus as you try to out-do all those other sites up there created by kids who stay up all night preparing graphics, sound clips, and so on.

One topic that I did want to touch on before I left the true BackOffice portion of this chapter is installation. One sign of the integration of the products is the fact that they have a common installation panel on those CD-ROMs where you buy the entire product family. (See Figure 29.23.) Note that they are all dependent on Windows NT Server and will require you to install that product first. You also need to have SQL Server before you can install SMS. Other than that, all the products can be selected individually based on your needs. Final reminders include the fact that you need to be running in a domain, not a workgroup for Exchange Server, and you need to have at least one NTFS disk for SMS.

FIGURE 29.23.

Common BackOffice installation screen.

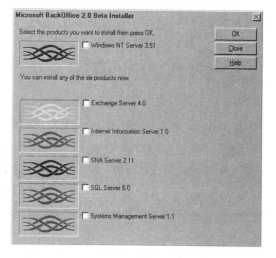

29

MICROSOFT
BACKOFFICE

The Windows NT Resource Kit

Next on our list of other items that are available to support you and your Windows NT Server is the Windows NT Resource Kit from Microsoft. This documentation and tool set may be a little bit expensive for the casual user who is just maintaining a small NT setup. However, if you are trying to do front-line development or maintain a larger or complicated NT network, this kit contains a wealth of detailed information for you. Figure 29.24 shows the utilities available under the Windows NT 3.51 Resource Kit (which is all that was available at press time and probably represents roughly what the NT 4 kit may contain).

FIGURE 29.24.

The Windows NT Resource Kit program group.

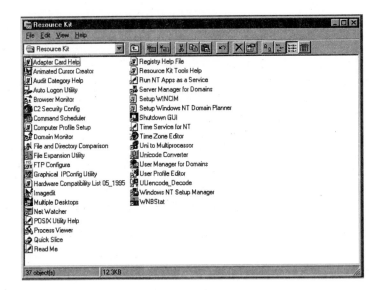

As you can see, there are a number of tools that take up only 23MB of hard disk space and often meet many of those needs that administrators have when trying to do something a little out of the ordinary on their system. Let me cover just one of them to give you an idea of what this tool kit can do. My favorite among this group is a utility that you run from the command line called SRVANY. I do not use it often (twice so far, actually), but it gives me a capability that I miss from the UNIX world—the ability to execute startup scripts. This is important when you have databases such as Oracle Workgroups server. While you can set the services associated with the Oracle instance to start when the system starts up, Oracle requires you to run a few commands (or use a graphical utility) to make the database available for users. I run SRVANY to create a service that I start up at system startup time. The SRVANY utility can make a service out of an NT executable program, including the simplest case, which is a good old batch file. Anyway, I call this batch file startup.bat and put it in a script directory. I run SRVANY to turn it into a service and then edit the Registry keys (read the instruction file that accompanies SRVANY) to specify the details. Once this is set up, you can modify the startup.bat file much like you would use the RC directories under UNIX to run a series of batch files on system startup.

There are a number of such utilities in the Resource Kit, and it can be fun exploring them. There are also at least four (by last count) books in the Resource Kit that go into some Windows NT topics in extreme detail (there is an entire book on tuning). Again, these may be a little bit too in depth for the average NT user. However, it is nice to have such a resource available in your shop for those times when everything starts to go wrong and you need some help.

Products Available from Microsoft on the Internet

Now for my favorite place to get information—the Internet. Yes, I know that I covered the technologies involved with Internet servers and intranet servers just a few sections ago, but this is different. I am not concerned with the technologies in this section. Instead, I want to cover some of the content of the Internet that can make your job so much easier. First, you need to have a Web browser and mail package combined with a connection to the Internet. Assuming you have an account with access to the Internet, you're in luck. Windows NT has the Microsoft Exchange Inbox, which is ready to get you started with Internet electronic mail. You also get the Microsoft Internet Explorer as part of your desktop (if you specified it as an installation option; if not, just go back and get it from your NT CD-ROM). This will enable you to surf the Web and read newsgroups to your heart's content. If you are feeling a little more ambitious, there are a number of other Web products that you can try out from Netscape, Delrina, NCSA, and others.

A couple of things might be of interest to you. The first is the Microsoft Web page (`http://www.microsoft.com`). Figure 29.25 shows the BackOffice page that is accessible from the main Microsoft page. Yes, Microsoft has even found a way to implement tab dialogs on a Web page. You can see a lot of text and also a number of underlined sections of text and also some buttons (like the tabs at the top of the page) that you can click to go exploring. This is a good experience, and you will quickly learn to move around on these pages. Let me go over a brief list of some of the resources that can be found on this Web site:

- Free downloads of trial versions or Beta copies of software (even the big products such as the Internet Information Server were offered in this format).
- Updated device drivers for devices that I am having problems with or new devices which are not on the distribution CD-ROM.
- Product information such as white papers on products that I am evaluating or implementing.
- Product technical specifications when I am putting together system configurations (this used to take weeks calling vendors, getting faxes or materials mailed out, but now you can get it when you need it).
- Access to some of the online technical support resources and other data that can help you solve problems that you might run into.

29
MICROSOFT BACKOFFICE

FIGURE 29.25.

The BackOffice page accessible from the main Microsoft Web page (http://www. microsoft.com).

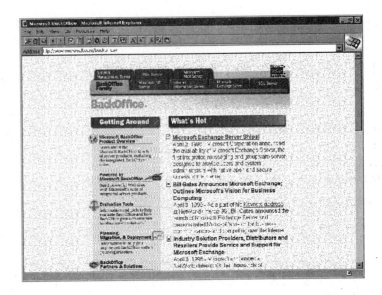

Microsoft updates its Web pages (both content and look and feel) more often than any of the places that I visit regularly. Therefore, it is useful to get over to this site every week or so to see what is happening. I tend to look for trends and new products that Microsoft seems to be pushing. I find it helpful to know something about what they are doing before they do it and I have to respond.

One final point: Microsoft is not the only company who has heard of the World Wide Web. As a matter of fact, I have found very few major computer vendors who do not have their own Web pages. Some of these are a little bit skimpy on some of the detailed technical information and device drivers, but almost all of them have product specifications and other information that helps to support sales and marketing. If you do not know the name, try accessing one of the Internet search engines such as www.lycos.com or www.Webcrawler.com, and fill in the blanks to search for the company that you are interested in. I always try www.[company name].com (www.oracle.com, for example) when I am searching for a company, and it usually works.

Future Directions

Most of the Microsoft products that I have observed are shaped by a combination of good ideas from the development team, guidance from Mr. Gates and his management/sales team, and the desires of the software consuming public who vote with their money. Being an author and therefore being entitled to at least a little artistic license (even though this is a computer book), I wanted to discuss a few ideas as to where BackOffice and the related Microsoft products might be headed over the next couple of years. This is not totally a random guessing game. Microsoft does routinely leak clues as to where it is heading in the form of the following:

■ Speeches by Mr. Gates and other top Microsoft executives at the major computer industry conferences.

■ Product announcements and other published material on their product directions.

■ The emphasis at Microsoft-sponsored conferences such as the recent professional developers conference in San Francisco. It is important not just to listen to the words in the keynote speech, but also to look at the topics that they consider important enough to emphasis over and over again (like intranets).

Gazing into this crystal ball, I see the following things on the horizon for these products:

■ Microsoft products will become one with the Internet and intranets. Some of their recently released products and published product directions show that they plan on making it as easy to open up a Web page in one of your office tools (such as MS Word) as it is to open a file on your local hard disk. In effect, the Internet will become an extension of your computer's storage and processing capabilities.

■ Internet applications will spring up that transmit little applets to the remote computers to execute (through Java).

■ More applications will learn how to use OLE, which will blur application boundaries.

■ Network-based multisystem management will become a reality.

■ BackOffice will become even more tightly integrated and will push towards domains as opposed to workgroups.

Realize that I cannot guarantee that any of this will come to pass. However, if you read enough predictions about the future, you can start to see trends. These trends probably indicate where the industry is going. You can rationalize this by saying that when enough computer types are talking about a concept, there is probably a market for it. If there is a market, Microsoft will probably be there with products (Bill did not become a billionaire wasting time on building things that no one wants). I hope that this section has stimulated your creative thought processes, even if just a little bit.

Summary

This chapter has tried to give an overview of a topic that could easily fill an entire book. As a matter of fact, Sams Publishing also offers *Microsoft BackOffice Administrator's Survival Guide*, and is also coming up with separate books devoted entirely to Microsoft Exchange and each of the other BackOffice components. This summary chapter was intended to give you enough information so that you know what the products in the BackOffice family can do for you. You do not know the details of tuning a SQL Server database, but you can learn that by reading one of the books devoted to the topic. I also tried to approach these products from the viewpoint of their impact on the NT Server and the system administrator. Hopefully, you will be able to answer your boss's questions about this BackOffice thing that he or she read about in a magazine last week.

Windows NT Server as a Database Server

by Joe Greene

IN THIS CHAPTER

No one I know of has ever accused Microsoft of lacking ambition. The Windows NT Server product is certainly no exception to this rule. Not only did the design team intentionally take on industry-leader Novell in the file server and print server markets, but they targeted the client/server database server market as well. About the only computer market Microsoft isn't in with NT Server is the "dumb" terminal market of the mainframes (although you can get Telnet servers that enable NT Servers to do some of this type of work). This chapter addresses the use of NT Servers to operate database management systems that are accessed by remote clients.

This is somewhat of a challenge. There are entire books written about the various database management systems you can purchase for Windows NT. These books cover topics such as database administration, application development, and even specialized topics such as database tuning. Obviously, I cannot cover all these topics in one chapter. Instead, I focus on the interaction between the more common database management systems (Oracle, Microsoft SQL Server, and Microsoft Access's JET) and the Windows NT system. The chapter is divided into the following parts:

- First impressions of databases under Windows NT
- Types of database management systems
- Interactions between the operating system and database management system
- Oracle under Windows NT
- Microsoft SQL Server under Windows NT
- Microsoft Access's JET database engine under Windows NT
- A quick discussion of ODBC and OLE

First Impressions of Databases Under Windows NT

My first exposure to Windows NT was when I was asked to serve as database administrator for an Oracle Workgroup Server database. The goal of this project was to store a fair amount of data within this database and to use some of the more advanced (and demanding) features of the database, such as storing audio in the database. I was more than a bit skeptical, coming from the large UNIX server environment. I was concerned that even if Microsoft had done a good job on the operating system, the limited processing and data transfer capabilities of a PC-based server would quickly overload the system and cause miserable response times.

The good news is that I was actually quite surprised. Even though the Windows NT product had not been out on the market very long, and its main focus at the time was combating NetWare as a file and print server, I was able to get more than adequate response times in my development environment. Don't get me wrong—I wouldn't try to put a multi-terabyte database on a Pentium PC server (although it might be interesting to see a DEC Alpha running NT trying this out). However, most databases are just not that big. Also, with distributed database and database replication technologies coming into their own, you can often design a series of smaller databases that accomplish the same functions as a single large database in traditional environments.

When you work on an NT Server for such functions as word processing, you will notice that it seems very slow when compared with the NT Workstation product on the same computer (or even a smaller computer with less memory). You might be the only one in the building, and there might be no other jobs running on the computer. This is actually an intentional design feature that distinguishes the server version of NT from the workstation version. The server version is tuned to respond to background server processes (services) that are designed to service other users who might want some of your server's computing capacity. The person on the server's keyboard gets leftover CPU cycles. This is a key feature that enables NT Server to function as a database server. Almost all the big, multiuser database management systems use a series of background processes to store and retrieve information from the database and perform all the necessary housekeeping functions. Therefore, when running a database management system, you need to have a system that gives these background processes the time they need to keep information flowing between the database and the users. Keep this in mind if your boss ever proposes that you can use the server as your personal PC to save money.

Types of Database Management Systems

I bet that title scared some of you. Fear of a lengthy discussion about the relative merits of the hierarchical model versus the relational model flashed through your head. What this section is actually devoted to is a discussion of the alternative architectures from the operating system's point of view. Database management systems are among the most challenging applications I have run across when it comes to using operating system resources. They are always demanding on memory, and depending on the types of processing, they often stress the input/output subsystems.

All too often, when a database server is performing poorly, the system administrator blames the database, and the database administrator blames the server and operating system. Of course, everybody blames the programmers who wrote the applications. With a little knowledge in the hands of the system administrators, many of these problems could be avoided. This section starts this discussion with a presentation of the various architectural alternatives for database management systems on NT Servers that you are likely to come across. These include the following:

- Client/server versus host/terminal processing
- File access versus background processes for data access
- Distributed databases
- Database replication

The first industry buzzwords I throw at you in this section are client/server computing. Quite simply, this process involves applications that divide their processing between two or more computers. This is a simplified discussion, but it is good enough for what I am working with here. The contrast to client/server computing is host/terminal computing. Figure 30.1 illustrates these two architectures.

FIGURE 30.1.

Host/terminal versus client/server computing.

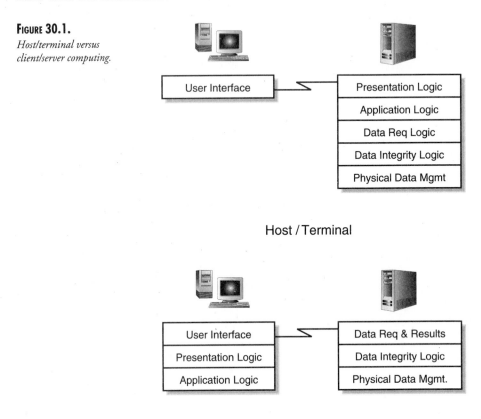

Host / Terminal

Client / Server

It is often easier to start with the host/terminal computing architecture. It was the first computer user access architecture to evolve after the days of punch cards. It involves hooking a controller to the big central computer that can take input from a number of terminals. These terminals are usually referred to as "dumb" terminals because they have very limited memory and almost no capacity to process information. They merely display information in the format the central computer has given them.

The alternative, client/server computing, splits the work between several computers, each of which has some degree of "smarts." This can be thought of as a divide-and-conquer approach for computer systems. The user sits at a workstation that performs most of the display functions and possibly some of the data analysis. The server is assigned the duties of data access and transmission.

Once you have grasped the basic concepts of client/server computing, I have another wrinkle to throw at you. There are actually multiple flavors of client/server computing. The differences lie primarily in how the labor is divided between the client and the server. Although the client is typically assigned the display functions and the server the database access, the question comes up as to where the business processing functions are performed. Although there are many minor variations between different vendor products, the key concepts to grasp are the two-tier and three-tier client/server architectures. There are books devoted to the intricate details of client/server architectures if you are interested; however, this is a Windows NT book, so you can get away with just understanding the basics. The two-tier and three-tier architectures are illustrated in Figure 30.2.

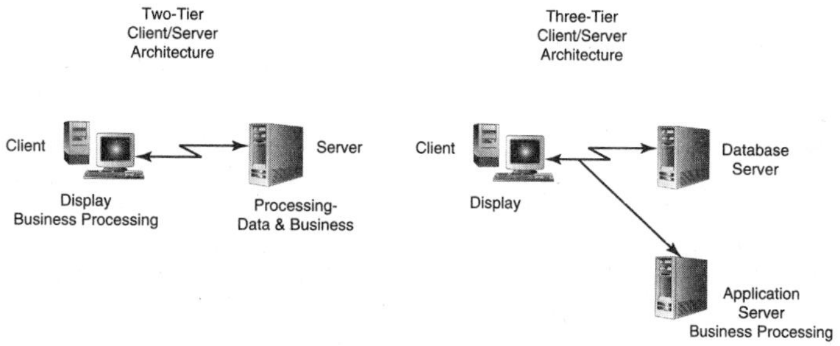

FIGURE 30.2.

Two-tier and three-tier client/server architectures.

The key point to pick up here is that the two-tier architecture splits business processing between the user's client workstations and the database server. The machines might become overloaded as you try to implement a large number of users running complex business processes. Remember, your poor NT Server might be asked to support dozens or hundreds of users at a given time. Also, many of your users might still have older client workstations (such as 80386-based PCs). You might also need a large degree of coordination at a central site between users of certain applications. This is where another server whose sole function is to implement business processing logic comes into play. It interfaces with clients and the database to coordinate the business activities and off-load the other processors.

Now tie these concepts to the Windows NT environment. (Yes, this is still an NT book.) Most of the Windows NT installations I have seen operate in a client/server mode. Although you can set up terminal functions under NT, it is really designed to use the built-in networking functions (NetBEUI, TCP/IP, and IPX/SPX, which are described in more detail in Chapter 6, "Integrated Networking") to enable free communication between client processes and server processes. You might have an NT workstation running your front-end database applications (the ones that the users actually see) and an NT Server running the database management system. The business logic can be split between the client and server as the developers see fit or even off-loaded to an applications server (which could also be running NT). In a sense, Microsoft designed NT around the same framework that Sun Microsystems made so popular in the UNIX world—that of the computer actually being a collection of computing devices located across a network that come together to serve the user's needs. This is actually fairly easy once you have a network of devices that can communicate easily with one another, which I have found in the NT, Windows 95, and UNIX environments. I like to imagine this environment something like that presented in Figure 30.3.

FIGURE 30.3.

Networked computers forming a virtual computer.

Now that you have the basics out of the way, I will introduce a few of the concepts that are creeping into real systems today. The basic theory presented earlier works well (divide and conquer to get the job done using client/server architectures). However, there are two circumstances that present problems when you actually try to implement these systems (see Figure 30.4):

- How do you provide adequate communications capabilities for remote locations in your organization?
- How do you link the various departmental databases to enable your organization to obtain an overall picture of what's going on?

If you have not done a lot of work with computer networks, the question of adequate communications for remote locations might seem strange. However, the reality of the current market is that it is relatively inexpensive to transmit data signals over a range of a few hundred yards, but it gets expensive when you have to transmit the same volume of data over hundreds or even thousands of miles. The transmission lines running to other cities, or even within your own city, are controlled by communications companies that are out to make a profit and have access to a limited commodity (the transmission system). It can cost hundreds or thousands of dollars, per month, to maintain communications circuits. You might have had communications circuits for years when you used mainframe links; however, the communications companies charge not only by the distance, but also by the transmission capacity. You might be impressed with the vast amount of data that is at your fingertips with your new client/server applications. However, this high volume of data multiplied by the large number of users that now have access to your system requires you to install a very robust communications system, and this can be expensive.

FIGURE 30.4.

*Problems with client/
server implementations.*

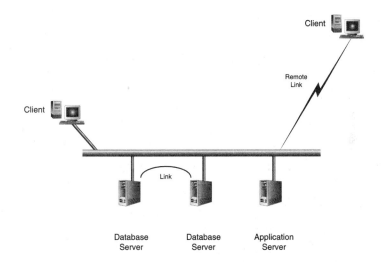

Now, permit me a slight diversion—the Internet. Almost everyone in the computer industry is talking about it (try to get Bill Gates or Larry Ellison to talk about anything else). The Internet can be thought of as a collection of networks someone else has already installed that you can connect to with just a local communications circuit. (See Figure 30.5.) The Internet could be the low-cost transmission system everyone has been dreaming about. Windows NT is very well integrated with TCP/IP (and therefore Internet) communications, and NT Server actually powers a fair number of the services you find on the Internet. However, a few issues need to be worked out before the Internet can be used as the solution to everyone's problems. First, many organizations are gun-shy about the idea of transmitting their critical business data over a public network. Anyone could detect the packets, and your competitors might even be used as key links to various parts of the Internet. Many people are working on security for the Internet, and they will probably solve this problem soon. The second problem is the transmission capacity of the system. Much of the current Internet transmission capacity is funded in the United States with government funds. The pressures of cost-cutting, desires to limit transmission of pornography, and, of course, a few suggestions from telephone company lobbyists might limit expansion of the current Internet transmission capacity. If a large number of companies start doing business on the already busy Internet, it might become overloaded, and performance might degrade. Anyway, it is something to consider if you are really strapped for communications capabilities to remote sites.

FIGURE 30.5.

An overly simplified picture of the Internet.

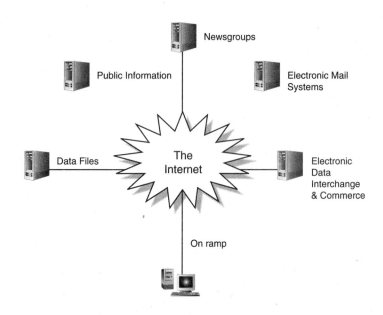

Now back to the main discussion. The second problem that creeps into many client/server systems is that of increased demand to integrate data from various departments. When everyone had to live with nightly mainframe printouts, they had enough trouble wading through their existing printouts and relied on weekly reports from other departments to integrate business functions. Once they realized how easy it was to get at their business data using computer networks, they usually got demanding and wanted access to all the business data that affected them so they could make the business function better as a whole. This put pressure on the information systems department to be able to link together a large number of databases that, taken together, were too large to fit on any single computer.

Seeing this trend in the market, the database and computer systems vendors have started to produce products to support the concept of distributed databases. This works out well for Windows NT because most NT Servers are relatively small (such as high-end PC servers) and can be linked together to form a powerful computing environment. The key components of a distributed database include the following:

- Good interfaces to operating system data transmission facilities (such as TCP/IP).

- Client and server tools that can communicate with multiple databases at the same time.

- Gateway products that link computers and database management systems from different vendors together in a relatively seamless manner from the user's point of view.

- Database management systems that can deal with the time delays that might be involved with writing data to remote systems.
- Efficient data transmission systems between the various computers and user workstations.

Windows NT supports this type of environment in a variety of ways. First, it is very network-friendly. Because networking was part of its base design (as opposed to being a product added decades after the first release of the operating system, as is the case in many mainframes), it supports efficient links between applications (including database management systems) and its networking utilities. Also, with its multitasking features, it is capable of supporting numerous background processes working together behind the scenes to take care of the communications functions while the user interacts with the front-end application.

Before I leave this topic, I want to extend the concept of distributed databases just a bit. This seems to be a direction that database vendors (Oracle and Microsoft in its SQL Server product) seem to be heading. The basic concept is that of replicated databases. Imagine that you want to have a single directory of employees and their associated personnel information synchronized throughout your entire multinational organization. You could have everybody log into the home office in Cleveland through an extensive corporate network to look up the phone number of the guy two floors up. However, there is another way. That way is that you have a master database in Cleveland that contains the verified and updated information as entered by the central personnel department. The computer network to Cleveland is very busy during the day, but it is used lightly at night. Because there is no great penalty for having telephone numbers that are a day old, why not transmit the updated personnel databases to all regional offices every night? This gets them the information they need and saves your limited communications bandwidth for important business processing.

Companies have been implementing applications that transfer selected bits of information between computers for years. They write code that transfers the information to tape or even transfers it across the network where another program loads up the information into the local database. Now imagine that you could tell your database management system to keep multiple tables in multiple databases in sync and have it take care of all the details. This is what database replication is all about. The database management systems build the utilities for you to take care of all those annoying details. This is especially attractive to many Windows NT installations, where you are running near capacity during normal business hours and don't have a lot of legacy software written in older development environments to hold you back. It is often worth spending some time investigating these technologies to save yourself weeks (that you might not have) developing complex routines or trying to justify additional network bandwidth to the central office.

Okay, so where am I now? The database administrator has laid a bit of database theory and product information on people who are interested in Windows NT, the operating system. This was not just an attempt to get sympathy from operating system proponents for the complexity of managing modern databases. Instead, it lays the foundation for the next section, which talks about the types of interactions between applications, database management systems, and the operating system, specifically Windows NT.

Interactions Between the Operating System and Database Management System

Perhaps you are in the position of having worked for a while using Windows NT as a file and print server. Someone tells you that he or she needs to use your server to host a database for a critical corporate function (such as coordinating arrangements for use of the executive condominium in Barbados). It is important to understand the demands placed on your operating system and server computer. You can then compare these requirements with your current capabilities and load to ensure that you can support this new requirement.

For the purposes of this discussion, I divide the interactions between the operating system and database management system into the following categories:

- Shared server memory areas
- Server background processes
- Server disk storage capacity
- Server input/output processing capacity
- Network communications processing capacity
- Network transmission capacity

I start with a discussion of shared server memory areas. This is the key to understanding the differences between your common print and file sharing functions under NT and database management systems. Most server database management systems use large areas of memory to store database and processing information. Why? The answer is simple: speed. Memory is several orders of magnitude faster to access than disk drives (even the good ones). Although it is okay to scan a small file of a few hundred kilobytes to find the information you need, you don't want to scan large database files of megabytes or even gigabytes.

With everyone wanting to get more for less, database vendors are in a big competition to see who can get more performance out of less hardware. They want to process more transactions per second or handle larger database warehouses. To do this, they have gotten extremely creative about devising ways to keep frequently accessed information readily available in memory and also using memory to cache information retrieved through efficient transfers from the disk storage files, as shown in Figure 30.6. This figure shows how Oracle uses memory areas. User processes interact with various memory areas while background processes transfer information from the disk drives to the memory areas. When the database management system developers do their jobs well, you will find that the data you want is usually located in the rapid-access memory areas, and you therefore do not have to wait for the data to be transferred from the slower disk drives. The bottom line is that the big database management systems such as Oracle and SQL Server ask for a lot more memory than PC people are used to. You can easily see requirements for 8MB to 32MB just for the database itself (in addition to the operating system and all the other services running on the system).

FIGURE 30.6.

Database shared memory areas.

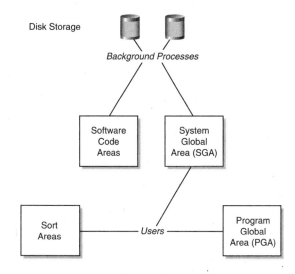

This can be critical if you are running NT on Intel-based platforms. Although NT supports a large amount of memory (4GB), you rarely find an Intel-based computer that can actually hold that amount. This is especially true of computers that were designed several years ago, when very few applications in the PC world dreamed of needing this kind of memory. There are two types of limitation on memory. The first is the capacity of your motherboard to recognize the memory (many have limitations of 128MB or less). The other is the number of slots you have to hold memory (often four slots). This can be a problem, because RAM chips are among the most expensive components in a PC and you always get some on the motherboard when you buy the computer. If you want to upgrade a computer to 64MB of RAM and you have 32MB already, all you have to do is buy 32MB more, right? Maybe. You might also find that you have four 8MB memory chips in your machine that are filling all four of your available slots. Then your only solution is to remove your existing four memory chips and install four 16MB memory chips. Perhaps you can reallocate your other memory chips to users who have recently upgraded their workstations from Windows 3.1 to Windows NT Workstation or Windows 95 (they probably need as much memory as they can get), or sometimes you can get a trade-in deal from vendors who are hungry for your business.

One final note is on the banking of memory slots on the motherboard. It might seem like an annoying hardware detail, but it can come around to bite you. Imagine you have four memory slots, two of which are filled with 16MB memory chips. Your database administrator works with you to determine the memory requirements for a new database, and it turns out that you need an additional 16MB of memory. You just order another one of those 16MB chips, and you'll still have room for future expansion, right? Once again, maybe. Computer motherboards often link two slots together in their logical designs and require that these two slots be filled with memory chips of the same size and type. Therefore, you might not be able to mix sizes or leave one slot in these banks empty.

The key to managing the database management system demands on your memory is to understand both the database's memory requirements and the capabilities of your system. The database administrator or vendor should be able to give you an idea of the required memory size. One thing I have always noted about databases is that they tend to grow rapidly, so it is good to allow yourself a little room to spare. You also need to understand the other needs and capabilities of your operating system. You might have to consult a hardware expert or crawl under the hood yourself to determine the amount of memory that is currently installed and the maximum amount of memory that can be installed in your computer. The Performance Monitor in the NT administrator utilities enables you to measure the usage of several resources, including memory, over a reasonable amount of time to understand the memory requirements of your operating system and other services. This tool is discussed in more detail in Chapter 20, "Performance Tuning and Optimization."

> **CAUTION**
>
> When you run out of memory, your system starts swapping applications and data to the hard drive, and performance degrades rapidly. Avoid swapping whenever possible. Trust me, it hurts.

Now that I have solved all the memory problems you might run into, it's time to discuss the next load a database management system places on your system: server background processes. You might have wondered how those memory areas that give the database management system all that speed get maintained. What writes the changes from the memory areas to the data files on disk (which stick around after you turn the power off) and gets the anticipated data from disk to memory before the user needs it? The answer for most database management systems is a series of background processes (services and threads under NT) that perform specialized functions when needed. (See Figure 30.7.) Some of these processes also service user requests. One of the keys to modern database management systems is that the users tell the system what they want and the system figures out the most efficient way to get it. This works well because teams of people work on efficient search algorithms that you would never have time to implement if you had to do it yourself. The end result is a complex series of processes that need to have computer processing capacity to get their jobs done.

FIGURE 30.7.
*Background database
services.*

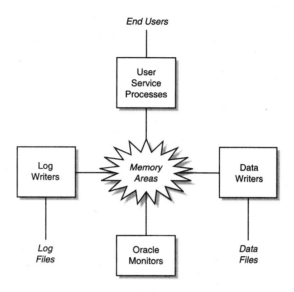

So how do these background processes impact the NT administrator? I would typically consider three key areas:

■ You have several CPU processes and threads that you can have running. Although NT is mostly a self-tuning operating system, you might have to get involved on larger servers that are running a number of applications.

■ You have to consider the interaction of the processes with one another. Your total throughput in a database management system is determined by the weakest link in the chain of processes that are used to complete the processing tasks. Many of these systems enable you to tune their background processes by allocating threads or creating additional server processes. It is important to understand your database management system and see where the processing bottlenecks are to determine where additional processing resources are required.

The next key resource to discuss is the disk storage system (see Figure 30.8). Databases with large volumes of information need to have a permanent home for the user data; this typically takes the form of an array of fixed disk drives. Databases often take up much more space than would ever be needed by print servers or file sharing. Therefore, it is important to get disk storage sizing estimates before starting a new database project.

It is also important to lay out the physical configuration of the disk drives. Many PC servers have a limited number of internal disk drive bays, and some of these bays are larger than others. You also have to consider the limitations of the number of drives on a given disk drive controlled (typically seven for SCSI disk drives and two for IDE disk drives). It turns into a bit of a puzzle to ensure that you have enough bays, cables, and controllers. Due to physical space

limitations or drive bay limitations, you might have to remove older, smaller disk drives and replace them with larger capacity drives, especially on Intel-based servers.

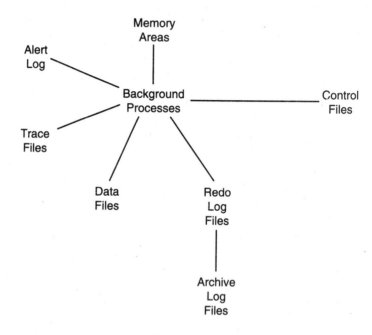

FIGURE 30.8.

A disk storage system.

Following are a few things you might not think of that might require some disk space:

- The database management system software. (It can consume several hundred megabytes.)

- Space for database management system log and dump files. (They can provide a lot of useful information. Don't forget to implement routines to clean them out every now and then.)

- Space for any server-based applications you might be writing (for example, business processing logic for an application server in the three-tier client/server architecture).

- Additional paging file space for the memory you might have added to accommodate your database.

- A disk drive to provide you with a place to copy files when you are rearranging other disk drives. (It is sometimes hard to justify but can make your job so much easier. Try selling it as a hot spare for reliability and quick recovery.)

Another key system resource that you have to be concerned with, especially in some Intel-based NT systems, is the disk input/output capacity. Basically, this is how quickly you can transfer information from memory to the disk drives. Although most UNIX systems are built with high-speed SCSI disk drives and controllers, many Intel-based servers have relatively slower data transfer subsystems. In many database servers (even large UNIX boxes or mainframes), the data transfer speeds can be the limiting factor in the overall performance of the database. Therefore, you need to know a few tricks to ensure that you are doing the best you can to provide adequate data transfer capabilities (see Figure 30.9).

FIGURE 30.9.

Keys to data transfer capacity.

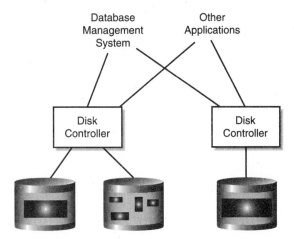

- ■ Understand the transfer capacity and configuration of the controllers and disk drives. Not all controllers are created equally. SCSI-2 is twice as fast as regular SCSI, and it is faster than the IDE controllers you typically find on PCs (and you have to consider an enhanced IDE). Also, these controllers are connected to different buses on your computer (PCI is much faster than the ISA bus for Intel-based computers). Anyway, it might pay off to talk with vendors or your favorite hardware guru to see what you can do to arrange things to put the most demanding files on the most capable controllers and drives.

- ■ You need to balance the transfer needs of the database against those of other operating system services. See where the hot operating system files (such as the Windows NT directory or your print server spool files) are and try to avoid putting your hot database files on the same drive. This can evolve over time, so it can be useful to routinely look at input/output loading to see if some disks are getting a little too warm.

- ■ Keep an eye on the fragmentation of your disk. NT 4.0 does not come with a built-in defragmentation utility for FAT partitions, unlike many other operating systems (such as Windows 95). As files are added, resized, and deleted from the disk, the operating system might have to use multiple small chunks of disk to store the data. (See Figure 30.10.) This causes problems for the disk drives and controllers because they have to read one section, reposition the heads on the disk drive, and then read the next section. Disk drives read data much more quickly than they move their heads, so this can really slow down performance. It might be useful to pick up a third-party defragmentation utility or use the NTFS file system for disk drives that are likely to become fragmented.

FIGURE 30.10.
Disk fragmentation.

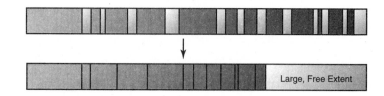

Large, Free Extent

■ Finally, even if you have a nicely defragmented disk drive storing your database files, you might have fragmentation within those data files. The database files on most database management systems contain many tables, which are stored in chunks. As you add rows to a table, it might have to get another chunk of data storage space within the data file that is not contiguous with the previous extent. Therefore, it is worthwhile to ask the database administrator if he has defragmented his database files recently if you are having input/output loading problems.

 Next on the list of interactions between the database management system and the operating system is the network communications processing load that the interaction places on your server. Typically, NT handles tuning the communications processes you use to connect your database servers, application servers, and workstations together. There are, however, two things for you to consider when implementing database client/server networking on your computers:

■ First, not all network cards are created equal. Some cards can process several times the data traffic of other cards, even on the same type of network (for example, 10 million bits per second Ethernet). Therefore, it might serve you to get a higher capacity card for your busy servers to ensure that they can keep up with all the workstations out there.

■ Second, some protocols are better for client/server communications than others. I have not had much luck using NetBEUI for Oracle databases. NetBEUI was designed to be a file and print server network protocol. It was not designed with the larger network features that you find in TCP/IP. Therefore, if you have a choice, try using TCP/IP, especially for larger client/server networks.

Last on the list of resources is something that is not in your NT computers and that the operating system lacks any control over. I'm talking about the transmission capacity of the network itself. Why mention it in a book on NT? Typically, when performance is poor, the users call the database administrator, system administrator, or developers. Eventually, the finger usually falls on the servers and the operating system. You should check out all the things mentioned earlier that you do have control over, but also check out the network as a possible problem. Remember, it takes all the components of a client/server system working efficiently together to achieve overall system performance.

To really see if the network itself is causing the problem, you have to be familiar with the over-all network topology. I have included Figure 30.11 as an example. You might have to fight like heck to get one of these drawings out of a network guru, but it is usually worth your effort. There are a few key items to look for when a problem occurs:

- If the problem exists only for a certain group that is physically separated from the other users, is there a bottleneck leading to that particular group, or is their network segment overloaded itself? Your network consultant should have or be able to get some network monitoring equipment that can investigate this issue. Also, you might be able to see the problem by visual inspection. For example, if you have 100 users located in a remote office that has a 56-kilobit-per-second line, and all your other offices have 10 users and communications lines several times faster, the problem might be the wide area network line to that first remote location. Remember, unless you do something special, your NT database server treats all connection requests equally.

- Next, look to see if there is a pattern to the problems. One classic example is when network performance becomes poor at 8 a.m., 1 p.m., and 4 p.m. This typically corresponds with everyone logging in to check their e-mail first thing in the morning, right after lunch, and right before they go home. You might also notice a problem that occurs every day at 2 p.m. that corresponds with the time the engineers are transfer-ring massive data files between computer systems. The solution to this type of problem is usually to try to juggle jobs (for example, moving the engineers' data transfer to 12 p.m. when everyone else is at lunch) to level the workload. Whatever the solution, this type of analysis combined with NT Performance Monitor data can save you many hours of work trying to figure out why your server is slowing down at certain times of the day.

FIGURE 30.11.
Network transmission capacity limitations.

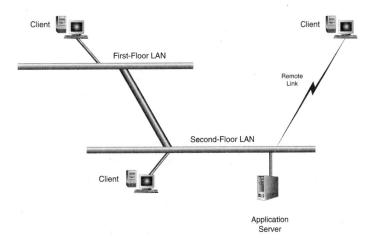

Did you ever feel like a database administrator has locked you in a room and hit you with more database information than you ever wanted to know? There has been a method to my madness. One of the biggest problems I have run across in computer environments is a lack of understanding of the needs of other specialty groups. On a database server, the database is the reason the server exists. If you know a bit about what the database is doing to your operating system and server, you are in a better position to react to those demands and keep things running smoothly. I hate sitting in a room where one techie says it's not his subsystem that's causing the problem, it's the other subsystem that's to blame, and vice versa. When asked why, they usually resort to "it's obvious" or "I've tested my system thoroughly." If nothing else, you are better armed to determine exactly where the problem is and explain why the other people have to take corrective actions and how you have already taken your corrective actions.

Oracle Under Windows NT

If every database management system were alike, I would be finished with this chapter. However, there are many vendors in the highly competitive computer world. Each of them tries to do some things just a little differently to achieve better performance or cost less or fill some special niche, such as decision support systems. Therefore, I have chosen to examine three of the most common types of database management systems you are likely to run across so that you can get a feel for these differences.

The first system I have chosen is the one with the largest share of the overall database market (depending on what you measure). Oracle runs on computers ranging from mainframes to personal computers running Windows 3.1. They also have a wide product family, ranging from the database management system itself to development tools to full-fledged applications such as financial and manufacturing systems. (See Figure 30.12.)

FIGURE 30.12.

The Oracle product family.

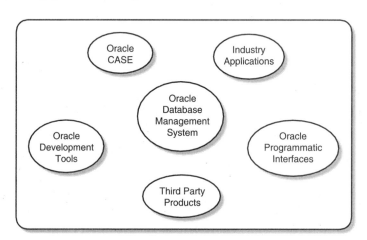

What would the average NT system administrator need to know about Oracle database management systems running on his server? I concentrate on the database because that is probably the most demanding component for most administrators. The basic architecture of the database management system consists of several memory areas (designated for different purposes and tunable by the DBA to be larger or smaller), a series of background processes (combined into one service per database instance under NT), and the database data files. (See Figure 30.13.)

FIGURE 30.13.

The basics of the Oracle architecture.

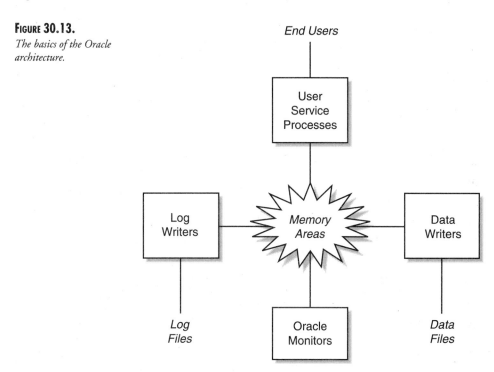

To facilitate communications with your Oracle database administrator, a few definitions are in order:

- **Oracle Instance:** This is a collection of background processes (in NT terms, it is a single service you are running) that performs all the interactions between the database and data files.

- **Oracle Database:** This is the collection of data files and supporting files that contain the data the users want to get at.

- **Alert Log:** This is a file that contains a record of activity (startups, shutdowns, problems, and so on) of your Oracle Instance. You should know where it is to help you when problems come up. The database administrator sets this up in the Oracle initialization file.

- **Trace Files:** When Oracle encounters a serious problem, it is almost always able to write a trace file that describes what the system was doing and what the problem was that caused it to crash.

■ **SQL*Net:** This is the Oracle utility that communicates with the underlying network software (such as TCP/IP). It must be located between both the application and the client networking software and the host networking software and the database. The versions have to match, as do the communication protocol options. SQL*Net version 2 has some network configuration files (TNSNAMES.ORA, SQLNET.ORA, and LISTENER.ORA) that must be created by the DBA and loaded on all systems that connect via SQL*Net.

■ **SQL*Net Listener:** This is the NT service that connects the networking transport services (such as TCP/IP) and the database instance processes. It has to be started with the database services in order to start the Oracle Instance.

■ **SQL*DBA:** This is an older tool that is still used in Oracle version 7.1. It is a command line with a pull-down menu interface to perform database administrative functions.

■ **Instance Manager:** This is a GUI-based tool that enables you to check the status of your Oracle instances and start or stop them. I recommend having this as an icon on your desktop to at least enable you to determine if the Oracle Instances are running. You need to have a special database password to start or stop the Oracle Instances (work this out with your database administrator).

■ **SQL*Plus:** This is a simple command-line interface that lets you get at the Oracle database and its data. It is quick for those who are familiar with Structured Query Language (SQL), but not of much use to others.

■ **Oracle Navigator:** This is a newer Oracle tool that first came out under Windows 95. It can be used across the network to query several databases and produce nice, tabular displays of the data in Oracle tables. This is good if you need to check on data (or verify that you can access the database) and are not a SQL guru.

Now that I have the definitions out of the way, here are a few tips on running Oracle under Windows NT:

■ If you have the Windows NT Resource Kit and Oracle RDBMS version 7.1, look for the SRVANY utility and read its online documentation. This enables you to start the Oracle database automatically when you start your Windows NT system. For whatever reason, Oracle enables you to start the database services (Instance, in Oracle terms) and the SQL*Net services, but it does not open up the database for general use. To do this, you have to use Instance Manager, SQL*DBA, or one of the other Oracle tools. However, you might be busy and forget to start the Instance manually, or your system might be recovering from a power outage and you don't have an uninterruptible power supply (please say it isn't so). Anyway, with the SRVANY utility you can turn a normal batch file into a service you can set for automatic startup. This batch file should run a SQL script using a utility such as SQL*DBA. (Setting up this file is covered in the Oracle documentation and might vary between releases, so it is best to look it up in the source for your version of Oracle.) The SQL script connects to the Oracle database and issues the database startup command. Anyway, this little utility can save you a lot of pain when you are hurrying to do maintenance and get the system back into operation. Note that this is not needed in Oracle RDBMS version 7.2, which provides its own startup process.

■ I have had very little luck trying to use SQL*Net NetBEUI across an Ethernet connection. When I switched to SQL*Net TCP/IP, I got significantly faster and more reliable connections.

■ Many of the Oracle memory areas are allocated only when needed. Therefore, if you have a system that works fine under 32MB of memory in your development environment, it might take significantly more memory to make it run for a larger number of users in production. Always err on the conservative side, because NT and Oracle production degrades severely when you start paging.

■ The Oracle tools that run under version 7.1 are somewhat strange by my standards. A few of the tools, such as SQL*DBA and Instance Manager, are 32-bit tools, and you can run them without setting up SQL*Net on your machine. However, if you want to run most of the other tools, such as SQL*Plus or the Import and Export utilities, you need to install SQL*Net for both the Windows and Windows NT systems on your NT Server. This is because most of these Oracle applications are 16-bit applications. The Oracle database is 32-bit, and Oracle uses SQL*Net to communicate between the 16- and 32-bit worlds. Also remember to load the network configuration files into both the Windows and Windows NT network administration directories to enable these two sides of the world to communicate with one another. However, the version 7.2 Oracle tools eliminate these problems.

This section was actually quite a challenge. You could write an entire book on Oracle database administration. (I know, I did it.) It can be a complex beast—powerful and a challenge to discipline. However, it is popular and works fairly well in the NT environment. In fact, Oracle has recently announced that it will add NT to the list of operating systems included in the initial wave of releases when it upgrades the product. This family of operating systems includes the more popular UNIX systems and is a sign that Oracle sees NT as a viable (and hence profitable) platform for its operating system. Anyway, this section should provide you with the basics you need to communicate with your database administrator and, combined with previous sections, help you understand what the Oracle database management system is doing to your operating system and server.

Microsoft SQL Server Under Windows NT

Microsoft has its own database management system that it would be glad to sell to you with your Windows NT operating system. It is called Microsoft SQL Server, to differentiate it from Sybase SQL Server, which runs under NT in addition to several flavors of UNIX. Microsoft originally teamed with Sybase to develop this product under Windows NT, but they have recently agreed to go their separate ways on development. Anyway, the Microsoft SQL Server product is something you might have to support on your NT Servers and workstations for the following reasons:

- It is the database that is bundled with, and is a prerequisite for, several of the other Microsoft BackOffice products, which are discussed in more detail in Chapter 29, "Microsoft BackOffice and Other Microsoft Products" (for example, Microsoft Systems Management Server).

- It is a cost-competitive database for the NT Server environment. For many organizations, it doesn't matter whether you have to select a single database management system that runs on a wide variety of platforms such as UNIX and VMS.

- Because it is part of Microsoft BackOffice, several third-party developers support it because it comes with their Microsoft Developer Network Level 3 subscriptions.

So what is Microsoft SQL Server like? Although the salespeople might stress the differences between the various products and underlying technologies (such as scalability), I tend to see the similarities. The Microsoft SQL Server architecture is somewhat similar to the Oracle architecture, at least from the operating system administrator's point of view. (See Figure 30.14.) It has the three key components found in most server database management systems: shared memory areas, background processes, and disk storage files.

FIGURE 30.14.
The basics of the Microsoft SQL Server architecture.

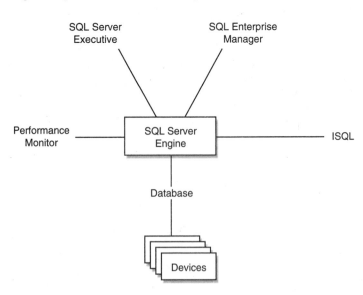

A few of the terms you might want to be familiar with for dealing with Microsoft SQL Server databases include the following:

- **Database:** A logical set of data, tables, and other related objects (such as views and indexes) that should share a common function and are stored together within a database device (see *device*).

- **Device:** A Windows NT disk file that stores databases. A database can take up more than one device. SQL Server defines two types of devices: database devices, which store databases, and dump devices, which store backups of databases.

- **SQL Server Engine:** The main service providing access to the SQL Server database and devices. This service can be tuned for the number of threads it utilizes.

- **SQL Executive:** A service that provides access to replication, task management, event management, and notification services to the users.

- **SQL Enterprise Manager:** A tool used to manage your servers and databases. It provides a graphical interface to perform a wide variety of management tasks with SQL Server, including database management, database object management (tables), and event scheduling.

- **ISQL/w:** A command-line interface with several GUI utilities that is used to interact with SQL Server (it is somewhat analogous to Oracle SQL*Plus).

- **SQL Performance Monitor:** A package that integrates with Windows NT Performance Monitor to enable you to monitor SQL Server similar to the way you monitor other NT resources. This is discussed in more detail in Chapter 20.

Now for a few final notes on dealing with Microsoft SQL Server as your database management system:

- Allow about an hour for installation of the product. It performs several configuration tasks while setting up your initial databases, and it requires a reboot before you can use SQL Server. This usually needs to be scheduled if you are using a production server.

- Take advantage of the performance monitoring capabilities that are integrated with those of Windows NT. It is always useful to be comfortable with how to find performance information before you have a performance problem and have a thousand managers breathing down your neck.

- Try to organize your database devices (files) in a common set of directories (such as \dbdata\production) on all disk drives when you use multiple disk drives for your data. This can make trying to work with problems or expand the system much easier.

Again, Microsoft SQL Server can fill an entire book by itself. Actually, it has an enormous documentation set stored online that comes with the product. (Some people are still not comfortable working with online documentation, but at least you never leave your copy at home.) The key components of SQL Server were discussed earlier, and you can apply the principles discussed earlier in the book for dealing with database interactions with the operating system to plan and manage your system more effectively. One side note: I have found that the system administrator is more likely to have to administer a SQL Server database than an Oracle database. That is because Microsoft often integrates its BackOffice system products (such as

Systems Management Server) with SQL Server. It is not a formally maintained application such as a general ledger, where you have a development group and a support group that contains a database administrator.

Microsoft Access's JET Database Engine Under Windows NT

A final topic that I want to discuss briefly is the concept of using a simple database file stored on a server to meet modest database needs. Back in the old days (which were not always good), people often stored dBASE files on servers that could be accessed from several PCs on the network. The locking mechanisms were primitive (locking mechanisms prevent one user from overwriting the changes of another user who is accessing the row at the same time), but they met many needs. I wanted to mention that you might consider using something like the Microsoft Access JET database engine (access to it comes bundled in Visual C++, Visual Basic, and Microsoft Query) to set up one of these simple databases.

If you use this approach, you have to provide a storage area on a shared directory that contains a database file (in Microsoft Access's case, a file with the .mdb extension). People use applications or access tools (such as MS Query) that use the Open Database Connectivity (ODBC) tool set to access this data file. When you create the ODBC data source, you use a standard browse window to select the .mdb file you want to access. It is simple and does not provide complex transaction logging, recovery, or locking services, but it is relatively simple to implement and might meet many modest user requirements.

A Quick Discussion of ODBC and OLE

One of the concepts you might have to deal with when supporting client/server databases is middleware. Middleware can be defined as the software products that are needed to make the applications talk to the operating system networking utilities. The complicating factor is that each database can support several different sets of middleware, and these products can come from several vendors. The middleware stacks are generally as depicted in Figure 30.15.

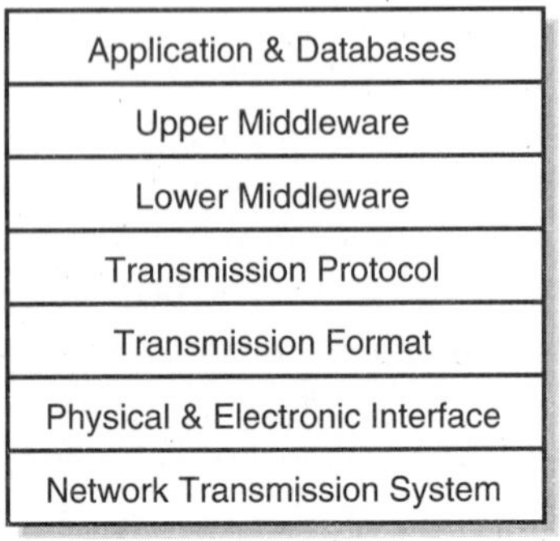

FIGURE 30.15.
Middleware and database access.

| Application & Databases |
| Upper Middleware |
| Lower Middleware |
| Transmission Protocol |
| Transmission Format |
| Physical & Electronic Interface |
| Network Transmission System |

I typically divide middleware into two components that I refer to as upper middleware and lower middleware. The upper middleware is responsible for interfacing with the database or applications. The lower middleware component is responsible for interfacing with the network drivers. In Oracle's case, you have SQL*Net. For Oracle tools (such as SQL*Forms), SQL*Net provides both upper and lower middleware services. However, if you are writing Visual C++ applications, you need to use something like the Open Database Connectivity (ODBC) drivers to link your applications to SQL*Net. Confused? There are also ODBC drivers for Oracle (such as Openlink) that integrate the two layers of middleware into one package.

Just when you get comfortable with the concepts behind ODBC, Microsoft comes out with the OLE 2 (Object Linking and Embedding) utilities that provide an alternative to ODBC. If you were one of the few people to get comfortable with developing for OLE, Microsoft has another database access technology (Database Access Objects, or DAO) that is optimized toward certain types of transactions to the JET database engine.

Why am I scaring you with all these terms, technologies, and options? What I wanted you to get from this brief discussion of access technologies is an understanding that client/server database environments consist of applications and databases that have been designed to work in client/server environments, along with a set of communications software (middleware) that links everything together. Vendors provide many options for middleware, and you have to take the time to figure out how to connect the various products that are standard in your organization before you field production client/server databases. This can take a fair amount of time and is always best done in a prototype environment before the pressure is on to deliver that system to the field. You might want to try several vendors' products to see which ones work best for the type of database you are deploying. Finally, be prepared for the fact that many middleware errors translate into "something somewhere is causing some kind of problem" (in other words, it can take you a bit of time to figure out and correct errors). However, once you get the hang of things, middleware works well and provides a level of service to database users that cannot be beat.

Summary

This chapter was devoted to the use of Windows NT Server to support databases. I covered the ways a database can impact the operating system and how to deal with these effects. Several of the more common database management systems were presented—not to make you an expert database administrator, but to give you a feel for a few of the implementations and their basic terminologies. I have found that database management systems can be a challenge even to the capacities of large UNIX, VMS, and mainframe computers. They use a lot of memory and try to use some complex tricks to increase their performance, and this can cause a few headaches for the system administrator. I hope you now understand the concepts behind these effects and know where to look to see what is happening and how to deal with it.

Using Windows NT as an Internet Server

by Joe Greene and Terry Ogletree

IN THIS CHAPTER

31

CHAPTER

Windows NT Server is perfectly suited to provide services on the Internet—not only because of its stability and scalability, but also because there are several good server products you can buy to set up an Internet site for Windows NT. Microsoft's Internet Information Server (IIS) wasn't the first of these to appear, but it has evolved to the point that it is now a first-class application that you can use to easily manage a simple or complex Internet site.

This chapter introduces you to the basic Internet services (such as WWW and FTP) and shows you how the IIS administrative tools can be used to manage these services. New applications that became available in IIS 3.0 and IIS 4.0, such as Microsoft NetShow Live and Microsoft Index Server, are too complex to deal with in a single chapter. You will learn how to install these applications and their documentation.

Introducing Internet Information Server (IIS)

This chapter discusses three different versions of IIS. IIS 2.0 is included with Windows NT Server 4 and is a simple yet effective way to manage a small or medium-sized Internet site. Here are the basic services that you will find in IIS 2.0:

- World Wide Web service: A graphical interface that can be used to download information from WWW servers on the Internet. With the addition of scripting, Java, and other technologies, the Web is becoming more than a static document reader. HyperText Transmission Protocol (HTTP) is used to transmit information, and HyperText Markup Language (HTML) is used to format text and graphics for display by the service. Users use Internet browsers (such as Netscape Navigator or Microsoft Internet Explorer) to interact with WWW servers.

- FTP service: File Transfer Protocol provides a simple method for sending or receiving files on the Internet. Anonymous FTP is supported by many FTP sites on the Internet. Anonymous sites allow anyone to log in and access files at the site. The FTP server will access the data for users using a user account assigned by the administrator for that purpose. You can also use user/password authentication methods to protect important files.

- Gopher service: Although not as popular as it used to be, the Gopher service can be used to provide information to users through text-based menus. This service was actually alive and well on the Internet before the WWW service was created. The graphical interface and expanded capabilities of the WWW service now provide a better technology for presenting information in most cases.

> **NOTE**
>
> Although the Gopher service is supported in IIS 2.0 and 3.0, it is not supported in IIS 4.0.

IIS 2.0

Although IIS 2.0 is not the oldest version of IIS, it is the oldest one still available from Microsoft. Why would you want to install this version of IIS when later versions have been released? There are two good reasons. First, IIS version 3.0 is built on top of IIS 2.0, or you can consider it an upgrade of 2.0. In order to install 3.0, you must first install 2.0.

Second, if you want to provide a simple WWW, FTP, or Gopher service (for example, to provide Human Resources information for employees on your local LAN) and you don't need the advanced applications or features that come with later versions of IIS, you might find that IIS 2.0 is a simple way to do just that. If you're already running Windows NT Server 4.0, you don't have to buy or download additional software, because IIS 2.0 is on the Windows NT source CD. IIS 2.0 also takes up much less space than its descendants, which might be a deciding factor in some cases.

Installing IIS 2.0

Windows NT 4.0 Server comes with the source code to install IIS 2.0. During the installation of Windows NT 4.0 Server, a dialog box will ask you if you want to install IIS. If you do, it is set up as part of the Windows NT installation process. If you do not elect to install IIS during the initial Windows NT installation, an icon will be placed on the desktop for that purpose so that you can perform the IIS installation later.

To begin the installation of IIS 2.0, double-click the Install Internet Information Server icon on the desktop. A dialog box will prompt you for the path to the Windows NT Server source files. You can specify your CD-ROM drive, a local path, or a network path for the files. The next dialog box will tell you that you should close any other applications that are running because the Setup program won't be able to update any files that are open and shared by other processes. Click the OK button to continue the installation.

Choosing the Internet Services to Install

The Setup dialog box shown in Figure 31.1 appears next. You can use it to select individual IIS components or all of them. In addition to the standard Internet services (WWW, FTP, and Gopher), you can also choose to install the following:

- Internet Service Manager (or its HTML version): This application is used to manage the IIS services. The HTML version can be used to remotely administer IIS 2.0 using a Web browser. If you want to run the Internet Service Manager on a node other than the one you install the services on, you can select only this component for installation.

- WWW Service Samples: This component will install sample code that you can use. It includes HTML code, ActiveX samples, and Internet Database Connector samples.

- ODBC Drivers & Administration: This component installs the necessary drivers for database connectivity.

Figure 31.1.

You can select any or all of the components of IIS for installation.

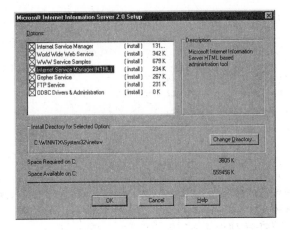

The default path for the IIS executable files is shown beneath the components. You can use the Change Directory button to edit this path to use another disk drive or directory. Note that next to each component whose checkbox is selected, you see the word *install* in parentheses. This indicates that the component will be installed. If this is your first installation, there should be no text following the component name. If you unselect a checkbox and the word *remove* appears in parentheses, this indicates that the component was previously installed on the computer. If you clear this checkbox, the component will be uninstalled if you continue.

After you have made your choices, click the OK button to continue. If the specified installation path doesn't exist, you will be prompted before Setup will create it.

Selecting the Service Publishing Directories

The Publishing Directories dialog box appears next (see Figure 31.2). Here you select a path to be used as the root directory for each of the services you choose to install. You can take the default, you can directly edit the directory field, or you can use the Browse button to specify another directory path. Click the OK button when you're ready to continue. Again, if the directories don't already exist, Setup will prompt you before creating them for you.

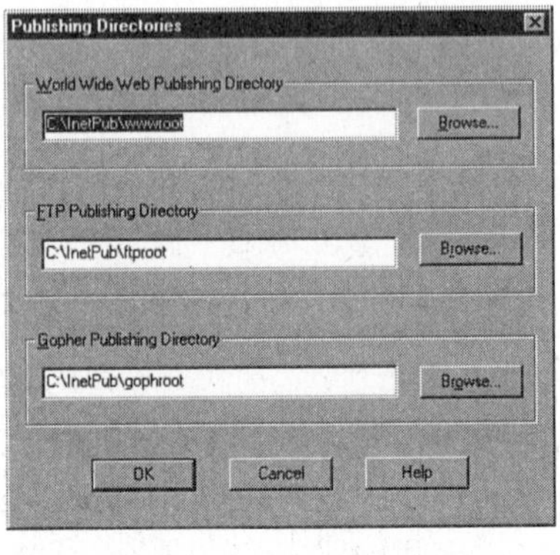

Figure 31.2.

Use the Publishing Directories dialog box to specify the directories used for each Internet service.

Setup will next copy the files necessary to install the selected services and attempt to start the services.

Installing ODBC Drivers

If you choose to install the ODBC drivers, Setup will prompt you with a list of available drivers using the Install Drivers dialog box, shown in Figure 31.3. Highlight those you want to use and click the OK button. You can use the Advanced button to bring up the Advanced Installation Options dialog box, shown in Figure 31.4, where you can decide to install Selected Driver(s), Driver Managers, or Translators on an individual basis.

FIGURE 31.3.

Select the ODBC driver to install or use the Advanced button to further customize the process.

FIGURE 31.4.

You can customize the installation of ODBC files using the Advanced Installation Options dialog box.

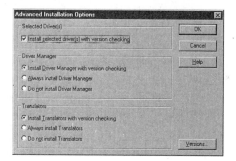

Finally, if you click the Versions button in the Advanced Installation Options dialog box, you can highlight each ODBC component selected for installation and view details about the particular version of the file.

When you're finished configuring ODBC drivers for IIS, click the OK button in the Install Drivers dialog box to continue. If you have a later version of an ODBC driver already installed on your computer, Setup will warn you and ask if you want to continue. If you get this warning, you should probably elect to keep the existing driver by clicking the No button. If you have a specific need to install the older driver, click the Yes button.

Finishing the Installation

After you click the OK button in the Install Drivers dialog box, Setup will copy more files to your hard disk and then display a dialog box telling you that the installation is complete. Click the OK button. To check to see if the installation was successful, you can start the Internet Service Manager by selecting Start | Programs | Microsoft Internet Server | Internet Service Manager. You should see the services you choose to install displayed, and under the State column you should see the word *Running*.

Alternatively, you can use the Services applet in the Control Panel to see if the services are running, or to change the startup mode (manual, automatic, or disabled) or the account under which the service runs. All three of the basic Internet services are run as Windows NT services, in the background, waiting to respond to network requests.

To administer your Web site, you will use the Internet Service Manager. The next section discusses using the IIS Manager to control the WWW, FTP, and Gopher services.

Using the Internet Service Manager for IIS 2.0

After you finish installing IIS 2.0, you will find a new program group in the Programs folder called Microsoft Internet Server (Common). In this folder you will find the Internet Service Manager (as well as an HTML counterpart) along with the Setup program, documentation, and the Key Manager to use for managing SSL (Secure Sockets Layer) certificates. Figure 31.5 shows the Microsoft Internet Service Manager utility. In this example, all three Internet services are running normally.

FIGURE 31.5.

The Internet Service Manager is used to control IIS 2.0 services.

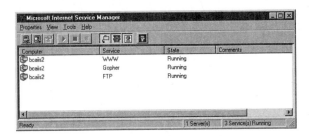

You view the properties of any service by double-clicking it or by highlighting it and selecting Properties | Service Properties. You can also use the Properties menu to start, stop, or pause the service. Figure 31.6 shows the properties page for the WWW service. There are four tabs on this property sheet that you can use to view or modify service characteristics. Each will be discussed in the following sections.

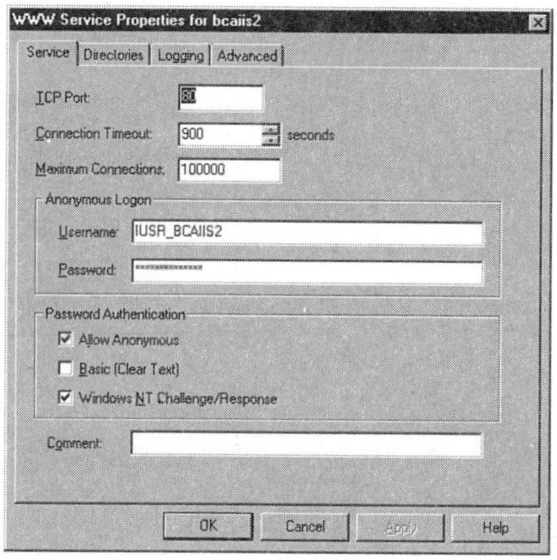

FIGURE 31.6.
*The WWW Service
Properties page allows
you to change specific
attributes of the service.*

NOTE

The Properties menu also lets you locate other IIS servers on your network so that you can administer multiple servers from one location. Select Properties | Find All Servers to do so. You can also use the Connect To Server option if you know the name of the specific IIS server you want to connect to.

Using the Service Tab

You can use the first tab, the Service tab, to change connection parameters, including the TCP port, timeout value, and maximum number of connections allowed. You can choose the method that will be used to authenticate users, allowing anonymous access or using more restrictive methods such as Windows NT Challenge/Response with NT clients. The username you see in the Anonymous Logon Username field is an account that the installation process creates and will use to access resources for anonymous clients. Do not give this account additional rights or access to any privileged information, because anonymous access allows *anyone* to access anything on your system that this account can get to.

Using the Directories Tab

This tab on the WWW Service Properties sheet is where you can specify directory paths used by the WWW Service. As shown in Figure 31.7, you will see listed the default directories that you allowed Setup to create during installation. At the bottom of the sheet you can select the Enable Default Document checkbox and then specify a filename. This file will be the document presented to users when they don't specify a document. You can place a file with this default name into each directory (or virtual directory) you create. You can have the WWW server send the user an HTML-formatted directory listing by selecting the Directory Browsing Allowed checkbox. Users can then navigate the directories and choose the documents to view.

FIGURE 31.7.

The Directories tab shows you the directory paths used by the WWW service.

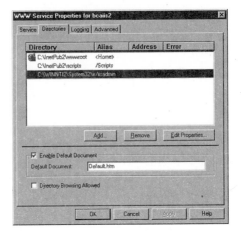

You can add new directories by using the Add button or change existing directory paths by double-clicking them. Either method will bring up the Directory Properties dialog box, shown in Figure 31.8. Here you can edit the Directory field to specify a new path or use the Browse button to locate one.

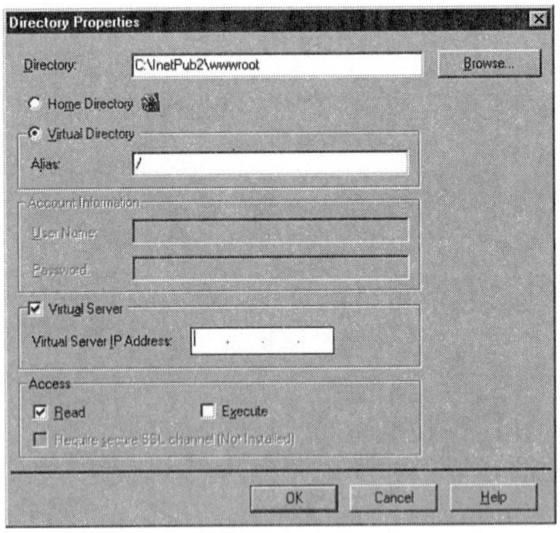

FIGURE 31.8.

The Directory Properties dialog box lets you add new directories or change existing ones.

The directory you specify for the service will become the root directory under which your HTML files will be located. By default, IIS uses the \Wwwroot subdirectory directly under your installation directory (that is, \Inetpub by default).

You can also make available to your WWW users subdirectories or other directory paths from remote servers by using the Virtual Directory radio button. You assign an alias that WWW users will use to access the directory. To use a virtual directory, enter the directory path in the Directory field, enable the Virtual Directory radio button, and fill in an alias to be used for the directory. If you are creating an alias for a directory on another server, use the UNC (Universal Naming Convention) method to specify the directory in the form of \\Server\path. When you specify the directory in this format, the Username and Password fields in the Account Information area become visible, and you can enter the access information for the directory share.

If you want to provide more than one Web site using the same server, you can create virtual servers by assigning multiple IP addresses to the server's network adapter and then using the Virtual Server checkbox on the Directory Properties sheet. When you select this checkbox, you must enter the home directory or virtual directory information for the Web root, as well as the IP address for the virtual server, so that IIS will be able to distinguish which virtual server's home directory needs to be accessed when it receives an HTTP request.

Finally, at the bottom of the Directories Properties sheet you can select Read or Execute access to be enabled for the directory. If you have installed SSL certificates, you can select the checkbox Require Secure SSL channel to further enhance security when users access the particular directory across the Internet or some other untrusted medium.

> **WARNING**
>
> When you use the Virtual Servers option, you must specify an IP address for each WWW root you create. If you have multiple addresses assigned to your network adapter, and you create directories that don't have an associated IP address, these directories will be visible to all the virtual servers you create. For example, when you install IIS, it creates three directories, which are not virtual servers. Therefore, these initial directories will be accessible to users who know they are there, no matter which virtual server they attach to. So, if you decide to use virtual servers, you might want to change these initial directories and bind them to an IP address.

Using the Logging Tab

IIS will provide feedback information in a log file for your server if you choose this option in the Logging tab (see Figure 31.9). Select the checkbox labeled Enable Logging. Then select either Log to File or Log to SQL/ODBC Database, depending on the method you want to use. By storing the log file data in a database, you will be able to manipulate it and produce precise reports that can help you tune a busy Web site.

If you elect to use a database, you will need to create the database table first and then supply information in this dialog box that allows the IIS server to access the table.

If you decide to use a log file, you can choose the format for the log file (standard or NCSA format) and set the server to create a new log on a timely basis or when the log file reaches a certain size.

The Log file directory field allows you to enter a directory path for the log files. Alternatively, you can use the Browse button to locate a directory.

FIGURE 31.9.

The Logging tab is where you set logging options.

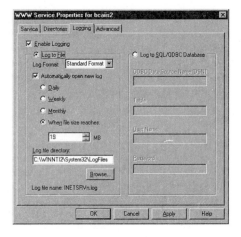

Using the Advanced Tab

As shown in Figure 31.10, the Advanced tab in the WWW Service Properties sheet can be used to grant or deny access to the WWW service. Use the radio buttons Granted Access or Denied Access to specify the default action for all computers, and then use the Add button to add exceptions to that rule. For example, you can click the Granted Access button to allow everyone access and then use the Add button to add a few computers that shouldn't be granted access.

FIGURE 31.10.

You can grant or deny access by computer using the Advanced tab.

Finally, at the bottom of this property sheet you can use the checkbox labeled Limit Network User by all Internet Services on this computer and then fill in a value in KB/second for the amount of network bandwidth to allow. This limitation applies to all of the IIS services combined, not just to this WWW service, so be careful when changing this value.

Using Windows NT as an Internet Server

CHAPTER 31

1029

31

USING WINDOWS
NT AS AN
INTERNET SERVER

Changing Properties for the Gopher Service

You can display or change properties for the Gopher service in much the same way you do for the WWW service (see Figure 31.11). In fact, the Directories, Logging, and Advanced tabs operate the same. The Service tab, however, solicits only a small amount of information, such as the TCP port (typically 70 for the Gopher service), connection timeout, and the maximum number of concurrent connections.

FIGURE 31.11.

The Service tab for the Gopher service.

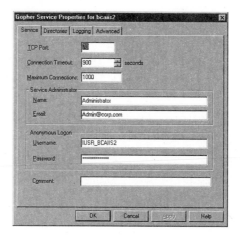

You can specify an administrator's name and email address that users of the service can use to communicate with you. If you allow anonymous logons, you will need to supply a user account and password, just as was required in the WWW properties sheets. The default is the IUSR_*computername* account that the Setup program created for you. Note again that this account can't have a blank password. Because the account is used by the service to gain access on behalf of the users, the users don't need to know about this account or its password.

You can place comment text in the last field of this property sheet; it will be displayed to users of the Gopher service. This can be a simple descriptive comment about the service offered by you or a warning or legal text regarding access to the data.

Changing Properties for the FTP Service

The FTP service has property sheets similar to the ones for the WWW and Gopher services. The Directories, Logging, and Advanced tabs are the same. The Service tab is almost the same, soliciting the same TCP and connection information along with anonymous access information. However, you will find a Current Sessions button that you can use to view connected users and, if necessary, disconnect them.

Notice that there is also a Messages tab, as shown in Figure 31.12. This tab lets you enter text that will be presented to the user as a welcome message. You also have room to display an exit message and a message that will be displayed when the maximum number of users is reached and no more connections are allowed.

FIGURE 31.12.

You can set a welcome message along with other text to be displayed by the FTP server.

As you can see, IIS 2.0 is all you need to create a simple Internet site. You can set up all the basic services (WWW, FTP, and Gopher) that are common to most sites. If you work for a small business and you just want to put marketing information or perhaps technical information online for your customers, IIS 2.0 is an excellent choice.

But the Web is changing. Many Web administrators want to add multimedia capabilities to their sites. Providing an index to your site's content can make it easier to navigate, making retrieving information easier for your clients. In Service Pack 2, Microsoft released IIS 3.0 as an upgrade to extend the basic Internet service capabilities offered by IIS 2.0. The next section shows you how to install components from IIS 3.0 so that you can enhance your Web site.

IIS 3.0

With release 3.0, IIS capabilities greatly expand with five new components that you can use to enhance your Web site, including a content indexing system, multimedia capabilities, and a reporting application to help improve Web site management. Here are the five new components (with the exception of Active Server Pages, they can be installed separately):

■ Active Server Pages (ASP): This is the only component that you need to install before you install any other component of IIS 3.0. The setup process for ASP will also install Service Pack 1a if it is not already installed. ASP provides ActiveX components that you can use with HTML pages to create applications for your Web site. Support is also included for VBScript and JScript.

■ Microsoft Index Server 1.1: Now you can index the content of your computer or your Web site to allow a full-text indexed search. Use Index Server to provide search capabilities to users of your Web site.

■ Microsoft FrontPage 97 Server Extensions: This module provides additional capabilities for users of FrontPage 97. Your business can use these to provide better access to information, such as creating links from HTML Web pages to Microsoft Office documents or spreadsheets.

■ Crystal Reports: This product is a great report writer that can now be used to create business presentation-quality reports using data from your IIS Web site log files, using templates included in this module.

■ Microsoft NetShow: If you want to add audio/video capabilities to your Web site, install NetShow.

The next section will walk you through installing IIS 3.0. For information on each component you can install, see product documentation available on the source.

Installing IIS 3.0

Before installing any of the IIS 3.0 components, be sure you have IIS 2.0 installed. IIS 3.0 contains components that upgrade an existing 2.0 installation. If you haven't already installed version 2.0, see the earlier section "Installing IIS 2.0." You should stop the IIS 2.0 services before you begin to install any of the new components. You can use the Internet Service Manager to stop each service (WWW, Gopher, and FTP). Simply highlight the service and then select Properties | Stop Service.

> **TIP**
>
> You can also use the Services applet in the Control Panel to start and stop IIS services, because these applications run as regular Windows NT services.

The first component you should install is the Active Server Pages component, because it contains Windows NT Service 1a. After you install ASP, you can choose to install any or all of the remaining components—whichever best suit the needs of your Web site.

You might want to consider installing a later service pack, though. Service packs are cumulative, and unless you have a specific hardware or software incompatibility, it's usually best to have the latest code. Also, if you install Service Pack 2 or later, support for Microsoft VM for Java will be included. This is required if you want to support ASP server components written using the Java language.

Active Server Pages (ASP)

Active Server Pages will give you the ability to use VBScript and JScript in your Web pages, and you won't have to worry whether the client browser will support them. Instead, installing ASP will allow IIS to process the script files for the client, thus making your Web site more compatible with a wider range of browsers.

When you execute the Setup program (ASP.EXE), it will first ask you to agree to the license. Read the text and click the I Agree button. The next Setup dialog box, shown in Figure 31.13, warns you to close all applications before continuing, because open files that are shared might not be updated correctly. Click the Next button to continue.

FIGURE 31.13.

Before beginning the installation of Active Server Pages, you should close all other running applications.

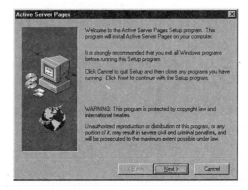

NOTE

You will need a minimum of 30 MB of free disk space to install ASP.

If you haven't remembered to stop the IIS 2.0 services currently running on your computer, you will see a warning dialog box asking if you want Setup to stop the services so that it can continue the installation. Click the Yes button to have Setup stop each service (WWW, FTP, or Gopher), or click No to cancel the installation and perform it at a later time.

Next you will see the Select Options dialog box, shown in Figure 31.14. The Active Server Pages Core will be selected by default. You can also select to install database drivers and online documentation and sample code. Use the checkboxes to make your choice, and click the Next button to continue.

FIGURE 31.14.

Select the ASP components to install.

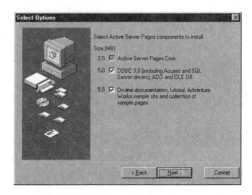

The Select Paths dialog box appears next with a default directory path displayed in the Destination Directory field. Use the Browse button to change this to a different disk or directory, and then use the Next button to continue the installation. Setup will copy files to your hard drive (the amount will depend on the options you elected to install), and then the Setup Is Complete dialog box will show you a list of the components that have been installed. Click the OK button, and you are finished with the setup. Setup will prompt you and then restart the IIS services for you.

After the installation of ASP is complete, you will find a new selection in the Microsoft Internet Server (Common) folder called Active Server Pages Roadmap. For your convenience, there is also a selection you can use to uninstall ASP. The roadmap option will bring up the product documentation in HTML format. You can read it online or print sections to use for later review. If you want to relocate the HTML files, you will find them on disk under the directory path `<IIS WWW root>\Iasdocs\aspdocs`.

You can use Internet Explorer 3.0 (or later) or any browser that supports frames to view the documentation.

Microsoft Index Server 1.1

You can use the Index Server to make Web site content more readily available to your users. You can manage the Index Server using HTML-based tools.

Run the Setup program, IS11ENU.EXE. The first dialog box will display the license agreement, which you must read and agree to before continuing. Click the Yes button when you're ready. Setup will extract files to your hard drive and then prompt you once more before continuing. Click the Continue button in the Setup dialog box, shown in Figure 31.15, to continue, or use the Exit button to halt the installation.

FIGURE 31.15.

After extracting the necessary files, Setup will prompt you before installing the index server.

The next two dialog boxes will ask you to enter directory paths to be used to store sample files, such as HTML or script files. The defaults used when installing IIS 2.0 are

`<drive>:\InetPub\wwwroot`

`<drive>:\inetpub\scripts`

A final dialog box will ask you to designate a path to the location that will be used to store the index file. You can use the default drive letter or enter a path. After you click the Continue button, Setup will stop the IIS services currently running and then copy files to the appropriate WWW or scripts directories. It will then update the Registry and install the Performance Monitor counter, a process that might take a few minutes. The Internet services will be restarted, and a dialog box will show you the URL to a sample search page that you can view with a browser (see Figure 31.16). Click the Exit to Windows button after you write down the URL, and the installation is complete.

FIGURE 31.16.

Write down this URL, which you'll use to activate a sample search page.

Figure 31.17 shows what the sample search page (Simple Content Query) looks like.

FIGURE 31.17.

The Simple Content Query HTML page can be found in the samples directory.

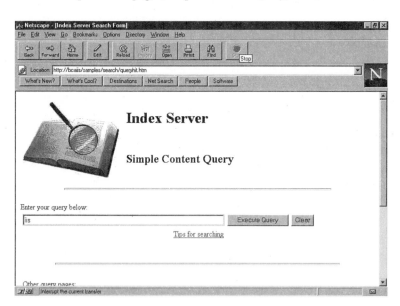

After the installation is complete, you will find a new folder under the Administrative Tools folder called Microsoft Index Server (Common). You will find four options in this folder:

■ Index Server Administration: This is a browser-based tool that you can use to manage your Index Server. For more information on index management tasks using this tool, see the documentation provided with the Index Server.

Using Windows NT as an Internet Server

CHAPTER **31**

1035

31

USING WINDOWS
NT AS AN
INTERNET SERVER

- Index Server Online Documentation: This option will bring up an HTML-based online documentation called Microsoft Index Server Guide. You can view individual sections of the guide or use the built-in search feature to look up specific portions of text.

- Index Server Release Notes: As with any application, you should always read the release notes after installation if you haven't already read them before the installation. Use the quick link to bring up the Release Notes in HTML format. There is no search engine here, but there are links you can use to remove the Index Server or visit the Microsoft Index Server home page.

- Index Server Sample Query Form: This option will bring up Microsoft Internet Explorer (or your installed browser) and display the Simple Content Query page. Use this option to perform quick searches.

Microsoft FrontPage97 Server Extensions

If you decide to install FrontPage97 Server Extensions on a FAT partition, you will get a warning at the end of the installation process, as shown in Figure 31.18.

FIGURE 31.18.

If you don't use an NTFS partition, you will be warned about the security implications when installation is complete.

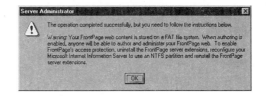

If security isn't an issue, you can use a FAT partition. Otherwise, you should always install on an NTFS partition to take advantage of the built-in file-level security access mechanisms.

As with the other components, when you execute the Setup program for the FrontPage97 Server Extensions, Setup will extract a few files and then prompt you to close any running applications before continuing. You will then need to read the license agreement and click the Yes button in that dialog box to continue the installation.

Next, the Setup program will display the Destination Path dialog box, shown in Figure 31.19, with a default path filled in for the Destination Directory field. You can use the Browse button to change this drive or directory. If the directory path you specify doesn't exist, Setup will create it for you.

The next dialog box, Installed Servers Detected (see Figure 31.20), displays a list of the Internet servers it has detected to be installed on the computer. If you have more than one (or more than one version of a particular server type) installed, you can select which one the extensions will be applied to. Use the Select All or Clear All buttons to aid in your choice, and then use the Next button to continue.

FIGURE 31.19.

Use the Browse button in the Destination Path dialog box to change the installation directory.

FIGURE 31.20.

If you have more than one Internet server installed, you can select the one to use with the FrontPage97 Extensions.

The Setup program will now display the Start Copying Files dialog box, which shows the component to be installed (Server Extensions) and the path for the installation. Click the Next button to start the file copy. When Setup is finished copying files and performing other setup tasks, you are prompted before the IIS WWW service is restarted. Click the Yes button. An informational dialog box appears, telling you that you must enable basic authentication on your Web server if you want to allow earlier versions of FrontPage Explorer and Editor to access FrontPage Web sites on your server. Click the Yes button to allow Setup to enable basic authentication. After it has made this change, another informational dialog box will tell you that the user account used to access that page will need the Log on Locally right granted to it using the User Manager utility.

A final Setup Complete dialog box will appear. You can click the Finish button to complete the installation.

Crystal Reports 4.5

This component lets you easily use a simple report writer application to create content for your Web site. You can use Crystal Reports 4.5 to place data directly into HTML pages without having to write SQL scripts or learn complicated database programming techniques. You can also use it to create reports based on the IIS log files so that you can use the data contained therein to direct your efforts at your Web site. Ten sample reports based on the log files are included to get you started.

After the Setup program (CRYSTAL.EXE) extracts files and presents you with the license agreement dialog box, you can customize the installation using the Select Components dialog box, shown in Figure 31.21.

FIGURE 31.21.

Select the optional installation components and installation directory.

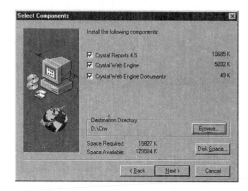

You can use the Browse button to change the installation path. Although you can use the Browse button to change the disk drive letter as well as the directory path, you can use the Disk Space button to change the disk drive if you want to see available space statistics for each drive while you make your choice. Figure 31.22 shows the Available Disk Space dialog box with the Drive drop-down menu expanded.

FIGURE 31.22.

Selecting the drive for installation is easier when you can view the free space statistics.

The components you can install are

- Crystal Reports 4.5
- Crystal Web Engine
- Crystal Web Engine Documents

The Select Components dialog box shows the amount of disk space each component will require. When you have selected an installation path and the components to install, click the Next button. The Setup program will copy files, perform other installation tasks, and prompt you to restart your IIS server. Click the Yes button to do so, or click the No button if it is inconvenient to perform these tasks at this time. The Setup Complete dialog box will finally appear. You can use the checkboxes in this dialog box to elect to view the ReadMe file or to run Crystal Reports. Click the Finish button to end the Setup program.

After the installation, you will find the Crystal Reports 4.5 entry in the Programs folder. Here you can view online documentation, the help file, or start the Crystal Reports 4.5 application. Sample reports based on data from the IIS log files are also available here.

NetShow

NetShow consists of several different multimedia components, each of which you can install separately. Those components include an on-demand and a live server for multicasting audio on the Internet. The installation of each of these components is covered in the following sections.

Installing the NetShow Live Server

This server can be used to multicast audio and perform file transfers to clients on the Internet. You can use it to multicast live audio or WAV sound files. WWW pages use ActiveX controls to provide playback for the network client. You can also record live audio in WAV format.

The Setup program for NetShow Live (`Nslservr.exe`) will let you accept the license agreement and then will extract files needed for the installation. The Welcome dialog box tells you that the NetShow Live Server is about to be installed. To proceed with the installation, click the Continue button. The Select Directory dialog box will allow you to accept the default installation path or to use the Browse button to locate another. When the path is correct, click the Continue button.

Next, Setup will prompt you to let it create a new Program Manager group called Microsoft NetShow or will let you choose another folder to put this application into. Click the Continue button when you have made your selection. The Setup program will conclude with a dialog box telling you the installation is complete. Click the OK button.

After the installation, you will find a new program group in the Programs folder called Microsoft NetShow. In this folder you will find the Live-Administrator program to manage NetShow Live, the Live SDK, as well as documentation.

Installing the NetShow On-Demand Server

When you run the `NSOSRV.EXE` Setup program, you will have to consent to the license agreement. Setup will then extract files and display the Welcome dialog box. Click the OK button to continue the installation. Figure 31.23 shows the next dialog box, in which you can choose which options to install. You can install the on-demand server by itself, or you can also install the administration tools for the server.

Next, the Select Directory dialog box lets you edit the default installation directory path or use the Browse button to search for a directory. After you choose a directory, Setup will copy files to the appropriate path and then display a dialog box allowing you to configure the server, as shown in Figure 31.24.

Using Windows NT as an Internet Server

CHAPTER 31

1039

31

USING WINDOWS
NT AS AN
INTERNET SERVER

FIGURE 31.23.

You can install the server or the management tools or both.

FIGURE 31.24.

You can configure the On-Demand Server.

The parameters you can configure here are

- Maximum Clients
- Maximum Network Bandwidth
- Maximum File Bandwidth

Click the OK button to continue. The next configuration dialog box lets you select a directory path to be used as the virtual root directory where NetShow On-Demand content will be stored. You can use the Browse button or edit the Path field directly.

Click the OK button to continue with the configuration process. Finally, a dialog box appears, telling you that the installation is finished. Click the Restart Now button to restart your Windows NT Server and to cause the changes made to your system to take effect. You can delay the reboot until a more convenient time by clicking the Exit to Windows NT button instead.

Installing the NetShow On-Demand Tools

The Setup program's Welcome dialog box for this component of NetShow lists the tools that will be installed and warns you that you should install the NetShow On-Demand Player before you continue installing the tools. If you have already installed the On-Demand Player, click the Continue button. Otherwise, use the Cancel Setup button and install the player before installing the tools.

The Setup program will then copy files to their destination directories. Click the OK button in the last dialog box to exit the Setup program. When the installation is finished, you can access the tools from the Internet Information Server program folder.

Installing the NetShow Demos

You can install the package of 17 NetShow demonstrations using the NSODEMOS.EXE Setup program. The first dialog box, shown in Figure 31.25, tells you that 20 MB of disk space will be required and that you will have to run another Setup program to finish the installation (this first program simply extracts the files from the compressed archive). Finally, a dialog box will ask you to enter or browse for a directory path to be used to install the demos, and Setup will create the directory you specify if it doesn't exist.

FIGURE 31.25.

Click the Yes button to install the NetShow demos.

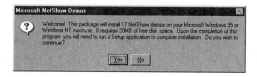

After Setup extracts a number of files, it informs you that the first part of the installation is complete. Click the OK button to continue.

To start the next phase of the installation process, you need to run the Setup.exe program, which you will now find in the directory that you chose for the installation during the first part of Setup. Figure 31.26 shows the Welcome dialog box for the Setup program. At this time, you should heed its warning and close other applications to prevent any file conflicts should the Setup program try to update a file currently on the system. Click the Next button to continue the installation. The Readme Information dialog box, shown in Figure 31.27, will then instruct you to use the START_HERE.HTM file to start the demo when the installation is finished.

FIGURE 31.26.

The opening Welcome dialog box for installing the NetShow demos.

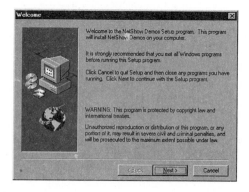

FIGURE 31.27.

The Readme Information dialog box shows you the installation directory and tells you how to run the demo after installation.

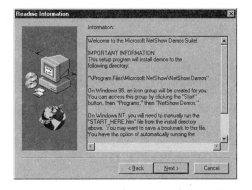

Setup will then check for the necessary disk space and make a list of files to be installed. It will then decompress the required files and create icons. When finished, the Setup Complete dialog box will allow you to read the Readme file if you wish. Click the Finish button to complete the installation.

To start any of the demos, use a browser and fill in the URL for the START_HERE.HTM file that Setup informed you of. Figure 31.28 shows the START_HERE page after it has been scrolled down to show the table of demos that you can run from it. Simply click any of the hyperlinks to run a demo.

FIGURE 31.28.

Run any demo by clicking the hyperlink on the START_HERE Web page.

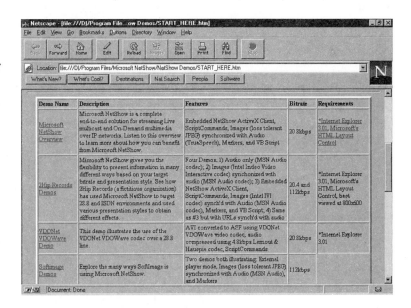

> **NOTE**
>
> You must first install the NetShow On-Demand Client to run the demos.

Installing the NetShow On-Demand Player

The Setup program NSOPLAY.EXE will make you consent to the license agreement and then extract files needed for the installation. A Welcome dialog box will appear, and you can start the installation by clicking the Continue button. The Select Directory dialog box will let you accept the default installation directory or edit it by placing the cursor in the Location field. You can also use the Browse button to search for a different path. Click the Continue button when you have chosen an installation directory.

The Select Start Menu Program Group dialog box lets you choose an existing group to place the player in or make Setup create a new program group called Microsoft NetShow. Make your selection and click the Continue button.

After Setup copies files to their target directories, a dialog box informs you that the installation is complete. Click the OK button to finish. Under the Microsoft NetShow folder you will now find entries for the On-Demand Player and its help file.

Installing the Microsoft On-Demand Documentation

Use the NSOPRNT.EXE file to create printable documentation in RTF format. You can then use WordPad or another word processor to read or print the files. After you run this program, it will prompt you to enter the location where you want to place the documentation files. You can enter the path directly or use the Browse button to locate one to use. After you select the directory and click the OK button, the files will be extracted from the compressed archive and placed into the directory you specified.

IIS 4.0

This version of IIS can be found in the Windows NT 4.0 Option Pack. The Option Pack consists of multiple components that can be used to add functionality to the base Windows NT 4.0 operating system, including the new IIS 4.0. Some components, such as the Microsoft Transaction Server and Microsoft Message Queue Server, can be used to enhance applications that are used on your LAN and also by applications that work with IIS.

The Option Pack consists of the following individual components. You can choose any or all of the different parts from this list:

- Internet Information Server 4.0
- Transaction Server
- Index Server
- Certificate Server

- Data Access Components
- Site Server Express
- Message Queue Server
- Internet Connection Services for RAS
- Administration
- Development Components

You can download trial copies of the Option Pack files from Microsoft's Web site. You can also get information about ordering the CD for the Option Pack. The URL for the home page for IIS 4.0 is

```
http://www.microsoft.com/iis/default.asp
```

If you want to install every component in the Option Pack, you would probably do better to order the CD than attempt the download. At the download Web page, you can select individual components to download, so you can minimize download time if you want to install only IIS 4.0 or just parts of the Option Pack.

Installing IIS 4.0

In order to start the installation of IIS 4.0 on Windows NT 4.0, you will need

- To install Windows NT Server 4.0 Service Pack 3
- To install Microsoft Internet Explorer 4.01 (IE 4.01)
- 32 MB of RAM (at least 64 MB is recommended)
- From 50 to 200 MB of free disk space, depending on the components you install
- An Internet connection if you're publishing on the Internet, or a network adapter card if you're publishing on a local intranet

You can also download the Service Pack and IE 4.01 from Microsoft's Web site. The general download page that has links todownloads for applications, betas, add-ons, and other files is

```
http://www.microsoft.com/msdownload/default.asp
```

If you haven't loaded Service Pack 3 or IE 4.01, you will get a warning message (see Figure 31.29), and the setup process will abort.

FIGURE 31.29.

You must install the Service Pack and IE 4.01 before you can install IIS 4.0.

> **WARNING**
>
> Before you perform any major upgrade to a running production system, you should be sure to have a good backup of the system disk and a recently updated copy of the Emergency Repair Disk (ERD). Do not install Service Pack 3 or IE4 until you have made an ERD. A good backup and an ERD might be your only way out should something catastrophic happen during the installation of several products, such as installing the Service Pack, IE4, and components of IIS 4.0 at the same time.

Starting the Option Pack Setup

IIS 4.0 is installed using an integrated Setup program that can be used to install any or all of the Option Pack components. After you have downloaded the components you want to install, be sure to download the SETUP.EXE program also. You run this program to start the Option Pack integrated setup application.

After initialization, the first dialog box that Setup displays (see Figure 31.30) lists the features you can add to your Windows NT 4.0 Server from the Option Pack. Click the Next button to continue.

FIGURE 31.30.

The first dialog box shows the components of the Option Pack you can install.

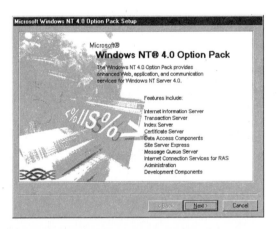

> **WARNING**
>
> If you're running the Microsoft Gopher service from a previous IIS installation, Setup will warn you at the start that the Microsoft Gopher service is no longer supported. It will also warn you that if you continue the installation, the service will be removed from your system. If you need this service, do not install 4.0 on your computer at this time. Click the OK button to continue.

The license agreement appears next. Scroll through and read this document and then click the Accept button. If you click the Decline button, the installation will end. After you accept the license agreement, a dialog box will prompt you for the installation type: minimum, typical, or custom. Because we are installing only IIS 4.0 components, use the Custom button in this dialog box to continue the installation.

> **NOTE**
>
> If you have a previous installation of IIS on your computer, you will have the option of performing an upgrade or an upgrade plus. The Upgrade option will simply upgrade existing IIS components on your system. The Plus option will let you install all of the IIS 3.0 components.

Selecting the Components to Install

Next you will see a dialog box that lets you select components, as shown in Figure 31.31. Here you can choose to install anything from the Option Pack, provided that you have the CD or you downloaded the files needed for your choices. To select a component, simply mark the checkbox next to it. If a box has a checkmark in it already but has a gray background instead of a white one, that component has options that you can select for it, and only some of the options have been selected. Use the Show Subcomponents button to see a listing of the optional parts of any component. Figure 31.32 shows the subcomponents for the Internet Information Server (IIS) component.

FIGURE 31.31.

Select the Option Pack components you want to install from this dialog box.

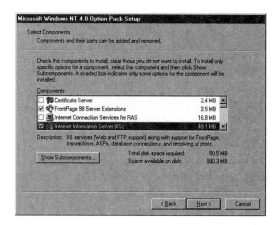

FIGURE 31.32.
You can select optional components for IIS.

If you elect to install all of the IIS 4.0 subcomponents, including documentation and supporting Option Pack files, you will need 78.6 MB of disk space. In addition to documentation, here are the subcomponents for IIS 4.0:

- World Wide Web Server
- File Transfer Protocol (FTP) Server
- Internet NNTP Service
- Internet Service Manager
- Internet Service Manager (HTML)
- SMTP Service
- World Wide Web Sample Site

You will notice that there is no longer a Gopher service. But you now have the NNTP service, which you can use to provide discussion group services for your clients. Microsoft Index Server, FrontPage 98 Extensions, and the Transaction Server are installed by default when you choose to install IIS 4.0 portions of the Data Access Components. In addition, the Windows Scripting Host and the Microsoft Script Debugger are included. You can elect to not install any of these additional components, but you won't be able to use all of the new features provided in IIS 4.0 if you don't install them.

Selecting Destination Directories

Figure 31.33 shows the next dialog box, which you use to specify the home directories for the WWW service and the FTP service, provided that you choose to install these services. You can also specify the root from which Option Pack applications will be installed. The default Application Installation Point is `<drive>:\Program Files`.

Each component you choose to install from the Option Pack will now bring up a dialog box to ask for configuration information. The following sections describe the user interaction required to install the default components.

FIGURE 31.33.
Use this dialog box to set home directories for Internet services and applications.

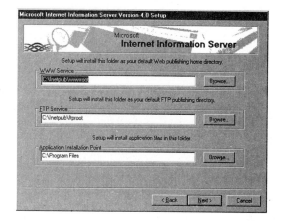

Transaction Server 2.0 (MTS)

The Microsoft Transaction Server 2.0 dialog box lets you specify the directory path for the installation of MTS. You can accept the default or use the MTS Install Folder field to make direct edits. Use the Browse button if you want to search your computer's resources to locate a place to put the files. The default path is `<drive>:\Program Files\Mts`.

After you finish, use the Next button to bring up the dialog box shown in Figure 31.34. By default, the installation will allow for local administration of MTS. If you want to allow for remote administration capabilities, select the Remote option and provide an administrator account and password.

FIGURE 31.34.
You need to provide an administrator-level account if you want to use remote administration features.

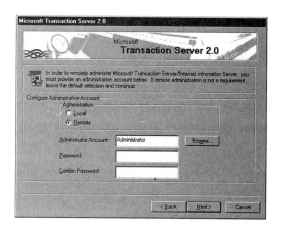

If you use the Browse button, a dialog box will appear from which you can select a user account from the accounts in your domain or the accounts in a domain that your domain trusts. Remember that you will have to provide the password for the account username that you select here. Click the Next button when you have selected the username.

Index Server

The next component to be installed by default is the Index Server. You can use it to index content on your computer or at your Web site and provide an easy search interface for users. The first dialog box for this component lets you specify the directory path under which the Index Server's catalog directory will be created. The default location is the \Inetpub IIS directory.

Microsoft SMTP and NNTP Service

The dialog box for these features alsolets you specify the directory path under which the SMTP and NNTP components will be installed. The directories that will be created and their defaults are the Mail directory, \Inetpub\Mailroot, and the NNTP file directory, \Inetpub\nntpfile.

Finishing the Installation

The integrated Setup application will now build a list of the files it needs to install based on the selections you have made during the first part of the setup. It will then extract files from their compressed archives and copy them to their target directories. This process might take some time, depending on how many components you are installing, so be patient.

When all the files have been copied and the services configured by Setup, the dialog box shown in Figure 31.35 will appear. Click the Finish button.

FIGURE 31.35.

Click the Finish button to finish setting up components from the Option Pack.

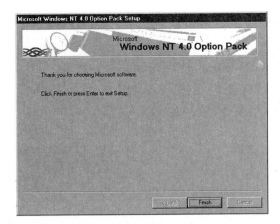

You will then be prompted to restart the computer before the changes that have been made to the system will take effect.

When the system has rebooted, you will notice under the Programs folder that you no longer have an entry for IIS. Instead, there is now an entry called Windows NT 4.0 Option Pack. In this folder you will find a folder for the Microsoft Internet Information Server. In this folder you will find the new Internet Service Manager, along with an HTML version. Although similar in function to the Internet Service Manager utility that you find in IIS 2.0, this new version is manifested as a *snap-in* for the Microsoft Management Console (MMC).

Another thing you will soon notice is that you will now have much more control over your Internet site. The degree of flexibility and granularity of control you can now achieve is much greater than in past IIS versions. The next section discusses using the IIS MMC tool and the expanded list of properties you can now configure.

Using the Internet Service Manager MMC Snap-In

The Microsoft Management Console (MMC) is designed to be a standard administrative application for which developers can write modules to snap in. It is a framework that can make management tasks have a common look and feel. MMC itself doesn't provide any administrative capabilities, just the environment. Snap-in modules (MMC files) provide the management capability within MMC. Microsoft has announced that it soon will be a BackOffice logo requirement that administration be done using a snap-in. It is interesting to note that you can have not only snap-ins, but also extension snap-ins that simply extend the functionality of a standalone snap-in.

Figure 31.36 shows the Internet Service Manager snap-in running under MMC. As you can see, it resembles Microsoft Explorer in that information is represented in a hierarchical manner. In this figure, the Internet Information Server folder has been expanded so that you can see the server, BCAIIS, and the Internet services it offers. You can click the box next to an entry to change it from plus to minus, and thus expand or collapse a particular branch of the structure. You can also double-click an entry to accomplish the same thing.

FIGURE 31.36.

The Internet Service Manager is now a snap-in for Microsoft Management Console.

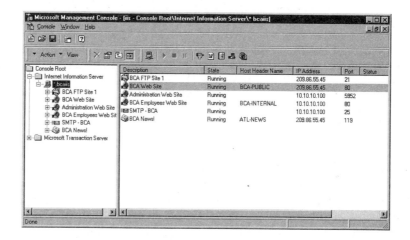

Also notice that you can manage multiple Web sites, using the same IP address or by using multiple IP addresses. In this example, the company BCA is offering a Web site (BCA Web Site) on the Internet for access by customers, and another (BCA Employees Web Site) for internal purposes.

Managing Properties for Your Web Site

The ability to localize information so that you don't have to use several different utilities, or even different actions in the same utility, is an important factor when you're trying to streamline administrative functions. IIS 4.0 makes it easy to access a host of properties for any Web site by simply right-clicking the site in the Internet Service Manager MMC snap-in (you can also highlight an object and then select Action | Properties). Figure 31.36 showed a typical Internet site being managed by IIS 4.0. Figure 31.37 shows the properties sheet for the BCA Web site. The Web Site tab is selected by default.

Figure 31.37.

The properties sheet for a Web site makes configuration easy.

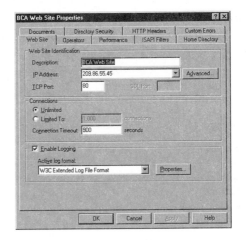

The properties you can change here include a description of the Web site and the IP address for this site, along with other items. You can change the IP address by editing that field on the property sheet, or you can use the pull-down menu to select one. Although TCP port 80 is the default port used by the WWW service, you can change this if you need to. Ports 0 through 1023 are known as *well-known ports* and are managed by the Internet Assigned Numbers Authority (IANA). Ports 1024 through 65535 are known as *registered ports* and are used by a variety of different processes but are not controlled by IANA. If you're operating a Web site for internal use and you don't care about standard ports on the Internet, you can choose a different port number. If you want to use host headers or add multiple identities to this Web site, use the Advanced button. The Advanced Multiple Web Site Configuration dialog box, shown in Figure 31.38, lets you add or remove IP addresses for this Web site.

FIGURE 31.38.

The Advanced button brings up a dialog box that you can use to assign multiple identities to your Web site.

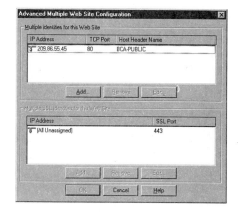

Other tabs in the Web Site Properties Sheet allow you to configure almost anything you can think of for your Web site. Each of these tabs is described in the following sections.

Designating the Home Directory for Your Web Site

On the Home Directory tab you can specify a local directory (on a hard drive attached to the computer), a network file share, or a redirection to another URL. Depending on which you choose, this tab's appearance will change. For example, if you choose a local directory, a Local Path field will appear under it, as shown in Figure 31.39.

FIGURE 31.39.

The Home Directory tab lets you specify where the content for this Web site will come from.

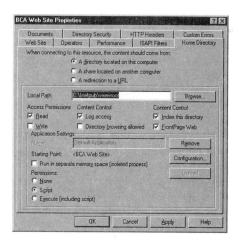

However, if you click the next radio button, A share located on another computer, to make the home directory for this Web site on a network share, the Local Path field changes to Network Directory, and the Browse button becomes the Connect As button (see Figure 31.40).

FIGURE 31.40.

The fields that appear on this property sheet depend on whether the home directory is local or on a network share.

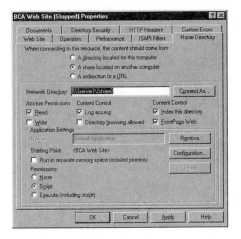

Regardless of whether the path is local or a network file share, you can set access permissions (read/write), but if the path is on an NTFS partition, you should be sure that the access you select here isn't further restricted by NTFS permissions. The rule is that the more-restrictive access setting wins. In other words, if NTFS denies access, setting it here won't grant access. Also, if you grant access via NTFS but deny it here, the user won't have access. Read access lets the user view or download a document. Write access lets the user upload to the Web server, but write access must be done with a browser that supports the Put feature found in the HTTP 1.1 protocol.

The Log access field should be checked if you want visits to this Web site recorded in the log file. The Directory browsing allowed option, if selected, lets users browse through a hypertext display of the files and subdirectories in this directory path. This is not necessarily a good idea if you're running a Web site where security is important.

You can control whether Microsoft Index Server indexes this directory by selecting the Index this directory checkbox. If it isn't selected, this directory won't be indexed.

Designating Web Site Operators

To allow for flexibility in managing multiple Web and FTP sites, IIS 4.0 lets you specify selected users to be Web Site Operators. These users will be able to manage properties for *their* Web site only and won't be able to access administrative tasks that apply to IIS as a whole. This localized control capability means that an Internet Service Provider, for instance, can let customers manage their own Web sites that the ISP hosts for them without compromising the security or integrity of other customers' sites hosted on the same server.

Web Site Operators don't have complete control over their sites. They can't change the site's identification or create virtual directories. They can't change the anonymous username or its password. Some of the duties Web Site Operators can perform include the following:

■ Control content expiration
■ Control content ratings
■ Change the default document for the Web site
■ Set access permissions
■ Manage logging for the Web site

You can designate ordinary users to be Web Site Operators, provided that their user account is not denied access to any NTFS directories they will need to work with. A Web Site Operator doesn't have to be a member of the Administrators group or have special privileges.

To add users to this special IIS group, click the Add button on the Operators tab. A dialog box called Add Users And Groups will appear to let you select usernames from your domain and domains you trust.

Managing Performance Properties

Figure 31.41 shows the Performance tab of the Web site properties sheet. Here you do not evaluate performance, but help to control it. You can use the Performance Tuning control to adjust memory requirements based on an estimate of the number of hits you expect per day for the Web site. The range is from Fewer than 10,000 to More than 100,000. You should set this value to be just a little larger than the number of hits you actually get when you have historical data to make such a determination. By setting the value slightly higher than necessary, you will improve performance. If you set it to an extremely large value over your actual usage, you will simply be wasting memory resources and possibly degrade performance.

FIGURE 31.41.
You can use the Performance tab to control how resources are allocated for this Web site.

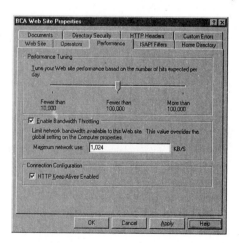

If you select the Enable Bandwidth Throttling checkbox, the value you specify for KB/second will override any value set at the computer level. You can use this option to allocate network bandwidth among multiple Web sites running on the same server. At the bottom of the property sheet is the HTTP Keep-Alives Enabled checkbox. If this is selected, the server will not open a new connection with a client each time it makes a request, but instead will maintain an open connection for multiple requests.

Working with ISAPI Filters

ISAPI filters are programs that are written to work with processing an HTTP request. Programmers can use this property sheet to add or remove ISAPI filters from the Web server. You can also modify the priority rating of the filter and view details about them.

Enabling Default Documents and Creating Footers for Web Pages

In the Documents tab you will notice that the Enable Default Document checkbox is selected by default. If a user's HTML request doesn't include a filename, the default document is used. You can add multiple default documents for the Web site if you want to by using the Add button. In this case, the server will return to the user the first file that it finds from this list (when it searches the directory for the files).

The second checkbox is called Enable Document Footer. This option, if selected, lets you specify a filename of an HTML file that will be appended to the bottom of each Web page your server sends out. There are many uses for footers, including having a common navigation bar at the bottom of each page. If you are hosting Web pages for a number of users, you might want to include a footer at the bottom of their pages referencing your Web-hosting services.

Setting Authentication and Security Properties

Figure 31.42 shows the Directory Security tab of the Web Site Properties sheet. You will find three categories of security controls:

- Anonymous Access and Authentication Control
- Secure Communications
- IP Address and Domain Name Restrictions

FIGURE 31.42.

Use this property sheet to control user access and other security controls.

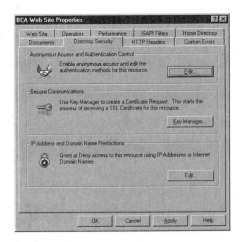

The Anonymous Access and Authentication Control section allows you to specify user authentication or allow anonymous access. Use the Edit button to bring up the Authentication Methods dialog box, shown in Figure 31.43. If you select Allow Anonymous Access, use the Edit button next to it to bring up a dialog box that will let you specify the user account that will be used to allow accesses by anonymous users.

FIGURE 31.43.

You can choose the method used to authenticate users accessing the Web site.

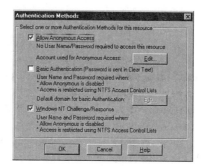

The Secure Communications section of this property sheet lets you set up this Web site to use secure communications using an SSL certificate. Before you can use the SSL features on your Web site, you will need to obtain a server certificate from a trusted third-party certificate authority. There are several operating on the Internet. When you have a valid certificate, you can use the Key Manager to create a public/private SSL key pair that can be used to establish encrypted secure communications with your clients.

You create a new key pair using the Create New Key Wizard (select Key | Create New Key). This wizard will prompt you for the information needed to create a file you can use to request a certificate.

After you create this key file, you will see your key listed in the main Key Manager dialog box. When you receive a valid certificate from an authority, you can use other options on the Key menu to install the certificate.

The last item you will see on the Directory Security tab allows you to grant or restrict access to Web sites running on this server. Use the Edit button in the IP Address and Domain Name Restrictions section to enforce restrictions. The method used is to either grant or deny access to all computers. After that, you can enter exceptions. In Figure 31.44, you can see that for this particular Web site, all computers are allowed to access the Web site except for computers that are in the ONO domain and the specific computer with the IP address of 159.110.123.59.

If you have a more restrictive site, you might want to use this feature in reverse: Select the Denied Access radio button in Figure 31.44 and then use the Add button to grant access to only a few specific computers or domains that you want.

FIGURE 31.44.

You can use the Add or Remove button to add to the list of those who are not allowed access to the site.

Using Content Expiration, Ratings, and HTTP Headers

The HTTP Headers tab lets you create HTTP headers. This feature is used to send values to a browser in the header portion of the HTML page. In addition, you can control other properties of your HTML documents on this page, including

- Enable Content Expiration
- Content Rating

If content expiration is selected, you will be allowed to specify that content on this Web site will expire after a certain amount of time or on a certain date. Expired content is no longer available to users. This feature could be used to be sure that important time-dependent information is not left on your site past its usefulness. By choosing the expiration time in advance, you won't have to be bothered with regularly reviewing your site to remove stale content.

Use the Edit Ratings button to provide information to users of your Web pages about their content. Figure 31.45 shows the Ratings tab selected in the Content Ratings dialog box.

FIGURE 31.45.

You can rate your Web pages using this dialog box.

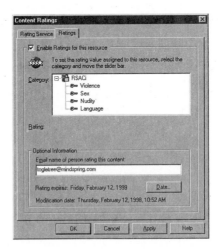

You can rate your Web pages by selecting the appropriate category (Violence, Sex, and so on) and then using the Rating control to set a level. Each category can be set to none or to one of four other levels, which become progressively more severe. For example, the rating categories for Violence are

- None
- Level 1: Fighting
- Level 2: Killing
- Level 3: Killing with blood and gore
- Level 4: Wanton and gratuitous violence

At the bottom of the Ratings tab you can enter an email address that users can use to comment on your ratings. This field is optional. You can use the Date button at the bottom to specify a date that the content rating will expire.

The Content Ratings dialog box will appear. The Rating Service tab will allow you to connect to the information page of the Recreational Software Advisory Council (using the More Info button), which uses a system to provide information about content based on the amount of nudity, violence, and offensive language. Click this button for more information about this organization. The Ratings Questionnaire button will take you to a page where you can register your Web site and complete a questionnaire that can be used to make recommendations for your ratings.

Managing Properties for Your FTP Site

Although the World Wide Web is what most people think of when you mention the Internet, the WWW service is quite new compared to other types of communication on the Net. The File Transfer Protocol (FTP) service has been used for over a decade to provide a simple method of transferring files between computers. Most browsers support FTP, so many users are unaware that they are even using the service when they point and click to download a file from a Web site.

Windows NT Server makes an excellent FTP server because of its ability to use Windows NT security authentication, although you can also set up an anonymous FTP service for the general public.

If you select an FTP site in the Internet Service Manager MMC tool, you will get a set of properties to choose from that is a little different from the properties you can manage for a WWW site. Figure 31.46 shows the FTP site properties sheet with the FTP Site tab selected. Here you can administer basic FTP site information such as the IP address and a description of the name you want to give the site. You can also specify the TCP port, limit the number of concurrent connections, and enable logging for the FTP site.

At the bottom of this property sheet you can use the Current Sessions button to bring up a display of the users connected to your server, along with the connect time. You can also use this to disconnect one or more users.

FIGURE 31.46.

The FTP Site tab contains basic information about the site.

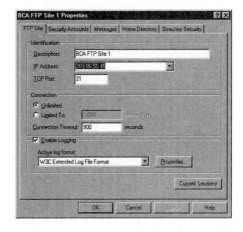

Assigning FTP Site Operators

The Security Accounts tab is used to assign FTP Site Operators in a manner similar to that used to make users Web Site Operators (see the earlier section "Designating Web Site Operators"). At the top of this sheet you can select the Allow Anonymous Connections checkbox and then specify a username and password that will be used to access resources for anonymous users. By default, IIS creates an account called IUSR_*computername*. Note that the user account you use for anonymous connections must have a password (it can't be "blank"), and it must possess the Log On Locally right.

If you select the next checkbox, Allow Only Anonymous Connections, users won't be able to log on using their regular Windows NT username and password. Use this to restrict users from accessing the computer from any account other than the one you choose for anonymous requests.

Creating a Welcome Message for an FTP Site

The Messages tab in the FTP Site Properties sheet lets you enter a text message that is displayed when users log into your FTP server. You can also specify an exit message and a message to be returned to users when the maximum number of users has been reached and no more logons can be handled.

Setting the FTP Home Directory

This is much like the method used to set the home directory for a WWW site. Use the Home Directory tab in the FTP Site Properties sheet. You can specify a directory that exists on a hard drive attached to the local computer, or you can specify a network file share. If you specify a file share, you will have to provide a username and password that are needed to connect to the share. Either way, you can also use the Read and Write checkboxes to control access. The Log Access checkbox (selected by default) will cause visits to this particular directory to be recorded in the log file, provided that you have enabled logging for the server on the FTP Site tab.

Using Windows NT as an Internet Server

CHAPTER 31

1059

31

USING WINDOWS
NT AS AN
INTERNET SERVER

In addition to specifying a path for the home directory, you can also use this tab to specify the UNIX or MS-DOS style for displaying the directory listing for clients.

Limiting Access by IP Address or Domain Name

You can specify a particular computer, group of computers, or domain name to grant or deny access to. Figure 31.47 shows the Directory Security tab. You can use the Granted Access or Denied Access radio button and then use the Add or Remove button to add entries to the type of access.

FIGURE 31.47.

You can grant or deny access to the FTP site by IP address or domain name.

When you click the Add button, you can grant or deny access based on

- ◼ A Single Computer: You will have to enter the IP address for the computer.
- ◼ Group of Computers: You will have to supply a network ID and a subnet mask.
- ◼ Domain Name: You will have to supply a domain name.

Note that the radio button you choose will determine the effect that the Add button will have. The text in the dialog box informs you that all users will be either granted access or denied access, with the exception of those you add to the list. For example, to let only a few specific users access this Web site, select the Denied Access button and then use the Add button to specify the users who will be exceptions and therefore will be allowed to access the site.

You can also do the opposite and select the Granted Access radio button to grant all computers access. Then you can use the Add button to deny access to those few computers that you don't want accessing your site.

Managing Properties for Other IIS Components

The preceding sections, which discussed the properties sheets for the WWW and FTP site objects, only scratched the surface. You can edit the properties for any object that falls underneath the Internet Information Server entry in the MMC console. For example, you can edit the top-level properties for the IIS site itself. Figure 31.48 shows the properties for the BCAIIS IIS site.

FIGURE 31.48.

You can control properties for the entire IIS site.

When you set properties at this level, all objects underneath will inherit these values unless you use their individual property sheets to make changes. In Figure 31.48 you can set the master properties for the WWW service or the FTP service by selecting either (use the pull-down menu and then click the Edit button). You will see a master properties sheet for the service, which looks almost exactly like the property sheets you would find for a specific instance of that service.

The difference is that if you change the property here, all Web sites or FTP sites you then create will inherit these properties as their defaults.

Each Web site and FTP site you create will have its own properties sheets that you can edit. Other Internet services you can add (such as the NNTP newsgroup service) also have properties sheets with information on them that is applicable to the particular service.

Managing Logging Properties for IIS 4.0

You can control whether a Web server or FTP server logs user accesses to an IIS log file by using the appropriate tab in the service's properties sheets. IIS supports three formats you can choose from when deciding to create log files:

- W3C Extended Log File Format
- Microsoft IIS Log File Format
- ODBC Logging

By default, W3C Extended Log File Format is selected. You can choose to use Microsoft's format or to log on to an ODBC database instead. You can also control other properties that define the behavior of logging on your system.

When you choose the ODBC option, you will first need to create a database table that contains the following fields:

- Client host name
- Username

- Log time
- Service (that is, WWW or FTP)
- Machine
- Server IP address
- Processing time
- Bytes received
- Bytes sent
- Service status
- Win32Status
- Operation
- Target
- Parameters

You can then use the Logging Properties page to fill in the information needed by IIS to access the database, such as the table name, a username, and a password.

If you want to have control over the types of data that are recorded in the log file, you should choose the W3C Extended Log File Format. Figure 31.49 shows the Extended Properties tab, with the different logging categories you can select to record in the log file.

FIGURE 31.49.
You can control logging information if you use the W3C Extended Log File Format.

Summary

With several versions of IIS to choose from, you should have no difficulty finding an appropriate solution to your Internet server needs using Windows NT 4.0 Server. The easy-to-use IIS 2.0 applications can be used for a departmental server on your local LAN or as a server on the Internet. If you want to add multimedia capabilities or transaction capabilities for your Internet applications, you can install components from IIS 3.0 or IIS 4.0. Whichever version you choose to use will provide you with a safe, effective presence on the Internet.

Programming Windows NT Server

by Weiying Chen

IN THIS CHAPTER

Developing applications on the Windows NT platform requires software developers to become well versed with many software development kits (SDKs), application programming interfaces (APIs), technologies, and at least one integrated development environment.

This chapter discusses current and evolving technologies and helps you properly use the available SDKs and APIs to implement them. Armed with the knowledge contained in this chapter, you can begin on an accelerated and correct path to successful development of robust Windows NT applications and services.

Software Development Toolkits

There are several software development toolkits in the suite of development support products Microsoft has released to this date. The Win32 SDK contains the libraries needed to develop OLE and Win32 applications on Windows NT. The Win32 SDK also includes extensions for telephony, electronic commerce, and database access.

Win32 SDK

Before you can begin to develop applications for Windows NT, you must obtain a Win32 SDK or one of the Microsoft products that include this SDK. The Win32 SDK contains the libraries, sample code, utilities, and Help files needed to successfully develop Win32 applications.

A recommended companion for any serious Win32 platform developer is the Microsoft Developers Network (MSDN) CD. The Professional Edition of the MSDN includes the Win32 SDK.

Win32 API

The Win32 API included with the Win32 SDK enables you to write virtually any kind of application under a full 32-bit environment. Many elaborate APIs for implementing specific technologies are also a part of the Win32 SDK.

The Microsoft Foundation Classes (MFC) object-oriented API, for example, exposes Windows 32 functions to any C++ or object-oriented language.

The Win32 API can be divided into the following categories:

■ **Windows management:** Includes a set of functions and messages to extensively manage the Windows operating system resources. These resources include the concepts of Windows, Carets, Clipboards, common dialog boxes, cursors, NT menus, hooks, icons, keyboard accelerators, keyboard inputs, multiple document interfaces, messages and message queues, mouse input, painting and drawing, rectangles, timers, the window class, window properties, and window procedures.

- **Window control:** Includes several interfaces to manage every aspect of window controls. Window controls include many subcontrols, such as an Animation control, drag listbox, Header control, hot-key control, Image lists, List View control, progress bar, property sheet, Rich Edit controls, status windows, tab control, toolbar, toolkit controls, track bar, Tree View control, up-down controls, combo box, controls, dialog box, Edit control, listbox, scrollbar, and Static control.

- **Console shell:** Includes a set of functions and messages to manage shell programming. The shell is an application that enables users to group, start, and control other applications for the Microsoft Windows operating systems.

  These functions and messages enable you to write Control Panel applications. They also support software version control, File Manager extensions, screen saver libraries, the Shell Dynamic Data Exchange interface for controlling Program Manager Resources, and even a Windows 95 shell extension on Windows NT.

- **Graphics device interface:** This gives you entire function sets to produce and animate advanced graphics objects.

- **System services:** Windows NT provides a variety of resources within the operating system. These resources provide a robust and standard method of working with files, network transports, application data, security, exception handling, processes, threads, IPC methods, application debugging, performance monitoring, and even server backups.

- **Network services:** Win32 network functions are network-independent. Applications can use these functions to add and cancel network connections, retrieve information about the current configuration of the network, or administrate a domain.

  The network service API includes support for LAN Manager functions, network DDE, and the Windows Socket interface.

- **Multimedia service:** Win32 API gives developers high-level and low-level interfaces for developing multimedia applications. It includes support for high-level audio, low-level audio, a media control interface, multimedia file input/output, multimedia services, a multimedia timer, and joystick services.

The OLE SDK

The OLE SDK exposes several powerful interfaces and models that enable developers to write platform-independent and language-independent objects. The OLE SDK contains a specification for the Component Object Model (COM), which is the fundamental model of OLE and ActiveX.

The OLE SDK supports the Microsoft Object Linking and Embedding interface, an incredibly broad and powerful abstraction for interfacing between objects. OLE can be used to implement client or server solutions that can utilize all resources within the Windows operating system. Developers who want to write incredibly powerful applications based on any computing abstracts need to consider OLE as the vehicle to do so.

The next sections describe the primary components of OLE in enough detail for developers to understand the basic concepts behind each. Any development effort should probably spend a good deal on prototyping or defining the problem domain before jumping directly into implementation. Many pieces of OLE are very complex. However, once you understand OLE, it is undoubtedly the most powerful software abstraction available on multiple platforms.

Component Object Model

The Component Object Model (COM) is the basic technology behind OLE. It specifies how objects interact within a single application or between applications.

COM defines certain basic interfaces that provide functions common to all COM-based technologies within OLE. You should put some time into understanding the COM standard before you write applications that use some of the more advanced OLE features.

Data Transfer Model

The data transfer model enables users to transfer data uniformly with a drag-and-drop operation, a copy/paste operation, or programmatically. This model is supported by the `IDataObject` interface.

The Structured Storage Model

The structured storage model specifies how data is saved and retrieved from storage. Two types of objects exist within this model: storages and streams. Many resources within the Windows operating system are accessible through the structured storage model.

The Compound Document Model

The compound document model is a document within another application (referred to as the *container application*) that seamlessly integrates various types of data or items, such as sound clips, spreadsheets, or bitmaps. OLE enables you to use compound documents without worrying about switching between the different applications.

OLE Automation

Automation is the capability of an application to control another application's objects programmatically. An integral part of OLE Automation is the capability of an object to describe its capabilities through type descriptions implemented by an *Object Description Language* (ODL). ODL is absolutely necessary in order to implement OLE controls.

Control

OLE objects that support the in-place activation features of OLE documents use OLE automation to expose properties and methods and to provide event support within applications.

RPC

Win32 API provides *remote procedure calls* (RPCs) to enable applications to call functions located remotely on another machine. This machine can be anywhere on the network.

Microsoft's implementation of RPC is compatible with the Open Software Foundation (OSF) Distributed Computing Environment (DCE) version. This means that RPC applications written using the Win32 API are able to communicate with other RPC applications on other operating systems that support DCE. You can find more information in the *Microsoft Win32 Remote Procedure Call Programmer's Guide and Reference*.

RPC can be configured to use one or more transports, one or more name services, and one or more security servers. It is designed to work with multiple service providers.

Microsoft RPC consists of runtime libraries, an Interface Definition Language (IDL), and its compiler.

IDL is a rich, complex language that enables you to define interface parameters carefully in terms of their direction and type. IDL files consist of two parts: the interface header and body. It must be compiled with the IDL compiler. The compiler takes the IDL files and generates proxy/stub code, an interface header file, and an interface identifier file.

After an IDL file is compiled successfully, the generated files are run through the standard C/C++ compile and link steps.

Microsoft Visual C++ 4.1 contains some RPC examples.

Multimedia

Win32 SDK gives developers both high-level and low-level services for developing multimedia applications that use the extended capabilities of a multimedia computer.

A sample program called SPEAKN that demonstrates this type of application programming is located in Microsoft Visual C++ 4.1.

OpenGL

OpenGL, originally developed by Silicon Graphics Incorporated (SGI) for its graphics workstations, enables applications to create high-quality color images and animated 3D graphics independent of the windowing system, operating system, or hardware.

OpenGL includes many components, such as a full set of current OpenGL commands, an OpenGL utility library (GLU), the OpenGL programming guide auxiliary library, Windows Graphic Library APIs, and the new Win32 APIs for pixel formats and double buffering.

Microsoft Visual C++ 4.1 contains some OpenGL examples.

Win32 Extensions

Microsoft has developed several powerful and robust extensions for providing programmatic control of Telephony (TAPI), asynchronous communications (RAS), database access (ODBS, DAO, RDO), and electronic commerce (Exchange SDK).

The TAPI Interface

The *Telephony Application Programming Interface* (TAPI) provides the API to program basic telephonic functionality using the line-device class functions. A *line device* is a physical device such as a fax board, a modem, or an ISDN card that is connected to an actual telephone line. Line devices support telephonic capabilities by enabling applications to send or receive information to or from a telephone network.

The API includes place, receive, drop a call, call hold, call transfer (blind and consultative transfer), and call-monitoring capabilities.

The MAPI Interface

You use the *Messaging Application Programming Interface* (MAPI) to communicate with electronic messaging systems such as fax, voice mail, public communication services AT&T EasyLink, CompuServe, and MCI Mail. MAPI is a component of the Windows 95 operating system and is part of NT 4. Because MAPI is an integrated part of the operating system, developers of 16-bit and 32-bit Windows applications can standardize on a consistent interface.

MAPI is a messaging architecture that enables multiple applications to interact with multiple messaging systems seamlessly across a variety of hardware platforms. MAPI consists of a few different interfaces of its own. Together, these interfaces offer an open programming standard that is separated into two independent parts. The first part supports front-end messaging for client applications. The second is a programming interface used by the back-end service providers.

MAPI is made up of a set of common application programming interfaces and dynamic link library (DLL) components. The interfaces are used to create and access diverse messaging applications and messaging systems.

The MAPI SDK includes tools to help in the development of MAPI-compliant client applications, service providers, and message services. Both a 16- and 32-bit version of MAPI are available.

The 32-bit version of the MAPI SDK also is included within the Win32 SDK. It contains a variety of examples and tools in C, C++, and Visual Basic. For more information regarding MAPI, see the *Messaging Application Programming Interface (MAPI) Programmer's Reference*. This reference is included in the documentation that accompanies the MAPI SDK.

ODBC SDK 2.1

The Microsoft *Open Database Connectivity* (ODBC) SDK version 2.1 is a set of software components, tools, and documentation designed to help you develop ODBC drivers and ODBC-enabled applications for the Windows operating systems.

The ODBC interface allows applications to access data stored in database management systems (DBMSs) by using the Structured Query Language (SQL) as a standard.

Additionally, a single application can access different database management systems. This enables you to develop, compile, and ship an application without targeting a specific DBMS. Users then can add modules called *database drivers* that link the application to their choice of database management systems.

The ODBC architecture has four components:

- **Application:** Performs processing and calls ODBC functions to submit SQL statements and retrieve results.
- **Driver Manager:** Loads drivers on behalf of an application.
- **Driver:** Processes ODBC function calls, submits SQL requests to a specific data source, and returns results to the application.
- **Data source:** Consists of the data the user wants to access.

For more information on ODBC, see the Microsoft ODBC SDK Programmer's Reference.

The DAO SDK

The *Database Access Objects* (DAOs) and collections provide a framework for using code to create and manipulate components of your database system. Objects and collections have properties that describe the characteristics of database components and methods that you use to manipulate them.

Objects and collections provide different types of containment relationships. Objects contain zero or more collections.

Microsoft Visual C++ 4.x contains an example using ODBC that shows how to use the MFC DAO classes to create databases, tables, queries, fields, and indexes. MFC and DAO use the Microsoft Jet Database Engine, currently version 3.0, to retrieve data from and store data in user and system databases. DAO can read any ODBC data source for which you have an ODBC driver.

The Microsoft Jet Database Engine is the data manager component on which various implementations are built, such as the MFC DAO classes, Microsoft Access, and Microsoft Visual Basic, and the Microsoft Desktop Database Drivers (currently version 3.0).

The example also shows how to map the properties of the database objects to user controls.

The RAS SDK

The *Remote Access Service* (RAS) enables remote users to work as if they are connected directly to a computer network. RAS supports accessing other machines on the network as if all machines are on the same physical network.

The RAS API exposes functions that enable an application to establish, communicate, and terminate remote access to other machines. Applications can use a static or a dynamic version of this API.

The Exchange SDK

The Microsoft Exchange Server SDK enables you to use a powerful new message and data-transport system. The SDK provides functions that support new technologies, such as public folders and signing and sealing.

You can use this SDK to develop client and Microsoft Exchange Server Administrator program extensions for Microsoft Exchange. The SDK also enables you to build client and server applications customized for an environment or to develop standalone client and server applications that use Microsoft Exchange Server.

Integrated Development Environment

Microsoft's Developers Studio is provided with Microsoft Visual C++ or many professional editions of other Microsoft languages. The Microsoft Developers Studio integrates source management and editing, project management, and debugging into a user interface that enables you to effectively manage the window real estate.

The following sections summarize a great deal of information about several new and improved products from Microsoft. All of the new capabilities integrate effectively into the Microsoft Developers Studio. Furthermore, most of the information within these sections are weighted toward C++ and higher-level language development.

Microsoft Visual C++ 4.1

C++ developers will need to purchase Microsoft Visual C++ 4.1 to get the most recent revisions to the following Microsoft products and standards.

Microsoft Developers Studio

Visual C++ 4.1 contains the Microsoft Developers Studio, which integrates Visual C++ with other Microsoft products through one common development environment. Visual C++ 4.1 includes many products, each of which integrates nicely into the Microsoft Developers Studio:

- Microsoft Development Library
- Microsoft FORTRAN PowerStation
- Microsoft Visual Test
- Microsoft Visual SourceSafe
- Microsoft Visual C++ Cross-Development Edition for Macintosh

The Microsoft Developers Studio provides new features, such as a Class Viewer, a Wizard bar, and an extensive editor emulator for Brief and Epsilon. The new online Help viewer, Infoview, supports the books online and the MSDN.

Visual C++ is a powerful and intuitive development environment that enables you to develop applications faster and better. Visual C++ makes software reuse easy because it provides many existing objects and classes, such as a component gallery, OLE controls, Custom AppWizards, and MFC extensions.

The compiler for Visual C++ 4.1 is state of the art. It supports the latest C++ language features and many new standards, including runtime type information (RTTI), standard template library (STL), name spaces, minimal rebuild, and incremental linking improvements.

Visual C++ 4.1 includes InstallSHIELD, which is the worldwide standard for software distribution of Windows applications.

In addition to performance improvements, Visual C++ 4.1 incorporates new features for developers targeting the Internet. The new features include Internet server classes, an AppWizard for creating Internet applications, and World Wide Web access within the Developers Studio.

With Visual C++ 4.1, you now can access your favorite World Wide Web sites from within Developers Studio. Simply choose the Web Favorites command from the Help menu. Developers Studio Web Favorites comes preloaded with a list of Microsoft Web sites for Visual C++ developer support. Using the Web Favorites dialog, you can edit this list of web sites and add your own favorite sites.

Microsoft Foundation Classes 4.0

The Microsoft Foundation Class Library (MFC) is an "application framework" (often called *framework*) for writing applications for Microsoft Windows and other platforms that support the Win32 API. The framework is implemented as a group of C++ classes, many of which represent common objects such as windows, documents, and so on. MFC 4.0 provides the following new classes.

32

PROGRAMMING
WINDOWS NT
SERVER

New Features

Visual C++ 4.1 provides an updated version of the industry standard, Microsoft Foundation Class Library 4.0, with many new features:

- Additional support for Windows 95 applications
- New MFC classes for data access objects (DAO)
- OLE control container support
- New common dialogs

Internet Server Classes

MFC has added five new classes that implement the Internet Server API (ISAPI). Using these classes, you can create DLLs that add functionality to Internet servers and Web pages:

- **CHtmlStream:** Called by CHttpServer to send a Hypertext Markup Language (HTML) stream back to the client.
- **CHttpFilter:** A class for creating an Internet server filter to screen messages sent to and from an Internet server.
- **CHttpFilterContext:** A class that CHttpFilter uses to handle concurrent, multiple requests.
- **CHttpServer:** A class for creating an Internet server extension. Internet server extensions provide a more efficient, DLL-based alternative to Common Gateway Interface (CGI) applications.
- **CHttpServerContext:** A class that CHttpServer uses to handle concurrent, multiple requests.

The new ISAPI Extension Wizard creates Internet server extensions and filters. Internet server extensions and filters are DLLs based on the new Internet Server API (ISAPI) MFC classes. To access the ISAPI Extension Wizard, open the New Project Workspace dialog by choosing the New command from the File menu and then choosing ISAPI Extension Wizard from the dialog.

Other MFC Classes

MFC classes shipping with Visual C++ 4.1 include some new classes:

- **CDockState:** A CObject class that can hold the state of a number of control bars. You can save the state to and load the state from the Registry, an INI file, or the binary contents of a CArchive object.
- **CRecentFileList:** A CObject class that supports the most recently used (MRU) file list.

■ **CSharedFile:** A `CMemFile` class that supports RAM-based shared memory files for fast temporary storage and for transferring raw bytes or serialized objects between independent processes.

New MFC Examples

The 4.1 release of Visual C++ has added many new MFC examples that show you how to perform the following tasks:

■ **ACDUAL:** Adding dual-interface support to an MFC-based OLE Automation server. The sample implements the normal dispatch interface and then adds a custom interface derived from `IDispatch`.

■ **BINDSCRB:** Writing an OLE document object for use with the Binder tool in Microsoft Office 95 applications. Based on the Scribble tutorial.

■ **DLGTEMPL:** Dynamically creating a dialog template and using the template with `CreateDialogIndirect` or `InitModalIndirect`.

■ **HTTPSVR:** Using MFC and the Windows Sockets (WinSock) classes to implement a simple World Wide Web HTTP server that supports form creation and execution of Common Gateway Interface (CGI) server applications by using the standard HTML constructs.

■ **MFCUCASE:** Using MFC classes to create Internet filter DLLs.

■ **ODBCINFO:** Determining ODBC driver capabilities at runtime by opening a selected ODBC data source and displaying information by using property pages.

■ **ROWLIST:** Implementing full-row selection in the Report mode of the `CListView` control class.

■ **WWWQUOTE:** Writing a World Wide Web application for retrieving information (in this case, stock quotes).

Visual C++ 4.1 consolidates methods for accessing samples in the InfoView tab. All examples, including the MFC examples, now are located under the `Samples` heading. MFC examples no longer can be found under the `Visual C++ Books/MFC 4.x` heading.

Alphabetical and subject lists of MFC examples now are available under `Key Visual C++ Topics` (under `MFC Samples` below the `MFC Topics` subheading).

Visual Basic 4.0

Microsoft Visual Basic gives you the power and the flexibility to develop everything from quick user interface (UI) prototypes to robust client/server solutions.

Analyzing the complexity and requirements of a solution beforehand often makes the implementation language decision for you due to limitations of the language. Today, almost all new

32

PROGRAMMING
WINDOWS NT
SERVER

Microsoft specifications such as ActiveX and DAO are available through either VB 4.0 or VC++ 4.1.

Microsoft Visual Basic Enterprise Edition CD-ROM is a programming system for the Windows platform. It contains Visual Basic 4.0 32-bit and 16-bit, MSDN starter kit (Microsoft Developers Network for Visual Basic users), and Visual SourceSafe 4.0 (a source control system for Visual Basic 4.0) that can be used only under NT 3.51 or later versions and Windows 95.

The Visual Basic Application Edition 2.0 has been added as the language engine in Visual Basic. This version is fully compatible with earlier versions of the standalone Visual Basic products and Visual Basic 1.0, which is included in Microsoft Excel 5.0 and Microsoft Project 4.0. It supports OLE Automation. With the OLE Automation, you can "borrow" the functionality of other applications by controlling their objects from within your Visual Basic applications. If the object is an OLE Automation object, you can use its properties and methods in your application.

Windows 95 custom controls such as list views, tree views, a status bar, toolbars, and tabbed dialog boxes enable you to create applications with the Windows 95 interface look and feel.

Visual Basic includes new features designed to give you the means to build client/server applications that manage business-critical data.

Remote automation enables you to create shared, reusable components that use the OLE Automation interface for network communication. Remote data objects (RDOs) and the `RemoteData` control (RDC) permit applications to access ODBC-accessible data sources without using a local query processor. Although RDO and RDC can access any ODBC data source, they are designed to take advantage of database servers that use sophisticated query engines, such as Microsoft SQL Server and Oracle.

Perl

The Windows NT 3.51 resource kit includes Perl 5. Perl is a free-form interpreted language optimized for scanning arbitrary text files, extracting information from text files, and printing reports based on the information. It combines some of the best features of C: `sed`, `awk`, and `sh`.

Windows NT Perl 5

Windows NT Perl 5 is based on the UNIX distribution of Perl 5, which supports packages. A package can function as a class with support for dynamic multiple inheritance and virtual methods. Perl 5 also supports multiple simultaneous DBM implementations and OLE Automation. You easily can imbed Perl 5 into your C or C++ applications.

To run Windows NT Perl 5, you need a computer running Windows NT Workstation 3.5 or Advanced Server 3.5 or later, with at least 2MB of free disk space.

Perl Script

A Perl script consists of a sequence of declarations and statements and a powerful set of keywords. Some of the keywords follow:

```
continue    goto      unless

do{}until   if        until

for         sub       while

foreach     switch
```

For more information on programming in Perl, refer to *Teach Yourself Perl in 21 Days* by Sams Publishing.

Perl scripts written under UNIX terminate lines with a line feed. In Windows NT, however, lines terminate with a carriage return and a line feed. If you are moving Perl scripts over to NT from UNIX, you might have to do some formatting.

Getting More Information About Perl

Information on Perl and extensions are available on the Internet through the World Wide Web, Usenet, or anonymous FTP.

On the Usenet, investigate the following newsgroups:

comp.lang.perl

comp.lang.perl.announce

comp.lang.perl.misc

World Wide Web:

Site: Perl Meta-FAQ:

http://www.khoros.unm.edu/staff/neilb/perl/metaFAQ/metaFAQ.html

Site: Perl 5 information, announcements, and discussion:

http://www.metronet.com/perlinfo/perl5.html

Site: Perl Man pages:

http://www.metronet.com/0/perlinfo/perl5/manual/perl.html

Site: Perl reference materials:

http://www.eecs.nwu.edu/perl/perl.html

Via anonymous FTP:

```
ftp://ftp.microsoft.com

ftp://ftp.khoros.unm.edu/pub/perl/

ftp://perl.com/pub/perl/

ftp://ftp.cs.ruu.nl/pub/perl/

ftp://ftp.funet.fi/pub/languages/perl/ports/

ftp://src.doc.ic.ac.uk/packages/perl5/
```

HTML

The *Hypertext Markup Language* (HTML) is the language of the World Wide Web. *Hypertext* refers to text containing connections to other documents.

Every web page is written in HTML. All the document formatting, clickable hyperlinks, graphical images, multimedia documents, and fill-in forms are supported through HTML commands.

A Word Internet Assistant is available on the MSDN. You can use it to create a home page and to get started on the web. You also can download it from `www.microsoft.com`.

Advanced Programming Under Windows NT 4

For the developer who designs custom operating system extensions, Microsoft provides several abstracts, APIs, and object interfaces.

Windows 95 Shell Extension

Within Windows NT 4, developers can make extensions to the Windows NT shell. This capability is through a set of interfaces that provide programmatic control over the shell through property sheets. For example, you can assign an icon to each file, add commands to the Context menu or File menu, or control many other parts of the shell.

The interface classes for shell extensions follow:

- **IShellExtInit:** Allocates an interface used to initialize a property sheet extension, a context menu extension, or a drag-and-drop handler.
- **IShellFolder:** Allocates an interface implemented by the shell and used to determine the contents of a folder.
- **IShellLink:** Allocates an interface that allows an application to create and resolve shell links.

■ **IShellPropSheetEx:** Allocates an interface that enables a property sheet handler to add or replace pages in the property sheet for a file object.

Microsoft Visual C++ 4.1 provides a sample SHELLEXT.

Distributed COM

The Distributed Component Object Model (DCOM), which formerly was known as Network OLE, extends the programming model and constructs introduced by OLE 2.0 to work seamlessly across the network.

DCOM includes features such as the following:

- **Location transparency:** An application need not know where objects it is using are located.
- **Packaging transparency:** A client application does not need to know how objects are packaged as in-process objects (in DLL), or as local or remote objects (in executable).
- **Free-threaded objects:** High-performance, scalable object services supporting simultaneous calls can be written for use by remote clients or by clients on the same machine. OLE (through the use of the RPC runtime) maintains a pool of threads to be used for incoming calls. As method calls on objects arrive from clients, they are dispatched to a thread that executes the method. Applications call CoInitializeEx(NULL, COINIT_MULTITHREADED) to establish multithreaded object concurrency for a thread—typically, during thread initialization.
- **Launch Security:** Launch Security enables only administrators to launch existing classes from a remote client.
- **Access Security:** Allows only administrators to access existing, published objects from a remote client.
- **Call Level Security:** Enforces security to operate at the per-call level between an established connection from a client to an object (server).

DCOM Advanced Application Programming Interfaces (API)

Free-Threaded API

The free-threaded API supports multithreaded concurrent access to objects. The model used to enforce concurrency is often referred to as the *apartment model.* In the apartment model, an object acquires the concurrency model from the thread in which the object was first marshalled, or from registry information as in the case of an in-proc server DLL.

- **CoInitializeEx:** Initializes COM for use by the current thread.

Activation API for Clients

The activation API exposes functions to a locally or remotely created instance of a specific class. The following list of functions and descriptions are commonly used APIs.

- **CoCreateInstanceEx:** Creates an instance of a specific class on a specific machine.
- **CoGetClassObject:** Retrieves the class object of a specific class.
- **CoGetInstanceFromFile:** Creates a new object and initializes it from a file by using IPersistFile::Load.
- **CoGetInstanceFromIStorage:** Creates a new object and initializes it from IStorage by using IPersistStorage::Load.

Call Security Interface and APIs

The COM model supports two mechanisms to secure calls. The first mechanism is similar to DCE-RPC, where an application can do its own security checking. The second mechanism is done automatically by the COM infrastructure. To use the second mechanism, applications must provide some set of information that will enable COM to make the necessary calls to secure the application's objects. The following list of functions and descriptions are commonly used APIs.

- **CoInitializeSecurity:** Initializes the security layer.
- **CoQueryAuthenticationServices:** Retrieves a list of the authentication services registered when the process invoked CoRegisterAuthenticationServices.
- **CoRegisterAuthenticationServices:** Establishes the list of authentication services that DCOM uses to authenticate incoming calls.
- **IClientSecurity:** Enables the client to control the security on calls to individual interfaces.
- **IServerSecurity:** Enables the server to retrieve security information about a call and to impersonate the call.

A couple DCOM examples are included with Win32 SDK.

OLECNFG

OLECNFG is used by the remote activation Registry configuration tool. The tool sets and creates all new Registry keys with the default Registry access control list (ACL). An ACL controls access to anything to which it is attached. Almost every entity that has a name can be configured to employ security. The ACLs for security keys can be modified manually by using regedt32.

If the tool runs without any parameters, it displays the current value for the global activation fields. The activation fields are EnableNetworkOLE, DefaultLaunchPermission, DefaultAccess Permission, and LegacyAuthenticationLevel.

Writing Custom Server Applications Under Windows NT

Complexity increases as an application is extended to include a customer server component across a network. The Win32 API offers full control over process and thread synchronization in either a console or network service capacity. In addition, the Win32 API provides application logging and real-time performance monitoring capabilities. Along with the system utilities provided within Windows NT, the Win32 API enables developers to implement robust and supportable as well as complex applications. Furthermore, the Win32 API is a platform-independent API that works on RISC, ALPHA, MIPS, and other platforms.

Because so many resources are available within Windows NT, you need to know a little about each resource type before you can design the application architecture. This section briefly explains the common resources that should be considered, if not used, in your Win32 application. Along with this explanation is a list of the most common functions and sample code using these functions.

Processes

The Win32 API provides support for creating, controlling, prioritizing, and synchronizing Windows NT processes. You can control the priority of the child process as well as its child threads. The following functions are the common functions used to control a Windows NT process:

- **CreateProcess:** Creates a new process and its primary thread. The new process executes the specified executable file.
- **ExitProcess:** Ends a process and all its threads.
- **GetPriorityClass:** Returns the priority class for the specified process.
- **SetPriorityClass:** Controls the priority of a class as scheduled by the Windows NT operating system.

In the case of manipulating a process priority, if no priority is specified, Windows NT uses a default priority.

Threads

Threads are very similar to processes, but they allow in some architectures more programmatic control than a process. The following functions commonly are used to control a Windows NT thread:

- **CreateRemoteThread:** Creates a thread that runs in the address space of another process.
- **CreateThread:** Creates a thread to execute within the address space of the calling process.

- ■ **ExitThread:** Terminates a thread.
- ■ **GetThreadPriority:** Returns the priority value for the specified thread.
- ■ **ResumeThread:** Decrements a thread's suspend count. When the suspend count is decremented to 0, the execution of the thread is resumed.
- ■ **SetThreadPriority:** Sets the priority value for the specified thread.
- ■ **Sleep:** Suspends the execution of the current thread for a specified interval.
- ■ **SleepEx:** Causes the current thread to enter a wait state until the specified interval of time has passed or until an I/O completion callback function is called.
- ■ **SuspendThread:** Suspends the specified thread.
- ■ **TerminateThread:** Terminates a thread.

Synchronization

The Win32 API provides several ways of enforcing mutual exclusion and synchronization. If you are writing a multithreaded process, you should be familiar with the following functions:

- ■ **CreateEvent:** Creates a named or unnamed event object.
- ■ **CreateMutex:** Creates a named or unnamed mutex object.
- ■ **CreateSemaphore:** Creates a named or unnamed semaphore object.
- ■ **ReleaseMutex:** Releases ownership of the specified mutex object.
- ■ **ReleaseSemaphore:** Increases the count of the specified semaphore object by a specified amount.
- ■ **ResetEvent:** Sets the state of the specified event object to `nonsignaled`.
- ■ **SetEvent:** Sets the state of the specified event object to `signaled`.
- ■ **WaitForMultipleObjects:** When anyone or all of the specified objects are in the signaled state or when the time-out interval elapses, this function fires.
- ■ **WaitForSingleObject:** Specifies that the function returns when the specified object is in the signaled state or when the time-out interval elapses.

Several examples of processes, threads, and events are included as sample code within Microsoft Visual C++ 2.x or 4.x.

Registry

Any server application that will run as a Windows NT service will need to make extensive use of the Windows Registry. The Registry functions support accessing the various keys and values located within it.

Server information and data for all Windows NT services are stored in the Registry in the following section:

```
HKEY_LOCAL_MACHINE\System\CurrentControlSet\Services
```

The following functions are used most frequently to access the Windows Registry:

- **RegConnectRegistry:** Establishes a connection to a predefined Registry handle on another computer.
- **RegCreateKeyEx:** Creates the specified key.
- **RegOpenKeyEx:** Opens the specified key.
- **RegQueryValueEx:** Retrieves the type and data for a specified value name associated with an open Registry key.
- **RegSetValueEx:** Sets the value associated with the specified key.

An example that uses the Registry is located in Microsoft Visual C++ 2.x or 4.x.

Event Log

Event logging in Windows NT provides a standard, centralized way for applications to record important software and hardware events. Using the Event log and functions removes the need to develop a similar logging mechanism for your Win32 application. Writing this type of mechanism can sometimes become complex in multithreaded, multiprocess application development.

The Event Viewer provides a standard user interface for viewing the logs and a programming interface for examining the logs. The more commonly used calls follow:

- **DeregisterEventSource:** Closes a handle returned by the RegisterEventSource.
- **RegisterEventSource:** Returns a handle that can be used with the ReportEvent function to log an event.
- **ReportEvent:** Writes an entry at the end of the specified Event log.

Windows NT Services

A service is an executable object installed in a Registry database maintained by the Service Control Manager (SCM) to provide a unified and secure means of controlling services. Each machine running Windows NT has a Service Control Manager process started by the system at startup. The Service Control Manager is an RPC server.

The functions in the Win32 API that access an SCM are provided through RPC so that service configuration and service control processes can manipulate services on a remote machine.

These functions are used to register and affect your application as an NT service:

- **CreateService:** Creates a service object and adds it to the specified Service Control Manager database.
- **RegisterServiceCtrlHandler:** Registers a function to handle service control requests for a service.
- **SetServiceStatus:** Updates the Service Control Manager's status information for the calling service.

A sample service is provided in Microsoft Visual C++ 2.x or 4.0.

Performance Monitor

Windows NT introduces the concepts of performance objects and counters, which enable you to apply performance monitoring to your application. Performance objects are a collection of counters used to measure attributes and activity in a system at a process or even more granular level.

The Windows NT Perfmon utility is a general-purpose monitor tool that is extensible and independent of other counters in the system. This enables developers to expose performance counters in their own applications for viewing locally or remotely. These are called *extended objects* rather than *system objects*, which are part of the operating system itself.

Several structures are provided with Win32 to make use of performance counters and object types:

- **PERF_COUNTER_DEFINITION:** Describes a performance counter.
- **PERF_DATA_BLOCK:** Contains the performance data provided by the RegQueryValueEx function.
- **PERF_INSTANCE_DEFINITION:** Contains the instance-specific information for a block of performance data.
- **PERF_OBJECT_TYPE:** Describes the object-specific performance information.

You can find an example on how to program performance objects in the NT Resource Kit (MSDN).

Summary

Programming for Windows NT can be both exciting and intimidating. Microsoft provides a comprehensive set of products to make the burden inviting.

Windows NT is a powerful operating system. To harness its power, you first need to harness the Win32 API. The Win32 API and its extensions provide a comprehensive set of functions to fully control Windows NT and its resources. These functions enable a developer to implement whatever solution the project requirements might call for. Platform-independent development has never been so extensive and easy.

Microsoft Language products give developers what they need to make application development for Windows NT a controllable and efficient work effort. The Microsoft Developers Studio manages the entire development through an extensive project and source management that integrates a debugging environment, help system, and editing environment all into the same user interface.

The utilities provided with Windows NT complement the development effort with a set of tools to manage application logging and real-time monitoring of system resources.

Introducing Microsoft Cluster Server

by Terry Ogletree

IN THIS CHAPTER

CHAPTER 33

Minimizing downtime in a computer network has always been a high priority for most network administrators. This is even more true today as more businesses connect private intranets to the Internet and computing is becoming a 24-hour global business. Protecting each component of the network, from communications lines to servers to disk storage, is necessary since the failure of any one component in the network could render resources unavailable to the user.

RAID (Redundant Array of Inexpensive Disks) disk subsystems can provide fault-tolerant data storage, and backup data paths can be used to provide a continuous connection to the Internet. Still, a single server can be a single point of failure. It doesn't matter if the data is stored on mirrored disks or a fault-tolerant stripe set if the server that is used to access that data isn't functioning. *Clustering* is the technology that is used to remedy this part of the problem. Clustering two Windows NT Servers lets both servers connect to a shared disk system in a coordinated manner so that if one server fails, the other can take over and continue to provide access to the resources. In this first release of Microsoft's Cluster Server, only two-node clusters are supported (each member server is often referred to as a *node* in the cluster). Support for clusters with more than two nodes is expected to be available in the next major release of the clustering software. This chapter gives you a brief overview of the installation process to create a two-node cluster and how to use the Cluster Administrator tool to configure resources and failover groups. First, however, we'll cover the benefits of clustering and see what constitutes a *resource* that can be supported by clustering.

Understanding the Benefits of Clustering

Clustering is not a total solution to providing computer uptime. However, it is a very good compromise. For a fraction of the cost of using a nonstop fault-tolerant computer (such as a Tandem), you can achieve an extremely high amount of reliable access to your network's resources. Here are some of the benefits you will get from using Windows NT in a clustered format:

- High availability with failover capability
- A single resource server name for resources offered by multiple computers
- Maximum use of all members of a cluster; no member needs to be in "stand-by" mode
- Scalability in that with future versions of Microsoft Cluster Server, you will be able to add more than two nodes to the cluster

A cluster appears to the network as a single system. Users don't have to be concerned with the identity of either of the computers involved in the cluster. A *cluster name* is used when browsing for shares, and users have a single point of departure to select resources from all computers active in the cluster.

When one member of the cluster fails for any reason, the cluster-monitoring software detects the failure and, provided it has been configured to do so, restarts the resource on another server in the cluster that has the ability to access the same data storage. When a server is brought back online, the cluster-monitoring software can automatically switch the resource back over to its original server, or the administrator can perform this function manually at a convenient time.

The downside of this is that you don't have *process failover*. If a user's session is reconnected to another server member of the cluster, the resources that the process was using (such as file shares) can be failed over, and the user can restart the application to access the failed-over resources. Unless an application is specifically written to be cluster-aware and transaction-oriented, users of some types of applications will notice that the failover has occurred.

For the purposes of this chapter, the term *failover* means restarting a process on another server when the original server fails. Depending on the particular application and how closely it is written to be integrated with the clustering software, users may barely notice that anything has happened, or they might be inconvenienced by having to restart a program after the clustering software reconnects their session to the remaining cluster node.

You can make the best use of cluster members by running applications on both servers and configuring the resources on each server to fail over to the other server in case of a problem. When a failover occurs, the remaining cluster member might be under a strain to support all the concurrent users, but you will still be able to provide resources to your client while you make repairs to the failed server. The alternative is to have one server set up to be the failover server and to use its capacity on the network until a failover occurs. This would be best applied in situations where performance is a critical factor.

The benefits of clustering are best seen in applications that are written to be cluster-aware—those that are written using the cluster APIs from Microsoft that are available in the Microsoft Platform SDK. However, not all BackOffice products are written this way. The standard editions of Microsoft Exchange Server (5.0) and Microsoft SQL Server (6.5) aren't cluster-aware, and Microsoft doesn't support setting them up as failover resources. However, Enterprise versions of both products will be released that will take advantage of clustering mechanisms to provide true failover capabilities.

Several other BackOffice components are not being migrated to take advantage of clustering due to their own inherent backup mechanisms. For example, failover won't be supported for a domain controller server since backup domain controllers already exist for that purpose. The Windows Internet Naming Service (WINS) already provides for backup WINS servers. Other components that are not cluster aware include Microsoft SNA Server, Microsoft Proxy Server, and Microsoft Systems Management Server (SMS).

Cluster Architecture

Some third-party clustering solutions are implemented in both hardware and software. Microsoft clustering is implemented only in software. The main benefit to be derived from this approach is that you don't have to purchase specialized additional hardware to connect the cluster members. Instead, members in an MSCS cluster need only an industry-standard shared SCSI bus and standard network connections to communicate (see Figure 33.1). For performance and security reasons, the best configuration is to use a separate network adapter on each computer for the cluster connection rather than using the adapter that connects the computers to the enterprise network.

33

INTRODUCING
MICROSOFT
CLUSTER SERVER

FIGURE 33.1.

A cluster consists of two Windows NT Servers connected by a private network card and a shared SCSI bus.

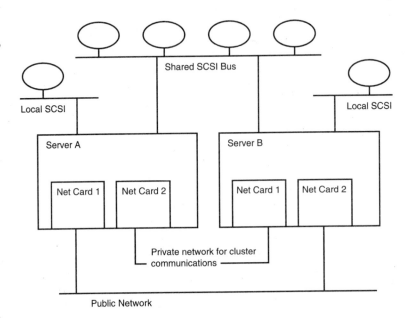

The basic components of the clustering software are the Cluster Service and the resource monitors. Resource monitors are implemented by Dynamic Link Libraries (DLLs) and are the interface to resources managed by the cluster. The Cluster Service communicates with the resource monitors to keep track of resources, failing them over to the other cluster member when necessary. The Cluster Service also communicates with the other cluster node to control cluster activity.

Each node in the cluster maintains a database that keeps track of the functioning of the cluster and its resources. When failover occurs, data stored in the cluster database is used by the remaining member to determine which resources need to be started, and on which node. When changes to the database occur, messages are sent to other nodes so that all databases can remain consistent. The log file, on the quorum disk (see "The Quorum Resource" later in this chapter), is used to record database changes to allow nodes coming online to be synchronized with the current database.

Communication between cluster nodes can occur on either of the network adapters installed in each server. The private network connection is intended to provide fast access between the servers, and also so that more than one connection will be available as a redundant safeguard. The User Datagram Protocol (UDP) is used for most messaging (such as the heartbeat packets and acknowledgments), and Remote Procedure Calls (RPC) are used for some cluster activities.

Communication between the Cluster Service and the resource monitors is accomplished using Interprocess Communications (IPC), since they each reside on the same computer. Other software components are involved, such as the Cluster Administrator program, which is used by the administrator to configure cluster activities, but the Cluster Resource and the resource monitors provide the most basic functionality of the cluster.

Understanding Resources and Virtual Servers

A file share offered by a network server is a resource to its users. So is a print share. Database applications and other types of resources can also be made available by a server. These types of computing resources are what the cluster software is designed to monitor and fail over in the case of failure. Here are the basic types of resources that MSCS (Microsoft Cluster Server) offers as built-in structures:

- DHCP Server: A DHCP service provided by using Microsoft's DHCP server in a clustered environment.

- Distributed Transaction Coordinator: A transaction-processing service provided by Microsoft's Distributed Transaction Coordinator in a clustered environment.

- File share: Regular file services that a server offers to clients.

- Generic application: A regular application that wasn't written to be *cluster-aware*. The administrator might have to write a script file for the cluster software to use in failing over resources of this type.

- Generic service: Services such as authentication that are normally provided by Windows NT.

- IIS virtual root: Internet Information Server (IIS) Web services, such as WWW and FTP.

- IP address: Services requiring a specific IP address (other than IIS virtual root).

- Microsoft message: A queue server. A message queuing service provided by Microsoft's Message Queue Server in a clustered environment.

- Network name: Similar to the IP address resource type, but this type of resource uses a unique computer name to provide a network service.

- Physical disk: Resources requiring disk access from disks that reside on the cluster's shared SCSI bus.

- Print spooler: A print-queuing service for printers that reside on the network.

- Time service: This resource type provides time synchronization between cluster server members.

As you can see from this list, a database application can be considered a resource when it's provided to the network by the cluster software. In this type of example, the actual database files are stored on disks connected to the shared SCSI bus and the database application itself is installed on both servers in the cluster. Either server will be able to run the application and access the shared data, although only one server will be able to access the data at any given time.

Some resources, such as a Web server, have an IP address (and possibly a unique network name) associated with them. Resources of this type are called *virtual servers*. They are virtual because they can be offered by one or more cluster server members to the network. Although an IP address is usually associated with a particular computer, virtual server resources can be failed over to another server and retain the same IP address for the service. Virtual servers eliminate the need to configure client software to use multiple IP addresses to locate information that can be offered by more than one server in the network.

Dynamic link libraries (DLLs) are used to support each type of resource in the cluster, and you can use the Microsoft Platform SDK to create custom resource types. Since these DLLs are usually run using a system account, you should be sure that any custom DLLs have been tested for integrity and safety.

Resource States

When the cluster software is up and running, each resource will be in one of the following states:

- Offline: This means that the resource is unavailable on this node. For example, when a disk resource is online on a cluster member, it is offline on the other cluster members because a physical disk resource can be available to only one cluster member at a time.

- Offline pending: This indicates that the resource was online and is now in the process of being taken offline. It is not available for new connections by clients at this time.

- Online pending: This resource state indicates that a resource that was offline is now being brought online by the cluster software. This doesn't guarantee that it will succeed and finally become available, only that the cluster software is trying to start it.

- Failed: This state means that the cluster software wasn't available to bring the resource online within the timeout period allowed. You should examine any application log files and the system Event Viewer logs to troubleshoot the cause of failure.

- Online: The resource is online when it is available for use by clients of the cluster.

You can use the Cluster Administrator to monitor the state of a particular resource at any time. When one of the cluster members fails and resources are taken offline and brought back online again on the remaining cluster member, it is the quorum disk that is used to record changes in resource states so that when the other server returns to the cluster, it can be updated.

The Quorum Resource

The quorum resource was added to clustering to help resolve issues that occur when network communications between cluster members become faulty and each node could try to project itself onto the network as the remaining cluster member. For example, if Node A in a two-node cluster lost contact with Node B in that cluster, it would believe that Node B had failed and would attempt to start any resources that should be failed over. After starting the resources, it would make them available on the network. But if Node B hasn't failed, it will assume the same and also try to take control of any resources it thinks have failed on Node A. Confusion would run rampant throughout the network, because clients couldn't make consistent connections to a resource.

Ownership of the quorum resource is what is used as a tie-breaker in these situations. The quorum resource in this release of MSCS is a disk that is on the shared SCSI bus that both cluster members can see. When communication breaks down between cluster members, the member that currently has the quorum disk online is the member that continues as the cluster. The other member recognizes that it doesn't have the quorum disk, and can't acquire ownership of it, and gracefully leaves the cluster.

When you install the cluster node on the first member of a cluster, you designate the quorum resource to *form* a cluster. When you add a node to the cluster, you join the cluster, and you don't have to designate a quorum resource, because one already exists for the cluster.

The quorum disk is also used as the storage medium for the cluster log file. This file is used for recording changes to the state of the cluster when communication between the cluster members fails. The cluster log file stored on the quorum resource is necessary for the cluster to operate. If the log file becomes unusable, the cluster won't start until you designate a new quorum resource so that the file can be re-created. After you designate the new resource, you must stop and restart the cluster service on the node that currently owns the resource. Alternatively, you can reboot both servers in the cluster.

Grouping Resources to Control Dependencies

When you run a database application, the application needs to access data storage on a physical disk device. For this reason, you can say that the database application is dependent on the physical disk resource in order to run.

Clustering software needs to be aware of such dependencies so that it can restart resources in the correct order if a failover occurs. It would do no good for the cluster software to attempt to make available a database application if the underlying disk storage prevented the users from accessing the data.

MSCS uses resource groups to group dependent resources and allow you to prioritize them in the startup order necessary for the particular resource types. There are three important points to remember about resources:

- A particular resource can belong to only one group.
- Each resource group can be offered by only one cluster server member at a time.
- All resources in a group must reside on the same server.

Based on these principles, if you maintain several SQL databases on the same physical disk (or stripe set or other RAID subsystem disk), all of those SQL databases will have to be placed into the same resource group.

Clients connect to a cluster service using a cluster name, not the computer name of the cluster server member that currently has the service online. For this reason, you must not give any two resources the same name, even if they are available on separate cluster members. The cluster software doesn't *load-balance* services between the two cluster server members. This doesn't mean that you can't offer the same *type* of resource, using a different name, from both servers at the same time. For example, you could offer a word processing application from Server A and call it WORDA, and offer the same application software from Server B, calling the service WORDB.

> **TIP**
>
> You aren't limited to using resource groups for applications and resources that have dependencies. You can also use them for administrative convenience. For example, an administrator might choose to group resources by organizational function instead, to make administrative chores easier.

Choosing Hardware for Clustered Configurations

Microsoft maintains a Hardware Compatibility List (HCL) for Windows NT Server. It also has another HCL for hardware that has been certified to be suitable for use in MSCS Windows NT clusters. You can find HCLs for Windows NT products at `http://www.microsoft.com/hwtest/hcl/`.

MSCS doesn't require any special hardware components from any particular manufacturer in order to function. Standard off-the-shelf components are used. However, because of the intricate nature of the cluster software and its monitoring and messaging functions, you would be best off using hardware components that are on the HCL.

For an MSCS cluster, you will need two Pentium-class servers that run at a speed of at least 90Mz. You can also use two RISC computers. The only one supported at this time is the Alpha chip from Digital Equipment Corporation. Each server must be of the same architecture. You can't have an Alpha- and an Intel-based server in the same cluster. You can, however, have Alpha or Intel clusters on the same network. Each server will have to have a PCI bus and at least 64MB of RAM, although you will probably need more than that to run a large database or other enterprise application that is worth the clustering effort.

For storage purposes, you will need to have at least one external, shared SCSI bus with enough disk storage attached to provide for the applications you will cluster. Each server will also need a local disk (500MB or larger) that is not on the shared SCSI bus to use as a boot disk.

Each server will require two network cards. One will connect the server to the public network so that clients can access the cluster, and the other will be connected to the other cluster server member to create a private network for cluster communications between the cluster members.

Finally, you will have to install Windows NT Server 4.0 on each server along with the MSCS software.

You should consider using a fault-tolerant disk subsystem on the shared SCSI bus, such as a RAID system. The clustering software will make the data available to the appropriate cluster member only if it can access it. So, to prevent a single point of failure in the cluster, all important shared data should be on a fault-tolerant disk system of some type.

Another important factor to consider when trying to prevent downtime is an uninterruptible power supply. More-powerful versions of these can be used to keep systems up and running during power outages. Inexpensive versions can be used to give a server time for an orderly shutdown, thus protecting data from corruption.

Making Data Available to Both Cluster Nodes with the Shared SCSI Bus

The clustering software mediates the ownership of the disk resources between nodes in the cluster. For this reason, these types of cluster resources must be on a shared bus so that either member can access them via the hardware interface. The SCSI bus is chosen for clustering purposes because of its reliability and performance considerations.

Resources in an NT cluster are considered to be unshared. In other words, only one node can own them at a time. In some other versions of clustering software, such as OpenVMS, a node that has a disk attached to it can offer the disk for mounting on multiple systems and mediate the different nodes' access to the disk using locking software mechanisms. MSCS doesn't support a distributed lock manager, which would be necessary for this type of access, so resources aren't shared. This is called the *shared-nothing* approach to clustering.

Since the cluster log file and the cluster database need to be available to both nodes, they can't reside on a disk that is local to either system, but must be on the shared SCSI bus. When one node in the cluster fails, the remaining node can proceed with the failover process, taking control of any disks that reside on the shared bus. When the failed cluster member returns to the cluster, it can read the cluster log file from the quorum disk to update its cluster database.

Improper termination on the SCSI bus can cause problems when you're implementing clustering. Be sure that no device in the SCSI chain has internal termination turned on. Also be sure to use the Disk Administrator to assign disk drive letters before installing the clustering software (as described in the later section "Installing Microsoft Cluster Server"), using the same drive letters for each disk on both of the cluster nodes.

The System Disk Can't Be Shared

Each server member of the cluster must have a separate system disk, and it can't reside on the shared SCSI bus. You can still use hardware RAID techniques to provide additional protection for each node's system disk, but these disks must be on separate controllers, private to each computer. Also, even though it's a good idea from a performance standpoint to put the paging file on a separate disk from the system files or application files, you can't use disks on the shared SCSI bus for paging files.

Using RAID on the Shared SCSI Bus

Although clustering will help you survive most hardware failures that involve the CPU and other board-level components, it won't do you any good at all if the data on your disk drives becomes unavailable. The shared SCSI bus gives both nodes in the cluster the ability to take control of a disk and serve the data to clients. However, it doesn't provide any fault tolerance for those disk drives. Thus, if you don't take precautions to keep your data safe, this will present a single point of failure in your system.

RAID techniques can be used to provide the necessary protection for your data. You can use disk mirroring (RAID level 1) or disk striping with parity (RAID level 5). Although Windows NT can provide both of these RAID levels, which you can configure by using the Disk Administrator, you will find that there is one disk that you can't use Windows NT itself to protect: the system disk. Because Windows NT Server must be up and running in order to run the software drivers necessary to provide RAID functions, the mirroring capability isn't present at boot time.

However, you can use hardware-level RAID subsystems on each computer's system boot disk and on the disks that reside on the shared SCSI bus. By providing this extra layer of protection in a way that is abstracted from the operating system, you can improve performance (with the hardware controllers performing the RAID work) while you provide fault tolerance at the same time. On any large system that will support important data (such as a large SQL database), such fault-tolerant measures will cost almost nothing compared to the cost of reloading a database from backup tapes in case of a major disaster.

Cluster Network Communications

Cluster members exchange messages during normal processing for many purposes. First, at regular intervals, a heartbeat message is sent to other members so they can track which nodes are still active in the cluster. Failure to receive this message from another node is what leads to a failover in the cluster. Second, the cluster members exchange messages concerning the state of resources, such as when the administrator performs a manual failover or failback of a resource group. Applications that are written to be cluster-aware can also exchange messages across this channel.

Determining Which Servers to Cluster

You must be running Windows NT Server (version 4.0 or above) to create an NT cluster using MSCS. The cluster members must both be in the same domain, and they can be primary or backup domain controllers. Note, however, that even though you can cluster a PDC, you can't designate both members of the cluster to be PDCs, because only one primary domain controller can exist in an NT network for any particular domain, and because both server members must belong to the same domain. You can, however, cluster a PDC with a BDC or cluster two BDCs together.

Because the purpose of having a BDC is to distribute the security database (SAM) to provide redundancy and to allow for the distribution of logon processing, it stands to reason that you would want to separate two domain controllers in the network rather than closely couple them in a cluster. Domain controllers would benefit little from a cluster when it comes to the work they do related to maintaining the domain database. Domain controllers already have a failover capacity built into them so that both can provide logon processing, and you can always promote a BDC to be the new PDC if necessary.

Installing Microsoft Cluster Server

You should plan ahead for the installation process and not consider it a simple upgrade to the operating system. For example, if you have users connecting to an SQL database that will now reside on a clustered system, you will need to plan to configure each client to locate the required resources using the new cluster name rather than the previous server names that have been used. Here are some other things you should take care of before installation:

■ Configure any disks and associated controller or subsystem hardware ahead of time. If you're going to use controller-based striped or mirrored sets, create those before you begin installing the cluster software. Some controllers let you connect a dumb terminal to a port for configuration, and others let you access the system using a graphical interface under Windows operating systems.

> **CAUTION**
>
> Perform disk maintenance with the shared SCSI drive attached to only one booted Windows NT computer. Do not boot both computers at the same time running Windows NT (or any other operating system that recognizes the SCSI bus) and try to access the disks at the same time.

■ Use the SCSI setup software to assign SCSI IDs to the devices on the bus, as well as to each server host that will be attached to the bus. Do not assign the same ID to both servers, because both will be active on the bus at the same time. For example, assign 6 to the first server and 7 to the second.

■ Disable the boot-time reset feature on each SCSI controller.

■ Connect both servers to the public network.

■ Connect both servers in a private network using a hub or a crossover cable.

■ Install Windows NT Server 4.0 on each server. Install the latest service pack (at least Service Pack 3) on each server.

■ Be sure that both computers are members of the same domain, not a workgroup. If they aren't, use an administrator-level password to bring them into the domain during installation, or use the Server Manager administrative tool to create a computer account in the domain for each server.

■ Decide ahead of time on a name to use for the cluster. It must be a unique NetBIOS name. That means that it can't be the same name that is already used as a computer or resource name on the network.

■ Decide on the static IP addresses that you will use for each node's network adapters. You can't use DHCP to assign IP information to members of the cluster. Remember that each node has two adapters, so each node will require two IP addresses.

After you have prepared the disk subsystem and configured the remaining hardware, and after you have installed Windows NT Server 4.0 and the latest service pack, you can proceed to install MSCS on the two servers.

It's important to carefully follow directions when performing the installation to avoid causing problems with disks on the shared SCSI bus. Until the clustering software is installed and operating on both servers, each can potentially access data stored on any disk on the bus, and the uncoordinated access of both servers can corrupt files and disk structures.

Starting the Installation

The first thing you need to do in order to begin the installation is connect both servers to the shared SCSI bus. The order in which you then boot the servers and install the clustering software is outlined in the following steps:

1. Boot the first server, but then stop it at the boot screen (by pressing the spacebar).

2. Boot the second server into Windows NT Server and use the Disk Administrator tool to assign drive letters to the disks on the shared SCSI bus.

3. Shut down the second computer (but don't power it off) after you have finished making adjustments using the Disk Administrator, and pause it at the boot menu using the spacebar.

4. Boot the first computer that has been paused at the boot screen.

5. Use the Disk Administrator to assign identical drive letters to the corresponding disks on the first server that you assigned drive letters to.

6. Leaving one server at the boot menu, log into the other (which is booted into Windows NT Server) using the administrator-level domain account you have decided to use for the installation. Begin the setup by running the program SETUP.EXE from the appropriate directory (for example, \I386 or \Alpha) on the cluster software CD or from a network share on which you have copied the source files.

7. You are prompted to form a new cluster or to join an existing cluster. For the first installation, enter the name you have decided to use for the cluster in the appropriate field, and choose to form a new cluster.

8. You will be given the option of placing the cluster software's files into the default installation directory (\Cluster, directly under the Windows NT installation directory), or you can choose to browse and select a different directory.

9. The next window will display the SCSI adapters that are connected to the computer. You should select any adapters that aren't shared with the other node and use the Remove button to move them out of the list of shared devices.

   Here you should also select one of the disks on a shared SCSI bus that will be designated as the quorum device.

10. The next setup window will display a list of the network adapters installed in the system. You can select the adapter that will be used for the private network between the two cluster nodes.

11. Finally, the last window prompts you to enter the IP address you are assigning to the cluster. This must be a static IP address, not a dynamic address from a DHCP server. Enter the correct subnet mask for this address. Click the Finish button to complete the process.

Bringing the Second Node into the Cluster

When you install the clustering software on the first node, you create a cluster. When you install the software on the second node, you will join a cluster.

To continue the process, leave the first node booted into Windows NT and go ahead and boot the second node. Follow these steps:

1. After the second node has booted, log into it using the same domain account you used to install MSCS on the first node.

2. Run the MSCS Setup program.

3. When the dialog box appears asking if you want to create a cluster or join a cluster, enter the name of the cluster you have already created, and then click Join.

4. Another dialog box will allow you to select the path for the cluster files.

5. After you have given the installation path, click the Finish button.

You have now finished installing MSCS. The next step you should take is to verify that the cluster software is operating properly by bringing up the Cluster Administrator program. From there you can begin to create resources and resource groups so that you can begin to use the cluster for production work.

Running the Cluster Administrator from Other Network Nodes

True to the distributed nature of a modern operating system such as Windows NT Server, you don't have to sit at the console of a cluster member in order to perform management tasks on the cluster. You can install the Cluster Administrator utility on other nodes in your network and monitor the cluster from different locations.

Even though MSCS runs only on Windows NT Server, you can run the Cluster Administrator not only on member servers in your network, but also on Windows NT Workstation nodes. Workstation can't partake of the cluster as a member node, but you can run the Cluster

Administrator on that platform with no problems. Before installing the software on other network nodes, be sure that the workstation or member server has been updated to Windows NT 4.0 Service Pack 3 first.

The installation process is simple: Run the Setup program from the MSCS CD. The first dialog box will give you the option of installing the Cluster Administrator or installing the clustering software. Choose to install the Cluster Administrator.

Cluster Administration

You use the Cluster Administrator utility to create resource groups and to set failover policies for resources. You also can use it to move resources from one node to another by performing a manual failover.

To start the Cluster Administrator, choose Start, Programs, Administrative Tools, Cluster Administrator. You will be prompted to enter the name or IP address of the cluster you want to administer. This is required because you can use the Cluster Administrator to administer more than one cluster residing on your network. Because you can install the Cluster Administrator on NT Workstations and other member servers in the network, you can remotely administer several clusters or divide administrative tasks among users in the network.

The Cluster Administrator window looks very similar to a directory display that you would see when using Microsoft Explorer. On the left is a window that lists one or more clusters to which you have attached the Cluster Administrator, along with expandable lists of resources, groups, nodes, and other entities related to the cluster. On the right side of the display are details about the entities selected from the other display.

The File menu at the top left of the Cluster Administrator window is used for many functions that you will carry out to perform the initial setup of resources and groups for the cluster. Wizards help make the configuration process more understandable.

Creating Resources and Resource Groups

You use the Cluster Administrator to create resource groups, and then you create the resources to put into those groups. The New Group Wizard will walk you through the process of creating the group, and the New Resource Wizard will help you create resources for those groups.

Using the New Group Wizard

To run the New Group Wizard, select File, New, Group. The wizard will prompt you to enter the following:

- The group name
- A description of the group
- A preferred node for the group

The preferred node for the group is the one that you want the resource group to execute during normal processing. Although you can set up resource groups to be able to fail over to either node in the cluster, the preferred node is the one on which you want the resource group to execute most of the time.

After you specify the preferred node, you can specify whether or not the resource group should fail back to preferred node after a failover. You might want to think about this one. For example, if the application you're running on the cluster causes clients to have to reconnect after a failover and restart processes (and perhaps re-enter data that was lost), you might want to have control over the failback process.

Why? Consider a situation in which Server A crashes and resources fail over to the other cluster member. The users are put through one session of having to reconnect and restart their processes. Then Server A automatically reboots a few minutes later. If the resource groups are set up to fail back, the users would get another unexpected interruption. Instead, after a failover, the administrator should control the failback process manually so that he can plan when it should happen and warn the users.

This gist of this is that whether or not you choose a preferred node, you can always use the Cluster Administrator to initiate a manual failover to move resource groups to any node in the cluster when you wish to do so.

Bringing a Group Online

After you have created a new group, you can create the resources to be put into the group. However, you must first bring the group online before you can add resources to it. By default, when you create a new group, it is offline. To bring a group online, highlight the group and select File, Bring Online.

Using the New Resource Wizard

To run the New Resource Wizard, select File, New, Resource. The prompts that you will receive from the wizard will depend on the type of resource you create. Here are some things that are common to most resources:

- Resource name: This must be a unique name in the cluster. You can't use the same resource on another node in the cluster. Also, remember that a resource can be a member of only one resource group.
- Resource type: See the earlier section "Understanding Resources and Virtual Servers" to determine what type of resource you will create.
- Name of resource group: This is the name of the group to which you will add the resource.
- Reference monitor preference: If you have an application that you're offering as a resource, and it is giving you problems, you should select the check box Run this resource in a separate resource monitor to make the troubleshooting process easier. Otherwise, the cluster software runs a single resource monitor for up to 15 resources.

■ Possible owners lists: Each resource you create must have at least one owner in the list of possible owners. For this list, you should specify each node in the cluster that the resource is capable of being run on. The failover process will allow resources to be failed over only to nodes that are listed in the possible owners list. If you list only one node here, the resource will not fail over to the other cluster node when this node fails.

■ Resource dependencies: If you're creating a resource and adding it to a resource group that already has resources, you will be prompted to indicate any dependencies within the group as you add new resources. Keep in mind that the order in which resources are placed online and taken offline is specified by the dependency order you establish.

Some resource types require other resources in order to run. For example, a file share resource needs to have a physical disk resource configured in the same group and is dependent on that physical disk resource starting before it does. Of the resource types that are supplied with the cluster software, the following types do not have any dependencies on other resources, by default:

■ Fault-tolerant disk set

■ Generic service

■ Physical disk

■ TCP/IP address

■ Time service

The following resource types are dependent on other resources in order to run:

■ File share: You need to specify a dependent physical disk or fault-tolerant disk set resource that contains the files offered by the file share.

■ IIS virtual root: This type of resource also needs to have a physical disk or fault-tolerant disk set associated with it. Additionally, you will need to configure a TCP/IP address for this type of resource.

■ Network name: This type of resource is dependent on a TCP/IP address.

■ Print spooler: This resource type needs a physical disk or fault-tolerant disk set, along with a network name resource.

The last dialog box that the New Resource Wizard will display will prompt you to enter IP address information. If your resource depends on an IP address for its functioning, you will need to supply information here for a static IP address for the resource. You can't use IP addresses or configuration information supplied by a DHCP server for this purpose.

For each network adapter that the resource will be offered on, you will need to supply a static IP address and the correct subnet mask for that address.

Adding Fault-Tolerant Disk Sets

Although you use the Disk Administrator to set up fault-tolerant disk sets, you must still make them known as a resource in the cluster.

Run the New Resource Wizard by selecting File, New, Resource. When you're prompted for the resource type, select Fault-Tolerant Disk Set.

When adding a fault-tolerant disk set to the cluster database as a resource, you don't have to specify the underlying details of the disk set. The cluster software will read the signature placed on the set by the Disk Administrator and use the information it finds to properly configure the resource.

Adding Cluster File Shares

Creating a file share to be offered as a cluster resource is similar to the usual method used to create file shares in Windows NT. When running the New Resource Wizard, you should select File Share as the resource type. The wizard will prompt you for a name for the share, the path, and the maximum number of users who can connect to the share at the same time.

Configuring Generic Applications and Services

A generic application is an application that is not cluster-aware. These types of applications don't communicate across the cluster's private network. Instead, a generic application runs on a cluster in the same way it runs on a single computer.

When you set up a generic application, the New Resource Wizard will ask you to enter the command line that is needed to start the application, as well as a path for a default directory to be used when the application runs.

If the generic application that you're setting up as a resource is one that users will connect to and use interactively, you should select the check box labeled Allow application to interact with desktop. If the application isn't used interactively by users, don't select this check box.

You can also add a service that runs under Windows NT as a resource in the cluster. When you run the New Resource Wizard, select Generic Service for the resource type. You will need to enter the exact name of the service as it appears when you view it using the Services applet in the Control Panel. You don't have to fill in the Command line field unless you need to supply command-line startup parameters for the service.

Resources for generic applications and generic services aren't automatically made available (online) to the cluster as are programs that are cluster-aware. You will need to use the Cluster Administrator to bring the application or service online the first time. After that, you can use the regular failover and failback capabilities of the cluster software to make the resources available to users.

Adding IIS Virtual Roots

An IIS virtual root type of resource needs to have an IP address configured. After you enter the typical resource information, the wizard will prompt you for the following information for each IIS virtual root that you set up:

- IIS service type: This can be FTP, WWW, or Gopher.
- Alias: Enter an alias name to be used to access the service.

33

INTRODUCING
MICROSOFT
CLUSTER SERVER

- Directory: This is a path to the files offered by the service. Note that to create an IIS virtual root on a cluster, this directory must reside on the shared disk system that both cluster members can see.

- Account information: Here you enter the Windows NT user account and password that the IIS service runs under.

- Access: You can specify that users have read access, execute access, or both.

Using Network Names to Create Virtual Servers

This type of resource is similar to an IIS virtual root in that you must configure an IP address for it. When a resource group contains this type of resource, the group can be browsed on the network using the name you supply. For example, if you create a network name resource called "Warehouse," users can see the group and its resources using Network Neighborhood, under the name "Warehouse." Under this virtual server, users would see other resources configured in the group.

The only additional configuration parameters you need to specify for this type of resource are the network name and the IP address.

Configuring a Print Spooler Resource

A resource group that offers a print spooler to users in the cluster must have three other types of resources configured in the same group. You will need to create an IP address resource, a network name resource, and a physical disk resource. When specifying the dependencies in this group, specify that the print spooler resource is dependent on the physical disk resource and the network name resource.

The other additional parameter you need to specify is a path to the print spooler folder.

Modifying Resource Group Properties

As mentioned earlier, you can easily make changes to the resources and groups that you set up in the cluster. Using the Cluster Administrator program, select the resource or group and then select File, Properties to bring up the properties sheet for the group or resource to make your changes. The information you need depends on the resource type or types.

The properties sheet has four tabs:

- General: This tab shows general information about a resource, such as its name, a list of possible owners, and the group in which it is found.

- Dependencies: This tab shows any other resources that a particular resource is dependent on.

- Advanced: This tab can be used to specify failover information for the resource. If you select the check box Affect the group, a failure of this resource will cause the group in which it resides to be failed over. Since a group typically has more than one resource in it, you should select this check box on the Advanced tab for each resource that is required for the group to be available. You also set the values for the number of times the cluster software will attempt to restart the resource, and how long it will attempt to do so. You also specify the amount of time a resource will remain in a pending state before the cluster software declares it to be offline or online.

■ Parameters: Not all resource types will have this tab on their property sheet. Only resources that have configurable parameters (such as a file share) will have this tab. For example, for an IIS Virtual Root resource, you can use this tab to specify the type of resource (WWW, FTP, Gopher), and the directory path used by the service.

When you create a group for resources, you aren't limited to putting dependent resources into a group. You can also put many unrelated resources into a single group, along with their dependent resources. By using the Advanced tab on the property sheet, you set up the failover policies for the resource. Remembering that the resource is part of a group, if you select the Affect the group check box, the *entire group* will be failed over if this resource fails.

If you have a group of unrelated resources, some of the resources might not be necessary for normal functioning. For those resources, which you can put into a failover group for administrative convenience, you shouldn't select the Affect the group check box. Thus, if the resource fails, the group remains online on the current server and the administrator can take remedial action on the resource or decide to manually fail the group over to the other node.

Testing the Cluster for Failover

The easiest way to test failover for cluster groups is to simply power-cycle the server. If you have correctly set up resources and dependencies into failover groups, the cluster software should, after the threshold time, restart the resources on the other node.

In most situations, however, this isn't practical. Suppose you have just finished modifying the dependencies in a group, and you need to test it on a server that is currently being accessed by users. In this case, you can right-click any group and then, from the menu that appears, select Move Group. You should wait for the failover to occur and then test the resources on the other node to be sure that they were started in the correct order and are functioning properly.

If you want to test failover for all resource groups on a node at the same time, you can select File, Bring Offline or File, Initiate Failure. If you select Bring Offline, the groups will be placed into the offline state and won't be available on the other cluster node member. If you select Initiate Failure, the cluster software will place the groups into the offline state and then will attempt to restart them on the other cluster node.

When testing failover policies, you should be intimately aquainted with the dependencies for any particular resource. If a file share resource doesn't come online on the other cluster node member when you initiate a failover, check to see if the other resources on which it depends are being started in the correct order. For example, a file share resource depends on disk storage (a physical disk or a fault-tolerant disk set) in order to work. If you don't set up the group to start the disk storage resources first, the file share resource will fail when the cluster software attempts to start it, because the requisite disk resource isn't available at that time.

For best results, test each resource group, one at a time, until you're confident that you have correctly identified the dependencies for the group. When you have tested each group, try initiating a manual failover for the server to be sure that all resource groups function correctly.

Programming for Cluster Capability

In addition to the Platform SDK that Microsoft provides for application development, samples used for clustering are also provided. You can get more information about Microsoft's SDKs by visiting the following URL:

```
http://www.microsoft.com/msdn/sdk/platform.htm
```

The SDK provides four sets of Application Programming Interfaces (APIs) that can be used to program cluster-aware applications:

- Cluster API: This API is used by the application to communicate with the Cluster Service and its associated database.
- Resource API: This API is used by the Cluster Service to communicate with the resource monitor.
- Cluster Administrator Extension API: When you're developing custom resource types, this API can be used to integrate the appropriate menus and property pages for the resource type for manipulation by the Cluster Administrator application.
- Cluster Automation Server API: This API can be used when writing an application that, like the Cluster Administrator application, can be used to administer the cluster and its resources.

If you decide to embark on a project to code your own cluster-aware applications, you will only have to worry about client software licenses to access Windows NT Server. If you decide to purchase software from established vendors, you should read the next section on licensing.

Understanding How Clustering Affects Software Licensing

At this time there is no special type of license you can get from Microsoft for applications that run on Windows NT clusters. If you install an application on both servers in a cluster—one on which it runs normally and one for failover purposes—you must purchase two licenses. It doesn't matter if you run the application on only one computer at a time, as in when you fail over and fail back. Two licenses are required.

When using the per-server licensing option with Windows NT, you will need to have as many licenses on each cluster server as you expect the maximum number of users to be during normal functioning or during a failover. If you use per-seat licensing, the per-seat license is used for each server member when a client connects to a server.

NOTE

Per-server licenses are specific to a computer. When a failover occurs, your software licenses don't fail over to the other cluster member. Evaluate your software licensing options carefully when deciding whether or not to use clustered servers in your network.

If you find that you are limited in the number of licenses you can buy, you might consider a situation in which a smaller number of users are licensed on the failover server. In that case, during failover, only selected users would be allowed to access the application until the main server had been repaired and the resource groups failed back to it.

Summary

The addition of clustering technology to Windows NT Server is one more step toward making the OS an enterprise-class network operating system. You can expect to see more applications being rewritten to adapt to the new cluster paradigm computing platform very soon. With larger computers (such as Digital's Alpha-based platforms) taking advantage of clustering technology, the scalability of Windows NT is being proved. As Microsoft continues to incorporate other parts of clustering technology that have been proven on other systems for years, you can expect to see improvements for years to come. The next release of MSCS is supposed to include the ability to cluster more than two servers, and this will probably greatly enhance its adoption in the business environment.

33

INTRODUCING
MICROSOFT
CLUSTER SERVER

Tips and Tricks with NT Server

by Jason Garms

IN THIS APPENDIX

No matter how much work you expend designing an outline for a book, you always realize somewhere during the writing process that there is a better way to do things—so you must go with the flow. Originally, this appendix was called "Ten Tips for Setting Up an NT Server," but when I started writing it, I realized that all the good tips and tricks on setting up an NT Server were covered in Chapter 4, "Installing Windows NT Server." I realized it would be better to include an appendix for all those nifty little things that don't easily fall into a particular chapter, but make using and administering an NT Server easier and more pleasurable. That's what this appendix has become.

1. Deleting Files with Reserved Names

There's nothing worse than running across a file on your system such as LPT1, PRN, or COM, and not being able to delete it. If you've never run into this problem, you might not even know it exists, so pay attention and you'll be able to fix it if it ever happens to you.

The problem is that there are certain reserved words that NT uses for addressing certain devices. It is possible to create an actual file using one of these names, but when you try to use any of the standard NT utilities to delete it, it can prove quite difficult.

> **NOTE**
>
> Some people might be wondering why you would want to create a file with a reserved name. You would probably rarely want to do this; however, there are many ways that one can accidentally be created. Others might be wondering why you can't just leave the file alone and ignore it. Well, that can work in many situations; however, if you need to delete a directory, you need to be able to delete all the files within the directory as well, so you're going to need to know how to delete this obnoxious file.

The reserved filenames are as follows:

- COMx—Where *x* is a number between 1 and 9, representing an installed serial device.
- AUX—This is the first available serial device.
- LPTx—Where *x* is a number between 1 and 9, representing an installed parallel print device.
- PRN—This is the first available printer device.
- CON—This filename is reserved for the input console—the keyboard.

Most Windows NT utilities honor these device names and will not permit you to create a file with a reserved name.

Let's take a look and see what happens when we use the command prompt to try working with a file that has a reserved filename. In this example I used a trick to create a file called com1 in the directory d:\users\default. In Figure A.1 I have brought up the command prompt and issued the dir command to display the directory.

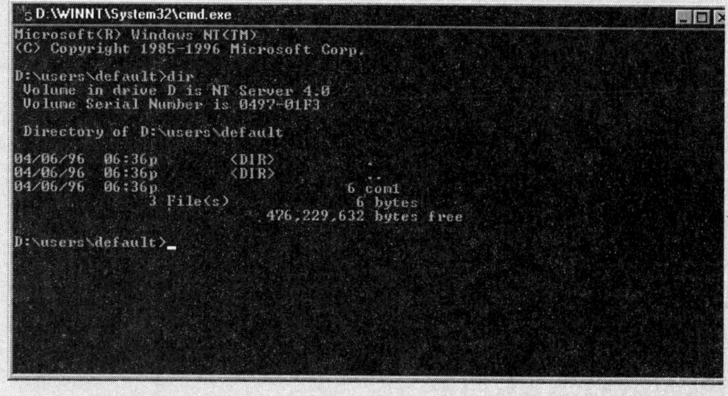

FIGURE A.1.

A directory showing the existence of a file with a reserved filename.

So what's so hard about deleting this file? Well, let's try to use the built-in command del to remove the file. The syntax we will use is del com1. Likewise, we could type del com1., or even del d:\users\default\com1, and we would get the same result. Figure A.2 shows what happens when you issue this command.

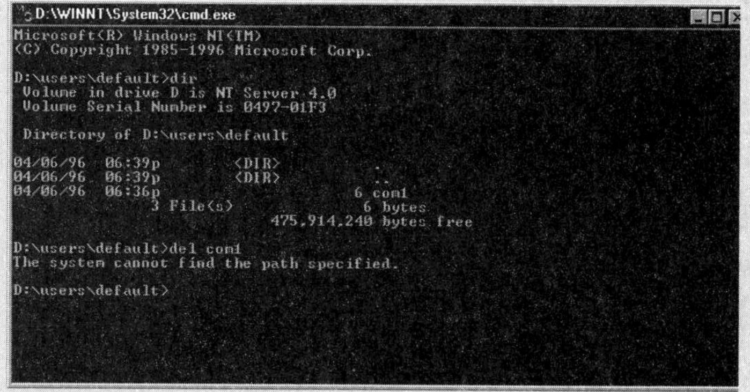

FIGURE A.2.

Trying to use the del command to delete a file with a reserved filename.

As you can see, the del command is ineffective in removing the file. To satisfy your curiosity, you could also try using the commands erase, rename, and move to manipulate the file. However, you will find these utilities are equally ineffective. Likewise, the Windows GUI tools such as Explorer and File Manager are unable to delete these files. In fact, in the beta release of Windows NT 4, which I am currently using, if you click on a file that has a reserved name, the current Explorer window goes off to la-la land, never to return. I've been assured this will be fixed in the shipping product.

So how do you delete these files? Actually there are three ways; one is the easiest and will always work. The other two have caveats. These three methods are as follows:

■ Use the file's direct system name, which bypasses reserved checking for reserved words.

■ Use an application from the POSIX subsystem.

■ Use a Macintosh client.

The first method takes advantage of a special direct naming convention that NT uses to bypass checking for reserved filenames. This convention is \\.*drive letter*:*path**filename*. For example, to delete the pesky file we created previously, we would type del \\.\d:\ users\default\com1. Figure A.3 shows the result of this command.

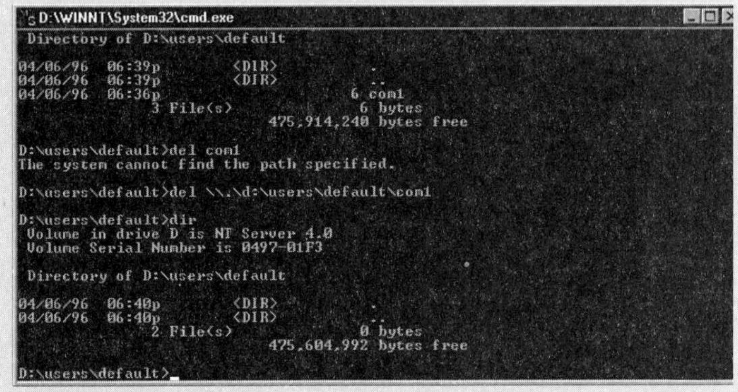

FIGURE A.3.

Using a direct file addressing mechanism to delete files with invalid filenames.

As you can see, the del command did not return an error, and in fact the dir command shows us that the file was actually removed. To tell the truth, the way I created that file for this example was by issuing the command string copy con \\.\d:\users\default\com1 and then typing a few characters into the file.

The second method for removing these pesky files is to take advantage of the POSIX subsystem. For those of you who don't really know much about the POSIX subsystem, there's not much to worry about. It is installed and enabled by default with Windows NT. The only problem is that the NT distribution CD-ROM does not include any POSIX commands. To get these commands, you need to install the Windows NT Resource Kit, which is available from Microsoft Press.

The reason you can delete these files with the POSIX subsystem is because they are not considered reserved words. The concept of these being reserved words is a legacy of DOS and only provided for backward compatibility with older software applications.

So how can you use POSIX to remove these files? The POSIX command rm is similar to the DOS command del or erase. If you have the Resource Kit installed, simply type rm com1 from the directory where the file resides and it will be deleted. Additionally you will find that all other POSIX utilities, such as mv, which is like the DOS command move, will work for manipulating files with reserved names.

The third method of deleting these files is using a Macintosh client. For Macintosh computers, COM, AUX, LPT, and the other names mentioned previously are not reserved words. This means that any Macintosh client can save a file called COM1, which is then inaccessible by Windows clients. In fact, this is the most common way that these annoying files get created. This is probably the most inconvenient way of deleting these files, but it is possible should you need to.

2. Connecting to a Remote Machine as a Different User

So what is this section all about? Well for me, one of the most annoying things about using Windows 3.x or Windows 95 is the inability to connect to different machines on the network using different user names. I've met many administrators who've never even tried this, but I find it invaluable, and once you start doing it, you'll never want to stop.

So why do it? Well, security for one, and convenience for another. In Chapter 28, "Advanced Security Guidelines," one of my recommendations is that you use a non-administrative user account for your day-to-day work at your workstation. The problem is, if you need to do a quick administrative task, you have to log out and back on, using another account, or you have to go to a different computer. If you come from a UNIX background where you could simply use SU to get administrative rights on-the-fly, the lack of a similar feature in NT can sometimes be a pain.

So how does this all work and why doesn't it work with Windows 3.x or Windows 95? It's quite simple. Windows NT can keep track of a different set of user credentials for each server you connect to. Windows 3.x and Windows 95 do not have this capability. They try to use the same username and password for connecting to all network devices.

So what? When, exactly, would I want to do this?

First and foremost would be for your daily activities. Let's give you a scenario. I administer a bunch of machines, both NT Workstations and NT Servers. I administer these machines from my NT Workstation in my office. We run a reasonable amount of security, and as such, I use a nonprivileged account, jgarms, for my daily work. Now I need to make some administrative changes on an NT Server called ROME. Let's say I want to add a user. My administrative account is called jg-admin. So, I need to logon to ROME using the account jg-admin. There are two methods of doing this.

The first, and most common, method is to establish a drive connection to the remote machine using the Connect As option. This is shown in Figure A.4.

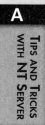

A

TIPS AND TRICKS
WITH NT SERVER

FIGURE A.4.

*Connecting to a
network drive using a
different user account.*

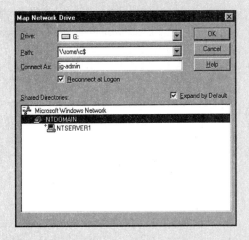

There are two disadvantages to this method. First, you might not want to connect to a share
on the remote system. While connecting to a drive share achieves the purpose of establishing a
user context between you and the remote system, it is unnecessary. Additionally, if persistent
connections are enabled, you will have to disconnect from the drive when you are finished or
the connection will be reestablished each time you log on. This is messy.

Second, and probably more important, the Connect As option does not enable you to specify
a different password. What will happen is that NT will try to connect to the remote system
using the username you entered into the Connect As box, but it will send the password from
your current user account. If the passwords for the two accounts are the same, the connection
will succeed. However, if the passwords are different, it will fail and you will be prompted with
a message to enter a correct username and password, as shown in Figure A.5.

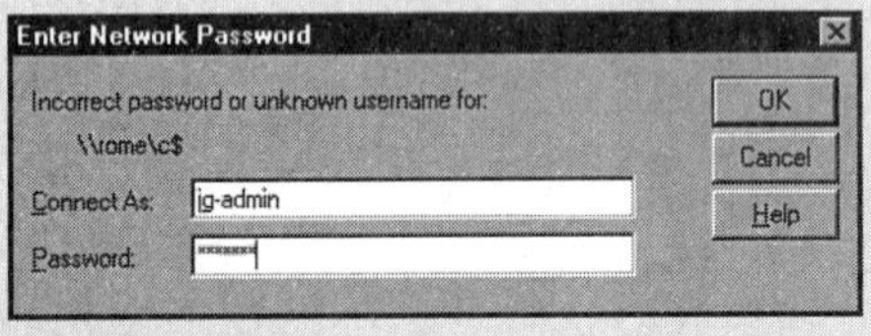

FIGURE A.5.

*You will receive a logon
failure if the passwords
don't match.*

This can really be a problem when you are using the intruder lockout features of Windows
NT. This connection failure is registered by the NT Server as a failed logon attempt, which
could result in accidentally locking out your account.

The cleanest method of establishing a session with a remote NT system using a different user
context is to use the command line. This enables you to create a session—without establishing
a drive share—which is all that is necessary. The command you want to use is net use *server
name*/user:*domain name**username* *, where *server name* is the name of the remote NT system
you are connecting to, *domain name* is the name of the domain where the user account you are

using comes from, and *username* is the account you want to use to connect. The * tells NT to prompt you for the correct password. You can leave the domain name empty if the user account comes from the domain of which the system you are connecting to is a member. This might be confusing, so let me explain by continuing our example.

I want to connect to the server ROME. ROME is a member of the domain SALES. If I want to connect to ROME using my account jg-admin, which is an account in domain SALES, I would type net use \\rome /user:jg-admin *. However, if the user account jg-admin does not exist in the domain SALES, but rather exists in the domain PROCUREMENT, which is trusted by SALES, I would type net use \\rome /user:procurement\jg-admin *. Notice the difference between the two commands.

Okay, so let's try this. First, I'll type net use, just to show that there are currently no connections to ROME. Then, I'll type net use \\rome /user:jg-admin * to create the connection to ROME. I'll be prompted for a password, which I'll enter. As I enter the password, nothing appears on the screen. Finally, I'll type net use one more time to confirm my connection to ROME. These transactions are shown in Figure A.6.

FIGURE A.6.

NET USE *can be used to create an Inter-Process Communication (IPC) link to a remote server.*

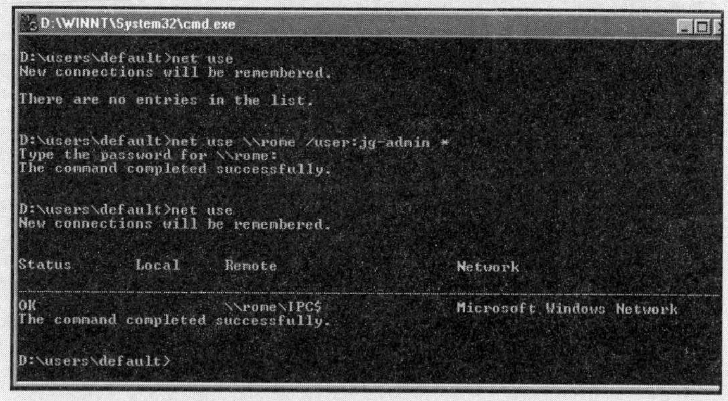

Notice, the connection to ROME shows up as \\ROME\IPC$. IPC stands for Inter-Process Communication, and is the remote procedure call (RPC) channel used to talk between the two NT systems.

Now, I can use the User Manager, Server Manager, Event Viewer, or any other administrative tools to remotely manage the server. Also, now that I have a channel between me and the remote server, I can open additional shared drive resources from it without having to re-enter the username and password. For example, because my current user context to ROME has administrative permissions, I can connect to the administrative share for ROME's drive C, as shown in Figure A.7.

A

TIPS AND TRICKS WITH NT SERVER

FIGURE A.7.

The administrative shares are created automatically.

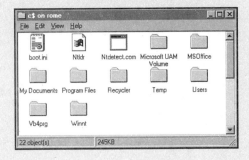

Note that you can only have a single user context between you and a remote system. What this means is that because I am currently connected to ROME as the user jg-admin, if I try to simultaneously create a new connection to ROME using a different user account, say my JGARMS account, I will get an error message, as shown in Figure A.8.

FIGURE A.8.

Trying to connect to a network server using multiple user accounts simultaneously results in an error message.

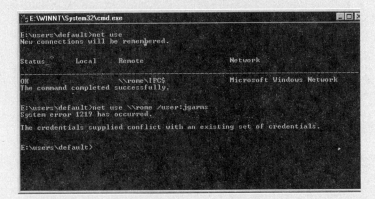

Now, when you are finished doing what you need to on the remote system, you can delete the IPC channel by using the command syntax net use \\<server name> /d, where <server name> is the name of the server connection you wish to disconnect from. In my example, I would type net use \\rome /d.

When else does this come in handy?

If you are using NT Workstation on your user's machine and you go out to help them, you can use it to get a connection to a secured resource without having to log them out. This can really come in handy.

Another time it can be useful is if you have a number of domains in your organization and don't necessarily have trusts set up between them.

I use it sometimes from a help desk. I get calls from users with NT Workstations and NT Servers that I don't have any connection to. Sometimes the easiest way to help them is to have them create a local user account for me with administrative capabilities. I then use the techniques described previously to connect using the account they created for me. When I'm finished, either they disable the account or delete it completely. Having this flexibility is quite a blessing.

3. What to Do If You Lose Your Administrative Password

Tough question. Many people think that because NT is "so secure," if you lose your administrator account's password, and you don't have any other accounts with administrative permissions, you're up the creek without a paddle. Actually, this is not true. I've talked to many people who have reinstalled NT from scratch and lost all their data because they were somehow locked out of their system. You don't have to do this!

I went through a lot of soul searching when I was deciding how to approach this topic. Essentially, I am describing a method of breaking into Windows NT. While it is normally considered bad taste by most people to provide detailed explanations of how to break into systems, I decided that this isn't the case here. This is not some procedure where someone can break into a system undetected over the network. Nor is it even a method of infiltrating NT without leaving a trace. While it is possible to set up scenarios where both of these tasks are possible, what I will describe in this scenario is a simple method of recovering important files from a system to which you have full physical access. Additionally, in the process of performing this procedure you will effectively destroy the system in order to get to data stored on the disk.

So why are we doing this? Well, if all other methods of accessing your NT Server fail, you would use this as a last resort. I've had people forget the only administrative password to a system. Or, even worse, a disgruntled administrator leaves your company and changes all the administrative passwords. If you keep backups, that might be fine. However, in case there is data on the system that cannot be recovered from backup, you could use this method to recover the necessary data before restoring the rest of the system from backup.

WARNING

While this procedure is a useful method for recovering data from an otherwise-inaccessible NT system, it will completely replace the user account, registry, and configuration information.

While the steps for performing this procedure are relatively simple, many people don't realize it can be done, because it is not fully explained in Microsoft's NT documentation.

You will need a copy of the NT distribution media. The example here assumes you have the NT Server CD-ROM and three accompanying setup disks. Here are the steps to perform this operation:

A

TIPS AND TRICKS WITH NT SERVER

1. Boot your system with the NT Setup Boot Disk in drive A.

2. When prompted, insert Disk 2.

3. NT Setup will load and present you with four options. You should press Enter, indicating you want to install Windows NT.

4. Allow NT Setup to detect any mass storage devices by pressing Enter when prompted. If you prefer, you can specify them yourself.

5. Insert Disk 3 when prompted.

6. At the bottom of the screen the setup program will indicate that it is searching the system for existing NT installations.

   A message indicating the existing NT installations will appear. At this point the NT Setup assumes that you are trying to upgrade one of these installations, which it will do if you press enter. *This is not what you want to do.* If you choose this option, the security account information will not be replaced, thus defeating our purpose.

7. Press N to indicate that you want to install a new installation of Windows NT.

8. A list of your hardware configuration will appear on the screen. If everything is correct, press Enter to continue.

9. Now a list of all the drives and existing partitions will appear on the screen. Use the up and down arrow keys to select the partition with the installation of Windows NT that you want to "break into." Press Enter when it is highlighted.

10. You will now be prompted about what you want to do with the file system. You should choose the option "Leave the current file system intact (no change)" and press Enter.

11. You will not be prompted to enter the path where you want the NT system files to be installed. You should enter the path for the existing system files, such as \WINNT or \WINNT35. Press Enter.

12. The setup program will display a message indicating that the directory you entered contains an existing NT installation, which will be overwritten, replacing the user account, security, and configuration information. Press Enter to continue.

13. The setup program will now copy files from the CD-ROM to the hard drive. Depending on the speed of your system, this could take 5 to 20 minutes.

    If someone played around with the NTFS security permissions on the system directory where you are reinstalling NT, you might get errors indicating that certain files could not be copied. This is fine. You can just choose the option to ignore it.

14. When it's finished, you will be prompted to remove the floppy disk and press Enter to reboot the system. Do this.

15. NT will reboot and enter the GUI part of the installation procedure. Depending on your goals here, you can just skip various parts of the system setup. I recommend that you do only what is necessary to recover your necessary files. If you have a tape drive,

you can backup the system to tape, reinstall a good, clean copy of Windows NT and recover the files you need.

If you get "access denied" errors when logging on or trying to access data, simply take ownership of everything on the drive and grant the administrator account full access permissions to everything.

Granted, this procedure is messy, but sometimes you need to recover files that might be otherwise unrecoverable. It's actually a good thing that this procedure does destroy the system. This way, you can tell if your system has been infiltrated. Also, by breaking into a system using this method, you replace the system's unique identifier token, which identifies itself to other systems in the NT domain. This means that if someone can gain physical access to a machine on your network and uses this method to break into it, he or she cannot use that to leverage an assault on other machines in the domain.

4. Using the Run Option in the Windows 95 Interface

I'm sure that by now you've played with the Start button down there on the bottom left of your screen. Have you noticed the Run command? It does basically the same thing as the Run command from the Program Manager in NT 3.x.

Well, actually there are some other neat things you can do with it, courtesy of the Windows 95 user interface.

Here's one example of why the Run command is useful:

I run around to lots of NT systems, many of which aren't mine. Because people love to customize their interface beyond recognition, it is usually easier to know what the names of various programs are and use the Run command to bring them up when necessary. Here are the executable names for some useful programs that I use all the time:

- eventvwr—Event Viewer
- srvmgr—Server Manager
- usrmgr—User Manager for Domains
- musrmgr—Local User Manager
- perfmon—Performance Monitor
- notepad—Notepad
- windisk—Disk Administrator
- winfile—File Manager
- control—Control Panel
- printman—Print Manager

- `winmsd`—Windows NT Diagnostics
- `regedt32`—Registry Editor for Windows NT
- `regedit`—Registry Editor for Windows 95
- `cmd`—NT Command Prompt

There is no difference between this and the way you could use the Run command in the Program Manager under Windows NT 3.x.

However, the Run command in NT 4 gives you an additional feature that makes navigating your system and the network easier. As nice as the Explorer is, occasionally it can be inconvenient. That's why it is always nice to know more than one way to access information.

From the Run command, you can type the universal naming convention name (UNC) of a resource you want to open, and it will be opened.

So what? Well, here are some examples.

If you need to see what's on the floppy drive, how would you do it? Well, one way would be to double-click on My Computer and double-click on the icon for drive A. Of course if you do this a lot, you might have a shortcut for drive A also. Well, the Run command gives you another way. I have lots of tricks like this up my sleeves, and people always think it's so I can work faster and get more accomplished. Actually, I think it comes from the fact that I'm fundamentally lazy. I want to do as little as possible to achieve a desired result.

I use this particular trick with the Run command all the time when I am typing and don't want to take my fingers from the keyboard to use the mouse. To get a directory of drive A, equivalent to using my computer as described previously, all I do is use Ctrl+Esc to get the Start menu. Then I press R, for Run. The Run window pops up. Then I type a:\ in the Run window, and press Return, and up pops a window with the contents of drive A. Net savings? Oh, a second or two. But if you're like me, you have your screen cluttered with dozens of windows that would have to be minimized or moved to even find My Computer.

So what else can you do? Well, anything with UNCs. If I want to access a shared resource from the network, I can type the path, and it pops up for me. For instance, if I want to access a shared directory called FIGURES from a server called ROME, I would do the following:

1. Press Ctrl+Esc. This will bring up the Start menu.
2. Press R. This will bring up the Run dialog box.
3. Type \\ROME\FIGURES into the dialog box and press Enter.

It's as simple as that. This is also very useful when you are connected to a machine over a slow link, such as a modem with RAS. If I were to use the Network Neighborhood icon to find my location, it might take a while, because lots of data will have to come over the slow link. However, if I know that I want to look in a particular directory on ROME, I could simply enter the full path into the Run command and gain quick access.

You can also use it to access directories on your local computer, just like we did previously to access the local A drive. If I want to see what's in the directory C:\USERS\DEFAULT, the navigation could take a few moments using the Explorer interface. However, using the Run command, you would simply bring up the Run window, type C:\USERS\DEFAULT, and you're there.

5. Using the Command Line

I've been using graphical user interface (GUI) systems for over ten years. They definitely have their place, and I would never give them up. However, there are also times where a good command-line interface can complement the GUI in a strong way.

In the previous section, I talked about using the Run command from the Start menu to quickly access Windows programs or network resources. What I'd like to talk about here is how to expand on this and use Windows NT's Command Prompt to make your NT experience richer and fuller.

Setting the Command Prompt to Automatically Start

The way I usually set my account is to automatically start a minimized Command Prompt session when I log on. I accomplish this is by using the following steps:

1. Right-click on the Start button. This will bring up a context-sensitive menu with the options Open, Explore, and Find.

2. Left-click on Explore.

3. This will bring up the Explorer browser focused on the items in your Start menu, as shown in Figure A.9.

FIGURE A.9.

Using the Explorer to see what's in the Start menu.

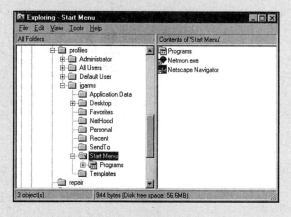

A

TIPS AND TRICKS
WITH NT SERVER

4. Double-click on Programs in the left-hand window pane. This will expand the Programs folder.

5. Double-click the Startup folder in the left-hand window pane. This will expand the Programs folder. If there is anything in the Startup folder, you will see it in the right side of the window. If there is currently nothing in the Startup folder, the right pane of the windows will be empty, as shown in Figure A.10.

FIGURE A.10.

Browsing the Startup folder.

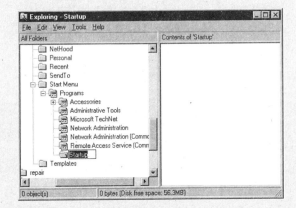

6. Now, we're going to create a shortcut to the Command Prompt. To do this, right-click on the right window pane. A context-sensitive list will appear, as shown in Figure A.11.

NOTE

The Start Menu folder is the folder that contains all the items that appear in the Start menu and is normally at the bottom left of your screen. The Startup folder contains all the items that automatically start when you log on. This folder is located off the Programs group under the Start menu.

7. Choose New from the list. A submenu will appear. Select Shortcut from this sub-menu, as shown in Figure A.12.

8. The Create Shortcut window will appear. Type CMD into the Command Line field, as shown in Figure A.13.

FIGURE A.11.

Right-clicking in the Startup folder brings up a context-sensitive options list.

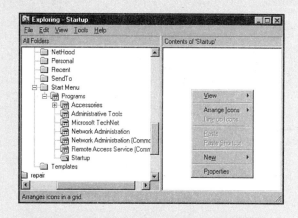

FIGURE A.12.

Creating a new shortcut in the Startup folder.

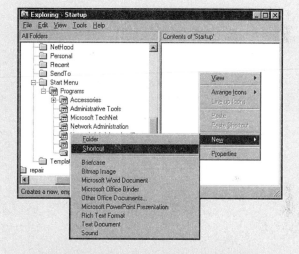

FIGURE A.13.

Specifying the program to be executed by the shortcut.

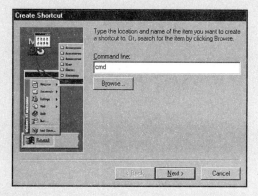

A

TIPS AND TRICKS WITH NT SERVER

> **NOTE**
>
> It is important to remember that `CMD.EXE` and `COMMAND.COM` are not the same thing. `CMD.EXE` is the Windows NT Command Prompt. It is a full 32-bit application that can be used to do a number of powerful things. `COMMAND.COM` is a 16-bit shell that runs in an NT virtual DOS machine (VMD) and is provided for compatibility with some older applications.

9. Click Next. You will now be asked to give the shortcut a name. By default, it should display `CMD.EXE`. Let's change this to "Command Prompt." Click the Finish button.

   You should now have a Command Prompt shortcut in your Startup folder, as shown in Figure A.14.

FIGURE A.14.

The Startup folder now contains a shortcut to the Command Prompt.

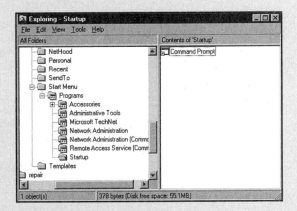

Now every time you log on to this machine, you will automatically get a command prompt. The problem is it gets annoying to have it pop up in your way every time. So, let's go ahead and make the Command Prompt pop up minimized so it will be there, without being in the way.

1. Right-click on the Command Prompt shortcut we created in the last section. Select Properties from the list that pops up. The Command Prompt Properties window will appear.

2. Click on the Shortcut tab at the top of the window. From the Run pick-list, select Minimized, as shown in Figure A.15.

3. Click OK to close the Shortcut properties window.

4. Close the Explorer window.

FIGURE A.15.

Selecting Minimized will cause the Command Prompt to appear minimized when it is started on logon.

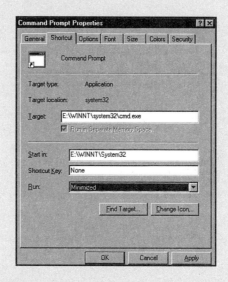

Using the Command Prompt

So now that we've gone through all this trouble to have the Command Prompt start up all the time, what are we going to do with it?

Well, one of the nice things about the Command Prompt is that it will usually respond, even when the rest of the system appears to be bogged down. This gives you a fairly surefire method of controlling your system. Because I tend to run my systems to their limit, it's nice to be able to regain control with relative ease. When you have a Command Prompt open, you can use the Alt+Tab keystroke combination to bring it to the foreground. Because NT is very responsive to Alt+Tab, this is usually possible, even in the worst-case scenarios.

Once you have the Command Prompt in the foreground, you can take back control of your system. To make this most effective, you should install the utilities that come with the Windows NT Resource Kit. This provides a number of command-line utilities to work with.

However, you can also use the Command Prompt as a place for launching your Windows applications by using the START command.

I often use the START command to launch applications I need. Also, you can create batch jobs that do a number of these activities for you. For example, from the command line you would type start eventvwr to bring up the Event Viewer, or start srvmgr \\ROME to bring up the Server Manager focused on ROME.

A

TIPS AND TRICKS WITH NT SERVER

The syntax for the START command is

```
START ["title"] [/Dpath] [/i] [/min] [/max] [/separate ¦ /shared] [/low ¦ /normal ¦
/high ¦ /realtime] [/wait] [/b] [command/program [parameters]]
```

`"title"`—This is the title that will appear in the window's title bar.

`/Dpath`—This is the switch that tells NT to set the default directory for the program or command to *path*.

`/i`—Normally when you use START, Windows NT uses the default, which passes the default environment variables to the new program. However, if you specify the /i switch, NT will pass the current environment variables instead.

`/min`—This switch specifies that the new program should be started minimized.

`/max`—This switch specifies that the new program should be started maximized.

`/separate`—Indicates that a 16-bit Windows program should be run in a separate memory space. This option is ignored unless the specified application is 16-bit.

`/shared`—Indicates that a 16-bit Windows program should be run in a shared memory space with other 16-bit Windows applications. This option is ignored unless the specified application is 16-bit.

`/low`—Tells NT to set the applications priority level to IDLE.

`/normal`—Tells NT to set the applications priority level to NORMAL.

`/high`—Tells NT to set the applications priority level to HIGH.

`/realtime`—Tells NT to set the applications priority level to REALTIME. You should use the REALTIME priority class with care, because it can cause the rest of your system, including responsiveness to the keyboard console interface, to grind to a halt.

`/wait`—Normally, an application that is launched with the START command is spawned off on its own and control is returned immediately to the Command Prompt. If you specify the /wait switch, the Command Prompt will wait for the spawned application to terminate before returning control. This is useful in batch jobs where the execution of subsequent pieces of the batch file depends on first completing a preceding event.

`/b`—When you use the START command to start applications that run in the character-based subsystem, NT spawns a new Command Prompt window in which to run the application. If you specify the /b option, however, a new window will not be created. Instead, the application will run in the existing window. Additionally, Ctrl+C handling is ignored. You must use Ctrl+Break to interrupt the application and return to the Command Prompt.

command/program—This is the name (and path, if necessary) of the program you want to start. If the program runs in the character-based subsystem, a new window is spawned and will disappear when the program is terminated. If you use START to run a command built into CMD.EXE, however, such as dir, or copy, the window will remain when the command is terminated.

parameters—You can specify parameters to pass to the program.

So what else can we do from the Command Prompt? Lots of things.

6. Using Nifty Features of the QuickView Applet

Have you ever used the QuickView applet? This is one of those nifty little utilities that came to Windows NT along with the Windows 95 user interface.

QuickView is a fairly straightforward program that is useful for viewing text documents, Word documents, and other kinds of files. There is more to this little application than meets the eye, however.

QuickView includes filters that enable you to view applications, Dynamic Link Libraries (DLLs), drives, and other forms of executable code. If you've ever tried to use a text editor to view an executable file and have seen how messy and unintelligible they can be, you might be asking yourself "so what?"

Well, one of the standard filters included with QuickView is able to read and decode these binary files and give us useful information that can be used for troubleshooting or just to help get a better understanding of how things work.

First, let's take a quick look at how to access the QuickView applet. The QuickView application and support files are located in the %systemroot%\system32\viewers folder. There is, however, an easier way to access it.

QuickView got its name because it was created to fill two niches. First, it is quick and handy. This means that Microsoft created an easy and quick method of getting to QuickView. Second, QuickView was designed for its quickness—meaning that it is quick to load, so you can get a quick idea of what the file is before possibly loading it with an application such as Microsoft Word, which is not always quick to load.

You can access QuickView from the Windows Explorer interface by right-clicking on a file. This brings up the context-sensitive options menu. If QuickView has an installed viewer for the file type you clicked on, the QuickView option will appear, as shown in Figure A.16.

FIGURE A.16.
*You can open a file
with QuickView by
right-clicking on a file
compatible with
QuickView's installed
viewers.*

Now that we know how to get to QuickView, what good is it? Well, to be quite honest, it's not
one of those applications that you will use everyday and change the course of your life. However, it has its time and its place. Let's take a look at an executable file using QuickView.

1. Open the system32 folder in your system root. For most people that's c:\winnt\
   system32. However, let's learn a new trick. From the Start menu, choose Run. In
   the Open box, type %systemroot%\system32, as shown in Figure A.17.

FIGURE A.17.
*You can take advantage
of the Run option to
quickly locate your
computer's system32
directory.*

The system32 folder should open in a window on your screen, as shown in Figure
A.18.

> **NOTE**
>
> By default, the Windows NT Explorer does not display system-related files, such as DLL,
> drv, vxd, and so on. In order to display these types of files, choose the View menu from an
> Explorer window and select Options. Click the View tab and select the option Show All
> Files.

FIGURE A.18.

The %SYSTEMROOT%\
SYSTEM32 *folder.*

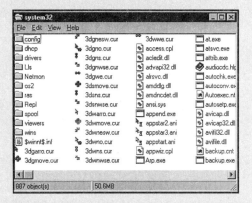

2. Scroll down to find the CACLS.EXE file and right-click on it.

3. Choose the QuickView option.

   The QuickView applet should bring up a window displaying information about the CACLS.EXE file, as shown in Figure A.19.

FIGURE A.19.

*You can use QuickView
to display internal
information about an
executable, such as*
CACLS.EXE.

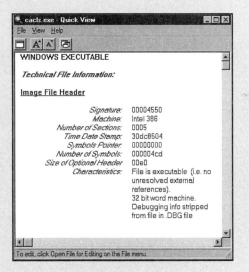

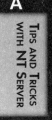

Don't be intimidated by the things you see in this file. Let's just take a look at some of the things that are interesting to the average administrator.

- ■ At the top, it tells you this is a Windows executable.

- ■ Under the Image File Header section, the machine type is displayed. This identifies the processor platform that this file was compiled for. If you are using an Intel architecture system, it will say Intel 386, regardless of the exact processor type you are using, i486 or Pentium, for example.

- Under Image Optional Header, it tells you the version of the code itself, as well as the version of the operating system for which it was compiled.

- Also, under Image Optional Header, it lists the Windows NT subsystem that the file runs under. In this case, CACLS.EXE runs in the Windows character subsystem. Other possible subsystems are the Windows GUI subsystem, the POSIX character subsystem, or no subsystem.

- Some of the other information you can find out when viewing a Win32 application with QuickView is what external DLL references are made, and you can even identify the name of the function called. This can be useful in tracking down missing DLL files or identifying what is causing certain General Protection Fault (GPF) errors.

To see some of the differences in information displayed, take a look at a 32-bit Windows program, such as the Notepad. For comparison, look at a 16-bit Windows program, such as Write. Yes, Write is still 16-bit and viewing it with QuickView will prove it! Also try viewing a DLL, a device driver, and even an MS-DOS program. If you have the Windows NT Resource Kit installed, try looking at one of the POSIX applications to see how it differs.

Each type of file has slightly different information. Don't expect to understand it all at once, but comparing these files with QuickView could help you to get a better understanding of what's really going on inside these binary files.

7. Ownership of Files as an Administrative User

Remember that discrete ownership of an object is one of the foundations of NT's security model. Under this model, every single object has an owner. Under normal circumstances, the owner of an object is almost always a user. However, if the user is an administrator, the owner of the object becomes the local administrator.

This concept is important to understand, because if you don't, it can seem as if NT is doing something wrong.

So why does NT assign the ownership of an object to the Administrators group instead of the individual administrative account? Well, the basic reason is that NT expects that the administrators of a local computer will work together and granting them joint ownership makes that easier.

Of course, the more complex reason has to do with the user's access token. When you take ownership of an object (or create an object), the system assigns a security identifier (SID) based on the value of the TOKEN_OWNER in the user's security token, which is assigned during the logon process. For normal users, the TOKEN_OWNER field identifies the user by using the user's SID. The exception to this rule is when the user is a member of the Administrators group. If this is the case, the TOKEN_OWNER field is set to the administrator's SID.

Windows NT does not provide a user interface that enables an administrator to take ownership of an object and set the new ownership to the user's SID, rather than the administrator's SID.

This is another reason why it is good practice to use non-privileged accounts for your daily work.

So what does this mean in the real world and how does it look? Let's look at an example. I am currently logged on my system using a user account JGARMS. This account is a member of the local Administrators group. I just created a blank text document, called blank.txt, in the directory e:\users\JGARMS, as shown in Figure A.20.

FIGURE A.20.

BLANK.TXT *was created in* E:\JGARMS\DEFAULT *by the administrative user account* JGARMS.

Let's look at the owner on that file. Right-click on blank.txt and choose Properties. Click the Security tab, and then on the Ownership button. This brings up the ownership information, as shown in Figure A.21.

FIGURE A.21.

The ownership information confirms that this file is owned by the Administrators group.

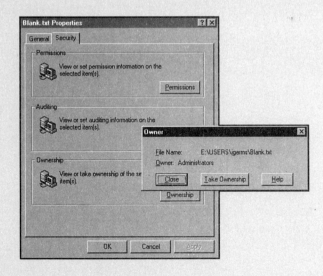

If you try to take ownership of the file to see if the ownership can be set to the user's account, rather than to the Administrators group, you will discover that it doesn't work.

Now, for the sake of understanding this better, I've removed the user account JGARMS from the Administrators group, logged off, and logged back on. Now, if I take ownership of the file using the exact same procedures as shown previously, the owner of the account will be JGARMS, as shown in Figure A.22.

FIGURE A.22.
The owner of the file is now JGARMS, not Administrators.

> **NOTE**
>
> Although the JGARMS account is no longer a member of the Administrators group, it can take ownership of this file because of the permissions on the file. The folder e:\users\jgarms is the home directory for the JGARMS account, and the permissions are set up such that JGARMS is granted full control of any file created in the directory.

As you can see, the owner of the file reflects the actual user, JGARMS, rather than the Administrators group.

8. Using OLE Properties to Identify Files Without Extensions

If you are familiar with the Windows 3.1x Program Manager style interface, you are probably acquainted with the way File Manager uses a file's extension to determine to what program it is linked. For example, if a file has the extension TXT, by default it is opened with Notepad. Likewise, DOC files are opened with Microsoft Word (if you have Word installed). However, this mapping of extensions to applications is neither consistent nor reliable. After all, what happens if the extension is removed, or if you have multiple programs that use the same three-character extension?

Well, the Explorer in Windows NT 4 inherits a useful feature from the Windows 95 interface. This interface tries to take full advantage of the OLE properties of a document to provide as much useful information as possible. Of course, this only applies to documents created by programs that save their documents as OLE containers, such as the Office 95 applications.

To see what this is all about, let's take a look at an OLE document. Figure A.23 shows a PowerPoint 95 document created by someone at Microsoft, which I downloaded from their Internet site.

FIGURE A.23.

DECUS.PPT *is a*
PowerPoint 95
document from the
Microsoft Internet site.

If we right-click on this document and choose Properties, the Properties window will appear as shown in Figure A.24.

FIGURE A.24.

The Properties window
for DECUS.PPT.

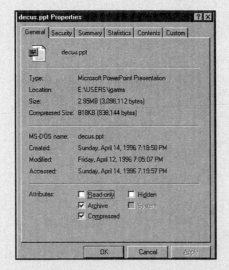

Notice that this Properties window includes tabs for the normal items you would expect, such as General and Security. It also includes tabs for Summary, Statistics, Contents, and Custom. These tabs come from the OLE properties of this document. If you've ever used an application from the Microsoft Office suite, you'll recognize the items listed under the Summary tab, as shown in Figure A.25.

As you can see, the summary information contains the title, subject, author, and other information about the document. We can even tell what file was used as the template for creating it.

From the Statistics tab, we can find out information such as when the document was created, modified, accessed, and last printed. This information is included internal to the document as an OLE property. It is completely independent of the file system date information. The Statistics tab for DECUS.PPT is shown in Figure A.26.

A

TIPS AND TRICKS
WITH NT SERVER

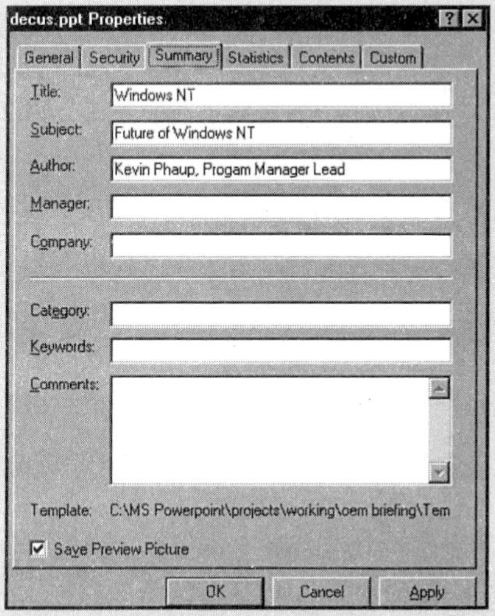

FIGURE A.25.

The entries in the Summary tab for DECUS.PPT *are taken from the OLE properties embedded in the document.*

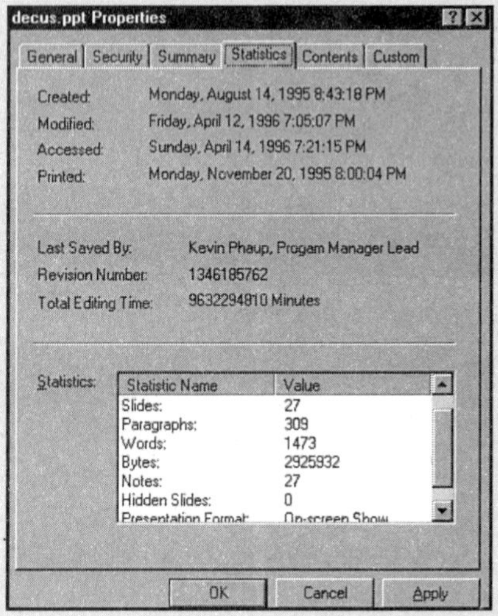

FIGURE A.26.

The Statistics tab shows information about the time the file was created, modified, accessed, and printed.

Different document types contain different information in the Statistics tab. For example, a Word 95 document gives information on the number of characters, lines, paragraphs, sections, and pages.

The Contents tab also contains some useful information about the document. For example, in a PowerPoint slide, it contains information such as what fonts are used in the document, what template was used, and the names of all the slides. In addition, it lists any embedded OLE servers, such as clip art, Word documents, Excel spreadsheets, and so on. Figure A.27 shows the Contents tab for the DECUS.PPT document.

A

TIPS AND TRICKS
WITH NT SERVER

FIGURE A.27.

The Contents tab shows information on font usage, document template, and slide titles.

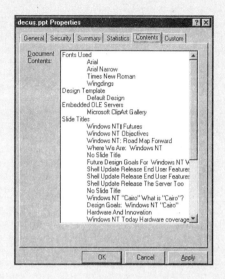

The Custom tab enables you to customize the type of information you want to gather by entering custom OLE properties.

OLE Documents without Extensions

So, as you've seen, the OLE properties of a file can be useful for gathering information from a file, such as statistics, contents, and summary information. However, there is one more interesting thing that these OLE properties enable you to do with the Windows 95–style interface.

Rather than explain it, let's take our example and I'll show you.

We know that in the traditional Windows environment, the file extension, in this case PPT, is what identifies the program that should be used to open the file. PPT means PowerPoint. As we mentioned previously, this can be quite inconvenient, because some programs use the same extension as other programs, thus confusing things. Well, the Windows 95 user interface, which NT inherited in NT 4, tries to improve on the methods used to identify documents. It does this by accessing this OLE property information we were just talking about. However, it retains the support for document extensions for backward compatibility. So let's take a look at what this means. We'll use the DECUS.PPT document to demonstrate. DECUS.PPT is shown in Figure A.28.

FIGURE A.28.

DECUS.PPT *is a PowerPoint 95 document that will be used to demonstrate extracting information from OLE properties.*

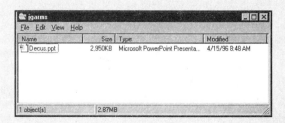

> **NOTE**
>
> As mentioned previously, I have set the Explorer's viewing option to display system-related files, such as DLL, drv, vxd, and so on. By default, these file types are hidden. In order to display these, choose the View menu from an Explorer window and select Options. Click the View tab and select the option Show All Files. Also, to make this demonstration effective, you also need to deselect the option Hide file extensions for known file types.

Notice that the Type listed for DECUS.PPT is Microsoft PowerPoint Presentation. If I didn't have Office 95 installed, or if it were installed incorrectly, the Type would be displayed as PPT Document. However, because I have Office 95 installed, I can double-click the DECUS.PPT icon, and PowerPoint will load and open the document. This is normal and to be expected; there is no trickery involved. The Explorer simply reads the PPT extension and knows to open PowerPoint.

So what? Well, I agree there is nothing special yet. However, what happens if we rename the document and remove the extension, as shown in Figure A.29.

FIGURE A.29.

When you remove the extension from DECUS.PPT, *the icon reverts to a plain file icon.*

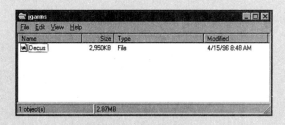

Note that the Type is now listed simply as File and the icon has changed to the simple file icon. However, if we right-click on DECUS, and choose Properties, we can still see the OLE information, such as Summary, Statistics, and Contents.

Now, let's double-click on DECUS. If you're not trying this yourself, you'll have to take my word that PowerPoint opens up and loads DECUS.

So how does this happen without a file extension? OLE magic. Now take note that this only works with applications that embed OLE properties into their documents. If you took an old Office document, such as a Word 6 file, stripped off the extension and double-clicked it, Word would not automatically load. This is because it is with Office 95 that files began including all the OLE information necessary to make this magic work.

While this might just seem like a cute feature for now, OLE properties represent ultimate doom for those inconvenient three-character file extensions. Now that we have long filename support in Windows 95 and on all file systems in Windows NT, and as more and more vendors begin to include OLE properties in their documents, it shouldn't be long before the often-confusing extensions go the way of the dodo bird.

9. Connecting to Machines Using Their TCP/IP DNS Names

What is the Internet? No, this is not one of those cheap riddles. The answer is really quite important. The Internet represents the ultimate wide-area network (WAN). This has been obvious to some people for quite some time, and believe it or not, Microsoft has been planning a lot more than some people realize.

In the winter of 1995, people complained that Microsoft was missing the game when it came to the Internet. In a burst of thunder that shook the very foundation of Redmond, Microsoft announced their Internet strategies that caused reverberating waves throughout their entire product line.

Well, actually, the game they were missing was the World Wide Web craze. While it was important for Microsoft to stake their claim in this race, they had really been preparing for other strategies on the Internet for many years. As we discussed earlier in this book, that is what led to Microsoft's deep commitment to a solid TCP/IP product on all their platforms, and what also led to the development of WINS and DHCP.

It's also what leads us to this tip. So what is the tip, you ask? Actually, I think it's one of the most incredibly useful improvements made in NT 4. It's the capability to connect to a network resource based on its TCP/IP DNS name—regardless of its location or NetBIOS/Windows name, and without WINS or LMHOSTS files.

So what? Well, this changes the nature of working over the Internet. I'll give you one good example and I think you'll appreciate it better. In fact, we'll use Microsoft's FTP server to demonstrate our point.

If you want to download a file from Microsoft, how do you do it? Assuming you know what file you want, you might FTP to ftp.microsoft.com, navigate through the FTP site and grab what you want. This is okay, right? Well, actually, it's a little archaic. Even some of the shareware and commercial FTP utilities leave a bit to be desired because FTP itself is the archaic factor here. How can we use some of the tools at our disposal to make this job easier? Well, one way, certainly, is to use a Web browser to locate and download the information. This is a compelling solution. But I want to show you one more. It's quite simple really, but very few people have tried it—get a standard Windows network connection to Microsoft's Internet site. We're going to bypass FTP altogether and use the built-in robust networking capabilities of NT to mount ftp.microsoft.com as we would any other network server. Of course, this will only work if you are connected to the Internet, have TCP/IP installed, and have Windows Networking bound to TCP/IP.

From the Start menu, choose Run and type \\ftp.microsoft.com. Depending on the speed of your network, a window will soon appear, showing the contents of ftp.microsoft.com, as shown in Figure A.30.

FIGURE A.30.

You can connect to
ftp.microsoft.com
using standard
Windows Networking
to treat it like any other
server on your network.

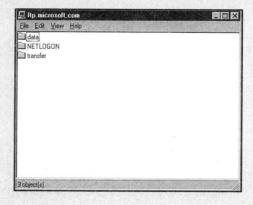

From here you can double-click on the data directory to look inside, as shown in Figure A.31.

FIGURE A.31.

Connecting to
\\ftp.microsoft.com\data
brings you to the same
place as using FTP to
connect to
ftp.microsoft.com,
except it has a better
interface.

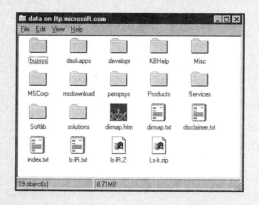

If you FTP to ftp.microsoft.com, you will end up in this directory. If you use FTP, however, you don't get all the neat features that come with Windows Networking.

Like what, you might ask? Well, you can use Find to locate any file on ftp.microsoft.com. Or, you can create shortcuts to frequently accessed locations on this server. Or, yet another useful thing would be to create a Briefcase on your local server and use it to automatically synchronize data from ftp.microsoft.com. Service Packs would be a good example of a useful application for this. The applications are limited only to the features of Windows Networking.

So why else would you want to connect in this manner, instead of using the standard FTP approach? Well, in this example we are connecting to Microsoft's Internet site, but you are not limited to that. You can actually use this method to connect to any Windows machines attached to the Internet, provided they have Microsoft Networking bound to their TCP/IP stack. Another advantage is while FTP has no secure form of user authentication (FTP passes passwords in clear text over the network) connecting to an NT Server like this over the Internet uses NT's secure challenge authentication protocol (CHAP). Furthermore, you can automate connections to these remote servers using standard Windows scripting tools. Also, when you copy files using FTP, the file's creation time and date get lost. Using the Windows Networking approach, however, these are preserved.

To get a better idea of a use for this, let's take a look at an application. Microsoft maintains its software library on `ftp.microsoft.com`. This software library contains patches, bug fixes, performance enhancements, and other utilities for all its applications and operating systems. There is an index file they use to record all files stored in the software library. The software library contains thousands of files in a single directory (2,148 files as of April 14, 1996). If you were to look in this directory over a slow network link, it would literally take all day. To solve this problem, and to let us know when Microsoft adds files to the software library, we can create a shortcut to the software library's index file and put that shortcut on our desktop.

The universal naming convention (UNC) for the index file is `\\ftp.microsoft.com\data\ Softlib\index.txt`. This file is shown in Figure A.32.

FIGURE A.32.

INDEX.TXT *contains an index of the files in Microsoft's online software library.*

Because we are working with standard Windows networking, simply right-click the `index.txt` icon and drag it to the desktop. Let go of the right mouse button wherever you want the shortcut to be, and a menu will pop up asking if you want to move the file, create a shortcut, copy the file, or cancel. Choose `Create Shortcut Here`. The shortcut icon will appear, as shown in Figure A.33.

Now, whenever you want to check to see the most recent additions to Microsoft's software library, simply double-click this icon. NT will establish the networking connection completely in the background and display the file as shown in Figure A.34.

FIGURE A.33.

"Shortcut to index.txt" is a shortcut that points to a file on `ftp.microsoft.com` *over the Internet.*

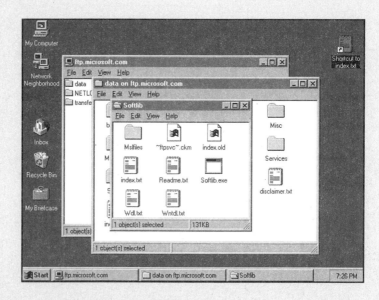

FIGURE A.34.

The `INDEX.TXT` *file shows all the files stored in Microsoft's online software library, with the most recent additions at the top of the list.*

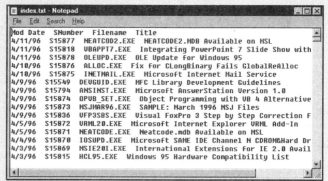

More Technical Stuff about Using DNS Names

So how does this all work, and what's so special about it?

Well, I'll address the second half of the question first. You can actually do something similar to this with Windows for Workgroups (WFW) 3.11 and Windows 95, but there is a big difference. With Windows for Workgroups and Windows 95, you need to create an LMHOSTS file and you cannot actually use the TCP/IP DNS name to address the remote server.

You would have to enter the NetBIOS name for the remote server and its static IP address into an LMHOSTS file on each workstation you wanted to connect to. The downside here is that Windows NetBIOS naming is not hierarchical, which could result in two machines on the Internet having the same names—something STS cannot account for. Additionally, the need to enter a static IP address in the LMHOSTS file on each client could result in a big problem if the IP address of the server changes.

This new feature of NT 4 enables you to address a machine using its DNS name without accounting for its NetBIOS name. This is important because I can have a machine with a NetBIOS name of jason, and you can have a machine with the NetBIOS name of jason somewhere else on the Internet. With the LMHOSTS file, we would have problems connecting, because a name must be unique. Under NT 4, your computer name and my computer name can both be jason, but as long as their fully qualified domain names (FQDN) are different, we don't have a problem. So my computer can be called jason.xyzcorp.com, and your computer can be jason.USACollege.edu and we can connect without a problem. Additionally, with traditional Windows naming, each computer can only have *one* name. For creating an extensible environment, this might not always be useful. However, because DNS enables you to alias multiple computer names to the same IP address, or host, you can give your system multiple names.

Let's use NET USE to see how NT treats this network connection. Figure A.35 shows the output of the NET USE command.

FIGURE A.35.

NET USE *shows that the network connection is in fact made to* \\ftp. microsoft.com.

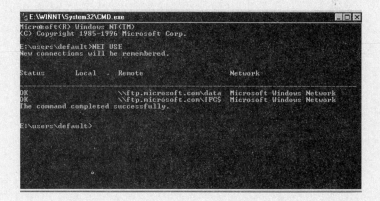

There is a command included in the Windows NT Resource Kit for 3.51 called INET. INET is a substitute for the NET command that enables you to enter DNS names or IP addresses instead of NetBIOS names. For example, you could type INET USE ftp.microsoft.com to get a connection to Microsoft's FTP server. However, there is an enormous difference between the way INET works and the integrated DNS functionality in NT 4. INET actually worked by resolving the DNS name, or IP address to a particular computer, and then querying that computer for its NetBIOS name, such as you can do with the NBTSTAT command with the -A or -a switches. It would then create an entry for this computer in your LMHOSTS file and address the computer based on its NetBIOS name. If you issued a plain NET USE command, you would only see the NetBIOS name of the computer. However, the new DNS lookup functionality of NT 4 does not work in such a roundabout and limited way.

Summary

This appendix looked at some tips and tricks for making more productive use of Windows NT. Some of these tips, such as examining file information based on their OLE properties, and using QuickView to view internal application code information, permit us to get a better understanding of how and why Windows NT works the way it does.

Other tricks such as recovering data on an NT Server when you lose the administrator's password, or deleting files with reserved names, can help you recover from common problems that could have very painful answers.

Some of the other tips in this section are just intended to make your administrative job simpler, such as making effective use of the Command Prompt and connecting to a remote NT system using a different user account.

Windows NT and Viruses

by Jason Garms

IN THIS APPENDIX

What Is a Computer Virus?

Computer virus is a phrase that strikes fear into the hearts of both computer professionals and end users. What is a virus, and, more importantly, how can it affect Windows NT?

To define what a computer virus is, let's start with the definition of a common virus taken from the *Oxford American Dictionary*: "a very simple organism…capable of causing disease." If you extrapolate this to the computer world, you get a good definition of a computer virus: "a very simple piece of software code, written with the intent of causing system malfunctions." This is fairly generalized, but it is an accurate description for our purposes.

Although today there are literally thousands of computer viruses, they have all sprung up in the last few years. It wasn't until the latter half of the 1980s that computer viruses began to appear. Many of the first viruses were written as proof of concept, not always with ill intent in mind.

How Do Computer Viruses Spread?

Just as human viruses spread with contact, so do computer viruses. If you want to avoid catching a virus, you could simply hide out in your house and have no interaction with other people. Similarly, if you want to prevent any chance of your computer catching a virus, you can keep it from communicating with other computers by never connecting it to a network and never inserting a floppy disk or CD-ROM. But, quite frankly, that takes most of the use, and all of the fun, out of using a computer. Computer connectivity is becoming an increasingly important medium in our information-based society, and simply disassociating yourself is not a solution.

How do viruses spread? I defined a virus as a simple piece of code that does unwanted and often malicious things. How does this code get into someone's computer? Usually this is accomplished by piggybacking onto another piece of useful, or good, code. For instance, you write a piece of virus code and then attach it to a game. Whenever the game is loaded, you have the viral code look around the hard drive for other programs. The code then copies parts of itself into the startup routines of these other programs. Now these other programs are infected. Attaching a piece of viral code onto a piece of software that is otherwise attractive is a common method of distribution.

To make matters worse, there are other ways of spreading viruses that many people don't know about. A piece of viral code can be stored anywhere where there are instructions that will be executed by a computer. This includes the boot record of a disk, as well as macro functions, including those in office automation applications such as Microsoft Office.

The Myth of Viruses and Windows NT

To set the record straight, Windows NT is not immune to viruses in any way. Too many people have to find this out the hard way before taking action. The misconceptions of NT's alleged virus resistance mostly come from exaggerated tales of NT's Hardware Abstraction Layer (HAL). The HAL prevents software routines from writing directly to hardware, thus making NT resistant to one of the more common techniques used by viruses to assist in their propagation. Also, because NT prevents one 32-bit application from accessing the memory space of another 32-bit application, Windows NT can prevent viruses that spread by loading into memory and then watching for other programs to load.

To many people, that might sound pretty good. The problem is viruses that employ additional schemes in their pursuit of mayhem. Even hinting that NT might in some way be virus-proof gives people the wrong impression. As Windows NT Server and NT Workstation become more prevalent in the marketplace, so will the number of NT-specific viruses.

What Is Protected in NT Server?

When you talk about protecting Windows NT Server against viruses, there are actually two distinct roles that need to be addressed: NT as a file server and NT as a workstation.

Most people use Windows NT Server in some capacity as a file server. Even systems that also act primarily as applications servers usually play at least a minor role as a file server. Because most viruses infect files and are transmitted by accessing or executing an infected file, one primary duty is to ensure that NT Server is not used as a medium to transmit viruses. It is also important to understand the consequences of viruses passing through NT Server and how it's done. For instance, imagine you are connected to an NT Server from a Windows 95 client and your system gets infected by a virus called X. If the task of virus X is to propagate by infecting all executables on all mounted volumes, it might first infect your local hard disk and then move to volumes mounted from the NT Server. If you have write permission to any executables on the server, such as in a public region, the virus could infect those files. Then when someone else on the network accesses the infected files from the server, their computer could become infected as well. So the virus spreads. In this instance, the NT Server is merely a host to the virus, and the virus cannot harm the NT Server.

However, because Windows NT Server can also be used as a workstation console to execute standard programs, you also have to worry about the possibility of infecting the server from the console. In this instance, you might install a utility on the NT Server console and not realize that the utility has been infected by a virus. Unlike the previous instance, you can actually harm the NT system itself. Additionally, depending on the rights of the user you were logged in as at the time of infection, the virus could infiltrate other files on the server. When a client accesses one of these infected files, it too could become infected. Thus the virus spreads.

Types of Computer Viruses

For these purposes, I classify viruses into five major types, based on the environment in which they were designed to function. They are MBR viruses, DOS viruses, Windows 3.x viruses, native Windows NT viruses, and macro viruses. In each of the sections, I address how the viruses in that area typically spread, and, more importantly, how they could possibly affect Windows NT.

Master Boot Record (MBR) Viruses

The vast majority of viral infections come from boot sector viruses. These are pieces of viral code that attach themselves to the boot sector of a floppy or hard disk. This boot sector normally contains a small piece of code that is executed when the disk is booted. A boot sector virus typically spreads by attaching a copy of itself onto the boot sector of all currently mounted local disks—such as your hard disk and any floppy disks. Additionally, the boot sector virus keeps a small piece of code resident in memory that is used to infect other disks that are inserted into the computer, thus spreading itself.

The boot sector virus is loaded before any operating system code, and therefore can be considered operating-system–independent, running on any Intel-compatible system designed for running MS-DOS.

However, there are problems with boot sector viruses and Windows NT. First, when you install Windows NT, it uses its own boot sector code, which differs from the standard DOS code. Most boot sector viruses expect a standard piece of boot code and make assumptions based on this expectation. The problem is when your NT system gets a boot sector virus and you try to boot your system. Depending on the virus, one of two things happens.

If the virus actually makes radical changes to the boot sector (such as encrypting the partition information) when it passes control to Windows NT for the operating system to begin loading, NT loads a virtualized piece of code that continues the boot process. This differs from traditional DOS methods, in which the operating system relies on BIOS-level calls, which the virus traps and then passes correct information back to the OS, enabling it to boot. However, because NT doesn't rely on these BIOS-level calls, the virus is cut out of the loop. Because the virus has altered the boot information, usually by encryption, NT is unable to continue the boot process and typically dies with a blue screen error message.

The second kind of boot sector virus is similar to the first, except it does not actually make changes to the boot information. In this case, when NT begins loading, it completely ignores the viral code, because it uses its own virtualized code, thus rendering the virus impotent. Unfortunately, this kind of boot sector virus is less common than the previous.

How can NT get infected by a boot sector virus? Typically, there are two ways to get infected by a boot sector virus. The first is by using an infected disk (usually a floppy disk) that drops the virus onto your system. However, when NT is alive, it cannot be infected in this manner because the infection process actually requires writing directly to the hardware, something that is disabled by NT's Hardware Abstraction Layer (HAL). The second way of spreading a boot sector virus is to boot a system from an infected disk. Unfortunately, this often happens because of a user's mistake. More often than not, a user works with a floppy disk, forgets the disk is in the drive, and restarts the system. If this disk is infected and the system reads the boot code, the virus is replicated onto your local hard drives, thus infecting your system. Because NT is not alive at this point, it cannot protect itself. To help guard against this, you might want to disable booting from floppy disks if your hardware supports such an option.

DOS Viruses

Although MBR viruses account for the largest number of infections, they don't account for the largest number of viruses. DOS-based viruses actually make up the largest segment of the virus population. You can further split DOS viruses into two categories: those that load a portion of code into memory, where it can continue to infect other programs, and those that perform their functions only when they are executed.

This distinction is made to identify what effects the viruses can have on Windows NT. The first group, which loads a memory-resident piece of code, was very effective under DOS and Windows 3.x. Because all applications shared a common memory space, which was fully accessible, a simple memory-resident virus could simply "hang out" and infect things at its leisure. This was often done by intercepting various DOS calls and manipulating them in some way. However, things work a little differently under Windows NT, so it is important to realize what can happen. Beginning with version 3.5, NT can run 16-bit programs in a shared address space with other 16-bit programs, or in its own 32-bit virtual DOS machine (VDM). By default, all 16-bit applications run together in a shared VDM. This means that a virus that loads itself as a memory-resident program can affect any other 16-bit application that runs in the shared memory space. However, the virus is completely unaware of any 32-bit processes that are also running on the system and is completely unable to interfere with their operation. Additionally, if you run all 16-bit applications in their own memory space, a virus of this type cannot do its job properly.

However, the situation is a little different with the second type of virus. This other kind of virus typically sits attached to a seemingly normal program or utility and spreads itself, or performs unwanted actions, only when you run the utility. These are often referred to as Trojan horse viruses. Although you can have viruses that work in a combination of these two ways, typically virus writers focus on one or the other distribution methods. Very often these viruses perform some sort of direct file manipulation. This takes the form of either corrupting data on the system or replicating its viral code onto other executable files, further spreading the infection. NT is very susceptible to this kind of attack. The main way to limit the impact of this kind of attack is to make sure you never use unknown programs when you are logged on as an administrative user. More importantly, you should limit the kinds of actions you perform at the server's console and limit the access you grant people from the network to the minimum level required. Additionally, you should be sure to install a good virus-scanning program to help watch for these kinds of viruses. See the section "Commercial Virus Detection Packages" later in this appendix for information on choosing an appropriate virus detection program.

Windows 3.x Viruses (16-Bit)

Several viruses out there are targeted for the Windows 3.x environment. Most of these work at least partially, even under Windows NT. This is because NT offers many services that provide down-level compatibility with Windows 3.x. For the most part, these viruses are limited in the same way as the DOS viruses mentioned in the previous section.

Windows 3.x viruses can directly affect only other 16-bit programs running in the same VDM. However, the virus can still alter data, as long as it doesn't try to do so by directly writing to the hardware and the current user has access permissions to modify the file targeted by the virus.

Native Windows NT Viruses (32-Bit)

As of this writing, there are no known viruses that specifically target Windows NT. This could mean either that none have yet been written or that someone has written and released one that was unsuccessful in propagating itself in the outside world.

A virus targeted for Windows NT could take many forms, including a device driver, a dynamic link library (DLL), or a standard executable. Because all these forms contain code segments that get executed, often by the operating system itself, infection through one of these avenues could spread rapidly.

From the server standpoint, it makes sense to set rules and limits as to who can log onto the server's console and what kinds of actions are permitted from the console. Remember, simply denying that NT can become infected does nothing but increase the likelihood that you will become infected.

Macro Viruses

Macro viruses are the fifth type of virus I discuss here. Until recently, the macro languages included with most applications were not powerful or robust enough to support writing an effective virus. However, many of the more advanced applications that are being developed today include built-in programming capabilities that rival some of the larger development packages. This has recently been demonstrated by the various strains of Microsoft Word viruses, including the so-called Word Concept and Word Nuclear viruses. These viruses transport themselves through Microsoft Word documents. When opened in Word, they perform various actions, including spreading themselves into the user's installation of Word, thus preparing to infect all future documents on the system.

An additional concern is that macro viruses can be cross-platform. The Word Concept virus has the claim to fame of being the first prominent cross-platform virus, because it can infect both Windows and Macintosh systems.

Because most application macro languages support passing execution to an external shell, such as COMMAND.COM or CMD.EXE, the power of the macro virus is not limited to the constraints of the macro language itself.

Additional Ways to Protect Against Viruses

Using a good anti-virus package is a defense against viruses. However, there is always the possibility that somehow a virus can sneak past your defenses. Following are some ways you can help reduce your risk of infection or help recover your data if your system does get infected by a virus.

Perform Regular Backups

One of the best ways to help protect your system against viruses is to implement an effective backup solution. No matter what kind of virus detection software you use, there is always the possibility that a virus could go undetected and you could lose all your data. By incorporating a virus protection strategy into your backup plans, you have a much greater chance of recovering your data if a virus does penetrate your server.

When planning for this contingency in your backup strategy, here are a few points you should note:

- Remember that most viruses (with the major exception of MBR viruses) live inside standard files. When you back up these files to tape, the virus tags along for the ride. This means that when you restore it from tape, the virus is restored as well. If you are recovering from tape after suffering a viral invasion, you should always check your system to make sure you are not re-infecting it.

- Make sure you don't recycle your tapes too often. Some people use simple tape rotation strategies where they use the same tapes each week. This can be dangerous if your files do get infected by a virus. Depending on the type of viral infection, you might not discover the infection for weeks, or even months. By then, the virus might have caused irrecoverable damage.

Create an Emergency Boot Disk

If your system is successfully attacked by a Master Boot Record (MBR) virus, NT most likely cannot boot. (For more information about why this is, see the earlier section on MBR viruses.) If your MBR is infected by a virus, you can use an emergency boot disk to get Windows NT up and running. Once NT has begun the boot process, a boot sector virus cannot cause any further damage. I repeat for emphasis: A boot sector virus cannot cause any further damage once NT is booted. This sentence pertains to boot sector viruses only. Other types of viruses can continue to cause further problems, even after NT has booted. Although this gives you the capability to get NT working again, and potentially keep it working until a more convenient time when you can take it down to remove the virus, you should remove the virus as soon as possible! After you have successfully booted NT with the emergency boot disk, you should back up the system before trying to remove the virus.

Keep Your Emergency Repair Disk Updated

Remember that the Emergency Repair Disk contains the most important files that give a unique identity to your NT system. It contains parts of the boot system, as well as key components of the Registry. If your system is attacked by a virus and rendered unable to boot properly, having an up-to-date Emergency Repair Disk is invaluable for getting your system back up and running. Use the RDISK.EXE program to update your Emergency Repair Disk or to create a new one.

Remember, there is a difference between the Emergency Repair Disk and the emergency boot disk referred to in the previous section.

The emergency boot disk contains the key components that enable NT to begin the load process and then hand off control to the appropriate NT installation on your system. It does not contain any of the key Registry components that could be useful in reconstructing a corrupted system. This disk is useful if somehow the bootstrap information cannot find a valid NT installation where it expects to.

In contrast, the Emergency Repair Disk is not a bootable disk. To use it, you must boot with the NT installation disk set and choose options to recover your system. This disk is invaluable if your NT installation itself is somehow corrupted.

Use NTFS

Using NTFS along with properly implemented security settings can help stop the spread of viruses. NTFS enables you to restrict a user's access to a single file or directory. This restriction is enforced if the file is accessed from the network or if it is accessed locally. However, NT cannot prevent access to FAT or HPFS partitions from the local system.

Additionally, when accessing HPFS and FAT volumes from a remote system, access restrictions can be assigned only for the entire share at a time. If a user needs to write to a single file on the share, the whole share must be created with write permissions for that user. If you use NTFS, you can restrict a user's write access to all the files except the one he or she needs to be able to write to.

Log On with an Unprivileged Account

If you want to protect yourself as much as possible from potential Trojan horse viruses, do not use a privileged user account for your day-to-day work. If you execute a Trojan horse virus, the virus has the same level of user privileges as you do. If you have administrative privileges, so does the virus. However, if you are using an unprivileged account, the virus's actions are more limited. For instance, if you were using a privileged account, the virus could potentially create a new user and grant it administrative rights. This account could later be used to further infiltrate your system. If you weren't using a privileged account, the virus could not have performed these actions.

If you must use a privileged user account, never run anything other than the standard administrative utilities or other utilities of known origin that you are sure you can trust!

> **WARNING**
>
> It's easy to write a WordBasic or Visual Basic macro that can make changes to the NT user database, so be careful about even opening seemingly innocuous files in Microsoft Word or Excel. To help protect yourself, you might want to use the Word Viewer or disable automatic macro execution in any program that supports macros.

Potential New Viruses

Unfortunately, the future promises more viruses, not less. With the number of computers increasing every day, as well as the increasing penetration of computers into the corporate environment, viruses will become the preferred method of espionage and revenge. More powerful multiplatform development tools, as well as prebuilt virus templates, make it easy for anyone with minimal knowledge to create a computer virus. Additionally, as you automate your computing environment through the use of macros, interactive online environments, and more complex personal agents that make your life easier, you also open yourself to new outside threats.

Commercial Virus Detection Packages

Unlike MS-DOS and Windows 3.x, Microsoft does not ship Windows NT with any type of anti-virus software. To make matters worse, until recently very few virus packages supported Windows NT. Fortunately, many vendors have come forward to help fill that gap. Today, several virus packages support Windows NT.

How to Evaluate an Anti-Virus Package

Before deciding what anti-virus package you want for your system, you should ask yourself a few questions to make sure you get a package that best fits your needs. When evaluating a virus package for Windows NT, here are some questions you will probably want to ask:

- **Is it a native Windows NT program?** Ideally, you want a package that was made specifically for Windows NT. Some 16-bit Windows- and DOS-based virus scanning packages run on Windows NT, with varying degrees of success. Make sure your package was specifically made for NT.

- **Does it run as a service?** What you really want is a virus detection engine that installs itself as a Windows NT service. This allows greater flexibility when configuring your system. If it does not install as a service, you need to leave a user logged on to the system for the virus scanner to run.

- **Is it intended for workstation or server operations, or both?** A package that provides both gives you the most security. What does this really mean? Windows NT Server is actually providing you with two functions. Its primary function is to provide file services for users on the network. You want a virus solution that constantly scans files as users access them from the network. Many virus products enable you to adjust the level of scanning separately for incoming and outgoing files, as well as specify what actions should be taken if a virus is discovered.

  The second function of NT Server is that of a workstation. You want a virus scanner that helps protect you when you log on to the NT Server console. Ideally, it automatically scans any disks you insert for viruses, as well as scanning any programs you run to ensure they are virus-free. Remember what I talked about earlier: If you're logged on as the administrator and run a program, if that program is infected with a virus, the virus is running with administrative privileges!

- **How does the licensing work?** Some virus scanners for NT make you pay a fee for each server you run it on. However, some also have additional costs per workstation that accesses the server. Make sure you understand and are willing to abide by the anti-virus maker pricing policy before choosing to go with its package. Remember, good virus protection can be costly!

- **How is the virus scanner going to impact the rest of your system's security?** Make sure you understand what permissions the virus scanner needs to do its job. Most virus scanners that install as an NT service create a special user account for their use. Find out what privileges this account needs and how this will impact the security of your system.

- **What kind of viruses does this package protect against?** Most of the virus protection vendors are fairly diligent about updating their software to detect the latest viruses. However, you need to understand the limitations of what it will not detect. For instance, many vendors still do not detect macro viruses, such as the cross-platform Word Concept virus that infects Microsoft Word documents. Also, many of the packages do not detect Macintosh viruses. If you are using NT Server to provide file services to Macintosh clients, you want to make sure to choose a package that provides support for Macintosh viruses.

■ **What kind of support and service will you get?** You want to look for a company that has a history of providing quality Windows NT software. Additionally, you should choose a company with a track record of regularly updating their virus detection database.

■ **What processor platforms does it support?** If you are using non-Intel platforms to run NT Server, make sure your platform is supported. You might be surprised how many work only on the Intel platform.

A List of Available Virus Protection Software for Windows NT

Following is a list of some of the more common packages on the market with Windows NT support. The level of functionality between the different products varies greatly, so use the questions listed here as a guideline when evaluating these packages for your use.

Vendor: Symantec

Product Name: Norton AntiVirus (NAV) for Windows NT

For more information: `http://www.symantec.com`

Vendor: McAfee

Product Name: VirusScan for Windows NT

For more information: `http://www.McAfee.com`

Vendor: S&S International PLC

Product Name: Dr. Solomon's Anti-Virus Kit for Windows NT

For more information: `http://www.drsolomon.com`

Vendor: Sophos

Product Name: SWEEP

For more information: `http://www.sophos.com`

Vendor: IBM Corporation

Product Name: IBM AntiVirus

For more information: `http://www.brs.ibm.com`

Vendor: Data Fellows

Product Name: F-PROT Professional for Windows NT

For more information: `http://www.datafellows.com`

Vendor: Intel Corporation

Product Name: LANDesk Virus Protect for Windows NT

For more information: `http://www.intel.com`

Vendor: Carmel Software Engineering

Product Name: Carmel Anti-Virus for Windows NT

For more information: `http://fbsolutions.com`

APPENDIX C

List of Default Groups, Privileges, and User Rights

by Jason Garms

IN THIS APPENDIX

This appendix lists the standard and advanced user rights that can be assigned in Windows NT. User rights are used to determine what types of special actions a user is permitted to perform. Most rights are assigned to a default group or groups, but additional users can be granted a right, either explicitly or by granting membership into a group that is granted the right.

Standard User Rights

Standard user rights are the rights that are usually of the most interest to NT administrators. These rights typically have to do with administrative capabilities on the server, such as backing up and restoring files or setting the time on the server.

The first column in Table C.1 lists the common name for the user right. Beneath this, listed in parentheses, is the internal name for this right. This is the name that shows up in the Event Viewer if you are auditing the use of user rights.

The second column gives a description of what the right entails, including any comments and caveats. Additionally, some of the rights that can be assigned in Windows NT have not yet been implemented. If this is the case, it is indicated in the Description column.

The third column lists the groups that by default are granted the particular right on an NT Server installed as a Primary Domain Controller (PDC) or a Backup Domain Controller (BDC).

The fourth column lists the default groups that are granted the particular right on an NT Server installed as a member server (nondomain controller) and on an NT Workstation.

Table C.1. Standard user rights.

NT Member User Right	Description Server and NT Workstation	Default on Server and NT Workstation	Domain Controller
Access this computer from network	This right enables specified users to log on to this computer over the network. Note that the abilities to log on to an NT system from the console and from the network are controlled independently by two different rights.	Administrators, everyone	Administrators, everyone, power users

NT Member User Right	Description Server and NT Workstation	Default on Server and NT Workstation	Domain Controller
Backup files and directories (SeBackup Privilege)	The holder of this right is permitted to circumvent NTFS file- and directory-level access permissions to back up any files on the computer. Note that utilities such as SCOPY also take advantage of this capability and can be used to circumvent security policy. Assign this right with caution.	Administrators, server operators, backup operators	Administrators, backup operators
Change the system time (SeSystemTime Privilege)	The specified users are permitted to set the computer's system clock.	Administrators, server operators, backup operators	Administrators, backup operators
Force shutdown from a remote system (SeRemote Shutdown Privilege)	The intent of this right is to permit the specified users to remotely initiate a system shutdown. However, this right is not yet implemented and has no effect in this version of Windows NT.	Administrators, server operators	Administrators, power users
Log on locally	This right enables the user to log on to the NT system using the console keyboard and gain interactive desktop access.	Administrators, server operators, backup operators, account operators, print operators	Administrators, backup operators, power users, users, guests

continues

Table C.1. continued

NT Member User Right	Description Server and NT Workstation	Default on Server and NT Workstation	Domain Controller
	Note that the abilities to log on to an NT system from the console and from the network are controlled independently by two different rights.		
Manage auditing and security log (SeSecurity Privilege)	This right permits the user to view and clear the security logs, as well as specify which object accesses are audited by the system. This right does not permit the users to enable or disable the system-wide auditing policy.	Administrators	Administrators
Restore files and directories (SeRestore Privilege)	The holder of this right is permitted to circumvent NTFS file- and directory-level access permissions to restore any files on the computer. It also permits the users to restore NTFS security attributes, including the file's owner information. Note that utilities such as SCOPY also take advantage of this capability and can be used to circumvent security policy. Assign this right with caution.	Administrators, server operators, backup operators	Administrators, backup operators

NT Member User Right	Description Server and NT Workstation	Default on Server and NT Workstation	Domain Controller
Shut down the system (SeShutdown Privilege)	This right permits the user to initiate a system shutdown if the user is interactively logged on to the system's console.	Administrators, server operators, backup operators, account operators, print operators	Administrators, backup operators, power users, users, guests
Take ownership of files or other objects (SeTake Ownership Privilege)	Possessing this right permits a user to take ownership of an NT object, including files, directories, and processes, regardless of the user's actual permissions on that resource.	Administrators	Administrators

Advanced User Rights

Advanced user rights are the rights that are typically of lesser interest to NT administrators. By this, I mean that they rarely need to be changed from their default values. However, in an environment in which you are writing and debugging programs on Windows NT, you will probably need to make some changes. However, you should be sure to fully understand what you are doing, because most of these rights provide the ability to circumvent different parts of NT's security system.

The first column in Table C.2 lists the common name for the user right. Beneath this, listed in parentheses, is the internal name for that right. This is the name that shows up in the Event Viewer if you are auditing the use of user rights.

The second column gives a description of what the right entails, including any comments and caveats. Additionally, some of the rights that can be assigned in Windows NT have not yet been implemented. If this is the case, it is indicated in the Description column.

The third column lists the groups that by default are granted the particular right on an NT Server installed as a Primary Domain Controller (PDC) or a Backup Domain Controller (BDC).

The fourth column lists the default groups that are granted the particular right on an NT Server installed as a member server (nondomain controller) and on an NT Workstation.

Table C.2. Advanced user rights.

NT Member User Right	Description Server and NT Workstation	Default on Server and NT Workstation	Domain Controller
Act as part of the operating system (`SeTcbPrivilege`)	This right enables the designated user to bypass certain operating system constraints and act as a trusted entity. The `SYSTEM` account can always do this. Additionally, some subsystems are given this capability. Some Win32API calls, such as `LogonUser()` and `CreateProcessAsUser()`, require that they be run with this right.	None	None
Add workstations to domain	This right enables the user to create NT Workstation or NT Server computer accounts in the NT domain. It is a built-in right for administrators and account operators, which cannot be removed. Note that the NT 3.5 and 3.51 documentation incorrectly lists the server operators as holding this right instead of the account operators. Additionally, many resources that are derived from this documentation also contain this error. See Microsoft's TechNote Q129116 for more information.	None	Not applicable

NT Member User Right	Description Server and NT Workstation	Default on Server and NT Workstation	Domain Controller
Bypass traverse checking (SeChangeNotify Privilege)	Permits a user to access a resource to which he or she is granted permissions even if the user does not have permission to access all the parent resources. For more information about this right, see Chapter 27, "Advanced Security Guidelines."	Everyone	Everyone
Create a pagefile (SeCreatePage- file Privilege)	This right enables the user to create a pagefile. However, it has no effect in the current version of Windows NT.	Administrators	Administrators
Create a token object (SeCreateToken Privilege)	This right enables the possessor to create security access tokens, which are normally built by the Local Security Authority whenever a user logs on to a Windows NT system. Normally only the Local Security Authority can create access tokens. You cannot audit the use of this right. Some Win32API calls, such as LogonUser() and CreateProcessAsUser(), require that they be run with this permission.	None	None

continues

Table C.2. continued

NT Member User Right	Description Server and NT Workstation	Default on Server and NT Workstation	Domain Controller
Create permanent shared objects (`SeCreatePermanentPrivilege`)	Possession of this right enables the user to create permanent shared objects. Note: Do not confuse this right with the ability to create network shares!	None	None
Debug programs (`SeDebugPrivilege`)	This right enables the user to gain full access to any system-level process, including the ability to view the process's memory space, terminate the process, and spawn additional processes and threads using the system's security context. It is intended for debugging only and should be handled with care. Use of this right is not auditable.	Administrators	Administrators
Generate security audits (`SeAuditPrivilege`)	Enabling this right for a user enables the user to run a process that creates entries in the system's security log, which can be viewed with the Event Viewer. You cannot audit the use of this right.	None	None

NT Member User Right	Description Server and NT Workstation	Default on Server and NT Workstation	Domain Controller
Increase quotas (`SeIncreaseQuota Privilege`)	This right is provided to enable the user to increase object quotas. However, it is not implemented in the current version of Windows NT.	Administrators (beginning in NT 3.51)	Administrators (beginning in NT 3.51)
Increase scheduling priority (`SeIncreaseBase PriorityPrivilege`)	Having this right enables a user to change the priority of a Win32 application. Note: Increasing the priority of a process can starve other processes, including the system.	Administrators	Administrators
Load and unload device drivers (`SeLoadDriver Privilege`)	This right enables the user to install and remove NT device drivers.	Administrators	Administrators
Lock pages in memory (`SeLockMemory Privilege`)	This enables a process owned by the user to lock pages in memory so they cannot be paged out. Note that locking a page in memory effectively reduces the amount of physical memory that can be allocated to other processes. Usually only the system processes should be allowed to be locked.	None	None

continues

Table C.2. continued

NT Member User Right	Description Server and NT Workstation	Default on Server and NT Workstation	Domain Controller
Log on as a batch job (SeBatchSid)	This right enables the user to log on using a batch queue facility that is not implemented in this version of Windows NT. Assigning this right currently has no effect.	None	None
Log on as a service (SeServiceSid)	This right enables a user to log on to NT as a service. By default, most services in NT run in the SYSTEM account user context. However, if you want to run a service, such as the scheduler service, in a different user context, you would need to assign this right to that user account.	None	None
Modify firmware environment variables (SeSystem Environment Privilege)	This right enables a user to change environment settings stored in nonvolatile RAM (NVRAM). This is applicable only on systems that have such a feature. Note that this right has nothing to do with the system's environmental variables or user variable, which can be set from the Control Panel's System icon.	Administrators	Administrators

NT Member User Right	Description Server and NT Workstation	Default on Server and NT Workstation	Domain Controller
Profile single process (SeProfileSingle ProcessPrivilege)	This right enables the user to use NT's performance monitoring tools to profile the performance of a single process. However, this right is not implemented in the current release of Windows NT. Assigning it does nothing.	Administrators	Administrators, power users
Profile system performance (SeSystemProfile Privilege)	This right enables the user to use NT's performance monitoring tools to profile the system's performance.	Administrators	Administrators
Replace a process-level token (SeAssignPrimary TokenPrivilege)	This right enables the user to modify a process's access token. Some Win32API calls, such as LogonUser() and CreateProcessAsUser(), require that they be run with this right.	None	None

I

INDEX

Get the best information and learn about latest developments in:

- Design
- Graphics and Multimedia
- Enterprise Computing and DBMS
- General Internet Information
- Operating Systems
- Networking and Hardware
- PC and Video Gaming
- Productivity Applications
- Programming
- Web Programming and Administration
- Web Publishing

Turn to the *Authoritative* Encyclopedia of Computing

You'll find over 150 full text books online, hundreds of shareware/freeware applications, online computing classes and 10 computing resource centers full of expert advice from the editors and publishers of:

- Adobe Press
- BradyGAMES
- Cisco Press
- Hayden Books
- Lycos Press
- New Riders
- Que
- Que Education & Training
- Sams Publishing
- Waite Group Press
- Ziff-Davis Press

The Authoritative Encyclopedia of Computing

When you're looking for computing information, consult the authority. The Authoritative Encyclopedia of Computing at mcp.com.